GW00362541

BRITAIN BED & BREAKFAST 2003

Publisher **Tim Stilwell**

Editor **Martin Dowling**

STILWELL

Publishing

Distributed by Orca Book Services, Stanley House, 3 Fleets Lane, Poole, Dorset BH15 3AJ
(Tel: 01202 665432).
Available from all good bookshops.

ISBN 1-900861-32-1

Published by Stilwell Publishing,
59 Charlotte Road, Shoreditch, London, EC2A 3QW.
Tel: 020 7739 7179.

Publisher: Tim Stilwell
Editor: Martin Dowling
Typesetting: Tradespools Ltd, Frome, Somerset

Printed in Great Britain by Stephens & George Print, Merthyr Tydfil, Mid Glamorgan.

Contents

Introduction

This directory is really very straightforward. It sets out to list as many B&Bs in as many places in Britain as possible, so that wherever you go, you'll be able to find one nearby.

The book was actually born out of frustration. In the summer of 1991, my wife and I walked a long distance footpath over several weekends. As neither of us are avid campers or wished to stay in expensive hotels, we decided on B&Bs for our overnight stays. But we encountered a major problem straightaway. One could not find good value bed and breakfast accommodation along the route without going to a lot of trouble. Local libraries, Directory Enquiries, six different Tourist Information Centres and a large pile of brochures yielded nothing but a hotchpotch of B&B addresses – most of them miles out of our way. In the end, we abandoned our research and did the walk in one-day stretches, high-tailing it back to our London home each evening on the train. Needless to say, the memory stayed with us.

As did this one. Earlier that year, my work for a large publishing company sent me to a conference at the National Exhibition Centre, in Birmingham. My colleagues and I wished to stay in the area together and had to book at short notice. Our office was typical of the times; the recession was in full swing and our budget did not stretch far. We asked for the local Tourist Information Centre's brochure, but it wasn't much help. It arrived three days later, had no area map and consisted mostly of hotels outside our price range. A 2-mile trek to the local reference library to trawl through the Birmingham Yellow Pages did yield a list of local guest house telephone numbers, but there was no way of knowing what facilities any of them had or how much they cost. It was like blind man's buff. Fortunately, we were lucky. We found what we wanted after only 20 calls – bed and breakfast in a thriving Coleshill pub, five miles from the Centre. We had to book our rooms unseen, though, on the landlord's word only – an uninformed decision. In their small ways, both experiences illustrated the need for a book such as Stilwell's **Britain: Bed & Breakfast**.

As the recession grew worse, I lost my job with the large publishing company. A year later, I set up my own small publishing company whose first project was this directory. Happily, it has been rather successful. The reason must be that many others have found themselves in similar straits – stuck for a place to stay for the evening. For lack of information, they've missed out on the good value offered by B&Bs. This book has been expressly designed with these people in mind. Its purpose is simple: to save the reader time and money. It suits anyone who wishes to plan a trip in Britain, who appreciates good value and who is open to ideas. The directory is quite deliberately not a guidebook. Its aim is that of any directory in any field: to be comprehensive, offering the widest possible choice. By this definition, Stilwell's **Britain: Bed & Breakfast** outstrips any guidebook. We publish the largest number of B&Bs of any book available in this country. What we don't do, though, is make up the reader's mind for them. There are plenty of other B&B books that push their particular premises as 'exclusive' or 'special'. We think that a simple glance over the salient details will allow the reader to be his or her own best judge.

We have two kinds of reader in mind. The first knows exactly where to go but not where to stay. The nearest B&B is often the best solution and a quick look at the right county map will provide the answer. The other kind of reader is not so sure where to go. A good browse through these pages, studying the colour pictures, the facilities lists and the short descriptions, will offer good ideas.

All the accommodation information in this book has been supplied by the B&B owners themselves. And all the entries are bona fide B&Bs: 99% are listed at the local Tourist Information Centre. We should make it clear that inclusion in these pages does not imply personal recommendation. We have not visited every B&B individually. What we have done is write to them. The directory lists over 6,500 entries in 4,000 locations throughout Britain. The vast majority offer B&B for under £30 per person per night.

Owners were canvassed in the summer of 2002 and responded by the middle of October. They were asked to provide their lowest and their highest rates per person per night for 2003. The rates are thus forecasts and are subject to seasonal fluctuations due to demand. Some information may already be out of date. Grades may go up or down or be removed. British Telecom may alter exchange numbers. Proprietors may decide to sell up and move out of the business altogether. This is why the directory is year specific, published annually. In general, though, the information published here will be accurate, pertinent and useful for many a year.

Each listing in **Britain: Bed & Breakfast** is an advertisement. The B&B owners decide on the type of entry they want – basic or highlighted in pink to stand out on the page; with or without a colour picture – and pay accordingly.

The chief aim is to provide details that are concise and easy to understand. The only symbols used are conventional tourist symbols, common to all travel books. Similarly, the abbreviations should be clear as to what they stand for without having to refer to the key on the first page.

The grades are perhaps more difficult as each inspecting organisation – the national Tourist Boards, the AA and the RAC – has its own classification system with its own definition of merit. Once again, though, the reader will soon pick out the exceptional establishments – many have high grades from each organisation. The general rule is that more facilities mean higher prices. But don't be misled into thinking that an ungraded establishment is inferior. Many B&Bs are locally registered but never apply for grades or do not wish to pay for one. They thrive on word-of-mouth and business from guests who return again and again because of the excellent hospitality. My advice is to ring around. A simple telephone call and some judicious questions will give you an impression of your host very effectively. If you write to a B&B for more details, it's a good idea to enclose a stamped, addressed envelope for a quick reply. The largest number of British B&Bs is now laid out before you – the greatest choice available on the market. We think that your tastes and preferences will do the rest.

We have deliberately arranged the book by administrative county in alphabetical order except in the cases where this would disrupt a perceived sequence (such as East, North, South and West Yorkshire). There is an exception to prove the rule – County Durham appears perversely under D, as most people look for it under this heading. Merseyside is merged into the adjacent Greater Manchester section. South, West and Mid-Glamorgan appear together under the heading of The Glamorgans. We hope this will delight those who show pride in their native or adopted counties. In April 1996, the government decided to rename administrative counties and revise many local government boundaries. Out went the 1974 creations of the Heath government – Avon, Cleveland, Hereford & Worcester, Humberside, Dyfed, Clwyd, Gwynedd, Strathclyde, Grampian, Central and Tayside – and in came older and much-loved names, such as Argyll & Bute or Pembrokeshire. While this has undoubtedly served to make many people happier (hatred of the 1974 regions was quite intense), it has proved rather a headache for travel book publishers. For example, North West Wales and North East Wales cover a plethora of unitary authorities. Also, since many of the new Scottish regions are too small to merit their own chapter, we have merged them into neighbouring regions, hence 'Edinburgh & Lothians' and 'Stirling & the Trossachs'. The Glasgow & District chapter mixes several unitary authorities. The same goes for our Glamorgan and Monmouthshire chapters.

One feature of the book is that we insist on using the proper postal address. Many entries may carry a county name different from the one they are listed under or a post town that is some miles from their village. These oddities arise from the Royal Mail's distribution system. They should not, under any circumstances, be used as a directional guide. In one case, the village of Laid, on Loch Eriboll, is 67 miles from its quoted post town – not a journey to make in error. Used on a letter though, this system does speed the mail up. If you need directions to a B&B (especially if you are travelling at night), the best solution is to telephone the owner and ask the way.

The county maps are intended to act as a general reference. They are intended to show the location of each entry in the directory. For a more accurate idea of the exact location of a particular B&B, use the six-figure National Grid reference published under each location's name. Used in tandem with an Ordnance Survey map (such as the excellent Landranger series) or any atlas that uses the National Grid, these numbers provide first-class route-planning references. The pubs that appear beneath each location heading are included on the recommendation of B&B owners themselves. The tankard symbol shows that they are local pubs where one can get a decent evening meal at a reasonable price.

This is the second edition of **Britain: Bed & Breakfast** to include colour pictures. This year, we have changed the design and colour scheme of the maps. Essentially, however, we present you with the same high-quality product our readers are accustomed to, with ease of use, geographical accuracy and excellent value.

The Publisher,
Stoke Newington, December 2002.

GREAT BRITAIN
SHETLAND ISLANDS
ISLES OF ORKNEY
WESTERN ISLES
Wick
Stornoway
Inverness
Aberdeen
SCOTLAND
Fort William
Glasgow
EDINBURGH
Newcastle upon Tyne
Durham
NORTHERN
IRELAND
ISLE OF MAN
Kendal
York
Manchester
Liverpool
REPUBLIC
OF
IRELAND
Norwich
Birmingham
Aberystwyth
ENGLAND
WALES
CARDIFF
Bristol
LONDON
Dover
Portsmouth
Exeter
Plymouth
ISLE OF WIGHT
ISLES OF SCILLY
CHANNEL ISLANDS
FRANCE

England & Wales – *Regions*

ENGLAND

1 Bedfordshire
2 Berkshire
3 Bristol
4 Buckinghamshire
5 Cambridgeshire
6 Cheshire
7 Cornwall
8 Cumbria
9 Derbyshire
10 Devon
11 Dorset
12 County Durham
13 Essex
14 Gloucestershire
15 Greater Manchester & Merseyside
16 Hampshire
17 Herefordshire
18 Hertfordshire
19 Isle of Wight
20 Kent
21 Lancashire
22 Leicestershire
23 Lincolnshire
24 London
25 Norfolk
26 Northamptonshire
27 Northumberland
28 Nottinghamshire
29 Oxfordshire
30 Rutland
31 Shropshire
32 Somerset
33 Staffordshire
34 Suffolk
35 Surrey
36 East Sussex
37 West Sussex
38 Teesside
39 Tyne & Wear
40 Warwickshire
41 West Midlands
42 Wiltshire
43 Worcestershire
44 East Yorkshire
45 North Yorkshire
46 South Yorkshire
47 West Yorkshire

48 Isle of Man

WALES

49 Anglesey
50 Carmarthenshire
51 Ceredigon
52 The Glamorgans
53 Monmouthshire
54 North East Wales
55 North West Wales
56 Pembrokeshire
57 Powys

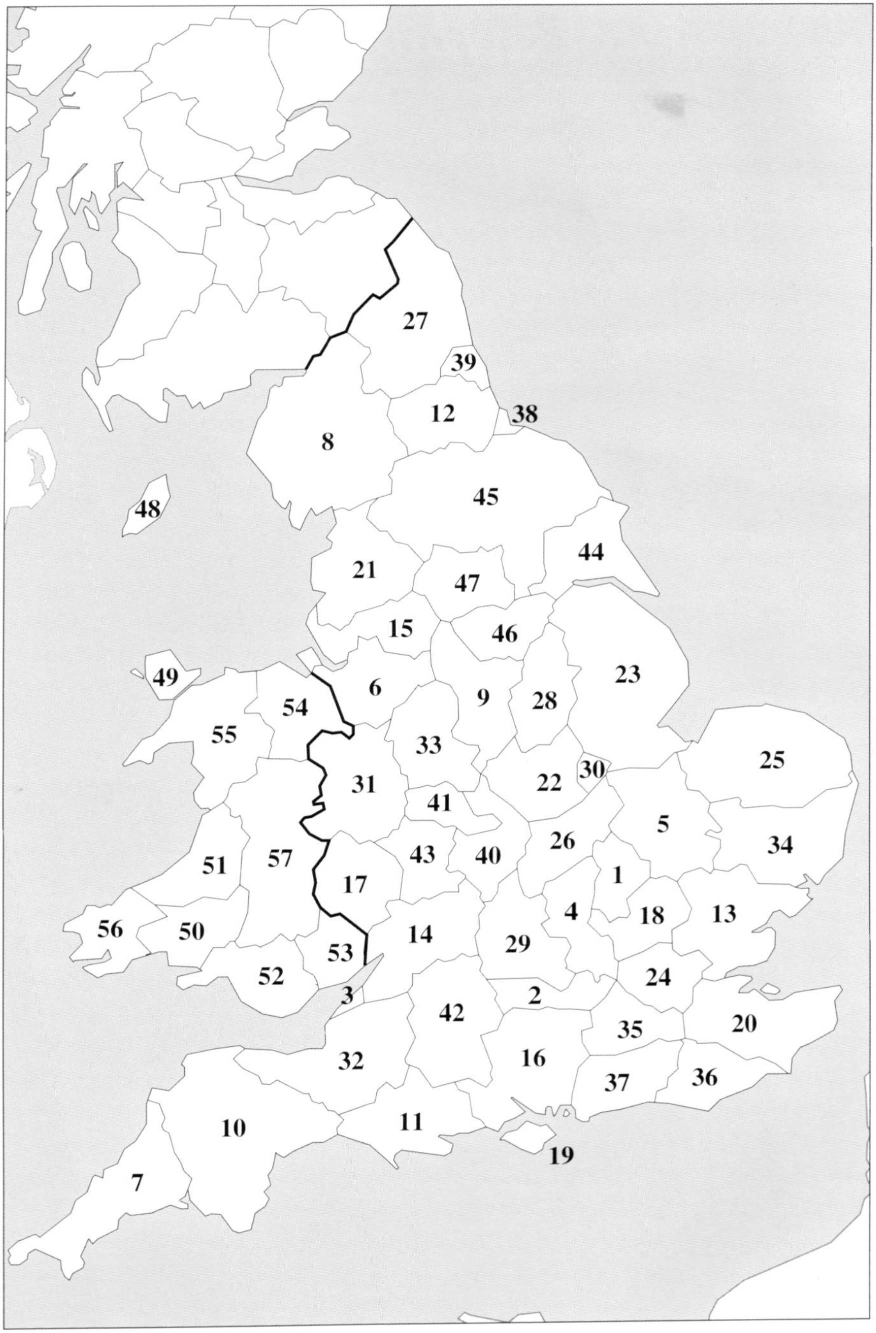
27
39
12
38
8
48
45
44
21
47
15
46
49
6
9
28
23
54
55
33
31
30
22
25
41
5
57
51
43
40
26
34
17
1
4
18
13
56
50
14
29
53
52
24
3
2
42
35
20
32
16
37
36
10
11
19
7

Scotland – *Regions*

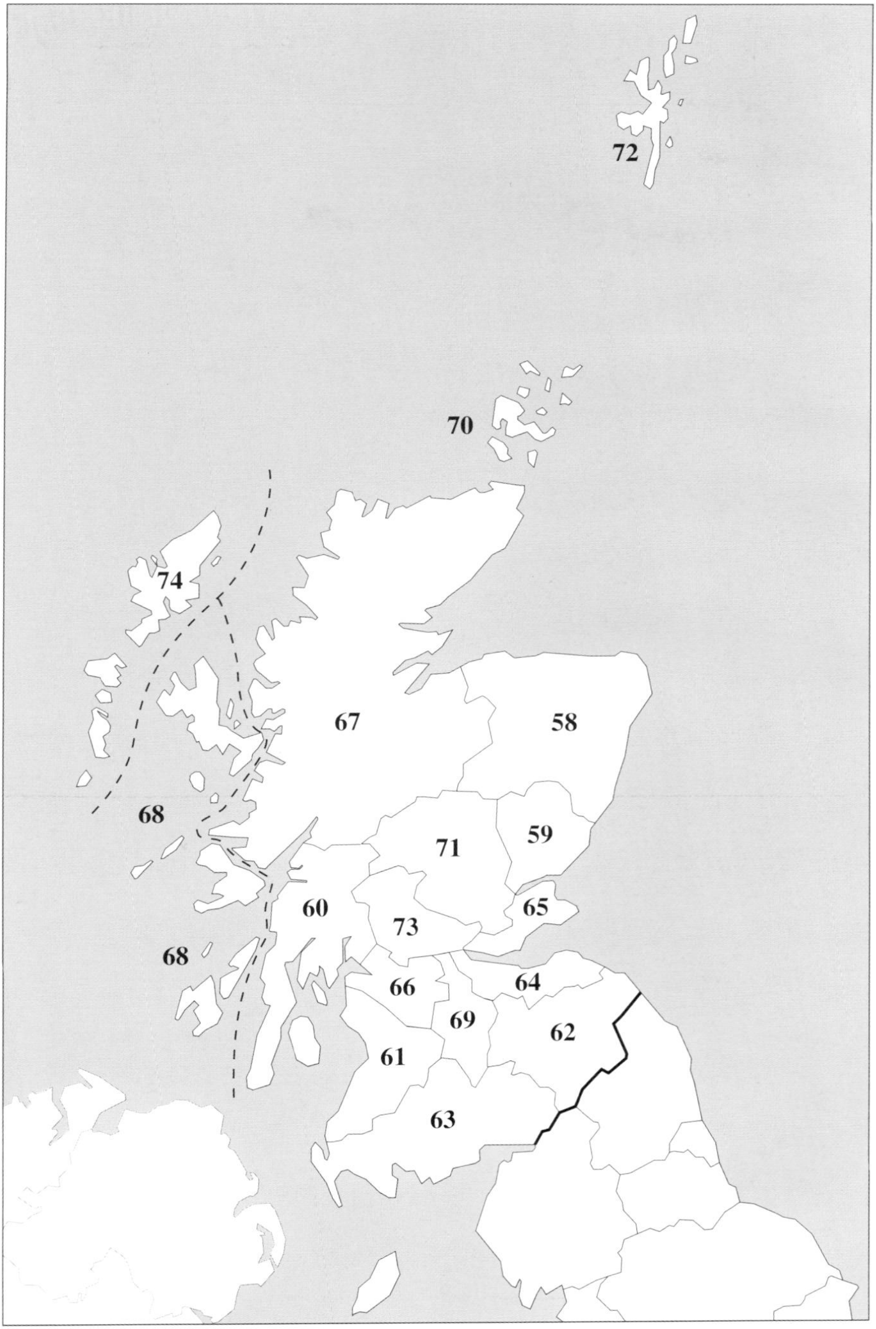
72
70
74
67
58
68
71
59
60
65
73
68
66
64
69
62
61
63

Channel Islands

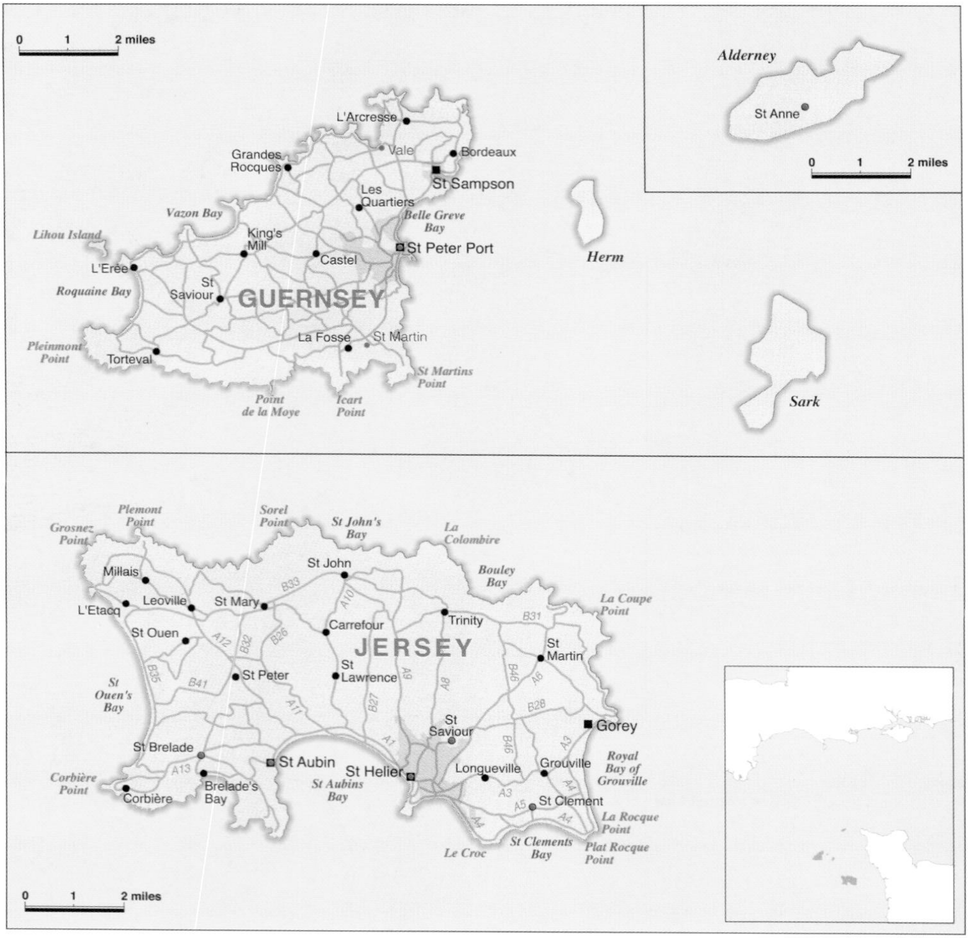

▼ ALDERNEY

St Anne

L'Haras, *Newtown Road, Alderney, Guernsey, C.I., GY9 3XP.* Quiet family-run guest house, close to harbour and town. **Open:** All year
01481 823174 (also fax) Mrs Jansen *lharas@internet.alderney.gg* www.internet.alderney.gg/lharas **D:** Fr £22.00–£30.00 **S:** Fr £22.00–£33.00 **Beds:** 1D 2T 2S **Baths:** 2 En 1 Sh (10)

▼ GUERNSEY

St Martin

Rosewood, *La Grand Rue, St Martin, Guernsey, Channel Islands, GY4 6RU.* Centrally situated in St Martins village - homely guest house, large garden. **Open:** Easter to Oct
01481 238329 Mr Sinkinson **Fax: 01481 239457 D:** Fr £16.00–£20.00 **S:** Fr £19.00–£23.00 **Beds:** 1F 2D 2T 1S **Baths:** 2 Sh (3) (8)

St Peter Port

Rosewood, *The Grange, St Peter Port, Guernsey, Channel Islands, GY1 1RQ.* 10 mins walking distance from town centre. Friendly & homely. **Open:** May to Oct
Grades: GTB 2 Diamond
01481 720606 (also fax) D: Fr £19.00–£25.00 **S:** Fr £21.00–£27.00 **Beds:** 1F 2T 1D **Baths:** 3 En 1 Sh (3) (2)

Marine Hotel, *Well Road, St Peter Port, Guernsey, C.I., GY1 1WS.* Friendly, comfortable hotel 30 meters from sea. Five mins walk to shops, harbour, leisure centre, theatre, etc. Lovely sun patio and relaxing lounge with sea views. Full choice English breakfast cooked fresh to order. Flexible bookings and package holidays aranged with substantial discounts. **Open:** All year
01481 724978 Mrs Clegg **Fax: 01481 711729**
D: Fr £17.95–£26.95 **S:** Fr £17.95–£28.95
Beds: 3F 3T 4D 1S **Baths:** 11 En
cc

St Saviour

Anneville, *Les Vallettes, St Saviour, Guernsey, C.I., GY7 9YW.* Small country cottage, all room with facilities. Ideal walking/cyclists base.
Open: All year
01481 263814 **D:** Fr £17.50–£18.50 **S:** Fr £18.50 **Beds:** 1F 1T 2D 1S **Baths:** 1 En 4 Pr

Vale

L'Ancresse View Guest House, *La Garenne, Vale, Guernsey, C.I., GY3 5SQ.* Bordering L'Ancresse Golf Course. Main bus route to St Peter Port. **Open:** All year
01481 243963 (also fax) Mr Peacegood *lancresse@hotmail.com* **D:** Fr £12.00–£18.50 **S:** Fr £12.00–£18.50 **Beds:** 1F 2D 1T

▼ JERSEY

St Aubin

Peterborough House, *Rue du Crocquet, High Street, St Aubin, Jersey, C.I., JE3 8BZ.* C17th house, personally-run, conservation area, some rooms sea view.
Open: Mar to Oct
01534 741568 Mr & Mrs Cabral **Fax: 01534 746787** *fernando@localdial.com* www.jerseyisland.com/staubin/peterborough **D:** Fr £19.00–£30.00 **S:** Fr £24.00–£35.00 **Beds:** 1F 4D 5T 4S **Baths:** 12 En 1 Sh (10) **cc**

RATES
D = Price range per person sharing in a double or twin room
S = Price range for a single room

Panorama, *Rue du Crocquet, St Aubin, Jersey, C.I., JE3 8BZ.* Gold merit award guest house. Exceptional standards, food, service, accommodation. **Open:** Easter to Oct
01534 742429 **Fax: 01534 745940**
www.jerseyisland.com/staubin/panorama
D: Fr £24.00–£46.00 **S:** Fr £24.00–£72.00
Beds: 12T 2D 3S **Baths:** 17 En

St Brelade

Au Caprice, *Route de la Haule, St Brelade, Jersey, C.I., JE3 8BA.* Small friendly establishment situated opposite a large safe sandy beach. **Open:** Apr to Dec
01534 722083 Ms Monpetit **Fax: 01534 280058** *aucaprice@jerseymail.co.uk*
www.jerseyisland.com/staubin/aucaprice
D: Fr £18.50–£28.00 **S:** Fr £20.00–£29.00
Beds: 2F 6D 4T **Baths:** 12 En (2) (20) **cc**

Lyndhurst, *Route de la Haule, St Brelade, Jersey, C.I., JE3 8BA.* Overlooking the golden sands of St Aubin's Bay. Superb food.
Open: All year
01534 720317 **Fax: 01534 613776** **D:** Fr £15.50–£25.50 **S:** Fr £25.50–£35.50 **Beds:** 4F 4D 3T **Baths:** 11 Pr (6) **cc**

St Clement

Rocqueberg View, *Rue de Samares, St Clement, Jersey, JE2 6LS.* Comfortable friendly quiet house in convenient quiet location near beach. **Open:** All year
01534 852642 L & S Monks **Fax: 01534 851694** **D:** Fr £15.00–£26.00 **S:** Fr £15.00–£46.00 **Beds:** 2F 5D 2T **Baths:** 9 En (9)

Planning a longer stay? Always ask for any special rates

St Helier

Millbrook House, *Rue de Trachy, Millbrook, St Helier, Jersey, C.I., JE2 3JN.* **Open:** May to Oct **Grades:** AA 4 Diamond
01534 733036 Mr Pirouet **Fax: 01534 724317** *millbrookhouse@jerseymail.co.uk*
www.millbrookhousehotel.com **D:** Fr £35.00–£39.00 **S:** Fr £35.00–£39.00 **Beds:** 5F 10D 9T 3S **Baths:** 27 En (20)
Where the air is clear, Millbrook House offers peace, quiet and character. Exceptional park and gardens with views of the sea. Each night a five course dinner is served, complemented by a wine list of some 80 wines.

Bromley Guest House, *7 Winchester Street, St Helier, Jersey, C.I., JE24TH.* **Open:** All year
01534 725045 & 01534 723948 Mrs Schillaci **Fax: 01534 769712** *lmcgrpe@aol.com*
www.jersey.co.uk/hotels/bromley **D:** Fr £18.00–£28.00 **S:** Fr £31.00–£45.00 **Beds:** 1F 3D 3T 2S **Baths:** 7 En 2 Sh
cc
Jersey town guest house, open all year. Double/twin/family rooms all ensuite, single rooms basic only. Colour TV, tea/coffee facilities. Situated only 3-4 minutes from shopping area and all amenities. Travel can be arranged from England, Scotland and Ireland.

Almorah, *Almorah Crescent, St Helier, Jersey, C.I., JE2 3GU.* Small family-run hotel in an elevated position overlooking the town of St Helier. **Open:** Easter to Oct
01534 721648 **Fax: 01534 509724** *hammond@ic24.net* **D:** Fr £26.00–£35.00 **S:** Fr £41.00–£50.00 **Beds:** 3F 9D 2T **Baths:** 14 En

Seacroft, *38 Green Street, St Helier, Jersey, Channel Islands, JE2 4UG.* Close to all amenities. Small, friendly home. **Open:** All year (not Xmas/New Year)
01534 732732 **D:** Fr £18.00–£20.00 **S:** Fr £20.00 **Beds:** 1F 5T 2D **Baths:** 3 Sh (2)

Bedfordshire

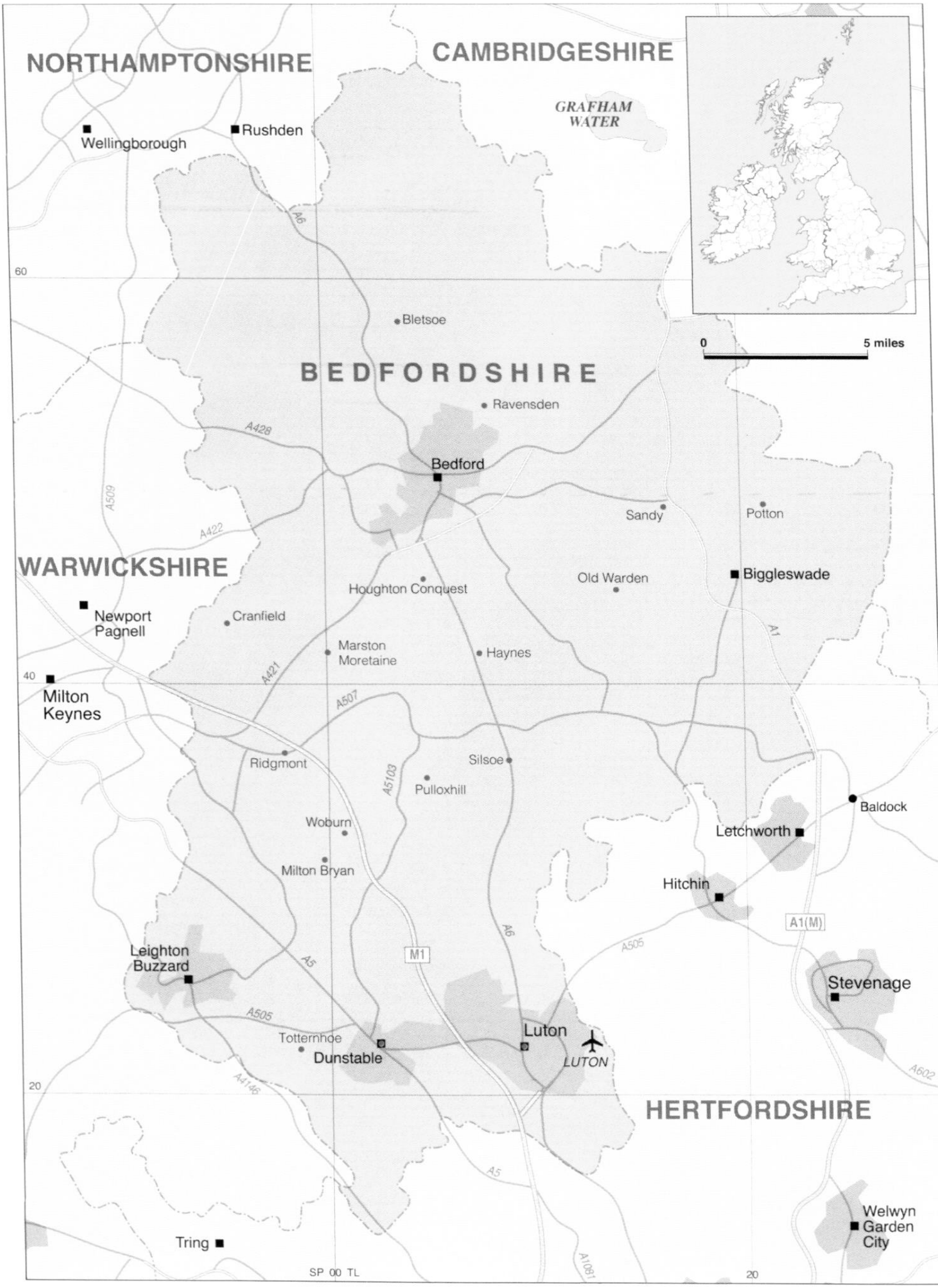
NORTHAMPTONSHIRE
CAMBRIDGESHIRE
GRAFHAM WATER
Wellingborough
Rushden
A6
60
Bletsoe
BEDFORDSHIRE
0
5 miles
Ravensden
A428
Bedford
A509
Sandy
Potton
A422
WARWICKSHIRE
Houghton Conquest
Old Warden
Biggleswade
Newport Pagnell
Cranfield
A1
Marston Moretaine
Haynes
A421
40
Milton Keynes
A507
Ridgmont
Silsoe
A5103
Pulloxhill
Baldock
Woburn
Letchworth
Milton Bryan
Hitchin
A1(M)
A6
A505
M1
Leighton Buzzard
A5
Stevenage
A505
Luton
Totternhoe
Dunstable
LUTON
A602
20
A4146
HERTFORDSHIRE
A5
Welwyn Garden City
Tring
SP 00 TL
A1081
20

Bletsoe

TL0357

North End Farm, *Riseley Road, Bletsoe, Bedford, MK44 1QT.* A beautiful barn conversion in quiet countryside on a farm. **Open:** All year
01234 781320 & 07979 596913 (M) Mr & Mrs Forster **Fax: 01234 781320 D:** Fr £25.00–£50.00 **S:** Fr £25.00–£30.00 **Beds:** 8T **Baths:** 48 En (5) (20) TV V cc

Cranfield

SP9542

The Queen Hotel, *40 Dartmouth Road, Olney, Buckinghamshire, MK46 4BH.* Enchanting Victorian house in bustling market town. **Open:** All year
01234 711924 (also fax) Mrs Elsmore **D:** Fr £27.50–£29.00 **S:** Fr £42.00–£44.50 **Beds:** 3T 4D 2S **Baths:** 7 En 1 Sh (9) TV cc

Dunstable

TL0121

Regent House Guest House, *79a High Street North, Dunstable, Beds, LU6 1JF.* Dunstable town centre, close to MI. **Open:** All year
01582 660196 Mr Woodhouse **D:** Fr £17.00 **S:** Fr £20.00 **Beds:** 5T 5S 1F **Baths:** 4 En (6) TV V

Haynes

TL1041

Westview, *Church End, Haynes, Bedford, Beds, MK45 3QS.* Situated within easy reach to M1 South - North + London Luton Airport. **Open:** All year
01234 742881 Mr & Mrs Baker *bevb123@hotmail.com* **D:** Fr £27.50–£30.00 **S:** Fr £27.50–£30.00 **Beds:** 1T 1D 1S **Baths:** 1 En 1 Sh (5) (4) TV

Luton

TL0921

Belzayne, *70 Lalleford Road, Luton, Beds, LU2 9JH.* Modern semi, near airport. Old fashioned hospitality. Close to M1. **Open:** All year (not Xmas/New Year)
01582 736591 (also fax) Mrs Bell **D:** Fr £15.00–£18.00 **Beds:** 1D 2T **Baths:** 2 Sh (12) (5)

Shannon Hotel, *40a Guildford Street, Luton, LU1 2PA.* Situated in heart of Luton. Personal friendly service. **Open:** All year
01582 482119 Fax: 01582 482818 *shannon@dial.pipex.com* www.shannonhotel.com **D:** Fr £40.00–£55.50 **S:** Fr £50.00–£65.00 **Beds:** 7F 7T 7D 7S **Baths:** 28 En TV V cc

Marston Moretaine

SP9941

The Coach House, *The Old Rectory, Marston Moretaine, Bedford, MK43 0NF.* Listed building, fully modernised, in 5 acres of mature gardens. **Open:** All year (not Xmas)
01234 767794 (also fax) G S Lake *isla.lake@uk.uumail.com* **D:** Fr £19.50 **S:** Fr £30.00 **Beds:** 1T 4D 1S **Baths:** 6 En (20) TV cc

Milton Bryan

SP9730

Town Farm, *Milton Bryan, Milton Keynes, Bucks, MK17 9HS.* Quiet, secluded farmhouse, good views, easy access Woburn and M1. **Open:** All year (not Xmas)
01525 210001 (also fax) Mrs Harris **D:** Fr £22.50 **S:** Fr £25.00 **Beds:** 2T **Baths:** 2 En (12) (4) TV V

Old Warden

TL1343

Old Warden Guest House, *Shop & Post Office, Old Warden, Biggleswade, Beds, SG18 9HQ.* Centre of quiet, picturesque village. **Open:** All year (not Xmas/New Year)
Grades: ETC 3 Diamond
01767 627201 Mr Bruton **D:** Fr £21.00–£23.00 **S:** Fr £25.00–£27.00 **Beds:** 2D 1T **Baths:** 3 En (5) TV V

Potton

TL2248

The Old Coach House, *12 Market Square, Potton, Sandy, Beds, SG19 2NP.* Former C17th coaching inn. Home-cooked food and real ales. **Open:** All year
01767 260221 Mr Cobb **D:** Fr £32.50 **S:** Fr £40.00–£50.00 **Beds:** 2F 4D 4T 4S **Baths:** 11 En TV V cc

BATHROOMS
En = Ensuite
Pr = Private
Sh = Shared

Pulloxhill

TL0633

Tower House B&B, *74 Church Road, Pulloxhill, Bedford, Beds., MK45 5HE.* Overlooking countryside. Quiet, rustic, original watercolours. Fresh flowers. Tasty breakfasts. **Open:** All year (not Xmas)
01525 714818 Mr Lawrence **D:** Fr £25.00–£26.00 **S:** Fr £30.00–£35.00 **Beds:** 1D 2T **Baths:** 3 En (6) TV V

Ravensden

TL0853

Tree-Garth, *Church End, Ravensden, Bedford, MK44 2RP.* Comfortable, warm family home, local pubs, home-made fayre. **Open:** All year (not Xmas/New Year)
01234 771745 (also fax) Mrs Edwards *treegarth@ukonline.co.uk* www.treegarth.co.uk **D:** Fr £22.00–£23.00 **S:** Fr £23.00–£30.00 **Beds:** 1T 1D 1S **Baths:** 1 Sh (12) (5) TV cc

Ridgmont

SP9736

Firs Guest House, *85 High Street, Ridgmont, Bedford, MK43 0TY.* Large, comfortable, family-run guest house. Close to Woburn Estate. **Open:** All year
01525 280279 Mr & Mrs Gladman *firsguesthouse@tiscali.co.uk* **D:** Fr £25.00 **S:** Fr £25.00 **Beds:** 2D 3T 3S (12) TV V

Sandy

TL1748

The Pantiles, *6 Swaden Everton Road, Sandy, Beds, SG19 2DA.* Converted barn in wooded valley overlooking lawns and flower gardens. **Open:** All year (not Xmas/New Year)
01767 680668 *pantiles@breathemail.net* **D:** Fr £25.00 **S:** Fr £35.00 **Beds:** 2D 1T **Baths:** 3 En TV V

Fairlawn Hotel, *70 Bedford Road, Sandy, Beds, SG19 1EP.* Small, friendly. Easy access A1 and main line railway station. **Open:** All year (not Xmas)
01767 680336 D: Fr £24.00–£30.00 **S:** Fr £25.00–£30.00 **Beds:** 1F 2D 2T 3S **Baths:** 2 Pr 1 Sh (10) TV V

Highfield Farm, *Great North Road, Sandy, Beds, SG19 2AQ.* Wonderfully comfortable farmhouse in delightful grounds. Ample safe parking. **Open:** All year
01767 682332 Mrs Codd **Fax: 01767 692503** *margaret@highfield.farm.co.uk* **D:** Fr £25.00–£30.00 **S:** Fr £25.00–£45.00 **Beds:** 2F 2D 2T **Baths:** 3 En 1 Pr 1 Sh (10) **cc**

Silsoe

TL0836

The Old George Hotel, *High Street, Silsoe, Bedford, Beds., MK45 4EP.* Old coaching inn. Village location, large garden, famous fish restaurant. **Open:** All year (not Xmas)
01525 860218 J C Bridge **D:** Fr £24.00–£35.00 **S:** Fr £35.00–£39.00 **Beds:** 5D 1T 1S **Baths:** 2 En 2 Sh (50) **cc**

Totternhoe

SP9821

Country Cottage, *5 Brightwell Avenue, Totternhoe, Dunstable, Beds, LU6 1QT.* Quiet village house in countryside with views of Dunstable Downs. **Open:** All year (not Xmas)
01582 601287 (also fax) Mrs Mardell **D:** Fr £25.00 **S:** Fr £25.00 **Beds:** 1T 1D 1S **Baths:** 2 En 1 Sh (3)

BATHROOMS
En = Ensuite
Pr = Private
Sh = Shared

Woburn

SP9433

11 George Street, *Woburn, Milton Keynes, Bucks, MK17 9PX.* Small, cosy, personally run, Grade II Listed cottage. Very near Woburn Abbey. **Open:** All year
01525 290405 (also fax) Mrs Tough **D:** Fr £20.00 **S:** Fr £20.00 **Beds:** 1D 4F 2T 1S **Baths:** 3 Sh 1 Pr

Please respect a B&B's wishes regarding children, animals and smoking

Berkshire

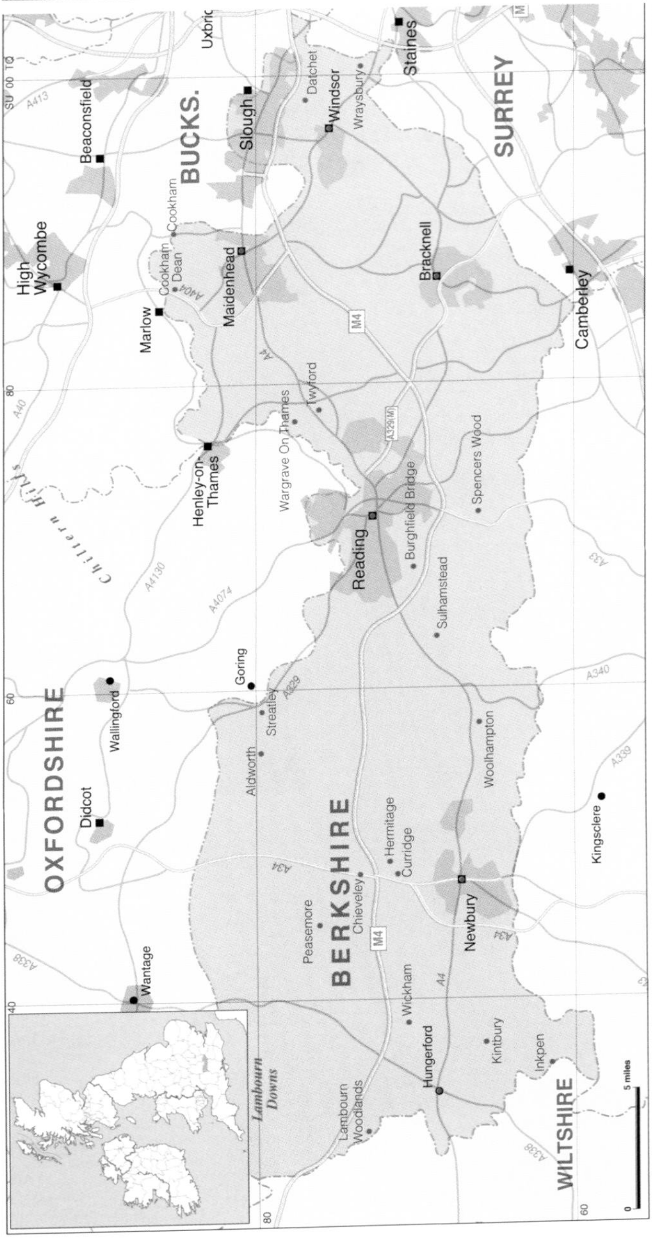

Aldworth

SU5679

Fieldview Cottage, *Aldworth, Reading, Berks, RG8 9SB.* Attractive residence in rural position on Berkshire Downs. Ideal for walking & cycling, close to M4. **Open:** All year (not Xmas/New Year)
01635 578964 Mrs Hunt *host@fieldview.freeserve.co.uk* **D:** Fr £25.00–£30.00 **S:** Fr £25.00–£30.00 **Beds:** 1F 1T 1D 1S **Baths:** 1 En 1 Pr 1 Sh (5)

Bracknell

SU8668

53 Swaledale, *Wildridings, Bracknell, Berks, RG12 7ET.* Near M3 and M4 also near town centre. **Open:** All year (not Xmas/New Year)
01344 421247 T Webber **D:** Fr £25.00 **S:** Fr £25.00 **Beds:** 1T 1S **Baths:** 1 Sh

Burghfield Bridge

SU6870

Kennet Houseboat, *Burghfield Bridge, Reading, Berks, RG30 3RA.* Luxury houseboat on Kennet and Avon Canal, accommodation only. **Open:** All year
0118 957 1060 Mrs Ogden **D:** Fr £20.00 **S:** Fr £20.00 **Beds:** 2D (3)

Chieveley

SU4773

19 Heathfields, *Chieveley, Newbury, Berks, RG20 8TW.* Quietly situated, but near A34/M4, shop, pub. Welcoming & friendly. **Open:** Feb to Dec **Grades:** ETC 3 Diamond
01635 248179 Mrs Wood **Fax: 01635 248799** *ingandco@aol.com* **D:** Fr £22.50–£27.50 **S:** Fr £25.00–£30.00 **Beds:** 1D 1T **Baths:** 1 Pr (3)

The Old Farmhouse, *Downend Lane, Chieveley, Newbury, Berks, RG20 8TN.* Old farmhouse in large gardens. Accommodation in ground floor annexe. **Open:** All year **Grades:** ETC 4 Diamond
01635 248361 & 07970 583373 (M)
Mrs Pallett *palletts@aol.com* **D:** Fr £28.00–£30.00 **S:** Fr £35.00–£38.00 **Beds:** 1F **Baths:** 1 En (4)

Cookham

SU8985 *The Harvester, Two Roses, Bel & The Dragon*

Wylie Cottage, *School Lane, Cookham, Maidenhead, Berks, SL6 9QJ.* Detached Victorian house in Cookham village. **Open:** All year (not Xmas/New Year)
01628 520106 *crowegc@ntlworld.com* **D:** Fr £25.00–£30.00 **S:** Fr £28.00–£40.00 **Beds:** 1T 1D **Baths:** 1 Sh (2)

Cookham Dean

SU8684

Cartlands Cottage, *King's Lane, Cookham Dean, Maidenhead, Berks, SL6 9AY.* Self-contained guest room in garden. Rural, very quiet. **Open:** All year
01628 482196 Mr & Mrs Parkes **D:** Fr £20.00–£27.50 **S:** Fr £23.50–£30.00 **Beds:** 1F **Baths:** 1 Pr (2)

Curridge

SU4871 *Bunk Inn*

Many Trees, *Curridge Road, Curridge, Thatcham, Berks, RG18 9DH.* Quiet, tranquil, perfectly situated near the A34/M4 for North, South, East and West. **Open:** All year (not Xmas/New Year)
01635 200872 Mrs Hendel **D:** Fr £35.00–£50.00 **S:** Fr £25.00–£35.00 **Beds:** 1T 1D 1S (6)

Hermitage

SU5173

The Granary, *Hermitage, Thatcham, Berks, RG18 9SD.* Charming converted barn with large garden in pretty rural hamlet. **Open:** All year (not Xmas/New Year)
01635 200249 (also fax) Mr & Mrs De Lisle-Bush **D:** Fr £20.00–£25.00 **S:** Fr £23.00–£26.00 **Beds:** 1T 1D 1S **Baths:** 1 Sh 1 En (12) (3)

Hungerford

SU3368

Anne's B&B, *59 Priory Avenue, Hungerford, Berks, RG17 0AS.* Family-run. Close to canal and railway. 5 mins M4. **Open:** All year (not Xmas/New Year)
01488 682290 Mrs Whittaker **Fax: 01488 686993** *anne@hungerfordberks.co.uk* www.hungerfordberks.co.uk **D:** Fr £40.00–£50.00 **S:** Fr £20.00–£25.00 **Beds:** 1T 1D 2S **Baths:** 1 En 1 Pr (4)

Plough House, *49 High Street, Hungerford, Berks, RG17 0NE.* Great location plus spacious, comfortable rooms with modern ensuite facilities. **Open:** All year
01488 686008 Mrs Greenslade *michael.greenslade@bt.com* **D:** Fr £25.00–£30.00 **S:** Fr £35.00–£40.00 **Beds:** 2T **Baths:** 2 En

Wilton House, *33 High Street, Hungerford, Berks, RG17 0NF.* Elegant ensuite bedrooms in classic, historic English town house predating 1450. **Open:** All year (not Xmas)
01488 684228 Mrs Welfare **Fax: 01488 685037** *welfares@hotmail.com* **D:** Fr £25.00–£27.50 **S:** Fr £35.00–£38.00 **Beds:** 1D 1T **Baths:** 2 En (8) (3)

Alderborne, *33 Bourne Vale, Hungerford, Berkshire, RG17 0LL.* Modern detached family house overlooking open country. Walking distance shops. **Open:** All year (not Xmas)
01488 683228 & 07808 184156 (M) Mr & Mrs Honeybone *honeybones@hungerford.co.uk* **D:** Fr £17.50–£18.50 **S:** Fr £17.50–£22.50 **Beds:** 2T 1S **Baths:** 1 Pr 1 Sh (5) (3)

Inkpen

SU3764

Beacon House, *Bell Lane, Upper Green, Inkpen, Hungerford, Berks, RG17 9QJ.* **Open:** All year **Grades:** AA 3 Diamond
01488 668640 Mr & Mrs Cave *l.g.cave@classicfm.net* **D:** Fr £25.00 **S:** Fr £25.00 **Beds:** 1T 2S **Baths:** 2 Sh (6)
A warm welcome awaits you at our home, Berks/Wilts/Hants border. Comfortable beds and wonderful home cooking. If the weather is inclement there are plenty of books and an artist's studio where you can try your hand at printmaking.

Kintbury

SU3866

The Forbury, *Crossways, Kintbury, Hungerford, Berks, RG17 9SU.* Extended C17th cottage. Lovely position facing south, overlooking own woodlands. **Open:** All year (not Xmas)
01488 658377 Mr Cubitt **D:** Fr £22.50–£27.50 **S:** Fr £22.50–£25.00 **Beds:** 1T 1S 1F **Baths:** 1 Pr 1 Sh (10)

Lambourn Woodlands

SU3175

Lodge Down, *Lambourn , Hungerford, Berks, RG17 7BJ.* Magnificent house with spacious rooms and extensive garden with woodland. **Open:** All year
01672 540304 (also fax) Mrs Cook **D:** Fr £22.50 **S:** Fr £30.00 **Beds:** 1F 2D 2T **Baths:** 3 En (6)

Maidenhead

SU8781

Laburnham Guest House, *31 Laburnham Road, Maidenhead, Berks, SL6 4DB.* Fine Edwardian house, near town centre, station and M4 motorway. **Open:** All year (not Xmas)
01628 676748 (also fax) Mrs Stevens *rdgs@waitrose.com* **D:** Fr £25.00–£30.00 **S:** Fr £35.00–£50.00 **Beds:** 1F 2D 1T 1S **Baths:** 5 En (5)

Copperfields Guest House, *54 Bath Road, Maidenhead, Berks, SL6 4JY.* Elegant Victorian Guest House **Open:** All year (not Xmas/New Year)
01628 674941 Mrs Lindsay **D:** Fr £27.00–£30.00 **S:** Fr £35.00–£40.00 **Beds:** 1T 4S **Baths:** 2 En 1 Sh (5)

Hillcrest Guest House, *19 Craufurd Rise, Maidenhead, Berks, SL6 7LR.* Near to town centre, Legoland, Henley-on-Thames, Windsor and Shire Horse Centre. **Open:** All year
01628 620086 & 01628 623572 Mrs Colligan **Fax: 01628 623572** *clifton@aroram.freeserve.co.uk* www.cliftonguesthouse.co.uk **D:** Fr £35.00–£60.00 **S:** Fr £35.00–£60.00 **Beds:** 2F 6T 7D 5S **Baths:** 10 En 3 Sh (20) cc

Newbury

SU4767

The Old Farmhouse, *Downend Lane, Chieveley, Newbury, Berks, RG20 8TN.* Old farmhouse in large gardens. Accommodation in ground floor annexe. **Open:** All year **Grades:** ETC 4 Diamond
01635 248361 & 07970 583373 (M) Mrs Pallett *palletts@aol.com* **D:** Fr £28.00–£30.00 **S:** Fr £35.00–£38.00 **Beds:** 1F **Baths:** 1 En (4)

15 Shaw Road, *Newbury, Berks, RG14 1HG.* Late Georgian terraced house near town centre, rail and canal. **Open:** All year
01635 44962 Mrs Curtis **D:** Fr £18.00–£20.00 **S:** Fr £18.00–£20.00 **Beds:** 1D 1T **Baths:** 1 Sh

Paddock House, *17 Derby Road, Newbury, Berks, RG14 6DA.* Situated near town centre. Conveniently close to main Basingstoke road. **Open:** All year (not Xmas/New Year)
01635 47444 Mr & Mrs Liddell *hotelhardel@claranet.com* **D:** Fr £20.00–£25.00 **S:** Fr £22.00–£28.00 **Beds:** 2T 2S **Baths:** 2 Sh

Laurel House, *157 Andover Road, Newbury, RG14 6NB.* A warm welcome awaits you in our delightful Georgian house. **Open:** All year (not Xmas)
01635 35931 Mr & Mrs Dixon **D:** Fr £18.00 **S:** Fr £18.00 **Beds:** 1D 1T **Baths:** 1 Sh (2)

125 Greenham Road, *Newbury, RG14 7JE.* Close to Newbury centre. Victorian home. Warm welcome. **Open:** All year
01635 47377 Mr & Mrs Kirke *a.kirke@cwcom.net* **D:** Fr £28.00 **S:** Fr £20.00–£30.00 **Beds:** 1D 1S **Baths:** 1 Pr 1 Sh

Peasemore

SU4576

Peasemore House, *Peasemore, Newbury, Berks, RG20 7JH.* Traditional family farmhouse with beautiful gardens set in arable downland. **Open:** All year (not Xmas/New Year)
01635 248505 (also fax) Mrs Brown *peasemorebrowns@hotmail.com* **D:** Fr £25.00 **S:** Fr £25.00–£30.00 **Beds:** 1T 1D **Baths:** 2 En

Reading

SU7173

Dittisham Guest House, *63 Tilehurst Road, Reading, Berks, RG30 2JL.* Centrally located quiet Georgian house, good public transport, motorway connections. **Open:** All year **Grades:** ETC 3 Diamond
0118 956 9483 Mr Harding *dittishamgh@aol.com* **D:** Fr £22.50–£30.00 **S:** Fr £27.50–£35.00 **Beds:** 2D 1T 2S **Baths:** 3 En 2 Sh cc

Donnington House B&B, *82-86 London Road, Reading, Berks, RG1 5AU.* Independently-run hotel which is centrally located near town centre. **Open:** All year (not Xmas/New Year)
0118 926 5258 Fax: 0118 926 4593 *reservations@comfortlodge.freeserve.co.uk* **D:** Fr £40.00–£50.00 **S:** Fr £75.00–£85.00 **Beds:** 2F 10T 9D 14S **Baths:** 17 En 5 Sh cc

St Hilda's, *24 Castle Crescent, Reading, Berkshire, RG1 6AG.* Quiet Victorian home near town centre. All rooms have colour TVs & fridges. **Open:** All year
0118 961 0329 Mr & Mrs Hubbard **D:** Fr £46.00–£52.00 **S:** Fr £25.00 **Beds:** 3F 2T **Baths:** 3 Sh (1)

Crescent Hotel, *35 Coley Avenue, Reading, Berks, RG30 3UN.* Near town centre & Oracle. All rooms ensuite. Special weekend rates. **Open:** All year (not Xmas/New Year) **Grades:** ETC 3 Diamond
0118 950 7980 Fax: 0118 957 4299 D: Fr £60.00–£75.00 **S:** Fr £40.00–£65.00 **Beds:** 2F 10T 3D 4S **Baths:** 14 En 1 Sh (18) cc

Greystoke Guest House, *10 Greystoke Road, Caversham, Reading, Berks, RG4 5EL.* Private home in quiet road, TV & tea/coffee making in lounge. **Open:** All year (not Xmas)
0118 947 5784 Mrs Tyler **D:** Fr £25.00–£30.00 **S:** Fr £28.00–£35.00 **Beds:** 1D 2S **Baths:** 1 Sh (3)

Spencers Wood

SU7166 *Swan Inn, Farriers' Arms*

Meadowview B and B, *Basingstoke Road, Spencers Wood, Reading, Berks, RG7 1AL.* Homely, welcoming country semi, 1/2 mile M4/J11. Garden view. **Open:** All year (not Xmas/New Year)
0118 988 3270 Mrs Patman **D:** Fr £25.00–£30.00 **S:** Fr £26.00–£30.00 **Beds:** 1D 1S **Baths:** 1 Sh (2)

Streatley

SU5980

Pennyfield, *The Coombe, Streatley, Reading, Berkshire, RG8 9QT.* Pretty village house with attractive terraced garden. Friendly, welcoming hosts. **Open:** All year (not Xmas/New Year)
01491 872048 (also fax) *mandrvanstone@hotmail.com* **D:** Fr £22.50–£25.00 **S:** Fr £22.50–£25.00 **Beds:** 1T 2D **Baths:** 2 En 1 Sh (4)

Sulhamstead

SU6368

The Old Manor, *Whitehouse Green, Sulhamstead, Reading, Berks, RG7 4EA.*
Open: All year (not Xmas/New Year)
0118 983 2423 Fax: 0118 983 6262 *rags-r@theoldmanor.fsbusines.co.uk* **D:** Fr £35.00–£50.00 **S:** Fr £35.00–£50.00 **Beds:** 2D **Baths:** 2 En (4)
C17th manor house with very large and beautiful beamed bedrooms. Every modern convenience in the ensuite bathrooms. Elegance and tranquillity with superb meals for the discerning guest.

Twyford

SU7975

Copper Beeches, *Bath Road, Kiln Green, Twyford, Reading, Berks, RG10 9UT.* Quiet house in large gardens with tennis court, warm welcome. **Open:** All year
0118 940 2929 (also fax) Mrs Gorecki **D:** Fr £22.50–£25.00 **S:** Fr £28.00–£35.00 **Beds:** 3F 4T 1D 1S **Baths:** 1 En 3 Sh (3) (14)

Somewhere To Stay, *c/o Loddon Acres, Bath Road, Twyford, Reading, Berks, RG10 9RU.* Self-contained, modern, detached ensuite accommodation. Full facilities. Lovely gardens. **Open:** All year
0118 934 5880 (also fax) R Fisher *reservations@somewhere-tostay.com* www.somewhere-tostay.com **D:** Fr £24.50–£29.00 **S:** Fr £39.00–£49.00 **Beds:** 1F 1D 1T 1S **Baths:** 3 En 1 Pr (6)

Wargrave-on-Thames

SU7978

Windy Brow, *204 Victoria Road, Wargrave-on-Thames, Reading, Berks, RG10 8AJ.* Victorian detached house, close M4/M40, 1 mile A4, 6 miles Reading & Maidenhead. **Open:** All year (not Xmas/New Year)
0118 940 3336 Mrs Carver **Fax: 0118 940 1260** *heathcar@aol.com* **D:** Fr £27.50–£35.00 **S:** Fr £37.00–£49.00 **Beds:** 1D 2T 2S **Baths:** 1 En 2 Sh (5)

Wickham

SU3971

St Swithins B & B, *3 St Swithins Close, Wickham, Newbury, Berks, RG20 8HJ.* A warm welcome awaits you in this home in outstanding countryside. **Open:** All year
01488 657566 & 07979 014634 (M) Mrs Edwards **Fax: 0870 1693325** *r.edwards@iee.org* **D:** Fr £20.00–£25.00 **S:** Fr £25.00–£28.00 **Beds:** 1T 1S **Baths:** 1 Pr (2)

Windsor

SU9676

Belmont House, *64 Bolton Road, Windsor, Berks, SL4 3JL.* **Open:** All year
01753 860860 Fax: 01753 830330 *bbs@orange.net* **D:** Fr £50.00–£55.00 **S:** Fr £45.00–£50.00 **Beds:** 1T 3D (4)
Elegant, comfortable & very friendly B&B overlooking Windsor Great Park. All rooms are ensuite & recently refurbished to a very high standard. 4 Diamonds award by Tourist Board inspections. Separate apartment with full office facilities in the town centre also available.

All details shown are as supplied by B&B owners in Autumn 2002

RATES

D = Price range per person sharing in a double or twin room

S = Price range for a single room

Allbrown House, *15 Princess Avenue, Windsor, Berks, SL4 3LU.* **Open:** All year **01760 441700** Mrs Blandford **Fax: 01760 440440** *info@b-and-b.uk.com* www.b-and-b.uk.com **D:** Fr £25.00–£40.00 **S:** Fr £25.00–£30.00 **Beds:** 1F 2T D 3S **Baths:** 2 Sh (9) cc

5 mins' walk Windsor, 1 min for bus to Legoland and London, mainline station to Waterloo 10 mins walk. Accommodation can be arranged to suit individual parties or family units. TV, lounge, open kitchen policy for the making of snacks 24 hours.

Elansey, *65 Clifton Rise, Windsor, Berks, SL4 5SX.* Modern, quiet, comfortable house. Garden, patio, Excellent breakfasts, highly recommended. **Open:** All year (not Xmas)
01753 864438 Mrs Forbutt **D:** Fr £25.00–£30.00 **S:** Fr £25.00–£35.00 **Beds:** 1D 1T 1S **Baths:** 1 En 1 Sh (3)

Langton House, *46 Alma Road, Windsor, Berks, SL4 3HA.* Victorian house, quiet tree-lined road, 5 minutes walk to town & castle. **Open:** All year (not Xmas)
01753 858299 (also fax) Paul & Sonja Fogg *bookings@langtonhouse.co.uk* www.langtonhouse.co.uk **D:** Fr £35.00–£37.00 **S:** Fr £55.00–£60.00 **Beds:** 2D 1T **Baths:** 2 En 1 Pr (2)

The Andrews, *77 Whitehorse Road, Windsor, Berks, SL4 4PG.* Modern, comfortable private house. **Open:** All year (not Xmas)
01753 866803 Mrs Andrews **D:** Fr £18.00–£22.50 **S:** Fr £23.00–£25.00 **Beds:** 1D 2T **Baths:** 2 Sh (5) (3)

Jean's, *1 Stovell Road, Windsor, Berks, SL4 5JB.* Quiet comfortable self-contained ground floor flat comprising 2 ensuite bedrooms. **Open:** All year
01753 852055 Ms Sumner **Fax: 01753 842932** *jeanlsumner@aol.com* **D:** Fr £25.00 **S:** Fr £50.00 **Beds:** 1D 1T **Baths:** 2 En (2)

The Laurells, *22 Dedworth Road, Windsor, Berks, SL4 5AY.* Pretty Victorian house 3/4 mile town centre. Heathrow 20 minutes. **Open:** All year (not Xmas)
01753 855821 Mrs Joyce **D:** Fr £22.00–£22.50 **S:** Fr £25.00–£30.00 **Beds:** 2T (5)

62 Queens Road, *Windsor, Berks, SL4 3BH.* Recommended, quiet. 10 mins walk castle/station. Large ground floor family room. **Open:** All year
01753 866036 (also fax) Mrs Hughes **D:** Fr £22.50–£25.00 **S:** Fr £30.00–£35.00 **Beds:** 1F 1D **Baths:** 2 En (1) 3

Woolhampton

SU5766

Bridge Cottage, *Station Road, Woolhampton, Reading, Berks, RG7 5SF.* Beautiful 300 year-old riverside home with secluded cottage garden. **Open:** All year (not Xmas/New Year)
01189 713138 Mrs Thornely **Fax: 01189 714331** *jthornely@talk21.com* **D:** Fr £28.00–£30.00 **S:** Fr £32.00–£36.00 **Beds:** 1D 1T 3S **Baths:** 2 En 1 Sh

Wraysbury

TQ0073

Honeysuckle Cottage, *61 Fairfield Approach, Wraysbury, Staines, TW19 5DR.* Picturesque cottage in the historic Thames-side village of Wraysbury. Excellent country pubs. **Open:** All year (not Xmas)
01784 482519 Mrs Vogel **Fax: 01784 482305** *B&B@berks.force9.co.uk* www.berks.force9.co.uk **D:** Fr £22.50–£27.50 **S:** Fr £30.00–£40.00 **Beds:** 2F 1D 1T 1S **Baths:** 4 En 1 Pr (3) (8) cc

Great Kimble

SP8205

The Swan, *Grave Lane, Great Kimble, Aylesbury, HP17 9TR.* Friendly Real Ale country inn close to historic Ridgeway walk. **Open:** All year
01844 275288 Mr Woolnough **Fax: 01494 837312 D:** Fr £25.00–£35.00 **S:** Fr £35.00–£45.00 **Beds:** 1F 2T 1D **Baths:** 4 En P (25) TV V cc

Great Kingshill

SU8798

Hatches Farm, *Hatches Lane, Great Kingshill, High Wycombe, Bucks, HP15 6DS.* Quiet, comfortable farmhouse. Rooms overlooking garden. Easy reach of Oxford/Windsor. **Open:** All year (not Xmas)
01494 713125 Mrs Davies **Fax: 01494 714666 D:** Fr £16.50–£17.50 **S:** Fr £22.00 **Beds:** 1D 1T **Baths:** 1 Sh (12) P (6)

Haddenham

SP7408

Cover Point, *19 The Croft, Haddenham, Aylesbury, Bucks, HP17 8AS.* Free transport to Ridgeway and Thames long distance paths. **Open:** All year (not Xmas)
01844 290093 Mrs Collins *maplegins@aol.com* **D:** Fr £20.00–£25.00 **S:** Fr £25.00–£30.00 **Beds:** 1F **Baths:** 1 En P TV

Hanslope

SP8046

Woad Farm, *Tathall End, Hanslope, Milton Keynes, Bucks, MK19 7NE.* Situated on edge of village, large garden, tennis court. Milton Keynes & Northampton accessible. **Open:** All year
01908 510985 (also fax) Mr & Mrs Stacey *mail@srahstacey.freeserve.co.uk* **D:** Fr £22.00–£24.00 **S:** Fr £22.00–£25.00 **Beds:** 2D 1T **Baths:** 3 Sh P TV V

Haversham

SP8243

The Bungalow, *The Crescent, Haversham, Milton Keynes, Bucks., MK19 7AW.* Village location within six minutes drive from central Milton Keynes. **Open:** All year
01908 311883 D: Fr £18.00–£20.00 **S:** Fr £18.00–£20.00 **Beds:** 2F 1T 1S P (2) TV

High Wycombe

SU8693

The Masons Arms, *Saffron Road, High Wycombe, Bucks, HP13 6AB.* Walking distance from town centre, train centre. Large car park opposite. **Open:** All year
01494 452204 (also fax) D: Fr £22.50 **S:** Fr £25.00 **Beds:** 5T 3S **Baths:** 3 Sh (10) P TV V

Harfa House, *Station Road, High Wycombe, Bucks, HP13 6AD.* **Open:** All year
01494 529671 & 07956 984321 (M) Mrs Foster-Brown **Fax: 01494 529671** *irena@harfahouse.co.uk* www.harfahouse.co.uk **D:** Fr £17.50–£25.00 **S:** Fr £20.00–£25.00 **Beds:** 1T 2S **Baths:** 1 Sh P TV
Private, self-contained annexe to Victorian house. Comfortable, pleasant rooms with fridge and microwave. Convenient for town centre, bus, railway stations. 30 minutes to London. Excellent location for touring lovely English countryside, Marlow, Oxford, Henley, Windsor. Good pubs, restaurants nearby.

Iver Heath

TQ0282

Oaklands, *Bangors Road South, Iver Heath, Slough, Bucks, SL10 0BB.* Large family house convenient for Heathrow, Windsor, Uxbridge and Slough. **Open:** All year (not Xmas)
01753 653005 Mrs Fowler **Fax: 01753 653003 D:** Fr £20.00 **S:** Fr £20.00–£25.00 **Beds:** 1F 1D 2T 1S **Baths:** 1 En 2 Sh P (4) TV

Jordans

SU9791

Old Jordans, *Jordans Lane, Jordans, Beaconsfield, Buckinghamshire, HP9 2SW.* Historic venue in large grounds. Traditional food and excellent hospitality. **Open:** All year
01494 874586 Fax: 01494 875657 *reception@oldjordans.org.uk* oldjordans.org.uk **D:** Fr £25.00–£31.00 **S:** Fr £31.00–£49.00 **Beds:** 1F 3T 9D 11S **Baths:** 15 En 4 Sh P V cc

Kingsey

SP7406

Foxhill, *Kingsey, Aylesbury, Bucks, HP17 8LZ.* Spacious and comfortable farmhouse with beautiful garden in rural setting. **Open:** Mar to Nov
01844 291650 (also fax) N M D Hooper **D:** Fr £25.00–£26.00 **S:** Fr £26.00–£29.00 **Beds:** 1D 2T **Baths:** 1 Sh (8) P (20) TV V

Little Chalfont

SU9997

Holmdale, *Cokes Lane, Little Chalfont, Chalfont St. Giles, Amersham, HP8 4TX.* Comfortable cottage in the Chilterns; easy access to London on trains. **Open:** All year
01494 762527 Fax: 01494 764701 *judy@holmdalebb.freeserve.co.uk* www.smoothhound.co.uk/hotels/holmdale.html **D:** Fr £30.00–£35.00 **S:** Fr £45.00–£50.00 **Beds:** 1D/F 1T 1S **Baths:** 3 En P (2) TV V

Marlow

SU8586

Merrie Hollow, *Seymour Court Hill, Marlow, Bucks, SL7 3DE.* **Open:** All year **Grades:** ETC 3 Diamond
01628 485663 (also fax) Mr Wells **D:** Fr £20.00–£25.00 **S:** Fr £30.00–£35.00 **Beds:** 1D 1T **Baths:** 1 Sh P (4) TV V
Secluded quiet country cottage in large garden 150 yds off B482 Marlow to Stokenchurch road, easy access to M4 and M25, 35 mins from Heathrow and Oxford, private off-road car parking.

Acha Pani, *Bovingdon Green, Marlow, Bucks, SL7 2JL.* Quiet location, easy access Thames Footpath, Chilterns, Windsor, London, Heathrow. **Open:** All year
01628 483435 (also fax) Mrs Cowling *mary@achapani.freeserve.co.uk* **D:** Fr £20.00 **S:** Fr £20.00 **Beds:** 1D 1T 1S **Baths:** 1 En 1 Sh (10) P (3) TV V

Glade End Guest House, *2 Little Marlow Road, Marlow, Bucks, SL7 1HD.* Delightful detached house, 3 minute walk from central Marlow and train. **Open:** All year **Grades:** ETC 4 Diamond
01628 471334 Mrs Peperell *sue@gladeend.com* www.gladeend.com **D:** Fr £40.00–£50.00 **S:** Fr £55.00–£80.00 **Beds:** 3D 3T 1S **Baths:** 1 Sh 4 En (10) P (7) TV

Sunnyside, *Munday Dean, Marlow, Bucks, SL7 3BU.* Comfortable, friendly, family home in Area of Outstanding Natural Beauty. **Open:** All year
01628 485701 Mrs O'Connor *ruthandtom@tinyworld.co.uk* **D:** Fr £17.50 **S:** Fr £20.00 **Beds:** 2D 1T **Baths:** 1 Sh P (5) TV

Milton Keynes

SP8636

Furtho Manor Farm, *Old Stratford, Milton Keynes, Bucks, MK19 6BA.* Dairy and arable farm, 10 mins to central Milton Keynes. **Open:** All year (not Xmas)
01908 542139 (also fax) Mrs Sansome *dsansome@farming.co.uk* **D:** Fr £20.00–£22.00 **S:** Fr £20.00–£25.00 **Beds:** 1D 2T **Baths:** 2 Sh P (6) TV V

Mill Farm, *Gayhurst, Newport Pagnell, Bucks, MK16 8LT.* C17th farmhouse on working farm. Fishing and hard tennis court available. **Open:** All year **Grades:** ETC 3 Diamond, AA 3 Diamond
01908 611489 (also fax) K Adams *adamsmillfarm@aol.com* **D:** Fr £20.00–£25.00 **S:** Fr £20.00–£25.00 **Beds:** 1F 1T 1D 1S **Baths:** 1 En 2 Sh P TV

Vignoble, *2 Medland, Woughton Park, Milton Keynes, Bucks, MK6 3BH.* Quiet, secluded, comfortable private house. **Open:** All year **Grades:** ETC 3 Diamond
01908 666804 Mrs Evans **Fax: 01908 666626** *vignoblegh@aol.com* **D:** Fr £24.00–£30.00 **S:** Fr £30.00–£48.00 **Beds:** 1S 1D 2T **Baths:** 1 En 1 Sh (7) P (3) TV V

Planning a longer stay? Always ask for any special rates

Kingfishers, *9 Rylstone Close, Heelands, Milton Keynes, Bucks, MK13 7QT.* Modern luxurious house. Near central Milton Keynes and station. **Open:** All year
01908 310231 Mrs Botterill **Fax: 01908 318601** *sheila-derek@m-keynes.freeserve.co.uk*
D: Fr £20.00 **S:** Fr £23.00–£28.00 **Beds:** 1F 1D 1S **Baths:** 2 En 1 Pr (2) (4)

Rovers Return, *49 Langcliffe Drive, Milton Keynes, Bucks, MK13 7LA.* Warm welcoming modern chalet-type house in tree-lined courtyard adjacent to Redway Cycle Track. **Open:** All year (not Xmas/New Year)
01908 310465 E Levins **D:** Fr £20.00–£25.00 **S:** Fr £23.00–£25.00 **Beds:** 1T 1S 1D **Baths:** 2 Sh (10)

Mursley

SP8128 *Swan Inn, Green Man*

Richmond Hill Farm, *Stewkley Lane, Mursley, Milton Keynes, Bucks, MK17 0JD.* Spacious, tranquil setting room overlooking landscaped gardens. 8 miles from the M1. **Open:** All year
01296 720385 (also fax) S J Oldham **D:** Fr £25.00 **S:** Fr £25.00–£28.00 **Beds:** 2T **Baths:** 2 Pr (10)

Naphill

SU8596

Wood-peckers, *244 Main Road, Naphill, High Wycombe, Bucks, HP14 4CX.* **Open:** All year
01494 563728 Mrs Brand *angela.brand@virgin.net* www.visitbritain.com **D:** £23.50–£25.00 **S:** £25.00 **Beds:** 1T 1D 1S **Baths:** 2 En 1 Pr (4)
Fully modernised cottage in heart of Chiltern Hills. Close to London, Windsor, Henley, Oxford, Heathrow, good public transport. Wonderful walks and scenery with places of historic interest nearby. Also can be rented as self-catering unit (6-8 people, prices on request).

Newport Pagnell

SP8743

Rectory Farm, *North Crawley, Newport Pagnell, Bucks, MK16 9HH.* Warm welcome on family farm. Convenient for Milton Keynes & Bedfordshire. **Open:** All year
01234 391213 (also fax) E Hobbs **D:** Fr £20.00 **S:** Fr £20.00–£25.00 **Beds:** 1T 1D **Baths:** 1 Sh (7) (4)

Mill Farm, *Gayhurst, Newport Pagnell, Bucks, MK16 8LT.* C17th farmhouse on working farm. Fishing and hard tennis court available. **Open:** All year **Grades:** ETC 3 Diamond, AA 3 Diamond
01908 611489 (also fax) K Adams *adamsmillfarm@aol.com* **D:** Fr £20.00–£25.00 **S:** Fr £20.00–£25.00 **Beds:** 1F 1T 1D 1S **Baths:** 1 En 2 Sh

The Clitheroes, *5 Walnut Close, Newport Pagnell, Bucks, MK16 8JH.* Homely atmosphere, comfortable rooms, full English breakfast, off-road parking. **Open:** All year (not Xmas)
01908 611643 (also fax) *shirleyderek.clitheroe@btinternet.com* **D:** Fr £19.00 **S:** Fr £22.00 **Beds:** 1D 1T 2S **Baths:** 2 Sh (5)

Olney

SP8851

Colchester House, *26 High Street, Olney, Bucks, MK46 4BB.* Georgian town house in market town near pubs and restaurants. **Open:** All year (not Xmas)
01234 712602 Fax: 01234 240564 *blenkinsops@compuserve.com* **D:** Fr £25.00 **S:** Fr £25.00 **Beds:** 2D 1T **Baths:** 2 En 1 Sh (4)

Poundon

SP6425

Manor Farm, *Poundon, Bicester, Oxon, OX6 0BB.* Extremely comfortable and welcoming. Delicious breakfasts and lovely surroundings. **Open:** All year (not Xmas)
01869 277212 Mrs Collett **Fax: 01869 277166** **D:** Fr £25.00–£30.00 **S:** Fr £25.00–£30.00 **Beds:** 1F 1D 1S **Baths:** 2 Sh (10)

Quainton

SP7419

Woodlands Farmhouse, *EdgcottRoad, Quainton, Aylesbury, Bucks, HP22 4DE.* C18th farmhouse offering peaceful accommodation in 11 acres of ground. **Open:** All year
01296 770225 Mrs Creed **D:** Fr £25.00–£30.00 **S:** Fr £25.00–£30.00 **Beds:** 1f 2T 1D **Baths:** 4 En (10)

Please respect a B&B's wishes regarding children, animals and smoking

St Leonards

SP9006

Field Cottage, *St Leonards, Tring, Herts, HP23 6NS.* Pretty secluded cottage near the Ridgeway & convenient for Wendover, Chesham & Great Missenden. **Open:** All year (not Xmas/New Year)
01494 837602 Mr & Mrs Jepson **D:** Fr £25.00–£30.00 **S:** Fr £25.00–£35.00 **Beds:** 1D 1T 1S (12) (4)

Stokenchurch

SU7695

Gibbons Farm Ltd., *Bigmore Lane, Stokenchurch, High Wycombe, Bucks, HP14 3UR.* **Open:** All year
01494 482385 Mrs McKelvey **Fax: 01494 485400** *gibbonsfarm@tiscali.co.uk* **D:** Fr £25.00–£30.00 **S:** Fr £25.00–£30.00 **Beds:** 2F 1D 1T 4S **Baths:** 6 En 1 Sh (20)
Traditional farm offering accommodation in converted barn. Set in courtyard surrounded by open countryside, this family-run B&B offers a warm and friendly welcome with Marlow and Oxford within half-hour drive, situated within 5 mins of M40, London is easily accessible.

Stony Stratford

SP7940

Fegans View, *119 High Street, Stony Stratford, Milton Keynes, Bucks, MK11 1AT.* C18th comfortable town house near local amenities. **Open:** All year
01908 562128 & 01908 564246 Mrs Levitt **D:** Fr £19.00–£21.00 **S:** Fr £22.00–£30.00 **Beds:** 3T 1S **Baths:** 1 En 2 Sh (1) (5)

Wendover

SP8608

46 Lionel Avenue, *Wendover, Aylesbury, Bucks, HP22 6LP.* Family home. Lounge, conservatory, garden. English/vegetarian breakfasts. Tea/coffee always available. **Open:** All year (not Xmas/New Year)
01296 623426 Mr & Mrs MacDonald **D:** Fr £24.00 **S:** Fr £25.00 **Beds:** 1T 2S **Baths:** 1 Sh (3)

Whitchurch

SP8020

3 Little London, *Whitchurch, Aylesbury, Bucks, HP22 4LE.* Quiet location near Waddesdon Manor; 1 hour London, Stratford. **Open:** All year (not Xmas)
01296 641409 Mrs Gurr **D:** Fr £22.00–£25.00 **S:** Fr £22.00–£25.00 **Beds:** 1D 1T 1S **Baths:** 2 Sh (3)

Winslow

SP7627

Tuckey Farm, *Winslow, Buckingham, Bucks, MK18 3ND.* C18th farmhouse, convenient for Stowe, Waddesdon Manor, Claydon House, Silverstone. **Open:** All year (not Xmas)
01296 713208 Mrs Haynes **D:** Fr £20.00 **S:** Fr £20.00 **Beds:** 1T 2S **Baths:** 1 Sh (5) P (4) TV

The Congregational Church, *15 Horn Street, Winslow, Buckingham, MK18 3AP.* Victorian church turned into fascinating home in old town centre. **Open:** All year **Grades:** ETC 3 Diamond
01296 715717 (also fax) Mrs Hood **D:** Fr £22.50 **S:** Fr £30.00 **Beds:** 1D 1T 1S **Baths:** 2 Sh TV V

The White Cottage, *Verney Junction, Buckingham, MK18 2JZ.* Lovely country house in small hamlet. Super breakfasts, log fires. Business guests only. **Open:** Jan to Dec
01296 714416 Mrs Gilchrist **D:** Fr £20.00 **S:** Fr £20.00 **Beds:** 2D 1S **Baths:** 1 Pr P (3) TV X V

National Grid References given are for villages, towns and cities – not for individual houses

B&B owners may vary rates – be sure to check when booking

Woughton Park

SP8737

Vignoble, *2 Medland, Woughton Park, Milton Keynes, Bucks, MK6 3BH.* Quiet, secluded, comfortable private house. **Open:** All year **Grades:** ETC 3 Diamond
01908 666804 Mrs Evans **Fax: 01908 666626** *vignoblegh@aol.com* **D:** Fr £24.00–£30.00 **S:** Fr £30.00–£48.00 **Beds:** 1S 1D 2T **Baths:** 1 En 1 Sh (7) P (3) TV V

Cambridgeshire

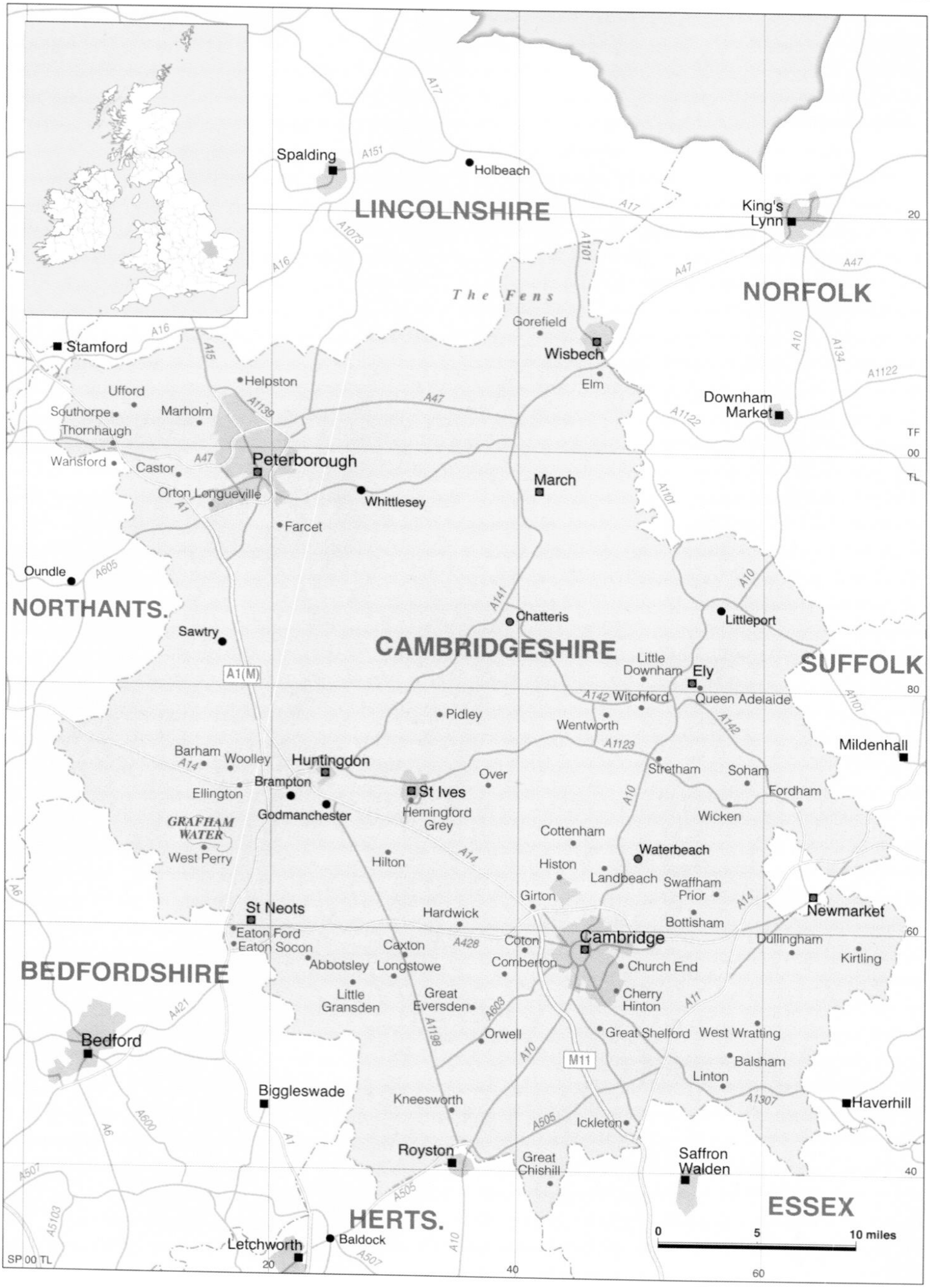

Abbotsley

TL2256

Rectory Farm, *High Street, Abbotsley, St Neots, Cambs, PE19 6UE.* Quiet Victorian farm house. Large gardens and ample private parking. Short stroll from centre of picturesque village with local pubs serving good food. Local countryside walks. Cambridge, Bedford, Huntingdon 30 mins' drive; London 1 hour by train from St Neots. **Open:** All year (not Xmas)
01767 677282 (also fax) Mr Hipwell **D:** Fr £20.00 **S:** Fr £20.00 **Beds:** 1D 2T 1S **Baths:** 1 Sh (6)

Balsham

TL5849

The Garden End, *10 West Wratting Road, Balsham, Cambridge, CB1 6DX.* Self-contained ground floor suite - children / pets welcome all year. **Open:** All year
01223 894021 (also fax) Mrs Gladstone **D:** Fr £18.00 **S:** Fr £20.00 **Beds:** 1F **Baths:** 1 En 1 Pr (2)

Barham

TL1374

Ye Olde Globe and Chequers, *The Village, Barham, Huntingdon, Cambs, PE28 5AB.* Former Victorian village inn offering true country hospitality in idyllic rural setting. Tastefully furnished rooms with excellent facilities. Easy access A1/A14 via Junction 18. Ideally situated for Cambridge, Ely, Huntingdon, Northampton, Thrapston, Peterborough. With Grafham Water closeby. Colour brochure available. **Open:** All year (not Xmas/New Year)
01480 890247 & 07860 268524 (M) Mrs Grove-Price *cheryll@globeandchequers.fsnet.co.uk* www.globeandchequers.fsnet.co.uk **D:** Fr £21.00–£22.50 **S:** Fr £28.00–£32.00 **Beds:** 1F 1T 1D **Baths:** 1 En 1 Sh (3)

Bottisham

TL5460

27 Beechwood Avenue, *Bottisham, Cambridge, CB5 9BG.* Modern house backing farmland near Cambridge city and Newmarket racecourse. **Open:** All year (not Xmas)
01223 811493 Mrs Knight **Fax: 0870 1312396** *mike.knight@home.cam.net.uk* **D:** Fr £22.50–£25.00 **S:** Fr £25.00 **Beds:** 1D 2T 1S **Baths:** 1 Sh (12) (3)

Cambridge

TL4658

Dykelands Guest House, *157 Mowbray Road, Cambridge, CB1 7SP.* **Open:** All year
01223 244300 Mrs Tweddell **Fax: 01223 566746** *dykelands@fsbdial.co.uk* www.dykelands.com **D:** Fr £20.00–£25.00 **S:** Fr £28.00–£30.00 **Beds:** 3F 3D 2T 1S **Baths:** 7 En 1 Sh (6) cc
Lovely detached guest house on south side of city. Easy access from M11 and A14, yet only 1.75 miles from historic city centre. Private parking. Spacious, well-furnished, comfortable rooms, 2 on ground floor, most ensuite. Good breakfasts, English/vegetarian.

Arbury Lodge, *82 Arbury Road, Cambridge, CB42JE.* **Open:** All year (not Xmas/New Year) **Grades:** ETC 3 Diamond
01223 364319 A J Celentano **Fax: 01223 566988** *arburylodge@ntlworld.com* www.guesthousecambridge.com **D:** Fr £23.00–£60.00 **S:** Fr £30.00–£50.00 **Beds:** 1F 2T 3D 1S **Baths:** 4 En 3 Sh (8)
A comfortable family-run guest house where we pride ourselves in offering excellent service, good home cooking, cleanliness and a friendly atmosphere. We are conveniently situated about 1.5 miles north of the city centre with easy access to A14/M11.

78 Milton Road, *Cambridge, CB4 1LA.* **Open:** All year **01223 323555** Mr Chapman **Fax: 01223 236078** *victoriahouse@ntlworld.com* www.smoothhound.co.uk/hotels/victori3.html **D:** Fr £19.00–£30.00 **S:** Fr £22.00–£49.00 **Beds:** 1F 1D 1T **Baths:** 1 En 1 Pr 1 Sh (4) cc
Victorian house - all rooms have TV, tea and coffee-making facilities, ensuite private or shared facilities. Ideally situated for city centre, colleges and River Cam. Easy access to A14 and M11. Self-catering apartments also available.

Tudor Cottage, *292 Histon Road, Cambridge, CB4 3HF.* **Open:** All year **Grades:** ETC 4 Diamond
01223 565212 & 07775 667512 (M) Mrs Celentano **Fax: 01223 565660** *tudor.cottage@ntlworld.com* **D:** Fr £25.00–£30.00 **S:** Fr £30.00–£35.00 **Beds:** 1D 1S **Baths:** 1 En 1 Sh (4)
Comfortable friendly Tudor-style cottage situated within walking distance of city centre and colleges. Ensuite or shared facilities, central heating, colour TV, tea/coffee making facilities, excellent food and friendly personal service, off street parking easy access to A14/M11.

Hamilton Hotel, *156/158 Chesterton Road, Cambridge, CB4 1DA.* **Open:** All year **Grades:** ETC 3 Diamond
01223 365664 Fax: 01223 314866 *hamiltonhotel@talk21.com* www.hamiltonhotelcambridge.co.uk **D:** Fr £30.00–£35.00 **S:** Fr £40.00–£50.00 **Beds:** 4F 8T 8D 5S **Baths:** 20 En 2 Sh (20) cc
Small hotel less than 1 mile from centre of city. Easy access from A14 & M11. Most rooms have ensuite shower & toilet. All rooms have TV, direct dial telephone & hospitality tray. 7 ground floor bedrooms. Large car park.

Home From Home, *78-80 Milton Road, Cambridge, Cambs, CB4 1LA.* Centrally located with access M11, A14 and Science Park. **Open:** All year **Grades:** ETC 4 Diamond
01223 323555 & 07740 594306 Mrs Fasano **Fax: 01223 236078** *homefromhome@tesco.net* www.accommodationcambridge.co.uk **D:** Fr £25.00–£30.00 **S:** Fr £40.00–£50.00 **Beds:** 1F 2D 1T **Baths:** 3 En 1 Pr (5) cc

Cristinas Guest House, *47 St Andrews Road, Cambridge, CB4 1DH.* Quiet location, 15 minutes' walk from city centre. Hairdryers. Radio alarm clocks. **Open:** All year (not Xmas)
01223 365855 & 01223 327700 Mrs Celentano **Fax: 01223 365855** *Cristinas.guesthouse@ntlworld.com* www.cristinasguesthouse.com **D:** Fr £25.00–£28.00 **S:** Fr £37.00 **Beds:** 1F 4D 4T **Baths:** 7 En 2 Sh (8) 2

Planning a longer stay? Always ask for any special rates

Hamden Guest House, *89 High Street, Cherry Hinton, Cambridge, CB1 9LU.* High standard of bed & breakfast accommodation. All rooms with ensuite shower. **Open:** All year
01223 413263 Mr Casciano **Fax: 01223 245960 D:** Fr £30.00 **S:** Fr £35.00 **Beds:** 1F 2D 1T 1S **Baths:** 5 En (10) (7)
cc

Carolina Bed & Breakfast, *148 Perne Road, Cambridge, CB1 3NX.* 1930s building located in a nice residential area. **Open:** All year **Grades:** ETC 4 Diamond
01223 247015 & 07789 431456 (M) Mrs Amabile **Fax: 01223 247015** *carolina.amabile@tesco.net* www.smoothhound.co.uk/hotels/carol/html **D:** Fr £25.00–£32.50 **S:** Fr £28.00–£48.00 **Beds:** 1D 1T **Baths:** 2 En (3) **cc**

Double Two, *22 St Margarets Road, Cambridge, CB3 0LT.* By Girton College, 1 1/2 miles Cambridge centre, near M11/A14. **Open:** All year (not Xmas/New Year)
01223 276103 (also fax) C Noble *carol.noble@ntlworld.com* **D:** Fr £24.00–£26.00 **S:** Fr £35.00–£50.00 **Beds:** 2T 1D **Baths:** 2 En 1 Sh (2)

Ashtrees Guest House, *128 Perne Road, Cambridge, Cambs, CB1 3RR.* Comfortable suburban residence with garden. Good bus to city centre. **Open:** Jan to Jan
01223 411233 (also fax) Mrs Hill **D:** Fr £20.00–£23.00 **S:** Fr £22.00–£38.00 **Beds:** 1F 3D 1T 2S **Baths:** 3 En 1 Sh (6) **cc**

El Shaddai, *41 Warkworth Street, Cambridge, Cambs, CB1 1EG.* Centrally located, within a ten minute walk to colleges, shops and other social amenities. **Open:** All year
01223 327978 Mrs Droy **Fax: 01223 501024** *pauline@droy.freeserve.co.uk* www.droy.freeserve.co.uk **D:** Fr £20.00–£22.50 **S:** Fr £23.00–£25.00 **Beds:** 1F 1D 2T 1S **Baths:** 1 Sh

Cam Guest House, *17 Elizabeth Way, Cambridge, CB4 1DD.* 15 mins' walk to city centre, 5 mins' to Grafton shopping centre. **Open:** All year (not Xmas/New Year)
01223 354512 Fax: 01223 353164 *camguesthouse@btinternet.com* **D:** Fr £21.00–£30.00 **S:** Fr £30.00 **Beds:** 3F 3D 4S **Baths:** 2 En 3 Sh (5)

National Grid References given are for villages, towns and cities – not for individual houses

Castor

TL1297

Cobnut Cottage, *45 Peterborough Road, Castor, Peterborough, PE5 7AX.* Cosy Listed stone cottage in pretty village close to Peterborough, A1 motorway and Stamford. **Open:** All year **Grades:** ETC 4 Diamond
01733 380745 (also fax) Mrs Huckle *huckle.cobnut@talk21.com* **D:** Fr £21.00–£25.00 **S:** Fr £28.00–£35.00 **Beds:** 1T 2D **Baths:** 1 En 1 Sh (4) (6)

Chatteris

TL3985

The George Hotel, *2 High Street, Chatteris, Cambs, PE16 6BE.* **Open:** All year
01354 692208 SarahThompson
D: Fr £25.00–£60.00 **S:** Fr £25.00 **Beds:** 1F 3T 4S **Baths:** 4 En 1 Pr 1 Sh (40)
Originally a coach house which offers quality accommodation, situated at the centre of an old market town in the heart of the Fenland countryside. Large fishing community within close distance of historic Ely and Cambridge.

Cherry Hinton

TL4855

Hamden Guest House, *89 High Street, Cherry Hinton, Cambridge, CB1 9LU.* High standard of bed & breakfast accommodation. All rooms with ensuite shower. **Open:** All year
01223 413263 Mr Casciano **Fax: 01223 245960 D:** Fr £30.00 **S:** Fr £35.00 **Beds:** 1F 2D 1T 1S **Baths:** 5 En (10) (7)
cc

Church End (Cambridge)

TL4856

The Ark, *30 St Matthews Street, Cambridge, CB1 2LT.* Centrally situated. Rail/coach stations, cinema, restaurants, shops nearby. Landlady speaks German/Spanish/French. **Open:** All year (not Xmas/New Year)
01223 311130 Alexander Bartow Wylie *bartow.wylie@iscs.org.uk* **D:** Fr £18.00–£22.00 **Beds:** 1T 1D **Baths:** 1 Sh (10)

Comberton

TL3856 *Three Horseshoes*

White Horse Cottage, *28 West Street, Comberton, Cambridge, CB3 7DS.* Restored C17th cottage near Cambridge. Pretty garden, many local attractions. **Open:** All year
01223 262914 J Wright **D:** Fr £22.00–£35.00 **Beds:** 1F 1D (3)

Coton

TL4058

Woodpeckers, *57-61 The Footpath, Coton, Cambridge, CB3 7PX.* Modern house, quiet village. Close to Cambridge and nearby attractions. **Open:** All year
01954 210455 & 07850 060688 (M) J Young **Fax: 01954 210733** *roy@woodpeckers61.freeserve.co.uk* **D:** Fr £40.00–£45.00 **S:** Fr £30.00–£33.00 **Beds:** 1T 2D **Baths:** 1 En 1 Pr 1 Sh (4)

Cottenham

TL4467

Denmark House, *58 Denmark Road, Cottenham, Cambridge, CB4 8QS.* Delightful detached residence in village 6 miles Cambridge. Also self-catering. **Open:** All year **Grades:** ETC 4 Diamond
01954 251060 & 01954 251629 (M) Mrs Whittaker **Fax: 01954 251629** *denmark@house33.fsnet.co.uk* www.denmarkhouse.fsnet.co.uk **D:** Fr £23.00–£25.00 **Beds:** 2D 1T **Baths:** 3 En (3)

Dullingham

TL6257

The Old School, *Dullingham, Newmarket, Suffolk, CB8 9XF.* Attractive conversion, spacious rooms, delightful village, nearby pub serves food. **Open:** All year
01638 507813 Mrs Andrews **Fax: 01638 507022** *gill.andrews@premeirhoildays.co.uk* **D:** Fr £23.00–£25.00 **Beds:** 1D **Baths:** 1 En (2)

Eaton Ford

TL1759

Home From Home, *1 Laxton Close, Eaton Ford, St Neots, Cambs, PE19 3AR.* Friendly family house, tea/coffee served. Ten minutes walk town. **Open:** All year
01480 383677 & 07974 969257 (M) Mrs Francis-Macrae **Fax: 01480 383677** *gillmacrae@cheerful.com* **D:** Fr £20.00–£22.00 **S:** Fr £16.00–£18.00 **Beds:** 1D 1S **Baths:** 1 Sh (2)

Eaton Socon

TL1758

North Laurels House, *206 Great North Road, Eaton Socon, St Neots, Cambs, PE19 8EF.* Comfortable and well presented Georgian family home. **Open:** All year
01480 385086 *jeffval@supanet.net* **D:** Fr £20.00–£28.00 **S:** Fr £20.00–£28.00 **Beds:** 1F 1T 1S **Baths:** 1 En 1 Sh (3)

Ellington

TL1671

Grove Cottage, *Malting Lane, Ellington, Huntingdon, PE28 0AA.* Peaceful, relaxing, self-contained suite in charming comfortable period cottage. **Open:** All year **01480 890167 (also fax)** Mr Silver *hr73@dial.pipex.com* **D:** Fr £20.00–£22.50 **S:** Fr £27.50–£30.00 **Beds:** 1D **Baths:** 1 En (2)

Elm

TF4606

Elm Manor, *Main Road, Elm, Wisbech, Cambs, PE14 0AG.* Charles II manor house. Beams, inglenooks, four-posters, gardens, adjacent to local inn. **Open:** All year (not Xmas)
01945 861069 (also fax) *sandynye.co.uk* www.sandynye.co.uk **D:** Fr £20.00–£22.50 **S:** Fr £30.00–£40.00 **Beds:** 1D 1T **Baths:** 1 En 1 Pr (8) (2)

Ely

TL5480

Rosendale Lodge, *223 Main Street, Witchford, Ely, Cambs, CB6 2HT.* Award-winning guest house. Adjacent historic Ely - Cambridge & Newmarket nearby. **Open:** All year
Grades: ETC 5 Diamond, Silver, AA 5 Diamond
01353 667700 Ms Pickford **Fax: 01352 667799** *val.pickford@rosendalelodge.co.uk* www.rosendalelodge.co.uk **D:** Fr £27.50–£32.50 **S:** Fr £40.00–£45.00 **Beds:** 1F 1T 2D **Baths:** 4 En (10) **cc**

82 Broad Street, *Ely, Cambs, CB7 4BE.* Comfortable rooms, central Ely. Near station, river, cathedral. Self-catering available. Jubilee gardens. **Open:** All year **01353 667609** Mr & Mrs Hull **Fax: 01353 667005** **D:** Fr £20.00 **S:** Fr £20.00 **Beds:** 1F 1T 1S **Baths:** 1 En 1 Pr 1 Sh

11 Chapel Street, *Ely, Cambs, CB6 1AD.* Comfortable Listed character cottage. Quiet, close to historical centre. Parking nearby. **Open:** All year
01353 668768 Daphne Mortimer *daffmort@talk21.com* **D:** Fr £21.00 **S:** Fr £21.00–£25.00 **Beds:** 1D 1S **Baths:** 1 Sh (5)

Greenways, *Prickwillow Road, Queen Adelaide, Ely, Cambs, CB7 4TZ.* Comfortable ground floor accommodation, 1 mile cathedral city of Ely. **Open:** All year
01353 666706 & 07811 92526 (M) Mr Dunlop-Hill **Fax: 01954 251629** *greenways.ely@tesco.net* **D:** Fr £23.00–£25.00 **S:** Fr £28.00–£30.00 **Beds:** 1F 1D 1T 1S **Baths:** 4 En (6)

Cathedral House, *17 St Mary's Street, Ely, Cambs, CB7 4ER.* Grade II Listed house, in shadow of cathedral, close to museums, restaurants, shops. **Open:** All year (not Xmas)
01353 662124 (also fax) Mr & Mrs Farndale *farndale@cathedralhouse.co.uk* www.cathedralhouse.co.uk **D:** Fr £25.00–£30.00 **S:** Fr £35.00–£45.00 **Beds:** 1F 1D 1T **Baths:** 3 En (4)

Sycamore House, *91 Cambridge Road, Ely, Cambs, CB7 4HX.* Newly renovated Edwardian family home set in acre of mature gardens. **Open:** All year (not Xmas/New Year)
01353 662139 Mrs Webster **Fax: 01353 662795** *sycamore_house@hotmail.com* **D:** Fr £25.00–£30.00 **S:** Fr £35.00–£40.00 **Beds:** 2T 2D **Baths:** 4 En (8)

Farcet

TL2094

Red House Farm, *Broadway, Farcet, Peterborough, PE7 3AZ.* Situated close to A1 and city centre with lovely views. **Open:** All year
01733 243129 (also fax) *gill.emberson@totalise.co.uk* **D:** Fr £18.00–£20.00 **S:** Fr £18.00–£20.00 **Beds:** 2T 1D (6)

Fordham

TL6270

Homelands, *1 Carter Street, Fordham, Ely, Cambs, CB7 5NG.* Comfort in a private house. Rooms of character. Garden & private parking. **Open:** All year (not Xmas)
01638 720363 Mrs Bycroft **D:** Fr £25.00–£30.00 **S:** Fr £22.00–£25.00 **Beds:** 1F 1D 1T **Baths:** 2 En (4)

Queensberry, *196 Carter Street, Fordham, Ely, Suffolk, CB7 5JU.* Country house comfort. First village off A14 Newmarket to Ely road. **Open:** All year
01638 720916 M D Roper **Fax: 01638 720233** **D:** Fr £25.00–£30.00 **S:** Fr £30.00–£40.00 **Beds:** 1D 1T 1S

Girton

TL4261

Finches, *144 Thorton Road, Girton, Cambridge, CB3 0ND.* A friendly welcome to our home, beautiful new ensuite rooms. **Open:** All year (not Xmas)
01223 276653 Mr & Mrs Green *liz.green.b-b@talk21.com* **D:** Fr £30.00–£50.00 **S:** Fr £30.00–£50.00 **Beds:** 1D 2T (4)

Planning a longer stay? Always ask for any special rates

Gorefield

TF4211

Maison De La Chien, *35 Churchill Road, Gorefield, Wisbech, Cambs, PE13 4NA.* Quiet village location overlooking farmland on the beautiful Cambridgeshire fens.
Open: All year
01945 870789 & 07990 575219 (M) Mrs Barnard **Fax: 01945 870789** *hols-maisonchien@faxvia.net* **D:** Fr £15.00 **S:** Fr £15.00 **Beds:** 1D 1T **Baths:** 1 Sh (2)

Grantchester

TL4355

Honeysuckle Cottage, *38 High Street, Grantchester, Cambridge, CB3 8PL.* Grantchester is a beauty spot, the home of politician Jeffrey Archer. **Open:** All year
01223 845977 & 07974 767807 (M) Mr & Mrs Salt **D:** Fr £38.00 **S:** Fr £38.00 **Beds:** 3F 3D 3T 3S **Baths:** 3 En

Great Chishill

TL4238

Hall Farm, *Great Chishill, Royston, Cambridgeshire, SG8 8SH.* Beautiful Manor house, secluded gardens, pretty hilltop village. **Open:** All year
01763 838263 (also fax) Mrs Wiseman www.hallfarmbb.co.uk **D:** Fr £25.00–£30.00 **S:** Fr £30.00–£35.00 **Beds:** 1F 1T 1D **Baths:** 1 En 1 Sh (4)

Great Eversden

TL3653

The Moat House, *Great Eversden, Cambridge, CB3 7HN.* Welcoming period family home. Easy access Cambridge and East Anglia. **Open:** All year (not Xmas)
01223 262836 Mr Webster **Fax: 01223 262979** *randjw@ntlworld.com* **D:** Fr £25.00 **S:** Fr £25.00 **Beds:** 1T 1D **Baths:** 1 Pr (4)

Great Shelford

TL4652

Norfolk House, *2 Tunwells Lane, Great Shelford, Cambridge, Cambs, CB2 5LJ.* Elegant Victorian residence retaining original character plus 21st-Century comforts. **Open:** All year (not Xmas/New Year)
01223 840287 Mrs Diver **D:** Fr £18.50–£22.50 **S:** Fr £25.00–£30.00 **Beds:** 2T 1D **Baths:** 1 En 1 Sh (10) (2)

Hardwick

TL3759

Wallis Farm, *98 Main Street, Hardwick, Cambridge, CB3 7QU.* Quiet location close to city of Cambridge. 6 ensuite rooms in converted barn with exposed beams decorated to high standard. Large gardens leading to meadows and woodland.
Open: All year
01954 210347 Mrs Sadler **Fax: 01954 210988** *wallisfarm@mcmail.com* **D:** Fr £22.50–£30.00 **S:** Fr £35.00–£40.00 **Beds:** 1F 2D 3T **Baths:** 6 En (8)

Helpston

TF1205

Helpston House, *Helpston, Peterborough, Cambs, PE6 7DX.* Grade II Listed stone manor house set in beautiful grounds, dating back to 1090. **Open:** All year
01733 252190 Mrs Orton **Fax: 01733 253853** *orton.helpstonhouse@btinternet.com* www.helpstonhouse.co.uk **D:** Fr £17.50–£20.00 **S:** Fr £22.00–£25.00 **Beds:** 1F 1D 1S **Baths:** 1 En 1 Sh (6)

Hemingford Grey

TL2970

Willow Guest House, *45 High Street, Hemingford Grey, Huntingdon, Cambs, PE28 9BJ.* Large, comfortable, quiet guest house in pretty riverside village. **Open:** All year
01480 494748 Mr Webster **Fax: 01480 464456 D:** Fr £24.00–£26.00 **S:** Fr £37.00–£42.00 **Beds:** 2F 2D 2T 1S **Baths:** 7 En (12)

Hilton

TL2866

Prince of Wales, *Potton Road, Hilton, Huntingdon, Cambridgeshire, PE18 9NG.* Traditional village inn offering fine ales and hearty meals. **Open:** All year (not Xmas/New Year)
01480 830257 D: Fr £32.00 **S:** Fr £45.00–£50.00 **Beds:** 1T 1D 2S **Baths:** 4 En (5) (6) cc

Histon

TL4363

Wynwyck, *55 Narrow Lane, Histon, Cambridge, CB4 9HD.* Comfortable peaceful; ideal for Cambridge, Ely, Newmarket, Duxford, Museum and East Anglia.
Open: All year (not Xmas)
01223 232496 (also fax) Mrs Torrens **D:** Fr £23.00–£30.00 **S:** Fr £32.00–£36.00 **Beds:** 1F 1D 2T **Baths:** 2 En 1 Sh (4)

Huntingdon

TL2472 *Victoria Inn, Dridge Hotel*

Sandwich Villas Guest House, *16 George Street, Huntingdon, Cambs, PE29 3BD.* Comfortable Victorian House, close to town centre, railway and bus station. **Open:** All year
01480 458484 Mrs Sturgeon **D:** Fr £22.50 **S:** Fr £25.00–£38.00 **Beds:** 1F 1T 1D 1S **Baths:** 1 En 1 Sh (4)

Ickleton

TL4843

New Inn House, *10 Brookhampton Street, Ickleton, Duxford, Cambs, CB10 1SP.* Picturesque village, ideal for Duxford, Cambridge and North Essex. Warm welcome. **Open:** All year (not Xmas)
01799 530463 Mrs Fletcher **Fax: 01799 531499** *jpinternational@nascr.net* www.newinnhouse.co.uk **D:** Fr £18.00–£20.00 **S:** Fr £25.00–£30.00 **Beds:** 1D 1T **Baths:** 1 Sh (5) (6)

Kirtling

TL6858

Hill Farm Guest House, *Kirtling, Newmarket, Suffolk, CB8 9HQ.* Delightful farm house in rural setting. **Open:** All year
01638 730253 (also fax) Mrs Benley **D:** Fr £25.00–£50.00 **S:** Fr £25.00 **Beds:** 1D 1T 1S **Baths:** 2 En 1 Pr (5)

Kneesworth

TL3444 *Queen Adelaide*

Fairhaven, *102 Old North Road, Kneesworth, Royston, Herts, SG8 5JR.* Comfortable country home near Cambridge, Wimpole Hall & Duxford War Museum. **Open:** All year (not Xmas/New Year)
01763 249471 (also fax) D Watson **D:** Fr £20.00 **S:** Fr £20.00–£25.00 **Beds:** 1T 1D 1S **Baths:** 1 Sh (3)

Landbeach

TL4765 *Travellers Rest*

New Farm, *Green End, Landbeach, Cambridge, CB4 8ED.* Recently renovated to a high specification, New Farm is located on the edge of the quiet village of Landbeach, situated between Ely and Cambridge. All rooms are beautifully decorated and equipped. A must for guests who appreciate attention to detail. **Open:** All year
01223 863597 & 07780 982734 (M) Mrs Matthews **Fax: 01223 860258** *new_farm@hotmail.com* www.smoothhound.co.uk/hotels/newfarm.html **D:** Fr £20.00–£30.00 **S:** Fr £30.00–£40.00 **Beds:** 1T 2D **Baths:** 2 En 1 Pr (6)

Linton

TL5646

Linton Heights, *36 Wheatsheaf Way, Linton, Cambridge, CB1 6XB.* Comfortable, friendly home, sharing lounge, convenient Duxford, Cambridge, Newmarket, Saffron Walden, Bury. **Open:** All year (not Xmas)
01223 892516 Mr & Mrs Peake **D:** Fr £18.00–£20.00 **S:** Fr £18.00–£20.00 **Beds:** 1T 1S **Baths:** 1 Sh (6) (2)

Cantilena, *4 Harefield Rise, Linton, Cambridge, CB1 6LS.* Quiet, spacious bungalow in historic village. Near Cambridge, Duxford, Newmarket, Stansted. **Open:** All year
01223 892988 (also fax) Mr & Mrs Clarkson **D:** Fr £20.00–£22.00 **S:** Fr £20.00–£25.00 **Beds:** 1F 1D 1T **Baths:** 1 Sh (3)

Little Downham

TL5283

Bury House, *11 Main Street, Little Downham, Ely, Cambs, CB6 2ST.* Grade II Listed, large comfortable bedrooms in friendly home. **Open:** All year
01353 698766 & 07748 378198 (M) Mrs Ambrose **D:** Fr £20.00 **Beds:** 1F 1T **Baths:** 1 Sh (2)

Casa Nostra Guest House, *6 Black Bank Road, Little Downham, Ely, Cambs, CB6 2UA.* Delightful modern country house, large landscaped garden, set in rural location ideal for exploring the Fens and the city of Ely. Family-run with a relaxed atmosphere. Comfortable ground-floor accommodation and an excellent breakfast. Good, secure, off-road parking.
Open: All year
01353 862495 Mrs Milan *casanostra@btinternet.com* **D:** Fr £25.00 **S:** Fr £35.00 **Beds:** 1F3T 3D **Baths:** 5 En 1 Sh (10)

Little Gransden

TL2754

Elms Farm, *52 Main Road, Little Gransden, Sandy, Beds, SG19 3DL.* Farm house, quiet, picturesque gardens and village. Central to many attractions.
Open: All year (not Xmas)
01767 677459 Mrs Bygraves *joan@elmsfarmbandb.fsnet.co.uk* **D:** Fr £20.00 **S:** Fr £25.00 **Beds:** 1F 1D 1T 1S **Baths:** 1 En 1 Pr 1 Sh (10)

Model Farm, *Little Gransden, Sandy, Beds, SG19 3EA.* Comfortable quiet farmhouse. 14 miles west of Cambridge. **Open:** All year (not Xmas/New Year)
01767 677361 (also fax) Mrs Barlow *bandb@modelfarm.org.uk* www.modelfarm.org.uk **D:** Fr £22.00 **S:** Fr £25.00 **Beds:** 3D **Baths:** 3 En (12) (6)

Longstowe

TL3055

Finch Farmhouse, *28 Fen Road, Bassingbourn, Royston, Herts, SG85 5PQ.* Charming Victorian family home 20 minutes drive from Cambridge. **Open:** All year (not Xmas/New Year)
01763 242019 (also fax) Mrs Murray *btmurray@dial.pipex.com* **D:** Fr £21.00 **S:** Fr £28.00 **Beds:** 1D **Baths:** 1 En (5) (3)

March

TL4197

Woodpecker Cottage Guest House, *20 Kingswood Road, March, Cambs, PE15 9RT.* Luxury house - landscaped gardens, hearty breakfast. Accessible London and Norfolk coast. **Open:** All year
01354 660188 Mr & Mrs Spencer **Fax: 01354 655866** *johnliz.spencer@talk21.com* **D:** Fr £18.50–£25.00 **S:** Fr £22.00–£27.00 **Beds:** 2T 1D **Baths:** 1 Sh (6)

Marholm

TF1402

Ancient Marholm Farm, *Woodcroft Road, Marholm, Peterborough, Cambs, PE6 7HU.* Ancient farmhouse with oak beams, stone walls, set in peaceful and pastoral surroundings. **Open:** All year
01733 262824 Mrs Scott www.s-systems.co.uk/hotels/marholm.html **D:** Fr £20.00–£35.00 **S:** Fr £20.00–£35.00 **Beds:** 3F 1T 1S 1D **Baths:** 1 Sh (20)

Orton Longueville

TL1795

Longueville Guest House, *411 Oundle Road, Orton Longueville, Peterborough, Cambs, PE2 7DA.* Small, family-owned guest house, offering a warm and friendly atmosphere. **Open:** All year
01733 233442 Glover **D:** Fr £25.00–£27.50 **S:** Fr £35.00–£40.00 **Beds:** 1F 2T 2D **Baths:** 5 En (6)

Orwell

TL3650

Northfields House, *8 Leaden Hill, Orwell, Royston, SG8 5QH.* Comfortable, period-style house. In peaceful village, near Cambridge. **Open:** All year (not Xmas/New Year)
01223 208097 *gillian@leadenhill.fsnet.co.uk* **D:** Fr £18.00–£25.00 **S:** Fr £18.00–£25.00 **Beds:** 2D **Baths:** 1 Sh (2)

Orchards End, *9 Greenford Close, Orwell, Royston, Herts, SG8 5QA.* Friendly, comfortable Tudor style family home in picturesque village. **Open:** All year (not Xmas/New Year)
01223 207202 C Sharman **Fax: 01763 208865** *sharman@lineone.net* **D:** Fr £22.50 **S:** Fr £25.00 **Beds:** 1D 1S **Baths:** 1 Pr (4)

Over

TL3770

Charter Cottage, *Horseware, Church End, Over, Cambridge, CB4 5NX.* Peaceful country cottage close to Cambridge, Ely & St Ives. **Open:** All year
01954 230056 Mr & Mrs Warren **Fax: 01954 232300** *charter.cottage@talk21.com* **D:** Fr £17.00 **S:** Fr £20.00 **Beds:** 1D 1T **Baths:** 1 Sh (3) (6)

Peterborough

TL1999

Montana, *15 Fletton Avenue, Peterborough, Cambs, PE2 8AX.* Clean, friendly, family home. Close city centre. Private car park. **Open:** All year (not Xmas)
01733 567917 (also fax) Mr & Mrs Atkins www.peterboroughaccommodation.co.uk **D:** Fr £17.50–£20.00 **S:** Fr £20.00–£25.00 **Beds:** 1D 2T 4S **Baths:** 2 Sh (6)

Aragon House, *75/77 London Road, Peterborough, Cambs, PE2 9BS.* Comfortable, friendly, easy parking and close to city centre. **Open:** All year (not Xmas)
01733 563718 (also fax) Mr & Mrs Spence *aragon@fsbdial.co.uk* www.aragonhouse.co.uk **D:** Fr £19.00–£22.00 **S:** Fr £20.00–£30.00 **Beds:** 1F 3D 2T 6S **Baths:** 3 En 2 Sh (8) cc

Rose-Marie, *14 Eastfield Road, Peterborough, Cambs, PE1 4AN.* The Rose Marie is a family-run guest house close to city centre. **Open:** All year
01733 557548 Mr Doyle **Fax: 01733 764801** **D:** Fr £15.00–£18.00 **S:** Fr £18.00–£20.00 **Beds:** 1F 2D 1T 2S **Baths:** 1 Sh

Pidley

TL3277

Lakeside Lodge, *Fen Road, Pidley, Huntingdon, Cambs, PE28 3DF.* Located on 42-hole golf complex. Ten-pin bowling, bar/restaurant. **Open:** All year
01487 740540 Mrs Hopkins **Fax: 01487 740852** *info@lakeside-lodge.co.uk* www.lakeside-lodge.co.uk **D:** Fr £25.00–£30.00 **S:** Fr £30.00–£35.00 **Beds:** 14T 3D **Baths:** 17 En cc

Queen Adelaide

TL5580

Greenways, *Prickwillow Road, Queen Adelaide, Ely, Cambs, CB7 4TZ.* Comfortable ground floor accommodation, 1 mile cathedral city of Ely. **Open:** All year
01353 666706 & 07811 92526 (M) Mr Dunlop-Hill **Fax: 01954 251629** *greenways.ely@tesco.net* **D:** Fr £23.00–£25.00 **S:** Fr £28.00–£30.00 **Beds:** 1F 1D 1T 1S **Baths:** 4 En (6)

Soham

TL5973

Greenbank, *111 Brook Street, Soham, Ely, Cambs, CB7 5AE.* Pleasant bungalow in a quiet street, convenient for Newmarket, Ely or Cambridge. **Open:** All year (not Xmas/New Year)
01353 720929 Mrs Rump **D:** Fr £16.00 **S:** Fr £16.00 **Beds:** 1T 1D **Baths:** 1 Sh (3) (2) cc

Southorpe

TF0803

Midstone Farm House, *Midstone House, Southorpe, Stamford, Lincs, PE9 3BX.* Beautiful stone Georgian house in quiet location. Meet George the pot-bellied pig. **Open:** All year
01780 740136 Mrs Harrison Smith **Fax: 01780 749294** *midstonehouse@amserve.net* **D:** Fr £25.00–£30.00 **S:** Fr £25.00–£30.00 **Beds:** 1D 1T **Baths:** 1 En 1 Pr

St Ives

TL3171 *The Aviator*

Forty Winks, *3 Laburnum Way, St Ives, Huntingdon, Cambs, PE17 6YW.* Central for Cromwell country. Perfect for Cambridge, East Anglia. **Open:** All year
01480 465117 & 07803 915100 (M) *40winks@waitrose.com* **D:** Fr £20.00–£23.00 **S:** Fr £25.00–£30.00 **Beds:** 1F 2D **Baths:** 2 En 1 Sh (2)

St Neots

TL1860

The Bays, *33-35 New Street, St Neots, Cambs, PE19 1AJ.* Tastefully decorated Edwardian house, close to town centre and railway. **Open:** All year (not Xmas/New Year)
01480 403701 (also fax) Mrs McKnight *thebaysguesthouse@hotmail.com* hometown.aol.co.uk/snmcknight/thebays.html **D:** Fr £22.00–£27.00 **S:** Fr £25.00–£38.00 **Beds:** 1F 1T 1D 1S **Baths:** 1 En 2 Sh (4)

All details shown are as supplied by B&B owners in Autumn 2002

The Ferns, *Berkley Street, Eynesbury, St Neots, Huntingdon, Cambs, PE19 2NE.* Welcoming family home: Picturesque C18th former farmhouse in cottagey gardens. **Open:** All year (not Xmas/New Year)
01480 213884 E Raggatt *raggatt@onetel.net.uk* www.webonetel.net.uk/~raggatt **D:** Fr £18.00–£20.00 **S:** Fr £20.00–£22.00 **Beds:** 1F 1D **Baths:** 1 En 1 Sh (2)

Stretham

TL5074

The Red Lion, *47 High Street, Stretham, Ely, Cambs, CB6 3JQ.* **Open:** All year (not Xmas)
01353 648132 Mrs Hayes **Fax: 01353 648327** *frank.hayes@ukgateway.net* **D:** Fr £25.00 **S:** Fr £40.00–£44.00 **Beds:** 3F 5D 2T 2S **Baths:** 12 En (18) cc
A C18th inn centrally situated for touring or business. 4 miles from Ely, 14 miles Newmarket, 12 miles Cambridge, 30 miles from Stansted Airport. Close to major motorways, M11, A14, A428 and A10. Conservatory restaurant for guests.

Bridge House, *Green End, Stretham, Ely, Cambs, CB6 3LF.* Period farmhouse, river frontage, in 13 acres. Relaxed atmosphere, wildlife in profusion. **Open:** All year (not Xmas)
01353 649212 Mr Whitmore **D:** Fr £20.00–£25.00 **S:** Fr £25.00–£35.00 **Beds:** 2F 1D 2T **Baths:** 3 En 1 Pr (6)

Swaffham Prior

TL5663

Sterling Farm, *Health Road, Swaffham Prior, Cambridge, CB5 0LA.* Convenient for visiting Newmarket, Cambridge and Ely. Anglesea Abbey 3 miles. **Open:** All year (not Xmas)
01638 741431 Mrs Harris **D:** Fr £20.00–£25.00 **S:** Fr £20.00–£25.00 **Beds:** 1D 1T 1S **Baths:** 1 Sh (8)

Thornhaugh

TF0700

Sacrewell Lodge Farm, *Thornhaugh, Peterborough, PE8 6HJ.* Farmhouse in quiet location surrounded by attractive gardens and farmland. **Open:** All year (not Xmas)
01780 782277 Mrs Armitage **D:** Fr £18.00–£20.00 **S:** Fr £15.00–£18.00 **Beds:** 1D 1T 1S **Baths:** 1 En 1 Sh (10)

Ufford

TF0904

Ufford Farm, *Ufford, Stamford, Lincs, PE9 3BP.* C18th farmhouse, comfortably furnished, with open fires on edge of peaceful village. **Open:** All year
01780 740220 (also fax) Mrs Vergette *vergette@ufford1.freeserve.co.uk* **D:** Fr £25.00–£30.00 **S:** Fr £25.00–£30.00 **Beds:** 1T 1S **Baths:** 1 Sh (3) (4)

Wansford

TL0799 *Haycock Hotel, Papermills*

Stoneacre, *Elton Road, Wansford, Peterborough, Cambs, PE8 6JT.* Near Peterborough and Stamford; self-catering available for long lets. **Open:** All year
01780 783283 (also fax) Mr Wilkinson **D:** Fr £21.00–£26.00 **S:** Fr £36.00–£46.00 **Beds:** 1F 1T 4D **Baths:** 4 En 1 Pr 1 Sh (10)

Waterbeach

TL4964 *The Slap Up*

Goose Hall Farm, *Ely Road, Waterbeach, Cambridge, CB5 9PG.* Modern farm house on 13 acres with a deer run & half acre lake. **Open:** All year (not Xmas)
01223 860235 (also fax) Mrs Lock **D:** Fr £20.00–£22.00 **S:** Fr £30.00–£35.00 **Beds:** 1F 1D 1T **Baths:** 3 En (5) (8)

Wentworth

TL4777

Desiderata, *44 Main Street, Wentworth, Ely, Cambs, CB6 3QG.* Large modern house in quiet country lane; ideal for disabled. **Open:** All year
01353 776131 & 07768 827901 (M) Mrs Graham *chips.1@virgin.net* **D:** Fr £20.00–£25.00 **S:** Fr £25.00 **Beds:** 2D 2T **Baths:** 2 En 1 Sh (6)

West Perry

TL1566

38 West Perry, *West Perry, Huntingdon, Cambs, PE28 0BX.* Victorian country cottage, peaceful, interesting garden. Close Grafham Water Reservoir. **Open:** All year (not Xmas/New Year)
01480 810225 Mrs Hickling **D:** Fr £20.00–£25.00 **S:** Fr £20.00–£25.00 **Beds:** 2T 1S **Baths:** 1 Sh (13) (3)

West Wratting

TL5951

The Old Bakery, *West Wratting, Cambridge, CB1 5LU.* Period cottage situated in quiet village with nice garden. **Open:** All year
01223 290492 Mr & Mrs Denny **Fax: 01223 290845** *ddtractors@zoom.co.uk* **D:** Fr £22.50 **S:** Fr £22.50 **Beds:** 2T 3D **Baths:** 1 En 1 Pr (2)

Whittlesey

TL2797

Cobwebs Guest House, *21 The Delph, Whittlesey, Peterborough, Cambs, PE7 1QH.* Close to diving centre, fishing, lakes. **Open:** All year (not Xmas/New Year)
01733 350960 Mrs Ekins **D:** Fr £17.50 **S:** Fr £18.00 **Beds:** 1F 4T **Baths:** 2 Sh (4)

Wicken

TL5670

Spinney Abbey, *Wicken, Ely, Cambs, CB7 5XQ.* Georgian Farmhouse with tennis court. Close to NT Nature Reserve. **Open:** All year (not Xmas/New Year)
01353 720971 V Fuller **Fax: 01353 720488** *spinney.abbey@tesco.net* www.spinneyabbey.co.uk **D:** Fr £23.00–£24.00 **Beds:** 1F 1T 1D **Baths:** 2 En 1 Pr (5) (4)

The Old School, *48 North Street, Wicken, Ely, Cambs, CB7 5XW.* Tastefully renovated Edwardian village school, with tea-room, gifts, Bygones shop. **Open:** All year (not Xmas/New Year)
01353 720526 Mrs Wright *wicken.oldschool@btinternet.com* **D:** Fr £20.00–£24.00 **S:** Fr £25.00–£30.00 **Beds:** 1F 1D **Baths:** 1 En 1 Pr

Wisbech

TF4609

Marmion House Hotel, *11 Lynn Road, Wisbech, Cambs, PE13 3DD.* Georgian town house hotel located in the capital of the Fens. **Open:** All year
01945 582822 Mrs Lilley **Fax: 01945 475889** **D:** Fr £19.50–£22.50 **S:** Fr £20.00–£25.00 **Beds:** 15F 5D 2T 3S **Baths:** 25 En cc

Algethi Guest House, *136 Lynn Road, Wisbech, Cambs, PE13 3DP.* Small, family-run guest house near town centre. Warm welcome. **Open:** All year
01945 582278 E McManus **Fax: 01945 466456** *lizalgethi@talk21.com* **D:** Fr £15.00–£17.00 **S:** Fr £15.00–£17.50 **Beds:** 2F 2T 1S **Baths:** 2 Pr

Ravenscourt, *138 Lynn Road, Wisbech, Cambs, PE13 3DP.* Quality accommodation, friendly atmosphere, easy walking distance to town centre. **Open:** All year (not Xmas/ New Year)
01945 585052 (also fax) Mr Parish
ravenscourt@rya-online.net
www.ravenscourtgh.fsnet.co.uk **D:** Fr £16.00 **S:** Fr £20.00 **Beds:** 1F 2D 1T **Baths:** 4 Pr (3)

RATES
D = Price range per person sharing in a double or twin room
S = Price range for a single room

Witchford

TL5078

Rosendale Lodge, *223 Main Street, Witchford, Ely, Cambs, CB6 2HT.* Award-winning guest house. Adjacent historic Ely - Cambridge & Newmarket nearby. **Open:** All year **Grades:** ETC 5 Diamond, Silver, AA 5 Diamond
01353 667700 Ms Pickford **Fax: 01352 667799** *val.pickford@rosendalelodge.co.uk*
www.rosendalelodge.co.uk **D:** Fr £27.50–£32.50 **S:** Fr £40.00–£45.00 **Beds:** 1F 1T 2D **Baths:** 4 En (10) **cc**

17 Common Road, *Witchford, Ely, Cambs, CB6 2HY.* Detached house and garden opposite village common. **Open:** All year (not Xmas/New Year)
01353 663918 R J Westell *rjwest@elyfl.freeserve.co.uk* **D:** Fr £20.00 **S:** Fr £20.00 **Beds:** 1T 1D 1S **Baths:** 1 Sh (1)

Woolley

TL1574

New Manor Farm, *Woolley, Huntingdon, Cambs, PE18 0YJ.* Large, comfortable, hospitable farmhouse. Idyllic rural setting. Colour brochure available. **Open:** All year
01480 890092 & 07855 611809 (M) Mrs Harris
newmanorfarm@aol.com **D:** Fr £22.50–£24.00 **S:** Fr £32.00–£35.00 **Beds:** 3T **Baths:** 2 En 1 Sh

Planning a longer stay? Always ask for any special rates

Cheshire

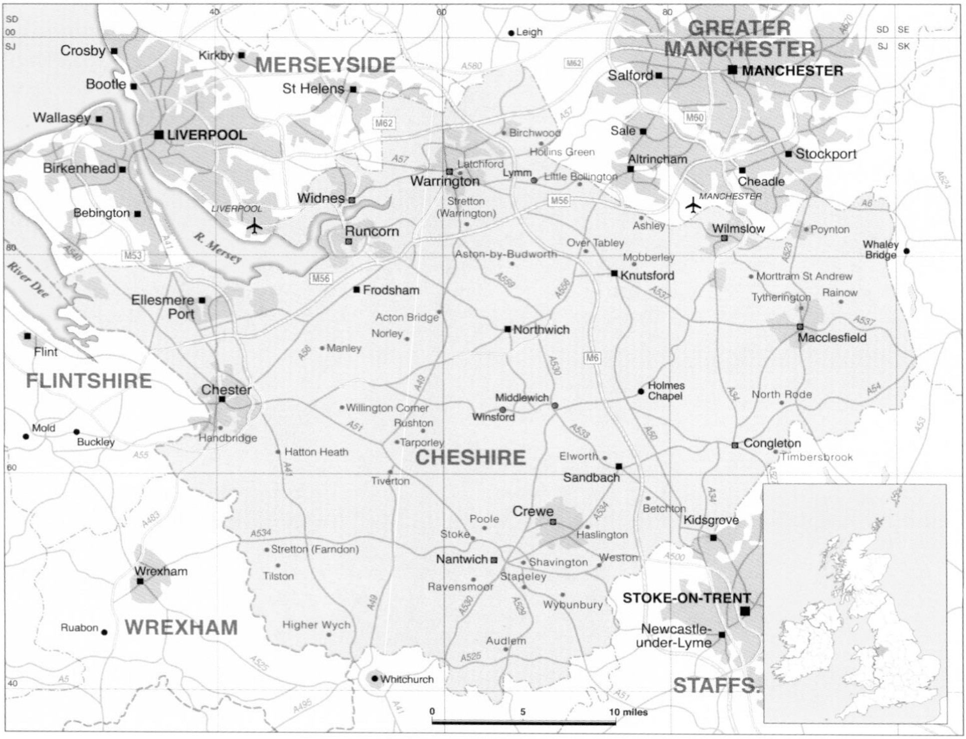

Acton Bridge

SJ5975

Manor Farm, *Cliff Road, Acton Bridge, Northwich, Cheshire, CW8 3QP.* Peaceful, elegantly furnished traditional country house. Large garden and views. **Open:** All year (not Xmas)
01606 853181 (also fax) Mrs Campbell
terri.mac.manorfarm@care4free.net **D:** Fr £24.00–£27.00 **S:** Fr £24.00–£27.00 **Beds:** 1F 1T 1S **Baths:** 1 En 2 Pr (1) (10)

BATHROOMS
En = Ensuite
Pr = Private
Sh = Shared

Ashley

SJ7784

Birtles Farm, *Ashley, Altrincham, Cheshire, WA14 3QH.* Delightful riverside farmhouse. Spacious bedrooms, beautifully decorated, every comfort. Peaceful yet close Manchester Airport. **Open:** All year
0161 928 0458 (also fax) Mrs Norbury
birtlesl@supanet.com **D:** Fr £22.00–£23.00 **S:** Fr £25.00–£26.00 **Beds:** 1F 1T 1D **Baths:** 2 En 1 Pr (10)

RATES
D = Price range per person sharing in a double or twin room
S = Price range for a single room

Aston-by-Budworth

SJ6976

Clock Cottage, *Hield Lane, Aston-by-Budworth, Northwich, Cheshire, CW9 6LP.* Lovely C17th thatched country cottage, beautiful, large, secluded garden, wooded countryside, open views. **Open:** All year (not Xmas/New Year)
01606 891271 T Tanner-Betts **D:** Fr £20.00–£25.00 **S:** Fr £20.00–£25.00 **Beds:** 1T 1S **Baths:** 1 Sh (4)

BEDROOMS
D = Double
T = Twin
S = Single
F = Family

All details shown are as supplied by B&B owners in Autumn 2002

Audlem

SJ6643

Little Heath Farm, *Audlem, Crewe, Cheshire, CW3 0HE.* Warm traditionally furnished oak beamed farmhouse in canal side village of Audlem. **Open:** All year (not Xmas/New Year)
01270 811324 (also fax) Mrs Bennion **D:** Fr £18.00–£24.00 **S:** Fr £22.00–£26.00 **Beds:** 1D 1T 1F **Baths:** 1 Pr 1 En (3)

Betchton

SJ7959

Yew Tree Farm, *Love Lane, Betchton, Sandbach, Cheshire, CW11 4TD.* Open plan bungalow - panoramic views - many local attractions - close to M6 J17. **Open:** All year
01477 500626 (also fax) Mrs Hollinshead **D:** Fr £23.00 **S:** Fr £25.00 **Beds:** 1F 1D **Baths:** 1 En 1 Pr (5) (10)

Yew Tree Farm, *Love Lane, Betchton, Sandbach, Cheshire, CW11 4TD.* M6 J17. Ideally situated for Cheshire's beauty spots. **Open:** All year
01477 500626 (also fax) Mrs Hollinshead **D:** Fr £18.00–£23.00 **S:** Fr £20.00–£25.00 **Beds:** 2D **Baths:** 1 En 1 Pr

Birchwood

SJ6492 *The Noggin*

14 Cadshaw Close, *Warrington, Warrington, Cheshire, WA3 7LR.* Modern residence situated in quiet cul-de-sac near M6 and M62. **Open:** All year
01925 818108 P Agarwal *patagarwal@hotmail.com* **D:** Fr £20.00–£22.00 **S:** Fr £20.00–£25.00 **Beds:** 1T 1D 2S **Baths:** 1 En 1 Sh (12)

Chester

SJ4066

Dee Heights Guest House, *23 City Walls, Chester, CH1 1SB.* **Open:** All year
01244 350386 Mrs Willis **D:** Fr £24.00–£25.00 **S:** Fr £30.00–£35.00 **Beds:** 1D **Baths:** 1 Pr
A charming riverside house situated on the Roman walls overlooking the River Dee and Old Dee Bridge. Fresh flowers and magnificent river views. Studio bed-sitting room with French window opening onto south-facing balcony. Three minutes from city centre.

The Curzon Hotel, *52/54 Hough Green, Chester, Cheshire, CH4 8JQ.* **Open:** All year (not Xmas/New Year) **Grades:** AA 2 Star
01244 678581 *curzon.chester@virgin.net* www.chestercurzonhotel.co.uk **D:** Fr £35.00–£40.00 **S:** Fr £45.00–£60.00 **Beds:** 2F 13D 1S **Baths:** 16 En (20) cc
Privately-owned & managed Victorian town house hotel with 16 individual ensuite guest bedrooms. Cosy lounge bar and monthly changing 'A La Carte' menu served in our delightful restaurant. Plenty of private parking and within walking distance of Chester.

Cotton Farmhouse, *Cotton Edmunds, Chester, CH3 7PT.* **Open:** All year (not Xmas/New Year)
01244 336616 & 07752 091025 (M) Fax: 01244 336699 *info@cottonfarm.co.uk* www.cottonfarm.co.uk **D:** Fr £26.00–£27.00 **S:** Fr £32.00–£33.00 **Beds:** 1F 1T 1D **Baths:** 3 En (20)
Complete peace at our family farmhouse set in 250 acres. Only 4 miles from the historic walled city of Chester, we offer extremely large and comfortable bedrooms with all the extras. Beeston Castle, Chirk, Liverpool and North Wales all nearby.

Devonia, *33-35 Hoole Road, Chester, CH2 3NH.* Large Victorian family run guest house. Same owner for 38 years. **Open:** All year
01244 322236 Fax: 01244 401511 D: Fr £17.50–£25.00 **S:** Fr £25.00 **Beds:** 4F 2D 2T 2S **Baths:** 3 En 3 Sh (20)

Planning a longer stay? Always ask for any special rates

Laburnum Guest House, *2 St Anne Street, Chester, CH1 3HS.* Warm, friendly, central townhouse. Just outside Roman city wall. **Open:** All year
01244 380313 (also fax) *laburnumhouse@bushinternet.com* **D:** Fr £22.00 **S:** Fr £22.00 **Beds:** 1T 1D 1S **Baths:** 3 En (2)

Holding Lodge Guest House, *81 Hoole Road, Hoole, Chester, Cheshire, CH2 3NJ.* Home from home, minutes from railway, city centre & motorways. **Open:** All year
01244 345815 (also fax) Mr & Mrs Holding *info@holdinglodge.co.uk* www.holdinglodge.co.uk **D:** Fr £17.50–£25.00 **S:** Fr £20.00–£27.50 **Beds:** 1F 1T 1S **Baths:** 3 En 1 Pr (4)

Grosvenor Place Guest House, *2-4 Grosvenor Place, Chester, CH1 2DE.* Excellent breakfast and very clean; proprietor: Alma Wood. **Open:** All year (not Xmas)
Grades: ETC 3 Diamond
01244 324455 Mrs Wood **Fax: 01244 400225 D:** Fr £19.00–£23.50 **S:** Fr £27.00 **Beds:** 2F 3D 2T 3S **Baths:** 6 En 2 Sh cc

Castle House, *23 Castle Street, Chester, CH1 2DS.* Pre-1580 Tudor house, plus Georgian front (1738). **Open:** All year
01244 350354 Mr Marl **D:** Fr £25.00 **S:** Fr £38.00 **Beds:** 1F 1D 1T 2S **Baths:** 3 En 1 Sh cc

Green Cottage, *Higher Kinnerton, Chester, CH4 9BZ.* 6 miles from historic Chester, relaxing atmosphere, good food, in a Welsh rural setting. **Open:** All year
01244 660137 & 01244 661369 Mrs Milner **D:** Fr £20.00 **S:** Fr £25.00 **Beds:** 1D 1T **Baths:** 1 Pr

Aplas Guest House, *106 Brook Street, Chester, Cheshire, CH1 3DU.* Family-run guest house, ideally located for historic Chester. 10 mins' walk city centre. **Open:** All year
01244 312401 Mr Aplas **D:** Fr £13.00–£17.50 **Beds:** 1F 4D 2T **Baths:** 5 En 2 Sh (7)

Stone Villa, *3 Stone Place, Hoole, Chester, CH2 3NR.* A haven of quiet relaxation with individual attention and warm hospitality. **Open:** All year (not Xmas)
01244 345014 Mr Pow *adam@stonevilla.freeserve.co.uk* **D:** Fr £25.00–£28.00 **S:** Fr £25.00–£32.00 **Beds:** 1F 6D 2T 1S **Baths:** 9 En 1 Pr (10) cc

Please respect a B&B's wishes regarding children, animals and smoking

Green Gables Guest House, *11 Eversley Park, Chester, Cheshire, CH2 2AJ.* Quietly situated yet 0.9 miles from town centre. Victorian property. **Open:** All year **01244 372243** Mrs Perruzza **Fax: 01244 376352 D:** Fr £19.00 **S:** Fr £26.00 **Beds:** 1F 1D 1T 1S **Baths:** 3 En (5)

Chester Court Hotel, *48 Hoole Road, Chester, CH2 3NL.* Set in its own grounds only 3/4 mile from city centre. **Open:** All year (not Xmas/New Year) **01244 320779** Mr Row **Fax: 01244 344795** *info@chestercourthotel.com* www.chestercourthotel.com **D:** Fr £32.50–£35.00 **S:** Fr £40.00–£45.00 **Beds:** 3F 3T 11D 3S **Baths:** 20 En (25) **cc**

Congleton

SJ8663

The Lamb Inn, *3 Blake Street, Congleton, Cheshire, CW12 4DS.* Central location convenient for Cheshire country houses and attractions. **Open:** All year **01260 272731** Mr Kelly *john.kelly5@tesco.net* www.lambinn.org.uk **D:** Fr £17.00–£21.00 **S:** Fr £19.00–£26.00 **Beds:** 1F 2D 2T 1S **Baths:** 4 En 2 Sh (40)

Cuttleford Farm, *Newcastle Road, Astbury, Congleton, Cheshire, CW12 4SD.* C16th farmhouse - working farm close to National Trust House. **Open:** All year **01260 272499** Mrs Downs **D:** Fr £15.00–£19.00 **S:** Fr £20.00–£25.00 **Beds:** 2D 1T **Baths:** 1 En 1 Sh

8 Cloud View, *Congleton, Cheshire, CW12 3TP.* Lovely family home, edge of countryside, good views, beautiful garden. **Open:** All year (not Xmas) **01260 276048** Mrs Stewart **D:** Fr £18.00–£25.00 **S:** Fr £20.00–£25.00 **Beds:** 1T 1D 1S **Baths:** 1 En 1 Sh (1)

Elworth

SJ7461

Poplar Mount Guest House, *2 Station Road, Elworth, Sandbach, Cheshire, CW11 9JG.* Friendly family-run guest house, convenient for M6 motorway. **Open:** All year **01270 761268 (also fax)** Mrs McDonald **D:** Fr £20.00 **S:** Fr £20.00–£28.00 **Beds:** 2F 3D 1T 2S **Baths:** 4 En 1 Sh (9) **cc**

Handbridge

SJ4065

Eaton House, *36 Eaton Road, Handbridge, Chester, CH4 7EY.* Victorian town house within close walking distance of city centre. **Open:** All year (not Xmas/New Year) **01244 680349 Fax: 01244 659021** *grahamd@aol.com* **D:** Fr £19.00–£24.00 **S:** Fr £20.00–£24.00 **Beds:** 1F 1D (8) (3) **cc**

Haslington

SJ7355

Ferndale House, *Gutterscroft, Haslington, Crewe, Cheshire, CW1 5RJ.* Victorian home, large rooms, excellent food, secure parking, convenient M6. **Open:** All year **01270 584048** L M Docherty *ferndalehouse@tinyworld.co.uk* www.ferndalehouse.co.uk **D:** Fr £20.00–£23.50 **S:** Fr £20.00 (7)

Hatton Heath

SJ4561

Golborne Manor, *Platts Lane, Hatton Heath, Chester, Cheshire, CH3 9AN.* Beautifully decorated C19th manor house with glorious views and garden. **Open:** All year **01829 770310 & 07850 265425 (M)** Mrs Ikin **Fax: 01829 770370** *ann.ikin@golbornemanor.co.uk* **D:** Fr £58.00–£68.00 **S:** Fr £28.00–£38.00 **Beds:** 1F 1T 1D **Baths:** 3 En (6)

Higher Wych

SJ4943

Mill House, *Higher Wych, Malpas, Cheshire, SY14 7JR.* Modernised mill house, peaceful valley. Convenient for Chester, Shrewsbury, Llangollen. **Open:** Jan to Nov **01948 780362** Mrs Smith **Fax: 01948 780566** *angela@videoactive.co.uk* **D:** Fr £20.00–£22.00 **S:** Fr £20.00–£22.00 **Beds:** 1D 1T **Baths:** 1 En 1 Sh (4)

Hollins Green

SJ6991 *Black Swan, Red Lion, Rhinewood Hotel*

Brook Farm, *Manchester Road, Hollins Green, Warrington, Cheshire, WA3 6HX.* Situated in a semi-rural location, close to M6, M62, M56 and 15 mins Manchester Airport. A working farm and equestrian centre. Central for Manchester and Warrington for business or leisure. Known for our 'big breakfast'. **Open:** All year (not Xmas/New Year) **0161 775 6053 (also fax)** Mr Hesford **D:** Fr £18.00–£20.00 **S:** Fr £21.00–£25.00 **Beds:** 2T 2D 2S **Baths:** 3 En 1 Sh (20)

Latchford

SJ6187

The Maples Private Hotel, *11 Longdin Street, Latchford, WA4 1PJ.* Family-run hotel. Close village/town. Good access motorways. Friendly welcome. **Open:** All year (not Xmas/New Year) **01925 637752** S M Savory **D:** Fr £15.00–£30.00 **S:** Fr £10.00–£20.00 **Beds:** 1F 3T 2D 2S **Baths:** 2 En 1 Pr 1 Sh

Little Bollington

SJ7286

Bollington Hall Farm, *Park Lane, Little Bollington, Altrincham, Cheshire, WA14 4TJ.* Close to Manchester, Dunham Massey Hall, Tatton Hall, Trans-Penine Trail & motorway network **Open:** All year (not Xmas/New Year) **0161 928 1760** Mrs Owen **D:** Fr £18.00 **S:** Fr £18.00 **Beds:** 1F 1D **Baths:** 1 Sh (10)

Macclesfield

SJ9173

Heaton House Farm, *Rushton Spencer, Macclesfield, Cheshire, SK11 0RD.* **Open:** All year **01260 226203 Fax: 01260 226562** *mick@heatonhouse.fsnet.co.uk* www.heatonhousefarm.co.uk **D:** Fr £22.50–£27.50 **S:** Fr £30.00 **Beds:** 2D **Baths:** 2 En (5)
Converted granary on edge of Staffordshire Moorlands provides two, quality double ensuite bedrooms with kingsize beds. One has kitchen & views over 3 counties. Near Alton Towers, Cheshire & Derbyshire borders. An area famous for antique shops, walking & scenery.

Penrose Guest House, *56 Birtles Road, Whirley, Macclesfield, Cheshire, SK10 3JQ.* Central for Wilmslow, Prestbury, Macclesfield. Close Intercity trains, motorway, airport. **Open:** All year **01625 615323 Fax: 01625 432284** *info@PenroseGuestHouse.co.uk* www.PenroseGuestHouse.co.uk **D:** Fr £20.00 **S:** Fr £20.00 **Beds:** 1T 2S (4) (6)

RATES
D = Price range per person sharing in a double or twin room
S = Price range for a single room

Manley

SJ5071

Rangeway Bank Farm, *Manley, Warrington, Cheshire, WA6 9EF.* Friendly traditional farmhouse in rural Cheshire, access to Delamere Forest. **Open:** All year (not Xmas)
01928 740236 J Challoner **Fax: 01928 740703** **D:** Fr £20.00–£25.00 **S:** Fr £22.00–£25.00 **Beds:** 1F 1D 1T **Baths:** 2 En 1 Sh (6)

Middlewich

SJ7066

Sandhurst Lodge, *69 Chester Road, Middlewich, Cheshire, CW10 9EW.* Charming Edwardian residence close to M6 in Cheshire heartland. **Open:** All year (not Xmas)
01606 834125 Mrs Fair **D:** Fr £22.00–£24.00 **S:** Fr £25.00–£30.00 **Beds:** 2F 5D 1T **Baths:** 8 En (8)

Mobberley

SJ7879

Laburnum Cottage, *Knutsford Road, Mobberley, Knutsford, Cheshire, WA16 7PU.* Country house close to Knutsford overlooking Tatton Park, award-winning food. **Open:** All year
01565 872464 (also fax) Mr & Mrs Messenger **D:** Fr £28.50 **S:** Fr £44.00 **Beds:** 1F 1t 1D 1S **Baths:** 4 En (10) **cc**

Mottram St Andrew

SJ8778 *Bull's Head*

Goose Green Farm, *Oak Road, Mottram St Andrew, Macclesfield, Cheshire, SK10 4RA.* Perfectly situated, comfortable, quiet location with lovely views. Warm welcome. **Open:** All year
01625 828814 (also fax) D Hatch *goosegreenfarm@talk21.com* **D:** Fr £22.00–£24.00 **S:** Fr £22.00 **Beds:** 1T 1D 2S **Baths:** 1 En 1 Sh (5) (8) **cc**

Nantwich

SJ6452

Oakland House, *252 Newcastle Road, Blakelow, Shavington, Nantwich, Cheshire, CW5 7ET.* **Open:** All year **Grades:** AA 5 Diamond
01270 567134 Mr & Mrs Groom **Fax: 01270 651752** **D:** Fr £21.50–£24.50 **S:** Fr £30.00–£34.00 **Beds:** 3T 5D 1S **Baths:** 9 En **cc**
5m from M6, 1.5m Nantwich on A500 J 16. Rural location.

Lea Farm, *Wrinehill Road, Wybunbury, Nantwich, Cheshire, CW5 7NS.* Charming farmhouse set in landscaped gardens where peacocks roam. **Open:** All year (not Xmas)
01270 841429 Mrs Callwood **Fax: 01270 841030** *contactus@leafarm.co.uk* **D:** Fr £20.00 **S:** Fr £25.00 **Beds:** 1F 1D 1T **Baths:** 2 Pr 1 Sh (22)

The Railway Hotel, *Pillory Street, Nantwich, Cheshire, CW5 5SS.* Historic 1890 building, on the edge of beautiful Nantwich town. **Open:** All year
01270 623482 J Hobson *jhobson@freeuk.com* **D:** Fr £25.00 **S:** Fr £30.00–£40.00 **Beds:** 2F 1T 1S **Baths:** 4 En **cc**

Norley

SJ5672

Wicken Tree Farm, *Blakemere Lane, Norley, Warrington, Cheshire, WA6 6NW.* High quality self-contained accommodation and B&B, surrounded by Delamere Forest. **Open:** All year
01928 788355 Mr Appleton *ches@williamj99.freeserve.co.uk* **D:** Fr £23.50–£25.00 **S:** Fr £23.50–£31.00 **Beds:** 1F 5D 7T 3S **Baths:** 6 En 1 Pr 2 Sh (14)

North Rode

SJ8866

Yew Tree Farm, *North Rode, Congleton, Cheshire, CW12 2PF.* Cosy farmhouse in wooded parkland, traditional home-cooked meals. **Open:** All year **Grades:** ETC 4 Diamond
01260 223569 Mrs Kidd **Fax: 01260 223328** *yewtreebb@hotmail.com* www.yewtreebb.co.uk **D:** Fr £22.00–£27.00 **S:** Fr £27.00–£30.00 **Beds:** 1D 1F **Baths:** 2 En (10)

Over Tabley

SJ7280

The Old Vicarage, *Moss Lane, Over Tabley, Knutsford, Cheshire, WA16 0PL.* Set in 2 acres of wooded gardens. A warm welcome awaits you. **Open:** All year (not Xmas/New Year)
01565 652221 Mrs Weston **Fax: 01565 755918** **D:** Fr £32.50 **S:** Fr £49.50 **Beds:** 1F 2T 2D **Baths:** 5 En (10) (20) **cc**

Poole

SJ6455

Poole Bank Farm, *Poole, Nantwich, Cheshire, CW5 6AL.* Charming C17th timbered farmhouse, surrounded by picturesque dairy farmland. **Open:** All year
01270 625169 Ms Hocknell **D:** Fr £18.00–£22.00 **S:** Fr £20.00–£24.00 **Beds:** 1D 1T 1F **Baths:** 1 Pr 2 Sh (10)

Poynton

SJ9283 *Vernon Arms*

Whitethorn, *1 Waters Reach, Poynton, Stockport, Greater Manchester, SK12 1XT.* Modern detached house. Quiet cul-de-sac close to village. **Open:** All year (not Xmas/New Year)
01625 871590 C P Williams **D:** Fr £18.00–£20.00 **S:** Fr £18.00–£20.00 **Beds:** 1D **Baths:** 1 Pr

Rainow

SJ9576

The Tower House, *Tower Hill, Rainow, Macclesfield, Cheshire, SK10 5TX.* Luxury accommodation in carefully restored C16th farmhouse. Superb breakfasts. **Open:** All year
01625 438022 (also fax) Mrs Buckley **D:** Fr £25.00 **S:** Fr £25.00–£35.00 **Beds:** 2T 1S **Baths:** 1 Pr (4)

Ravensmoor

SJ6250

Pujols, *Barracks Lane, Ravensmoor, Nantwich, Cheshire, CW5 8PR.* Quiet location, easy reach M6, railways, North Wales, Peak District. **Open:** All year
01270 626528 **D:** Fr £12.00–£15.00 **S:** Fr £15.00–£18.00 **Beds:** 1T 1D **Baths:** 1 Sh (2)

Runcorn

SJ5281

Fountains Hotel, *10 High Street, Runcorn, Cheshire, WA7 1AU.* Town centre Victorian building tastefully furnished. Convenient motorways and public transport. **Open:** All year
01928 569799 Mr & Mrs Gittins **Fax: 01928 830513** **D:** Fr £17.00 **S:** Fr £20.00–£27.00 **Beds:** 1F 4T 1D 2S **Baths:** 8 En

Please respect a B&B's wishes regarding children, animals and smoking

Rushton
SJ5863

Hill House Farm, *The Hall Lane, Rushton, Tarporley, Cheshire, CW6 9AU.* Beautiful Victorian former farmhouse, comfortable accommodation, 1.5 miles from Oulton Park. **Open:** All year (not Xmas/New Year) **Grades:** ETC 4 Diamond **01829 732238 & 07973 284863 (M)** Mrs Rayner **Fax: 01829 733929** *rayner@hillhousefarm.fsnet.co.uk* **D:** Fr £25.00–£30.00 **S:** Fr £30.00–£35.00 **Beds:** 1F 1T 1D **Baths:** 2 En 1 Pr (10)

Shavington
SJ6951

Oakland House, *252 Newcastle Road, Blakelow, Shavington, Nantwich, Cheshire, CW5 7ET.* 5m from M6, 1.5m Nantwich on A500 J 16. Rural location. **Open:** All year **Grades:** AA 5 Diamond **01270 567134** Mr & Mrs Groom **Fax: 01270 651752 D:** Fr £21.50–£24.50 **S:** Fr £30.00–£34.00 **Beds:** 3T 5D 1S **Baths:** 9 En **cc**

Stapeley
SJ6749

York Cottage, *82 Broad Lane, Stapeley, Nantwich, Cheshire, CW5 7QL.* Comfortable detached rural cottage, with garden, 2 miles from Nantwich. **Open:** All year **01270 629829** Mrs Orford **Fax: 01270 625404 D:** Fr £18.00–£20.00 **S:** Fr £18.00–£22.00 **Beds:** 2D 1F **Baths:** 1 Sh (3)

Stoke
SJ6552 *Dysart Arms, Boot & Slipper, Red Fox*

Stoke Grange Farm, *Chester Road, Stoke, Nantwich, Cheshire, CW5 6BT.* Canalside farmhouse. Wonderful views. Pets' Corner farmhouse. Peace and quiet. **Open:** All year **01270 625525 (also fax)** Mrs West *stokegrange@freeuk.com* **D:** Fr £25.00–£30.00 **S:** Fr £30.00–£35.00 **Beds:** 1F 1T 1D **Baths:** 3 En (10)

Stretton (Farndon)
SJ4452

Stretton Lower Hall, *Marsh Lane, Stretton, Tilston, Malpas, SY14 7HS.* C17th country house near Stretton Water Mill, Carden Park Golf Course, The Sandstone Trail and 15 minutes drive south of historic Chester. Comfortable and quiet. Large gardens and spacious parking area. 1m from Jacobean pub/restaurant. **Open:** All year (not Xmas/New Year) **01829 250641 Fax: 01829 250596** *dradel000@aol.com* **D:** Fr £25.00–£29.00 **S:** Fr £25.00–£29.00 **Beds:** 1F 1T 1D 1S **Baths:** 1 En 1 Pr 1 Sh (20)

Stretton (Warrington)
SJ6182

The School House, *Stretton Road, Stretton, Warrington, Cheshire, WA4 4NT.* Old headmaster's school house (1835). Now an upmarket B&B - semi-rural location. **Open:** All year (not Xmas/New Year) **01925 730826 D:** Fr £22.50 **S:** Fr £35.00 **Beds:** 4F 1T 3D **Baths:** 4 En

Tarporley
SJ5462

Hill House Farm, *The Hall Lane, Rushton, Tarporley, Cheshire, CW6 9AU.* Beautiful Victorian former farmhouse, comfortable accommodation, 1.5 miles from Oulton Park. **Open:** All year (not Xmas/New Year) **Grades:** ETC 4 Diamond **01829 732238 & 07973 284863 (M)** Mrs Rayner **Fax: 01829 733929** *rayner@hillhousefarm.fsnet.co.uk* **D:** Fr £25.00–£30.00 **S:** Fr £30.00–£35.00 **Beds:** 1F 1T 1D **Baths:** 2 En 1 Pr (10)

1 Bunbury Court, *Eaton Road, Tarporley, Cheshire, CW6 0DL.* Situated in lovely Cheshire village. Close to restaurants and inns. **Open:** All year **01829 733452** Mrs Spencer **D:** Fr £17.50 **S:** Fr £18.50 **Beds:** 1T 1D **Baths:** 1 Sh (1)

Foresters Arms, *92 High Street, Tarporley, Cheshire, CW6 0AX.* A traditional country inn offering fine ales and comfortable rooms. **Open:** All year (not Xmas/New Year) **01829 733151** Mr Hulse **Fax: 01829 730020 D:** Fr £18.00–£22.50 **S:** Fr £18.00–£22.50 **Beds:** 4T 2D **Baths:** 2 En 3 Sh (10) (20) **cc**

Tilston
SJ4551

Tilston Lodge, *Tilston, Malpas, Cheshire, SY14 7DR.* Handsome country house with spacious grounds. Luxuriously equipped quiet bedrooms. **Open:** All year (not Xmas/New Year) **01829 250223 (also fax)** Mrs Ritchie **D:** Fr £33.00–£35.00 **S:** Fr £43.00–£45.00 **Beds:** 1T 1D **Baths:** 2 En (10)

Timbersbrook
SJ8962 *Church House, Robin Hood*

Pedley House Farm, *Pedley Lane, Timbersbrook, Congleton, Cheshire, CW12 3QD.* Free range eggs, home-made jam for breakfast. **Open:** All year (not Xmas/New Year) **01260 273650 (also fax)** Mrs Gilman **D:** Fr £18.00 **S:** Fr £18.00–£20.00 **Beds:** 1F 1T 1D **Baths:** 3 Sh (3)

Tiverton
SJ5460

The Gables, *Tiverton, Tarporley, Cheshire, CW6 9NH.* Beautiful country cottage set amidst almost 1/2 acre of gardens. **Open:** All year **01829 733028** Mr Wilson **Fax: 01829 733399 D:** Fr £17.50–£19.00 **S:** Fr £25.00–£35.00 **Beds:** 3D **Baths:** 1 Sh (8)

Tytherington
SJ9175 *Cock & Pheasant*

Moorhayes House Hotel, *27 Manchester Road, Tytherington, Macclesfield, Cheshire, SK10 2JJ.* Warm welcome. Hearty breakfast. Half a mile north of Macclesfield. **Open:** All year (not Xmas/New Year) **01625 433228 (also fax)** Helen Wood *helen@moorhayeshouse.freeserve.co.uk* **D:** Fr £26.00–£30.00 **S:** Fr £35.00–£40.00 **Beds:** 1F 1T 5D 1S **Baths:** 8 En (14) **cc**

Warrington
SJ6088

New House Farm, *Hatton Lane, Stretton, Warrington, Cheshire, WA4 4BZ.* Fields surround cottages. 1 mile M56 J10, 4 miles south of Warrington. **Open:** All year **01925 730567 & 01925 264326** Mrs Delooze *newhousefarmcottage@talk21.com* **D:** Fr £18.00–£20.00 **S:** Fr £18.00–£20.00 **Beds:** 1D 2T 1S **Baths:** 1 En 1 Pr 1 Sh (30)

The Hollies, *1 Long Lane, Orford, Warrington, Cheshire, WA2 8PT.* Small & friendly. New bathroom & beds this year. Great cooked breakfasts. **Open:** All year (not Xmas/New Year) **01925 635416 (also fax)** Mrs Brown **D:** Fr £17.50–£20.00 **S:** Fr £20.00–£22.00 **Beds:** 1F 2T 1D **Baths:** 1 Sh (5) (8)

The Cottage Guest House, *37 Tanners Lane, Warrington, Cheshire, WA2 7NL.* Side street location, homely atmosphere, comfortable beds. 3 mins town centre. **Open:** All year (not Xmas/New Year) **01925 631524** Mr & Mrs Ramsdale **Fax: 01925 445400** *j.h.@3pigeons.fsnet.co.uk* **D:** Fr £16.00–£18.00 **S:** Fr £20.00–£22.00 **Beds:** 3T 1S **Baths:** 2 En 2 Sh (6)

Braemar Guest House, *274 Manchester Road, Woolston, Warrington, WA1 4PS.* Large family house on A57 1/2 mile from J21 on M6. **Open:** All year **01925 491683** Mr Freeman **Fax: 01244 836666 D:** Fr £20.00–£25.00 **Beds:** 2S **Baths:** 1 Sh (5)

Weston (Crewe)

SJ7352

Snape Farm, *Snape Lane, Weston, Crewe, Cheshire, CW2 5NB.* Quiet location within easy reach of M6. Superb farmhouse breakfasts. **Open:** All year (not Xmas/New Year) **Grades:** ETC 3 Diamond
01270 820208 (also fax) Mrs Williamson *jean@snapefarm.fsnet.co.uk* **D:** Fr £20.00–£25.00 **S:** Fr £22.00–£28.00 **Beds:** 2T 1D **Baths:** 1 En 2 Sh (6)

Willington Corner

SJ5366 *The Boot*

Roughlow Farm, *Willington Corner, Tarporley, Cheshire, CW6 0PG.* Sandstone farmhouse. Lovely views, peaceful location. Top quality accommodation. **Open:** All year
01829 751199 (also fax) Mrs Sutcliffe *sutcliffe@roughlow.freeserve.co.uk* www.roughlow.freeserve.co.uk **D:** Fr £25.00–£40.00 **S:** Fr £10.00 **Beds:** 12D **Baths:** 3 En (3) (6)

Wilmslow

SJ8480

The Grange, *Clay Lane, Handforth, Wilmslow, Cheshire, SK9 3NR.* Set in rural surroundings but close airport, motorway and trains. **Open:** All year
01625 523653 Mrs Godlee **Fax: 01625 530140** *alisongodlee@lineone.net* **D:** Fr £22.50 **S:** Fr £35.00 **Beds:** 3F 1T 2S **Baths:** 3 En (6)

Tulip Tree Guest House, *7 Longmeade Gdns, Wilmslow, SK9 1DA.* 2 minutes from train station. One stop Manchester airport. 40 restaurant/cafes nearby. **Open:** All year
01625 536709 & 01625 530654
Mrs Armstrong **D:** Fr £20.00–£30.00 **S:** Fr £25.00–£30.00 **Beds:** 1F 1T 1D 1S

Winsford

SJ6566

Hermitage House, *1 Hareswood Close, Winsford, Cheshire, CW7 2TP.* Close to Oulten Park, Delamere Forest. Warm, friendly house. **Open:** All year (not Xmas/New Year)
01606 550544 (also fax) Mrs Campbell **D:** Fr £30.00 **S:** Fr £20.00–£25.00 **Beds:** 1T 1D 1S **Baths:** 2 En 1 Sh (3)

Wybunbury

SJ6949

Lea Farm, *Wrinehill Road, Wybunbury, Nantwich, Cheshire, CW5 7NS.* Charming farmhouse set in landscaped gardens where peacocks roam. **Open:** All year (not Xmas)
01270 841429 Mrs Callwood **Fax: 01270 841030** *contactus@leafarm.co.uk* **D:** Fr £20.00 **S:** Fr £25.00 **Beds:** 1F 1D 1T **Baths:** 2 Pr 1 Sh (22)

Cornwall

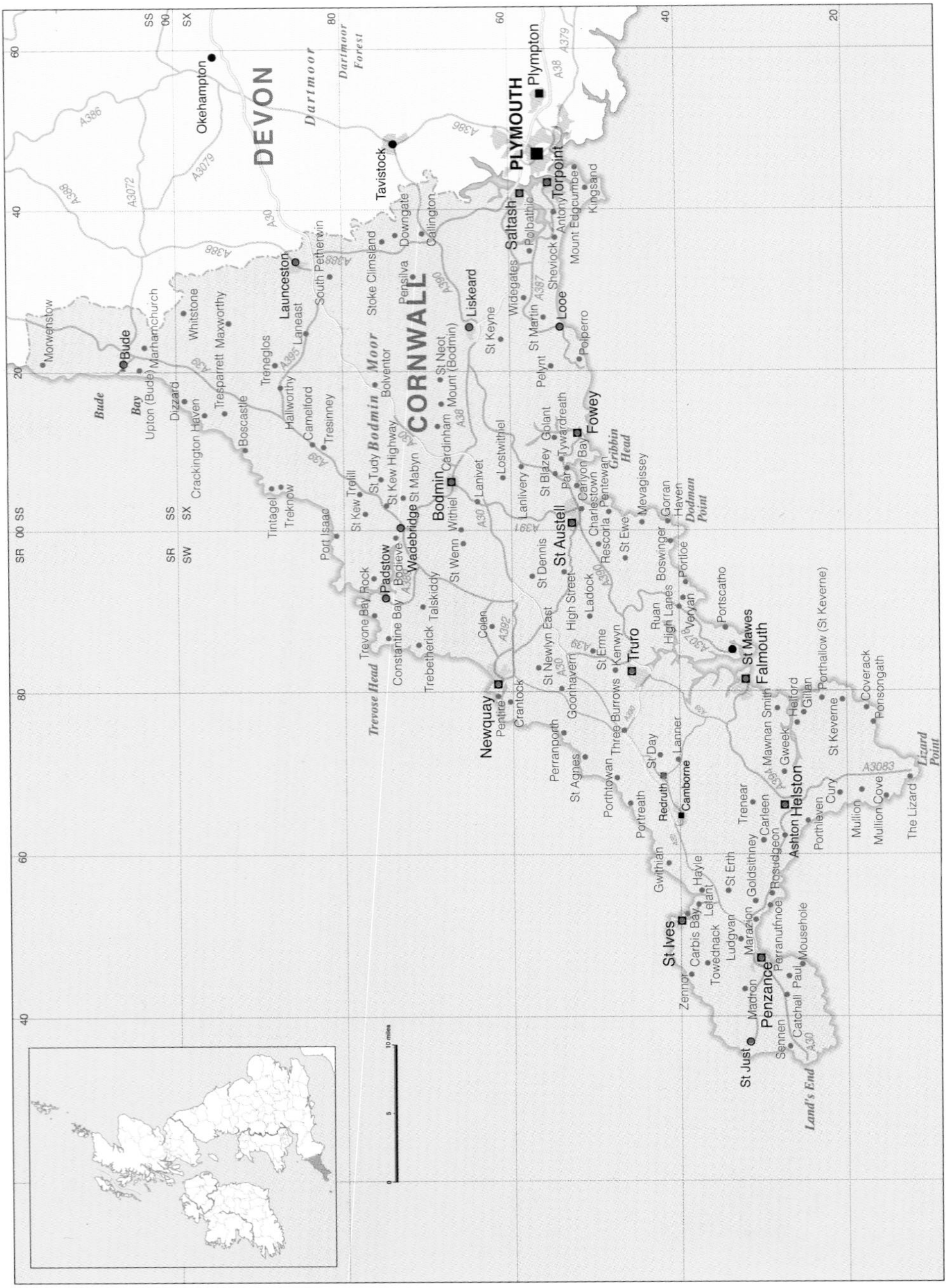
DEVON
CORNWALL
Dartmoor
Dartmoor Forest
Bodmin Moor
PLYMOUTH
Plympton
Okehampton
Tavistock
Launceston
Bude
Bude Bay
Morwenstow
Marhamchurch
Whitstone
Maxworthy
Treneglos
Laneast
Tresparrett
Upton (Bude)
Dizzard
Crackington Haven
Boscastle
Hallworthy
Camelford
Tresinney
Tintagel
Treknow
Port Isaac
St Kew
Trelill
St Tudy
St Kew Highway
St Mabyn
Wadebridge
Padstow
Rock
Bodieve
Trevone Bay
Constantine Bay
Trevose Head
Talskiddy
Trebetherick
St Wenn
Withiel
Bodmin
Lanivet
Cardinham
Mount (Bodmin)
St Neot
Bolventor
South Petherwin
Stoke Climsland
Downgate
Callington
Pensilva
Liskeard
St Keyne
Lostwithiel
Lanlivery
St Blazey
Par
Golant
Tywardreath
Fowey
Gribbin Head
Carlyon Bay
Pentewan
Charlestown
St Austell
Mevagissey
Gorran Haven
Dodman Point
St Ewe
Rescorla
Boswinger
Portloe
Veryan
Portscatho
St Mawes
Falmouth
Ruan High Lanes
St Dennis
High Street
Ladock
Colan
Newquay
Pentire
Crantock
St Newlyn East
Goonhavern
St Erme
Kenwyn
Truro
Three Burrows
Perranporth
St Agnes
Porthtowan
Portreath
St Day
Lanner
Redruth
Camborne
Gwithian
Hayle
Lelant
Carbis Bay
St Ives
Zennor
Towednack
Ludgvan
Marazion
St Erth
Goldsithney
Rosudgeon
Perranuthnoe
Penzance
Madron
Paul
Mousehole
Catchall
Sennen
St Just
Land's End
Helston
Ashton
Porthleven
Trenear
Carleen
Gweek
Mawnan Smith
Helford
Gillan
Porthallow (St Keverne)
St Keverne
Coverack
Ponsongath
Cury
Mullion
Mullion Cove
The Lizard
Lizard Point
Saltash
Polbathic
Torpoint
Antony
Sheviock
Kingsand
Mount Edgcumbe
Widegates
St Martin
Looe
Polperro
Pelynt
A30
A38
A39
A386
A388
A390
A391
A392
A394
A395
A3072
A3079
A3083
A379
A387
SS
SX
SR
SW
10 miles

Charlestown

SX0351 *Rashleigh Arms, Pier House, Polgooth Inn*

Ardenconnel, *179 Charlestown Road, Charlestown, St Austell, Cornwall, PL25 3NN.* Beautiful Victorian house situated in the unchanged C18th port of Charlestown. **Open:** All year
01726 75469 Mr Callis *ardenconnel@hotmail.com* **D:** Fr £21.00–£25.00 **S:** Fr £29.00–£33.00 **Beds:** 1F 1T 1D **Baths:** 1 En 1 Pr (2)

Colan

SW8661

Colan Barton Farmhouse, *Colan, Newquay, Cornwall, TR8 4NB.* C17th farmhouse set in stunning countryside. Self-contained cottage adjacent, sleeps 2 or 4. Warm welcome. **Open:** Apr to Sep
01637 874395 Mrs Machin-Weaver **Fax: 01637 881388** *colanbarton@yahoo.co.uk* **D:** Fr £25.00–£27.00 **S:** Fr £30.00–£32.00 **Beds:** 3F 1T 1D **Baths:** 1 En 1 Pr (6)

Constantine Bay

SW8574

Chyloweth, *Constantine Bay, Padstow, Cornwall, PL28 8JQ.* Quiet location close to sandy beaches and Trevose Golf Club. **Open:** All year **Grades:** ETC 3 Diamond
01841 521012 R & S Vivian *roger.vivian@ukgateway.net* **D:** Fr £25.00–£30.00 **S:** Fr £25.00–£45.00 **Beds:** 1T 1D **Baths:** 2 En (2)

Coverack

SW7818

Boak House, *Coverack, Helston, Cornwall, TR12 6SH.* Seaside guest house overlooking harbour and cove. Sea views from rooms. **Open:** Easter to Nov
01326 280608 Mrs Watters www.bedandbreakfastcornwall.com/members-house/boakhouse.htm **D:** Fr £18.50–£19.00 **S:** Fr £18.50–£19.00 **Beds:** 2F 1T 1D 1S **Baths:** 1 Sh (2)

Wych Elm, *Ponsongath, Coverack, Helston, Cornwall, TR12 6SQ.* Idyllic quiet setting close secluded Lankidden Cove. Backwoodsmen's bliss! **Open:** All year (not Xmas)
01326 280576 Mrs Whitaker **D:** Fr £18.00 **S:** Fr £20.00 **Beds:** 1T **Baths:** 1 En (8) (2)

Tamarisk Cottage, *North Corner, Coverack, Helston, Cornwall, TR12 6TG.* C18th cottage overlooking bay. On footpath. Parking and wash basin. **Open:** Easter to Oct
01326 280638 Mrs Carey **D:** Fr £17.00 **S:** Fr £17.00 **Beds:** 1T 1D 1S **Baths:** 1 Sh (8) (2)

Crackington Haven

SX1496

Venn Park Farm, *Crackington Haven, Bude, Cornwall, EX23 0LB.* Relaxation opportunity. Sea/countryside views. 2 miles beach. Coastal/moorland walks. Traditional farmhouse cooking, buffet breakfast. **Open:** All year
01840 230159 (also fax) Jane Wilson **D:** Fr £18.00–£24.00 **S:** Fr £20.00–£26.00 **Beds:** 1F 2D **Baths:** 2 En 1 Pr

Hallagather, *Crackington Haven, Bude, Cornwall, EX23 0LA.* Ancient farmhouse, warm, welcoming. Substantial buffet-style breakfast. Spectacular scenery. **Open:** Feb to Nov **Grades:** ETC 4 Diamond
01840 230276 (also fax) Mrs Anthony **D:** Fr £18.00–£27.00 **S:** Fr £18.00–£28.00 **Beds:** 1F 1D 1S **Baths:** 3 En (11) (6)

Crantock

SW7960

Carden Cottage, *Halwyn Hill, Crantock, Newquay, Cornwall, TR8 5RR.* **Open:** All year (not Xmas/New Year)
01637 830806 Mr Clark *bernie@cardencottage.fsnet.co.uk* members.lycos.co.uk/crantock2 **D:** Fr £22.00–£24.00 **S:** Fr £22.00–£26.00 **Beds:** 1T 2D **Baths:** 3 En (10) (4)
A beautiful place with king-size beds, tea and coffee, soap and towels and a full English breakfast, situated in the heart of the village, with two pubs, a church and a few minutes walk from a lovely sandy beach.

Highfield Lodge Hotel, *Halwyn Road, Crantock, Newquay, Cornwall, TR8 5TR.* Friendly non-smoking hotel in picturesque village with sandy beach. **Open:** All year (not Xmas/New Year) **Grades:** ETC 4 Diamond
01637 830744 Fax: 01637 830568 *info@highfieldlodge.co.uk* www.highfieldlodge.co.uk **D:** Fr £18.00–£24.00 **S:** Fr £18.00–£30.00 **Beds:** 1T 7D 1S **Baths:** 6 En 1 Sh (12) cc

Cury

SW6721 *Old Inn, Wheel Inn*

Tregaddra Farmhouse, *Cury, Helston, Cornwall, TR12 7BB.* Farmhouse B&B quiet, peaceful, set in Area of Outstanding Natural Beauty. **Open:** All year (not Xmas)
01326 240235 (also fax) Mrs Lugg www.tregaddra.freeserve.co.uk **D:** Fr £20.00–£25.00 **S:** Fr £20.00–£25.00 **Beds:** 2F 4D 1T **Baths:** 6 En 1 Pr (10) cc

Nanplough Farm, *Cury, Whitecross, Helston, Cornwall, TR12 7BQ.* Large Victorian farmhouse. Overlooking wooded valley. Beach 1 mile. **Open:** All year
01326 241088 Mr Lepper *william.lepper@btclick.com* **D:** Fr £22.00–£28.00 **Beds:** 1F 1D **Baths:** 2 En

Colvennor Farmhouse, *Cury, Helston, Cornwall, TR12 7BJ.* Delightful former farmhouse. Peaceful setting. Perfect location for exploring. Excellent hospitality. **Open:** All year (not Xmas/New Year)
01326 241208 Mrs Royds *colvennor@aol.com* **D:** Fr £20.00–£23.00 **S:** Fr £25.00–£28.00 **Beds:** 1T 2D **Baths:** 3 En (3)

Dizzard

SX1698 *Wainhouse Inn, Coombe Barton Inn*

Trengayor Farm, *Dizzard, Bude, Cornwall, EX23 0NX.* Secluded 1900 farmhouse, close Coastal Path, Cycle Route. Coastal views. **Open:** All year (not Xmas/New Year)
01840 230427 Mr Jackson **D:** Fr £18.00 **S:** Fr £18.00 **Beds:** 1D 1S **Baths:** 1 Sh (6)

Downgate

SX3672 *Springer Spaniel*

Niggles Nook Guest House, *Sandercock Close, Downgate, Callington, Cornwall, PL17 8JS.* Modern bungalow set in lovely countryside. Midway north/south coasts. **Open:** All year
01579 370813 S Bartlett **D:** Fr £15.00 **S:** Fr £15.00 **Beds:** 2D **Baths:** 1 Sh (2)

Falmouth

SW8032

Green Lawns Hotel, *Western Terrace, Falmouth, Cornwall, TR11 4QJ.* **Open:** All year (not Xmas) **Grades:** ETC 3 Star, AA 3 Star, RAC 3 Star
01326 312734 Mr Collings **Fax: 01326 211427** *info@greenlawnshotel.com* www.greenlawnshotel.com **D:** Fr £55.00–£85.00 **S:** Fr £60.00–£110.00 **Beds:** 8F 14T 11D 6S **Baths:** 39 En (50) cc
Chateau-style hotel set in prize-winning gardens only a short stroll to the main beaches and town. A la carte restaurant, leisure complex, honeymoon/executive suites, bargain breaks and special family terms. Close to Eden Project and Maritime Museum.

Melvill House Hotel, *52 Melvill Road, Falmouth, Cornwall, TR11 4DQ.* **Open:** All year (not Xmas) **Grades:** AA 4 Diamond
01326 316645 Mr & Mrs Crawford **Fax: 01326 211608** *enquiries@melvill.eurobell.co.uk* www.melvill-house-falmouth.co.uk **D:** Fr £20.00–£26.00 **S:** Fr £20.00–£26.00 **Beds:** 2F 3D 2T **Baths:** 7 En (9) cc
Friendly, family-run hotel. It has spacious, comfortable and attractive rooms with views of the sea and harbour. Excellent home cooking, table licence, special diets catered for. Lots of ideas for trips and visits for all ages.

Camelot, *5 Avenue Road, Falmouth, Cornwall, TR11 4AZ.* **Open:** All year (not Xmas/New Year)
01326 312480 (also fax) *camelotfalmouth@aol.com* **D:** Fr £22.00–£25.00 **S:** Fr £25.00–£30.00 **Beds:** 4F 3D 1S **Baths:** 8 En
We offer comfortable, homely accommodation with a high standard of decor. Falmouth is an ideal touring centre. Visit Eden Project, Maritime Museum or many of the beautiful private & National Trust houses and gardens. Close to town and beaches.

Wellington House, *26 Melvill Road, Falmouth, Cornwall, TR11 4AR.* Comfort and convenience, perfectly located for harbour, beaches, Maritime Museum, shops, road and rail access. **Open:** All year
01326 319947 Mrs Riddette-Gregory www.bedbreakfastcornwall.co.uk **D:** Fr £17.50–£25.00 **S:** Fr £20.00–£30.00 **Beds:** 1F 1T 1D 1S **Baths:** 3 En 1 Pr (4) cc

Telford Guest House, *47 Melvill Road, Falmouth, Cornwall, TR11 4DG.* Ideal base for Cornish holidays. Friendly, personal service assured. **Open:** Feb to Nov
01326 314581 (also fax) A Eschenauer *telford-falmouth@gofornet.co.uk* www.smoothhound.co.uk/hotels/telfordg.html **D:** Fr £18.00–£21.00 **Beds:** 1T 4D **Baths:** 5 En (5)

Ambleside Guest House, *9 Marlborough Road, Falmouth, Cornwall, TR11 3LP.* Victorian guest house. Relaxed and friendly. **Open:** All year
01326 319630 Mr Walker **D:** Fr £20.00 **S:** Fr £18.00 **Beds:** 1F 2D 1T 1S **Baths:** 1 Sh

Dolvean Hotel, *50 Melvill Road, Falmouth, Cornwall, TR11 4DQ.* For further information & special offers, check www.dolvean.co.uk. **Open:** All year (not Xmas)
01326 313658 Mrs Crocker **Fax: 01326 313995** *reservations@dolvean.freeserve.co.uk* www.dolvean.co.uk **D:** Fr £30.00–£45.00 **S:** Fr £30.00–£45.00 **Beds:** 7D 1T 3S **Baths:** 11 En (12) (11) cc

Beachwalk House, *39 Castle Drive, Falmouth, Cornwall, TR11 4NF.* Fabulous views, seafront position, overlooks Falmouth Bay, beaches and castle. **Open:** All year (not Xmas)
01326 319841 Mr & Mrs Clarke **D:** Fr £18.00–£20.00 **S:** Fr £20.00–£25.00 **Beds:** 3D 1T **Baths:** 4 En (4)

Trevu House Hotel, *45 Melvill Road, Falmouth, Cornwall, TR11 4DG.* Small select, non-smoking hotel. Superb for town, Princess Pavilion & beautiful gardens. **Open:** All year (not Xmas)
01326 312852 Mrs Eustice **Fax: 01326 318631** *elaine.eddy@lineone.net* www.trevu-house-hotel.co.uk **D:** Fr £17.50–£21.50 **S:** Fr £17.50–£21.50 **Beds:** 1F 2D 3T 3S **Baths:** 9 En (5)

Chelsea House Hotel, *2 Emslie Road, Falmouth, Cornwall, TR11 4BG.* Enjoy panoramic sea views, close to town and beaches. **Open:** Mar to Oct
01326 212230 Mr & Mrs Parkes **D:** Fr £20.00–£28.00 **S:** Fr £30.00–£40.00 **Beds:** 2F 1T 3D 1S **Baths:** 7 En (4) (4) cc

Trevaylor, *8 Pennance Road, Falmouth, Cornwall, TR11 4EA.* Close town and beaches, disabled facilities, sea views, table licence. **Open:** All year (not Xmas/New Year)
01326 313041 Fax: 01326 316899 *stay@trevaylor.co.uk* www.trevaylor.co.uk **D:** Fr £18.00–£25.00 **S:** Fr £20.00–£35.00 **Beds:** 2F 3T 3D 1S **Baths:** 9 En (9) cc

Rosemullion Hotel, *Gyllyngvase Hill, Falmouth, Cornwall, TR11 4DF.* Imposing Tudor-style building with balcony rooms, sea view, king-size beds. **Open:** All year
01326 314690 Mrs Jones **Fax: 01326 210098** **D:** Fr £21.50–£26.00 **S:** Fr £24.50–£26.00 **Beds:** 3T 9D 1S **Baths:** 1 En 2 Pr

Fowey

SX1251

St Keverne, *4 Daglands Road, Fowey, Cornwall, PL23 1JL.* Comfortable Edwardian house close to town centre, with river views. **Open:** All year (not Xmas)
01726 833164 Mrs Eardley *carol@stkeverne1.fsnet.co.uk* **D:** Fr £25.00 **S:** Fr £30.00 **Beds:** 2D **Baths:** 2 En

Pembroke, *12 Polvillion Road, Fowey, Cornwall, PL23 1HF.* Comfortable accommodation, short walk town. River, beach close. Eden Project. **Open:** Easter to Oct
01726 833560 **D:** Fr £20.00 **Beds:** 1D **Baths:** 1 Pr

Pendower, *11 Park Road, Fowey, Cornwall, PL23 1EB.* River views both rooms. 7 mins town. 5 miles Eden Project. **Open:** Apr to Oct
01726 833559 Mrs Dorkins **D:** Fr £21.00–£25.00 **S:** Fr £24.00–£26.00 **Beds:** 1T 1D **Baths:** 2 Pr (2)

Safe Harbour Hotel, *Lostwithiel Road, Fowey, Cornwall, PL23 1BD.* Friendly inn, river views, car parking, quiet lounge bar, full menu available. **Open:** All year
01726 833379 **D:** Fr £21.00–£25.00 **S:** Fr £25.00 **Beds:** 2F 2D 1T **Baths:** 5 En (8)

Gillan

SW7824 *New Inn, Shipwright's Arms, Five Pilchards, Three Tuns, White Hart*

Porthvean, *Gillan, Manaccan, Helston, Cornwall, TR12 6HL.* Specially suitable Coastal Footpath walkers. Views, Gillan Creek and Helford. **Open:** All year (not Xmas/New Year)
01326 231204 E A Whale **D:** Fr £16.50 **S:** Fr £16.50 **Beds:** 1T **Baths:** 1 En (2)

Planning a longer stay? Always ask for any special rates

Golant

SX1254 *Fisherman's Arms, Royal Oak*

Bellscat, *Golant, Fowley, Cornwall, PL23 1LA.* A gentleman's residence situated in stunning countryside overlooking the River Fowey. **Open:** All year (not Xmas/New Year)
01726 833404 *carol_white@bellscat.freeserve.co.uk* cornwall-online.co.uk
D: Fr £22.50–£25.00 **S:** Fr £15.00–£30.00 (12)

Goldsithney

SW5430

South Colenso Farm, *Goldsithney, Penzance, Cornwall, TR20 9JB.* **Open:** Mar to Oct
01736 762290 (also fax) D: Fr £21.00–£26.00 **S:** Fr £31.00–£36.00 **Beds:** 1F 1T 1D **Baths:** 3 En (6)
Spacious Georgian-style farmhouse on arable farm. Delightful, peaceful setting, secluded yet not isolated. Large ensuite bedrooms with lovely country views across our fields. A perfect central location for touring with pretty coves, sandy beaches & many other attractions nearby.

Goonhavern

SW7853

September Lodge, *Wheal Hope, Goonhavern, Truro, Cornwall, TR4 9QJ.* Modern house with countryside views. Ideally situated for touring Cornwall. **Open:** All year (not Xmas/New Year)
01872 571435 (also fax) Mr Philipps *jc.septlodge@virgin.net* **D:** Fr £20.00 **S:** Fr £25.00–£28.00 **Beds:** 1F 1D **Baths:** 2 En (10)

Gorran Haven

SX0041

Homestead, *Chute Lane, Gorran Haven, St Austell, Cornwall, PL26 6NU.* Cottage/beach 100m overlooking garden. Parking. Easy reach Heligan/Eden. **Open:** All year
01726 842567 Mr & Mrs Smith **D:** Fr £25.00–£30.00 **S:** Fr £50.00 **Beds:** 1T 1D **Baths:** 2 Pr

Piggys Pantry, *The Willows, Gorran Haven, St Austell, Cornwall, PL26 6JG.* Detached family bungalow. Close to beach, Heligan Gardens and Eden Project.
Open: All year
01726 843545 G Mott *piggyspantry@hotmail.com* www.piggypantry.co.uk **D:** Fr £20.00 **S:** Fr £25.00 **Beds:** 1T 1D 1S **Baths:** 1 Sh

Grampound

SW9348

Perran House, *Grampound, Truro, Cornwall, TR2 4RS.* Delightful C17th cottage in the pretty village of Grampound within a conservation area. Centrally located for touring, visiting the many nearby gardens including the Lost Gardens of Heligan and the Eden Project. Also within easy reach of the coastal footpaths. **Open:** All year
01726 882066 Mr Diboll **Fax: 01726 882936** *perran-house@faxvia.net* **D:** Fr £18.00–£20.00 **S:** Fr £16.00–£17.00 **Beds:** 3D 1T 2S **Baths:** 3 En 1 Sh (8)

Gweek

SW7026 *Sweet Inn*

1 Rose Terrace, *Gweek, Helston, Cornwall, TR12 6UG.* A delightful waterside terraced cottage. Seal Sanctuary within the village. **Open:** All year
01326 221345 Miss Jacobs **D:** Fr £23.00–£24.00 **S:** Fr £23.00–£24.00 **Beds:** 1T 1D **Baths:** 1 Sh (1)

Barton Farm, *Gweek, Helston, Cornwall, TR13 0QH.* Attractive open beamed farmhouse, a mile from Gweek the head of the beautiful Helford River. Ideal base for exploring all of South West Cornwall from the Lizard to Lands End with its lovely coves, beaches, gardens and coastal walks.
Open: All year (not Xmas/New Year)
01326 572557 *bartonfarm@talk21.com* www.cornwall-online.co.uk/barton-farm
D: Fr £16.00–£18.00 **S:** Fr £17.50–£20.00 **Beds:** 1T 2D **Baths:** 1 Pr 1 Sh (5)

Gwithian

SW5841

Nanterrow Farm, *Gwithian, Hayle, Cornwall, TR27 5BP.* **Open:** All year (not Xmas)
01209 712282 Mrs Davies *nanterrow@hotmail.com* www.nanterrowfarm.co.uk **D:** Fr £18.00–£22.00 **S:** Fr £18.00–£22.00 **Beds:** 1F 1D 1S **Baths:** 2 Sh (4)
Come and enjoy a relaxing stay on our traditional working farm situated in a quiet traffic-free valley 1.5 miles from St Ives Bay. 3 miles of sandy beaches; good area for coastal walks; many other local attractions. Good farmhouse fare.

Hallworthy

SX1887

Wilsey Down Hotel, *Hallworthy, Camelford, Cornwall, PL32 9SH.* Warm welcome, friendly hotel, views over Bodmin Moor, near to coast. **Open:** All year
01840 261205 J Bremdon **D:** Fr £18.00–£24.00 **S:** Fr £15.00–£18.00 **Beds:** 1F 2T 2D **Baths:** 2 En 1 Pr 1 Sh (50) cc

Hayle

SW5537 *Bluff Inn, Star Inn, Bucket of Blood*

54 Penpol Terrace, *Hayle, Cornwall, TR27 4BQ.* Large mid-terraced Victorian cottage. Close to Bird Paradise.
Open: Easter to Nov
01736 752855 A Cooper **D:** Fr £18.00–£22.00 **S:** Fr £20.00–£25.00 **Beds:** 1T 1D **Baths:** 1 Sh (2)

Helford

SW7526 *Shipwrights' Arms, New Inn*

Pengwedhen, *Helford, Helston, Cornwall, TR12 6JZ.* Riverbank gardens. Quay. Verandah with stunning sea and estuary views. **Open:** Easter to Oct
01326 231481 J Davies *nandjdavies@hotmail.com* **D:** Fr £22.00 **S:** Fr £22.00 **Beds:** 1T 1D 1S **Baths:** 1 Pr 1 Sh (3)

Helston

SW6627

Lyndale Guest House, *Greenbank, Meneage Road, Helston, Cornwall, TR13 8JA.*
Open: All year
01326 561082 Mr & Mrs Tucker **Fax: 01326 565813** *enquiries@lyndale1.freeserve.co.uk* www.lyndale1.freeserve.co.uk **D:** Fr £18.50–£22.50 **S:** Fr £24.00–£27.00 **Beds:** 1F 3D 2T 1S **Baths:** 3 En 1 Sh (6) cc
Pretty cottage guesthouse. 6 rooms of highest quality, most ensuite. Located at edge of ancient town of Helston, gateway to the beautiful Lizard Peninsula, and its unspoilt coves & countryside. Central for walking & touring in Cornwall.

Planning a longer stay? Always ask for any special rates

Longstone Farm, *Trenear, Helston, Cornwall, TR13 0HG.* **Open:** Mar to Nov **Grades:** ETC 3 Diamond
01326 572483 & 07971 240345 (M) Jane Martins *janemartins@longstone-farm.freeserve.co.uk* **D:** Fr £20.00–£24.00 **S:** Fr £20.00–£24.00 **Beds:** 3F 1T 1D **Baths:** 3 En 2 Pr (10)
Enjoy the warm and friendly atmosphere of our home, off the beaten track overlooking rolling fields and peaceful countryside. Ideal for touring, beaches and NT gardens. Enjoy walking on the beautiful Lizard peninsular. Relax in our TV lounge or sun-lounge.

High Street

SW9653

Manor Farm, *High Street, Burngullow, St Austell, Cornwall, PL26 7TQ.* Beautiful Grade II Listed manor house. Eden Project, Heligan 6 miles. **Open:** All year (not Xmas/New Year)
01726 72242 (also fax) S Manuell *suzannemanuell@tinyworld.co.uk* **D:** Fr £21.00–£22.00 **S:** Fr £25.00–£30.00 **Beds:** 1F 1D **Baths:** 2 En (10)

Kenwyn

SW8145

The Mowhay, *Coosebean, Truro, Cornwall, TR4 9EA.* Charming barn set in countryside, 10 mins walk to city. **Open:** All year
01872 272502 (also fax) **D:** Fr £20.00–£25.00 **S:** Fr £25.00–£28.00 **Beds:** 1F 1T 3D **Baths:** 3 En 1 Pr 1 Sh (10) (6)

Kingsand

SX4350

Cliff House, *Devon Port Hill, Kingsand, Torpoint, Cornwall, PL10 1NT.* Listed comfortable house. Sea and country views. Great wholefood cookery. **Open:** All year
01752 823110 Mrs Heasman **Fax: 01752 822595** *info@cliffhse.abel.co.uk* cliffhse.abel.co.uk **D:** Fr £21.00–£25.00 **S:** Fr £25.00–£35.00 **Beds:** 3F 3T 2D **Baths:** 3 En 3 Pr (3)

Ladock

SW8950

Swallows Court, *Treworyan, Ladock, Truro, Cornwall, TR2 4QD.* Beautifully converted stone barn, peaceful location, delicious breakfasts, friendly atmosphere. **Open:** Mar to Sept
01726 883488 Mrs Harvey **D:** Fr £19.00–£22.00 **S:** Fr £22.00–£25.00

Laneast

SX2284

Stitch Park, *Laneast, Launceston, Cornwall, PL15 8PN.* Situated close to Bodmin Moor with magnificent views towards Dartmoor. **Open:** All year
01566 86687 Mrs Handford **D:** Fr £16.50–£18.00 **S:** Fr £16.50–£18.00 **Beds:** 1T 1D **Baths:** 2 En (6)

Lanivet

SX0364

Bokiddick Farm, *Lanivet, Bodmin, Cornwall, PL30 5HP.* Georgian farmhouse and newly converted barn. Oak beams, wood panelling, full of character. **Open:** All year (not Xmas)
01208 831481 (also fax) Mrs Hugo *gillhugo@bokiddickfarm.co.uk* www.bokiddickfarm.co.uk **D:** Fr £25.00–£30.00 **S:** Fr £28.00–£38.00 **Beds:** 4D 1T **Baths:** 5 En (4)

High Cross Farm, *Lanivet, Bodmin, Cornwall, PL30 5JR.* Victorian farmhouse, set within 91 acres in geographical centre of Cornwall. **Open:** All year (not Xmas)
01208 831341 **D:** Fr £20.00–£24.00 **S:** Fr £30.00 **Beds:** 1F 1D 1T **Baths:** 1 En 1 Sh (6)

Tremeere Manor, *Lanivet, Bodmin, Cornwall, PL30 5BG.* Spacious farmhouse in lovely surroundings. Easy access coasts and moors. **Open:** Feb to Nov
01208 831513 Mrs Oliver **Fax: 01208 832417** *oliver.tremeere.manor@farming.co.uk* **D:** Fr £15.00–£20.00 **S:** Fr £16.00–£20.00 **Beds:** 2D 1T **Baths:** 1 En 1 Sh (6)

Lanlivery

SX0759 *Crown Inn*

Lynnwood, *Lanlivery, Bodmin, Cornwall, PL30 5BX.* Modern bungalow in landscaped gardens. 3 miles from Eden Project. **Open:** All year
01208 872326 A J Penk **D:** Fr £15.00–£20.00 **S:** Fr £15.00–£20.00 **Beds:** 1T 2D **Baths:** 1 En 1 Sh (3)

Longfield House, *Lanlivery, Bodmin, Cornwall, PL30 5BT.* Quiet family house. Panoramic countryside views. 4 miles Eden Project. **Open:** All year (not Xmas/New Year)
01208 873439 Mrs Haley **D:** Fr £20.00 **S:** Fr £30.00 **Beds:** 1F 2D **Baths:** 3 En

Higher Pennant, *Lanlivery, Bodmin, PL30 5DD.* Friendly, relaxed, rural accommodation. Ideal family break with horse-riding available. **Open:** All year
01208 873252 Mr Chester *dave@higherpennant.freeserve.co.uk* **D:** Fr £20.00 **S:** Fr £20.00–£30.00 **Beds:** 1F 1D 1S **Baths:** 2 En 1 Pr

Lanner

SW7140

Lanner Inn, *Lanner, Redruth, Cornwall, TR16 6EH.* Old traditional country inn, comfortable accommodation, a warm welcome in a true local. **Open:** All year (not Xmas/New Year)
01209 215611 J L Wilson **Fax: 01209 214065** *lannerinn@btconnect.com* lannerinn.com **D:** Fr £18.00–£25.00 **S:** Fr £20.00–£30.00 **Beds:** 2F 1T 2D **Baths:** 2 En 1 Sh (30) **cc**

Launceston

SX3384

Oakside, *South Petherwin, Launceston, Cornwall, PL15 7LJ.* **Open:** Mar to Nov
01566 86733 Mrs Crossman **D:** Fr £18.00–£22.00 **S:** Fr £18.00–£22.00 **Beds:** 1F 1D 1T **Baths:** 1 En 3 Sh (4)
Panoramic views of Bodmin Moor from bungalow nestling peacefully in beautiful surroundings 1 min from A30 trunk road, Exeter, M5. Ideal base for touring, Eden Project, all Cornwall. English breakfasts a speciality, attractively furnished, well-equipped rooms. Many legendary landmarks nearby.

11 Castle Street, *Launceston, Cornwall, PL15 8BA.* Georgian St. Town facilities. Castle views. Gourmet breakfasts. Parking. Period furnishings. **Open:** Easter to Oct **Grades:** ETC 4 Diamond
01566 773873 Mrs Bowles **D:** Fr £17.50–£25.00 **S:** Fr £25.00 **Beds:** 2T 1D **Baths:** 1 En 1 Sh

White Horse Inn, *14 Newport Square, Launceston, Cornwall, PL15 8EL.* Fine hostelry with accommodation in ancient capital of Cornwall. **Open:** All year
01566 772084 Mr & Mrs Howard **D:** Fr £20.00–£25.00 **S:** Fr £22.00–£25.00 **Beds:** 3D 1T **Baths:** 1 En 2 Sh (20)

Newport Villa Guest House, *34 St Stephens Hill, Launceston, Cornwall, PL15 8HW.* Old house near town, steam railway, golf course. Warm welcome. **Open:** All year
01566 775242 L Ackroyd **D:** Fr £18.00–£22.50 **S:** Fr £18.50–£22.00 **Beds:** 1F 1T 1D 2S **Baths:** 1 Pr 2 Sh (4)

Bradbridge Farm, *Boyton, Launceston, Cornwall, PL15 9RL.* On Devon/Cornwall border, fishing, walks, wildlife, golf, riding, beach nearby. **Open:** Easter to Oct
01409 271264 Mrs Strout **D:** Fr £16.00 **S:** Fr £16.00 **Beds:** 1D 1T 1S

Mousehole

SW4626

Carn Du Hotel, *Mousehole, Penzance, Cornwall, TR19 6SS.* Peaceful comfortable hotel. Superb views, food, accommodation overlooking Mount's Bay. **Open:** All year **01736 731233 (also fax)** Mr Field **D:** Fr £25.00–£35.00 **S:** Fr £35.00–£45.00 **Beds:** 4D 3T **Baths:** 6 En 1 Pr (12) **cc**

Mullion

SW6719

Campden House, *The Commons, Mullion, Helston, Cornwall, TR12 7HZ.* One acre of gardens. Home-grown vegetables when in season. **Open:** All year (not Xmas) **01326 240365** Mr & Mrs Hyde **D:** Fr £16.50–£17.50 **S:** Fr £16.50–£17.50 **Beds:** 2F 5D 1T 2S **Baths:** 2 Sh (9)

Meaver Farm, *Mullion, Helston, Cornwall, TR12 7DN.* Traditional 300 year old farmhouse; exposed beams, log fire, delightful breakfasts. **Open:** All year **01326 240128** J Stanland **Fax: 01326 240011** *meaverfarm@eclipse.co.uk* www.meaverfarm.freeserve.co.uk **D:** Fr £21.00–£24.00 **S:** Fr £25.00–£30.00 **Beds:** 1T 2D **Baths:** 3 En (3)

Mullion Cove

SW6617

Criggan Mill, *Mullion Cove, Helston, Cornwall, TR12 7EU.* Timber lodges 200 yards from fishing harbour and coastal footpath. **Open:** Easter to Oct **01326 240496** Mr Bolton **Fax: 0870 1640549** *info@criggan-mill.co.uk* www.crigganmill.co.uk **D:** Fr £17.00–£22.00 **S:** Fr £20.00–£25.00 **Beds:** 5F 6D 4T **Baths:** 3 En (1) **cc**

Newquay

SW8161

Pengilley, *12 Trebarwith Crescent, Newquay, Cornwall, TR7 1DX.* **Open:** All year **01637 872039** *jan@pengilley-guesthouse.com* www.pengilley-guesthouse.com **D:** Fr £17.00–£25.00 **S:** Fr £17.00–£25.00 **Beds:** 2F 2D 1T 1S **Baths:** 4 En 2 Sh (5)
A friendly atmosphere awaits you at Pengelley, one minute from town, beach, close to shops and Newquay's famous nightlife and restaurants. For those wishing to try surfing, an introduction to Newquay's coolest surf school - West Coast Surfari.

Dalswinton House, *St Mawgan-In-Pydar, Newquay, Cornwall, TR8 4EZ.* **Open:** All year **01637 860385 (also fax)** Stuart & Sal Hope *dalswinton@bigwig.net* www.dalswinton.com **D:** Fr £30.00–£32.00 **S:** Fr £40.00–£42.00 **Beds:** 2T 7D **Baths:** 9 En (10) **cc**
Glorious 10-acre rural setting overlooking St. Mawgan village with views to the sea at Mawgan Porth. Holidays for dogs & their owners in comfortable, friendly surroundings. Easy access to Newquay Airport, local walks & Coastal Path. Heated outdoor pool.

Alicia, *136 Henver Road, Newquay, Cornwall, TR7 3EQ.* Perfectly situated to explore the Cornish coastline & Newquay's golden sands. **Open:** All year **Grades:** ETC 4 Diamond **01637 874328** Mrs Limer *aliciaguesthouse@mlimer.fsnet.co.uk* www.alicia-guesthouse.co.uk **D:** Fr £18.00–£30.00 **S:** Fr £30.00–£45.00 **Beds:** 1T 3D 1F **Baths:** 3 En 2 Sh (6)

Blue Haven Guest House, *4 Godophin Way, Newquay, Cornwall, TR7 3BU.* Quality accommodation, ideal base for touring. Relaxing, quiet & welcoming. **Open:** All year (not Xmas/New Year) **01637 875840 (also fax)** *bluehavennewq@aol.com* **D:** Fr £18.50–£22.50 **S:** Fr £23.00–£27.50 **Beds:** 2F 2T 6D 2S **Baths:** 12 En (10) (4) **cc**

Trewinda Lodge, *17 Eliot Garden, Newquay, Cornwall, TR7 2QE.* Small, friendly, quiet. Close to beach, Trennance Gardens, Eden Project. **Open:** All year **01637 877533** *trewindalodge@yahoo.co.uk* www.trewindalodge.co.uk **D:** Fr £18.50–£28.00 **S:** Fr £18.50–£28.00 **Beds:** 1F 2T 1D 1S **Baths:** 5 En (1) **cc**

BATHROOMS
En = Ensuite
Pr = Private
Sh = Shared

Planning a longer stay? Always ask for any special rates

Chichester Guest House, *14 Bay View Terrace, Newquay, Cornwall, TR7 2LR.* Good coffee. We provide walking, mineral-collecting and archaeology weeks. **Open:** All year (not Xmas) **Grades:** ETC 1 Diamond **01637 874216 (also fax)** Miss Harper *sheila.harper@virgin.net* freespace.virgin.net/sheila.harper **D:** Fr £17.00 **S:** Fr £17.00 **Beds:** 2F 2D 2T 1S **Baths:** 2 Sh (6)

The Bangaroo Guest House, *23 Tolcarne Road, Newquay, Cornwall, TR7 2NQ.* Near town centre and beaches. Licensed. No restrictions. **Open:** All year **01637 874798 (also fax)** Ms Beechey www.bangaroo.free-online.co.uk **D:** Fr £30.00–£40.00 **S:** Fr £15.00–£20.00 **Beds:** 2F 3T

The Croft Hotel, *37 Mount Wise, Newquay, Cornwall, TR7 2BL.* Ideally situated close to beaches, pubs & clubs, coach & rail stations. **Open:** All year (not Xmas) **01637 871520** L Duffin www.the-crofthotel.co.uk **D:** Fr £14.00–£25.00 **S:** Fr £20.00–£40.00 **Beds:** 4F 2T 2D **Baths:** 4 En 2 Pr 1 Sh **cc**

Padstow

SW9175

Mother Ivey Cottage, *Trevose Head, Padstow, Cornwall, PL28 8SL.* **Open:** All year **01841 520329 (also fax)** Mrs Woosnam Mills *woosnammills@compuserve.com* **D:** Fr £25.00 **S:** Fr £30.00 **Beds:** 2T **Baths:** 2 En (6)
Traditionally-built Cornish clifftop house with stunning sea views, overlooking Trevose Head with a beach below. The area is renowned for swimming, fishing, surfing and walking. A championship golf course - Trevose - is nearby. The Cornwall Coastal Path is adjacent.

Althea Library B&B, *27 High Street, Padstow, Cornwall, PL28 8BB.* Converted library, short walk from harbour, old part of town. Credit cards including AmEx. **Open:** All year (not Xmas) **Grades:** ETC 5 Diamond, Silver **01841 532717** J Beare *enquiries@althealibrary.co.uk* www.althealibrary.co.uk **D:** Fr £30.00–£32.00 **Beds:** 2D 1T **Baths:** 3 En (3) **cc**

Hemingford House, *21 Grenville Road, Padstow, Cornwall, PL28 8EX.* Comfortable relaxed style. Hearty breakfast. 10 minute walk to harbour. **Open:** All year
01841 532806 (also fax) Mr Tamblin *peter@ptamblin.freeserve.co.uk* www.padstow-bb.co.uk **D:** Fr £22.50–£27.50 **S:** Fr £25.00–£30.00 **Beds:** 1T 2D **Baths:** 1 En 1 Pr 1 Sh (12) (1)

Par

SX0753

Hidden Valley Gardens, *Treesmill, Par, Cornwall, PL24 2TU.* Secluded location. Near Eden Project and Fowey, in own grounds. **Open:** Easter to Oct
01208 873225 **D:** Fr £20.00–£22.00 **S:** Fr £22.00–£24.00 **Beds:** 2D **Baths:** 2 En (7)

Paul

SW4527

Kerris Farm, *Paul, Penzance, Cornwall, TR19 6UY.* Peaceful dairy farm, rural views, central to Minack Theatre, St Ives. **Open:** Easter to Oct
01736 731309 *susangiles@btconnect.com* www.cornwall-online.co.uk/kerris-farm **D:** Fr £15.00–£20.00 **S:** Fr £16.00–£18.00 **Beds:** 1F 1D 1T **Baths:** 1 En 1 Sh (4)

Pelynt

SX2055 *Jubilee Inn*

Little Larnick Farm, *Pelynt, Looe, Cornwall, PL13 2NB.* Character farmhouse and barn accommodation in the beautiful Looe valley. **Open:** All year
01503 262837 (also fax) Mrs Eastley *littlelarnick@btclick.com* **D:** Fr £20.00–£24.00 **S:** Fr £25.00–£28.00 **Beds:** 1F 1T 4D **Baths:** 6 En (3) (6) cc

Colwells House, *Pelynt, Looe, Cornwall, PL13 2JX.* Family run country house. Polperro 3 miles. **Open:** All year (not Xmas/New Year)
01503 220201 Mrs Harvey **D:** Fr £17.00–£22.00 **S:** Fr £25.00 **Beds:** 1F 1T 2D **Baths:** 1 En 2 Sh (12) (7)

Talehay, *Tremaine, Pelynt, Looe, Cornwall, PL13 2LT.* Charming C17th former farmstead. Large ensuite rooms with beautiful views. A quiet haven with countryside/coastal walks nearby. Delicious breakfasts served with our own freerange eggs & home-made marmalade. An ideal comfortable base for exploring the delights of Cornwall & close to Eden Project. **Open:** All year
01503 220252 (also fax) Mr & Mrs Brumpton *pr.brumpton@ukonline.co.uk* www.talehay.co.uk **D:** Fr £23.00–£25.00 **S:** Fr £33.00 **Beds:** 1F 1D 1T **Baths:** 3 En (12)

Pensilva

SX2969

Wheal Tor Hotel, *Caradon Hill, Pensilva, Liskeard, Cornwall, PL14 5PJ.* Highest inn in Cornwall. Set in rugged Bodmin Moor location. **Open:** All year
01579 362281 Mr & Mrs Chapman **Fax: 01579 363401** *pdc@whealtorhotel.freeserve.co.uk* www.wheal-tor-hotel.co.uk **D:** Fr £22.50–£27.50 **S:** Fr £30.00–£32.50 **Beds:** 1F 2T 3D **Baths:** 4 En 2 Sh cc

Pentewan

SX0147 *Crown Inn, Ship Inn, Fountains, Polgooth Inn*

Piskey Cove, *The Square, Pentewan, St Austell, Cornwall, PL26 6DA.* Close to the Eden Project and Heligan Gardens. Family run and situated in peaceful, pretty coastal village. Ideal base for cosy winter, refreshing spring, British summer and beautiful autumn breaks, to visit Cornwall's sites. Complimentary and sports therapy in house. **Open:** All year (not Xmas/New Year)
01726 843781 (also fax) Ms Avery *gillian@averya.freeserve.co.uk* **D:** Fr £25.00–£35.00 **S:** Fr £25.00–£38.00 **Beds:** 1F 2T 3D **Baths:** 3 En 1 Pr (2) cc

Pentire

SW7861 *Lewinnick Lodge, Olde Dolphin*

Golden Bay Hotel, *Pentire Avenue, Pentire, Newquay, Cornwall, TR7 1PD.* Unwind and relax in this surprisingly affordable, small, quality hotel. **Open:** Feb to Oct
01637 873318 *enquires@goldenbayhotel.co.uk* www.goldenbayhotel.co.uk **D:** Fr £18.00–£30.00 **S:** Fr £24.00–£40.00 **Beds:** 2F 1T 7D **Baths:** 10 En (10) cc

Penzance

SW4730

Lynwood Guest House, *41 Morrab Road, Penzance, Cornwall, TR18 4EX.* **Open:** All year
01736 365871 (also fax) Mrs Stacey *Lynwoodpz@aol.com* www.lynwood-guesthouse.co.uk **D:** Fr £13.50–£17.50 **S:** Fr £13.50–£21.50 **Beds:** 2F 2D 2T 2S **Baths:** 4 En 2 Pr 2 Sh (5) cc
Family-run Victorian guest house. Internationally recommended for good food, cleanliness. Close to all amenities. Ideally situated for visiting Land's End, St Michael's Mount, Minack Theatre, art galleries and the Lizard Peninsula.

Trewella Guest House, *18 Mennaye Road, Penzance, Cornwall, TR18 4NG.* Large Victorian house. Recommended for good food. Ideal touring centre. **Open:** Mar to Oct **Grades:** ETC 3 Diamond
01736 363818 D Glenn *shan.dave@lineone.net* **D:** Fr £18.50–£19.50 **S:** Fr £16.50–£22.50 **Beds:** 2F 4D 2S **Baths:** 6 En 1 Sh (5)

Carnson House Private Hotel, *East Terrace, Market Jew Street, Penzance, Cornwall, TR18 2TD.* Centrally-located, friendly, small hotel near station and harbour. **Open:** All year **Grades:** ETC 2 Diamond
01736 365589 Mr & Mrs Smyth **Fax: 01736 365594** *carnson@netcomuk.co.uk* www.carnson-house.co.uk **D:** Fr £18.00–£24.50 **S:** Fr £20.00 **Beds:** 3D 2T 2S **Baths:** 3 Pr 1 Sh (6)

Menwidden Farm, *Ludgvan, Penzance, Cornwall, TR20 8BN.* Comfortable farmhouse, centrally situated in peaceful countryside. Friendly welcome guaranteed. **Open:** Easter to Oct **Grades:** ETC 3 Diamond
01736 740415 Mrs Quick **D:** Fr £18.00–£23.00 **S:** Fr £18.00 **Beds:** 3D 1T 1S **Baths:** 1 En 2 Sh (8)

Mount Royal Hotel, *Chyandour Cliff, Penzance, Cornwall, TR18 3LQ.* Small family-run hotel facing the sea & overlooking the entrance of Penzance harbour. **Open:** Mar to Oct **Grades:** AA 3 Diamond
01736 362233 (also fax) Mr Cox *mountroyal@talk21.com* **D:** Fr £22.50–£27.50 **S:** Fr £25.00–£27.50 **Beds:** 3F 3D 2T **Baths:** 5 En 2 Sh (1) (10)

Pendennis Hotel, *Alexandra Road, Penzance, Cornwall, TR18.* Victorian licensed hotel built 1830 in a quiet tree-lined residential area. **Open:** All year
01736 363823 (also fax) Mrs Cook *ray@pendennishotel.freeserve.co.uk* **D:** Fr £15.00–£22.00 **S:** Fr £15.00–£22.00 **Beds:** 5F 2D **Baths:** 7 En 1 Sh cc

Kimberley House, *10 Morrab Road, Penzance, Cornwall, TR18 4EZ.* Convenient bus and railway station. Minutes walk town and seafront. **Open:** Feb to Dec
01736 362727 Mr & Mrs Bashford **D:** Fr £15.00–£21.00 **S:** Fr £15.00–£18.00 **Beds:** 2F 2D 3T 1S **Baths:** 3 En 2 Pr 3 Sh (5) (3)

All details shown are as supplied by B&B owners in Autumn 2002

Saltash

SX4259

Mill Park House, *Pill, Saltash, Cornwall, PL12 6LQ.* Victorian farmhouse. Large comfortable rooms. Ideal base for touring. **Open:** All year (not Xmas/New Year)
01752 843234 Mrs Wadge *millpark_house@yahoo.co.uk* **D:** Fr £17.00–£20.00 **S:** Fr £18.00–£25.00 **Beds:** 1F 1T 1D **Baths:** 1 En 1 Sh (2)

The Old Cottage, *Barkers Hill, St Stephens, Saltash, Cornwall, PL12 4QA.* Charming old beamed cottage, hearty breakfasts. **Open:** All year (not Xmas)
01752 845260 Mrs Plant *roger.plant@virgin.net* **D:** Fr £15.00 **S:** Fr £15.00 **Beds:** 1D 2S **Baths:** 1 Sh (2)

Sennen

SW3525

Treeve Moor House, *Sennen, Penzance, Cornwall, TR19 7AE.* **Open:** All year (not Xmas/New Year)
01736 871284 & 07771 914660 (M) Miss Trenary **Fax: 01736 871284** *info@firstandlastcottages.co.uk* www.firstandlastcottages.co.uk **D:** Fr £18.00–£25.00 **S:** Fr £28.00–£35.00 **Beds:** 1F 1T 1D **Baths:** 2 En 1 Pr (3)
Located within sight of Land's End in a tranquil, secluded setting with uninterrupted sea views. Footpath direct from the house to the sandy beach at Sennen Cove. Minack Theatre and excellent pubs nearby. Haven for birdwatchers and walkers.

Sunny Bank Hotel, *Seaview Hill, Sennen, Lands End, Penzance, Cornwall, TR19 7AR.* Comfortable detached hotel, close beaches, Minack Theatre, good food, licensed. **Open:** Jan to Nov
01736 871278 Mr & Mrs Comber *sunnybanksennen@bushinternet.com* **D:** Fr £15.00–£20.00 **S:** Fr £15.00–£25.00 **Beds:** 2F 5D 2T 2S **Baths:** 2 Sh (15)

The Old Manor Hotel, *Sennen, Lands End, Penzance, Cornwall, TR19 7AD.* This C18th, granite built, Cornish manor house offers a warm welcome and comfortable accommodation. Located amidst coastal and rural scenery, less than a mile from Land's End and a short walk to Sennen Cove and the South West coastal path. **Open:** All year
01736 871280 Mr O'Grady **Fax: 01736871280** *info@oldmanor.net* www.oldmanor.net **D:** Fr £25.00–£30.00 **S:** Fr £20.00–£30.00 **Beds:** 2F 1T 2D 2S **Baths:** 6 En 1 Pr (2) (10) **cc**

Sheviock

SX3755

Sheviock Barton, *Sheviock, Torpoint, Cornwall, PL11 3EH.* **Open:** All year (not Xmas)
01503 230793 & 07775 688403 (M) Carol & Tony Johnson **Fax: 01503 230793** *thebarton@sheviock.freeserve.co.uk* www.sheviockbarton.co.uk **D:** Fr £25.00 **S:** Fr £30.00 **Beds:** 1F 1D 1T **Baths:** 2 En 1 Pr (10)
Beautifully restored 300 year old farmhouse in AONB. TV all rooms. Guests sitting room. Breakfast in large oak-beamed kitchen, games room, gardens. Beach/pub/restaurant 1/2 mile. Looe, Polperro, Plymouth 20 mins. Eden Project 35 mins. Come & go as you please.

South Petherwin

SX3181

Oakside, *South Petherwin, Launceston, Cornwall, PL15 7LJ.* Panoramic views of Bodmin Moor from bungalow nestling peacefully in beautiful surroundings. **Open:** Mar to Nov
01566 86733 Mrs Crossman **D:** Fr £18.00–£22.00 **S:** Fr £18.00–£22.00 **Beds:** 1F 1D 1T **Baths:** 1 En 3 Sh (4)

RATES
D = Price range per person sharing in a double or twin room
S = Price range for a single room

St Agnes

SW7250

Penkerris, *Penwinnick Road, St Agnes, Cornwall, TR5 0PA.* Enchanting Edwardian residence & garden. **Open:** All year
01872 552262 (also fax) Mrs Gill-Carey *info@penkerris.co.uk* www.penkerris.co.uk **D:** Fr £20.00–£25.00 **S:** Fr £25.00–£35.00 **Beds:** 2F 2D 2T 2S **Baths:** 3 En 3 Sh (9)

St Austell

SX0252

Sunnycroft, *28 Penwinnick Road, St Austell, Cornwall, PL25 5DS.* **Open:** All year (not Xmas/New Year)
01726 73351 Fax: 01726 879409 *info@sunnycroft.net* www.sunnycroft.net **D:** Fr £25.00–£35.00 **S:** Fr £25.00–£35.00 **Beds:** 1T 3D 1S **Baths:** 5 En **cc**
Centrally located large detached house on main road. 5 mins walk from bus/railway station. Situated between the Eden Project (3 miles) and the Lost Gardens of Heligan (3 miles). Beautiful South Coastal Path 1 1/2 miles. Telephone for brochure. Early booking recommended.

Crossways, *6 Cromwell Road, St Austell, Cornwall, PL25 4PS.* Beaches, golf, Heligan, Eden Project, coastal walks nearby. Contractors welcome. **Open:** All year
01726 77436 Mrs Nancarrow **Fax: 01726 66877** **D:** Fr £25.00 **Beds:** 3D 1T 1F **Baths:** 5 En

National Grid References given are for villages, towns and cities – not for individual houses

Tregilgas Farm, *Gorran, St Austell, Cornwall, PL26 6ND.* Farmhouse in quiet unspoilt countryside. 2 miles Heligan Gardens, 12 miles Eden Project. **Open:** Easter to Oct
01726 842342 & 07789 113620 (M) *dclemes88@aol.com* **D:** Fr £22.50–£25.00 **S:** Fr £27.00–£30.00 **Beds:** 1T 2D **Baths:** 2 En (5) (4) cc

Leeside, *16 Haddon Way, Carlyon Bay, St Austell, Cornwall, PL25 3QG.* Spacious, spotless, private & peaceful room. Lovely coastal area. Eden 3 miles. **Open:** Easter to Oct
01726 815566 Mrs Buckingham www.sbuckingham.fsbusiness.co.uk **D:** Fr £23.00–£29.00 **S:** Fr £33.00–£39.00 **Beds:** 1D **Baths:** 1 En (12) (2)

The Elms, *14 Penwinnick Road, St Austell, Cornwall, PL25 5DW.* Superior quality accommodation, close to Eden Project & Heligan Gardens. **Open:** All year (not Xmas/New Year)
01726 74981 & 07929 170631 (M) Fax: 01726 74981 *sue@edenbb.co.uk* www.cornwall-information.co.uk/edenbb **D:** Fr £25.00–£35.00 **S:** Fr £35.00–£50.00 **Beds:** 1D 2S **Baths:** 3 En (3) cc

Poltarrow Farm, *St Mewan, St Austell, Cornwall, PL26 7DR.* Charming farmhouse, with pretty ensuite rooms, delicious breakfast, indoor swimming pool. **Open:** All year (not Xmas/New Year)
01726 67111 (also fax) Mrs Nancarrow *enquire@poltarrow.co.uk* www.poltarrow.co.uk **D:** Fr £23.00–£25.00 **S:** Fr £28.00–£30.00 **Beds:** 1F 3D 1T **Baths:** 4 En 1 Pr (10) cc

Cornerways Guest House, *Penwinnick Road, St Austell, Cornwall, PL25 5DS.* Cornerways stands in its own grounds surrounded by garden/ large car park. **Open:** All year
01726 61579 B J Edwards **Fax: 01726 66871** *nwsurveys@aol.com* **D:** Fr £16.50–£19.00 **S:** Fr £16.50–£22.50 **Beds:** 1F 1T 1S **Baths:** 2 En 1 Sh (10)

BATHROOMS
En = Ensuite
Pr = Private
Sh = Shared

St Blazey

SX0655

Nanscawen Manor House, *Prideaux Road, St Blazey, Par, Cornwall, PL24 2SR.* Lovely Georgian home; peaceful countryside. 3 ensuite bedrooms, swimming pool. **Open:** All year
01726 814488 Mr & Mrs Martin *keith@nanscawen.com* www.nanscawen.com **D:** Fr £40.00–£45.00 **S:** Fr £70.00–£80.00 **Beds:** 2D 1T **Baths:** 3 En (12) (8) cc

St Day

SW7342

Lower Poldice Cottage, *St Day, Redruth, Cornwall, TR16 5PP.* High quality, comfortable, friendly accommodation. Central for touring/walks/cycling. **Open:** All year
01209 820438 (also fax) J K Oates **D:** Fr £18.00–£22.00 **S:** Fr £18.00–£22.00 **Beds:** 1T 2D **Baths:** 1 En 1 Sh (8)

St Dennis

SW9558

Boscawen Hotel, *Foe Street, St Dennis, St Austell, Cornwall, PL26 8AD.* Easy access north and south coast, near Cornwall's Eden Project. **Open:** All year
01726 822275 K Mason **D:** Fr £17.50–£25.00 **S:** Fr £15.00–£20.00 **Beds:** 1F 1T 1D 1S **Baths:** 1 En 2 Sh

St Erme

SW8449

Trevispian Vean Farm Guest House, *St Erme, Truro, Cornwall, TR4 9BL.* 300 old working farm - family-run - lovely views of Cornish countryside. **Open:** Feb to Nov
01872 279514 Mr & Mrs Dymond **Fax: 01872 263730** www.guesthousestruro.com **D:** Fr £20.00–£25.00 **S:** Fr £20.00–£24.00 **Beds:** 2F 2D 1T **Baths:** 9 Pr (12)

St Erth

SW5535

Lanuthnoe Barns, *St Erth Hill, St Erth, Hayle, Cornwall, TR27 6HX.* Picturesque converted barn, peaceful village location yet 1.5 miles to sea. **Open:** All year
01736 755529 Mrs Crutchfield **D:** Fr £18.00 **Beds:** 1F 1D **Baths:** 1 Pr (4)

St Ewe

SW9746

Corran Farm, *St Ewe, St Austell, Cornwall, PL26 6ER.* Quality B&B in open countryside, adjoining Heligan Gardens. Eden nearby. **Open:** All year (not Xmas)
01726 842159 Mrs Lobb *terryandkathy@corranfarm.fsnet.co.uk* **D:** Fr £17.00–£19.00 **S:** Fr £20.00–£22.00 **Beds:** 1T 1D **Baths:** 1 En 1 Pr (4)

St Ives

SW5140

Gowerton Guest House, *6 Sea View Place, St Ives, Cornwall, TR26 1PS.* **Open:** All year (not Xmas)
01736 796805 (also fax) Mr & Mrs Bennett *accommodation-st-ives@gowerton.freeserve.co.uk* **D:** Fr £22.50–£30.00 **Beds:** 3F 4D **Baths:** 3 En 1 Sh (12) (3)
Eddie & Zelda Bennett run this 7 bedroom guesthouse at the edge of the sea in St. Ives. A warm friendly atmosphere awaits you at our non-smoking sea front accommodation. We are ideally situated for visiting attractions such as the Eden Project to Land's End.

Rivendell, *7 Porthminster Terrace, St Ives, Cornwall, TR26 2DQ.* **Open:** All year **Grades:** RAC 4 Diamond **01736 794923** Ms Walker *rivendellstives@aol.com* www.rivendell-stives.co.uk **D:** Fr £16.00–£26.00 **S:** Fr £17.00–£23.00 **Beds:** 1F 4D 1T 1S **Baths:** 4 En 1 Sh (6)
Highly recommended family-run guest house. Superb sea views from many rooms. Close to town, beaches, bus and rail stations. Friendly hospitality, excellent food. As featured in the TV drama 'Wycliffe'.

Blue Hayes Private Hotel, *Trelyon Avenue, St Ives, Cornwall, TR26 2AD.*
Open: Feb to Nov
01736 797129 Mr Herring *malcolm@bluehayes.fsbusiness.co.uk* www.bluehayes.co.uk **D:** Fr £45.00–£65.00 **S:** Fr £65.00–£85.00 **Beds:** 6D **Baths:** 6 En (10) (10) cc
Country house by the sea. Recently completely refurbished to high standard. Six luxury rooms with full ensuite facilities. Master suite with balcony, and Godrevy & Bay suites with seaviews. Bar and dining room open to terrace with stunning views.

Downlong Cottage Guest House, *95 Back Road East, St Ives, Cornwall, TR26 1PF.*
Open: All year (not Xmas)
01736 798107 D: Fr £20.00–£25.00 **S:** Fr £25.00 **Beds:** 1F 4D 1T **Baths:** 4 En 1 Sh (11)
Ideally situated in the heart of Downlong, the old fishing quarter of picturesque St Ives, Downlong Cottage is only minutes away from the harbour and beaches. St Ives is famous for its artists and galleries including the Tate.

Monterey Guest House, *7 Clodgy View, St Ives, Cornwall, TR26 1JG.* Warm welcome. Outstanding sea views, near beautiful beaches, town, harbour Coastal Path, Tate & other galleries. **Open:** Feb to Nov
01736 794248 *info@monterey-stives.fsnet.co.uk* www.monterey-stives.co.uk **D:** Fr £20.00–£27.50 **S:** Fr £20.00–£27.50 **Beds:** 1F 3D 1S **Baths:** 2 En 1 Pr 2 Sh (2) cc

Carlill, *9 Porthminster Terrace, St Ives, Cornwall, TR26 2DQ.* Friendly, comfortable, licensed, family-run guest house. Good food. Highly recommended. **Open:** All year
01736 796738 Mrs Bowden *Lynne@lgpa.freeserve.co.uk* **D:** Fr £16.00–£25.00 **S:** Fr £18.00–£25.00 **Beds:** 2F 2D 2T 1S **Baths:** 3 En 2 Pr 2 Sh (5) (6) cc

Chy-An-Creet Hotel, *The Stennack, St Ives, Cornwall, TR26 2HA.* Warm welcome, relaxing home comfort, excellent touring and walking base. **Open:** Easter to Oct **Grades:** AA 4 Diamond
01736 796559 (also fax) Mr & Mrs Tremelling *judith@chy.co.uk* www.chy.co.uk **D:** Fr £23.00–£29.00 **S:** Fr £23.00–£29.00 **Beds:** 2F 4D 1T 1S **Baths:** 8 En (8) cc

The Primrose Valley Hotel, *St Ives, Cornwall, TR26.* A popular independent family friendly hotel with both stunning views over St Ives and on the level with direct access to Porthminster Beach (less than one minute!) Sun terrace, licensed bar, evening meals with home-made specials and fantastic handpicked wine list. **Open:** All year
01736 794939 (also fax) *info@primroseonline.co.uk* www.primroseonline.co.uk **D:** Fr £24.50–£40.00 **S:** Fr £24.50–£50.00 **Beds:** 4F 2T 4D **Baths:** 10 En (9) cc

The Old Vicarage Hotel, *Parc-An-Creet, St Ives, Cornwall, TR26 2ES.* Large Victorian vicarage, beautifully converted, peaceful location, wooded grounds.
Open: Easter to Nov
01736 796124 J Sykes **Fax: 01736 796343** *holidays@oldvicaragehotel.co.uk* www.oldvicaragehotel.co.uk **D:** Fr £23.00–£28.00 **S:** Fr £28.00–£49.00 **Beds:** 3F 4T 1S **Baths:** 3 En 4 Pr (8) cc

Whitewaves, *4 Sea View, St Ives, Cornwall, TR26 2DH.* Small, warm, friendly, family-run, non-smoking guest house in quiet private road. **Open:** All year (not Xmas)
01736 796595 (also fax) Mrs Webb *jan@whitewaves.in2home.co.uk* **D:** Fr £14.00–£20.00 **S:** Fr £14.00–£20.00 **Beds:** 1F 3D 1T 2S **Baths:** 3 Sh

St Just-in-Penwith

SW3631

Boscean Country Hotel, *St Just-in-Penwith, Penzance, Cornwall, TR19 7QP.*
Open: All year (not Xmas)
01736 788748 (also fax) Mr & Mrs Wilson *boscean@aol.com* www.connexions.co.uk/boscean/index.htm **D:** Fr £23.00–£26.00 **S:** Fr £31.00–£45.00 **Beds:** 3F 4D 5T **Baths:** 12 En (15) cc
A warm & hospitable welcome awaits you at Boscean - a magnificent country house in three acres of private walled garden, set amidst some the most dramatic scenery in West Cornwall. Home-cooking, using fresh local and home-grown produce.

All details shown are as supplied by B&B owners in Autumn 2002

Planning a longer stay? Always ask for any special rates

Roseudian, *Crippas Hill, St. Just-in-Penwith, Penzance, Cornwall, TR19 7RE.* **Open:** Mar to Oct **Grades:** ETC 4 Diamond
01736 788556 Mrs Mercer *roseudian@ukgateway.net* www.roseudian.co.uk **D:** Fr £22.00 **S:** Fr £32.00 **Beds:** 1T 2D **Baths:** 3 En (12) (4)
A small quiet guesthouse with a warm welcome in countryside near Lands End. Ideal for walking/prehistoric sites/beaches. Also within easy reach of the Minack Theatre, St Michael's Mount, St Ives & the Lizard. Delicious dinners using home-grown & local produce.

Boswedden House Hotel, *Cape Cornwall, St Just-in-Penwith, Penzance, Cornwall, TR19 7NJ.* Spacious Georgian mansion. Quiet country setting. Large garden, warm welcome. **Open:** All year
01736 788733 (also fax) Miss Griffiths *relax@boswedden.org.uk* www.boswedden.org.uk **D:** Fr £20.00–£25.00 **S:** Fr £20.00–£30.00 **Beds:** 1F 2D 3T 2S **Baths:** 8 En cc

St Keverne

SW7921

Trevinock, *St Keverne, Helston, Cornwall, TR12 6QP.* Excellent food & accommodation. Beautiful, unspoilt coastal area. Warm welcome. Parking.
Open: Easter to Oct
01326 280498 Mrs Kelly *ritakelly@talk21.com* **D:** Fr £19.00–£23.00 **S:** Fr £19.00–£23.00 **Beds:** 1D 2S **Baths:** 1 En 1 Sh (5)

St Kew

SX0177

Tregellist Farm, *Tregellist, St Kew, Bodmin, Cornwall, PL30 3HG.* Set in beautiful countryside with splendid views. Close to Camel Trail. **Open:** All year (not Xmas/New Year)
01208 880537 Mrs Cleave **Fax: 01208 881017** *jillcleave@tregellist.fsbusiness.co.uk* **D:** Fr £24.00 **S:** Fr £26.00–£30.00 **Beds:** 1F 3D 1T **Baths:** 5 En (6) cc

St Kew Highway

SX0375 *St Kew Inn, Maltsters' Arms, Red Lion*

Porchester House, *St Kew Highway, Bodmin, Cornwall, PL30 3ED.* In rural village, secluded detached house with large conservatory/aviary. **Open:** All year (not Xmas)
01208 841725 Mr Ashley **D:** Fr £25.00 **Beds:** 1D 1T **Baths:** 1 En 1 Pr (4)

Brookfields, *Hendra Lane, St. Kew Highway, Bodmin, Cornwall, PL30 3EQ.* Quality en-suite accommodation in picturesque North Cornwall. Modern country home with panoramic rural views. Wonderful setting, welcoming, fine rooms, great breakfasts. Centrally located for coasts, beaches, golf, walking, cycling, moors, towns, stately homes, attractions - and the Eden Project. Families welcome. **Open:** All year (not Xmas/New Year)
01208 841698 Mr Caswell **Fax: 01208 841174** *robbie.caswell@btinternet.co.uk* www.brookfields-stkew.co.uk **D:** Fr £20.00–£25.00 **S:** Fr £25.00 **Beds:** 1F 1T 1D **Baths:** 3 En (10)

St Keyne

SX2460 *Highwayman Inn, Old Plough*

Wallis Holiday Barn, *St Keyne, Liskeard, Cornwall, PL14 4RP.* Rural Victorian house in 3 acres. Breakfast in conservatory with views. **Open:** All year (not Xmas/New Year)
01579 345412 (also fax) Ms Sharp *wallisbarn@hotmail.com* **D:** Fr £16.00 **S:** Fr £21.00 **Beds:** 1T 1D **Baths:** 1 Sh (2)

St Mabyn

SX0473

Chrismar, *Wadebridge Road, St Mabyn, Bodmin, Cornwall, PL30 3BH.* Family house in village overlooking countryside. Well-positioned Camel Trail, Eden Project. **Open:** Easter to Oct **Grades:** ETC 2 Diamond
01208 841518 (also fax) Mrs Francis **D:** Fr £15.00–£18.00 **S:** Fr £13.00–£15.00 **Beds:** 1F 1D 1S **Baths:** 1 Sh (4)

Cles Kernyk, *Wadebridge Road, St Mabyn, Bodmin, Cornwall, PL30 3BH.* Relax in quiet North Cornwall village. Handy for beaches/moors. **Open:** All year (not Xmas) **Grades:** ETC 3 Diamond
01208 841258 Mrs Jago *sue@mabyn.freeserve.co.uk* **D:** Fr £15.00–£20.00 **S:** Fr £15.00–£20.00 **Beds:** 1F 1D **Baths:** 1 Sh (3)

St Martin

SX2655

Penvith Barn, *St Martin, Looe, Cornwall, PL13 1NZ.* **Open:** All year (not Xmas/New Year)
01503 240772 Mrs Alison Swann **Fax: 01503 240723** *penvith@btinternet.com* **D:** Fr £20.00–£25.00 **Beds:** 1F 1D **Baths:** 2 En
C16th converted barns set in rolling countryside, only a mile from Seaton Beach and Coastal Path. Themed bedrooms with sitting areas and video library. Breakfast includes full English with daily lighter or sweeter alternatives. Self-catering apartment available.

Tregoad Farm Camping and Caravanning Park, *St Martin, Looe, Cornwall, PL13 1PB.* Tregoad Farmhouse offers quiet and restful accommodation 1.5 miles from the heart of Looe. **Open:** May to Sept
01503 262718 Mr Werkmeister **Fax: 01503 264777** *www.tregoadfarmccp@aol.com* www.cornwall-online.co.uk/tregoad **D:** Fr £25.00–£30.00 **S:** Fr £25.00–£30.00 **Beds:** 1T 1D **Baths:** 2 En cc

St Neot

SX1867

Lampen Mill, *St Neot, Liskeard, Cornwall, PL14 6PB.* **Open:** All year
01579 321119 (also fax) Mrs Pearce *heather@lampen.ndo.co.uk* www.lampen.ndo.co.uk **D:** Fr £25.00–£28.00 **S:** Fr £28.00–£30.00 **Beds:** 1F 1T 1D **Baths:** 3 En
Lampen Mill is a lovingly converted cornmill nestling in complete seclusion in 8 acres of natural woodland. An ideal location for touring Cornwall and Devon, close to Bodmin Moor, the Eden Project and National Trust Properties. Warm welcome is assured.

Lampen Farm, *St Neot, Liskeard, Cornwall, PL14 6PB.* Delightful, spacious C16th farmhouse in a tranquil setting on edge of Bodmin Moor. **Open:** All year
01579 320284 **D:** Fr £17.00–£22.00 **S:** Fr £20.00–£25.00 **Beds:** 1F 1T 1D **Baths:** 2 En 1 Pr (4)

Dye Cottage, *St Neot, Liskeard, Cornwall, PL14 6NG.* Charming C17th cottage, oak beams, flagstone floors, lovely gardens by river. **Open:** All year (not Xmas)
01579 321394 S M Williams **Fax: 0870 169 2029** *dyecott@lineone.net* www.cornwall-info.co.uk/dye-cottage **D:** Fr £18.00 **S:** Fr £18.00 **Beds:** 1D 2S **Baths:** 1 Sh (1)

St Newlyn East

SW8256

Trewerry Mill, *Trerice, St Newlyn East, Newquay, Cornwall, TR8 5GS.* Picturesque C17th watermill in peaceful riverside gardens, 4m from coast. **Open:** Feb to Nov
01872 510345 (also fax) D & T Clark *trewerry.mill@which.net* www.trewerry.mill.co.uk **D:** Fr £20.00–£28.00 **S:** Fr £20.00–£45.00 **Beds:** 1F 2D 1T 1S **Baths:** 3 En 2 Sh (7) (12)

St Tudy

SX0676

Polrode Mill Cottage, *Allen Valley, St Tudy, Bodmin, Cornwall, PL30 3NS.* **Open:** All year
01208 850203 Mr Edwards *polrode@tesco.net* www.cornwall-online.co.uk/polrode-mill **D:** Fr £33.00–£40.00 **S:** Fr £66.00–£80.00 **Beds:** 3D **Baths:** 3 En (5) cc
C17th cottage set in 3 acres of garden & woodland. The cottage is sympathetically decorated in rustic style and combines the comfort of modern living with the romance of the past. Ideal base for Eden, Heligan, Padstow, Port Isaac.

Please respect a B&B's wishes regarding children, animals and smoking

St Wenn
SW9665

Tregolls Farm, *St Wenn, Bodmin, Cornwall, PL30 5PG.* **Open:** All year (not Xmas) **Grades:** ETC 4 Diamond
01208 812154 (also fax) Mrs Hawkey *tregollsfarm@btclick.com* tregollsfarm.co.uk **D:** Fr £18.00–£22.00 **S:** Fr £18.50–£20.00 **Beds:** 2D 1T 1S **Baths:** 1 En 1 Sh (10) cc
Tregolls is a Grade II Listed building, on a beef and sheep farm in mid Cornwall. We have a farm trail which links up to the Saints' Way Footpath. Convenient for visiting Padstow, Lanhydrock House, Heligan Garden and the Eden Project.

Stoke Climsland
SX3674

Penpill Farmhouse, *Stoke Climsland, Callington, Cornwall, PL17 8QE.* C18th farmhouse on A388 between Plymouth and Launceston. Within easy reach of the moors, Tamar Valley, famous gardens, north and south coasts. **Open:** All year **Grades:** AA 3 Diamond
01579 370540 S Thomas *penpill@btinternet.com* www.penpill.co.uk **D:** Fr £20.00–£25.00 **S:** Fr £25.00–£30.00 **Beds:** 1F 1T 2D **Baths:** 4 En (8)

Talskiddy
SW9165

Pennatillie Farm, *Talskiddy, St Columb Major, TR9 6EF.* Secluded delightful 450 acre dairy farm. Excellent accommodation and food. **Open:** All year
01637 880280 (also fax) Mrs Colgrove **D:** Fr £16.00–£18.00 **S:** Fr £16.00–£18.00 **Beds:** 3D **Baths:** 3 En

The Lizard
SW7012

Parc Brawse House, *Penmenner Road, The Lizard, Helston, Cornwall, TR12 7NR.* Relax, take time out in our high quality picturesque home. **Open:** All year (not Xmas/New Year) **Grades:** RAC 4 Diamond
01326 290466 Jo & Ben Charity **Fax: 01326 290894** *benjocharity@aol.com* **D:** Fr £17.50–£26.00 **S:** Fr £21.00–£37.00 **Beds:** 1F 2T 4D **Baths:** 5 Pr 2 Sh (7) cc

Three Burrows
SW7447

Lands Vue Country House, *Lands Vue, Three Burrows, Truro, Cornwall, TR4 8JA.* Special welcome for all our guests at a peaceful country home. **Open:** All year (not Xmas)
01872 560242 Mrs Hutchings **Fax: 01872 560950 D:** Fr £20.00–£24.00 **S:** Fr £25.00–£32.00 **Beds:** 1D 2T **Baths:** 3 En (12) (4)

Tintagel
SX0588

Polkerr Guest House, *Molesworth Street, Tintagel, Cornwall, PL34 0BY.* **Open:** All year (not Xmas) **Grades:** ETC 4 Diamond
01840 770382 & 01840 770132 Mrs Rundle *polkerr@tiscali.co.uk* **D:** Fr £20.00–£25.00 **S:** Fr £25.00–£35.00 **Beds:** 2F 2T 3D **Baths:** 5 En 1 Pr (9) cc
A family-run B&B offering a friendly atmosphere with a large dining room & separate guest lounge. Just 2 mins walk from the centre of Tintagel. The coastal walks are a ramblers' paradise with breathtaking scenery. Close to Eden Project.

Bosayne Guest House, *Atlantic Road, Tintagel, Cornwall, PL34 0DE.* Warm, friendly family-run guest house with sea views, serving a great breakfast. **Open:** All year **Grades:** ETC 3 Diamond
01840 770514 Mr & Mrs Sara & Jamie Hawkins *sarahawkins@sjhl.freeserve.co.uk* www.bosayne.co.uk **D:** Fr £20.00–£26.00 **S:** Fr £20.00–£26.00 **Beds:** 2D 2F 1T 3S **Baths:** 4 En 1 Pr 2 Sh

Bossiney Cottage, *Tintagel, Cornwall, PL34 0AY.* Character cottage, carefully restored. Good touring base, close Coastal Path. **Open:** All year (not Xmas)
01840 770327 D: Fr £17.50 **S:** Fr £20.00 **Beds:** 1F 2D **Baths:** 1 Sh (3) (4)

Planning a longer stay? Always ask for any special rates

Pendrin House, *Atlantic Road, Tintagel, Cornwall, PL34 0DE.* Beautiful Victorian house close to many amenities, castle and beaches. **Open:** Mar to Nov **Grades:** AA 4 Diamond
01840 770560 (also fax) Mrs Howe *pendrin@tesco.net* **D:** Fr £20.00–£22.00 **S:** Fr £20.00 **Beds:** 2F 2T 4D 1S **Baths:** 3 En 3 Sh (5)

Tintagel Arms Hotel, *Fore Street, Tintagel, Cornwall, PL34 0DB.* 200 year old stone building on site of Chapel of St Dennis. **Open:** All year
01840 770780 Mr Hunter **D:** Fr £20.00–£25.00 **S:** Fr £25.00–£30.00 **Beds:** 1F 4D 2T **Baths:** 7 En (8) cc

Towednack
SW4838

Chytodden Farm, *Towednack, St Ives, Cornwall, TR26 3AT.* Comfortable accommodation in peaceful surroundings, good food. Car essential. **Open:** Easter to Oct
01736 795029 Mr & Mrs Hollow **D:** Fr £15.00 **S:** Fr £15.00 **Beds:** 1F 1D **Baths:** 1 Sh

Trebetherick
SW9378 *St Kew Inn, Port Gaverne Hotel*

Daymer House, *Daymer Bay, Trebetherick, Wadebridge, PL27 6SA.* Large country house by the beach. Close famous golf course & lovely coastal walks. **Open:** All year (not Xmas/New Year)
01208 862639 Mrs Burrows **D:** Fr £27.50–£30.00 **S:** Fr £15.50–£27.50 **Beds:** 1T 2D 1S **Baths:** 1 En 1 Pr (11) (3)

Treknow
SX0586

Atlantic View Hotel, *Treknow, Tintagel, Cornwall, PL34 0E.* Victorian house, glorious position, set 300 yards from cliff top. **Open:** Feb to Dec.
01840 770221 Fax: 01840 770995 *atlantic-view@eclipse.co.uk* www.holidayscornwall.com **D:** Fr £28.00–£32.00 **S:** Fr £32.00 **Beds:** 2F 1T 6D **Baths:** 9 En (10) cc

Hillscroft, *Treknow, Tintagel, Cornwall, PL34 0EN.* Scenic views across Trebarwith Valley. Use of garden & summer house. **Open:** All year (not Xmas/New Year)
01840 770551 Mrs Nutt *Pat@bascastle.fsnet.co.uk* **D:** Fr £16.00–£20.00 **S:** Fr £16.00–£20.00 **Beds:** 1T 2D **Baths:** 2 En 1 Sh (8) (6)

Penallick, *Treknow, Tintagel, Cornwall, PL34 0EJ.* **Open:** All year
01840 770296 Claire & Jason Hayes www.penallickhotel.co.uk **D:** Fr £26.00–£29.00 **S:** Fr £26.00–£41.00 **Beds:** 1F 2T 7D **Baths:** 10 En (10) cc
Penallick is a quality and peaceful hotel. Probably one of the best situated hotels in Cornwall overlooking the magnificent coastline in between Tintagel (1 mile) and the sandy beach of Trebarwith Strand (1/2 mile). Set back just 300 yards from the National Trust Coast Path, with the connecting path starting at the private hotel car park.

Challoch Guest House, *Treknow, Tintagel, Cornwall, PL34 0EN.* Small friendly guest house, superb views, near beautiful surfing beach. **Open:** Easter to Oct
01840 770273 Mrs May **D:** Fr £17.00–£19.00 **S:** Fr £19.00–£20.00 **Beds:** 2D 1T

Trelill
SX0477

Trevorrian Farm, *Trelill, Bodmin, Cornwall, PL30 3HZ.* Dairy farm. Near Port Isaac. Wonderful views over peaceful countryside. **Open:** Easter to Oct
01208 850434 (also fax) Mrs Kingdon **D:** Fr £20.00–£25.00 **S:** Fr £30.00 **Beds:** 2D **Baths:** 1 En 1 Sh (4)

Trenear
SW6832

Longstone Farm, *Trenear, Helston, Cornwall, TR13 0HG.* Enjoy the warm and friendly atmosphere of our home, off the beaten track. **Open:** Mar to Nov **Grades:** ETC 3 Diamond
01326 572483 & 07971 240345 (M) Jane Martins *janemartins@longstone-farm.freeserve.co.uk* **D:** Fr £20.00–£24.00 **S:** Fr £20.00–£24.00 **Beds:** 3F 1T 1D **Baths:** 3 En 2 Pr (10)

National Grid References given are for villages, towns and cities – not for individual houses

Planning a longer stay? Always ask for any special rates

Treneglos
SX2088

The Old Vicarage, *Treneglos, Launceston, Cornwall, PL15 8UQ.* Renowned for hospitality and excellent food. Highest standards throughout. **Open:** Mar to Nov
01566 781351 (also fax) Mrs Fancourt *maggie@fancourt.freeserve.co.uk* www.fancourt.freeserve.co.uk **D:** Fr £25.00 **S:** Fr £25.00 **Beds:** 2D 1S **Baths:** 2 En (10)

Tresinney
SX1081

Higher Trezion, *Tresinney, Advent, Camelford, Cornwall, PL32 9QW.* **Open:** All year **Grades:** ETC 4 Diamond
01840 213761 Mr & Mrs Wood **Fax: 01840 212509** *higher.trezion@virgin.net* **D:** Fr £24.00–£26.00 **S:** Fr £24.00–£26.00 **Beds:** 1D 1T 1F **Baths:** 3 En
Peacefully situated in a quiet & secluded area on the edge of Bodmin Moor. Ideal base for visiting the Eden Project & the National Trust Properties & Gardens. Open all year. Farmhouse breakfast. Cats & dogs in residence.

Tresparrett
SX1491

Oaklands, *Tresparrett, Boscastle, Cornwall, PL32 9SX.* 2 miles north of picturesque Boscastle. Superb, quiet, spacious ground floor accommodation. **Open:** Easter to Sept
01840 261302 Mrs Routly **D:** Fr £16.00–£19.00 **S:** Fr £16.00–£20.00 **Beds:** 1T 2D **Baths:** 1 En 1 Sh (11) (4)

Trevone Bay
SW8876

Well Parc Hotel, *Trevone Bay, Padstow, Cornwall, PL28 8QN.* Family run hotel and inn. Friendly, excellent food, fine ales. **Open:** All year (not Xmas/New Year)
01841 520318 Mrs Mills **D:** Fr £23.00–£32.00 **S:** Fr £23.00–£32.00 **Beds:** 4F 1T 4D 1S **Baths:** 5 En 2 Sh

Truro
SW8244

The Donnington Guest House, *43 Treyew Road, Truro, Cornwall, TR1 2BY.* **Open:** All year
01872 222552 Fax: 01872 222394 *eathorne-gibbons@donnington-guesthouse.co.uk* donnington-guesthouse.co.uk **D:** Fr £20.00–£30.00 **S:** Fr £20.00 **Beds:** 2F 1T 2D 1S **Baths:** 4 En 2 Pr (6)
Elegant Victorian house with lovely views over cathedral and countryside, providing excellent accommodation, service and facilities for discerning visitors. Perfectly situated to explore the historic delights of Cornwall and the amazing Eden Project. Our mouth-watering breakfast will make your day.

Patmos, *8 Burley Close, Truro, Cornwall, TR1 2EP.* Beautiful friendly home, close to centre. River view. Excellent breakfast. **Open:** All year
01872 278018 Mrs Ankers *brian.ankers@lineone.net* **D:** Fr £17.50–£22.50 **S:** Fr £18.00–£25.00 **Beds:** 1D 1T **Baths:** 1 En 1 Pr (5)

Trevispian Vean Farm Guest House, *St Erme, Truro, Cornwall, TR4 9BL.* 300 old working farm - family-run - lovely views of Cornish countryside. **Open:** Feb to Nov
01872 279514 Mr & Mrs Dymond **Fax: 01872 263730** www.guesthousestruro.com **D:** Fr £20.00–£25.00 **S:** Fr £20.00–£24.00 **Beds:** 2F 2D 1T **Baths:** 9 Pr (12)

Tywardreath
SX0854

Polbrean House, *Woodland Avenue, Tywardreath, Par, Cornwall, PL24 2PL.* Comfortable Victorian house. Close to beaches, Fowey, Eden Project & Heligan Gardens. **Open:** All year (not Xmas)
01726 812530 Mrs Ball **D:** Fr £20.00–£22.50 **S:** Fr £25.00 **Beds:** 2D 1S **Baths:** 1 Sh (4)

Upton (Bude)
SS2004

Harefield Cottage, *Upton, Bude, Cornwall, EX23 0LY.* Luxurious cottage with outstanding views. Ideal for walking/touring holiday. **Open:** All year
01288 352350 Mrs Trewin **Fax: 01288 352712** *sally@coast-countryside.co.uk* www.coast-countryside.co.uk **D:** Fr £23.00–£25.00 **S:** Fr £22.00–£30.00 **Beds:** 2D 1T **Baths:** 3 En (4)

Veryan

SW9139

The New Inn, *Veryan, Truro, Cornwall, TR2 5QA.* **Open:** All year (not Xmas) **Grades:** AA 3 Diamond
01872 501362 Mr Gayton **Fax: 01872 501078** *jack@veryan44.freeserve.co.uk* www.veryan44.freeserve.co.uk **D:** Fr £25.00 **S:** Fr £25.00–£35.00 **Beds:** 1D 1T 1S **Baths:** 2 En 1 Pr cc
The inn is based on a pair of C16th cottages. The single bar is welcoming and unspoilt. Situated in a beautiful village close by safe bathing beaches. Renowned locally for a high standard of catering.

Wadebridge

SW9872

Keresen, *St Giles Drive, Wadebridge, PL27 6DS.* 6 miles from coastal walks and beautiful beaches. Comfortable accommodation. **Open:** All year (not Xmas/New Year)
01208 813975 & 07775 873364 Mr & Mrs Braithwaite **D:** Fr £18.00–£20.00 **S:** Fr £18.00–£20.00 **Beds:** 1T 2D **Baths:** 1 Sh (3)

Porteath Barn, *St Minver, Wadebridge, Cornwall, PL27 6RA.* Recently converted barn in 8 acres. Own path to beach. **Open:** All year
01208 863605 Ms Bloor *mbloor@ukonline.co.uk* **D:** Fr £22.00–£28.00 **S:** Fr £25.00–£30.00 **Beds:** 2T 1D **Baths:** 2 Sh (12)

Whitstone

SX2698

West Nethercroft, *Whitstone, Holsworthy, Devon, EX22 6LD.* Warm welcome. Relaxing home from home break. Delicious farmhouse foods. **Open:** All year (not Xmas/New Year)
01288 341394 Mrs Hopper **D:** Fr £15.00–£17.50 **S:** Fr £15.00–£17.50 **Beds:** 1F 1D 1S **Baths:** 1 Sh

Widegates

SX2857

Treveria Farm, *Widegates, Looe, Cornwall, PL13 1QR.* Delightful manor offering luxurious accommodation in spacious and elegant rooms. **Open:** Easter to Oct
01503 240237 (also fax) Mrs Kitto **D:** Fr £20.00–£22.00 **S:** Fr £25.00–£30.00 **Beds:** 2D 1T **Baths:** 3 Pr (3)

Tresorya, *Widegates, Looe, Cornwall, PL13 1QL.* Cottage conveniently situated, main Looe road. Enjoy beautiful landscaped gardens. **Open:** All year (not Xmas)
01503 240258 Mrs Southwood *info@tresorya.co.uk* www.tresorya.co.uk **D:** Fr £18.00–£25.00 **S:** Fr £20.00–£27.00 **Beds:** 1F 1T 1D 1S **Baths:** 1 En 1 Sh (10)

Withiel

SW9965

Tregawne, *Withiel, Bodmin, Cornwall, PL30 5NR.* C18th farmhouse lovingly restored and situated on beautiful Ruthern Valley, Eden Project 15 mins. **Open:** All year
01208 831552 Mr Jackson **Fax: 01208 832122** **D:** Fr £25.00–£35.50 **S:** Fr £35.00–£47.50 **Beds:** 1F 1T 1D cc

Zennor

SW4538

Boswednack Manor, *Zennor, St Ives, Cornwall, TR26 3DD.* Peaceful, vegetarian, non-smoking. Organic gardens, superb views, sea sunsets. **Open:** Easter to Oct
01736 794183 Mrs Gynn *boswednack-manor@cornwall.county.com* **D:** Fr £17.00–£22.00 **S:** Fr £18.00–£23.00 **Beds:** 1F 2D 1T 1S **Baths:** 2 En 1 Sh (6)

Trewey Farm, *Zennor, St Ives, Cornwall, TR26 3DA.* Working farm. Peaceful, attractive surroundings. Warm welcome, excellent food. **Open:** Feb to Nov
01736 796936 Mrs Mann **D:** Fr £19.00–£22.00 **S:** Fr £19.00–£22.00 **Beds:** 2F 2D 1T 1S **Baths:** 1 Sh (6) cc

Rosmorva, *Boswednack, Zennor, St Ives, Cornwall, TR26 3DD.* Beautiful coastal location. Superb walking on cliffs and moorland. **Open:** All year
01736 796722 Ms Hamlett www.rosmorva.freeuk.com **D:** Fr £18.00–£20.00 **S:** Fr £18.00–£20.00 **Beds:** 1F 1T **Baths:** 1 En 1 Pr (4) (3)

The Old Chapel Backpackers, *Zennor, St Ives, Cornwall, TR26 3BY.* Perfectly situated on SW Footpath between Land's End and St Ives. **Open:** All year
01736 798307 (also fax) Ms Whitelock *zennorbackpackers@btinternet.com* www.backpackers.co.uk/zennor **D:** Fr £12.50–£14.00 **S:** Fr £12.50–£14.00 **Beds:** 1F 5S **Baths:** 6 Sh

Cumbria

DUMFRIES
AND GALLOWAY
KIELDER
RESERVOIR
The Borders
Langholm
Bailey
Catlowdy
A74(M)
Longtown
Walton
Hadrian's Wall
Annan
Banks
A69
Westlinton
Blackford
Low Row
Hexham
A689
CARLISLE
Brampton
Bowness-on-
Solway
Stanwix
Talkin
Warwick
Bridge
NORTHUMBERLAND
Carlisle
Castle Carrock
Blackwell
Brisco
Cumwhinton
Solway Firth
Wigton
A689
A596
Ainstable
Alston
A595
A6
Renwick
Leadgate
Nenthead
Aspatria
Mealsgate
Ivegill
A686
Garrigill
Oughterside
Caldbeck
Crosscanonby
Plumbland
Bothel
M6
Whelpo
Hesket Newmarket
Maryport
Little Salkeld
A689
Melmerby
Bassenthwaite
DURHAM
Cockermouth
Greystoke
Newbiggin
Penrith
A66
BASSENTHWAITE LAKE
Workington
Embleton
Skiddaw
Mungrisdale
Eamont Bridge
Lorton
Tirril
Yanwath
Thornthwaite
Troutbeck
(Penrith)
High Harrington
Pardshaw
High Lorton
Portinscale
A66
Dalemain
Dufton
Graythwaite
Braithwaite
Keswick
Watermillock
Bolton
Moresby
Castlerigg
Morland
Whitehaven
Loweswater
DERWENT WATER
Appleby-in-
Westmorland
Newlands
Grange-in-
Borrowdale
Glenridding
ULLSWATER
Frizington
Bampton
St Bees
Head
Buttermere
A5086
Rosthwaite
Patterdale
Ennerdale
Bridge
ENNERDALE
WATER
Watendlath
Shap
Brough
Egremont
Borrowdale
Longthwaite
Helvellyn
Hartsop
HAWESWATER
Little Musgrave
St Bees
A591
Thornhill
Lake
District
Winton
CUMBRIA
Wasdale Head
Grasmere
Raisbeck
Scafell Pike
Under
Loughrigg
Rydal
Newbiggin-on-Lune
A685
Kirkby Stephen
WAST
WATER
Elterwater
Ambleside
Kentmere
Ravenstonedale
A595
Troutbeck
Tebay
Holmrook
Eskdale Green
NX NY
SC SD
High Wray
Windermere
Staveley
A6
Selside
Outhgill
Irton
Hawkshead
Hill
Hawkshead
Coniston
Ings
Garth Row
A591
Grayrigg
A683
Ravenglass
Little Arrow
Near Sawrey
Far
Sawrey
Bowness-on-
Windermere
Patton
Carleton
Ulpha
Crook
CONISTON
WATER
WINDERMERE
Kendal
Sedbergh
Grisedale
Satterthwaite
Underbarrow
New Hutton
Broughton in
Furness
A593
A592
Brigsteer
Helsington
Bootle
Lowick Bridge
Lakeside
Dent
Hawes
Duddon
Bridge
Old Hutton
Lowick
Newby Bridge
Levens
M6
Middleton
Cowgill
A5092
Witherslack
Endmoor
Barbon
Haverthwaite
Millom
Lindale
Ulverston
Arnside
Hale
Cartmel
Kirkby Lonsdale
A590
Cark-in-Cartmel
Grange-
over-
Sands
YORKSHIRE DALES
NATIONAL PARK
Dalton-in-Furness
Flookburgh
A6
A65
A5087
Baycliff
NORTH
YORKSHIRE
Carnforth
Barrow-in-Furness
Bolton-le-Sands
LANCS.
Leece
Roa Island
Morecambe
A683
Settle
Heysham
Lancaster
Isle of Walney
M6
0
5
10 miles
SC 00 SD
20
40
60
80
00
NY
80
60
40
20
NY
00
SD
80
60

Ainstable

NY5346

Bell House, *Ainstable, Carlisle, Cumbria, CA4 9RE.* Set in the Eden Valley. Explore the Lakes, Hadrian's Wall. **Open:** All year (not Xmas/ New Year) **Grades:** ETC 4 Diamond
01768 896255 Ms Robinson *mrobinson@ bellhouse.fsbusiness.co.uk* **D:** Fr £20.00–£22.50 **S:** Fr £20.00–£22.50 **Beds:** 1D **Baths:** 1 En (1)

Alston

NY7146

High Field, *Brunteley Meadows, Alston, Cumbria, CA9 3UX.* Beautiful views. Remedial massage. Home-made bread, oatcakes and jam. **Open:** All year (not Xmas)
01434 382182 Mrs Pattison *cath@ cybermoor.org* **D:** Fr £16.00–£18.00 **S:** Fr £16.00–£18.00 **Beds:** 1T 1D 1S **Baths:** 1 En 1 Sh (2)

Harbut Law, *Brampton Road, Alston, Cumbria, CA9 3BD.* Centrally situated to explore the Lakes, Hadrian's Wall and Northumberland. **Open:** All year (not Xmas/New Year)
01434 381950 Mrs Younger *thomas@ younger.fsnet.co.uk* www.cumbria-cottages.co.uk **D:** Fr £18.00–£21.00 **S:** Fr £20.00–£25.00 **Beds:** 2F 1T 3D **Baths:** 2 En (3)

Lowbyer Manor Country House Hotel, *Alston, CA9 3JX.* Georgian Manor House. Log fires. Library. Woodlands, gardens, secure parking. **Open:** All year
01434 381425 *stAy@lowbyer.com* www.lowbyer.com **D:** Fr £32.00–£36.00 **S:** Fr £32.00–£36.00 **Beds:** 3T 7D 1S **Baths:** 11 En (10) cc

The Cumberland Hotel, *Townfoot, Alston, Cumbria, CA9 3HX.* Central to walks, Hadrian's Wall and North East. Family-run. **Open:** All year
01434 381875 Fax: 01434 382035 *postweigh@ aol.com* www.cumbria1st.com/towns/hotel st **D:** Fr £22.00–£26.00 **S:** Fr £27.00–£31.00 **Beds:** 3F 2D **Baths:** 5 En cc

Ambleside

NY3704

How Head Barn, *Fairview Road, Ambleside, Cumbria, LA22 9ED.* Spectacular views over Lakeland fells, with easy access to Ambleside. **Open:** All year
015394 32948 Mrs Walker **D:** Fr £16.00–£18.00 **S:** Fr £16.50–£18.00 **Beds:** 1D 2S (1)

Lattendales, *Compston Road, Ambleside, Cumbria, LA22 9DJ.* Central Ambleside, comfortable en-suite accommodation. English or vegetarian breakfast. Discounted midweek breaks. **Open:** All year
015394 32368 *admin@latts.freeserve.co.uk* www.latts.freeserve.co.uk **D:** Fr £19.00–£26.00 **S:** Fr £19.00–£21.00 **Beds:** 4D 2S **Baths:** 4 En 1 Sh (10) cc

Fern Cottage, *6 Waterhead Terrace, Ambleside, Cumbria, LA22 0HA.* Homely Lakeland stone terraced cottage, two minutes from Lake Windermere. **Open:** All year (not Xmas) **Grades:** ETC 3 Diamond
015394 33007 S M Rushby **D:** Fr £16.00–£18.00 **S:** Fr £20.00–£22.00 **Beds:** 2D 1T **Baths:** 1 Sh (4)

Rothay House, *Rothay Road, Ambleside, Cumbria, LA22 2EE.* Quality establishment, professional care, first-class breakfast. Private car park. **Open:** Feb to Dec
015394 32434 (also fax) Mr & Mrs Lees *email@rothay-house.com* www.rothay-house.com **D:** Fr £25.00–£30.00 **S:** Fr £35.00–£40.00 **Beds:** 1T 5D **Baths:** 6 En (2) (9) cc

Claremont House, *Compston Road, Ambleside, Cumbria, LA22 9DJ.* Family-run Victorian guest house. Centrally situated in the heart of the Lake District. **Open:** All year
015394 33448 *enquiries@ claremontambleside.co.uk* **D:** Fr £18.00–£27.50 **S:** Fr £20.00–£25.00 **Beds:** 1F 4D 1T 1S **Baths:** 6 En 2 Sh

Broadview, *Lake Road, Ambleside, Cumbria, LA22 0DN.* Friendly Victorian guest house between lake & village. Walks from door. **Open:** All year **Grades:** ETC 3 Diamond
015394 32431 Mr & Mrs Clarke *enquiries@ broadviewguesthouse.co.uk* www.broadviewguesthouse.co.uk **D:** Fr £18.00–£25.00 **S:** Fr £20.00–£50.00 **Beds:** 2F 3D 1T **Baths:** 3 En 1 Pr 1 Sh cc

Hillsdale Guest House, *Church Street, Ambleside, Cumbria, LA22 0BT.* Situated in centre of Ambleside. Modern, stylish rooms. Great breakfast. **Open:** All year (not Xmas) **Grades:** ETC 4 Diamond
015394 33174 Mr Staley **Fax: 015394 31226** *stay@hillsdaleguesthouse.co.uk* www.hillsdaleguesthouse.co.uk **D:** Fr £22.00–£35.00 **S:** Fr £25.00 **Beds:** 1F 2T 5D 1S **Baths:** 8 En cc

Planning a longer stay? Always ask for any special rates

Mill Cottage Country Guest House, *Rydal Road, Ambleside, LA22 9AN.* **Open:** All year
015394 34830 (also fax) www.millcottage88.freeserve.co.uk **D:** Fr £23.00–£30.00 **S:** Fr £28.00–£34.00 **Beds:** 1F 1T 3D (2) cc
Mill Cottage is a Grade II Listed building, built in 1501. It was once used as a fulling mill, in the finishing process of cloth. it is now a family-run business which incorporates a tea-room. Situated by the river in the centre of Ambleside.

The Old Vicarage, *Vicarage Road, Ambleside, Cumbria, LA22 9DH.* **Open:** All year
015394 33364 Mrs Burt **Fax: 015394 34734** *the.old.vicarage@kencomp.net* www.oldvicarageambleside.co.uk **D:** Fr £30.00 **S:** Fr £30.00–£40.00 **Beds:** 2F 6D 2T **Baths:** 10 En (15)
Quality bed and breakfast accommodation in a peaceful location in central Ambleside. Large car park. Pets welcome. All bedrooms are well-appointed and have multi-channel TV, video, CD, hairdryers, radio alarm, mini fridge, kettle, private bath/shower and WC.

Ambleside Lodge, *Rothay Road, Ambleside, Cumbria, LA22 0EJ.* **Open:** All year
015394 31681 Fax: 015394 34547 *hmd@ ambleside-lodge.com* www.ambleside-lodge.com **D:** Fr £32.50–£60.00 **S:** Fr £35.00–£60.00 **Beds:** 1T 16D 1S **Baths:** 18 En cc
Ambleside Lodge is perfectly situated between Lake Windermere and the village of Ambleside. Set in 2.5 acres of garden, but yet only a small walk to the lake and over 25 restaurants, a cinema, country pubs, and all the amenities of the village.

The Howes, *Stockghyll Brow, Ambleside, Cumbria, LA22 0QZ.* We are close to the beautiful Stockghyll Waterfalls, but only 3 mins walk from Ambleside centre. Perfect for walkers and tourists alike. Our rooms are on the ground floor and breakfast is served within the privacy of your own room. **Open:** All year
015394 32444 *enquiries@ thehowes-ambleside.co.uk* www.thehowes-ambleside.co.uk **D:** Fr £22.00–£28.00 **Beds:** 1T 1D **Baths:** 2 En (5)

Melrose Guest House, *Church Street, Ambleside, Cumbria, LA22 0BT.* **Open:** All year **Grades:** ETC 3 Diamond
015394 32500 Fax: 015394 31495 *info@melrose-guesthouse.uk* www.melrose-guesthouse.co.uk **D:** Fr £18.00–£30.00 **S:** Fr £18.00–£30.00 **Beds:** 3F 2T 4D 1S **Baths:** 6 En 2 Pr
A comfortable warm and friendly clean family run, traditional Lakeland house recently refurbished to include a ensuite ground floor bedroom. Situated in a quiet location in the centre of Ambleside, minutes walking distance to shops, restaurants, cinema and Lake Windermere.

Borwick Lodge, *Hawkshead, Ambleside, Cumbria, LA22 0PU.* Award-winning 'accommodation of the highest standards'. A rather special C17th country house. **Open:** All year
015394 36332 (also fax) Margaret & Malcolm MacFarlane *borwicklodge@talk21.com* www.borwicklodge.com **D:** Fr £30.00–£39.00 **Beds:** 1F 4D 1T **Baths:** 6 En (8) (8)

Appleby-in-Westmorland

NY6820

Limnerslease, *Bongate, Appleby-in-Westmorland, Cumbria, CA16 6UE.* Family-run guest house 10 mins town centre. Lovely golf course and many walks. **Open:** All year (not Xmas)
017683 51578 Mrs Coward *limnerslease@fsmail.net* **D:** Fr £18.00–£19.00 **Beds:** 2D 1T **Baths:** 1 Pr 1 Sh (3)

Slakes Farm, *Milburn, Appleby-in-Westmorland, Cumbria, CA16 6DP.* Slakes Farm was built in 1734. It is situated in the beautiful Eden Valley, with views of the Pennines and Lake District Fells. Good local produce, own bread and preserves. A warm welcome with tea and homemade biscuits on arrival. Open fire. **Open:** Easter to Oct
017683 61385 C Braithwaite *oakleaves5491@aol.com* **D:** Fr £21.00–£22.00 **S:** Fr £25.00 **Beds:** 1T 1D **Baths:** 2 En (4)

Planning a longer stay? Always ask for any special rates

Wemyss House, *48 Boroughgate, Appleby-in-Westmorland, Cumbria, CA16 6XG.* Georgian house in small country town. **Open:** Easter to Oct
017683 51494 Mrs Hirst *nickhirst@aol.com* **D:** Fr £18.00–£20.00 **S:** Fr £18.00–£20.00 **Beds:** 1D 1T 1S **Baths:** 2 Sh (2)

Church View, *Bongate, Appleby-in-Westmorland, Cumbria, CA16 6UN.* C18th character house, near coaching inn and town facilities. **Open:** All year (not Xmas)
017683 51792 (also fax) Mrs Kemp **D:** Fr £17.50 **S:** Fr £20.00 **Beds:** 1F 1D 1S **Baths:** 1 Sh (5) (4)

Bongate House, *Appleby-in-Westmorland, Cumbria, CA16 6UE.* **Open:** Mar to Nov **Grades:** AA 4 Diamond
017683 51245 Mrs Dayson **Fax: 017683 51423** *bongatehouse@aol.com.* **D:** Fr £20.00–£23.50 **S:** Fr £20.00–£35.00 **Beds:** 1F 3T 3D 1S **Baths:** 5 En 1 Sh (5) (8)
This large Georgian guest house is in an acre of secluded gardens. Taste good food in a relaxed atmosphere, ideal base to tour Dales, Borders and, of course, the Settle to Carlisle Railway. Make your holiday one to remember.

Howgill House, *Bongate, Appleby-in-Westmorland, Cumbria, CA16 6UW.* Ideally situated for Lakes, Dales, Eden Valley. Comfortable. **Open:** Easter to Oct
017683 53459 & 07909 664705 (M) Mrs Pigney *linda@pigney.fsbusiness.co.uk* **D:** Fr £17.50–£25.00 **S:** Fr £17.50–£25.00 **Beds:** 1T 2D **Baths:** 1 Sh (6)

Arnside

SD4578

Willowfield Hotel, *The Promenade, Arnside, Carnforth, Lancs, LA5 0AD.* Non-smoking, family-run hotel in superb estuaryside location. **Open:** All year **Grades:** AA 4 Diamond
01524 761354 Mr Kerr *janet@willowfield.net1.co.uk* www.willowfield.uk.com **D:** Fr £27.00–£29.00 **S:** Fr £27.00–£42.00 **Beds:** 2F 3D 4T 2S **Baths:** 9 En 1 Pr 2 Sh (8) **cc**

Aspatria

NY1441 *The Beeches*

The Retreat, *Lakeside, Brayton, Aspatria, Carlisle, Cumbria, CA5 3PT.* Modern guest house. Central location, great view, bike hire. Patio, gardens. **Open:** All year
016973 21900 Mr & Mrs Stitt www.gstitt.fsnet.co.uk **D:** Fr £20.00–£22.00 **S:** Fr £20.00–£22.00 **Beds:** 1T 1D 1S **Baths:** 1 En (10)

Castlemont, *Aspatria, Carlisle, Cumbria, CA7 2JU.* Castlemont is a large Victorian family residence in 2 acres of garden. **Open:** All year
016973 20205 (also fax) Mr & Mrs Lines *castlemont@tesco.net* www.tuckedup.com/castlemont.html **D:** Fr £21.00–£25.00 **Beds:** 1F 1D 1T **Baths:** 1 En 2 Sh **cc**

Bailey

NY5179

Cleughside Farm, *Bailey, Newcastleton, Roxburghshire, TD9 0TR.* **Open:** All year **Grades:** ETC 3 Diamond
016977 48634 (also fax) *alicewhy@aol.com* www.cleughside.freeserve.co.uk **D:** Fr £20.00–£22.00 **S:** Fr £25.00–£30.00 **Beds:** 1F 1T/D 1D **Baths:** 1 En 1 Sh (3)
Independent traveller? Venture off the beaten track to Cleughside Farm. Share with us the atmosphere and tranquillity of the North Cumbrian countryside - steeped in Border Reiver history, abundant in wildlife. Enjoy the freedom to roam on foot, horseback or by bicycle.

Bampton

NY5218

Crown and Mitre, *Bampton Grange, Bampton, Penrith, Cumbria, CA10 2QR.* Family-run hotel set in undiscovered part of Lake District. **Open:** All year
01931 713225 Mrs Frith **D:** Fr £20.00 **S:** Fr £20.00 **Beds:** 2F 3T 5D 2S **Baths:** 5 En (5)

Banks

NY5664

South View, *Banks, Brampton, Cumbria, CA8 2JH.* Quiet location on Hadrian's Wall. Rooms have independent access. **Open:** All year (not Xmas/New Year) **Grades:** ETC 3 Diamond
016977 2309 Mrs Hodgson *sandrahodgson@southviewbanks.f9.co.uk* www.southviewbanks.f9.co.uk **D:** Fr £20.00–£24.00 **S:** Fr £22.00–£25.00 **Beds:** 1T 1D **Baths:** 2 En (12) (4)

Avondale, *3 St Aidans Road, Carlisle, Cumbria, CA1 1LT.* Attractive comfortable Edwardian house. Quiet central position convenient M6 J43. **Open:** All year (not Xmas) **Grades:** ETC 4 Diamond
01228 523012 (also fax) Mr & Mrs Hayes *beeanbee@hotmail.com* www.bed-breakfast-carlisle.co.uk **D:** Fr £20.00 **S:** Fr £20.00–£40.00 **Beds:** 1D 2T **Baths:** 1 En 1 Pr (3)

East View Guest House, *110 Warwick Road, Carlisle, Cumbria, CA1 1JU.* 10 minutes' walking distance from city centre, railway station & restaurants. **Open:** All year (not Xmas) **Grades:** ETC 3 Diamond, AA 3 Diamond
01228 522112 (also fax) Mrs Glease www.eastviewguesthouse.com **D:** Fr £19.00–£20.00 **S:** Fr £20.00–£25.00 **Beds:** 3F 2D 1T 1S **Baths:** 7 En (4)

Angus Hotel & Almonds Bistro, *14 Scotland Road, Stanwix, Carlisle, Cumbria, CA3 9DG.* **Open:** All year **Grades:** AA 4 Diamond
01228 523546 & 08000 262046 Mr Webster **Fax: 01228 531895** *angus@hadrians-wall.fsnet.co.uk* www.angus-hotel.fsnet.co.uk **D:** Fr £23.00–£30.00 **S:** Fr £30.00–£48.00 **Beds:** 4F 3D 4T 3S **Baths:** 11 En 3 Sh (6) **cc**
Victorian town house, foundations on Hadrian's Wall. Excellent food, Les Routiers Awards, local cheeses, home-baked bread. Genuine warm welcome from owners. Bar,bistro, lounge, meeting room, Internet cafe, direct dial telephones, secure garaging. Group rates for cyclists available.

Cartmel

SD3878

Bank Court Cottage, *The Square, Cartmel, Grange-over-Sands, Cumbria, LA11 6QB.* **Open:** All year (not Xmas)
015395 36593 (also fax) Mrs Lawson **D:** Fr £19.50–£26.00 **S:** Fr £22.50–£30.00 **Beds:** 1D 1T **Baths:** 1 Sh
We welcome visitors to our charming, character cottage situated in a pretty courtyard close to the centre of the beautiful historic South Lakeland village of Cartmel. Beams, log fire, views over the racecourse and park. Ideal walking & cycling country.

Castle Carrock

NY5455

Gelt Hall Farm, *Castle Carrock Brampton, Carlisle, Cumbria, CA4 9LT.* Farmhouse dating back to C17th. Near Hadrian's Wall, good stop-off on way to Scotland, near Gretna Green. Scenic walks and bird sanctuary, 2 miles golf course and Talkin Tarn boating lake. **Open:** All year
01228 670260 Ms Robinson **D:** Fr £17.50 **S:** Fr £16.00–£17.50 **Beds:** 1F 1D 1T **Baths:** 2 Sh

Castlerigg

NY2822

The Heights Hotel, *Rakefoot Lane, Castlerigg, Keswick, Cumbria, CA12 4TE.* Family-run hotel. Outstanding location, with panoramic views of lakes & fells. **Open:** All year (not Xmas/New Year)
017687 72251 Fax: 017687 75553 *enquiries@theheightshotel.co.uk* www.theheightshotel.co.uk **D:** Fr £24.00–£28.50 **S:** Fr £24.00–£26.50 **Beds:** 4F 1T 6D 1S **Baths:** 12 En (12) **cc**

Catlowdy

NY4576

Bessiestown, *Catlowdy, Longtown, Carlisle, Cumbria, CA6 5QP.* As featured on TV, multi-award winning Best Guest House, offering warm, lighthearted welcome, peace and quiet, delightful public rooms, beautiful ensuite bedrooms, luxury honeymoon suite, delicious food. Open all year with indoor heated swimming pool May-Sept. Easy access M6, M74, A7. **Open:** All year (not Xmas)
01228 577219 & 01228 577019 (also fax) Mr & Mrs Sisson *bestbb2000@cs.com* www.bessiestown.co.uk **D:** Fr £27.50–£30.00 **S:** Fr £35.00 **Beds:** 1F 2T 3D **Baths:** 6 Pr 3 **cc**

Cockermouth

NY1230

Riverside, *12 Market Street, Cockermouth, Cumbria, CA13 9NJ.* **Open:** All year (not Xmas/New Year)
01900 827504 D Meldrum **D:** Fr £18.50–£20.00 **S:** Fr £18.50–£20.00 **Beds:** 2T 1S **Baths:** 1 En 1 Sh
A welcoming Georgian terraced house, located in the quiet riverside conservation area of central Cockermouth. All main facilities, theatre and T.I.C. nearby. Bus, walking, cycling routes to exlore the unspoilt north-western Lakes! Comfortable ambience with excellent breakfasts using local produce.

The Rook Guest House, *9 Castlegate, Cockermouth, Cumbria, CA13 9EU.* Cosy C17th town house. Spiral staircase. Convenient for all amenities. **Open:** All year (not Xmas)
01900 828496 Mrs Waters www.therookguesthouse.gbr.cc **D:** Fr £16.00–£19.00 **S:** Fr £20.00–£22.00 **Beds:** 2D 1T **Baths:** 1 En 1 Pr 1 Sh (5)

Coniston

SD3097

Crown Hotel, *Coniston, Cumbria, LA21 8EA.* Situated in the picturesque village of Coniston within easy reach of the famous lake. **Open:** All year (not Xmas)
015394 41243 Mr Tiidus **Fax: 015394 41804** *info@crown-hotel-coniston.com* www.crown-hotel-coniston.com **D:** Fr £35.00–£40.00 **S:** Fr £40.00–£50.00 **Beds:** 6D 6T **Baths:** 12 En (20) **cc**

Lakeland House, *Tilberthwaite Avenue, Coniston, Cumbria, LA21 8ED.* Village centre, warm welcome for walkers/cyclists/groups. Internet access. **Open:** All year (not Xmas)
015394 41303 Mrs Holland *lakelandhouse_coniston@hotmail.com* www.lakelandhouse.com **D:** Fr £18.00–£35.00 **S:** Fr £18.00–£35.00 **Beds:** 5F 2D 1T 1S **Baths:** 3 En 3 Sh **cc**

Waverley, *Lake Road, Coniston, Cumbria, LA21 8EW.* Clean and friendly, excellent value. Large Victorian house. **Open:** All year (not Xmas)
015394 41127 (also fax) Mrs Graham **D:** Fr £16.00 **S:** Fr £16.00 **Beds:** 1F 1D 1T **Baths:** 1 Pr 1 Sh (3)

Thwaite Cottage, *Waterhead, Coniston, Cumbria, LA21 8AJ.* Beautiful C17th cottage. Peaceful location near head of Coniston Water. **Open:** All year (not Xmas)
015394 41367 Mrs Aldridge *m@thwaitcot.freeserve.co.uk* www.thwaitcot.freeserve.co.uk **D:** Fr £21.00–£24.00 **Beds:** 2D 1T **Baths:** 1 En 2 Pr (3)

Kirkbeck House, *Lake Road, Coniston, Cumbria, LA21 8EW.* Comfortable friendly accommodation close to lake and amenities. Yummy breakfast. **Open:** All year
015394 41358 Mrs Potter *ann@kirkbeckhouse.co.uk* www.kirkbeckhouse.co.uk **D:** Fr £16.00 **S:** Fr £16.00 **Beds:** 1F 1D 1T (3)

All details shown are as supplied by B&B owners in Autumn 2002

Planning a longer stay? Always ask for any special rates

Ship Inn, *Bowmanstead, Coniston, Cumbria, LA21 8HB.* Traditional Country Inn with original oak beams and real log fire. Perfectly situated for exploring Coniston Fells and surrounding areas of the Lake District. You can be assured of a warm welcome, comfortable accommodation and good food. **Open:** All year
015394 41224 Mrs Jackson **D:** Fr £22.50–£25.00 **S:** Fr £25.00–£30.00 **Beds:** 1F 3D **Baths:** 2 Sh (10) cc

Oaklands, *Yewdale Road, Coniston, Cumbria, LA21 8DX.* Beautiful spacious ensuite accommodation, near village centre, private parking. **Open:** All year (not Xmas/New Year)
015394 41245 (also fax) Mrs Myers *judithzeke@oaklandsguesthouse.fsnet.co.uk* www.geocities.com/oaklandsguesthouse **D:** Fr £22.00–£25.00 **S:** Fr £22.00–£25.00 **Beds:** 1T 2D **Baths:** 2 En 1 Sh (4)

Yewdale Hotel, *Coniston, Cumbria, LA21 8LU.* Owners long-distance walkers. Family-run, fresh produce catering only. **Open:** All year
015394 41280 Mr Barrow **Fax: 015394 41662** *mail@yewdalehotel.com* **D:** Fr £30.00–£34.50 **S:** Fr £37.50–£42.00 **Beds:** 4F 3D 5T **Baths:** 12 En (6)

Cowgill

SD7587

The Sportsman's Inn, *Cowgill, Dent, Sedbergh, Cumbria, LA10 5RG.* Family owned freehouse 1670, scenic location, rooms overlooking River Dee. **Open:** All year
015396 25282 Mr & Mrs Martin *ronmartin@bun.com* **D:** Fr £17.50–£23.50 **S:** Fr £17.50–£23.50 **Beds:** 1F 2D 3T **Baths:** 3 Sh (10)

Crook

SD4695

Mitchelland Farm Bungalow, *Crook, Kendal, Cumbria, LA8 8LL.* Wheelchair accessible spacious working farm bungalow. Wonderful views near Windermere. **Open:** All year
015394 47421 Mr Higham **D:** Fr £22.00–£26.00 **S:** Fr £25.00–£30.00 **Beds:** 1T 1D **Baths:** 1 En 1 Pr (5)

BEDROOMS
D = Double
T = Twin
S = Single
F = Family

Crosscanonby

NY0739

East Farm, *Crosscanonby, Maryport, Cumbria, CA15 6SJ.* Modernised, comfortable farmhouse, traditional breakfast. Aquaria, leisure centre, beach nearby. **Open:** All year (not Xmas)
01900 812153 Mrs Carruthers *carruthers_eastfarm@hotmail.com* **D:** Fr £18.00–£20.00 **S:** Fr £20.00–£24.00 **Beds:** 1F 1D **Baths:** 1 En 1 Pr (2) (2)

Cumwhinton

NY4552

Cringles, *Cumwhinton, Carlisle, Cumbria, CA4 8DL.* A quality cottage 3 miles from Carlisle, ideal touring/walking area. **Open:** All year (not Xmas/New Year) **Grades:** ETC 4 Star
01228 561600 Mrs Stamper **D:** Fr £25.00 **S:** Fr £35.00 **Beds:** 1T 1D **Baths:** 1 Sh (3)

Dalemain

NY4726

Park House Farm, *Dalemain, Penrith, Cumbria, CA11 0HB.* Idyllic, peaceful setting. Near Lake Ullswater. C18th farmhouse. Home-made fayre. **Open:** Mar to Nov **Grades:** ETC 3 Diamond
017684 86212 (also fax) Mrs Milburn *mail@parkhousedalemain.freeserve.co.uk* www.eden-in-cumbria.co.uk/parkhouse **D:** Fr £20.00–£23.00 **S:** Fr £25.00 **Beds:** 1F/T 1D **Baths:** 2 En cc

RATES
D = Price range per person sharing in a double or twin room
S = Price range for a single room

Dalton-in-Furness

SD2374

Park Cottage, *Park, Dalton-in-Furness, Cumbria, LA15 8JZ.* **Open:** All year
01229 462850 Mr & Mrs Nicholson *nicholson.parkcottage@quista.net* www.parkcottagedalton.co.uk **D:** Fr £18.50–£21.50 **S:** Fr £22.00–£26.00 **Beds:** 1F 2D **Baths:** 3 En (6)
Surrounded by woodland and farmland, this C17th beamed cottage enjoys a peaceful location and overlooks Burlington Lake. Birdwatchers' paradise. Excellent ensuite bedrooms have good views. Comfortable residents' lounge. Hearty Cumbrian breakfasts. Easy access to South Lakeland, fells and coast. Highly recommended, many repeat bookings.

Dent

SD7086

Rash House, *Dent Foot, Dent, Sedbergh, Cumbria, LA10 5SU.* Charming C18th farmhouse situated in picturesque Dentdale. **Open:** All year (not Xmas)
015396 20113 (also fax) Mrs Hunter *annehunter@msn.com* **D:** Fr £18.00–£20.00 **S:** Fr £20.00–£22.00 **Beds:** 1F 1D **Baths:** 1 Sh (2)

Garda View Guest House, *Dent, Sedbergh, Cumbria, LA10 5QL.* Village centre, friendly family house. Hearty breakfasts, walking information available. **Open:** All year (not Xmas)
015396 25209 Mrs Smith *rita@gardaview.co.uk* **D:** Fr £18.00–£20.00 **S:** Fr £18.00–£25.00 **Beds:** 1D 1T 1S **Baths:** 1 Sh 1 En (2)

Smithy Fold, *Whernside Manor, Dent, Sedbergh, Cumbria, LA10 5RE.* Relax in this beautiful setting and we'll make it memorable. **Open:** All year
015396 25368 A J Cheetham *cheetham@smithyfold.co.uk* www.smithyfold.co.uk **D:** Fr £18.00 **S:** Fr £18.00 **Beds:** 1F 1T 2D **Baths:** 1 Sh (3) (20)

All details shown are as supplied by B&B owners in Autumn 2002

Duddon Bridge

SD1988 *High Cross Inn, Black Cock, King's Head, Blacksmith's Arms*

The Dower House, *High Duddon, Duddon Bridge, Broughton In Furness, Cumbria, LA20 6ET.* Exceptional location, peaceful, secluded country house. Comfortable rooms & warm welcome. **Open:** All year (not Xmas/New Year) **01229 716279 (also fax)** Mrs Nichols **D:** Fr £23.00–£27.00 **S:** Fr £30.00 **Beds:** 1F 1T 3D 1S **Baths:** 4 En 1 Pr (8) cc

Dufton

NY6825

Sycamore House, *Dufton, Appleby-in-Westmorland, Cumbria, CA16 6DB.* Listed cottage, cosy living room, close to pub and shop. **Open:** Easter to Dec **017683 51296** Mrs O'Halloran *o_halloran@hotmail.com* www.sycamorehouse.org.uk **D:** Fr £18.00–£20.00 **S:** Fr £17.00–£20.00 **Beds:** 3D **Baths:** 1 En 1 Sh (2)

Eamont Bridge

NY5228

River View, *6 Lowther Glen, Eamont Bridge, Penrith, Cumbria, CA10 2BP.* Beautiful riverside bungalow near Lake Ullswater. Comfortable beds, good breakfasts. **Open:** All year **01768 864405** Mrs O'Neil **D:** Fr £18.00–£22.00 **S:** Fr £20.00–£22.00 **Beds:** 1T 2D 2S **Baths:** 1 En (4)

Egremont

NY0110 *White Mare*

Ghyll Farm Guest House, *Egremont, Cumbria, CA22 2UA.* Comfortable, clean, friendly farmhouse. Good breakfast, private off-road parking. Try a fishing holiday on River Irt at Holmrook and catch salmon and sea trout. Reasonable rates. While the men fish, the ladies can visit our beautiful lakes etc. **Open:** All year (not Xmas) **01946 822256** Mrs Holliday **D:** Fr £15.00 **S:** Fr £15.00 **Beds:** 2T 2S **Baths:** 2 Sh (6)

Elterwater

NY3204

Britannia Inn, *Elterwater, Langdale, Ambleside, Cumbria, LA22 9HP.* Traditional Lakeland inn overlooking village green. Cosy bars with log fires. **Open:** All year (not Xmas) **015394 37210** J A Fry **Fax: 015394 37311** *info@britinn.co.uk* www.britinn.co.uk **D:** Fr £24.00–£39.00 **S:** Fr £24.00–£30.00 **Beds:** 9D 3T **Baths:** 9 En 3 Sh (10) cc

Embleton

NY1630

Orchard House, *Embleton, Cockermouth, Cumbria, CA13 9XP.* Detached Edwardian country house with 3/4 acre garden. Mountain views. **Open:** All year **017687 76347 (also fax)** Mrs Newton *info@orchardhouse.uk.net* www.orchardhouse.uk.net **D:** Fr £18.00–£20.00 **S:** Fr £20.00–£25.00 **Beds:** 2D **Baths:** 2 En (7) (8)

Endmoor

SD5385

Summerlands Tower, *Summerlands, Endmoor, Kendal, Cumbria, LA8 0ED.* Victorian country house with fine rooms and gardens. 3 miles from M6/J36. **Open:** Easter to Nov **015395 61081 (also fax)** Mr & Mrs Green *m_.green@virgin.net* **D:** Fr £24.00–£29.50 **S:** Fr £29.00–£34.50 **Beds:** 2T 1D **Baths:** 1 En 1 Pr (12) (3)

Ennerdale Bridge

NY0715

The Shepherds Arms Hotel, *Ennerdale Bridge, Cleator, Cumbria, CA23 3AR.* Friendly refurbished inn situated in idyllic unspoilt Lake District valley. Bargain breaks! **Open:** All year **01946 861249 (also fax)** Mr Madden *enquiries@shepherdsarmshotel.co.uk* www.shepherdsarmshotel.co.uk **D:** Fr £29.50 **S:** Fr £32.00–£37.50 **Beds:** 1F 3D 3T 1S **Baths:** 6 En 2 Pr (6) cc

Eskdale Green

NY1400

The Ferns, *Eskdale Green, Holmrook, Cumbria, CA19 1UA.* Homely accommodation in large Victorian residence. Near lakes and mountains. **Open:** All year **019467 23217 (also fax)** Mr & Mrs Prestwood *j.prestwood@talk21.com* www.eskdalebreaks.com **D:** Fr £20.00–£25.00 **S:** Fr £22.00–£25.00 **Beds:** 2D 1T **Baths:** 1 En 2 Sh (4)

Far Sawrey

SD3895

Sawrey Hotel, *Far Sawrey, Ambleside, Cumbria, LA22 0LQ.* C18th country inn. Log fires. Bar in old stables. **Open:** All year (not Xmas) **015394 43425 (also fax)** Mr Brayshaw **D:** Fr £29.50 **S:** Fr £29.50 **Beds:** 3F 8D 5T 2S **Baths:** 18 Pr 1 Sh (30) cc

Flookburgh

SD3675

Fieldhead Farm House, *Flookburgh, Grange-over-Sands, Cumbria, LA11 7LN.* A C17th farmhouse on edge of ancient fishing village. **Open:** All year **015395 58651** Mrs Mardon *mardon@fieldheadcrafts.fsnet.co.uk* **D:** Fr £18.00–£20.00 **S:** Fr £18.00–£20.00 **Beds:** 2D 1S 1T 1F **Baths:** 1 Sh (3)

Frizington

NY0317

14 Lingley Fields, *Frizington, Cumbria, CA26 3RU.* Village house set in cottage-style garden. Choice of breakfast. **Open:** All year **01946 811779** Mrs Hall **D:** Fr £16.00–£20.00 **S:** Fr £16.00–£20.00 **Beds:** 1F 1T **Baths:** 1 En 1 Sh

Garrigill

NY7441

Ivy House, *Garrigill, Alston, Cumbria, CA9 3DU.* C17th converted farmhouse. Comfortable, friendly atmosphere. Picturesque North Pennines village. **Open:** All year **01434 382501** Mrs Humble **Fax: 01434 382660** *ivyhouse@garrigill.com* www.garrigill.com **D:** Fr £19.00–£24.00 **S:** Fr £27.00–£29.00 **Beds:** 2F 3T 2D 3S **Baths:** 3 En (10) cc

Garth Row

SD5297

Hollin Root Farm, *Garth Row, Kendal, Cumbria, LA8 9AW.* Peaceful farmhouse, decorated to high standards. Superb views, excellent breakfasts. **Open:** All year **Grades:** ETC 4 Diamond **01539 823638** Mrs Rowles *b-and-b@hollin-root-farm.freeserve.co.uk* www.hollinrootfarm.co.uk **D:** Fr £22.00–£28.00 **Beds:** 3D **Baths:** 3 En (6)

Glenridding

NY3816 *White Lion, Travellers' Rest, Ratchers Bar*

Beech House, *Glenridding, Penrith, Cumbria, CA11 0PA.* Very popular walking area next to Ullswater, close to Helvellyn. **Open:** All year **017684 82037 (also fax)** Mr & Mrs Reed *reed@beechhouse.com* www.beechhouse.com **D:** Fr £18.00–£25.00 **S:** Fr £18.00–£20.00 **Beds:** 1F 4D 2S **Baths:** 2 En (8) cc

Planning a longer stay? Always ask for any special rates

Grange-in-Borrowdale

NY2517

Grayrigg, *Grange-in-Borrowdale, Keswick, Cumbria, CA12 5UQ.* **Open:** All year (not Xmas)
017687 77607 Mrs Figg *judyfigg@supanet.com* www.grayrigg.biz **D:** Fr £19.00–£23.00 **S:** Fr £19.00–£30.00 **Beds:** 1F 1D 1T **Baths:** 2 En 1 Pr (4)
Ideally situated on outskirts of village in quiet location at foot of Maiden Moor, offering comfortable accommodation and quality breakfasts. All rooms have a view, including the loos! For further information visit www.grayrigg.biz. A warm welcome awaits you.

Scawdel, *Grange-in-Borrowdale, Keswick, Cumbria, CA12 5UQ.* Comfortable accommodation with magnificent mountain views. Ideal walking/touring base. **Open:** All year (not Xmas)
017687 77271 J Reinecke *info@scawdel.co.uk* www.scawdel.co.uk **D:** Fr £20.00–£22.50 **S:** Fr £20.00–£40.00 **Beds:** 2D 1S **Baths:** 2 En 1 Sh (4)

Grange-over-Sands

SD4077

Mayfields, *3 Mayfield Terrace, Kents Bank Road, Grange-over-Sands, Cumbria, LA11 7DW.* Perfectly situated for Lakes, Dales, Cartmel & Furness Peninsular. Very warm welcome. **Open:** All year **Grades:** ETC 4 Diamond, AA 4 Diamond
015395 34730 Mr Thorburn **D:** Fr £25.00 **S:** Fr £32.00 **Beds:** 1T 1D 1S **Baths:** 2 En 1 Pr (3)

Grasmere

NY3307

Ryelands, *Grasmere, Ambleside, Cumbria, LA22 9SU.* **Open:** Mar to Nov
015394 35076 (also fax) *kirkbride.ryelands@virgin.net* www.ryelandsgrasmere.co.uk **D:** Fr £30.00–£35.00 **Beds:** 3D **Baths:** 3 En (3)
A delightful Victorian Lakeland country house in 3 acres of peaceful gardens on the edge of one of the most beautiful villages in Lakeland. Elegant, spacious and comfortable accommodation for discerning guests, the perfect retreat from which to enjoy the Lake District.

Oak Lodge, *Easedale Road, Grasmere, Ambleside, Cumbria, LA22 9QJ.* Quiet location with open views of the Easedale Valley. **Open:** Feb to Dec
015394 35527 Mrs Dixon **D:** Fr £22.00–£26.00 **S:** Fr £30.00 **Beds:** 2D 1T **Baths:** 3 En (10) (3)

Ash Cottage, *Red Lion Square, Grasmere, Ambleside, Cumbria, LA22 9SP.* Detached guest house in central Grasmere. Gardens. **Open:** All year
015394 35224 *ashcottage@demon.co.uk* **D:** Fr £24.00–£30.00 **S:** Fr £25.00–£32.00 **Beds:** 1F 3T 3D 1S (8) (10)

Grayrigg

SD5797

Punchbowl House, *Grayrigg, Kendal, Cumbria, LA8 9BU.* Spacious and comfortable former Victorian farmhouse in the centre of the village. **Open:** Mar to Dec
01539 824345 (also fax) Mrs Johnson **D:** Fr £20.00–£25.00 **S:** Fr £20.00–£40.00 **Beds:** 2D 1T **Baths:** 1 En 1 Sh (4)

Grayrigg Hall Farm, *Grayrigg, Kendal, Cumbria, LA8 9BU.* An C18th farmhouse in beautiful open countryside. Working farm. Convenient M6 (J38). **Open:** Easter to Nov **Grades:** ETC 3 Diamond
01539 824689 Mrs Bindloss **D:** Fr £18.00–£20.00 **S:** Fr £18.00–£20.00 **Beds:** 1F 1D 1S **Baths:** 1 Sh (2)

National Grid References given are for villages, towns and cities – not for individual houses

Graythwaite

NY1123

Low Graythwaite Hall, *Graythwaite, Ulverston, Cumbria, LA12 8AZ.* Historic statesman's house, old panelling, fine furnishings, open log fires. **Open:** Feb to Jan
015395 31676 (also fax) **D:** Fr £22.00–£30.00 **S:** Fr £25.00–£30.00 **Beds:** 1F 1T 1D **Baths:** 2 En (20)

Greystoke

NY4430 *The Sportsman, Boot & Shoe, Clickham Inn*

Lattendales Farm, *Greystoke, Penrith, Cumbria, CA11 0UE.* Comfortable C17th farmhouse in pleasant quiet village. **Open:** Feb to Nov
017684 83474 Mrs Ashburner **D:** Fr £17.00–£18.00 **Beds:** 1T 2D **Baths:** 1 Sh (0)

Orchard Cottage, *Church Road, Greystoke, Penrith, Cumbria, CA11 0TW.* Comfortable, peaceful bedrooms overlooking gardens. M6/jct. 40 just 4 1/2 miles. **Open:** All year
017684 83264 Mrs Theakston **Fax: 017684 80015** **D:** Fr £22.00 **S:** Fr £22.00 **Beds:** 1F 1D **Baths:** 1 En 1 Pr

Grisedale

SD7792

Aldershaw, *Grisedale, Sedbergh, Cumbria, LA10 5PS.* Superb Daleside renovated farmhouse, oak-beamed. Delicious food. **Open:** All year (not Xmas)
015396 21211 Mr & Mrs Robinson **D:** Fr £17.50–£25.00 **S:** Fr £20.00–£27.00 **Beds:** 1D 1T 1S **Baths:** 1 En 1 Sh (3)

Hale

SD5078

Yewdale, *Hale, Milnthorpe, Cumbria, LA7 7BL.* **Open:** All year (not Xmas)
015395 62457 Mrs Westworth *t.westworth@virgin.net* **D:** Fr £24.00–£27.50 **S:** Fr £18.00–£22.50 **Beds:** 1D 2T 1S **Baths:** 1 En 2 Sh (4)
High-class accommodation in AONB, 180 degree spectacular views, excellent location for outdoor pursuits, RSPB reserve nearby, Windermere 15 min, Yorkshire Dales 20 min. Perfect midway break between England/Scotland. A warm welcome & superb breakfast assured. 5 miles from M6/J35.

Hartsop

NY4013

Patterdale, *Fellside, Hartsop, Penrith, Cumbria, CA11 0NZ.* C17th stone built farmhouse, close to lakes and high mountains. **Open:** All year (not Xmas/New Year)
017684 82532 Mrs Knight **D:** Fr £16.00–£18.00 **S:** Fr £20.00–£24.00 **Beds:** 2T **Baths:** 1 Sh (2)

Haverthwaite

SD3483

Rusland Pool Hotel and Restaurant, *Haverthwaite, Newby Bridge, Ulverston, Cumbria, LA12 8AA.* Friendly, informal atmosphere. Central to popular local walks. **Open:** All year
01229 861384 *enquiries@ruslandpool.co.uk* www.ruslandpool.co.uk **D:** Fr £26.00–£39.50 **S:** Fr £40.00–£59.00 **Beds:** 4F 4T 10D **Baths:** 18 En (35) **cc**

Hawkshead

SD3597 *The Outgate, Queen's Head, Red Lion, Drunken Duck, King's Arms*

School House Cottage, *Hawkshead, Ambleside, Cumbria, LA22 0NT.* A warm welcome to Hawkshead, said to be the prettiest village in the Lakes. Ideal for walking, touring, cycling. Close to Grizedale Forest, Tarn Hows, Beatrix Potter country. Quiet location, comfortable rooms, hearty breakfast, private garden with sun loungers. **Open:** All year
015394 36401 **D:** Fr £21.00 **Beds:** 2D **Baths:** 2 En (2)

Beechmount, *Near Sawrey, Hawkshead, Ambleside, Cumbria, LA22 0JZ.* **Open:** All year
015394 36356 Mrs Siddall *beechmount@supanet.com* www.beechmountcountryhouse.co.uk **D:** Fr £24.00–£26.00 **S:** Fr £30.00–£35.00 **Beds:** 3D 1T 1F **Baths:** 2 En 1 Pr (3)
Beechmount is a charming, spacious country house in Beatrix Potter's picturesque village Near Sawre, with its Olde Worlde Inn. Delightful appointed bedrooms with superb lake/country views. Relaxed friendly atmosphere. Delicious breakfasts. Excellent value. Brochure available or www.beechmountcountryhouse.co.uk.

Borwick Lodge, *Hawkshead, Ambleside, Cumbria, LA22 0PU.* Award-winning 'accommodation of the highest standards'. A rather special C17th country house. **Open:** All year
015394 36332 (also fax) Margaret & Malcolm MacFarlane *borwicklodge@talk21.com* www.borwicklodge.com **D:** Fr £30.00–£39.00 **Beds:** 1F 4D 1T **Baths:** 6 En (8) (8)

Hawkshead Hill

SD3398

Yewfield Vegetarian Guest House, *Hawkshead Hill, Ambleside, LA22 0PR.* Peaceful retreat in 30 acres grounds, impressive Gothic house overlooking Esthwaite Vale. **Open:** Feb to Nov
015394 36765 Mr Hook www.yewfield.co.uk **D:** Fr £20.00–£37.00 **S:** Fr £25.00–£33.00 **Beds:** 1T 2D **Baths:** 3 En (9) (6) **cc**

Helsington

SD5090

Helsington Laithes Manor, *Helsington, Kendal, Cumbia, LA9 5RJ.* Historic Listed Manor House in 3 acre grounds, 5 minutes M6/J36. **Open:** All year (not Xmas/New Year)
01539 741253 & 07767 342696 (M) Fax: 01539 741346 *themanor@helsington.uk.com* www.helsington.uk.com **D:** Fr £20.00–£25.00 **S:** Fr £25.00–£30.00 **Beds:** 1F 1T 3D **Baths:** 2 En 1 Pr (5) (5)

Hesket Newmarket

NY3338

Denton House, *Hesket Newmarket, Caldbeck, Wigton, Cumbria, CA7 8JG.* **Open:** All year
Grades: ETC 3 Diamond
016974 78415 Mrs Monkhouse *dentonhnm@aol.com* **D:** Fr £18.00–£22.00 **S:** Fr £20.00–£25.00 **Beds:** 3F 3T 2D 1S **Baths:** 4 En 1 Pr 4 Sh
A friendly atmosphere with home-cooking awaits you in our C17th house modernised to C20th comforts. Situated in the unspoilt village of Hesket Newmarket, ideal for touring the Lakes or stopover enroute to Scotland.

Newlands Grange, *Hesket Newmarket, Caldbeck, Wigton, Cumbria, CA7 8HP.* Comfortable, oak-beamed farmhouse offering all home-cooking. All welcome. **Open:** All year (not Xmas)
016974 78676 Mrs Studholme **D:** Fr £17.50–£20.50 **S:** Fr £18.00–£21.00 **Beds:** 1F 1D 1T 1S **Baths:** 1 En 1 Sh

High Harrington

NY0025

Riversleigh Guest House, *39 Primrose Terrace, High Harrington, Workington, Cumbria, CA14 5PS.* Riverside house overlooking gardens, 5 mins from station and marina. **Open:** All year
01946 830267 Mrs Davies **D:** Fr £15.00–£20.00 **S:** Fr £15.00–£20.00 **Beds:** 1F 1T 1D **Baths:** 2 En 1 Pr (5) (8)

High Lorton

NY1625

Owl Brook, *Whinlatter Pass, High Lorton, Cockermouth, Cumbria, CA13 9TX.* Green slate bungalow, designed by owners. Pine ceilings. Oak floors. **Open:** All year
01900 85333 Mrs Roberts **D:** Fr £16.50–£17.50 **S:** Fr £16.50–£17.50 **Beds:** 3D **Baths:** 1 Sh (0) (2)

High Wray

SD3799

Tock How Farm, *High Wray, Ambleside, Cumbria, LA22 0JF.* Traditional farmhouse overlooking to Lake Windermere and the surrounding Fells. **Open:** All year
015394 36106 & 07971 984232 (M) Mrs Irvine **D:** Fr £19.50–£23.00 **S:** Fr £21.00–£25.00 **Beds:** 1F 1D **Baths:** 2 En (4)

Holme

SD5279

Marwin House, *Duke Street, Holme, Carnforth, Cumbria, LA6 1PY.* Gateway to Lake District, Yorkshire Dales. M6 (J36) 5 minutes. **Open:** All year
01524 781144 (also fax) **D:** Fr £16.00–£18.00 **S:** Fr £17.00–£19.00 **Beds:** 1F 1T **Baths:** 1 Sh (3)

Holmrook

SD0799

Hill Farm, *Holmrook, Cumbria, CA19 1UG.* Working farm - beautiful views overlooking River Irt and Wasdale Fells. **Open:** All year (not Xmas)
019467 24217 Mrs Leak **D:** Fr £15.00 **S:** Fr £15.00 **Beds:** 2F **Baths:** 2 Sh

Ings

SD4498 *Watermill, Railway Hotel*

St Annes Farm, *Ings, Kendal, Cumbria, LA8 9QG.* Clean, friendly. Windermere 2 miles. Good breakfast. **Open:** Easter to Oct
01539 821223 Mrs Allen **D:** Fr £17.00 **Beds:** 2D **Baths:** 1 Sh (5) (2)

Irton

NY1000

Cookson Place Farm, *Irton, Holmrook, Cumbria, CA19 1YQ.* Working farm. Quiet area within easy reach of Wasdale, Eskdale. **Open:** All year (not Xmas)
019467 24286 Mrs Crayston **D:** Fr £15.00 **S:** Fr £15.00 **Beds:** 1F 1T **Baths:** 1 Sh

Ivegill

NY4143

Streethead Farm, *Ivegill, Carlisle, Cumbria, CA4 0NG.* Distant hills, real fires, home-baking, convenient for Lakes or Scotland. **Open:** All year (not Xmas)
016974 73327 (also fax) Mrs Wilson **D:** Fr £20.00–£22.00 **S:** Fr £22.00–£25.00 **Beds:** 2D **Baths:** 2 En (7) (2)

Croft End Hurst, *Ivegill, Carlisle, Cumbria, CA4 0NL.* Rural bungalow situated midway between J41/42 of M6. **Open:** All year
017684 84362 Mrs Nichol **D:** Fr £17.00–£19.00 **S:** Fr £17.00 **Beds:** 1D 1T **Baths:** 1 Sh (1) (4)

Kendal

SD5192

Riversleigh Guest House, *49 Milnthorpe Road, Kendal, Cumbria, LA9 5QG.* Victorian guest house. Town location. Ideal for all amenities. **Open:** All year
Grades: ETC 3 Diamond
015397 26392 Mrs King **D:** Fr £18.00–£25.00 **S:** Fr £18.00–£30.00 **Beds:** 1F 2T 3D 2S **Baths:** 2 En 2 Pr 2 Sh (6)

Bridge House, *65 Castle Street, Kendal, Cumbria, LA9 7AD.* **Open:** All year
015397 22041 & 07813 679411 (M)
Mrs Brindley *sheila@bridgehouse-kendal.co.uk* www.bridgehouse-kendal.co.uk **D:** Fr £20.00–£25.00 **S:** Fr £25.00–£30.00 **Beds:** 1D 1T **Baths:** 1 En 1 Sh
Beautiful Georgian Listed building a short walk from Kendal Castle and the River Kent. Home-made bread and preserves a speciality. Complimentary Kendal Mint Cake for our visitors. A lovely private garden for guests' use. A warm and friendly welcome.

Mitchelland House, *Off Crook Road, Kendal, Cumbria, LA8 8LL.* Delightful country location, only 5 minutes Lake Windermere and all attractions. **Open:** All year (not Xmas)
015394 48589 *marie.mitchelland@talk21.com* **D:** Fr £18.00–£24.00 **S:** Fr £21.00–£26.00 **Beds:** 1F 1D 1T **Baths:** 1 En 1 Sh (10)

The Headlands Hotel, *53 Milnthorpe Road, Kendal, Cumbria, LA9 5QG.* Family run (private) hotel. Ideal town location for all amenities. **Open:** All year
01539 732464 (also fax) Mr & Mrs Kellington *info@headlands-kendal.fsnet.co.uk* www.headlands-hotel.co.uk **D:** Fr £20.00–£24.00 **S:** Fr £20.00–£35.00 **Beds:** 2F 1T 3D **Baths:** 5 En 1 Pr cc

Magic Hills House, *123 Appleby Road, Kendal, Cumbria, LA9 6HF.* Late Victorian family house, comfortably furnished, tastefully decorated. 10 mins' walk to centre. **Open:** All year (not Xmas)
01539 736248 C.K Moseley *ckm@ukgateway.net* **D:** Fr £18.50–£22.50 **S:** Fr £21.00–£27.00 **Beds:** 2D 1T **Baths:** 1 En 1 Pr 1 Sh (12)

Hillside Guest House, *4 Beast Banks, Kendal, Cumbria, LA9 4JW.* Large Victorian guest house, town centre. Ideal for Lake District & Yorkshire Dales. **Open:** Mar to Nov
015397 22836 Mrs Denison **D:** Fr £18.00–£21.00 **S:** Fr £18.00–£22.00 **Beds:** 3D 1T 3S **Baths:** 5 En 4 Pr 1 Sh (4) (4)

Fairways, *102 Windermere Road, Kendal, Cumbria, LA9 5EZ.* Victorian guest house, ensuite rooms, TV. Edge of Lake District. **Open:** All year
015397 25564 Mrs Paylor *mp@fairwaysl.fsnet.co.uk* **D:** Fr £19.00–£20.00 **S:** Fr £20.00–£25.00 **Beds:** 1F 2D 1S **Baths:** 3 En 1 Pr (2) (4)

Airethwaite House, *1 Airethwaite, Horncop Lane, Kendal, Cumbria, LA9 4SP.* Spacious Victorian guest house. Original features, antique furniture. Lovely views. Town centre 5 mins. **Open:** All year
01539 730435 Mrs Dean *info@airethwaitehouse.co.uk* www.arethwaitehouse.co.uk **D:** Fr £20.00–£22.00 **S:** Fr £25.00 **Beds:** 3D/T **Baths:** 3 En (3)

Punchbowl House, *Grayrigg, Kendal, Cumbria, LA8 9BU.* Spacious and comfortable former Victorian farmhouse in the centre of the village. **Open:** Mar to Dec
01539 824345 (also fax) Mrs Johnson **D:** Fr £20.00–£25.00 **S:** Fr £20.00–£40.00 **Beds:** 2D 1T **Baths:** 1 En 1 Sh (4)

The Glen, *Oxenholme, Kendal, Cumbria, LA9 7RF.* **Open:** All year (not Xmas/New Year)
015397 26386 Mrs Green *greenintheglen@btinternet.com* www.glen-kendal.co.uk **D:** Fr £19.00–£26.00 **S:** Fr £25.00–£30.00 **Beds:** 1F 1T 3D **Baths:** 5 En (6) (10)
On the outskirts of Kendal in a quiet location under 'the Helm' (local walk and view point of Lakeland fells), but within a short walk of pub and restaurant. For that special occasion a four-poster, jacuzzi and spa (ensuite).

Highgate Hotel, *128 Highgate, Kendal, Cumbria, LA9 4HE.* Grade II* Listed town centre B&B, built 1769. Private car park. **Open:** All year (not Xmas/New Year)
01539 724229 (also fax) Mr Dawson *info@highgatehotel.co.uk* www.highgatehotel.co.uk **D:** Fr £21.50–£23.50 **S:** Fr £27.00–£29.00 **Beds:** 1F 4D 2T 3S **Baths:** 10 En (10) cc

Sundial House, *51 Milnthorpe Road, Kendal, Cumbria, LA9 5QG.* Quality guest house, private car park, 5 mins from town centre. **Open:** All year (not Xmas)
01539 724468 Mr & Mrs Richardson **Fax: 01539 736900** *sundialghouse@aol.com* **D:** Fr £17.50–£25.00 **S:** Fr £18.50–£22.50 **Beds:** 1F 1D 2T 3S **Baths:** 2 En 3 Sh (8)

Lakeland Natural Vegetarian Guest House, *Low Slack, Queens Road, Kendal, Cumbria, LA9 4PH.*
Open: All year **Grades:** ETC 3 Diamond
01539 733011 (also fax) Helen Charlton *relax@lakelandnatural.co.uk* www.lakelandnatural.co.uk **D:** Fr £30.00 **S:** Fr £35.00 **Beds:** 1F 2T 2D **Baths:** 5 En (7) cc
Spacious Victorian home, with stunning views overlooking Kendal and the surrounding fells. Adjacent woodland walks and golf course. Only 5 mins' walk from the town centre. Non-smoking. Brilliant breakfasts and imaginative evening meals using largely organic produce. Licensed.

Plumtree House, *Brigsteer, Kendal, Cumbria, LA8 8AR.* **Open:** All year (not Xmas/New Year)
015397 68774 & 07817 170908 (M)
plumtreehousebrigsteer@hotmail.com **D:** Fr £25.00–£30.00 **S:** Fr £30.00–£35.00 **Beds:** 1T 2D **Baths:** 3 En (5) (4)
Nestling under the local landmark of Scout Scar, Plumtree House offers the perfect base for walking or touring holidays. Being a Victorian country house, the rooms are large and airy with panoramic views across and along the renowned Lyth Valley, famous for the damson orchards.

Please respect a B&B's wishes regarding children, animals and smoking

RATES
D = Price range per person sharing in a double or twin room
S = Price range for a single room

Sonata, *19 Burnside Road, Kendal, Cumbria, LA9 4RL.* **Open:** All year
01539 732290 (also fax) Mr Wilkinson *chris@sonataguesthouse.freeserve.co.uk*
www.sonataguesthouse.co.uk **D:** Fr £23.00 **S:** Fr £27.00–£35.00 **Beds:** 1F 2D 1T **Baths:** 4 En cc
Sonata Guest House is located 4 mins walk to town centre. We are a friendly family run Georgian establishment. All our bedrooms are ensuite & contain remote controlled colour televisions, radio alarms, complimentary beverages, hairdryers & individually controlled central heating. Prices include breakfast of your choice.

Birslack Grange, *Hutton Lane, Levens, Kendal, Cumbria, LA8 8PA.* Converted farm buildings in rural setting overlooking the scenic Lyth Valley. **Open:** All year (not Xmas)
015395 60989 Mrs Carrington-Birch *birslackgrange@msn.com* www.birslackgrange.co.uk **D:** Fr £20.00–£22.00 **S:** Fr £22.00–£28.00 **Beds:** 1F 2D 2T 2S **Baths:** 4 En 2 Sh (3) (6)

Hollin Root Farm, *Garth Row, Kendal, Cumbria, LA8 9AW.* Peaceful farmhouse, decorated to high standards. Superb views, excellent breakfasts. **Open:** All year **Grades:** ETC 4 Diamond
01539 823638 Mrs Rowles *b-and-b@hollin-root-farm.freeserve.co.uk*
www.hollinrootfarm.co.uk **D:** Fr £22.00–£28.00 **Beds:** 3D **Baths:** 3 En (6)

Kentmere

NY4504

Maggs Howe, *Kentmere, Kendal, Cumbria, LA8 9JP.* Detached former farmhouse in beautiful, quiet, unspoilt cul-de-sac valley.
Open: All year (not Xmas)
01539 821689 Mrs Hevey
www.smoothhound.co.uk/hotels/maggs.html **D:** Fr £18.00–£25.00 **S:** Fr £18.00–£25.00 **Beds:** 1F 1D 1T **Baths:** 1 En 1 Sh (6)

Keswick

NY2623 *Station Inn, Punch Bowl, Derwentwater Hotel, Masons, King's Head, Two Dogs Inn, The George, Farmers' Arms, Four In Hand, Swan Hotel, Swinside Inn, Keswick Lodge, Bank Tavern*

Lynwood House, *35 Helvellyn Street, Keswick, Cumbria, CA12 4EP.* Victorian-style with modern comforts. Traditional or home-made organic breakfasts. **Open:** All year
017687 72398 Mr Picken *lynwoodho@aol.com*
D: Fr £17.00–£20.50 **S:** Fr £18.50–£23.00 **Beds:** 1F 2D 1S **Baths:** 1 En (3)

Anderville, *19 Helvellyn Street, Keswick, Cumbria, CA12 4EN.* 'Anderville' offers quiet comfortable guest house accommodation, situated just two minutes from the town centre. Parks and Lake Derwentwater are just a short stroll away as is the 'Theatre by the Lake'. Open all year with the exception of Xmas day. Evening meals available. Your hosts Paul and Anita Wilson welcome you.
Open: All year (not Xmas)
017687 72578 (also fax) *wpaul595@aol.com*
www.anderville.co.uk **D:** Fr £15.00–£18.00 **S:** Fr £15.00–£16.00 **Beds:** 1T 2D 1S **Baths:** 3 En 1 Pr

Glendale Guest House, *7 Eskin Street, Keswick, Cumbria, CA12 4DH.* Comfortable Victorian house. Close to town, lake, park and fells. **Open:** All year
017687 73562 Mr Lankester *info@glendalekeswick.co.uk* www.glendalekeswick.co.uk **D:** Fr £18.00–£22.00 **S:** Fr £19.00–£22.00 **Beds:** 1F 2T 2D 1S **Baths:** 3 En 2 Sh

Littlefield, *32 Eskin Street, Keswick, Cumbria, CA12 4DG.* Very conveniently situated for the centre of Keswick and Derwentwater. We have a very comfortable guests' lounge with many books, maps and walking guides available for visitors. A warm welcome is assured from Ali and Maureen the proprietors. **Open:** All year
017687 72949 Miss Maddock *littlefield@keswick98.fsnet.co.uk* keswick98.fsnet.co.uk
D: Fr £17.00–£18.00 **S:** Fr £17.00–£18.00 **Beds:** 1T 2D 2S **Baths:** 1 Sh (3)

Edwardene, *26 Southey Street, Keswick, Cumbria, CA12 4EF.* The Edwardene Hotel offers central, stylish, luxurious accommodation at affordable rates.
Open: All year
017687 73586 & 0800 163983 Mr Holman
Fax: 017687 73824 *info@edwardenehotel.com*
www.edwardenehotel.com **D:** Fr £26.00–£29.00 **S:** Fr £37.00–£43.00 **Beds:** 1F 2T 6D 2S **Baths:** 11 Pr (1) (2) cc

Daresfield, *Chestnut Hill, Keswick, Cumbria, CA12 4LS.* Warm welcome, splendid views, walks advice, doll-making studio.
Open: All year (not New Year)
017687 72531 V Spencer *daresfield@hotmail.com* **D:** Fr £16.00 **S:** Fr £16.00 **Beds:** 1T 1D 1S **Baths:** 2 Sh (3)

Berkeley Guest House, *The Heads, Keswick, Cumbria, CA12 5ER.* Friendly, relaxed guest house with superb mountain views from each comfortable room.
Open: Jan to Dec
017687 74222 Mrs Crompton *berkeley@tesco.net* berkeley_keswick.homepage.com
D: Fr £17.00–£24.00 **S:** Fr £20.00 **Beds:** 1F 2D 1T 1S **Baths:** 3 En 2 Sh (3)

The Paddock Guest House, *Wordsworth Street, Keswick, Cumbria, CA12 4HU.* Delightful 1800's residence. Close to town, lake, parks and fells. **Open:** All year
017687 72510 www.keswickguesthouse.com
D: Fr £19.00–£21.00 **S:** Fr £25.00–£40.00 **Beds:** 1F 1T 4D **Baths:** 6 En (5) cc

Watendlath, *15 Acorn Street, Keswick, Cumbria, CA12 4EA.* Few mins Keswick centre, quiet retreat, renowned superb traditional English breakfasts. **Open:** All year
017687 74165 D: Fr £17.00–£20.00 **Beds:** 2F 2D **Baths:** 3 En 1 Sh

Shemara Guest House, *27 Bank Street, Keswick, Cumbria, CA12 5JZ.* A warm, friendly welcome awaits you at our award-winning guest house. All rooms are furnished to a very high standard and have stunning views of the mountains. A full Cumbrian or continental breakfast is served in our cosy dining room. **Open:** All year
017687 73936 Fax: 017687 80785
shemaraguesthouse@yahoo.co.uk www.shemara.u.k.com **D:** Fr £19.50–£25.00 **S:** Fr £25.00 **Beds:** 1F 1T 5D **Baths:** 7 En (2) (4) cc

Claremont House, *Chestnut Hill, Keswick, Cumbria, CA12 4LT.* Built about 150 years ago as lodge house to Fieldside Estate, 1m Keswick. **Open:** Easter to Nov
017687 72089 Peter & Jackie Werfel
claremonthouse@btinternet.com
www.claremonthousekeswick.co.uk **D:** Fr £21.00–£25.00 **Beds:** 3D 1T **Baths:** 4 En (12) (5)

Ivy Lodge, *32 Penrith Road, Keswick, Cumbria, CA12 4HA.* Superb rooms. Convenient for parks, theatre and lake. **Open:** All year
017687 75747 *pdwells@compuserve.com* **D:** Fr £18.00–£23.00 **S:** Fr £25.00–£28.00 **Beds:** 1F 1T 1D **Baths:** 3 En (10)

Hedgehog Hill, *18 Blencathra Street, Keswick, Cumbria, CA12 4HP.* You are assured a warm welcome from your hosts Nel and Keith. Ideally situated for exploring the Lake District. Located in a quiet street close to all amenities, stunning fell views from most rooms. Freshly prepared breakfast with choice. **Open:** All year
017687 74386 Fax: 017687 80622 *info@hedgehoghill.co.uk* www.hedgehoghill.co.uk **D:** Fr £21.00–£24.00 **S:** Fr £17.50–£18.50 **Beds:** 4D 2S **Baths:** 4 En 1 Sh **cc**

Clarence House, *14 Eskin Street, Keswick, Cumbria, CA12 4DQ.* Lovely detached Victorian house, excellent ensuite accommodation. Cleanliness guaranteed. No smoking. **Open:** All year (not Xmas)
017687 73186 Mr & Mrs Robertson **Fax: 017687 72317** *clarenceho@aol.com* www.members.aol.com/clarenceho/index.html **D:** Fr £20.00–£28.00 **S:** Fr £20.00–£28.00 **Beds:** 1F 4D 3T 1S **Baths:** 8 Pr (5)

Brookfield, *Penrith Road, Keswick, Cumbria, CA12 4LJ.* A warm welcome awaits you at this family-run Victorian guest house. **Open:** All year
017687 72867 Mr Gregory *ronnie.sally@talk21.com* www.expage.com/ronniesally **D:** Fr £16.00–£20.00 **S:** Fr £16.00–£20.00 **Beds:** 2F 2D **Baths:** 4 En (4)

Harvington House, *19 Churh Street, Keswick, Cumbria, CA12 4DX.* **Open:** All year (not Xmas)
017687 75582 *info@harvingtonhouse.co.uk* www.harvingtonhouse.co.uk **D:** Fr £19.50–£23.50 **S:** Fr £19.50–£23.50 **Beds:** 1T 3D 2S **Baths:** 3 En 1 Sh
Hiking, biking, touring or relaxing. A warm welcome assured at Harvington House. Friendly ,relaxed, homely accommodation. Close to centre of Keswick and picturesque shores of Derwent Water. If you need an ideal base, give us a call.

Spooney Green, *Spooney Green Lane, Keswick, Cumbria, CA12 4PJ.* Only 15 minutes' walk into Keswick, foothills of Skiddaw, a relaxing country retreat. **Open:** All year
017687 72601 Ms Wallace *spooneygreen@beeb.net* **D:** Fr £20.00–£25.00 **S:** Fr £25.00–£40.00 **Beds:** 1T 1D **Baths:** 1 En 1 Pr (5)

Chaucer House Hotel, *Derwentwater Place, Keswick, Cumbria, CA12 4DR.* Lakeland hospitality at its best. Quiet setting, surrounded by spectacular mountains. Close to theatre, market place & lake. Relaxed, informal atmosphere. Freshly prepared evening meal available. Friendly, professional staff always available to help you enjoy your stay, plan tours and walks. **Open:** Feb to Dec
017687 72318 & 017687 73223 Mr Pechartscheck **Fax: 017687 75551** *enquiries@chaucer-house.demon.co.uk* www.chaucer-house.co.uk **D:** Fr £32.00–£46.00 **S:** Fr £32.00–£41.00 **Beds:** 4F 9D 12T 8S **Baths:** 29 En 4 Pr **cc**

Lairbeck Hotel, *Vicarage Hill, Keswick, Cumbria, CA12 5QB.* **Open:** Mar to Jan
017687 73373 Mr Coy **Fax: 017687 73144** *swell@lairbeckhotel-keswick.co.uk* www.lairbeckhotel-keswick.co.uk **D:** Fr £36.00–£42.00 **S:** Fr £36.00–£42.00 **Beds:** 1F 7D 2T 4S **Baths:** 14 En (5) (16)
Featured on television's 'Wish You Were Here', Lairbeck is a superb country house hotel in a secluded setting with magnificent mountain views. Lairbeck offers award-winning traditional dining and hospitality in a friendly, informal atmosphere. Special breaks available. Spacious parking.

Badgers Wood Guest House, *30 Stanger Street, Keswick, Cumbria, CA12 5JU.* **Open:** All year (not Xmas)
017687 72621 Ms Godfrey *enquiries@badgers-wood.co.uk* www.badgers-wood.co.uk **D:** Fr £18.00–£24.00 **S:** Fr £18.00 **Beds:** 3D 1T 2S **Baths:** 4 En 1 Sh
Comfortable, quiet, friendly, ideally-situated for walking, climbing and sightseeing. Badgers Wood is close to bus station, town centre and eating places. All our bedrooms have mountain views. We can offer you ensuite or standard rooms.

Cragside Guest House, *39 Blencathra Street, Keswick, Cumbria, CA12 4HX.* **Open:** All year **Grades:** AA 3 Diamond
017687 73344 & 017687 80410 *sue@cragsideguest-house.fsnet.co.uk* cragsideguest-house.fsnet.co.uk **D:** Fr £20.00 **Beds:** 1F 1T 2D **Baths:** 4 En (5)
Sue and Mike invite you to bring your family and pets to stay at our friendly Victorian home with views of the local fells and close to Keswick town centre. Enjoy easy access to great walks and stunning scenery.

Hazeldene Hotel, *The Heads, Keswick, Cumbria, CA12 5ER.* **Open:** Jan to Dec
017687 72106 Fax: 017867 75435 *info@hazeldene-hotel.co.uk* www.hazeldene-hotel.co.uk **D:** Fr £25.00–£40.00 **S:** Fr £25.00–£40.00 **Beds:** 2F 3T 11D 1S **Baths:** 17 En **cc**
At Hazeldene Hotel, our aim is simple:- to provide our guests with exceptional quality and value accommodation in an outstanding location. Large ensuite bedrooms, excellent food and a relaxed and peaceful atmosphere combine to make Hazeldene a perfect holiday haven.

Anworth House, *27 Eskin Street, Keswick, Cumbria, CA12 4DQ.* High quality accommodation, come and be spoilt at Anworth House. **Open:** All year **Grades:** ETC 4 Diamond, Silver
017687 72923 Mr & Mrs Johnson www.anworthhouse.co.uk **D:** Fr £23.00–£30.00 **S:** Fr £30.00 **Beds:** 2T 3D **Baths:** 5 En **cc**

The Heights Hotel, *Rakefoot Lane, Castlerigg, Keswick, Cumbria, CA12 4TE.* **Open:** All year (not Xmas/New Year)
017687 72251 Fax: 017687 75553 *enquiries@theheightshotel.co.uk* www.theheightshotel.co.uk **D:** Fr £24.00–£28.50 **S:** Fr £24.00–£26.50 **Beds:** 4F 1T 6D 1S **Baths:** 12 En (12) cc
Family-run hotel. Outstanding location, with panoramic views of lakes & fells. Superb walks from hotel. Residents' bar with evening meals. Ideal base for exploring the Northern Lakes. Special rates available. Ring for brochure or see our website at: www.theheightshotel.co.uk.

Hawcliffe House, *30 Eskin Street, Keswick, Cumbria, CA12 4DG.* Warm welcome assured. Short walk to lake and town centre. **Open:** All year
017687 73250 D McConnell *diane@hawcliffehouse.co.uk* www.hawcliffehouse.co.uk **D:** Fr £17.00–£18.00 **S:** Fr £17.00–£18.00 **Beds:** 2T 2D 2S **Baths:** 2 Sh

Bluestones, *7 Southey Street, Keswick, Cumbria, CA12 4EG.* Homely Victorian residence, comfortable accommodation. Try our walkers' 'big breakfast'. **Open:** All year
017687 74237 & 07866 883423 (M) Fax: 017687 74237 *mj.rackham@ntlworld.com* www.members.tripod.com/bluestoneskeswick **D:** Fr £18.00–£21.00 **S:** Fr £18.00–£21.00 **Beds:** 2F 1T 1D 1S **Baths:** 1 En 1 Sh cc

Derwentdale Guest House, *8 Blencathra Street, Keswick, Cumbria, CA12 4HP.* Close to shops, lake and parks. Walkers and cyclists welcome. **Open:** All year
017687 74187 (also fax) Mrs Riding **D:** Fr £18.00–£22.00 **S:** Fr £18.00–£18.50 **Beds:** 3D 1T 2S **Baths:** 2 En 3 Pr

Please respect a B&B's wishes regarding children, animals and smoking

Loch Villa, *34 Blencathra Street, Keswick, Cumbria, CA12 4HP.* Family-run, central, ideal for walking. Safe garage for cycles.
Open: All year **Grades:** ETC 3 Diamond
017687 73226 D: Fr £21.00–£23.00 **S:** Fr £21.00–£23.00 **Beds:** 1T 1D 1S **Baths:** 2 En 1 Pr (10)

Seven Oaks Guest House, *7 Acorn Street, Keswick, Cumbria, CA12 4EA.* Warm and friendly welcome. Maps, guide books and walking advice. **Open:** All year
017687 72088 C Firth & L Furniss *enquiries@keswicksevenoaksbb.co.uk* www.keswicksevenoaksbb.co.uk **D:** Fr £20.00–£25.00 **S:** Fr £18.00–£20.00 **Beds:** 1F 1T 3D 2S **Baths:** 2 En 1 Pr 4 Sh (4) cc

Guest House, *37 Brundholme Terrace, Keswick, Cumbria, CA12 4NB.* Comfy stay, excellent food, charming house, central.
Open: All year
017687 75186 *lse6889715@aol.com* **D:** Fr £18.00–£24.00 **S:** Fr £18.00–£25.00 **Beds:** 1F 1D **Baths:** 1 En 2 Pr

Birch How, *41 Brundholme Terrace, Station Road, Keswick, Cumbria, CA12 4NB.* **Open:** All year
017687 73404 *birchhow@aol.com* www.birchhow.com **D:** Fr £17.50–£23.00 **S:** Fr £20.00–£30.00 **Beds:** 1T 2D **Baths:** 2 En 1 Sh (3)
Birch How is a small, friendly guest house close to Fitz Park, and very convenient for town centre. Within easy reach of Derwent Water, the Borrowdale Valley, and many other local beauty areas. Advice can be given on local walks.

Kirkby Lonsdale

SD6178

Wyck House, *4 Main Street, Kirkby Lonsdale, Carnforth, Lancs, LA6 2AE.* Quality accommodation in a Victorian town house, close to amenities. **Open:** All year
015242 71953 (also fax) Pat & Brian Bradley *wyckhouse@studioarts.co.uk* www.studioarts.co.uk/wyckhouse.htm **D:** Fr £22.50 **S:** Fr £18.50–£30.00 **Beds:** 1F 1T 2D 2S **Baths:** 3 En 1 Sh (2)

Barnfield Farm, *Tunstall, Kirkby Lonsdale, Carnforth, Lancs, LA6 2QP.* 1702 family farmhouse on a 200-acre working farm. **Open:** All year (not Xmas/New Year)
015242 74284 (also fax) J Stephenson *jstephenson@barnfieldfarm.freeserve.co.uk* www.smoothhound.co.uk/hotels/barnfield.html **D:** Fr £17.00–£17.50 **S:** Fr £17.50–£20.00 **Beds:** 1F 1D **Baths:** 1 Sh (2)

Kirkby Stephen

NY7708

Lockholme, *48 South Road, Kirkby Stephen, Cumbria, CA17 4SN.* Victorian home, offering quality accommodation in lovely countryside. **Open:** All year (not Xmas/New Year)
017683 71321 (also fax) Mrs Graham *info@lockholme.co.uk* www.lockholme.co.uk **D:** Fr £18.00–£20.00 **S:** Fr £17.50–£25.00 **Beds:** 1F 1T 1D 1S **Baths:** 2 En 1 Sh

Old Croft House, *Market Street, Kirkby Stephen, Cumbria, CA17 4QW.* Unique, unusual Georgian townhouse, welcomes you for a memorable stay. **Open:** All year (not Xmas/New Year)
017683 71638 *oldcrofthouse@hotmail.com* www.oldcrofthouse.co.uk **D:** Fr £20.00–£28.00 **S:** Fr £25.00–£28.00 **Beds:** 2F 2D **Baths:** 3 En 1 Sh (4) (1)

Lakeside

SD3787

The Knoll Country Guest House, *Lakeside, Newby Bridge, Ulverston, Cumbria, LA12 8AU.* The Knoll - a delightful Victorian house, set amidst peaceful wooded countryside at the south end of Lake Windermere, offering a relaxed night's sleep and hearty breakfast. Only 5 minutes walk from main attractions, an ideal base for relaxing or exploring. **Open:** All year
015395 31347 Ms Meads and Ms T Watson *info@theknoll-lakeside.co.uk* www.theknoll-lakeside.co.uk **D:** Fr £26.00–£45.00 **S:** Fr £40.00 **Beds:** 6D 2T **Baths:** 8 En (9) cc

Leadgate

NY7043

Brownside House, *Leadgate, Alston, Cumbria, CA9 3EL.* Warm welcome awaits at peaceful house in the country with superb views. **Open:** All year
01434 382169 & 01434 382100 Mrs Le Marie **Fax: 01434 382169** *brownside_hse@hotmail.com* www.cumbria1st.com/brown_side/indexhtm **D:** Fr £18.00 **S:** Fr £18.00 **Beds:** 1D 2T 1S **Baths:** 1 Sh (4) cc

Leece

SD2469

Winander, *Leece, Ulverston, Cumbria, LA12 0QP.* Converted barn in quiet village location in Lake District peninsula.
Open: All year (not Xmas)
01229 822353 Mr Cockshott **D:** Fr £18.00–£23.00 **S:** Fr £21.00–£26.00 **Beds:** 1T 1D **Baths:** 1 Pr 1 Sh (5) (3)

Levens

SD4886

Glen Robin, *Church Road, Levens, Kendal, Cumbria, LA8 8PS.* Beautiful house with lovely views, delicious breakfasts, peace and quiet. **Open:** All year (not Xmas) **015395 60369 (also fax) D:** Fr £16.00–£20.00 **S:** Fr £16.00–£20.00 **Beds:** 1D 1T 1S **Baths:** 1 Sh (3) (3)

Lindale

SD4180

Greenacres Country Guest House, *Lindale, Grange-over-Sands, Cumbria, LA11 6LP.* Warm hospitality, lovely rooms, ideal for Lakes, Dales and coast. **Open:** All year (not Xmas/New Year) **Grades:** ETC 4 Diamond **015395 34578 (also fax)** *www.smoothhound.co.uk/hotels/greenacres* **D:** Fr £25.00–£29.00 **S:** Fr £25.00–£34.00 **Beds:** 1F 1T 2D **Baths:** 4 En (5) **cc**

Little Arrow

SD2895

Browside, *Little Arrow, Coniston, Cumbria, LA21 8AU.* Panoramic views across Coniston Water to Brantwood, Grizedale Forest & Ambleside Fells. **Open:** Feb to Nov **015394 41162** Mrs Dugdale **D:** Fr £18.00–£22.00 **S:** Fr £20.00–£25.00 **Beds:** 1T 1D **Baths:** 2 En

Little Musgrave

NY7513

Smithfield Barn, *Little Musgrave, Kirkby Stephen, Cumbria, CA17 4PG.* Modern barn conversion. Tranquil setting. beautiful views over unspoilt countryside. **Open:** All year **017683 41002** E Hodgson **D:** Fr £19.00 **S:** Fr £19.00 **Beds:** 2D **Baths:** 1 En 1 Pr

Little Salkeld

NY5636

Bankhouse Farm and Stables, *Bankhouse, Little Salkeld, Penrith, Cumbria, CA10 1NN.* Converted barns on stable yard. Village location in Eden Valley. **Open:** All year **01768 881257 D:** Fr £20.00–£30.00 **S:** Fr £25.00–£30.00 **Beds:** 3F 3T 3D **Baths:** 6 En 3 Sh (20)

Longthwaite

NY2514 *Scafell Hotel, Lanstrath Hotel*

Castle Lodge, *Peat Howe, Longthwaite, Borrowdale, Keswick, Cumbria, CA12 5XE.* Cosy, charming Lakeland cottage. Olde Worlde with modern conveniences. **Open:** All year (not Xmas/New Year) **017687 77346** Mrs Weir *www.castle-lodge.co.uk* **D:** Fr £18.00–£23.00 **S:** Fr £21.00 **Beds:** 1F 1T 1D 1S **Baths:** 1 En 1 Sh

Longtown

NY3868

New Pallyards, *Hethersgill, Carlisle, Cumbria, CA6 6HZ.* Ideal stopover or longer visit to explore our wonderful countryside. **Open:** All year **Grades:** ETC 4 Diamond **01228 577308 (also fax)** Mrs Elwen *info@newpallyards.freeserve.co.uk* www.newpallyards.freeserve.co.uk **D:** Fr £23.00–£25.00 **S:** Fr £27.00–£30.00 **Beds:** 1F 2T 2D 1S **Baths:** 6 En **cc**

Lorton

NY1525

Cragg End Farm, *Rogerscale, Lorton Vale, Cockermouth, Cumbria, CA13 0RG.* Beautiful views, ideal situation for walking. Quiet, working, family farm. **Open:** All year **01900 85658** Mrs Steel **D:** Fr £20.00 **S:** Fr £20.00 **Beds:** 1F 1D 2T **Baths:** 3 Sh

Low Row

NY5863 *Railway Inn*

High Nook Farm, *Low Row, Brampton, Cumbria, CA8 2LU.* Comfortable farmhouse built in 1857. **Open:** June to Oct **016977 46273** Mrs Foster **D:** Fr £28.00–£30.00 **S:** Fr £15.00 **Beds:** 1D **Baths:** 1 Sh (2)

Loweswater

NY1420

Askhill Farm, *Loweswater, Cockermouth, Cumbria, CA13 0SU.* Beef & sheep rearing farm, quiet valley, Loweswater. Ideal country walking area. **Open:** Easter to Oct **01946 861640** Mrs Vickers **D:** Fr £18.00–£20.00 **S:** Fr £19.00–£21.00 **Beds:** 1F 1D **Baths:** 1 Sh (3)

Brook Farm, *Thacktwaite, Loweswater, Cockermouth, Cumbria, CA13 0RP.* Comfortable, quiet, working farmhouse. Good food, open fire, pretty garden. **Open:** Easter to Nov **01900 85606 (also fax)** Mrs Hayton **D:** Fr £20.00–£21.00 **S:** Fr £20.00–£21.00 **Beds:** 1F 1D **Baths:** 1 Sh (3)

Lowick

SD2986

Garth Row, *Lowick Green, Ulverston, Cumbria, LA12 8EB.* Traditional Lakeland house. Warm welcome. Super, peaceful setting. Quality accommodation. **Open:** All year (not Xmas/New Year) **Grades:** ETC 3 Diamond **01229 885633** Mrs Wickens *b&b@garthrow.freeserve.co.uk* www.garthrow.co.uk **D:** Fr £18.00–£20.00 **S:** Fr £23.00–£25.00 **Beds:** 1F 1D **Baths:** 1 Sh (4)

Lowick Bridge

SD2986

Red Lion Inn, *Lowick Bridge, Ulverston, Cumbria, LA12 8EF.* In the unspoilt part of English Lake District. Cosy atmosphere. **Open:** All year **01229 885366 (also fax)** *redlion@lowick.fslife.co.uk* **D:** Fr £17.50–£25.00 **S:** Fr £25.00–£30.00 **Beds:** 2D **Baths:** 2 En **cc**

Maryport

NY0336

East Farm, *Crosscanonby, Maryport, Cumbria, CA15 6SJ.* Modernised, comfortable farmhouse, traditional breakfast. Aquaria, leisure centre, beach nearby. **Open:** All year (not Xmas) **01900 812153** Mrs Carruthers *carruthers_eastfarm@hotmail.com* **D:** Fr £18.00–£20.00 **S:** Fr £20.00–£24.00 **Beds:** 1F 1D **Baths:** 1 En 1 Pr (2) (2)

Mealsgate

NY2041

Appletree House, *Mealsgate, Wigton, Cumbria, CA7 1JP.* Conveniently situated for exploring Northern Lakes and Solway Coast. **Open:** All year (not Xmas) **016973 71200** Mrs Exley **D:** Fr £18.00 **S:** Fr £18.00 **Beds:** 1D 1T **Baths:** 1 Sh (3)

Melmerby

NY6137

Gale Hall Farm, *Melmerby, Penrith, Cumbria,* CA10 1HN. Large comfortable farmhouse near Pennines and Lake District. **Open:** June to Nov
01768 881254 Mrs Toppin **D:** Fr £16.00 **S:** Fr £16.00 **Beds:** 1F 1T 1S **Baths:** 1 Sh (3)

Bolton Farmhouse, *Melmerby, Penrith, Cumbria,* CA10 1HF. C17th oak-beamed farmhouse. Wonderful views. Friendly. Comfortable. Good sightseeing. **Open:** All year
01768 881851 & 07702 933952 (M)
www.eden-valley.net/boltonfarmhouse **D:** Fr £16.00 **S:** Fr £16.00 **Beds:** 1T 1D 1S **Baths:** 1 Sh (4)

Middleton

SD6286

Tossbeck Farm, *Middleton, Carnforth, Lancashire,* LA6 2LZ. A friendly welcome awaits you at Tossbeck, mixed farm in unspoilt Lune Valley. **Open:** Easter to Oct
015242 76214 D: Fr £17.00–£19.00 **S:** Fr £22.00–£25.00 **Beds:** 1F 1D **Baths:** 1 En 1 Pr (2)

Moresby

NX9921

Moresby Hall, *Moresby, Whitehaven, Cumbria,* CA28 6PJ. A Grade I Listed character building. Spacious and well-equipped rooms. **Open:** All year
01946 696317 Mrs Saxon **Fax: 01946 692666** *saxon@moresbyhall.co.uk* www.moresbyhall.co.uk **D:** Fr £22.50–£32.50 **S:** Fr £25.00–£35.00 **Beds:** 1F 1T 2D **Baths:** 2 En 2 Pr (10) (6) **cc**

Morland

NY5923

Mill Beck Cottage, *Water Street, Morland, Penrith, Cumbria,* CA10 3AY. Traditional riverside cottage, unspoilt village and countryside, comfortable rooms, good beds. Morning sun, excellent food. Perfectly situated for the Lakes, Pennines and Yorkshire Dales, 45 mins. M6 10 minutes. Tranquility supported by good pubs and peaceful villages, of which Morland is one of the oldest. **Open:** All year (not Xmas/New Year)
01931 714567 Mrs Jackson **Fax: 01931714567 D:** Fr £22.00–£25.00 **S:** Fr £22.00–£25.00 **Beds:** 1T 1D **Baths:** 1 Pr (12)

Mungrisdale

NY3630

Near Howe Hotel, *Mungrisdale, Penrith, Cumbria,* CA11 0SH. **Open:** All year (not Xmas) **Grades:** ETC 3 Diamond
017687 79678 Mrs Weightman **Fax: 017687 79462** *nearhowe@btopenworld.com* www.nearhowe.co.uk **D:** Fr £20.00–£25.00 **S:** Fr £20.00–£25.00 **Beds:** 3F 3D 1T **Baths:** 5 En 2 Sh (20)
Small hotel in beautiful area. Warm welcome awaits you.

Near Sawrey

SD3795

High Green Gate Guest House, *Near Sawrey, Ambleside, Cumbria,* LA22 0LF. Converted farmhouse in Beatrix Potter's village countryside, farm position. **Open:** Apr to Oct
015394 36296 Miss Fletcher **D:** Fr £23.00–£26.00 **S:** Fr £23.00 **Beds:** 4F 1D **Baths:** 3 Pr 1 Sh (7)

Nenthead

NY7843

Mill Cottage Bunkhouse, *Nenthead, Alston, Cumbria,* CA9 3PD. Bunkhouse in spectacular landscape, part of Nenthead Mines heritage site. **Open:** All year
01434 382037 *administration.office@virgin.net* www.np.ht.com **D:** Fr £12.00 **S:** Fr £8.00–£12.00 **Beds:** 2F (4)

The Miners Arms, *Nenthead, Alston, Cumbria,* CA9 3PF. Friendly family pub. Real ales, real food, real fires. **Open:** All year
01434 381427 Miss Clark www.theminersarms.org.uk **D:** Fr £15.00 **S:** Fr £15.00 **Beds:** 2F 2D 2T 2S **cc**

New Hutton

SD5691 *Station Inn*

Cragg Farm, *New Hutton, Kendal, Cumbria,* LA8 0BA. Situated 4 miles Kendal, warm welcome, excellent accommodation. Breakfast provided. **Open:** Mar to Nov
01539 721760 (also fax) Mrs Knowles *knowles.cragg@ukgateway.net* **D:** Fr £17.00–£19.00 **S:** Fr £17.00–£19.00 **Beds:** 1F 1D 1S **Baths:** 1 Sh

All details shown are as supplied by B&B owners in Autumn 2002

Newbiggin (Stainton)

NY4629

Tymparon Hall, *Newbiggin, Penrith, Cumbria,* CA11 0HS. Secluded farm house. 3/4 mile A66 close M6/J40 & Ullswater. **Open:** Feb to Nov
017684 83236 Ms Taylor *margaret@pearson.freeserve.co.uk* www.pearson.freeserve.co.uk **D:** Fr £21.00–£25.00 **S:** Fr £21.00–£25.00 **Beds:** 1F 1D 1T **Baths:** 2 En 1 Pr

Newbiggin-on-Lune

NY7005 *Black Swan*

Church View Farmhouse, *Newbiggin-on-Lune, Kirkby Stephen, Cumbria,* CA17 4NS. Comfortable, beamed C17th farmhouse in peaceful village. Good walking country. **Open:** All year (not Xmas/New Year)
015396 23283 (also fax) *kedwards@coultsinfo.com* **D:** Fr £17.00–£18.00 **S:** Fr £17.00–£18.00 **Beds:** 2D **Baths:** 1 Sh (2)

Tranna Hill, *Newbiggin-on-Lune, Kirkby Stephen, Cumbria,* CA17 4NY. Beautiful views from lovely rooms - good walking area, 5 miles M6. **Open:** Easter to Oct
015396 23227 & 07989 892368 (M)
B Boustead *trannahill@hotmail.com* **D:** Fr £18.00 **S:** Fr £20.00 **Beds:** 1T 1D **Baths:** 1 En 1 Pr (4)

Newby Bridge

SD3786 *Crown Inn, Swan Inn, Newby Bridge Hotel*

Alloa Guest House, *Newby Bridge, Cumbria,* LA12 8LZ. Secluded luxury bungalow with all amenities. Excellent home cooking. Superb lake views. **Open:** All year (not Xmas/New Year)
015395 30391 (also fax) D: Fr £20.00–£25.00 **S:** Fr £25.00–£30.00 **Beds:** 1F 1T 1D **Baths:** 2 En 1 Pr (2) (10)

Miller Beck, *Newby Bridge, Ulverston, Cumbria,* LA12 8NE. Typical Lakeland house from 1920, backing onto Lake Windermere. Warm welcome, good breakfasts. **Open:** All year (not Xmas)
015395 31329 E I Foster **D:** Fr £22.50–£25.00 **S:** Fr £30.00–£35.00 **Beds:** 1D 1T 1S **Baths:** 2 En (8) (10)

Old Barn Farm, *Fiddler Hall, Lake Windermere, Newby Bridge, Ulverston, Cumbria,* LA12 8NQ. Beautiful C17th house, large gardens, views, quiet. Lake Windermere nearby. **Open:** All year (not Xmas) **Grades:** ETC 4 Diamond
015395 31842 & 07754 048502 (M) Mr & Mrs Harforth *peter@oldbarnfarm.com* www.oldbarnfarm.com **D:** Fr £23.00–£25.00 **S:** Fr £28.00–£30.00 **Beds:** 1F 1D 1T **Baths:** 3 En (4)

Hill Crest, *Backbarrow, Newby Bridge, Ulverston, Cumbria, LA12 8QP.* Traditional Lakeland house, magnificent views, country location - quality accommodation, homely. **Open:** All year (not Xmas)
015395 31766 Mrs Jenkinson **Fax: 015395 31986** *enquiries@hillcrest.gbr.cc* www.hillcrest.gbr.cc **D:** Fr £20.00–£25.00 **S:** Fr £25.00–£35.00 **Beds:** 1F 3D 1T **Baths:** 2 En 1 Pr P (3) TV V

Lyndhurst Country House, *Newby Bridge, Ulverston, Cumbria, LA12 8ND.* A relaxing, friendly guesthouse set in lovely gardens. **Open:** All year **Grades:** RAC 4 Diamond
015395 31245 Mr & Mrs Douglas *christine@lyndhurstcountryhouse.co.uk* www.lyndhurstcountryhouse.co.uk **D:** Fr £25.00–£30.00 **S:** Fr £30.00 **Beds:** 1T 2D **Baths:** 3 En P (3) TV

Newlands

NY2420

Uzzicar Farm, *Newlands, Keswick, Cumbria, CA12 5TS.* Clean, cosy, comfortable farmhouse with character, situated in idyllic surroundings. **Open:** All year (not Xmas)
017687 78367 Mrs Simpson **D:** Fr £17.00–£19.00 **S:** Fr £20.00 **Beds:** 1D 1F **Baths:** 1 Sh P V

Old Hutton

SD5688

Blaven, *Middleshaw Head Barn, Old Hutton, Kendal, Cumbria, LA8 0LZ.* Peaceful, hilly location. Lovely streamside Lakeland house, very convenient for M6 J36/37. **Open:** All year
01539 734894 Mrs Beale & Mr Green **Fax: 01539 727447** *blaven@greenarrow.demon.co.uk* www.superdigs.co.uk **D:** Fr £25.00–£32.00 **S:** Fr £28.00–£42.00 **Beds:** 1S 1T 1F **Baths:** 1 En 1 Pr P (4) TV cc

RATES

D = Price range per person sharing in a double or twin room

S = Price range for a single room

B&B owners may vary rates – be sure to check when booking

Oughterside

NY1140

The Manor House Guest House, *Oughterside, Aspatria, Cumbria, CA7 2PT.* Georgian manor farmhouse. Spacious rooms and grounds. Peaceful. Comfortable. Welcoming. **Open:** All year
016973 22420 (also fax) Mr & Mrs Mortimer *richardandjudy@themanorhouse.net* www.themanorhouse.net **D:** Fr £21.00–£25.00 **S:** Fr £25.00–£30.00 **Beds:** 2F 1T 2D **Baths:** 3 En 1 Sh P (5) TV V

Outhgill

NY7801

Faraday Cottage, *Outhgill, Kirkby Stephen, Cumbria, CA17 4JU.* Historic cottage. Heart of Mallerstang Valley, walkers' paradise. **Open:** All year (not Xmas/New Year)
017683 72351 Mrs Porter **D:** Fr £15.00 **S:** Fr £15.00 **Beds:** 1T 1D **Baths:** 1 Sh P (2) TV V

Pardshaw

NY0924 *Old Posting House*

Pardshaw Hall, *Pardshaw, Cockermouth, Cumbria, CA13 0SP.* New barn conversion. Reduced rates. Children welcome. All ensuite. **Open:** All year
01900 822607 Mrs Richardson **D:** Fr £20.00 **S:** Fr £20.00 **Beds:** 1F 1D 1S **Baths:** 3 En (3) P (3) TV V

Patterdale

NY3915

Glebe House, *Patterdale, Penrith, Cumbria, CA11 0NL.* Comfortable accommodation in bungalow with beautiful views. Ideal touring/walking. **Open:** All year (not Xmas/New Year)
017684 82339 Mrs Pool **D:** Fr £22.00–£25.00 **Beds:** 1T 1D **Baths:** 2 En P (3) V

Greenbank Farm, *Patterdale, Penrith, Cumbria, CA11 0NR.* C16th farmhouse, centrally-heated, log fires, oak beams. Ideal touring/walking area. **Open:** All year (not Xmas)
017684 82292 Mrs Iredale *beverleyiredale@aol.com* **D:** Fr £18.00 **S:** Fr £20.00 **Beds:** 1D 1F 1T **Baths:** 1 Sh (1) P (4) TV V

Ullswater View, *Patterdale, Penrith, Cumbria, CA11 0NW.* **Open:** All year (not Xmas/New Year)
017684 82175 Fax: 017684 82181 *bookings@ullswater-view.co.uk* www.ullswater-view.co.uk **D:** Fr £20.00–£27.50 **S:** Fr £29.50–£37.50 **Beds:** 2F 2T 4D **Baths:** 3 En 1 Pr P (4) TV V cc
Elegant & welcoming, this B&B is beautifully situated on the banks of Goldrill Beck. Guests are welcome to enjoy the guest lounge & garden at any time during their stay. Telephone for a brochure or view the website.

Patton

SD5496

High Barn, *Shaw End, Patton, Kendal, Cumbria, LA8 9DU.* Beautiful barn conversion on the Dales Way. Peaceful setting. Home cooking. **Open:** All year
01539 824625 Mrs Sanderson *hibarn@hotmail.com* **D:** Fr £16.00 **S:** Fr £16.00 **Beds:** 2D **Baths:** 1 En 1 Pr P (2) TV V

Penrith

NY5130

Glendale, *4 Portland Place, Penrith, Cumbria, CA11 7QN.* **Open:** All year (not Xmas/New Year) **Grades:** ETC 4 Diamond, AA 4 Diamond
01768 862579 Fax: 01768 867934 *glendale@lineone.net* www.glendaleguesthouse.net **D:** Fr £19.00–£25.00 **S:** Fr £25.00–£35.00 **Beds:** 4F 4T 6D 1S **Baths:** 5 En 1 Pr P TV V
Julie and Mike invite you to enjoy a relaxing break in our family-run guest house. All our rooms are designed to provide comfortable accommodation for your stay. Ideal base for touring Lakes and Eden Valley.

Victoria Guest House, *3 Victoria Road, Penrith, Cumbria, CA11 8HR.* **Open:** All year (not Xmas/New Year)
01768 863823 *liz@vicguesthouse* www.vicguesthouse.co.uk **D:** Fr £20.00–£25.00 **S:** Fr £25.00–£38.00 **Beds:** 1F 1T 1D 1S **Baths:** 4 En (7)
Ideally situated for the M6 Jun. 40, A66 and Penrith town centre. Hearty English breakfast and diets confidently catered for. All rooms tastefully decorated, ensuite, TV, and hospitality tray. Large rear car park, secure cycle storage. Phone for brochure.

Albany House, *5 Portland Place, Penrith, Cumbria, CA11 7QN.* Friendly, comfortable Victorian house, mega breakfast, close town centre, M6 5 minutes. **Open:** All year
01768 863072 Ms Jackson **Fax: 01768 895527** *info@albany-house.org.uk* www.albany-house.org.uk **D:** Fr £18.50–£25.00 **S:** Fr £22.50–£27.50 **Beds:** 4F 1D **Baths:** 2 En 2 Sh (1)

Makalolo, *Barco Avenue, Penrith, Cumbria, CA11 8LU.* Spacious modern house, beamed lounge, conservatory, views of Lakeland hills. Local Authority Approved. **Open:** All year
01768 891519 Mrs Dawson **D:** Fr £20.00–£24.00 **S:** Fr £25.00–£28.00 **Beds:** 1T 1D **Baths:** 1 En 1 Pr (6)

Blue Swallow, *11 Victoria Road, Penrith, Cumbria, CA11 8HR.* Victorian town house situated in lovely market town of Penrith. **Open:** All year (not Xmas) **Grades:** ETC 3 Diamond
01768 866335 (also fax) Mrs Hughes *blueswallows@lineone.net* www.blueswallow.co.uk **D:** Fr £17.00–£20.00 **S:** Fr £22.00–£30.00 **Beds:** 1F 2D 2T **Baths:** 3 En 1 Sh (5)

Norcroft Guest House, *Graham Street, Penrith, Cumbria, CA11 9LQ.* Spacious, charming Victorian house with relaxed friendly atmosphere. Ideal for holiday centre or stop over for English Lakes and Scottish Borders (M6 Junction 40, 5 min drive away). Ample private parking and secure cycle storage. C2C route on doorstep. **Open:** All year
01768 862365 (also fax) Ms Simmons **D:** Fr £21.00–£23.00 **S:** Fr £22.00–£26.00 **Beds:** 2F 3T 3D 1S **Baths:** 9 En (9) 1 **CC**

Brooklands Guest House, *2 Portland Place, Penrith, Cumbria, CA11 7QN.* Fine Victorian town house 100m town centre, retaining many of the original features. **Open:** All year
01768 863395 Fax: 01768 864895 *leon.j.kirk@btinternet.com* **D:** Fr £18.00–£22.50 **S:** Fr £20.00–£22.00 **Beds:** 1F 2S 3D/T **Baths:** 2 Sh 3 En (1)

Plumbland

NY1439

Chapel House, *Plumbland, Aspatria, Carlisle, Cumbria, CA5 2HA.* Well-located between Keswick, Cockermouth & the Solway with excellent access to the Lakes. **Open:** All year (not Xmas/New Year)
01697 321480 Mr & Mrs Wells *gilda.wells@talk21.com* members.tripod.co.uk/wells-2/b-b.html **D:** Fr £17.50 **S:** Fr £17.50 **Beds:** 1T 1D **Baths:** 2 En (3)

Portinscale

NY2523

Rickerby Grange, *Portinscale, Keswick, Cumbria, CA12 5RH.* Set within own garden, private parking. In the pretty village of Portinscale. **Open:** All year
017687 72344 Mrs Bradley *val@ricor.demon.co.uk* www.ricor.demon.co.uk **D:** Fr £28.00–£30.00 **S:** Fr £28.00–£30.00 **Beds:** 3F 9D 2S **Baths:** 14 En (5) (14)

Skiddaw Croft, *Portinscale, Keswick, Cumbria, CA12 5RD.* Comfortable & friendly B&B in charming village. Splendid lake & mountain views. **Open:** All year
017687 72321 (also fax) J Downer *skiddawcroft@talk21.com* **D:** Fr £20.00–£25.00 **S:** Fr £20.00–£25.00 **Beds:** 1F 1T 2D 2S **Baths:** 4 En 1 Sh (6)

Raisbeck

NY6407

New House Farm, *Raisbeck, Orton, Penrith, Cumbria, CA10 3SD.* Quiet, picturesque. Panoramic views. For walking and camping and caravanning. **Open:** All year
015396 24324 Mrs Winder **D:** Fr £17.50–£18.50 **S:** Fr £18.50 **Beds:** 2T 1D 2S

Ravenglass

SD0896

Muncaster Country Guest House, *Ravenglass, Cumbria, CA18 1RD.* A very comfortable & welcoming country guest house adjoining Muncaster Estate & open countryside. **Open:** Mar to Oct
01229 717693 (also fax) Mr Putnam **D:** Fr £20.00–£24.00 **S:** Fr £22.00–£28.00 **Beds:** 1F 3D 2T 3S **Baths:** 2 En 2 Sh (1) (16)

Rosegarth, *Main Street, Ravenglass, Cumbria, CA18 1SQ.* Warm and friendly welcome, most rooms with estuary view. **Open:** All year (not Xmas/New Year)
01229 717275 Mrs Muxlow *rosegarth@talk21.com* **D:** Fr £18.00–£23.00 **S:** Fr £18.00–£23.00 **Beds:** 1F 2T 3D 1S **Baths:** 2 Sh (6)

Ravenstonedale

NY7203

Westview, *Ravenstonedale, Kirkby Stephen, Cumbria, CA17 4NG.* Quiet village with pubs, beautiful views; ideal touring & walking area. **Open:** All year
015396 23415 Mrs Ellis *enquiries@westview-cumbria.co.uk* www.westview-cumbria.co.uk **D:** Fr £21.00–£23.00 **S:** Fr £25.00–£30.00 **Beds:** 2D 1F 1T **Baths:** 4 En (5)

Bowber Head, *Ravenstonedale, Kirkby Stephen, Cumbria, CA17 4NL.* C17th farmhouse, open views, centre for classic coach tours. **Open:** All year
015396 23254 (also fax) Mr Hamer *hols@cumbriaclassiccoaches.co.uk* www.cumbriaclassiccoaches.co.uk **D:** Fr £20.00–£22.00 **S:** Fr £20.00–£22.00 **Beds:** 1F 2D 2T **Baths:** 1 En 2 Pr (6)

Renwick

NY5943

Scalehouse Farm, *Scalehouses, Renwick, Penrith, Cumbria, CA10 1JY.* Old farmhouse with period features, tastefully renovated. Peaceful, quiet location. **Open:** All year (not Xmas)
01768 896493 (also fax) Mrs Bonnick *pamela.bonnick@amserve.net* **D:** Fr £16.00–£22.00 **S:** Fr £20.00–£24.00 **Beds:** 2D 1T **Baths:** 1 Pr 1 Sh (6)

Roa Island

SD2364

Villa Marina, *Roa Island, Barrow-in-Furness, Cumbria, LA13 0QL.* Victorian gentleman's residence situated on Morecambe Bay. **Open:** All year (not Xmas/New Year)
01229 822520 Mrs Allen **D:** Fr £15.00–£20.00 **S:** Fr £20.00–£25.00 **Beds:** 1F 2T **Baths:** 1 En 1 Sh (4)

All details shown are as supplied by B&B owners in Autumn 2002

Rosthwaite (Borrowdale)

NY2514

Royal Oak Hotel, *Rosthwaite, Keswick, Cumbria, CA12 5XB.* A traditional family-run hotel. With good home-cooking, open fire and friendly service. **Open:** All year
017687 77214 (also fax) Mr Dowie *info@royaloakhotel.co.uk* www.royaloakhotel.co.uk
D: Fr £21.00–£37.00 **S:** Fr £25.00–£42.00 **Beds:** 6F 5D 2T 2S **Baths:** 12 En 3 Sh (15) cc

Yew Craggs, *Rosthwaite, Keswick, Cumbria, CA12 5XB.* Central Borrowdale, peaceful location. Private car park, stunning mountain scenery. **Open:** Mar to Oct
017687 77260 Mr & Mrs Crofts *yewcraggs@aol.com* www.members.aol.com/yewcraggs
D: Fr £18.00–£23.00 **S:** Fr £25.00–£35.00 **Beds:** 2F 3D **Baths:** 1 Sh (6) (6)

The How, *Rosthwaite, Keswick, Cumbria, CA12 5BX.* **Open:** Mar to Nov
017687 77692 *info@thehowborrowdale.co.uk* www.thehowborrowdale.co.uk **D:** Fr £22.00–£24.00 **S:** Fr £24.00 **Beds:** 1T 2D **Baths:** 2 Sh (4)
Rosthwaite is in the beautiful Borrowdale Valley about six miles from Keswick. Fell and riverside walking. Country house in well-kept garden. Comfortable lounge with television, log fire when required. Breakfast room. Superb views.

Hazel Bank, *Rosthwaite, Keswick, Cumbria, CA12 5XB.* Award-winning Victorian country house. Superb views. Ideal walking. No smoking/pets. **Open:** All year (not Xmas) **Grades:** ETC 5 Diamond, Gold, AA 5 Diamond, RAC 5 Diamond, Sparkling
017687 77248 Fax: 017687 77373 *enquiries@hazelbankhotel.co.uk* ww.hazelbankhotel.co.uk
D: Fr £35.00–£57.00 **S:** Fr £35.00–£57.00 **Beds:** 2T 6D **Baths:** 8 En (10) (12) cc

Rydal

NY3606

Glen Rothay Hotel, *Rydal, Ambleside, LA22 9LR.* Friendly coaching inn. Great food, quality accommodation. Beautiful views. Parking. **Open:** All year
015394 34500 D: Fr £30.00–£55.00 **S:** Fr £45.00–£70.00 **Beds:** 2T 6D **Baths:** 8 En (30) cc

Satterthwaite

SD3392

Eagles Head, *Satterthwaite, Ulverston, Cumbria, LA12 8LN.* C16th inn, heart of Grizedale Forest, log fire, good food. **Open:** All year (not Xmas/New Year)
01229 860237 D: Fr £19.50 **S:** Fr £25.00 **Beds:** 1D **Baths:** 1 En (6)

Force Mill Guest House, *Satterthwaite, Ulverston, Cumbria, LA12 8LQ.* Comfortable Lakeland house by waterfalls. Beautiful, secluded, ideal walking/touring. **Open:** All year (not Xmas/New Year)
01229 860205 (also fax) *forcemil@aol.com* www.forcemillfarm.co.uk **D:** Fr £20.00–£25.00 **S:** Fr £25.00–£30.00 **Beds:** 1F 1T 2D **Baths:** 4 En (6)

Sedbergh

SD6592

Bull Hotel, *Main Street, Sedbergh, Cumbria, LA10 5BL.* **Open:** All year
015396 20264 Fax: 015396 20212 *bullhotel@btinternet.com* www.bullatsedburgh.co.uk **D:** Fr £27.00–£32.00 **S:** Fr £32.00 **Beds:** 3F 4T 6D 2S **Baths:** 15 En 1 Sh (20) cc
C17th coaching inn, ideally situated between Yorkshire Dales & the Lake District. There is a large beer garden with play area & secure outbuildings for bikes , golf clubs etc. A friendly atmosphere awaits.

Holmecroft, *Station Road, Sedbergh, Cumbria, LA10 5DW.* Detached house, fell views, bright accommodation, wonderful walks, home-made preserves. **Open:** All year (not Xmas)
015396 20754 (also fax) Mrs Sharrocks *susan@holmecroftbandb.co.uk* www.holmecroftbandb.co.uk **D:** Fr £20.00 **S:** Fr £20.00 **Beds:** 1D 1T 1S **Baths:** 1 Sh (6)

Stable Antiques, *15 Back Lane, Sedbergh, Cumbria, LA10 5AQ.* C18th wheelwright's cottage with wonderful views of Howgill Fells. **Open:** All year
015396 20251 Miss Thurlby *antique.thurlby@amserve.net* ourworld.compuserve.com/homepages/sedbergh **D:** Fr £19.00–£20.00 **S:** Fr £20.00 **Beds:** 1D 1T **Baths:** 1 Sh (10) cc

Brantrigg, *Winfield Road, Sedbergh, Cumbria, LA10 5AZ.* Pleasantly-situated private house, above town centre, with extensive views. **Open:** All year (not Xmas/New Year)
015396 21455 Mrs Hopkins *brantrigg@aol.com*
D: Fr £20.00 **S:** Fr £22.00 **Beds:** 1T **Baths:** 1 Pr

Selside

SD5399

Hollowgate, *Selside, Kendal, Cumbria, LA8 9LG.* C16th comfortable farmhouse. **Open:** Easter to Oct
01539 823258 Mrs Knowles *hollowgate@talk21.com* **D:** Fr £17.00–£17.50 **S:** Fr £17.00–£17.50 **Beds:** 2D 1S

Shap

NY5615

The Crown Inn, *Main Street, Shap, Penrith, Cumbria, CA10 3NL.* A warm welcome awaits you at our charming C18th inn where your comfort is our priority. Historic Shap is ideally situated for the Lakes, Pennines and Howgills - just two miles from the M6 (Junction 39). Perfect for breaking long journeys! **Open:** Feb to Dec
01931 716229 Mrs Beardall *crowninnshap@totalise.co.uk* www.shap-cumbria.com. **D:** Fr £19.50–£22.50 **S:** Fr £19.50–£22.50 **Beds:** 1F 1D 1S **Baths:** 1 Sh (15)

Fell House, *Shap, Penrith, Cumbria, CA10 3NY.* Large Victorian house in small friendly village, ideal base for touring Lakes and Dales. **Open:** All year
01931 716343 Mr & Mrs Fletcher *fellhouse.shap@btopenworld.com* www.shapaccommodation.co.uk **D:** Fr £18.50–£24.50 **S:** Fr £21.00–£25.50 **Beds:** 3F 1D 1T **Baths:** 1 En 2 Sh

Brookfield, *Shap, Penrith, Cumbria, CA10 3PZ.* Renowned for good food, comfort and personal attention. Ensuite, licensed. **Open:** All year (not Xmas/New Year)
01931 716397 (also fax) Mrs Brunskill *info@brookfieldshap.co.uk* www.brookfieldshap.co.uk **D:** Fr £19.50–£26.00 **S:** Fr £20.00–£26.00 **Beds:** 5D 3T 1S **Baths:** 4 En 4 Pr 1 Sh (20)

St Bees

NX9711

Tomlin Guest House, *1 Tomlin House, St Bees, Cumbria, CA27 0EN.* Comfortable Victorian house convenient to beach and St Bees Head. **Open:** All year (not Xmas) **01946 822284** Mrs Whitehead **Fax: 01946 824243** *id.whitehead@which.net* **D:** Fr £16.00–£18.00 **S:** Fr £20.00 **Beds:** 1F 2D 1T **Baths:** 2 En 2 Sh (2)

Fairladies Barn Guest House, *Main Street, St Bees, CA27 0AD.* Large converted barn located in centre of seaside village. **Open:** All year **Grades:** ETC 3 Diamond **01946 822718** Mrs Carr **Fax: 01946 825838** *info@fairladiesbarn.co.uk* www.fairladiesbarn.co.uk **D:** Fr £18.00–£20.00 **S:** Fr £20.00–£25.00 **Beds:** 1F 5D 3T 1S **Baths:** 7 En 2 Sh (10)

Outrigg House, *St Bees, Cumbria, CA27 0AN.* Georgian house with unique character, situated in centre of village. **Open:** All year (not Xmas/New Year) **01956 822348 (also fax)** Mrs Moffat **D:** Fr £17.00–£18.00 **S:** Fr £17.00–£18.00 **Beds:** 1F 1T 1D 1S **Baths:** 1 Sh (2)

Stonehouse Farm, *Main Street, St Bees, Cumbria, CA27 0DE.* Modern Georgian farmhouse in centre of village, next to railway station. **Open:** All year (not Xmas) **01946 822224** Mrs Smith **D:** Fr £16.00–£20.00 **S:** Fr £20.00 **Beds:** 1F 2D 2T 1S **Baths:** 4 En 1 Sh (20)

Stanwix

NY3957

No. 1, *1 Etterby Street, Stanwix, Carlisle, Cumbria, CA3 9JB.* Homely accommodation in easy reach of Hadrian's Wall & Scotland, Lakes. **Open:** All year (not Xmas/New Year) **01228 547285** Ms Nixon **D:** Fr £17.00–£20.00 **S:** Fr £17.00–£20.00 **Beds:** 1D 2S (4) (1)

Staveley

SD4698

Stock Bridge Farm, *Staveley, Kendal, Cumbria, LA8 9LP.* Modernised comfortable C17th farmhouse in picturesque village close to Lakes. **Open:** Mar to Oct **01539 821580** Mrs Fishwick **D:** Fr £18.00–£19.00 **S:** Fr £19.00 **Beds:** 1F 4D 1T 1S **Baths:** 1 Sh (6)

Heywood, *Kentmere Road, Staveley, Kendal, Cumbria, LA8 9JF.* Peaceful spacious bungalow in hamlet with views of Kentmere Valley. **Open:** Feb to Nov **01539 821198** **D:** Fr £18.00–£20.00 **S:** Fr £20.00 **Beds:** 1D **Baths:** 1 En (1)

Sunny Wood, *Kentmere Road, Staveley, Kendal, Cumbria, LA8 9JF.* Away from the crowds. Friendly family home overlooking the Fells. **Open:** All year **01539 821236** **D:** Fr £16.00 **S:** Fr £20.00–£25.00 **Beds:** 1T 1D **Baths:** 1 Sh (3)

Talkin

NY5457

Blacksmith Arms, *Talkin, Brampton, Cumbria, CA8 1LE.* Village inn, restaurant, cask ales, open fire. **Open:** All year **016977 3452** Mrs Jackson **Fax: 016977 3396** *blacksmitharmstalkin@yahoo.co.uk* www.blacksmithsarmstalkin.co.uk **D:** Fr £25.00 **S:** Fr £35.00 **Beds:** 2T 3D **Baths:** 5 En (20) cc

Tebay

NY6104

Primrose Cottage, *Orton Road, Tebay, Penrith, Cumbria, CA10 3TL.* Adjacent M6 J38. Four-poster bed, jacuzzi bathroom, suitable for disabled visitors. **Open:** All year **Grades:** ETC 4 Diamond **015396 24791** Mrs Jones *primrosecottebay@aol.com* www.primrosecottagecumbria.co.uk **D:** Fr £20.00–£25.00 **S:** Fr £20.00–£30.00 **Beds:** 2D 1T **Baths:** 1 En 2 Pr (6)

Thornhill

NY0108

The Old Vicarage Guest House, *Thornhill, Egremont, Cumbria, CA22 2NY.* C19th vicarage of character, within easy reach Fells and Lakes. **Open:** All year (not Xmas) **01946 841577** Mrs Graham **D:** Fr £15.00–£17.00 **S:** Fr £15.00–£17.00 **Beds:** 3F **Baths:** 2 Sh (6)

Thornthwaite

NY2225 *Swan Inn, Coledale Inn, Royal Oak, Swinside Inn*

Thwaite Howe Hotel, *Thornthwaite, Keswick, Cumbria, CA12 5SA.* Beautiful small country house hotel backing onto Thornthwaite Forest, views over Derwent Valley. **Open:** Mar to Oct **017687 78281** Mr & Mrs Marshall **D:** Fr £28.00–£35.00 **S:** Fr £48.00–£58.00 **Beds:** 5D 3T 1F 1S **Baths:** 8 En (12) (10) cc

Tirril

NY5026

The Queens Head Inn, *Tirril, Penrith, Cumbria, CA10 2JF.* C1719, once owned by Wordsworth, own brewery, food awards. **Open:** All year (not Xmas) **01768 863219** **Fax: 01768 863243** *bookings@queensheadinn.co.uk* www.queensheadinn.co.uk **D:** Fr £22.50–£25.00 **S:** Fr £30.00–£35.00 **Beds:** 1F 5D 1T **Baths:** 4 En 1 Pr 1 Sh (40) cc

Troutbeck (Penrith)

NY3826

Greenah Crag Farm, *Troutbeck, Penrith, Cumbria, CA11 0SQ.* **Open:** Feb to Nov **017684 83233** *greenahcrag@lineone.net* **D:** Fr £17.50–£23.00 **S:** Fr £17.50–£25.00 **Beds:** 2D 1T **Baths:** 2 En 1 Sh Warm welcome to our old farmhouse. Guests' sitting room with woodburner. Oak-beamed dining room, memorable breakfast. Ideal for exploring Lakes, Eden Valley, Carlisle, Borders. Quiet secluded rural location, only 8 miles from motorway. Keswick 10, Ullswater 6.

Troutbeck (Windermere)

NY4002

Yew Grove, *Troutbeck, Windermere, Cumbria, LA23 1PG.* Comfortable C18th stone house, beautiful village, valley and mountain views. **Open:** All year (not Xmas) **015394 33304** Mr Pratt **D:** Fr £20.00–£24.00 **S:** Fr £22.00–£23.00 **Beds:** 1F 1D 1T 1S **Baths:** 1 En 1 Pr 1 Sh (3)

High Fold Farm, *Troutbeck, Windermere, Cumbria, LA23 1PG.* Unbeatable views of Troutbeck Valley. Well furnished comfortable accommodation of the highest standards in a tranquil setting. Excellent breakfasts. Ideal centre for walkers, for touring. Located in one of the Lakes' prettiest villages, only 3 miles from Ambleside and Windermere. **Open:** All year **015394 32200** **Fax: 015394 34970** **D:** Fr £20.00–£27.00 **S:** Fr £25.00–£35.00 **Beds:** 2F 1T 2D **Baths:** 3 En 1 Sh (6)

BATHROOMS

En = Ensuite

Pr = Private

Sh = Shared

Ulpha
SD1993

Oak Bank, *Ulpha, Duddon Valley, Broughton in Furness, Cumbria, LA20 6DZ.* Victorian house in peaceful valley; relax indoors or ramble. **Open:** All year (not Xmas)
01229 716393 Mrs Batten *soakbank@supanet.com* www.duddonvalley.co.uk **D:** Fr £20.00 **S:** Fr £22.00 **Beds:** 2D 1T **Baths:** 3 Sh (8)

Ulverston
SD2878

The Stables, *At The Derby Arms, Great Urswick, Ulverston, Cumbria, LA12 0SP.* Converted stable in friendly country village, within easy reach of Lake District. **Open:** All year
01229 586348 Mr Dickinson **Fax: 01229 585223** *thederbyarms@yahoo.co.uk* www.geocities.com/thederbyarms **D:** Fr £20.00–£25.00 **S:** Fr £30.00–£40.00 **Beds:** 2T 2D **Baths:** 4 En (10)

Sefton House, *Queen Street, Ulverston, Cumbria, LA12 7AF.* Georgian town house in the busy market town of Ulverston. **Open:** All year (not Xmas)
01229 582190 Mrs Glaister **Fax: 01229 581773** *romo@seftonhouse.co.uk* **D:** Fr £20.00–£22.50 **S:** Fr £27.50–£30.00 **Beds:** 1F 1D 1S 1T **Baths:** 4 En (15) **cc**

Church Walk House, *Church Walk, Ulverston, Cumbria, LA12 7EW.* Tastefully decorated Georgian house in town centre. Comfortable and relaxing. **Open:** All year (not Xmas/New Year)
01229 582211 M Chadderton *churchwalk@mchadderton.freeserve.co.uk* **D:** Fr £20.00–£26.00 **S:** Fr £20.00–£26.00 **Beds:** 1T 2D **Baths:** 2 En 1 Pr

Under Loughrigg
NY3404

Foxghyll, *Lake Road, Under Loughrigg, Ambleside, Cumbria, LA22 9LL.* Large country house. 2 acre garden, 4 poster bed, spa bath. **Open:** All year
015394 33292 Mrs Mann *foxghyll@hotmail.com* www.smoothhound.co.uk/hotels/foxghyll.html **D:** Fr £23.50–£27.00 **S:** Fr £23.50–£27.00 **Beds:** 1D 2T **Baths:** 3 En (5) (7)

Underbarrow
SD4692

Tranthwaite Hall, *Underbarrow, Kendal, Cumbria, LA8 8HG.* Tranthwaite Hall is something special dating back to C11th. Excellent accommodation. **Open:** All year
015395 68285 Mrs Swindlehurst *tranthwaitehall@hotmail.com* www.tranthwaitehall.freeserve.co.uk **D:** Fr £22.00–£25.00 **S:** Fr £25.00–£30.00 **Beds:** 1F 1D 1T **Baths:** 2 En (4)

Walton
NY5264

High Rigg Farm, *Walton, Brampton, Cumbria, CA8 2AZ.* Excellent accommodation near the Roman Wall; spacious rooms, beautiful views. **Open:** All year (not Xmas) **Grades:** ETC 3 Diamond
016977 2117 Mrs Mounsey *mounsey-highrigg@hotmail.com* www.waltonhighrigg.co.uk **D:** Fr £18.00–£20.00 **S:** Fr £20.00–£23.00 **Beds:** 1F **Baths:** 1 Pr 1 Sh (4)

Town Head Farm, *Walton, Brampton, Cumbria, CA8 2DJ.* Cosy 200 year old farmhouse with panoramic views. Near Hadrian's Wall. **Open:** All year (not Xmas/New Year)
016977 2730 Ms Armstrong *armstrong_townhead@hotmail.com* **D:** Fr £16.00–£17.00 **S:** Fr £17.00–£18.00 **Beds:** 1T 1D **Baths:** 1 Sh

Warwick Bridge
NY4756

Brookside B&B, *Warwick Bridge, Carlisle, Cumbria, CA4 8RE.* Delightful sandstone Listed building. Original miller's house, homely atmosphere, comfortable beds. **Open:** All year (not Xmas)
01228 560250 D Wearing *brookside@contactme.co.uk* **D:** Fr £17.00–£20.00 **S:** Fr £20.00–£24.00 **Beds:** 2D 1T **Baths:** 1 En 1 Sh (3)

Wasdale Head
NY1808

Burnthwaite Farm, *Wasdale Head, Seascale, Cumbria, CA20 1EX.* Perfectly situated for walkers and climbers, peaceful valley, farmhouse breakfast. **Open:** All year
019467 26242 Mrs Buchanan **D:** Fr £25.00–£27.50 **S:** Fr £27.50–£30.00 **Beds:** 2F 4D 1S **Baths:** 2 En 2 Sh (12)

Watendlath
NY2716

Fold Head Farm, *Watendlath, Keswick, Cumbria, CA12 5UN.* Comfortable friendly accommodation on working farm in beautiful unspoiled valley. **Open:** Mar to Nov
017687 77255 Mrs Richardson **D:** Fr £17.00–£18.00 **S:** Fr £17.00–£18.00 **Beds:** 1F 2D **Baths:** 1 Sh

Watermillock
NY4422

Land End Country Lodge, *Watermillock, Ullswater, Penrith, Cumbria, CA11 0NB.* **Open:** Apr to Dec
017684 86438 Miss Holmes **Fax: 017684 86959** *infolandends@btinternet.com* www.landends.co.uk **D:** Fr £28.00–£35.00 **S:** Fr £30.00–£33.00 **Beds:** 4D 2T 2S **Baths:** 8 En (15)
Tastefully-restored traditional farmhouse with pretty courtyard in 25 acres with 2 lakes, lovely trees and lots of wildlife, including red squirrels. Quality rooms, cosy lounge and honesty bar make this a perfect place to relax. Ullswater's dramatic scenery 1 mile.

Mellfell House Farm, *Watermillock, Penrith, Cumbria, CA11 0LS.* Beautiful old farmhouse high above Ullswater, log fires, relaxed atmosphere. **Open:** All year (not Xmas)
017684 86295 (also fax) Mrs Goddard www.mellfell.co.uk **D:** Fr £13.50–£17.50 **S:** Fr £13.50–£20.00 **Beds:** 1F 1D 1T **Baths:** 2 Sh (6)

Westlinton
NY3964

Lynebank, *Westlinton, Carlisle, Cumbria, CA6 6AA.* Family-run, excellent food, ideal stop for England/Scotland journey. **Open:** All year
01228 792820 (also fax) Mrs Butler *info@lynebank.co.uk* www.lynebank.co.uk **D:** Fr £18.00–£22.00 **S:** Fr £20.00–£24.00 **Beds:** 2F 3D 1T 3S **Baths:** 9 En (15) **cc**

Whelpo
NY3039

Swaledale Watch, *Whelpo, Caldbeck, Wigton, Cumbria, CA7 8HQ.* Enjoy great comfort, excellent home-cooking, warm, friendly farmhouse welcome. **Open:** All year (not Xmas)
016974 78409 (also fax) Mrs Savage *nan.savage@talk21.com* **D:** Fr £19.00–£22.00 **S:** Fr £21.00–£25.00 **Beds:** 2F 2D 1T **Baths:** 4 En 1 Pr (10)

Wigton

NY2548

Howbeck Farm Cottage, *Howbeck Farmhouse, Hesket Newmarket, Wigton, Cumbria, CA7 8JN.* **Open:** All year (not Xmas/ New Year)
01697 478306 Mr Topman *nick.topman@ virgin.net* www.howbeckfarmhouse.com **D:** Fr £23.00–£35.00 **S:** Fr £30.00–£40.00 **Beds:** 1T 1D **Baths:** 3 En (4)
The Northern Lake District National Park is a closely guarded secret with super fell walks, wonderful bike rides and little or no traffic. Explore the area and treat yourself to a great B&B experience in our lovely C17th home!

Windermere

SD4198

Meadfoot, *New Road, Windermere, Cumbria, LA23 2LA.* Detached house, large garden, patio and summerhouse. Warm welcome assured. **Open:** Jan to Dec
Grades: ETC 4 Diamond
015394 42610 T Shaw **Fax: 015394 45280** *enquiries@meadfoot-guesthouse.co.uk* www.meadfoot-guesthouse.co.uk **D:** Fr £20.00–£30.00 **S:** Fr £25.00–£30.00 **Beds:** 1F 4D 1T 1S **Baths:** 7 En (7)

Beckmead House, *5 Park Avenue, Windermere, Cumbria, LA23 2AR.* A warm, friendly welcome awaits you in our traditional stone-built Victorian house. **Open:** All year
Grades: ETC 3 Diamond
015394 42757 (also fax) *beckmead_house@ yahoo.com* www.beckmead.co.uk **D:** Fr £18.00–£24.00 **S:** Fr £18.00–£24.00 **Beds:** 1F 1T 2D 1S **Baths:** 2 En 1 Pr 1 Sh cc

Fir Trees, *Lake Road, Windermere, Cumbria, LA23 2EQ.* Perfectly situated midway between Windermere and the Lake. Scrumptious breakfasts. **Open:** All year
015394 42272 Fax: 015394 42512 *enquiries@ fir-trees.com* www.fir-trees.com **D:** Fr £20.00–£34.00 **S:** Fr £30.00–£45.00 **Beds:** 2F 1T 5D **Baths:** 7 En 1 Pr (8) cc

Glenthorne, *Princess Road, Windermere, Cumbria, LA23 2DD.* Friendly, quality accommodation in ideal location to explore the Lake District. **Open:** All year
015394 47558 Mrs Pirie *johnandgwen@ glenthorne23.fsnet.co.uk* www.glenthorne-guesthouse.co.uk **D:** Fr £19.00–£25.00 **S:** Fr £22.00–£25.00 **Beds:** 1T 3D **Baths:** 2 En 1 Sh (12)

Ivy Bank, *Holly Road, Windermere, Cumbria, LA23 2AF.* **Open:** All year (not Xmas/New Year)
Grades: ETC 4 Diamond
015394 42601 Mr Clothier *ivybank@clara.co.uk* www.ivybank.clara.co.uk **D:** Fr £19.00–£27.00 **Beds:** 1F 1T 3D **Baths:** 5 En (6) cc
Pretty Victorian stone-built home in quiet location close to village centre and station. Attractively decorated and comfortably furnished. Substantial choice for breakfast. Beautiful viewpoints within 30 minutes walk. Private car park, storage for cycles. Free use of local leisure club.

Newstead Guest House, *New Road, Windermere, Cumbria, LA23 2EE.* **Open:** All year (not Xmas/New Year) **Grades:** AA 5 Diamond, RAC 5 Diamond
015394 44485 Mrs Jackson *info@ newstead-guesthouse.co.uk* www.newstead-guesthouse.co.uk **D:** Fr £23.00–£32.50 **S:** Fr £30.00–£32.50 **Beds:** 1F 2T 5D **Baths:** 8 En (7) (10)
Ideal situation between Windermere village and the lake. In large grounds with secure private parking. Maintained to highest standards. All rooms ensuite. Beautiful woodwork. Hand-crafted bedroom furniture. Original fireplaces. Antiques etc. Freshly-cooked breakfasts, special diets etc. Friendly atmosphere.

Holly Lodge Guest House, *6 College Road, Windermere, Cumbria, LA23 1BX.* **Open:** All year (not Xmas)
015394 43873 (also fax) Tim & Alison Doyle *doyle@hollylodge20.fsnet.co.uk* www.hollylodge20.fsnet.co.uk **D:** Fr £19.00–£27.00 **S:** Fr £19.00–£27.00 **Beds:** 2F 5D 3T 1S **Baths:** 6 En 2 Sh (7)
Built in 1854, one of the oldest houses in Windermere. It's situated just off the main road in the village, in a quiet position, close to shops, restaurants, buses, trains. It's also well placed for bus tours & Lake Windermere.

Beckside Cottage, *4 Park Road, Windermere, LA23 2AW.* Comfortable B&B with full ensuite bedrooms in Windermere village. **Open:** All year
015394 42069 Mrs Cook **D:** Fr £17.00–£23.00 **S:** Fr £18.00–£25.00 **Beds:** 1F 2D 1T **Baths:** 4 En (6) (3)

Braemount House, *Sunny Bank Road, Windermere, Cumbria, LA23 2EN.* **Open:** All year (not Xmas)
015394 45967 (also fax) *enquiries@ braemount-house.co.uk* www.braemount-house.co.uk **D:** Fr £23.00–£30.00 **S:** Fr £23.00–£30.00 **Beds:** 3F 5D 1T **Baths:** 9 En (9) cc
Our guest book reads 'immaculate accommodation and lots of extras not normally available', 'excellent, especially breakfast in bed', 'great once again', 'wonderful', 'lovely room, brilliant hospitality, yummy breakfast', 'we will be back', and many more. Why not come and read it?

Ashleigh Guest House, *11 College Road, Windermere, Cumbria, LA23 1BU.* Comfortable Victorian guest house situated in the village of Windermere. **Open:** All year
015394 42292 Mr & Mrs Smith *ashleighhouse@windermere44.fsnet.co.uk* **D:** Fr £19.00–£21.00 **S:** Fr £23.00–£25.00 **Beds:** 2F 2D 1S **Baths:** 5 En

The Queens Cottage, *Queens Hotel, Victoria Street, Windermere, Cumbria, LA23 1AB.* Windermere, a beautiful area, is an ideal base for exploring nearby lake and fells and all the Lake District. The Queens Cottage and traditional pub - the Queens Hotel - with private parking are in the centre, close to buses and trains. **Open:** All year
015394 43713 Fax: 015394 44261 D: Fr £17.00–£28.00 **S:** Fr £20.00–£27.00 **Beds:** 1T 4D **Baths:** 5 En cc

Applegarth Hotel, *College Road, Windermere, LA23 1BU.* Victorian hotel of character. Excellent location, friendly bar, warm welcome. **Open:** All year
015394 43206 Mr & Mrs Hydes **Fax: 015394 46636** *enquiries@applegarthhotel.com* www.applegarthhotel.com **D:** Fr £20.00–£40.00 **S:** Fr £22.00–£40.00 **Beds:** 4F 3T 10D 3S **Baths:** 18 En cc

Villa Lodge, *Cross Street, Windermere, Cumbria, LA23 1AE.* Extremely comfortable traditional accommodation in peaceful area overlooking Windermere village.
Open: All year
015394 43318 (also fax) Mr Rooney *rooneym@btconnect.com* www.villa-lodge.co.uk
D: Fr £22.00–£35.00 **S:** Fr £22.00–£30.00 **Beds:** 5D 1T 2S **Baths:** 8 En (8) cc

Beech Hill Hotel, *Newby Bridge Road, Windermere, LA23 3LR.* Perfect lakeside setting ideal for business or leisure. Fantastic food. **Open:** All year
015394 42137 J Santanera **Fax: 015394 43745** *beechhill@richardsonshotels.co.uk* www.richardsonshotels.co.uk **D:** Fr £45.00–£100.00 **S:** Fr £45.00–£100.00 **Beds:** 2F 12T 38D 6S **Baths:** 58 En (80) cc

The Archway, *13 College Road, Windermere, Cumbria, LA23 1BU.* Comfortable Victorian guest house, choice of breakfasts, good touring base. **Open:** All year **Grades:** ETC 4 Diamond
015394 45613 (also fax) *archway@btinternet.com* www.communiken.com/archway **D:** Fr £20.00–£30.00 **S:** Fr £30.00–£45.00 **Beds:** 2T 2D **Baths:** 4 En (10)

Laurel Cottage, *Park Road, Windermere, Cumbria, LA23 2BJ.* A superb place to stay to tour this beautiful corner of England.
Open: All year (not Xmas/New Year)
015394 43053 W Taylor **D:** Fr £22.00–£26.00 **S:** Fr £22.00–£28.00 **Beds:** 1F 2T 2D 1S

Osborne Guest House, *3 High Street, Windermere, Cumbria, LA23 1AF.* Family-run guest house. Central Windermere. Excellent food, warm welcome. **Open:** All year
015394 46452 J Every *jennyevery@aol.com* **D:** Fr £18.00–£28.00 **S:** Fr £20.00–£28.00 **Beds:** 2F 2D **Baths:** 3 En 1 Sh

Kenilworth Guest House, *Holly Road, Windermere, Cumbria, LA23 2AF.* Comfortable Victorian house, two minutes centre Windermere. Convenient centre for exploring Lakeland's beautiful scenery.
Open: All year
015394 44004 Mr Roberts **Fax: 015394 46554 D:** Fr £16.00 **S:** Fr £16.00 **Beds:** 1F 2T 2D 1S **Baths:** 3 En 3 Sh (3)

Linthwaite House, *Crook Road, Windermere, Cumbria, LA23 3EZ.* Sublime hilltop setting. Beautiful gardens overlooking Lake Windermere. Delicious food. **Open:** All year
015394 44680 *riseholme215@aol.com* **D:** Fr £45.00–£125.00 **S:** Fr £90.00–£115.00 **Beds:** 1F 4T 12D 1S **Baths:** 12 En

Westbury House, *27 Broad Street, Windermere, Cumbria, LA23 2AB.* Victorian house, centre of Windermere. Near lake, shops, trains. Lovely food. **Open:** All year
015394 46839 & 015394 44575 Mrs Baker **Fax: 015394 42784** *westhouse@communndo.net* **D:** Fr £14.00–£23.00 **S:** Fr £16.00–£30.00 **Beds:** 2F 3D 1T **Baths:** 4 En 1 Sh (2) (5) cc

Annisgarth House, *2 Annisgarth, Bowness-on-Windermere, Windermere, Cumbria, LA23 2HF.* Views of lake and mountains. Private parking. Quiet location.
Open: Mar to Dec
015394 48049 (also fax) Mrs Erwig *2annisgarth@amserve.net* **D:** Fr £16.00–£22.00 **S:** Fr £21.00–£27.00 **Beds:** 1T 1D **Baths:** 1 En 1 Sh (3)

1 Park Road, *Windermere, Cumbria, LA23 2AW.* Beautiful, refurbished Victorian residence, great rooms, relaxed bar, candlelit dinners. **Open:** All year
015394 42107 Fax: 015394 48997 *enquiries@1parkroad.com* www.1parkroad.com **D:** Fr £27.50–£35.00 **S:** Fr £40.00–£50.00 **Beds:** 2F 1T 3D **Baths:** 6 En (1) (4) cc

Firgarth, *Ambleside Road, Windermere, Cumbria, LA23 1EU.* Comfortable Victorian country house, fine views, opposite riding stables. **Open:** All year **Grades:** ETC 3 Diamond, AA 3 Diamond
015394 46974 Mr & Mrs Lucking **Fax: 015394 42384** *thefirgarth@ktdinternet.com* **D:** Fr £18.50–£25.00 **S:** Fr £19.00–£27.00 **Beds:** 1F 3D 3T 1S **Baths:** 8 Pr (9) cc

Eastbourne Guest House, *Biskey Howe Road, Windermere, Cumbria, LA23 2JR.* Our traditional Lakeland guest house is situated below the Biskey Howe Viewpoint in a quiet, central location. Our aim is to offer you high quality well-furnished ensuite accommodation with excellent value for money. Joyce and John will ensure a warm, friendly welcome into a relaxed and cosy atmosphere. **Open:** Feb to Dec
015394 43525 (also fax) Mr Whitfield *mail@eastbourne-guesthouse.co.uk* www.eastbourne-guesthouse.co.uk **D:** Fr £22.00–£35.00 **S:** Fr £26.00–£35.00 **Beds:** 1F 1T 5D 1S **Baths:** 7 En 1 Pr (5) (6) cc

Winton

NY7811

South View Farm, *Winton, Kirkby Stephen, Cumbria, CA17 4HS.* Lovely farmhouse situated in quiet village, easy access to the Lakes and Dales. **Open:** All year
017683 71120 & 07801 432184 (M)
Mrs Marston *southviewwinton@hotmail.com*
D: Fr £17.00 **S:** Fr £17.00 **Beds:** 1F 1D 1S (2)

Witherslack

SD4384

Fernhill Vegetarian Country House, *Witherslack, Grange Over Sands, Cumbria, LA11 6RX.* Idyllic country house and garden. Excellent organic vegetarian food.
Open: All year
01359 552237 *alibramall@lineone.net* **D:** Fr £30.00–£35.00 **S:** Fr £30.00–£45.00 **Beds:** 2D 1S **Baths:** 1 En 1 Pr 1 Sh (10)

Workington

NX9927

Fernleigh House, *15 High Seaton, Workington, Cumbria, CA14 1PE.* Georgian house, lovely garden, warm and friendly welcome, excellent breakfasts. **Open:** All year
01900 605811 Ms Bewsher **D:** Fr £17.00–£45.00 **S:** Fr £17.00 **Beds:** 1F 2T 1S

Yanwath

NY5128

Yanwath Gate Farm, *Yanwath, Penrith, Cumbria, CA10 2LF.* Comfortable C17th farmhouse, good food, near a pub.
Open: All year
01768 864459 Mr & Mrs Donnelly
yanwathgatefarm@aol.com **D:** Fr £17.00–£20.00
S: Fr £17.00–£20.00 **Beds:** 1F 1D **Baths:** 2 En (9)

Derbyshire

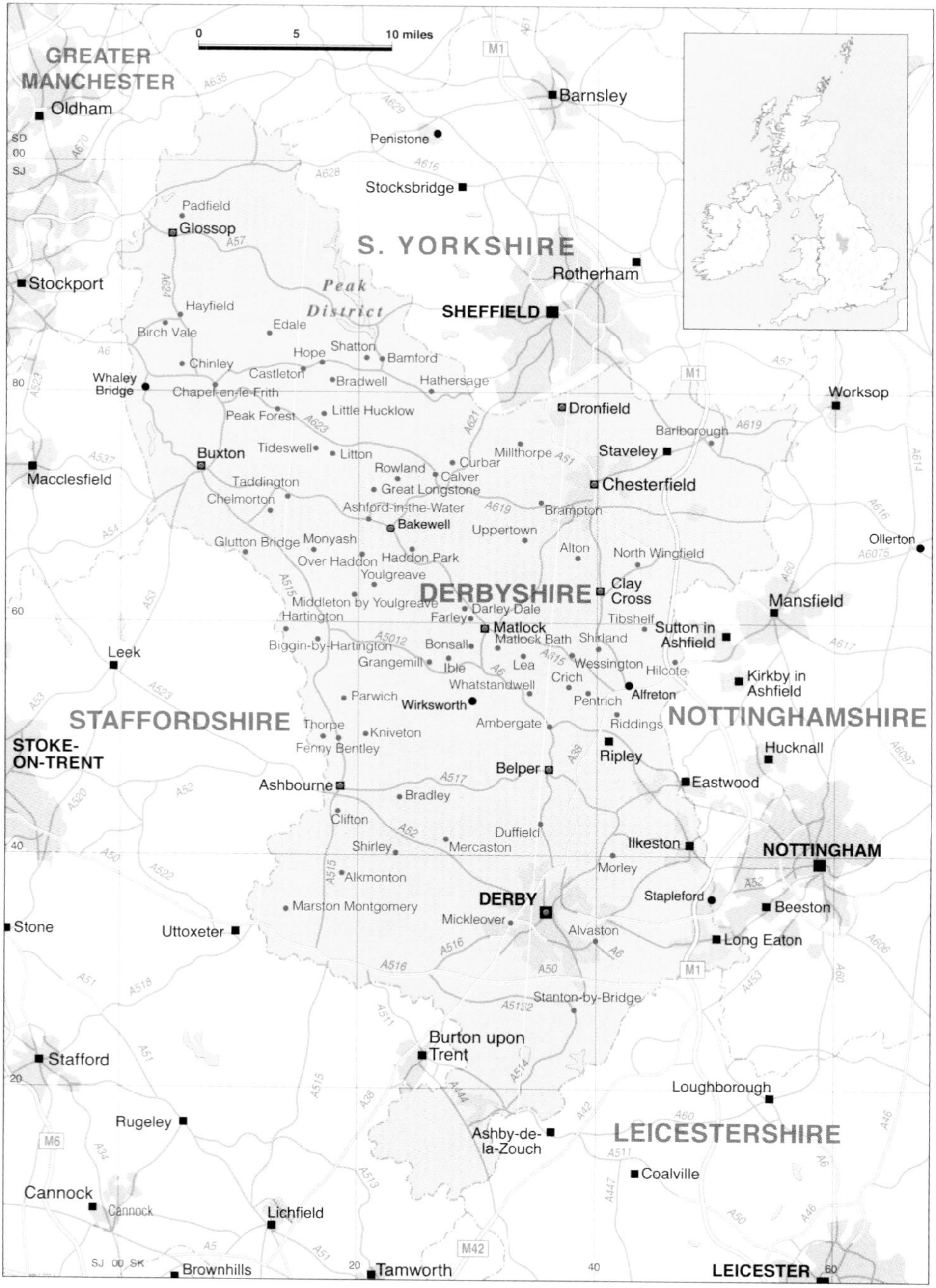

0 5 10 miles
GREATER MANCHESTER
Oldham
Barnsley
Penistone
Stocksbridge
S. YORKSHIRE
Rotherham
SHEFFIELD
Padfield
Glossop
Stockport
Peak District
Hayfield
Birch Vale
Edale
Hope
Shatton
Bamford
Chinley
Castleton
Bradwell
Hathersage
Whaley Bridge
Chapel-en-le-Frith
Peak Forest
Little Hucklow
Dronfield
Worksop
Barlborough
Staveley
Tideswell
Litton
Millthorpe
Buxton
Curbar
Rowland
Calver
Macclesfield
Taddington
Great Longstone
Chesterfield
Chelmorton
Ashford-in-the-Water
Brampton
Bakewell
Uppertown
Ollerton
Glutton Bridge
Monyash
Over Haddon
Haddon Park
Alton
North Wingfield
Youlgreave
DERBYSHIRE
Clay Cross
Middleton by Youlgreave
Darley Dale
Mansfield
Hartington
Farley
Tibshelf
Matlock
Sutton in Ashfield
Matlock Bath
Shirland
Biggin-by-Hartington
Bonsall
Leek
Grangemill
Ible
Lea
Wessington
Hilcote
Crich
Kirkby in Ashfield
Whatstandwell
Alfreton
Parwich
Pentrich
STAFFORDSHIRE
Wirksworth
Ambergate
Riddings
NOTTINGHAMSHIRE
Thorpe
Kniveton
STOKE-ON-TRENT
Fenny Bentley
Ripley
Hucknall
Belper
Ashbourne
Eastwood
Bradley
Clifton
Duffield
Ilkeston
Shirley
Mercaston
NOTTINGHAM
Morley
Alkmonton
DERBY
Stapleford
Marston Montgomery
Beeston
Stone
Uttoxeter
Mickleover
Alvaston
Long Eaton
Stanton-by-Bridge
Burton upon Trent
Stafford
Loughborough
Rugeley
Ashby-de-la-Zouch
LEICESTERSHIRE
Coalville
Cannock
Lichfield
Brownhills
Tamworth
LEICESTER
M1
M6
M42

The Smithy, *Biggin by Hartington, Buxton, Derbyshire, SK17 0DT.* **Open:** All year **Grades:** AA 5 Diamond
01298 84548 (also fax) Gary & Lynn Jinks-Lowe *thesmithy@newhavenderbyshire.freeserve.co.uk* **D:** Fr £30.00–£35.00 **S:** Fr £40.00–£45.00 **Beds:** 1F 3D **Baths:** 4 En (10)
Set peacefully in the Peak National Park, The Smithy, Grade II Listed and previously an inn, offers a warm personalised service. Ensuite rooms are privately located in the renovated barn, and breakfasts are served in the former blacksmith's workshop.

Birch Vale

SK0186

Spinney Cottage B&B, *Spinner Bottom, Birch Vale, High Peak, SK22 1BL.* Tastefully furnished country home, excellent walking & biking area, 1 mile Hayfield. **Open:** All year (not Xmas)
01663 743230 **D:** Fr £20.00–£22.00 **S:** Fr £20.00–£25.00 **Beds:** 1D 1T 1S **Baths:** 2 En 1 Pr

Bonsall

SK2758

Town Head Farmhouse, *70 High Street, Bonsall, Matlock, Derbyshire, DE4 2AR.* Converted friendly C18th farmhouse set in peaceful pretty village. **Open:** All year **Grades:** ETC 4 Diamond, Silver
01629 823762 Mrs Taylor **D:** Fr £23.00–£27.00 **S:** Fr £25.00–£30.00 **Beds:** 4D 2T **Baths:** 6 En (6)

Bradley

SK2246

Yeldersley Old Hall Farm, *Yeldersley Lane, Bradley, Ashbourne, Derbyshire, DE6 1PH.* Relax and unwind in peaceful surroundings at our Grade II Listed farmhouse. **Open:** Easter to Nov
01335 344504 (also fax) Mrs Hinds *janethindsfarm@yahoo.co.uk* **D:** Fr £20.00–£25.00 **S:** Fr £25.00–£26.00 **Beds:** 2D 1T **Baths:** 2 En 1 Pr (7)

Bradwell

SK1781

Ashbrook, *Brookside, Bradwell, Hope Valley, S33 9HF.* Idyllic, peaceful location lovely gardens with fish pond, stunning views. **Open:** All year (not Xmas)
01433 620803 J Maskrey **D:** Fr £16.00–£25.00 **S:** Fr £20.00–£25.00 **Beds:** 2D 1T **Baths:** 1 Sh 1 Pr (2)

Stoney Ridge, *Granby Road, Bradwell, Hope Valley, S33 9HU.* Our large split-level bungalow overlooks The Peakland Village of Bradwell with overviews of Hope Valley. Our heated indoor pool is available to guests teatime and before breakfast. **Open:** All year
01433 620538 Mrs Plant **Fax: 01433 623154** *toneyridge@aol.com* www.cressbrook.co.uk/hopev/stoneyridge **D:** Fr £28.00 **S:** Fr £31.00 **Beds:** 3D 1T **Baths:** 3 En 1 Pr (10) (4) cc

Brampton

SK3670

Brampton Guest House, *75 Old Road, Brampton, Chesterfield, Derbyshire, S40 2QU.* Victorian house in quiet cul-de-sac close to Chatsworth. **Open:** All year
01246 276533 Mr Thompson **Fax: 01246 211636** *guesthouse@oldroadbrampton.freeserve.co.uk* www.ztour.com/top/brampton.guesthouse.htm **D:** Fr £14.00–£16.00 **S:** Fr £14.00–£18.50 **Beds:** 2F 1D 1S **Baths:** 3 Pr 1 Sh (4)

Buxton

SK0573

The Old Manse Private Hotel, *6 Clifton Road, Silverlands, Buxton, Derbyshire, SK17 6QL.* Quietly situated Victorian hotel. Delicious food. Warm welcome. Friendly atmosphere. **Open:** All year **Grades:** AA 3 Diamond
01298 25638 (also fax) P A Cotton *old_manse@yahoo.co.uk* www.oldmanse.co.uk **D:** Fr £18.00–£25.00 **S:** Fr £18.00–£25.00 **Beds:** 2F 4D 1S **Baths:** 7 En 2 Sh (3) cc

Harefield, *15 Marlborough Road, Buxton, Derbyshire, SK17 6RD.* Elegant Victorian property set on its own grounds overlooking Buxton. Quiet location just a few minutes walk from the historic town centre. An ideal base for exploring the beautiful Peak District. Friendly atmosphere, delicious food and lovely gardens to enjoy. **Open:** All year (not Xmas/New Year)
01298 24029 (also fax) *hardie@harefield1.freeserve.co.uk* www.harefield1.freeserve.co.uk **D:** Fr £23.00–£25.00 **S:** Fr £23.00–£25.00 **Beds:** 2T 3D 1S **Baths:** 5 En 1 Pr (8)

Fairhaven, *1 Dale Terrace, Buxton, Derbyshire, SK17 6LU.* Victorian premises in historical Buxton, surrounded by picturesque Peak District. **Open:** All year
01298 24481 (also fax) *paulandcatherine@fairhavenguesthouse.freeserve.co.uk* www.fairhavenbedandbreakfast.com **D:** Fr £17.00–£19.00 **S:** Fr £19.00–£23.00 **Beds:** 1F 2T 2D 1S **Baths:** 1 Pr 2 Sh cc

Hilldeen, *97 Dale Road, Buxton, Derbyshire, SK17 6PD.* Family-run business, established 15 yrs. Pavilion, gardens, Opera House 10 mins walk. **Open:** All year (not Xmas/New Year)
01298 23015 Mrs Taylor **D:** Fr £19.00 **S:** Fr £20.00–£22.00 **Beds:** 1F 1T 1D 1S **Baths:** 5 En

Buxton Wheelhouse Hotel, *19 College Road, Buxton, Derbyshire, SK17 9DZ.* Elegant Victorian establishment. Refurbished spacious bedrooms. Central. Warm welcome, excellent value. **Open:** All year (not Xmas)
01298 24869 (also fax) Ms Thompson Price *lyndsie@buxton-wheelhouse.com* www.buxton-wheelhouse.com **D:** Fr £22.00–£27.00 **S:** Fr £27.00–£35.00 **Beds:** 3F 3D 2T 1S **Baths:** 9 En (10) cc

Abbey Guest House, *43 South Avenue, Buxton, Derbyshire, SK17 6NQ.* In the centre of Buxton. Small and friendly, great value. **Open:** All year
01298 26419 *aghbuxton@aol.com* **D:** Fr £15.00 **S:** Fr £15.00 **Beds:** 1F 1T **Baths:** 1 Sh (1)

Ford Side House, *125 Lightwood Road, Buxton, Derbyshire, SK17 6RW.* Peaceful elegant Edwardian house for non-smokers. Premier residential area. **Open:** Easter to Oct
01298 72842 Mr & Mrs Roberts **D:** Fr £19.00–£20.00 **S:** Fr £25.00–£30.00 **Beds:** 3D 1T **Baths:** 3 En (10) (3)

Compton House Guest House, *4 Compton Road, Buxton, Derbyshire, SK17 9DN.* Warm & friendly atmosphere. Comfortable rooms, good food, excellent value. **Open:** All year **Grades:** ETC 3 Diamond
01298 26926 (also fax) Mr Hesp *comptonbuxton@aol.com* **D:** Fr £20.00–£25.00 **S:** Fr £25.00–£30.00 **Beds:** 2F 2D 1T 1S **Baths:** 4 En 1 Sh

Nithen Cottage, *123 Park Road, Buxton, Derbyshire, SK17 6SP.* Beautiful Victorian house. Luxurious accommodation. Wonderful breakfasts. Close town centre. **Open:** All year (not Xmas/New Year)
01298 24679 & 07734 552362 (M) *therogersons@freeuk.com* **D:** Fr £23.00–£25.00 **S:** Fr £33.00–£35.00 **Beds:** 2D **Baths:** 1 En 1 Pr

Planning a longer stay? Always ask for any special rates

Grendon Guest House, *Bishops Lane, Buxton, Derbyshire, SK17 6UN.* **Open:** All year **Grades:** ETC 5 Diamond, Silver
01298 78831 Mrs Parker **Fax: 01298 79257** *parkerhl@talk21.com* www.grendonguesthouse.co.uk **D:** Fr £25.00–£35.00 **S:** Fr £33.00–£50.00 **Beds:** 2D 1T 1S **Baths:** 3 En 1 Pr (11) (6) cc
A quality experience of comfort, space, good food & hospitality awaits you in our beautiful home conveniently situated for the delights of Buxton and the Peak District. Lovely gardens & rural views, evening meals & four-poster available.

The Grosvenor House, *1 Broad Walk, Buxton, Derbyshire, SK17 6JE.* **Open:** All year
01298 72439 Patrick & Joan Chapman **Fax: 01298 214185** *grosvenor.buxton@btopenworld.com* www.smoothhound.co.uk/hotels/grosvenor.html **D:** Fr £25.00–£37.50 **S:** Fr £45.00–£50.00 **Beds:** 2F 5D 1T **Baths:** 8 En
Idyllically-set in the heart of historic spa town, overlooking Pavilion Gardens/Opera House. Bedrooms ensuite, non-smoking, hearty full English breakfast. Ideal centre for exploring Peak District & Derbyshire Dales. Within easy walking distance of numerous pubs & restaurants. 'Which?' Recommended.

The Victorian Guest House, *3a Broad Walk, Buxton, Derbyshire, SK17 6JE.* Unique quiet elegant home, refurbished 1999, overlooking Pavilion Gardens/Opera House. **Open:** All year
01298 78759 Mrs Whiston **Fax: 01298 74732** *buxvic@x-stream.co.uk* **D:** Fr £25.00–£32.50 **S:** Fr £35.00 **Beds:** 2F 5D 2T **Baths:** 9 En (10)

Calver

SK2374

Hydrangea Cottage, *Hall Fold, Main Street, Calver, Hope Valley, S32 3XL.* Luxurious accommodation, beautiful garden and views. Quiet location near Chatsworth. **Open:** All year (not Xmas)
01433 630760 Mrs Hall **D:** Fr £25.00 **S:** Fr £50.00 **Beds:** 1D **Baths:** 1 Pr (1)

Valley View, *67 Smithy Knoll Road, Calver, Hope Valley, S32 3XW.* **Open:** All year **Grades:** ETC 4 Diamond, AA 4 Diamond
01433 631407 (also fax) Mr Stone *sue@a-place-2-stay.co.uk* www.a-place-2-stay.co.uk **D:** Fr £15.00–£25.00 **S:** Fr £35.00–£40.00 **Beds:** 1F 1T 1D **Baths:** 3 En (4) (6)
EVER POPULAR-ideal for Chatsworth, Bakewell, Castleton & Eyam. Luxury ensuite rooms with glorious views. Private entrance, own key, local pubs serving excellent meals. Ideal base for walking, sightseeing & cycling. Off street parking! Hearty breakfasts - BOOK EARLY!

Castleton

SK1582

Bray Cottage, *Market Place, Castleton, Hope Valley, S33 8WQ.* Charming C18th cottage, excellent accommodation, hearty breakfast, very friendly atmosphere. **Open:** All year (not Xmas)
01433 621532 Mrs Heard *Chris.Waller4@btopenworld.com* **D:** Fr £22.50–£25.00 **S:** Fr £25.00–£30.00 **Beds:** 2D **Baths:** 1 En 1 Pr (1)

Bargate Cottage, *Market Place, Castleton, Hope Valley, Derbyshire, S33 8WQ.* Comfortable C17th cottage overlooking picturesque village green. Warm welcome. **Open:** All year (not Xmas) **Grades:** ETC 4 Diamond
01433 620201 F Saxon **Fax: 01433 621739** *fionasaxon@bargatecottage78.freeserve.co.uk* www.peakland.com/bargate **D:** Fr £25.00 **S:** Fr £40.00 **Beds:** 1T 2D **Baths:** 3 En (12) (5)

Hillside House, *Pindale Road, Castleton, Hope Valley, S33 8WU.* Peaceful location, panoramic views, hearty breakfasts. Clean, spacious family house. **Open:** All year (not Xmas) **Grades:** ETC 4 Diamond
01433 620312 (also fax) Mrs Webster **D:** Fr £23.50–£25.00 **Beds:** 2D **Baths:** 2 En (3)

National Grid References given are for villages, towns and cities – not for individual houses

Willow Croft, *Pindale Road, Castleton, Hope Valley, Derbyshire, S33 8WU.* Perfectly situated for exploring the area. Warm welcome, wonderful views. **Open:** All year (not Xmas/New Year)
01433 620400 D: Fr £22.50–£25.00 **S:** Fr £25.00–£30.00 **Beds:** 2D **Baths:** 2 En (6)

Cryer House, *Castleton, Hope Valley, S33 8WG.* C17th rectory; beautiful cottage garden & views of church and castle. **Open:** All year (not Xmas) **Grades:** ETC 3 Diamond
01433 620244 Mrs Skelton *FleeSkel@aol.com* **D:** Fr £24.50–£25.00 **Beds:** 2D **Baths:** 1 En 1 Pr

Chapel-en-le-Frith

SK0680 *Wanted Inn, New Inn, Roebuck, King's Arms, Devonshire Arms, Lamb Inn, Jolly Carter, Rose & Crown, Hanging Gate, Crown & Mitre*

Potting Shed, *Bank Hall, Chapel-en-le-Frith, High Peak, Derbyshire, SK23 9UB.* Breakfast in plant lovers' conservatory, gorgeous views, oak beams, antique furniture. **Open:** All year (not Xmas/New Year)
01298 812656 & 0161 338 8134 Mr Ashton **D:** Fr £22.50–£25.00 **S:** Fr £35.00–£40.00 **Beds:** 2D **Baths:** 2 En (3)

Slack Hall Farm, *Castleton Road, Chapel-en-le-Frith, High Peak, SK23 6QS.* C17th farmhouse on family-run working farm, comfortable friendly accommodation. **Open:** All year (not Xmas/New Year)
01298 812845 (also fax) Mrs Hayward **D:** Fr £19.00–£20.00 **Beds:** 1F 1D **Baths:** 2 En (2)

Chelmorton

SK1169

Ditch House, *Chelmorton, Buxton, Derbyshire, SK17 9SG.* Cottage with superb views. Close to Buxton, Bakewell and Chatsworth. **Open:** All year
01298 85719 (also fax) Ms Simmonds **D:** Fr £20.00–£30.00 **S:** Fr £25.00–£30.00 **Beds:** 1T 1D **Baths:** 2 En (4)

Chesterfield

SK3871

Locksley, *21 Tennyson Avenue, Chesterfield, Derbyshire, S40 4SN.* Comfortable friendly atmosphere; pleasant location near town centre. **Open:** All year (not Xmas)
01246 273332 Mrs Parker **D:** Fr £15.00 **S:** Fr £17.00 **Beds:** 1D 1T/S **Baths:** 1 Sh

All details shown are as supplied by B&B owners in Autumn 2002

Hathersage

SK2381

Cannon Croft, *Cannonfields, Hathersage, Hope Valley, Derbyshire, S32 1AG.* **Open:** All year
01433 650005 (also fax) Mrs Oates *soates@cannoncroft.fsbusiness.co.uk* www.cannoncroft.fsbusiness.co.uk **D:** Fr £23.00–£26.00 **S:** Fr £35.00–£46.00 **Beds:** 2T 2D **Baths:** 4 En (12) (5)
Enjoy panoramic views from the conservatory. Famous for our welcome, decor and varied menu (try our sundancer eggs, whiskey porridge etc.). Flower-arrangers' garden. Excellent choice of local dining within 10 mins' walk. Visit Chatsworth, walk, climb cycle, enjoy.

Hillfoot Farm, *Castleton Road, Hathersage, Hope Valley, Derbyshire, S32 1EG.* Originally C16th inn and toll house on the old Jaggers Pack Horse route. **Open:** All year
01433 651673 Mrs Wilcockson *lorna@wilcockson0.fsnet.co.uk* www.hillfootfarm.com **D:** Fr £20.00–£25.00 **S:** Fr £25.00–£50.00 **Beds:** 2D 2T **Baths:** 4 En (10)

Moorgate, *Castleton Road, Hathersage, Hope Valley, S32 1EH.* Fringe of Hathersage in Peak National Park - touring, walking, climbing. **Open:** All year
01433 650293 Mrs Veevers **D:** Fr £17.00 **S:** Fr £19.00–£22.00 **Beds:** 1D 1T 1S **Baths:** 1 Sh (3)

Polly's B&B, *Moorview Cottage, Cannonfields, Jaggers Lane, Hathersage, Hope Valley, S32 1AG.* Warm, friendly, first-class accommodation in quiet location, very imaginative breakfast menu. **Open:** All year
01433 650110 P Fisher **D:** Fr £19.00–£23.00 **S:** Fr £25.00–£28.00 **Beds:** 2D 1T **Baths:** 3 En (4) (3)

Hayfield

SK0386 *Pack Horse, Royal Hotel, Sportsman, Lantern Pike*

Pool Cottage, *Park Hall, Hayfield, High Peak, SK22 2NN.* Unusual Victorian greenhouse. Converted house, secluded. South facing woodland setting. **Open:** May to Dec
01663 742463 Mr Dean **D:** Fr £20.00–£22.00 **Beds:** 1F 1T 1S **Baths:** 2 En 1 Pr

Hilcote

SK4457

Hillcote Hall, *Hilcote Lane, Hilcote, Alfreton, Derbyshire, DE55 5HR.* Listed country house with easy access to M1 and Derbyshire. **Open:** Mar to Nov
01773 812608 Mrs Doncaster **D:** Fr £18.00 **S:** Fr £20.00 **Beds:** 1F 1D (4)

Hope

SK1683

Underleigh House, *off Edale Road, Hope, Hope Valley, S33 6RF.* A stunning, tranquil setting in the heart of magnificent walking country. **Open:** All year (not Xmas/New Year) **Grades:** ETC 5 Diamond, Silver, AA 5 Diamond
01433 621372 Mrs Taylor **Fax: 01433 621324** *underleigh.house@btinternet.com* www.underleighhouse.co.uk **D:** Fr £32.00–£34.50 **S:** Fr £40.00–£49.00 **Beds:** 4D 2T **Baths:** 6 En (12) (6) **cc**

Round Meadow Barn, *Parsons Lane, Hope , Hope Valley, Derbyshire, S33 6RA.* Converted barn, magnificent views all round. Ideal walking, hang-gliding, rock-climbing, mountain-biking. **Open:** All year
01433 621347 Fax: 01433 621 347 *rmbarn@bigfoot.com* **D:** Fr £20.00–£23.00 **S:** Fr £25.00–£28.00 **Beds:** 1F 1T **Baths:** 2 Sh (12)

Kniveton

SK2050

New House Farm, *Longrose Lane, Kniveton, Ashbourne, Derbyshire, DE6 1JL.* Working organic farm. Many local attractions. 'Peak Practice' country. Also camping, caravans, self-catering. **Open:** All year
01335 342429 Mrs Smail **D:** Fr £11.50–£20.00 **S:** Fr £13.50–£30.00 **Beds:** 2F 1T 1D (10)

Lea

SK3257

The Coach House, *Lea, Matlock, Derbyshire, DE4 5GJ.* Converted farm buildings, central location for walking and touring Derbyshire. **Open:** All year
01629 534346 (also fax) Mr & Mrs Hobson *alanandbarbara@coachhouselea.co.uk* www.coachhouselea.co.uk **D:** Fr £18.50–£27.50 **S:** Fr £22.50–£30.00 **Beds:** 2T 1D **Baths:** 1 En 1 Sh **cc**

Little Hucklow

SK1678

Ye Olde Bull's Head, *Little Hucklow, Tideswell, Buxton, Derbyshire, SK17 8RT.* Unspoilt C12th inn with cosy log fires and panoramic views. **Open:** All year
01298 871097 (also fax) Mr Denton *accom@yeoldebullshead.freeserve.co.uk* www.yeoldebullshead.freeserve.co.uk **D:** Fr £25.00–£30.00 **S:** Fr £30.00–£60.00 **Beds:** 2D **Baths:** 2 En **cc**

Litton

SK1675

Beacon House, *Litton, Buxton, Derbyshire, SK17 8QP.* Farm smallholding overlooking Tansley Dale. Quietly situated, walks from the door. **Open:** Feb to Nov
01298 871752 Mrs Parsons **D:** Fr £19.00–£21.00 **Beds:** 2D **Baths:** 2 En (4)

Marston Montgomery

SK1337

Waldley Manor, *Marston Montgomery, Doveridge, Ashbourne, Derbyshire, DE6 5LR.* Relax in this C16th manor farmhouse. Quiet location, access to commuter roads. **Open:** All year (not Xmas/New Year)
01889 590287 Ms Whitfield **D:** Fr £20.00–£25.00 **S:** Fr £20.00–£25.00 **Beds:** 1F 1D **Baths:** 2 En

Matlock

SK3060

Bank House, *12 Snitterton Road, Matlock, Derbyshire, DE4 3LZ.* Beamed C17th stone cottage, part in converted stable with private lounge. **Open:** All year (not Xmas/New Year) **Grades:** ETC 4 Diamond
01629 56101 Mrs Hill *jennyderbydales@hotmail.com* **D:** Fr £23.00–£25.00 **S:** Fr £35.00 **Beds:** 1F 1T **Baths:** 1 En 1 Pr (5) (2)

Ellen House, *37 Snitterton Road, Matlock, Derbys, DE4 3LZ.* Friendly hosts offer hospitality and comfort in attractively extended Edwardian home. **Open:** All year
01629 55584 Mrs Lewis **D:** Fr £21.00–£25.00 **S:** Fr £25.00–£30.00 **Beds:** 1T 2D **Baths:** 3 En

Farley Farm, *Farley, Matlock, Derbyshire, DE4 5LR.* Working farm, lovely countryside, easy access Chatsworth/walks. Pets welcome. **Open:** All year (not Xmas/New Year)
01629 582533 & 07801 756409 (M) M Brailsford **D:** Fr £20.00–£25.00 **S:** Fr £22.00–£25.00 **Beds:** 1F 1D **Baths:** 2 En (10)

Norden House, *Chesterfield Road, Two Dales, Matlock, Derbyshire, DE4 2EZ.* Converted barn, village outskirts. Friendly, cosy accommodation, pub nearby. Tasty home cooking. **Open:** All year (not Xmas) **01629 732074** Mrs Pope **Fax: 01629 735805** *david.a.pope@talk21.com* www.geocities.com/nordenhouse **D:** Fr £20.00–£26.00 **S:** Fr £37.00–£40.00 **Beds:** 2D **Baths:** 2 En (2)

Edgemount, *16 Edge Road, Matlock, Derbyshire, DE4 3NH.* Friendly hosts, pleasant location. Near bus/rail station. Records office. Parking. **Open:** All year (not Xmas) **Grades:** ETC 2 Diamond **01629 584787** Mrs Allen **D:** Fr £18.00–£20.00 **S:** Fr £18.00–£20.00 **Beds:** 1D 1F 1S **Baths:** 1 Sh 1 Pr (5) (2)

Sheriff Lodge, *51 Dimple Road, Matlock, Derbyshire, DE4 3JX.* **Open:** All year (not Xmas/New Year) **Grades:** ETC 4 Diamond **01629 760760 Fax: 01629 760860** *info@sherifflodge.co.uk* www.sherifflodge.co.uk **D:** Fr £25.00–£30.00 **S:** Fr £35.00–£39.00 **Beds:** 2T 2D **Baths:** 4 En (6) **cc** Luxurious accommodation in Edwardian surroundings, ideally situated for Chatsworth House, Haddon Hall & Bakewell. Views across the Derwent Valley to Riber Castle. Perfect spot for walkers & cyclists, bikers welcome. Drying room. Bargain breaks - call for details.

Riverbank House, *Derwent Avenue, Matlock, Derbyshire, DE4 3LX.* Victorian house nestling on the banks of the River Derwent. **Open:** All year (not Xmas/New Year) **Grades:** ETC 4 Diamond **01629 582593** Mr & Mrs Newberry **Fax: 01629 580885** *bookings@riverbankhouse.co.uk* **D:** Fr £23.50–£25.00 **S:** Fr £25.00–£32.00 **Beds:** 2F 1T 3D **Baths:** 6 En

Glendon, *Knowleston Place, Matlock, Derbyshire, DE4 3BU.* Conveniently situated, well-equipped accommodation in a relaxed atmosphere. **Open:** Jan to Nov **Grades:** AA 4 Diamond **01629 584732** Mrs Elliott **D:** Fr £21.50–£25.00 **S:** Fr £25.00–£29.00 **Beds:** 1F 2D 1T **Baths:** 2 En 2 Sh (3) (5)

Matlock Bath

SK2958

Ashdale Guest House, *92 North Parade, Matlock Bath, Matlock, Derbyshire, DE4 3NS.* Georgian villa, central Matlock Bath. Level walking to station/amenities. **Open:** All year **Grades:** ETC 2 Diamond **01629 57826** Mrs Lomas *ashdale@matlockbath.fsnet.co.uk* www.ashdaleguesthouse.co.uk **D:** Fr £22.00–£25.00 **S:** Fr £25.00–£30.00 **Beds:** 2F 1T 1D **Baths:** 4 En (4) **cc**

Sunnybank Guest House, *Clifton Road, Matlock Bath, Matlock, Derbyshire, DE4 3PW.* Spacious Victorian residence offering peace and comfort in wonderful location. **Open:** All year (not Xmas) **01629 584621** Mr & Mrs Ward *sunward@lineone.net* **D:** Fr £20.00–£33.00 **S:** Fr £20.00–£30.00 **Beds:** 1F 2D 1T 1S **Baths:** 4 En 1 Pr

Old Museum Guest House, *170-172 South Parade, Matlock Bath, Matlock, Derbyshire, DE4 3NR.* Friendly family-run guest house. Ensuite double rooms with four-poster beds. **Open:** All year (not Xmas) **01629 57783 (also fax)** Mr & Mrs Bailey *lindsayandstewartbailey@tinyworld.co.uk* **D:** Fr £15.00 **S:** Fr £20.00 **Beds:** 1F 2D **Baths:** 3 En

Mercaston

SK2643

Mercaston Hall, *Mercaston, Ashbourne, Derbyshire, DE6 3BL.* A warm welcome in comfortable historic farmhouse set in peaceful attractive countryside. **Open:** All year (not Xmas) **Grades:** AA 4 Diamonds **01335 360263** Mrs Haddon **Fax: 01335 361399** *Mercastonhall@btinternet.com* **D:** Fr £22.00–£24.00 **S:** Fr £28.00–£30.00 **Beds:** 2D 1T **Baths:** 2 En 1 Pr (8) (6)

Mickleover

SK3033

Bonehill Farm, *Etwall Road, Mickleover, Derby, DE3 5DN.* Comfortable Georgian farmhouse in countryside, 3 miles from centre of Derby. **Open:** All year **Grades:** ETC 3 Diamond **01332 513553** Mrs Dicken *bonehillfarm@hotmail.com* **D:** Fr £20.00–£25.00 **S:** Fr £20.00–£25.00 **Beds:** 1F 1D 1T **Baths:** 2 En 2 Sh (6)

Middleton by Youlgreave

SK1963

Castle Farm, *Middleton by Youlgreave, Bakewell, Derbyshire, DE45 1LS.* Quiet, beautiful Peak District village. Excellent farmhouse breakfast. Warm welcome. **Open:** All year (not Xmas/New Year) **Grades:** ETC 4 Diamond **01629 636746** Mrs Butterworth **D:** Fr £21.00 **S:** Fr £35.00 **Beds:** 1F 1D **Baths:** 2 En (6)

Millthorpe

SK3176

Carpenter House, *Millthorpe, Holmesfield, Dronfield, S18 7WH.* Ideal for Peak District and town alike. Local cricket within the grounds. **Open:** All year **0114 289 0307 Fax: 0114 289 0551** *paddy@mcghee44.freeserve.co.uk* **D:** Fr £22.50 **S:** Fr £30.00 **Beds:** 1F 1D **Baths:** 1 En 1 Pr (20)

Monyash

SK1566

Sheldon House, *Chapel Street, Monyash, Bakewell, Derbyshire, DE45 1JJ.* Recently renovated Grade II Listed house - a warm welcome awaits you. **Open:** All year (not Xmas) **01629 813067 (also fax)** Mr & Mrs Tyler *sheldonhouse@lineone.net* **D:** Fr £20.00–£22.00 **S:** Fr £30.00–£32.00 **Beds:** 3D **Baths:** 3 En (10) (2)

Rowson Farm, *Monyash, Bakewell, Derbyshire, DE45 1JH.* Clean and comfortable accommodation. Delicious Aga-cooked breakfasts are served daily. **Open:** All year **01629 813521** Mr Mycock *gm@rowson99.freeserve.co.uk* **D:** Fr £20.00–£25.00 **S:** Fr £15.00–£25.00 **Beds:** 5D/T **Baths:** 5 En (10)

Morley

SK3940

Alambie, *189 Main Road, Morley, Ilkeston, Derbyshire, DE7 6DG.* Warm welcome. Good food. Comfy beds. Spotlessly clean. Ensuite rooms. **Open:** All year **01332 780349 (also fax)** Mrs Green-Armytage *alambie@beeb.net* www.alambieguesthouse.co.uk **D:** Fr £20.00–£25.00 **Beds:** 1F 2D 1T **Baths:** 4 En (5)

North Wingfield

SK4165

South View, *95 Church Lane, North Wingfield, Chesterfield, Derbyshire, S42 5HR.* Peaceful farmhouse, 3 miles from M1/j29; easy to find. **Open:** All year **Grades:** ETC 3 Diamond
01246 850091 Mrs Hopkinson **D:** Fr £18.00–£30.00 **S:** Fr £18.00 **Beds:** 1D 1T 1S **Baths:** 1 Sh (4)

Over Haddon

SK2066

Mandale House, *Haddon Grove, Over Haddon, Bakewell, Derbyshire, DE45 1JF.* Peaceful farmhouse near Lathkilldale. Good breakfasts, packed lunches available. **Open:** Feb to Nov
01629 812416 Mrs Finney *julia.finney@virgin.net* www.mandalehouse.co.uk **D:** Fr £20.00–£25.00 **S:** Fr £25.00–£30.00 **Beds:** 2D 1T **Baths:** 3 En (5) (4)

Padfield

SK0296

The Peels Arms, *Temple Street, Padfield, Hyde, Cheshire, SK14 7ET.* Country inn, oak beams, log fires, real ale, fine foods. Manchester/Sheffield 40 minutes. **Open:** All year
01457 852719 Mrs Murray **Fax: 01457 850536 D:** Fr £20.00–£25.00 **S:** Fr £25.00 **Beds:** 3D 2T **Baths:** 3 En 1 Sh (20) **cc**

Parwich

SK1854 *The Sycamore, Old Gate*

Flaxdale House, *Parwich, Ashbourne, Derbyshire, DE6 1QA.* Delightful Georgian farmhouse in centre of attractive, unspoilt village of Parwich. Ideally placed for Dovedale, Tissington and High Peak Trails, Carsington Water, Arbor Low, Minninglow and Roystone Grange and an abundance of public footpaths across glorious open countryside. **Open:** All year
01335 390252 & 07740 626804 (M) Mr & Mrs Radcliffe **Fax: 01335 390644** *b&b@flaxdale.demon.co.uk* www.flaxdale.demon.co.uk **D:** Fr £25.00 **S:** Fr £30.00 **Beds:** 1T 1D **Baths:** 2 En (3)

Peak Forest

SK1179 *The Devonshire Arms*

Dam Dale Farm, *Peak Forest, Buxton, Derbyshire, SK17 8EF.* Working farm, homely, comfortable atmosphere, wonderful views, hearty breakfast, secure parking. **Open:** All year (not Xmas/New Year)
01298 24104 Mrs Fletcher **D:** Fr £20.00–£21.00 **S:** Fr £25.00 **Beds:** 1T 1D **Baths:** 2 Sh (10) (4)

B&B owners may vary rates – be sure to check when booking

Pentrich

SK3952

Coney Grey Farm, *Chesterfield Road, Pentrich, Ripley, Derbyshire, DE5 3RF.* Beautiful farmhouse with panoramic views. Ripley, Alfreton and Crich nearby. **Open:** All year (not Xmas/New Year)
01773 833179 D: Fr £14.00–£15.00 **S:** Fr £15.00 **Beds:** 1T 1D **Baths:** 1 Sh (6) (4)

Riddings

SK4252

1 Peveril Drive, *Riddings, Alfreton, Derbyshire, DE55 4AP.* Self-contained bungalow accommodation with private bathroom, lounge and parking. **Open:** All year
01773 607712 Mrs Brown **D:** Fr £15.00 **S:** Fr £20.00 **Beds:** 1D **Baths:** 1 Pr (3)

Rowland

SK2172

Rowland Cottage, *Rowland, Great Longstone, Bakewell, Derbyshire, DE45 1NR.* Hamlet C17th cottage, near Chatsworth, traffic free, quiet, relaxing, comfortable. **Open:** All year
01629 640365 (also fax) Mrs Scott *jgarde7@aol.com* **D:** Fr £17.50–£22.50 **S:** Fr £20.00–£22.50 **Beds:** 1F 1T **Baths:** 1 Pr 1 Sh (3)

Shatton

SK1982

The White House, *Shatton, Bamford, Hope Valley, S33 0BG.* Friendly, comfortable, private country house, lovely views, close to amenities. **Open:** All year (not Xmas) **Grades:** AA 3 Diamond
01433 651487 (also fax) Mrs Middleton **D:** Fr £18.00–£22.00 **S:** Fr £20.00–£25.00 **Beds:** 1D 1T 2S **Baths:** 2 Sh (4)

Shirland

SK4058

Park Lane Farm, *Park Lane, Shirland, Alfreton, Derbyshire, DE55 6AX.* Early C18th farmhouse, situated on the borders of the Peak National Park. **Open:** All year
01773 831880 Mrs Davis **D:** Fr £22.50–£25.00 **S:** Fr £25.00 **Beds:** 2F 2D 2T (8)

Shirley

SK2141

Shirley Hall Farm, *Shirley, Brailsford, Ashbourne, Derbyshire, DE6 3AS.* Few minutes walk from Shirley Village. Superb breakfasts with home-made bread & preserves. **Open:** All year
01335 360346 (also fax) Mrs Foster *sylviafoster@shirleyhallfarm.com* www.shirleyhallfarm.com **D:** Fr £21.00–£25.00 **S:** Fr £23.00–£27.00 **Beds:** 1F 1T 1D **Baths:** 2 En 1 Pr (6) (6)

Stanton by Bridge

SK3727

Ivy House Farm, *Stanton by Bridge, Derby, DE73 1HT.* **Open:** Mar to Oct **Grades:** ETC 4 Diamond, Silver
01332 863152 Mrs Kidd *mary@guesthouse.fsbusiness.co.uk* www.ivy-house-farm.com **D:** Fr £25.00–£45.00 **S:** Fr £25.00 **Beds:** 4D 2T **Baths:** 6 En (9) 3
These purpose-built B&B chalets are in this small quiet village, but close to lots of interesting things - Donington Park Racing, Calke Abbey, Alton Towers, Twycross Zoo, Swadlincote ski slopes, the National Forest.

Taddington

SK1470

Ade House, *Taddington, Buxton, Derbyshire, SK17 9TY.* Find peace, home-baking, organic produce, good walks & a warm welcome. **Open:** All year (not Xmas)
01298 85203 Mrs Elkington **D:** Fr £20.00 **S:** Fr £20.00 **Beds:** 1F 1T 3S **Baths:** 2 Sh (4)

Thorpe

SK1550 *Coach & Horses*

The Old Orchard, *Thorpe, Ashbourne, Derbyshire, DE6 2AW.* Quietly situated limestone home with colourful gardens. Ample car parking. **Open:** Mar to Nov
01335 350410 (also fax) Mrs Challinor **D:** Fr £20.00–£25.00 **S:** Fr £25.00–£30.00 **Beds:** 2D 2S **Baths:** 2 En 1 Sh (10)

Jasmine Cottage, *Thorpe, Ashbourne, Derbyshire, DE6 2AW.* Pretty stone cottage near Dovedale. Warm, peaceful, comfortable. Excellent food. **Open:** All year
01335 350465 Mrs Round **D:** Fr £20.00–£25.00 **S:** Fr £25.00–£35.00 **Beds:** 1D 1T (4)

National Grid References given are for villages, towns and cities – not for individual houses

BEDROOMS
D = Double
T = Twin
S = Single
F = Family

Tibshelf

SK4360

Rosvern House, *High Street, Tibshelf, Alfreton, Derbyshire, DE55 6AX.* Friendly, homely atmosphere. Comfortable rooms, convenient for business travellers/tourists. **Open:** All year
01773 874800 Mrs Byard *byard.tibshelf@lineone.net* **D:** Fr £16.00–£18.00 **S:** Fr £17.00–£18.00 **Beds:** 1F 1D (2)

Tideswell

SK1575

Poppies, *Bank Square, Tideswell, Buxton, Derbyshire, SK17 8LA.* Comfortable accommodation. Ideally located for Peak District activities and attractions. **Open:** All year (not Xmas/New Year) **Grades:** AA 3 Diamond
01298 871083 Mrs Pinnegar *poptidza@dialstart.net* **D:** Fr £18.00–£22.50 **S:** Fr £18.00–£22.50 **Beds:** 1F 1T 1D **Baths:** 1 En **cc**

Uppertown

SK3264

Old School Farm, *Uppertown, Ashover, Chesterfield, Derbyshire, S45 0JF.* Spacious, comfortable, working farm, home from home, peaceful and friendly. **Open:** Easter to Oct
01246 590813 Mrs Wooton **D:** Fr £22.00 **S:** Fr £22.00 **Beds:** 2F 1D 1T 1S **Baths:** 3 En 1 Pr 1 Sh (6)

Wessington

SK3757 *Horse & Jockey, Plough Inn*

Oaktree Farm, *Matlock Road, Oakerthorpe, Wessington, Alfreton, Derbyshire, DE55 7NA.* Modern stone farmhouse. Coarse fishing free to residents. Sky TV. **Open:** All year (not Xmas/New Year)
01773 832957 Mrs Prince *oaktree_farm@talk21.com* **D:** Fr £21.00–£25.00 **S:** Fr £23.00–£27.00 **Beds:** 2D 1T **Baths:** 3 En (10)

Crich Lane Farm, *Moorwood Moor Lane, Wessington, Alfreton, Derbyshire, DE55 6DU.* C17th farmhouse. Peaceful surroundings, friendly atmosphere. **Open:** All year (not Xmas)
01773 835186 & 07775 881423 (M) Mrs Green **D:** Fr £20.00–£25.00 **S:** Fr £20.00–£25.00 **Beds:** 2F 3D 2T 1S **Baths:** 5 En 1 Pr 1 Sh (8)

Whatstandwell

SK3354 *Holmesford Cottage, White Lion, Derwent Hotel*

Meerbrook Farm, *Wirksworth Road, Whatstandwell, Matlock, Derbyshire, DE4 5HU.* Lovely old stone farmhouse set in the scenic Derbyshire Dales. **Open:** All year (not Xmas/New Year)
01629 824180 & 07713 769074 (M) Mrs Johnson *jackie.johnson@tinyworld.co.uk* **D:** Fr £18.50 **S:** Fr £20.00 **Beds:** 1F 1T **Baths:** 1 Sh (4)

Riverdale Guest House, *Middle Lane, Whatstandwell, Matlock, Derbyshire, DE4 5EG.* Enjoy panoramic views of Derwent Valley from our cul-de-sac house. **Open:** All year
01773 853905 (also fax) Mrs Durbridge **D:** Fr £21.00–£26.00 **S:** Fr £26.00 **Beds:** 1T 2D **Baths:** 1 Pr (5) (4)

Youlgreave

SK2164 *Bull's Head, George Hotel, Farmyard Inn*

Fairview, *Bradford Road, Youlgreave, Bakewell, Derbyshire, DE45 1WG.* Small house with stunning views. Relaxed, friendly atmosphere. **Open:** All year
01629 636043 Mrs Bartlett **D:** Fr £16.50 **S:** Fr £18.00 **Beds:** 1F 1T 1D **Baths:** 1 Sh (4) (1)

Bulls Head Hotel, *Fountain Square, Church Street, Youlgreave, Bakewell, Derbyshire, DE45 1UR.* **Open:** All year
01629 636307 Mrs Atkinson *atkinsonm969@aol.com* **D:** Fr £15.00–£20.00 **S:** Fr £20.00 **Beds:** 2F 2T 3D **Baths:** 1 En 1 Sh (5) **cc**
A Grade II Listed building with lots of charm and a friendly welcome. Lying between two beautiful Dales, the Lathkill and Bradford. Great area for walking and touring the closeby Chatsworth House, Haddon Hall and market towns of Bakewell, Buxton, Chesterfield.

The Old Bakery, *Church Street, Youlgreave, Bakewell, Derbyshire, DE45 1UR.* Two bedroom guest wing or tasteful barn conversion for two. **Open:** All year
01629 636887 Ms Croasdell *croasdell@oldbakeryyoulgrave.freeserve.co.uk* www.cressbrook.co.uk/youlgve/oldbakery **D:** Fr £18.00–£27.00 **S:** Fr £24.00–£35.00 **Beds:** 1D 2T **Baths:** 1 En 1 Sh (2)

Bankside Cottage, *Youlgreave, Bakewell, Derbyshire, DE45 1WD.* Large stone cottage, unique off-road position, terrace garden overlooks secluded Bradford Dale. **Open:** All year
01629 636689 Mr Blackburn **D:** Fr £16.50 **S:** Fr £16.50 **Beds:** 1D 1T **Baths:** 1 Sh

Devon

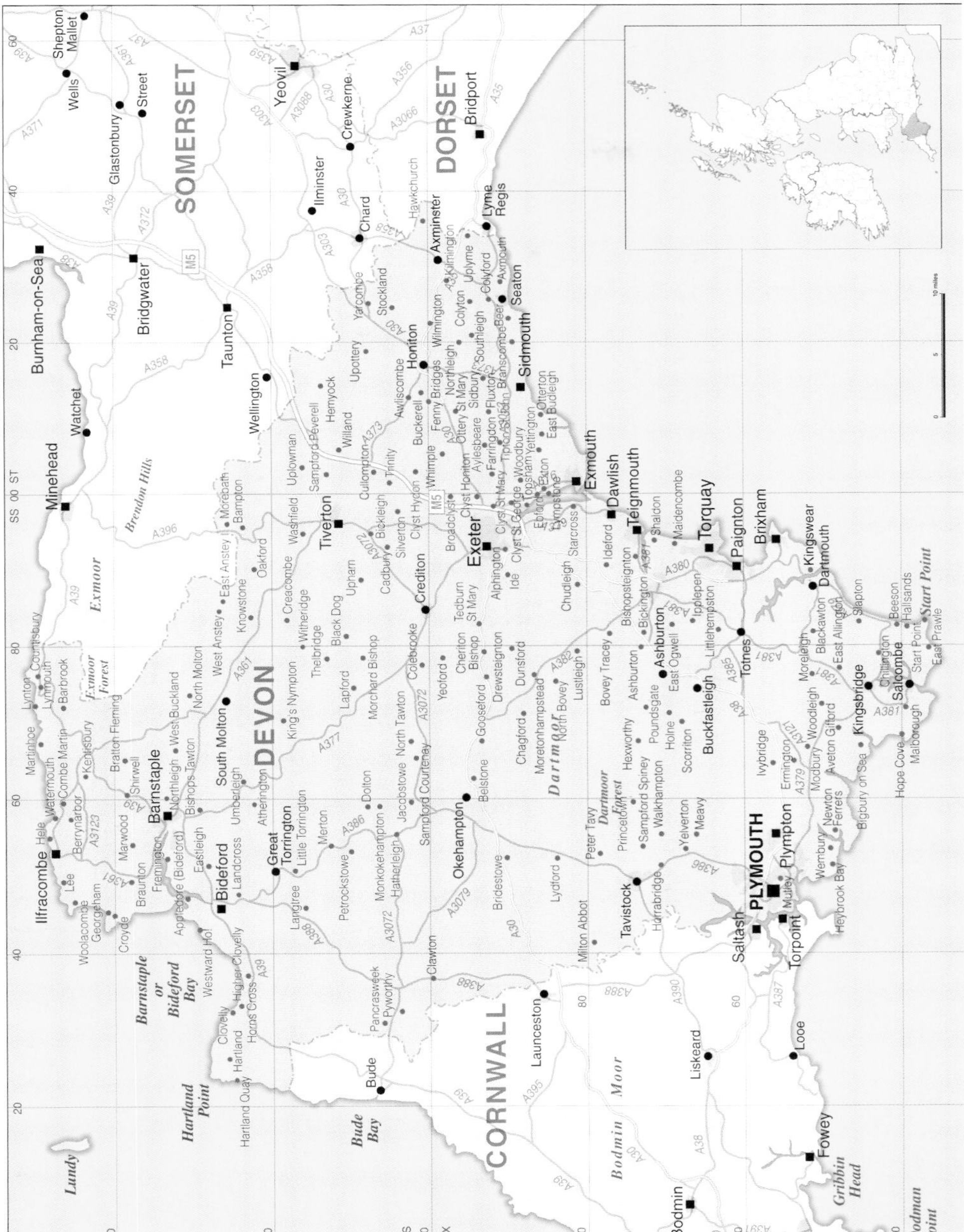

SOMERSET
DORSET
DEVON
CORNWALL
Exmoor
Dartmoor
Bodmin Moor
Brendon Hills
Lundy
Hartland Point
Barnstaple or Bideford Bay
Bude Bay
Gribbin Head
Dodman Point
Start Point
Ilfracombe
Minehead
Watchet
Burnham-on-Sea
Bridgwater
Taunton
Wellington
Glastonbury
Street
Wells
Shepton Mallet
Yeovil
Crewkerne
Ilminster
Chard
Bridport
Lyme Regis
Axminster
Seaton
Sidmouth
Honiton
Exmouth
Dawlish
Teignmouth
Torquay
Paignton
Brixham
Dartmouth
Kingswear
Totnes
Salcombe
Kingsbridge
Exeter
Tiverton
Crediton
Okehampton
Barnstaple
South Molton
Bideford
Great Torrington
Tavistock
PLYMOUTH
Plympton
Saltash
Torpoint
Ashburton
Buckfastleigh
Launceston
Liskeard
Looe
Fowey
Bodmin
Bude

BEDROOMS
D = Double
T = Twin
S = Single
F = Family

Alphington

SX9189

The Old Mill, *Mill Lane, Alphington, Exeter, Devon, EX2 8SG.* Historical premises in quiet area. Full farm breakfast. Recommended for 28 years. **Open:** All year **01392 259977** Mrs Marchant **D:** Fr £13.00–£15.00 **S:** Fr £13.00–£15.00 **Beds:** 2F 1D 1T 1S **Baths:** 1 Pr 1 Sh (8)

Appledore (Bideford)

SS4630

The Seagate Hotel, *The Quay, Appledore, Bideford, Devon, EX39 1QS.* C17th riverside inn. Quaint fishing village on Torridge Estuary. **Open:** All year **01237 472589 (also fax)** Mr & Mrs Gent **D:** Fr £25.00–£35.00 **S:** Fr £29.00–£35.00 **Beds:** 1F 5D 1T **Baths:** 7 Pr (10) cc

Ashburton

SX7570

Sladesdown Farm, *Landscove, Ashburton, Newton Abbot, Devon, TQ13 7ND.* Warm welcome, countryside views, farmhouse breakfast. Sea and moors nearby. **Open:** All year **Grades:** ETC 4 Diamond, Silver **01364 653973 (also fax)** *sue@sladesdownfarm.co.uk* www.sladesdownfarm.co.uk **D:** Fr £22.50–£25.00 **S:** Fr £25.00–£30.00 **Beds:** 1F 2D **Baths:** 2 En 1 Pr (6)

Gages Mill Farmhouse, *Buckfastleigh Road, Ashburton, Newton Abbot, Devon, TQ13 7JW.* C14th former wool mill, edge of Dartmoor. Award-winning food. **Open:** Mar to Nov **Grades:** ETC 4 Diamond, Silver, AA 4 Diamond **01364 652391 (also fax)** Mr & Mrs Moore *moore@gagesmill.co.uk* www.gagesmill.co.uk **D:** Fr £21.00–£30.00 **S:** Fr £21.00–£30.00 **Beds:** 1T 5D 1S **Baths:** 7 Pr (12) (9)

Rosary Mount House, *Ashburton, Newton Abbot, Devon, TQ13 7JL.* A luxuriously furnished country house (circa 1857) standing in its own landscaped gardens. **Open:** All year (not Xmas/New Year) **01364 653900** Mr Stone **Fax: 01364 653821** *annette@rosarymount.co.uk* www.roserymount.co.uk **D:** Fr £17.50–£20.00 **S:** Fr £25.00 **Beds:** 2D 1T **Baths:** 2 Sh (8) (6)

Atherington

SS5922

The Village Shop and Tea Rooms, *The Square, Atherington, Umberleigh, Devon, EX37 9HY.* C17th building in pretty North Devon village. Friendly comfortable atmosphere. **Open:** All year (not Xmas/New Year) **01769 560248** Mr & Mrs Hart **D:** Fr £20.00 **S:** Fr £20.00 **Beds:** 1T 1D **Baths:** 1 Sh

Aveton Gifford

SX6947

Marsh Mills, *Aveton Gifford, Kingsbridge, Devon, TQ7 4JW.* Mill house, pond, stream, gardens, orchard. Small farm, friendly animals. **Open:** All year (not Xmas/New Year) **01548 550549 (also fax)** Mrs Newsham *newsham@marshmills.co.uk* www.marshmills.co.uk **D:** Fr £22.00–£24.00 **S:** Fr £20.00–£22.00 **Beds:** 2T 2D 1S **Baths:** 2 En 1 Sh 1 Pr (6)

Awliscombe

ST1301

Threshays, *Awliscombe, Honiton, Devon, EX14 3QB.* Warm, friendly, delightful views. Ideal for exploring glorious East Devon. **Open:** All year **Grades:** AA 3 Diamond **01404 43551 & 07811 675800 (M)** Mrs Gillingham **Fax: 01404 43551** *threshays@tesco.net* **D:** Fr £18.00 **S:** Fr £18.00 **Beds:** 1F 1D **Baths:** 1 Sh (6)

Ridgeway Farm, *Awliscombe, Honiton, Devon, EX14 3PY.* C18th farmhouse, tucked away with country views, three miles North of Honiton. Tasteful decor and renovations have brought the accommodation up to a very high standard which is spotlessly clean. A superb English breakfast and a warm welcome await you. **Open:** All year (not Xmas/New Year) **01404 841331** Mrs Chamberlain *jessica@ridgewayfarm.co.uk* www.smoothhound.co.uk/hotels/ridgewayfarm.html **D:** Fr £20.00–£25.00 **S:** Fr £22.00–£25.00 **Beds:** 1T 2D **Baths:** 2 En 1 Pr (5) (3)

Wessington Farm, *Awliscombe, Honiton, Devon, EX14 3NU.* Elegant late-Victorian stone farmhouse in Area of Outstanding Natural Beauty. **Open:** All year **01404 42280 & 07989 300392 (M)** Mrs Summers **Fax: 01404 45271** *bandb@eastdevon.com* www.eastdevon.com/bedandbreakfast **D:** Fr £20.00–£25.00 **S:** Fr £20.00–£40.00 **Beds:** 1D 2T **Baths:** 2 En 1 Pr (10) cc

Birds Farm, *Awliscombe, Honiton, Devon, EX14 0PU.* Comfortable C16th beamed farmhouse. Near coast and moors. Lovely countryside. **Open:** Mar to Oct **01404 841620** Mrs Manley **D:** Fr £16.00–£17.00 **S:** Fr £16.00–£17.00 **Beds:** 2D **Baths:** 1 Sh (4)

Axminster

SY2998

Shamwari, *Musbury Road, Abbey Gate, Axminster, Devon, EX13 8TT.* **Open:** All year **Grades:** AA 4 Diamond **01297 32838 Fax: 01297 34465** *shamwariguesthouse@hotmail.com* **D:** Fr £22.00–£24.00 **S:** Fr £22.00–£30.00 **Beds:** 1T 1D 1S **Baths:** 3 En
Pat's award-winning hospitality, stylish, comfortable accommodation, breakfasts 'to leap out of bed for', 3 acres of gardens & wild flower meadow and panoramic views across Devon's beautiful Axe Valley will make it hard to leave this unique B&B.

Mount House, *Lyme Road, Axminster, Devon, EX13 5BL.* Large Regency family house. Warm welcome, good food, lovely countryside. **Open:** All year **01297 34630** Mrs Morrison **D:** Fr £17.00–£19.00 **S:** Fr £17.00–£20.00 **Beds:** 2F 1D **Baths:** 2 En 1 Sh

Millbrook Farmhouse, *Chard Road, Axminster, Devon, EX13 5EG.* Millbrook Farmhouse is a Grade II Listed building in rural surroundings. **Open:** All year (not Xmas) **01297 35351** Ms Gay **Fax: 01297 35739 D:** Fr £20.00 **S:** Fr £25.00 **Beds:** 1D 1T **Baths:** 1 En 1 Pr (3)

Axmouth

SY2591 *Ship Inn, Harbour Inn*

Stepps House, *Axmouth, Seaton, Devon, EX12 4AR.* Thatched medieval 'hall' house - star listed. Beautiful village on Axe Estuary. **Open:** Easter to Oct **01297 20679 (also fax)** Mrs Trezise **D:** Fr £20.00–£25.00 **S:** Fr £25.00–£30.00 **Beds:** 1T 1D **Baths:** 1 Sh (2)

Aylesbeare

SY0392

Livermore Farm, *Aylesbeare, Exeter, Devon, EX5 2DH.* Quality accommodation in peaceful setting. Stunning views. Close moors/beaches. **Open:** All year (not Xmas/New Year) **01395 232351 (also fax) D:** Fr £25.00 **S:** Fr £32.00–£34.00 **Beds:** 1T 2D **Baths:** 3 En (3) (6)

Bampton

SS9522

Manor Mill House, *Bampton, Devon, EX16 9LP.* Welcoming C17th home in historic Bampton. Ideal base, close to Exmoor. **Open:** All year
01398 332211 Mrs Ayres **Fax: 01398 332009** *stay@manormill.demon.co.uk* www.manormill.demon.co.uk **D:** Fr £21.00–£24.00 **Beds:** 2D 1T **Baths:** 3 En (20)

Barbrook

SS7147 *Beggars Roost Inn*

Manor Hotel, *Barbrook, Lynton, Devon, EX35 9BP.* A beautiful 300 year old manor house set in magnificent countryside offering luxury accommodation. Its own medieval-style function room and C17th Inn serving traditional home-cooked food, real ales, open fire and oak beams makes it a special place. **Open:** All year
01598 752404 Fax: 01598 753636 *Beggars.Roost.Inn@tinyworld.co.uk* www.smoothhound.co.uk/hotels/manorho1.html **D:** Fr £25.00–£30.00 **S:** Fr £39.00 **Beds:** 2F 5D **Baths:** 7 En (60) cc

Barnstaple

SS5633

Mount Sandford, *Landkey Road, Barnstaple, Devon, EX32 0HL.* Georgian house set in beautiful gardens, easy reach of all resorts. **Open:** All year (not Xmas/New Year)
01271 342354 (also fax) S White **D:** Fr £20.00–£25.00 **S:** Fr £22.50–£25.00 **Beds:** 1F 1T 1D **Baths:** 3 En (3)

Beer

SY2289

Pamber House, *Clapps Lane, Beer, Seaton, Devon, EX12 3HD.* **Open:** All year **01297 20722 (also fax)** Mrs Cummins *pamber-beer-dgr-@amserve.net* **D:** Fr £21.00–£24.00 **S:** Fr £28.00–£30.00 **Beds:** 3D **Baths:** 3 Pr (7) (3)
Set in idyllic fishing village. Quiet position, 2 minutes walk from village and beach. Stunning views, food cooked to order. Winter rates, ideal base.

Garlands, *Stovar Long Lane, Beer, Seaton, Devon, EX12 3EA.* Edwardian character house in an acre of ground - superb views sea and Devon countryside. **Open:** All year (not Xmas)
01297 20958 Ms Harding **Fax: 01297 23869** *nigelharding1@compuserve.com* **D:** Fr £20.00–£25.00 **S:** Fr £32.00–£35.00 **Beds:** 2F 2D 1T 1S **Baths:** 6 En (10) cc

Bay View Guest House, *Fore Street, Beer, Seaton, Devon, EX12 3EE.* Seafront location, coastal views, large comfortable rooms and great breakfasts! **Open:** Easter to Nov
01297 20489 Mr & Mrs Oswald **D:** Fr £15.50 **S:** Fr £15.50 **Beds:** 1F 1T 4D 2S **Baths:** 3 En 1 Pr 4 Sh

Beeson

SX8140

Marybank House, *Beeson, Kingsbridge, Devon, TQ7 2HW.* Beautifully located Victorian country house. Have delicious breakfast whilst enjoying sea views. 1 mile beach, coastal walks. **Open:** All year
01548 580531 Mrs Honeywill *marybankhouse@hotmail.com* www.marybankhouse.com **D:** Fr £22.50–£26.00 **S:** Fr £30.00–£34.00 **Beds:** 1T 2D **Baths:** 2 En 1 Pr

Belstone

SX6293

Moorlands House, *Belstone, Okehampton, Devon, EX20 1QZ.* Beautifully situated; edge of unspoilt Dartmoor village with superb moorland views. **Open:** All year
01837 840549 Mr Weaver **D:** Fr £18.00–£20.00 **S:** Fr £20.00–£25.00 **Beds:** 2T 2D **Baths:** 1 En 1 Pr 1 Sh (6)

Berrynarbor

SS5646

Tower Cottage, *Berrynarbor, Ilfracombe, Devon, EX34 9SE.* Charming cottage with beautiful garden in 'Best Kept Village Berrynarbor'. **Open:** All year (not Xmas/New Year)
01271 883408 *tombartlettbooks@berrynarbor.fsnet.co.uk* **D:** Fr £18.00–£22.00 **S:** Fr £25.00 **Beds:** 1F 1D **Baths:** 2 En

Bickington (Newton Abbot)

SX7972

Rentor, *Bickington, Newton Abbot, TQ12 6JW.* Refurbished former farmhouse, country views, between Dartmoor/Torbay. Brochure available. **Open:** Feb to Nov
01626 821213 Mrs Warren *rentor.bnb@talk21.com* **D:** Fr £17.50–£20.00 **S:** Fr £20.00–£22.00 **Beds:** 1D 1T **Baths:** 2 En (3)

Bickleigh (Tiverton)

SS9407

Willow Grove House, *The Orchard, Bickleigh, Tiverton, Devon, EX16 8RD.* Situated in beautiful garden, walking distance to thatched restaurants on river. **Open:** All year
01884 855263 D M Lock *mjhowes@bickleigh93freeserve.co.uk* **D:** Fr £20.00–£25.00 **S:** Fr £20.00–£25.00 **Beds:** 1T 1D 1S **Baths:** 2 En 1 Sh (5) (3)

The Old Post Office, *Bickleigh, Tiverton, Devon, EX16 8RH.* Stay somewhere special. Visit Exeter, Dartmoor, Exmoor, coast, beautiful Dunster, Bickleigh Castle. **Open:** All year
01884 855731 Mr Latchem **Fax: 07000 783845** *bickleighpostoffice@asgardltd.co.uk* **D:** Fr £20.00–£25.00 **S:** Fr £20.00 **Beds:** 1D 1T 1S **Baths:** 2 En 1 Pr 1 Sh

Bideford

SS4526

The Mount Hotel, *Northdown Road, Bideford, Devon, EX39 3LP.* **Open:** Jan to Dec
01237 473748 Mr & Mrs Laugharne *andrew@themountbideford.fsnet.co.uk* **D:** Fr £25.00–£27.00 **S:** Fr £27.00–£33.00 **Beds:** 2F 3D 1T 2S **Baths:** 7 En (4) cc
Charming Georgian licensed guest house only 5 minutes' walk to town centre, private lounge for guests' use, all rooms ensuite, attractive garden, car parking for guests. Convenient for touring North Devon coastline, Clovelly, Lundy, Exmoor and Dartmoor. No smoking.

Corner House, *14 The Strand, Bideford, Devon, EX39 2ND.* Family-run, C18th building, clean, comfortable, close to amenities. **Open:** All year
01237 473722 C and S Stone *ccornerhouse@aol.com* **D:** Fr £19.00–£21.00 **S:** Fr £20.00–£25.00 **Beds:** 1F 1D 1S **Baths:** 1 Sh

Bigbury on Sea

SX6544

Folly Foot, *Challaborough, Bigbury On Sea, Kingsbridge, Devon, TQ7 4JB.* 50m sandy beach/ South West Way. Warm welcome, bungalow. **Open:** Feb to Oct
01548 810036 *carolwalsh@freenet.co.uk* www.freenetpages.co.uk/hp/follyfoot **D:** Fr £22.50–£33.00 **S:** Fr £20.00–£25.00 **Beds:** 1F 2D 1S **Baths:** 2 En 1 Sh (6) (6)

Bishops Tawton

SS5630

Overton House, *Codden Hill, Bishops Tawton, Barnstaple, Devon, EX32 0DX.* C15th Devon longhouse, idyllic rural setting, luxury accommodation. **Open:** All year (not Xmas)
01271 342514 Mrs Bater **Fax: 01271 375971** *bater6@aol.com* **D:** Fr £19.00–£29.00 **S:** Fr £24.00–£34.00 **Beds:** 2D 1T **Baths:** 2 En 1 Pr

Bishopsteignton

SX9073

Cockhaven Manor, *Cockhaven Rd, Bishopsteignton, Teignmouth, Devon, TQ14 9RF.* Family-run freehouse for the best of West Country food. **Open:** All year
01626 775252 Fax: 01626 775572 *cockhaven.manor@virgin.net* **D:** Fr £25.00–£30.00 **S:** Fr £30.00–£40.00 **Beds:** 4T 7D 1S **Baths:** 12 En (40) cc

Black Dog

SS8009 *Thelbridge Cross Inn, Black Dog, London Inn, Mount Pleasant*

Lower Brownstone Farm, *Black Dog, Crediton, Devon, EX17 4QE.* Heart of Devon. Art gallery. Large lawn and fields. Painting holidays. **Open:** All year
01363 877256 H Wedlake **D:** Fr £15.00–£19.00 **S:** Fr £15.00–£19.00 **Beds:** 3D **Baths:** 2 Sh (10)

Oaklands, *Black Dog, Crediton, Devon, EX17 4RQ.* Friendly accommodation in peaceful countryside, central for coast and moors. **Open:** All year
01884 860645 Mrs Bradford **Fax: 01884 861030 D:** Fr £18.00–£20.00 **S:** Fr £20.00–£22.00 **Beds:** 1F 1D 1T **Baths:** 2 En 1 Pr (6)

Blackawton

SX8050

Woodside Cottage, *Blackawton, Totnes, Devon, TQ9 7BL.* C18th gamekeeper's lodge in peaceful valley with superb views from all rooms. **Open:** All year (not Xmas/ New Year) **Grades:** ETC 4 Diamond, Silver
01803 712375 T & S Adams **Fax: 01803 712761** *b&b@woodsidedartmouth.co.uk* www.woodsidedartmouth.co.uk **D:** Fr £25.00–£30.00 **S:** Fr £35.00–£60.00 **Beds:** 1T 2D **Baths:** 3 En (4)

Bovey Tracey

SX8178

Whitstone Farm, *Bovey Tracey, TQ13 9NA.* Luxury accommodation, gorgeous views overlooking Dartmoor. Excellent food. Warm welcome. **Open:** All year (not Xmas/ New Year)
01626 832258 Mrs Bunn **Fax: 01626 836494** *kate@reynolds2000.co.uk* **D:** Fr £25.00–£32.50 **S:** Fr £40.00–£45.00 **Beds:** 1T 2D **Baths:** 3 En (10)

Front House Lodge, *East Street, Bovey Tracey, Newton Abbot, Devon, TQ13 9EL.* Delightful C16th house, edge of Dartmoor. Antiques. Atmosphere. Delicious breakfasts. **Open:** All year (not Xmas) **Grades:** AA 5 Diamond
01626 832202 (also fax) Mr & Mrs Campbell *fronthouselodge@aol.com* **D:** Fr £24.00–£27.50 **S:** Fr £27.50–£35.00 **Beds:** 1F 3D 2T (6) cc

Branscombe

SY1988

Masons Arms, *Branscombe, Seaton, Devon, EX12 3DJ.* **Open:** All year **Grades:** AA 2 Star
01297 680300 Mr Inglis **Fax: 01297 680500** *reception@masonsarms.co.uk* www.masonsarms.co.uk **D:** Fr £24.00–£75.00 **S:** Fr £22.00–£125.00 **Beds:** 6T 19D 3S **Baths:** 25 En 3 Pr (45) cc
Enchanting 600-year-old creeper-clad inn - picturesque coastal village. Four-poster beds, antiques, designer furnishings. Good Pub Guide 2002 'Devon Dining Pub of the Year'. Ideal base for walks along the stunning Jurassic Coast or for touring Devon and Dorset.

National Grid References given are for villages, towns and cities – not for individual houses

Hole Mill, *Branscombe, Seaton, Devon, EX12 3BX.* **Open:** All year
01297 680314 Mr Hart www.users.globalnet.co.uk/~branscombe/hole1.htm **D:** Fr £20.00–£23.00 **S:** Fr £29.00–£37.00 **Beds:** 2D 1T **Baths:** 2 Sh (6) (6)
Old converted watermill providing comfortable accommodation in style of yesteryear. Beams, brass beds, inglenook lounge, garden, stream. No rush, no town noises - just peace/relaxation. Featured in 'Which? The Good Bed and Breakfast Guide' and 'Staying Off the Beaten Track'.

Bratton Fleming

SS6437

Haxton Down Farm, *Bratton Fleming, Barnstaple, Devon, EX32 7JL.* Secluded peaceful working farm set between coast and Exmoor. **Open:** Easter to Nov **Grades:** ETC 4 Diamond
01598 710275 Mrs Burge *pat@haxtondown.co.uk* www.haxtondownfarmholidays.co.uk **D:** Fr £18.00–£21.00 **S:** Fr £20.00–£22.00 **Beds:** 1F 1D **Baths:** 2 En (3)

Braunton

SS4936

St Merryn, *Higher Park Road, Braunton, Devon, EX33 2LG.* **Open:** Jan to Dec
01271 813805 Mrs Bradford **Fax: 01271 812097** *ros@st-merryn.co.uk* www.st-merryn.co.uk **D:** Fr £20.00–£22.00 **S:** Fr £20.00–£25.00 **Beds:** 1F 1T 1D **Baths:** 1 En 2 Pr (5)
Beautiful home set in delightful large garden. Many suntraps with seating. Swimming pool, tranquil setting, excellent parking and within easy walking distance of village. Excellent beaches, golf courses, Coastal Path, Marwood Garden and RHS Rosemoor within short drive.

North Cottage, *14 North Street, Braunton, Devon, EX33 1AJ.* Well-situated for local beaches, golf course & South West Coastal Path. **Open:** All year
01271 812703 Mrs Watkins **D:** Fr £18.00 **S:** Fr £18.00 **Beds:** 1T 2D 1S **Baths:** 2 En 1 Sh

Creacombe

SS8219

Creacombe Parsonage, *Parsonage Cross, Creacombe, Rackenford, Tiverton, Devon, EX16 8EL.* C17th farmhouse in open countryside, views of Dartmoor. Ideal spot to rest. **Open:** All year
01884 881441 Mrs Poole **Fax: 01884 881551** *creaky.parson@dial.pipex.com* **D:** Fr £18.00 **S:** Fr £18.00 **Beds:** 1F 2T **Baths:** 1 Sh 1 En cc

Crediton

SS8300

Taw Vale, *2 Crediton, Devon, EX17 3BU.* **Open:** All year **01363 777879 (also fax)** Mrs Whitby **D:** Fr £19.00–£21.00 **S:** Fr £20.00–£23.00 **Beds:** 1F 1D 1T **Baths:** 2 En 1 Pr (3) Listed Georgian-style family home on edge of Crediton. Ideal touring base for Dartmoor, Exmoor and both coasts. Easy access to Exeter and beyond, via bus and train. 6 National Trust properties within 30 minutes. Choice of Aga-cooked breakfasts.

Libbetts Cottage, *Church Street, Crediton, Devon, EX17 2AQ.* A great taste of Devon in lovely olde worlde cottage. **Open:** All year
01363 772709 Mrs Venn www.s-h-systems.co.uk/hotels/libbetts **D:** Fr £24.00 **S:** Fr £30.00 **Beds:** 1D 1T **Baths:** 1 Pr (6) (2)

Creedy Manor, *Long Barn, Crediton, Devon, EX17 4AB.* Victorian farmhouse, picturesque peaceful comfort. Town 0.5 mile. Also self-catering apartments. **Open:** All year
01363 772684 (also fax) Mrs Turner *creedymanor@eclipse.co.uk* **D:** Fr £18.00–£25.00 **S:** Fr £19.50 **Beds:** 1D 1T 1F **Baths:** 3 En (6)

Croyde

SS4439 *Thatched Barn, Billy Budds*

Oamaru, *Down End, Croyde, Braunton, Devon, EX33 1QE.* 400m from top surfing beach and village. Relaxed friendly atmosphere. **Open:** All year
01271 890765 Mr & Mrs Jenkins *philcroyde@hotmail.com* **D:** Fr £17.50–£25.00 **S:** Fr £17.50–£25.00 **Beds:** 1F 1D **Baths:** 1 En 1 Pr (6) cc

Moorsands, *Moor Lane, Croyde Bay, Braunton, Devon, EX33 1NP.* **Open:** All year **Grades:** ETC 3 Diamond
01271 890781 Mr & Mrs Davis www.croyde-bay.com/moorsands.htm **D:** Fr £21.00–£27.00 **S:** Fr £21.00–£32.00 **Beds:** 1F 1T 2D **Baths:** 4 En (6) Originally a large Victorian coast guard station with stunning views, Moorsands offers short walks to beach, village and local facilities. Surf, ride, cycle etc. or simply relax with our comfortable ensuite rooms, guest lounge, beautiful surroundings, warm welcome and superb breakfasts.

Vale Cottage Thatched B&B, *Cross, Croyde, Braunton, Devon, EX33 1PL.* One of the oldest character Devon thatched longhouses, offering quality ensuite. **Open:** All year (not Xmas)
01271 890804 Mrs Adey *mail@valecottage.co.uk* www.valecottage.co.uk **D:** Fr £25.00–£35.00 **S:** Fr £35.00 **Beds:** 3D **Baths:** 3 En (3)

Cullompton

ST0106

Oburnford Farm, *Cullompton, Devon, EX15 1LZ.* Georgian farmhouse. Within easy reach of exploring main Devon attractions. **Open:** All year
01884 32292 Mrs Chumbley **D:** Fr £20.00 **S:** Fr £23.00 **Beds:** 3F 3T 4D 5S **Baths:** 3 En 1 Pr (10)

Dartmouth

SX8751

Woodside Cottage, *Blackawton, Totnes, Devon, TQ9 7BL.* **Open:** All year (not Xmas/New Year) **Grades:** ETC 4 Diamond, Silver
01803 712375 T & S Adams **Fax: 01803 712761** *b&b@woodsidedartmouth.co.uk* www.woodsidedartmouth.co.uk **D:** Fr £25.00–£30.00 **S:** Fr £35.00–£60.00 **Beds:** 1T 2D **Baths:** 3 En (4) C18th gamekeeper's lodge in peaceful valley with superb views from all rooms towards Start Point Light. Short walk to village pubs, Dartmouth and the sea 4 miles. Beautifully furnished rooms, conservatory, fine terrace and lovely gardens.

Chapel House, *29 Clarence Street, Dartmouth, Devon, TQ6 9NW.* An interesting converted chapel, one min from river, gardens & park. **Open:** All year (not Xmas/New Year)
01803 834452 Mr & Mrs Legg www.dartmouth.org.uk/displays/b&b/Chapelhse/chapelhse.htm **D:** Fr £25.00 **S:** Fr £30.00 **Beds:** 2D **Baths:** 2 En (1)

Browns Norton Farm, *Dartmouth, Devon, TQ6 0ND.* Charming C17th farmhouse with sloping ceilings, modern bathroom shower etc. **Open:** All year (not Xmas/New Year)
01803 712321 Mrs Bond **D:** Fr £20.00–£25.00 **S:** Fr £20.00 **Beds:** 1T 1D 1S **Baths:** 1 Sh

Regency House, *30 Newcomen Road, Dartmouth, Devon, TQ6 9BN.* Overlooking the beautiful River Dart and Baynards Cove. **Open:** All year (not Xmas)
01803 832714 Mrs Shalders **D:** Fr £27.50 **S:** Fr £36.00–£52.00 **Beds:** 1F 2D **Baths:** 3 En

The Cedars, *79 Victoria Road, Dartmouth, Devon, TQ6 9RX.* The Cedars, level location, near town centre, friendly welcome. **Open:** All year (not Xmas)
01803 834421 Mrs Greeno **D:** Fr £20.00–£22.00 **S:** Fr £22.00 **Beds:** 2F 1D 2T 1S **Baths:** 1 Sh

Valley House, *46 Victoria Road, Dartmouth, Devon, TQ6 9DZ.* Comfortable, small, friendly guest house. **Open:** Feb to Dec
01803 834045 Mr & Mrs Ellis **D:** Fr £21.00–£25.00 **S:** Fr £25.00–£30.00 **Beds:** 2D 2T **Baths:** 4 En (4)

Sunnybanks, *1 Vicarage Hill, Dartmouth, Devon, TQ6 9EW.* Friendly atmosphere. Excellent breakfasts & just minutes from the River Dart. **Open:** All year
01803 832766 (also fax) *sue@sunnybanks.com* www.sunnybanks.com **D:** Fr £21.00–£25.00 **S:** Fr £20.00–£30.00 **Beds:** 2F 2T 5D 1S **Baths:** 8 En 1 Pr 1 Sh (2)

BEDROOMS
D = Double
T = Twin
S = Single
F = Family

BATHROOMS
En = Ensuite
Pr = Private
Sh = Shared

Greenswood Farm, *Greenswood Lane, Dartmouth, Devon, TQ6 0LY.* **Open:** All year (not Xmas)
01803 712100 Mrs Baron **D:** Fr £25.00–£32.00 **S:** Fr £30.00 **Beds:** 1T 2D **Baths:** 3 En (12) (8)
A C15th Devon longhouse set in its own secluded valley, with large sub-tropical gardens. A haven for wildlife. Only 4 miles to Dartmouth, Start Bay and Slapton Ley nature reserve. 2 miles to Dartmouth golf and country club.

Dawlish

SX9676

Acorn House, *15 Port Road, Dawlish, Devon, EX7 0NY.* High-quality accommodation, panoramic views. Access to Dartmoor/Devon attractions. **Open:** All year (not Xmas/New Year)
01626 867934 Ms Hughes **Fax: 01626 867336** **D:** Fr £23.50–£25.00 **S:** Fr £25.00–£30.00 **Beds:** 1T 1D **Baths:** 2 En (5)

Ocean's Guest House, *9 Marine Parade, Dawlish, Devon, EX7 9DJ.*
Open: Easter to Nov
01626 888139 **D:** Fr £20.00–£30.00 **S:** Fr £30.00–£45.00 **Beds:** 3F 3T 9D **Baths:** 15 En
Seafront location. Some sea views, all ensuite, TV, tea/coffee making facilities, balcony use overlooking sea. Full English breakfast. Rooms on ground floor for people with walking disabilities and ramp for wheelchairs. Non-smoking.

Dolton

SS5712

Robin Cottage, *Church Street, Dolton, Winkleigh, Devon, EX19 8QE.* Modernised cottage situated near church in attractive Devon village, near RHS Rosemoor Garden.
Open: All year
01805 804430 S Newman **D:** Fr £18.00–£20.00 **S:** Fr £18.00–£20.00 **Beds:** 1T 1S **Baths:** 1 En 1 Sh (12)

Drewsteignton

SX7390

The Old Inn Guest House & Restaurant, *The Square, Drewsteignton, Exeter, Devon, EX6 6QR.* **Open:** All year
01647 281276 (also fax) Mr & Mrs Gribble *oldgribb@amserve.com* www.smoothhound.co.uk/hotels/oldinn.html **D:** Fr £22.50–£30.00 **S:** Fr £35.00–£40.00 **Beds:** 1F 1T 2D **Baths:** 2 En 1 Pr 1 Sh (3)
Comfortable former C18th Inn in the village square. One mile south of A30 and from Castle Drogo and Fingle Bridge. Chagford 4 Miles, Okehampton 10 and Exeter 13. Fishing and superb walks. Former member of D.T.A. Renowned breakfasts. Three nights less 10%.

East Fingle Farm, *Drewsteignton, Exeter, Devon, EX6 6NJ.* Devon farm longhouse, beautiful views, friendly farm animals, warm welcome, children half-price. **Open:** All year
01647 281639 Mrs Cordy **D:** Fr £18.00–£21.00 **S:** Fr £18.00–£21.00 **Beds:** 3F 2T 1D **Baths:** 2 En 2 Pr (10)

Puddicombe House, *Drewsteignton, Exeter, Devon, EX6 6RD.* Converted apple store in Georgian house. Beautiful grounds. Dartmoor National Park. **Open:** All year (not Xmas/New Year)
01647 281206 Ms Hodge *judith.hodge@virgin.net* **D:** Fr £25.00 **S:** Fr £30.00 **Beds:** 1D **Baths:** 1 En

BEDROOMS
D = Double
T = Twin
S = Single
F = Family

Dunsford

SX8189

Royal Oak Inn, *Dunsford, Exeter, Devon, EX6 7DA.*
Open: All year
01647 252256 Mrs Arnold *mark@troid.co.uk* www.troid.co.uk **D:** Fr £20.00–£22.50 **S:** Fr £22.50–£27.50 **Beds:** 2F 1T 4D **Baths:** 5 En 2 Sh cc
Victorian Inn, Mark & Judy have been offering B&B for over 7 years. We serve good beer & food seven days a week. Listed in both 'The Good Beer Guide' & 'The Good Pub Guide'. Children & dogs welcome.

Oak Lodge, *The Court, Dunsford, Exeter, Devon, EX6 7DD.* Peacefully situated in picturesque Dartmoor village. Award winning breakfast. High quality accommodation with beautiful views. Ideal touring/walking area. Close to National Trust Properties. Eden Project one hour away. Exeter seven miles. Bargain breaks available. Telephone for brochure.
Open: All year (not Xmas/New Year)
01647 252829 Ms Hodge *shirley.hodge@virgin.net* www.oaklodge-devon.co.uk **D:** Fr £18.00–£24.00 **S:** Fr £25.00–£40.00 **Beds:** 1F 1T 1D **Baths:** 1 En 1 Pr (2)

East Allington

SX7648

The Fortescue Arms, *East Allington, Totnes, Devon, TQ9 7RA.* Delightful Devon inn with superb restaurant - CAMRA recommended real ales. **Open:** All year (not Xmas/New Year)
01548 521215 Mr Gledhill *steve_trish@talk21.com* www.webmachine.co.uk/fortescue/ **D:** Fr £17.50–£22.50 **S:** Fr £22.50–£30.00 **Beds:** 3D 1T **Baths:** 2 En 2 Sh (10) cc

Tor Cottage, *The Mounts, East Allington, Totnes, Devon, TQ9 7QJ.* Warm welcome. Beautiful country views, central location, superb breakfasts. **Open:** All year
01548 521316 (also fax) Mr Larner *john@torcottage.freeserve.co.uk* www.torcottage.freeserve.co.uk **D:** Fr £14.00–£19.00 **S:** Fr £14.00–£19.00 **Beds:** 2F **Baths:** 2 En 1 Pr (2) (5)

East Anstey

SS8626

Threadneedle, *East Anstey, Tiverton, Devon, EX16 9JH.* Built in the style of a Devon Longhouse, set in 3 acres, close Dulverton.
Open: All year
01398 341598 Mr & Mrs Webb **D:** Fr £23.00–£25.00 **S:** Fr £23.00–£25.00 **Beds:** 1D 1T **Baths:** 2 En (10)

East Budleigh

SY0684

Wynards Farm, *East Budleigh, Budleigh Salterton, Devon, EX9 7DQ.* Working farm in village centre, two miles from coast. **Open:** All year
01395 443417 (also fax) Mrs Smith *j.h.g.s@btinternet.com* **D:** Fr £18.00–£25.00 **S:** Fr £20.00–£30.00 **Beds:** 1F 1D 1T **Baths:** 1 En 1 Sh (1) (3)

East Ogwell

SX8370

Milton Farm, *East Ogwell, Newton Abbot, Devon, TQ12 6AT.* Bungalow in picturesque village - 7 miles Torbay, golf 3 miles. **Open:** Mar to Nov
01626 354988 **D:** Fr £16.50–£18.00 **S:** Fr £18.00–£20.00 **Beds:** 1T 1D **Baths:** 1 Sh (3)

East Prawle

SX7836

Stures Court, *East Prawle, Kingsbridge, Devon, TQ7 2BY.* C17th thatched cottage with C21st comfort. Highly commended by guests. **Open:** All year
01548 511261 Miss Benson **D:** Fr £18.00–£20.00 **S:** Fr £19.00–£21.00 **Beds:** 2D 2S **Baths:** 1 Sh (7)

Eastleigh

SS4927 *Crab Inn, Ale House*

Pillhead Farm, *Old Barnstaple Road, Bideford, Devon, EX39 4NF.* Extra special breakfasts in delightful, well-located period farmhouse. **Open:** All year
01237 479337 Mr & Mrs Hill *hill@pillheadfarm.fsnet.co.uk* **D:** Fr £17.00–£23.00 **S:** Fr £20.00 **Beds:** 1F 1T 2D **Baths:** 2 En 2 Pr (8)

Ebford

SX9887

Ebford Court, *Ebford, Exeter, Devon, EX3 0RA.* C15th peaceful thatched farmhouse. Close to sea and moors. **Open:** All year (not Xmas)
01392 875353 Mrs Howard **Fax: 01392 876776** *beegeehoward@aol.com* **D:** Fr £19.00 **S:** Fr £19.00 **Beds:** 1D 1T 1S **Baths:** 1 Sh (8) (7)

Little Holt, *Ebford Lane, Ebford, Exeter, Devon, EX3 0QX.* C18th coaching cottage, quiet hamlet, tranquil gardens: roses, honeysuckle, jasmine, pond & woodlands. **Open:** May to Oct
01392 876945 (also fax) Ms Schoenburg **D:** Fr £16.00–£20.00 **S:** Fr £18.00–£22.00 **Beds:** 1D **Baths:** 1 En

Ermington

SX6453 *Rose & Crown*

Waye Farm, *The Grange, Ermington, Ivybridge, Devon, PL21 9NU.* Offering high standard accommodation and a hearty English breakfast. **Open:** Mar to Dec
01752 830427 Mr & Mrs Livermore *andrea@livermore44.fsnet.co.uk* **D:** Fr £20.00–£22.00 **S:** Fr £28.00–£30.00 **Beds:** 1T 1D **Baths:** 2 En (2)

Exeter

SX9192

Raffles Hotel, *11 Blackall Road, Exeter, Devon, EX4 4HD.* Centrally-located Victorian townhouse, beautifully maintained with antique furniture. **Open:** All year
Grades: ETC 4 Diamond
01392 270200 (also fax) *raffleshtl@btinternet.com* www.raffles-exeter.co.uk **D:** Fr £26.00–£28.00 **S:** Fr £34.00–£38.00 **Beds:** 1F 2T 2D 2S **Baths:** 7 En (6) **cc**

St David's Guest House, *89 St David's Hill, Exeter, Devon, EX4 4DW.* Stations and city 10 mins walk. Good selection restaurants nearby. **Open:** All year
01392 434737 (also fax) Mr & Mrs Morris **D:** Fr £15.00–£17.50 **S:** Fr £15.00–£25.00 **Beds:** 1F 2D 2T 1S **Baths:** 4 En 1 Sh (4)

Hotel Maurice, *5 Bystock Terrace, Exeter, Devon, EX4 4HY.* Town house in quiet Georgian square in the heart of the city. **Open:** All year (not Xmas)
01392 213079 Mr Wenley *hotel.maurice@eclipse.co.uk* www.hotelmaurice.eclipse.co.uk **D:** Fr £17.00–£19.00 **S:** Fr £22.00 **Beds:** 1F 3D 2T 2S **Baths:** 8 En (3) (1) **cc**

Crossmead, *Barley Lane, Dunsford Hill, Exeter, Devon, EX4 1TF.* Comfortable bedrooms within beautiful landscaped grounds of attractive Victorian house. **Open:** All year (not Xmas)
01392 273703 Mrs Snow **Fax: 01392 422594** *crossmead@exeter.ac.uk* www.crossmead.com **D:** Fr £18.75–£27.50 **S:** Fr £19.95–£32.50 **Beds:** 33D 15T 39S **Baths:** 52 En 30 Sh **cc**

Marianne Pool Farm, *Clyst St George, Exeter, Devon, EX3 0NZ.* Thatched farmhouse amid peaceful countryside. Close M5 J30, Exeter & coast. **Open:** Mar to Nov
01392 874939 (also fax) Mrs Bragg **D:** Fr £19.00–£22.00 **S:** Fr £19.00–£25.00 **Beds:** 1F 1T **Baths:** 1 En 1 Sh (2)

The Old Mill, *Mill Lane, Alphington, Exeter, Devon, EX2 8SG.* Historical premises in quiet area. Full farm breakfast. Recommended for 28 years. **Open:** All year
01392 259977 Mrs Marchant **D:** Fr £13.00–£15.00 **S:** Fr £13.00–£15.00 **Beds:** 2F 1D 1T 1S **Baths:** 1 Pr 1 Sh (8)

Ebford Court, *Ebford, Exeter, Devon, EX3 0RA.* C15th peaceful thatched farmhouse. Close to sea and moors. **Open:** All year (not Xmas)
01392 875353 Mrs Howard **Fax: 01392 876776** *beegeehoward@aol.com* **D:** Fr £19.00 **S:** Fr £19.00 **Beds:** 1D 1T 1S **Baths:** 1 Sh (8) (7)

The Grange, *Stoke Hill, Exeter, Devon, EX4 7JH.* Country house in private grounds, wooded location overlooking Exeter, surrounding countryside. **Open:** All year
01392 259723 Mr Dudley *dudleythegrange@aol.com* **D:** Fr £18.00–£22.00 **S:** Fr £30.00 **Beds:** 4D **Baths:** 4 En (8)

Drakes Farm House, *Ide, Exeter, Devon, EX2 9RQ.* **Open:** All year
01392 256814 & 01392 495564
Mrs Easterbrook **Fax: 01392 495564** *drakesfarmhouse@hotmail.com* www.drakesfarm.fsnet.co.uk **D:** Fr £20.00–£22.50 **S:** Fr £22.50–£30.00 **Beds:** 1F 2D 1T **Baths:** 2 En 1 Pr 1 Sh (4) **cc**
C15th farmhouse with large garden in quiet village, 2 miles M5/city centre. 3 pubs/restaurants 5 mins walk. Close to National Trust/moors/coasts. Laundry. 2 nights minimum. Ensuite rooms shower/bath. Private parking. Eden Project 1 hr approx.

Wood Barton, *Farringdon, Exeter, Devon, EX5 2HY.* **Open:** All year
01395 233407 J D Bolt **Fax: 01395 277226** *jackie_bolt@hotmail.com* www.smoothhound.co.uk/hotels/woodbar.html **D:** Fr £21.00–£25.00 **S:** Fr £25.00–£30.00 **Beds:** 1F 1T 1D **Baths:** 3 En
Wood Barton is a C17th farmhouse with splendid views over quiet countryside. English breakfast cooked on Aga. Eating place half a mile away. Spacious bedrooms, convenient for Exeter, sandy beaches, Dartmoor. Good access. 3 miles M5 J30. 1.5 miles Westpoint.

Planning a longer stay? Always ask for any special rates

Montgomery House, *144 Fore Street, Exeter, Devon, EX4 3AN.* **Open:** All year
01392 424086 D: Fr £24.00 **S:** Fr £32.00
Beds: 2T 2D **Baths:** 4 En
Very large, well-furnished, quiet rooms in city centre, close cathedral, shops & quay.

Dunmore Hotel, *22 Blackall Road, Exeter, Devon, EX4 4HE.* Close to city centre, coach and railway stations and university. **Open:** All year **Grades:** AA 2 Diamond
01392 431643 (also fax) Mr & Mrs Gilderthorp *dunmorehtl@aol.com* **D:** Fr £19.00–£22.00 **S:** Fr £22.00–£27.00 **Beds:** 3F 2D 1T 2S **Baths:** 5 En 3 Sh **cc**

Exmouth
SY0081

Victoria Guest House, *131 Victoria Road, Exmouth, Devon, EX8 1DR.* **Open:** All year (not Xmas/New Year)
01395 222882 Mrs Woods *st@exmouth.net* www.exmouth.net **D:** Fr £20.00–£26.00 **S:** Fr £30.00–£36.00 **Beds:** 1T 2D **Baths:** 3 En (2) **cc**
Quality accommodation professionally run by ex-hoteliers. Very close to the seafront with direct access to Exmouth Quay. Just a short level walk from the town centre. bus and rail stations. Ideal for birdwatching and Jurassic Coast cruises.

Hope Cottage, *The Strand, Lympstone, Exmouth, Devon, EX8 5JS.* C15th cottage in beautiful village on Exe estuary (Mr & Mrs Clarke). **Open:** All year
01395 268349 Mr Clarke **D:** Fr £18.50 **S:** Fr £18.50 **Beds:** 3D 1T **Baths:** 1 En 1 Sh

The Swallows, *11 Carlton Hill, Exmouth, Devon, EX8 2AJ.* The Swallows Guest House is a late Georgian house tastefully converted and modernised whilst retaining its comfortable and peaceful atmosphere. Situated in attractive residential area close to the seafront and town centre. **Open:** All year
01395 263937 Fax: 01395 271040 *swallows@amserve.net* **D:** Fr £20.00–£25.00 **S:** Fr £30.00–£40.00 **Beds:** 1F 1T 2D **Baths:** 4 En 1 Pr (5) **cc**

Exton
SX9886

Chatfield, *Exmouth Road, Exton, Exeter, Devon, EX3 0PQ.* Edwardian house near Topsham, coast, motorway. Large garden. Comfortable rooms. **Open:** All year (not Xmas/New Year)
01392 874135 *chatfield@exton.freeserve.co.uk*
D: Fr £18.00–£22.00 **S:** Fr £20.00–£25.00
Beds: 1F 1T 2D **Baths:** 2 En 1 Sh (8)

Farringdon
SY0191

Wood Barton, *Farringdon, Exeter, Devon, EX5 2HY.* Wood Barton is a C17th farmhouse with splendid views over quiet countryside. **Open:** All year
01395 233407 J D Bolt **Fax: 01395 277226** *jackie_bolt@hotmail.com* www.smoothhound.co.uk/hotels/woodbar.html **D:** Fr £21.00–£25.00 **S:** Fr £25.00–£30.00 **Beds:** 1F 1T 1D **Baths:** 3 En

Fenny Bridges
SY1198

Little Ash Farm, *Fenny Bridges, Honiton, Devon, EX14 3BL.* **Open:** All year (not Xmas)
01404 850271 Mrs Reid **D:** Fr £16.00–£19.00 **S:** Fr £16.00–£19.00 **Beds:** 1F 1T 1D **Baths:** 1 En 2 Sh (4)
A warm welcome at a comfortable old farmhouse. Set in 3/4 acre peaceful garden with mini golf overlooked by the large conservatory/breakfast room. Close to new A30 and within easy reach of East Devon Coast, Exeter and Dartmoor.

Fluxton
SY0892

Fluxton Farm, *Fluxton, Ottery St Mary, Devon, EX11 1RJ.* Cat lovers' paradise in lovely open countryside. Ideal touring area. **Open:** All year **Grades:** AA 2 Diamond
01404 812818 Mrs Forth **Fax: 01404 814843**
D: Fr £25.00–£27.50 **S:** Fr £25.00–£27.50
Beds: 1F 5T 3D 2S **Baths:** 11 En (8) (15)

Fremington
SS5132

Lower Yelland Farm, *Yelland Road, Fremington, Barnstaple, Devon, EX31 3EN.* North Devon Coast beautifully situated period house on Taw Estuary. **Open:** All year (not Xmas/New Year)
01271 860101 (also fax) Mr Day **D:** Fr £20.00 **S:** Fr £20.00 **Beds:** 1T 2D **Baths:** 3 En (6)

Georgeham
SS4739

Georgeham Village Stores, *Chapel Street, Georgeham, Braunton, Devon, EX33 1JJ.* High-quality accommodation, peaceful countryside setting. Excellent surfing/walking area. **Open:** All year
01271 890534 *grahamkym@aol.com* **D:** Fr £25.00–£30.00 **S:** Fr £30.00–£50.00 **Beds:** 1F 1T 1D **Baths:** 1 En 1 Sh **cc**

Gooseford
SX6791

Fairhaven Farm, *Gooseford, Whiddon Down, Okehampton, Devon, EX20 2QH.* Magnificent views of patchwork fields with rising hills of Dartmoor beyond. **Open:** All year (not Xmas/New Year)
01647 231261 Mrs Scott www.guestbeds.com
D: Fr £20.00–£24.00 **S:** Fr £20.00–£24.00
Beds: 1F 1D **Baths:** 1 En 1 Sh (4)

Hallsands
SX8138

Widget, *Hallsands, Kingsbridge, Devon, TQ7 2EX.* **Open:** All year (not Xmas)
01548 511110 Mrs Wolstenholme **D:** Fr £20.00–£25.00 **S:** Fr £20.00–£25.00 **Beds:** 2D 1T **Baths:** 1 En 1 Pr (4)
A lovely new bungalow 50 yards from the beach and Coastal Path. In a wonderful, peaceful area, ideal for relaxing or exploring the beautiful South Hams. A warm welcome, lovely accommodation and unbeatable breakfast await you.

Hartland
SS2624

West Titchberry Farm, *Hartland Point, Bideford, Devon, EX39 6AU.* Typical Devon longhouse on traditional family-run coastal stock farm. **Open:** All year (not Xmas)
01237 441287 (also fax) Mrs Heard **D:** Fr £18.00–£22.00 **S:** Fr £20.00 **Beds:** 1F 1D 1T **Baths:** 1 En 2 Sh

Greenlake Farm, *Hartland, Bideford, Devon, EX39 6DN.* Warm welcome, old farmhouse on working farm in unspoilt countryside. **Open:** Easter to Nov
01237 441251 Mrs Heard **D:** Fr £16.00–£18.00 **S:** Fr £16.00–£18.00 **Beds:** 1F 1D **Baths:** 2 En

Hartland Quay
SS2224

Hartland Quay Hotel, *Hartland Quay, Hartland, Bideford, Devon, EX39 6DU.* An historic building on South West Coast Path. Fantastic views. **Open:** All year (not Xmas)
01237 441218 Mrs Johns **Fax: 01237 441371** *hartlandquayhotel@supanet.co.uk* www.hartlandquayhotel.com **D:** Fr £25.00–£27.00 **S:** Fr £25.00–£27.00 **Beds:** 5F 4T 6D 2S **Baths:** 12 En 3 Pr 2 Sh (50) **cc**

Hatherleigh

SS5404

Seldon Farm, *Monkokehampton, Winkleigh, Devon, EX19 8RY.* Charming C17th farmhouse in beautiful, tranquil, rural setting. **Open:** Easter to Oct **Grades:** ETC 3 Diamond
01837 810312 Mrs Case www.seldon-farm.co.uk **D:** Fr £20.00 **S:** Fr £23.00 **Beds:** 1T/F 1D **Baths:** 2 En

Pressland Country House Hotel, *Hatherleigh, Okehampton, Devon, EX20 3LW.* Delightful and spacious Victorian house set in 1.5 acres of landscaped garden, with glorious views of Dartmoor and surrounding countryside. The family-run hotel is licensed and there is a large, comfortable lounge, separate bar and a restaurant of growing repute. **Open:** Mar to Dec
01837 810871 Fax: 01837 810303 *accom@presslandhouse.co.uk* www.presslandhouse.co.uk **D:** Fr £25.00–£35.00 **S:** Fr £33.00–£38.00 **Beds:** 2T 3D **Baths:** 4 En 1 Pr (12) (6) cc

Hawkchurch

ST3300

Castle House, *Hawkchurch, Axminster, Devon, EX13 5UA.* Comfortable Grade II Listed house set in 2 acres of beautiful gardens. **Open:** All year (not Xmas/New Year)
01297 678291 Mrs Lewis **D:** Fr £18.00–£20.00 **S:** Fr £18.00–£20.00 **Beds:** 1T 2D **Baths:** 1 En 1 Pr 1 Sh (4)

Hele (Ilfracombe)

SS5347

Moles Farmhouse, *Old Berrynarbor Road, Hele, Ilfracombe, Devon, EX34 9RB.* Beautifully restored former farmhouse, situated in picturesque Hele Valley, near Ilfracombe. **Open:** All year
01271 862099 (also fax) Ms Grindlay *wendy@molesfarmhouse.freeserve.co.uk* www.molesfarmhouse.co.uk **D:** Fr £17.00–£20.00 **Beds:** 1F 1T 1D **Baths:** 2 En 1 Sh (4)

RATES
D = Price range per person sharing in a double or twin room
S = Price range for a single room

Hemyock

ST1313

Orchard Lea, *Culmstock Road, Hemyock, Cullompton, Devon, EX15 3RN.* Perfectly situated in the Blackdown Hills, ideally placed to explore Exmoor and Dartmoor. **Open:** All year (not Xmas/New Year)
01823 680057 (also fax) Mrs Sworn *anne@sworns.co.uk* **D:** Fr £19.00 **S:** Fr £19.00 **Beds:** 2T 1D **Baths:** 2 Sh (3)

Hexworthy

SX6572

The Forest Inn, *Hexworthy, Princetown, Devon, PL20 6SD.* Middle of Dartmoor, ideal for walking, fishing, riding, or just relaxing. **Open:** Feb to Dec
01364 631211 Mr Selwood **Fax: 01364 631515** *forestinn@hotmail.com* **D:** Fr £20.00–£29.50 **S:** Fr £25.00–£33.00 **Beds:** 5D 3T 2S **Baths:** 7 En 3 Pr (30) cc

Heybrook Bay

SX4948 *Eddystone Inn, Mussel Inn*

Heybrook Bay Private Hotel, *Beach Road, Heybrook Bay, Plymouth, Devon, PL9 0BS.* Small family run hotel on Coastal Footpath, stunning sea views. **Open:** Mar to Nov
01752 862345 D: Fr £17.50 **S:** Fr £20.00–£22.00 **Beds:** 2T 4D

Higher Clovelly

SS3124

Fuchsia Cottage, *Burscott Lane, Higher Clovelly, Bideford, Devon, EX39 5RR.* Situated in a quiet lane, beautiful coastal and countryside views. **Open:** All year (not Xmas/New Year) **Grades:** ETC 4 Diamond, AA 4 Diamond
01237 431398 Mrs Curtis *curtis@fuchsiacottage.fslife.co.uk* www.clovelly-holidays.co.uk **D:** Fr £20.00 **S:** Fr £17.00 **Beds:** 1T 1D 1S **Baths:** 2 En 1 Sh (3)

Holne

SX7069

Chase Gate Farm, *Holne, Newton Abbot, Devon, TQ13 7RX.* Comfortable, friendly farmhouse with lovely views and well-equipped rooms. **Open:** All year
01364 631261 Mr & Mrs Higman **D:** Fr £19.00–£20.00 **S:** Fr £19.00–£20.00 **Beds:** 2D 1T **Baths:** 1 En 1 Pr 1 Sh

Mill Leat Farm, *Holne, Ashburton, Newton Abbot, Devon, TQ13 7RZ.* C18th farmhouse offering great food, set off the beaten track. **Open:** All year (not Xmas)
01364 631283 (also fax) Mrs Cleave **D:** Fr £17.00–£19.00 **S:** Fr £19.00–£20.00 **Beds:** 2F **Baths:** 1 En 1 Pr

Hazelwood, *Holne, Newton Abbot, Devon, TQ13 7SJ.* Friendly home from home welcome with panoramic views of Devon. **Open:** Easter to Oct
01364 631235 Mrs Mortimore **D:** Fr £18.50–£19.00 **S:** Fr £18.50–£19.00 **Beds:** 2D 1S (3)

Honiton

ST1600

Wessington Farm, *Awliscombe, Honiton, Devon, EX14 3NU.* **Open:** All year
01404 42280 & 07989 300392 (M) Mrs Summers **Fax: 01404 45271** *bandb@eastdevon.com* www.eastdevon.com/bedandbreakfast **D:** Fr £20.00–£25.00 **S:** Fr £20.00–£40.00 **Beds:** 1D 2T **Baths:** 2 En 1 Pr (10) cc
Elegant late-Victorian stone farmhouse in Area of Outstanding Natural Beauty. Aga English breakfast served in stylish dining room with superb view overlooking open countryside. Honiton centre of antiques & lace 1 mile, historic Exeter 16 miles, picturesque East Devon coast 20 mins.

Threshays, *Awliscombe, Honiton, Devon, EX14 3QB.* Warm, friendly, delightful views. Ideal for exploring glorious East Devon. **Open:** All year **Grades:** AA 3 Diamond
01404 43551 & 07811 675800 (M) Mrs Gillingham **Fax: 01404 43551** *threshays@tesco.net* **D:** Fr £18.00 **S:** Fr £18.00 **Beds:** 1F 1D **Baths:** 1 Sh (6)

Hope Cove

SX6739

Hope Cove Hotel, *Hope Cove, Kingsbridge, Devon, TQ7 3HH.* On Coastal Path. Spectacular sea views to Eddystone Lighthouse. **Open:** Easter to Oct
01548 561233 (also fax) Mr Clarke **D:** Fr £23.50–£28.50 **S:** Fr £33.50–£38.50 **Beds:** 2T 5D **Baths:** 7 En (12) cc

Tanfield Hotel, *Hope Cove, Kingsbridge, Devon, TQ7 3HF.* **Open:** May to Sep **01548 561268 (also fax)** Mr & Mrs Anderton *hopecove@tanfieldhotel.com* www.tanfieldhotel.com **D:** Fr £28.00–£35.00 **S:** Fr £30.00–£35.00 **Beds:** 2T 4D 2S **Baths:** 8 En (9) × cc
A peaceful place, Hope Cove is ideal for a relaxing holiday away from the noise and bustle of town traffic. But there are plenty of places to visit within a short drive, such as Salcombe, Kingsbridge, Totnes and Buckfastleigh.

Horns Cross

SS3823

The Hoops Inn, *Horns Cross, Bideford, Devon, EX39 5DL.* Enjoy genuine hospitality at one of Devon's most famous inns. **Open:** All year
01237 451222 G P Marriott **Fax: 01237 451247** *reservations@hoopsinn.co.uk* www.hoopsinn.co.uk **D:** Fr £45.00–£80.00 **S:** Fr £40.00–£90.00 **Beds:** 1F 6T 6D **Baths:** 12 En (10) × cc

Horrabridge

SX5169

Overcombe Hotel, *Old Station Road, Horrabridge, Yelverton, Devon, PL20 7RA.* Homely, relaxed atmosphere. Comfortable ensuite bedrooms. Substantial breakfast. Beautiful views. **Open:** All year
01822 853501 JH & G Wright *enquiries@overcombehotel.co.uk* www.overcombehotel.co.uk **D:** Fr £23.00–£30.00 **S:** Fr £23.00–£35.00 **Beds:** 2F 2T 3D 1S **Baths:** 8 En (8) cc

Ide

SX9090

Drakes Farm House, *Ide, Exeter, Devon, EX2 9RQ.* C15th farmhouse with large garden in quiet village, 2 miles M5/city centre.
Open: All year
01392 256814 & 01392 495564
Mrs Easterbrook **Fax: 01392 495564**
drakesfarmhouse@hotmail.com
www.drakesfarm.fsnet.co.uk **D:** Fr £20.00–£22.50 **S:** Fr £22.50–£30.00 **Beds:** 1F 2D 1T **Baths:** 2 En 1 Pr 1 Sh (4) cc

Ideford

SX8977

Higher Rixdale Farm, *Ideford, Newton Abbot, TQ13 0BW.* Situated near Teignmouth, secluded surroundings. Visitors can enjoy lovely walks around the farm. **Open:** Feb to Nov
01626 866232 **D:** Fr £15.00–£17.00 **S:** Fr £15.00–£17.00 **Beds:** 1T 2D 1S **Baths:** 2 Sh (2) (8)

Ilfracombe

SS5147

Harcourt Hotel, *Fore Street, Ilfracombe, Devon, EX34 9DS.* Small family run hotel - home from home. **Open:** All year
01271 862931 JM Doorbar **D:** Fr £18.00–£24.00 **S:** Fr £18.00–£24.00 **Beds:** 3F 1T 3D 1S **Baths:** 9 En (4) × cc

Strathmore Hotel, *57 St Brannock s Road, Ilfracombe, Devon, EX34 8EQ.* **Open:** All year **Grades:** ETC 5 Diamond, AA 5 Diamond, RAC 5 Diamond
01271 862248 Mrs Metaxas **Fax: 01271 862243** *strathmore@ukhotels.com* www.strathmore.ukhotels.com **D:** Fr £25.00–£40.00 **S:** Fr £30.00–£45.00 **Beds:** 1F 5D 1T 1S **Baths:** 8 Pr (7) × cc
Delightful Victorian Hotel near Ilfracombe town centre, Bicclescombe Park, Cairn Nature Reserve and glorious beaches. All rooms ensuite with colour TV and hospitality trays. We offer varied and delicious menus. All meals are freshly prepared and cooked on the premises.

Beechwood Hotel, *Torrs Park, Ilfracombe, Devon, EX34 8AZ.* **Open:** Easter to Sep **Grades:** ETC 2 Star
01271 863800 (also fax) P Burridge *info@beechwoodhotel.co.uk* www.beechwoodhotel.co.uk **D:** Fr £23.00–£27.50 **S:** Fr £28.00–£32.50 **Beds:** 2T 5D **Baths:** 7 En (8) × cc
Peacefully situated non-smoking Victorian mansion, own woods bordering spectacular National Trust lands and Coast Path. Superb views over town and countryside to sea. Just 10 minutes walk to harbour and town. Spacious well-appointed guest rooms, good food. Licensed. Parking.

All details shown are as supplied by B&B owners in Autumn 2002

Varley House, *Chambercombe Park, Ilfracombe, Devon, EX34 9QW.* **Open:** All year (not Xmas/New Year) **Grades:** ETC 4 Diamond, AA 4 Diamond
01271 863927 Mrs O'Sullivan **Fax: 01271 879299** *info@varleyhouse.co.uk* www.varleyhouse.co.uk **D:** Fr £26.00–£27.00 **S:** Fr £30.00–£31.00 **Beds:** 2F 1T 4D 1S **Baths:** 7 En 1 Pr (5) (8) × cc
Built in the early 1900's to revitalise and refresh officers returning from the Boer War. Delightfully situated. All rooms have either sea or country views. Our aim is to offer a very friendly and personal atmosphere, combined with quality accommodation.

Lyncott House, *56 St Brannock's Road, Ilfracombe, Devon, EX34 8EQ.* **Open:** All year **Grades:** ETC 4 Diamond
01271 862425 (also fax) Mr & Mrs Holdsworth *david@ukhotels.com* www.lyncottdevon.com **D:** Fr £21.00–£26.00 **S:** Fr £21.00–£26.00 **Beds:** 2F 3D 1S **Baths:** 6 En (5)
Join David and Marianna in their charming, lovingly-refurbished Victorian house pleasantly situated near lovely Bicclescombe Park. Relax in elegant, smoke-free surroundings. Enjoy delightful, spacious, individually designed ensuite bedrooms and sample their delicious home-made breakfasts.

Combe Lodge Hotel, *Chambercombe Park, Ilfracombe, Devon, EX34 9QW.* Quiet position, overlooking harbour, ideal for walking, cycling, golf holidays. **Open:** All year (not Xmas) **Grades:** ETC 3 Diamond
01271 864518 Mr & Mrs Wileman *combelodgehotel@tinyworld.co.uk* **D:** Fr £19.50–£21.00 **S:** Fr £24.50–£26.00 **Beds:** 2F 4D 2S **Baths:** 4 En 1 Pr 1 Sh (1) (8) × cc

Glenville House, *2 Tors Road, Lynmouth, Devon, EX35 6ET.* **Open:** Feb to Nov **Grades:** AA 4 Diamond **01598 752202** Mr & Mrs Francis *tricia@glenvillelynmouth.co.uk* www.glenvillelynmouth.co.uk **D:** Fr £24.00–£28.00 **S:** Fr £24.00–£30.00 **Beds:** 4D 1T 1S **Baths:** 3 En 1 Pr 2 Sh (12)
Idyllic riverside setting. Delightful Victorian house full of character and charm. Licensed. Tastefully decorated bedrooms. Picturesque harbour, village and unique Cliff Railway nestled amidst wooded valley. Magnificent Exmoor scenery, spectacular coastline and beautiful walks. Peaceful, tranquil, romantic - a very special place.

Tregonwell The Olde Sea Captain's House, *1 Tors Road, Lynmouth, Devon, EX35 6ET.* **Open:** All year (not Xmas) **Grades:** ETC 3 Diamond **01598 753369** Mrs Parker www.smoothhound.co.uk/hotels/tregonwl.html **D:** Fr £22.00–£27.00 **S:** Fr £22.00–£25.00 **Beds:** 2F 5D 1T 1S **Baths:** 5 En 1 Pr 3 Sh (7)
Award-winning, romantic, elegant riverside (former sea captain's) stone-built guesthouse, snuggled amidst waterfalls, cascades, wooded valleys, soaring cliff tops, lonely beaches, enchanting harbourside 'Olde Worlde' smugglers' village. Shelley, Wordsworth, Coleridge stayed here. 'England's Switzerland'. Pretty bedrooms, dramatic views. Garaged parking.

Lynton

SS7149 *George & Dragon, Globe, Dolphin, Fo'c's'le, Castle, Pack of Cards*

The Turret, *33 Lee Road, Lynton, Devon, EX35 6BS.* Step back in time & experience old world hospitality. Cosy dining room. **Open:** All year **01598 753284 (also fax)** Mrs Wayman *nancy@theturret.fsbusiness.co.uk* www.exmoortourism.org/theturret.htm **D:** Fr £18.00–£23.00 **S:** Fr £25.00 **Beds:** 5D 1T **Baths:** 4 En (12) cc

Southcliffe, *Lee Road, Lynton, Devon, EX35 6BS.* **Open:** All year **Grades:** ETC 4 Diamond **01598 753328** Andy & Sue North *info@southcliffe.co.uk* www.southcliffe.co.uk **D:** Fr £23.00–£27.00 **S:** Fr £28.00–£30.00 **Beds:** 6D 2T **Baths:** 8 En (8) cc
Victorian gentleman's residence, set in picturesque Exmoor Village. Ideally situated for touring/walking. On Coastal Path, with Valley of Rocks, Waters Meet and North Walk close by. Friendly service. Substantial breakfast, with lighter options and vegetarians well catered for.

The North Cliff Hotel, *North Walk, Lynton, Devon, EX35 6HJ.* **Open:** Mar to Oct **01598 752357** Mr Hardy *holidays@northcliffhotel.co.uk* www.northcliffhotel.co.uk **D:** Fr £30.00–£34.00 **S:** Fr £30.00–£34.00 **Beds:** 3F 2T 8D 1S **Baths:** 14 En (3) (12) cc
Georgian Villa C1830, own grounds, magnificent sea/coastal views over Lynmouth Harbour and Countisbury Foreland Point. Ideal location for relaxing, comfortable stay in picturesque Lynton and for touring fascinating corners of Exmoor's Lorna Doone Country. Golf, riding, tennis, fishing nearby.

Woodlands, *Lynbridge Road, Lynton, Devon, EX35 6AX.* Ideal base for walkers. Beautiful views across Summerhouse Hill. **Open:** Mar to Nov **01598 752324** Mr & Mrs Kuczer **Fax: 01598 753828** *info@woodlandsguesthouse.co.uk* www.woodlandsguesthouse.co.uk **D:** Fr £18.00–£25.00 **S:** Fr £20.00–£25.00 **Beds:** 1T 5D 1S **Baths:** 6 En 1 Pr (12) (8) cc

Meadhaven, *12 Crossmead, Lynton, Devon, EX35 6DG.* Edwardian guest house. Traditional English cooking. Ideal ramblers/tourists. **Open:** All year **01598 753288** Ms Kirk **D:** Fr £18.00–£19.00 **S:** Fr £18.00–£19.00 **Beds:** 1T 2S **Baths:** 2 Sh

Please respect a B&B's wishes regarding children, animals and smoking

The Denes Guest House, *Longmead, Lynton, Devon, EX35 6DQ.* A warm friendly greeting awaits you at The Denes, with its Edwardian charm. Comfortable accommodation and home cooked food, evening meals served in our licensed dining room. Ideal base to explore Exmoor on the South West Coastal Path. An Exmoor Paths partner. **Open:** All year **01598 753573** Mr McGowan *j.e.mcgowan@btinternet.com* www.thedenes.com **D:** Fr £16.00–£22.50 **S:** Fr £16.00–£22.50 **Beds:** 3F 2D **Baths:** 3 En 2 Sh (5) cc

Malborough

SX7039

Quill View, *Well Hill Close, Malborough, Kingsbridge, Devon, TQ7 3SS.* Very quiet village position with views and patios, super lounge. **Open:** All year (not Xmas) **01548 562085** *willwrite@tesco.net* **D:** Fr £16.00–£20.00 **S:** Fr £19.00–£23.00 **Beds:** 1D 1T **Baths:** 1 En 1 Pr (7) (2)

Martinhoe

SS6648

Mannacott Farm, *Martinhoe, Parracombe, Barnstaple, Devon, EX31 4QS.* Within Exmoor National Park, ideal walking area, Coast Path 1/2 mile. **Open:** Apr to Oct **01598 763227** Mrs Dallyn **D:** Fr £16.00–£17.00 **Beds:** 1D 1T **Baths:** 1 Sh (2)

Marwood

SS5437

Lee House, *Marwood, Barnstaple, Devon, EX31 4DZ.* **Open:** Apr to Oct **01271 374345** Mrs Darling **D:** Fr £20.00–£22.00 **S:** Fr £20.00–£22.00 **Beds:** 1T 2D **Baths:** 3 En (8)
A stone-built Elizabethan Manor house standing in own secluded grounds, magnificent views over rolling countryside. Family-run, friendly, relaxing atmosphere. Easy access to beaches, moor. Walking distance to local pub with excellent food. Marwood Hill Gardens one mile.

Meavy

SX5467 *Rock Inn, Skylark, Burrator*

Greenwell Farm, *Meavy, Yelverton, Devon, PL20 6PY.* Working away from home? Try our new do-it-yourself B & B. **Open:** All year **01822 853563 (also fax)** Mrs Cole *greenwellfarm@btconnect.com* **S:** Fr £20.00–£30.00 **Beds:** 3S **Baths:** 3 En (6)

Merton

SS5212

Richmond House, *New Road (A386), Merton, Okehampton, Devon, EX20 3EG.* Country house within easy reach of beach, moors, gardens, Tarka Trail. **Open:** All year
01805 603258 Mrs Wickett **D:** Fr £15.00 **S:** Fr £15.00 **Beds:** 3F 1T 2D **Baths:** 1 Sh (5) (4) cc

Milton Abbot

SX4179 *Royal Inn*

Beera Farm, *Milton Abbot, Tavistock, Devon, PL19 8PL.* Come and relax on our working farm on the banks of the River Tamar. Abundant wildlife. Beautiful location. Stay in spacious well-appointed rooms with attention to detail. Wonderful hospitality. Romantic four-poster bedroom. Delicious food. Warm friendly atmosphere. **Open:** All year
01822 870216 (also fax) Mrs Tucker *robert.tucker@farming.co.uk* www.beera-farm.co.uk **D:** Fr £20.00–£25.00 **S:** Fr £25.00–£35.00 **Beds:** 1F 2D **Baths:** 3 En (5) cc

Modbury

SX6551

Orchard Cottage, *Palm Cross Green, Modbury, Ivybridge, Devon, PL21 0QZ.* Double ensuite garden room in private cottage. Views over Modbury. **Open:** All year
01548 830633 Mrs Ewen **D:** Fr £22.50 **S:** Fr £27.50 **Beds:** 1D **Baths:** 1 En

Monkokehampton

SS5805

Seldon Farm, *Monkokehampton, Winkleigh, Devon, EX19 8RY.* Charming C17th farmhouse in beautiful, tranquil, rural setting. **Open:** Easter to Oct **Grades:** ETC 3 Diamond
01837 810312 Mrs Case www.seldon-farm.co.uk **D:** Fr £20.00 **S:** Fr £23.00 **Beds:** 1T/F 1D **Baths:** 2 En

Morchard Bishop

SS7607 *London Inn, Thelbridge Cross, New Inn*

Oldborough Fishing Retreat, *Morchard Bishop, Crediton, Devon, EX17 6JQ.* Lakeside rural retreat. 40 minutes M5/j27. Nice place for Exeter city break. **Open:** All year (not Xmas/New Year)
01363 877437 Mrs Wilshaw *fishingretreat@eclipse.co.uk* **D:** Fr £16.00–£17.00 **S:** Fr £16.00–£17.00 **Beds:** 1F 1T **Baths:** 1 Sh (10) cc

Beech Hill House, *Morchard Bishop, Crediton, Devon, EX17 6RF.* Basic accommodation in rural community. Ideal for Two Moors Way. **Open:** All year (not Xmas/New Year)
01363 877228 www.beech-hill.org.uk **D:** Fr £15.00 **S:** Fr £15.00 **Beds:** 3F 1T **Baths:** 3 Sh

Morebath

SS9524 *The Anchor*

Lodfin Farm, *Morebath, Bampton, Devon, EX16 9DD.* Peaceful, welcoming farmhouse. Large gardens, hearty breakfast, ideal location for Exmoor. **Open:** All year (not Xmas/New Year)
01398 331400 (also fax) Mrs Goodwin *lodfin.farm@eclipse.co.uk* **D:** Fr £21.50–£23.50 **S:** Fr £22.00–£25.00 **Beds:** 1F 1D 1S **Baths:** 1 En 1 Sh (6) cc

Moreleigh

SX7652

Island Farm, *Moreleigh, Totnes, Devon, TQ9 7SH.* Situated in the heart of South Hams. Panoramic views of countryside. **Open:** All year (not Xmas/New Year)
01548 821441 Mrs Finch **D:** Fr £20.00–£22.00 **S:** Fr £20.00–£22.00 **Beds:** 1F 1T 2D **Baths:** 2 En 1 Pr (4)

Moretonhampstead

SX7586 *White Hart, Plymouth Inn, Bell Inn, Ring of Bells*

Great Wooston Farm, *Moretonhampstead, Newton Abbot, Devon, TQ13 8QA.* High above Teign Valley, a peaceful haven with views across the moors. **Open:** All year (not Xmas)
01647 440367 (also fax) Mrs Cuming **D:** Fr £20.00–£22.00 **S:** Fr £20.00–£25.00 **Beds:** 2D 1T **Baths:** 2 En 1 Pr (8) (3) cc

Moorcote Country Guest House, *Chagford Cross, Moretonhampstead, Newton Abbot, Devon, TQ13 8LS.* Victorian house set well back from the road in a mature garden, overlooking the town of Moretonhampstead with stunning views of Dartmoor and the surrounding countryside. Ideal centre from which to explore Dartmoor and beautiful Devon. Private parking in grounds. **Open:** Mar to Oct
01647 440966 (also fax) Mr Lambert *moorcote@smartone.co.uk* **D:** Fr £19.00–£21.00 **S:** Fr £25.00–£35.00 **Beds:** 2F 1T 2D **Baths:** 4 En 1 Pr (5) (6)

Little Wooston Farm, *Moretonhampstead, Newton Abbot, Devon, TQ13 8QA.* Working farm in beautiful countryside. Ideally situated for walking. Quiet location. **Open:** All year **Grades:** ETC 3 Diamond
01647 440551 & 07850 098789 (M) Mrs Cuming **Fax: 01647 440551** *jeannecuming@tesco.net* **D:** Fr £17.00–£18.00 **S:** Fr £17.00–£18.00 **Beds:** 1F 1D 1S **Baths:** 1 Sh (4)

Great Sloncombe Farm, *Moretonhampstead, Newton Abbot, Devon, TQ13 8QF.* C13th Dartmoor farmhouse, everything provided for an enjoyable stay. **Open:** All year
01647 440595 (also fax) Mrs Merchant *hmerchant@sloncombe.freeserve.co.uk* www.greatsloncombefarm.co.uk **D:** Fr £23.00–£24.00 **S:** Fr £30.00 **Beds:** 2D 1T **Baths:** 3 En (8) (3)

Newton Ferrers

SX5448

Crown Yealm, *Bridgend Hill, Newton Ferrers, Plymouth, Devon, PL8 1AW.* Beautiful riverside country house. All guest rooms overlook garden to water's edge. **Open:** All year
01752 872365 (also fax) Mrs Johnson **D:** Fr £17.00–£22.00 **S:** Fr £21.00–£30.00 **Beds:** 1F 1D 1T **Baths:** 2 En 1 Sh (7)

Wood Cottage, *Bridgend, Newton Ferrers, Plymouth, Devon, PL8 1AW.* Welcoming, modernised cottage, overlooking end of Yealm Estuary and farmland. **Open:** All year
01752 872372 Mrs Cross *jillx@wdcott.freeserve.co.uk* **D:** Fr £20.00–£22.50 **S:** Fr £22.50–£25.00 **Beds:** 1T 2D **Baths:** 1 En 1 Sh (2)

North Bovey

SX7383

The Ring of Bells Inn, *North Bovey, Newton Abbott, Devon, TQ13 8RB.* **Open:** All year
01647 440375 Mr Rix **Fax: 01647 207156** *info@ringofbellsinn.com* www.ringofbellsinn.com **D:** Fr £20.00–£30.00 **Beds:** 2T 3D **Baths:** 5 En cc
Famous thatched inn in the heart of Dartmoor, dating back to the C13th. The perfect pub in one of Devon's prettiest villages! Warm & friendly welcome, local ales, quality food & fine wine list. Great value all-inclusive tariffs available.

Planning a longer stay? Always ask for any special rates

Please respect a B&B's wishes regarding children, animals and smoking

North Molton
SS7329

Middle Poole, *North Molton, South Molton, Devon, EX36 3HL.* C15th thatched cottage. Wealth of Olde Worlde charm - a rare find. **Open:** All year
01598 740206 (also fax) Mrs Procter *ronandsueprocter@tiscali.co.uk* **D:** Fr £20.00 **S:** Fr £25.00 **Beds:** 1D 1T **Baths:** 1 En 1 Pr (10) P (2) TV V

North Tawton
SS6601

Kayden House Hotel, *High Street, North Tawton, Devon, EX20 2HF.* Devon heartland, ideal for moors and coasts. Warm welcome assured. **Open:** All year
01837 82242 Ms Waldron **D:** Fr £20.00 **S:** Fr £26.00 **Beds:** 1F 2T 2D 2S **Baths:** 5 En 2 Pr TV V cc

Northleigh (Honiton)
SY1996

Sunnyacre, *Rockerhayne Farm, Northleigh, Colyton, Devon, EX24 6DA.* Bungalow on working farm in beautiful scenic countryside close to coast. **Open:** All year (not Xmas)
01404 871422 N Rich **D:** Fr £15.00–£20.00 **S:** Fr £15.00–£20.00 **Beds:** 1F 1D 1T **Baths:** 1 Sh P (4) TV V

Smallicombe Farm, *Northleigh, Colyton, Devon, EX24 6BU.* Old world charm, idyllic rural setting with only the sights & sounds of the countryside. **Open:** All year
01404 831310 Mrs Todd **Fax: 01404 831431** *maggie_todd@yahoo.com* www.smallicombe.com **D:** Fr £20.00–£23.50 **S:** Fr £25.00 **Beds:** 1F 1D 1T **Baths:** 3 En P (10) TV V 3

Oakford
SS9021

Harton Farm, *Oakford, Tiverton, Devon, EX16 9HH.* Peaceful farmhouse. Home-grown additive-free meat, vegetables. Friendly animals. **Open:** All year (not Xmas/New Year)
01398 351209 (also fax) Mrs Head *harton@eclipse.co.uk* **D:** Fr £16.00–£17.00 **S:** Fr £16.00–£17.00 **Beds:** 1F 1T **Baths:** 1 Sh (4) P (2) TV V

Okehampton
SX5895

Bourna Farmhouse, *Okehampton, Devon, EX20 3EJ.* Traditional newly thatched Devon longhouse, many original features, very comfortable. **Open:** All year (not Xmas/New Year)
01805 804584 A Andrews **D:** Fr £15.00–£20.00 **S:** Fr £15.00–£20.00 **Beds:** 1F 1T 1D 1S **Baths:** 1 En 1 Sh P (20) TV V

Betty Cottles Inn, *Graddon Cross, Okehampton, Devon, EX20 4LR.* **Open:** All year
01837 55339 Mr & Mrs Wilson **Fax: 01837 55191** *cottles@eurobell.co.uk* www.cottles.eurobell.co.uk **D:** Fr £20.00–£50.00 **S:** Fr £20.00–£37.50 **Beds:** 2F 1T 3D 2S **Baths:** 4 En 1 Sh P (50) TV V cc
Edge of Dartmoor National Park. Charming country pub ideally placed for your holiday base in West Devon. With the coast only 20 mins away, Dartmoor over the road and the Eden Project within 50 mins' driving, there is plenty to do and see.

North Lake, *Exeter Road, Okehampton, Devon, EX20 1QH.* **Open:** All year **01837 53100** Mrs Jeffery *pamjeffery@northdevon.co.uk* www.northlakedevon.co.uk **D:** Fr £18.00–£24.00 **S:** Fr £20.00–£30.00 **Beds:** 2D 1T 1S **Baths:** 2 En 1 Sh (6) P (10) TV V
A warm welcome awaits you at this friendly bed and breakfast, set in its own grounds, with panoramic views across Dartmoor. Superbly sited for walking, cycling, riding & touring. Seperate facilities for dogs with day kennelling available.

Southey Farm, *Sampford Courtenay, Okehampton, Devon, EX20 2TE.* Comfortable farmhouse within easy reach of many attractions in Devon and Cornwall. **Open:** All year (not Xmas/New Year)
01837 82446 Mr & Mrs Townsend Green *tg@southeyfarm.freeserve.co.uk* **D:** Fr £15.00 **S:** Fr £15.00 **Beds:** 1T 1S/T **Baths:** 2 Pr P (4) TV

Otterton
SY0885

Ropers Cottage, *Ropers Lane, Otterton, Budleigh Salterton, Devon, EX9 7JF.* C17th cottage in picturesque village, near river and Coastal Path. **Open:** Easter to Oct
01395 568826 Mrs Earl **Fax: 01395 568206** **D:** Fr £19.50–£20.00 **S:** Fr £19.50–£20.00 **Beds:** 1T 1S **Baths:** 2 En (1) P (2) TV

Ottery St Mary
SY1095

Fluxton Farm, *Fluxton, Ottery St Mary, Devon, EX11 1RJ.* Cat lovers' paradise in lovely open countryside. Ideal touring area. **Open:** All year **Grades:** AA 2 Diamond
01404 812818 Mrs Forth **Fax: 01404 814843** **D:** Fr £25.00–£27.50 **S:** Fr £25.00–£27.50 **Beds:** 1F 5T 3D 2S **Baths:** 11 En (8) P (15) TV V

Holly Ridge, *West Hill, Ottery St Mary, Devon, EX11 1UX.* Holly Ridge is on the edge of the peaceful village of West Hill. **Open:** All year
01404 812776 (also fax) Mr Abel *hollyridge@aol.com* **D:** Fr £18.00–£26.00 **S:** Fr £18.00–£26.00 **Beds:** 1F 2D **Baths:** 1 En 1 Sh (12) P (8) TV V

Paignton
SX8960

Bella Vista, *5 Berry Square, Paignton, TQ4 6AZ.* On level adjacent to beach, town etc. Choice of menu. **Open:** Easter to Nov
01803 558122 *bellavista@berrysquare.co.uk* **D:** Fr £14.00–£21.00 **S:** Fr £14.00–£24.00 **Beds:** 2F 2T 3D 2S **Baths:** 4 En 2 Sh P (10) TV cc

Hotel Fiesta, *2 Kernou Road, Paignton, TQ4 6BA.* **Open:** All year **01803 521862** Mr Hawker **Fax: 01803 392978** *mark@hawker55.fsnet.co.uk* **D:** Fr £19.00–£25.00 **S:** Fr £20.00–£26.00 **Beds:** 8D 1S **Baths:** 8 En 1 Sh P TV cc
The Fiesta is close to Paignton's sea front. Train & bus station 10 min walk. Restaurants to suit all tastes. We now offer accommodation for adults only. Also available large spa, pool & sun deck, four-poster bedroom. Come & relax.

Devon House Hotel, *20 Garfield Road, Paignton, Devon, TQ4 6AX.* **Open:** All year **Grades:** ETC 3 Diamond **01803 559371** Mr Hallam *info@devonhousehotel.com* www.devonhousehotel.com **D:** Fr £16.00–£22.00 **S:** Fr £24.00–£33.00 **Beds:** 2F 1T 5D 3S **Baths:** 5 En 3 Sh (5) (11) cc

Devon House is a lovely Victorian building with a relaxed & friendly atmosphere. We have TVs & tea/coffee facilities in all our large bedrooms. 100 yards to the sea front & pier, plus all other amenities. We are a short walk from the town's bus/train station & opposite the lovely Victoria Park. We also have a licensed bar & separate TV lounge.

Cherwood Hotel, *26 Garfield Road, Paignton, TQ4 6AX.* **Open:** All year **Grades:** ETC 4 Diamond, Silver **01803 556515** J Alderson **Fax: 01803 555126** *james-pauline@cherwood-hotel.co.uk* www.cherwood-hotel.co.uk **D:** Fr £18.00–£22.00 **S:** Fr £20.00–£22.00 **Beds:** 3F 3D 2T 1S **Baths:** 9 En (4) cc

High quality licensed hotel. Ideal position by central seafront, 2 min walk town centre. Within yards of beaches & all amenities. All rooms ensuite, TV, video, clock radio alarm, hairdryer, tea/coffee, romantic four-poster rooms available. Friendly atmosphere.

South Sands Hotel, *Alta Vista Road, Paignton, Devon, TQ4 6BZ.* South-facing, licensed family-run hotel in peaceful location overlooking beach/park. **Open:** Mar to Oct **01803 557231 & 0500 432153 (ext 10)** Mr Cahill **D:** Fr £20.00–£25.00 **S:** Fr £20.00–£25.00 **Beds:** 7F 4D 6T 2S **Baths:** 17 En 2 Pr (17) cc

Hotel San Brelade, *3 Alta Vista Road, Paignton, Devon, TQ4 6DB.* Family hotel close to harbour. High standard accommodation, excellent food. **Open:** All year (not Xmas/New Year) **Grades:** ETC 3 Diamond **01803 553725** Mrs Brueton *hotelsanbrelade@aol.com* **D:** Fr £16.00–£22.00 **S:** Fr £20.00–£28.00 **Beds:** 1F 1T 4D 1S **Baths:** 4 En 3 Sh (5) (7) cc

Rosemead Guest House, *22 Garfield Road, Paignton, Devon, TQ4 6AX.* Superb position for the beach. Close to centre/railway station. **Open:** All year **Grades:** ETC 3 Diamond **01803 557944** *rosemeadhotel@aol.com* www.rosemeadpaignton.co.uk **D:** Fr £16.00–£20.50 **S:** Fr £16.00–£20.50 **Beds:** 2F 2T 3D 3S **Baths:** 6 En (4) cc

Park View Guest House, *19 Garfield Road, Paignton, Devon, TQ4 6AX.* Small friendly guest house - short level stroll town & sea front. **Open:** All year (not Xmas/New Year) **01803 528521** **D:** Fr £13.00–£16.00 **S:** Fr £13.00–£16.00 **Beds:** 3F 1D **Baths:** 1 Sh

Sundale Hotel, *10 Queens Road, Paignton, Devon, TQ4 6AT.* Quiet family run hotel, close to local amenities, highly recommended. **Open:** All year **01803 557431** Mr McDermott **D:** Fr £14.50–£17.50 **S:** Fr £14.50–£17.50 **Beds:** 2F 2T 3D 1S **Baths:** 4 En 1 Sh

Greenford Lodge Hotel, *56 Dartmouth Road, Paignton, Devon, TQ4 5AN.* Situated 5 mins from town centre/sea. Warm welcome. Ample Parking. **Open:** All year (not Xmas/New Year) **01803 553635** Mr & Mrs Nash **D:** Fr £16.00–£24.00 **S:** Fr £16.00–£18.00 **Beds:** 8F 2T 5D 1S **Baths:** 2 En 2 Pr 4 Sh

Pancrasweek

SS2906

The Barton, *Pancrasweek, Holsworthy, Devon, EX22 7JT.* Working farm. Peaceful position. Easy reach coast, moors, famous Clovelly. **Open:** Easter to Oct **01288 381315** Mrs Chant **D:** Fr £20.00 **S:** Fr £20.00 **Beds:** 2D 1T **Baths:** 3 En

All details shown are as supplied by B&B owners in Autumn 2002

Peter Tavy

SX5177

Churchtown, *Peter Tavy, Tavistock, Devon, PL19 9NP.* Detached Victorian house standing in own large quiet garden. **Open:** All year (not Xmas) **01822 810477** Mrs Lane **Fax: 01822 810630** *blane@swcg.co.uk* **D:** Fr £18.00–£19.00 **S:** Fr £18.00–£19.00 **Beds:** 2D 1S **Baths:** 1 En 1 Sh (10) (6)

Petrockstowe

SS5109

Aish Villa, *Petrockstowe, Okehampton, Devon, EX20 3HL.* Peaceful location, ideal for visiting moors, coast. Tarka Trail nearby. **Open:** All year **01837 810581** Ms Gordon *gillandtonygordon@hotmail.com* **D:** Fr £17.00 **S:** Fr £17.00 **Beds:** 1F 1T 1D **Baths:** 1 Sh (4)

Plymouth

SX4756

The Firs Guest House, *13 Pier Street, Plymouth, Devon, PL1 3BS.* **Open:** All year (not Xmas/New Year) **01752 262870** Leo & Polly Kirk **Fax: 01752 294003** *thefirsinplymouthuk@hotmail.com* www.thefirsinplymouthuk.co.uk **D:** Fr £19.00–£25.00 **S:** Fr £19.00–£25.00 **Beds:** 2F 1T 3D 3S **Baths:** 2 En 2 Sh

Be welcomed by us. Family-run & homely near the sea, Hoe, Pavilions, Barbican, Ferryport & city centre. Ideal for Dartmoor, Eden Project (35 miles) & Land's End (85 miles). It's very good- we vouch for it. Woof Woof Woof.

Bay Cottage, *150 Church Road, Wembury, Plymouth, Devon, PL9 0HR.* Victorian cottage by the sea, surrounded by National Trust land. **Open:** All year (not Xmas) **01752 862559 (also fax)** Mrs Farrington *TheFairies@aol.com* www.bay-cottage.com **D:** Fr £28.00–£31.00 **S:** Fr £28.00–£38.00 **Beds:** 2D 2T 1S **Baths:** 3 En 2 Sh (2)

Smeaton's Tower Hotel, *40-42 Grand Parade, Plymouth, Devon, PL1 3DJ.* **Open:** All year (not Xmas/New Year)
01752 221007 Fax: 01752 221664 *info@smeatonstowehotel.co.uk* www.smeatonstowerhotel.co.uk **D:** Fr £22.50–£27.50 **S:** Fr £30.00–£35.00 **Beds:** 4F 4D 2S **Baths:** 10 En cc
Smeaton's Tower Hotel is privately owned and operated, situated 20 yards from Plymouth Hoe foreshore, 15 minute walk from the famous Barbican and Mayflower Steps, city centre shopping, Theatre Royal, Pavilions, Marine Aquarium, Brittany Ferry port. Ideal base to explore Dartmoor and Cornwall.

Brittany Guest House, *28 Athenaeum Street, Plymouth, Devon, PL1 2RQ.* **Open:** All year (not Xmas/New Year)
01752 262247 *jcooper239@aol.com* www.brittanyguesthouse.co.uk **D:** Fr £17.00–£23.00 **S:** Fr £17.00–£30.00 **Beds:** 5F 1T 2D 1S **Baths:** 4 En 2 Sh (6) cc
A charming Victorian town house situated in the heart of the city on the famous Plymouth Hoe with an enviable reputation for comfort, cleanliness and a breakfast that will set you up for the day! Perfect for business or pleasure.

Mountbatten Hotel, *52 Exmouth Road, Stoke, Plymouth, Devon, PL1 4QH.* **Open:** All year
01752 563843 Mr Stretton-Downes **Fax: 01752 606014 D:** Fr £23.00–£25.00 **S:** Fr £20.00–£27.00 **Beds:** 3F 6D 2T 4S **Baths:** 7 En 2 Sh (4) cc
Small licensed Victorian hotel overlooking parkland with river views. Quiet cul-de-sac. Close city centre/ferryport. Good access Cornwall. Walking distance Naval base, Royal Fleet Club, FE College. Secure parking. Well-appointed rooms. Tea/coffee, CTVs, telephones. Credit cards accepted.

The Old Pier Guest House, *20 Radford Road, West Hoe, Plymouth, Devon, PL1 3BY.* Convenient for ferry, Barbican, city centre, sea front. Offers exceptional value. **Open:** All year (not Xmas/New Year) **Grades:** ETC 3 Diamond
01752 268468 Mrs Jones *enquiries@oldpier.co.uk* www.oldpier.co.uk **D:** Fr £16.00–£21.00 **S:** Fr £16.00–£30.00 **Beds:** 1F 3T 3D 1S **Baths:** 1 En 2 Sh cc

Cassandra Guest House, *13 Crescent Avenue, Plymouth, Devon, PL1 3AN.* Ideally situated for city centre, seafront, Barbican, Ferry Port, theatres, stations. **Open:** All year
01752 220715 (also fax) D: Fr £17.00–£22.00 **S:** Fr £17.00–£30.00 **Beds:** 3F 1T 1D 1S **Baths:** 2 En 1 Pr 1 Sh cc

Athenaeum Lodge, *4 Athenaeum St, Plymouth, Devon, PL1 2RQ.* A highly-commended guest house, recommended by 'Which Hotel Guide'. **Open:** All year (not Xmas) **Grades:** ETC 4 Diamond
01752 665005 (also fax) D Kewell *sales@athenaeumlodge.fsnet.co.uk* **D:** Fr £18.00–£23.00 **S:** Fr £25.00–£34.00 **Beds:** 3D 5T 1S **Baths:** 7 En 2 Sh (5) (5) cc

Sunray Hotel, *3/5 Alfred Street, The Hoe, Plymouth, Devon, PL1 2RP.* Centrally located, convenient for theatre, shops, Barbican and National Aquarium. **Open:** All year (not Xmas/New Year)
01752 669113 Mr Thomas **Fax: 01752 268969 D:** Fr £23.00–£26.00 **S:** Fr £28.00–£35.00 **Beds:** 6F 4D 5T 3S **Baths:** 16 En 2 Pr (6)

Poundsgate

SX7072

New Cott Farm, *Poundsgate, Newton Abbot, Devon, TQ13 7PD.* Lovely walking in Dartmoor National Park. Good food, beds, welcoming & peaceful. **Open:** All year
01364 631421 Mrs Phipps *newcott@ruralink.co.uk* **D:** Fr £20.00–£22.00 **Beds:** 1F 2D 1T **Baths:** 3 En 1 Pr (5) (4)

Princetown

SX5873

Duchy House, *Tavistock Road, Princetown, Yelverton, Devon, PL20 6QF.* Warm welcome assured. Central base for exploring Dartmoor. Memorable breakfasts. **Open:** Dec to Oct
01822 890552 Mr Trimble *duchyhouse@aol.com* **D:** Fr £20.00–£25.00 **S:** Fr £20.00–£30.00 **Beds:** 1T 2D **Baths:** 1 En 1 Sh (6) cc

RATES

D = Price range per person sharing in a double or twin room

S = Price range for a single room

B&B owners may vary rates – be sure to check when booking

Pyworthy

SS3103

Leworthy Farm, *Pyworthy, Holsworthy, Devon, EX22 6SJ.* **Open:** All year **Grades:** ETC 4 Diamond, Silver, AA 4 Diamond
01409 259469 Mrs Jennings **D:** Fr £22.00–£25.00 **S:** Fr £25.00–£40.00 **Beds:** 1F 1T 2D **Baths:** 3 En 1 Pr (8)
North Cornish Coast 20 minutes. Georgian farmhouse in tranquil, unspoilt location. Lawned gardens, orchard, wildlife haven and fishing lake. Fresh flowers, pretty bone china, fresh milk, hearty breakfasts. Homely atmosphere. Peaceful lounge. Exquisitely decorated with pictures, plates and china throughout.

Salcombe

SX7339 *The Victoria, Fortescue, King's Arms*

Motherhill Farm, *Salcombe, Devon, TQ8 8NB.* Peaceful and homely Victorian farmhouse on a mixed working farm. **Open:** Easter to Oct
01548 842552 (also fax) Mrs Weymouth *djw@dweymouth.fsnet.co.uk* **D:** Fr £17.00–£19.00 **S:** Fr £17.00–£19.00 **Beds:** 1F/D 1T 1S **Baths:** 1 Sh (7) (6)

Sampford Courtenay

SS6301

West Trecott Farm, *Sampford Courtenay, Okehampton, Devon, EX20 2TD.* **Open:** May to Oct
01837 82569 Mrs Horn **D:** Fr £17.50–£20.00 **S:** Fr £17.50–£20.00 **Beds:** 3D **Baths:** 2 En 1 Sh (2) (6)
Early C15th farmhouse situated in quiet hamlet in heart of Devon countryside close to Dartmoor National Park on A3072. High-quality accommodation, private off-road parking. Ideal touring, walking, fishing & Tarka Trail.

Please respect a B&B's wishes regarding children, animals and smoking

Langdale, *Sampford Courtenay, Okehampton, Devon, EX20 2SY.* Quietly situated on edge of Devon thatched village, country views. **Open:** All year (not Xmas/New Year)
01837 82433 Mrs Clayton *chrisclayton7@lineone.net* **D:** Fr £16.50 **S:** Fr £16.50 **Beds:** 1F 1D 1S **Baths:** 1 Sh (3)

Southey Farm, *Sampford Courtenay, Okehampton, Devon, EX20 2TE.* Comfortable farmhouse within easy reach of many attractions in Devon and Cornwall. **Open:** All year (not Xmas/New Year)
01837 82446 Mr & Mrs Townsend Green *tg@southeyfarm.freeserve.co.uk* **D:** Fr £15.00 **S:** Fr £15.00 **Beds:** 1T 1S/T **Baths:** 2 Pr (4)

Sampford Peverell

ST0314

Challis, *12 Lower Town, Sampford Peverell, Tiverton, Devon, EX16 7BJ.* Challis - accessible large period house in conservation village. High-quality accommodation, idyllic gardens, private canal access. Excellent walking/cycling base. **Open:** All year
01884 820620 & 07748 152232 (M) Mrs Dutson **D:** Fr £20.00 **S:** Fr £25.00–£30.00 **Beds:** 1F 1T 1S 2D **Baths:** 1 En 1 Sh (5)

Sampford Spiney

SX5372

Withill Farm, *Sampford Spiney, Yelverton, Devon, PL20 6LN.* Dartmoor. Small secluded farm - beautiful setting, central for Devon, Cornwall. **Open:** All year
01822 853992 (also fax) Mrs Kitchen *withillfarm1@aol.com* **D:** Fr £19.00–£22.00 **S:** Fr £20.00–£24.00 **Beds:** 2D 1T **Baths:** 1 En 1 Sh (6)

Eggworthy Farm, *Sampford Spiney, Yelverton, Devon, PL20 6LJ.* Relax in our home. Quiet location, ideal for walking on Dartmoor. **Open:** All year (not Xmas)
01822 852142 (also fax) Mrs Landick *bjandllandick@aol.com* **D:** Fr £19.00 **S:** Fr £23.00 **Beds:** 2D 1S **Baths:** 1 En 1 Pr (6)

Scorriton

SX7068

The Tradesmans Arms, *Scorriton, Buckfastleigh, Devon, TQ11 0JB.* Warm friendly village pub. within Dartmoor National Park, set in beautiful Devon lanes. **Open:** All year (not Xmas/New Year)
01364 631206 Mr Lunday *john.lunday@virgin.net* www.thetradesmansarms.com **D:** Fr £25.00 **S:** Fr £25.00 **Beds:** 2D **Baths:** 1 Sh (20)

Seaton

SY2490 Harbour Inn, Ship Inn

The Harbour House, *1 Trevelyan Road, Seaton, Devon, EX12 2NL.* Spacious and comfortable harbourside house, directly on SW Coast Path. **Open:** Mar to Nov
01297 21797 Linda & Roger Sandbrook **D:** Fr £20.00 **S:** Fr £25.00 **Beds:** 1T 1D **Baths:** 2 En (5)

Harbourside Guest House, *2 Trevelyan Road, Seaton, Devon, EX12.* Perfectly situated on the harbour and Southwest Coast Path. **Open:** Feb to Nov
01297 20085 **D:** Fr £21.00–£23.00 **S:** Fr £25.00–£28.00 **Beds:** 1T 1D **Baths:** 2 En (1) (3)

Shaldon

SX9372

Virginia Cottage, *Brook Lane, Shaldon, Teignmouth, Devon, TQ14 0HL.* Early C17th house in one acre garden near sea. Ample parking. **Open:** Easter to Oct
01626 872634 (also fax) Mr & Mrs Britton **D:** Fr £25.00 **S:** Fr £35.00 **Beds:** 2D 1T **Baths:** 2 En 1 Pr (4)

Ringmore House, *Brook Lane, Shaldon, Teignmouth, Devon, TQ14 0AJ.* Beautiful old house & cottage set in ancient gardens full of exotic & unusual plants. **Open:** All year (not Xmas/New Year)
01626 873323 Mr & Mrs Scull **Fax: 01626 873353** *hscull@aol.com* **D:** Fr £25.00–£35.00 **S:** Fr £30.00–£40.00 **Beds:** 3D 1T **Baths:** 2 Pr 1 En (9) (10)

Shirwell

SS5937

Waytown Farm, *Shirwell, Barnstaple, Devon, EX31 4JN.* Comfortable C17th spacious farmhouse with superb views, 3 miles from Barnstaple. **Open:** All year (not Xmas)
01271 850396 (also fax) Mrs Kingdon *hazel@waytown.enterprise-plc.com* www.waytownholidays.co.uk **D:** Fr £20.00–£22.00 **S:** Fr £18.50–£20.00 **Beds:** 2F 1T 1S **Baths:** 3 En 1 Sh (6)

Sidbury

SY1391 Red Lion

Old Orchard Cottage, *Cotford Road, Sidbury, Sidmouth, Devon, EX10 0SQ.* Set in a delightful Saxon Village. A haven for walkers & birdwatchers. The uniquely lovely coastal town of Sidmouth 3 miles away. Many places to visit. Breakfast on the terrace in fine weather overlooking the River Sid & orchard. A good local pub. **Open:** All year (not Xmas/New Year)
01395 597645 Ms Collings *collings.sidbury@btinternet.com* www.oldorchard.uk.com **D:** Fr £20.00–£25.00 **S:** Fr £20.00–£25.00 **Beds:** 1T 1D **Baths:** 1 En 1 Pr (2)

Sidmouth

SY1287

Bramley Lodge, *Vicarage Road, Sidmouth, Devon, EX10 8UQ.* 600 metres from sea. Garden overlooks river and Byes Parkland. **Open:** All year
01395 515710 Mr & Mrs Haslam *haslam@bramleylodge.fsnet.co.uk* **D:** Fr £20.00–£26.00 **S:** Fr £20.00–£26.00 **Beds:** 1F 1T 2D 2S **Baths:** 5 En 1 Sh (6)

Glendevon Hotel, *Cotmaton Rd, Sidmouth, Devon, EX10 8QX.* A lovely Victorian hotel in a quiet & convenient location. **Open:** All year
01395 514028 *enquiries@glendevon-hotel.co.uk* www.glendevon-hotel.co.uk **D:** Fr £25.00–£28.00 **S:** Fr £25.00–£28.00 **Beds:** 2T 6D 4S **Baths:** 12 Pr

Larkstone House, *22 Connaught Road, Sidmouth, Devon, EX10 8TT.* Detached, quiet surroundings yet adjacent shops. 1/3 mile beautiful Sidmouth seafront. **Open:** Easter to Nov
01395 514345 Mrs Lever **D:** Fr £17.50–£19.50 **S:** Fr £16.50–£18.00 **Beds:** 1F 1D 1S **Baths:** 1 En 1 Sh (3)

Woodlands Hotel, *Station Rd, Sidmouth, Devon, EX10 8HG.* C16th building. All modern conveniences in the heart of Sidmouth. **Open:** All year
01395 513120 (also fax) *info@woodlands-hotel.com* www.woodlands-hotel.com **D:** Fr £20.00–£44.00 **S:** Fr £24.00–£42.00 **Beds:** 3F 8T 8D 5S **Baths:** 24 En (20) cc

Avalon, *Vicarage Road, Sidmouth, Devon, EX10 8UQ.* Elegant town house, backing onto river and National Trust park. **Open:** All year (not Xmas)
01395 513443 Mrs Young *janetyoungavalon@aol.com* www.avalonsidmouth.co.uk **D:** Fr £20.00–£27.50 **S:** Fr £30.00–£40.00 **Beds:** 4D 1T **Baths:** 5 En (5)

Lynstead, *Lynstead Vicarage Road, Sidmouth, Devon, EX10 8UQ.* Cosy guest house backing onto The Byes NT park. **Open:** All year
01395 514635 Mr & Mrs Mair *lynstead@aol.com* **D:** Fr £20.00–£22.00 **S:** Fr £20.00–£30.00 **Beds:** 2F 2D 1T 1S **Baths:** 4 En 1 Sh (8)

Saltwynds Farm, *Saltwynds Lane, Bowd, Sidmouth, Devon, EX10 0NP.* The farmhouse is a hexagonal shape with large reception rooms. **Open:** All year (not Xmas/ New Year)
01395 579441 C Edwards *carol27-53@aol.com* **D:** Fr £20.00–£25.00 **S:** Fr £20.00 **Beds:** 2F 2T 2D 2S **Baths:** 1 Pr 1 Sh (8)

Cheriton Guest House, *Vicarage Road, Sidmouth, Devon, EX10 8UQ.* Private garden for guests' use to banks of River Sid. **Open:** All year
01395 513810 (also fax) Mrs Lee *su9129@eclipse.co.uk* **D:** Fr £18.00–£22.00 **S:** Fr £18.00–£22.00 **Beds:** 2F 4D 2T 2S **Baths:** 10 En (10)

Ryton Guest House, *52-54 Winslade Road, Sidmouth, Devon, EX10 9EX.* A warm welcome, superb 3-course breakfast. Good walking area. **Open:** Feb to Nov
Grades: ETC 4 Diamond, AA 3 Diamond
01395 513981 Mr & Mrs Bradnam **Fax: 01395 519210** *info@ryton-guest-house.co.uk* www.ryton-guest-house.co.uk **D:** Fr £20.00–£22.00 **S:** Fr £20.00–£24.00 **Beds:** 4F 3D 1T 2S **Baths:** 8 En 2 Sh (6)

Sidling Field, *105 Peaslands Road, Sidmouth, Devon, EX10 8XE.* Large bungalow on outskirts of town. Quiet location. Ample parking. **Open:** Jan to Nov
01395 513859 Mrs Shenfield *su1889@eclipse.co.uk* **D:** Fr £19.00–£22.00 **S:** Fr £25.00–£30.00 **Beds:** 1D 1T **Baths:** 1 Sh (8) (3)

Higher Coombe Farm, *Tipton St John, Sidmouth, Devon, EX10 0AX.* Friendly welcome, comfortable rooms. Relaxed atmosphere. Working farm, sheep/cattle. **Open:** Mar to Dec **Grades:** ETC 3 Diamond
01404 813385 (also fax) Mrs Farmer *kerstinfarmer@farming.co.uk* **D:** Fr £19.00–£23.00 **S:** Fr £19.00–£23.00 **Beds:** 1F 1T 1D 1S **Baths:** 1 En 1 Sh (4)

Silverton

SS9502

Hayne House, *Silverton, Exeter, Devon, EX5 4HE.* Georgian farmhouse, peacefully situated, overlooking farm & woods. Relax in style. **Open:** Apr to Oct
01392 860725 (also fax) Mrs Kelly *haynehouse@ukonline.co.uk* www.devonfarms.co.uk **D:** Fr £16.00–£20.00 **S:** Fr £16.00–£20.00 **Beds:** 1F 1T **Baths:** 2 Pr

National Grid References given are for villages, towns and cities – not for individual houses

Slapton

SX8245

Start House, *Start, Slapton, Kingsbridge, Devon, TQ7 2QD.* **Open:** All year (not Xmas)
Grades: ETC 3 Diamond
01548 580254 Mrs Ashby **D:** Fr £23.00–£25.00 **S:** Fr £21.00–£23.00 **Beds:** 2D 1T 1S **Baths:** 2 Pr 1 Sh (4)
Comfortable Georgian house. Situated in quiet hamlet 1 mile from Slapton. All bedrooms overlook a beautiful valley with Slapton Ley and the sea at the end. Large interesting garden. Ideal for wildlife and walking. Traditional or vegetarian breakfast.

Old Walls, *Slapton, Kingsbridge, Devon, TQ7 2QN.* Listed C18th house in beautiful village, near sea. Nature reserve close by. **Open:** All year
01548 580516 Mrs Mercer **D:** Fr £20.00–£22.00 **S:** Fr £20.00–£25.00 **Beds:** 2F 1T **Baths:** 1 En 2 Pr

South Molton

SS7125

Stumbles Hotel & Restaurant, *131-134 East Street, South Molton, Devon, EX36 3BU.* **Open:** All year
01769 574145 Mrs Colette Potter **Fax: 01769 572558** *info@stumbles.co.uk* www.stumbles.co.uk **D:** Fr £22.50–£35.00 **S:** Fr £35.00–£55.00 **Beds:** 1F 4T 5D **Baths:** 10 En **cc**
On the edge of Exmoor, in historical market town. Highly-acclaimed restaurant. Alfresco dining in pretty courtyard. Fishing on Mole and Taw rivers. Half-price golf on nearby spectacular 18-hole course with many leisure facilities. Fourth night free. Ample off-road private parking.

Southleigh

SY2093

South Bank, *Southleigh, Colyton, Devon, EX24 6JB.* Sunny house, beautiful garden, lovely views, relaxing walking/bird watching. **Open:** All year (not Xmas/New Year)
01404 871251 Mrs Connor *jconnor21@ic24.net* **D:** Fr £14.00–£15.00 **S:** Fr £14.00–£15.00 **Beds:** 2D **Baths:** 1 Sh (10) (4)

Starcross

SX9781 *Courtenay Arms*

The Croft Guest House, *Cockwood Harbour, Starcross, Exeter, Devon, EX6 8QY.* Set in an acre of secluded gardens overlooking Cockwood Harbour and River Exe. Convenient for Powderham Castle and Dawlish Warren Nature Reserve. 2 mins walk to two of Devon's finest seafood pub/ restaurants, discount card for our guests. **Open:** All year (not Xmas)
01626 890282 Mr Stewart **Fax: 01626 891768** www.smoothhound.co.uk/hotels/croft/1.html **D:** Fr £17.50–£23.00 **S:** Fr £22.00–£28.00 **Beds:** 2F 3D 4T 1S **Baths:** 7 En (5) (8)

Start Point

SX8237 *Fortescue Arms, Creeks End, Crabshell, Ashburton Arms, Globe Inn, Cricket Inn, Church House, California Cross*

Lamacraft House, *Start Point, Kingsbridge, Devon, TQ7 2NG.* Beautiful secluded position overlooking Start Bay, midway Dartmouth/Salcombe. Unspoilt coast and countryside. One nights and singles welcome. Rooms with balcony overlooking gardens or overlooking sea. Morning and afternoon tea, transport for walkers to evening meals (four venues). **Open:** All year (not Xmas/New Year)
01548 511291 Mr & Mrs Sainthill **D:** Fr £20.00 **S:** Fr £21.00 **Beds:** 1T 2D **Baths:** 1 En 1 Sh (6)

Stockland

ST2404

Barn Park Farm, *Stockland Hill, Cotleigh, Honiton, Devon, EX14 9JA.* Traditional old Devon dairy farm, excellent walking country, abundance of wildlife. **Open:** All year (not Xmas/New Year)
01404 861297 & 08003 282605 (freephone) Mrs Boyland **Fax: 01404 861297** *pab@barnparkfarm.co.uk* www.lymeregis.com/barn-park-farm **D:** Fr £17.00–£20.00 **S:** Fr £20.00 **Beds:** 1F 1T 1D 1S **Baths:** 2 En 1 Pr 1 Sh (10)

The Kings Arms Inn, *Stockland, Honiton, Devon, EX14 9BS.* C16th inn set in beautiful Devon countryside. **Open:** All year (not Xmas)
01404 881361 Fax: 01404 881732 *reserve@kingsarms.net* www.kingsarms.net **D:** Fr £25.00 **S:** Fr £30.00 **Beds:** 2D 1T **Baths:** 3 En ⛟ P (40) TV ✕ V cc

Tavistock

SX4874 *Mucky Duck, Dartmoor Inn*

Kingfisher Cottage, *Mount Tavy Road, Tavistock, Devon, PL19 9JB.* Riverside accommodation in Characterful cottage. Near beautiful Dartmoor. Weekly discounts! **Open:** All year
01822 613801 M Toland **D:** Fr £17.50–£22.00 **S:** Fr £25.50–£40.00 **Beds:** 1F 1T 1D **Baths:** 2 En 1 Pr P (4) TV V

Bush Park, *Tavistock, Devon, PL19 0NE.* Stunning views. Next to Lydford Gorge and Forest. **Open:** All year
01822 820345 A S Hepworth *stay@bushpark.co.uk* **D:** Fr £18.00 **S:** Fr £24.00 **Beds:** 1T 1D **Baths:** 1 Pr (3) P (4) TV V

Downhouse Farm, *Mill Hill Lane, Tavistock, Devon, PL19 8NH.* Great accommodation, ideal for walking, cycling, horse-riding, golf, etc. **Open:** All year
01822 614521 Fax: 01822 613675 *downhousefarm@aol.com* www.downhousefarm.co.uk **D:** Fr £22.50 **S:** Fr £33.00 **Beds:** 1D **Baths:** 1 En P (1) TV

Acorn Cottage, *Heathfield, Tavistock, Devon, PL19 0LQ.* **Open:** All year **Grades:** ETC 4 Diamond
01822 810038 Mrs Powell-Thomas *viv@acorncot.fsnet.co.uk* www.geocities.com/acorncottage **D:** Fr £15.00–£20.00 **S:** Fr £20.00–£35.00 **Beds:** 1D 2T **Baths:** 3 En 1 Pr (6) P (20) TV V
C17th Grade II Listed, many original features retained. Peaceful, rural location, beautiful views, just 3 miles from Tavistock on the Chillaton road. Quality accommodation near Lydford Gorge and Brentor medieval church. Central to many activities. Also self-catering accommodation available.

Bracken B & B, *36 Plymouth Road, Tavistock, Devon, PL19 8BU.* Comfortable Victorian town house. Adjacent Dartmoor National Park. Warm welcome. **Open:** All year
01822 613914 Ms Spartley *niklin@supanet.com* **D:** Fr £16.00–£20.00 **S:** Fr £20.00–£30.00 **Beds:** 1T 3D **Baths:** 1 En 1 Pr 1 Sh (5) P (4) TV V

Tedburn St Mary

SX8194

Fingle Glen Farm, *Tedburn St Mary, Exeter, Devon, EX6 6AF.* **Open:** All year (not Xmas/New Year)
01647 61227
D: Fr £19.00 **S:** Fr £20.00 **Beds:** 1T 1D **Baths:** 1 Sh P (4) TV V
A warm & friendly welcome, central for coasts & moors, panoramic views, adjacent to 18 hole golf course. Close to National Trust properties, Eden Project 1 hour away. Situated 1/4 mile from A30 carriageway, 5 miles west of Exeter.

Teignmouth

SX9473

Wytchwood, *West Buckeridge Road, Teignmouth, Devon, TQ14 8NF.* **Open:** All year
01626 773482 & 07971 783454 (M) Mrs Richardson Brown *wytchwood@yahoo.com* www.messages.to/wytchwood **D:** Fr £28.50–£35.00 **S:** Fr £35.00–£45.00 **Beds:** 1F 1T 1D **Baths:** 1 En 2 Pr P TV cc
Award-winning Wytchwood has an outstanding reputation for lavish hospitality & traditional home cooking. To stay here is to be fully pampered! Panoramic views, beautiful garden & produce. Home made breads, jams, preserves & orchard honey. Delicious cream teas, sponges/cakes.

Leicester House, *2 Winterbourne Road, Teignmouth, Devon, TQ14 8JT.* Imposing towered Victoriana. Garden, parking and 5 mins to town and beach. **Open:** All year (not Xmas/New Year)
01626 773043 S Pickup **D:** Fr £18.00–£20.00 **Beds:** 1T 3D **Baths:** 4 En (6) P (3) TV V

The Bay Hotel, *Sea Front, Teignmouth, Devon, TQ14 8BL.* Overlooking the sea, previously summer house of Earl of Devon. **Open:** All year
01626 774123 Mrs Dumont **Fax: 01626 777794 D:** Fr £23.00–£26.00 **S:** Fr £23.00–£26.00 **Beds:** 4F 6T 6D 2S **Baths:** 18 En P (14) TV ✕ V ❄ cc

BATHROOMS
En = Ensuite
Pr = Private
Sh = Shared

Thelbridge

SS7911 *Thelbridge Cross Inn*

Hele Barton, *Thelbridge Cross, Thelbridge, Black Dog, Crediton, Devon, EX17 4QJ.* Comfortable, friendly thatched farmhouse accommodation. Ideal base for exploring Devon. **Open:** Easter to Nov
01884 860278 (also fax) Mrs Gillbard *gillbard@eclipse.co.uk* www.eclipse.co.uk/helebarton **D:** Fr £16.00–£21.00 **Beds:** 2T 1D **Baths:** 1 En 1 Sh P TV

Tipton St John

SY0991

Higher Coombe Farm, *Tipton St John, Sidmouth, Devon, EX10 0AX.* Friendly welcome, comfortable rooms. Relaxed atmosphere. Working farm, sheep/cattle. **Open:** Mar to Dec **Grades:** ETC 3 Diamond
01404 813385 (also fax) Mrs Farmer *kerstinfarmer@farming.co.uk* **D:** Fr £19.00–£23.00 **S:** Fr £19.00–£23.00 **Beds:** 1F 1T 1D 1S **Baths:** 1 En 1 Sh P (4) TV

Tiverton

SS9512

Angel Guest House, *13 St Peter Street, Tiverton, Devon, EX16 6NU.* Town centre Georgian house, large cycle shed, ideal touring centre. **Open:** All year **Grades:** AA 3 Diamond
01884 253392 Mr & Mrs Evans **Fax: 01884 251154** *cerimar@eurobell.co.uk* **D:** Fr £19.00–£23.00 **S:** Fr £19.00–£25.00 **Beds:** 2F 3D 1T 1S **Baths:** 3 Pr 2 Sh P (4) TV V

The Mill, *Lower Washfield, Washfield, Tiverton, Devon, EX16 9PD.* Relax, unwind, enjoy the peace and tranquillity of our idyllic riverside location. **Open:** All year
01884 255297 (also fax) Mrs Arnold **D:** Fr £23.00–£25.00 **S:** Fr £22.00–£26.00 **Beds:** 1F 1T 2D **Baths:** 4 En P (8) TV ✕ V ❄

Topsham

SX9688

Broadway House, *33 High Street, Topsham, Exeter, Devon, EX3 0ED.* **Open:** All year (not Xmas/New Year)
01392 873465 H & G Knee **Fax: 01392 666103** *heather@broadwayhouse.com* www.broadwayhouse.com **D:** Fr £22.00–£28.00 **S:** Fr £22.00–£28.00 **Beds:** 1F 2T 3D 2S **Baths:** 7 En 1 Sh P (6) TV V cc
A warm welcome awaits you at Broadway Home. Spacious ensuite rooms in Listed Georgian property (1776 II*). Traditional English breakfast. Near M5 & Westpoint. Off-street parking. 200 yards rail. 10 yards bus. Non-smoking. Contact Gerald or Heather Knee.

Westward Ho!

SS4329 *Country Cousins, Potwallopers*

Brockenhurst, *11 Atlantic Way, Westward Ho!, Bideford, Devon, EX39 1HX.* Comfortable, detached house. Views of Lundy Island and vast beach. **Open:** All year (not Xmas)
01237 423346 (also fax) Mrs Snowball **D:** Fr £22.50–£25.00 **S:** Fr £27.00–£30.00 **Beds:** 2D 1T **Baths:** 3 En (4)

Eversley, *1 Youngaton Road, Westward Ho!, Bideford, Devon, EX39 1HU.* Victorian gentleman's residence. Superb accommodation. Sea views, beach 2 mins. **Open:** All year
01237 471603 Mr Sharratt **D:** Fr £18.00–£20.00 **S:** Fr £24.00–£29.00 **Beds:** 1F 1D 1T **Baths:** 1 En 1 Sh (3)

Seadrift, *72 Atlantic Way, Westward Ho!, Bideford, Devon, EX39 1JG.* Comfortable family home. Hearty breakfast, lovely sea views, coastal walks. **Open:** All year
01237 421174 Mrs Shadbolt *chruth.shadalak@zoom.co.uk* **D:** Fr £17.50–£20.00 **S:** Fr £20.00–£22.00 **Beds:** 2T 1D **Baths:** 3 En

Whimple

SY0497

Busy Bee, *Mellifera, Church Road, Whimple, Exeter, Devon, EX5 2TF.* Friendly, lovely views, bungalow. Ideal for coast, city or airport. **Open:** All year
01404 823019 (also fax) Mr & Mrs Janaway *bandb.busybee@virgin.net* www.whimple.swest.co.uk **D:** Fr £19.00 **S:** Fr £21.00–£22.00 **Beds:** 1T 2D **Baths:** 3 En (5) (6)

Holway Barton, *Whimple, Exeter, Devon, EX5 2QY.* Elegant country home. Attractive gardens surrounded by open farmland. **Open:** All year (not Xmas/New Year)
01404 822477 Mr Brown **D:** Fr £20.00 **S:** Fr £25.00 **Beds:** 1F 2T 2D **Baths:** 1 En 1 Pr 1 Sh (6)

The Jays, *The Square, Whimple, Exeter, Devon, EX5 2SL.* C16th village square cottage. Ideal for Dartmoor and coast. **Open:** All year (not Xmas/New Year)
01404 823614 J & J Discombe **Fax: 01404 823629** *jaydiscombe@supanet.com* **D:** Fr £17.50 **Beds:** 1T 2D 1S **Baths:** 2 Sh

Willand

ST0310

Pitfield House, *Willand Old Village, Cullompton, Devon, EX15 2RL.* Charming family home. Large secluded garden. Small outdoor swimming pool. **Open:** All year (not Xmas/New Year)
01884 32304 Mrs Armstrong **D:** Fr £25.00–£30.00 **S:** Fr £20.00–£25.00 **Beds:** 2T 1D **Baths:** 2 Sh

Wilmington

ST2000

The Crest Guest House, *Moorcox Lane, Wilmington, Honiton, Devon, EX14 9JU.* A modern chalet style house nestling in the picturesque Unborne valley. **Open:** All year
01404 831419 Mrs Kidwell **D:** Fr £19.00–£21.00 **S:** Fr £26.00–£27.00 **Beds:** 1F 1D 1T (8)

Witheridge

SS8014

Mitre Inn, *Two Moors Way, Witheridge, Tiverton, Devon, EX16 8AH.* Large Victorian coaching inn. **Open:** All year (not Xmas/New Year)
01884 861263 Mr & Mrs Parsons **D:** Fr £18.00–£25.00 **S:** Fr £20.00–£27.00 **Beds:** 3F 1D 5T **Baths:** 1 En 3 Sh (5) **cc**

Woodbury

SY0187 *Digger's Rest*

Rydon Farm, *Woodbury, Exeter, Devon, EX5 1LB.* C16th Devon longhouse, dairy farm. Perfect retreat, highly recommended. **Open:** All year
01395 232341 (also fax) Ms Glanvill *sallyglanvill@hotmail.com* **D:** Fr £25.00–£28.00 **S:** Fr £27.00–£30.00 **Beds:** 1F 1T 1D **Baths:** 2 En 1 Pr

Cottles Farm, *Woodbury, Exeter, Devon, EX5 1ED.* Wonderful views, ideally situated for coast and Exeter. Farmhouse breakfast. **Open:** All year (not Xmas/New Year)
01395 232547 Mrs Brown **D:** Fr £20.00–£22.00 **S:** Fr £23.00–£25.00 **Beds:** 1F 1T 1D **Baths:** 2 En 1 Pr (3)

Greenacre, *Couches Lane, Woodbury, Exeter, EX5 1HL.* Secluded, comfortable country accommodation near village. Large stream-bordered gardens. **Open:** All year (not Xmas)
01395 233574 (also fax) Mrs Price *price@woodburystone.fsnet.co.uk* **D:** Fr £20.00–£25.00 **S:** Fr £25.00–£30.00 **Beds:** 1D 2T **Baths:** 2 En 1 Pr (5)

Woodleigh

SX7448

Yeo Farm, *Topsham Bridge, Woodleigh, Kingsbridge, Devon, TQ7 4DR.* C14th farm house in 86 acres of woods & pasture. Mile of riverbank. **Open:** All year
01548 550586 Mrs Smith *yeomary@appleonline.net* **D:** Fr £20.00–£25.00 **S:** Fr £20.00–£25.00 **Beds:** 1T **Baths:** 1 En (2)

Woolacombe

SS4543

Barton Lea, *Beach Road, Woolacombe, Devon, EX34 7BT.* **Open:** Easter to Oct
01271 870928 Mrs Vickery *lynda@bartonlea.fsnet.co.uk* **D:** Fr £20.00–£25.00 **S:** Fr £30.00 **Beds:** 1F 1D 1T **Baths:** 3 En (7)
Delightful home with wonderful sea views. Big breakfast menu, 5 mins walk from beach, main shops, restaurants and Coastal Path. Close to Exmoor, horse riding, cycling, golf, surfing and many more. Relaxed dining room, air garden and patio.

Ossaborough House, *Woolacombe, Devon, EX34 7HJ.* **Open:** All year **Grades:** AA 4 Diamond
01271 870297 Mr & Mrs Day *info@ossaboroughhouse.co.uk* www.ossaboroughhouse.co.uk **D:** Fr £24.00–£33.00 **S:** Fr £24.00–£34.00 **Beds:** 2F 2T 2D **Baths:** 6 En (8)
Escape to our lovely C17th country house originating in the days of Saxon England - rustic beams. Thick stone walls, inglenook fireplaces, candlelit dinners. All rooms sympathetically restored. Explore rolling hills, rugged cliffs, picturesque villages, stunning golden beaches and secluded coves.

Sunny Nook, *Beach Road, Woolacombe, Devon, EX34 7AA.* Delightful home in lovely situation, wonderful views and excellent breakfasts. **Open:** All year (not Xmas)
01271 870964 Mrs Morgan *kate@sunnynook.co.uk* **D:** Fr £25.00 **S:** Fr £35.00 **Beds:** 1F 1D 1T **Baths:** 3 En (5)

Clyst House, *Rockfield Road, Woolacombe, Devon, EX34 7DH.* Friendly, comfortable guest house close Blue Flag beach. Delicious English breakfast. Beautiful walking area. **Open:** Mar to Nov
01271 870220 Mrs Braund **D:** Fr £20.00–£22.00 **S:** Fr £20.00–£22.00 **Beds:** 1F 1D 1T **Baths:** 1 Sh (7)

RATES
D = Price range per person sharing in a double or twin room
S = Price range for a single room

Camberley, *Beach Road, Woolacombe, Devon, EX34 7AA.* Large Victorian house with views to sea & NT land. Use of indoor pool. **Open:** All year (not Xmas) **01271 870231** Mr & Mrs Riley *camberley@tesco.net* **D:** Fr £21.00–£27.00 **S:** Fr £21.00–£27.00 **Beds:** 2F 3D 1T **Baths:** 5 En 1 Pr (6) **cc**

Yarcombe

ST2408

The Belfry Country Hotel, *Yarcombe, Honiton, Devon, EX14 9BD.* Converted Victorian school, offering en-suite accommodation. Superb food. Fine wines. **Open:** All year **01404 861234** Mr Pierce **Fax: 01404 861579** www.westcountryhotels.com **D:** Fr £36.00 **S:** Fr £44.00 **Beds:** 2T 4D **Baths:** 1 En (12) (10) **cc**

All details shown are as supplied by B&B owners in Autumn 2002

Yelverton

SX5267

The Rosemont, *Greenbank Terrace, Yelverton, Devon, PL20 6DR.* **Open:** All year (not Xmas) **01822 852175** Mr & Mrs Eastaugh *office@rosemontgh.fsnet.co.uk* www.therosemont.co.uk **D:** Fr £22.50–£25.00 **S:** Fr £30.00–£40.00 **Beds:** 1F 3D 2T 1S **Baths:** 7 En (5) **cc**
Sunny, spacious Victorian house overlooking the village green. Safe garage for bicycles. Excellent free-range breakfast using local produce. Quality B&B on Dartmoor. See website for more information. www.therosemont.co.uk.

Overcombe Hotel, *Old Station Road, Horrabridge, Yelverton, Devon, PL20 7RA.* **Open:** All year **01822 853501** JH & G Wright *enquiries@overcombehotel.co.uk* www.overcombehotel.co.uk **D:** Fr £23.00–£30.00 **S:** Fr £23.00–£35.00 **Beds:** 2F 2T 3D 1S **Baths:** 8 En (8) **cc**
Homely, relaxed atmosphere. Comfortable ensuite bedrooms. Substantial breakfast. Beautiful views. Situated within Dartmoor National Park - walks from hotel. Buckland Abbey, the Garden House, Cotehele, historic Plymouth and Tavistock attractions are nearby. Totally non-smoking. No animals. Near Route 27(Cyclepath).

Rettery Bank, *Harrowbeer Lane, Yelverton, Devon, PL20 6EA.* Quiet house, central, wonderful views, pocket-sprung beds, jacuzzi, English breakfast. **Open:** All year (not Xmas) **01822 855088 (also fax)** Ms Leavey *bandtleavey@aol.com* **D:** Fr £18.00–£25.00 **S:** Fr £16.00–£20.00 **Beds:** 1D 1T **Baths:** 1 En 1 Sh (5) (2)

Stokehill Farmhouse, *Yelverton, Devon, PL20 6EW.* Beautiful country house in lovely grounds in a quiet, rural setting. **Open:** All year (not Xmas/New Year) **01822 853791** Mrs Gozzard **D:** Fr £22.50–£25.00 **S:** Fr £27.00–£30.00 **Beds:** 1T 2D **Baths:** 1 En 1 Pr (10)

Yeoford

SX7898

Warrens Farm, *The Village, Yeoford, Crediton, Devon, EX17 5JD.* C16th Devon longhouse. Antique furniture. Good meals. Prime touring position. **Open:** All year **01363 84304 (also fax)** W Brimacombe Nelissen **D:** Fr £18.00 **S:** Fr £20.00 **Beds:** 1F 2D **Baths:** 2 En (4)

Yettington

SY0585

Lufflands, *Yettington, Budleigh Salterton, Devon, EX9 7BP.* Comfortable C17th farmhouse in rural location. **Open:** All year **01395 568422** Mrs Goode **Fax: 01395 568810** *lufflands@compuserve.com* **D:** Fr £20.00–£22.00 **S:** Fr £20.00–£27.00 **Beds:** 1F 1D 1S **Baths:** 1 En 1 Pr (10)

Wrenwood Hotel, *11 Florence Road, Bournemouth, Dorset, BH5 1HH.* Small Victorian family hotel. Close to sea, shops and transport. **Open:** All year
01202 395086 Mr Masson *bookings@wrenwood.co.uk* www.wrenhood.co.uk **D:** Fr £18.00–£25.00 **S:** Fr £23.00–£35.00 **Beds:** 5F 1T 5D **Baths:** 11 En P (8) cc

West Cliff Sands Hotel, *9 Priory Road, West Cliff, Bournemouth, Dorset, BH2 5DF.* Prime position on popular West Cliff. Two mins' walk pier, theatres, International Conference Centre. **Open:** All year
01202 557013 (also fax) Mr & Mrs Pannell www.westcliffsands.sageweb.co.uk **D:** Fr £24.00–£35.00 **S:** Fr £35.00–£45.00 **Beds:** 5F 11D **Baths:** 16 En P (16) cc

Chelsea Hotel, *32 St Swithuns Road, Bournemouth, Dorset, BH1 3RH.* Popular family run hotel. Great atmosphere. Near train/coach station. **Open:** Easter to Oct
01202 290111 (also fax) Mr & Mrs Beere *info@chelseahotel32.co.uk* www.chelseahotel32.co.uk **D:** Fr £20.00–£25.00 **S:** Fr £20.00–£25.00 **Beds:** 5F 2T 2D 1S **Baths:** 7 En 2 Pr cc

Avonwood Hotel, *20 Owls Road, Bournemouth, Dorset, BH5 1AF.* A friendly, family-run hotel close to sandy beach, pier, shops and gardens. **Open:** All year
01202 394704 Mr & Mrs Hutchinson *avonwood.hotel@tinyworld.co.uk* **D:** Fr £19.00–£26.00 **S:** Fr £19.00–£26.00 **Beds:** 4F 3T 8D 1S **Baths:** 11 En P (14) cc

Golden Sovereign Hotel, *97 Alumhurst Road, Bournemouth, Dorset, BH4 8HR.* Excellent hotel, 5 mins from award-winning beaches. You will return! **Open:** All year
01202 762088 (also fax) Mr & Mrs Weetman *scott.p@talk21.com* **D:** Fr £25.00 **S:** Fr £25.00–£40.00 **Beds:** 2F 3T 2D 2S **Baths:** 7 En 2 Pr P (8) cc

Shoreline Hotel, *7 Pinecliffe Avenue, Southbourne, Bournemouth, BH6 3PY.* Close to new Forest, Beaulieu Motor Museum, Salisbury Wilton House. **Open:** Easter to Dec
01202 429654 (also fax) **D:** Fr £13.00–£21.00 **S:** Fr £13.00–£24.00 **Beds:** 2F 4D 2T 2S **Baths:** 5 En 2 Sh (5) P (5)

Chilterns Hotel, *44 Westby Road, Bournemouth, Dorset, BH5 1HD.* Excellent location. Few minutes to pier, glorious golden sandy beaches, wooded cliff top walks, shopping precinct, T/Operators. Comfortable, welcoming. Highly recommended for short or long stay. Level walking, AMPLE PARKING. Parties welcome. **Open:** Apr to Sept
01202 396539 (also fax) Mr Whitney *bwhit@tinyworld.co.uk* **D:** Fr £20.00–£25.00 **S:** Fr £18.50 **Beds:** 3F 8D 4T 2S **Baths:** 9 En 1 Pr 7 Sh P (10)

West Cliff Hall Hotel, *14 Priory Road, West Cliff, Bournemouth, BH2 5DN.* Superb central location, beautiful Westcliff. Close beaches and shops, entertainment. **Open:** All year
01202 299715 *info@bournehall.co.uk* www.bournehall.co.uk **D:** Fr £25.00–£39.00 **S:** Fr £30.00–£49.00 **Beds:** 7F 15T 9S **Baths:** 48 En P (35) cc

Cremona Hotel, *61 St Michaels Road, West Cliff, Bournemouth, Dorset, BH2 5DP.* Friendly 'home from home' hotel. Close to beach/town centre. **Open:** All year
01202 290035 (also fax) Mr Bird *Enquiries@cremona.co.uk* www.cremona.co.uk **D:** Fr £20.00–£25.00 **S:** Fr £18.00–£25.00 **Beds:** 4F 1T 5D **Baths:** 7 En 2 Sh cc

Whateley Hall Hotel, *7 Florence Road, off Sea Road, Bournemouth, BH5 1HH.*
Open: All year (not Xmas/New Year) **Grades:** AA 4 Diamond
01202 397749 (also fax) *whateleyhall.hotel@virgin.net* **D:** Fr £23.00–£28.00 **S:** Fr £25.00–£31.00 **Beds:** 3F 2T 5D **Baths:** 10 En (8) P (7)
Small, friendly, family-run, non-smoking hotel with residential licence. The hotel is situated a few minutes' walk from either Boscombe's sandy beach, Blue Flag, or shopping centre. Traditional English cooking. Ideal base for excursions to the New Forest, Poole, Christchurch.

Cransley Hotel, *11 Knyveton Road, East Cliff, Bournemouth, Dorset, BH1 3QG.* **Open:** All year (not Xmas) **Grades:** ETC 4 Diamond, AA 4 Diamond
01202 290067 Mr Goodwin **Fax: 0709 2381721** *info@cransley.com* www.cransley.com **D:** Fr £25.00–£32.00 **S:** Fr £35.00–£42.00 **Beds:** 4T 5D 2S **Baths:** 10 En 1 Pr P (8) cc
A comfortable and elegant house for non-smokers, set in a quiet pine avenue. Close to the town centre and beach. Conveniently placed for all major road and rail links. Sorry, no children & no pets.

Sandy Bay Guest House, *3 Westby Road, Bournemouth, BH5 1HA.* Probably one of the best B&Bs in the area. **Open:** All year
01202 309245 (also fax) Mr Villiers *sandybayhotel@lineone.net* www.sandybay.gbr.cc **D:** Fr £23.00 **S:** Fr £30.00–£40.00 **Beds:** 2T 3D 1S **Baths:** 5 En P (3) cc

St Michaels Friendly Guest House, *42 St Michaels Road, Westcliffe, Bournemouth, Dorset, BH2 5DY.* Home-cooking. Five minutes walk to town or sea and international conference centre. **Open:** All year
01202 557386 Mrs Davies *eileend@42stmichaels.fsworld.co.uk* www.stmichaelsfriendlyguesthouse.co.uk **D:** Fr £18.00–£22.00 **S:** Fr £20.00–£25.00 **Beds:** 1F 2D 2T 1S **Baths:** 2 Sh

Shady Nook Guest House, *3 Upper Terrace Road, Bournemouth, Dorset, BH2 5NW.* Town centre guest house near beach and entertainment. Excellent food and service. **Open:** All year (not Xmas)
01202 551557 Mr Holdaway *shady.nook@btinternet.com* **D:** Fr £21.00–£29.00 **S:** Fr £24.00–£32.00 **Beds:** 2F 3D 2T 1S **Baths:** 5 En 1 Sh P (4)

Southernhay Hotel, *42 Alum Chine Road, Bournemouth, Dorset, BH4 8DX.* Warm, homely and comfortable accommodation, perfectly situated for all amenities.
Open: All year **Grades:** ETC 3 Diamond
01202 761251 (also fax) Mrs Derby *enquiries@southernhayhotel.co.uk* www.southernhayhotel.co.uk **D:** Fr £21.00–£25.00 **S:** Fr £18.00–£30.00 **Beds:** 2F 1T 2D 1S **Baths:** 4 En 1 Sh P (12)

The Chines Hotel, *9 Rosemount Road, Alum Chine, Bournemouth, Dorset, BH4 8HB.* Quality B&B, near beach, heated indoor pool, overlooking Alum Chine. **Open:** All year
01202 761256 *chinehotel@aol.com* **D:** Fr £21.00–£28.00 **S:** Fr £21.00–£28.00 **Beds:** 4F 2T 4D 2S **Baths:** 12 En P (6) cc

All details shown are as supplied by B&B owners in Autumn 2002

Balincourt Hotel, *58 Christchurch Road, Bournemouth, Dorset, BH1 3PF.* Elegant Victorian residence, luxury spacious rooms. Close to sea front, town centre. **Open:** All year
01202 552962 Mr & Mrs Gandolfi **D:** Fr £25.00–£30.00 **S:** Fr £30.00–£45.00 **Beds:** 5D 5T 2S **Baths:** 12 En 1 Sh (11) **cc**

Moordown, *1031 Wimborne Road, Bournemouth, Dorset, BH9 2BX.* Accommodation near to shops/bus route. Rooms have hot and cold wash handbasin. **Open:** All year (not Xmas)
01202 527419 Miss Barton **D:** Fr £15.00–£30.00 **S:** Fr £25.00–£40.00 **Beds:** 2D 1S **Baths:** 1 Sh

Tenby House Hotel, *23 Pinecliffe, Southbourne, Bournemouth, Dorset, BH6 3PY.* Delightful, Edwardian-style private hotel. Superbly located for shops, pubs, restaurant and beach. **Open:** Jan to Dec
01202 423696 Carol Davis **D:** Fr £17.00–£22.00 **S:** Fr £19.00–£24.00 **Beds:** 2F 3D 3T 2S **Baths:** 5 En 3 Sh (2) (5)

Redlands Hotel, *79 St Michaels Road, Bournemouth, Dorset, BH2 5DR.* Family-run hotel near town centre and sea, private parking. **Open:** All year
01202 553714 Mr & Mrs Littlewort *enquiries@redlandshotel.co.uk* www.redlandshotel.co.uk **D:** Fr £22.00–£30.00 **S:** Fr £22.00–£30.00 **Beds:** 3F 1T 6D 2S **Baths:** 10 En 2 Sh (10) **cc**

Tivoli Private Hotel, *8 Southcote Road, Bournemouth, Dorset, BH1 3SR.* Quality accommodation. Walking distance rail/coach station - beach - town centre. **Open:** All year
01202 554491 (also fax) www.tivolihotel.co.uk **D:** Fr £25.00–£30.00 **S:** Fr £25.00–£30.00 **Beds:** 1F 1T 2D 1S **Baths:** 5 En (9) **cc**

Mayfield Guest House, *Knyveton Gardens, 46 Frances Road, Bournemouth, Dorset, BH1 3SA.* Friendly guest house opposite Knyveton Gardens. Central sea, shops, rail, coach. **Open:** Jan to Nov **Grades:** ETC 4 Diamond, Silver
01202 551839 (also fax) Mrs Barling *accom@mayfieldguesthouse.com* www.mayfieldguesthouse.com **D:** Fr £20.00–£24.00 **S:** Fr £20.00–£24.00 **Beds:** 1F 5D 1T 1S **Baths:** 7 En 1 Pr (5) (5)

Victoria, *120 Parkwood Road, Southbourne, Bournemouth, Dorset, BH5 2BN.* A friendly, comfortable private house near beach, shops and buses. **Open:** May to Sep
01202 423179 Mrs Rising **D:** Fr £15.00 **S:** Fr £15.00 **Beds:** 1D 1T **Baths:** 1 Sh (4) (2)

Fircroft Hotel, *Owls Road, Boscombe, Bournemouth, BH5 1AE.* Friendly family hotel close sea and shops (cycle friendly). Free entry to health club. **Open:** All year
01202 309771 Fax: 01202 395644 D: Fr £26.00–£34.00 **S:** Fr £26.00–£34.00 **Beds:** 14F 12D 18T 6S **cc**

Bridport

SY4693

Britmead House, *West Bay Road, Bridport, Dorset, DT6 4EG.* **Open:** All year **Grades:** ETC 4 Diamond, AA 4 Diamond
01308 422941 Mr Hardy **Fax: 01308 422516** *britmead@talk21.com* www.britmeadhouse.co.uk **D:** Fr £23.00–£33.00 **S:** Fr £26.00–£42.00 **Beds:** 2F 3D 2T **Baths:** 7 En (12) **cc**
An elegant Edwardian house situated between Bridport and West Bay Harbour, with its beaches, golf course and the Dorset Coast Path, all just a short walk away. We offer comfortable ensuite rooms with many thoughtful extras and a warm welcome. Non-smoking.

The Old Dairy House, *Walditch, Bridport, Dorset, DT6 4LB.* **Open:** All year
01308 458021 Mrs Long **D:** Fr £20.00 **S:** Fr £20.00 **Beds:** 1D 1T **Baths:** 1 Sh (4)
A friendly welcome to relax in this peaceful corner of West Dorset. Enjoy full English breakfast. Guests' TV lounge with log fire. Gardens, abundant wildlife. Rural/coastal walks. 18-hole golf 2 miles. Good selection country pubs nearby. Adults only.

Green Lane House, *Bridport, Dorset, DT6 4LH.* Welcoming, spacious home in own grounds. 1.5 miles from coast. **Open:** All year (not Xmas/New Year)
01308 422619 (also fax) Mrs Prideaux **D:** Fr £22.50 **S:** Fr £20.00–£23.00 **Beds:** 1S 1T 2D **Baths:** 3 En 1 Sh (5)

Saxlingham House, *West Road, Symondsbury, Bridport, Dorset, DT6 6AA.* Extensive country views many local attractions warm friendly welcome. **Open:** Easter to Sep
01308 423629 Mrs Nicholls *saxlingham@freezone.co.uk* **D:** Fr £18.00 **S:** Fr £18.00 **Beds:** 1T 2D **Baths:** 3 En

Broadstone

SZ0095

Ashdell, *85 Dunyeats Road, Broadstone, Poole, Dorset, BH18 8AF.* Central, comfortable, secluded. Breakfast/EM choice. Historic countryside/beaches, short breaks. **Open:** All year **Grades:** ETC 2 Diamond
01202 692032 Mrs Critchley *ian@ashdell.fsnet.co.uk* www.ashdell.co.uk **D:** Fr £17.00–£20.00 **S:** Fr £19.00–£23.00 **Beds:** 1F 1D 1T 1S **Baths:** 1 Sh (5) (3)

Planning a longer stay? Always ask for any special rates

Buckland Newton

ST6805

Holyleas House, *Buckland Newton, Dorchester, Dorset, DT2 7DP.* The family Labrador will welcome you to this typical period country house set in 1/2 acre lovely garden. Rooms are beautifully decorated with antique furniture and enjoy fine views. Relax in the guests sitting room with log fire burning in winter. **Open:** All year (not Xmas/New Year)
01300 345214 Mrs Bunkall **Fax: 01305 264488** *tiabunkall@holyleas.fsnet.co.uk* **D:** Fr £22.50–£27.00 **S:** Fr £25.00–£35.00 **Beds:** 1T 1D 1S **Baths:** 2 En 1 Pr (6)

Rew Cottage, *Buckland Newton, Dorchester, DT2 7DN.* Lovely views, good walking, easy reach Dorchester, Sherborne and sea. **Open:** Jan to Dec
01300 345467 (also fax) Mrs McCarthy **D:** Fr £22.50–£27.00 **S:** Fr £29.00–£35.00 **Beds:** 1D 1T 1S **Baths:** 2 Pr (6)

Whiteways Farmhouse Accommodation, *Bookham Farm, Buckland Newton, Dorchester, Dorset, DT2 7RP.* Warm welcome awaits at hamstone and flint farmhouse. Head of Blackmore Vale. **Open:** All year (not Xmas/New Year)
01300 345511 (also fax) *bookhamfarm@netscapeonline.co.uk* **D:** Fr £20.00–£25.00 **S:** Fr £20.00–£25.00 **Beds:** 1F 1S **Baths:** 1 En 1 Pr (3)

Burton Bradstock

SY4889

Burton Cliff Hotel, *Cliff Road, Burton Bradstock, Bridport, Dorset, DT6 4RB.* On cliff top, superb sea views, surrounded by NT countryside. Many rooms overlook beach. **Open:** All year
01308 897205 Mr Hoare **Fax: 01308 898111 D:** Fr £21.00–£39.00 **S:** Fr £24.50–£36.00 **Beds:** 8T 7D 3S **Baths:** 12 En 12 Pr 3 Sh (40) **cc**

Cerne Abbas

ST6601

Cowden House, *Frys Lane, Godmanstone, Dorchester, Dorset, DT2 7AG.* Vegetarian B&B. Spacious, peaceful house surrounded by beautiful downland. **Open:** All year (not Xmas)
01300 341377 Mr Mills www.cowdenhouse.co.uk **D:** Fr £22.00–£25.00 **S:** Fr £26.00–£30.00 **Beds:** 1D 1F 1T 1D **Baths:** 1 En 1 Sh (2)

Charminster
SY6892

Slades Farm, *North Street, Charminster, Dorchester, Dorset, DT2 9QZ.* Superb accommodation and every comfort in recently converted barn. **Open:** All year **Grades:** ETC 4 Diamond
01305 265614 Mr & Mrs Woods **Fax: 01305 265713** www.sladesfarm.co.uk **D:** Fr £23.00–£25.00 **S:** Fr £32.00 **Beds:** 1F 2D **Baths:** 3 En (8)

Charmouth
SY3693

Hensleigh Hotel, *Lower Sea Lane, Charmouth, Bridport, Dorset, DT6 6LW.* Great food, fish specialities, 300 metres Coastal Paths & beach. **Open:** Feb to Nov
01297 560830 (also fax) Mr & Mrs Davis *davis2000@skynow.net* **D:** Fr £35.00–£43.00 **S:** Fr £35.00–£43.00 **Beds:** 1F 4D 3T 2S **Baths:** 10 En (20) cc

Clifton, *Five Acres, Charmouth, Bridport, Dorset, DT6 6BE.* Views over beach and bay. Excellent food. Easy walk to beach. **Open:** All year
01297 560574 (also fax) Mrs Dedman **D:** Fr £22.50–£25.00 **S:** Fr £27.50–£30.00 **Beds:** 1F 1T 1D **Baths:** 3 En (2)

Chickerell
SY6480

Heathwick House, *Knights in the Bottom, Chickerell, Weymouth, Dorset, DT3 4EA.* **Open:** All year (not Xmas/New Year)
01305 777272 *r+r@heathwickhouse.com* www.heathwickhouse.com **D:** Fr £25.00–£35.00 **S:** Fr £40.00–£50.00 **Beds:** 2T 3D **Baths:** 5 En (10) cc
Quality ensuite accommodation with beautiful views of Dorset's rolling countryside. All rooms decorated & furnished to a very high standard. Ideal touring, walking, golfing area. 3 miles from Weymouth town centre. Phone now for brochure & availability. Stay & enjoy!

Stonebank, *14 West Street, Chickerell, Weymouth, Dorset, DT3 4DY.* Charming C17th former farmhouse ideally situated for exploring coast and country. **Open:** Apr to Sep **Grades:** ETC 5 Diamond, Gold
01305 760120 Mrs Westcott **Fax: 01305 760871** *stw@stonebank-chickerell.co.uk* www.stonebank-chickerell.co.uk **D:** Fr £25.00 **S:** Fr £40.00 **Beds:** 2D **Baths:** 2 En (2) cc

Chideock
SY4292 *Royal Oak, New Inn, George Inn, Clockhouse, Anchor Inn*

Chimneys Guest House, *Main Street, Chideock, Bridport, Dorset, DT6 6JH.* Warm welcome, comfortable bedrooms, guest lounge and dining room. Private parking. **Open:** All year (not Xmas)
01297 489368 D Backhouse & J M Backhouse **D:** Fr £22.50–£25.00 **S:** Fr £25.00 **Beds:** 1F 1T 3D **Baths:** 4 En (5)

Chideock House Hotel, *Main St, Chideock, Bridport, DT6 6JN.* 10-min walk to the sea and coastal path with stunning scenery. 'Harbour Lights' filmed locally. Abbots Swannery, Mapperton Gardens and Athelhampton House all nearby. Stunning food in candle lit restaurant. Close to Lyme Regis and Charmouth. Weymouth 20 mins. **Open:** Feb to Jan
01297 489242 Mr Dunn **Fax: 01297 489184** *still@chideockhousehotel.com* www.chideockhousehotel.com **D:** Fr £30.00–£42.50 **S:** Fr £50.00–£80.00 **Beds:** 9D **Baths:** 8 En 1 Pr cc

Betchworth House, *Chideock, Bridport, Dorset, DT6 6JW.* Very friendly C17th guest house has been refurbished to a very high standard. **Open:** All year
01297 489478 Jill & John Lodge **Fax: 01297 489932 D:** Fr £22.00–£25.00 **S:** Fr £27.00–£30.00 **Beds:** 1F 2D 2T **Baths:** 3 En 2 Pr (10) (6) cc

Frogmore Farm, *Chideock, Bridport, Dorset, DT6 6HT.* C17th farmhouse overlooking Lyme Bay. Adjoining South West Coast Path. **Open:** All year
01308 456159 Mrs Norman **D:** Fr £16.00–£20.00 **S:** Fr £20.00–£23.00 **Beds:** 1F 1D 1T 1S **Baths:** 2 En 2 Pr (8) (6)

Planning a longer stay? Always ask for any special rates

Chilcombe
SY5291

Rudge Farm, *Chilcombe, Bridport, Dorset, DT6 4NF.* **Open:** All year (not Xmas) **Grades:** ETC 5 Diamond, Silver
01308 482630 Mrs Diment *sue@rudgefarm.co.uk* www.rudgefarm.co.uk **D:** Fr £26.00–£28.00 **Beds:** 1F 2D 1T **Baths:** 4 En (4) cc
Relax at Rudge farm, peacefully situated in Area of Outstanding Natural Beauty, 2 miles from Dorset's 'Jurassic Coastline'. Comfortable Victorian farmhouse has spacious bedrooms with far-reaching views, and a cosy book-lined sitting room. Large family suite in adjacent barn.

Child Okeford
ST8312

Bartley House, *Upper Street, Child Okeford, Blandford Forum, Dorset, DT11 8EF.* Beautiful, spacious Victorian house in quiet village location. Great breakfasts! **Open:** All year
01258 860420 Mrs Langley *rmw@ukf.net* www.scalelink.co.uk **D:** Fr £17.50–£25.00 **S:** Fr £20.00–£25.00 **Beds:** 2F 1D 1T **Baths:** 2 En 1 Pr (6)

Christchurch
SZ1693

Beverly Glen, *1 Stuart Road, Highcliffe, Christchurch, Dorset, BH23 5JS.* 5 mins walk to seafront, shops, restaurants, etc. 10 mins car to New Forest. **Open:** All year (not Xmas) **Grades:** ETC 4 Diamond
01425 273811 Mr Welch **D:** Fr £25.00–£30.00 **S:** Fr £22.00–£35.00 **Beds:** 1F 3D 1T 1S **Baths:** 6 En (6) cc

Well Cottage, *15 Sopley, Christchurch, Dorset, BH23 7AX.* Ideally situated between New Forest and beach; warm welcome assured. **Open:** All year (not Xmas)
01425 674668 Mrs Ramm *well.cottage@care4free.net* **D:** Fr £18.00–£20.00 **S:** Fr £20.00–£25.00 **Beds:** 1D 1T 1S **Baths:** 1 Sh (3)

Please respect a B&B's wishes regarding children, animals and smoking

B&B owners may vary rates – be sure to check when booking

Lyndhurst Lodge Guest House, *Lyndhurst Road, Christchurch, Dorset, BH23 4SD.* Perfectly situated for beaches, forest, leisure activities and business parks. **Open:** All year (not Xmas/New Year)
01425 276796 Mrs Green **Fax: 01425 276499** *lynlodge1@aol.com* www.lyndhurstlodge.co.uk **D:** Fr £18.00–£26.00 **S:** Fr £19.00–£25.00 **Beds:** 1F 1T 3D 2S **Baths:** 4 En 3 Sh (8) TV ×

Ashbourne Guest House, *47 Stour Road, Christchurch, Dorset, BH23 1LN.* Perfectly situated for exploring Christchurch. Warm welcome, delicious breakfast. **Open:** All year
01202 475574 Ms Hamilton **Fax: 01202 482905** *ashcroft@hotmail.com* **D:** Fr £20.00–£28.00 **S:** Fr £20.00–£40.00 **Beds:** 2F 2T 3D 0S **Baths:** 4 En 1 Pr 2 Sh TV V

Bure Farmhouse, *107 Bure Lane, Friar's Cliff, Christchurch, Dorset, BH23 4DN.* Edwardian farmhouse, beautiful, peaceful surroundings, sea and New Forest. **Open:** All year
01425 275498 Mrs Erhardt **D:** Fr £18.00–£23.00 **S:** Fr £20.00–£25.00 **Beds:** 2D 1T **Baths:** 3 En (4) (4) TV V

Church Knowle

SY9381

Bradle Farmhouse, *Church Knowle, Corfe Castle, Wareham, Dorset, BH20 5NU.* Relax and unwind in our picturesque farmhouse in the heart of Purbeck. **Open:** All year (not Xmas) **Grades:** ETC 4 Diamond, Silver
01929 480712 Mrs Hole **Fax: 01929 481144** *bradlefarmhouse@farmersweekly.net* www.bradlefarmhouse.co.uk **D:** Fr £23.00–£26.00 **S:** Fr £25.00–£42.00 **Beds:** 2D 1T **Baths:** 3 En (5) (3) TV V

Compton Abbas

ST8617 *The Cricketers*

The Old Forge, *Fanners Yard, Chapel Hill, Compton Abbas, Shaftesbury, Dorset, SP7 0NQ.* Charming converted C18th wheelwright's with views to National Trust downland. Ideal for relaxing, walking, wildlife etc. Guests have their own private sitting/dining room. A traditional farmhouse breakfast is served using local organic produce. We offer a warm welcome all year round. **Open:** All year
01747 811881 (also fax) Mrs Kerridge *theoldforge@hotmail.com* www.smoothhound.co.uk/oldforge **D:** Fr £22.50–£27.50 **S:** Fr £40.00 **Beds:** 1F 1D 1S **Baths:** 1 En 1 Pr (8) (3) TV

Coombe Keynes

SY8484 *Weld Arms*

West Coombe Farmhouse, *West Farm, Coombe Keynes, Wool, Wareham, Dorset, BH20 5PS.* Relax in our period farmhouse situated in a quiet village close to Lulworth Cove. Spectacular walking or borrow our bikes, central to all Dorset has to offer. Private sitting room with log fires in winter, excellent selection of local pubs. **Open:** All year (not Xmas/New Year)
01929 462889 Mr & Mrs Brachi **Fax: 01929 405863** *westcoombefarmhouse@btinternet.com* www.westcoombefarmhouse.co.uk **D:** Fr £20.00–£27.50 **S:** Fr £20.00–£35.00 **Beds:** 1T 1D 1S **Baths:** 1 En 1 Pr 1 Sh (12) (7) TV V

Corfe Castle

SY9682

Lower Lynch House, *Kingston Hill, Corfe Castle, Wareham, Dorset, BH20 5LG.* Comfortable country house, quiet location in the heart of Purbeck. **Open:** All year (not Xmas/New Year)
01929 480089 Mrs Burt **D:** Fr £25.00 **Beds:** 1T 1D **Baths:** 1 En 1 Pr (6) TV

Bradle Farmhouse, *Church Knowle, Corfe Castle, Wareham, Dorset, BH20 5NU.* Relax and unwind in our picturesque farmhouse in the heart of Purbeck. **Open:** All year (not Xmas) **Grades:** ETC 4 Diamond, Silver
01929 480712 Mrs Hole **Fax: 01929 481144** *bradlefarmhouse@farmersweekly.net* www.bradlefarmhouse.co.uk **D:** Fr £23.00–£26.00 **S:** Fr £25.00–£42.00 **Beds:** 2D 1T **Baths:** 3 En (5) (3) TV V

Knitson Old Farm House, *Corfe Castle, Wareham, Dorset, BH20 5JB.* **Open:** All year **01929 422836** Mrs Aktas *mark@knitson.freeserve.co.uk* **D:** Fr £20.00–£22.00 **S:** Fr £20.00–£22.00 **Beds:** 1F 1D 1S **Baths:** 2 Sh (6) TV × V
C16th farmhouse, 3 miles from Corfe, 1 from Swanage. Ridgeway and footpaths in all directions. Plantsman's garden, long views, wholefood in season, wood stove, carpeted comfortable rooms, traditional breakfasts, years of experience, featured in the Best of British.

Cranborne

SU0513

La Fosse Restaurant, *London House, The Square, Cranborne, Wimborne, Dorset, BH21 5PR.* Small, family run restaurant with rooms, super food, comfortable accommodation. **Open:** All year
01725 517604 Mr La Fosse **Fax: 01725 517778** **D:** Fr £32.50–£35.00 **S:** Fr £35.00–£37.50 **Beds:** 2D 1T **Baths:** 3 En (10) TV × V cc

Dorchester

SY6890

Slades Farm, *North Street, Charminster, Dorchester, Dorset, DT2 9QZ.* Superb accommodation and every comfort in recently converted barn. **Open:** All year **Grades:** ETC 4 Diamond
01305 265614 Mr & Mrs Woods **Fax: 01305 265713** www.sladesfarm.co.uk **D:** Fr £23.00–£25.00 **S:** Fr £32.00 **Beds:** 1F 2D **Baths:** 3 En (8) TV

Churchview Guest House, *Winterbourne Abbas, Dorchester, Dorset, DT2 9LS.* **Open:** All year (not Xmas) **Grades:** ETC 4 Diamond, AA 4 Diamond
01305 889296 (also fax) Mr Deller *stay@churchview.co.uk* www.churchview.co.uk **D:** Fr £25.00–£31.00 **S:** Fr £29.00–£36.00 **Beds:** 1F 4D 3T 1S **Baths:** 8 En 1 Pr (5) (10) TV × V cc
Delightful C17th village guest house near Dorchester offers comfort, delicious breakfasts.

Higher Came Farmhouse, *Higher Came, Dorchester, DT2 8NR.* **Open:** All year **Grades:** ETC 4 Diamond
01305 268908 & 07970 498773 (M) Mrs Bowden **Fax: 01305 268908** *highercame@eurolink.ltd.net* www.highercame.co.uk **D:** Fr £25.00–£30.00 **S:** Fr £28.00–£32.00 **Beds:** 1F 2D **Baths:** 1 En 2 Pr (4) TV V cc
Beautiful C17th farmhouse nesting at the foot of the Ridgeway in the heart of Hardy country. Spacious rooms, lovely gardens, great breakfast, relaxing atmosphere. Close to Maiden Castle, Dorchester and the spectacular Dorset coastline; discover and explore.

Yellowham Farmhouse, *Yellowham Wood, Dorchester, Dorset, DT2 8RW.* **Open:** All year **Grades:** ETC 4 Diamond, Silver, AA 4 Diamond
01305 262892 *b+b@yellowham.freeserve.co.uk* www.yellowham.freeserve.co.uk **D:** Fr £25.00–£30.00 **S:** Fr £30.00–£50.00 **Beds:** 1F 1T 2D 1S **Baths:** 4 En (8)
Situated on the edge of idyllic Yellowham Wood at the end of a long tarmac drive in 120 acres of farmland and 130 acres of woodland, where peace and tranquillity are guaranteed. 1.5 miles east of Dorchester off the A35 road.

Maumbury Cottage, *9 Maumbury Road, Dorchester, Dorset, DT1 1QW.* Homely accommodation, Thomas Hardy country, local produce, 8 mins town centre, museums, transport. **Open:** All year
01305 266726 **D:** Fr £18.00 **S:** Fr £18.00–£25.00 **Beds:** 1D 1T 1S **Baths:** 1 Sh (3)

The Old Rectory, *Winterbourne Steepleton, Dorchester, Dorset, DT2 9LG.* Quiet hamlet in Hardy country. Peaceful night's sleep, copious English, vegetarian or Continental breakfast. **Open:** All year (not Xmas/New Year)
01305 889468 M Tree **Fax: 01305 889737** *trees@eurobell.co.uk* www.trees.eurobell.co.uk **D:** Fr £25.00–£55.00 **Beds:** 3T **Baths:** 3 En (6)

Maiden Castle Farm, *Dorchester, Dorset, DT2 9PR.* Nestling beneath the famous prehistoric earthwork, from which we take our name, in the heart of Hardy country, 1m Dorchester, 7m Weymouth. Museums, fossil hunting, beaches, Abbotsbury Swannery all within a few miles. **Open:** All year
01305 262356 Mrs Hoskin **Fax: 01305 251085** *maidencastlefarm@euphony.net* www.maidencastlefarm.co.uk **D:** Fr £25.00 **S:** Fr £25.00 **Beds:** 1F 2D 1T 2S **Baths:** 3 En 1 Pr (10)

Joan's B and B, *119 Bridport Road, Dorchester, Dorset, DT1 2NH.* Comfortable relaxed atmosphere. Excellent breakfast, beautiful wildlife garden. **Open:** All year (not Xmas/New Year)
01305 267145 (also fax) J Cox *b_and_b@joancox.freeserve.co.uk* **D:** Fr £20.00–£22.00 **S:** Fr £20.00–£24.00 **Beds:** 1T 1D 1S **Baths:** 2 Sh (3)

BATHROOMS
En = Ensuite
Pr = Private
Sh = Shared

Planning a longer stay? Always ask for any special rates

Sunrise Guest House, *34 London Road, Dorchester, Dorset, DT1 1NE.* County town near Hardy's cottage. excellent breakfast and friendly welcome. **Open:** All year (nox Xmas/New Year) **Grades:** ETC 4 Diamond
01305 262425 **D:** Fr £20.00–£30.00 **S:** Fr £25.00–£40.00 **Beds:** 1F 2D **Baths:** 2 En 1 Pr (8) (4)

East Lulworth

SY8682

Botany Farm House, *East Lulworth, Wareham, Dorset, BH20 5QH.* Ancient, atmospheric, tranquil. Fresh, robust, simple food. Birds, wildlife & "Mrs Tiggywinkle" garden. **Open:** All year (not Xmas/New Year)
01929 400427 Mrs Hemsley *hemsleys@lineone.net* www.botany-farmhouse.com **D:** Fr £20.00–£25.00 **S:** Fr £25.00 **Beds:** 1T 2D **Baths:** 2 En

East Stour

ST7922

Aysgarth, *Back Street, East Stour, Gillingham, Dorset, SP8 5JY.* Ground floor accommodation. Good touring centre. Discount 3 night stay. **Open:** All year (not Xmas)
01747 838351 Mrs Dowding *aysgarth@lineone.net* **D:** Fr £17.50–£19.00 **S:** Fr £20.00–£22.00 **Beds:** 1T 2D **Baths:** 2 En 1 Pr (3)

Eype

SY4491

Eypes Mouth Country Hotel, *Eype, Bridport, Dorset, DT6 6AL.* In a secret spot down a leafy lane, 5-min walk from the sea. **Open:** All year
01308 423300 Ms Tye **Fax: 01308 420033** **D:** Fr £29.50–£38.00 **S:** Fr £29.50–£38.00 **Beds:** 18F 3T 13D 2S **Baths:** 18 En cc

Ferndown

SU0700

Pennington Copse, *11 Denewood Road, West Moors, Ferndown, Dorset, BH22 0LX.* Quiet Edwardian house, 5 min walk to village pubs and restaurants. **Open:** All year (not Xmas)
01202 894667 Mrs Hedley **D:** Fr £18.00–£20.00 **S:** Fr £25.00–£30.00 **Beds:** 2D **Baths:** 1 Sh

Fifehead St Quintin

ST7710 *Crown Inn*

Lower Fifehead Farm, *Fifehead St Quintin, Sturminster Newton, Dorset, DT10 2AP.* Beautiful listed farmhouse situated countryside, warm welcome. **Open:** All year
01258 817335 (also fax) Mrs Miller **D:** Fr £17.50–£25.00 **S:** Fr £20.00–£25.00 **Beds:** 1T 1D **Baths:** 1 En 1 Pr

Fleet

SY6380

Highfield, *Fleet, Weymouth, Dorset, DT3 4EB.* Ideal location, beautiful countryside, excellent accommodation, wonderful walks, relaxation. **Open:** All year (not Xmas)
01305 776822 Mrs Weeden *highfield.fleet@lineone.net* **D:** Fr £22.00–£25.00 **Beds:** 1F 1D 1T **Baths:** 3 En (4)

Gillingham

ST8026

Bugley Court Farm, *Gillingham, Dorset, SP8 5RA.* Peaceful location with wonderful views in comfortable family home. **Open:** All year
01747 823242 Mrs Lewis **D:** Fr £18.00 **Beds:** 1D 1T **Baths:** 1 Pr (2)

Godmanstone

SY6696

Cowden House, *Frys Lane, Godmanstone, Dorchester, Dorset, DT2 7AG.* Vegetarian B&B. Spacious, peaceful house surrounded by beautiful downland. **Open:** All year (not Xmas)
01300 341377 Mr Mills www.cowdenhouse.co.uk **D:** Fr £22.00–£25.00 **S:** Fr £26.00–£30.00 **Beds:** 1D 1F 1T 1D **Baths:** 1 En 1 Sh (2)

Hamworthy

SY9991 *Yachtsman Inn*

Individual Touristik Poole, *53 Branksea Avenue, Hamworthy, Poole, Dorset, BH15 4DP.* Select accommodation for those seeking something special. Luxury double/twin bed suite, facing Poole Harbour, Brownsea Island, Purbeck Hills, Park Beach. Own balcony, optional kitchen/diner or twin/double room facing pretty garden. Baths/separate showers. Walking distance Quay/Town. **Open:** All year
01202 673419 Renate Wadham **Fax: 01202 667260** *johnrenate@lineone.net* **D:** Fr £28.00–£32.00 **S:** Fr £32.00–£40.00 **Beds:** 2D/T **Baths:** 2 En (9) (3)

Please respect a B&B's wishes regarding children, animals and smoking

Seashells, *4 Lake Road, Hamworthy, Poole, Dorset, BH15 4LH.* Perfectly situated for Dorset coastline, countryside. Poole Quay, beautiful beaches. Warm welcome. **Open:** All year (not Xmas/New Year) **Grades:** ETC 3 Diamond
01202 671921 Mrs Hockey **D:** Fr £16.00–£20.00 **S:** Fr £25.00–£30.00 **Beds:** 1T 2D **Baths:** 1 En 1 Pr 1 Sh (5) (3)

Hazelbury Bryan
ST7408

The Old Malthouse, *Droop, Hazelbury Bryan, Sturminster Newton, Dorset, DT10 2ED.* C17th malt house renowned for its peaceful rural location and traditional hospitality. **Open:** All year
01258 817735 Mr Bleathman **D:** Fr £18.00–£20.00 **S:** Fr £20.00–£25.00 **Beds:** 1F 2D **Baths:** 1 En

Hermitage
ST6406 *Rose & Crown*

Almshouse Farm, *Hermitage, Sherborne, Dorset, DT9 6HA.* Listed farmhouse, retaining age and beauty with every modern convenience. **Open:** Feb to Dec
01963 210296 (also fax) Mrs Mayo **D:** Fr £22.00–£26.00 **S:** Fr £30.00 **Beds:** 1T 2D **Baths:** 2 En 1 Pr (10) (6)

Highcliffe
SZ2094

The White House, *428 Lymington Road, Highcliffe, Christchurch, Dorset, BH23 5HF.* Beautiful Victorian house. 5 min walk beach, shops, restaurants. Short drive New Forest. **Open:** All year (not Xmas/New Year)
01425 271279 F G White **Fax: 01425 276900** *thewhitehouse@themail.co.uk* www.thewhite-house.co.uk **D:** Fr £22.00–£25.00 **S:** Fr £25.00–£35.00 **Beds:** 6F 2T 3D 1S **Baths:** 5 En 5 Pr 1 Sh **cc**

Higher Came
SY6987

Higher Came Farmhouse, *Higher Came, Dorchester, DT2 8NR.* Beautiful C17th farmhouse, foot of the Ridgeway, heart of Hardy country. **Open:** All year **Grades:** ETC 4 Diamond
01305 268908 & 07970 498773 (M) Mrs Bowden **Fax: 01305 268908** *highercame@eurolink.ltd.net* www.highercame.co.uk **D:** Fr £25.00–£30.00 **S:** Fr £28.00–£32.00 **Beds:** 1F 2D **Baths:** 1 En 2 Pr (4) **cc**

Hooke
ST5300

Watermeadow House, *Bridge Farm, Hooke, Beaminster, Dorset, DT8 3PD.* Part of a working dairy farm, large Georgian-style house on edge of small village. **Open:** Easter to Oct
01308 862619 (also fax) Mrs Wallbridge *enquiries@watermeadowhouse.co.uk* www.watermeadowhouse.co.uk **D:** Fr £22.00–£24.00 **S:** Fr £24.00–£28.00 **Beds:** 1F 1D **Baths:** 1 En 1 Pr (4)

Horton
SU0307

Treetops, *Wigbeth, Horton, Wimborne, Dorset, BH21 7JH.* Rural, light airy rooms, large garden, ideally situated for touring. **Open:** All year
01258 840147 Mr Purchase *treetops.bandb@virgin.net* **D:** Fr £18.00 **S:** Fr £20.00 **Beds:** 1T 1D **Baths:** 2 En (3)

Ibberton
ST7807

Manor House Farm, *Ibberton, Blandford Forum, Dorset, DT11 0EN.* C16th comfortable farmhouse. Also working dairy and sheep farm. **Open:** All year
01258 817349 Mrs Old **D:** Fr £16.00–£18.00 **S:** Fr £17.00–£20.00 **Beds:** 2D 1T **Baths:** 2 En 1 Sh (3)

Iwerne Courtney or Shroton
ST8512

Lattemere, *Frog Lane, Iwerne Courtney, Blandford Forum, Dorset, DT11 8QL.* Comfortable welcoming home in quiet picturesque village. Outstanding countryside walks. **Open:** All year **Grades:** AA 3 Diamond
01258 860115 (also fax) Mrs Wright **D:** Fr £20.00–£22.00 **S:** Fr £20.00–£25.00 **Beds:** 1D 1T **Baths:** 1 En 1 Sh (3)

Foxhangers, *4 Old Mill Cottages, Iwerne Courtney or Shroton, Blandford Forum, Dorset, DT11 8TW.* Modern cottage in quiet and peaceful village. Excellent breakfast. **Open:** All year (not Xmas)
01258 861049 Mrs Moss **Fax: 01258 860785** *jane_moss@talk21.com* **D:** Fr £20.00 **S:** Fr £25.00 **Beds:** 1D **Baths:** 1 En (1)

Planning a longer stay? Always ask for any special rates

RATES
D = Price range per person sharing in a double or twin room
S = Price range for a single room

Iwerne Minster
ST8614

The Talbot Hotel, *Blandford Road, Iwerne Minster, Blandford Forum, Dorset, DT11 8QN.* Country inn offering comfortable rooms, good food, ale, affordable prices. **Open:** All year
01747 811269 Mr & Mrs Richardson **D:** Fr £13.75–£19.25 **S:** Fr £15.00–£35.00 **Beds:** 2F 2D 1T 1S **Baths:** 2 En 2 Sh (30)

Kimmeridge
SY9179

Kimmeridge Farmhouse, *Kimmeridge, Wareham, Dorset, BH20 5PE.* Picturesque farmhouse with views of Kimmeridge Bay - spacious and attractively furnished ensuite bedrooms. **Open:** All year (not Xmas)
01929 480990 Mrs Hole **D:** Fr £22.00–£23.00 **S:** Fr £25.00–£35.00 **Beds:** 2D 1T **Baths:** 3 En (10) (3)

Kingston (Swanage)
SY9579

Kingston Country Courtyard, *Greystone Court, Kingston, Wareham, Dorset, BH20 5LR.* Character guest rooms in a courtyard setting. Magnificent views of Corfe Castle from our gardens. **Open:** All year (not Xmas/New Year)
01929 481066 Mrs Fry **Fax: 01929 481256** *annfry@kingstoncountrycourtyard.co.uk* www.kingstoncountrycourtyard.co.uk **D:** Fr £24.00–£35.00 **S:** Fr £26.00–£35.00 **Beds:** 1T 4D 2S **Baths:** 7 En (20) 2

Kington Magna
ST7623

Kington Manor Farm, *Church Hill, Kington Magna, Gillingham, Dorset, SP8 5EG.* Attractive farmhouse. Peaceful, pretty village overlooking Blackmore Vale. Heated pool. **Open:** All year (not Xmas)
01747 838371 (also fax) Mrs Gosney **D:** Fr £22.00 **S:** Fr £24.00 **Beds:** 1F 1D 1T **Baths:** 3 Pr

Langton Matravers

SY9978

Maycroft, *Old Malthouse Lane, Langton Matravers, Swanage, Dorset, BH19 3JA.* Quiet position with lovely views. Close to sea and Coastal Path. Recommended by 'Which?'. **Open:** Feb to Nov
01929 424305 (also fax) Mrs Bjorkstrand *janet.bjorkstrand@btinternet.com* **D:** Fr £17.50–£21.00 **S:** Fr £25.00–£30.00 **Beds:** 1D 1T **Baths:** 1 Sh (3) (4)

Seacombe, *54 High Street, Langton Matravers, Swanage, Dorset, BH19 3HB.* Comfortable, friendly, stone cottage in beautiful countryside. 2 miles Swanage. **Open:** All year (not Xmas/New Year)
01929 426066 *stella@seacombeholidays.fsnet.co.uk* **D:** Fr £17.50 **Beds:** 1F 1D **Baths:** 1 Sh

Lulworth Cove

SY8279

Mill House Hotel, *Lulworth Cove, West Lulworth, Wareham, Dorset, BH20 5RQ.* 9-bedroom country house-style hotel in heart of Lulworth Cove, 150 yards water's edge. **Open:** Feb to Dec
01929 400404 & 01929 400261 Mr Payne **Fax: 01929 400508** *dukepayne@hotmail.com* millhousehotel.tripod.com **D:** Fr £25.00–£40.00 **S:** Fr £35.00–£40.00 **Beds:** 2F 6D 1T **Baths:** 9 En (9) cc

Shirley Hotel, *West Lulworth, Wareham, Dorset, BH20 5RL.* Comfortable bedrooms, delicious food. Super indoor pool. Magnificent coastal walks. **Open:** Feb to Nov
01929 400358 Mr Williams **Fax: 01929 400167** *durdle@aol.com* www.shirleyhotel.co.uk **D:** Fr £37.00–£48.00 **S:** Fr £37.00–£38.00 **Beds:** 1F 4T 9D 1S **Baths:** 15 En (22) cc

Lyme Regis

SY3392

Kersbrook Hotel, *Pound Road, Lyme Regis, Dorset, DT7 3HX.* C18th thatched country house hotel. **Open:** All year
01297 442596 D: Fr £30.00–£35.00 **S:** Fr £40.00 **Beds:** 6D 4T **Baths:** 10 En (14)

The Old Monmouth Hotel, *12 Church Street, Lyme Regis, Dorset, DT7 3BS.* C17th building, centrally situated for beaches, harbour and all amenities. **Open:** All year (not Xmas)
01297 442456 (also fax) Mr & Mrs Brown *enquiries@lyme-regis-hotel.co.uk* www.lyme-regis-hotel.co.uk **D:** Fr £22.00–£25.00 **S:** Fr £30.00–£34.00 **Beds:** 2F 4D 1T **Baths:** 5 En 1 Sh cc

Tudor House Hotel, *3/5 Church Street, Lyme Regis, Dorset, DT7 3BS.* An historic Elizabethan house, c1580, 1 min's level walk to sea. **Open:** All year (not Xmas/New Year)
01297 442472 Mr Ray www.thetudorhousehotel.co.uk **D:** Fr £24.00–£49.00 **S:** Fr £28.00–£38.00 **Beds:** 9F 5D 1T 1S **Baths:** 14 En 2 Pr (15)

Mayflower Cottage, *39 Sherborne Lane, Lyme Regis, Dorset, DT7 3NY.* Quiet, traffic-free. Secluded garden. Town centre. Free parking nearby. **Open:** All year (not Xmas)
01297 445930 & 01297 442452 Mr Snowsill **D:** Fr £20.00–£25.00 **S:** Fr £25.00 **Beds:** 1F 1D 1T **Baths:** 3 En (3)

Charnwood Guest House, *21 Woodmead Road, Lyme Regis, Dorset, DT7 3AD.* **Open:** All year **Grades:** ETC 4 Diamond
01297 445281 Mr & Mrs Bradbury *charnwood@lymeregis62.freeserve.co.uk* www.lymeregisaccommodation.com **D:** Fr £22.00–£26.00 **S:** Fr £22.00–£26.00 **Beds:** 1F 4D 2T 1S **Baths:** 7 En 1 Pr (5) (7) cc
World heritage 'Jurassic' coastline. Attractive Edwardian house modernised inside to a high standard of comfort. Close to restaurants, shops and pubs. Onsite parking. Walk, fossil and enjoy the beach/coast/history. Midweek discounts. Hearty English breakfast/vegetarian. Ideal touring base.

Coombe House, *41 Coombe Street, Lyme Regis, Dorset, DT7 3PY.* **Open:** All year **Grades:** ETC 3 Diamond
01297 443849 (also fax) Mrs Duncan *duncs@hughduncan.freeserve.co.uk* www.coombe-house.co.uk **D:** Fr £19.00–£20.00 **Beds:** 1D 1T **Baths:** 2 En (1)
Situated in one of Lyme's oldest streets, this old stone house offers two delightful,comfortable ensuite rooms. Come and go as you please and enjoy the luxury of a wholefood breakfast brought to your room. One minute walk to the sea.

Marnhull

ST7718 *Blackmore Vale*

Moorcourt Farm, *Moorside, Marnhull, Sturminster Newton, Dorset, DT10 1HH.* Friendly, welcoming, happy farmhouse. Central touring. Ginormous breakfast menu. **Open:** Easter to Oct
01258 820271 (also fax) Mrs Martin **D:** Fr £18.00–£20.00 **S:** Fr £18.00–£20.00 **Beds:** 2D 1T **Baths:** 2 Sh (10) (6)

Martinstown

SY6488

The Old Post Office, *Martinstown, Dorchester, Dorset, DT2 9LF.* Good rural base in small village. **Open:** All year
01305 889254 (also fax) Mrs Rootham **D:** Fr £17.50–£25.00 **S:** Fr £25.00 **Beds:** 1D 2T **Baths:** 1 Sh (3)

Middlemarsh

ST6706

White Horse Farm, *Middlemarsh, Sherborne, Dorset, DT9 5QN.* In beautiful Thomas Hardy country, conservatory, patio/gardens/duck pond. Ideal touring base. **Open:** All year (not Xmas/New Year) **Grades:** ETC 4 Diamond
01963 210222 (also fax) Mr & Mrs Wilding *enquiries@whitehorsefarm.co.uk* www.whitehorsefarm.co.uk **D:** Fr £26.00–£30.00 **S:** Fr £31.00–£45.00 **Beds:** 3D **Baths:** 3 En (10) cc

Morcombelake

SY3994 *Ship Inn, Five Bells*

Wisteria Cottage, *Taylors Lane, Morcombelake, Bridport, Dorset, DT6 6ED.* Country cottage, panoramic views in area of outstanding natural beauty. **Open:** All year (not Xmas/New Year)
01297 489019 Mrs Ellis **D:** Fr £20.00–£25.00 **S:** Fr £30.00–£35.00 **Beds:** 1T 1D **Baths:** 2 En (3)

Moreton

SY8089

Frampton Arms, *Moreton, Dorchester, Dorset, DT2 8BB.* Traditional country pub with two bars, two restaurants and function room. **Open:** All year (not Xmas)
01305 852253 Mr Paulson **Fax: 01305 854586** *john_paulson@framptonarms.fsnet.co.uk* **D:** Fr £20.00–£27.50 **S:** Fr £30.00–£35.00 **Beds:** 1F 2D **Baths:** 2 En 1 Sh (40) cc

Netherbury

SY4699

Southview, *Whitecross, Netherbury, Bridport, Dorset, DT6 5NH.* Detached country cottage, lovely views and gardens in picturesque village. **Open:** All year
01308 488471 Mr Kennedy website.lineone.net/~southviewbb **D:** Fr £22.50–£25.00 **S:** Fr £25.00 **Beds:** 1F 1T 1D **Baths:** 1 En 1 Sh (5) (4)

North Wootton

ST6514

Stoneleigh Barn, *North Wootton, Sherborne, Dorset, DT9 5JW.* Beautiful stone barn close to Sherborne. A special place. **Open:** All year (not Xmas/New Year)
01935 815964 Mrs Chant *stoneleigh@ic24.net* **D:** Fr £23.00–£25.00 **S:** Fr £30.00–£37.50 **Beds:** 1F 1D **Baths:** 1 En 1 Pr (6) (4)

Okeford Fitzpaine

ST8010

Etheridge Farm, *Darknoll Lane, Okeford Fitzpaine, Blandford Forum, Dorset, DT11 0RP.* In the heart of the Blackmore Vale, close to Lulworth. **Open:** Feb to Dec
01258 860037 Ms Thorne **D:** Fr £17.00 **Beds:** 1F 1T 1D **Baths:** 2 Sh

Osmington

SY7283

Rosedale, *Church Lane, Osmington, Weymouth, Dorset, DT3 6EW.* Very attractive cottage. Large, comfortable rooms, warm friendly atmosphere. **Open:** Mar to Oct **Grades:** ETC 2 Diamond
01305 832056 Mrs Legg **D:** Fr £18.00–£20.00 **S:** Fr £18.00–£19.00 **Beds:** 1D 1T **Baths:** 1 En 1 Pr (5) (3)

Rosthwaite, *Church Lane, Osmington, Weymouth, Dorset, DT3 6EW.* Bungalow set in picturesque village, comfortable beds and excellent breakfasts. **Open:** All year
01305 833621 Ms Leigh **D:** Fr £15.00–£17.00 **S:** Fr £15.00–£20.00 **Beds:** 1D 1T **Baths:** 1 Sh (2)

Pimperne

ST9008

The Old Bakery, *Church Road, Pimperne, Blandford Forum, Dorset, DT11 8UB.* A warm welcome awaits, in this former shop and bakery. **Open:** All year
01258 455173 P J Tanner **D:** Fr £12.50–£15.00 **S:** Fr £15.00–£20.00 **Beds:** 1T 1D 1S **Baths:** 2 Sh (3) (2)

Poole

SZ0191

Melbury Guest House, *101 Parkstone Road, Poole, Dorset, BH15 2NZ.* Comfortable Edwardian home opposite Poole Park, near beaches, ferries, town. **Open:** All year
01202 749015 Mrs Lloyd **D:** Fr £16.00–£20.00 **S:** Fr £16.00–£20.00 **Beds:** 1F 1D 1T 1S **Baths:** 2 Sh (5) (4)

Sarnia Cherie, *375 Blandford Road, Hamworthy, Poole, Dorset, BH15 4JL.* A warm welcome offering excellent B&B only 5 mins to town centre. **Open:** All year (not Xmas)
01202 679470 & 01585 319931 C Collier **Fax: 01202 679470 D:** Fr £20.00–£22.50 **S:** Fr £25.00–£30.00 **Beds:** 2D 1T **Baths:** 3 En (3)

Highways Bed & Breakfast, *29 Fernside Road, Poole, Dorset, BH15 2QU.* 1920's house, very comfortable. Fire hygiene certificate, all ensuite & parking. **Open:** All year
01202 677060 Mr & Mrs Bailey **D:** Fr £22.50–£25.00 **S:** Fr £25.00–£30.00 **Beds:** 2D 2T **Baths:** 5 En (6)

Shalimar, *14 Burngate, Hamworthy, Poole, Dorset, BH15.* Stair lift available. Quiet cul-de-sac. Homely atmosphere. Lovely Dorset coastline. Continental breakfast. **Open:** All year (not Xmas/New Year)
01202 680070 Mrs Batten **D:** Fr £18.00 **S:** Fr £18.00 **Beds:** 1T 1D 1S **Baths:** 1 Sh (2)

Seashells, *4 Lake Road, Hamworthy, Poole, Dorset, BH15 4LH.* Perfectly situated for Dorset coastline, countryside. Poole Quay, beautiful beaches. Warm welcome. **Open:** All year (not Xmas/New Year) **Grades:** ETC 3 Diamond
01202 671921 Mrs Hockey **D:** Fr £16.00–£20.00 **S:** Fr £25.00–£30.00 **Beds:** 1T 2D **Baths:** 1 En 1 Pr 1 Sh (5) (3)

Ashdell, *85 Dunyeats Road, Broadstone, Poole, Dorset, BH18 8AF.* Central, comfortable, secluded. Breakfast/EM choice. Historic countryside/ beaches, short breaks. **Open:** All year **Grades:** ETC 2 Diamond
01202 692032 Mrs Critchley *ian@ashdell.fsnet.co.uk* www.ashdell.co.uk **D:** Fr £17.00–£20.00 **S:** Fr £19.00–£23.00 **Beds:** 1F 1D 1T 1S **Baths:** 1 Sh (5) (3)

Portesham

SY6085

Lavender Cottage, *9 Malthouse Meadow, Portesham, Weymouth, Dorset, DT3 4NS.* Lovely scenery, quiet location, birdwatchers' and walkers' paradise, hearty breakfast. **Open:** All year (not Xmas)
01305 871924 Mrs Haine **D:** Fr £17.50 **S:** Fr £17.50 **Beds:** 1D 1T **Baths:** 1 Sh

Corfe Gate House, *2 Coryates, Portesham, Weymouth, Dorset, DT3 4HW.* Victorian house peacefully situated in Waddon Valley near beautiful West Dorset coastline. **Open:** Easter to Oct
01305 871483 Mrs Adams **Fax: 01305 264024** *adams@corfegatehouse.co.uk* www.corfegatehouse.co.uk **D:** Fr £20.00–£25.00 **S:** Fr £35.00 **Beds:** 1F 1T 1D **Baths:** 3 En (4) (3)

Manor Farm House, *Portesham, Weymouth, Dorset, DT3 4ET.* **Open:** All year (not Xmas/New Year)
01305 871025 Mr Gargrave **Fax: 01305 871031** *bbportesham@yahoo.co.uk* **D:** Fr £25.00 **S:** Fr £25.00–£35.00 **Beds:** 2D 1S **Baths:** 1 Sh (4)
Beautiful Georgian farmhouse, superb location close to the spectacular Chesil Beach. Ideally situated for Dorchester, Weymouth and the historic village of Abbotsbury. Spacious south-facing accommodation. Relaxed, informal atmosphere in a quiet village setting. Private drive and parking.

Portland

SY6874

The Old Vicarage, *Grove Road, Portland, Dorset, DT5 1DB.* Substantial Victorian vicarage. Spacious, comfortable rooms, good food, friendly atmosphere. **Open:** All year (not Xmas/New Year)
01305 824117 Carolyn Robb *mccormicksmith@oldvicarage.fsnet.co.uk* **D:** Fr £22.00–£25.00 **S:** Fr £25.00–£30.00 **Beds:** 1F 1T 1D **Baths:** 3 En (3)

Poyntington

ST6420

Welgoer, *Poyntington, Sherborne, Dorset, DT9 4LF.* Comfortable accommodation in quiet village near Sherborne. Ideal touring base. **Open:** All year
01963 220737 Mrs Neville **D:** Fr £20.00–£25.00 **S:** Fr £20.00–£25.00 **Beds:** 1T 1D **Baths:** 1 En 1 Pr (5) (2)

Puddletown

SY7594

Zoar House, *Puddletown, Dorchester, Dorset, DT2 8SR.* **Open:** All year **01305 848498** Mrs Stephens **D:** Fr £16.00–£19.00 **S:** Fr £16.00–£20.00 **Beds:** 1F 1D 1T **Baths:** 1 En 1 Sh (6) Victorian house & garden situated close to Jurassic coastline, Hardy's cottage, forest walks, Roman history, market towns. Trout fishing. Horse livery whilst you're away, schooling, hacking & training holidays. Indoor, outdoor schools. BHSAI qualified trainer, specialising in dressage. Horse transport available.

Sandford

SY9289

Foresters, *14 Keysworth Drive, Sandford, Wareham, Dorset, BH20 7BD.* Modern spacious bungalow. Peaceful location. Wildlife garden, private off-road parking. Large breakfasts. **Open:** All year (not Xmas/New Year) **01929 556090** Mrs Harris *foresters@keysworth14.freeserve.co.uk* www.keysworth14.freeserve.co.uk **D:** Fr £16.50–£20.00 **S:** Fr £16.50–£22.50 **Beds:** 1T 1D 1S (5)

Shaftesbury

ST8622

Maple Lodge, *Christys Lane, Shaftesbury, Dorset, SP7 8DL.* Within 5 mins walk of shops, restaurants and famous Gold Hill. **Open:** All year (not Xmas/New Year) **01747 853945** Mr & Mrs Jameson *maplelodge@tesco.net* www.maplelodgebb.com **D:** Fr £18.00–£22.00 **S:** Fr £20.00–£25.00 **Beds:** 1F 1T 1D **Baths:** 2 En 1 Pr (8)

Sunridge Hotel, *Bleke Street, Shaftesbury, Dorset, SP7 8AW.* Warm welcome, friendly service, tastefully furnished, telephone for brochure. **Open:** All year **01747 853130** Michael Lodwick **Fax: 01747 852139** *sunridgehotel@talk21.com* **D:** Fr £32.50–£35.00 **S:** Fr £45.00–£47.50 **Beds:** 9F 4T 5D **Baths:** 9 En (9) cc

Charnwood Cottage, *Charlton, Shaftesbury, Dorset, SP7 9LZ.* C17th thatched cottage with lovely garden. Good base for touring. **Open:** All year (not Xmas/New Year) **01747 828310 (also fax)** Mr & Mrs Morgan **D:** Fr £19.00–£20.00 **Beds:** 1T 1D **Baths:** 1 Sh (2)

Ye Olde Wheelwrights, *Birdbush, Ludwell, Shaftesbury, Dorset, SP7 9NH.* Accommodation in separate annexe. Children and families welcome. Hearty breakfast. **Open:** All year (not Xmas) **Grades:** RAC 3 Diamond, Sparkling **01747 828955** C Dieppe *chris@cdieppe.freeserve.co.uk* **D:** Fr £19.00–£22.00 **S:** Fr £22.00–£25.00 **Beds:** 1T 1D **Baths:** 1 Sh

Sherborne

ST6316

Clatcombe Grange, *Bristol Road, Sherborne, Dorset, DT9 4RH.* Charming Listed converted barn. Spacious accommodation/garden. Ample parking. Warm welcome. Peaceful and friendly. **Open:** All year **01935 814355 & 07773 969145 (M)** Hellyar **D:** Fr £26.00 **S:** Fr £36.00 **Beds:** 1T 1D 1S **Baths:** 2 En 1 Pr

Britannia Inn, *Sherborne, Dorset, DT9 3EH.* Listed building, town centre, 300 years old. **Open:** All year **01935 813300** Mr Blackmore www.thebritanniainn.co.uk **D:** Fr £20.00–£35.00 **S:** Fr £20.00–£35.00 **Beds:** 2F 1D 2T 2S **Baths:** 1 En 3 Sh (6) cc

Bridleways, *Oborne Road, Sherborne, Dorset, DT9 3RX.* Comfortable house overlooking castle, 10 mins' walk to historic town centre. **Open:** All year (not Xmas) **Grades:** ETC 3 Diamond **01935 814716 (also fax)** Mr & Mrs Dimond *bridleways@tiscali.co.uk* **D:** Fr £22.00–£25.00 **S:** Fr £22.00–£25.00 **Beds:** 1D 2T **Baths:** 1 En 1 Pr (5)

Shillingstone

ST8211

The Willows Tea Rooms, *5 Blandford Road, Shillingstone, Blandford Forum, Dorset, DT11 0SG.* C18th cottage & tearooms in beautiful countryside. Blandford 5 miles. **Open:** Feb to Xmas **01258 861167** C A Dicker & H L Haycock *colindicker@aol.com* **D:** Fr £35.00–£40.00 **S:** Fr £25.00 **Beds:** 1D **Baths:** 1 En (6)

BEDROOMS
D = Double
T = Twin
S = Single
F = Family

Shipton Gorge

SY4991

Cairnhill, *Shipton Gorge, Bridport, DT6 4LL.* Beautiful countryside, warm welcome. Comfortable, spacious rooms, heated indoor pool. **Open:** Easter to Oct **01308 898203 (also fax)** R W Waite *cairnhill@talk21.com* **D:** Fr £25.00 **S:** Fr £25.00–£30.00 **Beds:** 1D 1T 1S **Baths:** 2 En 1 Pr (7)

Sixpenny Handley

ST9918

Town Farm Bungalow, *Sixpenny Handley, Salisbury, Wilts., SP5 5NT.* Excellent friendly accommodation. Magnificent views and peaceful surrounding. Superb breakfasts. **Open:** All year **01725 552319 (also fax)** Mrs Inglis **D:** Fr £17.50–£20.00 **S:** Fr £22.50–£35.00 **Beds:** 1T 2D **Baths:** 1 En 1 Sh (6)

Stapehill

SU0500

Pear Tree Cottage, *248 Wimborne Road West, Stapehill, Wimborne, Dorset, BH21 2DZ.* Charming thatched cottage, set in large, secluded gardens. **Open:** All year (not Xmas/New Year) **01202 890174** *ca.whiteman@ntlworld.com* **D:** Fr £22.50–£25.00 **S:** Fr £25.00–£35.00 **Beds:** 1T 1D 1S **Baths:** 1 Pr 2 Sh (3)

Stour Row

ST8221 *King's Arms, Crown Inn*

Beechmead, *Stour Row, Shaftesbury, Dorset, SP7 0QF.* Bungalow in a tiny village - surrounded by fields **Open:** All year **01747 838405** Mrs Slingerland **D:** Fr £15.00–£17.00 **S:** Fr £17.00–£19.00 **Beds:** 1T 1D **Baths:** 1 Pr 1 Sh (3)

Studland

SZ0382 *Manor House Hotel, Bankes Arms, Village Inn*

Bankers Arms Hotel, *Manor Road, Studland, Swanage, Dorset, BH19 3AU.* Lovely old country inn overlooking the sea in beautiful NT area. Log fires, ensuite accommodation, extensive homemade bar menu. AA fish & seafood recommended. CAMRA joint Pub of the Year for Dorset, real ale award, also outright winner for autumn CAMRA Pub of the Season. **Open:** All year **01929 450225** **D:** Fr £27.00–£36.00 **S:** Fr £27.00–£36.00 **Beds:** 1F 2T 4D 1S **Baths:** 6 En 1 Sh (4) (10) cc

Sutton Poyntz

SY7083

Upwater Barn, *Sutton Road, Sutton Poyntz, Weymouth, Dorset, DT3 6LW.* Excellent accommodation in beautiful village setting. Come & explore Dorset. **Open:** All year (not Xmas/New Year)
01305 835710 Mrs Anderson *chrstina@upwater.fsnet.co.uk* **D:** Fr £25.00–£30.00 **S:** Fr £30.00–£35.00 **Beds:** 1T 1D **Baths:** 2 Pr (4)

Swanage

SZ0278

Perfick Piece, *Springfield Road, Swanage, Dorset, BH19 1HD.* Small family guest house in quiet cul-de-sac near shops, beach and steam railway. **Open:** All year **Grades:** ETC 3 Diamond
01929 423178 Fax: 01929 423558 *perfick-piece@supanet.com* www.perfick-piece.co.uk **D:** Fr £15.00–£20.00 **S:** Fr £16.00–£20.00 **Beds:** 1F 1T 1D 1S **Baths:** 1 En 1 Pr 1 Sh (3)

Glenlee Hotel, *6 Cauldon Avenue, Swanage, Dorset, BH19 1PQ.* Friendly family run hotel in delightful position close to beach. **Open:** Mar to Oct
01929 425794 Mr Jones **Fax: 01929 421530** *info@glenleehotel.co.uk* www.glenleehotel.co.uk **D:** Fr £22.50–£27.50 **S:** Fr £35.00–£40.00 **Beds:** 2F 2T 3D **Baths:** 7 En (3) (7) cc

Plum Tree Cottage, *60 Bell Street, Swanage, Dorset, BH19 2SB.* Comfortable rooms, generous breakfasts, in area of outstanding natural beauty. **Open:** All year
01929 421601 & 07971 552082 (M) Mr & Mrs Howells **Fax: 01929 421601 D:** Fr £22.50–£30.00 **S:** Fr £30.00–£40.00 **Beds:** 3D **Baths:** 1 En 2 Pr (2)

Bearsden House, *15 Walrond Road, Swanage, Dorset, BH19 1PB.* Very close to sea and town in premier residential area. **Open:** All year (not Xmas/New Year)
01929 426359 Mrs Ely **Fax: 01929 426989** *carterely@eurobell.co.uk* **D:** Fr £23.00–£25.00 **S:** Fr £23.00–£25.00 **Beds:** 1T **Baths:** 1 En (2)

1 Drummond Road, *Swanage, Dorset, BH19 2DX.* Old family home, views sea/downs, lovely gardens. Peaceful area. **Open:** All year (not Xmas/New Year)
01929 427044 & 07766 418329 (M) *scottbyrne@btinternet.com* **D:** Fr £19.00–£23.00 **S:** Fr £30.00–£35.00 **Beds:** 2D **Baths:** 1 Sh (10) (2)

Hermitage Guest House, *1 Manor Road, Swanage, Dorset, BH19 2BH.* Quiet central location, relaxed atmosphere, bay views. 2 mins beach, Coastal Path.
Open: Easter to Nov
01929 423014 Mrs Pickering **D:** Fr £18.50–£19.50 **S:** Fr £20.00 **Beds:** 4F 2D 1T **Baths:** 2 Sh (5) (7)

Sydling St Nicholas

SY6399

Lamperts Cottage, *Sydling St Nicholas, Dorchester, Dorset, DT2 9NU.* Traditional C16th thatched cottage, stream at front, beams, inglenook, flagstones. **Open:** All year **Grades:** AA 3 Diamond
01300 341659 Mr Wills **Fax: 01300 341699** *nickywillis@tesco.net* **D:** Fr £22.00–£23.00 **S:** Fr £25.00–£26.00 **Beds:** 1F 1D 1T **Baths:** 2 Sh (8) (3) cc

Magiston Farm, *Sydling St Nicholas, Dorchester, Dorset, DT2 9NR.* C16th farmhouse, 400 acre working farm, large garden. Very peaceful. **Open:** All year (not Xmas)
01300 320295 Mrs Barraclough **D:** Fr £20.00 **S:** Fr £20.00 **Beds:** 1D 3T 1S **Baths:** 1 Pr 1 Sh (10) (12)

City Cottage, *Sydling St Nicholas, Dorchester, Dorset, DT2 9NX.* Country cottage, comfortable and a warm welcome assured. **Open:** All year (not Xmas)
01300 341300 Mrs Wareham **D:** Fr £18.00 **S:** Fr £18.00 **Beds:** 1D 1S **Baths:** 1 Sh (12) (2)

Symondsbury

SY4493

Saxlingham House, *West Road, Symondsbury, Bridport, Dorset, DT6 6AA.* Extensive country views many local attractions warm friendly welcome.
Open: Easter to Sep
01308 423629 Mrs Nicholls *saxlingham@freezone.co.uk* **D:** Fr £18.00 **S:** Fr £18.00 **Beds:** 1T 2D **Baths:** 3 En

RATES
D = Price range per person sharing in a double or twin room
S = Price range for a single room

Planning a longer stay? Always ask for any special rates

Thorncombe

ST3703

Upperfold House, *Thorncombe, Chard, Somerset, TA20 4PY.* Quiet Georgian country house, on major walks & near sea. **Open:** All year (not Xmas/New Year)
01460 30209 Mrs Bicknell *pbatupperfold@onetel.net.uk* **D:** Fr £22.00–£25.00 **S:** Fr £25.00–£28.00 **Beds:** 2T **Baths:** 1 En 1 Pr (9)

Tincleton

SY7791

Clyffe Farm, *Tincleton, Dorchester, DT2 8QR.* **Open:** All year (not Xmas)
01305 848252 Mrs Coleman **Fax: 01305 848702** *coleman.clyffe@virgin.net* www.heartofdorset.easynet.co.uk **D:** Fr £25.00–£32.50 **S:** Fr £37.50 **Beds:** 1D **Baths:** 1 Pr
Delightful farmhouse accommodation for two discerning guests. Something a little different. A warm welcome awaits but privacy prevails. Guests' own access to private apartment with lounge/diner, fridge/toaster. Continental breakfast provided, cooked on request. Beautiful surroundings, ideal situation for coast, culture or country pursuits. 2 nights minimum.

Toller Porcorum

SY5698

Colesmoor Farm, *Toller Porcorum, Dorchester, Dorset, DT2 0DU.* Small family farm in quiet setting with excellent views.
Open: May to Feb
01300 320812 Mrs Geddes **Fax: 01300 321402** *geddes.colesmoor@eclipse.co.uk* **D:** Fr £20.00 **S:** Fr £25.00 **Beds:** 1D 1T **Baths:** 2 En (4) 3

Planning a longer stay? Always ask for any special rates

Tolpuddle

SY7994

Lawrences Farm, *Southover, Tolpuddle, Dorchester, DT2 7HF.* **Open:** All year (not Xmas/New Year) **01305 848460** Mrs Slocock *sally.slocock@virgin.net* www.goflyfishing.co.uk **D:** Fr £23.00 **S:** Fr £28.00 **Beds:** 1F 1T 1D **Baths:** 2 En 1 Pr (8) (6)
Lawrences farm nestles in Dorset's famous Piddle Valley. In the 1830s the Tolpuddle Martyrs ensured world-wide fame for the village. Explore other Piddle and Puddle villages and Thomas Hardy countryside. Marvellous bird watching. Our own lake and river trout fishing.

Uploders

SY5093 *Loders Arms*

Uploders Farm, *Uploders, Bridport, Dorset, DT6 4NZ.* Quiet position. Ideal for touring. Beautiful countryside. Good English breakfast. **Open:** Easter to Oct **01308 423380** **D:** Fr £18.00–£20.00 **Beds:** 1F 1D **Baths:** 2 En (7) (3)

Upton (Poole)

SY9793

Tideway, *Beach Road, Upton, Poole, Dorset, BH16 5NA.* Please look at our website for further detail & pictures - www.maidinwessex.com/tideway. **Open:** All year (not Xmas) **01202 621293 (also fax)** Mr & Mrs Yates *tidewaybb@aol.com* www.maidinwessex.com/tideway **D:** Fr £20.00–£25.00 **S:** Fr £23.00–£25.00 **Beds:** 1D 1T **Baths:** 1 Sh (3)

Wareham

SY9287

Anglebury House, *15/17 North Street, Wareham, BH20 4AB.* Beautiful C16th building, comfortable, full of character. Lawrence of Arabia was a guest here. **Open:** All year **01929 552988** **D:** Fr £25.00–£30.00 **S:** Fr £30.00–£35.00 **Beds:** 2F 3D 1T 1S **Baths:** 6 En 1 Pr (6) cc

Ashcroft Bed & Breakfast, *64 Furzebrook Road, Wareham, Dorset, BH20 5AX.* Friendly, comfortable, good food. Convenient for bird watching and walking. **Open:** All year (not Xmas) **01929 552392** Mrs Cake **Fax: 01929 552422** *cake@ashcroft-bb.co.uk* www.ashcroft-bb.co.uk **D:** Fr £20.00–£25.00 **S:** Fr £20.00–£26.00 **Beds:** 1F 1D 1T **Baths:** 3 En (6)

West Bay

SY4690

Egdon, *Third Cliff Walk, West Bay, Bridport, Dorset, DT6 4HX.* Panoramic views over Lyme Bay. 5 Mins from beach/ cliff walks. **Open:** All year **01308 422542** Mrs Vallard **D:** Fr £18.00–£20.00 **S:** Fr £25.00–£30.00 **Beds:** 1F 1T 1D **Baths:** 1 Sh (3)

West Lulworth

SY8280 *Castle Inn*

Rose Cottage, *Main Road, West Lulworth, Wareham, Dorset, BH20 5RJ.* Beautiful thatched cottage situated 2 mins walk from Lulworth Cove. **Open:** All year (not Xmas/New Year) **01929 400150** B Clarke *barbara@rosecottage.fsworld.co.uk* www.rosecottage.fsworld.co.uk **D:** Fr £20.00–£25.00 **S:** Fr £20.00–£22.00 **Beds:** 1T 2D 1S **Baths:** 1 En 1 Sh (3)

The Copse, *School Lane, West Lulworth, Wareham, Dorset, BH20 5SA.* **Open:** All year (not Xmas) **01929 400581 (also fax)** Mr & Mrs Johari *ullajohari@aol.com* **D:** Fr £15.00–£17.50 **S:** Fr £15.00–£17.50 **Beds:** 1D 1T 1S **Baths:** 1 Sh (3)
Detached house in picturesque coastal village. Quiet location off main road overlooking field in Area of Outstanding Natural Beauty. Close to Lulworth Cove and beaches. Coastal walks, restaurants and village pub. Generous Continental breakfast.

Graybank Bed & Breakfast, *Main Road, West Lulworth, Wareham, Dorset, BH20 5RL.* Victorian house, World Heritage location, peaceful, warm welcome, excellent breakfast. **Open:** Feb to Nov **Grades:** ETC 3 Diamond **01929 400256** Mr & Mrs Burrill **D:** Fr £17.00–£20.00 **S:** Fr £17.00–£20.00 **Beds:** 2F 3D 1T 1S **Baths:** 3 Sh (4) (7)

West Down Farm, *West Lulworth, Wareham, Dorset, BH20 5PU.* Beautiful coastal area. Outstanding views. Ideal riding, cycling and walking. **Open:** All year **01929 400308 (also fax)** Ms Weld *william.weld@saqnet.co.uk* **D:** Fr £20.00–£25.00 **S:** Fr £25.00–£30.00 **Beds:** 1T 1D **Baths:** 1 Sh

Gatton House, *West Lulworth, Wareham, Dorset, BH20 5RU.* Picturesque guest house with spectacular views, near Lulworth Cove and Coastal Path. **Open:** Mar to Oct **01929 400252 (also fax)** Mr Dale *mike@gattonhouse.co.uk* www.gattonhouse.co.uk **D:** Fr £25.00–£38.00 **S:** Fr £40.00–£60.00 **Beds:** 1F 1T 6D **Baths:** 8 En (9) cc

Tewkesbury Cottage, *28 Main Road, West Lulworth, Wareham, Dorset, BH20 5RL.* C1600 thatched cottage 8 minutes walk to beach, coastal paths. Full English breakfast. **Open:** All year **01929 400561 (also fax)** Mrs Laing **D:** Fr £18.00–£20.00 **S:** Fr £20.00–£25.00 **Beds:** 2D 1T 1S **Baths:** 1 En 2 Sh (12) (6)

West Stafford

SY7289 *Wise Man*

Long Barn House, *1 Barton Mews, West Stafford, Dorchester, Dorset, DT2 8UB.* Converted byre/granary between pub and church in tranquil ancient village. **Open:** All year **01305 266899** *pessame@amserve.net* **D:** Fr £20.00–£27.00 **S:** Fr £25.00–£32.00 **Beds:** 1T 1D 1S **Baths:** 1 En 1 Pr (10) (2) cc

Weymouth

SY6779 *The Lodmoor, Ferrybridge, Wyke Smugglers*

Morven Hotel, *2 Westerhall Road, Weymouth, Dorset, DT4 7SZ.* Family hotel. 150 yards from sea and beautiful green hill gardens. **Open:** Easter to Oct **01305 785075** Mr Lambley **D:** Fr £20.00–£22.00 **S:** Fr £20.00–£25.00 **Beds:** 2T 7D 1S **Baths:** 7 En 3 Sh (10)

Molyneux Guest House, *9 Waterloo Place, Weymouth, Dorset, DT4 7PD.* Quality Georgian accommodation adjacent to seafront. Comfortable, friendly, with bar. **Open:** All year **01305 774623 & 07986 568938 (M)** Denise & Vic Davis *vgddavis@ntlworld.com* **D:** Fr £20.00–£27.00 **S:** Fr £30.00–£40.00 **Beds:** 1F 1T 3D **Baths:** 5 En (6)

Homelea, *9 St Helens Road, Weymouth, Dorset, DT4 9DY.* Warm friendly welcome, near Chesil Beach, Granby Estate, Weymouth Centre. **Open:** All year (not Xmas/New Year)
01305 778826 Mrs Jowett *saj@svmsm1.freeserve.co.uk* **D:** Fr £18.00–£20.00 **S:** Fr £20.00 **Beds:** 1T 1S (3)

Galway Guest House, *7 Abbotsbury Road, Weymouth, Dorset, DT4 0AD.* Ten mins walk to town beach and bird sanctuary, next to Portland cycle path. Secure garaging. **Open:** All year (not Xmas/New Year)
01305 783319 Evelyn Wilcox *galway@onetel.net.uk* **D:** Fr £16.00–£25.00 **S:** Fr £20.00 **Beds:** 3F 1T 2D 1S **Baths:** 2 Sh (7)

Beulah, *58 Rodwell Road, Weymouth, Dorset, DT4 8QU.* Between Weymouth & Portland. Easy walk to Weymouth & beaches. Lovely garden. **Open:** All year (not Xmas)
01305 772895 Mrs Sheppard *stella@beulah.dabsol.co.uk* **D:** Fr £21.00–£25.00 **S:** Fr £25.00–£30.00 **Beds:** 1D 1T **Baths:** 2 Pr (3)

Greenlands Guest House, *8 Waterloo Place, The Esplanade, Weymouth, Dorset, DT4 7PR.* Family-run guest house, on the sea front. Good wholesome breakfast. **Open:** All year
01305 776368 (also fax) Mrs Vogts **D:** Fr £20.00–£26.00 **S:** Fr £20.00–£26.00 **Beds:** 2F 5D (7) **cc**

Kings Acre Hotel, *140 The Esplanade, Weymouth, Dorset, DT4 7NH.* Lovely, privately run hotel in a grand Victorian terrace, offering friendly, courteous service, good food. **Open:** Feb to Nov
01305 782534 Mrs Mears **Fax: 01305 732354** **D:** Fr £25.00–£35.00 **S:** Fr £32.50–£40.00 **Beds:** 2F 7D 2T **Baths:** 10 En 1 Pr (9) **cc**

Seaways, *5 Turton Street, Weymouth, Dorset, DT4 7DU.* Victorian Building close to all amenities, beach, town and parking. **Open:** All year (not Xmas/New Year)
01305 771646 Mr & Mrs Seward *seasew@supanet.com* **D:** Fr £16.00 **S:** Fr £16.00 **Beds:** 5D 1T 1S **Baths:** 2 Sh

Hotel Mon Ami, *143/145 The Esplanade, Weymouth, Dorset, DT4 7NN.* Seafront, lift to all floors, licensed entertainment. On Jurassic coast. **Open:** Feb to Dec
01305 786917 **Fax: 01305 785911** **D:** Fr £23.00–£30.00 **S:** Fr £23.00–£30.00 **Beds:** 8S 16T 7D 11S **Baths:** 42 En (4) **cc**

Esplanade Hotel, *141 The Esplanade, Weymouth, Dorset, DT4 7NJ.* Sea front 1835 Georgian terrace hotel. Superior ensuite accommodation with car parking. **Open:** Easter to Oct
01305 783129 Mr & Mrs Paul **D:** Fr £25.00–£35.00 **S:** Fr £32.00–£35.00 **Beds:** 1F 7D 2T 1S **Baths:** 11 En (6) (9)

Mar Jun Guest House, *32 Lennox Street, Weymouth, Dorset, DT4 7HD.* Pretty guest house, two minutes Weymouth Bay, good home cooking. **Open:** All year
01305 761320 Mr & Mrs Edmondson **D:** Fr £18.00–£20.00 **Beds:** 1F 1T 4D **Baths:** 6 En (5)

Birchfields Hotel, *22 Abbotsbury Road, Weymouth, Dorset, DT4 0AE.* Close to beach and town, short breaks welcome, ideal touring base. **Open:** Easter to Oct
01305 773255 (also fax) Mr & Mrs Dutton *birchfieldshotel@lineone.net* www.smoothhound.co.uk/hotels/birchfields.html **D:** Fr £20.00–£25.00 **S:** Fr £16.00–£25.00 **Beds:** 2F 3D 2T 2S **Baths:** 3 En 7 Sh (3) **cc**

Whitchurch Canonicorum

SY3995

Cardsmill Farm, *Whitchurch Canonicorum, Bridport, Dorset, DT6 6RP.* Comfortable farmhouse on working family farm 3 miles from coast. **Open:** All year (not Xmas)
01297 489375 (also fax) Mrs Johnson *cardsmill@aol.com* **D:** Fr £18.00–£24.00 **S:** Fr £19.00–£23.00 **Beds:** 1F 1D 1S **Baths:** 2 En (6)

Wimborne Minster

SU0100 *Willett Arms*

Crab Apple Corner, *40 Lacy Drive, Wimborne, Dorset, BH21 1DG.* Situated close to town centre. Warm welcome. Full English breakfast. **Open:** All year (not Xmas/New Year)
01202 840993 Mrs Curry *Andrew.Curry@virgin.net* **D:** Fr £20.00–£22.00 **S:** Fr £22.00 **Beds:** 1D **Baths:** 1 Sh (1)

Sunnysides, *18 Victoria Road, Wimborne Minster, Dorset, BH21 1EW.* Warm, friendly, good touring centre close to town centre and eating places. **Open:** All year
01202 886953 Mrs Randall **D:** Fr £16.50 **S:** Fr £16.50 **Beds:** 1D 1T **Baths:** 1 Sh (2)

Heatherlands, *13 Wimborne Road, Colehill, Wimborne Minster, Dorset, BH21 2RS.* A large Victorian house where guests are treated as friends. **Open:** All year (not Xmas/New Year)
01202 882032 Mrs Gibbs **D:** Fr £18.00 **S:** Fr £18.00 **Beds:** 2F 1D **Baths:** 1 Sh

Turi, *21 Grove Road, Wimborne Minster, Dorset, BH21 1BN.* Victorian house with garden, off main road between Minster and market. **Open:** All year
01202 884818 Mrs Joyner *joyturi@care4free.net* **D:** Fr £14.00–£16.00 **S:** Fr £14.00–£16.00 **Beds:** 1F 1T **Baths:** 2 Sh

Peacehaven, *282 Sopwith Crescent Merley, Wimborne Minster, Dorset, BH21 1XL.* Perfectly situated with bus stops outside for Poole, Wimborne and Bournemouth. In easy reach of Dorset coast, New Forest, health clubs, fishing, golf, and many places of historical interest, museums, houses and gardens to visit, churches. All rooms on ground floor. **Open:** All year
01202 880281 Mr & Mrs Justice **D:** Fr £20.00–£22.50 **S:** Fr £22.50–£25.00 **Beds:** 2D **Baths:** 1 Sh

Moor Allerton, *Holtwood, Wimborne Minster, Dorset, BH21 7DU.* Tranquillity amidst glorious countryside, beaches, New Forest. Warmest Christian welcome. **Open:** All year (not Xmas/New Year)
01258 840845 (also fax) Mrs Oliver *martinoliver1@talk21.com* **D:** Fr £18.00–£23.00 **S:** Fr £20.00–£24.00 **Beds:** 1T 1D 1S **Baths:** 2 Pr

Winfrith Newburgh

SY8084

The Manor House, *Winfrith Newburgh, Dorchester, Dorset, DT2 8JR.* Historic manor house with luxury rooms near Lulworth Cove. **Open:** All year (not Xmas)
01305 854987 Mr & Mrs Smith **Fax: 01305 854988** *jennie@dorsetcoastalcottages.com* **D:** Fr £23.00–£25.00 **Beds:** 1D 1T **Baths:** 1 En 1 Pr

Marleywood House, *Winfrith Newburgh, Dorchester, Dorset, DT2 8UQ.* Converted Downland barn, one mile from sea, cliffs and country walks. **Open:** All year
01929 400582 Mr & Mrs Wintrip *info@marleywoodhouse.com* www.marleywoodhouse.com **D:** Fr £22.50 **S:** Fr £27.50–£30.00 **Beds:** 1T 3D **Baths:** 1 En 2 Sh (20)

Winterborne Kingston

SY8697

West Acres, *West Street, Winterbourne Kingston, Blandford Forum, Dorset, DT11 9AT.* Quiet spacious rural bungalow, large garden, excellent walking/riding paths. **Open:** All year
01929 471293 Mrs Jenkins **D:** Fr £20.00 **S:** Fr £23.00 **Beds:** 1F 1T 1D **Baths:** 1 En 1 Sh (10) (8)

Please respect a B&B's wishes regarding children, animals and smoking

Winterborne Zelston

SY8997

Brook Farm, *Winterborne Zelston, Blandford Forum, Dorset, DT11 9EU.* In quiet pretty hamlet, comfortable farmhouse accommodation, river and farmland views. Numerous country inns. **Open:** All year (not Xmas) **Grades:** ETC 3 Diamond
01929 459267 (also fax) Mrs Kerley *kerleybrookfarmzelston@yahoo.co.uk* **D:** Fr £20.00–£22.00 **S:** Fr £20.00–£22.00 **Beds:** 2D 1T **Baths:** 2 En 1 Pr (10)

Winterbourne Abbas

SY6190

Churchview Guest House, *Winterbourne Abbas, Dorchester, Dorset, DT2 9LS.* Delightful C17th village guest house near Dorchester offers comfort, delicious breakfasts. **Open:** All year (not Xmas) **Grades:** ETC 4 Diamond, AA 4 Diamond
01305 889296 (also fax) Mr Deller *stay@churchview.co.uk* www.churchview.co.uk **D:** Fr £25.00–£31.00 **S:** Fr £29.00–£36.00 **Beds:** 1F 4D 3T 1S **Baths:** 8 En 1 Pr (5) (10) cc

Winterbourne Steepleton

SY6289

The Old Rectory, *Winterbourne Steepleton, Dorchester, Dorset, DT2 9LG.* Quiet hamlet in Hardy country. Peaceful night's sleep, copious English, vegetarian or Continental breakfast. **Open:** All year (not Xmas/New Year)
01305 889468 M Tree **Fax: 01305 889737** *trees@eurobell.co.uk* www.trees.eurobell.co.uk **D:** Fr £25.00–£55.00 **Beds:** 3T **Baths:** 3 En (6)

Wool

SY8486

Fingle Bridge, *Duck Street, Wool, Wareham, Dorset, BH20 6DE.* Warm welcome. Close Monkey World, Tank Museum, coast and countryside. **Open:** All year
01929 462739 Mrs Baker **D:** Fr £20.00–£25.00 **S:** Fr £20.00 **Beds:** 1F 1T 1D **Baths:** 1 En 1 Sh (3)

East Burton House, *East Burton, Wool, Wareham, Dorset, BH20 6HE.* Relax and enjoy real food in our peaceful country house. **Open:** All year
01929 463857 Mr Francis **Fax: 01929 463026** *mikefr@ntlworld.com* **D:** Fr £22.00–£23.00 **S:** Fr £32.00–£36.00 **Beds:** 2D 1T **Baths:** 2 Sh (6)

Worth Matravers

SY9777

The Haven, *Worth Matravers, Swanage, Dorset, BH19 3LF.* Friendly welcome to comfortable modern house with pleasant sea views. **Open:** All year
01929 439388 & 01929 439388 Mr & Mrs Taylor **D:** Fr £20.00–£25.00 **S:** Fr £20.00–£25.00 **Beds:** 1D 1T **Baths:** 1 En 1 Pr

Yetminster

ST5910

Manor Farm House, *High Street, Yetminster, Sherborne, Dorset, DT9 6LF.* Interesting manor farmhouse rebuilt in C17th, with many architectural features. **Open:** All year (not Xmas)
01935 872247 & 0800 0566761 Mr & Mrs Partridge **Fax: 01935 872247** www.nsl.co.uk/shogun/manor/manpics.htm **D:** Fr £30.00–£35.00 **S:** Fr £35.00 **Beds:** 2T 1D 1S **Baths:** 4 En (20) cc

BEDROOMS
D = Double
T = Twin
S = Single
F = Family

County Durham

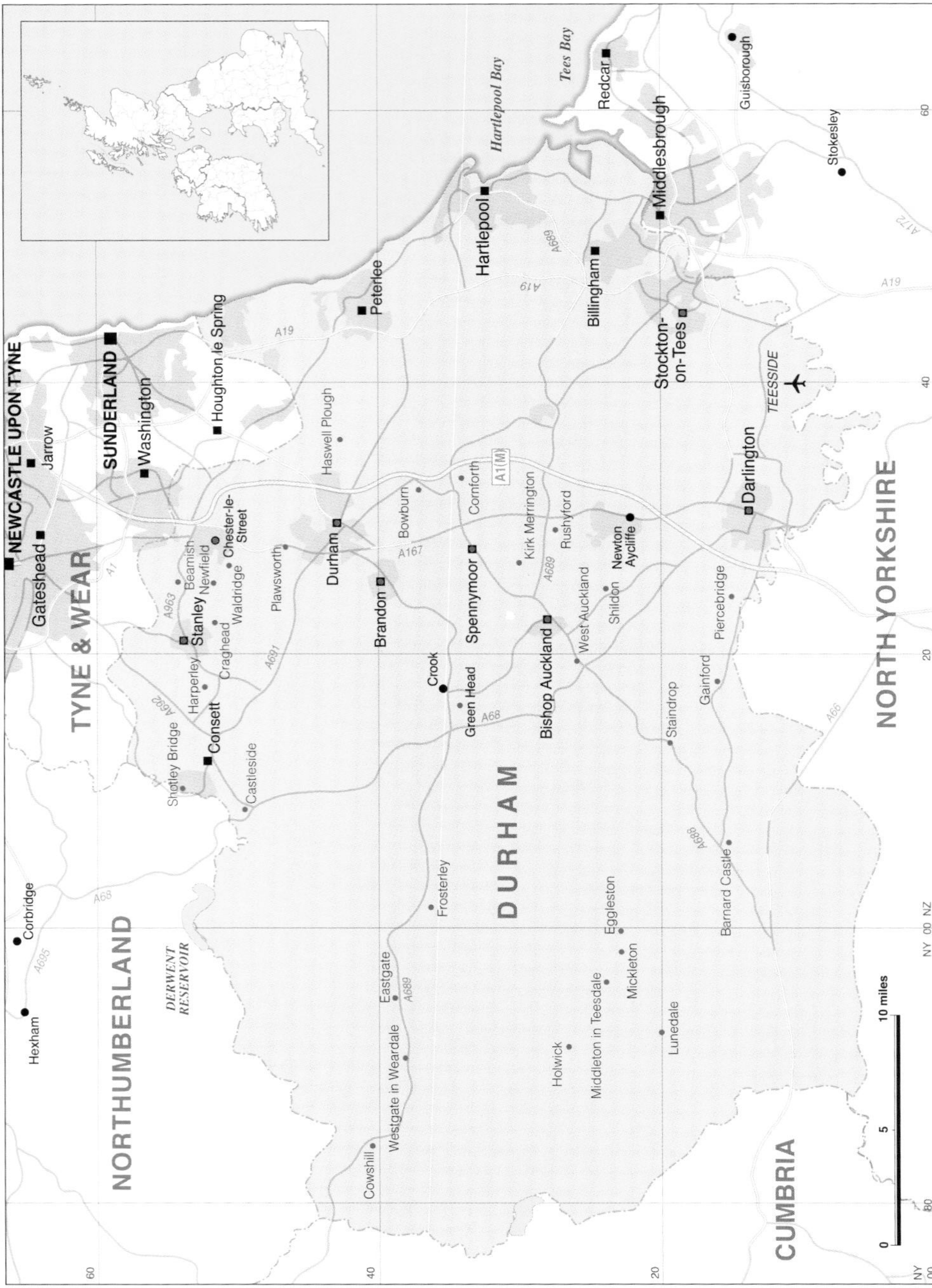

Barnard Castle

NZ0516 Kirk Inn

Old Well Inn, *21 The Bank, Barnard Castle, Co Durham, DL12 8PH.* Recommended by the Times and Sunday Telegraph, this C17th tavern in Teesdale boasts spacious ensuite rooms, freshly prepared local produce, antique shops, museums, castles. Beautiful scenery, wonderful walks, river and reservoir fishing and riding. **Open:** All year
01833 690130 Mrs Rabley **Fax: 01833 690140** *reservations@oldwellinn.co.uk* www.oldwellinn.co.uk **D:** Fr £30.00–£35.00 **S:** Fr £48.00–£57.00 **Beds:** 2F 6D 2T **Baths:** 10 En **cc**

Cloud High, *Eggleston, Barnard Castle, Co Durham, DL12 0AU.* Luxurious accommodation and hospitality, gourmet breakfasts, a delight. Sheer indulgence! **Open:** All year (not Xmas/New Year)
01833 650644 (also fax) Mr & Mrs Bell *cloudhigh@btinternet.com* www.cloudhigh-teesdale.co.uk **D:** Fr £23.00–£25.00 **S:** Fr £30.00 **Beds:** 2D 1T **Baths:** 3 En (4)

Beamish

NZ2253

No Place House, *Beamish, Stanley, Co Durham, DH9 0QH.* Converted co-operative store, close to Beamish Museum. Friendly warm welcome. **Open:** All year
Grades: ETC 2 Diamond
0191 370 0891 Mrs Wood *gaz@nobeam.fsnet.co.uk* www.noplace.co.uk **D:** Fr £20.00–£22.00 **S:** Fr £23.00–£26.00 **Beds:** 2D 1T **Baths:** 2 En 1 Sh (3) (5)

The Coach House, *High Urpeth, Beamish, Stanley, Co Durham, DH9 0SE.* Country hamlet location, near Durham City, Beamish, Metro Centre and A1(M).
Open: All year
0191 370 0309 Kim Foreman **Fax: 0191 370 0046** *coachhouse@foreman25.freeserve.co.uk* www.coachhousebeamish.ntb.org.uk **D:** Fr £20.00–£25.00 **S:** Fr £30.00–£35.00 **Beds:** 1F 1T 1D **Baths:** 1 En 2 Pr (6) **cc**

Bishop Auckland

NZ1928

Five Gables, *Binchester, Bishop Auckland, DL14 8AT.* Recommended by 'Which? Good B&B Guide'. 15 mins from Durham.
Open: All year (not Xmas/New Year)
Grades: ETC 3 Diamond
01388 608204 P.M.I Weston **Fax: 01388 663092** *book.in@fivegables.co.uk* www.fivegables.co.uk **D:** Fr £24.00–£25.00 **S:** Fr £28.00–£30.00 **Beds:** 1T 2D 1S **Baths:** 3 En 1 Pr (2) **cc**

Bowburn

NZ3038

Hillrise Guest House, *13 Durham Road West, Bowburn, Durham, DH6 5AU.* Recommended standard of accommodation in large ensuite rooms.
Open: All year **Grades:** ETC 4 Diamond, AA 4 Diamond
0191 377 0302 G B Webster **Fax: 0191 377 0898** *hillrise.guesthouse@btinternet.com* www.hill-rise.com **D:** Fr £25.00–£30.00 **S:** Fr £30.00 **Beds:** 3F 2D **Baths:** 5 En (4) **cc**

Brandon

NZ2439

Bay Horse Inn, *Brandon, Durham, DH7 8ST.* Situated in the quaint village of Brandon only 3 miles from the historical city of Durham. The Inn offers comfortable and friendly accommodation for the business person or the holiday maker. Nearby attractions include countryside walks, cathedral, museums and castles.
Open: All year
0191 378 0498 Mr & Mrs Maddock **D:** Fr £25.00–£30.00 **S:** Fr £40.00 **Beds:** 1F 6T 3D **Baths:** 10 En **cc**

Castleside

NZ0849

Castleneuk Guest House, *18/20 Front Street, Castleside, Consett, Co Durham, DH8 9AR.* Castleneuk is a family-run friendly guest house. **Open:** All year (not Xmas)
01207 506634 J McGuigan *jan@castleneuk.co.uk* **D:** Fr £18.00–£20.00 **S:** Fr £18.00–£20.00 **Beds:** 1F 1D 2T **Baths:** 4 Pr (4) (5)

Chester-le-Street

NZ2751

Waldridge Fell Guest House, *Waldridge Lane, Old Waldridge Village, Chester-le-Street, Co Durham, DH2 3RY.* Three minutes from Chester-le-Street Centre. Panoramic views. Friendly, relaxed atmosphere. **Open:** All year (not Xmas/New Year) **Grades:** AA 4 Diamond
0191 389 1908 Mrs Sharratt *bbchesterlestreet@btinternet.com* www.smoothhound.co.uk/hotels/waldridgefell.html **D:** Fr £24.00–£25.00 **S:** Fr £28.00–£30.00 **Beds:** 3F 2D 1S **Baths:** 6 En (8)

Hollycroft, *11 The Parade, Chester-le-street, County Durham, DH3 3LR.* Ideally located: A1(m), Country cricket, Beamish museum, Lumley Castle, Durham.
Open: All year (not Xmas/New Year)
0191 388 7088 & 07932 675069 (M) Mr Cutter *cutter@hollycroft11.freeserve.co.uk* **D:** Fr £22.50 **S:** Fr £27.00 **Beds:** 1T 2D (2)

Cornforth

NZ3134 Poacher's Pocket

Ash House, *24 The Green, Cornforth, Co Durham, DL17 9JH.* On village green, tastefully decorated, carved four-posters, adjacent A1M (motorway). **Open:** All year (not Xmas/New Year)
01740 654654 & 07711 133574 (M) Mrs Slack *delden@easicom.com* **D:** Fr £20.00–£22.50 **S:** Fr £25.00–£30.00 **Beds:** 1F 1T 1D

Cowshill

NY8540

Low Cornriggs Farm, *Cowshill, Wearhead, Bishop Auckland, Co Durham, DL13 1AQ.* Magnificent views, excellent location, quality accommodation, good breakfast. Riding school. Near to C2C.
Open: All year
01388 537600 Mrs Elliott **Fax: 01388 537777** *enquiries@lowcornriggsfarm.fsnet.co.uk* www.alstonandkillhoperidingcentre.co.uk **D:** Fr £22.00 **S:** Fr £25.00–£28.00 **Beds:** 1T 1D 1F **Baths:** 4 Pr (6)

Craghead

NZ2151

The Punch Bowl, *Craghead, Stanley, County Durham, DH9 6EF.* Village public house. Near Beamish Museum and Durham City. **Open:** All year (not Xmas/New Year)
01207 232917 **D:** Fr £15.00–£20.00 **S:** Fr £15.00–£20.00 **Beds:** 1T 1D 2S **Baths:** 1 Sh (15)

Darlington

NZ2814

Aberlady Guest Hotel, *51 Corporation Road, Darlington, Co Durham, DL3 6AD.* Victorian house close to town centre, Railway Museum, cinema and restaurants.
Open: All year (not Xmas)
01325 461449 Mrs Chaplin **D:** Fr £15.00–£20.00 **S:** Fr £15.00–£20.00 **Beds:** 2F 3T 2S **Baths:** 2 Sh (2)

Balmoral Guest House, *63 Woodland Road, Darlington, Co Durham, DL3 7BQ.* Excellent B&B accommodation, 5 mins town centre, ideal for business/leisure. **Open:** All year (not Xmas/New Year) **Grades:** AA 3 Diamond
01325 461908 Mr Hawke www.balmoral-darlington.co.uk **D:** Fr £21.00–£23.00 **S:** Fr £28.00–£35.00 **Beds:** 3F 1D 1T 4S **Baths:** 4 Pr 2 Sh

Durham

NZ2742

Littletown Lodge, *Littletown, Durham, DH6 1PZ.* **Open:** All year (not Xmas) **Grades:** ETC 3 Diamond
0191 372 3712 R Sutton *littletownlodge@aol.com* **D:** Fr £20.00–£40.00 **S:** Fr £30.00 **Beds:** 2F 1T 2D **Baths:** 5 En (7)
Quiet location guest house in a beautiful country location yet only 5 mins from Durham city. Ideal for a family holiday or touring/walking base. All bedrooms have ensuite bathrooms whilst the four-poster suites are particularly luxuriously appointed.

The Pink House, *16 Gilesgate, Durham, DH1 1QW.* Small Georgian house. Homely, central. **Open:** All year
0191 386 7039 Mrs Miles **D:** Fr £16.00 **S:** Fr £20.00 **Beds:** 1F 1D **Baths:** 1 Sh

Castle View Guest House, *4 Crossgate, Durham, DH1 4PS.* City centre Georgian guest house, close to castle and cathedral. **Open:** All year (not Xmas)
0191 386 8852 (also fax) Mrs Williams *castle_view@hotmail.com* **D:** Fr £30.00 **S:** Fr £45.00 **Beds:** 3D 2T 1S **Baths:** 6 En (2) cc

Hillrise Guest House, *13 Durham Road West, Bowburn, Durham, DH6 5AU.* Recommended standard of accommodation in large ensuite rooms. **Open:** All year **Grades:** ETC 4 Diamond, AA 4 Diamond
0191 377 0302 G B Webster **Fax: 0191 377 0898** *hillrise.guesthouse@btinternet.com* www.hill-rise.com **D:** Fr £25.00–£30.00 **S:** Fr £30.00 **Beds:** 3F 2D **Baths:** 5 En (4) cc

Queens Head Hotel, *2-6 Sherburn Road, Gilesgate Moor, Durham, DH1 2JR.* Comfortable, clean, friendly. Full breakfast. English, Cantonese food. 2 minutes A1. **Open:** All year
0191 386 5649 P Collins **Fax: 0191 386 7451** **D:** Fr £17.50–£27.50 **S:** Fr £22.00 **Beds:** 2F 1D 2T 2S **Baths:** 2 Sh (7) cc

14 Gilesgate, *Durham, DH1 1QW.* Central, spacious C18th town house with four-poster beds and antiques. **Open:** All year (not Xmas/New Year)
0191 384 6485 Mr Nimmins **Fax: 0191 386 5173** *bb@nimmins.co.uk* www.nimmins.co.uk **D:** Fr £20.00 **S:** Fr £20.00 **Beds:** 1F 1D 1T 1S **Baths:** 2 Sh (1)

9 Leazes Place, Claypath, *Durham, DH1 1RE.* Situated in charming period cul-de-sac. Short walk from market place. **Open:** Easter to Oct
0191 386 8479 Miss Thomas **D:** Fr £15.00 **S:** Fr £15.00 **Beds:** 2T **Baths:** 1 Sh (3) (1)

Eastgate

NY9539

Rose Hill Farm, *Eastgate, Bishop Auckland, County Durham, DL13 2LB.* Spacious barn conversion on working hill farm offering a warm welcome together with a high standard of accommodation. Panoramic views of Weardale from the large enclosed garden. Ideal base for visiting Durham, Beamish, Hexham, Barnard Castle. Ground floor rooms available. **Open:** All year
01388 517209 & 07808 402425 (M) Ms Wearmouth **Fax: 01388 517209** *june@rosehillfarm.fsnet.co.uk* www.rosehillfarmholidays.co.uk **D:** Fr £22.50–£25.00 **S:** Fr £30.00 **Beds:** 2F 1T 2D **Baths:** 5 En (5)

Eggleston

NZ0023

Moorcock Inn, *Hill Top, Gordon Bank, Eggleston, Co Durham, DL12 0AU.* Country inn with scenic views over Teesdale ideal for walking. Cosy ensuite bedrooms. **Open:** All year
01833 650395 Mr & Mrs Zacharias **Fax: 01833 650052** **D:** Fr £32.00–£37.00 **S:** Fr £20.00–£25.00 **Beds:** 6D 6S **Baths:** 4 En 3 Sh (30) cc

Frosterley

NZ0237

High Laithe, *Hill End, Frosterley, Bishop Auckland, County Durham, DL13 2SX.* Small working farm. Peacefully situated. Splendid views. Ideal touring, walking. **Open:** All year (not Xmas)
01388 526421 Mr Moss **D:** Fr £18.00 **S:** Fr £18.00 **Beds:** 1D 1S **Baths:** 1 Pr (5) (2)

BATHROOMS
En = Ensuite
Pr = Private
Sh = Shared

Gainford

NZ1617

Queens Head Hotel, *11 Main Road, Gainford, Darlington, DL2 3DZ.* Inn/restaurant/bar meals. A67 between Darlington and Barnard Castle. **Open:** All year
01325 730958 Mrs Batty **D:** Fr £22.50 **S:** Fr £35.00 **Beds:** 2F 1T 2D **Baths:** 5 En (30) cc

Green Head

NZ1434 *The Victoria, Duke of York, Helm Park, Fir Tree*

Greenhead Country Caravan Park, *Fir Tree, Crook, Co Durham, DL15 8BL.* Private hotel with all en-suite bedrooms restricted to resident guests. **Open:** All year
01388 763143 (also fax) Mr Birkbeck *info@thegreenheadhotel.co.uk* www.thegreenheadhotel.co.uk **D:** Fr £30.00–£35.00 **S:** Fr £45.00–£55.00 **Beds:** 2T 4D 2S **Baths:** 8 En (14) cc

Harperley

NZ1753

Bushblades Farm, *Harperley, Stanley, County Durham, DH9 9UA.* Georgian farmhouse, rural setting. Close Beamish Museum and Durham City. **Open:** All year (not Xmas) **Grades:** ETC 3 Diamond
01207 232722 Mrs Gibson **D:** Fr £18.50–£21.00 **S:** Fr £25.00–£30.00 **Beds:** 2D 1T **Baths:** 1 En 2 Sh (12) (4)

Haswell Plough

NZ3742

The Gables Hotel, *Haswell Plough, Durham, DH6 2EW.* Small family run hotel 5 miles east of Durham city on the B1283. **Open:** All year
0191 526 2982 (also fax) Mr Milner *johngables@aol.com* www.powow.com/thegables/index.htm. **D:** Fr £17.50–£28.00 **S:** Fr £19.00–£30.00 **Beds:** 1F 2D 2T **Baths:** 2 Sh 3 En (30)

Holwick

NY9027

The Strathmore Arms, *Holwick, Middleton-in-Teesdale, Barnard Castle, Co Durham, DL12 0NJ.* Idyllic C17th Teesdale Inn, near High Force Waterfalls on the Pennine Way. **Open:** All year
01833 640362 (also fax) *hojo@supanet.com* **D:** Fr £22.50–£25.00 **S:** Fr £30.00–£35.00 **Beds:** 1F 1T 2D **Baths:** 4 En

Kirk Merrington

NZ2631

Highview Country House, *Kirk Merrington, Spennymoor, DL16 7JT.* Set in one acre panoramic countryside, good pubs, safe parking, peaceful. **Open:** All year **01388 811006 (also fax)** *highview house@genie.co.uk* **D:** Fr £23.00 **S:** Fr £25.00 **Beds:** 1F 1T 4D 1S **Baths:** 7 En

Lunedale

NY9221

Wemmergill Hall Farm, *Lunedale, Middleton in Teesdale, Barnard Castle, County Durham, DL12 0PA.* Traditional farmhouse, views over moorland and reservoir. Walkers/ birdwatchers paradise! **Open:** Jan to Nov **01833 640379 (also fax)** Mrs Stoddart **D:** Fr £18.00–£20.00 **S:** Fr £20.00–£25.00 **Beds:** 1F 1D (4) (2)

Mickleton

NY9623

Pine Grove, *Lowside, Mickleton, Barnard Castle, Co Durham, DL12 0JQ.* Situated on quiet back road with fine views of Teesdale. **Open:** All year (not Xmas) **01833 640886** Mr & Mrs Gillings *chris@cgillings.freeserve.co.uk* **D:** Fr £16.00–£18.00 **S:** Fr £17.00–£19.00 **Beds:** 1F 1D 1T **Baths:** 1 Sh (4)

Middleton in Teesdale

NY9425

Brunswick House, *55 Market Place, Middleton in Teesdale, Barnard Castle, Co Durham, DL12 0QH.* Charming C18th guest house, excellent food. Many beautiful walks. **Open:** All year **01833 640393 (also fax)** Mr & Mrs Milnes *enquiries@brunswickhouse.net* www.brunswickhouse.net **D:** Fr £20.00–£24.00 **S:** Fr £24.00–£32.00 **Beds:** 3D 2T **Baths:** 5 En (5) cc

Belvedere House, *54 Market Place, Middleton-in-Teesdale, Barnard Castle, Co Durham, DL12 0QA.* Enjoy a warm welcome, English breakfast and explore Teesdale's beautiful countryside. **Open:** All year **Grades:** ETC 4 Diamond **01833 640884 (also fax)** Mrs Finn *belvedere@thecoachhouse.net* www.thecoachhouse.net **D:** Fr £18.00 **S:** Fr £19.00 **Beds:** 1T 2D **Baths:** 3 En (3)

Ivy House, *Stanhope Road, Middleton in Teesdale, Barnard Castle, Co Durham, DL12 0RT.* Victorian house overlooking lovely countryside. Friendly welcome to all guests. **Open:** Apr to Oct **01833 640603** M Ebdon **D:** Fr £17.00–£18.00 **S:** Fr £18.00–£20.00 **Beds:** 1T 1D **Baths:** 1 En 1 Pr (5) (2)

Bluebell House, *Market Place, Middleton in Teesdale, Barnard Castle, Co Durham, DL12 0GG.* Former inn, beautiful walks, good food, friendly family atmosphere guaranteed. **Open:** All year (not Xmas) **01833 640584** Ms Northey **D:** Fr £16.00–£17.00 **S:** Fr £21.00–£25.00 **Beds:** 2D 2T **Baths:** 3 En 1 Pr (2)

Newfield

NZ2452

Malling House, *1 Oakdale Terrace, Newfield, Chester-le-Street, County Durham, DH2 2SU.* Heather, your host, has extensive knowledge of area and attractions. **Open:** All year **0191 370 2571** Ms Rippon **Fax: 0191 370 1391** www.mallingguesthouse.freeserve.co.uk **D:** Fr £36.00–£46.00 **S:** Fr £20.00–£26.00 **Beds:** 1F 1T 1S (3)

Piercebridge

NZ2015

Holme House, *Piercebridge, Darlington, Co Durham, DL2 3SY.* Attractive C18th farmhouse surrounded by beautiful countryside, spacious comfortable accommodation. **Open:** All year (not Xmas) **Grades:** ETC 3 Diamond **01325 374280 (also fax)** Mrs Graham *graham@holmehouse22.freeserve.co.uk* **D:** Fr £22.50–£25.00 **S:** Fr £22.50–£30.00 **Beds:** 1F 1T **Baths:** 2 En (4)

Plawsworth

NZ2647

Lilac Cottage, *Wheatley Well Lane, Plawsworth, Chester-le-Street, Co Durham, DH2 3LD.* Stone built Georgian cottage just off A167. Very conveniently situated for Durham city. **Open:** All year (not Xmas) **0191 371 2969** Mrs Prizeman **D:** Fr £17.50 **S:** Fr £17.50 **Beds:** 1D 1T 1S **Baths:** 2 Sh (2)

Rushyford

NZ2829

Garden House, *Windlestone Park, Windlestone, Rushyford, Ferryhill, County Durham, DL17 0LZ.* House with stunning walled garden. Haven of peace and tranquillity. **Open:** All year **01388 720217 & 07979 297374 (M)** Ms Cattell **D:** Fr £20.00–£22.00 **S:** Fr £25.00–£28.00 **Beds:** 1T 2D **Baths:** 2 En 1 Pr

Shildon

NZ2227

101 Main Street, *Shildon, Co Durham, DL4 1AW.* 8 miles from A1(m). Ample parking. Georgian mid terrace. **Open:** All year (not Xmas/New Year) **01388 772646** Mr Walton **D:** Fr £17.00 **S:** Fr £17.00 **Beds:** 1F 1T 1D (18)

Shotley Bridge

NZ0852

Crown & Crossed Swords Hotel, *Shotley Bridge, Consett, Co Durham, DH8 0NH.* Historic country hotel. Meals all day 12-9.30 Mon-Sat. Sunday lunch 12-3. **Open:** All year **01207 502006** Mrs Suddick **D:** Fr £18.00–£23.00 **S:** Fr £20.00–£25.00 **Beds:** 2F 4D 3T 1S **Baths:** 4 En 2 Sh (40) cc

Spennymoor

NZ2533

Idsley House, *4 Green Lane, Spennymoor, Co Durham, DL16 6HD.* Warm welcome assured. Local knowledge. Close to Durham A167/A688 Junction. **Open:** All year **Grades:** ETC 4 Diamond **01388 814237** Mrs Dartnall **D:** Fr £24.00 **S:** Fr £35.00–£38.00 **Beds:** 1F 2D 2T 1S **Baths:** 4 En 1 Pr (5) (8) cc

Staindrop

NZ1220

Malvern House, *7 Front Street, Staindrop, Darlington, Co Durham, DL2 3LZ.* Georgian town house, overlooking the green in conservation village. **Open:** All year **01833 660846** Mrs Young **D:** Fr £18.00 **S:** Fr £18.00 **Beds:** 2T **Baths:** 1 Sh

Stanley

NZ1952

Bushblades Farm, *Harperley, Stanley, County Durham, DH9 9UA.* Georgian farmhouse, rural setting. Close Beamish Museum and Durham City. **Open:** All year (not Xmas) **Grades:** ETC 3 Diamond **01207 232722** Mrs Gibson **D:** Fr £18.50–£21.00 **S:** Fr £25.00–£30.00 **Beds:** 2D 1T **Baths:** 1 En 2 Sh (12) (4)

Waldridge

NZ2550

Waldridge Fell Guest House, *Waldridge Lane, Old Waldridge Village, Chester-le-Street, Co Durham, DH2 3RY.* Three minutes from Chester-le-Street Centre. Panoramic views. Friendly, relaxed atmosphere. **Open:** All year (not Xmas/New Year) **Grades:** AA 4 Diamond
0191 389 1908 Mrs Sharratt *bbchesterlestreet@btinternet.com* www.smoothhound.co.uk/hotels/waldridgefell.html **D:** Fr £24.00–£25.00 **S:** Fr £28.00–£30.00 **Beds:** 3F 2D 1S **Baths:** 6 En (8)

West Auckland

NZ1726

Country Style, *Etherley Bank, West Auckland, Bishop Auckland, Co Durham, DL14 0LG.* All rooms are ground floor, each with separate entry from off-road car park. **Open:** All year
01388 832679 Ms Walton **D:** Fr £18.50–£20.00 **S:** Fr £20.00–£25.00 **Beds:** 1F 1D 1T 1S **Baths:** 4 En (1) (8)

Westgate in Weardale

NY9038 *Hare & Hounds, Cross Keys*

Lands Farm, *Westgate in Weardale, Bishop Auckland, Co Durham, DL13 1SN.* Peaceful location, ideal for exploring Durham and the Pennines. **Open:** All year
01388 517210 Mrs Reed **D:** Fr £22.50–£23.00 **S:** Fr £27.00 **Beds:** 1F 1D **Baths:** 2 En (4)

Essex

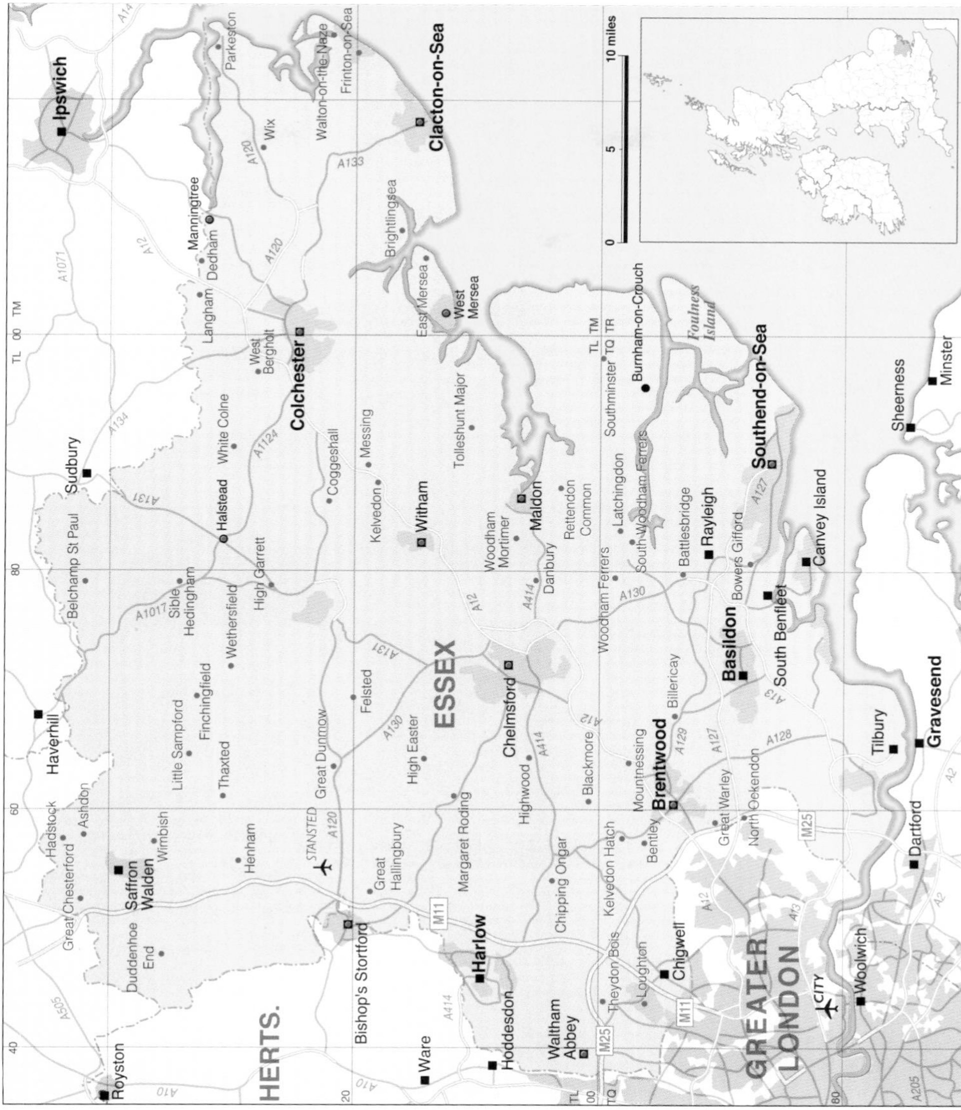
ESSEX
HERTS.
GREATER LONDON
Ipswich
Clacton-on-Sea
Colchester
Sudbury
Haverhill
Saffron Walden
Royston
Bishop's Stortford
Harlow
Hoddesdon
Ware
Waltham Abbey
Chelmsford
Witham
Halstead
Maldon
Brentwood
Chigwell
Basildon
Rayleigh
Southend-on-Sea
Burnham-on-Crouch
Canvey Island
South Benfleet
Tilbury
Gravesend
Dartford
Woolwich
Sheerness
Minster
Manningtree
Dedham
Langham
West Bergholt
White Colne
Coggeshall
Messing
Kelvedon
Tolleshunt Major
West Mersea
East Mersea
Brightlingsea
Wix
Walton-on-the-Naze
Frinton-on-Sea
Parkeston
Belchamp St Paul
Sible Hedingham
Wethersfield
High Garrett
Finchingfield
Little Sampford
Thaxted
Great Dunmow
Felsted
High Easter
Margaret Roding
Great Hallingbury
Henham
Wimbish
Hadstock
Ashdon
Great Chesterford
Duddenhoe End
Woodham Mortimer
Danbury
Rettendon Common
Latchingdon
South Woodham Ferrers
Woodham Ferrers
Southminster
Battlesbridge
Bowers Gifford
Billericay
Mountnessing
Blackmore
Highwood
Chipping Ongar
Kelvedon Hatch
Bentley
Great Warley
North Ockendon
Theydon Bois
Loughton
Foulness Island
STANSTED
CITY
M11
M25
A12
A120
A131
A130
A133
A134
A1124
A1017
A414
A127
A128
A129
A13
A2
A10
A505
A1071
A14
A205
0
5
10 miles
TL
TM
TQ
TR
00
20
40
60
80

Ashdon

TL5842

Cobblers, *Bartow Road, Ashdon, Saffron Walden, Essex, CB10 2HR.* Peaceful place, warm welcome, relaxing rooms, bountiful breakfasts, great garden! **Open:** All year (not Xmas)
01799 584666 Mrs Slater *cobblers@ashdon2000.freeserve.co.uk* **D:** Fr £20.00 **S:** Fr £20.00–£25.00 **Beds:** 2D **Baths:** 1 En 1 Pr (3) (4)

Battlesbridge

TQ7794

The Cottages Guest House, *Beeches Road, Battlesbridge, Wickford, Essex, SS11 8TJ.* Rural, cosy, licensed guest house. Easy reach Southend, Chelmsford, Basildon. Licensed bar. **Open:** All year (not Xmas) **Grades:** ETC 2 Diamond
01702 232105 Miss Carr *cottages2000@totalise.co.uk* **D:** Fr £20.00–£25.00 **S:** Fr £20.00–£29.00 **Beds:** 3D 1T 1S 2F **Baths:** 1 En 1 Sh (10)

Belchamp St Paul

TL7942

The Plough, *Belchamp St Paul, Sudbury, Suffolk, CO10 7BT.* Charming former pub. Peaceful village. Comfortable friendly atmosphere. Centrally located. **Open:** All year **Grades:** ETC 4 Diamond, Silver
01787 278882 Mrs Stormont *info@theplough-belchamp.co.uk* www.theplough-belchamp.co.uk **D:** Fr £24.00–£26.00 **S:** Fr £28.00–£36.00 **Beds:** 1T 1D **Baths:** 2 En (6) (6)

Bentley

TQ5696

The Coach House, *Mores Lane, Bentley, Brentwood, Essex, CM14 5PZ.* 200 year old coaching house in 1 acre grounds.
Open: All year (not Xmas/New Year)
01277 375015 S Mead **Fax: 01277 372954** *sheilaghandroger@aol.com* **D:** Fr £22.00–£25.00 **S:** Fr £22.00–£25.00

Billericay

TQ6794 *Kings Head*

Badgers' Rest, *2 Mount View, Billericay, Essex, CM11 1HB.* 'Badgers Rest' is in a pleasant, select area of Billericay. **Open:** All year
01277 625384 & 07778 444169 (M) C J Parker **Fax: 01277 633912 D:** Fr £23.00–£25.00 **S:** Fr £23.00–£25.00 **Beds:** 3S 1D **Baths:** 2 Sh 1 En (10) (6)

Planning a longer stay? Always ask for any special rates

Blackmore

TL6001

Little Lampetts, *Hay Green Lane, Blackmore, Ingatestone, Essex, CM4 0QE.* Secluded period house. Easy access to M25, mainline stations, towns. **Open:** All year
01277 822030 Mrs Porter *shelagh.porter@btinternet.com* **D:** Fr £25.00–£30.00 **S:** Fr £25.00–£35.00 **Beds:** 2T **Baths:** 1 Pr (5)

Bowers Gifford

TQ7588

38 Kelly Road, *Bowers Gifford, Basildon, Essex, SS13 2HL.* Self contained apartment. Train to London 45 minutes. Country setting and views. **Open:** All year
01268 726701 Ms Jenkinson *patricia.jenkinson@tesco.net* **D:** Fr £28.00–£40.00 **S:** Fr £22.00–£25.00 **Beds:** 2D (8)

Brentwood

TQ6093

Brentwood Guesthouse, *77 Rose Valley, Brentwood, Essex, CM14 4HJ.* Family run, recently refurbished. Close to town centre/station. 25 mins London, 1m M25.
Open: All year
01277 262713 Mr & Mrs Corbo **Fax: 01277 211146** *info@brentwoodguesthouse.com* www.brentwoodguesthouse.com **D:** Fr £25.00–£35.00 **S:** Fr £40.00–£60.00 **Beds:** 4F 2T 2D 1S **Baths:** 8 En 2 Pr cc

Brightlingsea

TM0817 *Cherry Tree, Red Lion*

Paxton Dene, *Church Road, Brightlingsea, Essex, CO7 0QT.* Attractive spacious cottage-style accommodation set in 1/2 acre grounds **Open:** All year
01206 304560 Mr & Mrs Reynolds **Fax: 01206 302877** *nora@paxtondene.freeserve.co.uk* **D:** Fr £20.00–£22.50 **S:** Fr £30.00–£40.00 **Beds:** 3F **Baths:** 3 Pr (4)

Chelmsford

TL7006 *Black Bull*

Aarandale, *9 Roxwell Road, Chelmsford, Essex, CM1 2LY.* Charming friendly B&B in large Victorian House, close town centre.
Open: All year (not Xmas/New Year)
01245 251713 (also fax) M Perera *aarandaleuk@aol.com* **D:** Fr £22.00 **S:** Fr £25.00–£35.00 **Beds:** 1F 1T 4S **Baths:** 1 En 1 Pr 1 Sh (6)

Clacton-on-Sea

TM1715

The Hamelin Hotel, *20 Penfold Road, Clacton-on-Sea, Essex, CO15 1JN.* A Christian family-run hotel close to sea and shops.
Open: All year (not Xmas)
01255 474456 Mrs Baker **Fax: 01255 428053** *hamelincentre@aol.com* **D:** Fr £19.00–£24.00 **S:** Fr £20.00–£28.00 **Beds:** 3F 2D 2T 1S **Baths:** 3 En 1 Sh (3) cc

Coggeshall

TL8522

White Heather Guest House, *19 Colchester Road, Coggeshall, Colchester, Essex, CO6 1RP.* Modern, family-run guest house, overlooking farmland. **Open:** All year (not Xmas)
01376 563004 Mrs Shaw **D:** Fr £22.00–£22.50 **S:** Fr £22.00–£25.00 **Beds:** 2D 2S **Baths:** 2 En 1 Sh (8)

Colchester

TL9925

Apple Blossom House, *8 Guildford Road, Colchester, Essex, CO1 2YL.* Detached house convenient town, sports. Healthy breakfasts. Parking. Weekly rates.
Open: All year
01206 512303 Ms Harris **Fax: 01206 870260** *patricia.appleblossom@virgin.net* **D:** Fr £20.00–£23.00 **S:** Fr £24.00 **Beds:** 1D 1S 1T **Baths:** 2 En 1 Pr (4)

St John's Guest House, *330 Ipswich Road, Colchester, Essex, CO4 4ET.* Well-situated close to town, convenient to A12 and A120 Harwich. **Open:** All year
01206 852288 E Knight **D:** Fr £20.00–£30.00 **S:** Fr £30.00–£50.00 **Beds:** 2F 2T 2D 1S **Baths:** 6 En 1 Sh

Salisbury Hotel, *112 Butt Road, Colchester, Essex, CO3 3DL.* Situated in the historical garrison town of Colchester and within easy reach of 3 cathedral cities. Despite being in the centre of town this pub has a relaxed and informal atmosphere. The in-house bar and restaurant serve delicious and innovative meals **Open:** All year
01206 508508 Fax: 01206 797265 www.thesalisburyhotel.co.uk **D:** Fr £25.00–£35.00 **S:** Fr £30.00–£40.00 **Beds:** 2F 4T 3D 3S **Baths:** 12 En cc

Please respect a B&B's wishes regarding children, animals and smoking

Danbury
TL7705

Southways, *Copt Hill, Danbury, Chelmsford, Essex, CM3 4NN.* House with large attractive garden adjoining National Trust common land. **Open:** All year
01245 223428 Mrs Deavin **D:** Fr £20.00–£22.00 **S:** Fr £22.00 **Beds:** 2T **Baths:** 1 Sh (2)

Wych Elm, *Mayes Lane, Danbury, Chelmsford, Essex, CM3 4NJ.* Welcoming, convenient central village location, quiet aspect. Extensive woods nearby. **Open:** All year **Grades:** ETC 3 Diamond
01245 222674 Mrs Axon *axonwychelm@tiscali.co.uk* **D:** Fr £22.50–£24.00 **S:** Fr £25.00–£27.00 **Beds:** 2T 1D 1S **Baths:** 1 En 1 Sh (6)

Dedham
TM0533

Mays Barn Farm, *Mays Lane, off Long Road West, Dedham, Colchester, Essex, CO7 6EW.* A comfortable well-furnished old house with wonderful views of Dedham Vale. **Open:** All year **Grades:** ETC 4 Diamond, Silver
01206 323191 Mrs Freeman *maysbarn@talk21.com* www.mays.barn.btinternet.co.uk
D: Fr £21.00–£24.00 **S:** Fr £25.00–£30.00 **Beds:** 1D 1T **Baths:** 1 En 1 Pr (10) (3)

Duddenhoe End
TL4636

Rockells Farm, *Duddenhoe End, Saffron Walden, Essex, CB11 4UY.* Georgian farmhouse with lake view. **Open:** All year (not Xmas/New Year)
01763 838053 Mrs Westerhuis **D:** Fr £20.00–£25.00 **S:** Fr £20.00–£25.00 **Beds:** 1F 1T 1S **Baths:** 3 En (4)

East Mersea
TM0514

Bromans Farm, *East Mersea, Colchester, Essex, CO5 8UE.* Grade II Listed C14th farmhouse, 5 minutes from sea & 9 miles Colchester. **Open:** All year
01206 383235 (also fax) Mrs Dence **D:** Fr £20.00–£25.00 **S:** Fr £25.00–£30.00 **Beds:** 1D 1T 1S **Baths:** 2 Pr (3)

Felsted
TL6720

Yarrow, *Felsted, Great Dunmow, Essex, CM6 3HD.* Near Stansted Airport in quiet historic village with pubs & restaurants.
Open: All year
01371 820878 (also fax) Mr & Mrs Bellingham Smith *bookings@yarrowbandb.co.uk* www.yarrowbandb.co.uk
D: Fr £18.00–£23.00 **S:** Fr £20.00–£29.00 **Beds:** 1D 1T 1S **Baths:** 1 En 1 Sh (6)

Frinton-on-Sea
TM2318

Uplands Guest House, *41 Hadleigh Road, Frinton-on-Sea, Essex, CO13 9HQ.* Quiet and comfortable. Just three minutes sea, shops. Ample parking. **Open:** All year (not Xmas)
01255 674889 Mrs Fitzgerald **D:** Fr £22.00–£28.00 **S:** Fr £22.00–£28.00 **Beds:** 1D 3S 2T **Baths:** 4 En 2 Sh (5)

Russell Lodge, *47 Hadleigh Road, Frinton-on-Sea, Essex, CO13 9HQ.* Home comfort and Edwardian elegance near seafront and town centre. **Open:** All year
01255 675935 J M Russell www.russell-lodgefsnet.co.uk **D:** Fr £20.00 **S:** Fr £20.00 **Beds:** 1T 1D 1S **Baths:** 1 En 1 Sh

Great Chesterford
TL5042

White Gates, *School Street, Great Chesterford, Saffron Walden, Essex, CB10 1PH.* C18th timber framed cottage in heart of historic village. **Open:** All year
01799 530249 Mrs Mortimer **D:** Fr £19.00–£25.00 **S:** Fr £23.00–£25.00 **Beds:** 1F 1T 1S **Baths:** 1 En 1 Sh (3)

Great Dunmow
TL6221

Homelye Farm, *Homelye Chase, Braintree Road, Great Dunmow, Essex, CM6 3AW.* Good quality motel-style accommodation close to Stansted Airport. **Open:** All year
01371 872127 Mrs Pickford **Fax: 01371 876428** *homelye@supanet.com* www.homelyefarm.co.uk **D:** Fr £27.50 **S:** Fr £35.00 **Beds:** 1F 3D 2T 3S **Baths:** 9 En (9) **cc**

Planning a longer stay? Always ask for any special rates

Great Hallingbury
TL5019

Yew Tree Farmhouse, *Tilekiln Green, Great Hallingbury, Bishops Stortford, Herts, CM22 7TQ.* Family-run C17th farmhouse in 2 acres, close M11 & Stansted Airport.
Open: All year (not Xmas)
01279 758875 (also fax) **D:** Fr £27.50–£45.00 **S:** Fr £45.00–£65.00 **Beds:** 1F 1D 1T 1S **Baths:** 4 Pr (5) (10)

Great Warley
TQ5890

Chestnut Tree Cottage, *Great Warley Street, Great Warley, Brentwood, Essex, CM13 3JF.* Attractive country cottage. Conveniently located M25, A127, A12. 1 mile to London. **Open:** All year
01277 221727 Mrs Malyon **D:** Fr £25.00–£35.00 **S:** Fr £25.00–£35.00 **Beds:** 1F 1T 1D **Baths:** 3 En (31)

Hadstock
TL5544

Yardleys, *Orchard Pightle, Hadstock, Cambridge, CB1 6PQ.* Peace and quiet in pretty village only 20 mins Cambridge, 10 mins Saffron Walden. **Open:** All year (not Xmas/New Year)
01223 891822 (also fax) Mrs Ludgate *yardleys@waitrose.com* **D:** Fr £22.00–£25.00 **S:** Fr £25.00–£32.00 **Beds:** 2T 1D **Baths:** 1 En 2 Pr (5) **cc**

Halstead
TL8130

Mill House, *The Causeway, Halstead, Essex, CO9 1ET.* Listed town house in the market town, private parking, Brochure available. **Open:** All year (not Xmas)
01787 474451 Mr & Mrs Stuckey **Fax: 01787 473893** *stuckey@townsford.freeserve.co.uk* **D:** Fr £24.00–£25.00 **S:** Fr £30.00–£48.00 (12) (18) **cc**

Henham
TL5428

Pleasant Cottage, *Woodend Green, Henham, Bishops Stortford, Essex, CM22 6AZ.*
Open: All year
01279 850792 (also fax) Mr & Mrs Griffiths *george@pleasantcott.fsnet.co.uk* www.henham.org/accommodation **D:** Fr £30.00–£32.50 **S:** Fr £40.00–£45.00 **Beds:** 1T 2D **Baths:** 3 En (10)
Grade II Listed thatched cottage on village green, excellent accommodation with warm welcome. Well-positioned for Cambridge, London and Stansted Airport only 5 miles. Plus charming countryside with many delightful villages and market towns of Thaxted and Saffron Walden.

High Easter

TL6214

The Cock & Bell, *The Street, High Easter, Chelmsford, Essex, CM1 4QW.* C14th former coaching inn, operating as charming Guest House. **Open:** All year (not Xmas/New Year)
01245 231296 A Steel **D:** Fr £19.50–£24.50 **S:** Fr £22.50–£27.50 **Beds:** 2D 1F 1S **Baths:** 2 En 1 Sh

High Garrett

TL7726

Hare & Hounds, *High Garrett, Braintree, Essex, CM7 5NT.* **Open:** All year (not Xmas/New Year)
01376 324430 (also fax) Steve Watling *info@hare-and-hounds.com* www.hare-and-hounds.com **D:** Fr £22.50–£25.00 **S:** Fr £25.00–£30.00 **Beds:** 1F 3T 1D **Baths:** 3 En 1 Pr 1 Sh (20) cc
The Hare & Hounds is located in the village of High Garrett, 5 minutes from Braintree town centre on the A131. Recently refurbished, it offers a comfortable b&b throughout the year, and has an excellent reputation for high quality food.

Highwood

TL6404

Wards Farm, *Loves Green, Highwood Road, Highwood, Chelmsford, Essex, CM1 3QJ.* Traditional oak-beamed C16th farmhouse, moated grounds, log fires. **Open:** Mar to Dec **Grades:** ETC 2 Diamond
01245 248812 Mrs Barton **D:** Fr £22.50 **S:** Fr £23.00–£25.00 **Beds:** 1T 1D (8)

Kelvedon

TL8518

Highfields Farm, *Kelvedon, Colchester, Essex, CO5 9BJ.* Farmhouse in quiet countryside location, convenient for A12 and London. **Open:** All year **Grades:** ETC 3 Diamond
01376 570334 (also fax) Mrs Bunting *HighfieldsFarm@farmersweekly.net* www.highfieldsfarm.20m.com **D:** Fr £23.00–£24.00 **S:** Fr £26.00–£28.00 **Beds:** 1D 2T **Baths:** 2 En 1 Pr (4)

Kelvedon Hatch

TQ5799

57 Great Fox Meadow, *Kelvedon Hatch, Brentwood, Essex, CM15 0AX.* Homely, friendly, clean, comfortable. Overlooking farmlands. 4 miles from Brentwood and Ongar. **Open:** All year (not Xmas)
01277 374659 Mrs Maguire **D:** Fr £16.00–£21.00 **S:** Fr £16.00–£21.00 **Beds:** 1D 1S **Baths:** 1 Sh (3) (2)

Langham

TM0233

Oak Apple Farm, *Greyhound Hill, Langham, Colchester, Essex, CO4 5QF.* Comfortable farmhouse tastefully decorated with large attractive garden. **Open:** All year (not Xmas)
01206 272234 Mrs Helliwell *rosie@oakapplefarm.fsnet.co.uk* www.smoothhound.co.uk/hotels/oak.html **D:** Fr £22.00 **S:** Fr £22.00 **Beds:** 2T 1S **Baths:** 1 Sh (6)

Latchingdon

TL8800

Neptune Cafe Motel, *Burnham Road, Latchingdon, Chelmsford, Essex, CM3 6EX.* **Open:** All year
01621 740770 Mr Lloyd **D:** Fr £17.50 **S:** Fr £25.00 **Beds:** 4F 4D 2T 10S **Baths:** 10 En 2 Pr 1 Sh (40) 1
Cafe motel, luxury chalets adjoining. Close to boating and fishing areas, golfing and horse-riding close by. Lovely rural setting with grand views.

Little Sampford

TL6533

Bush Farm, *Little Sampford, Saffron Walden, Essex, CB10 2RY.* Oak-beamed period residence situated amidst rolling acres of farmland. **Open:** All year
01799 586636 (also fax) Mrs Freeman *aimreso@aol.com* **D:** Fr £25.00–£30.00 **S:** Fr £30.00–£35.00 **Beds:** 2D **Baths:** 1 En 1 Pr (5) (10)

Loughton

TQ4396

Forest Edge, *61 York Hill, Loughton, Essex, IG10 1HZ.* Quiet location. Off-street parking. Convenient for Central Line. **Open:** All year (not Xmas/New Year)
020 8508 9834 E Catterall **Fax: 020 8281 1894** *arthur@catterallarthur.fsnet.co.uk* **D:** Fr £19.00–£20.00 **S:** Fr £22.25–£25.00 **Beds:** 2T 1S

Maldon

TL8407

The Jolly Sailor, *Hythe Quay, Maldon, Essex, CM9 5HP.* Good pub grub and a la carte menu. **Open:** All year
01621 853463 D: Fr £20.00–£25.00 **S:** Fr £20.00–£25.00 **Beds:** 2F 2D **Baths:** 1 En

Manningtree

TM1031

Dairy House Farm, *Bradfield Road, Wix, Manningtree, Essex, CO11 2SR.* Spacious, quality, rural accommodation. A really relaxing place to stay. **Open:** All year (not Xmas) **Grades:** AA 5 Diamond
01255 870322 Mrs Whitworth **Fax: 01255 870186** *bridgetwhitworth@hotmail.com* **D:** Fr £22.00–£24.00 **S:** Fr £28.00–£30.00 **Beds:** 1D 1T **Baths:** 2 En (12) (4)

Margaret Roding

TL5912

Greys, *Ongar Road, Margaret Roding, Great Dunmow, Essex, CM6 1QR.* Old beamed cottage, surrounded by our farmland, tiny village. Good B&B. **Open:** All year (not Xmas) **Grades:** ETC 3 Diamond, AA 3 Diamond
01245 231509 Mrs Matthews **D:** Fr £22.50 **S:** Fr £25.00 **Beds:** 2D 1T **Baths:** 1 Sh (3)

Messing

TL8918

Crispin's, *The Street, Messing, Colchester, CO5 9TR.* Elizabethan building with garden in pretty village. Close to Constable country. **Open:** All year
01621 815868 D: Fr £27.00 **S:** Fr £35.00–£40.00 **Beds:** 2F 1T 2S **Baths:** 2 En (5) cc

Mountnessing

TQ6297

Millers, *Thoby Lane, Mountnessing, Brentwood, Essex, CM15 0TD.* Beautiful house and garden overlooking countryside close to A12, 10 mins M25. **Open:** All year
01277 354595 Mrs Stacey **D:** Fr £25.00 **S:** Fr £30.00 **Beds:** 1F 2T **Baths:** 1 Pr

National Grid References given are for villages, towns and cities – not for individual houses

Gloucestershire

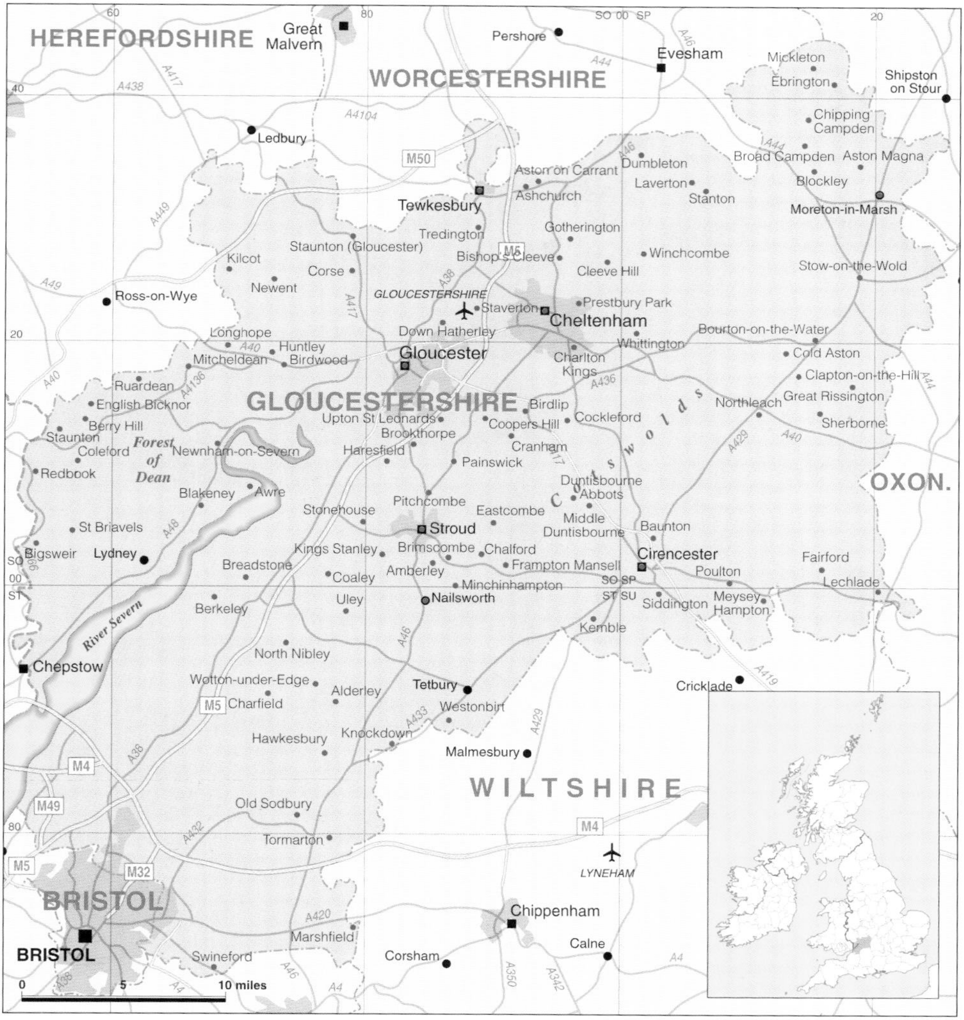

Alderley

ST7690

Hillesley Mill, *Alderley, Wotton-under-Edge, Glos, GL12 7QT.* Converted mill with lake in undulating fields and prolific woodland. **Open:** All year (not Xmas/New Year) **Grades:** ETC 3 Diamond **01453 843258** Mrs James **D:** Fr £22.00–£24.00 **S:** Fr £22.00–£24.00 **Beds:** 1F 1D 1T **Baths:** 1 En 1 Sh (8)

Amberley

SO8501

High Tumps, *St. Chloe Green, Amberley, Stroud, Glos, GL5 5AR.* Modest family home offers B&B in self contained annexe. **Open:** All year **Grades:** ETC 4 Diamond **01453 873584 Fax: 01453 873587** *dakavic@high-tumps.freeserve.co.uk* **D:** Fr £15.00–£17.00 **S:** Fr £15.00–£17.00 **Beds:** 1T **Baths:** 1 En

Ashchurch

SO9233

Newton Farm, *Ashchurch, Tewkesbury, Glos, GL20 7BE.* Traditional farmhouse B&B, 1/2 mile from M5 J9 & railway station. **Open:** All year **01684 295903 (also fax) D:** Fr £20.00 **S:** Fr £22.00 **Beds:** 5F **Baths:** 5 En

Aston Magna

SP1935

Bran Mill Cottage, *Aston Magna, Moreton in Marsh, Glos, GL56 9QW.* Small traditional B&B in peaceful Cotswold cottage. Friendly, welcoming, homely. **Open:** All year (not Xmas) **Grades:** ETC 3 Diamond
01386 593517 Mr & Mrs Baggaley *enquiries@branmillcottage.co.uk* www.branmillcottage.co.uk **D:** Fr £18.00–£21.00 **S:** Fr £19.00–£25.00 **Beds:** 1D 1T 1S **Baths:** 1 Pr 1 Sh (3)

Aston on Carrant

SO9434

Wistaria Cottage, *Aston on Carrant, Tewkesbury, Glos, GL20 8HL.* Pretty rural hamlet, traditional country breakfast, excellent walking/touring area.
Open: Easter to Oct
01684 772357 Mrs Allen **D:** Fr £20.00–£22.00 **S:** Fr £25.00–£30.00 **Beds:** 1D 1T **Baths:** 1 En 1 Pr (3)

Awre

SO7008

Yew Trees, *Awe, Newnham, Glos, GL14 1EW.* **Open:** All year **01594 516687 & 07970 921686 (M)** Mrs Solari **Fax: 01594 517209** *b&b@yewtrees.uk.com* www.yewtrees.uk.com **D:** Fr £25.00 **S:** Fr £25.00 **Beds:** 1F 1T 2D **Baths:** 1 En 2 Sh (8)
Friendly welcome. Relaxed atmosphere. Quiet village location. Organic breakfasts. Close to Forest of Dean and Severn Estuary. Walking. Bird watching. Bell-ringing in church. Cycling. Pub serving food and real ale.

Baunton

SP0204

Windrush, *Baunton, Cirencester, Glos, GL7 7BA.* Detached house in large gardens. Beautiful views over Cotswold countryside.
Open: All year (not Xmas)
01285 655942 (also fax) S J Rees **D:** Fr £20.00–£25.00 **S:** Fr £20.00–£30.00 **Beds:** 1F 1D 1T **Baths:** 1 En 1 Pr 1 Sh (4)

Berkeley

ST6899

The Old Swan, *High Street, Berkeley, Glos, GL13 9BJ.* Beautiful town house very close to Berkeley Castle & Jenner Museum
Open: All year (not Xmas/New Year)
01453 810273 Mr & Mrs Stump **D:** Fr £12.50–£40.00 **S:** Fr £15.00–£20.00 **Beds:** 1F 2D 1S **Baths:** 1 Sh

Berry Hill

SO5712

Westlands House, *20 Grove Road, Berry Hill, Coleford, Glos, GL16 8QY.* Cottage close to forest walks, historic sites, outdoor pursuits. **Open:** All year (not Xmas)
01594 837143 Mrs Atherley **D:** Fr £15.00 **S:** Fr £15.00 **Beds:** 1D 1T **Baths:** 1 Sh (2)

Bigsweir

SO5304

Florence Country Hotel, *Bigsweir, St Briavels, Lydney, Glos, GL15 6QQ.* **Open:** All year
01594 530830 Mr Sabin *enquiries@florencehotel.co.uk* florencehotel.co.uk **D:** Fr £30.00–£36.00 **S:** Fr £36.00–£50.00 **Beds:** 5D 2T 1S **Baths:** 8 Pr (13)
A traditional C16th house on the bank of the river Wye on the English/Welsh border, surrounded by 5 acres of woodland & shrub garden. Ideal walking centre, enjoy a freshly-prepared dinner in our Riverview dining room.

Birdlip

SO9214

Beechmount, *Birdlip, Gloucester, GL4 8JH.*
Open: All year
01452 862262 (also fax) Mrs Carter *thebeechmount@breathemail.net* www.thebeechmount.co.uk **D:** Fr £19.00–£25.00 **S:** Fr £19.00–£32.00 **Beds:** 2F 2D 2T **Baths:** 2 En 3 Sh (7) cc
Warm hospitality. Personal attention. Family-run guest house. Ideal centre for exploring Cotswolds. All bedrooms individually decorated having many extras including hairdryers and welcome pack of toiletries etc. Large choice of menu for breakfast. Unrestricted access. Minutes from M5. Highly recommended.

Birdwood

SO7418

Birdwood Villa Farm, *Main Road, Birdwood, Huntley, Gloucester, GL19 3EQ.* A warm welcome awaits you at our 60-acre arable farm. **Open:** All year
01452 750451 M King **D:** Fr £20.00–£25.00 **S:** Fr £21.00–£26.00 **Beds:** 1F 1D **Baths:** 2 En (8) cc

Bishop's Cleeve

SO9527

Manor Cottage Guest House, *41 Station Road, Bishop's Cleeve, Cheltenham, Glos, GL52 8HH.* Conveniently located. Friendly and relaxed accommodaion in a Tudor cottage.
Open: All year (not Xmas/New Year)
Grades: ETC 2 Diamond
01242 673537 R Torpy **D:** Fr £20.00 **S:** Fr £30.00 **Beds:** 1T 2D **Baths:** 2 En 1 Pr (4)

Blakeney

SO6706

Viney Hill Country Guesthouse, *Blakeney, Glos, GL15 4LT.* A period house bordering the Forest of Dean between the Severn & Wye. **Open:** All year (not Xmas/New Year)
01594 516000 Mr Parsons **Fax: 01594 516018** *info@vineyhill.com* www.vineyhill.com **D:** Fr £24.00–£38.00 **S:** Fr £38.00 **Beds:** 3D 1T **Baths:** 4 En (4) cc

Blockley

SP1634

Tudor House, *High Street, Blockley, Moreton in Marsh, Glos, GL56 9EX.* Excellent walking, gardens to visit. Warm welcome. Own sitting room. **Open:** All year (not Xmas)
01386 700356 Mrs Thompson **D:** Fr £25.00–£30.00 **S:** Fr £25.00–£30.00 **Beds:** 1D 1T **Baths:** 1 Sh (10) (2)

The Malins, *21 Station Road, Blockley, Moreton In Marsh, Glos, GL56 9ED.* Attractive Cotswold stone house, many facilities, friendly hosts. **Open:** All year **Grades:** ETC 3 Diamond
01386 700402 (also fax) Mrs Malin *johnmalin@btinternet.com* www.chippingcampden.co.uk/themalins.htm **D:** Fr £20.00–£22.00 **S:** Fr £30.00–£35.00 **Beds:** 1D 2T **Baths:** 3 Pr (5)

Park Farmhouse, *Blockley, Moreton in Marsh, Glos, GL56 9TA.* Beautiful old farmhouse; idyllic location, easy walk village. Warm welcome. **Open:** All year
01386 700266 Mr & Mrs Dee **D:** Fr £18.00 **S:** Fr £18.00 **Beds:** 1D 1T 2S **Baths:** 1 Sh (6)

Arreton Guest House, *Station Road, Blockley, Moreton-in-Marsh, Glos, GL56 6DT.* Arreton is situated in the north Cotswold in the village of Blockley. **Open:** All year
01386 701077 (also fax) *bandb@arreton.demon.co.uk* www.arreton.demon.co.uk **D:** Fr £20.00–£22.00 **S:** Fr £28.00–£30.00 **Beds:** 1F 1D 1T **Baths:** 3 En

Bourton-on-the-Water

SP1620

Lansdowne House, *Lansdowne, Bourton-on-the-Water, Cheltenham, Glos, GL54 2AT.* Tastefully furnished ensuite accommodation. Combination of old and antique furniture. **Open:** All year (not Xmas)
01451 820812 Mrs Garwood **Fax: 01451 822484** *stilwell@lansdownehouse.co.uk* www.lansdownehouse.co.uk **D:** Fr £25.00 **S:** Fr £35.00–£40.00 **Beds:** 1F 2D **Baths:** 3 En (4)

Breadstone

SO7100

Green Acres Farm Guest House, *Breadstone, Berkeley, Glos, GL13 9HF.* Tranquil setting in large garden overlooking Welsh Hills and Cotswolds. Full English breakfast. **Open:** All year
01453 810348 Ms Evans **Fax: 01453 810799** *barbara@greenacresfarm.co.uk* **D:** Fr £23.50–£26.00 **S:** Fr £24.50–£26.50 **Beds:** 2T 2D 2S **Baths:** 6 En **cc**

Brimscombe

SO8702

Brandon Quarhouse, *Brimscombe, Chalford, Stroud, Glos, GL5 2RS.* Cotswold hillside house, pretty/productive garden, exquisite walks, warm welcome. **Open:** All year (not Xmas/New Year)
01453 883664 Mrs Clapham **D:** Fr £20.00 **S:** Fr £16.00–£20.00 **Beds:** 1T 1S **Baths:** 1 En 1 Sh (8) (4)

The Yew Tree, *Walls Quarry, Brimscombe, Stroud, Glos, GL5 2PA.* C17th Cotswold stone house overlooks the Golden Valley. **Open:** All year
01453 883428 (also fax) Mrs Peters **D:** Fr £20.00–£30.00 **S:** Fr £20.00–£30.00 **Beds:** 1F 1T 1D **Baths:** 1 En 1 Pr

Broad Campden

SP1537

Marnic House, *Broad Campden, Chipping Campden, Glos, GL55 6UR.* Comfortable, friendly and well furnished family home. Peacefully situated, scenic views. **Open:** All year (not Xmas/New Year)
01386 840014 Mrs Rawlings **Fax: 01386 840441** *marnic@zoom.co.uk* **D:** Fr £24.00–£25.00 **S:** Fr £38.00–£40.00 **Beds:** 2D 1T **Baths:** 2 En 1 Pr (10) (4)

Brookthorpe

SO8312

Brookthorpe Lodge, *Stroud Road, Brookthorpe, Gloucester, GL4 0UQ.* Licensed family-run three storey Georgian house in lovely countryside at foot of Cotswold escarpment. **Open:** All year
01452 812645 Mr Bailey *enq@brookthorpelodge.demon.co.uk* **D:** Fr £23.50–£25.00 **S:** Fr £30.00–£35.00 **Beds:** 2F 2D 3T 3S **Baths:** 6 En 2 Pr 1 Sh (15)

Chalford

SO8902

Ashleigh House, *Bussage, Chalford, Stroud, Glos, GL6 8AZ.* Peaceful village location. Attractive gardens overlooking valley. Convenient Westonbirt, Slimbridge. **Open:** Mar to Nov **Grades:** ETC 4 Diamond
01453 883944 Mr Dunsford **Fax: 01453 886931** *stilwell@ashleighgh.co.uk* www.ashleighgh.co.uk **D:** Fr £24.00–£27.00 **S:** Fr £32.00–£35.00 **Beds:** 3F 3D 3T **Baths:** 9 En (8) (9) **cc**

Beechcroft, *Brownshill, Chalford, Stroud, Glos, GL6 8AG.* Quietly situated Edwardian house. Home made bread and preserves. Good walking. **Open:** All year
01453 883422 Mrs Salt **D:** Fr £20.00–£25.00 **S:** Fr £24.00–£30.00 **Beds:** 1T 1D (2)

Charfield

ST7191

Falcon Cottage, *15 Station Road, Charfield, Wotton-under-Edge, Glos, GL12 8SY.* Convenient for M5, Bath, Bristol, Cheltenham, Cotswolds, Cotswold Way. **Open:** All year (not Xmas) **Grades:** ETC 4 Diamond
01453 843528 Mrs Haddrell **D:** Fr £22.00 **S:** Fr £22.00 **Beds:** 1T 1D **Baths:** 1 Sh (2)

Charlton Kings

SO9620 Waterside

Langett, *London Road, Cheltenham, Glos, GL54 4HG.* Perfect stop for walkers on the Cotswold Way. **Open:** Easter to Oct
01242 820192 (also fax) Mr Cox *cox.langett@btopenworld.com* **D:** Fr £20.00–£25.00 **S:** Fr £25.00 **Beds:** 1T 1D **Baths:** 1 Pr

Cheltenham

SO9422

Parkview, *4 Pittville Crescent, Cheltenham, Glos, GL52 2QZ.* Regency house in Cheltenham - nicest area. Cotswolds, Sudeley Castle, Stratford are nearby. **Open:** All year
01242 575567 Mrs Sparrey *jospa@tr250.freeserve.co.uk* **D:** Fr £22.50–£28.00 **S:** Fr £35.00–£55.00 **Beds:** 1F 1T 1S **Baths:** 2 En 2 Sh

Clun House, *4 The Oaks, Up Hatherley, Cheltenham, Glos, GL51 5TS.* Spacious, attractive, quiet house; lounge available, easy access M5. **Open:** All year (not Xmas)
01242 523255 & 07703 798230 (M) Mrs Hyde **D:** Fr £18.00 **S:** Fr £18.00 **Beds:** 1D 2S 1T **Baths:** 1 Pr 1 Sh (5)

Heron Haye, *Cleeve Hill, Cheltenham, Glos, GL52 3PW.* Quiet location, 1/4 mile Cotswold Way. Comfortable home. Full English breakfast. Superb views. **Open:** All year
01242 672516 & 07941 215390 (M) Mr Saunders *dick.whittamore@virgin.net* **D:** Fr £22.50–£30.00 **S:** Fr £25.00–£30.00 **Beds:** 2D 1S **Baths:** 1 Sh (4)

Crossways Guest House, *Oriel Place, 57 Bath Road, Cheltenham, Glos, GL53 7LH.* Fine Regency house in the centre of Cheltenham. **Open:** All year
01242 527683 Mr Lynch **Fax: 01242 577226** *cross.ways@btinternet.com* www.cross.ways.btinternet.co.uk **D:** Fr £22.00–£25.00 **Beds:** 3F 1T 1D 1S **Baths:** 3 En 1 Sh **cc**

Beaumont House Hotel, *Shurdington Road, Cheltenham, Glos, GL53 0JE.* Relaxed, friendly, peaceful, comfortable, totally non-smoking. Four poster rooms. Garden. **Open:** All year (not Xmas/New Year)
01242 245986 Fax: 01242 520044 *rocking.horse@virgin.net* **D:** Fr £30.00–£40.00 **S:** Fr £42.00–£56.00 **Beds:** 1F 3T 10D 2S **Baths:** 16 En (10) (16) **cc**

Central Hotel, *7-9 Portland Street, Cheltenham, Glos, GL52 2NZ.* Grade II Listed building in town centre, one block from shops and Regent Arcade. **Open:** All year
01242 582172 Mr Rouse **D:** Fr £22.00–£28.50 **S:** Fr £27.00–£37.00 **Beds:** 2F 3D 5T 4S **Baths:** 6 En 2 Sh (8) **cc**

Chipping Campden

SP1539

Folly Farm Cottage, *Back Street, Ilmington, Warwickshire, CV36 4LJ.* **Open:** All year (not Xmas/New Year) **Grades:** ETC 4 Diamond, Gold
01608 682425 (also fax) *slowe@follyfarm.co.uk* www.follyfarm.co.uk **D:** Fr £26.00–£41.00 **S:** Fr £39.00–£45.00 **Beds:** 3D (7)
Large country cottage surrounded by pretty cottage gardens, situated in delightful Cotswold village near Stratford-upon-Avon. We are providing superb quality B&B, double or king size four posters, one with whirlpool bath. All rooms have TV & video.

Holly House, *Ebrington, Chipping Campden, Glos, GL55 6NL.* **Open:** All year (not Xmas) **Grades:** AA 4 Diamond
01386 593213 Mrs Hutsby **Fax: 01386 593181** *hutsby@talk21.com* www.stratford-upon-avon.co.uk/hollyhouse.htm **D:** Fr £24.00–£26.00 **S:** Fr £35.00–£50.00 **Beds:** 3F/D/T **Baths:** 3 En (5)
Situated in centre of picturesque Cotswold village, 2 miles Chipping Campden and Hidcote Gardens, 11 miles Stratford, 20 miles Warwick. All rooms spaciously appointed with ensuite facilities. Lovely garden room at guests disposition. Private parking. Local pub serves meals.

Nineveh Farm, *Campden Road, Mickleton, Chipping Campden, Glos, GL55 6PS.* Award-winning Cotswold B&B & convenient for Stratford-upon-Avon/Warwick. Free use cycles. **Open:** All year **Grades:** ETC 4 Diamond, Silver, RAC 4 Diamond, Sparkling
01386 438923 *stay@ninevehfarm.co.uk* www.ninevehfarm.co.uk **D:** Fr £27.50 **S:** Fr £45.00 **Beds:** 2T 3D 1F **Baths:** 5 En 1 Pr (5) (6) CC

The Guest House, *Lower High Street, Chipping Campden, Glos, GL55 6DZ.* Period Cotswold stone cottage, easy walking to local beauty spots and shops. **Open:** Easter to Nov
01386 840163 Mrs Benfield **D:** Fr £19.00–£22.00 **S:** Fr £25.00 **Beds:** 1D 1T **Baths:** 2 En

Cirencester

SP0202

Sunset, *Baunton Lane, Cirencester, Glos, GL7 2NQ.* Quiet, small family house conveniently situated for touring the Cotswolds. **Open:** Easter to Oct
01285 654822 Mrs Castle **D:** Fr £17.00 **S:** Fr £17.00 **Beds:** 1T 2S **Baths:** 1 Sh (5) (5)

Chesil Rocks, *Baunton Lane, Cirencester, Glos, GL7 2LL.* Pleasant friendly home, quiet lane. Access town and country walks. **Open:** All year (not Xmas)
01285 655031 Mrs Clayton **D:** Fr £20.00 **S:** Fr £20.00 **Beds:** 1T 2S **Baths:** 1 Sh (2) (2)

Sprucewood, *Elf Meadow, Poulton, Cirencester, Glos, GL7 5HQ.* Quiet, homely, comfortable. Open views. Warm, friendly welcome awaits you. **Open:** All year (not Xmas) **Grades:** ETC 4 Diamond
01285 851351 (also fax) Mr & Mrs Walker **D:** Fr £17.00–£22.00 **S:** Fr £25.00–£30.00 **Beds:** 1D 1T 1S **Baths:** 1 Sh (4)

Clapton-on-the-Hill

SP1617

Farncombe, *Clapton-on-the-Hill, Bourton-on-the-Water, Cheltenham, Glos, GL54 2LG.* Come and share our peace and tranquillity with superb views. **Open:** All year (not Xmas)
01451 820120 & 07714 703142 (M) Mrs Wright **Fax: 01451 820120** *jwrightbb@aol.com* www.farncombecotswolds.com **D:** Fr £20.00–£23.00 **S:** Fr £25.00–£30.00 **Beds:** 2D 1T **Baths:** 1 En 2 Sh (4)

Cleeve Hill

SO9826

Heron Haye, *Cleeve Hill, Cheltenham, Glos, GL52 3PW.* Quiet location, 1/4 mile Cotswold Way. Comfortable home. Full English breakfast. Superb views. **Open:** All year
01242 672516 & 07941 215390 (M) Mr Saunders *dick.whittamore@virgin.net* **D:** Fr £22.50–£30.00 **S:** Fr £25.00–£30.00 **Beds:** 2D 1S **Baths:** 1 Sh (4)

Planning a longer stay? Always ask for any special rates

Planning a longer stay? Always ask for any special rates

Coaley

SO7701

Silver Street Farm House, *Silver Street, Coaley, Dursley, Glos, GL11 5AX.* Period farmhouse, tastefully furnished enjoying outstanding countryside, village location. **Open:** All year (not Xmas/New Year)
01453 860514 **D:** Fr £20.00–£22.50 **S:** Fr £25.00–£35.00 **Beds:** 1D **Baths:** 1 Pr

Cockleford

SO9614

Butlers Hill Farm, *Cockleford, Cowley, Cheltenham, Glos, GL53 9NW.* A secluded farm set in the upper Churn Valley with easy access to rivers & footpaths. **Open:** All year (not Xmas/New Year)
01242 870455 Mrs Brickell **D:** Fr £20.00–£25.00 **S:** Fr £25.00–£30.00 **Beds:** 3T 1D **Baths:** 2 Sh (3) (5)

Cold Aston

SP1220

Bangup Cottage, *Bang Up Lane, Cold Aston, Cheltenham, Glos, GL54 3BQ.* Spacious comfortable accommodation. Set in lovely countryside. Ideal touring Cotswolds. **Open:** Mar to Nov **Grades:** ETC 4 Diamond
01451 810127 Mrs Armer *chrisarmer@yahoo.com* **D:** Fr £25.00–£30.00 **S:** Fr £30.00–£35.00 **Beds:** 1T 1D **Baths:** 1 En 1 Pr (2)

Coleford

SO5710 *The Crown, Angel Hotel, Tudor Farmhouse*

Perouges, *31 Newland Street, Coleford, Glos, GL16 8AJ.* Several nearby children and adult attractions. Central location. Comfortable, modern. **Open:** All year (not Xmas/New Year)
01594 834287 **D:** Fr £14.00–£17.00 **Beds:** 1T 1D **Baths:** 1 Pr (1)

Coopers Hill

SO8914 *Royal William, Air Balloon, 12 Bells*

The Haven Tea Garden, *Coopers Hill, Brockworth, Gloucester, GL3 4SB.* Green wooden bungalow. Country garden. Wonderful walks - woodland or fields. **Open:** Easter to Sept
01452 863213 R Hellerman **D:** Fr £20.00 **Beds:** 1F 1T **Baths:** 1 Sh (2)

Corse
SO7826

Kilmorie, *Gloucester Road, Corse, Staunton, Gloucester, GL19 3RQ.* Grade II Listed (c1848) smallholding. Quality all ground floor accommodation. **Open:** All year (not Xmas) **Grades:** ETC 4 Diamond
01452 840224 Ms Barnfield **D:** Fr £18.00–£20.00 **S:** Fr £18.00–£20.00 **Beds:** 1F 2D 1T 1S **Baths:** 3 En 1 Pr 1 Sh (5) (8)

Cranham
SO8913

Pound Cottage, *Cranham, Gloucester, GL4 8HP.* Old Cotswold cottage. Quiet village - good walking, beechwoods and grassland. **Open:** All year (not Xmas/New Year)
01452 812581 Ms Dann **Fax: 01452 814380** *ddann@globalnet.co.uk* **D:** Fr £22.00 **S:** Fr £25.00 **Beds:** 1T 1D **Baths:** 1 Sh (2)

Down Hatherley
SO8622

Frog Furlong Cottage, *Frog Furlong Lane, Down Hatherley, Gloucester, GL2 9QE.* In the Green Belt, standing quietly alone, surrounded by fields. Swimming pool. **Open:** All year (not Xmas/New Year)
01452 730430 (also fax) Mrs Rooke *notalgia.frogs@ukonline.co.uk* **D:** Fr £22.00–£24.00 **S:** Fr £28.00–£30.00 **Beds:** 1D 1T **Baths:** 2 En (3)

Dumbleton
SP0136

Raymeadow Farm, *Dumbleton, Evesham, Worcs, WR11 7TR.* Peaceful farmhouse nestling within the Cotswolds between Stratford/ Cheltenham and Worcester. **Open:** Mar to Oct
01242 621215 Ms Alvis **D:** Fr £20.00–£25.00 **S:** Fr £20.00–£25.00 **Beds:** 1F 1T 1S **Baths:** 1 Sh

BATHROOMS
En = Ensuite
Pr = Private
Sh = Shared

Duntisbourne Abbots
SO9608

Dixs Barn, *Duntisbourne Abbots, Cirencester, Glos, GL7 7JN.* Converted barn on family-run farm, edge of village with magnificent views. **Open:** All year
01285 821249 & 07817 778110 (M)
Mrs Wilcox *wilcox@dixsbarn.freeserve.co.uk*
D: Fr £25.00–£30.00 **S:** Fr £30.00–£35.00 **Beds:** 1D 1T **Baths:** 1 En 1 Pr (8)

Eastcombe
SO8804

Pretoria Villa, *Wells Road, Eastcombe, Stroud, Glos, GL6 7EE.* Enjoy luxurious bed and breakfast in relaxed family country house. **Open:** All year (not Xmas) **Grades:** ETC 4 Diamond
01452 770435 Mrs Solomon *glynis@gsolomon.freeserve.co.uk* **D:** Fr £25.00 **S:** Fr £25.00 **Beds:** 1D 1T 1S **Baths:** 2 En 1 Pr (3)

Ebrington
SP1840

Home Farm, *Ebrington, Chipping Campden, Glos, GL55 6NL.* **Open:** All year (not Xmas/New Year)
Grades: ETC 4 Diamond
01386 593309 Mrs Stanley *willstanley@farmersweekly.net*
homefarminthecotswolds.co.uk **D:** Fr £27.50 **S:** Fr £40.00 **Beds:** 1F 2T 1D **Baths:** 4 En (6)
A warm, friendly welcome awaits you at our completely refurbished C15th Listed farmhouse, in the heart of this beautiful village. Spacious beamed rooms, inglenook fireplace in dining room where a full farmhouse breakfast is served. Hidcote Gardens 1 mile.

Holly House, *Ebrington, Chipping Campden, Glos, GL55 6NL.* Situated in centre of picturesque Cotswold village, 2 miles Chipping Campden. **Open:** All year (not Xmas) **Grades:** AA 4 Diamond
01386 593213 Mrs Hutsby **Fax: 01386 593181** *hutsby@talk21.com* www.stratford-upon-avon.co.uk/hollyhouse.htm **D:** Fr £24.00–£26.00 **S:** Fr £35.00–£50.00 **Beds:** 3F/D/T **Baths:** 3 En (5)

English Bicknor
SO5815

Dryslade Farm, *English Bicknor, Coleford, Glos, GL16 7PA.* Daphne and Philip ensure a relaxed, friendly atmosphere at their C17th farmhouse. **Open:** All year
01594 860259 (also fax) Mrs Gwilliam *dryslade@agriplus.net* www.drysladefarm.co.uk
D: Fr £22.00–£25.00 **S:** Fr £25.00 **Beds:** 1F 1T 1D **Baths:** 2 En 1 Pr (6)

Fairford
SP1500

Waiten Hill Farm, *Mill Lane, Fairford, Glos, GL7 4JG.* Imposing C19th farmhouse overlooking River Coln and famous church. **Open:** All year **Grades:** ETC 2 Diamond
01285 712652 (also fax) Mrs Rymer **D:** Fr £17.50–£20.00 **S:** Fr £20.00–£25.00 **Beds:** 1F 1D 1T **Baths:** 2 En

Milton Farm, *Fairford, Glos, GL7 4HZ.* Georgian farmhouse with individualised spacious ensuite bedrooms. Quiet pleasant outlook. **Open:** All year (not Xmas/New Year)
01285 712205 Mrs Suzie Paton **Fax: 01285 711349** *milton@farmersweekly.net* www.milton-farm.co.uk **D:** Fr £20.00–£25.00 **S:** Fr £25.00–£35.00 **Beds:** 1F 1T 1D **Baths:** 3 En

Frampton Mansell
SO9202

Crown Inn and Hotel, *Frampton Mansell, Stroud, Glos, GL6 8JG.* Picturesque Inn. Ideally situated. Walks, real ales, log wood. Hot meals. **Open:** All year
01285 760601 **D:** Fr £64.00–£72.00 **S:** Fr £44.00–£52.00 **Beds:** 1F 7T 4D **Baths:** 12 En
cc

Gloucester
SO8318

Alston Field Guest House, *88 Stroud Road, Gloucester, GL1 5AJ.* Conveniently located for city and countryside. Street parking. Rail & bus stations 3/4 mile. **Open:** All year (not Xmas/New Year)
01452 529170 & 01452 526625 Mrs Currie **D:** Fr £18.00–£25.00 **S:** Fr £18.00–£25.00 **Beds:** 1F 1T 1S **Baths:** 2 En 1 Sh
cc

Georgian Guest House, *85 Bristol Road, Gloucester, GL1 5SN.* Part-Georgian terraced house, 20 minutes walk city centre. **Open:** All year
01452 413286 (also fax) J W Nash **D:** Fr £15.00–£16.50 **S:** Fr £15.00 **Beds:** 4F 3T 2S **Baths:** 5 En 1 Sh (3)

Gotherington
SO9629

Moat Farm, *Malleson Road, Gotherington, Cheltenham, Glos, GL52 4ET.* Situated in the heart of the Cotswolds between Cheltenham and Tewkesbury. **Open:** All year (not Xmas)
01242 672055 & 01242 676807 Mr & Mrs Tilley **Fax: 07050 665639 D:** Fr £18.00–£19.00 **S:** Fr £18.00–£19.00 **Beds:** 2D 2T

Pardon Hill Farm, *Prescott, Gotherington, Cheltenham, Glos, GL52 4RD.* Modern, comfortable farmhouse, lovely views. **Open:** All year
01242 672468 (also fax) Mrs Newman *janet@pardonhillfarm.freeserve.co.uk* www.margintrip co.uk/pardonhill.shtml **D:** Fr £22.00–£50.00 **S:** Fr £27.00–£35.00 **Beds:** 1D 1T 1S **Baths:** 3 En (6)

Great Rissington
SP1917 *Lamb Inn*

Lower Farmhouse, *Great Rissington, Bourton on the Water, Cheltenham, Glos, GL54 2LH.* Listed Georgian house with guest annexe in Cotswold barn conversion. **Open:** All year
01451 810163 Mr & Mrs Fleming **Fax: 01451 810187** *kathryn@lowerfarmhouse.co.uk* www.lowerfarmhouse.co.uk **D:** Fr £18.00–£22.00 **S:** Fr £18.00–£30.00 **Beds:** 1D 1S **Baths:** 1 Sh

Haresfield
SO8110

Lower Green Farmhouse, *Haresfield, Stonehouse, Glos, GL10 3DS.* C18th Listed Cotswold stone farmhouse with countryside views. **Open:** All year (not Xmas/New Year)
01452 728264 (also fax) Mrs Reed *lowergreen@lineone.net* **D:** Fr £18.50 **S:** Fr £20.00 **Beds:** 1F 1T **Baths:** 2 Sh (6)

Hawkesbury
ST7686

Ivy Cottage, *Inglestone Common, Hawkesbury, Badminton, GL9 1BX.* Comfortable cottage surrounded by ancient woodland on edge of Cotswolds. **Open:** All year (not Xmas/New Year)
01454 294237 Mrs Canner **D:** Fr £19.00–£20.00 **S:** Fr £22.00–£25.00 **Beds:** 1F 1D 1T 1S **Baths:** 2 Sh (3)

Huntley
SO7219

Forest Gate, *Huntley, Gloucester, GL19 3EU.* Spacious Victorian rectory ideal for visiting Royal Forest of Dean, great breakfasts. Also camping. **Open:** All year (not Xmas) **Grades:** ETC 3 Diamond
01452 831192 (also fax) Mr Blakemore *forest.gate@huntley-glos.demon.co.uk* www.forestgate-huntley.co.uk **D:** Fr £25.00–£28.00 **S:** Fr £25.00–£28.00 **Beds:** 1F 2D 1S **Baths:** 1 En 2 Sh (6) **cc**

Kemble
ST9897

Smerrill Barns, *Kemble, Cirencester, Glos, GL7 6BW.* C18th converted barn, guest lounge with log fires in winter, drinks licence. **Open:** All year (not Xmas)
01285 770907 Mrs Sopher **Fax: 01285 770706 D:** Fr £27.50 **S:** Fr £45.00 **Beds:** 1F 5D 1T **Baths:** 7 En 1 Sh (8)

Kilcot
SO6925

Cherry Grove B&B, *Ford Lane, Kilcot, Newent, Glos, GL18 1NY.* Peaceful rural situation near Wye Valley, good cycling and walking. **Open:** All year (not Xmas)
01989 720126 Mr & Mrs Inwood **D:** Fr £15.00–£17.00 **S:** Fr £16.00–£18.00 **Beds:** 1F 1D **Baths:** 1 Pr 1 Sh (5) (6)

Kings Stanley
SO8103

Old Chapel House, *Broad Street, Kings Stanley, Stonehouse, Glos, GL10 3PN.* Converted chapel on Cotswold Way, ideal touring/walking area. **Open:** All year (not Xmas)
01453 826289 Mrs Richards Hanna *jeanhannaoldchapelhouse@hotmail.com* **D:** Fr £21.50 **S:** Fr £20.00 **Beds:** 1F 1D 2T 1S **Baths:** 2 En 1 Sh (5) (4)

Knockdown
ST8388

Avenue Farm, *Knockdown, Tetbury, Glos, GL8 8QY.* 300-year-old farmhouse in farm adjoining Westonbirt Arboretum. Bath, Bristol, Gloucester easy reach. **Open:** All year
01454 238207 Mrs King **Fax: 01454 238033** *sonjames@breathemail.net* **D:** Fr £25.00 **S:** Fr £30.00 **Beds:** 1F 1D 2T **Baths:** 2 En 1 Sh (6)

Laverton
SP0735

Gunners Orchard, *Laverton, Broadway, Glos, WR12 7NA.* Comfortable private house in quiet and beautiful setting personal attention. **Open:** All year (not Xmas/New Year)
01386 584213 Mrs Stephenson **D:** Fr £18.00–£20.00 **S:** Fr £25.00–£30.00 **Beds:** 1D 1T **Baths:** 1 Sh (6)

Lechlade
SU2199

The New Inn Hotel, *Market Square, Lechlade On Thames, Glos, GL7 3AB.* C17th fully modernised coaching inn on River Thames in the Cotswolds. **Open:** All year
01367 252296 Mr Sandhu **Fax: 01367 252315** *info@newinnhotel.co.uk* www.members.aol.com/newinnlech **D:** Fr £20.00–£32.50 **S:** Fr £40.00–£55.00 **Beds:** 2F 10D 10T 4S **Baths:** 26 En (40)

Cambrai Lodge Guest House, *Oak Street, Lechlade On Thames, Glos, GL7 3AY.* Modern comfortable house off the road. Ideal for touring Cotswolds. **Open:** All year
01367 253173 & 07860 150467 Mr Titchener **D:** Fr £24.00–£30.00 **S:** Fr £29.00–£40.00 **Beds:** 3D 2T 2S **Baths:** 5 En 1 Sh (9)

Longhope
SO6818 *Farmer's Boy, Nag's Head, Moody Cow*

The Old Farm, *Barrell Lane, Longhope, Glos, GL17 OLR.* Charming C16th farmhouse full of character, beams and fireplaces. Set in an idyllic rural location, within easy reach of the Cotswolds, Oxford, Cheltenham and Stratford. Royal Forest of Dean nearby. Excellent walking/cycling from the farm. Or just come to relax! **Open:** All year
01452 830252 Mrs Rodger **Fax: 01452 830255** *lucy@the-old-farm.co.uk* www.the-old-farm.co.uk **D:** Fr £20.00–£26.00 **S:** Fr £29.00 **Beds:** 2D 1T **Baths:** 3 En (12) (6) **cc**

Marshfield
ST7773

Knowle Hill Farm, *Beeks Lane, Marshfield, Chippenham, Wilts, SN14 8BB.* Modern farmhouse accommodation on outskirts of Marshfield. Peaceful location. **Open:** All year
01225 891503 C Bond **D:** Fr £20.00–£24.00 **S:** Fr £20.00–£24.00 **Beds:** 1F 1T 1D **Baths:** 1 En 1 Sh (4)

National Grid References given are for villages, towns and cities – not for individual houses

Meysey Hampton

SU1199

The Masons Arms, *High Street, Meysey Hampton, Cirencester, Glos, GL7 5JT.* Origins date C17th beside village green in award-winning village. **Open:** All year
01285 850164 (also fax) Mr O'Dell *jane@themasonsarms.freeserve.co.uk* www.smoothhound.co.uk/hotels/masons.html **D:** Fr £28.00–£32.00 **S:** Fr £38.00–£42.00 **Beds:** 1F 5D 2T 1S **Baths:** 9 En (3) (4) **cc**

Mickleton

SP1643

Nineveh Farm, *Campden Road, Mickleton, Chipping Campden, Glos, GL55 6PS.* Award-winning Cotswold B&B & convenient for Stratford-upon-Avon/Warwick. Free use cycles. **Open:** All year **Grades:** ETC 4 Diamond, Silver, RAC 4 Diamond, Sparkling
01386 438923 *stay@ninevehfarm.co.uk* www.ninevehfarm.co.uk **D:** Fr £27.50 **S:** Fr £45.00 **Beds:** 2T 3D 1F **Baths:** 5 En 1 Pr (5) (6) **cc**

Old Barn House, *Mill Lane, Mickleton, Chipping Campden, Glos, GL55 6RT.* Quiet location. Heart of conservation area. Ground floor, twin room. **Open:** All year (not Xmas/New Year)
01386 438668 (also fax) J Lodge **D:** Fr £23.00 **S:** Fr £35.00–£40.00 **Beds:** 1T 1D **Baths:** 2 Pr (10) (3)

Middle Duntisbourne

SO9806

Manor Farm, *Middle Duntisbourne, Cirencester, Glos, GL7 7AR.* Farmhouse set in beautiful Duntisbourne. **Open:** All year (not Xmas/New Year)
01285 658145 Mrs Barton **Fax: 01285 641504** *tina.barton@farming.co.uk* www.smoothhound.co.uk/hotels.manorfarm.html **D:** Fr £20.00–£25.00 **S:** Fr £40.00–£45.00 **Beds:** 1D 1T **Baths:** 1 En 1 Pr (8)

Minchinhampton

SO8600

Hyde Crest, *Cirencester Road, Minchinhampton, Stroud, Glos, GL6 8PE.* Beautiful country house. All bedrooms have own patio into gardens. **Open:** All year **Grades:** AA 4 Diamond
01453 731631 Mrs Rhoton *hydecrest@compuserve.com.com* www.hydecrest.co.uk **D:** Fr £25.00 **S:** Fr £30.00 **Beds:** 2D 1T **Baths:** 3 En (7) (6)

Burleigh Farm, *Minchinhampton, Stroud, Glos, GL5 2PF.* Attractive Cotswold stone farmhouse in 38 acres of parkland. Breathtaking views. **Open:** All year (not Xmas)
01453 883112 (also fax) Mr & Mrs Vines **D:** Fr £24.00–£28.50 **S:** Fr £39.00 **Beds:** 2D 1T **Baths:** 2 En 1 Pr (10) (5)

Mitcheldean

SO6618

Gunn Mill House, *Lower Spout Lane, Mitcheldean, Glos, GL17 0EA.* **Open:** All year **Grades:** ETC 4 Diamond, Silver
01594 827577 (also fax) *info@gunnmillhouse.co.uk* www.gunnmillhouse.co.uk **D:** Fr £25.00–£40.00 **S:** Fr £30.00–£45.00 **Beds:** 1F 5D 2T **Baths:** 8 En (14) **cc**
The Lucas family offer great hospitality and food in their Georgian home set in the 27000 acres of the Royal Forest of Dean. Enjoy trips to Tintern Abbey, Gloucester and Hereford Cathedrals or walking, cycling, pony trekking through the Forest.

Moreton-in-Marsh

SP2032

Jasmine Cottage, *Stretton-on-Fosse, Moreton-in-Marsh, Glos, GL56 9SA.* **Open:** All year (not Xmas)
01608 661972 Mrs Campbell Smith **D:** Fr £20.00 **S:** Fr £25.00 **Beds:** 1D 1T **Baths:** 1 Sh
A warm welcome awaits you in my cosy country cottage in a peaceful village, three miles from Chipping Campden. Ideal for touring The Cotswolds, Stratford-upon-Avon, Warwick Castle & Hidcote Gardens.

Treetops, *London Road, Moreton-in-Marsh, Glos, GL56 0HE.* Family-run guest house set in secluded gardens, 5 minutes' walk village centre. **Open:** All year
01608 651036 E Dean *treetops1@talk21.com* www.treetopscotswolds.co.uk **D:** Fr £45.00–£50.00 **S:** Fr £35.00 **Beds:** 1F 3D 2T **Baths:** 6 Pr (8)

Bran Mill Cottage, *Aston Magna, Moreton in Marsh, Glos, GL56 9QW.* Small traditional B&B in peaceful Cotswold cottage. Friendly, welcoming, homely. **Open:** All year (not Xmas) **Grades:** ETC 3 Diamond
01386 593517 Mr & Mrs Baggaley *enquiries@branmillcottage.co.uk* www.branmillcottage.co.uk **D:** Fr £18.00–£21.00 **S:** Fr £19.00–£25.00 **Beds:** 1D 1T 1S **Baths:** 1 Pr 1 Sh (3)

Planning a longer stay? Always ask for any special rates

Warwick House, *London Road, Moreton-in-Marsh, Glos, GL56 0HH.* A perfect touring base for the Cotswolds. Facilities include washing/ironing, VCR, phone. **Open:** All year
01608 650773 (also fax) Mr & Mrs Grant *charlie@warwickhousebnb.demon.co.uk* www.snoozeandsizzle.com **D:** Fr £17.50–£20.00 **S:** Fr £20.00–£25.00 **Beds:** 1T 2D **Baths:** 2 En 1 Pr (3)

Fourshires, *Great Wolford Road, Moreton-in-Marsh, Glos, GL56 0PE.* Beautiful country house set in 3 acres of garden, 1 mile from Moreton-in-Marsh. **Open:** All year (not Xmas)
01608 651412 & 01608 652069 Mrs Affron **Fax: 01608 651412** *m1aff@aol.com* www.fourshires.com **D:** Fr £20.00–£22.00 **S:** Fr £25.00–£30.00 **Beds:** 2D 1T **Baths:** 2 En 1 Pr (10) (6)

Nailsworth

ST8499

Aaron Farm, *Nympsfield Road, Nailsworth, Stroud, Glos, GL6 0ET.* Panoramic views. Ideal for touring Cotswolds. Warm welcome. **Open:** All year
01453 833598 (also fax) Mrs Mulligan *aaronfarm@compuserve.com* **D:** Fr £21.00–£22.00 **S:** Fr £30.00 **Beds:** 2T 1D **Baths:** 3 En (5)

The Vicarage, *Nailsworth, Stroud, Glos, GL6 0BS.* Large, comfortable, quiet Victorian vicarage. Beautiful garden. Good breakfast. **Open:** All year
01453 832181 Mrs Strong **D:** Fr £23.00 **S:** Fr £22.00 **Beds:** 1T 3S **Baths:** 1 Pr 1 Sh (4)

Newent

SO7225

The Old Winery, *Welsh House Lane, Newent, Gloucestershire, GL18 1LR.* Comfortable, very attractive former winery, overlooking pretty countryside and vineyards. **Open:** All year (not Xmas)
01531 890824 Mr & Mrs Kingham **Fax: 01594 890824** **D:** Fr £28.00–£32.00 **S:** Fr £28.00–£32.00 **Beds:** 1T **Baths:** 1 En (20)

RATES
D = Price range per person sharing in a double or twin room
S = Price range for a single room

Newnham-on-Severn

SO6911

Swan House, *High Street, Newnham-on-Severn, Glos, GL14 1BY.* **Open:** All year (not Xmas/New Year) **Grades:** ETC 4 Diamond
01594 516504 Fax: 01594 516177 *enquiries@swanhousenewnham.co.uk* www.swanhousenewnham.co.uk **D:** Fr £25.00–£35.00 **S:** Fr £30.00–£40.00 **Beds:** 1F 1T 4D **Baths:** 6 En (4) cc
A warm welcome to our family guest house, C17th merchant's house which is tastefully furnished, all rooms individually decorated, and carefully tended garden. Picturesque village and nearby beautiful Forest of Dean offers much, especially for those who enjoy the outdoors.

North Nibley

ST7395

Nibley House, *North Nibley, Dursley, Glos, GL11 6DL.* Magnificent Georgian manor house, centrepiece of 200 acre farm. **Open:** All year (not Xmas)
01453 543108 Mrs Eley **D:** Fr £22.00–£25.00 **S:** Fr £22.00–£25.00 **Beds:** 1F 1D 1T **Baths:** 2 En 1 Pr (12)

Northleach

SP1114

Northfield Bed & Breakfast, *Cirencester Road, Northleach, Cheltenham, Glos, GL54 3JL.* **Open:** All year (not Xmas/New Year) **Grades:** ETC 4 Diamond, AA 4 Diamond
01451 860427 (also fax) Ms Loving *nrthfield0@aol.com* **D:** Fr £25.00–£30.00 **S:** Fr £35.00–£40.00 **Beds:** 1F 2D **Baths:** 3 En (10) cc
Beautifully located in the Cotswolds, this delightful property is set in immaculate gardens. It offers tastefully furnished bedrooms with good home comforts & plenty of extras in the spacious bathrooms. Breakfast & dinner are served in the elegant dining room.

Old Sodbury

ST7581

Dornden Guest House, *Church Lane, Old Sodbury, Bristol, BS37 6NB.* Former vicarage, quietly situated, views to Welsh hills. **Open:** All year (not Xmas)
01454 313325 Mrs Paz **Fax: 01454 312263** *dorndenguesthouse@tinyworld.co.uk* **D:** Fr £29.00–£35.00 **S:** Fr £29.00–£48.00 **Beds:** 5F 2T 2S **Baths:** 6 En 2 Sh (15)

Elmgrove, *Badminton Road, Old Sodbury, Bristol, BS17 6LR.* Large airy rooms. Homely, friendly accommodation. Lovely gardens. **Open:** All year
01454 313276 E V Arney **D:** Fr £16.00 **S:** Fr £16.00 **Beds:** 2T 2S **Baths:** 1 Sh (4)

1 The Green, *Old Sodbury, Bristol, BS37 6LY.* Close M4, M5. Ideal location for Cotswold Way, Bath and Bristol. **Open:** All year (not Xmas)
01454 314688 Mr & Mrs Rees **D:** Fr £22.00–£26.00 **S:** Fr £22.00–£26.00 **Beds:** 2D 1T 3S **Baths:** 1 En 2 Sh (4)

Painswick

SO8609

Thorne, *Friday Street, Painswick, Stroud, Glos, GL6 6QJ.* **Open:** Easter to Nov
01452 812476 Fax: 01452 810925 D: Fr £25.00–£27.00 **S:** Fr £25.00–£30.00 **Beds:** 2T **Baths:** 2 Pr
Tudor merchant's house with market hall pillars 'in situ' on Cotswold Way. In centre of village, with good pubs for evening meal. Central heating, drying facilities for walkers. 3 miles from station. Wonderful walking area - all points compass. Near 'Cider with Rosie' valley.

Wheatleys, *Cotswold Mead, Painswick, Stroud, Glos, GL6 6XB.* **Open:** All year (not Xmas) **Grades:** ETC 5 Diamond, Gold
01452 812167 Mrs Burgess **Fax: 01452 814270** *wheatleys@dial.pipex.com* www.wheatleys-b-and-b.co.uk **D:** Fr £25.00–£27.50 **S:** Fr £35.00–£37.50 **Beds:** 1D 1T **Baths:** 2 En (10) (4)
Set in a beautiful Cotswold village, close to the Cotswold Way. This Gold Award-winning accommodation comprises a ground-floor suite with connecting sitting room & a first floor double overlooking the pleasant, secluded garden. Breakfast can be served on the terrace.

Upper Doreys Mill, *Edge, Painswick, Stroud, Glos, GL6 6NF.* Rural, peaceful streamside idyll. Log fires, good walking, lovely garden! **Open:** All year
01452 812459 S Marden **Fax: 01452 814756** *sylvia@doreys.co.uk* www.doreys.co.uk **D:** Fr £25.00–£28.00 **S:** Fr £30.00–£35.00 **Beds:** 1T 2D **Baths:** 3 En (4) cc

Cardynham House, *The Cross, Painswick, Glos, GL6 6XA.* Charming C16th house. All rooms have 4-poster beds. **Open:** All year
01452 814006 Ms Keyes **Fax: 01 452 812321** *iijo@cardynham.co.uk* www.cardynham.co.uk **D:** Fr £30.00–£60.00 **S:** Fr £47.00–£64.00 **Beds:** 3F 6D **Baths:** 3 En 1 Pr cc

Pitchcombe

SO8508

Gable End, *Pitchcombe, Stroud, Glos, GL6 6LN.* C16th - C17th house commands an elevated position overlooking Painswick Valley. **Open:** All year (not Xmas/New Year)
01452 812166 Mrs Partridge **Fax: 01452 812719 D:** Fr £22.50 **S:** Fr £30.00 **Beds:** 2D **Baths:** 2 En (5) (4)

Poulton

SP1001

Sprucewood, *Elf Meadow, Poulton, Cirencester, Glos, GL7 5HQ.* Quiet, homely, comfortable. Open views. Warm, friendly welcome awaits you. **Open:** All year (not Xmas) **Grades:** ETC 4 Diamond
01285 851351 (also fax) Mr & Mrs Walker **D:** Fr £17.00–£22.00 **S:** Fr £25.00–£30.00 **Beds:** 1D 1T 1S **Baths:** 1 Sh (4)

Prestbury Park

SO9524

Hunters Lodge, *Cheltenham Race Course, Prestbury Park, Cheltenham, Glos, GL50 4SH.* Hunters Lodge is a friendly hotel situated within the grounds of Cheltenham Racecourse. **Open:** May to Sept
01242 513345 Ms Clark **Fax: 01242 527306 D:** Fr £18.50 **S:** Fr £21.00 **Beds:** 31F 31T 51S **Baths:** 18 Sh cc

BEDROOMS
D = Double
T = Twin
S = Single
F = Family

Redbrook

SO5310

Tresco, *Redbrook, Monmouth, NP5 4LY.* Beautiful Wye Valley riverside house, fishing, pony trekking, walking, canoeing. **Open:** All year
01600 712325 Mrs Evans **D:** Fr £16.50 **S:** Fr £16.50 **Beds:** 1F 1D 1T 2S **Baths:** 2 Sh

Ruardean

SO6217

The Malt Shovel Inn, *Ruardean, Glos, GL17 9TW.* Close to River Wye, Symonds Yat and the Forest of Dean. **Open:** All year
01594 543028 *mark@maltshovel.u-net.com* www.maltshovel.u-net.com **D:** Fr £25.00–£29.00 **S:** Fr £25.00–£29.00 **Beds:** 2F 3D 2T **Baths:** 7 En cc

Sherborne

SP1714 *The Fox*

The Mead House, *Sherborne, Cheltenham, Gloucs, GL54 3DR.* Welcoming, comfortable, peaceful old house. Charming garden, views. Exceptional breakfast.
Open: Mar to Oct
01451 844239 Mrs Medill **D:** Fr £20.00–£25.00 **S:** Fr £25.00 **Beds:** 1T 1D 1S **Baths:** 1 Pr (10) (1)

Siddington

SU0399

Coleen B&B, *Ashton Road, Siddington, Cirencester, Glos, GL7 6HR.* Choice accommodation in the Cotswolds. Pub with character 50 metres. **Open:** All year
01285 642203 Mrs Proctor *proprietor@coleen.co.uk* www.coleen.co.uk **D:** Fr £20.00–£25.00 **S:** Fr £30.00–£40.00 **Beds:** 2D 1T **Baths:** 1 En 1 Pr (4)

St Briavels

SO5604

Offas Mead, *The Fence, St Briavels, Lydney, Glos, GL15 6QG.* Large country home on Offa's Dyke Path. Ensuite available.
Open: Easter to Oct
01594 530229 (also fax) Mrs Lacey **D:** Fr £18.00–£20.00 **S:** Fr £18.00–£20.00 **Beds:** 1D 2T **Baths:** 21 En 1 Pr (10) (6)

B&B owners may vary rates – be sure to check when booking

BATHROOMS
En = Ensuite
Pr = Private
Sh = Shared

Stanton

SP0634 *Mount Inn*

Shenberrow Hill, *Stanton, Broadway, Worcs, WR12 7NE.* Charming house and cottage accommodation in beautiful unspoilt village. Unforgettable. **Open:** All year (not Xmas)
01386 584468 (also fax) Mrs Neilan **D:** Fr £25.00–£27.50 **S:** Fr £30.00 **Beds:** 1F 1D 1T **Baths:** 2 En 1 Pr (5) (5)

The Vine, *Stanton, Broadway, Worcs, WR12 7NE.* Cotswold farmhouse set in the heart of Stanton. **Open:** All year
01386 584250 Mrs Carenza **Fax: 01368 584385** *info@cotswoldsriding.co.uk* www.cotswoldsriding.co.uk **D:** Fr £28.00 **S:** Fr £40.00–£56.00 **Beds:** 2F 3D 2T

Staunton (Coleford)

SO5412

Graygill, *Staunton, Coleford, Glos, GL16 8PD.* Quietly situated off A4136. Ideal for Forest of Dean, Wye Valley. **Open:** All year (not Xmas)
01600 712536 Mrs Bond **D:** Fr £17.50 **S:** Fr £17.50 **Beds:** 1D 1T **Baths:** 2 En (4)

Staunton (Gloucester)

SO7829

Kilmorie, *Gloucester Road, Corse, Staunton, Gloucester, GL19 3RQ.* **Open:** All year (not Xmas)
Grades: ETC 4 Diamond
01452 840224 Ms Barnfield **D:** Fr £18.00–£20.00 **S:** Fr £18.00–£20.00 **Beds:** 1F 2D 1T 1S **Baths:** 3 En 1 Pr 1 Sh (5) (8)
Grade II Listed (c1848) smallholding. Quality all ground floor accommodation. Tea trays, toiletries, TVs in all rooms, mainly ensuite. Rural location. Large garden to relax - watch birds, butterflies, wildlife we encourage, meet our pony, free-range hens, ramble countryside footpaths, safe parking.

Staverton

SO8823

Hope Orchard, *Gloucester Road, Staverton, Cheltenham, Glos, GL51 0TF.* Attractive rooms overlooking old orchard and paddock. Picnic area available.
Open: All year (not Xmas/New Year)
01452 855556 Mrs Parker **Fax: 01452 530037** *info@hopeorchard.com* www.hopeorchard.com **D:** Fr £20.00–£45.00 **S:** Fr £25.00–£30.00 **Beds:** 3F 2T 3D **Baths:** 8 En (12) cc

Stonehouse

SO8005

Tiled House Farm, *Oxlynch, Stonehouse, Glos, GL10 3DF.* C16th black and white half-timbered farmhouse, with oak beams and inglenook fireplace. **Open:** All year (not Xmas)
01453 822363 Mrs Jeffrey *nigel.jeffery@ukgateway.net* **D:** Fr £19.00–£21.00 **S:** Fr £19.00–£20.00 **Beds:** 1D 1T 1S **Baths:** 1 Pr 1 Sh (10) (2)

Stow-on-the-Wold

SP1826

South Hill Farmhouse, *Fosseway, Stow-on-the-Wold, Cheltenham, Glos, GL54 1JU.* Listed Cotswold farmhouse. Warm welcome. Ideal for walking or touring. **Open:** All year **Grades:** ETC 3 Diamond
01451 831888 Mr & Mrs Cassie **Fax: 01451 832255** *info@southhill.co.uk* www.southhill.co.uk **D:** Fr £25.00 **S:** Fr £37.00 **Beds:** 1F 2D 2T 1S **Baths:** 1 Pr 5 En (10) cc

Corsham Field Farmhouse, *Bledington Road, Stow-on-the-Wold, Cheltenham, Glos, GL54 1JH.* Traditional farmhouse with breathtaking views. Ideally situated for exploring Cotswolds. **Open:** All year
01451 831750 Mr Smith **D:** Fr £22.00–£25.00 **S:** Fr £25.00–£35.00 **Beds:** 3F 2D 2T **Baths:** 5 En 1 Sh (10)

All details shown are as supplied by B&B owners in Autumn 2002

The Limes, *Evesham Road, Stow-on-the-Wold, Cheltenham, Glos, GL54 1EN.* Large Victorian house, attractive garden. Guests made welcome, town 4 mins. **Open:** All year (not Xmas) **Grades:** AA 3 Diamond, RAC 3 Diamond
01451 830034 (also fax) Mr Keyte **D:** Fr £21.50–£22.00 **S:** Fr £25.00–£42.00 **Beds:** 1F 4D 2T **Baths:** 4 En 1 Pr (5)

Fifield Cottage, *Fosse Lane, Stow-on-the-Wold, Cheltenham, Glos, GL54 1EH.* Cottage on private road, peaceful situation. Close to town. Attractive garden. **Open:** All year (not Xmas)
01451 831056 Mrs Keyte **D:** Fr £21.00–£22.00 **S:** Fr £25.00 **Beds:** 1F 1D 1T **Baths:** 2 En 1 Pr (4)

Stroud

SO8405

The Downfield Hotel, *Cainscross Road, Stroud, Glos, GL5 4HN.* Stunning views of the hills and valleys. An unforgettable holiday. **Open:** All year
01453 764496 Fax: 01453 753150 *info@downfieldhotel.co.uk* www.downfieldhotel.co.uk **D:** Fr £25.00–£30.00 **S:** Fr £30.00–£45.00 **Beds:** 2F 9D 6T 4S **Baths:** 11 En 10 Sh (25) cc

Fir Tree House, *Rodborough Common, Stroud, Glos, GL5 5BJ.* Be warm and comfortable, have fabulous views, explore The Cotswolds. **Open:** All year (not Xmas/ New Year)
01453 762591 (also fax) Mrs Peters *cip@virgin.net* **D:** Fr £20.00 **S:** Fr £20.00 **Beds:** 1T **Baths:** 1 En

Clothiers Arms, *Bath Road, Stroud, Glos, GL5 3JJ.* Within walking distance of Stroud town centre, trains and bus station. **Open:** All year
01453 763801 Mrs Close **Fax: 01453 757161** *luciano@clothiersarms.demon.co.uk* www.clothiersarms.co.uk **D:** Fr £20.00–£33.00 **S:** Fr £23.00–£35.00 **Beds:** 7F 3D 2T **Baths:** 6 En 1 Pr (50) cc

Swineford

ST6969

Crofton Cottage, *Bath Road, Swineford, Bitton, Bristol, BS30 6LW.* Pretty 1800s cottage, 4 miles Bath, 6 miles Bristol, on A431. **Open:** All year
0117 932 3671 Mr and Mrs Marsh *crofton.cott@virgin.net* www.smoothhound.co.uk/croftoncottage **D:** Fr £20.00–£25.00 **S:** Fr £30.00–£35.00 **Beds:** 1T 1D **Baths:** 2 En (6)

Tewkesbury

SO8933

Carrant Brook House, *Rope Walk, Tewkesbury, Glos, GL20 5DS.* Excellent accommodation. Breakfast to die for! Quiet town centre location. **Open:** All year
01684 290355 Mrs Bishop *lorraine@carrantbrookhouse.co.uk* www.carrantbrookhouse.co.uk **D:** Fr £25.00–£35.00 **S:** Fr £27.50–£35.00 **Beds:** 1D 1T 1S **Baths:** 3 En (4)

Barton House Guesthouse, *5 Barton Road, Tewkesbury, Glos, GL20 5QG.* Regency house close to town centre, abbey, rivers and M5. **Open:** All year
01684 292049 M J Green *bartonhouse@hotmail.com* **D:** Fr £18.00–£25.00 **S:** Fr £20.00–£30.00 **Beds:** 2F 1T 1D 1S **Baths:** 2 En 1 Sh (4)

Hoo Farm, *Gloucester Road, Tewkesbury, Glos, GL20 7DD.* Superior hospitality in beautiful farmhouse, six acre grounds, glorious countryside. **Open:** All year
01684 292185 & 07801 506083 (M) Mrs Mitchell **Fax: 01684 292185** *hoofarm@ukonline.co.uk* **D:** Fr £20.00–£25.00 **S:** Fr £25.00–£40.00 **Beds:** 2T 1S **Baths:** 1 Pr 1 Sh (10)

Two, Back of Avon, *Riverside Walk, Tewkesbury, Glos, GL20 5BA.* Lovely Queen Anne house, Grade II Listed, overlooking river. **Open:** All year
01684 298935 Mr & Mrs Leach **D:** Fr £19.00–£22.00 **S:** Fr £22.00–£25.00 **Beds:** 1F 1D 1T **Baths:** 2 En

Tormarton

ST7678

Chestnut Farm, *Tormarton, Badminton, GL9 1HS.* Small Georgian farmhouse. **Open:** All year
01454 218563 (also fax) Ms Cadei www.chestnut.farm.co.uk **D:** Fr £30.00–£45.00 **S:** Fr £30.00–£45.00 **Beds:** 1F 4D 2T **Baths:** 7 Pr (8)

The Portcullis, *Tormarton, Badminton, GL9 1HZ.* Traditional ivy-clad inn and restaurant in pretty Cotswold village. **Open:** All year (not Xmas)
01454 218263 Fax: 01454 218094 D: Fr £20.00–£25.00 **S:** Fr £28.00–£30.00 **Beds:** 1F 2D 4T **Baths:** 7 En (6) (40) cc

All details shown are as supplied by B&B owners in Autumn 2002

Tredington

SO9029

Gothic Farm, *Tredington, Tewkesbury, Glos, GL20 7BS.* Friendly, comfortable, character farmhouse with wonderful views of the Cotswolds. **Open:** All year (not Xmas)
01684 293360 Mr Coleman *molliecoleman@saintmail.net* **D:** Fr £18.00–£25.00 **S:** Fr £20.00–£30.00 **Beds:** 1D 1T **Baths:** 1 Pr 2 Sh (2) (10)

Uley

ST7898 *King's Head, Crown Inn*

Hill House, *Crawley Hill, Uley, Dursley, Glos, GL11 5BH.* Very warm welcome. Cotswold stone house, beautiful views, quiet location. **Open:** All year (not Xmas)
01453 860267 Mrs V Coates **D:** Fr £18.50–£22.00 **S:** Fr £17.00–£30.00 **Beds:** 1F 1D 1T 1S **Baths:** 2 En 1 Sh (5)

Upton St Leonards

SO8614 *King's Head, Four Mile House, Royal William, Black Horse*

Bullens Manor Farm, *Portway, Upton St Leonards, Gloucester, GL4 8DL.* Beautiful views. Lovely walks. **Open:** All year (not Xmas/New Year)
01452 616463 Mrs Warner **D:** Fr £21.00–£22.00 **S:** Fr £23.00–£25.00 **Beds:** 2T 3D 3S **Baths:** 3 En (6)

Westonbirt

ST8589

Avenue Farm, *Knockdown, Tetbury, Glos, GL8 8QY.* 300-year-old farmhouse in farm adjoining Westonbirt Arboretum. Bath, Bristol, Gloucester easy reach. **Open:** All year
01454 238207 Mrs King **Fax: 01454 238033** *sonjames@breathemail.net* **D:** Fr £25.00 **S:** Fr £30.00 **Beds:** 1F 1D 2T **Baths:** 2 En 1 Sh (6)

RATES
D = Price range per person sharing in a double or twin room
S = Price range for a single room

National Grid References given are for villages, towns and cities – not for individual houses

Whittington

SP0021

Whittington Lodge Farm, *Whittington, Cheltenham, Glos, GL54 4HB.* Beautiful Cotswold stone farmhouse. Perfect for relaxing, walking, town, racecourse. **Open:** All year (not Xmas/New Year) **Grades:** ETC 4 Diamond, Silver
01242 820603 & 07976 691589 (M) C Boyd **Fax: 01242 820603** *cathy@whittlodgefarm.fslife.co.uk* www.whittlodgefarm.fslife.co.uk **D:** Fr £23.00–£25.00 **S:** Fr £30.00–£35.00 **Beds:** 2T 1D **Baths:** 1 En 1 Pr 1 Sh (12) (4)

Winchcombe

SP0228

Ireley Farm, *Ireley Road, Winchcombe, Cheltenham, Glos, GL54 5PA.* C18th Cotswold stone character farmhouse. Relaxed. Excellent breakfasts. **Open:** Jan to Nov
01242 602445 Mrs Warmington *warmingtonmaggot@aol.com* **D:** Fr £22.50–£26.00 **S:** Fr £25.00–£30.00 **Beds:** 1F 1D 1T **Baths:** 2 En 1 Pr

Manor Farm, *Winchcombe, Cheltenham, Glos, GL54 5BJ.* Luxurious Cotswold manor on family farm. Camping and caravan space on farm, with facilities. **Open:** All year (not Xmas)
01242 602423 (also fax) Mr & Mrs Day *janet@dickandjanet.fsnet.co.uk* **D:** Fr £25.00–£30.00 **S:** Fr £30.00–£35.00 **Beds:** 2D 1T **Baths:** 3 En (20)

Gower House, *16 North Street, Winchcombe, Cheltenham, Glos, GL54 5LH.* Ideally situated for exploring Cotswolds. Close to shops, pubs, restaurants. **Open:** All year (not Xmas)
01242 602616 Mrs Simmonds **D:** Fr £22.50–£24.00 **S:** Fr £35.00–£45.00 **Beds:** 1D 2T **Baths:** 2 En 1 Pr (3)

Blair House, *41 Gretton Road, Winchcombe, Cheltenham, Glos, GL54 5EG.* Georgian house in historic town. Warm friendly welcome, excellent breakfasts. **Open:** All year **Grades:** ETC 4 Diamond
01242 603626 Mrs Chisholm **Fax: 01242 604214** *chissurv@aol.com* **D:** Fr £47.50 **S:** Fr £27.50 **Beds:** 1D 1T 1S **Baths:** 1 En 1 Sh (1)

Sudeley Hill Farm, *Winchcombe, Cheltenham, Glos, GL54 5JB.* Comfortably furnished C15th farmhouse. **Open:** All year (not Xmas)
01242 602344 (also fax) Mrs Scudamore **D:** Fr £22.00–£25.00 **S:** Fr £30.00–£32.00 **Beds:** 1F 1D 1T **Baths:** 3 En (10)

Ireley Grounds, *Barnhouse, Broadway Road, Winchcombe, Cheltenham, Glos, GL54 5NY.* Stunning Cotswold house in 6 acres of attractive gardens, magnificent views of the countryside. **Open:** All year (not Xmas)
01242 603736 Mr Wright **D:** Fr £22.50–£32.50 **S:** Fr £22.50–£32.50 **Beds:** 1F 3D **Baths:** 4 En (20)

Wotton-under-Edge

ST7692

Wotton Guest House, *31a Long Street, Wotton-under-Edge, Glos, GL12 7BX.* **Open:** All year
01453 843158 Mrs Nixon **Fax: 01453 842410** **D:** Fr £24.00 **S:** Fr £30.00 **Beds:** 1F 2D 2T 2S **Baths:** 7 En (12)
C17th Manor house. Superb food in adjoining coffee shop. Walled garden for guests' use. Comfortable bedrooms and a warm welcome for ramblers.

Under-the-Hill-House, *Adeys Lane, Wotton-under-Edge, Glos, GL12 7LY.* C18th listed period house overlooking National Trust Land. **Open:** Mar to Oct
01453 842557 Mrs Forster **D:** Fr £20.00–£22.00 **S:** Fr £20.00–£22.00 **Beds:** 1T 1D **Baths:** 1 Sh (13) (2)

National Grid References given are for villages, towns and cities – not for individual houses

Greater Manchester & Merseyside

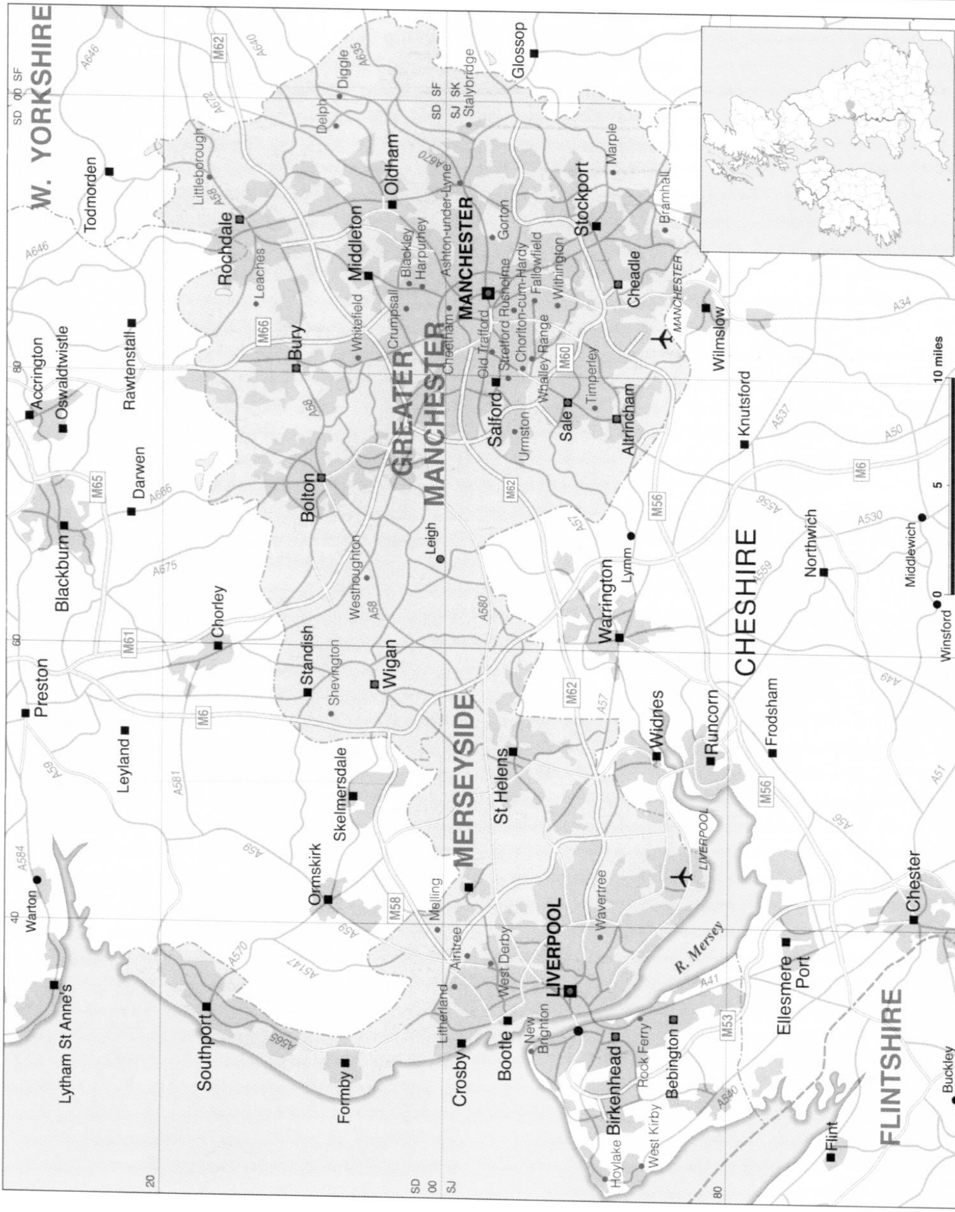

Altrincham

SJ7687

Belvedere Guest House, *58 Barrington Road, Altrincham, Cheshire, WA14 1HY.* Close to tram, restaurants, pubs. Manchester Airport 12 minutes away. **Open:** All year
0161 941 5996 Mr Kelly **Fax: 0161 929 6450**
D: Fr £18.00 **S:** Fr £20.00 **Beds:** 2F 1T
Baths: 4 Pr (5) 1

Acorn Of Oakmere, *6 Wingate Drive Timperley, Altrincham, Greater Manchester, WA15 7PX.* Warm comfortable family home, attractive walled garden. Relax with sunken spa bath. **Open:** All year
0161 980 8391 Mrs Moore *oakmere6@cwctv.net*
D: Fr £25.00–£30.00 **S:** Fr £25.00–£30.00
Beds: 1T 1S **Baths:** 1 En 1 Sh (2)

Oasis Hotel, *46-48 Barrington Road, Altrincham, Cheshire, WA14 1HN.* With warm and friendly welcome, ideally located in South Manchester and Manchester airport. **Open:** All year
0161 928 4523 **D:** Fr £20.00–£24.00 **S:** Fr £30.00–£36.00 **Beds:** 4F 9T 10D 10S
Baths: 33 En cc

Ashton-under-Lyne

SJ9399

Lynwood Hotel, *3 Richmond Street, Ashton-under-Lyne, Greater Manchester, OL6 7TX.* A friendly family-run hotel in a quiet location. A warm welcome guaranteed. **Open:** All year **Grades:** ETC 3 Diamond
0161 330 5358 (also fax) Mrs Lindsay **D:** Fr £20.00–£24.00 **S:** Fr £25.00–£30.00 **Beds:** 1F 1T 2S **Baths:** 2 En 1 Sh

King William IV Hotel, *Stamford Street West, Ashton-under-Lyne, Lancashire, OL6 7QU.* Mainly for commercial traveller seeking good clean accommodation at reasonable rates. **Open:** All year (not Xmas/New Year)
0161 339 6016 **D:** Fr £15.00 **S:** Fr £15.00
Beds: 5T 2D 1S **Baths:** 5 Pr cc

Bebington

SJ3383

Bebington Hotel, *24 Town Lane, Bebington, Wirral, Merseyside, CH63 5JG.* **Open:** All year (not Xmas) **Grades:** ETC 3 Diamond
0151 645 0608 (also fax) Mrs Vaghena *vaghena@aol.com* **D:** Fr £25.00–£27.00 **S:** Fr £29.50–£35.00 **Beds:** 1F 5D 1T 8S **Baths:** 15 En (12)
This professionally-run family hotel guarantees a warm welcome. All rooms of high standard, tastefully decorated, home from home comforts. Well-lit car park. Residents licence. Only five minutes from Bebington station and within easy reach of Liverpool and Chester.

Birkenhead

SJ3088

Ashgrove Guest House, *14 Ashville Road, Claughton, Prenton, Birkenhead, Merseyside, CH43 8SA.* **Open:** All year
0151 653 3794 Mr Lupton *brilupis@hotmail.com*
D: Fr £20.00–£24.00 **S:** Fr £20.00–£24.00
Beds: 1F 2D 2T 2S **Baths:** 1 En 3 Sh (6)
Family-run with artistic & musical ties, overlooking parkland. Mileage: underground trains 0.33, main shops 1, Liverpool 4, Chester 17, Southport 23, Blackpool 80. Games room. Play parkland, sport & swimming facilities all within 1 mile. Self-catering available.

Bolton

SD7108

Jumbles Country Park Guest House, Grange Farm, *Grange Road, Bromley Cross, Bolton, BL7 0BX.* **Open:** All year **Grades:** AA 5 Diamond
01204 303612 Mrs Sobey **Fax: 01204 303618**
office@jumbles.info www.jumbles.info **D:** Fr £25.00–£27.50 **S:** Fr £25.00–£30.00 **Beds:** 1F 1T 1D **Baths:** 3 En (5) cc
Stone farmhouse, tastefully decorated in picturesque setting, nestling on the banks of the Jumbles Country Park Reservoir. Stunning views over the water. Close to Bolton, Bury and East Lancs. Railway. Convenient for the North-West motorway network, Manchester and Liverpool.

Heyesleigh, *98 Castle Street, Bolton, Lancs, BL2 1JL.* Situated off main A58. Bury-Bolton Road. 7-minute walk town centre. **Open:** All year (not Xmas)
01204 523647 (also fax) Mrs Daley **D:** Fr £16.00–£18.00 **S:** Fr £17.00–£22.00 **Beds:** 3F 2D 1T 3S **Baths:** 5 En 1 Sh

RATES
D = Price range per person sharing in a double or twin room
S = Price range for a single room

Please respect a B&B's wishes regarding children, animals and smoking

Bramhall

SJ8984 Ladybrook

280 Bramhall Lane South, *Bramhall, Stockport, Cheshire, SK7 3DJ.* Close to South Manchester. Luxury accommodation. Warm, friendly. English breakfast. **Open:** All year
0161 439 5600 Mrs Hurd *guests@brookfieldguesthouse.co.uk* www.brookfieldguesthouse.co.uk **D:** Fr £19.00–£24.00 **S:** Fr £28.00–£30.00 **Beds:** 1F 1T 2D 1S **Baths:** 2 En 2 Sh
cc

Bury

SD8010

Pennine View, *8 Hunstanton Drive, Brandlesholme, Bury, Greater Manchester, BL8 1EG.* **Open:** All year
0161 763 1249 Mrs McKeon *j.mckeon@tinyworld.co.uk* **D:** Fr £17.50–£20.00 **S:** Fr £25.00–£30.00 **Beds:** 2D 1T/F 1S **Baths:** 1 En 1 Sh (3)
Attractive detached residence in a quiet, safe area. Adjacent to Bury town centre and easy access to motorways, Metrolink to Manchester city centre, Pennines & East Lancashire Railway. Quiet comfortable rooms. Excellent breakfasts, vegetarians catered for. Phone for further details.

Ashbury Guest House, *235 Rochdale Road, Bury, Greater Manchester, BL9 7BX.* Relax in a warm friendly family-run guest house. All rooms have TV/radio alarm. Tea/coffee, en-suite rooms available. Direct access to Manchester via Metro approximately 20 mins situated main road position directly off M66 motorway Junction 2. **Open:** All year
0161 762 9623 G Woodall **Fax: 0161 763 3887**
D: Fr £20.00–£22.00 **S:** Fr £20.00–£25.00
Beds: 1D 1T 2S **Baths:** 1 En 1 Sh

Cheadle Hulme

SJ8786

Spring Cottage, *60 Hulme Hall Road, Cheadle Hulme, Cheadle, Cheshire, SK8 6JZ.* Beautiful Victorian house adjacent to the C17th Hulme Hall. **Open:** All year
0161 485 1037 (also fax) Mr & Mrs Buckley
D: Fr £30.00–£42.00 **S:** Fr £23.00–£28.00
Beds: 2T 1S 1F **Baths:** 3 Pr 1 Sh (6) cc

Delph
SD9807 *Great Western*

Globe Farm Guest House, *Huddersfield Road, Delph, Oldham, Lancashire, OL3 5LU.* Former coaching house converted into comfortable ensuite bed & breakfast. **Open:** All year (not Xmas/New Year)
01457 873040 (also fax) *globefarm@amserve.com* www.globefarm.co.uk **D:** Fr £22.50 **S:** Fr £25.00 **Beds:** 1F 4T 5D 4S **Baths:** 14 En (30) **cc**

Diggle
SE0008

Sunfield, *Diglea, Diggle, Saddleworth, Oldham, Lancs, OL3 5LA.* Warm welcome, countryside views, farmhouse breakfast. Experience the Pennine moods. **Open:** All year
01457 874030 Mr & Mrs Francis *sunfield.accom@lineone.net* **D:** Fr £17.50–£20.00 **S:** Fr £25.00–£28.00 **Beds:** 1F 3D 2T 1S **Baths:** 7 En (8)

New Barn, *Harrop Green Farm, Diggle, Oldham, Lancs, OL3 5LW.* Working farm, lovely views over Saddleworth villages. Close to Standedge Canal Tunnel. **Open:** All year (not Xmas)
01457 873937 & 07979 598232 Mr Rhodes **Fax: 01457 873937 D:** Fr £17.00–£18.00 **S:** Fr £17.00–£18.00 **Beds:** 1F 1D 1T 1S **Baths:** 1 Pr 1 Sh (10)

Hoylake
SJ2188

Rockland, *70 Birkenhead Road, Hoylake, Wirral, Merseyside, CH47 0LA.* **Open:** All year
0151 632 4249 Mrs Hardman *rockland@nu-net.co.uk* **D:** Fr £20.00–£25.00 **S:** Fr £25.00–£35.00 **Beds:** 3F 3T **Baths:** 3 En (10)
Large Victorian House, friendly atmosphere. Close to Royal Liverpool Golf Club. Ideal for coastal & country walks. A wonderful beach 150 yards away. Near to wind surfing, sand-yachting and sailing centre. Ample parking. Heated pool in season.

Leigh
SD6500

Three Crowns, *188 Chapel Street, Leigh, Lancashire, WN7 2DW.* Three Crowns, Leigh, pub/restaurant open all year round.
Open: All year
01942 673552 D: Fr £15.00 **S:** Fr £15.00 **Beds:** 1T 1S **cc**

Litherland
SJ3498

Litherland Park, *34 Litherland, Bootle, L21 9HP.* Victorian detached house, spacious lounge, three bedrooms. Warm welcome assured. **Open:** All year (not Xmas/New Year)
0151 928 1085 B Harper **D:** Fr £19.00 **S:** Fr £20.00 **Beds:** 2D 1S **Baths:** 2 Sh (4)

Littleborough
SD9316

Hollingworth Lake B&B, *164 Smithybridge Road, Hollingworth Lake, Littleborough, Lancashire, OL15 0DB.* 5 Diamond Gold Award with NWTB at Hollingworth Lake Country Park. **Open:** All year **Grades:** ETC 5 Diamond, Gold
01706 376583 Ms Wood *hollingworthlakebb@hotmail.com* **D:** Fr £15.00–£22.50 **S:** Fr £25.00–£30.00 **Beds:** 1F 2D 1T 1S **Baths:** 5 En (5) 3 **cc**

Swing Cottage Guest House, *31 Lakebank, Hollingworth Lake Country Park, Littleborough, Greater Manchester, OL15 0DQ.* 'North West Best B&B' winner 2000 - beautiful countryside. **Open:** All year
01706 379094 C Dean **Fax: 01706 379091** *swingcottage@aol.com* www.hollingworthlake.com **D:** Fr £22.50 **S:** Fr £35.00 **Beds:** 2F 1T **Baths:** 3 En **cc**

LIVERPOOL Central
SJ3490

Embassie Youth Hostel, *1 Falkner Square, Liverpool, L8 7NU.* Town house in beautiful Georgian Falkner Square. Head towards Anglican cathedral, up Canning St. **Open:** All year
0151 707 1089 Mr Murphy **D:** Fr £12.50 **S:** Fr £9.50–£11.50 **Beds:** 20S **Baths:** 5 Sh (12)

Planning a longer stay? Always ask for any special rates

LIVERPOOL Orrell
SJ3496

Orrell Park Hotel, *109 Orrell Lane, Liverpool, Merseyside, L9 8BL.* **Open:** All year
0151 525 4018 (also fax) *alan.cousins2@virgin.net* **D:** Fr £20.00–£25.00 **S:** Fr £25.00 **Beds:** 3F 5T 2D 1S **Baths:** 4 Sh (5) (8) **cc**
Beautiful family-run hotel, licensed bar & TV lounge. City centre 3.5 miles, short distance from Aintree Racecourse home of the Grand National. Close to Anfield & Goodison football grounds. Close to all major transport links. Ring for brochure.

LIVERPOOL Wavertree
SJ3889

Holmeleigh Guest House, *93 Woodcroft Road, Wavertree, Liverpool, L15 2HG.* Family-run, continental breakfast, only 2.5 miles from city centre. **Open:** All year **Grades:** ETC 2 Diamond
0151 734 2216 (day) & 0151 726 9980 (eve) Mrs Bridge **Fax: 0151 728 9521** *bridges01@blueyonder.co.uk* **D:** Fr £15.00–£25.00 **S:** Fr £15.00–£30.00 **Beds:** 4T 2D 4S **Baths:** 6 En 1 Sh

LIVERPOOL West Derby
SJ3993

Parkland, *38 Coachman's Drive, Croxteth Park, Liverpool, L12 0HX.* Quiet residential house in country park. 5 miles from city centre. **Open:** All year (not Xmas/New Year)
0151 259 1417 R Todd **D:** Fr £20.00 **S:** Fr £25.00 **Beds:** 1T 1D **Baths:** 1 Sh (2)

MANCHESTER Blackley
SD8602

Bentley Guest House, *64 Hill Lane, Blackley, Manchester, M9 6PF.* A private homely semi-detached house, personal service, comfortable quality accommodation. **Open:** All year
Grades: ETC 3 Diamond
0161 795 1115 R Kerassites **D:** Fr £15.00–£20.00 **S:** Fr £20.00–£25.00 **Beds:** 2D 1S **Baths:** 1 En 1 Sh (9) (3)

New White Lion, *7 Middleton Old Road, Blackley, Manchester, M9 3DS.* Pleasant location, 7 mins city centre, 4 mins Commonwealth Stadium. Licensed bar on site. **Open:** All year
0161 720 7218 D: Fr £13.00–£15.00 **S:** Fr £13.00–£15.00 **Beds:** 2F 3T 1D **Baths:** 6 En

B&B owners may vary rates – be sure to check when booking

MANCHESTER Central

SJ8397

Monroes Hotel, *38 London Road, Manchester, M1 1PE.* Small family hotel in city centre opposite Piccadilly Station. Showers in most rooms. **Open:** All year (not Xmas/New Year)
0161 236 0564 Mr Ryan **D:** Fr £16.00 **S:** Fr £16.00 **Beds:** 4T 1D 2S **Baths:** 2 Sh

MANCHESTER Cheetham

SD8400

New Central Hotel, *144-146 Heywood Street, Cheetham, Manchester, M8 7PD.* Small, comfortable, friendly hotel. **Open:** All year
0161 205 2169 (also fax) Mrs Greenwood *newcentral@talk21.com* **D:** Fr £16.50–£17.50 **S:** Fr £18.50–£21.50 **Beds:** 1F 1D 2T 7S **Baths:** 5 Pr 2 Sh (2) (7)

MANCHESTER Chorlton-cum-Hardy

SJ8193

Kempton House Hotel, *400 Wilbraham Road, Chorlton-cum-Hardy, Manchester, M21 0UH.* Friendly, family-run hotel, comfortable, good food, and children very welcome. **Open:** All year (not Xmas/New Year) **Grades:** ETC 3 Diamond
0161 881 8766 Mr Marrow *kempton.house@virgin.net* **D:** Fr £20.00–£25.00 **S:** Fr £25.00–£35.00 **Beds:** 1F 2T 5D 3S **Baths:** 6 En 2 Sh (6) cc

Abbey Lodge Hotel, *501 Wilbraham Road, Chorlton-cum-Hardy, Manchester, M21 0UJ.* Elegant Edwardian house. Large, comfortable ensuite rooms. Centrally located. Breakfast served. **Open:** All year (not Xmas/New Year)
0161 862 9266 D: Fr £25.00–£40.00 **S:** Fr £30.00–£50.00 **Beds:** 1T 3D **Baths:** 4 En

MANCHESTER Crumpsall

SD8402

Cleveland Lodge, *117 Cleveland Road, Crumpsall, Manchester, M8 4GX.* Nearby Metrolink station, serves city centre and places of interest. **Open:** All year
0161 795 0007 (also fax) A Musgrove **D:** Fr £17.00 **S:** Fr £25.00 **Beds:** 2D 1S

MANCHESTER Fallowfield

SJ8593

Luther King House, *Brighton Grove, Manchester, M14 5JP.* Comfortable and value for money, overnight and short stay accommodation. **Open:** All year (not Xmas/New Year)
0161 224 6404 Fax: 0161 248 9201 *reception@lkh.co.uk* www.lkh.co.uk **D:** Fr £18.00–£20.00 **S:** Fr £24.50 **Beds:** 3F 8T 3D 35S **Baths:** 25 En 12 Sh (46) cc

Wilmslow Hotel, *356 Wilmslow Road, Fallowfield, Manchester, M14 6AB.* Family run, helpful staff, pubs and restaurants 5 minutes walk. **Open:** All year
0161 225 3030 Fax: 0161 257 2854 D: Fr £15.32–£20.62 **S:** Fr £19.95–£25.95 **Beds:** 4F 6T 9D 9S **Baths:** 14 En 3 Sh (10) cc

MANCHESTER Gorton

SJ8896

Clyde Mount Guest House, *866 Hyde Road Debdale Park, Gorton, Manchester, M18 7LH.* Large Victorian house overlooking park, friendly, comfortable, convenient city centre. **Open:** All year
0161 231 1515 *clydemount.sw@amserve.net* **D:** Fr £18.00 **S:** Fr £18.00 **Beds:** 1F 3D 3T 3S **Baths:** 3 Sh (8) cc

MANCHESTER Harpurhey

SD8601

Harpers Hotel, *745 Rochdale Road, Harpurhey, Manchester, M9 5SB.* Rooms ensuite. 2 miles city centre, Manchester Arena, Velodrome, 2002 Stadium. **Open:** All year
0161 203 5475 (also fax) D: Fr £22.00–£30.00 **S:** Fr £32.00–£40.00 **Beds:** 13F **Baths:** 13 En

MANCHESTER Old Trafford

SJ8295

Trafford Hall Hotel, *Talbot Road, Old Trafford, Manchester, M16 0PE.* Comfortable hotel, convenient for Old Trafford. **Open:** All year
0161 848 7791 Fax: 0161 848 0219 *traffordhallhotel@msn.com* **D:** Fr £19.50–£36.50 **S:** Fr £39.00–£49.50 **Beds:** 4F 6T 22D 4S **Baths:** 36 En (64) cc

MANCHESTER Rusholme

SJ8695

Elton Bank Hotel, *62 Platt Lane, Rusholme, Manchester, M14 5NE.* Peaceful parkside setting. Fast access to Manchester city centre. **Open:** All year (not Xmas/New Year)
0161 224 6449 *eltonbank@dial.pipex.com* **D:** Fr £39.00–£43.00 **S:** Fr £28.00–£33.00 **Beds:** 3T 3S **Baths:** 1 En 1 Pr 1 Sh (6) cc

MANCHESTER Stretford

SJ8095

Greatstone Hotel, *843-845 Chester Road, Gorse Hill, Stretford, Manchester, M32 0RN.* Family-run . Five minute walk Manchester Utd football ground. **Open:** All year
0161 865 1640 Mr Sill **D:** Fr £18.00–£20.00 **S:** Fr £20.00–£22.00 **Beds:** 1F 5T 6D 12S **Baths:** 2 En 4 Pr 3 Sh (50) cc

MANCHESTER Whalley Range

SJ8294

Polex Hotel, *70-78 Dudley Road, off Withington Road, Whalley Range, Manchester, M16 8DE.* 2m city centre, 1.5m Old Trafford, 3m airport. Continental breakfast, CH, 4 languages spoken. **Open:** All year
0161 881 4038 Mr Klocek **Fax: 0161 881 1567 D:** Fr £26.00–£30.00 **S:** Fr £25.00–£30.00 **Beds:** 2F 10D 24S **Baths:** 38 En (6) (24) cc

MANCHESTER Withington

SJ8592

The Drop Inn Hotel, *393 Wilmslow Road, Withington, Manchester, M20 4WA.* Pub/hotel separate buildings. Satellite television. Pool room. Very warm and cosy. **Open:** All year
0161 286 1919 G Wood **Fax: 0161 286 8880** *thedropinn@maileaseynet.co.uk* www.maileaseynet.co.uk **D:** Fr £25.00–£45.00 **Beds:** 15F 23T 7D 1S (50) cc

Marple

SJ9588

Sinclair Lodge, *84 Strines Road, Marple, Stockport, SK6 7DU.* Modern bungalow, countryside setting, yet convenient for town and airport. **Open:** All year (not Xmas)
0161 449 9435 (also fax) M Scott *mscott144@aol.com* www.members.aol.com/mscott144 **D:** Fr £20.00–£28.00 **S:** Fr £20.00–£25.00 **Beds:** 1D 1S **Baths:** 1 En (6)

New Brighton

SJ3093

Sherwood Guest House, *55 Wellington Road, New Brighton, Wallasey, Wirral, CH45 2ND.* Family run guest house close to train/bus station/ motorway. **Open:** All year (not Xmas/New Year)
0151 639 5198 Mrs Brereton *frankbreo@btinternet.com* **D:** Fr £15.00–£18.00 **S:** Fr £18.00–£20.00 **Beds:** 2F 3T 1S **Baths:** 3 En 3 Sh

Wellington House Hotel, *65 Wellington Road, New Brighton, Wirral, Merseyside, CH45 2NE.* Sea views, ground floor rooms available, bar, enclosed car park, CCTV. **Open:** All year (not Xmas/New Year)
0151 639 6594 (also fax) L Edwards www.wellington-house-hotel.freeserve.co.uk **D:** Fr £20.00–£22.50 **S:** Fr £22.00–£25.00 **Beds:** 4F 3T 2D 2S **Baths:** 8 En 2 Sh (14) cc

Rochdale

SD8913 *Egerton Arms, Owd Bets*

Harridge End Homestay, *Shawclough Road, Rochdale, Lancs, OL12 7HL.* Large, comfortable, friendly and quiet house, private parking. **Open:** All year
01706 645272 M Whiteley **D:** Fr £22.50–£25.00 **S:** Fr £25.00 **Beds:** 1F 1T **Baths:** 2 Sh (6)

Britannia Inn, *4 Lomax Street, Rochdale, Lancs, OL12 0DN.* Friendly local public house serving real ale, CAMRA listed. **Open:** All year
01706 646391 Mr Ainsworth **D:** Fr £13.00–£15.00 **S:** Fr £15.00 **Beds:** 3T **Baths:** 1 Sh

Sale

SJ7891

Cornerstones, *230 Washway Road, Sale, M33 4PA.* **Open:** All year (not Xmas/New Year)
0161 283 6909 (also fax) Mrs Casey *Toncasey@aol.com* www.cornerstoneshotel.com **D:** Fr £25.00–£29.00 **S:** Fr £27.50–£41.00 **Beds:** 3F 3T 3D **Baths:** 7 En 1 Pr 1 Sh cc
Located on the main A56 road into the city and 5 mins away from Brooklands Metro Station. This fine Victorian building built by Sir William Cunliff Brooks was totally restored in 1985 reproducing the splendour of the Victorian era.

Brooklands Luxury Lodge, *208 Marsland Road, Sale, Cheshire, M33 3NE.* Convenient for all major venues including the fabulous Trafford Centre. **Open:** All year **Grades:** AA 4 Diamond
0161 973 3283 Mr Bowker **D:** Fr £24.00–£29.00 **S:** Fr £27.00–£33.00 **Beds:** 2F 2D 1T 4S **Baths:** 5 En 2 Sh (1) (7) cc

Shevington

SD5408

Wilden, *11a Miles Lane, Shevington, Wigan, Lancashire, WN6 8EB.* Large bungalow. Secluded large gardens. 1 mile M6. Off road parking. **Open:** All year (not Xmas/New Year)
01257 251516 D Axon **D:** Fr £17.50–£20.00 **S:** Fr £17.50–£20.00 **Beds:** 1T 2D **Baths:** 1 En 1 Sh (5) cc

Southport

SD3317

The Sidbrook Hotel, *14 Talbot Street, Southport, Lancashire, PR8 1HP.* Family-run hotel close to town centre and amenities. **Open:** All year (not Xmas) **Grades:** ETC 3 Diamond, AA 3 Diamond
01704 530608 (also fax) Mrs Barker *sidbrookhotel@tesco.net* www.thesidbrooksouthport.co.uk **D:** Fr £21.00–£26.50 **S:** Fr £28.50 **Beds:** 1F 5D 2T **Baths:** 8 En (8) cc

Rosedale Hotel, *11 Talbot Street, Southport, Merseyside, PR8 1HP.* Friendly family-run hotel close to all Southport's main attractions. **Open:** All year (not Xmas/New Year) **Grades:** ETC 4 Diamond, AA 4 Diamond, RAC 4 Diamond
01704 530604 (also fax) Mr & Mrs Beer *info@rosedalehotelsouthport.co.uk* www.rosedalehotelsouthport.co.uk **D:** Fr £25.00 **S:** Fr £25.00 **Beds:** 2F 2T 2D 3S **Baths:** 8 En 1 Pr (6) cc

Aaron Hotel, *18 Bath Street, Southport, Lancashire, PR9 0DA.* Family run hotel located in the centre of Southport. **Open:** All year
01704 530283 Mr Urbanowski **Fax: 01704 501055** *info@aaronhotel.co.uk* www.aaronhotel.co.uk **D:** Fr £23.00–£28.00 **S:** Fr £28.00–£35.00 **Beds:** 2F 2T 2D 2S **Baths:** 8 En (2) (6) cc

The White Lodge, *12 Talbot Street, Southport, PR8 1HP.* Small select hotel offering high standards in food, cleanliness and service. **Open:** All year (not Xmas)
01704 536320 (also fax) Mr McKee **D:** Fr £25.00–£30.00 **S:** Fr £25.00–£40.00 **Beds:** 2F 2D 1T 2S **Baths:** 6 En 1 Sh (6)

Stalybridge

SJ9698

The Wharf Tavern, *Staley Wharf, Stalybridge, SK15 1PD.* Canal mooring facilities, family run. Warm welcome. Explore Cheshire countryside. **Open:** All year (not Xmas/New Year)
0161 338 2662 **D:** Fr £45.00 **S:** Fr £25.00 **Beds:** 3T 1S **Baths:** 4 En

Timperley

SJ7889

Beech Bank, *27 Bloomsbury Lane , Timperley, Altrincham, Greater Manchester, WA15 6LU.* Spacious rooms in Victorian home, quiet, airport parking/courtesy transport. **Open:** All year (not Xmas/New Year)
0161 980 7001 & 07747 865018 (M) Mrs Davidson *yvonne@beechbank.co.uk* **D:** Fr £25.00–£30.00 **S:** Fr £25.00–£30.00 **Beds:** 1F 1T **Baths:** 2 En (5)

Urmston

SJ7594

Beech Cottage, *80 Bent Lanes, Davyhulme, Urmston, Manchester, M41 8WY.* C16th black and white cottage, large gardens with natural pond and orchard. **Open:** All year (not Xmas)
0161 748 4649 Mr & Mrs Pollington **D:** Fr £18.00 **S:** Fr £20.00 **Beds:** 1D **Baths:** 1 Pr (1)

West Kirby

SJ2086

120 Frankby Road, *West Kirby, Wirral, Merseyside, CH48 9UX.* Perfectly situated for Wirral Pennisula. Farmhouse breakfast. Very warm welcome. **Open:** All year
0151 625 6215 Mrs Halliwell **D:** Fr £25.00–£30.00 **S:** Fr £25.00–£30.00 **Beds:** 1S 2F **Baths:** 1 Sh (2)

Caldy Warren Cottage, *42 Caldy Road, West Kirby, Wirral, Merseyside, CH48 2HQ.* Spectacular river views. Exceptional accommodation, close to Chester, Liverpool. **Open:** All year
0151 625 8740 Mrs Graves **Fax: 0151 625 4115** *sue@warrencott.demon.co.uk* www.warrencott.demon.co.uk **D:** Fr £20.00–£30.00 **S:** Fr £25.00–£35.00 **Beds:** 1D 1F 1S **Baths:** 2 En 1 Sh (2)

Westhoughton

SD6506

Daisy Hill Hotel, *3 Lower Leigh Road, Daisy Hill, Westhoughton, Bolton, BL5 2JP.* Village pub close to motorway and train station, rooms, separate building to pub. **Open:** All year
01942 812096 J Nuttal *daisy.hill@cwcom.net* www.daisyhillhotel.co.uk **D:** Fr £17.50–£20.00 **S:** Fr £25.00–£27.50 **Beds:** 2 T 2S **Baths:** 4 Pr **cc**

Whitefield

SD8106

Burke's Guest House, *122 Radcliffe New Road, Whitefield, Manchester, M45 7RW.* Ideally situated for Manchester and exploring Lancashire towns and countryside. **Open:** All year (not Xmas/New Year)
0161 766 5161 A P Burke **D:** Fr £20.00 **S:** Fr £20.00 **Beds:** 1T 1D 1S **Baths:** 2 Sh

Wigan

SD5805

Hotel Bel-Air, *236 Wigan Lane, Wigan, Lancs, WN1 2NU.* Family-run hotel and restaurant close to Wigan centre and M6 J27. **Open:** All year **Grades:** AA 2 Star, RAC 2 Star
01942 241410 Mr Lacaille **Fax: 01942 243967** *belair@hotelwigan.freeserve.co.uk* www.belairhotel.co.uk **D:** Fr £22.50–£25.00 **S:** Fr £35.00–£39.50 **Beds:** 11F **Baths:** 11 En (12)

Hampshire

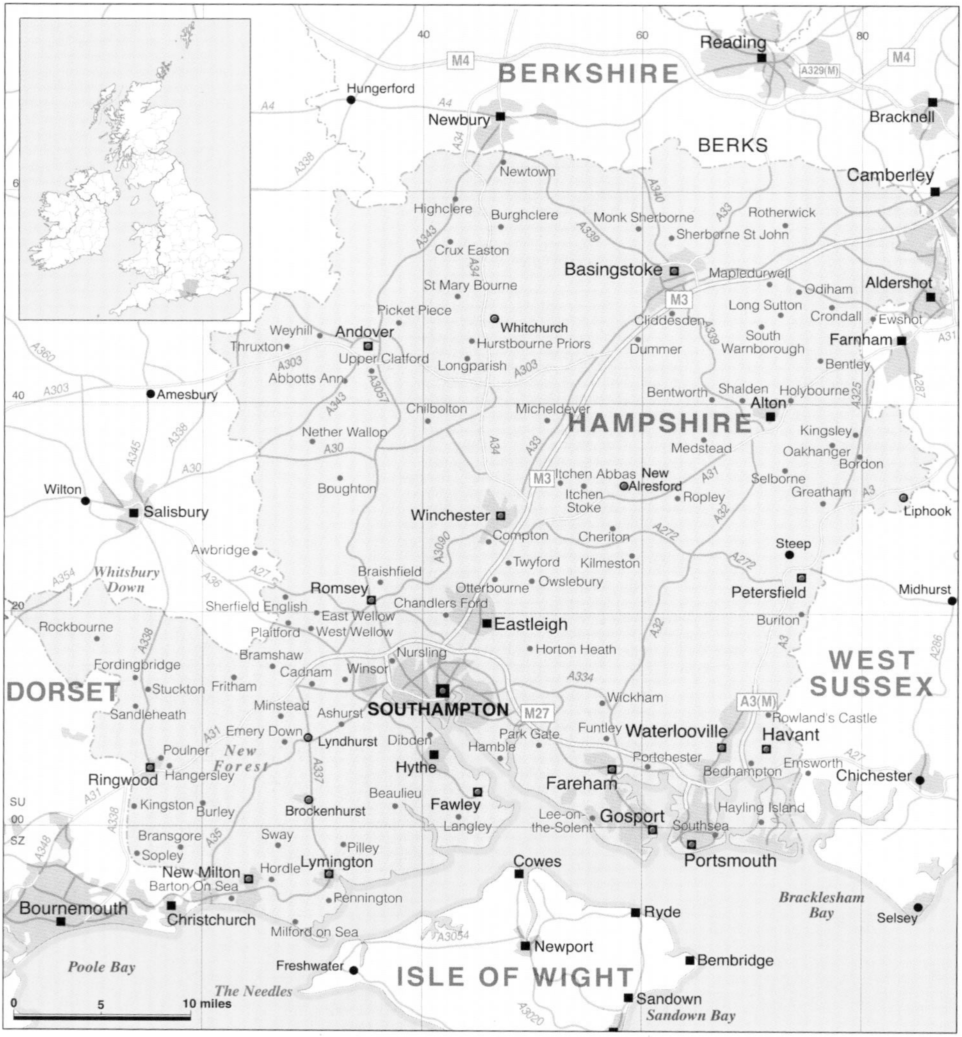

Abbotts Ann

SU3243

Carinya Farm, *Cattle Lane, Abbotts Ann, Andover, Hampshire, SP11 7DR.* Working stock farm, modern farmhouse with traditional values. Wildlife pond, large patio and conservatory. **Open:** All year
01264 710269 D W Fergusson *carinya.farm@virgin.net* carinyafarm.co.uk **D:** Fr £20.00 **S:** Fr £25.00 **Beds:** 1T 1D **Baths:** 2 En (4)

Aldershot

SU8750 *The Goose, Railway Tavern*

Alexandra Hotel, *Barrack Road, Aldershot, Hants, GU11 3NP.* Town centre, close to bars, restaurants, nightclubs and army military museum. **Open:** All year
01252 312550 D: Fr £20.00–£30.00 **S:** Fr £25.00–£40.00 **Beds:** 1F 4T 2D **Baths:** 2 Sh

Alton

SU7139

Walnut Tree Barn, *Bentworth, Alton, Hampshire, GU34 5JT.* Recently converted detached barn in peaceful location on edge of charming village. **Open:** All year (not Xmas)
01420 561281 & 07767 497482 (M) J Crawford *jackiecrawfor25@hotmail.com* **D:** Fr £22.00–£25.00 **S:** Fr £25.00–£30.00 **Beds:** 1D 1T **Baths:** 1 En 1 Pr (4)

Planning a longer stay? Always ask for any special rates

Andover

SU3645

Salisbury Road Bed & Breakfast, *99 Salisbury Road, Andover, Hants, SP10 2LN.* Virtually self-contained ground floor with access to beautiful garden. **Open:** All year (not Xmas)
01264 362638 Mrs Targett **D:** Fr £20.00–£25.00 **S:** Fr £20.00–£30.00 **Beds:** 1F **Baths:** 1 Pr (2)

Ashurst

SU3411

Forest Gate Lodge, *161 Lyndhurst Road, Ashurst, Southampton, SO40 7AW.* New Forest location. Excellent standard of accommodation, all Forest attractions. Special rates Oct, Apr. **Open:** All year **Grades:** ETC 4 Diamond, Silver
023 8029 3026 Mr & Mrs Hanlon *forestgatelodge@ukworld.net* **D:** Fr £23.00 **S:** Fr £23.00 **Beds:** 3D 1F 1T **Baths:** 5 En (2) (6)

Awbridge

SU3324

Crofton Country B and B, *Kents Oak, Awbridge, Romsey, Hants, SP51 0HH.* Nestled in 2 acres of gardens including a vineyard, Luxury, hotel-quality accommodation. **Open:** All year (not Xmas/New Year) **Grades:** ETC 4 Diamond, Silver
01794 340333 (also fax) Mrs Lightfoot *pauline@croftonbanb.com* www.croftonbandb.com **D:** Fr £25.00 **S:** Fr £25.00–£30.00 **Beds:** 1F 1T 1S **Baths:** 3 En (3) **cc**

Barton on Sea

SZ2393

Cleeve House, *58 Barton Court Avenue, Barton on Sea, New Milton, Hants, BH25 7HG.* Large character family home, close to sea, non-smoking house. **Open:** All year (not Xmas) **Grades:** ETC 4 Diamond, AA 4 Diamond
01425 615211 (also fax) Mrs Carter *cleeve.house@btinternet.com* **D:** Fr £22.50–£25.00 **S:** Fr £25.00–£50.00 **Beds:** 1F 1D 1T 1S **Baths:** 2 En 1 Sh (8)

Tower House, *Christchurch Road, Barton on Sea, New Milton, Hants, DH25 6QQ.* Between New Forest and sea, spacious comfortable rooms. Comprehensive breakfast menu. **Open:** All year (not Xmas)
01425 629508 (also fax) Mrs Steenhuis *bandb@towerhouse-newforest.co.uk* www.towerhouse-newforest.co.uk **D:** Fr £20.00–£25.00 **S:** Fr £20.00–£25.00 **Beds:** 2D 1T **Baths:** 3 En (7) (7)

Basingstoke

SU6352

The Carroll's Guesthouse, *104 Gershwin Road, Brighton Hill, Basingstoke, Hants, RG22 4HJ.* Basing House; Cromwell battle, many other historical places around. **Open:** All year
01256 410024 & 07786 105020 Mr Carroll **D:** Fr £17.50–£18.50 **S:** Fr £15.50–£17.50 **Beds:** 1F 2T 2S **Baths:** 1 Sh (5) (4)

Graham's Place, *3 Irwell Close, Riverdene, Basingstoke, Hampshire, RG21 4DG.* Informal theatrical atmosphere, short walk to town, restaurants, theatres. **Open:** All year
01256 325610 (also fax) Mr Bye *graham@ozuk.demon.co.uk* www.ozuk.demon.co.uk **S:** Fr £15.00–£18.00 **Beds:** 1S **Baths:** 1 Sh (1)

20 Lilac Way, *Basingstoke, Hampshire, RG23 8AQ.* Accommodation, local to shops, trains, buses, leisure park. **Open:** All year (not Xmas/New Year)
01256 417227 & 07941 071793 (M) Mrs Doidge *valarie.doidge@ntlworld.com* **D:** Fr £20.00 **S:** Fr £20.00 **Beds:** 1D **Baths:** 1 Sh (11) (1)

Beaulieu

SU3802

Leygreem Farm House, *Lyndhurst Road, Beaulieu, Brockenhurst, Hants, SO42 7YP.* **Open:** All year (not Xmas) **Grades:** ETC 3 Diamond
01590 612355 (also fax) Mr Helyer **D:** Fr £22.00–£25.00 **S:** Fr £25.00–£30.00 **Beds:** 2D 1T **Baths:** 3 En (6)
Victorian farmhouse in rural setting 1 mile from Beaulieu village ideal for Motor Museum, Buckler's Yard, New Forest and Exbury Gardens. Mountain bikes available for guests' use. Off-road private parking. Discounts 3 days or more. A warm welcome assured.

Bedhampton

SU7006 *Belmont Inn*

Green Cottage Guest House, *23 Park Lane, Bedhampton, Havant, Hampshire, PO9 3HG.* Organic ingredients used where possible in breakfasts and dinners. **Open:** All year (not Xmas/New Year)
023 9247 5670 Mrs Henning **D:** Fr £22.50–£25.00 **S:** Fr £25.00–£30.00 **Beds:** 1T 1D **Baths:** 2 En (2)

Bentley

SU7844

Pittersfield, *Hole Lane, Bentley, Farnham, Surrey, GU10 5LT.* Mews style accommodation in converted stables. Separate from main house. **Open:** All year
01420 22414 (also fax) Mrs Coulton **D:** Fr £25.00–£30.00 **S:** Fr £30.00–£40.00 **Beds:** 1T 1D 1S **Baths:** 2 Pr (3)

Vine Farmhouse, *Isington, Bentley, Alton, Hants, GU34 4PW.* Beautiful secluded riverside setting. Enchanting view over meadows & pasture. **Open:** All year (not Xmas)
01420 23262 (also fax) Mrs Sinclair *vinefarm@aol.com* **D:** Fr £17.50–£25.00 **S:** Fr £25.00–£35.00 **Beds:** 1F 1D 1S **Baths:** 1 En 1 Pr (4)

Bentworth

SU6640

Newmans Cottage, *Drury Lane, Bentworth, Alton, Hampshire, GU34 5RJ.* C17th cottage of great character in lovely gardens overlooking countryside. **Open:** All year (not Xmas/New Year)
01420 563707 *AdmiralD@aol.com* **D:** Fr £20.00–£22.50 **S:** Fr £25.00–£30.00 **Beds:** 1D **Baths:** 1 Pr (2)

Bordon

SU7935 *Robin Hood*

Bunga Raya, *36 Forest Road, Bordon, Hants, GU35 0PT.* Bungalow. Suitable for less abled. Situated close to main A3 trunk road. **Open:** All year (not Xmas/New Year)
01420 473835 & 01420 474191 Mrs Morrish **D:** Fr £30.00 **S:** Fr £15.00 **Beds:** 2F 2T 2D 1S **Baths:** 3 Sh (3)

Braishfield

SU3725

Cranford Farm, *Rudd Lane, Braishfield, Romsey, Hants, SO51 0PY.* **Open:** All year
01794 368216 (also fax) Mr Brooks **D:** Fr £22.50–£32.50 **S:** Fr £35.00 **Beds:** 3F 1T 2D **Baths:** 6 En
Cranford Farm is a large secluded farmhouse set in 3 acres of farmland in the beautiful Test Valley. Just off A3057 between Braishfield and Michelmersh. All rooms are comfortably furnished with colour TV, tea and coffee. All ensuite.

Springwood, *Crook Hill, Braishfield, Romsey, Hants, SO51 0QB.* Opposite Hillier gardens/arboretum. 2.5 acres includes copse. French spoken. **Open:** All year
01794 368134 Mrs Dickens **D:** Fr £20.00–£22.00 **S:** Fr £22.00–£24.00 **Beds:** 1D **Baths:** 1 Pr (4)

Bramshaw

SU2716

Forge Cottage, *Stocks Cross, Bramshaw, Lyndhurst, SO43 7JB.* Private rooms situated within the beautiful gardens of Listed cottage. **Open:** All year (not Xmas/New Year)
023 8081 3873 Mr & Mrs Davies *idavies1@aol.com* www.newforest-uk.com/forgecottage.htm **D:** Fr £22.50–£27.50 **S:** Fr £45.00
Beds: 1D 1T **Baths:** 2 En (3)

Bransgore

SZ1998

The Corner House, *Betsy Lane, Bransgore, Christchurch, Hants., BH23 8AQ.* Family house, edge of village, close to forest and pubs. **Open:** All year (not Xmas/New Year)
01425 673201 J Staniland **D:** Fr £20.00 **S:** Fr £22.00 **Beds:** 1F 1T **Baths:** 2 En (3)

Brockenhurst

SU2902

Little Heathers, *13 Whitemoor Road, Brockenhurst, Hants, SO42 7QG.* Friendly comfortable spacious bungalow, quiet location, 3-7 days special breaks. **Open:** All year
01590 623512 Mrs Harris **Fax: 01590 624255** *little_heathers@hotmail.com* www.newforest.demon.co.uk/littleheathers.htm **D:** Fr £24.00–£30.00 **S:** Fr £30.00–£35.00 **Beds:** 1T 1D **Baths:** 2 En (5)

Seraya Guest House, *8 Grigg Lane, Brockenhurst, Hants, SO42 7RE.* Family-run B&B in heart of New Forest. Easy reach Portsmouth, Stonehenge, Bournemouth, IOW. **Open:** All year
01590 622426 Mrs Ward *edwin.ward@btinternet.com* **D:** Fr £20.00–£28.00 **S:** Fr £22.00–£25.00 **Beds:** 2D 1T **Baths:** 1 Sh 1 En (4)

Crossings, *Lyndhurst Road, Brockenhurst, Hampshire, SO42 7RL.* Comfortable family home near railway, shops, forest. Good hearty breakfast. **Open:** All year **Grades:** AA 2 Diamond
01590 622478 Mrs Ferguson **D:** Fr £20.00–£23.00 **S:** Fr £25.00–£30.00 **Beds:** 1T 2D **Baths:** 1 Sh (2)

Hilden, *Southampton Road, Boldre, Brockenhurst, Hampshire, SO41 8PT.* Large, comfortable Edwardian house, 50 yards open New Forest, 2.5m sea. **Open:** All year
01590 623682 Mrs Arnold-Brown **Fax: 01590 624444** www.newforestbandb-hilden.co.uk **D:** Fr £20.00–£25.00 **S:** Fr £20.00–£35.00
Beds: 3F **Baths:** 3 En (6)

Goldenhayes, *9 Chestnut Road, Brockenhurst, Hants, SO42 7RF.* Owner-occupied home in central but quiet situation, large garden. **Open:** All year **Grades:** ETC 2 Diamond
01590 623743 B Curtis **D:** Fr £18.00–£20.00 **S:** Fr £20.00–£24.00 **Beds:** 1F 1S **Baths:** 1 Sh

Brookside Cottage, *Collyers Road, Brockenhurst, Hants, SO42 7SE.* Picturesque cottage, secluded area. Golf, riding, walking, famous gardens nearby. **Open:** All year (not Xmas) **Grades:** ETC 3 Diamond
01590 623973 Mrs Branfoot *mbranfoot@tiscali.co.uk* **D:** Fr £27.00–£28.00 **S:** Fr £27.00–£28.00 **Beds:** 1T 1S **Baths:** 1 Pr (2)

Thatched Cottage Hotel, *16 Brookley Road, Brockenhurst, Hampshire, SO42 7RR.* 400 year old cottage with double deluxe bedrooms. Superlative cuisine. **Open:** Feb to Dec
01590 623090 *sales@thatchedcottage.co.uk* www.thatchedcottage.co.uk **D:** Fr £45.00–£85.00 **S:** Fr £70.00–£90.00 **Beds:** 5D **Baths:** 5 En (12) (12) **cc**

Porthilly House, *Armstrong Road, Brockenhurst, Hants, SO42 7TA.* Luxurious king size suites in lovely, spacious 1920s house in heart of New Forest. **Open:** All year
01590 623182 Mrs Brown **Fax: 01590 622178** *sue@bandbnewforest.co.uk* www.bandbnewforest.co.uk **D:** Fr £29.00–£32.00 **S:** Fr £40.00–£50.00 **Beds:** 2D **Baths:** 2 En (8) (4)

Briardale, *11 Noel Close, Brockenhurst, Hants., SO42 7RP.* Friendly comfortable home - quiet yet close to village & forest. **Open:** Feb to Dec
01590 623946 (also fax) Mrs Parkin **D:** Fr £22.50–£27.00 **S:** Fr £32.00–£40.00 **Beds:** 2D **Baths:** 2 En (3)

Broughton

SU3133

Kings, *Salisbury Road, Broughton, Stockbridge, SO20 8BY.* Standing in half acre of garden, surrounded by open countryside. **Open:** All year (not Xmas/New Year)
01794 301458 Mrs Heather **D:** Fr £18.00 **S:** Fr £18.00 **Beds:** 1T 1S **Baths:** 1 Pr (3)

The Old Plough, *High Street, Broughton, Stockbridge, Hampshire, SO20 8AE.* Charming Listed cottage in idyllic village between Winchester and Salisbury. **Open:** All year (not Xmas)
01794 301598 Mrs Paul *paul_family@broughton26.freeserve.co.uk* **D:** Fr £20.00 **S:** Fr £25.00 **Beds:** 1D **Baths:** 1 Pr (1)

Burghclere

SU4761

The Old Station, *Spring Lane, Burghclere, Newbury, Berks, RG20 9JP.* **Open:** All year (not Xmas/New Year)
01635 278560 Mrs Saint *chris.saint@btopenworld.com* **D:** Fr £18.00–£28.00 **S:** Fr £20.00–£40.00 **Beds:** 1T 1D 1S **Baths:** 1 En 1 Sh (10) (3)
Victorian railway station in 2.5 acre garden. High quality accommodation three miles south of Newbury 1/2 mil from A34. Ideal for touring/walking. Oxford, Winchester, Reading, Salisbury within one hour drive. Near Highclere Castle, Sandham Memorial Chapel. Brochure available.

Buriton

SU7320

Nursted Farm, *Buriton, Petersfield, Hants, GU31 5RW.* Relax in the atmosphere of our 300-year-old farmhouse. **Open:** May to Feb
01730 264278 Mrs Bray **D:** Fr £20.00 **S:** Fr £20.00 **Beds:** 3T **Baths:** 1 Pr 1 Sh

Burley

SU2103

Charlwood, *Longmead Road, Burley, Ringwood, Hants, BH24 4BY.* Country house. Lovely gardens, views, quiet. Rural - off main road. **Open:** Feb to Nov
01425 403242 Mrs Russell *charlwoodbnb@aol.com* www.newforest.demon.co.uk/charlwood.htm **D:** Fr £24.00–£26.00 **S:** Fr £28.00–£32.00 **Beds:** 1D 1T **Baths:** 1 Sh (3)

Great Wells House, *Beechwood Lane, Burley, Ringwood, Hants, BH24 4AS.* Beautiful period property in the heart of the New Forest. **Open:** Feb to Nov **Grades:** ETC 5 Diamond
01425 402302 (also fax) Mrs Stewart *carolestewart@pobox.com* www.greatwells.com
D: Fr £25.00–£40.00 **S:** Fr £35.00–£60.00
Beds: 3D **Baths:** 3 En (10)

Bay Tree House, *1 Clough Lane, Burley, Ringwood, Hants, BH24 4AE.* Large garden, lovely walks, cycle hire, riding, fishing nearby. Good English breakfast, home produce. **Open:** Mar to Oct
01425 403215 (also fax) Mrs Allen *baytreehousebandb@burleyhants.freeserve.co.uk* www.smoothhound.co.uk/hotels/baytree
D: Fr £23.00–£26.00 **S:** Fr £23.00–£26.00
Beds: 1F 1S **Baths:** 1 Sh (4)

Toad Hall, *The Cross, Burley, Ringwood, Hampshire, BH24 4AB.* Spectacularly at the heart of the new forest. **Open:** All year
01425 403448 Fax: 01425 402058 D: Fr £23.00–£45.00 **S:** Fr £40.00–£50.00 **Beds:** 2T 6D 2S **Baths:** 10 En **cc**

Cadnam

SU2913

Bushfriers, *Winsor Road, Winsor, Southampton, SO40 2HF.* Forest cottage, peaceful surroundings, New Forest Heritage Area, highly rated breakfasts. **Open:** All year (not Xmas)
023 8081 2552 Mr & Mrs Wright *bushfriers@bushinternet.com* www.smoothhound.co.uk/hotels/bushfriers.html **D:** Fr £25.00 **S:** Fr £30.00 **Beds:** 2D **Baths:** 1 Pr 1 En (2)

Chandlers Ford

SU4320

133 Bournemouth Road, *Chandlers Ford, Eastleigh, Hants, SO53 3HA.* Comfortable accommodation, choice of breakfast. Easy access to M3/M27.
Open: All year
023 8025 4801 (also fax) Mr Lanham **D:** Fr £20.00–£21.00 **S:** Fr £20.00–£21.00 **Beds:** 1F 1S **Baths:** 1 Sh

Blackbird Hill, *24 Ashbride Rise, Chandlers Ford, Eastleigh, Hampshire, SO53 1SA.* Detached bungalow in quiet residential area. Easy access to M3 and M27. **Open:** All year (not Xmas)
023 8026 0398 D: Fr £20.00–£22.00 **S:** Fr £20.00–£22.00 **Beds:** 1D 1S **Baths:** 1 Sh (5) (1)

Cheriton

SU5828

The Garden House, *Cheriton, Alresford, Hampshire, SO24 0QQ.* Edge of pretty village. Tennis court. Near Cheriton Battle Field. Personal tour by arrangement. **Open:** All year
01962 771352 & 01962 771666 Mrs Verney **Fax: 01962 771667** *verney@standrewsball.co.uk*
D: Fr £20.00–£24.00 **S:** Fr £20.00–£24.00
Beds: 2T 1D **Baths:** 1 Pr 1 Sh (4)

Chilbolton

SU3940

Tefilah House, *10 Test Rise, Chilbolton, Stockbridge, Hants, SO20 6AF.* Comfortable, homely accommodation. Picturesque village. Ideal touring/walking/fishing.
Open: All year (not Xmas/New Year)
01264 860553 & 07803 913272 (M) Mr & Mrs Burberry *roland.burberry@lineone.net* **D:** Fr £20.00 **S:** Fr £25.00 **Beds:** 1T **Baths:** 1 En (1)

The Rectory, *Chilbolton, Stockbridge, SO20 6BA.* Large bungalow situated centrally near pub in beautiful village. **Open:** All year
01264 860258 (also fax) Mrs Williams *errolw@compuserve.com* **D:** Fr £20.00 **S:** Fr £20.00–£25.00 **Beds:** 1F 1S **Baths:** 1 En 1 Pr

Cliddesden

SU6348

The Hatchings, *Woods Lane, Cliddesden, Basingstoke, Hampshire, RG25 2JF.* Warm welcome. Breakfast served in own large bedrooms overlooking garden.
Open: All year **Grades:** AA 4 Diamond
01256 465279 Mr & Mrs Hatchaman **D:** Fr £29.50–£33.00 **S:** Fr £29.50–£33.00 **Beds:** 1D 2S **Baths:** 1 En 2 Pr (10) (10)

Compton

SU4625 *The Otter*

Wood Ridge, *Field Close, Compton Down, Compton, Winchester, Hampshire, SO21 2AP.* Rural area, convenient for Winchester, New Forest and South Coast.
Open: All year (not Xmas/New Year)
01962 711226 *attufnell@hotmail.com* **D:** Fr £20.00–£25.00 **S:** Fr £20.00–£30.00 **Beds:** 1T 2S **Baths:** 1 En 1 Sh (3)

RATES
D = Price range per person sharing in a double or twin room
S = Price range for a single room

Crondall

SU7948

Peperstiche, *Itchel Lane, Crondall, Farnham, Surrey, GU10 5PT.* Beautiful family house overlooking farmland. Friendly welcome. Memorable breakfasts. **Open:** All year (not Xmas)
01252 850156 Mr & Mrs Thomas *peperstich@aol.com* **D:** Fr £25.00–£30.00 **S:** Fr £25.00–£35.00 **Beds:** 2D 1S **Baths:** 1 En 2 Sh (5) (8)

Crux Easton

SU4256

Manor House, *Crux Easton, Newbury, Hants, RG20 9QF.* Historic farmhouse in quiet village, lovely views, near Highclere Castle.
Open: All year
01635 254314 Mrs O'Shaughnessy **Fax: 01635 254246 D:** Fr £25.00 **S:** Fr £25.00
Beds: 3T **Baths:** 2 Sh (8)

Dibden

SU4008

Dale Farm Guest House, *Manor Road, Applemore Hill, Dibden, Southampton, SO45 5TJ.* Olde world farmhouse with direct access to the New Forest, horse riding next door.
Open: All year **Grades:** ETC 3 Diamond
023 8084 9632 Mrs Archdeacon **Fax: 023 8084 0285** *info@dalefarmhouse.co.uk* www.dalefarmhouse.co.uk **D:** Fr £19.50–£26.00 **S:** Fr £25.50–£32.00 **Beds:** 1F 1T 3D 1S **Baths:** 4 Pr 2 Sh

Dummer

SU5845

Oakdown Farm, *Dummer, Basingstoke, Hants, RG23 7LR.* Secluded modern farm bungalow next to M3 J7 on Wayfarers' Walk. **Open:** All year **Grades:** ETC 3 Diamond
01256 397218 Mrs Hutton **D:** Fr £20.00–£25.00 **S:** Fr £20.00 **Beds:** 1D 2T **Baths:** 1 Sh (12) (4)

BEDROOMS
D = Double
T = Twin
S = Single
F = Family

East Wellow
SU3020

Roselea, *Hamdown Crescent, East Wellow, Romsey, Hampshire, SO51 6BJ.* Quiet mainly ground floor accommodation, near New Forest and M27. **Open:** All year (not Xmas) **Grades:** ETC 4 Diamond
01794 323262 (also fax) Mr & Mrs Cossburn *beds@roselea.info* www.roselea.info **D:** Fr £20.00–£22.50 **S:** Fr £18.00–£25.00 **Beds:** 1D 1T 1S **Baths:** 2 En 1 Sh (8) (2)

Emery Down
SU2808

Stable End Guest House, *Mill Lane, Emery Down, Lyndhurst, Hants, SO43 7FJ.* Lovely forest views and usually ponies outside the gate. **Open:** All year
023 8028 2504 (also fax) Mrs Dibben *dibbenfam@aol.com* **D:** Fr £25.00–£30.00 **S:** Fr £25.00–£30.00 **Beds:** 1D 1T **Baths:** 2 En (4)

Emsworth
SU7406

Bunbury Lodge, *10 West Road, Emsworth, Hampshire, PO10 7JT.* Perfect location 250 yards from Emsworth Harbour Foreshore. Superb breakfast. **Open:** All year **Grades:** ETC 4 Diamond
01243 432030 Mr & Mrs Knight *bunbury.lodge@breathemail.net* **D:** Fr £25.00–£30.00 **S:** Fr £35.00–£40.00 **Beds:** 1D 1F **Baths:** 1 En 1 Pr (5) (4)

Ewshot
SU8149

The Oast House, *Ewshot, Farnham, Hampshire, GU10 5BP.* Charming oasthouse c1850, peaceful rural village, 10 mins M3. **Open:** All year
01252 850474 (also fax) Mrs Morgan **D:** Fr £20.00–£25.00 **S:** Fr £25.00–£30.00 **Beds:** 1F 1T 1D 1S **Baths:** 1 En 1 Sh (6)

Fareham
SU5606

Beaulieu, *67 Portchester Road, Fareham, Hants, PO16 8AP.* Detached house, pleasant gardens, non-smoking, near golf club. M27 (J11) 1m. **Open:** All year
01329 232461 (also fax) Mrs Wycherley **D:** Fr £22.50 **S:** Fr £20.00–£30.00 **Beds:** 1D 1T 1S **Baths:** 1 Sh (3)

Planning a longer stay? Always ask for any special rates

Irish Shebeen, *63 Laburnum Road, Fareham, Hants, PO16 0SN.* Friendly place near HMS Collingwood and Fleetland, Fort Fareham, New Gate Lane. **Open:** All year
01329 232643 Mrs McGuinness *aneta_mcguinness@hotmail.com* **D:** Fr £15.00–£18.00 **S:** Fr £15.00–£18.00 **Beds:** 1T 1D 2S **Baths:** 1 En 1 Pr

Fawley
SU4603

Walcot House, *Blackfield Road, Fawley, Southampton, SO45 1ED.* Home from home. Good location for touring the area. **Open:** All year
023 8089 1344 Fax: 023 8089 0748 **D:** Fr £18.50–£20.00 **S:** Fr £19.00–£22.00 **Beds:** 1T 1D 5S **Baths:** 1 En 1 Sh (13) cc

Fordingbridge
SU1414

Hillbury, *2 Fir Tree Hill, Camel Green, Alderholt, Fordingbridge, Hants, SP6 3AY.* Large modern bungalow in peaceful surroundings. Warm welcome and comfortable. **Open:** All year **Grades:** ETC 3 Diamond
01425 652582 Mrs Sillence **Fax: 01425 657587** www.newforest.demon.co.uk/hillbury.htm **D:** Fr £19.00–£25.00 **S:** Fr £19.00–£25.00 **Beds:** 1F 1T 1S **Baths:** 1 Pr 1 Sh (4)

Fritham
SU2314

Primrose Cottage, *Fritham, Nr Lyndhurst, Hants, SO43 7HH.* Victorian cottage, forest access, your own lounge with views, garage. **Open:** Mar to Nov
023 8081 2272 Mr & Mrs Penfound www.smoothhound.co.uk/hotels/primrose.html **D:** Fr £19.00–£21.00 **S:** Fr £24.00–£26.00 **Beds:** 1D/T **Baths:** 1 Pr (8) (1)

Amberwood Cottage, *Fritham, Lyndhurst, Hants, SO43 7HL.* Self-contained. Off no through road, direct access into forest. **Open:** Mar to Oct
023 8081 2359 A Borrelli **D:** Fr £21.00 **Beds:** 1D **Baths:** 1 En

Funtley
SU5608

17 Lakeside, *Funtley, Fareham, Hants, PO17 5EP.* Lakeside location. Modern family house. Fishing, walking, horseriding all nearby. **Open:** All year (not Xmas/New Year)
01329 236128 L Moore **D:** Fr £17.00–£20.00 **S:** Fr £17.00–£20.00 **Beds:** 1T 2S **Baths:** 1 Sh (3)

Gosport
SU5900 *North Star, Bridgemary Manor Hotel*

Raysal, *90a Fareham Road, Gosport, Hants, PO13 0AG.* Family run guest house, large landscaped garden and sun lounge. **Open:** All year
01329 280093 Mrs Rolls **D:** Fr £19.00–£24.00 **S:** Fr £20.00–£25.00 (5) (6)

Greatham
SU7831

The Silver Birch Inn, *Petersfield Road (A325), Greatham, Liss, Hampshire, GU33 6AS.* Village Inn on three counties borders - Hampshire, Surrey, W Sussex. **Open:** All year
01420 538262 (also fax) *michelle@thesilverbirch.co.uk* **D:** Fr £24.00–£35.00 **S:** Fr £25.00–£29.50 **Beds:** 2F 2T 2D 2S **Baths:** 2 Pr 1 Sh (20) cc

Hamble
SU4706

Honeysuckle, *Flowers Close, Hamble, Southampton, Hants, SO31 4LU.* Bed and breakfast close to Hamble River, Marinas, pubs, yacht clubs. **Open:** All year (not Xmas)
023 8045 3209 (also fax) **D:** Fr £18.00–£20.00 **S:** Fr £20.00–£25.00 **Beds:** 2D **Baths:** 1 Sh (10) (2)

Hangersley
SU1706

Dunain Farm, *Hangersley, Ringwood, Hants, BH24 3JN.* Secluded bungalow, situated on high ground, 1.5 miles from Ringwood. **Open:** Mar to Oct
01425 472611 Mrs Griffin *dunain@aol.com* www.smoothhound.co.uk/hotels/dunain1.html **D:** Fr £19.00–£20.00 **S:** Fr £22.00–£24.00 **Beds:** 1F 1T 1D **Baths:** 1 Sh (8)

Havant
SU7107

Church View, *107 West Street, Havant, Hampshire, PO9 1LE.* Close town centre. Friendly welcome. Suit holiday/business visitors. Families accommodated. Full English breakfast. **Open:** Feb to Nov
023 9247 2405 Mrs Bryant **D:** Fr £20.00 **S:** Fr £25.00 **Beds:** 1D **Baths:** 1 Pr (5) (1)

Hayling Island

SU7201

Ravensdale, *19 St Catherines Road, Hayling Island, Hampshire, PO11 0HF.* Friendly welcome, quiet location, close to beach, excellent home cooking. **Open:** All year
023 9246 3203 & 07802 188259 Mr & Mrs Taylor **Fax: 023 9246 3203 D:** Fr £24.00–£27.00 **S:** Fr £32.00 **Beds:** 1F 3D **Baths:** 2 En (8) (6)

The Old Vine, *67 Havant Road, Hayling Island, Hampshire, PO11 0PT.* Easy access, beach, country, windsurfing, marinas. peaceful gardens. Warm welcome. **Open:** All year
023 9246 2543 Mrs Panagiotidis *theoldvine@aol.com* **D:** Fr £20.00–£24.00 **S:** Fr £25.00–£30.00 **Beds:** 1F 1T 1D **Baths:** 2 Pr (8)

Maidlings, *55 Staunton Avenue, Hayling Island, Hants, PO11 0EW.* Delightful family home close to beach with a great breakfast. **Open:** All year (not Xmas/New Year) **Grades:** ETC 3 Diamond
023 9246 6357 Mrs Harper **D:** Fr £20.00–£25.00 **S:** Fr £25.00 **Beds:** 2D 1T (3)

Anns Cottage, *45 St Andrews Road, Hayling Island, Hants, PO11 9JN.* Quiet location opposite open parkland. Good English breakfast, 60 yards seafront. **Open:** All year
023 9246 7048 Mrs Jay *ann.jay@virgin.net* **D:** Fr £20.00–£25.00 **S:** Fr £20.00–£25.00 **Beds:** 1F 1D 1T **Baths:** 1 Sh 1 En (3)

Autumn Cottage, *12 St Mary's Road, Hayling Island, Hants, PO11 9BY.* Friendly seaside quality accommodation. Attractive gardens. Midway Chichester & Portsmouth. **Open:** All year
023 9246 3296 Mrs Hooper **D:** Fr £23.00–£25.00 **S:** Fr £28.00–£30.00 **Beds:** 1F 1T **Baths:** 1 Sh (2)

Redwalls, *66 Staunton Avenue, Hayling Island, Hampshire, PO11 0EW.* Non-smoking superior, quiet accommodation close to the sea. Extensive breakfasts. **Open:** All year (not Xmas/New Year) **Grades:** RAC 3 Diamond
023 9246 6109 Mr & Mrs Grover *daphne@redwalls66.co.uk* www.redwalls.co.uk **D:** Fr £20.00–£22.50 **S:** Fr £25.00–£30.00 **Beds:** 2T 1D **Baths:** 2 En 1 Pr (4)

Farmhouse, *23 Sandy Point Road, Hayling Island, Hampshire, PO11 9RP.* 1900s farmhouse close to beach and sailing club. Warm welcome. **Open:** All year (not Xmas/New Year)
023 9246 9287 *penny-bennet@madasafish.com* **D:** Fr £13.00–£19.00 **S:** Fr £18.00–£24.00 **Beds:** 2T 1D **Baths:** 1 Sh (4)

Highclere

SU4360

Highclere Farm, *Highclere, Newbury, Hampshire, RG20 9PY.* Situated in designated Area of Outstanding Natural Beauty. Close to Highclere Castle & Newbury Racecourse. **Open:** All year (not Xmas/New Year)
01635 255013 Mrs Walsh *walshhighclere@newburyweb.com* **D:** Fr £25.00 **S:** Fr £40.00 **Beds:** 1F 1D **Baths:** 1 En

Holybourne

SU7340

25 Downs View, *Holybourne, Alton, Hants, GU34 4HY.* Good quality accommodation, semi-rural location. Ideal walking/touring South Downs and South Coast. **Open:** All year (not Xmas/New Year)
01420 541723 Ms Honnor **Fax: 01420 541920** *bethanyhonnor@yahoo.co.uk* **D:** Fr £25.00–£30.00 **S:** Fr £27.50–£30.00 **Beds:** 1T 1D **Baths:** 1 En 1 Pr (8) (5)

Hordle

SZ2795

Spinney Cottage, *219 Everton Road, Hordle, Lymington, Hants, SO41 0HE.* Welcome, charming, New Forest Home. Rural setting, superb breakfasts. **Open:** Jan to Oct
01590 644555 (also fax) Mrs Blackwell *spinneycottage@aol.com* www.spinneycottage.co.uk **D:** Fr £22.00–£25.00 **S:** Fr £22.00–£26.00 **Beds:** 2D 1S **Baths:** 2 Pr (3)

Horton Heath

SU4916

Sandelwood, *Knowle Lane, Horton Heath, Eastleigh, Hants, SO50 7DZ.* Quiet country house, extensive rural views. Friendly. Comfortable attractive rooms. **Open:** All year
023 8069 3726 Mrs Phipp **D:** Fr £44.00–£48.00 **S:** Fr £22.00–£26.00 **Beds:** 1F 1D **Baths:** 2 En (3)

Hurstbourne Priors

SU4346

The Hurstbourne, *Hurstbourne Priors, Whitchurch, Hants, RG28 7SE.* Public house, offering good food and quality ales. **Open:** All year
01256 892000 Mr & Mrs Essen **Fax: 01256 895351 D:** Fr £20.00–£25.00 **S:** Fr £25.00 **Beds:** 3F 2D 1T **Baths:** 1 Sh cc

Itchen Abbas

SU5332

The Trout, *Itchen Abbas, Winchester, Hampshire, SO21 1BQ.* Set in the heart of the Itchen Valley, a stone's throw away from the beautiful River Itchen. Ideal for the keen fisherman. We have a superb non-smoking restaurant with excellent food, real ales and wines of the world. **Open:** All year
01962 779537 Emma Howe **Fax: 01962 791046** *thetroutinn@freeuk.com* **D:** Fr £35.00 **S:** Fr £40.00 **Beds:** 2T 3D **Baths:** 5 En cc

Itchen Stoke

SU5532

The Parsonage, *Itchen Stoke, Alresford, Hants, SO24 0QU.* Modern house, quiet rural setting, very central for touring. **Open:** All year (not Xmas)
01962 732123 Mrs Pitt **D:** Fr £22.00 **S:** Fr £22.00 **Beds:** 1T **Baths:** 1 Sh (20)

Kilmeston

SU5926

Dean Farm, *Kilmeston, Alresford, Hants, SO24 0NL.* C18th working farm. Comfortable lounge with log fires. Nearby pubs. **Open:** All year (not Xmas)
01962 771286 Mrs Warr *warrdeanfarm@aol.com* **D:** Fr £22.50 **S:** Fr £25.00–£30.00 **Beds:** 2D 1T **Baths:** 1 Sh (10) (3)

Kingsley

SU7838 *Cricketers*

30 Churchfields, *Kingsley, Bordon, Hants, GU35 9PJ.* Modern village house adjoining commonland. Close Selborne, Chawton, Watercress Line. **Open:** All year (not Xmas/New Year)
01420 472271 Mrs Clack **D:** Fr £20.00–£22.50 **S:** Fr £22.50–£25.00 **Beds:** 1D 1S **Baths:** 1 Pr (2)

Kingston

SU1402

Greenacres Farmhouse, *Christchurch Road, Kingston, Ringwood, Hants, BH24 3BJ.* Comfortable Victorian family home near New Forest and River Avon. **Open:** All year (not Xmas)
01425 480945 Mrs Armstrong **D:** Fr £18.00 **S:** Fr £20.00 **Beds:** 1D 2T **Baths:** 1 En 1 Sh (5)

Planning a longer stay? Always ask for any special rates

Please respect a B&B's wishes regarding children, animals and smoking

Langley

SU4400

Langley Village Restaurant & Guest House, *Lepe Road, Langley, Southampton, SO45 1XR.* Close to Motor Museum, Beaulieu, Exbury Gardens and Calshot Castle. **Open:** All year (not Xmas)
023 8089 1667 Mrs McEvoy *alexismcevoy@tinyworld.co.uk* www.langley-hampshire.co.uk **D:** Fr £22.50 **S:** Fr £22.50 **Beds:** 1D 1T 2S **Baths:** 1 Sh (12) (8)

Lee-on-the-Solent

SU5600

Chester Lodge, *20 Chester Crescent, Lee-on-the-Solent, Gosport, Hampshire, PO13 9BH.* Family-run, quiet location, convenient for exploring the Solent area. **Open:** All year (not Xmas/New Year)
023 9255 0894 Mrs Jeffery **Fax: 023 9255 6291 D:** Fr £19.00 **S:** Fr £25.00 **Beds:** 1D 1F 1S **Baths:** 2 Sh (6)

Liphook

SU8431

The Bailiffs Cottage, *Hollycombe, Liphook, Hants, GU30 7LR.* **Open:** All year **Grades:** ETC 3 Diamond
01428 722171 Mr & Mrs Jenner **Fax: 01428 729394** *jenner@bailiffs.fsnet.co.uk* **D:** Fr £21.00–£23.00 **S:** Fr £21.00–£23.00 **Beds:** 1T 1S **Baths:** 1 Sh (3)
Quiet friendly comfortable C18th cottage with beautiful views and garden. Easy access to London, Portsmouth, Chichester, Farnham. On Hants/Sussex/Surrey border. 2 miles Liphook station. Min rate for more than two nights. Special rates for 4 weekday nights. Long term.

RATES
D = Price range per person sharing in a double or twin room
S = Price range for a single room

Long Sutton

SU7447

Four Horseshoes Country Inn, *The Street, Long Sutton, Hook, Hampshire, RG29 1TA.* **Open:** All year
01256 862488 & 01256 862441 Mr Brooks **Fax: 01256 862488** *tony.brooks@bun.com* www.fourhorseshoes.com **D:** Fr £30.00–£35.00 **S:** Fr £30.00–£35.00 **Beds:** 2T 2S **Baths:** 4 En (30) **cc**
Tony & Sheila Brooks welcome visitors of all ages to their charming country free house, situated on the Harrow Way. Customers come on foot, by bicycle and in cars to this homely 200-year-old pub, not far from Junction 5 of the M3. Inside the main area are low beamed ceilings, wheel back chairs and open fires, with an array of brass and copper ornaments, prints and photographs. The kitchen serves bar snacks to full meals, with a popular Sunday carvery. The pub's regular quiz nights are always well attended. For something more active there is pétanque in the large beer garden or the monthly Sunday morning off road mountain bike ride. Lots of play equipment for the children to enjoy. Long Sutton, a village of brick and timber cottages, lies South of Odiham in open countryside off the B3349. The parish church of All Saints dates from C13th, with a set of C16th bells.

Longparish

SU4344

Yew Cottage, *Longparish, Andover, Hampshire, SP11 6QE.* Cosy thatched cottage in beautiful village on the River Test. **Open:** All year
01264 720325 Mr & Mrs Lowry *yewcottage@ukgateway.net* **D:** Fr £20.00–£25.00 **S:** Fr £22.50–£27.50 **Beds:** 2T 1S **Baths:** 1 En 1 Sh (3)

Lymington

SZ3295 *Chequers, Red Lion, Mayflower, Ship Inn, Musketeers*

Monks Pool, *Waterford Lane, Lymington, Hants, SO41 3PS.* Unique spacious home. Centre Lymington. Large, sunny garden, private lake. **Open:** Jan to Dec
01590 678850 (also fax) M C Otten *cam@monkspool.swinternet.co.uk* **D:** Fr £20.00–£30.00 **S:** Fr £25.00–£35.00 **Beds:** 2D 1T **Baths:** 2 En 1 Sh (4)

Jevington, *47 Waterford Lane, Lymington, Hants, SO41 3PT.* Comfortable family-run B&B, in quiet lane yet only few minutes' walk to town. **Open:** All year
01590 672148 (also fax) Mr & Mrs Carruthers *jevingtonbb@lineone.net* www.caruthers.co.uk **D:** Fr £22.00–£25.00 **S:** Fr £22.00–£35.00 **Beds:** 1F 1D 1T **Baths:** 3 En (4) (4)

Admiral House, *3 Stanley Road, Lymington, Hants, SO41 3SJ.* Comfortable accommodation near pubs, shops, coastal walk, marinas and forest. **Open:** All year
01590 674339 Mrs Wild *bill@wild27.freeserve.co.uk* **D:** Fr £12.00–£14.00 **S:** Fr £12.00–£14.00 **Beds:** 3S 1T **Baths:** 1 Sh

Acorn Shetland Pony Stud, *Meadows Cottage, Arnewood Bridge Road, Lymington, Hampshire, SO41 6DA.* In 6.5 acres. Gr/fl rooms onto patios. Indoor splashpool. **Open:** All year
04590 682000 Mrs Oakhill **Fax: 01590 682000** *meadows.cottage@virgin.net* **D:** Fr £20.00–£25.00 **S:** Fr £25.00–£30.00 **Beds:** 1F 1T 1D **Baths:** 3 En (2)

The Rowans, *76 Southampton Road, Lymington, Hants, SO41 9GZ.* Delightful detached period house, 5 mins' walk to High Street. **Open:** All year
01590 672276 & 07860 630361 (M) Mrs Baddock **Fax: 01590 688610 D:** Fr £20.00–£25.00 **S:** Fr £20.00–£27.00 **Beds:** 3F 3D 3T **Baths:** 3 En (5) (6)

Lyndhurst

SU2908

Forest Cottage, *High Street, Lyndhurst, Hants, SO43 7BH.* Delightful 300-year-old cottage. Warm, comfortable and friendly. **Open:** All year (not Xmas) **Grades:** ETC 4 Diamond, SIlver
023 8028 3461 Mrs Rowland www.forestcottage.i12.com **D:** Fr £23.00–£25.00 **S:** Fr £23.00–£25.00 **Beds:** 1D 1T 1S **Baths:** 2 Sh (3)

Owl Cottage, *Clayhill, Lyndhurst, Hants, SO43 7DE.* Off beaten track, direct access to forest - escape for a while. **Open:** All year
023 8028 3800 Mr & Mrs Lowe **D:** Fr £20.00 **Beds:** 1D 1S **Baths:** 1 En (6)

Planning a longer stay? Always ask for any special rates

The Laurels, *9 Wellands Road, Lyndhurst, Hants, SO43 7AB.* Excellent accommodation, quiet, central, New Forest location. Warm welcome guaranteed. **Open:** All year (not Xmas)
023 8028 2545 Mrs Kennard *kennard.laurels@virgin.net* www.smoothhound.co.uk/hotels/laur.html **D:** Fr £20.00–£22.00 **S:** Fr £20.00 **Beds:** 1D/T **Baths:** 1 Pr (8) (1)

The Penny Farthing Hotel, *Romsey Road, Lyndhurst, Hampshire, SO43 7AA.* **Open:** All year (not Xmas) **Grades:** ETC 4 Diamond
023 8028 4422 Mr & Mrs Saqui **Fax: 023 8028 4488** *stay@pennyfarthinghotel.co.uk* www.pennyfarthinghotel.co.uk **D:** Fr £29.50–£45.00 **S:** Fr £35.00–£45.00 **Beds:** 2F 12D 3T 3S **Baths:** 20 En (15)
Welcome to our cheerful hotel, ideally situated in Lyndhurst village centre. We offer a variety of rooms that are all ensuite with colour TV, tea/coffee tray and telephones. Large car park, secure bike store. New Forest Visitor Centre 5 mins' walk.

Rose Cottage, *Chapel Lane, Lyndhurst, Hants, SO43 7FG.* Charming cottage set in beautiful, peaceful garden, close to forest and village. **Open:** All year **Grades:** ETC 4 Diamond
023 8028 3413 (also fax) Mrs Dawson *cindy@rosecottageb-b.freeserve.co.uk* www.rosecottageb-b.freeserve.co.uk **D:** Fr £22.00–£25.00 **S:** Fr £25.00–£30.00 **Beds:** 1F 2D **Baths:** 1 En 1 Sh (6)

Clarendon Villa, *Gosport Lane, Lyndhurst, Hants, SO43 7BL.* Victorian family house, village centre, breakfast served in your room. **Open:** All year (not Xmas)
023 8028 2803 M Preston **Fax: 023 8028 4303** *clarendonvilla@i12.com* www.clarendonvilla.i12.com **D:** Fr £22.50–£30.00 **S:** Fr £25.00–£35.00 **Beds:** 1F 2D **Baths:** 3 En (4) cc

Whitemoor House Hotel, *Southampton Road, Lyndhurst, Hants, SO43 7BU.* Friendly, relaxed atmosphere; opposite open forest, mins from village centre. **Open:** All year
023 8028 2186 Ms Scregg *whitemoor@aol.com* www.smoothhound.co.uk/hotels/whitemoo.html **D:** Fr £27.50–£35.00 **S:** Fr £35.00–£45.00 **Beds:** 2F 4D 2T **Baths:** 8 En (8) cc

Mapledurwell

SU6951

Eastside Coach House, *Frog Lane, Mapledurwell, Basingstoke, Hants, RG25 2LP.* A unique very attractive property sitting in the bed of the Basingstoke Canal. **Open:** All year
01256 465559 & 01256 363311 Mr & Mrs Cashmore **Fax: 01256 465559** *eastside@breathmail.net* **D:** Fr £20.00–£25.00 **S:** Fr £25.00–£30.00 **Beds:** 2F 1D 4T 2S **Baths:** 3 En 1 Pr 2 Sh (12)

Medstead

SU6537

Orchard View, *High Street, Medstead, Alton, Hants., GU34 5LN.* Modern bungalow secluded ample parking central for touring bus route. **Open:** All year (not Xmas)
01420 562480 Mrs Westbrook *debbie0001@hotmail.com* **D:** Fr £20.00–£25.00 **S:** Fr £20.00–£25.00 **Beds:** 1D 1T **Baths:** 1 En 1 Sh

Micheldever

SU5139

Orchard Close, *The Highways, Micheldever, Winchester, Hampshire, SO21 3BP.* Quiet spacious accommodation overlooking lawns and garden. Private off-road parking. 6m city centre. **Open:** All year
01962 774470 & 0585 482654 Mrs Holmes **D:** Fr £18.00–£20.00 **S:** Fr £25.00–£30.00 **Beds:** 1T 2D **Baths:** 1 En 1 Sh

Milford on Sea

SZ2891 *Smugglers, Red Lion*

Compton Hotel, *59 Keyhaven Road, Milford on Sea, Lymington, Hants, SO41 0QX.* Small private hotel with ensuite rooms and TV. Outdoor swimming pool. **Open:** All year (not Xmas/New Year)
01590 643117 Mr Emberson **D:** Fr £21.00–£24.00 **S:** Fr £30.00–£32.00 **Beds:** 1F 1T 4D 2S **Baths:** 4 En 1 Sh (8)

The Bay Trees, *8 High Street, Milford on Sea, Lymington, Hants, SO41 0QD.* **Open:** All year (not Xmas/New Year)
01590 642186 **D:** Fr £35.00–£40.00 **S:** Fr £40.00–£80.00 **Beds:** 1F 1T 2D **Baths:** 2 En 1 Sh cc
Lovely C17th home - a poorhouse in a previous life. Beautiful garden, a four poster room and superb bathrooms - only a short walk from the sea. Ideal for the New Forest and the coast.

Cherry Trees, *Lymington Road, Milford on Sea, Lymington, Hants, SO41 0QL.* Warm welcome assured at this lovely character retreat. Pretty rooms, delightful garden. **Open:** All year
01590 643746 & 07976 382828 (M) S Gadd *cherrytrees@beeb.net* **D:** Fr £20.00–£25.00 **S:** Fr £22.00–£35.00 **Beds:** 1F 1T 1D **Baths:** 2 En 1 Pr

Minstead

SU2811

Grove House, *Minstead, Lyndhurst, Hants, SO43 7GG.* New Forest small holding. Excellent comfort, varied breakfast, superb walking/riding. **Open:** All year
023 8081 3211 Mrs Dixon **D:** Fr £22.00–£25.00 **Beds:** 1T **Baths:** 1 Pr

Monk Sherborne

SU6056

Manor Farm, *Monk Sherborne, Basingstoke, Hants, RG26 5HW.* Traditional old farmhouse in a rural setting. **Open:** All year (not Xmas/New Year)
01256 850889 Mrs Dalgarno **D:** Fr £16.00 **S:** Fr £20.00–£22.00 **Beds:** 1D 1F **Baths:** 1 Sh (6)

Nether Wallop

SU3036 *Five Bells, George Inn*

Halcyon, *Church Hill, Nether Wallop, Stockbridge, Hants, SO20 8EY.* Extensive modern bungalow in quiet country lane with delightful views. **Open:** All year
01264 781348 Mrs Ayers **D:** Fr £22.00–£23.00 **S:** Fr £28.00–£30.00 **Beds:** 1F 1T 1S **Baths:** 1 En 1 Sh (6)

RATES

D = Price range per person sharing in a double or twin room

S = Price range for a single room

York Lodge, *Nether Wallop, Stockbridge, Hants, SO20 8HE.* **Open:** All year **Grades:** ETC 4 Diamond, AA 4 Diamond
01264 781313 Mrs Bradley *bradley@yorklodge.fslife.co.uk* www.york-lodge.co.uk **D:** Fr £25.00–£30.00 **S:** Fr £30.00–£35.00 **Beds:** 2D 2T **Baths:** 2 En (8)
Comfortable, self-contained accommodation in peaceful garden in picturesque village used as setting for Agatha Christie's 'Miss Marple' series. Ideal base for exploring Southern England (easy reach Winchester, Salisbury, Stonehenge). Excellent stopover for West Country. Adjacent A343/A30, 10 minutes A303.

New Alresford

SU5832

Tangletrees, *Broad Street, New Alresford, SO24 9AN.* High quality accommodation. Beautiful lake views. 2 mins town centre. Can be self-catering. **Open:** All year
01962 733174 Mrs Grey **Fax: 01962 734778** *roycepud@aol.com* **D:** Fr £25.00 **S:** Fr £30.00 **Beds:** 1T **Baths:** 1 En (3)

New Milton

SZ2395

Willy's Well, *Bashley Common Road, Wootton, New Milton, Hants, BH25 5SF.* **Open:** All year **Grades:** ETC 3 Diamond
01425 616834 *moyramac2@hotmail.com* **D:** Fr £22.50–£25.00 **S:** Fr £25.00–£30.00 **Beds:** 1T 1D **Baths:** 1 En 1 Pr
A warm welcome awaits you at our C18th thatched cottage. We are ideally situated for exploring the New Forest and coastal towns in the area. The cottage is set in 7 acres with 1 acre of garden. Bargain breaks available.

Saint Ursula, *30 Hobart Road, New Milton, Hants, BH25 6EG.* Ideal for New Forest/coast. Large comfortable house. Central. Disabled facilities. **Open:** All year **Grades:** ETC 3 Diamond
01425 613515 Mrs Pearce **D:** Fr £22.00–£25.00 **S:** Fr £40.00–£45.00 **Beds:** 1D 2T 1S **Baths:** 3 En 2 Pr 1 Sh (4) 3

RATES

D = Price range per person sharing in a double or twin room

S = Price range for a single room

Newtown (Newbury)

SU4763

White Cottage, *Newtown, Newbury, Berks, RG20 9AP.* Delightful semi-rural cottage on the edge of Watership Down. **Open:** All year (not Xmas)
01635 43097 & 07721 613224 (M) Mrs Meiklejohn *meiklejohn@onetel.co.uk* **D:** Fr £25.00–£30.00 **S:** Fr £27.00–£30.00 **Beds:** 1D 1T 1S **Baths:** 1 Sh (3)

Nursling

SU3716

Conifers, *6 Nursling Street Cottages, Nursling, Southampton, Hants, SO16 0XH.* Attractive 1930s cottage. Comfortable beds. Family Garden. Country pubs nearby. **Open:** All year **Grades:** ETC 3 Diamond
023 8034 9491 (also fax) Mrs Hinton **D:** Fr £20.00–£28.00 **S:** Fr £20.00–£28.00 **Beds:** 1F 1D 1S **Baths:** 1 En (2)

Oakhanger

SU7635

Ivanhoe, *Oakhanger, Bordon, Hants., GU35 9JG.* Comfortable accommodation with rural views. Small village central for walking. **Open:** All year (not Xmas/New Year)
01420 473464 Mrs Britton **D:** Fr £18.00 **S:** Fr £25.00 **Beds:** 1T **Baths:** 1 Pr (1)

Odiham

SU7451

Newlands Farm, *Odiham, Hook, Hampshire, RG29 1JD.* Period farmhouse, businessmen welcome. Quiet. Basins rooms, home-made bread, marmalade. **Open:** All year (not Xmas)
01256 702373 (also fax) Mrs Saunders **D:** Fr £16.00 **S:** Fr £16.00 **Beds:** 2S 1D **Baths:** 2 Sh (3)

Otterbourne

SU4623

8 Poles Lane, *Otterbourne, Winchester, Hampshire, SO23 2DS.* Modern accommodation, convenient for M3/New Forest. Ideal touring & ferries. **Open:** All year
01962 713048 Mrs Healey *the_healys@lineone.net* **D:** Fr £18.00–£22.00 **S:** Fr £18.00–£22.00 **Beds:** 1D 1S **Baths:** 1 Sh (12) (2)

Owslebury

SU5123

Mays Farmhouse, *Longwood Dean, Owslebury, Winchester, Hants, SO21 1JS.* Lovely C16th farmhouse, beautiful countryside; peaceful with good walks. **Open:** All year
01962 777486 Mrs Ashby **Fax: 01962 777747** *rosalieashby@maysfarm.fsnet.co.uk* **D:** Fr £22.50–£25.00 **S:** Fr £25.00–£30.00 **Beds:** 1F 1D 1T **Baths:** 3 Pr (7) (5)

Park Gate

SU5108

60 Southampton Road, *Park Gate, Southampton, Hants., SO31 6AF.* Quiet peaceful situation in lovely garden convenient to motorway. **Open:** All year (not Xmas/New Year)
01489 573994 Mrs White **D:** Fr £18.00–£20.00 **S:** Fr £18.00–£20.00 **Beds:** 1F 1S **Baths:** 1 Sh (5)

Pennington

SZ3194

Restormel, *Sway Road, Pennington, Lymington, Hants, SO41 8LJ.* Picturesque cottage, adjoining family farm. Varied breakfasts. Forest, coast nearby. **Open:** All year **Grades:** ETC 4 Diamond
01590 673875 (also fax) Mrs Morgan *judy@restormel-newforest.co.uk* www.restormel-newforest.co.uk **D:** Fr £20.00–£25.00 **S:** Fr £25.00–£30.00 **Beds:** 1F 1D **Baths:** 1 En 1 Pr (4)

Our Bench Guest House, *9 Lodge Road, Pennington, Lymington, Hants, SO41 8HH.* Large non-smoking bungalow between the forest and coast. Garden with heated indoor pool. **Open:** All year (not Xmas)
01590 673141 (also fax) Mrs Lewis *ourbench@newforest.demon.co.uk* www.ourbench.co.uk **D:** Fr £22.00–£27.50 **S:** Fr £22.00–£30.00 **Beds:** 1D 1T 1S **Baths:** 3 En (14) (6) 3 cc

Petersfield

SU7423

Heath Farmhouse, *Sussex Road, Petersfield, Hants, GU31 4HU.* Georgian farmhouse, lovely views, large garden, quiet surroundings, near town. **Open:** All year **Grades:** ETC 3 Diamond
01730 264709 Mrs Scurfield *info@heathfarmhouse.co.uk* www.heathfarmhouse.co.uk **D:** Fr £19.00–£20.00 **S:** Fr £20.00–£25.00 **Beds:** 1F 1D 1T **Baths:** 1 En 1 Sh (5)

Twyford House, *Main Road, Twyford, Winchester, Hampshire, SO21 1NJ.* Family home in Queen Anne House, large grounds, country walks. **Open:** All year (not Xmas/New Year)
01962 713114 Mrs Hawkes **D:** Fr £20.00 **S:** Fr £25.00 **Beds:** 1F 1D **Baths:** 1 Pr 1 Sh (3)

Upper Clatford

SU3543 *Crook & Shears*

Malt Cottage, *Upper Clatford, Andover, Hants, SP11 7QL.* Beautiful old country house with modern facilities in idyllic setting. **Open:** All year (not Xmas/New Year)
01264 323469 Mrs Mason **Fax: 01264 334100** *info@maltcottage.co.uk* www.maltcottage.co.uk **D:** Fr £30.00–£35.00 **S:** Fr £35.00–£45.00 **Beds:** 1T 2D **Baths:** 3 En

Waterlooville

SU6809 *George Inn, Hampshire Rose*

Corner House Hotel, *9 London Road, Waterlooville, Hants, PO8 8HH.* Craig and Lesley assure you of a warm welcome to our family run establishment. Near the top of Portsdown Hill with its fabulous views over Portsmouth and surrounding areas. Close to Portsmouth with its maritime heritage. Short walk to rolling heathland. Bus stop outside. **Open:** All year
023 9237 4079 *thebar@fishjuice.net* www.corner-house.net **D:** Fr £20.00–£25.00 **S:** Fr £20.00–£25.00 **Beds:** 1T 2D 3S **Baths:** 2 Sh cc

West Wellow

SU2919

Lukes Barn, *Maukys Lane, West Wellow, Romsey, Hampshire, SO51 6DA.* **Open:** All year (not Xmas/New Year)
01794 324431 **D:** Fr £20.00 **S:** Fr £25.00–£30.00 **Beds:** 2F **Baths:** 1 Sh (4)
Peaceful and unusual converted wooden barn, overlooking unspoilt countryside with use of garden. It is in easy reach of Salisbury, Winchester and New Forest. Comfortable bedrooms, good local pubs, you can expect a friendly atmosphere.

Weyhill

SU3146

Juglans, *Red Post Lane, Weyhill, Andover, Hampshire, SP11 0PY.* Large cottage garden, food/ale, 5 minutes Thruxton Circuit Close. **Open:** All year
01264 772651 & 07808 369464 (M) Mrs Rotherham **D:** Fr £22.00–£27.00 **S:** Fr £22.00–£27.00 **Beds:** 1D 1S **Baths:** 1 Sh (12) (4)

Whitchurch

SU4647

Long Barrow House, *Cole Henley, Whitchurch, Hants, RG28 7QJ.* **Open:** All year **Grades:** ETC 4 Diamond
01256 895980 Mrs Stevens *info@longbarrowhouse.co.uk* www.longbarrowhouse.co.uk **D:** Fr £25.00–£30.00 **S:** Fr £25.00–£35.00 **Beds:** 1D 1T **Baths:** 2 En (20)
Come and relax in our peaceful, comfortable farmhouse on our dairy farm, nestled in glorious unspoilt countryside yet only 2 miles from A34. Charming ensuite bedrooms with lovely views. Ample parking. Very tranquil. Many repeat bookings.

Wickham

SU5711

The Willows, *Fareham Road, Wickham, Fareham, Hampshire, PO17 5BY.* Close to twelve golf courses, sea and main cities/attractions. **Open:** All year (not Xmas)
01329 833742 & 07879 298103 (M) Mr Barnatt **Fax: 01329 833742** **D:** Fr £20.00 **S:** Fr £25.00 **Beds:** 1F 3D 1S **Baths:** 2 Sh (6) (10)

Wickhaven, *23 School Road, Wickham, Fareham, Hants, PO17 5AA.* Quality B&B in peaceful, friendly, comfortable house. Free tea/coffee. **Open:** All year (not Xmas)
01329 832457 Mrs Toogood **D:** Fr £18.00 **S:** Fr £18.00 **Beds:** 1F 1D 1T 1S **Baths:** 1 Sh (12) (2)

RATES
D = Price range per person sharing in a double or twin room
S = Price range for a single room

Winchester

SU4829

Giffard House Hotel, *50 Christchurch Road, Winchester, Hants, SO23 9SU.* **Open:** All year (not Xmas/New Year) **Grades:** ETC 4 Diamond, Silver
01962 852628 **Fax: 01962 856722** **D:** Fr £38.50–£47.50 **S:** Fr £59.00–£90.00 **Beds:** 1F 2T 6D 4S **Baths:** 13 En (13) cc
Recently restored to a very high standard, to recreate the atmosphere of a prosperous Victorian home. Situated in a leafy part of the city, just 10 minutes' walk from the centre. Cathedral, Winchester College and watermeadows are nearby.

Langhouse, *27 Chilbolton Avenue, Winchester, Hampshire, SO22 5HE.* **Open:** All year (not Xmas/New Year)
01962 860620 (also fax) Mrs Hooper *sheila@langhouse0.demon.co.uk* **D:** Fr £25.00–£30.00 **S:** Fr £40.00–£50.00 **Beds:** 1T 3D **Baths:** 3 En 1 Pr (10)
Spacious, elegant family home, set in 1 acre, overlooking Royal Winchester Golf Course. Extremely comfortable quality accommodation with splendid breakfasts. Perfectly situated for exploring historic Winchester and surrounding Hampshire countryside. 15 mins' walk or 5-min drive to city centre.

The Farrells, *5 Ranelagh Road, Winchester, Hants, SO23 9TA.* **Open:** All year (not Xmas) **Grades:** ETC 3 Diamond
01962 869555 (also fax) Mr Farrell *thefarrells@easicom.com* **D:** Fr £20.00–£25.00 **S:** Fr £22.00–£23.00 **Beds:** 1F 1D 1T 1S **Baths:** 1 En 1 Pr 2 Sh (5)
Turn-of-the-20th-Century Victorian villa, furnished in that style. We are close to the Cathedral and local inns which provide excellent meals. It is our pleasure to help our visitors to enjoy Winchester.

Planning a longer stay? Always ask for any special rates

8 Salters Acres, *Winchester, Hants, SO22 5JW.* Quality accommodation, well situated for both delightful countryside and historic city. **Open:** All year (not Xmas/New Year) **Grades:** ETC 4 Diamond
01962 856112 Mr & Mrs Cater *accommodation@8salters.freeserve.co.uk* **D:** Fr £24.00–£26.00 **S:** Fr £28.50–£32.00 **Beds:** 1T 1D **Baths:** 2 Pr (8) P (8) TV V

85 Christchurch Road, *Winchester, Hants, SO23 9QY.* Comfortable detached Victorian family house. Convenient base for Hampshire sightseeing. **Open:** All year **Grades:** ETC 4 Diamond, Silver
01962 868661 (also fax) Mrs Fetherston-Dilke *dilke@waitrose.com* **D:** Fr £27.00–£28.00 **S:** Fr £27.00–£33.00 **Beds:** 1D 1T 1S **Baths:** 2 En 1 Sh P (3) TV

Rocquaine, *19 Downside Road, Winchester, SO22 5LT.* Spacious welcoming detached family home in quiet residential area. **Open:** All year (not Xmas/New Year)
01962 861426 Mrs Quick *quick@rocq.fsnet.co.uk* **D:** Fr £19.00–£20.00 **S:** Fr £20.00–£25.00 **Beds:** 1D 1T 1S **Baths:** 1 Sh (8) P (4) TV

St Margaret's, *3 St Michael's Road, Winchester, Hampshire, SO23 9JE.* Comfortable rooms in Victorian house, close to cathedral and colleges. **Open:** All year (not Xmas) **Grades:** ETC 3 Diamond
01962 861450 & 07802 478926 (M) Mrs Brett *brigid.brett@amserve.net* www.winchesterbandb.com **D:** Fr £22.50 **S:** Fr £25.00–£40.00 **Beds:** 1D 1T 2S **Baths:** 2 Sh (4) P (1) TV V

The Orchard, *12 Hampton Lane, Weeke, Winchester, Hampshire, SO22 5LF.* Quality comfortable accommodation, easy access to city's historic centre. **Open:** All year (not Xmas/New Year)
01962 620673 Mrs McNeil *bobbiemcneil@yahoo.co.uk* **D:** Fr £20.00–£22.00 **S:** Fr £26.00–£28.00 **Beds:** 1T 1D **Baths:** 1 Sh (8) P (4) TV

Highfield Cottage, *Old Rectory Lane, Twyford, Winchester, Hampshire, SO21 1NS.* Pretty country cottage. Accommodation in self-contained barn annexe. **Open:** All year
01962 712921 C Rees *reescj@hotmail.com* **D:** Fr £25.00 **S:** Fr £30.00–£40.00 **Beds:** 1D 1T 1S **Baths:** 3 En P (3) TV

Sycamores, *4 Bereweeke Close, Winchester, Hants, SO22 6AR.* Well-maintained, peaceful, easily accessible. Approximately, 2km/1m north-west of city centre. **Open:** All year **Grades:** ETC 4 Diamond
01962 867242 Mrs Edwards **Fax: 01962 620300** *sycamores.b-and-b@virgin.net* **D:** Fr £20.00–£25.00 **Beds:** 2D 1T **Baths:** 3 Pr P (3) TV V

The Lilacs, *1 Harestock Close, off Andover Road North, Winchester, Hants, SO22 6NP.* Attractive Georgian style family home. Clean, comfortable, friendly. Excellent cooking. **Open:** All year (not Xmas/New Year)
01962 884122 & 01962 622387 & 07890 307245 (M) Mrs Pell **Fax: 01962 884122** *susan@rbpell.freeserve.co.uk* www.smoothhound.co.uk/hotels/lilacs.html **D:** Fr £20.00–£21.00 **S:** Fr £28.00–£30.00 **Beds:** 1D 1T **Baths:** 1 Sh P (2) TV V

Winsor

SU3114

Bushfriers, *Winsor Road, Winsor, Southampton, SO40 2HF.* Forest cottage, peaceful surroundings, New Forest Heritage Area, highly rated breakfasts. **Open:** All year (not Xmas)
023 8081 2552 Mr & Mrs Wright *bushfriers@bushinternet.com* www.smoothhound.co.uk/hotels/bushfriers.html **D:** Fr £25.00 **S:** Fr £30.00 **Beds:** 2D **Baths:** 1 Pr 1 En P (2) TV V

All details shown are as supplied by B&B owners in Autumn 2002

Herefordshire

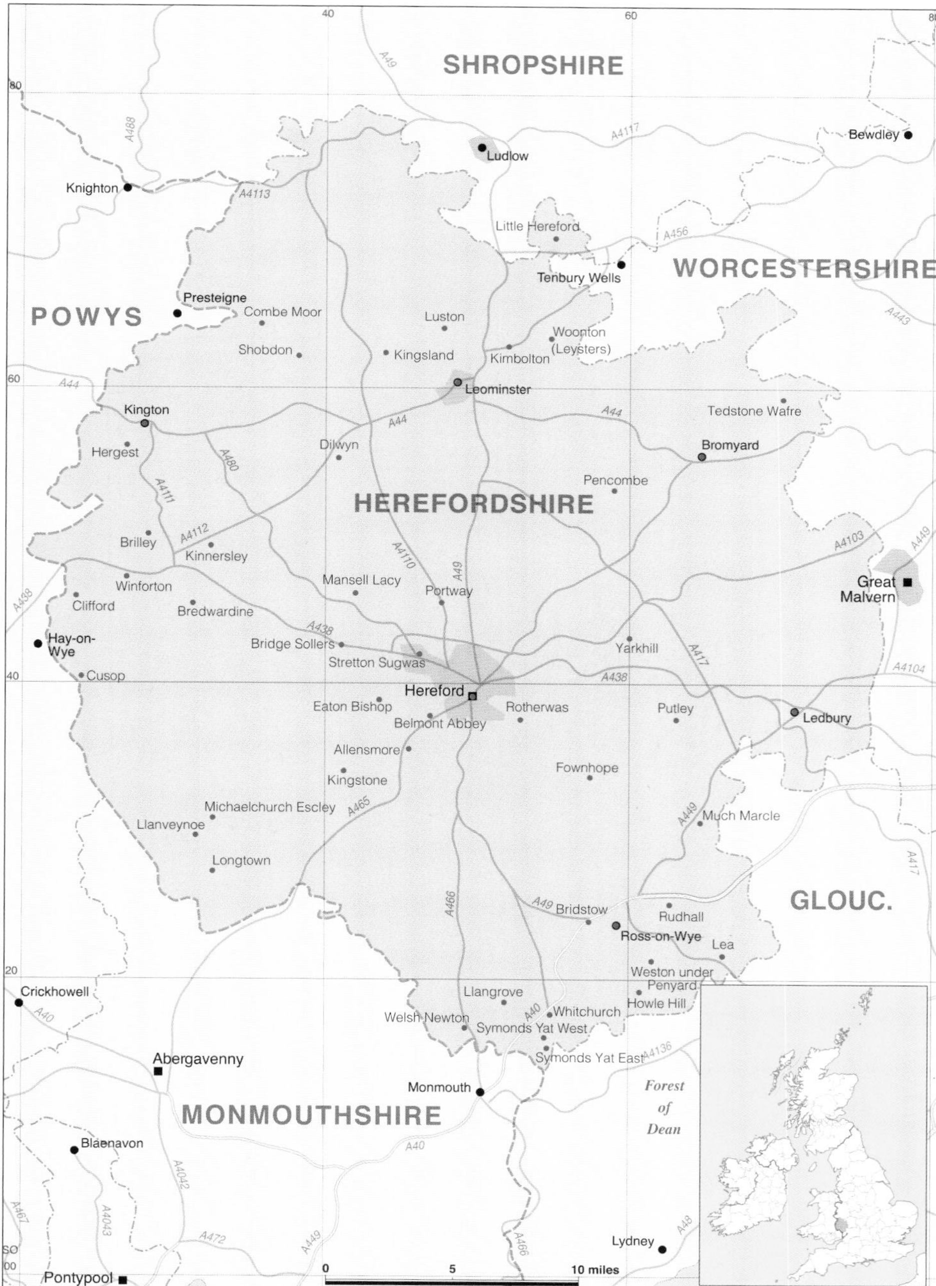

RATES
D = Price range per person sharing in a double or twin room
S = Price range for a single room

Allensmore

SO4635

Holly House Farm, *Allensmore, Hereford, HR2 9BH.* Delightful family country farmhouse in beautiful and peaceful open countryside. **Open:** All year (not Xmas) **01432 277294** Mrs Sinclair **Fax: 01432 261285** *hollyhousefarm@aol.com* **D:** Fr £20.00–£25.00 **S:** Fr £25.00 **Beds:** 1D 2T 1S **Baths:** 1 En 2 Pr 1 Sh (30)

Belmont Abbey

SO4838

Hedley Lodge, *Belmont Abbey, Belmont, Hereford, HR2 9RZ.* **Open:** All year **Grades:** ETC 4 Diamond **01432 374747 Fax: 01432 277318** *hedleylodge@aol.com* www.hedleylodge.com **D:** Fr £27.50 **S:** Fr £35.00 **Beds:** 1F 4D 12T **Baths:** 17 En (200) **cc** Superbly located on the edge of historic Hereford and within the beautiful grounds of Belmont Abbey, Hedley Lodge offers a warm friendly welcome in its comfortable modern guest house. Fully licensed restaurant open to all visitors.

Bredwardine

SO3344

Red Lion Hotel, *Bredwardine, Hereford, HR3 6BU.* C17th inn in heart of Wye Valley. Warm friendly atmosphere, good food. **Open:** All year **01981 500303 Fax: 01981 500400** www.hay-on-wye.co.uk/redlion **D:** Fr £20.00–£29.50 **S:** Fr £28.00–£40.00 **Beds:** 2F 5T 2D **Baths:** 9 En (15) **cc**

Bridge Sollers

SO4142

The Salmon, *Bridge Sollers, Hereford, Herefordshire, HR4 7JH.* Idyllic secluded location on banks of River Wye. Hereford 6 miles. **Open:** All year (not Xmas/New Year) **01981 590605 & 07775 751122 (M)** Mr Cotterell **Fax: 01981 590605** *cotterell@salmonbridge.co.uk* **D:** Fr £25.00 **S:** Fr £30.00 **Beds:** 1T **Baths:** 1 Pr (2)

Bridstow

SO5824

Lavender Cottage, *Bridstow, Ross-on-Wye, Herefordshire, HR9 6QB.* Part C17th house in tranquil countryside with delightful views. **Open:** Easter to Sep **01989 562836** Mrs Nash **Fax: 01989 762129** *barbara_lavender@yahoo.co.uk* **D:** Fr £19.00 **S:** Fr £25.00 **Beds:** 1D 2T **Baths:** 2 En 1 Pr (8) (3)

Brilley

SO2649

Pentwyn Farm, *Brilley, Hereford, HR3 6HW.* Victorian stone farmhouse. Fantastic views on Offa's Dyke path. **Open:** Easter to Oct **01497 831337** Mrs Price **D:** Fr £16.00 **S:** Fr £16.00 **Beds:** 2D 2S **Baths:** 1 Sh

Bromyard

SO6554

The Old Cowshed, *Avenbury Court, Bromyard, Herefordshire, HR7 4LA.* **Open:** All year **Grades:** ETC 4 Diamond, Silver **01885 482384** Mr & Mrs Combe **Fax: 01885 482367** *combes@cowshed.uk.com* www.cowshed.uk.com **D:** Fr £25.00–£30.00 **S:** Fr £25.00–£35.00 **Beds:** 1T 2D **Baths:** 2 Pr (4) **cc** Come & relax in our peaceful home. Tastefully furnished private suites, comfort assured. Ground floor rooms. Inglenook fireplace, beamed gallery, large garden, ample off-road parking. High level of personal service. Set in beautiful countryside with views over the Frome Valley.

BATHROOMS
En = Ensuite
Pr = Private
Sh = Shared

All details shown are as supplied by B&B owners in Autumn 2002

Littlebridge, *Tedstone Wafre, Bromyard, Herefordshire, HR7 4PN.* Tastefully decorated country house with panoramic views, ideal base for touring. **Open:** All year **Grades:** ETC 4 Diamond **01885 482471 (also fax)** Mrs Williams **D:** Fr £24.00–£35.00 **S:** Fr £25.00–£35.00 **Beds:** 1F 1D 1T **Baths:** 3 En (6)

Park House, *28 Sherford Street, Bromyard, Herefordshire, HR7 4DL.* Enjoy the country without the crowds. Great walks, superb pubs and really friendly people. **Open:** All year **01885 482294 (also fax)** Mr Gardiner *parkhouse@callnetuk.com* www.bromyard.co.uk/parkhouse **D:** Fr £20.00–£25.00 **S:** Fr £22.50–£30.00 **Beds:** 1F 1T 2D **Baths:** 3 En 1 Pr (6)

Clifford

SO2445

Cottage Farm, *Middlewood, Clifford, Hereford, HR3 5SX.* Quiet location, birds, walking, working farm, families welcome, good value. **Open:** All year (not Xmas) **01497 831496 (also fax)** Mrs Jones *julie@hgjmjones.freeserve.co.uk* www.smoothhound.co.uk/hotels/cottagef.html **D:** Fr £18.00 **S:** Fr £18.00 **Beds:** 1F 1T **Baths:** 1 Sh (4)

Combe Moor

SO3663

Brick House Farm, *Combe Moor, Presteigne, Powys, LD8 2HY.* Comfortable farmhouse on small holding. Beautiful countryside. Warm welcome. Memorable meals. **Open:** All year **01544 267306** Mr & Mrs Johnstone **Fax: 01544 260601** *dmfj@johnstone.kc3.co.uk* www.kc3.co.uk/chamber/brickhouse/index.html **D:** Fr £17.50–£20.00 **S:** Fr £20.00 **Beds:** 3D 1T 1S **Baths:** 2 Sh (4)

Cusop

SO2341

Fernleigh, *Hardwick Road, Cusop, Hay-on-Wye, Hereford, HR3 5QX.* Quiet location walking distance of the famous book town of Hay-on-Wye. **Open:** Easter to Oct **01497 820459** Mr Hughes **D:** Fr £17.00–£20.00 **S:** Fr £19.00–£20.00 **Beds:** 2D 1S **Baths:** 1 En 1 Sh (4)

Dilwyn

SO4154

Bedford House, *Dilwyn, Hereford, HR4 8JJ.* Small friendly farm offering excellent accommodation, peace and quiet. **Open:** All year (not Xmas/New Year) **01544 388260** Mrs Anthony **D:** Fr £18.00–£20.00 **S:** Fr £20.00 **Beds:** 1F 1T 1D **Baths:** 1 En 1 Sh (4)

Eaton Bishop

SO4339

The Ancient Camp Inn, *Ruckhall, Eaton Bishop, Hereford, HR2 9QX.* **Open:** All year (not Xmas/New Year) **Grades:** AA 2 Star **01981 250449** Dr Tomlinson **Fax: 01981 251581** *reservations@cwefarnham.worldonline.co.uk* **D:** Fr £30.00–£45.00 **S:** Fr £45.00–£80.00 **Beds:** 4D 1T **Baths:** 5 En (30) **cc** Come and be pampered! Peace and tranquillity in historic inn with stunning views above the Wye Valley. Delicious meals prepared with local seasonal produce. Fully licensed and totally non-smoking. Ideal base from which to explore Herefordshire's delights.

Fownhope

SO5834

Pippins, *Capler Lane, Fownhope, Hereford, HR1 4PJ.* Comfortable spacious accommodation with lovely views of River Wye and rolling countryside. **Open:** All year (not Xmas/New Year) **01432 860677** Mrs Corby **D:** Fr £20.00–£22.00 **S:** Fr £23.00–£25.00 **Beds:** 2T **Baths:** 1 Pr (4)

Hereford

SO5140

Sink Green Farm, *Rotherwas, Hereford, HR2 6LE.* **Open:** All year (not Xmas) **01432 870223** Mr Jones *sinkgreenfarm@msn.com* **D:** Fr £23.00–£27.00 **S:** Fr £23.00–£27.00 **Beds:** 2D 1T **Baths:** 3 En (10) We welcome you to our C16th farmhouse set in the picturesque Wye Valley, yet only 3 miles from Hereford. Relax in our tastefully decorated ensuite rooms, one 4 poster, all having tea/coffee facilities, colour TV and central heating.

Cedar Guest House, *123 White Cross Road, Hereford, HR4 0LS.* Family-run former Victorian gentleman's residence, many original features. Spacious centrally-heated accommodation. **Open:** All year **01432 267235 (also fax)** Mr & Mrs Williams *www.cedarguesthouse.com* **D:** Fr £18.00–£20.00 **S:** Fr £25.00–£35.00 **Beds:** 2F 1T 2D **Baths:** 1 En 1 Sh (8)

Hergest

SO2753

Bucks Head House, *Upper Hergest, Hergest, Kington, Herefordshire, HR5 3EW.* Situated on south side of Hergest Ridge and Offa's Dyke Path. **Open:** All year **01544 231063** Mrs Protheroe **D:** Fr £22.00–£24.00 **S:** Fr £22.00–£24.00 **Beds:** 2F 2D 1T 1S **Baths:** 2 Sh (6)

Howle Hill

SO6020

Old Kilns, *Howle Hill, Ross-on-Wye, Herefordshire, HR9 5SP.* Stay as our guests at our privately owned country house. **Open:** All year **01989 562051 (also fax)** Mrs Smith **D:** Fr £15.00–£30.00 **Beds:** 1F 1T 2D **Baths:** 1 En 1 Pr 1 Sh (8)

Kimbolton

SO5261 *Stockton Cross Inn, Roebuck*

The Fieldhouse Farm, *Bache Hill, Kimbolton, Leominster, Herefordshire, HR6 0EP.* A warm welcome awaits you in our traditional farmhouse with oak beams, log fires, stunning views and delicious breakfasts. **Open:** Apr to Nov **01568 614789** Mrs Franks **D:** Fr £20.00–£23.00 **S:** Fr £22.00–£24.00 **Beds:** 1T **Baths:** 1 Pr (4)

Kingsland

SO4461

Holgate Farm, *Kingsland, Leominster, Herefordshire, HR6 9QS.* Attractive farmhouse. Delicious breakfasts. Near Leominster, Ludlow and Welsh Marches. **Open:** All year (not Xmas/New Year) **01568 708275** Mrs Davies **D:** Fr £18.00 **S:** Fr £20.00 **Beds:** 1F 1T **Baths:** 1 Sh (3)

B&B owners may vary rates – be sure to check when booking

Planning a longer stay? Always ask for any special rates

Kingstone

SO4235

Mill Orchard, *Kingstone, Hereford, HR2 9ES.* Superior accommodation and warm welcome. Discounts available. Hereford 6 miles. **Open:** Feb to Nov **Grades:** ETC 4 Diamond, Gold **01981 250326** Mrs Cleveland *cleveland@millorchard.co.uk* *www.millorchard.co.uk* **D:** Fr £26.00–£30.00 **S:** Fr £32.00–£36.00 **Beds:** 1T 2D **Baths:** 2 En 1 Pr (12) (5)

Kington

SO2956

Bredward Farm, *Kington, Herefordshire, HR5 3HP.* **Open:** All year (not Xmas/New Year) **01544 231462** Mrs Wright **D:** Fr £16.00 **S:** Fr £16.00–£20.00 **Beds:** 1D 1S **Baths:** 1 Sh (2) (4) Bredward Farm dates back to C16th. Tastefully decorated sitting room, dining room, two bedrooms, shower room/WC. Car parking. Lovely garden. 1 mile from Offa's Dyke. Farmhouse breakfast and evening meal provided 3 miles from the Welsh Border.

Dunfield Cottage, *Kington, Herefordshire, HR5 3NN.* Friendly, relaxed; lovely views; large garden; log fires; H&C in bedrooms. **Open:** All year **01544 230632 (also fax)** Mr & Mrs Titley *robann@dunfieldcottage.kc3.co.uk* **D:** Fr £19.00 **S:** Fr £19.00 **Beds:** 1T 1D 1S **Baths:** 1 Sh (10) (6)

Bucks Head House, *Upper Hergest, Hergest, Kington, Herefordshire, HR5 3EW.* Situated on south side of Hergest Ridge and Offa's Dyke Path. **Open:** All year **01544 231063** Mrs Protheroe **D:** Fr £22.00–£24.00 **S:** Fr £22.00–£24.00 **Beds:** 2F 2D 1T 1S **Baths:** 2 Sh (6)

Cambridge Cottage, *19 Church Street, Kington, Herefordshire, HR5 3BE.* C17th cottage, tea-tray welcome, many return visits, comfortable beds, camping. **Open:** All year (not Xmas/New Year) **01544 231300** Hooton *gerry@kington.softnet.co.uk* **D:** Fr £18.00 **S:** Fr £18.00 **Beds:** 1F 1S **Baths:** 1 En 1 Sh (3) (2)

Church House, *Church Road, Kington, Herefordshire, HR5 3AG.* Large rooms with fine views in elegant Georgian family home. **Open:** All year (not Xmas) **01544 230534** Mrs Darwin **Fax: 01544 231100** *darwin@kc3.co.uk* www.churchhousekington.co.uk **D:** Fr £25.00 **S:** Fr £30.00–£40.00 **Beds:** 1D 1T **Baths:** 1 Sh (2)

Bollingham House, *Kington, Herefordshire, HR5 3LE.* Period residence with glorious views. Gracious rooms. Delightful English garden. **Open:** All year **01544 327326** Mrs Grant **Fax: 01544 327880** *bollhouse@bigfoot.com* **D:** Fr £25.00–£28.50 **S:** Fr £27.50 **Beds:** 2D 1T 1S **Baths:** 2 Pr (10)

Southbourne, *Newton Lane, Kington, Herefordshire, HR5 3NF.* Warm welcome by well travelled couple. Walking/mountain bike guide. **Open:** All year **01544 231706** Mr & Mrs Cooper **D:** Fr £16.00–£18.00 **S:** Fr £16.00–£18.00 **Beds:** 1F 1T 1S **Baths:** 2 Sh (5)

Kinnersley

SO3449

Upper Newton Farmhouse, *Kinnersley, Hereford, HR3 6QB.* C17th award-winning timbered farmhouse on working farm. Always a warm welcome. **Open:** All year **01544 327727 (also fax)** Mrs Taylor *enquiries@bordertrails.u-net.com* www.uppernewton.herefordshire.com **D:** Fr £25.00 **S:** Fr £25.00 **Beds:** 2D 1T **Baths:** 3 Pr (6)

Lea

SO6521 *Penny Farthing*

Forest Edge, *4 Noden Drive, Lea, Ross-on-Wye, HR9 7NB.* A friendly welcome awaits you at our modern home. Situated in a quiet rural area with beautiful views from garden. Rooms furnished and equipped to a high standard. Quality breakfasts. Ideal base for picturesque Wye Valley and Forest of Dean. **Open:** All year (not Xmas/New Year) **01989 750682** Mr & Mrs Wood *don@wood11.freeserve.co.uk* www.wood11.freeserve.co.uk **D:** Fr £21.00–£25.00 **S:** Fr £31.00–£35.00 **Beds:** 1T 1D **Baths:** 2 En (10) (4)

Ledbury

SO7137

Leadon House Hotel, *Ross Road, Ledbury, Herefordshire, HR8 2LP.* **Open:** All year **Grades:** ETC 2 Star, Silver **01531 631199** M H J Williams **Fax: 01531 631476** *leadon.house@amserve.net* www.leadonhouse.co.uk **D:** Fr £28.00–£38.00 **S:** Fr £38.00–£60.00 **Beds:** 2F 1T 2D 1S **Baths:** 6 En (8) **cc** Elegant Edwardian house in picturesque setting, approx 1 mile from historic Ledbury, convenient to Malvern Hills, Wye Valley and Herefordshire's renowned black and white villages. Refurbished in period style with comfortable accommodation, attractive gardens. Good home-cooked food. Non-smoking.

The Royal Oak Hotel, *The South End, Ledbury, Herefordshire, HR8 2EY.* Situated 15 Miles equidistant from Hereford, Gloucester, Worcester. Real beer. Real breakfasts. **Open:** All year **01531 632110** Mr Barron *royaloak@ukonline.co.uk* **D:** Fr £30.00 **S:** Fr £30.00 **Beds:** 3F 3T 9D 3S **Baths:** 7 En 1 Sh **cc**

Leominster

SO4959

Highfield, *Newtown Ivington Road, Leominster, Herefordshire, HR6 8QD.* Comfortable Edwardian house, pleasant rural location, delicious home-prepared food. **Open:** Mar to Oct **Grades:** ETC 4 Diamond **01568 613216** M & C Fothergill *info@stay-at-highfield.co.uk* www.stay-at-highfield.co.uk **D:** Fr £19.50–£25.00 **Beds:** 2T 1D **Baths:** 1 En 2 Pr (3)

Woonton Court Farm, *Woonton, Leysters, Leominster, Hereford, HR6 0HL.* Comfortable Tudor farmhouse, own produce. Freedom to walk and enjoy wildlife. Rural peace. **Open:** All year (not Xmas) **01568 750232 (also fax)** Mrs Thomas *thomas.woontoncourt@farmersweekly.net* **D:** Fr £22.00–£25.00 **S:** Fr £24.00–£25.00 **Beds:** 1F 1D 1T **Baths:** 3 En (3)

Copper Hall, *South Street, Leominster, Herefordshire, HR6 8JN.* An attractive and comfortable C17th house with a warm welcome. **Open:** All year **01568 611622** Mr & Mrs Crick *sccrick@copperhall.freeserve.co.uk* **D:** Fr £20.00–£22.00 **S:** Fr £20.00–£25.00 **Beds:** 2D 2T **Baths:** 3 En 1 Pr (4)

Rossendale Guest House, *46 Broad Street, Leominster, Herefordshire, HR6 8BS.* Friendly traditional town centre establishment welcoming tourists and business visitors. **Open:** All year **01568 612464** Mr Hosegood **D:** Fr £20.00–£25.00 **S:** Fr £20.00 **Beds:** 3D 2T 6S **Baths:** 1 En 1 Sh (10)

Little Hereford

SO5568

Haynall Villa, *Haynall Lane, Little Hereford, Ludlow, Shropshire, SY8 4BG.* 1820s farmhouse with original features, attractive garden in peaceful location. **Open:** All year (not Xmas/New Year) **01584 711589 (also fax)** Mrs Edwards **D:** Fr £18.00–£24.00 **S:** Fr £18.00–£28.00 **Beds:** 1F 1D 1T **Baths:** 1 En 1 Sh (6) (3)

Llangrove

SO5219

Thatch Close, *Llangrove, Ross-on-Wye, Herefordshire, HR9 6EL.* Secluded, quiet Georgian farmhouse, set in panoramic countryside, sympathetically modernised. **Open:** All year **Grades:** ETC 4 Diamond **01989 770300** Mrs Drzymalski *thatch.close@virgin.net* **D:** Fr £20.00–£23.00 **S:** Fr £25.00–£28.00 **Beds:** 2D 1T **Baths:** 2 En 1 Pr (8)

Llanveynoe

SO3031

Olchon Court, *Llanveynoe, Hereford, HR2 0NL.* Romantic medieval farmhouse in beautiful secluded valley. **Open:** All year (not Xmas/New Year) **01873 860356 (also fax)** Mrs Carter **D:** Fr £25.00–£27.00 **S:** Fr £30.00–£32.00 **Beds:** 2T 2D **Baths:** 2 En (12) (15)

Longtown

SO3228

Olchon Cottage Farm, *Turnant Road, Longtown, Hereford, HR2 0NS.* Warm welcome to explore Herefordshire and Marches. Farmhouse breakfasts. **Open:** All year **01873 860233 (also fax)** Mrs Pritchard www.golden-valley.co.uk/olchon **D:** Fr £21.00–£22.00 **S:** Fr £21.00–£22.00 **Beds:** 2F **Baths:** 2 En (6)

Luston

SO4863

Ladymeadow Farm, *Luston, Leominster, Herefordshire, HR6 0AS.* Large, friendly, comfortable C17th farmhouse near two NT properties. **Open:** Easter to Nov **01568 780262** Mrs Ruell **D:** Fr £19.00–£22.00 **S:** Fr £19.00–£22.00 **Beds:** 1F 1D 1S **Baths:** 1 En 1 Sh (20)

Little Bury Farm, *Luston, Leominster, Herefordshire, HR6 0EB.* Secluded country cottage in seven acres of gardens and paddocks. **Open:** Apr to Oct
01568 611575 Mrs Field **D:** Fr £20.00–£22.00 **S:** Fr £22.00–£24.00 **Beds:** 2D **Baths:** 1 Pr (4)

Mansell Lacy
SO4245

Apple Tree Cottage, *Mansell Lacy, Hereford, HR4 7HH.* C15th cottage in a peaceful situation surrounded by fields. **Open:** All year
01981 590688 Mrs Barker *monica.barker@tesco.net* **D:** Fr £17.00–£20.00 **S:** Fr £17.00–£20.00 **Beds:** 2T 1S **Baths:** 1 Pr (14) (4)

Michaelchurch Escley
SO3134

Grove Farm, *Michaelchurch Escley, Hereford, Herefordshire, HR2 0PT.* Situated near Black Mountains. Lovely and peaceful, warm welcome, farmhouse breakfasts. **Open:** All year (not Xmas/New Year)
01981 510229 (also fax) Mrs Lloyd **D:** Fr £20.00 **S:** Fr £18.00 **Beds:** 1F 1D 1S **Baths:** 1 En 1 Pr

Much Marcle
SO6532

New House Farm, *Much Marcle, Ledbury, Herefordshire, HR8 2PH.* Comfortable farmhouse and cottage, log fire, swimming pool, good food. **Open:** All year
01531 660604 A Jordan **D:** Fr £18.00–£20.00 **S:** Fr £18.00–£20.00 **Beds:** 1F 1T 1D **Baths:** 1 En 1 Sh (6)

Pencombe
SO5952

Hennerwood Farm, *Pencombe, Bromyard, Herefordshire, HR7 4SL.* Traditional dairy farm, quiet position. Panoramic views of beautiful Herefordshire. **Open:** Easter to Oct
01885 400245 (also fax) Mrs Thomas *hennerwood@farming.co.uk* **D:** Fr £20.00 **S:** Fr £20.00 **Beds:** 1F 1D (2)

Portway
SO4845

Heron House, *Canon Pyon Road, Portway, Hereford, HR4 8NG.* Relaxing house, near Hereford City, with spacious rooms and country views. **Open:** All year
01432 761111 R F Huckle **Fax: 01432 760603** *bb.hereford@tesco.net* homepages.tesco.net/~bb.hereford/heron.htm **D:** Fr £19.00–£21.00 **S:** Fr £16.00–£17.50 **Beds:** 1F 1D **Baths:** 1 En 1 Sh (10) (4)

Putley
SO6337

The Coach House, *Putley, Ledbury, Herefordshire, HR8 2QP.* The Coach House is an C18th coaching stable set in gorgeous Herefordshire. **Open:** All year
01531 670684 (also fax) Mrs Born *wendyborn@putley-coachhouse.co.uk* www.putley-coachhouse.co.uk **D:** Fr £16.00–£17.50 **S:** Fr £22.00–£25.00 **Beds:** 1T 2D 1S

Ross-on-Wye
SO6024

Rowan Lea, *Ponts Hill, Ross-on-Wye, Herefordshire, HR9 5SY.* Friendly, peaceful, detached dormer bungalow. Lovely views, gardens, big breakfast. **Open:** All year
01989 750693 Ms Griffiths **D:** Fr £16.00 **S:** Fr £16.00 **Beds:** 1F 1D **Baths:** 1 Sh (2)

Thatch Close, *Llangrove, Ross-on-Wye, Herefordshire, HR9 6EL.* Secluded, quiet Georgian farmhouse, set in panoramic countryside, sympathetically modernised. **Open:** All year **Grades:** ETC 4 Diamond
01989 770300 Mrs Drzymalski *thatch.close@virgin.net* **D:** Fr £20.00–£23.00 **S:** Fr £25.00–£28.00 **Beds:** 2D 1T **Baths:** 2 En 1 Pr (8)

Sunnymount Hotel, *Ryefield Road, Ross-on-Wye, Herefordshire, HR9 5LU.* Small family-run hotel, quiet, comfortable, excellent home-cooked meals. **Open:** All year
01989 563880 Mr & Mrs Robertson **Fax: 01989 566251** *sunnymount@tinyworld.co.uk* **D:** Fr £23.00–£26.00 **S:** Fr £23.00–£28.00 **Beds:** 4D 2T **Baths:** 2 En 1 Sh (6) cc

Rotherwas
SO5338

Sink Green Farm, *Rotherwas, Hereford, HR2 6LE.* We welcome you to our C16th farmhouse set in the picturesque Wye Valley. **Open:** All year (not Xmas)
01432 870223 Mr Jones *sinkgreenfarm@msn.com* **D:** Fr £23.00–£27.00 **S:** Fr £23.00–£27.00 **Beds:** 2D 1T **Baths:** 3 En (10)

Rudhall
SO6225

Rudhall Farm, *Rudhall, Ross-on-Wye, Herefordshire, HR9 7TL.* Elegant country house. Warm welcome. Aga cooked breakfasts. Highly recommended by guests. **Open:** All year (not Xmas)
01989 780240 Mrs Gammond **D:** Fr £25.00–£50.00 **S:** Fr £25.00–£30.00 **Beds:** 2D **Baths:** 1 Pr 1 Sh (10)

Shobdon
SO3961

The Paddock, *Shobdon, Leominster, Herefordshire, HR6 9NQ.* **Open:** All year (not Xmas)
Grades: ETC 4 Diamond, Gold
01568 708176 Mrs Womersley **Fax: 01568 708829** *thepaddock@talk21.com* **D:** Fr £23.00–£25.00 **S:** Fr £36.00 **Beds:** 4D 1T **Baths:** 5 En (5)
Delightful ground floor ensuite accommodation, situated in the beautiful border region between England and Wales. Large garden and patio, delicious home cooked food. Popular walking area, local National Trust attractions.

Stretton Sugwas
SO4642

New Priory Hotel, *Stretton Sugwas, Hereford, HR4 7AR.* A comfortable, friendly family-run hotel on the edge of Hereford. **Open:** All year
01432 760264 Mr Benjamin **Fax: 01432 761809** *newprioryhotel@ukonline.co.uk* www.newprioryhotel.co.uk **D:** Fr £27.50–£40.00 **S:** Fr £35.00–£65.00 **Beds:** 1F 1T 4D 1S **Baths:** 7 En cc

Symonds Yat East
SO5616

Rose Cottage, *Symonds Yat East, Ross-on-Wye, Herefordshire, HR9 6JL.* Comfortable riverside accommodation with spectacular views. **Open:** All year
01600 890514 Mrs Whyberd **Fax: 01600 890498** www.smoothhound.co.uk/hotels/rose2.html **D:** Fr £17.50–£27.50 **S:** Fr £30.00–£35.00 **Beds:** 3D **Baths:** 2 En 1 Pr (3)

Planning a longer stay? Always ask for any special rates

Symonds Yat West

SO5516

Norton House, *Whitchurch, Ross-on-Wye, Herefordshire, HR9 6DJ.* **Open:** All year **01600 890046** Mr & Mrs Jackson **Fax: 01600 890045** *enquiries@norton.wyenet.co.uk* www.Norton-House.com **D:** Fr £24.00–£26.00 **S:** Fr £30.00–£34.00 **Beds:** 1T 2D **Baths:** 3 En (12)
C17th Listed building, with a wealth of character, and all the modern comforts our guests could wish for. Freshly prepared, locally produced food, cooked on the Aga and served in the beautiful oak-beamed dining room. River Wye and Symonds Yat nearby.

Old Court Hotel, *Symonds Yat West, Ross-on-Wye, Herefordshire, HR9 6DA.* **Open:** All year (not Xmas) **01600 890367** Mr & Mrs Slade **Fax: 01600 890964** *oldcour@aol.com* www.oldcourthotel.com **D:** Fr £36.50–£45.00 **S:** Fr £46.50–£55.00 **Beds:** 3T 15D **Baths:** 18 En (12) (50) cc
C16th ancestral home set in the glorious Wye Valley. Excellent comfort and service, yet retaining the charm and character of a bygone era. Superb cuisine. Ideal for walking in the Wye Valley, Forest of Dean and Offa's Dyke Path.

Riversdale Lodge Hotel, *Symonds Yat West, Ross-on-Wye, Herefordshire, HR9 6BL.* Family run country house hotel, Riverside setting overlooking Wye Rapids. **Open:** Feb to Dec **01600 890445** Mr & Mrs Armsden **Fax: 01600 890443** *info@riversdale.uk.com* **D:** Fr £35.00 **S:** Fr £50.00 **Beds:** 1F 1T 3D **Baths:** 5 En (1) (11) cc

Tedstone Wafre

SO6759

Littlebridge, *Tedstone Wafre, Bromyard, Herefordshire, HR7 4PN.* Tastefully decorated country house with panoramic views, ideal base for touring. **Open:** All year **Grades:** ETC 4 Diamond **01885 482471 (also fax)** Mrs Williams **D:** Fr £24.00–£35.00 **S:** Fr £25.00–£35.00 **Beds:** 1F 1D 1T **Baths:** 3 En (6)

Welsh Newton

SO5017

The Lower Cwm, *Welsh Newton, Monmouth, NP25 5RW.* Stone farmhouse with terrace and vine-shaded conservatory, unusual garden. **Open:** All year (not Xmas/New Year) **01600 713040 (also fax)** Mrs Kelly **D:** Fr £20.00–£25.00 **S:** Fr £25.00 **Beds:** 1F 1D **Baths:** 2 Pr (3)

Weston under Penyard

SO6223

Wharton Farm, *Weston under Penyard, Ross-on-Wye, Herefordshire, HR9 5SX.* Excellent C17th/18th farmhouse accommodation in beautiful countryside, quiet & peaceful. **Open:** All year (not Xmas) **Grades:** ETC 4 Diamond **01989 750255 (also fax)** Mrs Savidge *je.savage@breathemail.net* **D:** Fr £20.00–£23.00 **S:** Fr £25.00–£27.50 **Beds:** 2D 1T **Baths:** 1 En 2 Pr (5)

BATHROOMS
En = Ensuite
Pr = Private
Sh = Shared

Whitchurch

SO5417

Norton House, *Whitchurch, Ross-on-Wye, Herefordshire, HR9 6DJ.* C17th Listed building, wealth of character, all modern comforts. **Open:** All year **01600 890046** Mr & Mrs Jackson **Fax: 01600 890045** *enquiries@norton.wyenet.co.uk* www.Norton-House.com **D:** Fr £24.00–£26.00 **S:** Fr £30.00–£34.00 **Beds:** 1T 2D **Baths:** 3 En (12)

Winforton

SO2947 *Sun Inn*

Winforton Court, *Winforton, Hereford, HR3 6EA.* Romantic C16th manor. King size, 4-posters. Log fires. Gardens. Relax and be pampered. **Open:** All year (not Xmas) **01544 328498 (also fax)** J Kingdon **D:** Fr £27.00–£36.00 **S:** Fr £42.00–£52.00 **Beds:** 3D **Baths:** 3 En (10) (10)

Woonton (Leysters)

SO5462

Woonton Court Farm, *Woonton, Leysters, Leominster, Hereford, HR6 0HL.* Comfortable Tudor farmhouse, own produce. Freedom to walk and enjoy wildlife. Rural peace. **Open:** All year (not Xmas) **01568 750232 (also fax)** Mrs Thomas *thomas.woontoncourt@farmersweekly.net* **D:** Fr £22.00–£25.00 **S:** Fr £24.00–£25.00 **Beds:** 1F 1D 1T **Baths:** 3 En (3)

Yarkhill

SO6043

Garford Farm, *Yarkhill, Hereford, HR1 3ST.* Peaceful farmhouse within easy reach of Worcester, Malvern & Hereford. **Open:** All year (not Xmas/New Year) **Grades:** AA 4 Diamond **01432 890226 Fax: 01432 890707** *garfordfarm@lineone.net* **D:** Fr £20.00–£22.00 **S:** Fr £22.00 **Beds:** 1F 1T **Baths:** 1 En 1 Pr (2) (6)

Hertfordshire

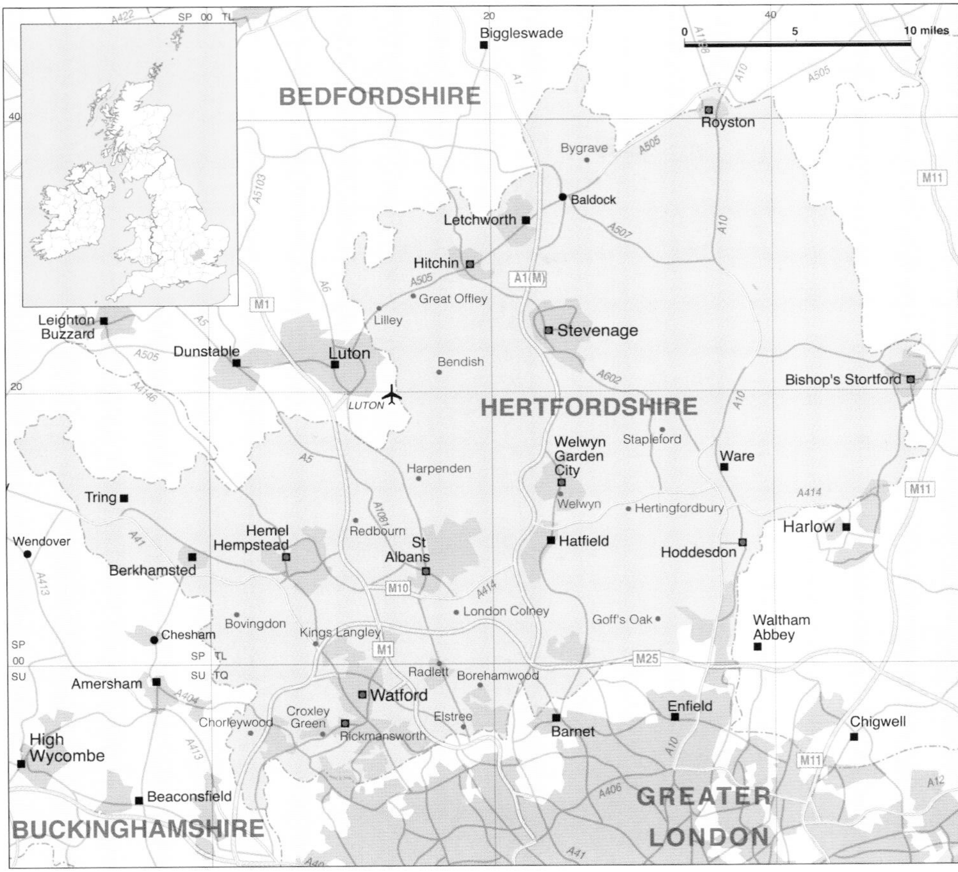

Bendish

TL1621

Bendish House, *Bendish, Hitchin, Hertfordshire, SG4 8JA.* Hilltop location, stunning views overlooking Mimram Valley. **Open:** All year (not Xmas) **01438 871519 Fax: 01438 871499 D:** Fr £20.00–£25.00 **S:** Fr £20.00–£25.00 **Beds:** 1D 1T 1S (6)

Bishop's Stortford

TL4921

Broadleaf Guest House, *38 Broadleaf Avenue, Bishop's Stortford, Herts, CM23 4JY.* Close to Stansted Airport; fast trains into London and Cambridge. **Open:** All year (not Xmas) **01279 835467** Mrs Cannon *paula@broadleaf63.freeserve.co.uk* **D:** Fr £25.00 **S:** Fr £25.00–£30.00 **Beds:** 1F 1D 1T **Baths:** 1 Pr (2)

Pearse House Conference & Trng Centre, *Parsonage Lane, Bishop's Stortford, Herts, CM23 5BQ.* Victorian mansion housing excellent conference facilities and ensuite bedrooms. **Open:** All year (not Xmas/New Year) **01279 757400** D Doyle **Fax: 01279 506591** *pearsehouse@route56.co.uk* www.pearsehouse.co.uk **D:** Fr £35.00–£40.00 **S:** Fr £60.00–£70.00 **Beds:** 2F 5T 7D 23S **Baths:** 35 En 2 Pr cc

Borehamwood

TQ1996

84 Stevenage Crescent, *Borehamwood, Herts, WD6 4NS.* Luxury, modern private house. **Open:** All year
020 8207 3320 M Feehily *miriamfeehily@aol.com* **D:** Fr £25.00 **S:** Fr £30.00 **Beds:** 3T
Baths: 1 Sh (4)

Bovingdon

TL0103

Rose Farm, *Water Lane, Bovingdon, Hemel Hempstead, Herts, HP3 0NA.* Country situated, newly-built farmhouse convenient M1, M25, trains, London. **Open:** All year (not Xmas)
01442 834529 Mrs Mills **D:** Fr £30.00 **S:** Fr £40.00 **Beds:** 6T **Baths:** 5 En 1 Pr (3) (10)

Bygrave

TL2636

Bygrave B&B, *59 Ashwell Road, Bygrave, Baldock, Hertfordshire, SG7 5DY.* Friendly family home, rural location. Guests' room, use of garden. **Open:** All year (not Xmas)
01462 894749 Mrs Spaul **D:** Fr £22.00–£25.00 **S:** Fr £22.00–£25.00 **Beds:** 2D 2T 1S **Baths:** 2 En 1 Sh (5)

Chorleywood

TQ0296

Kennels Cottage, *Common Road, Chorleywood, Herts, WD3 5LW.* A quiet oasis. A mellow brick cottage. A warm welcome. **Open:** All year (not Xmas)
01923 282927 Mrs Smethurst **D:** Fr £22.50 **S:** Fr £25.00 **Beds:** 2F 2S **Baths:** 1 Sh (4)

Croxley Green

TQ0695

Farthings, *Copthorne Road, Croxley Green, Rickmansworth, Hertfordshire, WD3 4AE.* Situated in private road. Close to station and M25 Motorway. **Open:** All year (not Xmas/New Year)
01923 771431 Mrs Saunders *bazmau@barclays.net* **D:** Fr £22.50 **S:** Fr £22.50 **Beds:** 1T 2S **Baths:** 1 Sh (6) (6)

Elstree

TQ1795

North Medburn Farm, *Watlin Street, Elstree, Herts, WD6 3AA.* Easy access to London. **Open:** All year (not Xmas)
020 8953 1522 Mrs Williams **D:** Fr £20.00–£25.00 **S:** Fr £20.00–£25.00 **Beds:** 1F 3T 1S **Baths:** 1 En 1 Sh (4)

Goff's Oak

TL3203

329 Goffs Lane, *Goff's Oak, Cheshunt, Herts, EN7 5QH.* Detached house close to countryside, walks drives, country pubs. **Open:** All year
01992 628524 (also fax) Mrs Morgan **D:** Fr £30.00–£32.00 **S:** Fr £28.00–£30.00 **Beds:** 2F 3D 1T **Baths:** 6 En (5)

Great Offley

TL1426

Church View, *Kings Walden Road, Great Offley, Hitchin, Herts, SG5 3DU.* **Open:** All year (not Xmas)
01462 768719 Mrs Maybury **D:** Fr £25.00–£27.50 **S:** Fr £30.00–£35.00 **Beds:** 1D 1T **Baths:** 1 En 1 Pr (10) (2)
Ideally situated between Luton (M1) and Hitchin (A1(M)), Airport 3 miles. You are assured of a warm welcome with well-equipped and comfortable accommodation. Full English breakfast. The village includes two pubs and a restaurant. Good surrounding country walks.

Harpenden

TL1314

The Old Cottage, *417 Luton Road, Harpenden, Herts, AL5 3QE.* Comfortable C18th cottage, convenient London and airports, warm welcome. **Open:** All year (not Xmas)
01582 762257 Mr & Mrs Horn **D:** Fr £20.00–£25.00 **S:** Fr £20.00–£30.00 **Beds:** 1F 1D 1S **Baths:** 1 En 1 Sh (3)

Hemel Hempstead

TL0607

Southville Private Hotel, *9 Charles Street, Hemel Hempstead, Herts, HP1 1JH.* Detached small hotel, near town centre. Car park. Near M1 and M25. **Open:** All year
01442 251387 Mr Davis **D:** Fr £20.50 **S:** Fr £29.50 **Beds:** 2F 1D 6T 10S **Baths:** 6 Sh (7) cc

Hertingfordbury

TL3011

Orchard Cottage, *East End Green, Hertingfordbury, Hertford, SG14 2PD.* Cosy country cottage, rural setting, 5 mins' drive Hertford, Hatfield, Welwyn Garden City. **Open:** All year (not Xmas/New Year)
01992 583494 (also fax) Mrs Adms **D:** Fr £45.00 **S:** Fr £25.00–£30.00 **Beds:** 3T
Baths: 2 Sh

Hitchin

TL1828

Firs Hotel, *83 Bedford Road, Hitchin, Herts, SG5 2TY.* Comfortable hotel with relaxed informal atmosphere. Excellent rail/road links and car parking. **Open:** All year
01462 422322 M Girgenti **Fax: 01462 432051** *info@firshotel.co.uk* www.firshotel.co.uk **D:** Fr £31.00 **S:** Fr £52.00 **Beds:** 3F 3D 8T 16S
Baths: 30 En (30) cc

Hoddesdon

TL3708

The Bell Inn, *Burford Street, Hoddesdon, Herts, EN11.* Close to M25 and A10. Contractors welcome. Entertainment weekends. **Open:** All year
01992 463552 Mr & Mrs Corrigan **Fax: 01992 450400** welcome.to/thebellinn **D:** Fr £17.00–£22.00 **S:** Fr £21.00–£26.00 **Beds:** 5F 5T 4S
Baths: 2 En cc

Kings Langley

TL0702

Woodcote House, *7 The Grove, Chipperfield Road, Kings Langley, Herts, WD4 9JF.* Detached timber-framed house in acre of gardens. **Open:** All year (not Xmas)
01923 262077 Mr & Mrs Leveridge **Fax: 01923 266198** *leveridge@btinternet.com* **D:** Fr £24.00–£30.00 **S:** Fr £26.00–£30.00 **Beds:** 1D 1T 2S **Baths:** 4 En (1) (6)

71 Hempstead Road, *Kings Langley, Herts, WD4 8BS.* Ideally situated M1, M25 near Watford, Hemel Hempstead, St Albans. Village centre within walking distance. **Open:** All year (not Xmas/New Year)
01923 270925 Mrs Fulton **D:** Fr £22.50–£25.00 **S:** Fr £22.50–£25.00 **Beds:** 1D
Baths: 1 Sh

Lilley

TL1126

Lilley Arms, *West Street, Lilley, Luton, Beds, LU2 8LN.* Early C18th coaching inn. **Open:** All year
01462 768371 Mrs Brown **D:** Fr £20.00–£30.00 **Beds:** 1F 1D 3T **Baths:** 3 En 1 Sh cc

London Colney

TL1804

The Conifers, *42 Thamesdale, London Colney, St Albans, Herts, AL2 1TL.* Modern detached house. Historic city St Albans 3 miles. Easy access motorway network. **Open:** All year **Grades:** ETC 3 Diamond
01727 823622 **D:** Fr £22.00–£26.00 **S:** Fr £22.00–£26.00 **Beds:** 1D 1T 1S **Baths:** 1 Sh (12)

Radlett

TL1600

The Turners, *43 Craigweil Avenue, Radlett, Hertfordshire, WD7 7ET.* Warm welcome. Ideally situated for Herts, Beds and Bucks. 20 mins to London. **Open:** All year
07776 132416 & 01923 469245 Mrs Turner **D:** Fr £20.00–£22.50 **S:** Fr £20.00–£25.00 **Beds:** 1T 1S **Baths:** 1 En 1 Sh (4)

Redbourn

TL1012

20 Cumberland Drive, *Redbourn, Herts, AL3 7PG.* Comfortable quiet home in village; easy access to M1/M25, London. **Open:** All year (not Xmas)
01582 794283 Mrs Tompkins **D:** Fr £22.00 **S:** Fr £22.00 **Beds:** 1T 1S **Baths:** 1 Pr 1 Sh (10)

Rickmansworth

TQ0494

The Millwards Guest House, *30 Hazelwood Road, Croxley Green, Rickmansworth, Herts, WD3 3EB.* Family run, quiet, pleasant canalside location. Convenient motorways, Watford/Croxley business centres, London trains. **Open:** All year (not Xmas/New Year)
01923 226666 & 07881 658870 (M) Mrs Millward **Fax: 01923 252874** *bandb@millwards.com* **D:** Fr £20.00–£22.50 **S:** Fr £25.00–£30.00 **Beds:** 3T **Baths:** 2 Sh (2) (2)

Tall Trees, *6 Swallow Close, Nightingale Road, Rickmansworth, Herts, WD3 7DZ.* Situated in quiet cul-de-sac near underground station. Home-made bread and preserves. **Open:** All year
01923 720069 Mrs Childerhouse **D:** Fr £28.00–£30.00 **S:** Fr £28.00–£30.00 **Beds:** 1D 3S **Baths:** 1 Sh (10) (4)

Royston

TL3541

Jockey Inn, *31-33 Baldock Street, Royston, Herts, SG8 5BD.* Traditional public house, real ales. Comfortable rooms - ensuite/cable TV. Hearty breakfast. **Open:** All year
01763 243377 **D:** Fr £26.50–£28.50 **S:** Fr £29.95–£34.00 **Beds:** 3T 1F **Baths:** 5 En (5)

Planning a longer stay? Always ask for any special rates

Hall Farm, *Great Chishill, Royston, Cambridgeshire, SG8 8SH.* **Open:** All year **01763 838263 (also fax)** Mrs Wiseman www.hallfarmbb.co.uk **D:** Fr £25.00–£30.00 **S:** Fr £30.00–£35.00 **Beds:** 1F 1T 1D **Baths:** 1 En 1 Sh (4)
Beautiful Manor house in secluded gardens on the edge of this pretty hilltop village 11 miles south of Cambridge, wonderful views and footpaths. Duxford Air Museum 4 miles. Good local food. Working arable farm. Comfortable new beds.

St Albans

TL1507

2 The Limes, Spencer Gate, *St Albans, Herts, AL1 4AT.* A modern, comfortable home, quiet cul de sac, 10 mins town centre. Home-baked bread. **Open:** All year **Grades:** ETC 3 Diamond
01727 831080 Mrs Mitchell *hunter.mitchell@virgin.net* **D:** Fr £20.00 **S:** Fr £20.00–£25.00 **Beds:** 1T 1S **Baths:** 1 Sh (3) (2)

7 Marlborough Gate, *St Albans, Herts, AL1 3TX.* Detached house close to station. **Open:** All year (not Xmas/New Year)
01727 865498 Mrs Jameson **Fax: 01727 812966** *michael.jameson@btinternet.com* **D:** Fr £20.00–£24.00 **S:** Fr £20.00–£24.00 **Beds:** 1T 2S (3)

76 Clarence Road, *St Albans, Herts, AL1 4NG.* Spacious Edwardian house opposite park. Easy walking to trains (London). **Open:** All year (not Xmas/New Year)
01727 864880 (also fax) Mr & Mrs Leggatt *pat.leggatt@talk21.com* www.twistedsilicon.co.uk/76/index.htm **D:** Fr £23.00–£25.00 **S:** Fr £26.00–£30.00 **Beds:** 1T 1S **Baths:** 1 Sh (2)

Stapleford

TL3116

Little Pipers, *1 Church Lane, Stapleford, Hertford, Herts, SG14 3NB.* Quiet riverside village location. Good transportation links to London. **Open:** All year
01992 589085 Mrs Lewis **D:** Fr £18.00–£25.00 **S:** Fr £20.00–£30.00 **Beds:** 4D **Baths:** 1 En 1 Sh (6)

All details shown are as supplied by B&B owners in Autumn 2002

Stevenage

TL2424

Abbington Hotel, *23 Hitchin Road, Stevenage, Herts, SG1 3BJ.* Old town location. All ensuite, telephone, remote CTV, hairdryer etc. **Open:** All year (not Xmas/New Year)
01438 315241 Fax: 01438 745043 *bookings@abbingtonhotel.co.uk* www.abbingtonhotel.co.uk **D:** Fr £22.50–£29.50 **S:** Fr £35.00–£54.00 **Beds:** 1F 2T 10D 7S **Baths:** 20 En (24) cc

Watford

TQ1097

33 Courtlands Drive, *Watford, Herts, WD1 3HU.* Detached house, warm and friendly. Convenient London, canal, motorways M1, M25. **Open:** All year (not Xmas)
01923 220531 A Troughton **D:** Fr £20.00–£22.50 **S:** Fr £25.00 **Beds:** 2T 1S **Baths:** 1 Sh (2) (6)

Applecrust B&B, *52 Rickmansworth Road, Watford, Herts, WD1 7HT.* Friendly, comfortable, centrally located accommodation with high quality home cooking. **Open:** All year
01923 223125 Mrs Spicer **Fax: 01923 211652** **D:** Fr £22.50–£27.50 **S:** Fr £30.00–£40.00 **Beds:** 1F 1T 1D **Baths:** 1 En 1 Sh (4)

Midmar, *12a Nascot Wood Road, Watford, Herts, WD17 4SA.* Tastefully furnished, spacious accommodation, centrally situated in quiet road. **Open:** All year (not Xmas/New Year)
01923 242015 *factform@aol.com* www.midmar-bed-breakfast.co.uk **D:** Fr £22.50–£25.00 **S:** Fr £30.00–£35.00 **Beds:** 3D 1S **Baths:** 2 En 1 Sh (10) (7)

The Millwards Guest House, *30 Hazelwood Road, Croxley Green, Rickmansworth, Herts, WD3 3EB.* Family run, quiet, pleasant canalside location. Convenient motorways, Watford/Croxley business centres, London trains. **Open:** All year (not Xmas/New Year)
01923 226666 & 07881 658870 (M) Mrs Millward **Fax: 01923 252874** *bandb@millwards.com* **D:** Fr £20.00–£22.50 **S:** Fr £25.00–£30.00 **Beds:** 3T **Baths:** 2 Sh (2) (2)

Grey s Bed & Breakfast, *1 Wellington Road, Watford, Herts, WD1 1QU.* Ideally located for railway station, town centre and business parks. **Open:** Jan to Dec
07990 956260 (M) M-L Grey **Fax: 01923 492446** *greysbnb@bigfoot.com* www.users.globalnet.co.uk/~outpost/bnb/home.html **D:** Fr £22.50 **S:** Fr £25.00 **Beds:** 2T 1S **Baths:** 2 Sh (4)

Welwyn

TL2316

Christmas Cottage, *3 Ayot Green, Welwyn, Herts, AL6 9AB.* **Open:** All year **01707 321489** Mr & Mrs Sherriff **Fax: 01707 392659** *janesherriff@tesco.net* **D:** Fr £30.00 **S:** Fr £55.00 **Beds:** 1D 1T 1S **Baths:** 2 En 1 Pr (10)
Charming 300-year-old cottage on village green, comfortable bedrooms overlooking garden and swimming pool, close to Hatfield and Welwyn Garden City stations. Rich local interest including cathedral city of St Albans and Hatfield House.

Welwyn Garden City

TL2413

L G Hotels, *Homestead Court Hotel, Homestead Lane, Welwyn Garden City, Herts, AL7 4LX.* Newly refurbished contemporary hotel in peaceful parklands. Next to A1(M) J4. **Open:** All year **Grades:** AA 3 Star **01707 324336** Mr Lababedi **Fax: 01707 326447** *enquiries@homesteadcourt.co.uk* www.homesteadcourt.co.uk **D:** Fr £92.00–£102.00 **S:** Fr £82.00–£92.00 **Beds:** 32T 20D 6S **Baths:** 58 En (70) **cc**

The Seven Bees, *76 Longcroft Lane, Welwyn Garden City, Herts, AL8 6EF.* Peaceful detached house, beautiful garden, short walk to town centre. **Open:** All year (not Xmas) **01707 333602** Mrs Bunyan **D:** Fr £25.00 **S:** Fr £25.00 **Beds:** 1T 1S **Baths:** 1 Sh (1)

RATES

D = Price range per person sharing in a double or twin room

S = Price range for a single room

Isle of Wight

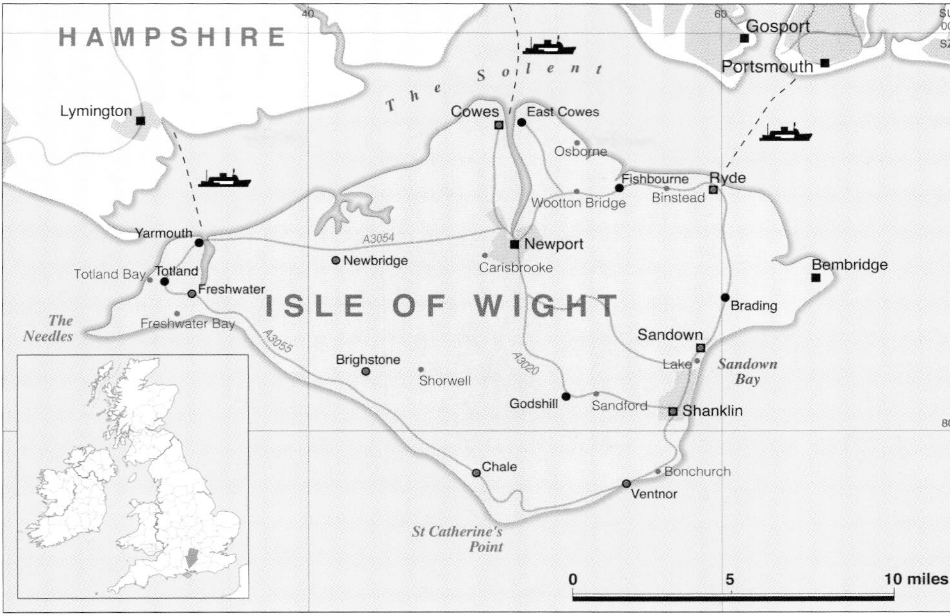

Binstead

SZ5791 *Fishbourne Inn*

Elm Close Cottage, *Ladies Walk, Binstead, Isle of Wight, PO33 3SY.* Converted stables to C18th mansion. Tranquil coastal footpath setting. **Open:** All year (not Xmas/ New Year)
01983 567161 *elm_cottage@hotmail.com* **D:** Fr £20.00–£25.00 **S:** Fr £22.50–£25.00 **Beds:** 1T 2D **Baths:** 3 En P (3)

Bonchurch

SZ5777

The Lake Hotel, *Shore Road, Bonchurch, Ventnor, Isle of Wight, PO38 1LF.* Country house hotel, 2-acre garden in Bonchurch seaside village. **Open:** Mar to Nov
01983 852613 (also fax) Mr Wyatt *richard@lakehotel.co.uk* www.lakehotel.co.uk **D:** Fr £26.00–£30.00 **Beds:** 3F 8T 8D 1S **Baths:** 20 En (3) P (20)

Brighstone

SZ4382

Buddlebrook Guest House, *Moortown Lane, Brighstone, Newport, Isle of Wight, PO30 4AN.* Peaceful country guest house. Adults only. Non-smokers. Super breakfast. **Open:** All year
01983 740381 & 07816 573843 (M) Mr & Mrs Woodford *patanddavid@onetel.net.uk* www.buddlebrookguesthouse.co.uk **D:** Fr £20.00–£25.00 **S:** Fr £22.00–£25.00 **Beds:** 2D 1T **Baths:** 3 En P (3)

Carisbrooke

SZ4888 *Eight Bells*

The Mount, *1 Calbourne Road, Carisbrooke, Newport, Isle of Wight, PO30 5AP.* Large Victorian private house in the beautiful village of Carisbrooke.
Open: Easter to Oct
01983 522173 & 01983 524359 Mrs Skeats **D:** Fr £16.00–£17.00 **S:** Fr £16.00–£17.00 **Beds:** 1T 1D **Baths:** 1 Sh P (2)

Chale

SZ4877

Cortina, *Gotten Lane, Chale, Ventnor, Isle of Wight, PO38 2HQ.* Modern comfortable bungalow. **Open:** All year (not Xmas)
01983 551292 Mrs Whittington **D:** Fr £17.00 **S:** Fr £20.00 **Beds:** 1D 1T **Baths:** 1 Sh P (6)

RATES
D = Price range per person sharing in a double or twin room
S = Price range for a single room

Cowes

SZ4996

Royal Standard Antiques, *70-72 Park Road, Cowes, Isle of Wight, PO31 7LY.* Interesting Victorian building; friendly relaxing atmosphere. 5 mins High Street. **Open:** All year
01983 281672 Mrs Bradbury *caroline@royalstandardantiques.fsbusiness.co.uk* royalstandardantiques.fsbusiness.co.uk **D:** Fr £23.00–£28.00 **S:** Fr £25.00–£30.00 **Beds:** 1T 1D 1S **Baths:** 1 Pr 1 Sh (2) cc

Halcyone Villa, *Grove Road, off Mill Hill Road, Cowes, Isle of Wight, PO31 7JP.* Small friendly Victorian guest house situated near marinas and town. **Open:** All year
01983 291334 Miss Fussell *sandra@halcyone.freeserve.co.uk* www.halcyonevilla.freeuk.com **D:** Fr £17.50–£35.00 **S:** Fr £17.50–£35.00 **Beds:** 1F 2D 2T 1S **Baths:** 1 En 1 Pr 1 Sh

Gurnard Pines Holiday Village, *Cockleton Lane, Cowes, Isle of Wight, PO31 8QE.* Countryside location close to yachting haven of Cowes. Luxury pine lodges or bungalows. **Open:** All year
01983 292395 Fax: 01983 299415 *mail@pines.tcp.co.uk* www.gurnardpines.co.uk **D:** Fr £25.00–£40.00 **S:** Fr £35.00–£50.00 **Beds:** 20F 30T 30D **Baths:** 40 En 40 Pr (200) cc

Freshwater

SZ3486

Royal Standard Hotel, *15 School Green Road, Freshwater, Isle of Wight, PO40 9AJ.* **Open:** All year **Grades:** ETC 3 Diamond
01983 753227 Mrs & Ms R Stephenson *beccy@stephenson84.freeserve.co.uk* **D:** Fr £24.00 **S:** Fr £24.00 **Beds:** 3F 3D 1T 4S **Baths:** 11 En
The Royal Standard is a family-run 11-bedroom hotel & free house which offers a warm & friendly welcome. Situated in the centre of Freshwater at the western end of the island, an ideal location for walking, cycling & golf.

Brookside Forge Hotel, *Brookside Road, Freshwater, Isle of Wight, PO40 9ER.* Small family-run hotel. Centre of village, yet quiet location. **Open:** All year
01983 754644 J Chettle **D:** Fr £24.00–£26.00 **S:** Fr £26.00–£28.00 **Beds:** 2F 2T 2D 1S **Baths:** 6 En 1 Pr (7) cc

Freshwater Bay

SZ3485

Wight Haven, *Afton Road, Freshwater Bay, Freshwater, Isle of Wight, PO40 9TT.* Ideal for walking/cycling holidays, 400 yards from Bay. **Open:** All year
01983 753184 Mr & Mrs Searle *wighthaven@btinternet.com* **D:** Fr £25.00 **S:** Fr £35.00 **Beds:** 1T 2D **Baths:** 3 En

Lake

SZ5883

Cliff Lodge, *13 Cliff Path, Lake, Isle of Wight, PO36 8PL.* Edwardian house. Gardens access coastal path. Warm welcome. English breakfast. **Open:** Feb to Nov **Grades:** ETC 3 Diamond
01983 402963 Mrs Grinstead **D:** Fr £19.00–£22.00 **S:** Fr £19.00–£22.00 **Beds:** 2F 6D 1S **Baths:** 8 En (2) (8)

Osterley Lodge, *62 Sandown Road, Lake, Sandown, Isle of Wight, PO36 9JX.* Between Sandown/Shanklin. Close to all amenities/transport/beach. **Open:** All year
01983 402017 Horton *osterley_lodge@netguides.co.uk* **D:** Fr £16.00–£25.00 **S:** Fr £16.00–£25.00 **Beds:** 1F 1T 5D **Baths:** 6 En 1 Pr (5) (7) cc

Newbridge

SZ4187

Homestead Farm, *Newbridge, Yarmouth, Isle of Wight, PO41 0TZ.* New wing of modern farmhouse. **Open:** Jan to Dec
01983 531270 Mrs Priddle **D:** Fr £20.00 **S:** Fr £25.00 **Beds:** 1F 1T 1D 1S **Baths:** 2 En

Osborne

SZ5194

The Doghouse, *Crossways Road, Osborne, East Cowes, Isle of Wight, PO32 6LJ.* Somewhere special. Popular friendly comfortable ensuite rooms near Osborne House. **Open:** All year
01983 293677 **D:** Fr £20.00–£30.00 **S:** Fr £30.00–£35.00 **Beds:** 1T 1D **Baths:** 2 En (3)

Planning a longer stay? Always ask for any special rates

BEDROOMS
D = Double
T = Twin
S = Single
F = Family

Ryde

SZ5992 *Thatcher's*

Seaward, *14 & 16 George Street, Ryde, Isle of Wight, PO332EW.* Close to beach, ferry terminals, town centre and local amenities. **Open:** All year
01983 563168 & 0800 9152966 *seaward@fsbdial.co.uk* **D:** Fr £15.00–£22.00 **S:** Fr £18.00–£24.00 **Beds:** 2F 1T 3D 1S **Baths:** 2 En 4 Sh

Rowantrees, *63 Spencer Road, Ryde, Isle of Wight, PO33 3AF.* Modern detached house, quiet rural setting, minutes from town centre & sea front. **Open:** All year (not Xmas/New Year)
01983 568081 **D:** Fr £15.00–£16.00 **S:** Fr £16.00 **Beds:** 1D/F 2S **Baths:** 1 Sh (4)

Dorset Hotel, *Dover Street, Ryde, Isle of Wight, PO33 2BW.* Centrally located, close to the beach. **Open:** All year (not Xmas/New Year)
01983 564327 *hoteldorset@aol.com* www.thedorsethotel.co.uk **D:** Fr £19.00–£21.00 **S:** Fr £25.00–£28.00 **Beds:** 2F 8T 8D 4S **Baths:** 18 En 4 Sh (3) (16) cc

Sandford

SZ5481 *Cask & Taverners, Griffin, White Horse*

The Barn, *Pound Farm, Shanklin Road, Sandford, Isle of Wight, PO38 3AW.* 1816 converted barn in 6 acres - golf, cycling. Farmhouse breakfast. **Open:** All year
01983 840047 (also fax) Mr & Mrs Squire *barnpoundfarm@free-online.co.uk* **D:** Fr £20.00 **S:** Fr £25.00 **Beds:** 1F 1T 1D **Baths:** 3 En

Sandown

SZ5984

Fernside Private Licensed Hotel, *30 Station Road, Sandown, Isle of Wight, PO36 9BW.* Family-run licensed hotel close to beach and town of Sandown. **Open:** Mar to Nov
01983 402356 Mr & Mrs Moore **Fax: 01983 403647** *enquiries@fernsidehotel.co.uk* www.fernsidehotel.co.uk **D:** Fr £20.00–£25.00 **S:** Fr £20.00–£25.00 **Beds:** 2F 3T 4D 1S **Baths:** 10 En (6) cc

Willow Dene Guest House, *110 Station Avenue, Sandown, Isle of Wight, PO36 8HD.* Near all amenities, home cooking, friendly atmosphere. **Open:** Feb to Oct
01983 403100 S Ratcliffe **D:** Fr £17.00–£20.00 **S:** Fr £17.00–£20.00 **Beds:** 3T 1D 1S **Baths:** 1 Sh

Rayles Hotel, *Yaverland Road, Sandown, Isle of Wight, PO36 8QP.* Secluded hotel, own grounds, sea views, ideal for walking/touring. **Open:** Easter to Nov
01983 402266 D: Fr £17.00–£27.50 **S:** Fr £17.00–£27.50 **Beds:** 3F 5T 11D 2S **Baths:** 15 En 1 Pr 1 Sh (15)

Shangri La, *30 Broadway, Sandown, Isle of Wight, PO36 8BY.* Friendly and informal detached hotel, licensed. Close to all amenities. **Open:** All year **Grades:** RAC 3 Diamond
01983 403672 (also fax) *shangrilahotel@aol.com* www.shangrilahotel.co.uk **D:** Fr £24.00–£27.00 **S:** Fr £24.00–£27.00 **Beds:** 4F 2T 6D 2S **Baths:** 1 Pr 1 Sh (1) (9) **cc**

Hazelwood Hotel, *19 Carter Street, Sandown, Isle of Wight, PO36 8BL.* Victorian hotel. near sea and nightclub. Home cooking, relaxed family atmosphere.
Open: All year
01983 402536 Mrs Wright **D:** Fr £18.00–£24.00 **S:** Fr £20.00 **Beds:** 3F 1T 1D **Baths:** 1 Sh (8)

The Iona Private Hotel, *44 Sandown Road, Sandown, Isle of Wight, PO36 9JT.* 9-room guest house, few mins' walk from beautiful cliff path and sandy beach.
Open: All year
01983 402741 (also fax) Mr Joy & Nora Dempsey *ionahotel@netscapeonline.co.uk*
D: Fr £15.00–£19.00 **S:** Fr £15.00–£19.00 **Beds:** 3F 4D 2T 3S **Baths:** 4 Pr 2 Sh (6) **cc**

Mount Brocas Guest House, *15 Beachfield Road, Sandown, Isle of Wight, PO36 8LT.* Beach, pier, shops, buses, coastal walks. 2 mins from Mount Brocas. **Open:** All year (not Xmas)
01983 406276 Mrs King *brocas@netguides.co.uk*
D: Fr £15.00–£20.00 **S:** Fr £16.00–£22.00 **Beds:** 2F 3D 2T 1S **Baths:** 4 En 2 Pr

Montpelier Hotel, *Pier Street, Sandown, Isle of Wight, PO36 8JR.* Situated in one of the finest positions in Sandown. **Open:** All year
01983 403964 S Birks **Fax: 0709 2212734** *still@montpelier-hotel.co.uk* www.montpelier-hotel.co.uk **D:** Fr £18.00–£25.00 **S:** Fr £18.00–£25.00 **Beds:** 2F 1T 3D 1S **Baths:** 5 En 1 Pr **cc**

Shanklin

SZ5881

Culham Lodge Hotel, *31 Landguard Manor Road, Shanklin, Isle of Wight, PO37 7HZ.* **Open:** Feb to Dec **Grades:** ETC 4 Diamond
01983 862880 (also fax) Mr Metcalf *metcalf@culham99.freeserve.co.uk* **D:** Fr £24.00–£25.00 **S:** Fr £24.00–£25.00 **Beds:** 4D 5T 1S **Baths:** 10 En (12) (8) **cc**
This delightful small hotel perfect for breaks is well known for good value, with lovely gardens, heated swimming pool, conservatory. All rooms ensuite, satellite TV, hairdryers, teamakers. Ferry-inclusive packages available. We can book your ferry and save you money.

Somerton Lodge Hotel, *Victoria Avenue, Shanklin, Isle of Wight, PO37 6LT.*
Open: All year
01983 862710 Fax: 01983 863841 *somerton@talk21.com* www.wight-holidays.co.uk **D:** Fr £23.00–£28.00 **S:** Fr £23.00–£28.00 **Beds:** 4F 7T 7D 2S **Baths:** 18 En 1 Pr (1) (20) **cc**
This warm & friendly well run family Victorian hotel lies in a beautiful tree-lined street just a short walk from Shanklin Chine. Offers traditional home cooked food in a non-smoking spacious luxury dining room. Special breaks available.

Ryedale Private Hotel, *3 Atherley Road, Shanklin, Isle of Wight, PO37 7AT.* Small and friendly. Near station and beach, children welcome. **Open:** All year
01983 862375 & 07816 812349 (M) Mrs & Mr J.D. Clark **Fax: 01983 862375** *ryedale@dottydots.co.uk* www.smoothhound.co.uk/hotels/ryedalep.html **D:** Fr £18.50–£23.50 **S:** Fr £18.50–£23.50 **Beds:** 3F 1T 2D 2S **Baths:** 5 En 1 Pr 1 Sh **cc**

Glendene Hotel, *7 Carter Avenue, Shanklin, Isle of Wight, PO37 7LQ.* **Open:** All year
01983 862924 Mr & Mrs Finch *janderekglendenehotel.fsnet.co.uk* www.glendenefreeserve.com **D:** Fr £18.00–£22.00 **S:** Fr £18.00–£22.00 **Beds:** 2F 2T 2D 1S **Baths:** 4 En 2 Sh (5) **cc**
Relax in our small friendly hotel situated in the heart of Shanklin, close to the shops, public transport, RBL and 10 minutes' walk to Shanklin's sandy beach & the picturesque old village of Shanklin with its ancient chine.

St George's House Hotel, *St Georges Road, Shanklin, Isle of Wight, PO37 6BA.* 2 minutes from glorious beaches and the 'old village'. **Open:** All year
01983 863691 Jon & Hazel Cain **Fax: 01983 861597** *info@stgeorgesiow.com* www.stgeorgesiow.com **D:** Fr £22.00–£27.00 **S:** Fr £25.00–£30.00 **Beds:** 2F 3T 3D **Baths:** 7 En 1 Pr **cc**

Hambledon Hotel, *Queens Road, Shanklin, Isle of Wight, PO37 6AW.* Family licensed hotel offers genuine personal service. All bedrooms ensuite and tastefully decorated. **Open:** All year
01983 862403 Mr Sewell www.hambledon-hotel.co.uk **D:** Fr £23.00–£26.00 **S:** Fr £25.00 **Beds:** 4F 4D 1T 1S **Baths:** 10 En (8)

The Hazelwood, *14 Clarence Road, Shanklin, Isle of Wight, PO37 7BH.* Friendly hotel, own grounds close to cliff path, station, town. **Open:** All year (not Xmas)
01983 862824 (also fax) Mr & Mrs Tubbs *barbara.tubbs@thehazelwood.free-online.co.uk* www.thehazelwood.free-online.co.uk **D:** Fr £19.00–£21.00 **S:** Fr £19.00–£21.00 **Beds:** 2F 3D 2T 1S **Baths:** 8 En (5) (3) **cc**

Shorwell

SZ4682

Northcourt, *Shorwell, Newport, Isle of Wight, PO30 3JG.* Historic manor house in outstanding 15-acre garden. **Open:** All year
01983 740415 Mr Harrison **Fax: 01983 740409** *john@north-court.demon.co.uk* www.wightfarmholidays.co.uk/northcourt
D: Fr £25.00–£30.00 **S:** Fr £34.00–£40.00 **Beds:** 3T 3D 1S **Baths:** 6 En

Planning a longer stay? Always ask for any special rates

Totland Bay

SZ3186

Lomarick, *Church Hill, Totland Bay, Isle of Wight, PO39 0EU.* Wonderful sea views, homely welcome, good breakfast, relaxing, touring/ walking area. **Open:** All year **Grades:** ETC 3 Diamond

01983 753364 & 01983 755140 *lomarick.iow@virgin.net* www.wightonline.co.uk/lomarick **D:** Fr £23.00–£25.00 **S:** Fr £25.00–£35.00 **Beds:** 1F 1T **Baths:** 1 En 1 Pr (1) (3)

Ventnor

SZ5677

Cornerways, *39 Medeira Road, Ventnor, Isle of Wight, PO38 1QS.* Quiet location with magnificent views over sea and Downs. **Open:** Mar to Oct **Grades:** AA 3 Diamond

01983 852323 Mr & Mrs Layburn *palmer99@supanet.com* www.cornerwaysventnor.co.uk **D:** Fr £21.00–£26.00 **S:** Fr £21.00–£39.00 **Beds:** 2F 3D 2T **Baths:** 7 En (4) cc

Picardie Hotel, *Esplanade, Ventnor, Isle of Wight, PO38 1JX.* Welcoming small seafront family hotel for lovers of country pursuits. **Open:** All year

01983 852647 (also fax) *hostmaster@picardie.f9.co.uk* www.picardie.f9.co.uk **D:** Fr £35.00–£45.00 **S:** Fr £30.00–£40.00 **Beds:** 3F 1T 4D 1S **Baths:** 5 En 4 Pr

Wootton Bridge

SZ5491

Briddlesford Lodge Farm, *Wootton Bridge, Ryde, Isle of Wight, PO33 4RY.* Friendly family farm with 150 Guernsey Dairy herd. Good breakfasts. **Open:** All year (not Xmas/ New Year)

01983 882239 Mrs Griffin **D:** Fr £20.00–£22.00 **S:** Fr £20.00–£22.00 **Beds:** 1F 1D 1T **Baths:** 1 En1 Sh (3)

Isles of Scilly

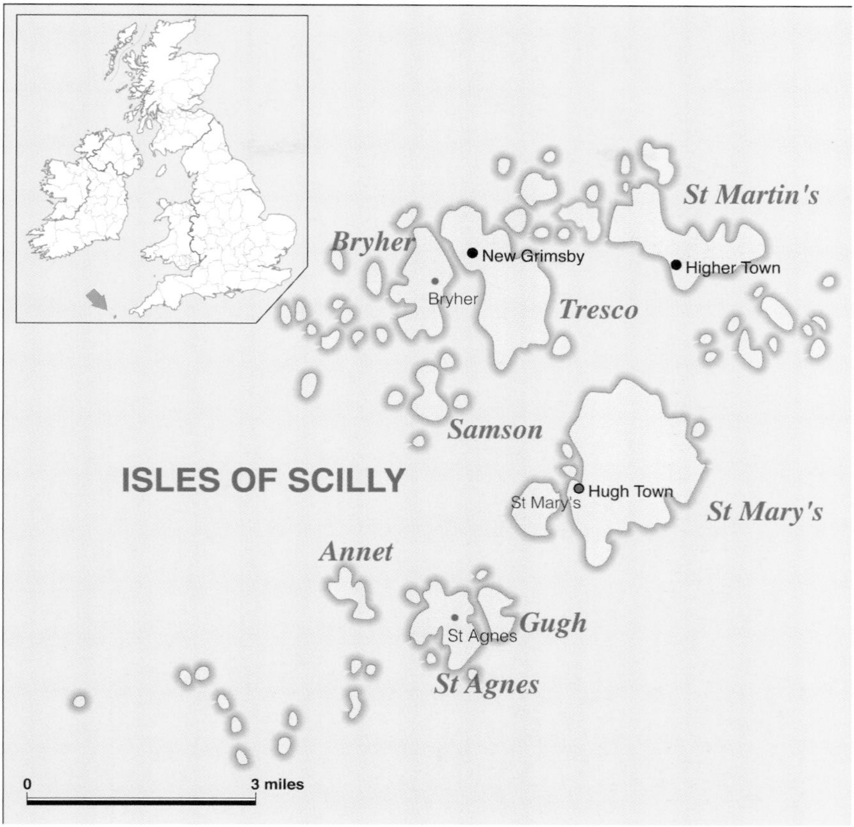

Bryher

SV8715

Soleil d'Or, *Bryher, Isles of Scilly, TR23 0PR.* Soleil d'Or, the perfect base to enjoy the tranquillity of Bryher. **Open:** Easter to Oct **01720 422003** Mrs Street **D:** Fr £22.00–£26.00 **S:** Fr £22.00–£40.00 **Beds:** 2D 1T **Baths:** 3 En (3)

St Agnes

SV8807

Covean Cottage, *St Agnes, Isles of Scilly, TR22 0PL.* Attractive granite cottage set in subtropical garden. Highly recommended. **Open:** Easter to Nov **01720 422620 (also fax)** Mrs Sewell **D:** Fr £26.00–£32.50 **S:** Fr £30.00–£35.00 **Beds:** 2D 2T **Baths:** 3 En 1 Sh (9)

St Mary's

SV9010

Lyonnesse House, *The Strand, St Mary's, Isles of Scilly, TR21 0PT.* Magnificent sea views and imaginative Aga-cooked cuisine, great hospitality. **Open:** Mar to Oct **Grades:** ETC 3 Diamond **01720 422458** Mrs Woodcock **D:** Fr £27.00–£28.00 **S:** Fr £27.00–£28.00 **Beds:** 1F 3D 3T 2S **Baths:** 5 Sh (5)

Marine House, *Church Street, Hugh Town, St Mary's, Isles of Scilly, TR21 0JT.* A very comfortable guest house, near harbour, beaches and shops. **Open:** Easter to Sept **01720 422966** Mrs Rowe *peggy@rowe55.freeserve.co.uk* **D:** Fr £22.00–£25.00 **S:** Fr £22.00–£25.00 **Beds:** 1D 1T 1S **Baths:** 1 En (9)

Kent

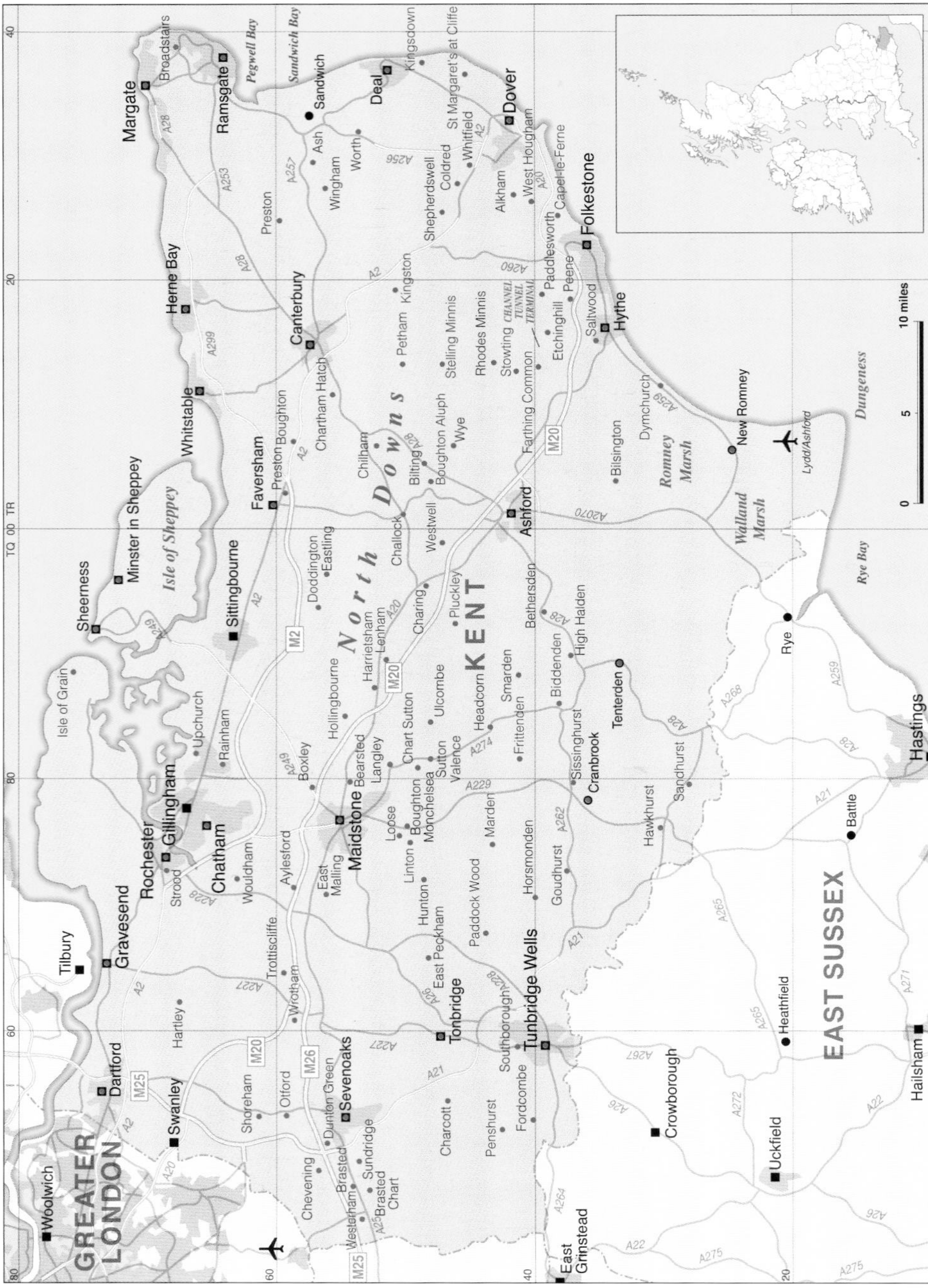
KENT
EAST SUSSEX
GREATER LONDON
North Downs
Isle of Sheppey
Romney Marsh
Walland Marsh
Dungeness
Rye Bay
Pegwell Bay
Sandwich Bay
CHANNEL TUNNEL TERMINAL
Margate
Broadstairs
Ramsgate
Herne Bay
Whitstable
Canterbury
Sandwich
Deal
Dover
Folkestone
Hythe
Ashford
Faversham
Sittingbourne
Sheerness
Minster in Sheppey
Rochester
Gillingham
Chatham
Gravesend
Dartford
Swanley
Sevenoaks
Tonbridge
Tunbridge Wells
Maidstone
Cranbrook
Tenterden
New Romney
Rye
Hastings
Battle
Hailsham
Heathfield
Crowborough
Uckfield
East Grinstead
Tilbury
Woolwich
Isle of Grain
Lydd/Ashford
10 miles

Alkham

TR2542

Alkham Court, *Meggett Lane, South Alkham, Dover, Kent, CT15 7DG.* **Open:** All year **Grades:** ETC 4 Diamond
01303 892056 & 07798 518387 (M) Mrs Burrows *wendy.burrows@alkhamcourt.co.uk* www.alkhamcourt.co.uk **D:** Fr £23.00–£27.50 **S:** Fr £30.00–£35.00 **Beds:** 1F 1D **Baths:** 1 En 1 Pr (4)
Beautiful location in area of outstanding natural beauty overlooking Alkham Valley with horses/sheep on family farm with homely atmosphere. Hearty English breakfasts with local produce in conservatory enjoying spectacular views. 5 mins from Channel Tunnel & ferries. 20 mins Canterbury.

Owler Lodge, *Alkham Valley Road, Alkham, Dover, Kent, CT15 7DF.* High quality accommodation, picturesque village. Ideal for touring East Kent. **Open:** All year (not Xmas) **Grades:** ETC 4 Diamond
01304 826375 Mrs Owler **Fax: 01304 829372** *owlerlodge@aol.com* **D:** Fr £22.00–£27.00 **S:** Fr £35.00–£38.00 **Beds:** 1F 1D 1T **Baths:** 3 En (5) (3)

Ash (Sandwich)

TR2758 *Lion Inn, Chequers*

55 Guilton, *Ash, Canterbury, Kent, CT3 2HR.* Between Canterbury and Sandwich, Victorian cottage, log fires, Victorian type dining room with original features, cottage garden, ideal touring Kent nature reserves, wildlife park, historic buildings, wine trails, Dover ferries, Manston airport and coast within easy reach. **Open:** All year (not Xmas)
01304 812809 Mrs Smith **D:** Fr £17.00 **S:** Fr £20.00 **Beds:** 2D **Baths:** 1 En (2)

Ashford

TR0042

Quantock House, *Quantock Drive, Ashford, Kent, TN24 8QH.* Quiet residential area. Easy walk to town centre. Comfortable and welcoming. **Open:** All year (not Xmas) **Grades:** ETC 3 Diamond
01233 638921 Mr & Mrs Tucker *tucker100@madasafish.com* **D:** Fr £22.00–£25.00 **S:** Fr £25.00–£26.00 **Beds:** 1F 1D 1T 1S **Baths:** 3 En (5) (3)

Ashford Warren Cottage Hotel, *136 The Street, Willesborough, Ashford, Kent, TN24 0NB.* **Open:** All year
01233 621905 Mrs Jones **Fax: 01233 623400** *general@warrencottage.co.uk* www.warrencottage.co.uk **D:** Fr £25.00–£35.00 **S:** Fr £20.00–£45.00 **Beds:** 1F 3D 1T 1S **Baths:** 6 En (20) cc
The Channel Tunnel terminal is just a few miles' drive south with direct access from the M20. Ashford is also an ideal location for travelling into London or to the Ports of Dover or Folkestone where regular ferry and hovercraft services are available.

Vickys Guest House, *38 Park Road North, Ashford, Kent, TN24 8LY.* Town centre, close to international station, Canterbury, Folkestone and Dover nearby. **Open:** All year
01233 631061 Mrs Ford **Fax: 01233 640420** *vicky@ford27.freeserve.co.uk* **D:** Fr £22.50–£25.00 **S:** Fr £25.00 **Beds:** 1F 1D 1S 1T **Baths:** 3 Pr 1 Sh cc

Glenmoor, *Maidstone Road, Ashford, Kent, TN25 4NP.* Victorian gamekeeper's cottage close to international station and motorway. **Open:** All year (not Xmas/New Year)
01233 634767 Mrs Rowlands **D:** Fr £17.00 **S:** Fr £20.00 **Beds:** 2D 1T **Baths:** 1 Sh (5) (3)

Heather House, *40 Burton Road, Kennington, Ashford, Kent, TN24 9DS.* Heather House offers a warm, friendly welcome in quiet residential area. Near Eurostar. **Open:** All year (not Xmas/New Year)
01233 661826 Mrs Blackwell **Fax: 01233 635183** **D:** Fr £20.00 **S:** Fr £20.00 **Beds:** 1T 1D 1S **Baths:** 2 Sh

Aylesford

TQ7258

Court Farm, *High Street, Aylesford, Maidstone, Kent, ME20 7AZ.* Beams, four poster, spa, antiques, drawing room. Sorry, no children. **Open:** All year
01622 717293 (also fax) Mrs Tucker *enquiries@courtfarm.com* www.courtfarm.com **D:** Fr £25.00 **S:** Fr £25.00 **Beds:** 2D 1T 1S **Baths:** 3 En 1 Pr (6) cc

Wickham Lodge, *The Quay, High Street, Aylesford, Kent, ME20 7AY.* **Open:** All year **Grades:** ETC 4 Diamond
01622 717267 Mrs Bourne **Fax: 01622 792855** *wickhamlodge@aol.com* www.wickhamlodge.com **D:** Fr £25.00–£30.00 **S:** Fr £30.00 **Beds:** 1F 1D 1S **Baths:** 2 En 1 Pr (4) cc
Historic Georgian/Tudor house in Aylesford village on bank of the River Medway, close to the old bridge. Recently terraced and landscaped walled garden at rear. Individually furnished accommodation to a high standard. Self-catering stable cottage also available.

The Guest House, *The Friars, Aylesford Priory, Aylesford, Kent, ME20 7BX.* Picturesque priory home to a community of Carmelite friars, founded in 1242. **Open:** All year (not Xmas/New Year)
01622 717272 M Larcombe **Fax: 01622 715575** *friarsreception@hotmail.com* www.carmelite.org **D:** Fr £19.00–£24.00 **S:** Fr £19.00–£24.00 **Beds:** 2F 1D **Baths:** 2 Pr (50) cc

Bearsted

TQ7955

Cherwell, *88 Ashford Road, Bearsted, Maidstone, Kent, ME14 4LT.* **Open:** All year **Grades:** ETC 3 Diamond
01622 738278 Ms Basley-Jones **Fax: 01622 738346** **D:** Fr £22.00 **S:** Fr £22.00 **Beds:** 1T 2D 1S **Baths:** 1 En 1 Pr 1 Sh (10) (12)
Good quality accommodation convenient for Leeds Castle, Maidstone. Excellent motorway connection for Channel Tunnel, ferries & airports. Picturesque gardens, ample parking facilities and excellent food within walking distance.

Tollgate House, *Ashford Road, Bearsted, Maidstone, Kent, ME14 4NS.* **Open:** All year (not Xmas/New Year)
01622 738428 Mrs Wise **D:** Fr £20.00–£25.00 **S:** Fr £25.00–£30.00 **Beds:** 1F 1T **Baths:** 2 En (3)
Detached house with friendly atmosphere and large garden. Situated on A20 convenient for Leeds Castle, M20 J8, Channel Tunnel and Dover Ferries. Rooms have ensuite bathrooms, TV and tea and coffee making facilities. Guests' sitting room, off-street parking.

Planning a longer stay? Always ask for any special rates

The Hazels, *13 Yeoman Way, Bearsted, Maidstone, Kent, ME15 8PQ.* Large, comfortable family home in quiet location, easy access M20 and A20. **Open:** All year **Grades:** ETC 4 Diamond
01622 737943 Mr & Mrs Buse *ianbuse@hotmail.com* www.aspwebspace.com/thehazels **D:** Fr £21.00–£23.00 **S:** Fr £24.00–£25.00 **Beds:** 1T **Baths:** 1 En (2) TV

Bethersden

TQ9240

The Coach House, *Oakmead Farm, Bethersden, Ashford, Kent, TN26 0NB.* Rural, well back off road in 5 acres gardens and paddocks. **Open:** Mar to Oct
01233 820583 (also fax) B Broad **D:** Fr £20.00 **S:** Fr £25.00 **Beds:** 1F 1D 1T **Baths:** 2 En 1 Pr (10) TV V

Biddenden

TQ8438 *Three Chimneys, Red Lion*

Drayton House Farm, *Stede Quarter, Biddenden, Ashford, Kent, TN27 8JQ.* Small working farm within easy reach of many tourist attractions. **Open:** Apr to Oct
01580 291931 (also fax) Mrs Lidgett **D:** Fr £13.00–£18.00 **Beds:** 2T **Baths:** 2 Sh (3) TV

Frogshole Oast, *Sissinghurst Road, Biddenden, Ashford, Kent, TN27 8LW.* Attractively located C18th oasthouse, 1.5 acre garden, adjacent Sissinghurst Castle. **Open:** Easter to Oct
01580 291935 (also fax) D Hartley *hartley@frogsholeoast.freeserve.co.uk* www.geocities.com/frogsholeoast/sissinghurst.html **D:** Fr £23.00–£26.00 **S:** Fr £30.00–£40.00 **Beds:** 2T 1D **Baths:** 1 En 1 Sh (9) (4) TV V

Bilsington

TR0434

Willow Farm, *Stone Cross, Bilsington, Ashford, Kent, TN25 7JJ.* Organic smallholding in rural setting. Home-made bread but no chintz. **Open:** All year (not Xmas)
01233 721700 Mrs Hopper *renee@willow-farm.freeserve.co.uk* **D:** Fr £18.50–£20.00 **S:** Fr £20.00–£25.00 **Beds:** 1F 1D 1T 1S **Baths:** 1 Pr 1 Sh (6) TV X V

BEDROOMS
D = Double
T = Twin
S = Single
F = Family

National Grid References given are for villages, towns and cities – not for individual houses

Bilting

TR0449

The Old Farm House, *Soakham Farm, White Hill, Bilting, Ashford, Kent, TN25 4HB.* Beautiful rolling countryside on North Downs Way, working farm ideal for walking, touring. **Open:** All year (not Xmas)
01233 813509 Mrs Feakins **D:** Fr £18.00–£20.00 **S:** Fr £20.00–£27.00 **Beds:** 1F 1D 1T TV V

Boughton

TR0659

Tenterden House, *209 The Street, Boughton, Faversham, Kent, ME13 9BL.* Half-acre garden in historic village with two pubs. **Open:** All year
01227 751593 Mrs Latham **D:** Fr £20.00–£22.00 **S:** Fr £30.00–£35.00 **Beds:** 1D 1T **Baths:** 2 En (4) TV

Boughton Aluph

TR0348 *Flying Horse, Chequers, Half Way House*

Warren Cottage, *Boughton Aluph, Ashford, Kent, TN25 4HS.* Quiet cottage with garden, fantastic view! **Open:** All year
01233 740483 B K Fearne **D:** Fr £20.00 **S:** Fr £20.00 **Beds:** 1T 1D (5) (4) TV

Boughton Monchelsea

TQ7651

Hideaway, *Heath Road, Boughton Monchelsea, Maidstone, Kent, ME17 4HN.* Chalet bungalow edge of village. Pub meals 1-minute walk. **Open:** Jan to Dec
01622 747453 (also fax) Mrs Knight **D:** Fr £16.00 **S:** Fr £20.00 **Beds:** 1D **Baths:** 1 Pr (2) TV V

Boxley

TQ7757

Barn Cottage, *Harbourland, Boxley, Maidstone, Kent, ME14 3DN.* Converted C16th barn, convenient for M2, M20 and Channel. **Open:** All year (not Xmas/New Year)
01622 675891 (also fax) Mrs Munson **D:** Fr £18.00–£20.00 **S:** Fr £18.00–£20.00 **Beds:** 1T 1D 1S **Baths:** 2 En 1 Pr (5) (6) TV

Brasted

TQ4755

Lodge House, *High Street, Brasted, Westerham, Kent, TN16 1HS.* Conveniently situated character property, a short walk from popular pubs. **Open:** All year **Grades:** ETC 3 Diamond
01959 562195 Mr & Mrs Marshall *lodgehouse@brastedbb.freeserve.co.uk* **D:** Fr £24.00–£29.00 **S:** Fr £30.00–£37.50 **Beds:** 1T 1D **Baths:** 1 En 1 Sh (3) TV

Holmesdale House, *High Street, Brasted, Westerham, Kent, TN16 1HS.* Delightful Victorian house (part C17th). Chartwell, Hever, Knole and mainline station. **Open:** All year
01959 564834 (also fax) Mr Jinks **D:** Fr £22.00–£29.00 **S:** Fr £36.00–£48.00 **Beds:** 1F 3D 1T **Baths:** 3 En 1 Sh (7) TV V

Brasted Chart

TQ4653

The Orchard House, *Brasted Chart, Westerham, Kent, TN16 1LR.* Family home, quiet, rural surroundings, near Chartwell, Hever, Knole, Gatwick. **Open:** All year (not Xmas) **Grades:** ETC 3 Diamond
01959 563702 Mrs Godsal *David.Godsal@tesco.net* **D:** Fr £24.00 **S:** Fr £26.00 **Beds:** 2T 1S **Baths:** 2 Sh (4) TV

Broadstairs

TR3967

Keston Court Hotel, *14 Ramsgate Road, Broadstairs, Kent, CT10 1PS.* Pleasant hotel with hospitality to match, 5 mins' walk to town, beach, most amenities. **Open:** All year
01843 862401 Mr & Mrs McVicker *kestoncourt@tinyonline.co.uk* **D:** Fr £17.00–£20.00 **S:** Fr £18.00 **Beds:** 5D 2T 1S **Baths:** 3 En 2 Sh (8) TV X V

Devonhurst Hotel, *Eastern Esplanade, Broadstairs, Kent, CT10 1DR.* Overlooking sandy beach and English Channel. Residential licensed family-run. **Open:** All year
01843 863010 Mr & Mrs Payne **Fax: 01843 868940** *info@devonhurst.co.uk* www.devonhurst.co.uk **D:** Fr £26.50–£29.50 **S:** Fr £29.50 **Beds:** 1F 7D 1T **Baths:** 9 En (5) TV X V **cc**

Goodwin Sands Guest House, *15 Wrotham Road, Broadstairs, Kent, CT10 1QG.* Close to amenities and sea front. Substantial breakfast. Warm, friendly atmosphere. **Open:** Feb to Dec
01843 862309 Mr & Mrs Hills **D:** Fr £19.00–£21.00 **S:** Fr £23.00–£28.00 **Beds:** 3F 3D 2S **Baths:** 5 En 1 Sh (2) TV V

Planning a longer stay? Always ask for any special rates

Canterbury

TR151560

Clare Ellen Guest House, *9 Victoria Road, Canterbury, Kent, CT1 3SG.* **Open:** All year
01227 760205 Mrs Williams **Fax: 01227 784482** *loraine.williams@clareellenguesthouse.co.uk* www.clareellenguesthouse.co.uk **D:** Fr £24.50–£29.00 **S:** Fr £28.00–£40.00 **Beds:** 2F 3D 2T 1S **Baths:** 6 En (8)
Large elegant ensuite rooms with TV, hairdryer, clock/radio and tea/coffee facilities. Full English breakfast. Vegetarian and special diets catered for on request. Six minutes walk to town centre, bus and train station. Parking/garage available. Credit cards accepted.

Chaucer Lodge, *62 New Dover Road, Canterbury, Kent, CT1 3DT.* **Open:** All year
01227 459141 (also fax) Mr Wilson *wchaucerldg@aol.com* www.thechaucerlodge.co.uk **D:** Fr £21.00–£25.00 **S:** Fr £25.00–£35.00 **Beds:** 2F 2T 3D 2S **Baths:** 9 En (10)
Family-run friendly guest house close to city centre, cathedral, cricket club and hospitals. Fridges in all rooms and telephone. Breakfast menu. High standard of cleanliness and service provided in a relaxed atmosphere. Secure off-road parking. Ideal base for visiting Canterbury and touring Kent.

Abberley House, *115 Whitstable Road, Canterbury, Kent, CT2 8EF.* Abberley House is a short walk to the town. Warm welcome. **Open:** All year (not Xmas)
01227 450265 Mr Allcorn **Fax: 01227 478626 D:** Fr £21.00–£24.00 **S:** Fr £25.00–£28.00 **Beds:** 2D 1T **Baths:** 1 En 2 Sh (3)

Please respect a B&B's wishes regarding children, animals and smoking

Cathedral Gate Hotel, *36 Burgate, Canterbury, Kent, CT1 2HA.* Family-run medieval hotel next to Canterbury Cathedral. Warm welcome. **Open:** All year **Grades:** ETC 3 Diamond
01227 464381 Mrs Jubber **Fax: 01227 462800** *cgate@cgate.demon.co.uk* **D:** Fr £23.50–£42.00 **S:** Fr £23.50–£55.50 **Beds:** 5F 9D 7T 6S **Baths:** 12 En 3 Sh cc

Little Courtney Guest House, *5 Whitstable Road, St Dunstans, Canterbury, Kent, CT2 8DG.* Warm welcome awaits you at our small family-run guest house. Close to Canterbury. **Open:** All year
01227 454207 Mrs Mercer **D:** Fr £17.50–£20.00 **S:** Fr £20.00–£25.00 **Beds:** 2T 1S **Baths:** 1 Sh (1)

Abbey Lodge Guest House, *8 New Dover Road, Canterbury, Kent, CT1 3AP.* Cathedral city centre 10 mins' walk, Dover 20 mins' ride. **Open:** All year
01227 462878 Mrs Gardner **D:** Fr £17.00–£20.00 **S:** Fr £20.00–£25.00 **Beds:** 1F 1T 1S **Baths:** 2 En 1 Sh (16)

London Guest House, *14 London Road, Canterbury, Kent, CT2 8LR.* Recommended by 'Let's Go' and 'Which?' Good B&B guides. **Open:** All year
01227 765860 Mrs Cabrini **Fax: 01227 456721** *londonguesthousecabnkz@supanet.com* **D:** Fr £20.00–£25.00 **S:** Fr £20.00–£40.00 **Beds:** 1F 1D 2T 2S **Baths:** 2 Sh

Castle Court Guest House, *8 Castle Street, Canterbury, Kent, CT1 2QF.* Friendly family house offering comfortable and clean accommodation. 2 mins' walk shops, buses, trains. **Open:** All year
01227 463441 (also fax) Mr Turner *guesthouse@castlecourt.fsnet.co.uk* **D:** Fr £21.00–£26.00 **S:** Fr £21.00–£24.00 **Beds:** 3F 2D 3T 1S **Baths:** 4 En 3 Sh (3) cc

Ashton House, *129 Whitstable Road, Canterbury, Kent, CT2 8EQ.* Beautifully refurbished Edwardian house. Warm, relaxed ambience. Superb breakfast, excellent location. Individual requirements our priority. **Open:** All year
01227 455064 Mrs Nimmons *ashtonbnb@hotmail.com* **D:** Fr £20.00–£22.50 **S:** Fr £25.00–£30.00 **Beds:** 1T 1D **Baths:** 2 En (2)

Capel-le-Ferne

TR2538 Lighthouse, Valiant Sailor

Xaipe, *18 Alexandra Road, Capel-le-Ferne, Folkestone, Kent, CT18 7LD.* Comfortable, detached bungalow. **Open:** All year (not Xmas/New Year)
01303 257956 D Strutt **D:** Fr £18.00 **S:** Fr £18.00 **Beds:** 1T 1D (2)

Challock

TR0150

Hegdale Farm House, *Hegdale Lane, Challock, Ashford, Kent, TN25 4BE.* C16th farmhouse, good food,relaxing atmosphere. Comfortable lounge and peaceful garden. **Open:** All year (not Xmas)
01233 740224 Mrs Baxter **D:** Fr £20.00–£22.50 **S:** Fr £22.50 **Beds:** 1F 1D 1T **Baths:** 1 En 2 Sh (8)

Charcott

TQ5247

Charcott Farmhouse, *Charcott, Leigh, Tonbridge, Kent, TN11 8LG.* Family home in glorious rural setting. Home-made bread. Free-range eggs. Guests' lounge. **Open:** All year (not Xmas/New Year)
01892 870024 Mr & Mrs Morris **Fax: 01892 870158** *nicholasmorris@charcott.freeserve.co.uk* www.smoothhound.co.uk/hotels/charcott.html **D:** Fr £45.00 **S:** Fr £30.00 **Beds:** 3T **Baths:** 2 En 1 Pr (5) (4)

Charing

TQ9549

Barnfield, *Charing, Ashford, Kent, TN27 0BN.* Romantic C15th Kent Hall farmhouse in English garden by lake. **Open:** All year (not Xmas)
01233 712421 (also fax) Mrs Pym *phillada@pym2.co.uk* **D:** Fr £28.00–£30.00 **S:** Fr £28.00–£30.00 **Beds:** 2D 1T 3S **Baths:** 1 Sh (99)

23 The Moat, *Charing, Ashford, Kent, TN27 0JH.* On North Downs Way. Shops, buses, trains, London, Canterbury, Eurostar. **Open:** Apr to Sep
01233 713141 Mrs Micklewright **D:** Fr £20.00 **S:** Fr £25.00 **Beds:** 1T **Baths:** 1 En (1)

Timber Lodge, *Charing Hill, Charing, Ashford, Kent, TN27 0NG.* Unusual upside down house. Tea/coffee on terrace. Ensuite. Near Pilgrim's Way. **Open:** All year (not Xmas/New Year)
01233 712822 (also fax) Mrs Bigwood **D:** Fr £20.00–£25.00 **S:** Fr £20.00–£35.00 **Beds:** 1F 1T 1S **Baths:** 2 En (8)

All details shown are as supplied by B&B owners in Autumn 2002

Planning a longer stay? Always ask for any special rates

Chart Sutton

TQ8049

White House Farm, *Green Lane, Chart Sutton, Maidstone, Kent, ME17 3ES.* C15th farmhouse, good home-cooking, near Leeds and Sissinghurst Castles and M20. **Open:** All year (not Xmas)
01622 842490 (also fax) Mrs Spain *sue.spain@totalise.co.uk* **D:** Fr £20.00–£25.00 **S:** Fr £25.00–£30.00 **Beds:** 2D 1T **Baths:** 1 En 2 Pr (8) (4)

Chartham Hatch

TR1056

The Willows, *Howfield Lane, Chartham Hatch, Canterbury, Kent, CT4 7HG.* Quiet country lane - garden for enthusiasts, 2 miles Canterbury. **Open:** All year
01227 738442 (also fax) Mrs Gough *thegoughs@hotmail.com* **D:** Fr £23.00–£27.00 **Beds:** 1D 1T **Baths:** 2 Pr (5)

Chatham

TQ7665

Normandy House, *143 Maidstone Road, Chatham, ME4 6JE.* Family-run establishment close to Chatham Dockyard & historic Rochester. **Open:** All year (not Xmas/New Year)
01634 843047 Mr & Mrs Rands *rands@normandyhouse.fsnet.co.uk* **D:** Fr £19.00–£24.00 **S:** Fr £20.00–£25.00 **Beds:** 1T 1D 2S **Baths:** 2 Sh (5)

Chevening

TQ4857

Crossways House, *Chevening Road, Chevening, Sevenoaks, Kent, TN14 6HF.* Beautiful Kentish ragstone c1760 in 5 acres. Small exclusive conferences. **Open:** All year (not Xmas/New Year)
01732 456334 Mrs Weavers **Fax: 01732 452312** *lelaweavers@hotmail.com* **D:** Fr £25.00 **S:** Fr £25.00–£30.00 **Beds:** 4D **Baths:** 3 En 1 Pr (4)

Chilham

TR0653

Maynard Cottage, *106 Wincheap, Canterbury, Kent, CT1 3RS.* Newly refurbished luxury accommodation. Ensuite. Hearty breakfasts and evening meals. **Open:** All year (not Xmas/New Year)
07951 496836 (M) Mrs Ely *fionaely@onetel.co.uk* **D:** Fr £20.00–£27.50 **S:** Fr £25.00–£55.00 **Beds:** 1T 1D cc

Coldred

TR2746

Colret House, *The Green, Coldred, Dover, Kent, CT15 5AP.* Garden rooms in grounds of detached Edwardian property facing village green. **Open:** All year **Grades:** ETC 4 Diamond
01304 830388 (also fax) Mrs White *jackie.colret@evnet.co.uk* **D:** Fr £25.00–£30.00 **S:** Fr £25.00–£30.00 **Beds:** 2F **Baths:** 2 En (6)

Cranbrook

TQ7736

Cordons, *Round Green Lane, Colliers Green, Cranbrook, Kent, TN17 2NB.* **Open:** All year
01580 211633 Mrs Johnstone **D:** Fr £22.50–£25.00 **S:** Fr £25.00–£30.00 **Beds:** 1D 1T 1S **Baths:** 2 Pr (4)
House situated off quiet country road in woodland surroundings. Close to Goudhurst in garden of England. Beautiful & tranquil plantsman's garden. Golden Award for wildlife gardening. Excellent walking country. Close to Sissinghurst, Finchcocks, Scotney and Leeds Castle. French spoken.

The Hollies, *Old Angley Road, Cranbrook, Kent, TN17 2PN.* Well-appointed comfortable bungalow, delightful garden, close to town centre and Sissinghurst Gardens. **Open:** All year (not Xmas)
01580 713106 Mrs Waddoup **D:** Fr £25.00 **S:** Fr £25.00 **Beds:** 1F 1T 1S **Baths:** 1 En 1 Pr (2) 1

Dartford

TQ5273

Royal Victoria & Bull Hotel, *1 High Street, Dartford, Kent, DA1 1DU.* An C18th inn. Easy access to town centre and motorways. **Open:** All year
01322 224415 Fax: 01322 289474 D: Fr £48.00 **S:** Fr £48.00 **Beds:** 2F 5D 9T 8S **Baths:** 25 En cc

Deal

TR3752

The Roast House Lodge, *224 London Road, Deal, Kent, CT14 9PW.* Lodge accommodation, garden and sunbathing patio. 1 mile Deal seafront, golf courses nearby. **Open:** All year
01304 380824 M Stokes **D:** Fr £25.00–£30.00 **S:** Fr £35.00–£40.00 **Beds:** 2F 2D 1T 1S **Baths:** 6 En cc

Sparrow Court, *Chalk Hill Road, Kingsdown, Deal, Kent, CT14 8DP.* Kingsdown, quiet seaside village between Deal and Dover. Bathing, walking, golf. **Open:** All year **Grades:** ETC 3 Diamond
01304 389253 Mrs Maude **Fax: 01304 389016** *www.farmstaykent.com* **D:** Fr £25.00–£30.00 **S:** Fr £25.00–£30.00 **Beds:** 1T 1D **Baths:** 2 Pr

Sondes Lodge, *14 Sondes Road, Deal, Kent, CT14 7BW.* Close to seafront, town, castles, golf courses. Warm welcome. **Open:** All year
01304 368741 (also fax) J Hulme *sondeslodge@aol.com* **D:** Fr £25.00–£28.00 **S:** Fr £35.00–£40.00 **Beds:** 2D 1T **Baths:** 3 En cc

Doddington

TQ9357 *Red Lion, George*

Palace Farmhouse, *Chequers Hill, Doddington, Sittingbourne, Kent, ME9 0AU.* C19th farmhouse. Comfortably furnished, pleasant gardens. Well situated. Warm welcome. **Open:** All year
01795 886820 Leake **D:** Fr £18.00–£22.00 **S:** Fr £15.00–£25.00 **Beds:** 1F 1T 2S **Baths:** 1 En 2 Sh (6)

Dover

TR3141

Colret House, *The Green, Coldred, Dover, Kent, CT15 5AP.* **Open:** All year **Grades:** ETC 4 Diamond
01304 830388 (also fax) Mrs White *jackie.colret@evnet.co.uk* **D:** Fr £25.00–£30.00 **S:** Fr £25.00–£30.00 **Beds:** 2F **Baths:** 2 En (6)
Garden rooms in grounds of detached Edwardian property facing the village green of Coldred - twice recently voted the Best Kept Village in Kent. Easy access from A2 - Canterbury/Sandwich/Dover all within 15 mins' drive. Ideal overnight stop for ferries/shuttle.

Bleriot's, Belper House, *47 Park Avenue, Dover, Kent, CT16 1HE.* One night 'stopovers' and 'mini-breaks'. Ensuite rooms, off-road parking. **Open:** All year (not Xmas) **Grades:** ETC 3 Diamond
01304 211394 Mrs Casey **D:** Fr £19.00–£25.00 **S:** Fr £20.00–£46.00 **Beds:** 2F 3D 2T 1S **Baths:** 6 En 2 Sh (8) cc

Owler Lodge, *Alkham Valley Road, Alkham, Dover, Kent, CT15 7DF.* High quality accommodation, picturesque village. Ideal for touring East Kent. **Open:** All year (not Xmas) **Grades:** ETC 4 Diamond
01304 826375 Mrs Owler **Fax: 01304 829372** *owlerlodge@aol.com* **D:** Fr £22.00–£27.00 **S:** Fr £35.00–£38.00 **Beds:** 1F 1D 1T **Baths:** 3 En (5) (3)

Hubert House, *9 Castle Hill Road, Dover, Kent, CT16 1QW.* Comfortable Georgian house with parking; ideally situated for local attractions and ferries. **Open:** Nov to Sep **Grades:** AA 3 Diamond, RAC 3 Diamond
01304 202253 Mr Hoynes *huberthouse@btinternet.com* www.huberthouse.co.uk **D:** Fr £20.00–£25.00 **S:** Fr £30.00–£34.00 **Beds:** 2F 2D 2T 1S **Baths:** 6 En (6) **cc**

Tower Guest House, *98 Priory Hill, Dover, Kent, CT17 0AD.* Old water tower now fully modernised into high standard accommodation. **Open:** All year
01304 208212 (also fax) D Wraight *enquiries@towerhouse.net* www.towerhouse.net **D:** Fr £20.00–£25.00 **Beds:** 1F 1D **Baths:** 2 En (2)

Valjoy Guest House, *237 Folkestone Road, Dover, Kent, CT17 9SL.* Victorian family house situated near rail, ferry and tunnel terminals. **Open:** All year (not Xmas)
01304 212160 Mr Bowes **D:** Fr £15.00–£20.00 **S:** Fr £15.00–£20.00 **Beds:** 3F 1S **Baths:** 1 Sh (5)

Number One Guest House, *1 Castle Street, Dover, Kent, CT16 1QH.* Georgian town house. All rooms ensuite. GARAGE PARKING. Port nearby **Open:** All year
01304 202007 Ms Reidy **Fax: 01304 214078** *res@number1guesthouse.co.uk* www.number1guesthouse.co.uk **D:** Fr £20.00–£25.00 **S:** Fr £25.00–£30.00 **Beds:** 1F 2D 2T **Baths:** 5 En (4)

Beulah House, *94 Crabble Hill, Dover, Kent, CT17 0SA.* Welcome to this imposing award-winning guest house in 1 acre of magnificent toparied gardens. **Open:** All year
01304 824615 Mrs Owen **Fax: 01304 828850** *owen@beulahhouse94.freeserve.co.uk* **D:** Fr £22.00–£25.00 **S:** Fr £30.00–£35.00 **Beds:** 2F 4D 3T **Baths:** 9 En **cc**

Dunton Green

TQ5156

15 Pounsley Road, *Dunton Green, Sevenoaks, Kent, TN13 2XP.* Pretty cottage in quiet private road. Easy access all Kent. **Open:** All year (not Xmas/New Year) **Grades:** ETC 3 Diamond
01732 469898 Mr & Mrs Hurrell *lilac_cottage@msn.com* **D:** Fr £20.00–£21.00 **S:** Fr £21.00 **Beds:** 1D 1S **Baths:** 1 Sh (1)

Dymchurch

TR1029

Waterside Guest House, *15 Hythe Road, Dymchurch, Romney Marsh, Kent, TN29 0LN.* **Open:** All year
01303 872253 Mrs Tinklin *info@watersideguesthouse.co.uk* www.watersideguesthouse.co.uk **D:** Fr £20.00–£22.50 **S:** Fr £25.00–£30.00 **Beds:** 1F 2D 2T **Baths:** 5 En (7)
Cottage-style house offering comfortable rooms, attractive gardens. Ideally situated for Channel crossings and exploring Kent and E Sussex. Experience the R H & D railway or stroll along nearby sandy beaches, finally enjoying a drink or meal chosen from our varied menu.

The Ship Inn, *118 High Street, Dymchurch, Romney Marsh, Kent, TN29 0LD.* Family-run C15th inn on the South Coast of Kent. **Open:** All year
01303 872122 Mr Sharp *stilwells@theshipinn.co.uk* www.theshipinn.co.uk **D:** Fr £19.00–£21.00 **S:** Fr £19.00–£31.00 **Beds:** 4F 2D 2S **Baths:** 2 Sh

East Malling

TQ7057

Hawthorn Cottage, *Easterfields, East Malling, West Malling, ME19 6BE.* Quiet country setting ideally situated for touring Kent, 3 miles M20 J5. **Open:** All year (not Xmas)
01732 843805 (also fax) Mrs Horvath *easterfields@talk21.com* www.easterfields.co.uk **D:** Fr £18.00 **S:** Fr £18.00 **Beds:** 1T 1S **Baths:** 1 Pr (3)

East Peckham

TQ6648

Roydon Hall, *Roydon Hall Road, East Peckham, Tonbridge, Kent, TN12 5NH.* Very attractive C16th manor in 10 acres of woodlands and gardens, peaceful atmosphere. **Open:** All year (not Easter or Xmas/New Year)
01622 812121 Mrs Bence **Fax: 01622 813959** *roydonhall@btinternet.com* www.southeastengland.uk.com **D:** Fr £22.50–£32.50 **S:** Fr £30.00–£50.00 **Beds:** 1F 3D 5T 1S **Baths:** 7 En 1 Pr 2 Sh **cc**

All details shown are as supplied by B&B owners in Autumn 2002

Eastling

TQ9656

The Carpenters' Arms, *The Street, Eastling, Faversham, Kent, ME13 0AZ.* C14th inn, candlelit restaurant, adjoining lodge, 30 mins Channel Ports. **Open:** All year (not Xmas/New Year)
01795 890234 Mrs O'Regan **Fax: 01795 890654** www.swale.gov.uk **D:** Fr £24.75–£26.00 **S:** Fr £41.50 **Beds:** 3D **Baths:** 3 En (12) (20) **cc**

Etchinghill

TR1639

One Step Beyond, *Westfield Lane, Etchinghill, Folkestone, Kent, CT18 8BT.* Quiet village. Channel Tunnel 4 mins. Dover 20 mins. Walks. **Open:** All year (not Xmas/New Year)
01303 862637 (also fax) J Holden *johnosb@rdplus.net* **D:** Fr £17.50–£20.00 **S:** Fr £20.00–£22.00 **Beds:** 1D **Baths:** 1 En

Farthing Common

TR1340

Southfields, *Farthing Common, Lyminge, Folkestone, Kent, CT18 8DH.* **Open:** Mar to Oct
01303 862391 Ms Wadie **D:** Fr £18.00 **S:** Fr £18.00 **Beds:** 1F 1T **Baths:** 1 Sh (6)
A peaceful home on the North Downs with a spectacular sea view. Ideal walking country dotted with village pubs. Central by car to Kent's many places of historic interest and France, through the Tunnel barely an hour away. Cyclists welcome.

Faversham

TR0161

Albion House, *11 South Road, Faversham, Kent, ME13 7LR.* Large family house adjacent to town centre. 1 mile M2. **Open:** All year (not Xmas/New Year)
01795 538748 (also fax) J & E Newfield *june.newfield@tesco.net* **D:** Fr £15.00–£25.00 **S:** Fr £25.00–£45.00 **Beds:** 1F 1S **Baths:** 1 Sh (5) (2)

Tanners Cottage, *37 Tanner Street, Faversham, Kent, ME13 7JP.* Attractive old cottage in quiet area of lovely old market town. **Open:** All year (not Xmas)
01795 536698 M Jameson **D:** Fr £15.00 **S:** Fr £15.00 **Beds:** 1D 1T **Baths:** 1 Sh (5) **cc**

Preston Lea, *Canterbury Road, Faversham, Kent, ME13 8XA.* **Open:** All year **Grades:** ETC 4 Diamond, Silver
01795 535266 Mr Turner **Fax: 01795 533388** *preston.lea@which.net* homepages.which.net/~alan.turner10 **D:** Fr £28.00–£30.00 **S:** Fr £40.00 **Beds:** 1T 2D **Baths:** 2 En 1 Pr (10) **cc**
A warm welcome in this large elegant house with unique architectural features set in beautiful secluded gardens. The sunny, spacious bedrooms furnished with antiques offer every comfort. Afternoon tea on arrival and delicious breakfast grilled in the Aga, to order.

Folkestone

TR2136

Wycliffe Hotel, *63 Bouverie Road West, Folkestone, Kent, CT20 2RN.* Clean, comfortable, affordable accommodation near shuttle, Seacat, 15 mins Dover Port.
Open: All year
01303 252186 (also fax) Mr & Mrs Sapsford *sapsford@wycliffhotel.freeserve.co.uk* www.wycliffehotel.com **D:** Fr £19.00–£22.00 **S:** Fr £19.00–£22.00 **Beds:** 2F 5D 4T 1S **Baths:** 1 Pr 2 Sh (8) **cc**

Bramble Hill Cottage, *Meggett Lane, West Hougham, Dover, Kent, CT15 7BS.* Warm welcome, beautiful rural setting, 15 mins tunnel and ferries. **Open:** Mar to Nov
01303 253180 Mrs Hughes **D:** Fr £18.00–£20.00 **Beds:** 1T 2D **Baths:** 2 En 1 Pr

Banque Hotel, *4 Castle Hill Avenue, Folkestone, Kent, CT20 2QT.* Small comfortable hotel. Near town centre, Channel Tunnel. Breakfast served.
Open: All year
01303 253797 *banquehotel4@hotmail.com* www.banquehotel.com **D:** Fr £20.00–£25.00 **S:** Fr £25.00–£30.00 **Beds:** 3F 3T 3D 3S **Baths:** 12 En (2) **cc**

Folkestone Kentmere Guest House, *76 Cheriton Road, Folkestone, Kent, CT20 1DG.* Situated near Channel Tunnel terminal. Close to town centre and sea front. **Open:** All year
01303 259661 *kentmere.guesthouse@ntlworld.com* www.smoothhound.co.uk/hotels/kentmore **D:** Fr £18.00–£25.00 **S:** Fr £18.00–£25.00 **Beds:** 4T 1D 2S **Baths:** 3 En 4 Sh (2) **cc**

Frittenden

TQ8141

Tolehurst Barn, *Knoxbridge, Cranbrook Road, Frittenden, Cranbrook, Kent, TN17 2BP.* Quiet, rural environment, near to many fine houses, castles & gardens. **Open:** All year (not Xmas/New Year)
01580 714385 (also fax) Mrs Tresilian **D:** Fr £20.00 **S:** Fr £25.00 **Beds:** 1F 1T 1D **Baths:** 2 En 1 Pr (4)

Gillingham

TQ7767

178 Bredhurst Road, *Wigmore, Gillingham, Kent, ME8 0QX.* Large chalet bungalow 4 minutes M2.
Open: All year
01634 233267 Mrs Penn **D:** Fr £16.00–£20.00 **S:** Fr £22.00–£24.00 **Beds:** 2T **Baths:** 2 En (2)

Abigails, *17 The Maltings, Rainham, Gillingham, Kent, ME8 8JL.* Friendly service, family establishment, central location, rural views, water garden. **Open:** All year
01634 365427 Ms Penfold **D:** Fr £15.00 **S:** Fr £15.00 **Beds:** 1F 1D 1S **Baths:** 2 En (4)

Ramsey House, *228a Barnsole Road, Gillingham, Kent, ME7 4JB.* Established 15 years. Friendly atmosphere, close A2, M2, maritime museums, Kent. **Open:** All year
01634 854193 Mrs Larssen **D:** Fr £16.00–£18.00 **S:** Fr £20.00–£25.00 **Beds:** 1S 2T **Baths:** 1 En 1 Sh (3) (2)

King Charles Hotel, *Brompton Road, Gillingham, Kent, ME7 5QT.* Modern, family-run hotel, set in the heart of maritime Kent.
Open: All year
01634 830303 Mr DeGiorgio **Fax: 01634 829430** *enquiries@kingcharleshotel.co.uk* **D:** Fr £20.00 **S:** Fr £34.00 **Beds:** 20F 30T 30D 1S **Baths:** 81 En **cc**

4 The Rise, *Gillingham, Kent, ME7 3SF.* Close to Exit 4 Gillingham M2. Coach stop to London and coast. Shopping centre close by. Friendly and welcoming household. Rural location ideal for ramblers. Transport to/from railway station if required. Rochester Dickens Experience nearby.
Open: All year
01634 388156 Mrs Haddow **D:** Fr £18.00 **S:** Fr £18.00 **Beds:** 1F 1T 1S **Baths:** 1 En 1 Pr

BATHROOMS
En = Ensuite
Pr = Private
Sh = Shared

All details shown are as supplied by B&B owners in Autumn 2002

Goudhurst

TQ7237

West Winchet, *Winchet Hill, Goudhurst, Cranbrook, Kent, TN17 1JX.* High quality accommodation. Beautifully located in secluded setting with stunning views.
Open: All year
01580 212024 Mrs Parker **Fax: 01580 212250** *annieparker@jpa-ltd.co.uk* **D:** Fr £27.50–£30.00 **S:** Fr £40.00 **Beds:** 1D 1T **Baths:** 1 En 1 Pr (5) (5)

Gravesend

TQ6574

48 Clipper Crescent, Riverview Park, *Gravesend, Kent, DA12 4NN.* Comfortable bedrooms. Close to A2/M2 frequent trains to London. **Open:** All year (not Xmas)
01474 365360 Mrs Jeeves **D:** Fr £17.00–£17.50 **S:** Fr £17.50 **Beds:** 1T 1S **Baths:** 1 Sh (3) (1)

Groombridge

TQ5336

Crown Inn, *Groombridge, Tunbridge Wells, Kent, TN3 9QH.* **Open:** All year
01892 864742 *crowngroombridge@aol.com* www.crowngroombridge.co.uk **D:** Fr £20.00–£30.00 **S:** Fr £35.00–£45.00 **Beds:** 1F 3T 1D **Baths:** 1 En 1 Sh (6) **cc**
C16th inn on village green, restaurant situated on Wealden Way. Ideal touring area, Gatwick Airport 40 mins. Walkers/cyclists welcome. Local climbing. Bargain breaks, ring for details. Full English breakfast, B&B recently upgraded.

Harrietsham

TQ8752

Homestay, *14 Chippendayle Drive, Harrietsham, Maidstone, Kent, ME17 1AD.* Close to Leeds Castle and ideally situated for exploring Kent.
Open: All year **Grades:** ETC 4 Diamond
01622 858698 (also fax) Mrs Beveridge *4homestay@lineone.net* www.kent-homestay.info **D:** Fr £21.00–£22.00 **S:** Fr £25.00–£26.00 **Beds:** 2T

All details shown are as supplied by B&B owners in Autumn 2002

Hartley (Meopham)

TQ6067

Kaye Cottage, *18 Old Downs, Hartley, Longfield, Kent, DA3 7AA.* Picturesque cottage. Friendly accommodation. All rooms to high standard. Lovely gardens. **Open:** All year (not Xmas) **Grades:** ETC 4 Diamond
01474 702384 (also fax) Mrs Smith *b-b@kaye-cottage.freeserve.co.uk* **D:** Fr £22.50–£35.00 **S:** Fr £25.00–£30.00 **Beds:** 1F 2D 1T 1S **Baths:** 2 En 2 Sh (5)

Hawkhurst

TQ7630 *The Curlew*

Southgate Little Fowlers, *Rye Road, Hawkhurst, Kent, TN18 5DA.* C17th country house Kent/Sussex border. Amidst many NT properties and gardens. **Open:** Easter to Nov
01580 752526 (also fax) Mrs Woodard *susan.woodard@btinternet.com* www.southgate.uk.net/ **D:** Fr £24.00–£30.00 **S:** Fr £30.00–£40.00 **Beds:** 1T 1D **Baths:** 2 En (10) (4)

The Wren's Nest, *Hasting Road, Hawkhurst, Cranbrook, Kent, TN18 4RT.* Spacious, beautifully appointed hotel-style suites, with character, comfortable lounge area in all rooms. Peaceful, delightful views, safe private parking. Ideal base for Sissinghurst, Great Dixter, Batemans, Bodiam Castle and many more places of interest. Perfect accommodation for longer stays. **Open:** All year
01580 754919 (also fax) Mrs Rodger **D:** Fr £27.50–£29.50 **S:** Fr £45.00–£49.00 **Beds:** 3D **Baths:** 3 En (10) (10)

Headcorn

TQ8344

Four Oaks, *Four Oaks Road, Headcorn, Ashford, Kent, TN27 9PB.* Restored 500-year-old farmhouse. Quiet location. Close Leeds Castle, Sissinghurst, Eurolink. **Open:** All year
01622 891224 Mrs Thick **Fax: 01622 890630** *info@fouroaks.uk.com* www.fouroaks.uk.com **D:** Fr £19.00–£21.00 **S:** Fr £20.00–£25.00 **Beds:** 2F 1T **Baths:** 1 En 1 Sh (4) cc

Curtis Farm, *Waterman Quarter, Headcorn, Ashford, Kent, TN27 9JJ.* Peaceful farmhouse setting, between Leeds, Sissinghurst, Euroports, Tunnel, M20. **Open:** All year **Grades:** ETC 3 Diamond
01622 890393 Ms Ray *curtis.farm@btopenworld.com* www.kent-esites.co.uk/curtisfarm **D:** Fr £20.00–£50.00 **S:** Fr £25.00–£30.00 **Beds:** 1F 1T 1D **Baths:** 2 En 1 Pr (5) (4)

Waterkant Guest House, *Moat Road, Headcorn, Ashford, Kent, TN27 9NT.* Detached house in beautiful landscaped gardens of Old Wealden village. **Open:** All year
01622 890154 & 07779 487519 (M) Dorothy Burbridge **D:** Fr £18.00–£23.00 **S:** Fr £25.00 **Beds:** 2D 1S **Baths:** 1 En 1 Sh (6)

Herne Bay

TR1768

'Hobbit Hole', *41a Pigeon Lane, Herne Bay, Kent, CT6 7ES.* **Open:** All year (not Xmas) **Grades:** ETC 3 Diamond
01227 368155 (also fax) Mrs Herwin *hobhole@aol.com* www.hobbithole.co.uk **D:** Fr £20.00–£23.00 **S:** Fr £22.00–£27.00 **Beds:** 1F 1T 1D **Baths:** 1 En 1 Pr (7)
After a long journey, you have finally found 'Hobbit-Hole'. Then rest with abandonment on super transcendental beds! Enjoy 'Bilbo Baggins breakfasts'. 'The Huntsman' tavern is a short gallop away and various spectacular places of interest within 25 miles radius.

High Halden

TQ8937

Draylands, *High Halden, Ashford, Kent, TN23 3JG.* Secluded location in Garden of England. Ground floor bedrooms with extensive views. **Open:** All year (not Xmas/ New Year)
01233 850048 (also fax) Mrs Russell *sallyrussell30@hotmail.com* **D:** Fr £23.00–£25.00 **S:** Fr £28.00–£30.00 **Beds:** 1D 1T **Baths:** 2 En (3)

11 The Martins, *High Halden, Ashford, Kent, TN26 3LD.* Quiet rural modern house. Safe parking. Good food. Homely atmosphere. **Open:** Mar to Nov
01233 850013 Mr & Mrs Thorowgood **Fax: 01233 850549** *bobandsandy@thorowgood.fsnet.co.uk* **D:** Fr £22.50–£25.00 **S:** Fr £27.50 **Beds:** 1F 1D 1T **Baths:** 1 En 1 Pr 1 Sh (4)

Planning a longer stay? Always ask for any special rates

Hollingbourne

TQ8455

Woodhouses, *49 Eyhorne Street, Hollingbourne, Maidstone, Kent, ME17 1TR.* C17th interconnected cottages close to village pubs and Leeds Castle. **Open:** All year
01622 880594 (also fax) Mr & Mrs Woodhouse *woodhouses@supanet.com* **D:** Fr £22.00–£23.00 **S:** Fr £24.00–£25.00 **Beds:** 3T **Baths:** 3 En (3)

Horsmonden

TQ7040

Forge House, *Brenchley Road, Horsmonden, Tonbridge, Kent, TN12 8DN.* Friendly house, ideal touring base, washbasins in all bedrooms. **Open:** All year
01892 723584 Mrs Brett *thebretts@amserve.com* **D:** Fr £16.00–£17.00 **S:** Fr £16.00–£17.00 **Beds:** 1D 1T 1S **Baths:** 1 Sh (5)

Hunton

TQ7149

The Woolhouse, *Grove Lane, Hunton, Maidstone, Kent, ME15 0SE.*
Open: All year (not Xmas/New Year)
01622 820778 A Wetton **Fax: 01622 820645** www.wetton.info **D:** Fr £28.00–£33.00 **S:** Fr £28.00–£33.00 **Beds:** 1T 1D 2S **Baths:** 4 En (10) (10)
Lovely 300-year-old Grade II Listed brick barn conversion, in quiet country lane in conservation area. Exposed beams, open fireplace, farmhouse kitchen, conservatory, very comfortable and pretty bedrooms all with private bathrooms. TV sitting room for guest use only. Friendly atmosphere.

Hythe

TR1634

Maccassil, *50 Marine Parade, Hythe, Kent, CT21 6AW.* A warm and friendly B&B in an idyllic peaceful location. **Open:** All year
01303 261867 **D:** Fr £18.00–£21.00 **S:** Fr £20.00–£25.00 **Beds:** 1F 1D 1T **Baths:** 2 En 1 Sh (3)

Hill View, *4south Road, Hythe, Kent, CT21 6AR.* Late Victorian house close to sea swimming pool and town. **Open:** All year (not Xmas)
01303 269783 Mrs Warbuton *beewarb@tesco.net* **D:** Fr £16.00–£18.00 **S:** Fr £18.00–£20.00 **Beds:** 1F 1T **Baths:** 1 Sh (5)

RATES
D = Price range per person sharing in a double or twin room
S = Price range for a single room

Isle of Grain

TQ8875 *Hogarth Inn*

Grayne Lodge, *Chapel Road, Isle of Grain, Rochester, Kent, ME3 0BZ.* Near the sea, close to London and the Channel Ports. **Open:** All year (not Xmas/New Year)
01634 271576 D: Fr £16.00–£18.00 **S:** Fr £19.00–£22.00 **Beds:** 4T 2D 6S **Baths:** 1 En 3 Sh (10)

Kingsdown

TR3648

Sparrow Court, *Chalk Hill Road, Kingsdown, Deal, Kent, CT14 8DP.* Kingsdown, quiet seaside village between Deal and Dover. Bathing, walking, golf. **Open:** All year **Grades:** ETC 3 Diamond
01304 389253 Mrs Maude **Fax: 01304 389016** www.farmstaykent.com **D:** Fr £25.00–£30.00 **S:** Fr £25.00–£30.00 **Beds:** 1T 1D **Baths:** 2 Pr

Kingston

TR1851 *Black Robin, Duke of Cumberland*

Oast Cottage, *13 The Street, Kingston, Canterbury, Kent, CT4 6JB.* Comfortable, clean, quiet, attractive and tastefully furnished period cottage situated in a pretty village near Canterbury. Amenities close by include castles, gardens and countryside walks plus easy access to the continent. Enjoy a relaxing stay in the heart of Kent. **Open:** All year
01227 830929 Mrs Simpson *oastcotts@aol.com* oastcottage-bedandbreakfast.co.uk **D:** Fr £17.50–£22.50 **Beds:** 1F 1T 1S **Baths:** 1 En 1 Sh (0) (4)

Langley

TQ8051

Langley Oast, *Langley Park, Langley, Maidstone, Kent, ME17 3NQ.* Luxuriously converted oast off A274 south of Maidstone in open countryside overlooking a lake. **Open:** All year (not Xmas)
01622 863523 (also fax) Mrs Clifford *margaret@langleyoast.freeserve.co.uk* **D:** Fr £22.50–£35.00 **S:** Fr £28.00–£50.00 **Beds:** 1F 1D 2T 1S **Baths:** 2 En 1 Sh (2) (5)

Lenham

TQ8951

East Lenham Farm, *Lenham, Maidstone, Kent, ME17 2DP.* Superb country views. Sitting room, garden and tennis court. 5 miles Leeds Castle. **Open:** Mar to Jan **Grades:** ETC 4 Diamond, Silver
01622 858686 Mrs Barr **Fax: 01622 859474** *eastlenham@farmline.com* www.eastlenhamfarm.co.uk **D:** Fr £25.00–£32.50 **S:** Fr £45.00–£50.00 **Beds:** 2D **Baths:** 1 En 1 Pr (3)

Linton

TQ7549

Clock House, *Linton, Maidstone, Kent, ME17 4PG.* **Open:** All year (not Xmas/New Year)
01622 743679 Ms Allfrey **Fax: 01622 743899** *antonia@allfrey.net* **D:** Fr £25.00–£30.00 **S:** Fr £25.00–£30.00 **Beds:** 2T **Baths:** 1 En 1 Pr (4)
Beautiful Grade II Listed house set in the middle of a 200-acre fruit farm. Lovely garden & fantastic view over the Weald of Kent. Pretty bedrooms, lovely walks, very quiet. Leeds Castle, Sissinghurst 15 mins. Hever, Rye, Great Dixter 40 mins.

Loose

TQ7551

Vale House, *Old Loose Hill, Loose, Maidstone, Kent, ME15 0BH.* Vale House stands in a secluded garden in the pretty historic village of Loose. **Open:** All year (not Xmas)
01622 743339 Mrs Gethin **Fax: 01622 743103** **D:** Fr £25.00–£27.50 **S:** Fr £26.00–£30.00 **Beds:** 2D 2T 1S **Baths:** 1 Pr 1 Sh

BATHROOMS
En = Ensuite
Pr = Private
Sh = Shared

Planning a longer stay? Always ask for any special rates

Maidstone

TQ7655

172 Tonbridge Road, *Maidstone, Kent, ME16 8SR.* **Open:** All year (not Xmas/New Year)
01622 720427 Mr Tindle *metindle@dialstart.net* **D:** Fr £19.00–£22.00 **S:** Fr £19.00–£22.00 **Beds:** 2T 1D 1S **Baths:** 2 Sh (5)
Perfectly situated for exploring the 'Garden of England' and yet within easy walking distance of Maidstone town centre. Easy access from the M20 and good rail links to London. Comfortable accommodation and a warm welcome await all our guests.

Langley Oast, *Langley Park, Langley, Maidstone, Kent, ME17 3NQ.* **Open:** All year (not Xmas)
01622 863523 (also fax) Mrs Clifford *margaret@langleyoast.freeserve.co.uk* **D:** Fr £22.50–£35.00 **S:** Fr £28.00–£50.00 **Beds:** 1F 1D 2T 1S **Baths:** 2 En 1 Sh (2) (5)
Luxuriously converted oast off A274 south of Maidstone in open countryside overlooking a lake.

Court Farm, *High Street, Aylesford, Maidstone, Kent, ME20 7AZ.* Beams, four poster, spa, antiques, drawing room. Sorry, no children. **Open:** All year
01622 717293 (also fax) Mrs Tucker *enquiries@courtfarm.com* www.courtfarm.com **D:** Fr £25.00 **S:** Fr £25.00 **Beds:** 2D 1T 1S **Baths:** 3 En 1 Pr (6) cc

10 Fant Lane, *Maidstone, Kent, ME16 8NL.* A character cottage with beams, quiet area, friendly accommodation. **Open:** All year
01622 729883 Mrs Layton **D:** Fr £20.00–£30.00 **S:** Fr £16.00–£25.00 **Beds:** 1F 1S **Baths:** 1 Sh (4) (1)

Grove House, *Grove Green Road, Weavering, Maidstone, Kent, ME14 5JT.* Attractive front garden for guests to enjoy quiet peaceful surroundings. **Open:** All year
01622 738441 S Costella **D:** Fr £22.50–£25.00 **S:** Fr £25.00–£35.00 **Beds:** 1T 2D **Baths:** 1 En 1 Sh (6) **cc**

Aylesbury Hotel, *56-58 London Road, Maidstone, Kent, ME16 8QL.* Built in 1861, the house has 8 individually decorated bedrooms. Walking distance to town centre and stations. Ideal touring base for the beautiful South East. Close to Leeds Castle. French and German spoken. **Open:** All year (not Xmas/New Year)
01622 762100 *aylesbury@onetel.net.uk* **D:** Fr £23.00–£26.00 **S:** Fr £42.00 **Beds:** 4T 4D 2S **Baths:** 6 En 1 Sh (8) **cc**

Marden

TQ7444

Tanner House, *Tanner Farm, Goudhurst Road, Marden, Tonbridge, Kent, TN12 9ND.* Secluded Tudor farmhouse, also with camping. Ideal for stopover or holiday. **Open:** All year (not Xmas) **Grades:** ETC 4 Diamond
01622 831214 Mrs Mannington **Fax: 01622 832472** *enquiries@tannerfarmpark.co.uk* www.tannerfarmpark.co.uk **D:** Fr £22.50–£25.00 **S:** Fr £40.00 **Beds:** 1D 2T **Baths:** 3 En (3) **cc**

Margate

TR3570

Carnforth, *103 Norfolk Road, Cliftonville, Margate, Kent, CT9 2HX.* Small Victorian hotel. Spacious, comfortable rooms, 1 min to shops. **Open:** All year **Grades:** ETC 4 Diamond
01843 292127 Mrs Heffer *carnforth-hotel@cwcom.net* www.carnforth-hotel.co.uk **D:** Fr £20.00–£28.00 **S:** Fr £25.00–£33.00 **Beds:** 2F 3D 1T 1S **Baths:** 6 En 1 Pr

Malvern Hotel, *Eastern Esplanade, Cliftonville, Margate, Kent, CT9 2HL.* Small, seafront hotel, close to indoor bowls, Winter Gardens, amenities etc. **Open:** All year
01843 290192 (also fax) **D:** Fr £20.00–£22.50 **S:** Fr £22.50–£30.00 **Beds:** 2F 5D 2T 1S **Baths:** 8 En 1 Sh **cc**

Somerville Hotel, *9 Canterbury Road, Margate, Kent, CT9 5AQ.* Family-run hotel overlooking sea close to all amenities. **Open:** All year (not New Year)
01843 224401 Mr Hubbard **D:** Fr £15.00–£20.00 **S:** Fr £20.00–£25.00 **Beds:** 1F 5D 2T **Baths:** 2 En 2 Sh

The Happy Dolphin, *11 Buenos Ayres, Margate, Kent, CT9 5AE.* Victorian private guest house overlooking beach. CTV, radio/cassette, fridge, phone, iron, hairdryer. **Open:** All year
01843 296473 (also fax) Ms Stratford **D:** Fr £15.00–£35.00 **S:** Fr £20.00–£35.00 **Beds:** 4F 1D 1T 2S **Baths:** 6 En 2 Pr **cc**

Fulwood Hotel, *2-4 Surrey Road, Margate, Kent, CT9 2LA.* Situated in Margate - a leisure destination. Easy access to Margate beaches. **Open:** All year
01843 293977 Mr Haiwad *haiwad_a@hotmail.com* www.fulwoodhotel.co.uk **D:** Fr £40.00–£50.00 **S:** Fr £20.00–£25.00 **Beds:** 1F 9T 6D 6S **Baths:** 8 En 9 Pr 10 Sh **cc**

Vienna Guest House, *28 Canterbury Road, Margate, Kent, CT9 5BN.* 300 yards to seafront. 17 miles to the city of Canterbury. **Open:** All year
01843 224522 Mr & Mrs Mullin **D:** Fr £16.00–£25.00 **S:** Fr £16.00–£25.00 **Beds:** 4F 3T 10D 4S **Baths:** 17 En (16) **cc**

Minster in Sheppey

TQ9573

Mia Crieff, *Mill Hill, Chequers Road, Minster in Sheppey, Sheerness, ME12 3QL.* Detached house with large garden. Comfortable accommodation and full breakfast. **Open:** All year (not Xmas)
01795 870620 Mrs White **D:** Fr £19.00–£20.00 **S:** Fr £23.00–£25.00 **Beds:** 3D **Baths:** 3 En (5)

Otford

TQ5159

9 Warham Road, *Otford, Sevenoaks, Kent, TN14 5PF.* Modern detached house in centre of village. London 35 mins. **Open:** All year (not Xmas/New Year) **Grades:** ETC 2 Diamond
01959 523596 Mrs Smith **D:** Fr £20.00 **S:** Fr £20.00 **Beds:** 1T 1D 1S **Baths:** 1 Sh

Darenth Dene, *Shoreham Road, Otford, Sevenoaks, Kent, TN14 5RP.* Quiet location. Half mile from Otford. Reduced rates 4 nights plus. **Open:** All year (not Xmas/New Year)
01959 522293 Mrs Reid **D:** Fr £25.00–£30.00 **S:** Fr £25.00–£30.00 **Beds:** 1T 2S **Baths:** 1 En 1 Sh

Paddlesworth

TR1940

Pigeonwood House, *Arpinge, Folkestone, Kent, CT18 8AQ.* Ancient homely farmhouse in beautiful downland spectacular views, rural tranquillity. **Open:** Apr to Oct
01303 891111 Mr & Mrs Martin **Fax: 01303 891019** *samandmary@aol.com* www.arpinge.com **D:** Fr £20.00–£25.00 **S:** Fr £25.00–£35.00 **Beds:** 1F 1D 1T **Baths:** 2 En 1 Pr (5) (5)

Paddock Wood

TQ6744

Little Fowle Hall Oast, *Lucks Lane, Paddock Wood, Tonbridge, Kent, TN12 6PA.* London: train 1 hour. **Open:** All year (not Xmas)
01892 832602 Mr Lumley **D:** Fr £20.00 **S:** Fr £20.00 **Beds:** 1F 2T **Baths:** 1 En 2 Sh (8)

Peene

TR1837

West Lodge, *Peene, Folkestone, Kent, CT18 8BA.* Grade II Listed property set in 3 acres in quiet village. **Open:** All year (not Xmas)
01303 274762 *john@gredley.freeserve.co.uk* **D:** Fr £17.50 **S:** Fr £25.00 **Beds:** 2F **Baths:** 1 Sh (3)

Penshurst

TQ5243 *Leicester Arms, Spotted Dog, Bottle House*

Well Place Farm, *Penshurst, Tonbridge, Kent, TN11 8BY.* Comfortable, secluded Victorian farmhouse with stunning views over Penshurst. **Open:** All year
01892 870894 Mrs Scott *scottswpf@aol.com* **D:** Fr £22.50 **S:** Fr £22.50 **Beds:** 1T 1D **Baths:** 1 Pr 1 Sh

Petham

TR1351

South Wootton House, *Capel Lane, Petham, Canterbury, Kent, CT4 5RG.* A beautiful farmhouse with conservatory set in extensive gardens, surrounded by fields and woodland. **Open:** All year (not Xmas/New Year)
01227 700643 F Mount **Fax: 01227 700613** **D:** Fr £20.00–£25.00 **S:** Fr £25.00–£30.00 **Beds:** 1F 1T **Baths:** 1 Pr

Upper Ansdore, *Duckpit Lane, Petham, Canterbury, Kent, CT4 5QB.* Medieval house overlooking nature reserve, very secluded views. Canterbury 15 mins. **Open:** All year (not Xmas/New Year)
01227 700672 R Linch **Fax: 01227 700840** www.smoothhound.co.uk/hotels/upperans.html **D:** Fr £21.00–£22.50 **S:** Fr £30.00–£38.00 **Beds:** 1F 1T 3D **Baths:** 3 En (5) (5) **cc**

National Grid References given are for villages, towns and cities – not for individual houses

Pluckley

TQ9245 *Rose & Crown, Swan Inn, Dering Arms*

Glebelands Bed and Breakfast, *Station Road, Pluckley, Ashford, Kent, TN27 0QU.* A warm, friendly welcome awaits you. Enjoy a Kentish breakfast with our own eggs and fresh local produce. Situated near the Greensand Way in the heart of 'Darling Buds of May' countryside, with easy access to Ashford International Station and the Channel crossings. **Open:** All year
01233 840089 (also fax) Mrs MacDonald *enquiries@glebelands-bedandbreakfast.co.uk* www.glebelands-bedandbreakfast.co.uk **D:** Fr £22.50–£25.00 **S:** Fr £30.00–£35.00 **Beds:** 1T 1D 1S **Baths:** 1 Sh (3)

Preston (Faversham)

TR0261

The Windmill Inn, *Canterbury Road, Preston, Faversham, ME13 8LT.* Typical English pub, two bars, dining area, warm friendly welcome. **Open:** All year
01795 536505 D: Fr £22.00–£36.00 **S:** Fr £18.00 **Beds:** 2T 2S **Baths:** 1 Sh (8)

Preston (Wingham)

TR2561

Forstal House, *The Forstal, Preston, Canterbury, Kent, CT3 1DT.* Secluded C18th country house near river and orchards. Beautiful walled garden. **Open:** All year (not Xmas)
01227 722282 Mrs Scott **Fax: 01227 722295 D:** Fr £20.00 **S:** Fr £22.00 **Beds:** 1D 1T **Baths:** 1 En 1 Pr (4)

Rainham

TQ8165

Irwin Grange, *Meresborough Road, Rainham, Gillingham, Kent, ME8 8PN.* Farm house set in 13 acres, good view of River Medway. **Open:** All year (not Xmas)
01634 232801 Mrs Knight **D:** Fr £17.50 **S:** Fr £20.00 **Beds:** 1F 2T **Baths:** 2 Sh (10)

Ramsgate

TR3864

The Royale Guest House, *7 Royal Road, Ramsgate, Kent, CT11 9LE.* Friendly, family-run guest house; close to all amenities. **Open:** All year **Grades:** ETC 3 Diamond
01843 594712 (also fax) Mrs Barry *theroyaleguesthouse@talk21.com* **D:** Fr £17.00–£23.00 **S:** Fr £17.00–£23.00 **Beds:** 1F 2D 2T 4S **Baths:** 3 En 2 Sh (2)

Glendevon Guest House, *8 Truro Road, Ramsgate, Kent, CT11 8BD.* Comfortable ensuite rooms with own well-equipped kitchen/eating areas. **Open:** All year **Grades:** ETC 4 Diamond
01843 570909 (also fax) S & A Everix *adrian.everix@btopenworld.com* **D:** Fr £18.00–£20.00 **S:** Fr £20.00–£24.00 **Beds:** 1F 2T 3D **Baths:** 6 En (5) cc

The Regency Hotel and School Of English, *Royal Crescent, Ramsgate, Kent, CT11 9PE.* Facing English Channel on west cliffs of Ramsgate. Glorious sea views. **Open:** All year
01843 591212 Fax: 01843 850035 *regency.school@btinternet.com* **D:** Fr £17.00–£19.00 **S:** Fr £24.00–£34.00 **Beds:** 3F 58T 26S **Baths:** 16 En 11 Sh (3) cc

Ramsgate Abbeygail Guest House, *17 Penshurst Road, Ramsgate, Kent, CT11 8EG.* 10 mins from award-winning sandy beach. **Open:** All year
01843 594154 D: Fr £18.00–£25.00 **S:** Fr £18.00 **Beds:** 3F 2T 2D 1S **Baths:** 3 En 2 Sh

Rhodes Minnis

TR1443

Monsoon Lodge, *Rhodes Minnis, Canterbury, Kent, CT4 6XX.* Family home, quiet, relaxing. Rural location near Channel Tunnel and Canterbury. **Open:** All year (not Xmas/New Year) **Grades:** ETC 3 Diamond
01303 863272 Mrs Mills **Fax: 01303 863215** *jm@farmersweekly.net* www.monsoonlodge.co.uk **D:** Fr £20.00–£25.00 **S:** Fr £20.00–£30.00 **Beds:** 1F 1T 1D **Baths:** 3 En (4) cc

Rochester

TQ7468

St Martin, *104 Borstal Road, Rochester, Kent, ME1 3BD.* Comfortable Victorian home overlooking river, easy walk to city centre. **Open:** All year (not Xmas) **Grades:** ETC 3 Diamond
01634 848192 Mrs Colvin *icolvin@stmartin.freeserve.co.uk* **D:** Fr £18.00 **S:** Fr £18.00 **Beds:** 1D 2T **Baths:** 2 Sh

255 High Street, *Rochester, Kent, ME1 1HQ.* Victorian family house near station. Antique 4-poster bed. **Open:** All year (not Xmas)
01634 842737 (also fax) Mrs Thomas **D:** Fr £15.00–£17.00 **S:** Fr £18.00–£25.00 **Beds:** 1F 1D 1T **Baths:** 1 Pr 1 Sh

52 Borstal Street, *Rochester, Kent, ME1 3HL.* Comfortable Victorian Terraced house. Suitable for cat lovers. Smokers welcome. **Open:** All year
01634 812347 Ms Walker **D:** Fr £12.50 **S:** Fr £20.00 **Beds:** 1D **Baths:** 1 Sh

Wouldham Court Farmhouse, *246 High Street, Wouldham, Rochester, Kent, ME1 3TY.* Beamed Grade II Listed farmhouse, inglenook fireplace, overlooking River Medway. **Open:** All year (not Xmas)
01634 683271 (also fax) Ms Parnell *wouldham.b-b@virgin.net* **D:** Fr £22.00–£24.00 **S:** Fr £18.00–£24.00 **Beds:** 1F 1D 1S **Baths:** 2 Sh (1) cc

11 Ethelbert Road, *Rochester, Kent, ME1 3EU.* Large family home 10 mins' walk from historic city centre. **Open:** All year (not Xmas)
01634 403740 Mrs Jenkinson **D:** Fr £18.00–£20.00 **S:** Fr £20.00 **Beds:** 1D 1T

Saltwood

TR1536 *Castle Hotel*

The Shrubsoles, *62 Brockhill Road, Saltwood, Hythe, Kent, CT21 4AG.* Victorian home in village setting, 5m Channel Tunnel entrance. **Open:** Nov to Sept
01303 238832 Mrs Shrubsole *marion_shrubsole@lineone.net* **D:** Fr £20.00–£25.00 **S:** Fr £22.00–£35.00 **Beds:** 1T 1D **Baths:** 1 En 1 Pr (2)

Sandhurst

TQ7928 *Bull Inn*

Hoads Farm, *Crouch Lane, Sandhurst, Cranbrook, Kent, TN18 5PA.* Comfortable C16th farmhouse on working farm. **Open:** All year
01580 850296 (also fax) A Nicholas *ca.nicholas@btinternet.com* **D:** Fr £20.00 **S:** Fr £20.00–£25.00 **Beds:** 3T **Baths:** 2 Sh (10) cc

Sevenoaks

TQ5255

Green Tiles, *46 The Rise, Sevenoaks, Kent, TN13 1RJ.* Quiet annexe in lovely garden, own entrance, for 1-5 guests. **Open:** All year
01732 451522 (also fax) Mrs Knoops **D:** Fr £20.00–£22.00 **S:** Fr £30.00–£35.00 **Beds:** 1F **Baths:** 1 En (2)

40 Robyns Way, *Sevenoaks, Kent, TN13 3EB.* Quiet location, station 10 mins' walk. French spoken, self-catering available. **Open:** All year **Grades:** ETC 3 Diamond
01732 452401 Mrs Ingram *ingram7oaks@onetel.net.uk* web.onetel.net.uk/~ingram7oaks **D:** Fr £25.00–£28.00 **S:** Fr £27.00–£30.00 **Beds:** 1D 1T 1S **Baths:** 1 En 1 Sh (3)

56 The Drive, *Sevenoaks, Kent, TN13 3AF.* Lovely Edwardian house and garden close to station and town. Peaceful. **Open:** All year (not Xmas)
01732 453236 Mrs Lloyd *jwlloydsks@aol.com* **D:** Fr £19.00–£24.50 **S:** Fr £22.00–£28.00 **Beds:** 2T 2S **Baths:** 2 Sh (4)

Sheerness

TQ9175

Sheppey Guest House, *214 Queenborough Road, Sheerness, Kent, ME12 3DF.* Friendly family guest house, which has served the public for 26 years. **Open:** All year
01795 665950 Ms Allen **Fax: 01795 661200** **D:** Fr £15.00 **S:** Fr £20.00 **Beds:** 5F 1T 2D 1S **Baths:** 9 En 2

The Whitehouse, *The Leas, Sheerness, Isle of Sheppey, ME12 2TE.* Small, friendly B&B with restaurant. All rooms with river views. **Open:** All year
01795 872266 & 0800 9230158 **Fax: 01708 404508** *pat@leas.co.uk* www.leas.co.uk **D:** Fr £23.00–£29.00 **S:** Fr £25.00–£28.00 **Beds:** 4D 1S **Baths:** 1 Sh (15) **cc**

Shepherdswell

TR2547

Sunshine Cottage, *The Green, Mill Lane, Shepherdswell, Dover, Kent, CT15 7LQ.* C17th cottage on village green, beautifully restored. Pretty garden/courtyard. **Open:** All year
01304 831359 Mrs Popple *sunshinecottage@shepherdswell.fsnet.co.uk* www.sunshine-cottage.co.uk **D:** Fr £25.00–£29.00 **S:** Fr £25.00–£35.00 **Beds:** 1F 4D 1T **Baths:** 2 Pr 2 Sh **cc**

Shoreham

TQ5261

Church House, *Church Street, Shoreham, Sevenoaks, Kent, TN14 7SB.* Georgian house; large garden and tennis court in picturesque village. **Open:** All year (not Xmas/New Year)
01959 522241 (also fax) Mrs Howie *katehowie@compuserve.com* www.heartofkent.org.uk **D:** Fr £22.00–£28.00 **S:** Fr £30.00–£35.00

Sissinghurst

TQ7937

Hillview Cottage, *Starvenden Lane, Sissinghurst, Cranbrook, Kent, TN17 2AN.* Total peace. Attractive, comfortable house close NT properties. **Open:** All year
01580 712823 & 07850 909838 (M) Mrs Lloyd Jones *rmlj@starlaine.freeserve.co.uk* **D:** Fr £20.00–£30.00 **S:** Fr £20.00–£30.00 **Beds:** 1D 1T **Baths:** 2 En 1 Pr

Smarden

TQ8842

Chequers Inn, *Smarden, Ashford, Kent, TN27 8QA.* C14th village inn. Renowned for good food and ambience. **Open:** All year (not Xmas)
01233 770217 **Fax: 01233 770623** **D:** Fr £25.00 **S:** Fr £26.00 **Beds:** 1F 2T 2D 1S **Baths:** 3 En 2 Pr (18)

Gate Cottage, *Maltmans Hill, Smarden, Ashford, Kent, TN27 8RD.* C17th tollhouse. Superb food. Ideal touring Kent/Sussex/Channel crossings. **Open:** All year (not Xmas/New Year)
01233 770226 (also fax) Mr & Mrs Ralph **D:** Fr £25.00–£27.50 **S:** Fr £35.00–£37.50 **Beds:** 2D **Baths:** 2 En (12) (4)

Southborough

TQ5842

10 Modest Corner, *Southborough, Tunbridge Wells, Kent, TN4 0LS.* Warm welcome in very comfortable, tastefully decorated B&B. **Open:** All year (not Xmas/New Year) **Grades:** ETC 3 Diamond
01892 522450 (also fax) Mr Leemhuis *modestanneke@lineone.net* **D:** Fr £22.50–£25.00 **S:** Fr £30.00–£35.00 **Beds:** 2T 1D **Baths:** 1 Pr 1 Sh (2)

St Margaret's at Cliffe

TR3644

Wallets Court Manor, *West Cliffe, St Margaret's at Cliffe, Dover, Kent, CT15 6EW.* C17th hotel. Restaurant and spa in White Cliffs country. **Open:** All year
01304 852424 Mr Oakley *stay@wallettscourt.com* www.wallettscourt.com **D:** Fr £45.00–£75.00 **S:** Fr £75.00 **Beds:** 1F 3T 12D **Baths:** 16 En (50) **cc**

BATHROOMS
En = Ensuite
Pr = Private
Sh = Shared

Stelling Minnis

TR1346

Bower Farm House, *Bossingham Road, Stelling Minnis, Canterbury, Kent, CT4 6BB.* Breakfast on fresh bread and new laid eggs in a charming heavily beamed C17th Kentish farmhouse on the edge of a medieval common. Visit historic Canterbury, walk in the beautiful countryside or see Dover Castle and the White Cliffs. **Open:** All year (not Xmas/New Year)
01227 709430 *book@bowerbb.freeserve.co.uk* **D:** Fr £22.00–£25.00 **S:** Fr £28.00–£30.00 **Beds:** 1T 1D **Baths:** 1 En 1 Pr (5)

Stowting

TR1241

Water Farm, *Stowting, Ashford, Kent, TN25 6BA.* Lakeside farm; homely and comfortable, beautiful scenery, trout fishing. **Open:** All year (not Xmas/New Year)
01303 862401 C Cole **D:** Fr £22.50–£25.00 **S:** Fr £22.50–£25.00 **Beds:** 1T 1D **Baths:** 1 En 1 Pr (12) (2)

Strood

TQ7268

3 Hillside Avenue, Frindsbury, *Strood, Rochester, ME2 3DB.* Friendly family Victorian home in quiet road, close to amenities. **Open:** All year
01634 713642 Mrs Firmin **D:** Fr £15.00–£18.00 **S:** Fr £15.00–£18.00 **Beds:** 1F 1T 1S **Baths:** 2 Sh

Sundridge

TQ4855

The Red House, *Church Road, Sundridge, Sevenoaks, Kent, TN14 6EA.* Queen Anne House in Beautiful gardens near Hever, Chartwell, London. **Open:** All year (not Xmas/New Year)
01959 565444 Mrs Belle **Fax: 01732 452312** *balles@waitrose.com* **D:** Fr £25.00 **S:** Fr £25.00 **Beds:** 3D **Baths:** 1 En 1 Sh (4)

Sutton Valence

TQ8149 *King's Head*

West Belringham, *Chart Road, Sutton Valence, Maidstone, Kent, ME17 3AW.* Spacious bungalows, panoramic views. Breakfast. Complimentary tea/coffee with home-made cakes. **Open:** All year (not Xmas/New Year)
01622 843995 (also fax) Mrs King *west.belringham@tesco.net* **D:** Fr £21.00 **S:** Fr £27.00 **Beds:** 2T **Baths:** 1 Pr (7) (5)

The Queens Head, *High Street, Sutton Valence, Maidstone, Kent, ME17 3AG.* Spectacular countryside views of Weald of Kent. Excellent home cooked food in countryside style. **Open:** All year
01622 843225 J Pilcher **Fax: 01622 842651**
D: Fr £22.50–£25.00 **S:** Fr £22.50–£25.00
Beds: 2F 1T 1D **Baths:** 1 Sh
cc

Tenterden

TQ8833

The White Cottage, *London Beach, St Michael's, Tenterden, Kent, TN30 6SR.* 2 miles north of Tenterden on A28 road, rural position.
Open: All year **Grades:** ETC 3 Diamond
01233 850583 Mrs Matthews
www.smoothhound.co.uk/shs.html **D:** Fr £16.50–£18.50 **S:** Fr £20.00–£25.00 **Beds:** 2D 1T **Baths:** 1 En 2 Sh (3)

Old Burren, *25 Ashford Road, Tenterden, Kent, TN30 6LL.* C17th home where a warm friendly welcome awaits you. **Open:** All year
01580 764442 Ms Pooley *poo@burren.fsbusiness.co.uk* www.oldburren.co.uk
D: Fr £20.00–£25.00 **S:** Fr £25.00–£45.00
Beds: 2D 1S **Baths:** 1 En 1 Pr (2)

Draylands, *High Halden, Ashford, Kent, TN23 3JG.* Secluded location in Garden of England. Ground floor bedrooms with extensive views. **Open:** All year (not Xmas/New Year)
01233 850048 (also fax) Mrs Russell
sallyrussell30@hotmail.com **D:** Fr £23.00–£25.00 **S:** Fr £28.00–£30.00 **Beds:** 1D 1T
Baths: 2 En (3)

Tonbridge

TQ5946

Starvecrow Place, *Starvecrow Hill, Shipbourne Road, Tonbridge, Kent, TN11 9NL.* Relaxed luxury accommodation set in delightful woodlands. Heated outdoor swimming pool. **Open:** All year (not Xmas)
01732 356863 Mrs Batson **D:** Fr £19.00–£22.00 **S:** Fr £30.00 **Beds:** 2D 1T **Baths:** 2 En 1 Pr (13) (6)

Trottiscliffe

TQ6460

Bramble Park, *Church Lane, Trottiscliffe, West Malling, Kent, ME19 5EB.* Secluded tranquil Victorian rectory in beautiful private parkland. Spacious comfortable.
Open: All year
01732 822397 Mrs Towler **D:** Fr £25.00 **S:** Fr £25.00 **Beds:** 1F 1D 1S **Baths:** 1 Pr 2 Sh (6)

Tunbridge Wells

TQ5839

Vale Royal Hotel, *54-57 London Road, Tunbridge Wells, Kent, TN1 1DS.*
Open: All year
01892 525580
V Constantine *reservations@valeroyalhotel.co.uk* www.valeroyalhotel.co.uk
D: Fr £33.00–£38.00 **S:** Fr £52.00–£65.00
Beds: 2F 6D 6T 6S **Baths:** 20 En (3) **cc**
Situated in the lovely spa town, overlooking the common. All rooms have courtesy beverage tray, TV, direct dial telephones. Relax in the countryside, visit stately homes, formal gardens, close to M25 and Gatwick Airport.

10 Modest Corner, *Southborough, Tunbridge Wells, Kent, TN4 0LS.*
Open: All year (not Xmas/New Year)
Grades: ETC 3 Diamond
01892 522450 (also fax) Mr Leemhuis
modestanneke@lineone.net **D:** Fr £22.50–£25.00
S: Fr £30.00–£35.00 **Beds:** 2T 1D **Baths:** 1 Pr 1 Sh (2)
You will experience a warm welcome in this very comfortable, tastefully decorated B&B situated on the outer edge of Tunbridge Wells in a little hamlet away from noisy traffic. Easy access M25 and main station. Ideally placed for visiting the SE.

Ash Tree Cottage, *Eden Road, Tunbridge Wells, Kent, TN1 1TS.* Delightful cottage-style house, short walk to the famous Pantiles. **Open:** All year (not Xmas/New Year)
01892 541317 Mrs Rogers **Fax: 01892 616770**
D: Fr £22.50–£25.00 **S:** Fr £35.00–£42.00
Beds: 1D 1T **Baths:** 2 En (9) (4)

Blundeston, *Eden Road, Tunbridge Wells, Kent, TN1 1TS.* Beautiful period house in quiet secluded part of the old village area of Tunbridge Wells. Within five minutes walk of many restaurants, the old High Street, Pantiles and railway station. **Open:** All year (not Xmas/New Year)
01892 513030 Mrs Day **Fax: 01892 540255**
D: Fr £23.00–£26.00 **S:** Fr £23.00–£26.00
Beds: 1T 1D **Baths:** 2 En

Ford Cottage, *Linden Park Road, Tunbridge Wells, Kent, TN2 5QL.* Picturesque and charming Victorian cottage, 3 mins' walk to Pantiles. **Open:** Feb to Nov
01892 531419 Mrs Cusdin *fordcottage@tinyworld.co.uk* **D:** Fr £21.00–£25.00 **Beds:** 3T
Baths: 2 En 1 Pr (5) (5)

66 Tunnel Road, *Tunbridge Wells, Kent, TN1 2BX.* Comfortable, modest accommodation. Centre beautiful town. Many interesting places nearby. **Open:** All year (not Xmas/New Year)
01892 529125 Mrs Harrison **D:** Fr £16.00–£18.00 **S:** Fr £17.00–£19.00 **Beds:** 1D
Baths: 1 Sh

Ulcombe

TQ8448

Bramley Knowle Farm, *Eastwood Road, Ulcombe, Maidstone, Kent, ME17 1ET.* Modern farmhouse, 10 mins M20 J8, near Leeds castle. **Open:** All year (not Xmas)
01622 858878 D Leat **Fax: 01622 851121**
www.bramleyknowlefarm.co.uk **D:** Fr £19.00–£22.50 **S:** Fr £20.00–£25.00 **Beds:** 2D 1S
Baths: 1 En 1 Sh (3) (6)

Upchurch

TQ8467

Suffield House, *The Street, Upchurch, Sittingbourne, Kent, ME9 7EU.* **Open:** All year (not Xmas) **Grades:** ETC 4 Diamond, Silver
01634 230409 & 07715 691683 (M) Mr & Mrs Newbery **D:** Fr £27.00 **S:** Fr £27.00 **Beds:** 2D 1T (10) (10)
Suffield House - a Victorian house set in the rural village of Upchurch, between Rainham and Sittingbourne. Easy access to historic Faversham, Rochester and the Saxon Shore Way. Village pub and golf course. Welcome and a superb breakfast. Reservations held until 7pm.

West Hougham

TR2540

Bramble Hill Cottage, *Meggett Lane, West Hougham, Dover, Kent, CT15 7BS.* Warm welcome, beautiful rural setting, 15 mins Tunnel and ferries. **Open:** Mar to Nov
01303 253180 Mrs Hughes **D:** Fr £18.00–£20.00 **Beds:** 1T 2D **Baths:** 2 En 1 Pr

BATHROOMS
En = Ensuite
Pr = Private
Sh = Shared

Westerham

TQ4454

Lodge House, *High Street, Brasted, Westerham, Kent, TN16 1HS.* Conveniently situated character property, a short walk from popular pubs. **Open:** All year **Grades:** ETC 3 Diamond
01959 562195 Mr & Mrs Marshall *lodgehouse@brastedbb.freeserve.co.uk* **D:** Fr £24.00–£29.00 **S:** Fr £30.00–£37.50 **Beds:** 1T 1D **Baths:** 1 En 1 Sh (3)

The Orchard House, *Brasted Chart, Westerham, Kent, TN16 1LR.* Family home, quiet, rural surroundings, near Chartwell, Hever, Knole, Gatwick. **Open:** All year (not Xmas) **Grades:** ETC 3 Diamond
01959 563702 Mrs Godsal *david.godsal@tesco.net* **D:** Fr £24.00 **S:** Fr £26.00 **Beds:** 2T 1S **Baths:** 2 Sh (4)

Holmesdale House, *High Street, Brasted, Westerham, Kent, TN16 1HS.* Delightful Victorian house (part C17th). Chartwell, Hever, Knole and mainline station. **Open:** All year
01959 564834 (also fax) Mr Jinks **D:** Fr £22.00–£29.00 **S:** Fr £36.00–£48.00 **Beds:** 1F 3D 1T **Baths:** 3 En 1 Sh (7)

Corner Cottage, *Toys Hill, Westerham, Kent, TN16 1PY.* Attractive self-contained accommodation in Laura Ashley fabrics. Spectacular panoramic views. **Open:** All year
01732 750362 Mrs Olszowska **Fax: 01959 561911** *olszowskiathome@jshmanco.com* **D:** Fr £45.00–£50.00 **S:** Fr £30.00–£35.00 **Beds:** 1F (1)

Westwell

TQ9847

Dean Court Farm, *Challock Lane, Westwell, Ashford, Kent, TN25 4NH.* Period rural farmhouse, central for Channel ports and touring Kent. **Open:** All year (not Xmas) **Grades:** ETC 3 Diamond
01233 712924 Mrs Lister **D:** Fr £20.00–£25.00 **S:** Fr £20.00–£25.00 **Beds:** 1D 2T **Baths:** 1 Sh (3)

Whitfield

TR2945

Rolles Court, *Church Whitfield Road, Whitfield, Dover, Kent, CT16 3HY.* Country home 3 miles Dover. Picturesque gardens. Very friendly atmosphere. **Open:** All year
01304 827487 Mrs Montgomery **Fax: 01304 827877** *rollescourt@tesco.net* **D:** Fr £25.00–£30.00 **S:** Fr £25.00–£30.00 **Beds:** 1F 1T 1D 1S **Baths:** 4 En

Whitstable

TR1066

Alliston House, *1 Joy Lane, Whitstable, Kent, CT5 4LS.* Comfortable spacious airy rooms. 10 mins town/beach, excellent breakfast. **Open:** All year **Grades:** ETC 3 Diamond
01227 779066 Mr Gough *allistonhouse@aol.com* **D:** Fr £22.50–£27.50 **S:** Fr £35.00–£45.00 **Beds:** 1T 2D **Baths:** 1 En 1 Pr 2 Sh (4)

Wingham

TR2357

Twitham Court Farm, *Staple Road, Wingham, Canterbury, Kent, CT3 1LP.* Enjoy our friendly, peaceful, comfortable farmhouse, organic breakfasts and beautiful gardens. **Open:** All year
01227 720265 M Duck & D Bowden *flower@twitham.fsnet.co.uk* **D:** Fr £20.00–£40.00 **S:** Fr £25.00–£40.00 **Beds:** 1F 2D 1T **Baths:** 1 En 1 Sh (8)

The Dog Inn, *Canterbury Road, Wingham, Canterbury, Kent, CT3 1BB.* Quaint C13th village inn near historic Canterbury. Warm welcome. **Open:** All year
01227 720339 (also fax) **D:** Fr £25.00 **S:** Fr £30.00 **Beds:** 2F 1T 3D **Baths:** 6 En cc

Worth

TR3355

Ilex Cottage, *Temple Way, Worth, Deal, Kent, CT14 0DA.* Lovely, secluded C18th village house, guest conservatory, pretty rural views. **Open:** All year (not Xmas/New Year) **Grades:** ETC 4 Diamond
01304 617026 Mrs Stobie **Fax: 01304 620890** *info@ilexcottage.com* www.ilexcottage.com **D:** Fr £20.00–£27.50 **S:** Fr £30.00–£35.00 **Beds:** 1F 1T 1D **Baths:** 3 En cc

Wouldham

TQ7164

Wouldham Court Farmhouse, *246 High Street, Wouldham, Rochester, Kent, ME1 3TY.* Beamed Grade II Listed farmhouse, inglenook fireplace, overlooking River Medway. **Open:** All year (not Xmas)
01634 683271 (also fax) Ms Parnell *wouldham.b-b@virgin.net* **D:** Fr £22.00–£24.00 **S:** Fr £18.00–£24.00 **Beds:** 1F 1D 1S **Baths:** 2 Sh (1) cc

Wrotham

TQ6059

Hillside House, *Gravesend Road, Wrotham, Sevenoaks, Kent, TN15 7JH.* Ideally situated for touring, Channel Ports, M20, M25, Gatwick, London. **Open:** All year (not Xmas/New Year)
01732 822564 J Thomas *clive@broteham.freeserve.co.uk* **D:** Fr £20.00–£22.00 **S:** Fr £20.00–£25.00 **Beds:** 1T 1D 1S **Baths:** 1 Sh (3)

Wye

TR0546

Mistral, *3 Oxenturn Road, Wye, Ashford, Kent, TN25 5BH.* Comfortable and well appointed house, mature garden, secluded but readily accessible to Wye village. **Open:** Jan to Dec
01233 813011 Mr & Mrs Chapman **Fax: 01233813011** *geoff@chapman.invictanet.co.uk* www.wye.org **D:** Fr £25.00 **S:** Fr £25.00 **Beds:** 1T 1S **Baths:** 1 Sh (2)

Lancashire

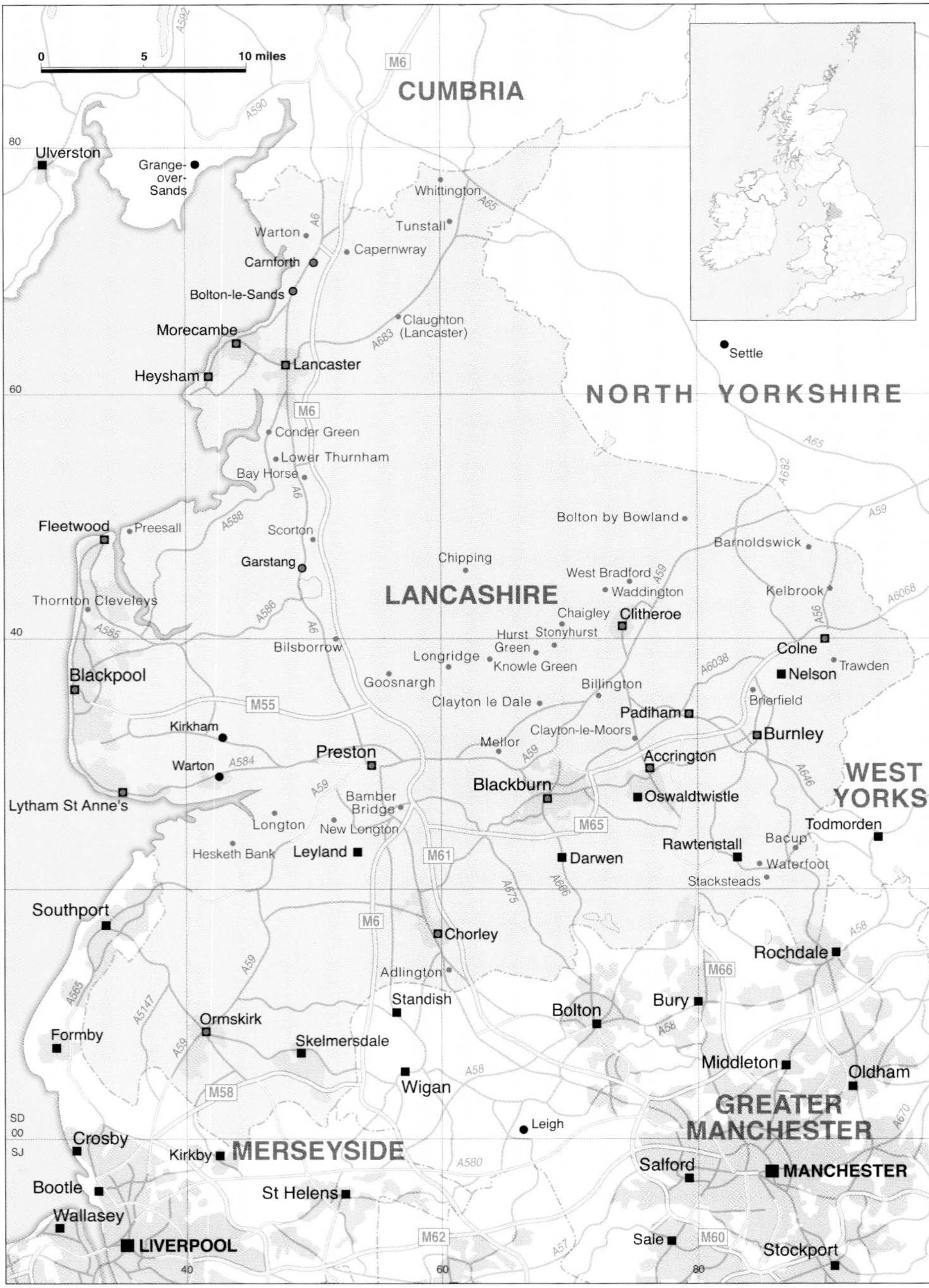

0
5
10 miles
CUMBRIA
NORTH YORKSHIRE
LANCASHIRE
WEST YORKS.
GREATER MANCHESTER
MERSEYSIDE
Ulverston
Grange-over-Sands
Whittington
Tunstall
Warton
Capernwray
Carnforth
Bolton-le-Sands
Claughton (Lancaster)
Morecambe
Lancaster
Heysham
Settle
Conder Green
Lower Thurnham
Bay Horse
Fleetwood
Preesall
Scorton
Garstang
Chipping
Bolton by Bowland
Barnoldswick
West Bradford
Waddington
Kelbrook
Thornton Cleveleys
Chaigley
Clitheroe
Hurst Green
Stonyhurst
Bilsborrow
Longridge
Knowle Green
Colne
Trawden
Nelson
Blackpool
Goosnargh
Billington
Brierfield
Clayton le Dale
Padiham
Kirkham
Clayton-le-Moors
Burnley
Mellor
Preston
Accrington
Warton
Blackburn
Oswaldtwistle
Lytham St Anne's
Bamber Bridge
Longton
New Longton
Todmorden
Bacup
Rawtenstall
Hesketh Bank
Leyland
Darwen
Waterfoot
Stacksteads
Southport
Chorley
Rochdale
Adlington
Standish
Bury
Bolton
Ormskirk
Formby
Skelmersdale
Middleton
Oldham
Wigan
Leigh
Crosby
Kirkby
Salford
MANCHESTER
Bootle
St Helens
Wallasey
LIVERPOOL
Sale
Stockport
M6
M55
M61
M65
M66
M58
M62
M60
A6
A65
A683
A588
A586
A585
A584
A59
A682
A6068
A56
A6038
A646
A666
A675
A58
A565
A5147
A580
A57
A670
A590
A592
80
60
40
SD 00
SJ

Accrington

SD7528

Maple Lodge Hotel, *70 Blackburn Road, Clayton-le-Moors, Accrington, BB5 5JH.* Friendly family-run licensed hotel off M65 J7. Home cooking. **Open:** All year
01254 301284 Fax: 01254 388152 *maplelod@aol.com* www.maplelodgehotel.co.uk **D:** Fr £25.00–£28.00 **S:** Fr £37.50–£42.50 **Beds:** 2T 6D **Baths:** 8 En (8) cc

Wendys B&B, *139 Whalley Road, Accrington, Lancs, BB5 1BX.* Friendly welcome; close to town centre and motorway networks. **Open:** All year
01254 871060 Mrs Walsh **D:** Fr £18.00 **S:** Fr £18.00 **Beds:** 2F 1T 1S **Baths:** 1 En 1 Sh

Adlington

SD6013

Briarfield House, *Bolton Road, Anderton, Adlington, Chorley, Lancs, PR6 9HW.* In own grounds, beautiful views over open countryside. Private parking. **Open:** All year
01257 480105 & 07831 651704 (M) Mrs Baldwin *briarfieldhouse@aol.com* **D:** Fr £20.00–£21.00 **S:** Fr £25.00–£26.00 **Beds:** 1D 2T **Baths:** 2 En 1 Pr

Bacup

SD8622

Pasture Bottom Farm, *Bacup, Lancs, OL13 0UZ.* Comfortable farmhouse B&B in a quiet rural area on a working beef farm. **Open:** All year (not Xmas)
01706 873790 (also fax) A Isherwood *ha.isherwood@zen.co.uk* **D:** Fr £17.00–£18.00 **S:** Fr £17.00–£18.00 **Beds:** 1D 2T **Baths:** 2 En 1 Pr 1 Sh (4)

Oakenclough Farm, *Oakenclough Road, Bacup, Lancashire, OL13 9ET.* Peaceful farmhouse. Cast iron fires. **Open:** All year
01706 879319 & 07973 314489 (M) Mr & Mrs Worswick **Fax: 01706 879319** *wharflenwickle@aol.com* **D:** Fr £29.00–£46.00 (4)

Bamber Bridge

SD5626

Anvil Guest House, *321 Station Road, Bamber Bridge, Preston, Lancs, PR5 6EE.* Comfortable, friendly, near M6, M61, M65. Central heating, TV lounge. **Open:** All year (not Xmas)
01772 339022 J C Arkwright **D:** Fr £14.50 **S:** Fr £16.00 **Beds:** 2F 4D 3T **Baths:** 2 Sh

Barnoldswick

SD8746

Foster's House, *203 Gisburn Road, Barnoldswick, Lancs, BB18 5JU.* A warm welcome awaits at our beautiful home from home. **Open:** All year
01282 850718 Mr & Mrs Edwards www.hotpots.com/fostershouse.htm **D:** Fr £20.00 **S:** Fr £20.00 **Beds:** 2D 2T **Baths:** 3 En 1 Sh (4)

Bay Horse

SD4953

Stanley Lodge Farmhouse, *Cockerham Road, Bay Horse, Lancaster, Lancs., LA2 0HE.* Rural area, Lancaster canal nearby. Lakes, Yorkshire Dales, golfing, horse riding nearby. **Open:** All year (not Xmas/New Year)
01524 791863 D: Fr £18.00–£20.00 **S:** Fr £18.00–£20.00 **Beds:** 1F 2D **Baths:** 1 Sh (4)

Billington

SD7235

Rosebury, *51 Pasturelands Drive, Billington, Clitheroe, Lancs, BB7 9LW.* Quality family accommodation, guest rooms overlook the beautiful Ribble Valley. **Open:** All year (not Xmas/New Year)
01254 822658 C P Hamer *enquiries_rosebury@yahoo.co.uk* www.rosebury-guest-house.co.uk **D:** Fr £20.00–£22.50 **S:** Fr £20.00–£22.50 **Beds:** 1F 1T **Baths:** 2 Sh

Bilsborrow

SD5139

Olde Duncombe House, *Garstang Road, Bilsborrow, Preston, Lancs, PR3 0RE.* **Open:** All year
01995 640336 (also fax) Mr Bolton *oldedunc@aol.com* www.geocities.com/oldeduncombehouse **D:** Fr £25.00 **S:** Fr £37.50 **Beds:** 1F 2T 5D 1S **Baths:** 9 En cc
An attractive, traditional, cottage style family-run B&B. It is believed to date back to the 1500s and that some of Bonnie Prince Charlie's men slept in the attached barn on the way back from the Battle of Preston.

BATHROOMS
En = Ensuite
Pr = Private
Sh = Shared

Blackburn

SD6827

The Chimneys, *139 Preston New Road, Blackburn, Lancs, BB2 6BJ.* Family-run Victorian property, central location, comfortable accommodation, friendly service. **Open:** All year (not Xmas/New Year)
01254 665026 D: Fr £18.00–£20.00 **S:** Fr £18.00–£25.00 **Beds:** 2F 4T 3D 2S **Baths:** 2 En 3 Sh (8)

Blackpool

SD3136

Raffles Hotel, *73-75 Hornby Road, Blackpool, Lancashire, FY1 4QJ.* **Open:** All year **Grades:** ETC 4 Diamond
01253 294713 Fax: 01253 294240 www.rafflesshotelblackpool.co.uk **D:** Fr £21.00–£28.00 **S:** Fr £27.00–£34.00 **Beds:** 2F 3T 11D 1S **Baths:** 17 En (10) cc
5 mins Winter Gardens, Theatre, Tower. ETC 3 Diamonds, licensed, parking, fully ensuite with colour TV, tea/coffee facilities, daily housekeeper. Imaginative choice menus. Full entry in the Good Hotel Guide 2000-2002. As featured on BBC's 'Summer Holiday'.

The Arncliffe Hotel, *24 Osborne Road, South Shore, Blackpool, Lancs, FY4 1HJ.* **Open:** All year **Grades:** ETC 3 Diamond
01253 345209 (also fax) Mr & Mrs Naisbett *arncliffe.hotel@virgin.net* www.blackpool-internet.co.uk/HOMEarncliffe.html **D:** Fr £16.00–£20.00 **S:** Fr £15.00–£18.00 **Beds:** 1F 5D 1T 1S **Baths:** 5 En 1 Sh (3) cc
Voted 'Hotel of the Year 2000' in Blackpool Tourism Awards. Small licensed, family-run hotel, catering for couples and families only. Close to Pleasure Beach, Promenade and all road/rail/air links. Discounted tickets available for Pleasure Beach, Tower and Zoo.

Planning a longer stay? Always ask for any special rates

The Carlton, *64 Albert Road, Blackpool, Lancs, FY1 4PR.* **Open:** All year (not Xmas/New Year)
01253 622693 (also fax) *Enquire@thecarlton.com* www.thecarlton.com **D:** Fr £16.00–£30.00 **S:** Fr £16.00–£30.00 **Beds:** 4F 2T 7D **Baths:** 13 En cc
Centrally located within walking distance of Blackpool's most famous landmarks including Winter Gardens, Tower, theatres & main shopping area. This licensed family hotel offers all modern ensuite bedrooms with colour TV, teasmade, central heating & double glazing.

Pembroke Private Hotel, *11 King Edward Avenue, Blackpool, Lancashire, FY2 9TD.* **Open:** Mar to Nov **Grades:** ETC 4 Diamond
01253 351306 (also fax) *stay@pembrokehotel.com* www.pembrokehotel.com
D: Fr £20.00–£26.00 **S:** Fr £23.00–£29.00
Beds: 1F 2T 5D 3S **Baths:** 11 En (6) cc
One of the very best small hotels in Blackpool, providing quality ensuite accommodation. Situated in a select area of North Shore, just off the Queen's Promenade and close to Gynn Gardens and North Shore Golf Course.

Ingledene Hotel, *44 Reads Avenue, Blackpool, Lancashire, FY1 4DE.* **Open:** All year
01253 625679 (also fax) Mr Norman *booking@4blackpool.co.uk* www.4blackpool.co.uk **D:** Fr £20.00–£27.50 **S:** Fr £22.50–£30.00 **Beds:** 5F 4T 17D 2S **Baths:** 26 En (3) cc
A professionally run hotel in the heart of Blackpool. Within 5 mins walk of the town centre, Tower and the Winter Gardens. With a bronze host accreditation, offering good standard of accommodation at a reasonable price. Coach parties welcome.

RATES
D = Price range per person sharing in a double or twin room
S = Price range for a single room

St Ives Hotel, *10 King George Avenue, North Shore, Blackpool, Lancs, FY2 9SN.*
Open: All year **Grades:** ETC 2 Diamond
01253 352122 (also fax) Mrs Dempsey *june@stiveshotel-blackpool.co.uk* **D:** Fr £16.00–£22.00
Beds: 3F 4D 2T **Baths:** 5 En 4 Sh (2) (2) cc
A highly recommended hotel situated just off Queen's Promenade, within easy reach of all amenities, including golf course. Most rooms ensuite with tea/coffee making facilities and full central heating throughout. Excellent food and a high standard of cleanliness.

Fairway Hotel, *34/36 Hull Road, Blackpool, Lancs, FY1 4QB.* **Open:** All year
Grades: ETC 3 Diamond
01253 623777 Mr Hodges **Fax: 01253 753455** *bookings@fairway.gb.com* www.come.to/fairway
D: Fr £20.00–£25.00 **S:** Fr £31.00–£33.00
Beds: 10F 8D **Baths:** 18 En cc
Family-run licensed hotel, close to Tower, Winter Gardens, shops and night life. No hidden extras. Deposit refundable if not satisfied on arrival. New Year breaks a speciality.

The Carlis Private Hotel, *34 Charnley Road, Blackpool, Lancs, FY1 4PF.* **Open:** All year
01253 622586 (also fax) Mrs Boyd *alan.boyd5@btinternet.com* www.carlis-hotel.co.uk **D:** Fr £13.00–£25.00 **S:** Fr £16.00–£30.00
Beds: 5F 9D 3T 2S **Baths:** 12 En 7 Sh cc
Licensed, good food and cleanliness assured. Central to beach, shops, shows, Tower and Winter Gardens. TV lounge, pool table. Hygiene certificate. Weekly rates from £69 B&B, e/s extra. All rooms have tea/coffee making facilities, central heating, TV.

May-Dene Private Hotel, *10 Dean Street, Blackpool, Lancs, FY4 1AU.* Clean, comfortable, 50 yards off Promenade. Close to entertainments and attractions. **Open:** All year **Grades:** ETC 3 Diamond
01253 343464 Mrs Duxbury-Campbell *may_dene_hotel@hotmail.com* www.may-dene.com **D:** Fr £21.00–£35.00 **S:** Fr £25.00–£60.00
Beds: 4F 1T 5D **Baths:** 8 En 2 Pr (8) cc

Knowlsley Hotel, *68 Dean Street, Blackpool, Lancs, FY4 1BP.* 5-minute walk from Pleasure Beach, South Pier & Promenade.
Open: Easter to Nov **Grades:** RAC 3 Diamond
01253 343414 *clntown@aol.com* **D:** Fr £18.00–£25.00 **S:** Fr £20.00–£27.00 **Beds:** 3F 1T 5D 2S **Baths:** 11 En (7) (9) cc

Clifton Court Hotel, *12 Clifton Drive, Blackpool, Lancs, FY4 1NX.* Comfortable, affordable accommodation, next to Blackpool Pleasure Beach. Unbeatable cleanliness. Lounge bar. **Open:** All year (not Xmas/New Year)
01253 342385 (also fax) *enquiries@clifton-court-hotel.co.uk* www.clifton-court-hotel.co.uk **D:** Fr £20.00–£28.00 **S:** Fr £20.00–£29.00 **Beds:** 4F 4T 4D 4S **Baths:** 16 En (20) cc

Westcliffe Private Hotel, *46 King Edward Avenue, Blackpool, Lancs, FY2 9TA.* Homely hotel in select area adjacent Queen's Promenade; comfort assured.
Open: All year (not Xmas)
01253 352943 Mr Carter **D:** Fr £18.00–£25.00 **S:** Fr £18.00–£25.00 **Beds:** 2D 2T 3S 1F **Baths:** 8 Pr (7)

The Beverley Hotel, *25 Dean Street, Blackpool, Lancashire, FY4 1AU.* Near Promenade, South Pier, Pleasure Beach, Sandcastle/Casino leisure complex. **Open:** All year **Grades:** ETC 3 Diamond
01253 344426 Mrs Yarnell *beverley.hotel@virgin.net* beverleyhotel-blackpool.co.uk **D:** Fr £19.00–£30.00 **S:** Fr £24.00–£34.00 **Beds:** 1S 1T 5D 4F **Baths:** 11 En cc

Trevine Hotel, *4 Havelock Street, Blackpool, FY1 4BN.* Perfectly situated for theatres, clubs, shopping and all main attractions.
Open: All year
01253 620897 Mrs Ainsworth *Ttrevine@btinternet.com* **D:** Fr £16.00–£20.00 **S:** Fr £18.00–£22.00 **Beds:** 4F 1T 4D 1S **Baths:** 10 En 10 Pr cc

BATHROOMS
En = Ensuite
Pr = Private
Sh = Shared

The Aberford, *12/14 Yorkshire Street, Blackpool, Lancs, FY1 5BG.* A mid-Victorian building, convenient for central attractions and town shops. Hairdryers, radio/alarm, personal safe, non-smoking dining-room, telephone in bedrooms. **Open:** All year
01253 625026 Mr & Mrs Goddard **Fax: 01253 622248** *admin@aberfordhotel.co.uk* www.smoothhound.co.uk/hotels/aberford.html **D:** Fr £15.00–£24.00 **S:** Fr £18.00–£27.00 **Beds:** 9F 3T 8D 1S **Baths:** 21 En (3) **cc**

Norfolk House, *51 St Chads Road, Blackpool, Lancs, FY1 6BP.* Off Promenade, Midway Tower/Pleasure Beach. Close many attractions and clubs. **Open:** All year
01253 344132 *hotel@st-chads.fsnet.co.uk* **D:** Fr £12.00–£25.00 **S:** Fr £18.00–£25.00 **Beds:** 4F 1T 6D **Baths:** 4 En 1 Pr 1 Sh

Langworthy Hotel, *5 Lonsdale Road, Blackpool, Lancs, FY1 6EE.* Family-run guest house. Children welcome. Licensed bar, centrally situated. **Open:** All year
01253 345914 Roger & Maggie Holdoway **D:** Fr £12.00–£25.00 **S:** Fr £12.00–£25.00 **Beds:** 5F 1T 4D **Baths:** 4 En 3 Sh

Clarron House, *22 Leopold Grove, Blackpool, Lancs, FY1 4LD.* Welcome Host Silver graded. Adjacent Winter Gardens, theatres, shops, piers. **Open:** All year
01253 623748 Mr & Mrs O'Donnell **Fax: 01253 653748** **D:** Fr £14.00–£23.00 **S:** Fr £17.00–£26.00 **Beds:** 3F 3D 1S **Baths:** 6 En 1 Sh **cc**

Astoria Hotel, *118-120 Albert Road, Blackpool, Lancs, FY1 4PN.* Excellent food & accommodation, all ensuite. Adjacent Winter Gardens, shops & theatres. **Open:** All year
01253 621321 Ann Brown **Fax: 01253 293203** *abnw15916@blueyonder.co.uk* **D:** Fr £20.00–£29.00 **S:** Fr £20.00–£29.00 **Beds:** 11F 10D 3T 3S **Baths:** 27 En (4) **cc**

Grasmere Hotel, *51 Palatine Road, Blackpool, FY1 4BX.* Friendly, family-run hotel. Good food and a warm welcome. **Open:** All year
01253 294887 Mrs Curtis *dave.jill@ukonline.co.uk* www.grasmerehotel.net **D:** Fr £15.00–£25.00 **S:** Fr £15.00–£25.00 **Beds:** 4F 2T 2D **Baths:** 2 En 3 Sh

Newlands Private Hotel, *14 Napier Avenue, Blackpool, FY4 1PA.* Friendly, family, licensed accommodation. Pleasure beach, Sandcastle, airport, golf minutes. **Open:** All year (not Xmas/New Year)
01253 341596 *newlandsprivatehotel@btinternet.com* **D:** Fr £10.00–£25.00 **S:** Fr £10.00–£25.00 **Beds:** 4F 4D 3S **Baths:** 1 En 3 Sh (6)

This'l Do Me Guest House, *67 Alexandra Road, Blackpool, FY1 6HW.* Small, friendly. 2 mins Promenade between Central and South Piers. **Open:** Easter to Nov
01253 408787 Mrs Jackson **D:** Fr £13.00–£15.00 **S:** Fr £14.00 **Beds:** 2F 4D 2S **Baths:** 2 En 2 Sh

Dale House, *16 Dale Street, Blackpool, FY1 5BP.* Friendly house. Central location near sea front. Home cooked food, personal service. **Open:** All year
01253 620548 (also fax) **D:** Fr £15.00–£18.00 **S:** Fr £15.00–£18.00 **Beds:** 2F 2D 1T **Baths:** 3 En 1 Pr 1 Sh (3)

Beachcomber Hotel, *78 Reads Avenue, Blackpool, FY1 4DE.* Comfortable centrally situated hotel; all rooms ensuite, off-road parking. **Open:** All year
01253 621622 Mr & Mrs Mcphail **Fax: 01253 299254** *info@beachcomberhotel.net* **D:** Fr £19.00–£24.00 **S:** Fr £19.00–£24.00 **Beds:** 2F 4D 3T 1S **Baths:** 10 En (10) **cc**

Ashcroft Hotel, *42 King Edward Avenue, Blackpool, Lancashire, FY2 9TA.* Select north shore area. 2 mins from Queen's Promenade tram stops. **Open:** All year (not Xmas/New Year) **Grades:** ETC 3 Diamond
01253 351538 *dave@ashcroftblackpool.freeserve.co.uk* www.smoothhound.co.uk/hotels/ashcroft.html **D:** Fr £19.00–£23.00 **S:** Fr £19.00–£23.00 **Beds:** 2F 1T 4D 3S **Baths:** 7 En 2 Sh

Cardoun Hotel, *15 St Chads Road, Blackpool, Lancs, FY1 6BP.* Very clean family-run hotel, 30 seconds from sea front. **Open:** All year
01253 344056 **Fax: 01253 344068** *cardoun.hotel@virgin.net* **D:** Fr £15.00–£30.00 **S:** Fr £20.00–£35.00 **Beds:** 3F 3T 3D **Baths:** 9 En

The Hatton, *10 Banks Street, Blackpool, Lancs, FY1 1RN.* Ideally situated 3 doors from Promenade adjacent North Pier. **Open:** All year
01253 624944 (also fax) Mrs Bliss www.hattonhotel.com **D:** Fr £16.00–£30.00 **S:** Fr £20.00–£35.00 **Beds:** 4F 2T 6D **Baths:** 12 En

Lynton House, *24 St Bedes Avenue, Blackpool, Lancs, FY4 1AQ.* Family guest house, close to all amenities, Piers, shops, Promenade. **Open:** All year
01253 345784 D Halloran **D:** Fr £10.00–£20.00 **S:** Fr £10.00–£20.00 **Beds:** 6F 2T 5D 1S **Baths:** 2 En 2 Sh **cc**

Kingsway Hotel, *68 Charnley Road, Blackpool, Lancs, FY1 4PF.* Small family-run hotel. **Open:** All year
01253 627696 Mr Armstrong **D:** Fr £20.00–£40.00 **S:** Fr £30.00–£50.00 **Beds:** 4F 2T 10D **Baths:** 16 En (1) (10) **cc**

The Belgrave Hotel, *313-315 South Promenade, Blackpool, Lancs, FY1 6AN.* Rooms with sea views. Late bar. Winter cabarets. Xmas/New Year parties. Breakfast upto 10am. **Open:** All year
01253 346581 Mr Woolley **D:** Fr £22.00–£30.00 **S:** Fr £25.00–£32.00 **Beds:** 5F 5T 28T 1S **Baths:** 40 En (27) **cc**

Robin Hood Hotel, *100 Queens Promenade, Blackpool, Lancs, FY2 9NS.* A quality no smoking hotel overlooking the Irish Sea. **Open:** Easter to Nov
01253 351599 www.robinhoodhotel.co.uk **D:** Fr £18.50–£26.50 **S:** Fr £20.50–£28.50 **Beds:** 3F 1T 6D **Baths:** 10 Pr **cc**

Berwick Hotel, *23 King Edward Avenue, Blackpool, Lancs, FY2 9TA.* Small, friendly. No smoking. Home cooking, choice breakfast. Adjacent Promenade. **Open:** All year
01253 351496 *chris@berwickhotel.fsnet.co.uk* **D:** Fr £17.00–£21.00 **S:** Fr £20.00–£24.00 **Beds:** 1F 2T 5D **Baths:** 8 En (4) **cc**

Sheron House, *21 Gynn Avenue, Blackpool, Lancs, FY1 2LD.* In a word - 'Quality'. Good food, good company, comfortable bed! **Open:** Feb to Dec
01253 354614 D. Atkinson & S. Fellows *sheronhouse@amserve.net* www.usefulblackpool.com/ghouses/sheron **D:** Fr £16.50–£22.00 **S:** Fr £16.50–£27.00 **Beds:** 2F 1T 3D **Baths:** 6 En **cc**

Wescoe Private Hotel, *14 Dean Street, Blackpool, Lancs, FY4 1AU.* Quality hotel near to sea front. Friendly welcome and cleanliness assured. **Open:** All year
01253 342772 Ms McClelland *wescoe@amserve.net* www.wescoehotel.co.uk **D:** Fr £15.00–£26.00 **S:** Fr £15.00–£26.00 **Beds:** 4F 1T 5D **Baths:** 8 En 1 Sh (4) **cc**

Regency Hotel, *50 Charnley Road, Blackpool, Lancs, FY1 4PE.* Family-run hotel ideally situated in heart of Blackpool. Near shops, Tower, Winter Gardens, Promenade. **Open:** All year (not Xmas/New Year)
01253 625186 (also fax) Mr Wyers *regency.hotel@talk21.com* **D:** Fr £14.00–£35.00 **S:** Fr £20.00–£45.00 **Beds:** 8F 9D **Baths:** 14 En 2 Sh (1) (3) **cc**

Cresta Hotel, *85 Whithnell Road, Blackpool, FY4 1HE.* Family-run, all ensuite hotel adjacent to the pleasure beach. **Open:** All year
0800 0745584 (also fax) J Snelson *john@snelly.co.uk* www.snelly.co.uk **D:** Fr £14.00–£25.00 **S:** Fr £16.00–£25.00 **Beds:** 1F 4D 3S **Baths:** 8 En (3) **cc**

Cherry Blossom Hotel, *2 Warley Road Corner, North Promemade, Blackpool, FY1 2JU.* Large Victorian house, overlooking Irish sea, 15-bedroom hotel with large public bar. **Open:** All year
01253 355533 **Fax: 01253 355534** **D:** Fr £17.00–£30.00 **S:** Fr £17.00–£30.00 **Beds:** 4F 4D 6T 1S **Baths:** 15 En (14) **cc**

The Blue Royale, *11 Charles Street, Blackpool, FY1 3HD.* Small friendly guest house caters for all. **Open:** All year
01253 628107 **D:** Fr £13.00–£20.00 **S:** Fr £13.00–£20.00 **Beds:** 3F 4D 3T 1S **Baths:** 4 En 1 Pr

All details shown are as supplied by B&B owners in Autumn 2002

Sandylands Guest House, *47 Banks Street, North Shore, Blackpool, Lancashire, FY1 2BE.* Clean, comfortable, good food, friendly. Ideal for over 40s. **Open:** Mar to Nov
01253 294670 D: Fr £13.00–£15.00 **S:** Fr £13.00–£15.00 **Beds:** 1F 5D 2S **Baths:** 1 Sh (8)

Granville Hotel, *12 Station Road, Blackpool, Lancashire, FY4 1BE.* Close to Pleasure Beach, South Pier, and all amenities etc. **Open:** Easter to Nov
01253 343012 Mr Taylor **Fax: 01253 408594** *wilft@thegranvillehotel.co.uk* **D:** Fr £18.00–£26.00 **S:** Fr £19.00–£26.00 **Beds:** 5F 5D 2S **Baths:** 11 En 1 Pr (2) cc

Bolton by Bowland
SD7849

Middle Flass Lodge, *Settle Road, Bolton by Bowland, Clitheroe, Lancashire, BB7 4NY.* Idyllic countryside location. Chef prepared cuisine. Cosy rooms. Friendly welcome. **Open:** All year **Grades:** ETC 4 Diamond, AA 4 Diamond
01200 447259 Mrs Simpson **Fax: 01200 447300** *info@middleflasslodge.fsnet.co.uk* www.middleflasslodge.co.uk **D:** Fr £24.00–£32.00 **S:** Fr £34.00–£42.00 **Beds:** 1F 3D 3T **Baths:** 7 En (24) cc

Brierfield
SD8436

179 Reedley Road, *Brierfield, Nelson, Lancs, BB9 5ES.* Situated in a quiet residential area offering warm comfortable accommodation. **Open:** All year (not Xmas/New Year)
01282 616284 Mrs Leedham **D:** Fr £16.50–£19.00 **S:** Fr £16.50–£19.00 **Beds:** 1T 1S **Baths:** 1 Sh (3)

Burnley
SD8332

Windsor House, *71 Church Street, Padiham, Burnley, Lancs, BB12 8JH.* Spacious Victorian house, in conservation area. Non smoking, hearty breakfast. **Open:** All year (not Xmas)
01282 773271 Mrs Stinton **D:** Fr £19.00 **S:** Fr £20.00 **Beds:** 1D 3T 3S **Baths:** 1 Pr 3 Sh (10)

Capernwray
SD5371

Capernwray House, *Capernwray, Carnforth, Lancs, LA6 1AE.* Beautiful country house. Panoramic views. Tastefully decorated throughout. Close Lakes, Dales, Lancaster. **Open:** All year (not Xmas)
01524 732363 (also fax) Mrs Smith *thesmiths@capernwrayhouse.com* www.capernwrayhouse.com **D:** Fr £22.00–£24.00 **S:** Fr £22.00–£30.00 **Beds:** 2D 1T 1S **Baths:** 3 En 1 Sh (5) (8) cc

Carnforth
SD4970

High Bank, *Hawk Street, Carnforth, Lancs, LA5 9LA.* Charming Victorian house. Panoramic views. Convenient for M6. RSPB Lakes. **Open:** All year **Grades:** ETC 4 Diamond
01524 733827 D: Fr £19.00 **S:** Fr £19.00–£22.00 **Beds:** 1F 2T 1D **Baths:** 2 Sh (4)

Galley Hall Farm, *Shore Road, Carnforth, Lancashire, LA5 9HZ.* C17th farm house, lovely coastal and Lakeland views and friendly welcome. **Open:** All year (not Xmas/New Year)
01524 732544 V Casson **D:** Fr £18.00 **S:** Fr £18.00–£20.00 **Beds:** 1T 1D 1S **Baths:** 1 Sh

26 Victoria Street, *Carnforth, Lancs, LA5 9ED.* Small, homely B&B adjacent canal walk. 6 miles Lancaster or Morecambe. **Open:** All year (not Xmas/New Year)
01524 732520 D Dickinson **D:** Fr £15.00 **S:** Fr £16.00 **Beds:** 1F 1T **Baths:** 1 Sh (2)

Chaigley
SD6941

Rakefoot Farm, *Chaigley, Clitheroe, Lancs, BB7 3LY.* Peacefully situated, ideal touring (motorway 8 miles). Holiday/business. Farmhouse meals. **Open:** All year
01995 61332 P Gifford **Fax: 01995 61296 D:** Fr £16.50–£20.50 **S:** Fr £16.50–£25.00 **Beds:** 3F 2T 4D 1S **Baths:** 6 En 2 Pr 1 Sh (10)

Chipping
SD6243

Carrside Farm, *Chipping, Preston, Lancs, PR3 2TS.* Working sheep farm with hill views in the forest of Bowland. **Open:** All year
01995 61590 J Cowgill **D:** Fr £25.00–£30.00 **S:** Fr £25.00–£30.00 **Beds:** 1D 1F 1S **Baths:** 2 En 1 Pr 1 Sh (5) (8)

Chorley
SD5817

Crowtress Cottage Guest House, *190 Preston Road, Chorley, Lancashire, PR6 7AZ.* C18th country cottage complemented by Lancashire hospitality. **Open:** All year
01257 269380 J Wrenall **D:** Fr £20.00–£30.00 **S:** Fr £25.00 **Beds:** 1D 1T 1S **Baths:** 1 En 1 Sh

Claughton (Lancaster)
SD5666

Low House Farm, *Claughton, Lancaster, Lancs., LA2 9LA.* Working mixed dairy farm in the heart of the picturesque Lune Valley. **Open:** All year (not Xmas/New Year)
015242 21260 Mrs Harvey *shirley@lunevalley.freeserve.co.uk* **D:** Fr £20.00 **S:** Fr £20.00–£25.00 **Beds:** 1F 1D 1S **Baths:** 1 En 1 Pr 1 Sh (4)

Clayton Le Dale
SD6733

2 Rose Cottage, *Longsight Road, Clayton le Dale, Blackburn, Lancs, BB1 9EX.* Picturesque cottage, gateway to Ribble Valley. Comfortable, fully-equipped rooms. **Open:** All year
01254 813223 M Adderley **Fax: 01254 813831** *bbrose.cott@talk21.com* www.smoothhound.co.uk/hotels/rosecott.html **D:** Fr £21.00 **S:** Fr £25.00 **Beds:** 2D 1T **Baths:** 3 En 1 Pr (4) cc

Clayton-le-Moors
SD7431

Maple Lodge Hotel, *70 Blackburn Road, Clayton-le-Moors, Accrington, BB5 5JH.* Friendly family-run licensed hotel off M65 J7. Home cooking. **Open:** All year
01254 301284 Fax: 01254 388152 *maplelod@aol.com* www.maplelodgehotel.co.uk **D:** Fr £25.00–£28.00 **S:** Fr £37.50–£42.50 **Beds:** 2T 6D **Baths:** 8 En (8) cc

Clitheroe
SD7441

Selborne House, *Back Commons, Kirkmoor Road, Clitheroe, Lancs, BB7 2DX.* Detached house on quiet lane giving peace and tranquillity. Excellent for walking, birdwatching, fishing. **Open:** All year **Grades:** ETC 4 Diamond
01200 423571 & 01200 422236 J V Barnes **Fax: 01200 423571** *judithv.barnes@lineone.net* www.selbornehouse.co.uk **D:** Fr £22.50 **S:** Fr £25.00 **Beds:** 3D 1T **Baths:** 4 En (1) (4)

Colne

SD8940

Higher Wanless Farm, *Red Lane, Colne, Lancs, BB8 7JP.* Beautifully situated, canalside, lovely walking, ideal for business people. Mill, shops etc. **Open:** Jan to Nov
01282 865301 C Mitson **Fax: 01282 865823** *wanlessfarm@bun.com* www.stayinlancs.co.uk
D: Fr £23.00–£30.00 **S:** Fr £25.00–£35.00
Beds: 1F 1T 1S **Baths:** 1 En 1 Sh (10) (4)

Wickets, *148 Keighley Road, Colne, Lancs, BB8 0PJ.* Edwardian family home overlooking open countryside, comfortable and attractive bedrooms. **Open:** Mar to Dec **Grades:** ETC 4 Diamond
01282 862002 Mrs Etherington **Fax: 01282 859675** *wickets@colne148.fsnet.co.uk* **D:** Fr £21.00–£25.00 **S:** Fr £25.00–£27.00 **Beds:** 1D 1T **Baths:** 2 En (11) (1)

Conder Green

SD4656

Stork Hotel, *Conder Green, Lancaster, Lancashire, LA2 0AN.* Traditional country inn 3 miles from Lancaster and close to Glasson Dock. **Open:** All year
01524 751234 A Cragg **D:** Fr £20.00 **S:** Fr £24.50 **Beds:** 1F 3D 3T 2S **Baths:** 9 Pr (20)

Fleetwood

SD3247

Chavock Guest House, *116 London Street, Fleetwood, Lancs, FY7 6EU.* Licensed guest house. **Open:** All year (not Xmas/ New Year)
01253 771196 (also fax) Mr McEvoy *suemcevoy@justtalk21.com* **D:** Fr £14.00–£19.00 **S:** Fr £15.00–£20.00 **Beds:** 1F 2D 1S 1T **Baths:** 1 En

Garstang

SD4945

Sandbriggs, *Lancaster Road, Garstang, Preston, Lancs, PR3 1JA.* Comfortable, convenient, secluded private house and gardens with secure parking. **Open:** All year
01995 603080 (also fax) Mr Wilkinson **D:** Fr £15.00–£18.00 **S:** Fr £15.00 **Beds:** 1D 2T **Baths:** 1 Pr 2 Sh (4) (10)

Guys Thatched Hamlet, *Canal Side, St Michael's Road, Bilsborrow, Preston, Lancs, PR3 0RS.* Picturesque thatched hamlet complex with country-style tavern and continental restaurant. **Open:** All year (not Xmas)
01995 640010 R Wilkinson **Fax: 01995 640141** *info@guysthatchedhamlet.com* www.guysthatchedhamlet.co.uk **D:** Fr £21.00–£24.00 **S:** Fr £42.50–£52.00 **Beds:** 8F 10T 50D **Baths:** 68 En (200) cc

Ashdene, *Parkside Lane, Garstang, Preston, Lancs, PR3 0JA.* Large family-run house, warm welcome, comfortable home, good food. **Open:** All year **Grades:** ETC 3 Diamond
01995 602676 J Wrathall *ashdene@supanet.com* www.ashdenebedandbreakfast.gbr.cc **D:** Fr £19.00–£20.00 **S:** Fr £26.00–£30.00 **Beds:** 2D 1T **Baths:** 3 En (5)

Goosnargh

SD5536

Isles Field Barn, *Syke House Lane, Goosnargh, Preston, Lancs, PR3 2EN.* Spacious accommodation surrounded by beautiful countryside. Hearty breakfast, friendly welcome. **Open:** All year
01995 640398 Mr McHugh *susan.mchugh@telinco.co.uk* **D:** Fr £22.00 **S:** Fr £22.00 **Beds:** 1F 1D 1T **Baths:** 3 En (6)

Hesketh Bank

SD4423

The Becconsall Hotel, *25 Station Road, Hesketh Bank, Preston, PR4 6SP.* Friendly local pub/restaurant in semi-rural location. **Open:** All year
01772 815313 **D:** Fr £17.50 **S:** Fr £22.50 **Beds:** 3D (20) cc

Heysham

SD4161

It'll Do, *15 Oxcliffe Road, Heysham, Morecambe, Lancs., LA3 1PR.* Ideal for touring Lake District, Heysham Port. Lancaster M6. **Open:** Jan to Dec
01524 850763 Mrs Peter **D:** Fr £14.00 **S:** Fr £15.00 **Beds:** 1T 1D **Baths:** 1 Sh (4)

Hurst Green

SD6838

Shireburn Arms Hotel, *Whalley Road, Hurst Green, Clitheroe, Lancs, BB6 9QJ.* A warm friendly welcome, excellent inn and restaurant, unrivalled views. **Open:** All year
01254 826518 S J Alcock **Fax: 01254 826208** *sales@shireburnarms.fsnet.co.uk* www.shireburn-hotel.co.uk **D:** Fr £32.50–£42.50 **S:** Fr £45.00–£65.00 **Beds:** 1S 2F 12D 3T **Baths:** 18 En (50) cc

Knowle Green

SD6338 *New Drop Inn*

Oak Lea, *Clitheroe Road, Knowle Green, Longridge, Preston, Lancs, PR3 2YS.* Ribble Valley Victorian country house, gardens, views, welcoming family atmosphere. **Open:** All year (not Xmas/New Year)
01254 878486 (also fax) Mrs Mellor **D:** Fr £21.00–£24.00 **S:** Fr £21.00–£26.00 **Beds:** 2T 1D 1S **Baths:** 2 En 1 Pr (4)

Lancaster

SD4761

Farmhouse Tavern, *Morecambe Road, Lancaster, LA1 5JB.* **Open:** All year **Grades:** ETC 3 Diamonds
01524 69255 **Fax: 01524 845823** **D:** Fr £25.00–£65.00 **S:** Fr £37.00–£65.00 **Beds:** 2F 8T 8D 1S **Baths:** 10 En (50) cc
Originally built as a farmhouse some three and a half centuries ago. Wood panelling, antique furniture and dressers. Well stocked bars & charismatic lounge with welcoming log fire. Convenient centre from which to explore Lake District, Fylde Coast and Yorkshire Dales.

Lancaster Town House, *11/12 Newton Terrace, Caton Road, Lancaster, LA1 3PB.* Award-winning guest house, close to city centre, minutes from M6 J34. **Open:** All year
01524 65527 Mrs Hedge-Holmes *hedge-holmes@talk21.com* www.lancastertownhouse.co.uk **D:** Fr £21.00–£23.00 **S:** Fr £26.00–£30.00 **Beds:** 1F 3D 1T 3S **Baths:** 8 En cc

BATHROOMS
En = Ensuite
Pr = Private
Sh = Shared

Longridge

SD6037

14 Whittingham Road, *Longridge, Preston, Lancs, PR3 2AA.* Homely, hearty breakfasts, scenic area, walking, sports, shopping, motorway accessibility. **Open:** All year
01772 783992 D Morley *dimorley@talk21.com*
D: Fr £19.00–£20.00 **S:** Fr £19.00–£20.00
Beds: 1F 1T 1S **Baths:** 1 Sh (4)

Longton

SD4726

Willow Cottage, *Longton Bypass, Longton, Preston, Lancs, PR4 4RA.* Old cottage set in beautiful gardens and countryside with its own horse stud farm. **Open:** All year (not Xmas/New Year)
01772 617570 Mrs Caunce *info@lancashirebedandbreakfast.co.uk* www.lancashirebedandbreakfast.co.uk **D:** Fr £23.00–£24.00 **S:** Fr £25.00 **Beds:** 2T 3D 4S **Baths:** 1 En 1 Sh (8)

Lower Thurnham

SD4655

Thurnham Mill Hotel, *Thurnham, Lancaster, LA2 0BD.* Located in the heart of a picturesque and historical area close to Lancaster. **Open:** All year
01524 752852 Fax: 01524 752477 D: Fr £27.25 **S:** Fr £39.50 **Beds:** 6F 3T 8D **Baths:** 17 En (80) cc

Lytham St Annes

SD3327

Monarch Hotel, *29 St Annes Road East, Lytham St Annes, Lancs, FY8 1TA.* Clean, comfortable hotel with great food, licensed. Aromatherapy, reflexology available. **Open:** All year
01253 720464 Mr Churchill *churchill@monarch91.freeserve.co.uk* www.monarch-st-annes.co.uk **D:** Fr £21.00–£27.00 **S:** Fr £21.00–£27.00 **Beds:** 2F 2D 3T 3S **Baths:** 7 En 1 Pr (8)

Sea Croft Hotel, *5 Eastbank Road, Lytham St Annes, Lancs, FY8 1ND.* A warm welcome in friendly, family-run licensed hotel adjacent to promenade and town centre. **Open:** All year (not Xmas)
01253 721806 (also fax) Mrs Bradshaw *seacrofthotel@aol.com* www.sea-croft.co.uk **D:** Fr £20.00–£21.00 **S:** Fr £15.00–£22.00 **Beds:** 5F 1D 1T 2S **Baths:** 8 En 1 Sh (5)

Harcourt, *21 Richmond Road, Lytham St Annes, Lancs, FY8 1PE.* Small private family hotel, town centre. 200 yds to beach and attractions. **Open:** All year
01253 722299 D: Fr £16.00–£19.00 **S:** Fr £16.00–£18.00 **Beds:** 3F 3D 1T 3S **Baths:** 5 En 5 Sh (6)

Mellor

SD6531

2 Rose Cottage, *Longsight Road, Clayton le Dale, Blackburn, Lancs, BB1 9EX.* Picturesque cottage, gateway to Ribble Valley. Comfortable, fully-equipped rooms. **Open:** All year
01254 813223 M Adderley **Fax: 01254 813831** *bbrose.cott@talk21.com* www.smoothhound.co.uk/hotels/rosecott.html **D:** Fr £21.00 **S:** Fr £25.00 **Beds:** 2D 1T **Baths:** 3 En 1 Pr (4) cc

Morecambe

SD4364

Sea Lynn Licensed Hotel, *29 West End Road, Morecambe, Lancs, LA4 4DJ.* Friendly, family run. Sea views, ideal base for touring/walking. **Open:** All year
01524 411340 *thesealynn@hotmail.com* **D:** Fr £15.00–£18.00 **S:** Fr £15.00–£18.00 **Beds:** 3F 1T 7D 3S **Baths:** 2 En 2 Sh

Roxbury, *78 Thornton Road, Morecambe, Lancashire, LA4 5PJ.* Small, friendly family hotel, quiet but close to all amenities. **Open:** All year **Grades:** ETC 2 Diamond
01524 410561 Ms Gerrard **Fax: 01524 420286** *ritall@bigfoot.com* www.roxburyhotelmorecambe.com **D:** Fr £18.00–£19.00 **S:** Fr £17.00–£19.00 **Beds:** 1F 1T 2D 3S **Baths:** 6 En 1 Sh

Westleigh Licensed Hotel, *9 Marine Road, Morecambe, Lancs, LA3 1BS.* Overlooks Morecambe Bay and Lakeland Hills. **Open:** All year (not Xmas/New Year)
01524 418352 Mr & Mrs Harrison **D:** Fr £17.00 **S:** Fr £17.00 **Beds:** 7T 4D 3S **Baths:** 14 En

Warwick Hotel, *394 Marine Road East, Morecambe, Lancs, LA4 5AN.* Non-smoking hotel overlooking bay and South Lakeland Hills. Victorian terraced property on the promenade. **Open:** All year (not Xmas/New Year)
01524 418151 A & A Leach **Fax: 01524 427235** www.smoothhound.co.uk/ms.html **D:** Fr £23.00–£27.00 **S:** Fr £25.00–£30.00 **Beds:** 3T 7D 3S **Baths:** 13 Pr

Harwood House Hotel, *1 Chatsworth Road, Westminster Road, Morecambe, Lancs, LA4 4JG.* Central for Lakes, Lune Valley. 2 mins' walk from sea front, licensed. **Open:** All year
01524 412845 J R Whitworth **Fax: 01524 409138** *hhhotel@supanet.com* www.harwoodhousehotel.co.uk **D:** Fr £15.00–£22.00 **S:** Fr £15.00–£22.00 **Beds:** 1F 2T 6D 4S **Baths:** 2 En 1 Pr 2 Sh (4)

The Trevelyan, *27 Seaview Parade, West End Road, Morecambe, Lancs, LA4 4DJ.* Comfortable guest house. Glorious Morecambe Bay. Ideal touring base. **Open:** All year
01524 412013 G Catterall *thetrevelyan@supanet.com* www.thetrevelyan.freeserve.co.uk **D:** Fr £15.00–£17.50 **S:** Fr £15.00 **Beds:** 2F 1T 4D 4S **Baths:** 1 En 4 Sh

The Channings, *455-456 Marine Road East, Morecambe, Lancs, LA4 6AD.* Victorian building, tastefully modernised. Situated on Promenade. Leisure centres adjacent. **Open:** All year
01524 417925 *channings.hotel@ukgateway.net* www.channingshotel.co.uk **D:** Fr £19.00–£23.00 **S:** Fr £21.00–£25.00 **Beds:** 4F 2T 9D 4S **Baths:** 17 En 2 Sh cc

New Longton

SD5125 *Farmers' Arms, Midge Hall*

Pleasant View, *Long Moss Lane, New Longton, Preston, Lancs, PR4 4XN.* Warm welcome, quiet area, close motorways, overlooking fields/gardens. **Open:** All year (not Xmas/New Year)
01772 615863 *sarah@dalgleish615.freeserve.co.uk* **D:** Fr £23.00–£26.00 **S:** Fr £30.00–£35.00 **Beds:** 2T **Baths:** 2 Pr (3)

Ormskirk

SD4108

The Meadows, New Sutch Farm, *Sutch Lane, Ormskirk, Lancashire, L40 4BU.* Beautiful C17th farmhouse. Ground floor guest rooms. Excellent breakfasts. **Open:** All year (not Xmas)
01704 894048 D: Fr £19.50 **S:** Fr £22.00 **Beds:** 2D 1S **Baths:** 2 En 1 Pr

All details shown are as supplied by B&B owners in Autumn 2002

Padiham

SD7933

Windsor House, *71 Church Street, Padiham, Burnley, Lancs, BB12 8JH.* Spacious Victorian house, in conservation area. Non smoking, hearty breakfast. **Open:** All year (not Xmas)
01282 773271 Mrs Stinton **D:** Fr £19.00 **S:** Fr £20.00 **Beds:** 1D 3T 3S **Baths:** 1 Pr 3 Sh (10)

Preesall

SD3647

Townfoot Cottage, *Back Lane, Preesall, Poulton le Fylde, Lancs., FY6 0NG.* Country cottage, comfortable accommodation, good food, picturesque setting, relaxing break. **Open:** All year (not Xmas/New Year)
01253 812681 C Richards **D:** Fr £17.00–£19.00 **S:** Fr £20.00–£25.00 **Beds:** 1F 1D **Baths:** 1 Sh (3)

Preston

SD5329

Stanley Guest House, *7 Stanley Terrace, Preston, PR1 8JE.* 5 mins' walk to town centre, overlooking quiet bowling area. **Open:** All year
01772 253366 Fax: 01772 252802
stanley.guest.house@prestonlancs.freeserve.co.uk www.prestonlancs.freeserve.co.uk **D:** Fr £16.00–£18.00 **S:** Fr £20.00–£25.00 **Beds:** 3F 2D 2S **Baths:** 2 En 1 Sh (5) cc

Scorton

SD5049

Woodacre Hall Farm, *Scorton, Preston, Lancs., PR3 1BN.* Working farm built in the late 1600s, comfortable and friendly. **Open:** Easter to Nov
01995 602253 (also fax) Ms Whitaker **D:** Fr £17.00–£19.00 **S:** Fr £20.00–£22.00 **Beds:** 2D 1T **Baths:** 2 En 1 Pr (4)

Stacksteads

SD8421

Glen Heights, *190 Booth Road, Stacksteads, Bacup, Lancs, OL13 0TH.* Warm welcome. Near motorways, Ski Rossendale, steam railways, hillwalking. **Open:** All year (not Xmas/New Year)
01706 875459 D Graham **D:** Fr £16.00 **S:** Fr £19.50 **Beds:** 1T 1D 1S **Baths:** 1 Sh (3) (3)

Stonyhurst

SD6939

Alden Cottage, *Kemple End, Birdy Brow, Stonyhurst, Clitheroe, Lancashire, BB7 9QY.* **Open:** All year (not Xmas/New Year) **Grades:** ETC 4 Diamond, Gold
01254 826468 (also fax) Mrs Carpenter *carpenter@aldencottage.f9.co.uk* fp.aldencottage.f9.co.uk **D:** Fr £27.00 **S:** Fr £32.00 **Beds:** 1T 2D **Baths:** 1 En 2 Pr (3)
Luxury accommodation in an idyllic C17th beamed cottage. Situated in Area of Outstanding Natural Beauty, overlooking the Ribble & Hodder Valleys. Charmingly furnished rooms include bath robes, fresh flowers, chocolates with private facilities including jacuzzi bath, shower.

Thornton Cleveleys

SD3442

Esperance Villa Guest House, *30 Ellerbeck Road, Thornton-Cleveleys, Lancs, FY5 1DH.* Family-run hotel, close to shops, Blackpool and Fleetwood bingo and clubs. **Open:** All year (not Xmas/New Year)
01253 853513 Mrs Duckett **D:** Fr £15.00–£17.00 **S:** Fr £15.00–£17.00 **Beds:** 1F 4D 1T 1S **Baths:** 2 Sh (3)

Beacholme Guest House, *38 Beach Road, Thornton Cleveleys, Lancs, FY5 1EQ.* Small, friendly, non-smoking guest house, close to tramline and seashore. **Open:** All year
01253 855350 *beach_holme@hotmail.com* **D:** Fr £15.00 **S:** Fr £15.00 **Beds:** 2D 1T 2S **Baths:** 1 En 1 Sh (2)

Trawden

SD9138

Middle Beardshaw Head Farm, *Trawden, Colne, Lancs, BB8 8PP.* C18th beamed farmhouse in picturesque setting of woodland, pools and meadows. **Open:** All year (not Xmas)
01282 865257 Mrs Mann **D:** Fr £20.00–£25.00 **S:** Fr £20.00–£25.00 **Beds:** 1F 2D 3S **Baths:** 1 En 1 Sh (10)

Tunstall

SD6073

Barnfield Farm, *Tunstall, Kirkby Lonsdale, Carnforth, Lancs, LA6 2QP.* 1702 family farmhouse on a 200-acre working farm. **Open:** All year (not Xmas/New Year)
015242 74284 (also fax) J Stephenson *jstephenson@barnfieldfarm.freeserve.co.uk* www.smoothhound.co.uk/hotels/barnfield.html **D:** Fr £17.00–£17.50 **S:** Fr £17.50–£20.00 **Beds:** 1F 1D **Baths:** 1 Sh (2)

Waddington

SD7243

Moorcock Inn, *Slaidburn Road, Waddington, Clitheroe, Lancs, BB7 3AA.* A warm welcome awaits at this friendly country inn. **Open:** All year **Grades:** ETC 2 Star
01200 422333 F M Fillary **D:** Fr £65.00 **S:** Fr £38.00 **Beds:** 3D 8T **Baths:** 11 Pr (150) cc

Peter Barn Country House, *Cross Lane, Waddington, Clitheroe, Lancs, BB7 3JH.* Explore Ribble Valley then sink into sumptuous sofas! Home-made jams. **Open:** All year (not Xmas/New Year)
01200 428585 Mrs Smith *jean@peterbarn.fsnet.co.uk* **D:** Fr £25.00–£26.00 **S:** Fr £29.00 **Beds:** 1T 2D **Baths:** 2 En 1 Pr (12) (6)

Backfold Cottage, *The Square, Waddington, Clitheroe, Lancs, BB7 3JA.* Luxury mini country hotel. **Open:** All year
01200 422367 D Forbes **D:** Fr £21.00–£23.00 **S:** Fr £21.00–£31.00 **Beds:** 1T 1D 1S **Baths:** 3 En (5) (4)

Warton

SD5072

Cotestone Farm, *Sand Lane, Warton, Carnforth, Lancs, LA5 9NH.* Near Leighton Moss RSPB Reserve, Lancaster/Morecambe, Lakes & Dales. **Open:** All year (not Xmas)
01524 732418 G Close **D:** Fr £16.00 **S:** Fr £17.00 **Beds:** 1F 1D 1T 1S **Baths:** 2 Sh (4)

Waterfoot

SD8322

729 Bacup Road, *Waterfoot, Rossendale, Lancs, BB4 7EU.* In the heart of the picturesque Rossendale Valley. Food everyday. **Open:** All year
01706 214493 P Stannard **Fax: 01706 215371** *info@theroyal-hotel.co.uk* www.theroyal-hotel.co.uk **D:** Fr £23.50–£30.00 **S:** Fr £25.00–£35.00 **Beds:** 1F 5D 2T 5S **Baths:** 13 En (10) cc

West Bradford

SD7444 *Buck Inn, Duke of York*

Old Hall, *Back Lane, West Bradford, Clitheroe, Lancs, BB7 4SN.* Elegant friendly family home in own grounds near Ribble Way. **Open:** All year (not Xmas/New Year) **01200 423282** E H Gretton *argettm@aol.com* **D:** Fr £19.00–£20.00 **S:** Fr £20.00–£22.00 **Beds:** 2T 1S **Baths:** 1 Sh (4)

Whittington

SD6076

The Dragon's Head, *Main Street, Whittington, Carnforth, LA6 2NY.* Small country pub in Lune Valley 2 miles west of Kirkby Lonsdale, B6254. **Open:** All year **015242 72383** **D:** Fr £20.00–£25.00 **S:** Fr £20.00–£25.00 **Beds:** 1F 1D 1S **Baths:** 1 Sh (5) (10)

Leicestershire

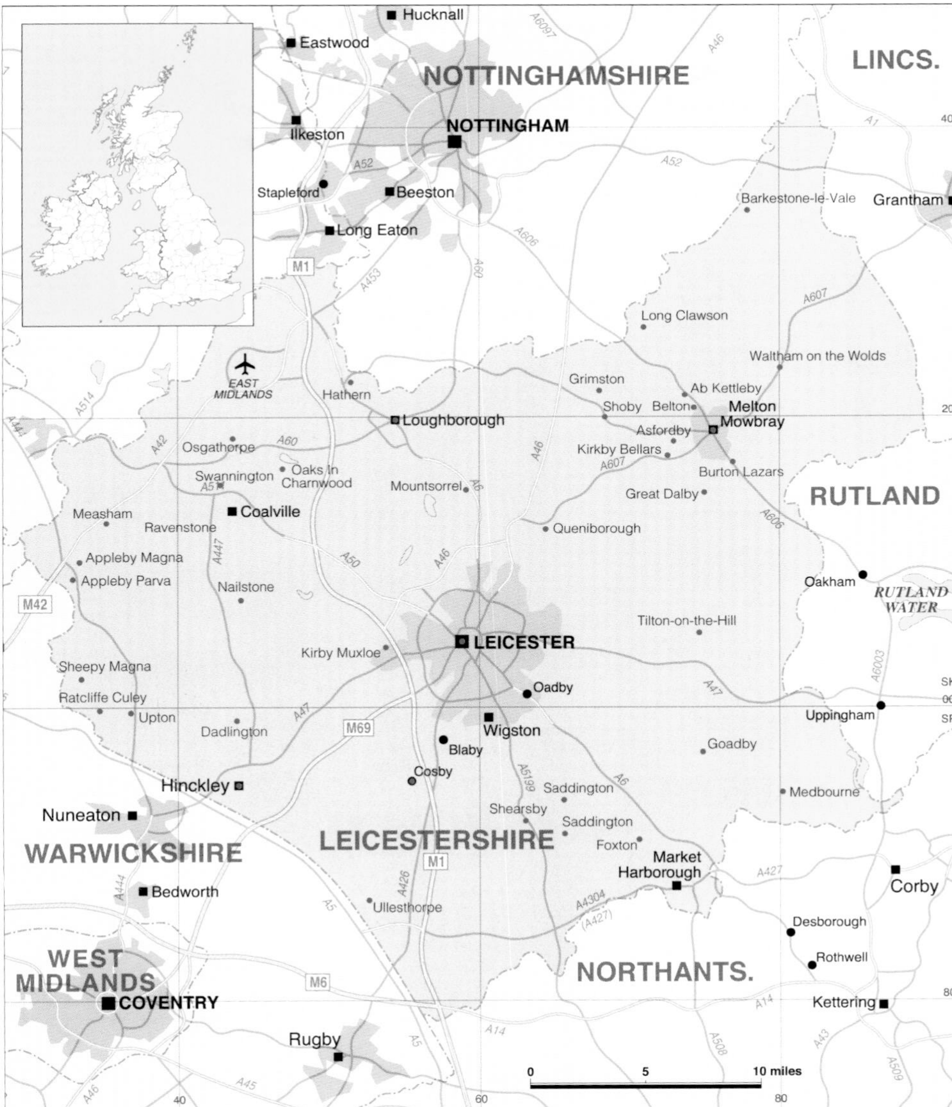

Ab Kettleby
SK7222

White Lodge Farm, *Nottingham Road, Ab Kettleby, Melton Mowbray, Leicestershire, LE14 3JB.* Farm buildings tastefully converted into self-contained rooms overlooking garden. **Open:** All year **01664 822286** Mrs Spencer **D:** Fr £19.00 **S:** Fr £22.00 **Beds:** 1F 1D 1T **Baths:** 3 En (9) (4)

Appleby Magna
SK3110

Ferne Cottage, *5 Black Horse Hill, Appleby Magna, Swadlincote, Derbyshire, DE12 7AQ.* C18th beamed cottage in Appleby Magna. Homely, friendly, comfortable. Historic village, 0.5m M42 J11. **Open:** All year (not Xmas) **01530 271772** G A Bird **Fax: 01530 270652** *gbirdapplebymag@aol.com* **D:** Fr £19.00–£25.00 **S:** Fr £22.00–£25.00 **Beds:** 1F 1D 1T 1S **Baths:** 1 En 1 Sh (5)

Appleby Parva
SK3109

Elms Farm, *Atherstone Road, Appleby Parva, Swadlincote, Leicestershire, DE12 7AG.* Pleasant farmhouse in rural position within 1.5 miles of M42. **Open:** All year (not Xmas) **01530 270450** Ms Frisby **D:** Fr £20.00–£22.00 **S:** Fr £20.00–£22.00 **Beds:** 1D 1T 1S **Baths:** 2 En 1 Pr (4) (4)

Asfordby
SK7019

Amberley Gardens, *4 Church Lane, Asfordby, Melton Mowbray, Leics, LE14 3RU.* Beautiful riverside bungalow. Idyllic floodlit lawns/gardens. Enjoy breakfast in garden room. **Open:** All year **Grades:** ETC 4 Diamond **01664 812314** B P Brotherhood **Fax: 01664 813740** *doris@amberleygardens.net* www.amberleygardens.net **D:** Fr £19.00–£25.00 **S:** Fr £20.00–£25.00 **Beds:** 1T 1D 1S **Baths:** 3 En

Barkestone-le-Vale
SK7834 *Windmill Inn*

Little Orchard, *Chapel Street, Barkestone-le-Vale, Nottingham, NG13 0HE.* Pretty village bungalow near Belvoir Castle, Nottingham, Metro and Motorway. **Open:** All year (not Xmas/New Year) **01949 842698** M A Fisher **D:** Fr £18.00 **S:** Fr £18.00 **Beds:** 1T 1D **Baths:** 1 Pr (3)

Belton (Loughborough)
SK4420

George Hotel, *17 Market Place, Belton, Loughborough, Leics, LE12 9UH.* Old C18th coaching inn with bar and restaurant facilities. **Open:** All year (not Xmas) **01530 222426** Mr Houston **Fax: 01530 223661** *thegeorgehotelbelton@hotmail.com* www.thegeorgehotelbelton.com **D:** Fr £50.00–£60.00 **S:** Fr £30.00–£45.00 **Beds:** 2F 8T 8D 4S **Baths:** 16 En 6 Sh **cc**

Burton Lazars
SK7717

Hillside House, *27 Melton Road, Burton Lazars, Melton Mowbray, Leics, LE14 2UR.* Overlooking rolling countryside, this converted old farm building is comfortable and tastefully furnished. **Open:** All year (not Xmas/New Year) **Grades:** ETC 4 Diamond **01664 566312** Mrs Goodwin **Fax: 01664 501819** *Hillhs27@aol.com* www.hillside-house.co.uk **D:** Fr £19.00–£22.00 **S:** Fr £27.00–£29.00 **Beds:** 1D 2T **Baths:** 2 En 1 Pr (10) (3)

Cosby
SP5494

The Vineries, *Cosby, Leicester, LE9 1UL.* Lovely period house in 1.5 acre gardens. All rooms tastefully furnished, overlooking gardens, countryside. **Open:** All year (not Xmas/New Year) **0116 2750817** Mrs Warren **D:** Fr £25.00–£27.50 **S:** Fr £35.00 **Beds:** 2D 1S **Baths:** 3 En (16) (8)

Dadlington
SP4098

Apple Orchard Farm, *Fenn Lane, Dadlington, Nuneaton, CV13 6DR.* C17th farmhouse set in heart of Bosworth battlefield site. **Open:** All year (not Xmas) **01455 213186 Fax: 01455 212500** *b&b@appleorchardfarm.co.uk* **D:** Fr £20.00 **S:** Fr £25.00 **Beds:** 1D 1T **Baths:** 2 En

Foxton
SP7089

The Old Manse, *Swingbridge Street, Foxton, Market Harborough, Leics, LE16 7RH.* Period house in conservation village. Canals, locks, local inns nearby. **Open:** All year (not Xmas) **Grades:** ETC 4 Diamond, Silver **01858 545456** Mrs Pickering **Fax: 01858 540030** *theoldmanse37@hotmail.com* **D:** Fr £25.00 **S:** Fr £32.00 **Beds:** 3T/D **Baths:** 3 En (6)

Goadby
SP7598

The Hollies, *Goadby, Leicester, LE7 9EE.* Beautiful Listed house in quiet village in pretty Leicestershire countryside. **Open:** All year (not Xmas) **0116 259 8301** Mrs Parr **Fax: 0116 259 8491** *j.parr@btinternet.com* **D:** Fr £22.50 **S:** Fr £25.00 **Beds:** 1F 1D 1S **Baths:** 1 En 1 Sh (5) (3)

Great Dalby
SK7414

Dairy Farm, *8 Burrough End, Great Dalby, Melton Mowbray, Leics, LE14 2EW.* Working dairy farm 30 minutes from Leicester, Nottingham, 5 mins Melton. **Open:** All year **01664 562783** Mrs Parker **D:** Fr £18.00–£20.00 **S:** Fr £20.00–£25.00 **Beds:** 2D 1T **Baths:** 2 En 1 Pr (5)

Grimston
SK6821

Gorse House, *33 Main Street, Grimston, Melton Mowbray, Leicestershire, LE14 3BZ.* **Open:** All year **Grades:** ETC 4 Diamond, Silver **01664 813537 & 07780 600792 (M)** Mr & Mrs Cowdell **Fax: 01664 813537** *cowdell@gorsehouse.co.uk* www.gorsehouse.co.uk **D:** Fr £22.50 **S:** Fr £27.50 **Beds:** 1F 1T 1D **Baths:** 3 En (12) (4)

Well furnished, extended C17th cottage, with attractive garden in peaceful conservation village 2 miles from A46. Convenient for Leicester, Nottingham & East Midlands Airport. Good pub food within 100 Yards. Beautiful countryside for walking, riding (stables available) & touring.

Hathern
SK5022

Leys Guest House, *Loughborough Road, Hathern, Loughborough, Leics, LE12 5JB.* Situated in small village. Close to Derbyshire, Leicestershire and Nottinghamshire. **Open:** All year **01509 844373 (also fax)** Mrs Hudson *leysab2@talk21.com* **D:** Fr £17.00–£19.00 **S:** Fr £17.00–£19.00 **Beds:** 3F 3T 2S **Baths:** 3 En 2 Sh (8) **cc**

RATES
D = Price range per person sharing in a double or twin room
S = Price range for a single room

Hinckley
SP4294

The Guest House, *45 Priesthills Road, Hinckley, Leics, LE10 1AQ.* Edwardian period house set in quiet pleasant area of Hinckley. **Open:** All year (not Xmas)
01455 619720 & 01455 446602 S Farmer *priest@hills45.freeserve.co.uk* **D:** Fr £20.00 **S:** Fr £22.00 **Beds:** 3T 1S **Baths:** 1 Sh 2 En

Kirby Muxloe
SK5104

Faith Cottage, *400 Ratby Lane, Kirby Muxloe, Leicester, Leics, LE9 9AQ.* Quaint spotlessly clean cottage type accommodation, easy access to M1. **Open:** All year (not Xmas)
0116 238 7435 Mrs Saunders *james@faithcottage.co.uk* www.faithcottage.co.uk **D:** Fr £20.00 **S:** Fr £22.00 **Beds:** 2T 1S **Baths:** 1 En 1 Pr (7) (6)

Kirkby Bellars
SK7117

Tole Cottage, *10 Main Street, Kirby Bellars, Melton Mowbray, Leicestershire, LE14 2EA.* Charming early C19th cottage, inspirational garden, rooms containing unique decorative effects. Picturesque Wreake Valley. **Open:** All year
01664 812932 & 07748 924617 (M) *michael@handjean.freeserve.co.uk* **D:** Fr £20.00–£21.00 **S:** Fr £25.00 **Beds:** 1F 1D 1S **Baths:** 1 En 1 Sh (7) (3)

Leicester
SK5804 *Merry Monarch, Old Horse, Varsity*

Cumbria Guest House, *16 Westcotes Drive, Leicester, LE3 0QR.* Friendly accommodation. One mile city centre, two miles from M1 and M69. **Open:** All year (not Xmas/New Year)
0116 254 8459 Mrs Ball **D:** Fr £15.00–£17.00 **S:** Fr £18.00–£20.00 **Beds:** 4T 4S **Baths:** 1 Sh (1)

Craigleigh Hotel, *17-19 Westleigh Road, Leicester, LE3 0HH.* Victorian house, pleasant location, close to city and sports venues. **Open:** All year (not Xmas)
0116 254 6875 (also fax) S T Pattison **D:** Fr £19.00–£22.00 **S:** Fr £18.00–£28.00 **Beds:** 4D 3T 4S **Baths:** 8 En 2 Sh cc

The Craft Hotel, *3 Stanley Road, Leicester, LE2 1RF.* Situated close to the city centre, Leicester University and De Montfort Hall. **Open:** All year
0116 270 3220 *crofthotel@hotmail.com* **D:** Fr £17.50–£22.50 **S:** Fr £25.00–£35.00 **Beds:** 3F 6T 2D 1S **Baths:** 7 En 4 Sh (18) cc

Long Clawson
SK7227

Elms Farm, *52 East End, Long Clawson, Melton Mowbray, Leics, LE14 4NG.* Warm comfortable old farmhouse village setting in Vale of Belvoir. **Open:** All year (not Xmas)
01664 822395 Mrs Whittard **Fax: 01664 823399** *jwhittard@ukonline.co.uk* **D:** Fr £17.00–£21.00 **S:** Fr £18.00–£26.00 **Beds:** 1F 1D 1S **Baths:** 1 En 1 Sh (4)

Loughborough
SK5319

Peachnook Guest House, *154 Ashby Road, Loughborough, Leics, LE11 3AG.* Ideally situated 5 miles from all amenities. Good breakfast, vegetarian/vegan catered for. **Open:** All year **Grades:** ETC 2 Diamond
01509 264390 & 01509 217525 Ms Wood www.smoothhound.co.uk/hotels/peachno.html **D:** Fr £19.00–£22.50 **S:** Fr £15.00–£30.00 **Beds:** 2F 2D 2T 1S (5)

Charnwood Lodge Guest House, *136 Leicester Road, Loughborough, Leics, LE11 2AQ.* Spacious Victorian licensed guest house in quiet surroundings, 5 mins town centre. **Open:** All year (not Xmas)
01509 211120 Mrs Charwat **Fax: 01509 211121** *charnwoodlodge@charwat.freeserve.co.uk* www.charnwoodlodge.com **D:** Fr £20.00–£35.00 **S:** Fr £30.00–£45.00 **Beds:** 1T 6D 2F 1S **Baths:** 10 En (8) cc

New Life Guest House, *121 Ashby Road, Loughborough, Leics, LE11 3AB.* Family-run Victorian villa. 5 minutes centre, university, M1. Parking outside house. **Open:** All year **Grades:** ETC 3 Diamond
01509 216699 Mrs Burnard **Fax: 01509 210020** *jean-of-newlife@assureweb.com* **D:** Fr £23.00–£25.00 **S:** Fr £18.00–£25.00 **Beds:** 1F 1T 2S **Baths:** 2 En 1 Sh

De Montfort Hotel, *88 Leicester Road, Loughborough, Leics, LE11 2AQ.* Attractive rooms. Homely atmosphere, hearty breakfasts. Centrally located. Warm welcome. **Open:** All year (not Xmas/New Year)
01509 216061 Mrs Howard **Fax: 01509 233667** *thedemontfordhotel@amserve.com* thedemonhotel.co.uk **D:** Fr £20.00–£25.00 **S:** Fr £30.00–£40.00 **Beds:** 3F 2T 3D 1S **Baths:** 4 En 1 Pr 2 Sh cc

Measham
SK3312

Laurels Guest House, *17 Ashby Road, Measham, Swadlincote, Derbyshire, DE12 7JR.* High class accommodation. Rural surroundings. Orchard, pond. Parking. Motorway access. **Open:** All year
01530 272567 (also fax) Mrs Evans *evanslaurels@onetel.net.uk* www.thelaurelsguesthouse.com **D:** Fr £22.00–£25.00 **S:** Fr £22.00–£25.00 **Beds:** 1D 2T **Baths:** 2 En 1 Pr (1) (8)

Measham House Farm, *Gallows Lane, Measham, Swadlincote, Derbyshire, DE12 7HD.* Large Georgian farmhouse on working farm close to heart of the National Forest. **Open:** All year (not Xmas)
01530 270465 (also fax) Mr Lovett **D:** Fr £21.00 **S:** Fr £21.00 **Beds:** 1F 2T **Baths:** 3 En 1 Pr (20)

Medbourne
SP7993

Medbourne Grange, *Nevill Holt, Market Harborough, Leics, LE16 8EF.* Comfortable farmhouse with breathtaking views; quiet location and heated pool. **Open:** All year (not Xmas)
01858 565249 Mrs Beaty **Fax: 01858 565257** **D:** Fr £20.00–£22.00 **S:** Fr £20.00–£25.00 **Beds:** 2D 1T **Baths:** 1 Sh 2 En (6)

Melton Mowbray
SK7519

The Noel Arms, *31 Burton Street, Melton Mowbray, Leics, LE13 1AE.* Ensuite B&B. Real ale. Clean, friendly atmosphere. **Open:** All year
01664 562363 Mrs Ling **D:** Fr £22.00 **S:** Fr £22.00 **Beds:** 2F 2T 2S **Baths:** 4 En 1 Sh

Please respect a B&B's wishes regarding children, animals and smoking

Shoby Lodge Farm, *Shoby, Melton Mowbray, Leics, LE14 3PF.* **Open:** All year (not Xmas/New Year) **Grades:** ETC 4 Diamond, Silver
01664 812156 Mrs Lomas **D:** Fr £22.50 **S:** Fr £25.00 **Beds:** 1T 2D **Baths:** 2 En 1 Pr (6)
Assured a warm welcome. Relax in the comfortable lounge with open log fire. Enjoy the garden and unspoilt countryside beyond from the conservatory. Ideally situated for Ragdale Hall, Six Hills Golf, jet-ski, Prestwold Hall for the Ferrari Experience.

Dairy Farm, *8 Burrough End, Great Dalby, Melton Mowbray, Leics, LE14 2EW.* Working dairy farm 30 minutes from Leicester, Nottingham, 5 mins Melton. **Open:** All year
01664 562783 Mrs Parker **D:** Fr £18.00–£20.00 **S:** Fr £20.00–£25.00 **Beds:** 2D 1T **Baths:** 2 En 1 Pr (5)

Amberley Gardens, *4 Church Lane, Asfordby, Melton Mowbray, Leics, LE14 3RU.* Beautiful riverside bungalow. Idyllic floodlit lawns/gardens. Enjoy breakfast in garden room. **Open:** All year **Grades:** ETC 4 Diamond
01664 812314 B P Brotherhood **Fax: 01664 813740** *doris@amberleygardens.net* www.amberleygardens.net **D:** Fr £19.00–£25.00 **S:** Fr £20.00–£25.00 **Beds:** 1T 1D 1S **Baths:** 3 En

Hillside House, *27 Melton Road, Burton Lazars, Melton Mowbray, Leics, LE14 2UR.* Overlooking rolling countryside, this converted old farm building is comfortable and tastefully furnished. **Open:** All year (not Xmas/New Year) **Grades:** ETC 4 Diamond
01664 566312 Mrs Goodwin **Fax: 01664 501819** *Hillhs27@aol.com* www.hillside-house.co.uk **D:** Fr £19.00–£22.00 **S:** Fr £27.00–£29.00 **Beds:** 1D 2T **Baths:** 2 En 1 Pr (10) (3)

Kirmel Guesthouse, *23 Mill Street, Melton Mowbray, Leics, LE13 1AY.* Competitively priced first class accommodation situated close to all amenities. **Open:** All year
01664 564374 Mrs Hardy **D:** Fr £19.00–£25.00 **S:** Fr £20.00 **Beds:** 1T 1S 1F 1D **Baths:** 1 Sh 1 En

Mountsorrel

SK5814

Barley Loft Guest House, *33a Hawcliffe Road, Mountsorrel, Loughborough, Leics, LE12 7AQ.*
Open: All year
01509 413514 Mrs Pegg **D:** Fr £20.00–£22.00 **S:** Fr £21.00–£25.00 **Beds:** 2F 1D 1T 2S **Baths:** 2 Sh (12)
Spacious bungalow close A6 Leicester/Loughborough, 10 mins M1. Quiet location, riverside walks, historical attractions. Comfortable working base: guests' fridge, microwave, toaster, with 24-hour use of dining area. Excellent nearby takeaways, supermarket, pubs, restaurants. Traditional hearty breakfast from 7am.

Nailstone

SK4107

Glebe Farm, *Rectory Lane, Nailstone, Nuneaton, Warks, CV13 0QQ.* Comfortable farmhouse on working farm near Bosworth Battlefield and Mallory Park. **Open:** All year (not Xmas)
01530 260318 Mrs Payne **D:** Fr £17.00 **S:** Fr £17.00 **Beds:** 1D 1T 1S **Baths:** 2 Sh (5)

Oaks in Charnwood

SK4716

St Josephs, *Abbey Road, Oaks in Charnwood, Coalville, Leics, LE67 4UA.* Old country house where hosts welcome you to their home.
Open: Apr to Oct
01509 503943 Mrs Havers *m.havers@virgin.net* **D:** Fr £20.00 **S:** Fr £20.00 **Beds:** 2T 1S **Baths:** 1 Sh (3)

Lubcloud Farm, *Charley Road, Oaks in Charnwood, Loughborough, Leics, LE12 9YA.* Organic working dairy farm. Peaceful rural location on Charnwood Forest. **Open:** All year
01509 503204 Mr & Mrs Newcombe **Fax: 01509 651267** www.lubcloudbednbreakfast.co.uk **D:** Fr £20.00–£22.00 **S:** Fr £22.50–£25.00 **Beds:** 1F 2D **Baths:** 3 En (10)

Osgathorpe

SK4219

The Royal Oak Guest House, *20 Main Street, Osgathorpe, Loughborough, Leicestershire, LE12 9TA.* High standard picturesque countryside. Secured parking, close M1, M42, EM Airport. **Open:** All year **Grades:** ETC 3 Diamond
01530 222443 V A Jacobs **D:** Fr £20.00–£22.50 **S:** Fr £30.00–£35.00 **Beds:** 2T 1D **Baths:** 3 En (50)

Queniborough

SK6412 *Britannia Inn, Horse & Groom*

Three Ways Farm, *Melton Road, Queniborough, Leicester, Leics, LE7 3FN.* Comfortable and attractive bungalow surrounded by fields. Good food and beds. **Open:** All year (not Xmas/New Year)
0116 260 0472 J S Clarke **D:** Fr £19.00–£20.00 **S:** Fr £19.00–£20.00 **Beds:** 1F 1T 1D 1S **Baths:** 1 Sh (5) (6)

Ratcliffe Culey

SP3299

Manor Farm, *Ratcliffe Culey, Atherstone, Warks, CV9 3NY.* Victorian house located in small quiet friendly village in beautiful countryside. **Open:** All year
01827 712269 Mrs Trivett *jane@ousbey.com* **D:** Fr £17.00–£18.00 **S:** Fr £20.00–£25.00 **Beds:** 3D **Baths:** 2 Sh (3) cc

Ravenstone

SK4013

Church Lane Farm House, *Ravenstone, Coalville, Leicester, LE67 2AE.* Queen Anne farmhouse. Interior designer and artist's home, antique furnishings throughout. **Open:** All year (not Xmas)
01530 810536 & 01530 811299 Mrs Thorne *annthorne@ravenstone-guesthouse.co.uk* www.ravenstone-guesthouse.co.uk **D:** Fr £27.50–£31.50 **S:** Fr £29.50–£35.00 **Beds:** 2D 2T **Baths:** 4 En (6)

Saddington

SP6591 *Queen's Head*

Breach Farm, *Shearsby Road, Saddington, Leicester, Leics, LE8 0QU.* Modern comfortable farmhouse. Panoramic views. Breakfast served in large conservatory. **Open:** All year
0116 240 2539 Mrs Thornton **D:** Fr £18.00–£20.00 **S:** Fr £20.00 **Beds:** 1T 2D **Baths:** 1 Sh

Shearsby

SP6290

The Greenway, *Knaptoft House Farm, Bruntingthorpe Road, Shearsby, Lutterworth, Leics, LE17 6PR.* Farmhouse B&B at its best. Set deep in Leicestershire countryside. **Open:** All year (not Xmas/New Year)
0116 247 8388 (also fax) Mr Hutchinson *info@knaptoft.com* www.knaptoft.com **D:** Fr £21.00–£24.00 **S:** Fr £27.00–£38.00 **Beds:** 2D 1T **Baths:** 2 Pr 1 Sh (5) (5)
cc

Sheepy Magna

SK3201

Elmsdale, *Ratcliffe Lane, Sheepy Magna, Atherstone, Leicestershire, CV9 3QY.*
Open: All year (not Xmas)
01827 718810 & 07971 668509 (M)
Mrs Calcott *sue@elmsdalehouse.fsnet.co.uk*
D: Fr £18.00 **S:** Fr £18.00 **Beds:** 1F 2S **Baths:** 1 Sh (5)
Modern family farmhouse set in 200 acres of farmland. River and pool fishing, clay pigeon shooting (by arrangement) country paths. A warm welcome awaits you. Well equipped rooms with extras.

Shoby

SK6820

Shoby Lodge Farm, *Shoby, Melton Mowbray, Leics, LE14 3PF.* Assured a warm welcome. Relax in the comfortable lounge with open log fire. **Open:** All year (not Xmas/New Year) **Grades:** ETC 4 Diamond, Silver
01664 812156 Mrs Lomas **D:** Fr £22.50 **S:** Fr £25.00 **Beds:** 1T 2D **Baths:** 2 En 1 Pr (6)

Swannington

SK4115

Hillfield House, *52 Station Hill, Swannington, Coalville, Leicestershire, LE67 8RH.*
Open: All year
01530 837414
Ms Nicholls **Fax: 01530 458233** *molly@hillfieldhouse.co.uk* www.hillfieldhouse.co.uk
D: Fr £20.00 **S:** Fr £25.00 **Beds:** 3T **Baths:** 2 En 1 Pr (5)
Perfectly located to explore National Forest/Middle England. In easy reach of EMA/Birmingham Airports and motorway network. Family home purposely extended with spacious and tastefully decorated rooms. Large, pleasant garden for the enjoyment of guests. Warm welcome. Hearty breakfasts.

Tilton on the Hill

SK7405

Knebworth House, *Loddington Lane, Launde, Tilton on the Hill, Leicester, LE7 9DE.* Comfortable accommodation in secluded countryside. **Open:** All year (not Xmas)
0116 259 7257 Mrs Setaycor **D:** Fr £15.00 **S:** Fr £15.00 **Beds:** 1F 1T 1S **Baths:** 1 Sh (10)

Please respect a B&B's wishes regarding children, animals and smoking

Ullesthorpe

SP5087

Forge House, *College Street, Ullesthorpe, Lutterworth, Leics, LE17 5BU.* Quiet village accommodation. Ideal for business and pleasure. Restaurants nearby. **Open:** All year
01455 202454 (also fax) *s.silvester@virgin.net*
D: Fr £20.00–£22.50 **S:** Fr £20.00–£25.00 **Beds:** 1D 1T **Baths:** 1 En 1 Sh (10) (3)

Upton

SP3699

Sparkenhoe Farm, *Upton, Nuneaton, Warks, CV13 6JX.* Beautiful Georgian farmhouse, fabulous countryside views. Large comfortable rooms recently refurbished to high standard. **Open:** All year
01455 213203 Mrs Clarke **D:** Fr £25.00 **S:** Fr £25.00–£30.00 **Beds:** 1D 2T **Baths:** 2 En 1 Pr (10)

Waltham on the Wolds

SK8025

Bryn Barn, *38 High Street, Waltham on the Wolds, Melton Mowbray, Leics, LE14 4AH.* Charmingly converted stables & barn, original timber beams, picturesque conservation village in Vale of Belvoir.
Open: All year (not Xmas)
01664 464783 Mr & Mrs Rowlands **D:** Fr £19.00–£21.00 **S:** Fr £25.00–£28.00 **Beds:** 1F 2D 1T **Baths:** 2 En 2 Sh (4)

Lincolnshire

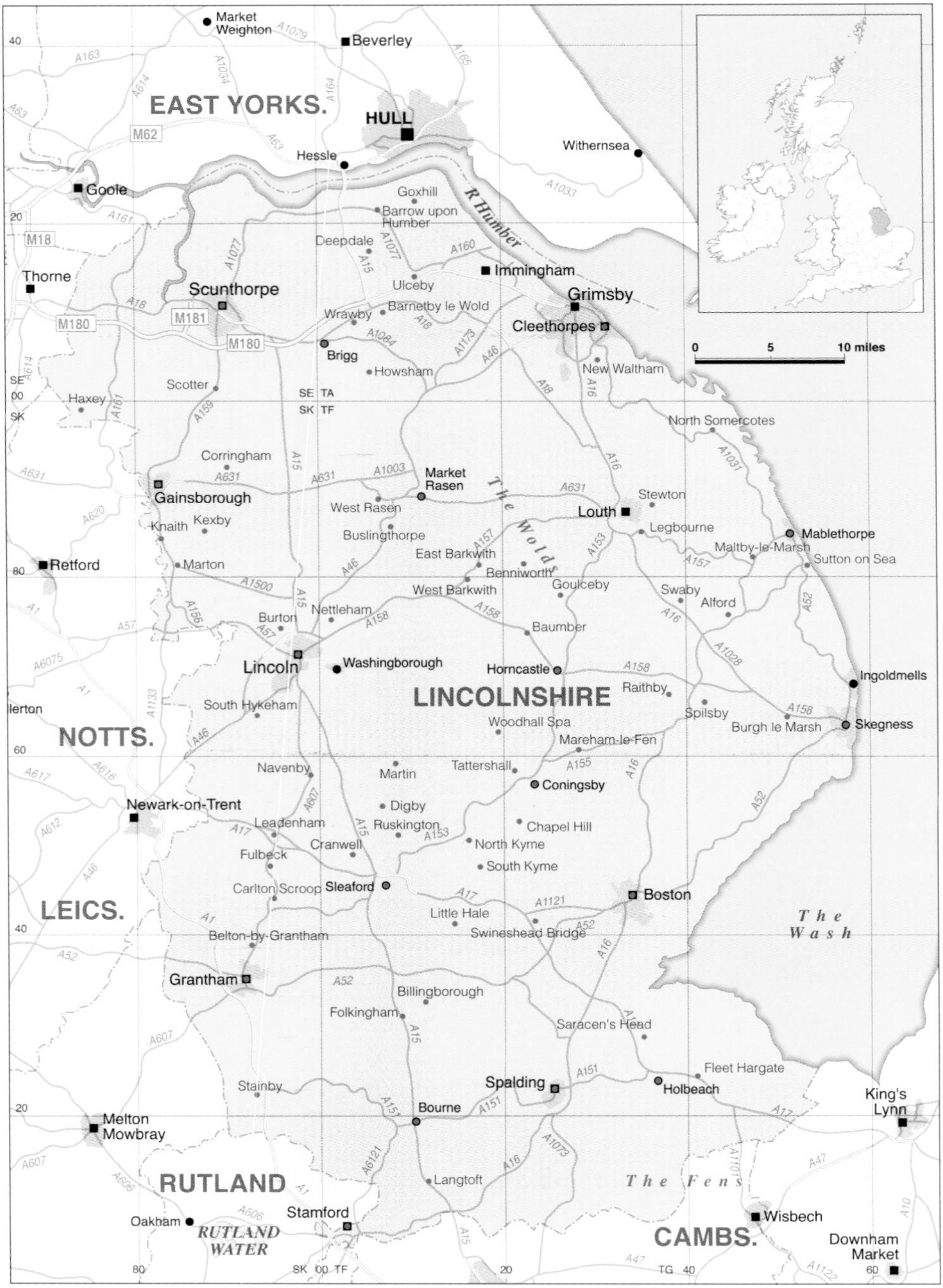

Alford

TF4575

Halton House, *50 East Street, Alford, Lincs, LN13 9EH.* Comfortable relaxing accommodation. Ideal for coast & country. **Open:** All year (not Xmas)
01507 462058 Mrs Mackey *tjmackey@aol.com* **D:** Fr £19.00 **S:** Fr £19.00 **Beds:** 1D 1T **Baths:** 1 Sh (3)

White Horse Hotel, *29 West Street, Alford, Lincs, LN13 9DG.* Thatched property with C13th charm, including original beams & fireplaces. **Open:** All year
01507 462218 Mrs Laskowski **Fax: 01507 469241** *whorsealford@aol.com* **D:** Fr £25.00–£35.00 **S:** Fr £35.00–£45.00 **Beds:** 3F 3T 3D 2S **Baths:** 20 En **cc**

Barnetby le Wold

TA0509

Holcombe Guest House, *34 Victoria Road, Barnetby le Wold, Lincs, DN38 6JR.* First class accommodation and a warm welcome await you. **Open:** All year
01652 680655 & 07850 764002 (M) Mrs Vora **Fax: 01652 680841** *holcombe.house@virgin.net* www.holcombeguesthouse.co.uk **D:** Fr £16.25–£20.00 **S:** Fr £20.00 **Beds:** 2F 1T 5S **Baths:** 4 Pr 2 Sh (7) **cc**

Barrow upon Humber

TA0720

Glengarth, *South End, Goxhill, Barrow-upon-Humber, Lincs, DN19 7LZ.* Comfortable, modernised farmhouse, open fires, quiet location in beautiful countryside, warm welcome. **Open:** All year
01469 530991 (also fax) Mrs Monro *home@monoracing.go-plus.net* **D:** Fr £20.00 **S:** Fr £20.00 **Beds:** 1D 1T **Baths:** 1 Pr 1 Sh (8)

Glebe Farm, *Cross Street, Barrow upon Humber, North Lincolnshire, DN19 7AL.* Spacious accommodation in village location. Superb for walking, cycling, sightseeing. **Open:** All year (not Xmas/New Year) **Grades:** ETC 3 Diamond
01469 531548 Mrs Styles **Fax: 01469 530034** *glebe_farm@lineone.net* **D:** Fr £19.00–£20.00 **S:** Fr £20.00–£22.00 **Beds:** 1D 1S **Baths:** 1 Pr (5) (2)

Kingswell, *Howe Lane, Goxhill, Barrow upon Humber, Lincs., DN19 7HU.* 300-year-old house. Many miles of walks. Birdwatching, riding, fishing nearby. **Open:** All year (not Xmas/New Year)
01469 532471 (also fax) **D:** Fr £17.50 **S:** Fr £18.00 **Beds:** 1T 1D 1S **Baths:** 1 Pr (4)

Baumber

TF2274

Baumber Park, *Baumber, Horncastle, Lincs, LN9 5NE.* Spacious period farmhouse, fine views, colourful gardens, walking, cycling, golf. **Open:** All year (not Xmas)
01507 578235 & 07977 722776 (M) Mrs Harrison **Fax: 01507 578417** uk.geocities.com/baumberpark/thehouse **D:** Fr £22.50–£27.50 **S:** Fr £22.50–£35.00 **Beds:** 1D 1T 1S **Baths:** 1 En 1 Pr 1 Sh (4)

Belton-by-Grantham

SK9239 *The Stag*

Coach House, *Belton-by-Grantham, Grantham, Lincs, NG32 2LS.* Centre of Belton NT village. Extensive gardens, private parking. **Open:** All year (not Xmas/New Year)
01476 573636 (also fax) Mrs Norton *coachhousebandb@yahoo.co.uk* www.smoothhound.co.uk/hotels/coachhouse **D:** Fr £22.00–£23.00 **S:** Fr £30.00–£35.00 **Beds:** 1F 2D **Baths:** 3 En (10)

Benniworth

TF2081

Glebe Farm, *Church Lane, Benniworth, Market Rasen, Lincolnshire, LN8 6JP.* C18th Listed farmhouse in Lincolnshire Wolds. Welcome Host. Taste of Lincolnshire. **Open:** All year **Grades:** ETC 4 Diamond, Silver
01507 313231 & 07802 309206 (M) Mrs Selby **Fax: 01507 313231** *info@glebe-farm.com* www.glebe-farm.com **D:** Fr £25.00 **S:** Fr £27.00 **Beds:** 2D 1T **Baths:** 3 En (6)

Billingborough

TF1134

Tiffany House, *2a Station Road, Billingborough, Sleaford, NG34 0NR.* Warm welcome awaits, friendly atmosphere, light airy rooms, pine furnishings. **Open:** All year
01529 240543 Mrs Abbott **D:** Fr £20.00–£24.00 **S:** Fr £22.00–£24.00 **Beds:** 1T 1D 1S **Baths:** 2 Sh (2) (2)

St Boswells, *10 Vine Street, Billingborough, Sleaford, Lincs, NG34 0QE.* Old detached attractive house and secluded garden overlooking village church. **Open:** All year
01529 240413 Fax: 01529 241413 *john.hockin@btinternet.com* www.btinternet.com/~john.hockin/ **D:** Fr £20.00 **S:** Fr £20.00 **Beds:** 1D 2T **Baths:** 1 Sh (1)

Boston

TF3344

Lochiel Guest House, *69 Horncastle Road, Boston, Lincs, PE21 9HY.* Comfortable, friendly, picturesque waterside setting. Large garden. Working windmill view. **Open:** All year
01205 363628 Mr & Mrs Lynch **D:** Fr £18.00 **S:** Fr £20.00–£25.00 **Beds:** 1D 1T 1S **Baths:** 1 Sh (3)

Bourne

TF0920

The Old Mill, *16 Victoria Place, Bourne, Lincs, PE10 9LJ.* Spacious family home where a warm and friendly welcome awaits. **Open:** All year (not Xmas/New Year)
01778 394893 Mr Davison *oldmill@bourne1.screaming.net* **D:** Fr £15.00 **S:** Fr £15.00 **Beds:** 2T **Baths:** 1 Sh

Brigg

TA0007

Hamsden Garth, *Cadney Road, Howsham, Market Rasen, Lincolnshire, LN7 6LA.* **Open:** All year (not Xmas) **Grades:** AA 3 Diamond
01652 678703 Mrs Robinson *reservations@hamsden.co.uk* www.hamsden.co.uk **D:** Fr £18.00 **S:** Fr £20.00 **Beds:** 1T 1S **Baths:** 1 Sh (10)
Warm friendly welcome, substantial English breakfast and very comfortable accommodation, in pleasant rural setting. Convenient for Humberside Airport, M18/M180 & Humber Bank industries. Enjoy Rasen Races, Forest Pines/Elsham golf courses, Viking Way long distance footpath, Eastern cycle route.

Planning a longer stay? Always ask for any special rates

Planning a longer stay? Always ask for any special rates

The Woolpack Hotel, *Market Place, Brigg, Lincs., DN20 8HA.* A Grade II Listed building and a fully licensed public house, with comfortable accommodation. **Open:** All year (not Xmas)
01652 655649 (also fax) *harry@woolpack488.freeserve.co.uk* **D:** Fr £15.00–£20.00 **S:** Fr £18.00–£25.00 **Beds:** 2F 3T 1S **Baths:** 2 En 1 Pr 1 Sh (20)

Burgh le Marsh

TF5064

The Old Mill, *West End, Burgh le Marsh, Skegness, Lincs, PE24 5EA.* Tastefully converted windmill set in lovely countryside, near the coast. **Open:** All year (not Xmas)
01754 810081 (also fax) Mr & Mrs Southward *oldmillburgh@talk21.com* www.skegness-resort.co.uk/oldmillburgh **D:** Fr £16.00–£26.00 **S:** Fr £25.00–£30.00 **Beds:** 1F 1D 1T **Baths:** 2 En 1 Sh (6)

Burton

SK9674

New Farm, *Burton, Lincoln, Lincs, LN1 2RD.* 328-acre working farm, open countryside, Lincoln Cathedral nearby. **Open:** Easter to Nov
01522 527326 Mrs Russon **D:** Fr £19.00 **S:** Fr £22.50 **Beds:** 2T **Baths:** 1 Pr 1 Sh (5) (3)

Buslingthorpe

TF0885 *White Hart*

East Farm House, *Middle Rasen Road, Buslingthorpe, Market Rasen, Lincs, LN3 5AQ.* Oak-beamed farmhouse, built 1750. Peaceful location 2 miles south of Middle Rasen. **Open:** All year (not Xmas/New Year)
01673 842283 Mrs Grant **D:** Fr £23.00–£24.50 **S:** Fr £28.00 **Beds:** 1T 1D **Baths:** 1 En 1 Pr (10)

Carlton Scroop

SK9545

Churchfield House, *Hough Lane, Grantham, Lincs., NG32 3AX.* Stylish peaceful accommodation with views over pretty sunny gardens. Close to NT properties. **Open:** All year (not Xmas/New Year)
01400 250387 Mrs Hankinson **Fax: 01400 250241** **D:** Fr £39.50 **S:** Fr £39.50 **Beds:** 1T **Baths:** 1 Pr (2)

Chapel Hill

TF2054

The Crown Lodge, *Chapel Hill, Tattershall, Lincoln, LN4 4PX.* Ensuite rooms, varied menu, walks, fishing, boating, real ale, entertainment. **Open:** All year
01526 342262 (also fax) Mr Harrington *barryharrington@hotmail.com* **D:** Fr £20.00 **S:** Fr £20.00 **Beds:** 1F 2T 1S (15)

Cleethorpes

TA3008

Hotel 77, *77 Kingsway, Cleethorpes, Lincs, DN35 0AB.* **Open:** All year (not Xmas/New Year)
01472 692035 (also fax) Mr & Mrs Knox *hotel77@knox24.fsbusiness.co.uk* **D:** Fr £19.50 **S:** Fr £25.00 **Beds:** 3F 3T 4D 4S **Baths:** 14 En cc
Situated near leisure centre, leisure park. Overlooking seafront. Car park with CCTV.

Ginnie's, *27 Queens Parade, Cleethorpes, N E Lincs, DN35 0DF.* A warm welcome awaits you at Ginnie's non-smoking guest house. **Open:** All year (not Xmas)
01472 694997 Mr Wood **Fax: 01472 693971** *kimkwood@aol.com* www.ginniesguesthousecleethorpes.co.uk **D:** Fr £17.00–£20.00 **S:** Fr £17.00–£20.00 **Beds:** 2F 4D 1T 1S **Baths:** 8 En (3) (2)

Lindenthorpe Guest House, *19 Grant Street, Cleethorpes, Lincs, DN35 8AT.* Comfortable accommodation, 5 mins to rail station, sea front, attractions. **Open:** All year
01472 313005 & 01472 312070 Mrs Richardson **Fax: 01472 312070** *lindenthorpe@fsbdial.co.uk* www.lindenthorpe.co.uk **D:** Fr £12.50–£14.00 **S:** Fr £14.00 **Beds:** 1F 1T 1T/D 2S **Baths:** 1 Sh

Pelham View Guest House, *12 Isaacs Hill, Cleethorpes, Lincs, DN35 8JS.* A warm welcome awaits all guests to Pelham View Guest House. **Open:** All year (not Xmas)
01472 690781 Mr Sharpe **D:** Fr £14.00 **S:** Fr £16.00 **Beds:** 3F 1D 1T **Baths:** 1 Pr

Gladson Guest House, *43 Isaacs Hill, Cleethorpes, Lincs, DN35 8JT.* Licensed family guest house, personal attention. Close to seafront. **Open:** All year
01472 694858 & 01472 239642 Mrs Pearce **Fax: 01472 239642** *enquiries@gladsonguesthouse.co.uk* www.gladsonguesthouse.co.uk **D:** Fr £15.00–£16.00 **S:** Fr £17.00–£18.00 **Beds:** 2F 1D 2S (3)

Holmhirst Hotel, *3 Alexandra Road, Cleethorpes, Lincs, DN35 8LQ.* Family-run seafront hotel. Good food a speciality. **Open:** All year (not Xmas)
01472 692656 (also fax) Mr Barrs *holmhirst@aol.com* **D:** Fr £20.00 **S:** Fr £18.00–£25.00 **Beds:** 1D 2T 5S **Baths:** 5 En 1 Sh (3) cc

Abbeydale Guest House, *39 Isaacs Hill, Cleethorpes, NE Lincs, DN35 8JT.* Clean comfortable accommodation. Excellent base for touring. Friendly welcome. **Open:** All year
01472 692248 & 01472 311088 Mr Inskip **Fax: 01472 311088** *enquiries@abbeydaleguesthouse.co.uk* www.abbeydaleguesthouse.co.uk **D:** Fr £14.00–£15.00 **S:** Fr £16.00–£22.00 **Beds:** 2F 1D 2S **Baths:** 2 Sh cc

Alpine Guest House, *55 Clee Road, Cleethorpes, Lincs., DN35 8AD.* Welcoming comfortable accommodation at realistic prices. **Open:** All year (not Xmas)
01472 690804 (also fax) W M Sanderson *w.sanderson@ntlworld.com* **D:** Fr £13.00–£15.00 **S:** Fr £15.00–£16.00 **Beds:** 2F 1T 2S **Baths:** 2 Sh (2) (3)

Adelaide Hotel, *41 Isaacs Hill, Cleethorpes, Lincs, DN35 8JT.* Small delightful family-run hotel. Superb accommodation, friendliness, cleanliness, home quality cooked food. **Open:** All year
01472 693594 **Fax: 01472 329717** *robert.callison@dtn.ntl.com* **D:** Fr £15.00–£18.50 **S:** Fr £16.00–£25.00 **Beds:** 2F 5T 4D 2S **Baths:** 3 En 2 Sh (3) (4)

Coningsby

TF2258

The White Bull, *High Street, Coningsby, Lincoln, Lincs, LN4 4RB.* Friendly pub, real ale, riverside beer garden, large children's playground. Open for food 11am to 11pm. **Open:** All year
01526 342439 Mr & Mrs Gordon **Fax: 01526 342818** *whitebullinn@hotmail.com* www.thewhitebullconingsby.co.uk **D:** Fr £15.00–£19.00 **S:** Fr £15.00–£20.00 **Beds:** 2F **Baths:** 2 En (35)

Corringham

SK8791

The Beckett Arms, *25 High Street, Corringham, Gainsborough, Lincolnshire, DN21 5QP.* Centrally located accommodation offering a warm welcome and home-cooked meals. **Open:** All year
01427 838201 **D:** Fr £17.00–£20.00 **S:** Fr £20.00–£24.00 **Beds:** 2F 1T 1D **Baths:** 4 En (30) cc

Cranwell

TF0349

Byards Leap Cottage, *Cranwell, Sleaford, Lincs, NG34 8EY.* Comfortable country cottage, beautiful garden, home cooking with home-grown produce. **Open:** All year (not Xmas) **Grades:** ETC 3 Diamond
01400 261537 Mrs Wood *lustacottage@supanet.com* **D:** Fr £20.00 **S:** Fr £20.00 **Beds:** 1D 1T **Baths:** 1 Sh (6)

Deepdale

TA0418

West Wold Farmhouse, *Deepdale, Barton-upon-Humber, Lincs., DN18 6ED.* Welcoming, friendly farmhouse. Home cooking. Peaceful surroundings, near historic Barton. **Open:** All year
01652 633293 (also fax) P Atkin **D:** Fr £17.50–£19.50 **S:** Fr £17.50–£19.50 **Beds:** 1T 1D **Baths:** 1 Sh

Digby

TF0855

The Shepherd's Cottage, *40 North Street, Digby, Lincoln, LN4 3LY.* Traditional cottage in delightful village. Short walk to local pub. **Open:** All year (not Xmas/New Year)
01526 323151 **D:** Fr £16.00–£20.00 **S:** Fr £22.00–£25.00 **Beds:** 1D 1S **Baths:** 1 Pr (2)

Woodend Farm, *Digby, Lincoln, LN4 3NG.* Homely farmhouse overlooking paddock. Accessible all day, own sitting room. **Open:** All year
01526 860347 Mrs Gillatt **D:** Fr £17.00–£19.00 **S:** Fr £17.00–£19.00 **Beds:** 1F 1T 1D **Baths:** 1 En 1 Pr

East Barkwith

TF1681

The Grange, *Torrington Lane, East Barkwith, Market Rasen, Lincs, LN8 5RY.* Warm welcome at Georgian farmhouse. Ideal for exploring Lincoln and the Wolds. **Open:** All year (not Xmas)
01673 858670 *sarahstamp@farmersweekly.net* www.thegrange-lincolnshire.co.uk **D:** Fr £23.50 **S:** Fr £30.00 **Beds:** 2D **Baths:** 2 En

Fleet Hargate

TF3925

Willow Tea Rooms And B&B, *Old Main Road, Fleet Hargate, Spalding, Lincs, PE12 8LL.* Pretty English tea rooms renowned for good food. Comfortable accommodation. **Open:** All year
01406 423112 **D:** Fr £16.00–£18.00 **S:** Fr £20.00–£22.00 **Beds:** 2F 3D 1T **Baths:** 5 En 1 Pr (6)

Folkingham

TF0733 *Fortesque Arms, Red Lion, Three Kings*

6 Sleaford Road, *Folkingham, Sleaford, Lincs, NG34 0SB.* Comfortable family home with pleasant meadow views in conservation village. **Open:** All year (not Xmas/New Year)
01529 497277 W H Lack **D:** Fr £16.00–£18.00 **S:** Fr £18.00–£20.00 **Beds:** 3T **Baths:** 1 Sh (3)

Fulbeck

SK9450

Hare & Hounds, *The Green, Fulbeck, Grantham, Lincs, NG32 3JJ.* C17th inn. Real ales, food all week. Patio garden. 10 mins A1. **Open:** All year
01400 272090 A Nicholas **Fax: 01400 273663** **D:** Fr £20.00–£27.50 **S:** Fr £30.00–£40.00 **Beds:** 4D 2T 2F **Baths:** 8 En **cc**

Gainsborough

SK8190

Ivy Lodge Hotel, *4 Messingham Road, Scotter, Gainsborough, Lincs, DN21 3UQ.* **Open:** All year
01724 763723 Mrs Mewis *hotel@choxx.co.uk* **D:** Fr £25.00 **S:** Fr £29.00–£40.00 **Beds:** 1F 1D 1T 2S **Baths:** 5 En (8)
Quality accommodation with friendly atmosphere & large garden. Situated in picturesque village on A159 between Gainsborough & Scunthorpe. Licensed. Summer ice cream parlour & all-year Continental chocolaterie. Close to Blyton Raceway, several golf courses, horseracing & Lincolnshire Wolds.

Goulceby

TF2579

Holly House, *Watery Lane, Goulceby, Louth, Lincs, LN11 9UR.* Comfortable accommodation in peaceful village setting. French, Hebrew, German spoken. **Open:** All year (not Xmas/New Year)
01507 343729 Mrs Lester **D:** Fr £16.00–£18.00 **S:** Fr £16.00–£18.00 **Beds:** 1D 1T **Baths:** 1 Sh (2)

Goxhill

TA1021

Glengarth, *South End, Goxhill, Barrow-upon-Humber, Lincs, DN19 7LZ.* Comfortable, modernised farmhouse, open fires, quiet location in beautiful countryside, warm welcome. **Open:** All year
01469 530991 (also fax) Mrs Monro *home@monoracing.go-plus.net* **D:** Fr £20.00 **S:** Fr £20.00 **Beds:** 1D 1T **Baths:** 1 Pr 1 Sh (8)

Grantham

SK9136

Beechleigh Guest House, *55 North Parade, Grantham, Lincs, NG31 8AT.* **Open:** All year **Grades:** ETC 4 Diamond
01476 572213 **Fax: 01476 566058** *beechleighgh@aol.com* www.beechleigh.co.uk **D:** Fr £27.50 **S:** Fr £27.50–£40.00 **Beds:** 1F 1T 1D 1S **Baths:** 2 En 1 Pr (3) **cc**
A warm welcome for all at our attractive Edwardian home. Delicious breakfast choices. Easy walking to town centre restaurants, pubs and businesses. Excellent touring and business base, close to A1 as well as historic sites and ancient buildings of Lincolnshire.

Church View, *12 North Parade, Grantham, Lincs, NG31 8AN.* A well-appointed Listed Georgian town house. Town centre location. **Open:** All year
01476 560815 Mr & Mrs Waldren *churchview@excite.com* **D:** Fr £18.00–£20.00 **S:** Fr £22.00–£25.00 **Beds:** 1D 1T 1F **Baths:** 2 En 1 Pr

Park Lodge Guest House, *87 Harrowby Road, Grantham, Lincolnshire, NG31 9ED.* A Victorian town house decorated in the William Morris style. **Open:** All year (not Xmas)
01476 567330 (also fax) Mr & Mrs Parkes *kath@parkes.org* www.parklodge.co.uk **D:** Fr £20.00 **S:** Fr £24.00 **Beds:** 2D 1T 1S **Baths:** 2 En 1 Pr (12) (7)

Haxey

SK7799

Duke William, *Church Street, Haxey, Doncaster, South Yorkshire, DN9 2HY.* C18th inn refurbished to provide accommodation in a warm and friendly atmosphere **Open:** All year
01427 752210 (also fax) **D:** Fr £22.50 **S:** Fr £32.00 **Beds:** 2T 4D (36) **cc**

B&B owners may vary rates – be sure to check when booking

Holbeach
TF3625

Elloe Lodge, *37 Barrington Gate, Holbeach, Spalding, Lincs, PE12 7LB.* Spacious house, old market town, close pubs and restaurants. Drawing room, delightful gardens. **Open:** All year (not Xmas)
Grades: AA 4 Diamond
01406 423207 (also fax) Mrs Vasey *bandbholbeach@lineone.net* **D:** Fr £20.00 **S:** Fr £25.00 **Beds:** 1F 1D 1T **Baths:** 1 En 2 Pr (10)

Horncastle
TF2669

Milestone Cottage, *42 North Street, Horncastle, Lincs, LN9 5DX.* Comfortable, self contained accommodation in Georgian town cottage. Self-catering option available. **Open:** All year
01507 522238 **D:** Fr £20.00 **S:** Fr £20.00 **Beds:** 1T **Baths:** 1 En (2)

Howsham
TA0403

Hamsden Garth, *Cadney Road, Howsham, Market Rasen, Lincolnshire, LN7 6LA.* Warm friendly welcome, substantial English breakfast and very comfortable accommodation. **Open:** All year (not Xmas)
Grades: AA 3 Diamond
01652 678703 Mrs Robinson *reservations@hamsden.co.uk* www.hamsden.co.uk **D:** Fr £18.00 **S:** Fr £20.00 **Beds:** 1T 1S **Baths:** 1 Sh (10)

Kexby
SK8785

Kexby Grange, *Kexby, Gainsborough, Lincs, DN21 5PJ.* Victorian farmhouse in pleasant countryside, convenient for Hemswell antiques, Lincoln and Wolds.
Open: All year (not Xmas)
01427 788265 Mrs Edwardson **D:** Fr £18.00 **S:** Fr £18.00 **Beds:** 1D 1S **Baths:** 1 Pr 1 Sh (4)

Langtoft
TF1212

Courtyard Cottage, *2 West End, Langtoft, Peterborough, PE6 9LS.* A tastefully refurbished C18th stone cottage providing a warm welcome. **Open:** All year
01778 348354 (also fax) *david_tinegate@ic24.net* **D:** Fr £22.50–£30.00 **S:** Fr £30.00–£50.00 **Beds:** 1F 1D 1T **Baths:** 2 En 1 Pr

Leadenham
SK9552

George Hotel, *High Street, Leadenham, Lincoln, LN5 0PN.* The George is a small country hotel, homely atmosphere and reputation for fine food. **Open:** All year
Grades: ETC 3 Diamond
01400 272251 Mr Willgoose **Fax: 01400 272091** **D:** Fr £15.00–£21.00 **S:** Fr £25.00–£32.00 **Beds:** 1F 2D 2T 1S **Baths:** 6 En 1 cc

Legbourne
TF3684

Boothby House, *Legbourne, Louth, Lincolnshire, LN11 8LH.* Situated at the edge of the picturesque Lincolnshire Wolds.
Open: All year (not Xmas)
01507 601516 (also fax) Mrs Wilson *boothbyhouse@freeuk.com* www.boothbyhouse.freeuk.com **D:** Fr £18.00–£21.00 **S:** Fr £18.00 **Beds:** 1D 1T 1S **Baths:** 1 En 1 Sh

Lincoln
SK9771

Edward King House, *The Old Palace, Minster Yard, Lincoln, LN2 1PU.*
Open: All year (not Xmas)
01522 528778 Rev Adkins **Fax: 01522 527308** *enjoy@ekhs.org.uk* www.ekhs.org.uk **D:** Fr £19.50–£21.50 **S:** Fr £20.00–£22.00 **Beds:** 1F 11T 5S **Baths:** 8 Sh (12) cc
A former residence of the Bishops of Lincoln at the historic heart of the city and next to the Cathedral and medieval Bishops' Palace. We offer a peaceful haven with a secluded garden and superb views.

South Park Guest House, *11 South Park, Lincoln, LN5 8EN.*
Open: All year
01522 528243 Mr Bull **Fax: 01522 524603** www.southpark-lincoln.co.uk **D:** Fr £20.00 **S:** Fr £22.00–£25.00 **Beds:** 1F 2T 2D 1S **Baths:** 6 En (1) (6)
Fine Victorian detached house, recently refurbished to provide excellent quality accommodation, while maintaining many original features and character. Situated overlooking the South Common, only a short walk to shops, pubs, restaurants, city centre and tourist attractions. Ensuite rooms. Private parking.

Planning a longer stay? Always ask for any special rates

National Grid References given are for villages, towns and cities – not for individual houses

Admiral Guest House, *16/18 Nelson Street, Lincoln, LN1 1PJ.* **Open:** All year (not Xmas)
01522 544467 (also fax) Mr Major *tony@admiral63.freeserve.co.uk* **D:** Fr £18.00–£20.00 **S:** Fr £25.00 **Beds:** 1F 4D 2T 3S **Baths:** 7 En 2 Pr (12) cc
Admiral Guest House, also known as Nelsons Cottages, situated just off main A57 close to city centre and Lincoln University, offering large floodlit car park, also close to Brayford pool, cathedral and castle and all amenities. All rooms ensuite and private bathrooms.

The Old Rectory, *19 Newport, Lincoln, LN1 3DQ.* Large Edwardian home near cathedral, castle, pubs and restaurants.
Open: All year (not Xmas)
01522 514774 Mr Downes **D:** Fr £20.00 **S:** Fr £20.00–£25.00 **Beds:** 2F 4D 1T 1S **Baths:** 6 En 1 Sh (8)

Hamiltons Hotel, *2 Hamilton Road, St Catherines, Lincoln, LN5 8ED.* Modernised Victorian residence offering homely accommodation with modern facilities. Close to town.
Open: All year
01522 528243 Stephen Bull **Fax: 01522 524603** *enquiries@southpark-lincoln.co.uk* www.hamiltonhotel.co.uk **D:** Fr £20.00 **S:** Fr £25.00 **Beds:** 2F 2T 2D 3S **Baths:** 5 En 2 Sh (9)

Westlyn House, *67 Carholme Road, Lincoln, LN1 1RT.* Late Georgian house close to university, marina, cathedral, castle, city centre. **Open:** All year (not Xmas)
01522 537468 (also fax) Mrs Shelton *westlyn.bblincoln@easicom.com* www.smoothhound.co.uk/hotels/westlyn.html **D:** Fr £17.50–£20.00 **S:** Fr £20.00–£25.00 **Beds:** 1F 1T 2D 1S **Baths:** 5 En (3) (4)

Newport Guest House, *26-28 Newport, Lincoln, LN1 3DF.* A high standard establishment 500 metres from historic city centre. **Open:** All year (not Xmas)
01522 528590 Mr Clarke **Fax: 01522 542868** *info@newportguesthouse.co.uk* www.newportguesthouse.co.uk **D:** Fr £16.00–£20.00 **S:** Fr £16.00–£28.00 **Beds:** 3D 4T 1S **Baths:** 7 En 2 Sh (6) (5)

Carline Guest House, *3 Carline Road, Lincoln, LN1 1HL.* Perfectly situated for castle, cathedral, town centre. Individually decorated bedrooms. **Open:** All year (not Xmas/New Year)
01522 530422 D: Fr £21.00–£22.00 **S:** Fr £30.00–£35.00 **Beds:** 2T 6S **Baths:** 8 En (2) (6)

A B C Charisma Guest House, *126 Yarborough Road, Lincoln, LN1 1HP.* Beautiful views overlooking Trent valley 10 mins' walk to tourist area. **Open:** All year
01522 543560 (also fax) D: Fr £20.00–£22.50 **S:** Fr £20.00–£25.00 **Beds:** 1F 2T 6D 2S **Baths:** 3 En 4 Sh (10) (10)

The Old Bakery Guest House, *26-28 Burton Road, Lincoln, LN1 3LB.* Converted Victorian bakery. Two mins from Lincoln Cathedral and Castle. **Open:** All year
01522 576057 (also fax) Mr Pearson **D:** Fr £20.00–£25.00 **S:** Fr £30.00–£35.00 **Beds:** 1F 2D 1T **Baths:** 3 En 1 Pr cc

Little Hale

TF1441

Bywell, *20 Chapel Lane, Little Hale, Sleaford, Lincs, NG34 9BE.* Bungalow backing onto farmland. Heckington Windmill & tea-room 1.5 miles. **Open:** All year
01529 460206 Mrs Downes **D:** Fr £17.50 **Beds:** 1D 1T **Baths:** 1 En 1 Sh (5) (3)

Mablethorpe

TF5085

Park View Guest House, *48 Gibralter Road, Mablethorpe, Lincs, LN12 2AT.* Clean and comfortable licensed guest house with some ground floor bedrooms. **Open:** All year
01507 477267 (also fax) Mr Dodds *malcolm@pvgh.fsnet.co.uk* **D:** Fr £17.00–£20.00 **S:** Fr £17.00–£20.00 **Beds:** 1F 1T 3D **Baths:** 2 En 2 Sh (6)

Maltby-le-Marsh

TF4681 *Turk's Head*

Old Mill Restaurant and Guest House, *Main Road, Maltby-le-Marsh, Alford, Lincs, LN13 0JP.* Excellent village location. Peaceful, good food. Comfortable. Warm welcome. **Open:** All year
01507 450504 *ros-harris@lineone.net* www.maltbymill.co.uk **D:** Fr £20.00–£23.00 **S:** Fr £25.00–£30.00 **Beds:** 1F 2D **Baths:** 2 En 1 Sh (20)

Mareham le Fen

TF2761

Barn Croft, *Main Street, Mareham le Fen, Boston, Lincs, PE22 7QJ.* Ensuite facilities in rural setting. Ideal for coast, Lincoln, Boston. **Open:** All year
01507 568264 Mrs Shaw **D:** Fr £17.50 **S:** Fr £25.00 **Beds:** 2D 1T **Baths:** 2 En 1 Pr (4)

Market Rasen

TF1089

Waveney Cottage Guest House, *Willingham Road, Market Rasen, Lincs, LN8 3DN.* Recommended for its warm, friendly welcome and delicious food. **Open:** All year
01673 843236 Mrs Bridger www.waveneycottage.co.uk **D:** Fr £18.00–£20.00 **S:** Fr £21.00–£23.00 **Beds:** 1D 2T **Baths:** 3 En (6)

Martin

TF1260

The Stables Studio, *94 High Street, Martin, Lincoln, LN4 3QT.* Stylish quality accommodation, gallery & garden. Ideal golfing/walking area. **Open:** All year (not Xmas/New Year) **Grades:** ETC 4 Diamond
01526 378528 (also fax) *kenjo@stablestudio.fsnet.co.uk* www.stables-studio.co.uk **D:** Fr £18.00–£19.00 **S:** Fr £25.00 **Beds:** 2T 2D **Baths:** 3 En 1 Sh (10) cc

Marton

SK8482

The Black Swan Guest House, *High St, Marton, Gainsborough, Lincolnshire, DN21 5AH.* A beautifully restored C18th coaching inn offering high quality ensuite accommodation. Much favoured stop for business travellers, British and international tourists and family groups. Excellent breakfasts in house, and superb choice of dinners only 5 minutes away. booking advisable. **Open:** All year
01427 718878 (also fax) A & V Ball *info@blackswan-marton.co.uk* www.blackswan-marton.co.uk **D:** Fr £25.00–£30.00 **S:** Fr £30.00 **Beds:** 2F 4D 1T 1S **Baths:** 8 En (8) cc

Navenby

SK9858

The Barn, *North Lane, Navenby, Lincoln, LN5 0EH.* Quality accommodation, superb breakfasts. Convenient Newark, Lincoln. 3/5/7 day breaks. **Open:** All year (not Xmas/New Year) **Grades:** ETC 4 Diamond, Silver
01522 810318 (also fax) Mr & Mrs Gill *gill@barnbb.fsnet.co.uk* **D:** Fr £20.00–£24.00 **S:** Fr £27.00–£35.00 **Beds:** 1F 1T **Baths:** 1 En 1 Pr (7) (6)

Planning a longer stay? Always ask for any special rates

Nettleham

TF0075

The Old Vicarage, *25 East Street, Nettleham, Lincoln, LN2 2SL.* **Open:** All year
01522 750819 Mrs Downs *susan@oldvic.net*
D: Fr £20.00 **S:** Fr £24.50 **Beds:** 1T 1D **Baths:** 1 En 1 Pr (2)
Welcome to our listed Georgian farmhouse near the centre of an attractive village with traditional 'village green' and 'beck'. A warm welcome, tastefully furnished rooms and excellent location make us an ideal base when visiting historic Lincoln and surrounding counties.

Haymans Ghyll, *9 Church Street, Nettleham, Lincoln, LN2 2PD.* C18th cottage situated centre village, private lounge. Lincoln 10 mins. **Open:** All year (not Xmas/New Year)
01522 751812 (also fax) Mr Dawkins *dawkins_net@talk21.com* **D:** Fr £20.00–£22.00 **S:** Fr £25.00–£30.00 **Beds:** 2D **Baths:** 1 En 1 Pr

New Waltham

TA2904

Peaks Top Farm, *Hewitts Avenue, New Waltham, Grimsby, DN36 4RS.* Our converted barns offer stylish, comfortable accommodation, farmhouse breakfasts. **Open:** Mar to Dec
01472 812941 *lmclayton@tinyworld.co.uk* **D:** Fr £18.00 **S:** Fr £18.00–£25.00 **Beds:** 2F 1D 2S **Baths:** 5 En (6)

North Kyme

TF1552

Old Coach House Tea Rooms & Cafe, *Church Lane, North Kyme, Lincoln, LN4 4DJ.* Beautifully refurbished old Georgian house offering warm and friendly welcome. **Open:** All year
01526 861465 Mr & Mrs Grice **Fax: 01526 861658 D:** Fr £18.00–£22.00 **Beds:** 3D 3T 1S **Baths:** 3 En

North Somercotes

TF4296

Pigeon Cottage, *Conisholme Road, North Somercotes, Louth, Lincolnshire, LN11 7PS.* Fishing lake on site, craft studio, pets area, 4 acres of playing field together. **Open:** All year
01507 359063 Ms Hill **D:** Fr £20.00–£22.00 **S:** Fr £20.00–£22.00 **Beds:** 3F 1T 1D 1S **Baths:** 6 En (6)

Raithby (Spilsby)

TF3767

Red Lion Inn, *Raithby, Spilsby, Lincs, PE23 4DS.* Old world inn in centre of pretty Wolds village. Real ales, log fires in the winter, char grilled steaks, fish, home-made curries and Sunday roasts. Regular Lincoln coast buses. Pretty ensuite rooms. Great English breakfasts. **Open:** All year
01790 753727 Mrs Smith *alcaprawn@aol.com*
D: Fr £18.50–£20.00 **S:** Fr £27.00–£30.00
Beds: 2D 1T **Baths:** 3 En (20) cc

Ruskington

TF0851

Sunnyside Farm, *Leasingham Lane, Ruskington, Sleaford, Lincolnshire, NG34 9AH.* Perfectly located base for historic centres, golf, walking, cycling. Horseriding.
Open: All year
01526 833010 D A Luke **D:** Fr £20.00–£22.00
S: Fr £20.00–£22.00 **Beds:** 1F 1T **Baths:** 2 En

Saracen's Head

TF3427

Pipwell Manor, *Washaway Road, Saracen's Head, Holbeach, Spalding, Lincs, PE12 8AL.* Tastefully furnished rooms. Beautiful grounds featuring a miniature railway. Free use of cycles. **Open:** All year (not Xmas/New Year)
01406 423119 (also fax) Mrs Honnor **D:** Fr £44.00–£46.00 **S:** Fr £30.00–£32.00 **Beds:** 2D 1T 1S **Baths:** 3 En 1 Pr (6)

Scotter

SE8800

Ivy Lodge Hotel, *4 Messingham Road, Scotter, Gainsborough, Lincs, DN21 3UQ.* Quality accommodation with friendly atmosphere & large garden. Situated in picturesque village. **Open:** All year
01724 763723 Mrs Mewis *hotel@choxx.co.uk*
D: Fr £25.00 **S:** Fr £29.00–£40.00 **Beds:** 1F 1D 1T 2S **Baths:** 5 En (8)

Scunthorpe

SE8910

Lindsey Hotel, *26-28 Normanby Road, Scunthorpe, Lincs., DN15 6AL.* Family-run hotel close to town centre and local amenities. **Open:** All year
01724 844706 Fax: 01724 343629 *steve@lindseyhotel.freeserve.co.uk* **D:** Fr £14.00–£18.00
S: Fr £18.00–£26.00 **Beds:** 2F 2D 3T 5S
Baths: 3 En 3 Sh (1) (10)

Skegness

TF5663

Westdene Hotel, *1 Trafalgar Avenue, Skegness, Lincs, PE25 3EU.* **Open:** All year
01754 765168 *tyrrellyn@aol.com* **D:** Fr £19.00–£23.00 **S:** Fr £19.00–£23.00 **Beds:** 4F 3D
Baths: 7 En (4)
Originally built for the Lady Mayoress, Westdene is run by award winning ex Royal Marine Chef Ashley & wife Sarah. Situated south of the town, Westdene offers fine dining and comfortable surroundings. Close to beaches, amusements, bowling & golf courses.

The Tudor Lodge Licensed Guest House, *61 Drummond Road, Skegness, Lincolnshire, PE25 3BB.* Close to all amenities. B&B and eve meals, col TV, tea/coffee machines. **Open:** All year
01754 766487 M Lowe **D:** Fr £15.00–£20.00
S: Fr £18.00–£22.00 **Beds:** 3F 2D 3T 1S (12) cc

Glynvale Hotel, *101 Drummond Road, Skegness, Lincs, PE25 3EH.* Small family-run hotel, close to beach and all amenities.
Open: All year
01754 767190 Mrs Wood **D:** Fr £14.00–£20.00
Beds: 4F 3T 2D **Baths:** 3 Sh (5)

Craigside Hotel, *26 Scarborough Avenue, Skegness, Lincs, PE25 2SY.* Family run hotel, close to sea front, theatre and town centre. **Open:** Easter to Sept
01754 763307 (also fax) Mrs Milner
kenanddeb@craigside69.freeserve.co.uk
www.skegness-resort.co.uk/craigside **D:** Fr £20.00–£22.00 **S:** Fr £20.00–£22.00 **Beds:** 5F 5D 3T 3S **Baths:** 12 En 1 Sh (10) cc

Merlewood Hotel, *61 Park Avenue, Skegness, PE25 1BL.* Situated on tree lined avenue. Walking distance from beaches, town centre. **Open:** All year
01754 762942 **D:** Fr £18.00–£20.00 **S:** Fr £23.00–£25.00 **Beds:** 3F 6D **Baths:** 9 En (6)

Mayfair Hotel, *10 Saxby Avenue, Skegness, PE25 3JZ.* The Mayfair is well situated in quiet location close to sea front/town centre. **Open:** All year (not Xmas/New Year)
01754 764687 **D:** Fr £14.00–£20.00 **S:** Fr £14.00–£20.00 **Beds:** 1F 5T 2D **Baths:** 8 En (5)

The Carlton Hotel and Holiday Flats, *70 Drummond Road, Skegness, Lincs, PE25 3BR.* Family hotel and flats near to sea front and town centre. **Open:** All year (not Xmas)
01754 765340 Mr & Mrs Parker **Fax: 0870 1115700** *carltonhotel@yahoo.co.uk*
www.carltonpp.freeserve.co.uk **D:** Fr £14.00–£19.00 **S:** Fr £28.00–£38.00 **Beds:** 3F 4D 2T
Baths: 4 En 4 Sh (2) (9) cc

Sleaford

TF0645

Anna Farmhouse, *Holdingham, Sleaford, Lincs, NG34 8NR.* **Open:** All year (not Xmas)
01529 307292 Mrs Wiles **D:** Fr £19.00 **S:** Fr £25.00 **Beds:** 1F 1D 1T **Baths:** 2 Sh (6)
Friendly atmosphere in C16/17th farmhouse. Ideal stop London airports to York and Edinburgh also Scotland and the North to Norfolk Broads and Gt Yarmouth. Ample parking, large English breakfast served after 7.30, continental earlier. Quiet position close to A15/17.

The Mallards Hotel, *6 Eastgate, Sleaford, Lincolnshire, NG34 7DJ.* 10 rooms, family hotel, riverside location, central Sleaford. **Open:** All year (not Xmas)
01529 413758 Mr & Mrs Smith **D:** Fr £25.00–£40.00 **S:** Fr £25.00 **Beds:** 6T 2D 2S
Baths: 10 En cc

South Hykeham

SK9364

The Hall, *Meadow Lane, South Hykeham, Lincoln, Lincs, LN6 9PF.* Quiet rural setting close to Lincoln. Breakfasts prepared using local produce. **Open:** All year
01522 686432 Mrs Phillips **Fax: 01522 696496** **D:** Fr £22.00–£25.00 **S:** Fr £22.00–£25.00 **Beds:** 1F 2D **Baths:** 1 En

South Kyme

TF1749

Hume Arms Hotel, *High Street, South Kyme, Lincoln, LN4 4AD.* Home cooked food and traditional beers. Fishing lake. Caravans welcome. **Open:** All year
01526 861004 Mr Leggat **D:** Fr £15.00–£16.00
S: Fr £20.00 **Beds:** 1D 1T **Baths:** 1 En 1 Sh (20)

Please respect a B&B's wishes regarding children, animals and smoking

Spalding

TF2422 *Red Lion*

High Bridge House, *9 London Road, Spalding, Lincs, PE11 2TA.* Georgian House situated along riverside next to town centre. Friendly. **Open:** All year (not Xmas/New Year)
01775 725810 Mrs Marshall **D:** Fr £38.00–£40.00 **S:** Fr £19.00–£25.00 **Beds:** 2T 4S 6F **Baths:** 3 Sh (10)

88 Winsover Road, *Spalding, Lincs, PE11 1HA.* Victorian family house; very good area for fishing. **Open:** All year
01775 714465 Mrs Rae **D:** Fr £15.00 **S:** Fr £15.00 **Beds:** 2T 1S **Baths:** 1 Sh

Spilsby

TF4066

Hethersett House, *3 The Terrace, Spilsby, Lincolnshire, PE23 5JR.* Listed Georgian townhouse in small market town, antiques, log fires, walled garden, home-cooked food. **Open:** All year
01790 752666 C M Morgan **D:** Fr £17.50 **S:** Fr £17.50 **Beds:** 1T 2D **Baths:** 1 Sh (10)

Stainby

SK9022

The Old Blue Dog, *Colsterworth Road, Stainby, Grantham, Lincs, NG33 5QT.* Beautiful stone residence in lovely rural countryside. Leicestershire/Lincolnshire border. **Open:** All year
01476 861010 Mrs Jones **Fax: 01476 861645** *fiona@thinkingstyles.co.uk* **D:** Fr £25.00 **S:** Fr £25.00 **Beds:** 1F 1D (7)

Stamford

TF0207

Birch House, *4 Lonsdale Road, Stamford, Stamford, Lincs, PE9 2RW.* Established, well-presented large comfortable house on outskirts of Stamford. **Open:** All year (not Xmas/New Year)
01780 754876 (also fax) J Headland *birchhouse@hotmail.com* **D:** Fr £20.00–£25.00 **S:** Fr £20.00–£25.00 **Beds:** 1T 1D 2S **Baths:** 1 Sh (5) (3)

Stewton

TF3586

The Old Rectory, *Stewton, Louth, Lincs, LN11 8SF.* An old rectory in peaceful garden. Come and see! **Open:** All year
01507 328063 *ajp100@postmaster.co.uk* **D:** Fr £22.50 **S:** Fr £25.00 **Beds:** 2T 2D **Baths:** 3 En 1 Pr (6)

Sutton on Sea

TF5281 *Bacchus Hotel*

Walnut End, *53a Alford Road, Sutton on Sea, Mablethorpe, Lincs, LN12 2HQ.* Modern bungalow. Quiet location. Close to shops and Blue Flag Beach. **Open:** All year (not Xmas/New Year)
01507 443451 (also fax) Mrs Smith **D:** Fr £20.00–£24.00 **S:** Fr £24.00–£28.00 **Beds:** 3D (4)

Swaby

TF3876

Jasmine Cottage, *Church Lane, Swaby, Alford, Lincolnshire, LN13 0BQ.* Peaceful village, excellent accommodation in an Area of Outstanding Natural Beauty. **Open:** All year (not Xmas/New Year) **Grades:** ETC 4 Diamond
01507 480283 (also fax) P Fieldsend *fieldsend@btinternet.com* **D:** Fr £22.00–£24.00 **S:** Fr £24.00–£27.00 **Beds:** 2T **Baths:** 2 En (2)

Swineshead Bridge

TF2242

Boston Lodge, *Browns Drove, Swineshead Bridge, Boston, Lincs, PE20 3PX.* Ideally situated for touring the Fens and South Lincolnshire. **Open:** All year (not Xmas)
01205 820983 S Humphreys **Fax: 01205 820512** *info@bostonlodge.co.uk* www.bostonlodge.co.uk **D:** Fr £18.00 **S:** Fr £22.00 **Beds:** 2F 3D 2T 2S **Baths:** 9 En (12) 2

Tattershall

TF2158

Lodge House, *Market Place, Tattershall, Lincoln, LN4 4LQ.* Clean comfortable accommodation. Close RAF Coningsby. Walking, Cycling, Angling, Golf. **Open:** All year
01526 342575 (also fax) Mr Palethorpe **D:** Fr £15.00–£17.00 **S:** Fr £15.00–£20.00 **Beds:** 1D 1T 2S **Baths:** 2 En 2 Sh (3)

Ulceby (Immingham)

TA1014

Gillingham Court, *Spruce Lane, Ulceby, Lincolnshire, DN39 6UL.* Quiet extremely comfortable high class guest house situated 4 miles from Humberside International Airport. **Open:** All year (not Xmas)
01469 588427 Ms Connole www.awentsbury.co.uk **D:** Fr £20.00 **S:** Fr £23.00 **Beds:** 2T 2S **Baths:** 2 En 2 Pr (12)

West Barkwith

TF1580

The Manor House, *West Barkwith, Market Rasen, Lincs., LN8 5LF.* Beautiful C18th manor house overlooking extensive landscaped gardens and lake. **Open:** All year (not Xmas/New Year)
01673 858253 (also fax) J A HObbins **D:** Fr £22.50 **S:** Fr £25.00–£28.00 **Beds:** 1T 1D **Baths:** 2 En

West Rasen

TF0689

Chuck Hatch, *Kingerby Road, West Rasen, Market Rasen, Lincs, LN8 3NB.* Superb facilities, hospitality, quiet country lakeside garden location, coarse fishing. **Open:** All year
01673 842947 (also fax) *chuck.hatch@btinternet.com* **D:** Fr £22.50–£27.50 **S:** Fr £32.50–£40.00 **Beds:** 2D 2T **Baths:** 4 En (4)

Woodhall Spa

TF1963

Claremont Guest House, *9-11 Witham Road, Woodhall Spa, Lincs, LN10 6RW.* Friendly personal service in a traditional unspoilt Victorian guest house. **Open:** All year
01526 352000 Mrs Brennan **D:** Fr £15.00–£20.00 **S:** Fr £15.00–£20.00 **Beds:** 4F 2D 1T 3S **Baths:** 4 En 2 Sh (4)

The Vale, *Tor-o-Moor Road, Woodhall Spa, Lincolnshire, LN10 6SB.* Edwardian house, private lake. National Golf Centre, Aviation Heritage nearby. **Open:** All year **Grades:** AA 3 Diamond
01526 353022 Mr & Mrs Mills **Fax: 01526 354949** *thevale@amserve.net* **D:** Fr £16.00–£20.00 **S:** Fr £24.00–£27.00 **Beds:** 1F 1T 1D **Baths:** 2 En 1 Pr (3)

BEDROOMS
D = Double
T = Twin
S = Single
F = Family

Newlands Guest House, *56 Woodland Drive, Woodhall Spa, Lincs, LN10 6YG.* Luxury accommodation in quiet tree-lined lane. Very convenient for village and international golf courses. **Open:** All year (not Xmas)
01526 352881 **D:** Fr £20.00 **S:** Fr £25.00 **Beds:** 1D 2T **Baths:** 2 En 1 Pr (8)

Planning a longer stay? Always ask for any special rates

Wrawby

TA0308

Wish-u-well Guest House, *Brigg Road, Wrawby, Brigg, Lincolnshire, DN20 8RH.* Modern bungalow in extensive private grounds. Country pub short walk. **Open:** All year **Grades:** ETC 3 Diamond
01652 652301 (also fax) Mrs Jobson *wishwell@talk21.com* **D:** Fr £17.00–£25.00 **S:** Fr £18.00–£25.00 **Beds:** 2S 2D 2F 2T **Baths:** 8 En (10)

London

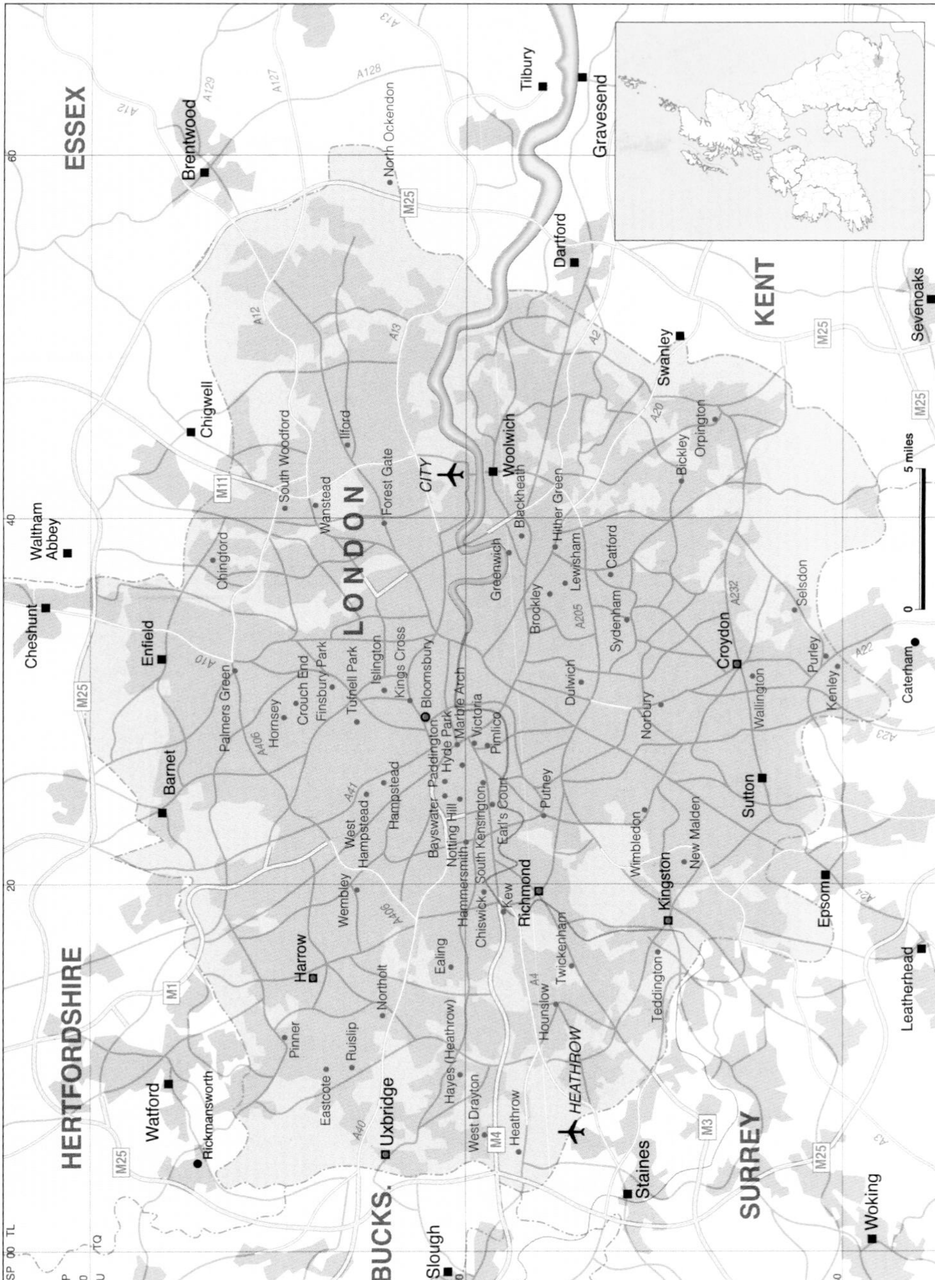
ESSEX
HERTFORDSHIRE
BUCKS.
SURREY
KENT
LONDON
Brentwood
Chigwell
Waltham Abbey
Cheshunt
Enfield
Barnet
Watford
Rickmansworth
Harrow
Uxbridge
Slough
Staines
Woking
Kingston
Richmond
Epsom
Leatherhead
Sutton
Croydon
Caterham
Sevenoaks
Swanley
Dartford
Gravesend
Tilbury
Woolwich
North Ockendon
South Woodford
Ilford
Forest Gate
Wanstead
Chingford
CITY
Blackheath
Greenwich
Hither Green
Lewisham
Catford
Brockley
Sydenham
Dulwich
Norbury
Bickley
Orpington
Selsdon
Purley
Kenley
Wallington
Palmers Green
Hornsey
Crouch End
Finsbury Park
Tufnell Park
Islington
Kings Cross
Bloomsbury
Marble Arch
Victoria
Pimlico
Paddington
Hyde Park
Bayswater
Notting Hill
Hampstead
West Hampstead
South Kensington
Earl's Court
Putney
Hammersmith
Chiswick
Kew
Wimbledon
New Malden
Wembley
Ealing
Northolt
Pinner
Ruislip
Eastcote
Hayes (Heathrow)
West Drayton
Heathrow
HEATHROW
Hounslow
Twickenham
Teddington
M25
M11
M1
M4
M3
A12
A13
A2
A20
A10
A406
A41
A40
A4
A205
A232
A22
A23
A24
A3
A127
A128
A129
0
5 miles

▼ CENTRAL LONDON

Bayswater
TQ2580

Caring Hotel, *24 Craven Hill Gardens, Bayswater, London, W2 3EA.* Comfortable budget B&B near Paddington. Hearty English breakfast. Great value. **Open:** All year **Grades:** ETC 2 Diamond
020 7262 8708 Mr Kalcov *caring@lineone.net*
D: Fr £22.00–£36.00 **S:** Fr £38.00–£50.00
Beds: 4F 11D 10T **Baths:** 12 En 4 Sh

Prince William Hotel, *42-44 Gloucester Terrace, Bayswater, London, W2 3DA.* Newly refurbished hotel, central location, close Hyde Park and shopping centres, cinemas, Soho. **Open:** All year
020 7724 7414 Fax: 020 7706 2411
princewilliamhotel@tiscali.co.uk **D:** Fr £27.50–£37.50 **S:** Fr £35.00–£55.00 **Beds:** 4F 15T 15D 13S **Baths:** 13 En cc

Bloomsbury
TQ3082

Garth Hotel, *69 Gower Street, Bloomsbury, London, WC1E 6HJ.* **Open:** All year
020 7636 5761 Mr Hoare *garth.hotel@virgin.net* www.garthhotel-london.com **D:** Fr £25.00–£40.00 **S:** Fr £35.00–£48.00 **Beds:** 5F 5T 4D 3S **Baths:** 8 En 4 Sh cc
The hotel, in the heart of London, has a friendly, peaceful atmosphere with clean comfortable rooms. All seventeen rooms have central heating, colour TV, tea/coffee facilities and direct-dial telephones. It has recently been refurbished to a very high standard.

Cosmo/ Bedford House Hotel, *27 Bloomsbury Square, Bloomsbury, London, WC1A 2QA.* Small family run C17th town house providing affordable accommodation, heart of London. **Open:** All year
020 7636 4661 Fax: 020 7636 0577
cosmo.bedford.hotel@dial.pipex.com
www.cosmobedfordhotel.com **D:** Fr £22.50–£28.00 **S:** Fr £28.00–£38.00 **Beds:** 3F 4T 5D 5S **Baths:** 4 En 4 Sh

Acorns Hotel, *42 Tavistock Place, Bloomsbury, London, WC1H 9RE.* Listed building near Russell Square, Euston Square. **Open:** All year
020 7837 3077 & 020 7837 2856 Mr Grover
D: Fr £19.00 **S:** Fr £25.00 **Beds:** 1F 6D 4T 1S
Baths: 4 Sh

Mentone Hotel, *54-55 Cartwright Gardens, Bloomsbury, London, WC1H 9EL.* Long a popular choice with tourists, due to pleasant surrounding and central location. **Open:** All year
020 7387 3927 Mr Tyner **Fax: 020 7388 4671**
mentonehotel@compuserve.com
www.mentonehotel.com **D:** Fr £74.00–£79.00
S: Fr £74.00–£79.00 **Beds:** 10F 10D 10T 10S
Baths: 40 En cc

Earl's Court
TQ2578

Windsor House, *12 Penywern Road, Earl's Court, London, SW5 9ST.* **Open:** All year
020 7373 9087 J Wardle **Fax: 020 7385 2417**
bookings@windsor-house-hotel.com
www.windsor-house-hotel.com **D:** Fr £20.00–£30.00 **S:** Fr £28.00–£46.00 **Beds:** 6F 5D 5T 2S **Baths:** 12 En 5 Pr 1 Sh
Central London: friendly, family-run B&B. Walk to Olympia/Earl's Court. Super-comfortable, super-affordable! Use of hotel kitchen for own meals! Single rooms £29–£46, Doubles £36–£65, 3/4/5 family studios £16–£26pppn. Great reductions for families with children. Group discounts.

Lord Jim Hotel, *23-25 Penywern Road, Earl's Court, London, SW5 9TT.* Attractive, well-appointed, moderately priced hotel close to city, airports, Earl's Court, Olympia. **Open:** All year
020 7370 6071 Mr Tayeb **Fax: 020 7373 8919**
ljh@lgh-hotels.com www.lgh-hotels.com **D:** Fr £15.00–£30.00 **S:** Fr £25.00–£50.00 **Beds:** 12F 10D 15T 8S **Baths:** 30 En 22 Sh cc

Rasool Court Hotel, *19-21 Penywern Road, Earl's Court, London, SW5 9TT.* The hotel is ideally located in fashionable Kensington close to the heart of the city. **Open:** All year
020 7373 8900 Mr Younis **Fax: 020 7244 6835**
rasool@rasool.demon.co.uk
www.rasoolcourthotel.com **D:** Fr £24.00–£28.00 **S:** Fr £33.00–£45.00 **Beds:** 8F 16D 8T 25S **Baths:** 38 En cc

Mowbray Court Hotel, *28-32 Penywern Road, Earl's Court, London, SW5 9SU.* Centrally located B&B hotel, 60% ensuite rooms, bar, lift, satellite TV. **Open:** All year
020 7370 2316 & 020 7370 3690 Fax: 020 7370 5693 *mowbraycrthot@hotmail.com*
www.m-c-hotel.mcmail.com **D:** Fr £28.00–£34.00 **S:** Fr £23.00–£26.00 **Beds:** 15F 18T 18D 25S **Baths:** 30 En 20 Pr 26 Sh cc

Ramsees Hotel, *32-36 Hogarth Road, Earl's Court, London, SW5 0PU.* The hotel is ideally located in fashionable Kensington close to the heart of the city. **Open:** All year
020 7370 1445 Mr Younis **Fax: 020 7244 6835**
ramsees@rasool.demon.co.uk
www.ramseeshotel.com **D:** Fr £24.00–£28.00
S: Fr £33.00–£42.00 **Beds:** 13F 27D 11T 15S
Baths: 56 En cc

Merlyn Court Hotel, *2 Barkston Gardens, Earl's Court, London, SW5 0EN.* This is a clean, friendly, good value hotel in a quiet garden square in Kensington. Family rooms are also available, very central with easy connections to all motorways and trains - direct links to Heathrow and Gatwick airports. **Open:** All year
020 7370 1640 Fax: 020 7370 4986 *london@merlyncourt.demon.co.uk* www.smoothhound.co.uk/hotels/merlyn.html **D:** Fr £28.00–£40.00 **S:** Fr £30.00–£60.00 **Beds:** 5F 4D 6T 4S **Baths:** 10 En 2 Pr cc

Oliver Plaza Hotel, *33 Trebovir Road, Earl's Court, London, SW5 0LR.* A nice value for money property in the heart of London. Good access to all public transport facilities and helpful staff to make your stay an enjoyable experience. Family run with emphasis on comfort. **Open:** All year
020 7373 7183 Fax: 020 7244 6021
oliverplaza@capricornhotels.co.uk
www.capricornhotels.co.uk **D:** Fr £20.00–£35.00 **S:** Fr £15.00–£25.00 **Beds:** 6F 20T 10D 2S **Baths:** 38 En (3) cc

Hyde Park
TQ2780

Classic Hotel, *92 Sussex Gardens, Hyde Park, London, W2 1UY.* Beautifully decorated, ideal for business, shopping, leisure. Paddington station close by. **Open:** All year
020 7706 7776 Mrs Hassan *classichotel@compuserve.com* **D:** Fr £30.00–£36.00 **S:** Fr £45.00–£52.00 **Beds:** 3F 3D 4T 2S (2) cc

Islington
TQ3184

Kandara Guest House, *68 Ockendon Road, Islington, London, N1 3NW.* **Open:** All year **Grades:** ETC 3 Diamond
020 7226 5721 Mrs Harmon **Fax: 020 7226 3379** *admin@kandara.co.uk* www.kandara.co.uk **D:** Fr £25.50–£32.00 **S:** Fr £41.00–£49.00
Beds: 3F 3D 1T 4S **Baths:** 5 Sh cc
Small family-run guest house near the Angel, Islington. Excellent public transport to the West End and City. All our bedrooms and bathrooms have recently been decorated and refitted to a high standard. Rooms are quiet, clean and comfortable.

Planning a longer stay? Always ask for any special rates

Kings Cross

TQ3083

A Fairway Hotel, *13-15 Argyle Street, Kings Cross, London, WC1H 8EJ.* Comfortable family-run B&B close to all major tourist attractions and shopping centres. **Open:** All year
020 7278 8682 (also fax) Mrs Caruana *fairway@cyberlobby.com* www.hotellondon.tv **D:** Fr £19.00–£22.00 **S:** Fr £28.00–£35.00 **Beds:** 7F 10T 10D 6S **Baths:** 3 En 8 Sh **cc**

Marble Arch

TQ2881

Lincoln House Hotel, *33 Gloucester Place, Marylebone, London, W1U 8HY.* **Open:** All year
020 7486 7630 Mr Shariff **Fax: 020 7486 0166** *reservations@lincoln-house-hotel.co.uk* www.lincoln-house-hotel.co.uk **D:** Fr £39.50–£44.50 **S:** Fr £59.00–£79.00 **Beds:** 3F 7D 3T 9S **Baths:** 22 En **cc**
Built in the days of George III, this hotel offers Georgian charms & character. Ensuite rooms with modern comforts. Competitively priced. Located in the heart of London's West End, next to Oxford Street and most famous shopping attractions, close to Theatreland.

Marble Arch Inn, *49-50 Upper Berkeley Street, Marble Arch, London, W1H 7PN.* Small, friendly, clean, comfortable hotel near Oxford Street and Hyde Park. **Open:** All year **Grades:** ETC 2 Diamond
020 7723 7888 Fax: 020 7723 6060 *sales@marblearch-inn.co.uk* www.marblearch-inn.co.uk **D:** Fr £32.50–£37.50 **S:** Fr £45.00–£75.00 **Beds:** 9F 7T 13D 2S **Baths:** 26 En 3 Sh **cc**

Notting Hill

TQ2480

Manor Court Hotel, *7 Clanricarde Gardens, Notting Hill Gate, London, W2 4JJ.* Only a few minutes away from Kensington and Hyde Park. **Open:** All year **Grades:** ETC 1 Diamond
020 7727 5407 & 020 7792 3361 Mr Zaidi **Fax: 020 7229 2875 D:** Fr £25.00–£30.00 **S:** Fr £35.00–£45.00 **Beds:** 3F 9D 3T 5S **Baths:** 17 En 3 Sh **cc**

Paddington

TQ2681

Europa House Hotel, *151 Sussex Gardens, Paddington, London, W2 2RY.* **Open:** All year **Grades:** ETC 2 Diamond
020 7723 7343 Fax: 020 7224 9331 *europahouse@enterprise.net* www.europahousehotel.com **D:** Fr £28.00–£33.00 **S:** Fr £32.00–£48.00 **Beds:** 2F 4T 10D 3S **Baths:** 19 En (1) **cc**
Family-run hotel, Central London, in a tree-lined avenue near Hyde Park and within walking distance of Oxford Street, Marble Arch. Reasonable prices, provide good value for money. Do give us a call and check our prices before trying anywhere else.

Albro House Hotel, *155 Sussex Gardens, Paddington, London, W2 2RY.* Near Hyde Park, public transport. Ideal location. Comfortable rooms, all with TV. **Open:** All year
020 7724 2931 G A Caruso **Fax: 020 7262 2278** *joe@albrohotel.freeserve.co.uk* **D:** Fr £28.00–£36.00 **S:** Fr £38.00–£56.00 **Beds:** 4F 6D 6T 2S **Baths:** 18 En (4) (1)

Ruddimans Hotel, *160 Sussex Gardens, Paddington, London, W2 1UD.* A warm and friendly atmosphere with a bit of a difference. **Open:** All year
020 7723 1026 Mr Charalambols **Fax: 020 7262 2983** *reservations@ruddimonshotel.co.uk* www.ruddimonshotel.co.uk **D:** Fr £25.00–£32.00 **S:** Fr £35.00–£48.00 **Beds:** 15F 15D 6T 5S **Baths:** 32 Pr 3 Sh **cc**

Barry House Hotel, *12 Sussex Place, Paddington, London, W2 2TP.* Family-run B&B offering warm and friendly welcome. Ensuite rooms with phones, TV, hairdryers, tea/coffee facilities. Convenient Madame Tussaud's, Buckingham Palace, Oxford St, Hyde Park and other sight-seeing places. Paddington Station 5 mins' walk. Heathrow Airport 15 mins by train. **Open:** All year
020 7723 7340 R S Bhasin **Fax: 020 7723 9775** *bh-hotel@bigfoot.com* Barryhouse.co.uk **D:** Fr £39.00–£43.00 **S:** Fr £38.00–£45.00 **Beds:** 4F 6T 4D 4S **Baths:** 14 En **cc**

RATES
D = Price range per person sharing in a double or twin room
S = Price range for a single room

Pimlico

TQ2978

Elizabeth House Hotel, *118 Warwick Way, Pimlico, London, SW1 4JB.* B&B close Victoria Station. Underground, BR, coach station. 24 hour reception. **Open:** All year
020 7630 0741 Mr Hussain **Fax: 020 7630 0740 D:** Fr £25.00–£30.00 **S:** Fr £30.00–£35.00 **Beds:** 8F 13T 3D 11S **Baths:** 10 En **cc**

South Kensington

TQ2678

Swiss House Hotel, *171 Old Brompton Road, South Kensington, London, SW5 0AN.* The hotel knows guests' priorities and aims to meet them all. **Open:** All year
020 7373 2769 Mr Vincenti **Fax: 020 7373 4983** *recep@swiss-hh.demon.co.uk* www.swiss-hh.demon.co.uk **D:** Fr £42.50–£49.50 **S:** Fr £48.00–£68.00 **Beds:** 8F 11D 10T 4S **Baths:** 1 Sh **cc**

Victoria

TQ2878

Edward House B&B, *5 St George's Drive, Victoria, London, SW1V 4DP.* **Open:** All year
020 7834 5207 Fax: 020 7976 5428 *edwardhouse@hotmail.com* **D:** Fr £30.00–£35.00 **S:** Fr £37.50–£50.00 **Beds:** 21F 4D 8T **Baths:** 15 En 3 Pr 4 Sh
Conveniently situated, walking distance famous landmarks - Buckingham Palace, Westminster Abbey, Houses of Parliament, Trafalgar Square, Piccadilly Circus, Leicester Square, many more. Victoria rail, bus, tube and Victoria Coach Station, serving London and the whole country, just a few minutes away.

Marne Hotel, *34 Belgrave Road, Victoria, London, SW1V 1RG.* Comfortable family-run B&B in the heart of London. **Open:** All year
020 7834 5195 & 07771 950095 Mr Montagnani **Fax: 020 7976 6180** *marnehotel@34belgraveroad.fsnet.co.uk* www.freepages.co.uk/marne_hotel **D:** Fr £21.00–£35.00 **S:** Fr £35.00–£55.00 **Beds:** 3F 5D 1T 3S **Baths:** 8 En 1 Sh **cc**

BATHROOMS
En = Ensuite
Pr = Private
Sh = Shared

Alexander House Hotel, *32 Hugh Street, Victoria, London, SW1V 1RT.* **Open:** All year
020 7834 5320 *stay@alexanderhousehotel.co.uk* www.alexanderhousehotel.co.uk **D:** Fr £20.00–£25.00 **S:** Fr £30.00–£45.00 **Beds:** 3F 3T 3D 2S **Baths:** 7 En 3 Sh cc
The Alexander House Hotel is a family-run business where personal care and attention are paramount. Its proximity to various transport systems and the delights of London's main tourist attractions will help to make your stay both enjoyable and convenient.

Stanley House Hotel, *19-21 Belgrave Road, Victoria, London, SW1V 1RB.* Stanley House Hotel, central location in elegant Belgravia, 4/5 mins' walk Victoria Station. **Open:** All year
020 7834 5042 Mr Shah **Fax: 020 7834 8439** *cmahotel@aol.com* www.affordablehotel.com
D: Fr £25.00–£31.00 **S:** Fr £42.00–£52.00 **Beds:** 11F 25D 8T **Baths:** 11 En 26 Pr 6 Sh cc

Dover Hotel, *44 Belgrave Road, Victoria, London, SW1V 1RG.* Friendly, clean, comfortable hotel in Victoria. Near Gatwick Express, Buckingham Palace. **Open:** All year **Grades:** ETC 2 Diamond
020 7821 9085 Fax: 020 7834 6425 *reception@dover-hotel.co.uk* www.dover-hotel.co.uk **D:** Fr £25.00–£30.00 **S:** Fr £40.00–£50.00 **Beds:** 8F 7T 14D 4S **Baths:** 29 En 4 Sh cc

St George's Hotel, *25 Belgrave Road, Victoria, London, SW1V 1RB.* Comfortable, clean, spacious bright rooms. Handy for Gatwick and Heathrow. Great central location. **Open:** All year
020 7828 2061 & 020 7828 3605 Mr Zaidi **Fax: 020 7834 8439** *cmahotel@aol.com* www.londonbudgethotels.co.uk **D:** Fr £25.00–£30.00 **S:** Fr £30.00–£45.00 **Beds:** 4D 4T 2F 1S **Baths:** 3 En 8 Pr

Holly House Hotel, *20 Hugh Street, Victoria, London, SW1V 1RP.* Bed and breakfast in the heart of London. Affordable accommodation perfectly situated.
Open: All year
020 7834 5671 Mr Jessa **Fax: 020 7233 5154** *hhhotel@ukgateway.net* www.hollyhousehotel.co.uk **D:** Fr £40.00–£50.00 **S:** Fr £30.00–£45.00 **Beds:** 2F 10D 7T 6S **Baths:** 11 En 7 Sh cc

Melita House Hotel, *35 Charlwood Street, Victoria, London, SW1V 2DU.* Excellent location and value, extensive facilities for category, recommended. **Open:** All year
020 7828 0471 Mr Gabrielle **Fax: 020 7932 0988** *reserve@melita.co.uk* www.melitahotel.com **D:** Fr £42.50–£50.00 **S:** Fr £55.00–£70.00 **Beds:** 4F 6T 10D **Baths:** 22 En cc

Alexander Hotel, *13 Belgrave Road, Victoria, London, SW1V 1RB.* Clean, comfortable, affordable family-run B&B situated in the centre of London. **Open:** All year (not Xmas)
020 7834 9738 Mr Montagnani **Fax: 020 7630 9630** www.alexanderhotel.co.uk **D:** Fr £22.50–£65.00 **S:** Fr £30.00–£60.00 **Beds:** 3F 7D 2T 1S **Baths:** 13 En cc

Collin House, *104 Ebury Street, Victoria, London, SW1W 9QD.* Centrally located providing an ideal base for visiting London's many attractions. **Open:** All year (not Xmas/New Year)
020 7730 8031 (also fax) Mr Thomas **D:** Fr £32.50–£40.00 **S:** Fr £52.00–£60.00 **Beds:** 1F 5D 4T 3S **Baths:** 8 En 3 Sh

▼ EAST LONDON

Forest Gate

TQ4085

Newham Hotel, *349-353 Romford Road, London, E7 8AA.* **Open:** All year
020 8534 8400 (also fax) **D:** Fr £21.00–£25.00 **S:** Fr £25.00–£48.00 **Beds:** 1F 13T 4D 8S **Baths:** 17 En 4 Sh (30) cc
East London's best value. Happily situated on the A118. 1 mile from Stratford Tube station, 2 miles from Ilford, the North Circular Road and the M11. Ideal for Docklands, the City and West End. 24-hour reception; secure off-street parking; comfortable rooms with direct dial phone, etc.

Grangewood Lodge Hotel, *104 Clova Road, Forest Gate, London, E7 9AF.* 5-minute walk Forest Gate station for easy access central London & Docklands. **Open:** All year
020 8534 0637 Mr Downing **Fax: 020 8503 0941** *grangewoodlodgehotel@talk21.com* www.grangewoodlodgehotel.co.uk **D:** Fr £18.00–£22.00 **S:** Fr £23.00–£40.00 **Beds:** 4F 1D 4T 9S **Baths:** 2 En 4 Sh (10) (2) cc

All details shown are as supplied by B&B owners in Autumn 2002

Ilford

TQ4486

Woodville Guest House, *10/12 Argyle Road, Ilford, Essex, IG1 3BQ.* Private family-run business for 25 years. Extremely friendly, minutes from shops and trains. **Open:** All year (not Xmas/New Year)
020 8478 3779 Mrs Murray **Fax: 020 8478 6282** *info@cassewoodville-guesthouse.co.uk* www.cassewoodville-guesthouse.co.uk **D:** Fr £20.00–£30.00 **S:** Fr £30.00–£45.00 **Beds:** 3F 6T 4D 3S **Baths:** 5 En 2 Pr 5 Sh (12)

North Ockendon

TQ5984 Old White Horse

Corner Farm, *Fen Lane, North Ockendon, Upminster, Essex, RM14 3RB.* Detached bungalow in rural setting. 4 Miles Upminster station. Breakfast served in conservatory. **Open:** All year (not Xmas/New Year)
01708 851310 Fax: 01708 852025 *corner.farm@virgin.net* **D:** Fr £17.50–£18.75 **S:** Fr £25.00–£35.00 **Beds:** 1F 1T 2S **Baths:** 1 En 1 Sh (8) cc

South Woodford

TQ4090

Grove Hill Hotel, *Grove Hill, South Woodford, London, E18 2JG.* Quiet, central location. Good breakfast. **Open:** All year (not Xmas/New Year)
020 8989 3344 Mr Mamelok **Fax: 0208 530 5286** **D:** Fr £53.00–£61.00 **S:** Fr £33.00–£45.00 **Beds:** 3F 4T 13D 8S **Baths:** 11 En 11 Pr 3 Sh (12) cc

Wanstead

TQ4088

The Fosters, *71 Grosvenor Road, Wanstead, London, E11 2ES.* Edwardian house; friendly welcome, excellent accommodation. Unrestricted parking/close Tube. **Open:** All year (not Xmas)
020 8530 6970 (also fax) Mrs Foster *fosters71@aol.com* **D:** Fr £22.00–£24.00 **S:** Fr £40.00–£45.00 **Beds:** 1F 1D 1T **Baths:** 2 En 1 Sh cc

Sunningdale Guest House, *35 Lonsdale Road, Wanstead, London, E11 2PH.* Friendly, family-run hotel. Close Green Belt. Five mins' walk direct line to central London. **Open:** All year
020 8989 3435 I A Novlis *irenenovlis@lineone.net* **D:** Fr £17.50–£20.00 **S:** Fr £23.00–£25.00 **Beds:** 2F 1T 6D 3S (4)

▼ NORTH LONDON

Chingford

TQ3894

22 Castle Avenue, *London, E4 9QD.* High quality accommodation, convenient for transport to centre & countryside. **Open:** All year
020 8527 7756 Ms Phare *phare@btinternet.com* www.btinternet.com/~budgetlondon **D:** Fr £25.00 **S:** Fr £30.00 **Beds:** 2T 2D **Baths:** 2 Sh (1) **cc**

Crouch End

TQ3089

22 Trinder Road, *(off Shaftesbury Road), Crouch Hill, London, N19 4QU.* Quiet, rustic, terraced house near lively bars, cafes, leafy area. Longer stays negotiated. **Open:** All year
020 7686 4073 Ms Shrive **D:** Fr £17.50–£20.00 **S:** Fr £20.00–£25.00 **Beds:** 2D 1S **Baths:** 2 Sh

Mount View, *31 Mount View Road, Crouch End, London, N4 4SS.* Near Finsbury Park Underground - Piccadilly and Victoria lines. **Open:** All year
020 8340 9222 O Hendrickx *mountviewbb@aol.com* www.mountviewguesthouse.com **D:** Fr £25.00–£35.00 **S:** Fr £40.00–£60.00 **Beds:** 2D 1T **Baths:** 1 En **cc**

Finsbury Park

TQ3086

Spring Park Hotel, *400 Seven Sisters Road, Manor House, London, N4 2LX.* Edwardian villa style hotel, overlooking scenic Finsbury Park. **Open:** All year
Grades: ETC 2 Diamond
020 8800 6030 Fax: 020 8802 5652 *sphotel400@aol.com* www.springparkhotel.co.uk **D:** Fr £20.00–£40.00 **S:** Fr £30.00–£50.00 **Beds:** 3F 21T 22D 4S **Baths:** 38 En 6 Sh (50) **cc**

Hampstead

TQ2685

Dillons Hotel, *21 Belsize Park, Hampstead, London, NW3 4DU.* Handy for central London - budget B&B between Hampstead and Camden. **Open:** All year
Grades: ETC 2 Diamond
020 7794 3360 Mr Dillon **Fax: 020 7431 7900** *desk@dillonshotel.com* www.dillonshotel.com **D:** Fr £24.00–£30.00 **S:** Fr £32.00–£44.00 **Beds:** 3F 5D 4T 1S **Baths:** 8 En 3 Sh **cc**

Hornsey

TQ3088

White Lodge, *1 Church Lane, Hornsey, London, N8 7BU.* **Open:** All year **Grades:** ETC 3 Diamond
020 8348 9765 Mrs Neocleous **Fax: 020 8340 7851 D:** Fr £30.00 **S:** Fr £40.00–£46.00 **Beds:** 3F 4T 5D 4S **Baths:** 8 En 8 Pr 3 Sh **cc**
Family-run guest house, located in North London close to train, tube or bus to all parts of London. Our motto: 'Cleanliness & friendliness'. A warm welcome for all our guests, home from home comfort.

Palmers Green

TQ3093

71 Berkshire Gardens, *Palmers Green, London, N13 6AA.* Private house with garden. **Open:** All year
020 8888 5573 Mr Clark **D:** Fr £18.00–£22.00 **S:** Fr £18.00–£22.00 **Beds:** 1T 1D 1S **Baths:** 1 Sh

Tufnell Park

TQ2986

Five Kings Guest House, *59 Anson Road, Tufnell Park, London, N7 0AR.* Five Kings is a family-run guest house in a quiet residential area. Only 15 minutes to Central London and tourist attractions. Camden Lock, London Zoo, Kings Cross, St Pancras station are only 2 miles away. No parking restrictions in Anson Road. **Open:** All year
020 7607 3996 Mr Poulacheris **Fax: 020 7609 5554 D:** Fr £19.00 **S:** Fr £24.00–£28.00 **Beds:** 4F 3D 3T 6S **Baths:** 16 En 7 Pr 3 Sh (4) **cc**

West Hampstead

TQ2585

Charlotte Guest House, *195-197 Sumatra Road, West Hampstead, London, NW6 1PF.* Central London. Accessible transport. Free London travel card for 7 nights' stay. **Open:** All year
020 7794 6476 L Koch **Fax: 020 7431 3584** *enquiries@charlotteguesthouse.co.uk* www.charlotteguesthouse.co.uk **D:** Fr £23.00–£28.00 **S:** Fr £35.00–£45.00 **Beds:** 2F 12T 12D 12S **Baths:** 20 En 6 Sh **cc**

▼ SOUTH LONDON

Bickley

TQ4269

Glendevon House Hotel, *80 Southborough Road, Bickley, Bromley, Kent, BR1 2EN.* 3 Crown hotel near Bromley town centre. All rooms ensuite. **Open:** All year
020 8467 2183 D: Fr £34.00 **S:** Fr £35.00–£46.00 **Beds:** 4T 4D 2S 2F **Baths:** 12 En 1 Pr (2) (8) **cc**

Blackheath

TQ3976

The Grovers, *96 Merriman Road, Blackheath, London, SE3 8RZ.* High quality accommodation in family home hotel for Greenwich & Central London. **Open:** All year **Grades:** ETC 3 Diamond
020 8488 7719 (also fax) Mr & Mrs Grover **D:** Fr £25.00 **S:** Fr £25.00 **Beds:** 2T 1S **Baths:** 1 Sh (2) (3)

29 Tellson Avenue, *Blackheath, London, SE18 4PD.* Situated in quiet tree lined avenue opposite bus stop. Leisure and shopping centres nearby. **Open:** All year (not Xmas/ New Year)
020 8856 9213 P T Nagalingham *ptndedicatedservices@compuserve.com* **S:** Fr £21.00 **Beds:** 2S **Baths:** 1 Sh (3)

Numbernine Blackheath Ltd., *9 Charlton Road, Blackheath, London, SE3 7EU.* Number Nine is a friendly, non-smoking guest house located at The Royal Standard, within twenty minutes walking distance of the historic town of Greenwich. This recently fully refurbished Victorian guest house provides warm, comfortable, safe, fully Fire Certificated surroundings. Individual Sky TV. Free video library. **Open:** All year
020 8858 4175 & 020 8293 0351 Fax: 020 8858 4175 *derek@numbernineblackheath.com* www.numbernineblackheath.com **D:** Fr £37.50 **S:** Fr £45.00 **Beds:** 1F 4D **Baths:** 5 Pr (5) (4) **cc**

Brockley

TQ3674

Geoffrey Road B & B, *66 Geoffrey Road, Brockley, London, SE4 1NT.* Friendly and relaxed Victorian family home in Brockley conservation area. **Open:** All year
020 8691 3887 (also fax) Ms Dechamps *b&bgeoffrey@woodin.u-net.com* **D:** Fr £20.00–£22.50 **S:** Fr £20.00–£25.00 **Beds:** 1T **Baths:** 1 Sh

Catford

TQ3873

Hazeldene Bed & Breakfast, *75 Brownhill Road (South Circular Road), Catford, London, SE6 2HF.* Traditional English B&B, Victorian house. Greenwich 3 miles/ Zone 3. **Open:** All year
020 8697 2436 Fax: 020 8473 9601 *hazeldene@zoo.co.uk* **D:** Fr £19.00–£22.50 **S:** Fr £20.00–£35.00 **Beds:** 1F 1D 2T 2S **Baths:** 1 En 2 Sh (8) (1)

All details shown are as supplied by B&B owners in Autumn 2002

Croydon
TQ3265

Croydon Friendly Guest House, *16 St Peters Road, Croydon, CR0 1HD.* Large character full detached house enjoying a warm friendly atmosphere. **Open:** All year
020 8680 4428 Mr Hasan **D:** Fr £20.00–£30.00 **S:** Fr £25.00–£30.00 **Beds:** 1T 5S **Baths:** 2 En 2 Sh (1) (6)

Dulwich
TQ3472

Diana Hotel, *88 Thurlow Park Road, West Dulwich, London, SE21 8HY.* Comfortable hotel near Dulwich Village, a pleasant London suburb. **Open:** All year
020 8670 3250 Fax: 020 8761 8300 *dihotel@aol.com* www.dianahotel.com **D:** Fr £25.00–£30.00 **S:** Fr £30.00–£60.00 **Beds:** 1F 13D/T 2S **Baths:** 7 En 2 Sh

Greenwich
TQ3977

78 Vanbrugh Park, Blackheath, *Greenwich, London, SE3 7JQ.* **Open:** All year
020 8858 0338 Mrs Mattey **D:** Fr £25.00 **S:** Fr £25.00 **Beds:** 1F 2T **Baths:** 1 En 1 Pr (3)
Lovely Victorian house near Greenwich Park and Heath. Close to Blackwall tunnel, trains and buses. Suit holidaymakers, weekly workers and weekenders. Rooms organised as flats with living-kitchen areas with cooker/fridge. Bedrooms overlook beautiful south-facing garden.

Dover House, *155 Shooters Hill, Greenwich, London, SE18 3HP.* Victorian family house opposite famous Oxleas Wood, 8 miles Central London. Warm welcome awaits. **Open:** All year (not Xmas)
020 8856 9892 (also fax) Mrs Araniello *joan.araniello@lineone.net* **D:** Fr £20.00–£25.00 **S:** Fr £25.00 **Beds:** 2T 1S 1F **Baths:** 1 Sh

Greenwich Parkhouse Hotel, *1 & 2 Nevada Street, Greenwich, London, SE10 9JL.* Small hotel, beautifully situated within World Heritage site by gates of Royal Greenwich Park. **Open:** All year
020 8305 1478 Mrs Bryan **D:** Fr £20.00–£25.00 **S:** Fr £33.00 **Beds:** 21F **Baths:** 2 En 1 Pr 2 Sh (8)

Hither Green
TQ3974

13 Wellmeadow Road, *Hither Green, London, SE13 6SY.* 3 mins BR Station, 6 mins A2 to Dover or M25. **Open:** All year
020 8697 1398 Mrs Noonan **Fax: 020 8 697 1398 D:** Fr £22.00 **S:** Fr £25.00 **Beds:** 2F 2D **Baths:** 2 Sh (2)

Kenley
TQ3259

Appledore, *6 Betula Close, Kenley, Surrey, CR8 5ET.* Comfortable detached house in quiet wooded location. Near M25, Gatwick. **Open:** All year
020 8668 4631 (also fax) Mrs Wilmshurst **D:** Fr £22.00–£24.00 **S:** Fr £25.00 **Beds:** 1D 1T 1S **Baths:** 1 Sh (12) (2)

Kingston
TQ1869

40 The Bittoms, *Kingston, KT1 2AP.* Very close to town centre & River Thames. Quiet location. **Open:** All year
020 8541 3171 Mrs Lefebvre **D:** Fr £22.50–£27.50 **S:** Fr £25.00–£35.00 **Beds:** 1T 1D 1S **Baths:** 1 Sh (4)

Lewisham
TQ3875

8 Yeats Close, Eliot Park, *Lewisham, London, SE13 7ET.* **Open:** All year **Grades:** ETC 2 Diamond
020 8318 3421 (also fax) Ms Hutton **D:** Fr £22.50–£25.00 **S:** Fr £25.00–£28.00 **Beds:** 1D 1T 1S **Baths:** 1 Sh
Homely base in quiet tree-lined road convenient for Greenwich, Docklands and Central London, yet only 5 mins from the Heath. Easy access to all bus, train and DLR connections taking you to Central London in 15 mins.

Manna House, *320 Hither Green Lane, Lewisham, London, SE13 6TS.* Family home, warm welcome, 20 mins train to Central London. **Open:** All year **Grades:** ETC 3 Diamond
020 8461 5984 Mrs Rawlins **Fax: 020 8695 5316** *mannahouse@aol.com* **D:** Fr £22.00–£25.00 **S:** Fr £25.00–£35.00 **Beds:** 1F 1D 1S **Baths:** 2 Sh (5) (2) **cc**

Family Stay, *2 Crofton Gateway, Lewisham, London, SE4 2DL.* Easy transport access. South East London, connected train. Buses accessible. **Open:** All year
020 8694 0011 D: Fr £15.00 **S:** Fr £15.00 **Beds:** 1D 1S **Baths:** 1 Sh (3)

All details shown are as supplied by B&B owners in Autumn 2002

New Malden
TQ2167

30 Presburg Road, *New Malden, Surrey, KT3 5AH.* Easy 20-min rail journey Central London or Hampton Court; 10 mins Kingston-upon-Thames, Wimbledon. **Open:** All year (not Xmas)
020 8949 4910 Mr & Mrs Evans **D:** Fr £22.50–£25.00 **S:** Fr £25.00–£30.00 **Beds:** 1F 1D 1S **Baths:** 2 Sh (6) (1)

Norbury
TQ3169

The Konyots, *95 Pollards Hill South, Norbury, London, SW16 4LS.* Located in a quiet residential area with a park nearby. **Open:** All year
020 8764 0075 Mrs Konyot **D:** Fr £15.00 **S:** Fr £15.00 **Beds:** 1F 1S **Baths:** 1 Sh (1)

Orpington
TQ4565

20 The Avenue, *St Pauls Cray, Orpington, Kent, BR5 3DL.* Detached family house in cul-de-sac. Excellent full English breakfast. Good road and rail connections. **Open:** All year (not Xmas/New Year)
020 8300 1040 (also fax) Mrs Tomkins *tomkinsbandb@20theavenue.freeserve.co.uk* **D:** Fr £21.00 **S:** Fr £21.00–£25.00 **Beds:** 1D 1T 1S **Baths:** 1 Sh (1)

Purley
TQ3161

The Nook, *12 Grasmere Road, Purley, Surrey, CR8 1DU.* Edwardian house, near to Purley station, small house with personal attention. **Open:** Jan to Dec
020 8660 1742 Mrs Andrews **D:** Fr £18.00–£20.00 **S:** Fr £18.00–£20.00 **Beds:** 1D 2S **Baths:** 1 Sh (5)

Putney
TQ2374

One Fanthorpe Street, *Putney, London, SW15 1DZ.* **Open:** All year (not Xmas)
020 8785 7609 Mr & Mrs Taylor **Fax: 020 8789 5584** *bbputney@btinternet.com* www.bbputney.btinternet.co.uk **D:** Fr £30.00 **S:** Fr £40.00 **Beds:** 1D 1T **Baths:** 1 En 1 Sh
A warm welcome awaits you to our comfortable family home, which is close to Thames, and convenient for bus, Underground and BR Mainline. No smoking. Evening meals by arrangement. Bed and excellent Continental breakfast £30–£40 per person per night.

Selsdon

TQ3461

Owlets, *112 Arundel Avenue, Selsdon, Croydon, Surrey, CR2 8BH.* Situated within easy reach of Croydon, Purley, London, Gatwick Airport. **Open:** All year (not Xmas/New Year) **020 8657 5213 & 07946 282562 (M) Fax: 020 8657 5213 D:** Fr £20.00–£25.00 **S:** Fr £25.00–£30.00 **Beds:** 3T **Baths:** 1 Sh

Sydenham

TQ3471

97 Wiverton Road, *Sydenham, London, SE26 5JB.* We offer bed and breakfast accommodation in our charming Victorian home in South-East London. **Open:** All year (not Xmas/New Year) **020 8778 8101** Dr & Mrs Tegner *henrytegner@sydenham2.demon.co.uk* www.sydenham2.demon.co.uk/b-and-b.htm **D:** Fr £30.00–£40.00 **S:** Fr £30.00–£40.00 **Beds:** 2T **Baths:** 1 Pr 1 Sh

Wallington

TQ2864

17 Osmond Gardens, *Wallington, Surrey, SM6 8SX.* Quiet road, near station - London Bridge/Victoria 33 mins direct. **Open:** All year (not Xmas/New Year) **020 8647 1943** Mrs Dixon **Fax: 020 8773 0617** *dixonguest@jennifer22.fsnet.co.uk* **D:** Fr £25.00–£29.00 **S:** Fr £50.00–£60.00 **Beds:** 1F 1D **Baths:** 1 En 1 Sh (1)

Wimbledon

TQ2471

22 Mayfield Road, *Wimbledon, London, SW19 3NF.* Artist's detached house. Warm welcome. Near BR, Underground, A3 and M25. **Open:** All year **020 8543 2607 (also fax)** Mr & Mrs Daglish **D:** Fr £25.00–£28.00 **S:** Fr £28.00–£30.00 **Beds:** 1D 1T **Baths:** 1 En 1 Pr (2)

131 Queens Road, *London, SW19 8NS.* Family Edwardian house, ten minutes from Underground/railway. Warm welcome. **Open:** All year **020 8542 9835** Mrs Crundall *teresacrundall@waitrose.com* **D:** Fr £23.00–£25.00 **S:** Fr £25.00–£26.00 **Beds:** 1T 1D **Baths:** 1 En 1 Sh

▼ WEST LONDON

Chiswick

TQ2078

Fouberts Hotel, *162-166 Chiswick High Road, Chiswick, London, W4 1PR.* Family-run hotel, continental atmosphere. Ice-cream parlour, café, restaurant & bar. **Open:** All year **020 8994 5202 & 020 8995 6743** Mr Lodico **D:** Fr £32.50–£35.00 **S:** Fr £45.00–£50.00 **Beds:** 6F 6D 4T 16S **Baths:** 32 En cc

Ealing

TQ1780

68 Cleveland Road, *Ealing, London, W13 8AJ.* **Open:** All year **020 8991 5142 (also fax)** Mrs McHugh **D:** Fr £25.00–£27.50 **S:** Fr £30.00–£35.00 **Beds:** 2F 1D 1T 1S **Baths:** 1 En 2 Pr 1 Sh (4) (4)
Large luxury house overlooking parkland, 30 mins to Central London or Heathrow.

Abbey Lodge Hotel, *51 Grange Park, Ealing, London, W5 3PR.* Halfway between Heathrow and Central London. Home from home atmosphere. **Open:** All year (not Xmas) **020 8567 7914** Mrs Grindrod **Fax: 020 8579 5350** *enquiries@londonlodgehotels.com* www.londonlodgehotels.com **D:** Fr £28.50 **S:** Fr £45.00 **Beds:** 3F 3D 1T 9S **Baths:** 16 En cc

Grange Lodge Hotel, *48/50 Grange Road, Ealing, London, W5 5BX.* Home away from home - close to 3 tube stations and lines. **Open:** All year (not Xmas) **Grades:** ETC 3 Diamond **020 8567 1049 Fax: 020 8579 5360** *enquiries@londonlodgehotels.com* www.londonlodgehotels.com **D:** Fr £24.00–£28.50 **S:** Fr £35.00–£45.00 **Beds:** 2F 3D 2T 7S **Baths:** 9 En 5 Sh (7) cc

4 Carlton Gardens, *Ealing, London, W5 2AN.* Lovely Victorian house, quiet conservation area. Easy access central London, theatres, tourist attractions. **Open:** All year (not Xmas/New Year) **020 8997 7712** Mrs Lynch **Fax: 020 8998 2590** *acc@bblondon.demon.co.uk* **D:** Fr £22.50 **S:** Fr £35.00 **Beds:** 1T 2D **Baths:** 2 Pr 1 Sh (10)

Eastcote

TQ1088

7 Eastfields, *Eastcote, Pinner, HA5 2SR.* Access to places of interest, many excellent restaurants, transport nearby. **Open:** All year (not Xmas) **020 8429 1746** Mrs Mash **D:** Fr £23.00 **S:** Fr £23.00 **Beds:** 2T **Baths:** 1 Sh

Hammersmith

TQ2279

67 Rannoch Road, *Hammersmith, London, W6 9SS.* **Open:** All year **020 7385 4904** Mr & Mrs Armanios **Fax: 020 7610 3235** www.thewaytostay.co.uk **D:** Fr £24.00 **S:** Fr £34.00 **Beds:** 1F 1D 1T **Baths:** 1 Sh
Comfortable, central, Edwardian family home. Quiet, close river, pubs, restaurants. Great base for sightseeing/courses/business. Excellent transport facilities. Direct lines to theatres, shopping, Harrods, museums, Albert Hall, Earls Court/Olympia exhibitions; Heathrow, Gatwick (Victoria), Eurostar. Children's reductions. Continental breakfast.

Harrow

TQ1488

Crescent Hotel, *58-60 Welldon Crescent, Harrow, Middx, HA1 1QR.* **Open:** All year **020 8863 5491** Mr Jivraj **Fax: 020 8427 5965** *jivraj@crsnthtl.demon.co.uk* www.crsnthtl.demon.co.uk **D:** Fr £27.50–£32.50 **S:** Fr £40.00–£50.00 **Beds:** 2F 2D 4T 13S **Baths:** 18 En 3 Sh (7) cc
Modern, friendly hotel in quiet crescent in heart of Harrow, yet only a short drive to Wembley and the West End with Heathrow easily accessible. 21 rooms all ensuite, comfortable and well furnished, with colour TV, satellite, fridge, telephone and tea/coffee making facilities.

Harrow Guest House, *48 Butler Road, Harrow, Middx, HA1 4DR.* Small town centre B&B near all travel facilities, pubs, restaurants, shops, hospitals and Harrow School. In quiet residential road. Non-smoking. **Open:** All year **020 8621 9090** Mrs Chaplin **D:** Fr £18.50 **S:** Fr £25.00 **Beds:** 1T 1D 2S **Baths:** 2 Sh (6)

Hayes (Heathrow)

TQ0880 *Grapes, Crown*

Balmoral Guest House, *262 Balmoral Drive, Hayes, Middx, UB4 8DQ.* Newly decorated family home, 10 mins from Heathrow. Use of kitchen. **Open:** All year
020 8848 3882 & 07973 875312 (M) Ms Dodder *mdodder@hotmail.com* **D:** Fr £35.00–£40.00 **S:** Fr £20.00–£30.00 **Beds:** 2T 2D 2S **Baths:** 1 En (4)

Heathrow

TQ0980

Shepiston Lodge, *31 Shepiston Lane, Heathrow, Middx, UB3 1LJ.* Character house near Heathrow. Comfortable & friendly. **Open:** All year
020 8573 0266 Mr Dhawan **Fax: 020 8569 2536** *shepistonlodge@aol.com* **D:** Fr £30.00 **S:** Fr £45.00 **Beds:** 2F 11T 3D 6S **Baths:** 22 En cc

Hounslow

TQ1475

Lampton Guest House, *47 Lampton Road, Hounslow, Middx, TW3 1JG.* Ideal for Heathrow airport and central London, stopover, superbly located. **Open:** All year
020 8570 0056 Fax: 020 8570 1220 *ppadda@talk21.com* www.paddahotels.com **D:** Fr £25.00–£30.00 **S:** Fr £40.00–£48.00 **Beds:** 4F 4D 4T 8S **Baths:** 20 En 1 Pr 1 Sh (3) (10) cc

Kew

TQ1876

34 Forest Road, *Kew, Richmond, Surrey, TW9 3BZ.* **Open:** All year
020 8332 6289 (also fax) Mrs Royle *ShirleyRoyle2@activemail.co.uk* **D:** Fr £21.00–£23.00 **S:** Fr £25.00–£30.00 **Beds:** 1F 1D 1T **Baths:** 1 Sh (12)
A comfortable Edwardian era family home. 5 mins' walk from Kew Gardens station, 35 mins to Westminster. 5 mins to Richmond, Kew Botanical Gardens and Public Records Office. Pleasant walks along Thames river bank. Good selection of pubs and restaurants nearby.

58 Ennerdale Road, *Kew Gardens, Richmond, Surrey, TW9 2DL.* **Open:** All year
020 8948 0021 W O'Sullivan **D:** Fr £35.00 **S:** Fr £45.00 **Beds:** 1D **Baths:** 1 Pr
West London - Kew. Select B&B in attractive town house. Lovely near rural surroundings yet only 7 mins walk to tube, with central London 20 mins away. Botanic Gardens & Public Records Office 10 mins' walk.

Melbury, *33 Marksbury Avenue, Kew, Richmond, Surrey, TW9 4JE.* Friendly and welcoming, refurbished private home, close to Richmond and Kew Gardens Underground. **Open:** All year
020 8876 3930 (also fax) Mrs Allen **D:** Fr £27.50–£35.00 **S:** Fr £32.00–£38.00 **Beds:** 1T 1D/S 1F **Baths:** 2 En 1 Sh (2) (1)

1 Chelwood Gardens, *Kew, Richmond, Surrey, TW9 4JG.* Situated in quiet cul-de-sac. Friendly house near Kew Gardens Station. **Open:** All year
020 8876 8733 L J Gray **Fax: 020 8255 0171** *MrsLJGray@aol.com* **D:** Fr £30.00–£32.00 **S:** Fr £34.00–£36.00 **Beds:** 2T 2S **Baths:** 2 Sh (5)

179 Mortlake Road, *Kew, Richmond, Surrey, TW9 4AW.* Georgian house close to Kew Gardens, PRO and Underground. **Open:** All year **Grades:** ETC 3 Diamond
020 8876 0584 (also fax) Mrs Butt **D:** Fr £25.00 **S:** Fr £35.00 **Beds:** 1T **Baths:** 1 En (5)

Northolt

TQ1283 *Crown Inn*

5 Doncaster Drive, *Northolt, Middx., UB5 4AS.* Leafy suburban Northolt - 15 mins Heathrow, 25 mins Central London. Ideal base for Stratford, Brighton, Oxford etc. All these destinations available on a daytrip basis. Our local knowledge will save you money and ensure that you get the mostest for the leastest. **Open:** All year
020 8423 5072 Mr & Mrs Wooster **D:** Fr £25.00–£30.00 **S:** Fr £25.00–£30.00 **Beds:** 1T 1S **Baths:** 1 Pr 1 Sh (2)

Pinner

TQ1189

Pinner B&B, *9 Cranbourne Drive, Pinner, Middx, HA5 1BX.* Family home, peaceful leafy setting. Short walk Pinner tube station. **Open:** All year (not Xmas)
020 8866 5308 Mrs Mckee **D:** Fr £20.00–£25.00 **S:** Fr £25.00 **Beds:** 2T **Baths:** 1 Sh (3)

Goodmans, *11 Meadow Road, Pinner, Middx, HA5 1EB.* Modern family house, 2 twin rooms, open all year, from £15 pppn. **Open:** All year
020 8868 1074 S Goodman **D:** Fr £15.00 **Beds:** 2T **Baths:** 2 Sh

Richmond

TQ1874

Ivy Cottage, *Upper Ham Road, Ham Common, Richmond, TW10 5LA.* Ten mins from river, Queen Anne family room. **Open:** All year
020 8940 8601 Fax: 020 8940 3865 *taylor@dbta.freeserve.co.uk* www.dbta.freeserve.co.uk **D:** Fr £22.50–£25.00 **S:** Fr £30.00–£32.50 **Beds:** 1D 1T **Baths:** 1 Pr

8 Maze Road, *Kew, Richmond, Surrey, TW9 3DA.* Refurbished Victorian house, close to Kew Gardens, PRO, mainline & Underground stations. **Open:** All year
020 8286 6681 Mrs Gill **Fax: 020 8948 6697** *cgill@easynet.co.uk* **D:** Fr £30.00–£40.00 **S:** Fr £28.00–£35.00 **Beds:** 2D 1S **Baths:** 1 En 1 Sh

Ruislip

TQ0987

2 Cornwall Road, *Ruislip, Middx, HA4 6RS.* Small friendly private house. Short walk underground stations. Near M40/M25. **Open:** All year
01895 636676 (also fax) Mrs Glanvill **D:** Fr £25.00 **S:** Fr £30.00 **Beds:** 1D 2S **Baths:** 1 Sh

Teddington

TQ1670

93 Langham Road, *Teddington, Middx, TW11 9HG.* Sympathetically restored Edwardian house with original features and brass beds. **Open:** All year (not Xmas)
020 8977 6962 Mrs Norris *lesleyanorris@aol.com* **D:** Fr £22.50–£25.00 **S:** Fr £30.00–£45.00 **Beds:** 1D 1T **Baths:** 1 Sh

Twickenham

TQ1573

11 Spencer Road, *Strawberry Hill, Twickenham, Middx, TW2 5TH.* Stylish Edwardian house near Richmond and Hampton Court. Excellent transport, easy parking. **Open:** All year
020 8894 5271 Mrs Duff **D:** Fr £20.00–£25.00 **S:** Fr £20.00–£25.00 **Beds:** 2D 1T **Baths:** 1 En 1 Sh

Uxbridge

TQ0583

Spackman Guest House, *14 Hillingdon Road, Uxbridge, Middx, UB10 0AD.* Listed house near town centre, Heathrow, M4, M40. English breakfast. **Open:** All year (not Xmas)
01895 237994 Mrs Spackman **Fax: 01895 234953 D:** Fr £20.00–£25.00 **S:** Fr £25.00 **Beds:** 1D 1T 1S **Baths:** 1 Sh (3)

Cleveland Hotel, *4 Cleveland Road, Uxbridge, Middx, UB8 2DW.* Clean and comfortable accommodation; free car-parking available. **Open:** All year
01895 257618 Mrs Sabathy **Fax: 01895 239710 D:** Fr £27.50–£30.00 **S:** Fr £35.00–£40.00 **Beds:** 5F 3D 1T 5S **Baths:** 9 En 3 Sh (10) **cc**

Hillbenn House, *235 Park Road, Uxbridge, Middx, UB8 1NS.* 10 mins from Heathrow Airport. 10 mins' walk to tube station. **Open:** All year
01895 850787 Fax: 01895 814909 *hillbenn.house@btinternet.com* **D:** Fr £22.50–£25.00 **S:** Fr £35.00–£40.00 **Beds:** 1F 3T 1S **Baths:** 5 En (4)

RATES
D = Price range per person sharing in a double or twin room
S = Price range for a single room

Wembley

TQ1785

Elm Hotel, *1-7 Elm Road, Wembley, Middx, HA9 7JA.* **Open:** All year (not Xmas)
020 8902 1764 Mr Gosden **Fax: 020 8903 8365** *info@elmhotel.co.uk* www.elmhotel.co.uk **D:** Fr £32.50–£36.00 **S:** Fr £45.00 **Beds:** 9F 7D 11T 6S **Baths:** 33 En (7) **cc**
Wembley Stadium, Arena and Conference Centre 1200 yds. Wembley Central (main line and underground) 150 yards. M1 2.5 miles, Heathrow Airport 8 miles. Comfortable family run 33 bedroom hotel. Get into hot water with your wife, some double rooms have Jacuzzi jet spa baths.

Adelphi Hotel, *4 Forty Lane, Wembley, Middlesex, HA9 9EB.* Close to Wembley complex. Warm, friendly atmosphere. Free car park. **Open:** All year
020 8904 5629 Mr Bajaj **Fax: 020 8904 5314** *enquiry@adelphihotel.fsnet.co.uk* www.hoteladelphi.co.uk **D:** Fr £22.50–£27.50 **S:** Fr £35.00–£49.00 **Beds:** 2F 3T 5D 3S **Baths:** 11 En 9 Pr 2 Sh **cc**

Please respect a B&B's wishes regarding children, animals and smoking

Aaron, Wembley Park Hotel, *8 Forty Lane, Wembley, Middx, HA9 9EB.* We are a small family-run hotel. We are within easy reach of the Wembley Stadium Arena, Conference Centre and exhibition halls. Park Royal, Harrow are close by. Wembley Park Tube Station is 10 minutes walk away, West End 20 minutes by tube. Visit www.aaronhotel.com **Open:** All year
020 8904 6329 Mr Patel **Fax: 020 8385 0472** *enquiries@aaronhotel.com* www.aaronhotel.com **D:** Fr £22.50–£35.00 **S:** Fr £29.00–£49.00 **Beds:** 6F 2D 1T 1S **Baths:** 9 En 1 Sh (11)

West Drayton

TQ0679

Oakwood Guest House, *121-123 Station Road, West Drayton, London, UB7 7DA.* Excellent location for Heathrow airport, motorways and London. English breakfast. **Open:** All year
07720 074800 & 01895 421314 *oakwood121@yahoo.co.uk* www.oakwood121.co.uk **D:** Fr £20.00–£30.00 **S:** Fr £30.00–£43.00 **Beds:** 1F 4T 2D 6S **Baths:** 13 En 2 Sh

Norfolk

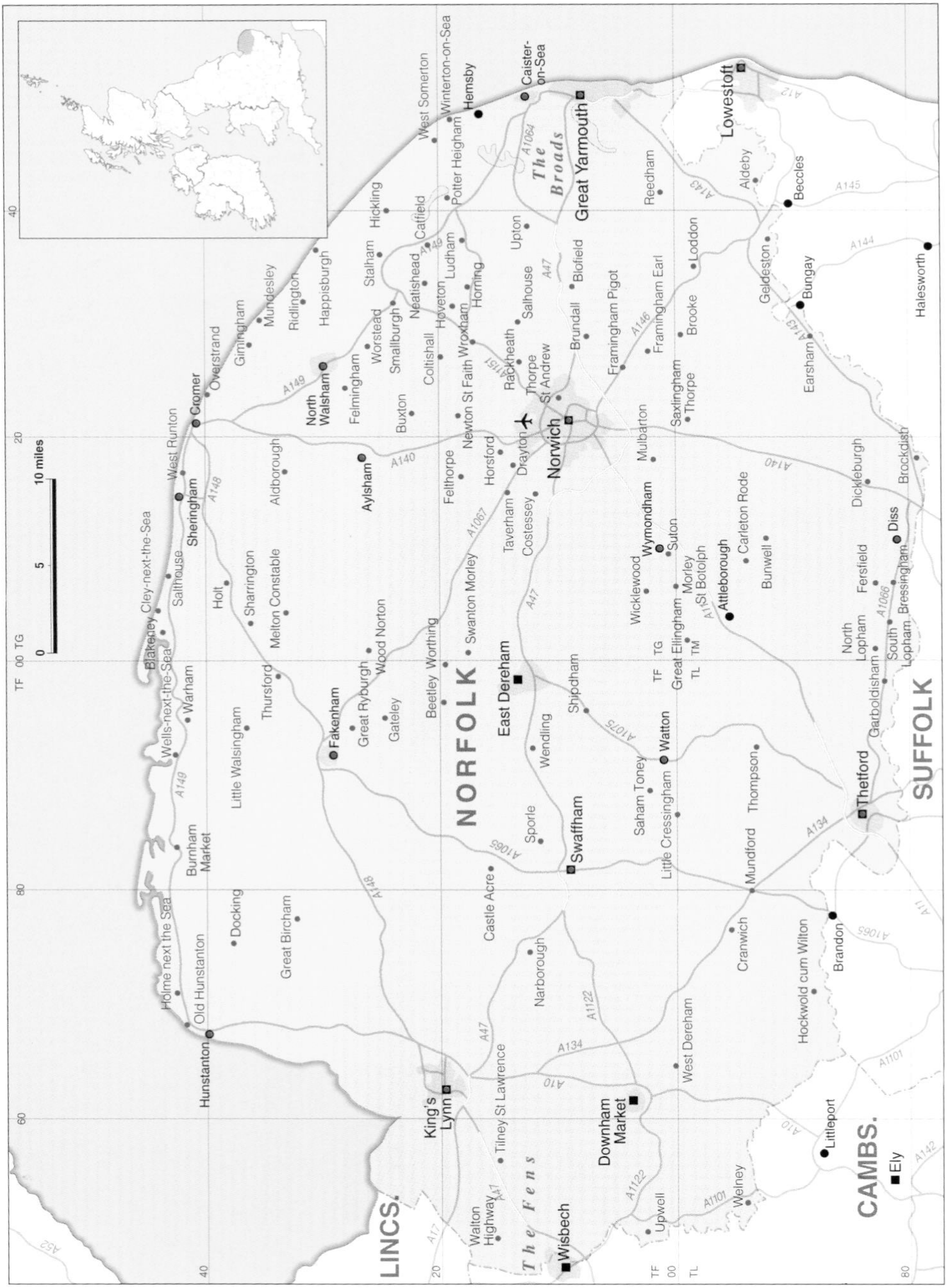

NORFOLK
SUFFOLK
LINCS.
CAMBS.
10 miles
The Broads
The Fens
Norwich
Great Yarmouth
Lowestoft
King's Lynn
Hunstanton
Cromer
Sheringham
North Walsham
Aylsham
Fakenham
East Dereham
Swaffham
Thetford
Diss
Wymondham
Attleborough
Watton
Downham Market
Wisbech
Brandon
Bungay
Beccles
Halesworth
Hemsby
Caister-on-Sea
Holt
Blakeney
Cley-next-the-Sea
Salthouse
Wells-next-the-Sea
Burnham Market
Holme next the Sea
Old Hunstanton
West Runton
Overstrand
Mundesley
Happisburgh
Hickling
Potter Heigham
Winterton-on-Sea
West Somerton
Reedham
Loddon
Ludham
Horning
Coltishall
Wroxham
Hoveton
Blofield
Brundall
Thorpe St Andrew
Drayton
Taverham
Costessey
Horsford
Mulbarton
Saxlingham Thorpe
Framingham Earl
Framingham Pigot
Ely
Littleport
Upwell
Welney
West Dereham
Narborough
Castle Acre
Sporle
Little Cressingham
Saham Toney
Thompson
Mundford
Cranwich
Hockwold cum Wilton
Garboldisham
North Lopham
South Lopham
Bressingham
Fersfield
Bunwell
Carleton Rode
Dickleburgh
Brockdish
Earsham
Geldeston
Aldeby
Wicklewood
Morley St Botolph
Great Ellingham
Suton
Shipdham
Wendling
Beetley
Worthing
Swanton Morley
Gateley
Great Ryburgh
Wood Norton
Thursford
Little Walsingham
Warham
Docking
Great Bircham
Melton Constable
Sharrington
Aldborough
Felthorpe
Buxton
Felmingham
Newton St Faith
Rackheath
Salhouse
Upton
Smallburgh
Worstead
Neatishead
Stalham
Catfield
Ridlington
Gimingham
Tilney St Lawrence
Walton Highway
A47
A10
A134
A11
A140
A146
A149
A148
A1065
A1067
A1075
A1122
A1101
A143
A144
A145
A12
A1064
A1151
A1066
A17
A52
A142
TF
TG
TL
TM

Please respect a B&B's wishes regarding children, animals and smoking

Aldborough

TG1834

Butterfly Cottage, *The Green, Aldborough, Norwich, Norfolk, NR11 7AA.* Idyllic location overlooking village green. High quality accommodation on Weavers Way. **Open:** All year **Grades:** ETC 3 Diamond
01263 768198 Ms Davidson *butterflycottage@btopenworld.com* www.butterflycottage.com
D: Fr £22.50–£25.00 **S:** Fr £25.00–£27.00
Beds: 1F 1T 1D 1S **Baths:** 3 En 1 Pr (4)

Aldeby

TM4493

The Old Vicarage, *Rectory Road, Aldeby, Beccles, Suffolk, NR34 0BJ.* Spacious old vicarage, tranquil 3-acre garden within open countryside. **Open:** All year (not Xmas) **Grades:** ETC 3 Diamond
01502 678229 Mrs Butler *butler@beccles33.freeserve.co.uk* **D:** Fr £20.00–£22.00 **S:** Fr £20.00–£22.00 **Beds:** 1D 2T **Baths:** 1 En 2 Pr (3)

Aylsham

TG1927

The Old Pump House, *Holman Road, Aylsham, Norwich, NR11 6BY.* **Open:** All year (not Xmas) **Grades:** ETC 4 Diamond
01263 733789 (also fax) Mr & Mrs Richardson **D:** Fr £20.00–£24.00 **S:** Fr £22.00–£30.00 **Beds:** 1F 2D 2T 1S **Baths:** 4 En 1 Sh (6)
Warm, welcoming Georgian farmhouse full of character and near to the Broads, Norwich, stately houses (Blickling Hall 1 mile) and the coast. Breakfasts freshly cooked to order in the pine-shuttered Red Room overlooking the peaceful garden.

Birchdale House, *Blickling Road, Aylsham, Norwich, NR11 6ND.* Charming house in conservation area, attractive gardens, close town centre. **Open:** All year
01263 734531 Mrs Blake *jillmblake@hotmail.com* **D:** Fr £22.00–£24.00 **S:** Fr £22.00–£24.00 **Beds:** 1T 1D 1S **Baths:** 1 En 1 Sh (5)

Beetley

TF9718

Peacock House, *Peacock Lane, Beetley, Dereham, Norfolk, NR20 4DG.* Beautifully restored farmhouse, lovely views. Perfect location for exploring Norfolk. **Open:** All year **Grades:** ETC 4 Diamond, Gold
01362 860371 Mrs Bell *PeackH@aol.com* www.smoothhound.co.uk/hotels/peacockh.html **D:** Fr £22.00–£24.00 **S:** Fr £28.00–£30.00 **Beds:** 1F 1T 1D **Baths:** 3 En (4)

Blakeney

TG0243

White Barn, *Back Lane, Blakeney, Norfolk, NR25 7NP.* Delightful ensuite annexe with individual access near Blakeney Quay. **Open:** All year (not Xmas)
01263 741359 (also fax) Mr & Mrs Millard *millard@clara.co.uk* members.tripod.co.uk/raymillard **D:** Fr £20.00–£25.00 **S:** Fr £25.00–£35.00 **Beds:** 1D 1D/T **Baths:** 2 En (5)

Blofield

TG3309

Aldwin, *Woodbastwick Road, Blofield, Norwich, NR13 4QH.* Large detached bungalow convenient for Norwich and Broads. Norwich 7 miles. **Open:** Easter to Oct
01603 713059 Mr Key **D:** Fr £15.00–£20.00 **S:** Fr £16.00–£20.00 **Beds:** 1D 1T **Baths:** 1 Sh (3)

Bressingham

TM0780

Poplar Farm, *Fersfield Road, Bressingham, Diss, Norfolk, IP22 2AP.* Quiet countryside, close Bloom's Gardens and steam museums, Norwich, Ipswich and coast. **Open:** All year (not Xmas)
01379 687261 Mrs Soar **D:** Fr £18.00–£20.00 **S:** Fr £18.00–£20.00 **Beds:** 1D 1T 2S **Baths:** 1 En 2 Sh (10)

Brockdish

TM2079

Grove Thorpe, *Grove Road, Brockdish, Diss, IP21 4JE.* Country house built 1610 nestling in 9 acres private fishing lake. **Open:** Jan to Dec
01379 668305 Mr & Mrs Morrish **Fax: 01379 688305 D:** Fr £25.00–£32.00 **S:** Fr £40.00 **Beds:** 1T 2D (12) (20)

Brooke

TM2899

The Old Vicarage, *48 The Street, Brooke, Norwich, Norfolk, NR15 1JU.* Beautiful house, beautiful garden, totally secluded, peace perfect peace. **Open:** All year (not Xmas/New Year) **Grades:** ETC 4 Diamond, Silver
01508 558329 D: Fr £21.00 **Beds:** 2D **Baths:** 2 En (3)

Brundall

TG3208

Braydeston House, *9 The Street, Brundall, Norwich, NR13 5JY.* Elegant house in wooded gardens only 10 minutes from Norwich. **Open:** All year (not Xmas/New Year) **Grades:** ETC 4 Diamond
01603 713123 Mrs Knox *ann@braydeston.freeserve.co.uk* **D:** Fr £25.00 **S:** Fr £30.00 **Beds:** 2T **Baths:** 1 Pr 1 Sh (2)

Bunwell

TM1293

The Cottage, *Rectory Lane, Bunwell, Norwich, Norfolk, NR16 1QU.* Picturesque C18th thatched cottage set in peaceful country gardens. **Open:** All year
01953 789226 & 07719 596070 (M) P M Jenkins **D:** Fr £17.00–£20.00 **S:** Fr £28.00–£30.00 **Beds:** 1F 2D **Baths:** 3 En (4)

Burnham Market

TF8342

Wood Lodge, *Millwood, Herrings Lane, Burnham Market, King's Lynn, Norfolk, PE31 8DP.* Peaceful, luxurious coastal lodge. **Open:** All year (not Xmas)
01328 730152 Mrs Leftley **Fax: 01328 730158 D:** Fr £27.50–£30.00 **S:** Fr £35.00–£45.00 **Beds:** 1D 1T (8)

Buxton

TG2322

Belair, *Crown Road, Buxton, Norwich, NR10 5EN.* Belair, central North Norfolk accommodation amid peaceful village of Buxton. **Open:** All year
01603 279637 (also fax) Mr Blake *johnblake1234@aol.com* **D:** Fr £18.00–£21.00 **S:** Fr £18.00 **Beds:** 1T 2D 1S **Baths:** 1 En 1 Sh

Caister-on-Sea

TG5112

Old Hall, *High Street, Caister-on-Sea, Great Yarmouth, Norfolk, NR30 5JL.* **Open:** All year **01493 720400 D:** Fr £25.00–£27.50 **S:** Fr £37.50–£42.50 **Beds:** 1T 4D **Baths:** 5 En cc
Warm family welcome, luxurious accommodation, bar & restaurant open daily. Perfectly situated for exploring the bright lights of Great Yarmouth, the serene splendour of the Norfolk Broads & miles of golden beaches. 20 miles from the majestic city of Norwich.

Carleton Rode

TM1193

Upgate Farm, *Carleton Rode, Norwich, NR16 1NJ.* Friendly homely accommodation offered in comfortable farmhouse set in rural location. **Open:** All year (not Xmas) **01953 860300 (also fax)** Mr Wright **D:** Fr £20.00 **S:** Fr £20.00 **Beds:** 1D 1T **Baths:** 1 Sh (2)

Castle Acre

TF8115

Gemini House, *Pyes Lane, Castle Acre, Kings Lynn, Norfolk, PE32 2XB.* Well situated for all Norfolk sights. **Open:** All year **01760 755375** Mrs Clark **D:** Fr £15.00–£17.50 **S:** Fr £15.00 **Beds:** 2D 2T **Baths:** 1 En 1 Sh (4)

3 Stocks Green, *Castle Acre, Kings Lynn, Norfolk, PE32 2AE.* Ancient cottage in centre of historic village of Castle Acre. **Open:** All year **01328 820044** Mr Guinness **D:** Fr £18.00–£20.00 **S:** Fr £20.00–£22.00

Willow Cottage Tea Rooms & B&B, *Stocks Green, Castle Acre, Kings Lynn, Norfolk, PE32 2AE.* Attractive beamed tea rooms and guest bedrooms, delicious home-cooked cakes, soups and puddings. Warm friendly welcome. Within walking distance of Cluniac Priory, Castle and River Nar. Ideal base for visiting local attractions in North and West Norfolk. **Open:** All year (not Xmas) **01760 755551** Mr Moister **Fax: 01760 755799** *willowcottage@webwise.fm* **D:** Fr £35.00 **S:** Fr £20.00 **Beds:** 2D 2T **Baths:** 1 Sh (4)

Catfield

TG3821

Grebe Cottage, *New Road, Catfield, Great Yarmouth, Norfolk, NR29 5DQ.* Situated in Norfolk Broads National Park. Ideal for sailing, fishing, walking, wildlife. **Open:** All year (not Xmas/New Year) **01692 584179** Mrs Wickens *jill@wickens61.freeserve.co.uk* **D:** Fr £18.00–£20.00 **S:** Fr £18.00–£20.00 **Beds:** 1T 2D **Baths:** 1 En 1 Sh (3)

The Limes, *Limes Road, Catfield, Great Yarmouth, Norfolk, NR29 5DG.* Heart of the Broads. Naturalists' paradise. Comfortable rooms. Real food. **Open:** All year **01692 581221** Simon & Jean Partridge *thelimes@catfield.fsbusiness.co.uk* www.catfield.fsbusiness.co.uk **D:** Fr £25.00 **S:** Fr £35.00 **Beds:** 1T 2D **Baths:** 2 En 1 Pr (6)

Cley-next-the-Sea

TG0443

Cley Windmill, *Cley-next-the-Sea, Holt, Norfolk, NR25 7NN.* Historic windmill overlooking beautiful unspoilt Norfolk coastal marshes. Wonderfully atmospheric. **Open:** All year **01263 740209 (also fax)** Mr Bolam **D:** Fr £37.00–£56.00 **S:** Fr £70.00 **Beds:** 4D 3T **Baths:** 7 Pr (12) cc

Coltishall

TG2720

Broadgates, *1 Wroxham Road, Coltishall, Norwich, NR12 7DU.* Comfortable accommodation in Broadland village. **Open:** All year (not Xmas) **01603 737598** Mrs Dack *broad1gates@tesco.net* www.norfolkbroads.com/broadgates **D:** Fr £21.00 **S:** Fr £21.00 **Beds:** 1F 1T **Baths:** 1 En 1 Pr (8)

BEDROOMS
D = Double
T = Twin
S = Single
F = Family

All details shown are as supplied by B&B owners in Autumn 2002

Costessey

TG1711

St Edmundsbury, *146 The Street, Costessey, Norwich, NR8 5DG.* **Open:** All year **01603 745959 (also fax)** *smiths@stedmundsbury.fsbusiness.co.uk* www.stedmundsbury.co.uk **D:** Fr £24.00 **S:** Fr £28.00 **Beds:** 1F 2T 3D 2S **Baths:** 4 En 1 Pr 2 Sh (10) cc
Surrounded by 8 golf courses, close to the Royal Norwich Showground, St Edmundsbury stands in a large attractive garden with ample on-site parking. Situated within easy reach of historic city of Norwich. Most rooms are ground floor and extremely comfortably furnished.

Cranwich

TL7794

Old Bottle House, *Cranwich, Mundford, Thetford, Norfolk, IP26 5JL.* 275-year-old former coaching inn, edge of Thetford Forest. Dining room with inglenook fireplace. **Open:** All year **01842 878012** Mrs Ford **D:** Fr £20.00–£22.00 **S:** Fr £20.00–£22.00 **Beds:** 1F 2T 1D **Baths:** 1 Sh (5) (10)

Cromer

TG2142

Cambridge House, *Sea Front, East Cliff, Cromer, Norfolk, NR27 9HD.* Superb, uninterrupted sea views above the promenade and beach. Good touring base. **Open:** All year (not Xmas/New Year) **Grades:** ETC 4 Diamond **01263 512085** Mrs Wass www.broadland.com/cambridgehouse **D:** Fr £21.00–£26.00 **S:** Fr £21.00–£26.00 **Beds:** 3F 1D 1S **Baths:** 3 En 1 Pr 1 Sh (5)

The Grove Guest House, *95 Overstrand Road, Cromer, Norfolk, NR27 0DS.* Ideal for North Norfolk. Beautiful, spacious, C18th guest house. **Open:** Easter to Sept **01263 512412** Mrs Graveling **Fax: 01263 513416 D:** Fr £26.00 **S:** Fr £26.00 **Beds:** 2F 2T 4D 1S **Baths:** 9 En

Planning a longer stay? Always ask for any special rates

Beachcomber Guest House, *17 Macdonald Road, Cromer, Norfolk, NR27 9AP.* Visiting North Norfolk? Excellent accommodation, well-placed for exploring entire area **Open:** All year (not Xmas/New Year)
01263 516698 Mrs Weinle *www.beachcomber-guesthouse.co.uk* **D:** Fr £19.00–£25.00 **S:** Fr £19.00–£38.00 **Beds:** 1F 1T 4D **Baths:** 5 En 1 Sh (6)

Dickleburgh

TM1682 *Half Moon*

Blacksmiths Cottage, *Langmere, Dickleburgh, Diss, Norfolk, IP21 4AQ.* Detached country cottage. Close to A140. Friendly environment. **Open:** Easter to Oct
01379 740982 J A Potterton **Fax: 01379 741917** *pottertonj@aol.com* **D:** Fr £17.00 **S:** Fr £17.00 **Beds:** 1D 1S **Baths:** 1 Sh (4)

Diss

TM1180

Park Hotel, *29 Denmark Street, Diss, IP22 4LE.* Friendly run market town hotel, ideal for touring Norfolk and Suffolk. **Open:** All year
01379 642244 R Twigge **Fax: 01379 644218** *park.hotel@btinternet.com* **D:** Fr £27.50–£40.00 **S:** Fr £25.00–£30.00 **Beds:** 2F 8D 4T 2S cc

Docking

TF7637

Jubilee Lodge, *Station Road, Docking, King's Lynn, Norfolk, PE31 8LS.* Comfortable Tudor-style house. Pleasant village between Fakenham and the seaside resort of Hunstanton. **Open:** Dec to Oct
01485 518473 (also fax) Mrs Howard *eghoward62@hotmail.com* www.jubilee-lodge.com **D:** Fr £20.00 **S:** Fr £25.00 **Beds:** 2D 1T **Baths:** 3 En (3)

Drayton

TG1813 *Red Lion, Cock*

The Chestnuts, *27 Fakenham Road, Drayton, Norwich, NR8 6PS.* Bungalow accommodation, central for touring Norfolk/coastal areas. **Open:** All year
01603 868860 M Howard **D:** Fr £18.00–£19.00 **S:** Fr £20.00–£25.00 **Beds:** 1T 2D **Baths:** 1 En 1 Sh (3) (10)

Earsham

TM3289

Park Farm, *Harleston Road, Earsham, Bungay, Norfolk, NR35 2AQ.* Spacious farmhouse, unique hand decoration, fantastic views with every comfort. **Open:** All year
01986 892180 Mrs Watchorn **Fax: 01986 894796** *watchorn_s@freenet.co.uk* **D:** Fr £23.00–£35.00 **S:** Fr £32.00–£46.00 **Beds:** 2D 1T **Baths:** 3 En (10) cc

Fakenham

TF9230

Highfield Farm, *Great Ryburgh, Fakenham, Norfolk, NR21 7AL.* Elegant farmhouse, welcoming hosts, comfortable rooms, peaceful and quiet. **Open:** All year (not Xmas/New Year)
01328 829249 Mrs Savory **Fax: 01328 829422** *jegshighfield@onet.co.uk* www.broadland.com/highfield **D:** Fr £20.00–£25.00 **S:** Fr £25.00–£35.00 **Beds:** 2T 1D **Baths:** 1 En 1 Sh (8)

Yew Tree House, *2 East View, Hempton, Fakenham, Norfolk, NR21 7LW.* Open spaces, birdwatching area. Close to Sandringham, North Norfolk Coast. **Open:** All year
01328 851450 Mr Beales **D:** Fr £15.00–£18.00 **S:** Fr £15.00–£18.00 **Beds:** 1F 1D 1T 1S **Baths:** 1 Sh (1) (5)

Felmingham

TG2529

Larks Rise, *North Walsham Road, Felmingham, North Walsham, Norfolk, NR28 0JU.* **Open:** Jan to Nov **Grades:** ETC 2 Diamond
01692 403173 Mrs Rudd www.broadland.com/larksrise **D:** Fr £16.00–£20.00 **S:** Fr £18.00–£22.00 **Beds:** 1F 1D 1T **Baths:** 1 En 1 Sh (2) 2
Traditionally-built family home with half acre secluded gardens in quiet rural area full of wildlife and historical interest. Superb centre for exploring North Norfolk and the Broads. Close to Weavers Way and Norfolk Coastal footpaths. Riding and fishing nearby.

All details shown are as supplied by B&B owners in Autumn 2002

Felthorpe

TG1618

Spinney Ridge, *Hall Lane, Felthorpe, Norwich, NR10 4BX.* **Open:** All year (not Xmas)
01603 754833 Mr & Mrs Thompson **D:** Fr £20.00–£22.00 **S:** Fr £20.00–£22.00 **Beds:** 2D 2T 1S **Baths:** 2 En 1 Sh (1) (6)
Characterful quiet house in a wooded rural setting with a warm and friendly welcome and service 6 miles north of Norwich off the A1149. Centre for North Norfolk and the Broads, convenient for recommended restaurants. No smoking, no dogs, please.

Lodge Farmhouse, *89 The Street, Felthorpe, Norwich, NR10 4BY.* Comfortable friendly family house, edge of village location, good breakfast. **Open:** All year (not Xmas)
01603 754896 Mrs Howe **D:** Fr £17.00 **S:** Fr £17.00 **Beds:** 1D 1T 1S **Baths:** 1 Sh (4)

Fersfield

TM0683

Strenneth, *Airfield Road, Fersfield, Diss, Norfolk, IP22 2B.* Close to Bressingham Gardens and Snetterton Circuit. C17th courtyard wing. **Open:** All year
01379 688182 K Webb **Fax: 01379 688260** *pdavey@strenneth.co.uk* www.strenneth.co.uk **D:** Fr £25.00–£35.00 **S:** Fr £28.00–£50.00 **Beds:** 4D 2T 1S **Baths:** 7 En (9) cc

Flint Barn, Fenners Farm, *Fersfield, Diss, IP22 2AW.* Converted barn in rural setting of 2 acres. NT properties, Norfolk Broads. **Open:** All year (not Xmas/New Year)
01379 687794 Mr & Mrs Green *joan.green@tesco.net* **D:** Fr £18.00–£19.00 **S:** Fr £18.00–£20.00 **Beds:** 1F 1S **Baths:** 1 Sh (10) (4)

Framingham Earl

TG2702

The Old Rectory, *Hall Road, Framingham Earl, Norwich, NR14 7SB.* Beautifully restored period family house in large country garden. **Open:** All year (not Xmas)
01508 493590 Mr & Mrs Wellings **Fax: 01508 495110** *brucewellings@drivedevice.freeserve.co.uk* **D:** Fr £21.00–£25.00 **S:** Fr £25.00–£28.00 **Beds:** 1D 1T **Baths:** 1 Sh (4)

Framingham Pigot

TG2703

The Old Rectory, *Rectory Lane, Framingham Pigot, Norwich, NR14 7QQ.* Friendly Victorian rectory. Large garden. 10 mins Norwich centre. **Open:** All year (not Xmas)
01508 493082 Mrs Thurman **D:** Fr £22.00 **S:** Fr £22.00 **Beds:** 1F 1D 1T **Baths:** 2 En 1 Sh (6)

RATES
D = Price range per person sharing in a double or twin room
S = Price range for a single room

Garboldisham

TM0081

Ingleneuk Lodge, *Hopton Road, Garboldisham, Diss, Norfolk, IP22 2RQ.* Pretty rural location with all rooms overlooking partly wooded grounds. **Open:** All year
01953 681541 Mr & Mrs Stone **Fax: 01953 681138** *info@ingleneuklodge.co.uk* **D:** Fr £27.50 **S:** Fr £33.00 **Beds:** 3D 3T 1S 1F **Baths:** 8 En
(15) cc

Gateley

TF9624

Centre Farm, *Gateley, Fakenham, Norfolk, NR20 5EF.* Beautiful Georgian farm house set in quiet country village. **Open:** All year
01328 829618 Mrs Savory *gill@savoryfarm.co.uk* www.savoryfarm.co.uk **D:** Fr £20.00–£25.00 **Beds:** 1D 2T **Baths:** 2 Pr (8)

Geldeston

TM3992

Archway Cottage, *Geldeston, Beccles, Suffolk, NR34 0LB.* Clean comfortable cottage with a warm welcome to all our guests. **Open:** All year
01508 518056 Mrs Dean *archwaycottage@btinternet.com* www.archwaycottage.co.uk **D:** Fr £20.00 **S:** Fr £25.00–£28.00 **Beds:** 2D **Baths:** 1 Sh (2)

Gimingham

TG2836

Bridge Farm Stables, *Mill Lane, Gimingham, Mundesley, Norwich, NR11 8AB.* Riding, reiki, golf, fishing. Rural views near beach. Tourers. **Open:** All year
01263 720028 Mr & Mrs Harris **D:** Fr £18.00–£20.00 **S:** Fr £24.00–£26.00 **Beds:** 1T 1D **Baths:** 1 Pr (4)

Great Bircham

TF7632

Kings Head Hotel, *Great Bircham, Kings Lynn, Norfolk, PE31 6RJ.* Friendly village inn and restaurant close to Sandringham, King's Lynn and the coast, Italian restaurant. Fresh Norfolk seafood and produce. Six ensuite rooms with colour TV, tea/coffee making facilities. English and Italian cuisine. Breaks available, for two nights and over. **Open:** All year
01485 578265 I Verrando **D:** Fr £29.50–£35.00 **S:** Fr £39.00 **Beds:** 1F 2T 2D 1S **Baths:** 6 En
(1) (40) cc

Great Ellingham

TM0197

Manor Farm Bed and Breakfast, *Hingham Road, Great Ellingham, Attleborough, Norfolk, NR17 1JE.* Relaxed atmosphere, excellent accommodation. Centrally located, Norwich 20 mins. Near to Snetterton racing circuit. **Open:** All year (not Xmas/New Year)
01953 453388 (also fax) *rivett.and.son@farmline.com* **D:** Fr £22.50–£25.00 **S:** Fr £20.00–£25.00 **Beds:** 1T 1D 1S **Baths:** 1 En 2 Pr (12) (3)

Home Cottage Farm, *Penhill Road, Great Ellingham, Attleborough, Norfolk, NR17 1LS.* Spacious self-contained B&B accommodation at period farmhouse in rural seclusion. **Open:** All year
01953 483734 M Jacobs *royandmaureen@mail.com* **D:** Fr £18.00–£20.00 **S:** Fr £18.00–£20.00 **Beds:** 2T 1D 1S **Baths:** 1 Pr 1 Sh
(4)

Great Ryburgh

TF9527

Highfield Farm, *Great Ryburgh, Fakenham, Norfolk, NR21 7AL.* Elegant farmhouse, welcoming hosts, comfortable rooms, peaceful and quiet. **Open:** All year (not Xmas/New Year)
01328 829249 Mrs Savory **Fax: 01328 829422** *jegshighfield@onet.co.uk* www.broadland.com/highfield **D:** Fr £20.00–£25.00 **S:** Fr £25.00–£35.00 **Beds:** 2T 1D **Baths:** 1 En 1 Sh
(8)

Please respect a B&B's wishes regarding children, animals and smoking

Great Yarmouth

TG5207

Clover Court Hotel, *15 Princes Road, Great Yarmouth, NR30 2DG.* **Open:** All year
01493 842175 **D:** Fr £15.00–£25.00 **S:** Fr £15.00–£25.00 **Beds:** 3F 2T 5D 2S **Baths:** 12 En
Ideal location, 1 min beach, shops and attractions. Relax in Schooners Bar while you plan the next days events. Our small friendly hotel has lots to offer, full English breakfast and choice of three course evening dinner. Short or long breaks available.

Lynden House, *102 Wellesley Road, Great Yarmouth, Norfolk, NR30 2AR.* Assured a warm welcome 3 mins from beach and shops. **Open:** All year (not Xmas/New Year)
01493 844693 Mrs Hinckley **D:** Fr £12.00–£18.00 **S:** Fr £12.00–£18.00 **Beds:** 3F 2S 1T **Baths:** 3 En 1 Sh

Sliverstone House, *29 Wellesley Road, Great Yarmouth, NR30 1EU.* All rooms ensuite, residential bar, close to all amenities. **Open:** All year (not Xmas)
Grades: ETC 3 Diamond
01493 844862 Mr Parker **D:** Fr £15.00–£19.50 **S:** Fr £15.00–£19.50 **Beds:** 5F 5D **Baths:** 10 En cc

The White House, *14 Camperdown, Great Yarmouth, NR30 3JB.* Friendly, run by family, 2 mins to seafront. Home cooking. **Open:** All year (not Xmas/New Year)
01493 857278 **D:** Fr £80.00–£95.00 **S:** Fr £80.00–£95.00 **Beds:** 10F 1T 1D 8S **Baths:** 1 Sh (1)

Taunton House, *9 Nelson Road South, Great Yarmouth, NR30 3JL.* Warm welcome, good food. 2 mins' walk to seafront/attractions. Children and senior citizens' discount. Phone for brochure. **Open:** All year
01493 850043 Mrs Hurd **D:** Fr £18.00–£25.00 **S:** Fr £18.00–£25.00 **Beds:** 3F 1T 3D 1S **Baths:** 8 En

Britannia Guest House, *119 Wellesley Road, Great Yarmouth, NR30 2AP.* Comfortable rooms, good breakfasts, close to beach, shops, restaurants, amusements. **Open:** All year
01493 856488 (also fax) **D:** Fr £14.00–£20.00 **S:** Fr £14.00–£20.00 **Beds:** 1F 3D 1T 2S **Baths:** 1 En 1 Sh (3)

Marlborough Guest House, *8 Trafalgar Road, Great Yarmouth, Norfolk, NR30 2LD.* Family run, friendly near to sea and town. Quality accommodations. **Open:** All year
01493 844542 Mr & Mrs Tillbrook *johnuk1@supanet.com* www.marlborough.topcities.com **D:** Fr £18.00–£25.00 **S:** Fr £16.00–£20.00 **Beds:** 2F 2T 2D 1S **Baths:** 5 En 2 Sh (2)

Senglea Lodge, *7 Euston Road, Great Yarmouth, Norfolk, NR30 1DX.* Family run. Voted to be best guest house by Which magazine. **Open:** All year (not Xmas/New Year)
01493 859632 Mrs Formosa *info@senglealodge.freeserve.co.uk* **D:** Fr £14.00–£17.00 **S:** Fr £5.00–£20.00 **Beds:** 2F 2T 2D 1S **Baths:** 4 En 1 Sh cc

Armani Hotel, *14-15 Sandown Road, Great Yarmouth, Norfolk, NR30 1EY.* 50 yards from the beach. Licensed bar, car park. **Open:** All year
01493 843870 (also fax) R Boon *armani-hotel@faxvia.net* www.armanihotel.co.uk **D:** Fr £25.00–£30.00 **S:** Fr £25.00–£35.00 **Beds:** 10F 6T 2D 4S **Baths:** 22 En (3) (50)

Holland House, *13 Apsley Road, Great Yarmouth, Norfolk, NR30 2HG.* Friendly family run guest house, one minute from sea. **Open:** All year (not Xmas/New Year)
01493 859534 Mr & Mrs Simmons **D:** Fr £12.00–£15.00 **S:** Fr £12.00–£15.00 **Beds:** 2F 4D 1S

The Collingwood Hotel, *25/26 Princes Road, Great Yarmouth, NR30 2DG.* Princes Road is the best road for hotels. We are at the seafront and 100 yds from Britannia Pier and all the shows and amusements. Walking distance from main shops at the heart of the Norfolk Broads - no hills to walk up. Guest lounge, licensed bar. **Open:** Mar to Nov
01493 844398 (also fax) Mr & Mrs Mills www.smoothhound.co.uk/hotels/collingwood.html **D:** Fr £19.00–£25.00 **S:** Fr £18.00–£22.00 **Beds:** 2F 9D 2T 6S **Baths:** 10 En 9 Sh cc

Seamore Guest House, *116 Wellesley Road, Great Yarmouth, NR30 2AR.* Family guest house. One minute from beach, five minutes from shops. **Open:** All year (not Xmas/New Year)
01493 857389 **D:** Fr £13.00–£18.00 **S:** Fr £13.00–£18.00 **Beds:** 2F 2T 3D 1S **Baths:** 2 Sh (4)

Strathclyde Guest House, *6 Paget Road, Great Yarmouth, NR30 2DN.* 24 hour bar/games room. 100 yards from sea front. **Open:** All year
01493 851596 Zoe Cook *strathclyde-yarmouth@hotmail.com* **D:** Fr £13.00–£17.00 **S:** Fr £12.00–£16.00 **Beds:** 2F 2T 2D 1S **Baths:** 1 En, 3 Sh

Barnard House, *2 Barnard Crescent, Great Yarmouth, Norfolk, NR30 4DR.* Delightful family home. Bedrooms overlooking gardens. Excellent Aga cooked breakfast. **Open:** All year (not Xmas/New Year)
01493 855139 J Norris **Fax: 01493 843143** *barnardhouse@btinternet.com* www.barnardhouse.com **D:** Fr £22.00–£24.00 **S:** Fr £25.00–£30.00 **Beds:** 1F 2D **Baths:** 2 En 1 Pr (3)

Happisburgh

TG3731

Cliff House Guest House, *And Tea Shop, Beach Road, Happisburgh, Norwich, NR12 0PP.* Comfortable Edwardian guest house and teashop on cliff top in attractive village. **Open:** All year (not Xmas)
01692 650775 Ms Wrightson **D:** Fr £18.00 **S:** Fr £18.00 **Beds:** 1D 1T 2S **Baths:** 2 Sh (4)

Manor Farmhouse, *Happisburgh, Norwich, NR12 0SA.* The best of both worlds - C21st luxury in a stunningly converted thatched C16th barn. Hearty Norfolk breakfasts, warm welcome, rural location. 5 mins sea, 5 miles Broads, yet only 1/2 hour Norwich - the perfect rural retreat. **Open:** All year (not Xmas/New Year)
01692 651262 Mr & Mrs Eldridge **Fax: 01692 650220** www.northnorfolk.co.uk/manorbarn **D:** Fr £20.00–£25.00 **S:** Fr £25.00 **Beds:** 1T/D 2D **Baths:** 3 En (7) (4)

Hickling

TG4123

Paddock Cottage, *Staithe Road, Hickling, Norwich, NR12 0YJ.* Comfortable modern cottage, quiet location, close nature reserve, sailing, fishing. **Open:** Mar to Oct **Grades:** ETC 4 Diamond
01692 598259 Mrs Parry **D:** Fr £20.00–£25.00 **S:** Fr £25.00–£30.00 **Beds:** 1F 1D 1T **Baths:** 2 En 2 Pr (4)

Hockwold cum Wilton

TL7388

Junipers, *18 South Street, Hockwold cum Wilton, Thetford, Norfolk, IP26 4JG.* Village near Mildenhall, Thetford. Forest, fishing, touring, historic sites. **Open:** All year
01842 827370 Mrs Waddington **D:** Fr £20.00 **S:** Fr £20.00 **Beds:** 2T 1S **Baths:** 2 Sh (4)

Planning a longer stay? Always ask for any special rates

Holme next the Sea

TF7043

Hawks Wind, *1 Kirkgate Street, Holme Next Sea, Hunstanton, Norfolk, PE36 6LY.* Delightful cottage in conservation village. Ideal for all rural pursuits. **Open:** All year (not Xmas)
01485 525695 Mrs Rutland **D:** Fr £25.00–£35.00 **S:** Fr £35.00–£45.00 **Beds:** 1F/D 1T **Baths:** 2 En (8)

Holt

TG0739

Hempstead Hall, *Holt, Norfolk, NR25 6TN.* **Open:** All year (not Xmas) **Grades:** ETC 4 Diamond
01263 712224 www.broadland.com/hempsteadhall **D:** Fr £22.00–£28.00 **S:** Fr £35.00–£38.00 **Beds:** 1F 1D **Baths:** 1 En 1 Pr (8)
Enjoy a relaxing holiday in beautiful surroundings on our 300-acre arable farm with ducks, donkey and large gardens. Spot the wild deer or the barn owl on the meadows. Close to the North Norfolk Coast and its many attractions.

Horning

TG3417

Keppelgate, *Upper Street, Horning, Norwich, NR12 8NG.* Delightful rural Broadland views. Boating, fishing, windmills. Convenient for coast. **Open:** All year (not Xmas/New Year)
01692 630610 Mrs Freeman **D:** Fr £17.00–£18.00 **S:** Fr £20.00 **Beds:** 1F 1D 1T **Baths:** 1 En 1 Sh (2) (3)

Horsford

TG1916

Church Farm Guest House, *Church Street, Horsford, Norwich, NR10 3DB.* Modern comfortable farmhouse, large garden. **Open:** All year
01603 898020 Mrs Hinchley **Fax: 01603 891649** **D:** Fr £25.00–£30.00 **S:** Fr £25.00–£30.00 **Beds:** 2F 2D 2T **Baths:** 6 Pr 6 En 1 Sh (20) cc

Hoveton

TG3018

The Vineries, *72 Stalham Road, Hoveton, Norwich, NR12 8DU.* Self-contained granny annexe, 1/2 mile from shops and Broads. **Open:** All year
01603 782514 S Meacock **D:** Fr £25.00–£30.00 **S:** Fr £25.00–£30.00 **Beds:** 1D **Baths:** 1 En (2)

Please respect a B&B's wishes regarding children, animals and smoking

The Beehive, *Riverside Road, Hoveton, Norwich, NR12 8UD.* Beautiful thatched riverside cottage overlooking River Bure and the Broads. **Open:** All year (not Xmas/ New Year)
01603 784107 R J Wendrop **D:** Fr £20.00–£22.00 **S:** Fr £25.00–£30.00 **Beds:** 1F 1T 2D **Baths:** 1 En 1 Sh (15) (7) cc

Hunstanton

TF6740

Rosamaly Guest House, *14 Glebe Avenue, Hunstanton, Norfolk, PE36 6BS.* Cosy ensuite bedrooms, ground floor/four poster available. Traditional hearty breakfasts, candlelit evening meals. **Open:** All year (not Xmas) **Grades:** ETC 3 Diamond
01485 534187 Mrs Duff Dick *vacancies@rosamaly.co.uk* www.rosamaly.co.uk **D:** Fr £20.00–£25.00 **S:** Fr £22.00–£30.00 **Beds:** 1F 3D 1T 1S **Baths:** 5 En

Peacock House, *28 Park Road, Hunstanton, Norfolk, PE36 5BY.* A large warm and comfortable Victorian house serving memorable breakfasts. **Open:** All year **Grades:** ETC 4 Diamond
01485 534551 Mrs Sandercock *peacockhouse@onetel.net.uk* web.onetel.net.uk/~peacockhouse **D:** Fr £22.00–£27.00 **S:** Fr £24.00–£30.00 **Beds:** 1F 1T 1D **Baths:** 3 En (5)

Kiama Cottage, *23 Austin Street, Hunstanton, Norfolk, PE36 6AN.* A warm welcome awaits you at our Victorian-style cottage, quiet residential area. **Open:** All year (not Xmas) **Grades:** ETC 3 Diamond
01485 533615 Mr & Mrs Gardiner *kiamacottage@btopenworld.com* **D:** Fr £18.00–£25.00 **S:** Fr £20.00–£25.00 **Beds:** 1F 1T 2D **Baths:** 3 En 1 Pr

The Gables, *28 Austin Street, Hunstanton, PE36 6AW.* Recently refurbished attractive Edwardian home retaining many original features. **Open:** All year
01485 532514 Mrs Bamfield *bbathegables@aol.com*www.thegableshunstanton.co.uk **D:** Fr £18.00–£26.00 **Beds:** 5F 1D 1T **Baths:** 5 En cc

King's Lynn

TF6120

Maranatha Havana Guest House, *115 Gaywood Road, King's Lynn, Norfolk, PE30 2PU.* Friendly family run. Special rates for children, groups catered for. **Open:** All year
01553 774596 Mr Bastone **D:** Fr £15.00–£20.00 **S:** Fr £20.00 **Beds:** 2F 2D 3T 2S **Baths:** 4 En 2 Sh (9)

Twinson Lee, *109 Tennyson Road, King's Lynn, Norfolk, PE30 5PA.* Friendly family run guest house, within walking distance of town centre. **Open:** All year (not Xmas/New Year)
01553 762900 Ms Thomas **Fax: 01553 769944 D:** Fr £25.00 **S:** Fr £20.00–£25.00 **Beds:** 1F 1T 1S **Baths:** 1 En 1 Sh (3)

The Old Rectory, *33 Goodwins Road, King's Lynn, Norfolk, PE30 5QX.* Well-appointed, high quality ensuite accommodation. Quietly situated, near centre of historic market town. **Open:** All year
01553 768544 C Faulkner **D:** Fr £21.00 **S:** Fr £32.00 **Beds:** 2F 2T **Baths:** 4 En (5)

Little Cressingham

TF8700

Sycamore House, *Little Cressingham, Thetford, Norfolk, IP25 6NE.* Large country home, tranquil village, luxurious jacuzzi bathroom, numerous attractions. **Open:** All year
01953 881887 (also fax) Mr Wittridge **D:** Fr £25.00 **S:** Fr £25.00 **Beds:** 2D 1T 1S **Baths:** 1 En 1 Sh (10)

Little Walsingham

TF9337

St Davids House, *Friday Market, Little Walsingham, Walsingham, Norfolk, NR22 6BY.* Tudor house in medieval village; 5 miles from coast. **Open:** All year
01328 820633 Mrs Renshaw **D:** Fr £23.00–£26.00 **S:** Fr £28.00–£31.00 **Beds:** 2F 1D 2T **Baths:** 2 En 2 Sh

Loddon

TM3698

Poplar Farm, *Sisland, Loddon, Norwich, NR14 6EF.* Working farm pigs, cows. Quiet, rural setting near Broads. **Open:** All year (not Xmas)
01508 520706 Mrs Hemmant *milly@hemmant.myhome.org.uk* **D:** Fr £17.00–£25.00 **S:** Fr £18.00–£25.00 **Beds:** 1F 1D 1T **Baths:** 1 En 1 Pr

Melton Constable

TG0433

Burgh Parva Hall, *Melton Constable, Norfolk, NR24 2PU.* Listed C16th farmhouse with country views, near coast, large bedrooms. **Open:** All year
01263 862569 (also fax) Mrs Heal *judyheal@talk21.com* **D:** Fr £18.00 **S:** Fr £20.00 **Beds:** 1D 1T **Baths:** 1 Sh (4)

Morley St Botolph

TM0799

Home Farm, *Morley St Botolph, Wymondham, Norfolk, NR18 9SU.* Set in 4 acres of secluded grounds, 3 miles from 2 towns. **Open:** All year (not Xmas)
01953 602581 Mrs Morter **D:** Fr £20.00–£22.00 **S:** Fr £20.00–£22.00 **Beds:** 1T 1D 1S **Baths:** 1 Sh (5) (5)

Mulbarton

TG1901

Richmond Lodge, *The Common, Mulbarton, Norwich, Norfolk, NR14 8JW.* Beautiful setting, games room, outdoor heated swimming pool, palm trees, barbecue area. **Open:** All year (not Xmas/ New Year)
01508 570449 Mrs Freeman **Fax: 01508 570372** *gillandpaul.freeman@ukgateway.net* **D:** Fr £39.50–£41.00 **S:** Fr £23.50–£25.00 **Beds:** 1F 3D 1S **Baths:** 2 En 2 Sh (20)

Mundesley

TG3136

Bridge Farm Stables, *Mill Lane, Gimingham, Mundesley, Norwich, NR11 8AB.* Riding, reiki, golf, fishing. Rural views near beach. Tourers. **Open:** All year
01263 720028 Mr & Mrs Harris **D:** Fr £18.00–£20.00 **S:** Fr £24.00–£26.00 **Beds:** 1T 1D **Baths:** 1 Pr (4)

Mundford

TL7993

Treetops, *6 Swaffham Road, Mundford, Thetford, Norfolk, IP26 5HR.* Comfortable bungalow on A1065. Guests own entrance, sitting/dining room. **Open:** All year (not Xmas/New Year)
01842 878557 Mrs Edmunds **Fax: 01842 879078 D:** Fr £18.00 **S:** Fr £18.00 **Beds:** 1T 1D **Baths:** 1 En 1 Pr (8)

Planning a longer stay? Always ask for any special rates

Narborough

TF7413

Paget, *Old Main Road, Narborough, Kings Lynn, Norfolk, PE32 1TE.* Lounge available - log fire; coarse fishing - trout, water sports, lakes nearby. **Open:** All year (not Xmas)
01760 337734 Mrs Green **D:** Fr £16.50 **S:** Fr £18.00 **Beds:** 1T 1D 1S **Baths:** 1 Pr 1 Sh (7)

Neatishead

TG3420

Allens Farmhouse, *School Lane, Neatishead, Norwich, NR12 8BU.* **Open:** All year
Grades: ETC 4 Diamond
01692 630080 Mr & Mrs Smerdon **D:** Fr £18.00–£22.00 **Beds:** 2D 1T **Baths:** 1 En 1 Sh (3)
Allens Farmhouse, built in early 1700s, was a working farm until early 1980s when it was extensively modernised. Large walled garden, landscaped to create a beautiful lawn surrounded by flower beds with the added attraction of a well, fish pond and orchard.

The Barton Angler Country Inn, *Instead Road, Neatishead, Norwich, NR12 8XP.* Once a rectory from which Nelson sailed as a boy, adjacent to Barton Broad. **Open:** All year (not Xmas/New Year)
01692 630740 Fax: 01692 631122 D: Fr £30.00 **S:** Fr £25.00 **Beds:** 4D 3S **Baths:** 5 En 2 Sh (40) cc

Newton St Faith

TG2117

Elm Farm Country House, *Horsham St Faith, Norwich, NR10 3HH.* Country house in village of Horsham St Faith, 4 miles from Norwich. **Open:** All year
01603 898366 Fax: 01603 897129 D: Fr £26.00–£29.00 **S:** Fr £31.00–£38.00 **Beds:** 2F 5T 4D 3S **Baths:** 14 En (20) cc

North Lopham

TM0382

Belgate, *The Street, North Lopham, Diss, Norfolk, IP22 2LR.* Peaceful bungalow. Large secluded garden, benefit of own front door. **Open:** All year
01379 687346 Mrs Hogg **Fax: 01379 688489 D:** Fr £20.00–£22.50 **S:** Fr £20.00–£25.00 **Beds:** 1T **Baths:** 1 En (2)

North Walsham

TG2830

Green Ridges, *104 Cromer Road, North Walsham, Norfolk, NR28 0HE.* Excellent ensuite accommodation in attractive setting, walking distance town centre. **Open:** All year
01692 402448 & 07748 542964 (M)
Mrs Mitchell *enquiries@greenridges.com* **D:** Fr £20.00–£30.00 **S:** Fr £20.00–£35.00 **Beds:** 1F 1T 1D **Baths:** 2 En 1 Pr (5)

Toll Barn, *Heath Rd, Norwich Road, North Walsham, Norfolk, NR28 0JB.* Private lodges in a quiet rural setting, adjacent to grazing farmland with horses & sheep. **Open:** All year (not Xmas)
01692 403638 Fax: 01692 500993 *nola@toll-barn.fsbusiness.co.uk* **D:** Fr £18.00–£25.00 **S:** Fr £25.00 **Beds:** 1F 1D 1T 1S **Baths:** 4 En (6)

Pine Trees, *45 Happisburgh Road, North Walsham, Norfolk, NR28 9HB.* Lovely house, guest bedrooms overlooking garden with grass tennis court. **Open:** All year (not Xmas/New Year)
01692 404213 (also fax) Mrs Blaxell **D:** Fr £20.00 **S:** Fr £20.00 **Beds:** 1T 1D **Baths:** 2 Sh (10) (2)

Norwich

TG2308

Earlham Guest House, *147 Earlham Road, Norwich, NR2 3RG.* **Open:** All year (not Xmas)
Grades: ETC 4 Diamond, AA 4 Diamond
01603 454169 (also fax) Mr & Mrs Wright *earlhamgh@hotmail.com* **D:** Fr £23.00–£26.00 **S:** Fr £25.00–£42.00 **Beds:** 1F 3D 1T 3S **Baths:** 2 En 2 Sh (12) cc
Susan and Derek Wright offer welcoming and friendly hospitality with comfortable modern facilities, close historic Norwich, University and Norfolk Broads. Vegetarian choices, personal keys. Short break rates available 1 Oct - 31 Mar. No smoking throughout. All cards welcome.

Trebeigh House, *16 Brabazon Road, Hellesdon, Norwich, NR6 6SY.* Warm welcome to quiet friendly house, convenient city, country, airport. **Open:** All year (not Xmas)
01603 429056 Mrs Jope **Fax: 01603 414247** *trebeigh@madasafish.com* **D:** Fr £20.00–£21.00 **S:** Fr £22.00–£24.00 **Beds:** 1D 1T **Baths:** 1 Sh (3)

Rosedale, *145 Earlham Road, Norwich, NR2 3RG.* Comfortable, family-run guest house. Easy access to city, coast and university. **Open:** All year (not Xmas)
01603 453743 Mrs Curtis **Fax: 01603 259887** *drcbac@aol.com* members.aol.com/drcbac **D:** Fr £20.00–£40.00 **S:** Fr £20.00–£25.00 **Beds:** 2F 2T 2S **Baths:** 2 Sh (4) cc

EdMar Lodge, *64 Earlham Road, Norwich, NR2 3DF.* Family run guest house. Ten minutes walk from city centre. **Open:** All year
01603 615599 Mr & Mrs Lovatt **Fax: 01603 495599** *edmar@cwcom.net* **D:** Fr £20.00–£24.00 **S:** Fr £28.00–£34.00 **Beds:** 1F 1T 3D **Baths:** 5 En (8) cc

Aylwyne House, *59 Aylsham Road, Norwich, NR3 2HF.* Quiet, spacious modern house, walking distance city and cathedral. **Open:** All year
01603 665798 Mrs Adams **D:** Fr £19.00–£21.00 **S:** Fr £22.00–£26.00 **Beds:** 1F 1D 1S **Baths:** 2 En 1 Pr (3) (3)

Arbor Linden Lodge, *Linden House, 557 Earlham Road, Norwich, NR4 7HW.* Family run for quality and warmth of welcome. Free parking near city centre. **Open:** All year
01603 451303 Mr Betts **Fax: 01603 250641** *info@guesthouses.uk.com* www.guesthouses.uk.com **D:** Fr £20.00–£25.00 **S:** Fr £26.00–£35.00 **Beds:** 1F 1T 3D 1S **Baths:** 6 En (10) cc

Wedgewood House, *42 St Stephens Road, Norwich, NR1 3RE.* Comfortable city centre house. Close to Norwich's shops and attractions. **Open:** All year (not Xmas/New Year)
01603 625730 *stay@wedgewoodhouse.co.uk* www.wedgewoodhouse.co.uk **D:** Fr £24.00–£26.00 **S:** Fr £34.00–£36.00 **Beds:** 3F 2T 5D 2S **Baths:** 9 En (7) cc

Beaufort Lodge, *62 Earlham Road, Norwich, NR2 3DF.* Spacious Victorian house with ample parking. Within easy walking distance of city centre. **Open:** All year (not Xmas/New Year)
01603 627928 (also fax) Mr Dobbins **D:** Fr £25.00 **S:** Fr £35.00–£40.00 **Beds:** 3D 1S **Baths:** 3 En 1 Pr

Pine Lodge, *518 Earlham Road, Norwich, NR4 7HR.* Distinctive, cheerful and comfortable accommodation between university and the city centre. **Open:** All year
01603 504834 Mr & Mrs Tovell *tovell@tovell.fsnet.co.uk* www.smoothhound.co.uk/hotels/pinelodge1.html **D:** Fr £18.00–£20.00 **S:** Fr £25.00

Old Hunstanton

TF6842

Cobblers Cottage, *3 Wodehouse Road, Old Hunstanton, Hunstanton, Norfolk, PE36 6JD.* Quietly situated 500 yards to sea, coastal path, pubs. Fantastic breakfasts. **Open:** Mar to Oct
01485 534036 Ms Poore *st.crispins@btinternet.com* **D:** Fr £23.00–£28.00 **S:** Fr £28.00–£39.00 **Beds:** 2T 1D **Baths:** 3 En (8)

Overstrand

TG2440 *Saracen's Head, Walpole Arms, Sea Marge Hotel, White Horse*

Cliif Cottage, *18 High Street, Overstand, Cromer, Norfolk, NR27 0AB.* C18th cottage. Two minutes from sandy beach. **Open:** All year
01263 578179 R & M Cooper *roymin@btinternet.com* **D:** Fr £18.00–£22.00 **S:** Fr £23.00–£27.00 **Beds:** 1T **Baths:** 2 En (2)

Potter Heigham

TG4119

Red Roof Farmhouse, *Ludham Road, Potter Heigham, Great Yarmouth, Norfolk, NR29 5NB.* Modern, friendly comfortable centrally-heated farmhouse close to sea and Broads. **Open:** All year
01692 670604 Mrs Playford *gplayford@farming.co.uk* **D:** Fr £18.00–£20.00 **S:** Fr £20.00–£25.00 **Beds:** 1F 1D 1T **Baths:** 1 Sh (10)

Hazelden, *Bridge Road, Potter Heigham, Great Yarmouth, NR29 5JB.* Ideal for coast, Broads, nature reserve, walking, boating, cycling, fishing. **Open:** All year (not Xmas) **Grades:** ETC 4 Diamond
01692 670511 Mr & Mrs Girling **D:** Fr £20.00 **S:** Fr £25.00 **Beds:** 1D/F **Baths:** 1 En (3) (2)

Rackheath

TG2813

Manor Barn House, *Back Lane, Rackheath, Norwich, NR13 6NN.* Traditional C17th Norfolk barn, exposed beams and cottage in garden. **Open:** All year
01603 783543 Mrs Lebbell www.manorbarnhouse.co.uk **D:** Fr £22.00–£25.00 **S:** Fr £23.00–£29.00 **Beds:** 3D 2T 1S **Baths:** 4 En 1 Pr (5) (6)

Barn Court, *Back Lane, Rackheath, Norwich, NR13 6NN.* Spacious accommodation built around a courtyard. Ideal for exploring Norfolk. **Open:** All year (not Xmas)
01603 782536 (also fax) Mrs Simpson **D:** Fr £18.00–£21.00 **S:** Fr £20.00–£25.00 **Beds:** 2D 1T **Baths:** 1 En 2 Sh (3)

Reedham

TG4201 *Ferry Inn, Ship Inn*

The Railway Tavern, *17 The Havaker, Reedham, Norwich, NR13 3HG.* A slice of rural heaven, close to the Norfolk Broads. **Open:** All year
01493 700340 I Swan Cuders *thetophouse@aol.com* www.reedham.net **D:** Fr £25.00–£30.00 **S:** Fr £30.00 **Beds:** 1F 1T 1D **Baths:** 3 En cc

The Pyghtie, *26A The Hills, Reedham, Norwich, NR13 3AR.* Perfectly situated for exploring Norwich and Norfolk countryside. Superb accommodation. **Open:** All year
01493 701262 M M Blanche **Fax: 01493 701635** *Blanches@Reedham.co.uk* **D:** Fr £22.50–£25.00 **S:** Fr £30.00–£35.00 **Beds:** 1D **Baths:** 1 En (6)

Ridlington

TG3431 *Butchers' Arms*

The Old Rectory, *Ridlington, North Walsham, Norfolk, NR28 9NZ.* Perfectly situated; ideal for exploring Norfolk. Home-made breakfast. Tennis court. **Open:** All year
01692 650247 Mr Black *blacks7@email.com* **D:** Fr £20.00–£25.00 **S:** Fr £25.00–£30.00 **Beds:** 1D **Baths:** 1 En

Saham Toney

TF8902

The Croft, *69 Hills Road, Saham Toney, Thetford, Norfolk, IP25 7EW.* Beautiful creeper covered Victorian farmhouse. Delightful garden, quiet position. **Open:** All year
01953 881372 Mrs Baldwin **D:** Fr £20.00–£22.00 **S:** Fr £22.00–£24.00 **Beds:** 1T 1D **Baths:** 1 En 1 Sh (12) (4)

Salhouse

TG3114

Brooksbank, *Lower Street, Salhouse, Norwich, NR13 6RW.* C18th house Broadland village within easy reach of Norfolk coast. **Open:** All year (not Xmas)
01603 720420 (also fax) Mr & Mrs Coe *ray@brooksbanks.freeserve.co.uk* **D:** Fr £18.00–£20.00 **S:** Fr £25.00–£28.00 **Beds:** 2D 1T **Baths:** 3 En (4)

Salthouse

TG0843

Cumfus Bottom, *Purdy St, Salthouse, Holt, Norfolk, NR25 7XA.* Rooms set in country garden, only minutes away from the beach and heathland. **Open:** All year
01263 741118 Mrs Holman **D:** Fr £20.00–£22.50 **S:** Fr £20.00–£30.00 **Beds:** 1D 1T **Baths:** 2 En

Saxlingham Thorpe

TM2197

Foxhole Farm, *Windy Lane, Foxhole, Saxlingham Thorpe, Norwich, NR15 1UG.* Friendly welcome. Spacious farmhouse. Comfortable bedrooms. Generous English breakfasts. **Open:** All year (not Xmas) **Grades:** ETC 4 Diamond, AA 4 Diamond
01508 499226 (also fax) *foxholefarm@hotmail.com* **D:** Fr £19.00–£22.50 **S:** Fr £25.00 **Beds:** 1D 1T **Baths:** 2 En (8)

Sharrington

TG0336

Daubeney Hall, *Sharrington, Melton Constable, Norfolk, NR24 2PQ.* Attractive Listed farmhouse in quiet village. Splendid breakfast. Warm welcome. **Open:** Easter to Oct **Grades:** RAC 4 Diamond
01263 861412 N Ogier *ninaogier@hotmail.com* **D:** Fr £22.00 **S:** Fr £20.00–£25.00 **Beds:** 2T 1D **Baths:** 2 En 1 Pr

Sheringham

TG1543

Sheringham Lodge, *50 Cromer Road, Sheringham, Norfolk, NR26 8RS.* **Open:** All year **Grades:** ETC 3 Diamond
01263 821954 Mr & Mrs Walker *mikewalker19@hotmail.com* **D:** Fr £22.00–£24.00 **S:** Fr £22.00–£24.00 **Beds:** 1F 2D 1T 1S **Baths:** 1 Sh (5) (5)
Sheringham Lodge, run by Mike and Maggie Walker, is an attractive Edwardian house offering a warm welcome and accommodation with ensuite facilities to most rooms. We are a few minutes walk from the centre of Sheringham and the sea front.

Planning a longer stay? Always ask for any special rates

Holly Cottage, *14a The Rise, Sheringham, Norfolk, NR26 8QB.* Beamed cottage, upstairs seaview. Ideal touring/ walking, birdwatching. Christian welcome. **Open:** All year
01263 822807 Chrissy Foster *hollyperks@aol.com* www.sheringham-network.co.uk **D:** Fr £15.00–£25.00 **S:** Fr £25.00–£34.00 **Beds:** 1T 2D **Baths:** 3 En

Canton House, *14 Cliff Road, Sheringham, Norfolk, NR26 8BJ.* Warm welcome. Comfortable surroundings. Excellent breakfast. Home made bread. **Open:** All year (not Xmas/New Year)
01263 824861 Ms Rayment *chrissy@toomemt.freeserve.co.uk* **D:** Fr £20.50–£21.00 **S:** Fr £20.50–£21.00 **Beds:** 1T 2D **Baths:** 2 En 1 Sh

Highfield Guest House, *5 Montague Road, Sheringham, Norfolk, NR26 8LN.* Peaceful residence of character and quality. Luxury ensuites. Choice menus. **Open:** All year
01263 825524 Mr & Mrs Caldwell **D:** Fr £18.00–£25.00 **Beds:** 2F 2T 3D **Baths:** 6 En 1 Sh (7) (2)

The Birches, *27 Holway Road, Sheringham, Norfolk, NR26 8HW.* Small guest house conveniently situated for town and sea front. **Open:** Apr to Oct
01263 823550 Ms Pearce www.broadland.com/thebirches **D:** Fr £20.00–£25.00 **S:** Fr £25.00 **Beds:** 1D 1T **Baths:** 2 En (12) (2)

The Bay-Leaf Guest House, *10 St Peters Road, Sheringham, Norfolk, NR26 8QY.* Charming Victorian licensed guest house, nestled between steam railway and sea. **Open:** All year
01263 823779 Mr Pigott **Fax: 01263 820041** **D:** Fr £22.00–£25.00 **S:** Fr £25.00 **Beds:** 2F 3D 2T **Baths:** 7 En (4)

Whelk Coppers, *Westcliff, Sheringham, Norfolk, NR26 8LD.* Traditional English tea rooms panelled in Indian teak from old sailing ship. **Open:** All year (not Xmas/New Year)
01263 825771 S & P Foster *peter.foster@ic24.net* **D:** Fr £17.00–£20.00 **S:** Fr £17.00–£20.00 **Beds:** 1F 1D **Baths:** 1 En 1 Pr

Shipdham

TF9507

Pound Green Hotel, *Pound Green Lane, Shipham, Thetford, Norfolk, IP25 7LS.* An acre of own grounds. Peaceful rural setting. **Open:** All year
01362 820940 Mr Hales & Ms S Woods **Fax: 01362 821253** *poundgreen@aol.com* www.poundgreen.co.uk **D:** Fr £22.50–£25.00 **S:** Fr £25.00–£35.00 **Beds:** 1F 8D 1S **Baths:** 8 En 2 Pr (50) cc

Smallburgh

TG3324

The Crown Inn, *Smallburgh, Norwich, NR12 9AD.* **Open:** All year (not Xmas/New Year)
01692 536314 (also fax) **D:** Fr £22.50–£25.00 **S:** Fr £30.00–£35.00 **Beds:** 1T 1D **Baths:** 2 En (20) cc
C15th thatched & beamed village inn which has been recommended in the CAMRA Good Beer guide since 1990. 5 traditional cask ales, good selection of wines by the glass & bottle. Well recommended freshly prepared home-cooked food available.

Bramble House, *Catts Common, Smallburgh, Norfolk, NR12 9NS.* Friendliness and comfort guaranteed in our large country house, in 1.5 acres **Open:** All year (not Xmas)
01692 535069 (also fax) S Ross *bramblehouse@tesco.com* **D:** Fr £22.00–£24.00 **S:** Fr £30.00 **Beds:** 1F 1T 1D 1S **Baths:** 4 En (4)

South Lopham

TM0481

Malting Farm, *Blo Norton Road, South Lopham, Diss, Norfolk, IP22 2HT.* Elizabethan timber-framed farmhouse on working farm. Patchwork and quilting. **Open:** Jan to Dec
01379 687201 Mrs Huggings www.farmstayangela.co.uk **D:** Fr £21.00–£25.00 **S:** Fr £25.00–£30.00 **Beds:** 1D 1T **Baths:** 1 En 1 Sh

Sporle

TF8411

Corfield House, *Sporle, Swaffham, Norfolk, PE32 2EA.* Visit our website for full details and pictures. **Open:** Feb to Dec **Grades:** ETC 4 Diamond, Silver, AA 4 Diamond
01760 723636 Mr & Mrs Hickey *corfield.house@virgin.net* www.corfieldhouse.co.uk **D:** Fr £24.50 **S:** Fr £30.00 **Beds:** 2D 2T **Baths:** 4 Pr

B&B owners may vary rates – be sure to check when booking

Stalham

TG3725

The White House, *Wayford Bridge, Stalham, Norwich, Norfolk, NR12 9LH.* Comfortable detached family home close to the Broads. **Open:** All year
01692 583316 Mr Blowers **D:** Fr £22.00–£25.00 **S:** Fr £25.00 **Beds:** 1D 2T

Suton

TM0999

Rose Farm, *School Lane, Suton, Wymondham, Norfolk, NR18 9JN.* C17th farmhouse in 5 acres where our donkeys graze. Convenient Norwich, Broads. **Open:** All year (not Xmas)
01953 603512 Mrs Durrant **D:** Fr £20.00–£22.00 **S:** Fr £20.00–£25.00 **Beds:** 1F 1D 2S **Baths:** 3 Sh (4)

Avalon Farm, *Suton, Wymondham, Norfolk, NR18 9JQ.* Traditional farmhouse, quiet country location, few mins A11. All rooms decorated to high standard. **Open:** All year
01953 602339 Mrs Reynolds **D:** Fr £24.00–£27.00 **S:** Fr £24.00–£27.00 **Beds:** 8F **Baths:** 5 En 3 Sh (8)

Swaffham

TF8109

Purbeck House, *Whitsands Road, Swaffham, Norfolk, PE37 7BJ.* Friendly family house, warm welcome. Full breakfast, large garden. **Open:** All year
01760 721805 & 01760 725345 Mrs Webster **D:** Fr £18.00–£20.00 **S:** Fr £20.00 **Beds:** 2F 2T 2S **Baths:** 1 En 2 Sh (3)

Swanton Morley

TG0217 *Darby's, Angel Inn*

Kesmark House, *Gooseberry HIll, Swanton Morley, Dereham, Norfolk, NR20 4PP.* Beautiful listed house. Aga breakfasts. Breckland, Coast, Norwich. Also cottage. **Open:** All year (not Xmas/ New Year)
01362 637663 Mr & Mrs Willis **Fax: 01362 637800** *kesmark@netcomuk.co.uk* www.northnorfolk.co.uk/kesmark/ **D:** Fr £20.00–£25.00 **S:** Fr £29.00–£40.00 **Beds:** 1F 1T 2D **Baths:** 1 En 2 Pr (3)

Taverham

TG1514

Taverham Mill, *Costessey Road, Taverham, Norwich, Norfolk, NR8 6TA.* Quiet riverside location, fishing available. Private entrance, bathroom, sitting room with TV. **Open:** All year
01603 869495 & 01603 868200 Mr Watts **Fax: 01603 869495** **D:** Fr £22.50 **S:** Fr £30.00 **Beds:** 1D **Baths:** 1 Pr cc

Thetford

TL8783

43 Magdalen Street, *Thetford, Thetford, Norfolk, IP24 2BP.* House built in 1575 close to town centre. **Open:** All year (not Xmas/New Year)
01842 764564 Mrs Findlay **D:** Fr £36.00 **S:** Fr £18.00 **Beds:** 2T 1S **Baths:** 1 Sh (1)

Thompson

TL9196

The Thatched House, *Pockthorpe Corner, Thompson, Thetford, Norfolk, IP24 1PJ.* **Open:** All year
01953 483577 Mrs Mills **D:** Fr £20.00 **S:** Fr £25.00 **Beds:** 1D 2T **Baths:** 2 Sh 1 Pr (6) (4)
C16th, delightful village on the edge of the Brecklands.

College Farm, *Thompson, Thetford, Norfolk, IP24 1QG.* Converted C14th college of priests; 3-acre garden, wonderful breakfasts. **Open:** All year
01953 483318 (also fax) Mrs Garnier *collegefarm@amserve.net* **D:** Fr £25.00 **S:** Fr £25.00 **Beds:** 2D 1T **Baths:** 1 Pr 1 Sh 2 En (7) (10)

Thorpe St Andrew

TG2609

Norwood House, *14 Stanmore Road, Thorpe St Andrew, Norwich, Norfolk, NR7 0HB.* Detached house with attractive garden in peaceful cul-de-sac, 2 miles from historic Norwich. **Open:** All year (not Xmas)
01603 433500 Mrs Simpson **D:** Fr £20.00–£22.50 **S:** Fr £20.00–£22.50 **Beds:** 2D 1S **Baths:** 2 Sh (10) (4)

Thursford

TF9734

Old Coach House, *Thursford, Fakenham, Norfolk, NR21 0BD.* Peaceful farmhouse. 8m beautiful coastline. Suit birdwatchers and country lovers. **Open:** All year (not Xmas/New Year) **Grades:** AA 3 Diamond
01328 878273 Mrs Green **D:** Fr £20.00–£25.00 **S:** Fr £23.00–£25.00 **Beds:** 3T 1D **Baths:** 2 En 1 Sh (6)

Tilney St Lawrence

TF5514

The Garden House, *27 Magdalen Road, Tilney St Lawrence, King's Lynn, Norfolk, PE34 4QX.* Open countryside, fishing, Sandringham House and Historic Lynn nearby. **Open:** Easter to Oct
01945 880610 Mr & Mrs Swain **D:** Fr £16.00 **S:** Fr £20.00 **Beds:** 1T 1D **Baths:** 1 En 1 Sh (8)

Upton

TG3912 *White Horse*

Cherry Tree Cottage, *Marsh Road, Upton, Norwich, NR13 6BS.* Comfortably converted cottage, close Broads. Coasts: Norwich and Yarmouth. **Open:** All year (not Xmas/New Year)
01493 750509 **D:** Fr £23.00 **S:** Fr £23.00 **Beds:** 1T 1S **Baths:** 1 Pr (3)

Upwell

TF5002

Five Bells Inn, *1 New Road, Upwell, Wisbech, Cambs, PE14 9AA.* Attractive riverside village inn, comfortable rooms and award-winning restaurant. **Open:** All year
01945 772222 **Fax: 01945 774433** **D:** Fr £20.00–£25.00 **S:** Fr £25.00–£30.00 **Beds:** 1F 3D 3T **Baths:** 7 En (20) **cc**

Walton Highway

TF4912

Homeleigh Guest House, *Lynn Road, Walton Highway, Wisbech, Cambs, PE14 7DE.* Homeleigh guest house built 1880s. All rooms ensuite. **Open:** All year
01945 582356 Mrs Wiseman **Fax: 01945 587006** **D:** Fr £20.00 **S:** Fr £20.00 **Beds:** 2D 2T 2S **Baths:** 6 En (6) **cc**

Warham

TF9441

The Three Horseshoes / The Old Post Office, *69 Bridge Street, Warham, Wells-next-the-Sea, Norfolk, NR23 1NL.* Dream country cottage adjoining award-winning village pub. **Open:** All year (not Xmas)
01328 710547 Mr Salmon **D:** Fr £24.00–£26.00 **S:** Fr £24.00 **Beds:** 3D 1S **Baths:** 1 En 1 Sh (10)

Watton

TF9100

The Hare & Barrel Hotel, *80 Brandon Road, Watton, Thetford, Norfolk, IP25 6LB.* A family-run country house hotel, 'home from home'. **Open:** All year
01953 882752 Mr Raveh **Fax: 01953 882312** *manager@hare-and-barrel-hotel-norfolk.co.uk* **D:** Fr £24.50 **S:** Fr £35.00 **Beds:** 2F 4D 5T 5S **Baths:** 16 Pr (40)

BEDROOMS
D = Double
T = Twin
S = Single
F = Family

Wells-next-the-Sea

TF9143

Wingate, *Two Furlong Hill, Wells-next-the-Sea, Norfolk, NR23 1HQ.*
Open: All year
01328 711814 Ms Richards *Anne.Teresa.Richards@virgin.net*
D: Fr £34.00–£37.00 **S:** Fr £49.00–£52.00 **Beds:** 1T 2D **Baths:** 2 En 1 Pr (10)
Built as a wedding present for wildlife artist Frank Southgate, this lovely Edwardian house stands in an acre of gardens with ample parking. It offers excellent accommodation in a peaceful atmosphere. Delicious organic breakfast. Vegetarians/vegans catered for.

St Heliers Guest House, *Station Road, Wells-next-the-Sea, Norfolk, NR23 1EA.* Comfortable accommodation, excellent breakfasts, walk to quay, marshes, beach, shops. **Open:** Feb to Nov
01328 710361 (also fax) Mrs Kerr *bookings@st-heliers.co.uk* st-heliers.co.uk **D:** Fr £18.00–£26.00 **S:** Fr £20.00–£32.00 **Beds:** 1D 1T 1S **Baths:** 2 Sh 1 En (4)

East House, *East Quay, Wells-next-the-Sea, Norfolk, NR23 1LE.* Old house overlooking marsh, creeks and boats to distant sea. **Open:** All year (not Xmas)
01328 710408 Mrs Scott *scottseasthousewells@talk21.com* **D:** Fr £22.50 **S:** Fr £26.00–£30.00 **Beds:** 2T **Baths:** 2 En (7) (2)

Hideaway, *Red Lion Yard, Wells-next-the-Sea, Norfolk, NR23 1AX.* Evening meals supplied on special out of season weekends. **Open:** All year (not Xmas/New Year)
01328 710524 Miss Higgs *hideaway.wells@btinternet.com* **D:** Fr £21.00–£22.50 **S:** Fr £25.00–£35.00 **Beds:** 2T 1D **Baths:** 3 En

Brambledene, *Warham Road, Wells-next-the-Sea, Norfolk, NR23 1NE.* Homely bungalow near the Wells and Washington miniature railway. **Open:** Easter to Sept
01328 711143 Mr & Mrs Bramley **D:** Fr £16.00 **S:** Fr £16.00 **Beds:** 1F **Baths:** 1 Sh (2)

Planning a longer stay? Always ask for any special rates

BEDROOMS
D = Double
T = Twin
S = Single
F = Family

Welney

TL5294 *Lamb & Flag*

Stockyard Farm, *Wisbech Road, Welney, Wisbech, Cambs, PE14 9RQ.* Comfortable former Fenland farmhouse, rurally situated between Ely and Wisbech. **Open:** All year (not Xmas/New Year)
01354 610433 Mrs Bennett **D:** Fr £18.00 **S:** Fr £23.00–£25.00 **Beds:** 1T 1D **Baths:** 1 Sh (5) (2)

Wendling

TF9213

Greenbanks Country Hotel, *Wendling, Dereham, Norfolk, NR19 2AR.* Central touring, NT properties, private fishing, 5 ground floor suites. Meadow gardens. **Open:** All year
01362 687742 *greenbanks@skynow.com* **D:** Fr £28.00–£36.00 **S:** Fr £36.00–£50.00 **Beds:** 3F 3T 2D **Baths:** 8 En cc

West Dereham

TF6500

Bell Barn, *Lime Kiln Road, West Dereham, King's Lynn, PE33 9RT.* Quality accommodation with rustic charm, quiet rural setting. **Open:** All year (not Xmas)
01366 500762 (also fax) Mrs Wood *chris@woodbarn.freeserve.co.uk* **D:** Fr £20.00 **S:** Fr £25.00 **Beds:** 1F 1D **Baths:** 1 En 1 Pr (4)

West Runton

TG1842

Corner Cottage, *Water Lane, West Runton, Cromer, Norfolk, NR27 9QP.* Beach 300 metres, golf, horseriding, sea views. Great breakfast, peaceful. **Open:** All year
01263 838180 Mrs Powell **D:** Fr £20.00 **S:** Fr £30.00 **Beds:** 1F 1T 1D **Baths:** 1 Sh (8) (6)

West Somerton

TG4620

The White House Farm, *The Street, West Somerton, Great Yarmouth, Norfolk, NR29 4EA.* **Open:** All year (not Xmas)
01493 393991 Mr Dobinson *gc_dobinson@btopenworld.com* **D:** Fr £19.00–£22.00 **S:** Fr £23.00–£25.00 **Beds:** 2D 1T **Baths:** 1 En 1 Sh (4)
Welcoming, peaceful old farmhouse close to Broads (rowing dinghy) and lovely beach. Enjoyable walks and bike rides. Substantial breakfasts. Private/ensuite shower/bath rooms. Comfortable bedrooms overlooking sunny walled garden. Guest lounge and conservatory for space and relaxation.

Wicklewood

TG0702

Witch Hazel, *Church Lane, Wicklewood, Wymondham, NR18 9QH.* Peter and Eileen welcome you to Witch Hazel - a spacious detached house. **Open:** All year
01953 602247 (also fax) Mr & Mrs Blake **D:** Fr £20.00 **S:** Fr £26.00 **Beds:** 3D **Baths:** 3 En (15) (3)

Winterton-on-Sea

TG4919

Tower Cottage, *Black Street, Winterton-on-Sea, Great Yarmouth, Norfolk, NR29 4AP.* Pretty flint cottage. Excellent breakfast. Peaceful village, unspoilt sandy beach. **Open:** All year (not Xmas)
01493 394053 Mr Webster *towercott@aladdinscave.net* www.towercottage.co.uk **D:** Fr £20.00–£24.00 **S:** Fr £26.00 **Beds:** 2D 1T **Baths:** 2 En 1 Pr (3)

Wood Norton

TG0127

Manor Farm, *Wood Norton, Dereham, Norfolk, NR20 5BE.* A warm welcome awaits you at large Grade II Listed farmhouse. **Open:** All year (not Xmas/New Year)
01362 683231 Mrs Crowe **D:** Fr £20.00–£25.00 **Beds:** 1T 2D **Baths:** 2 En 1 Pr (10) (4)

Planning a longer stay? Always ask for any special rates

Worstead

TG3026 *New Inn*

Geoffrey The Dyer House, *Church Plain, Worstead, North Walsham, Norfolk, NR28 9AL.* C17th Listed building. Centre conservation village **Open:** All year
01692 536562 Mrs O'Hara *vacarie@bun.com* **D:** Fr £25.00 **S:** Fr £25.00–£28.00 **Beds:** 1F 1T 1D 1S **Baths:** 4 En (4)

Worthing

TG0019

Tannery House, *Church Road, Worthing, Dereham, Norfolk, NR20 5HR.* **Open:** All year (not Xmas/New Year)
01362 668202 Mr & Mrs Eve *georgebelindaeve@tesco.net* www.thetanneryhouse.co.uk **D:** Fr £22.00–£26.00 **S:** Fr £30.00 **Beds:** 2T 2D **Baths:** 2 En 1 Sh
Quietly situated C18th house in the heart of rural Norfolk. In unspoilt hamlet convenient to the coast, Broads, Norwich and Sandringham. The beautiful 4-acre garden with riverside setting includes a swimming pool and well-stocked fishing lake and water.

Wroxham

TG3017

Wroxham Park Lodge, *142 Norwich Road, Wroxham, Norwich, NR12 8SA.* Victorian house with garden, ideal touring Norfolk and the Broads. **Open:** All year **Grades:** ETC 4 Diamond
01603 782991 K Jackman *prklodge@nascr.net* **D:** Fr £20.00–£24.00 **S:** Fr £22.00–£30.00 **Beds:** 1T 2D **Baths:** 3 En (4)

Wymondham

TG1101

Turret House, *27 Middleton Street, Wymondham, Norfolk, NR18 0AB.* Victorian town house of considerable character - close to historic abbey. **Open:** All year
01953 603462 (also fax) Mrs Morgan **D:** Fr £20.00 **S:** Fr £20.00 **Beds:** 1F 1T 1S **Baths:** 1 Sh (2) cc

Rose Farm, *School Lane, Suton, Wymondham, Norfolk, NR18 9JN.* **Open:** All year (not Xmas)
01953 603512 Mrs Durrant **D:** Fr £20.00–£22.00 **S:** Fr £20.00–£25.00 **Beds:** 1F 1D 2S
Baths: 3 Sh (4)
C17th farmhouse in 5 acres where our donkeys graze. Convenient for Norwich, Norfolk Broads, coast & Snetterton race circuit. All bedrooms on ground floor overlooking fishing pond. All Trunk Road-Norwich to London half mile away. But very quiet location.

Avalon Farm, *Suton, Wymondham, Norfolk, NR18 9JQ.* Traditional farmhouse, quiet country location, few mins A11. All rooms decorated to high standard. **Open:** All year
01953 602339 Mrs Reynolds **D:** Fr £24.00–£27.00 **S:** Fr £24.00–£27.00 **Beds:** 8F
Baths: 5 En 3 Sh (8)

Home Farm, *Morley St Botolph, Wymondham, Norfolk, NR18 9SU.* Set in 4 acres of secluded grounds, 3 miles from 2 towns. **Open:** All year (not Xmas)
01953 602581 Mrs Morter **D:** Fr £20.00–£22.00 **S:** Fr £20.00–£22.00 **Beds:** 1T 1D 1S
Baths: 1 Sh (5) (5)

Northamptonshire

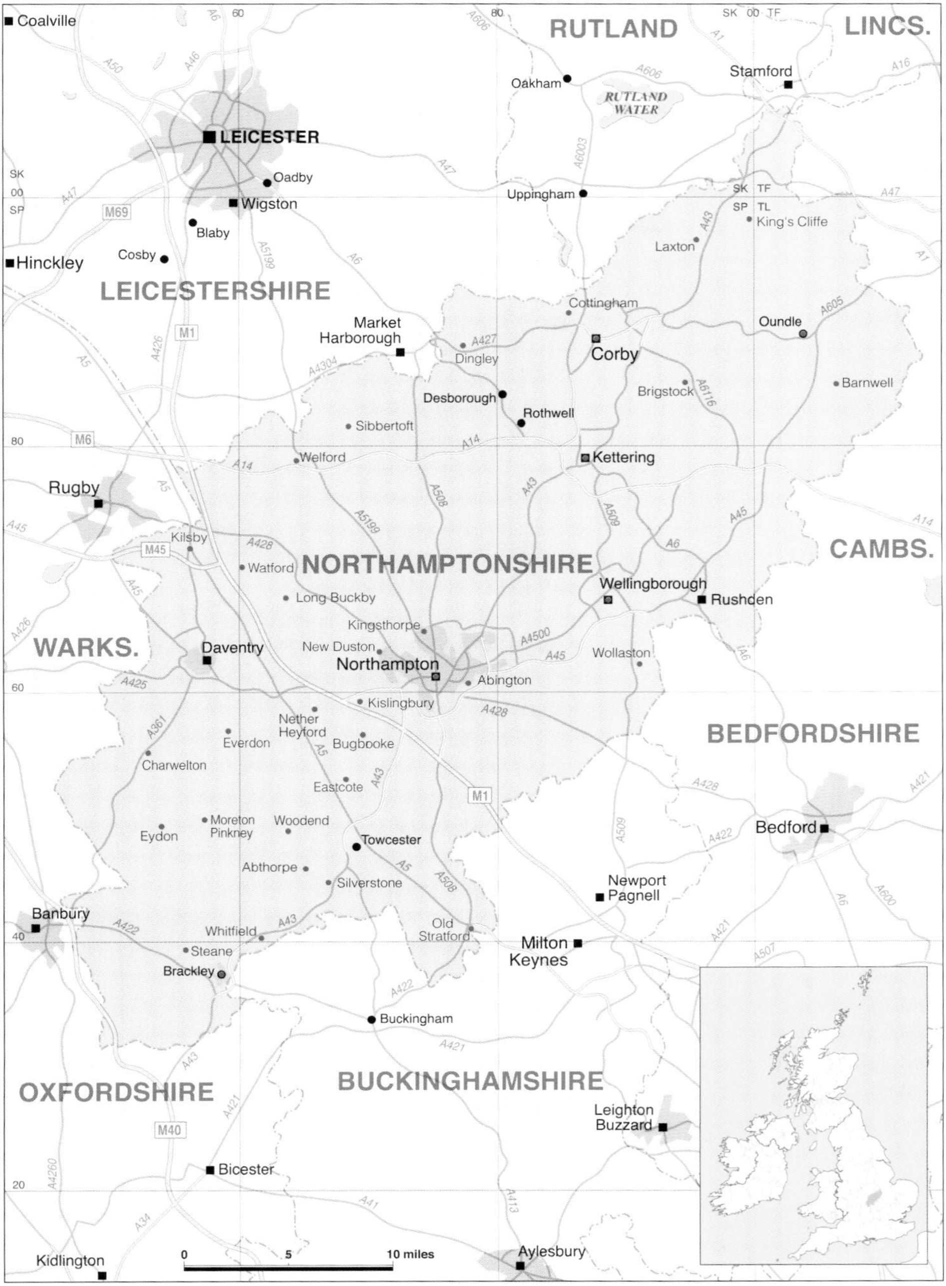

Abington

SP7761

Pembroke House, *36 Garrick Road, Abington, Northampton, NN1 5ND.* Beautiful Victorian property, all facilities, near park, town and M1. **Open:** Jan to Nov
01604 621858 Mr Thomas **D:** Fr £17.00–£19.00 **S:** Fr £17.50–£19.50 **Beds:** 1D 1T 1S **Baths:** 1 Sh

Abthorpe

SP6446 *Crown Inn, The New Inn*

Hilltop House, *Wappewham Road, Helmdow, Brackley, Northants, NN13 5QA.* Modern stone house convenient to Silverstone, Oxford Cotswolds and M40. **Open:** All year
01295 760560 Mrs Brodie **Fax: 01295 760 485** **D:** Fr £30.00–£35.00 **S:** Fr £30.00–£35.00 **Beds:** 2T **Baths:** 1 En 1 Pr (4)

Barnwell

TL0484

Lilford Lodge Farm, *Barnwell, Oundle, Peterborough, Cambridgeshire, PE8 5SA.* C19th farmhouse and adjoining barn recently converted. Set in the Nene Valley. **Open:** All year (not Xmas) **Grades:** AA 4 Diamond
01832 272230 (also fax) Mrs Dijksterhuis *trudy@lilford-lodge.demon.co.uk* www.lilford-lodge.demon.co.uk **D:** Fr £19.00–£22.00 **S:** Fr £19.00–£22.00 **Beds:** 1F 1D 1T 1S **Baths:** 4 En (20)

Brackley

SP5837

Walltree House Farm, *Steane, Brackley, Northants, NN13 5NS.* Central touring & business base. Comfortable warm converted stables. Ground-floor bedrooms and cottages. **Open:** All year (not Xmas)
01295 811235 Mrs Harrison **Fax: 01295 811147** *info@walltreehousefarm.co.uk* **D:** Fr £27.50–£37.50 **S:** Fr £37.50–£40.00 **Beds:** 2F 2D 2T **Baths:** 5 En 1 Pr (15) **cc**

Brigstock

SP9485

Bridge House, *3 Grafton Road, Brigstock, Kettering, Northants, NN14 3EY.* Quiet modern home in pretty village. Warm welcome. Full breakfast. **Open:** All year (not Xmas)
01536 373297 **D:** Fr £16.50–£20.00 **S:** Fr £16.50–£18.00 **Beds:** 1T 1S **Baths:** 1 Sh 1 En (3)

Bugbrooke

SP6757

Cherry Tree Cottage, *26a Camphill, Bugbrooke, Northampton, NN7 3PH.* Cleanliness, warm hospitality, hearty breakfast and pleasant surrounding are our speciality. **Open:** All year
01604 830929 Mrs Corben **D:** Fr £20.00–£25.00 **S:** Fr £20.00–£25.00 **Beds:** 1T 1D **Baths:** 1 Sh (2) (5)

Charwelton

SP5356 *Fox & Hounds*

Foxhall Farmhouse, *Charwelton, Daventry, Northants, NN11 6YY.* Self contained comfort, easily located, family run old traditional farmhouse. **Open:** All year
01327 261817 **Fax: 01327 264445** *drawit@globalnet.co.uk* **D:** Fr £20.00 **S:** Fr £25.00 **Beds:** 1T 1S **Baths:** 1 Pr (6)

Corby

SP8889

The Arches Guest House, *13 Croyde Avenue, Corby, Northants, NN18 8EG.* Near Rockingham Castle, Rockingham Speedway, Kirby Hall, Kettering Leisure Village. A14 nearby. **Open:** All year (not Xmas/New Year)
01536 268414 **D:** Fr £17.50 **S:** Fr £17.50 **Beds:** 3T 3S **Baths:** 3 Sh (6)

16 Dixon Walk, *Corby, Northants, NN17 1UR.* Near Rockingham Castle, Indy race track (opening Sept 2001). **Open:** All year
01536 402649 Mrs MacLeod **D:** Fr £15.00–£18.00 **S:** Fr £15.00–£18.00 **Beds:** 2S 1T

The Raven Hotel, *Rockingham Road, Corby, Northants, NN17 1UG.* The quality of a travel lodge plus that extra personal touch **Open:** All year
01536 202313 **Fax: 01536 203159** *ravenhotel@hotmail.com* www.mrbip.com **D:** Fr £21.50–£26.50 **S:** Fr £34.00–£44.00 **Beds:** 3F 12T 2D **Baths:** 5 En **cc**

Cottingham

SP8490

Bancroft House, *34 Bancroft Road, Cottingham, Market Harborough, Leics, LE16 8XA.* Friendly atmosphere. Quiet location. Basins in all bedrooms. Huge breakfast if required. **Open:** All year (not Xmas/New Year)
01536 770799 Mrs Evans *judy@bancroft88.fsnet.co.uk* **D:** Fr £20.00 **S:** Fr £20.00 **Beds:** 1D 2S **Baths:** 1 Sh (6)

Dingley

SP7787

Dingley Grange, *Sutton Lane, Dingley, Market Harborough, Leicestershire, LE16 8HL.* Elegant farmhouse in peaceful rolling countryside. Ideal walking/country pursuits. **Open:** All year (not Xmas/New Year)
01858 467387 Mr Elliott **Fax: 01848 434640** **D:** Fr £25.00 **S:** Fr £30.00 **Beds:** 1F 1D **Baths:** 1 En 1 Pr

Eastcote

SP6853

West Farm, *Gayton Road, Eastcote, Towcester, Northamptonshire, NN12 8NS.* **Open:** All year (not Xmas/New Year) **Grades:** ETC 4 Diamond, Silver
01327 830310 *west.farm@eastcote97.fsnet.co.uk* **D:** Fr £25.00–£30.00 **S:** Fr £25.00–£35.00 **Beds:** 1T 2D **Baths:** 3 En (10) (10)
Enjoy the peace, tranquillity and wonderful views of open countryside from our recently built stone farmhouse which is set in a beautiful garden with a small lake. Conveniently situated for Silverstone Circuit, Towcester Racecourse, Althorp, Canons Ashby and Sulgrave Manor.

Everdon

SP5957

Threeways House, *Everdon, Daventry, Northants, NN11 6BL.* Comfortable accommodation, peaceful conservation village, 5 mins' walk to pub meal. **Open:** All year **Grades:** ETC 4 Diamond, Silver
01327 361631 Mrs Barwood *elizabethbarwood@hotmail.com* www.threewayshouse.com **D:** Fr £25.00–£35.00 **S:** Fr £30.00–£40.00 **Beds:** 1F 1T 1D **Baths:** 4 En (6)

Please respect a B&B's wishes regarding children, animals and smoking

Eydon

SP5450

Crockwell Farm, *Eydon, Daventry, Northants, NN11 3QA.* Individually furnished accommodation in beautiful C17th barns. All bedrooms views over open countryside. **Open:** All year **01327 361358 & 07850 050716 (M)** J B Harper **Fax: 01327 361573** *info@crockwellfarm.co.uk* www.crockwellfarm.co.uk **D:** Fr £25.00–£30.00 **S:** Fr £30.00 **Beds:** 2F 2T 1D **Baths:** 4 En 1 Pr (6) cc

Kettering

SP8778

Hawthorn House Private Hotel, *2 Hawthorn Road, Kettering, Northants, NN15 7HS.* Victorian town house private hotel. Short drive A14 J9. **Open:** All year **Grades:** ETC 3 Diamond **01536 482513** Mrs McQuade **Fax: 01536 513121 D:** Fr £25.00 **S:** Fr £30.00 **Beds:** 1D 4T **Baths:** 3 En 2 Pr (4) cc

Pennels Guest House, *175 Beatrice Road, Kettering, Northants, NN16 9QR.* Quality accommodation, well-maintained, some ground room bedrooms overlooking private garden, quiet area. **Open:** All year **01536 481940** Mrs Green **Fax: 01536 410798** *pennelsgh@aol.com* www.members.aol.com/pennelsgh **D:** Fr £20.00–£22.00 **S:** Fr £22.50–£25.00 **Beds:** 1D 3T 3S **Baths:** 5 En 1 Sh (6) cc

Kilsby

SP5570

The Hollies Farmhouse, *Main Road, Kilsby, Rugby, Warks, CV23 8XR.* Comfortable farmhouse, conveniently central for leisure or business activities. **Open:** All year **01788 822629** Mrs Liddington **D:** Fr £20.00–£25.00 **S:** Fr £25.00–£35.00 **Beds:** 2D 1T **Baths:** 1 En 1 Sh (8)

King's Cliffe

TL0097

19 West Street, *King's Cliffe, Peterborough, Northamptonshire, PE8 6XB.* Grade II Listed 500-year-old house, beautiful walled garden, a King John hunting lodge. **Open:** All year (not Xmas) **01780 470365** J Dixon **Fax: 01780 470623** *100537.156@compuserve.com* www.kingjohnhuntinglodge.com **D:** Fr £20.00–£25.00 **S:** Fr £25.00–£30.00 **Beds:** 1S 1D 1T **Baths:** 3 Pr (2)

Freestone Lodge, *Bridge Street, King's Cliffe, Peterborough, PE8 6XH.* Traditional stone house in countryside. Rooms overlook garden and stables. **Open:** All year **01780 470213 (also fax)** Mr & Mrs Blunt *freesto@aol.com* **D:** Fr £20.00–£25.00 **S:** Fr £20.00–£25.00 **Beds:** 1F 2T **Baths:** 1 Sh (8) (6)

Kingsthorpe

SP7563

The Old Church Institute, *Kingsthorpe Village, Northampton, NN2 6QB.* Tastefully converted detached Edwardian property, attractive gardens. Close pubs/shops etc. **Open:** All year **01604 715500 (also fax)** E Bergin **D:** Fr £20.00–£25.00 **S:** Fr £20.00–£25.00 **Beds:** 2D 2T **Baths:** 2 En 1 Sh

Kislingbury

SP6959

The Elms, *Kislingbury, Northampton, NN7 4AH.* Victorian house overlooking our farm land. Close to Nene Way Walk. **Open:** All year **01604 830326** Mrs Sanders **D:** Fr £19.00 **S:** Fr £19.00 **Beds:** 1D 1T 1S 3F **Baths:** 1 Sh (4)

Laxton

SP9496 *Queen's Head*

The Old Vicarage, *Laxton, Corby, Northants, NN17 3AT.* Beautiful, C19th old-fashioned family home. Animals, art and lots more. **Open:** All year **01780 450248** Mrs Hill-Brookes **Fax: 01780 450398** *susan@marthahill.co.uk* **D:** Fr £21.00 **S:** Fr £21.00 (5) cc

Long Buckby

SP6267 *Globe Hotel, Stag's Head, Pytchley Hotel*

Murcott Mill, *Murcott, Long Buckby, Northampton, NN6 7QR.* Brilliant location for visiting Northamptonshire. Luxurious farmhouse accommodation. Friendly hosts. **Open:** All year **01327 842236** Mrs Hart **Fax: 01327 844524** *bhart6@compuserve.com* www.farmhohdap.co.uk **D:** Fr £22.00–£25.00 **S:** Fr £25.00–£30.00 **Beds:** 1F 2T **Baths:** 3 En (12)

Moreton Pinkney

SP5749

The Old Vicarage, *Moreton Pinkney, Daventry, Northants, NN11 3SQ.* Comfortable, pretty C18th house with walled garden in rural village. **Open:** All year (not Xmas) **01295 760057 (also fax)** Col & Mrs Eastwood *tim@tandjeastwood.fsnet.co.uk* www.tandjeastwood.fsnet.co.uk **D:** Fr £27.50–£30.00 **S:** Fr £30.00–£35.00 **Beds:** 1D 1T **Baths:** 1 En 1 Pr (7) (3)

Nether Heyford

SP6658

Heyford B&B, *27 Church Street, Nether Heyford, Northampton, NN7 3LH.* Lovely village, 1.5 miles M1 J16. Quiet, friendly and comfortable. **Open:** All year **01327 340872** Mrs Clements **D:** Fr £16.00–£20.00 **S:** Fr £20.00–£25.00 **Beds:** 3T 2S **Baths:** 2 En 1 Sh (8)

Northampton

SP7561

Castilian House, *34 Park Avenue North, Northampton, NN3 2JE.* Family run, easy access to main routes, town centre amenities. **Open:** All year (not Xmas) **01604 712863 (also fax)** Mrs Smith **D:** Fr £21.00 **S:** Fr £21.00 **Beds:** 1D 1S 1T

Rowena, *569 Harlestone Road, New Duston, Northampton, NN5 6NX.* Full of Victorian charm and character, close to city centre. **Open:** All year (not Xmas/New Year) **Grades:** ETC 4 Diamond **01604 755889** P Adcock *pat&bob@rowenabb.co.uk* www.rowenabb.co.uk **D:** Fr £22.50–£25.00 **S:** Fr £22.50–£25.00 **Beds:** 1D 1T 1S **Baths:** 1 Sh (3)

Old Stratford

SP7741

Furtho Manor Farm, *Old Stratford, Milton Keynes, Bucks, MK19 6BA.* Dairy and arable farm, 10 mins to central Milton Keynes. **Open:** All year (not Xmas) **01908 542139 (also fax)** Mrs Sansome *dsansome@farming.co.uk* **D:** Fr £20.00–£22.00 **S:** Fr £20.00–£25.00 **Beds:** 1D 2T **Baths:** 2 Sh (6)

Oundle

TL0487

Lilford Lodge Farm, *Barnwell, Oundle, Peterborough, Cambridgeshire, PE85SA.* **Open:** All year (not Xmas) **Grades:** AA 4 Diamond **01832 272230 (also fax)** Mrs Dijksterhuis *trudy@lilford-lodge.demon.co.uk* www.lilford-lodge.demon.co.uk **D:** Fr £19.00–£22.00 **S:** Fr £19.00–£22.00 **Beds:** 1F 1D 1T 1S **Baths:** 4 En (20) C19th farmhouse and adjoining barn recently converted. Set in the Nene Valley, 3 miles south of Oundle, 5 miles north of A14. Peterborough, Stamford, Kettering, Wellingborough and Corby are within easy reach. Coarse fishing available. Quiet, rural location.

Ashworth House, *75 West Street, Oundle, Peterborough, Northamptonshire, PE8 4EJ.* Grade II Listed town house with attractive walled gardens, in historic Oundle, close to the town centre and amenities, country park and the famous public school. Very comfortable ensuite accommodation with colour TV. Imaginative, traditional Aga cooking. **Open:** All year
01832 275312 (also fax) Mrs Crick **D:** Fr £20.00–£25.00 **S:** Fr £25.00–£30.00 **Beds:** 1D 1T **Baths:** 2 En (1)

Sibbertoft

SP6882

The Wrongs, *Welford Road, Sibbertoft, Market Harborough, Leics, LE16 9UJ.* Modern bungalow in open countryside. Carp fishing lake, working farm. **Open:** All year
01858 880886 Mrs Hart **Fax: 01858 880485** *maryhart@farming.co.uk* **D:** Fr £18.00–£20.00 **S:** Fr £18.00–£20.00 **Beds:** 1D 1S **Baths:** 1 Sh **cc**

Silverstone

SP6644

Silverthorpe Farm, *Abthorpe Road, Silverstone, Towcester, Northants, NN12 8TW.* Spacious, family-run rural bungalow, 1.5 miles Silverstone Circuit. **Open:** All year (not Xmas)
01327 858020 Mrs Branch **D:** Fr £25.00 **S:** Fr £25.00–£30.00 **Beds:** 1F 1D 1T 1S **Baths:** 2 Sh (8)

Steane

SP5539

Walltree House Farm, *Steane, Brackley, Northants. NN13 5NS.* Central touring & business base. Comfortable warm converted stables. Ground-floor bedrooms and cottages. **Open:** All year (not Xmas)
01295 811235 Mrs Harrison **Fax: 01295 811147** *info@walltreehousefarm.co.uk* **D:** Fr £27.50–£37.50 **S:** Fr £37.50–£40.00 **Beds:** 2F 2D 2T **Baths:** 5 En 1 Pr (15) **cc**

Watford

SP6068

Pandock Cottage, *Watford, Northampton, NN6 7UE.* Close to M1 (J18), spacious and traditionally furnished, rural - car essential. **Open:** All year (not Xmas)
01788 823615 D: Fr £20.00–£30.00 **S:** Fr £20.00–£25.00 **Beds:** 3F 1D 1T 1S **Baths:** 2 En (3)

Welford

SP6480

West End Farm, *5 West End, Welford, Northampton, NN6 6HJ.* Comfortable 1848 farmhouse. Quiet village street. 2 miles A14 J1. **Open:** All year **Grades:** ETC 4 Diamond
01858 575226 Mrs Bevin *bevin@uklynx.net* **D:** Fr £18.00–£20.00 **S:** Fr £18.00–£24.00 **Beds:** 1D 1T **Baths:** 1 Sh (2)

Wellingborough

SP8967

Euro-Hotel, *90-92 Midland Road, Wellingborough, Northamptonshire, NN8 1NB.* Modernised new hotel. **Open:** All year
01933 228761 D: Fr £18.00–£42.00 **S:** Fr £20.00–£35.00 **Beds:** 2F 3T 6D 5S **Baths:** 6 En 3 Sh (15) **cc**

High View Hotel, *156 Midland Road, Wellingborough, Northants, NN8 1NG.* Large detached brick building near town centre and railway station. **Open:** All year (not Xmas/New Year)
01933 278733 Fax: 01933 225948 *hotelhighview@hotmail.com* **D:** Fr £22.50–£29.50 **S:** Fr £29.95–£45.00 **Beds:** 2F 3T 4D 5S **Baths:** 14 En (3) (10) **cc**

Duckmire, *1 Duck End, Wollaston, Wellingborough, Northants, NN29 7SH.* Old stone house full of character, accessible for Wellingborough, Northampton, Milton Keynes. **Open:** All year (not Xmas)
01933 664249 (also fax) Mrs Woodrow *kerry@foreverengland.freeserve.co.uk* **D:** Fr £22.00 **S:** Fr £22.00 **Beds:** 1T **Baths:** 1 Pr (2)

Whitfield

SP6039 *Sun Inn*

The Thatches, *Whitfield, Brackley, Northants, NN13 5TQ.* Close to Silverstone NT Gardens, Sulgrave Manor, overlooking beautiful countryside. **Open:** All year (not Xmas/New Year)
01280 850358 Field **D:** Fr £20.00–£22.50 **S:** Fr £20.00–£25.00 **Beds:** 1F 1T 1D **Baths:** 1 Sh (2)

Wollaston

SP9162

45 Eastfield Road, *Wollaston, Wellingborough, Northamptonshire, NN29 7RS.* Friendly, helpful accommodation offering quality rooms and excellent breakfasts. **Open:** All year
01933 665266 Mr & Mrs Childs *eastfield.wollaston@talk21.com* **D:** Fr £20.00–£25.00 **S:** Fr £25.00–£30.00 **Beds:** 1F 1T **Baths:** 1 En 1 Pr

Woodend

SP6149

Christacorn House, *Main Street, Woodend, Towcester, Oxon, NN12 8RX.* Period house in rural village. Parking. 5 miles from Silverstone. **Open:** All year (not Xmas/New Year)
01327 860968 Ms Manners **Fax: 01327 860452** *mannersfam@ntlworld.com* **D:** Fr £22.50–£25.00 **S:** Fr £22.50–£25.00 **Beds:** 1S 2D 1T **Baths:** 2 Sh (6)

Northumberland

Acomb

NY9366

Mariner's Cottage Hotel, *Fallowfield Dene Road, Acomb, Hexham, Northd, NE46 4RP.* **Open:** All year
01434 603666 Miss Darling **D:** Fr £18.00–£20.00 **S:** Fr £18.00–£20.00 **Beds:** 1F 1D 1T 2S **Baths:** 3 Pr 2 Sh (5) (60)
Hotel set in country, 3 miles from market town of Hexham, within easy reach of Kielder Water & Hexham racecourse. Reduced rates for 2 nights or more, tea & coffee, television all rooms.

Allendale

NY8355

Thornley House, *Allendale, Hexham, Northd, NE47 9NH.* Beautiful country house in spacious grounds near Hadrian's Wall. **Open:** All year
01434 683255 Mr Finn *e.finn@ukonline.co.uk* **D:** Fr £18.50–£19.50 **S:** Fr £18.50–£19.50 **Beds:** 2D 1T **Baths:** 2 En 1 Pr (9) (4)

Allensford

NZ0750

Willerby Grange Farm, *Allensford, Castleside, Consett, County Durham, DH8 9BA.* Willerby Grange, quality accommodation, beautiful views. Ideal walking, biking, history. **Open:** All year
01207 508752 (also fax) Mr & Mrs Jopling *stay@willerbygrange.co.uk* www.willerbygrange.co.uk **D:** Fr £19.50–£22.50 **S:** Fr £22.50–£25.00 **Beds:** 2T 4D **Baths:** 6 En (10) cc

Alnmouth

NU2410

Saddle Hotel & Grill, *24/25 Northumberland Street, Alnmouth, Northd, NE66 2RA.* Small family run hotel in idyllic Northumbrian coastal village. **Open:** All year **Grades:** ETC 2 Star
01665 830476 **D:** Fr £30.00–£35.00 **S:** Fr £35.00–£40.00 **Beds:** 1F 3T 4D **Baths:** 8 En

Hipsburn Farm, *Lesbury, Alnmouth, Alnwick, Northd, NE66 3PY.* Large Georgian farmhouse, centrally located on heritage coast line, superb views over Aln Estuary. Ideally situated for golfers, walkers and bird watchers. Northumberland National Park offers a wonderful opportunity for those wishing to walk and explore also Farne Islands famous for colonies of seals and seabirds. **Open:** Easter to Oct
01665 830206 (also fax) Ms Tulip **D:** Fr £24.00–£30.00 **S:** Fr £24.00–£30.00 **Beds:** 2D 1T **Baths:** 3 En

Beaches B&B, *56 Northumberland Street, Alnmouth, Northd, NE66 2RJ.* Cosy oak-beamed former granary, bright spacious bedrooms above popular BYO restaurant. **Open:** All year
01665 830443 Mrs Hall **D:** Fr £18.00–£25.00 **S:** Fr £18.00–£30.00 **Beds:** 1D 1T **Baths:** 2 En

Alnwick

NU1813

Charlton House, *2 Aydon Gardens, Alnwick, Northd, NE66 2NT.*
Enjoy Northumberland Coast and Castles from our delightful Victorian house.
Open: All year (not Xmas/New Year)
Grades: ETC 4 Diamond
01665 605185 K & R J Bateman www.smoothhound.co.uk/hotels/charlt2.html **D:** Fr £21.00–£25.00 **S:** Fr £30.00–£40.00 **Beds:** 1T 3D 1S **Baths:** 5 En (4)

Aydon House, *South Road, Alnwick, Northd, NE66 2NT.* Comfortable and clean accommodation offered. Large private car park. **Open:** Easter to Oct
01665 602218 Mr Carroll **D:** Fr £19.00–£25.00 **S:** Fr £19.00–£25.00 **Beds:** 2F 2D 2T 2S **Baths:** 8 En (9)

Reighamsyde, *The Moor, Alnwick, Northd, NE66 2AJ.* Large detached house and gardens overlooking moors and Dukes Park. **Open:** Easter to Oct
01665 602535 Mrs Temple *reighamsyde@aol.com* **D:** Fr £20.00–£22.00 **S:** Fr £30.00–£35.00 **Beds:** 2D 1T **Baths:** 3 En (3)

Rooftops, *14 Blakelaw Road, Alnwick, Northd, NE66 1AZ.* Spacious accommodation panoramic views. Friendly, hospitality tray with home baking, fresh fruit. **Open:** Jan to Nov **Grades:** ETC 4 Diamond, Silver
01665 604201 Mrs Blair *rooftops.alnwick@talk21.com* www.rooftops.ntb.org.uk **D:** Fr £19.00 **Beds:** 1D **Baths:** 1 En (1)

The Georgian Guest House, *Hotspur Street, Alnwick, Northd, NE66 1QE.* Friendly, family-run stone guest house only yards from C14th Hotspur Tower. **Open:** All year
01665 602398 (also fax) Mr Gibb *georgianguesthouse@eggconnect.net* **D:** Fr £15.00–£20.00 **S:** Fr £20.00–£25.00 **Beds:** 2T 2D **Baths:** 4 En (3)

National Grid References given are for villages, towns and cities – not for individual houses

Bamburgh

NU1734

Greengates, *34 Front Street, Bamburgh, Northumberland, NE69 7BJ.* Castle views (100 metres away). Breakfast all local produce. **Open:** All year **Grades:** ETC 3 Diamond
01668 214535 Claire Sundin *greengatesbamburgh@amserve.com* **D:** Fr £19.50–£35.00 **S:** Fr £25.00–£45.00 **Beds:** 2T 1D **Baths:** 2 En 1 Pr cc

Broome, *22 Ingram Road, Bamburgh, Northumberland, NE69 7BT.* Peaceful location on edge of village - 5 mins' walk to beach/castle. **Open:** All year (not Xmas/New Year)
01668 214287 Ms Dixon *MDixon4394@aol.com* **D:** Fr £25.00–£28.00 **S:** Fr £30.00–£35.00 **Beds:** 1T 1D **Baths:** 1 Sh (12) (2)

Bardon Mill

NY7865 *Milecastle Inn*

Carrsgate East, *Bardon Mill, Hexham, Northumberland, NE47 7EX.* Relaxing, comfortable C17th home. Great views, good exploration base. **Open:** Feb to Nov
01434 344376 & 07710 981533 (M) Mrs Armstrong **Fax: 01434 344011** *lesley@armstrongrl.freeserve.co.uk* **D:** Fr £23.00–£27.00 **S:** Fr £25.00–£27.00 **Beds:** 2D **Baths:** 2 En (6)

Beadnell

NU2329

Beach Court, *Harbour Road, Beadnell, Northd, NE67 5BJ.* Magnificent turreted beachside home offering an atmosphere of timeless tranquillity. **Open:** All year **Grades:** ETC 5 Diamond, SIlver
01665 720225 Mrs Field **Fax: 01665 721499** *info@beachcourt.com* www.beachcourt.com **D:** Fr £29.50–£49.50 **S:** Fr £44.50–£64.50 **Beds:** 2D 1T **Baths:** 3 Pr (4)

Beadnell Bay

NU2327

Low Dover, *Harbour Road, Beadnell Bay, Chathill, Northd, NE67 5BJ.*
Open: All year (not Xmas)
01665 720291 & 07971 444070 (M) Mrs Thompson **Fax: 01665 720291** *kathandbob@lowdover.co.uk* www.lowdover.co.uk **D:** Fr £27.00–£35.00 **Beds:** 2D 1T **Baths:** 3 En (12) (2) cc
Virtually encompassed by the sea, superior beachside accommodation. Restful ground floor suites, each with private lounge & patio door. Beautiful garden. Breakfast with sea views. Sandy beach 50 metres. Superb website. 'Which?' B&B Guide. Also 4 Star s/c. Farne Islands 3 miles.

B&B owners may vary rates – be sure to check when booking

Beal

NU0643

Brock Mill Farmhouse, *Brock Mill, Beal, Berwick-upon-Tweed, Northumberland, TD15 2PB.* Quality accommodation opposite Lindisfarne. Perfect for discovering Northumbria and Borders. **Open:** Feb to Mar
01289 381283 (also fax) Ms Rogerson www.lindisfarnelinks.co.uk **D:** Fr £20.00–£25.00 **S:** Fr £20.00–£30.00 **Beds:** 1F 1T 1D 1S **Baths:** 2 Sh (6) cc

Bedlington

NZ2582

Woodside, *Hartford Bridge Farm, Hartford Bridge, Bedlington, Northumberland, NE22 6AL.* Centrally situated for rural or urban businesses. Guests' comfort our main aim. **Open:** All year (not Xmas/New Year)
01670 822035 Mrs Hoskins **D:** Fr £20.00–£22.00 **S:** Fr £18.00–£25.00 **Beds:** 1T 1S **Baths:** 1 En 1 Pr (5)

Belford

NU1033 *Apple Inn, Black Swan, Bluebell Hotel, Warenford Lodge*

The Farmhouse Guest House, *24 West Street, Belford, Northumberland, NE70 7QE.* Central village location quiet comfortable accommodation home cooking speciality. **Open:** All year (not Xmas)
01668 213083 Mr & Mrs Wood **D:** Fr £18.00–£23.00 **S:** Fr £23.00–£28.00 **Beds:** 1F 2D **Baths:** 2 En 1 Pr (1)

Oakwood House, *3 Cragside Avenue, Belford, Northumberland, NE70 7NA.* A quality country-style home with panoramic views over open countryside. **Open:** All year
01668 213303 Ms Allan **D:** Fr £21.00–£23.00 **S:** Fr £26.00–£28.00 **Beds:** 2D 1T **Baths:** 2 En 1 Pr (3)

Bellingham

NY8383

Lynn View, *Bellingham, Hexham, Northd, NE48 2BL.* Comfortable friendly accommodation in village. Close to all amenities. **Open:** All year (not Xmas)
01434 220344 Mrs Batey **D:** Fr £18.00–£20.00 **S:** Fr £20.00–£24.00 **Beds:** 2D 1T **Baths:** 1 Sh (2) (3)

Lyndale Guest House, *Bellingham, Hexham, Northd, NE48 2AW.* Explore Borderlands and Nature Trails and Hadrian's Wall, Pennine Way, Kielder Water or Cycleways including 'Reivers' Route. Enjoy a welcome break. Relax in our walled garden. Sun lounge. Panoramic views. Excellent dinners. Superb Breakfasts. Quality ground-floor ensuites. **Open:** All year (not Xmas)
01434 220361 & 07778 925479 (M) Mrs Gaskin **Fax: 01434 220361** *joy@lyndalegh.fsnet.co.uk* www.s-h-systems.co.uk/hotels/lyndalehtm/ **D:** Fr £23.50–£25.00 **S:** Fr £25.00–£30.00 **Beds:** 1F 2D 1T 1S **Baths:** 2 En 1 Pr 1 Sh (5) cc

Belsay

NZ1078 *Highlander*

Bounder House, *Belsay, Newcastle-upon-Tyne, NE20 0JR.* Comfortable B&B. Newcastle Airport nearby. Convenient for exploring Northumberland. **Open:** All year
01661 881267 Mrs Fearns **Fax: 01661 881266** *k.fearns@bigfoot.com* **D:** Fr £20.00 **S:** Fr £25.00 **Beds:** 1F 1T 1D **Baths:** 2 En 1 Pr cc

Berwick-upon-Tweed

NT9953

40 Ravensdowne, *Berwick-upon-Tweed, Northumberland, TD15 1DQ.* **Open:** All year (not Xmas) **Grades:** ETC 4 Diamond, Silver, RAC 4 Diamond
01289 306992 Mrs Muckle **Fax: 01289 331606** *petedot@dmuckle.freeserve.co.uk* www.secretkingdom.com/40 **D:** Fr £22.50–£27.50 **Beds:** 1F 2D 1T **Baths:** 4 En
A warm welcome awaits you, 3 luxury ensuite rooms furnished to a very high standard. Hearty breakfast with fresh local produce and real coffee. 1 minute to Elizabethan walls. 2 minutes to town centre. Resident parking tickets supplied. No smoking.

Rob Roy Pub & Restaurant, *Dock Road, Tweedmouth, Berwick-upon-Tweed, Northumberland, TD15 2BQ.* **Open:** All year (not Xmas)
01289 306428 Mr Wilson **Fax: 01289 303629** *therobroy@btinternet.com* www.therobroy.co.uk **D:** Fr £26.00 **S:** Fr £35.00 **Beds:** 1D 1T **Baths:** 2 En
Stone-built cosy riverside pub with open coal fire. Bar/restaurant menus offer fresh Northumbrian salmon and seafood, lobster, crab, oysters etc. 2 mins Berwick centre or sea front. Excellent situation to explore Northumberland. Celebrating 22 years this year with the Wilsons.

The Old Vicarage Guest House, *Church Road, Tweedmouth, Berwick-upon-Tweed, Northumberland, TD15 2AN.* Attractive C19th detached house, refurbished to highest standards. 10 mins' walk from town centre. **Open:** All year (not Xmas) **Grades:** ETC 4 Diamond, AA 4 Diamond
01289 306909 Mrs Richardson **Fax: 01289 309052** *stay@oldvicarageberwick.co.uk* www.oldvicarageberwick.co.uk **D:** Fr £17.00–£27.00 **S:** Fr £17.00–£19.00 **Beds:** 1F 4D 1T 1S **Baths:** 4 En 1 Sh (5)

West Sunnyside House, *Tweedmouth, Berwick-upon-Tweed, Northd, TD15 2QN.* C19th farmhouse, adjacent to Swan Leisure Centre on the A1167. **Open:** All year **Grades:** ETC 4 Diamond
01289 305387 (also fax) Ms Jamieson **D:** Fr £20.00–£25.00 **S:** Fr £25.00–£30.00 **Beds:** 1T 2D **Baths:** 2 En 1 Pr

Cobbled Yard Hotel, *40 Walkergate, Berwick-upon-Tweed, Northumberland, TD15 1DJ.* Surrounded by Berwick's Elizabethan walls, 2 mins' walk town centre. Food for all tastes. **Open:** All year **Grades:** ETC 3 Diamond
01289 308407 Ms Miller **Fax: 01289 330623** *cobbledyardhotel@berwicks35.fsnet.co.uk* www.cobbledyardhotel.com **D:** Fr £30.00 **S:** Fr £40.00 **Beds:** 3F 2D **Baths:** 5 En cc

Queens Head Hotel, *6 Sandgate, Berwick-upon-Tweed, TD15 1EP.* Family-run hotel, situated in town centre near historic town walls. **Open:** All year
01289 307852 Mr Kerr **Fax: 01289 307858** **D:** Fr £35.00–£40.00 **S:** Fr £35.00–£40.00 **Beds:** 2F 1D 2T 1S **Baths:** 6 En cc

Dervaig Guest House, *1 North Road, Berwick-upon-Tweed, TD15 1PW.* Large Victorian guest house, close railway station/town centre ample private parking. **Open:** All year
01289 307378 Mrs Tait **Fax: 01289 332321** *dervaig@talk21.com* www.dervaig-guesthouse.co.uk **D:** Fr £20.00–£27.00 **S:** Fr £25.00–£45.00 **Beds:** 1F 2D 2T **Baths:** 5 En (8)

Planning a longer stay? Always ask for any special rates

51 Church Street, *Berwick-upon-Tweed, Northumberland, TD15 1EE.* Situated within town walls, near shops and amenities. **Open:** All year
01289 306666 Mr Silvester *silprops@aol.com*
D: Fr £18.00–£22.00 **S:** Fr £20.00–£25.00
Beds: 1T 1D **Baths:** 2 En

Hillend, *4 The Crescent, Berwick-upon-Tweed, TD15 1RT.* Victorian family home over looking sea. Lindisfarne/Holy Island nearby. **Open:** Easter to Oct
01289 304454 Ms Law **D:** Fr £17.00–£20.00
Beds: 1T 1D **Baths:** 1 Pr 1 Sh (2)

6 North Road, *Berwick-upon-Tweed, Northumberland, TD15 1PL.* Beautiful Edwardian house; spacious, comfortable rooms near town centre, railway station. **Open:** All year (not Xmas)
01289 308949 (also fax) Ms Booth **D:** Fr £17.00–£19.00 **Beds:** 1F 1D **Baths:** 1 Sh

Bridge View, *14 Tweed Street, Berwick-upon-Tweed, Northumberland, TD15 1NG.* Centrally situated 200-year-old house, three minutes from town centre and railway station. **Open:** All year
01289 308098 Mrs Weatherley **D:** Fr £20.00–£25.00 **S:** Fr £25.00–£28.00 **Beds:** 1F 1S **Baths:** 1 En 1 Sh

The Friendly Hound, *Ford Common, Berwick-upon-Tweed, Northumberland, TD15 2QD.* Sympathetically restored to create a welcoming home, comfortable accommodation, good food, super views. **Open:** All year
01289 388554 Mrs Maycock *friendlyhound.b.b.@talk21.com* **D:** Fr £21.50–£23.00 **S:** Fr £21.50–£23.00 **Beds:** 1F 2D **Baths:** 3 En (5)

Blacka Burn

NY8278

Hetherington Farm, *Blacka Burn, Wark, Hexham, Northd, NE48 3DR.* Comfortable farmhouse on Pennine Way. Friendly atmosphere. Ideal walking, cycling. **Open:** All year (not Xmas/New Year)
01434 230260 (also fax) Mrs Nichol *a-nichol@hotmail.com* **D:** Fr £20.00–£26.00 **S:** Fr £22.00–£26.00 **Beds:** 3F 1T 1D 2S **Baths:** 2 En 1 Sh (8) (2)

Boulmer

NU2614

21 Boulmer Village, *Alnwick, Northumberland, NE66 3BS.* Charming fisherman's cottage. Log fire. Beautiful views overlooking the sea. **Open:** Mar to Nov
01665 577262 M H Campbell **D:** Fr £20.00–£25.00 **S:** Fr £20.00–£27.00 **Beds:** 2D **Baths:** 2 En 1 Pr (5)

Chatton

NU0528

The Old Manse, *New Road, Chatton, Alnwick, Northumberland, NE66 5PU.* Beautiful Victorian Manse, NTB B&B of Year 1999 & 2000. **Open:** All year
01668 215343 C Brown *chattonbb@aol.com* www.oldmansechatton.ntb.org.uk **D:** Fr £25.00–£30.00 **S:** Fr £25.00–£45.00 **Beds:** 1T 1D **Baths:** 2 En (10) (4)

Cheswick

NU0246

Ladythorne House, *Cheswick, Berwick-upon-Tweed, TD15 2RW.* Beautiful Georgian country house, wonderful views, central rural location, unspoilt beaches. **Open:** All year **Grades:** ETC 3 Diamond
01289 387382 Mrs Parker **Fax: 01289 387073** *valparker@ladythorneguesthouse.freeserve.co.uk* www.ladythorneguesthouse.freeserve.co.uk
D: Fr £17.00–£18.00 **S:** Fr £17.00–£18.00
Beds: 2F 2T 1D 1S **Baths:** 3 Sh (8)

The Cat Inn, *Cheswick, Berwick-upon-Tweed, TD15 2RL.* Ideally situated for Lindisfarne golf, fishing, beaches and castles. **Open:** All year (not Xmas/New Year)
01289 387251 (also fax) D: Fr £18.00–£20.00 **S:** Fr £18.00–£25.00 **Beds:** 2F 5T **Baths:** 4 En 3 Sh (20)

Chollerford

NY9170

Brunton Water Mill, *Chollerford, Hexham, Northd, NE46 4EL.* Beautifully converted water mill on the doorstep of Brunton Turrett. **Open:** All year
01434 681002 Mrs Pesarra *pessara@bruntonmill.freeserve.co.uk* **D:** Fr £24.00–£26.00 **S:** Fr £40.00 **Beds:** 1D 1T **Baths:** 2 En 1 Sh (8)

Corbridge

NY9964

Dilston Mill, *Dilston, Corbridge, Northumberland, NE45 5QZ.* Historic converted mill. Private suite: sleeps 2-6. Beautiful riverside setting. **Open:** All year
01434 633493 Mrs Ketelaar **Fax: 01434 633513** *susan@dilstonmill.com* www.dilstonmill.com **D:** Fr £25.00–£28.00 **S:** Fr £35.00–£40.00 **Beds:** 1F 1T 1D **Baths:** 1 Pr (3)

Priorfield, *Hippingstones Lane, Corbridge, Northd, NE45 5JP.* Elegantly furnished family house. Peaceful location. Whirlpool bath in double room. **Open:** All year
01434 633179 (also fax) Mrs Steenberg
D: Fr £18.00–£25.00 **S:** Fr £25.00–£32.00
Beds: 1D 1T **Baths:** 2 En (5) (2)

Cottonshopeburnfoot

NT7801

Border Forest Caravan Park, *Cottonshopeburnfoot, Otterburn, Newcastle-upon-Tyne, NE19 1TF.* Attractive motel, chalet rooms situated in picturesque Kielder Forest Park. **Open:** All year (not Xmas)
01830 520259 Mr & Mrs Bell **D:** Fr £19.00 **S:** Fr £21.00 **Beds:** 2F **Baths:** 2 En (1) (10)

Craster

NU2519

Howick Scar Farm House, *Craster, Alnwick, Northd, NE66 3SU.* Comfortable farmhouse with views towards the sea. Explore coast, castles. **Open:** Easter to Nov **Grades:** ETC 3 Diamond
01665 576665 & 07855 604701 (M) Mrs Curry **Fax: 01665 576665** *howick.scar@virgin.net* www.howickscar.co.uk **D:** Fr £19.00–£20.00 **S:** Fr £25.00–£28.00 **Beds:** 2D **Baths:** 1 Sh (3)

Stonecroft, *Dunstan, Craster, Alnwick, Northd, NE66 3SZ.* Friendly family home. Spacious comfortable. Rural. Hearty breakfasts. Wonderful coastline. **Open:** All year (not Xmas/New Year)
01665 576433 Mrs Stafford **Fax: 01665 576311** *sally@stonestaff.freeserve.co.uk* www.stonecroft.ntb.org.uk **D:** Fr £20.00 **Beds:** 2D **Baths:** 2 En (1) (4)

Cresswell

NZ2993 *Plough Inn*

Cresswell House, *Cresswell, Morpeth, Northumberland, NE61 5LA.* Hearty breakfast. Welcoming-overlooking 7 miles of golden beach. **Open:** All year
01670 861302 Ms Murdy **D:** Fr £18.00–£19.50 **S:** Fr £18.00 **Beds:** 2D 2S **Baths:** 1 En 1 Pr 1 Sh (8)

All details shown are as supplied by B&B owners in Autumn 2002

Crookham
NT9138

The Coach House, *Crookham, Cornhill-on-Tweed, Northd, TD12 4TD.* Spacious warm accommodation, excellent fresh food. Free afternoon tea. **Open:** Easter to Oct
01890 820293 Mrs Anderson **Fax: 01890 820284** *stay@coachhousecrookham.com* www.coachhousecrookham.com **D:** Fr £25.00–£43.00 **S:** Fr £25.00–£47.00 **Beds:** 2D 5T 2S **Baths:** 7 En (15) × 1 **cc**

Dilston
NY9862

Dilston Mill, *Dilston, Corbridge, Northumberland, NE45 5QZ.* Historic converted mill. Private suite: sleeps 2-6. Beautiful riverside setting. **Open:** All year
01434 633493 Mrs Ketelaar **Fax: 01434 633513** *susan@dilstonmill.com* www.dilstonmill.com **D:** Fr £25.00–£28.00 **S:** Fr £35.00–£40.00 **Beds:** 1F 1T 1D **Baths:** 1 Pr (3)

Eachwick
NZ1171

Hazel Cottage, *Eachwick, Newcastle-upon-Tyne, NE18 0BE.* Peaceful Northumbrian farmhouse in own grounds. Warm welcome, lovely rooms. **Open:** All year **Grades:** ETC 4 Diamond, Silver
01661 852415 Mrs Charlton **Fax: 01661 854797** *hazelcottage@eachwick.fsbusiness.co.uk* www.hazel-cottage.co.uk **D:** Fr £22.00–£24.00 **S:** Fr £26.00 **Beds:** 2T 2D **Baths:** 4 En (4) × **cc**

East Ord
NT9751

Fairholm, *East Ord, Berwick-upon-Tweed, Northumberland, TD15 2NS.* Stone-built bungalow, peaceful village 1.5 miles from Berwick. Lovely riverside/village walks. **Open:** All year (not Xmas/New Year) **Grades:** ETC 4 Diamond
01289 305370 Ms Welsh **D:** Fr £18.50–£22.50 **S:** Fr £20.00–£25.00 **Beds:** 1T 1D **Baths:** 1 En 1 Pr ×

Eglingham
NU1019

Ash Tree House, *The Terrace, Eglingham, Alnwick, Northd, NE66 2UA.* Warm Northumbrian welcome in our lovely home between hills and coast. **Open:** All year
01665 578533 Mrs Marks www.secretkingdom.com/ashtree/house.htm **D:** Fr £22.00 **S:** Fr £27.00 **Beds:** 1D 1T **Baths:** 1 Sh (3) ×

Ellington
NZ2791

Hagg Farmhouse, *Ellington, Ashington, Northd, NE61 5JW.* Old farmhouse, open aspect coast and country. **Open:** All year (not Xmas/New Year)
01670 860514 Mrs Nixon **D:** Fr £15.00–£18.00 **S:** Fr £16.00–£20.00 **Beds:** 1F 1D 1T 1S **Baths:** 1 En 1 Pr 2 Sh (6)

Falstone
NY7387

The Blackcock Inn, *Falstone, Hexham, Northd, NE48 1AA.* Country village inn, comfortable accommodation. Ideal for walking, fishing, cycling, touring. **Open:** All year **Grades:** ETC 3 Diamond, AA 3 Diamond
01434 240200 *blackcock@falstone.fsbusiness.co.uk* www.theblackcockinn.com **D:** Fr £25.00 **S:** Fr £28.00 **Beds:** 1F 2T 2D 1S **Baths:** 4 En 2 Sh (20) × **cc**

Fenwick (Holy Island)
NU0640

Cherry Trees, *Fenwick, Berwick-upon-Tweed, TD15 2PJ.* Detached house, large comfortable bedrooms. Holy Island approx 6m. **Open:** May to Aug
01289 381437 **D:** Fr £20.00–£25.00 **S:** Fr £25.00–£30.00 **Beds:** 1F 1D 1T 1S **Baths:** 2 Sh (6) ×

Great Tosson
NU0200

Tosson Tower Farm, *Great Tosson, Rothbury, Morpeth, Northd, NE65 7NW.* Spacious, warm, wonderful views, good food, friendly welcome. Free fishing. **Open:** All year (not Xmas/New Year)
01669 620228 (also fax) Mrs Foggin *ann@tossontowerfarm.com* www.tossontowerfarm.com **D:** Fr £22.00–£22.50 **S:** Fr £30.00–£35.00 **Beds:** 1F 1D 1T **Baths:** 3 En (4)

Greenhead
NY6665

Holmhead Licensed Guest House, *Thirlwall Castle Farm, Hadrian's Wall, Greenhead, Brampton, CA8 7HY.* Enjoy fine food, hospitality & Hadrian's Wall expertise. **Open:** All year (not Xmas) **Grades:** ETC 4 Diamond
016977 47402 (also fax) Mr & Mrs Staff *Holmhead@hadrianswall.freeserve.co.uk* www.bandbhadrianswall.com **D:** Fr £29.00–£30.00 **S:** Fr £34.00–£38.00 **Beds:** 1F 1D 2T **Baths:** 4 En (6) × **cc**

Greenhead Hotel, *Greenhead, Carlisle, Cumbria, CA6 7HB.* Friendly village inn, in beautiful surroundings, excellent food and accommodation. **Open:** All year
016977 47411 Mr Jones **D:** Fr £22.00 **S:** Fr £25.00 **Beds:** 1F 1T 1S **Baths:** 3 En (30) ×

Braeside, *Banktop, Greenhead, Brampton, CA8 7HA.* Perfect location on Hadrian's Wall. Extensive views from spacious bedroom. **Open:** Easter to Nov
016977 47443 Mrs Potts *smpotts@talk21.com* **D:** Fr £22.00–£24.00 **S:** Fr £30.00 **Beds:** 1F **Baths:** 1 En (4) (2)

Haltwhistle
NY7064

Hall Meadows, *Main Street, Haltwhistle, Northd, NE49 0AZ.* Large comfortable C19th private house, central for Hadrian's Wall. **Open:** All year (not Xmas)
01434 321021 (also fax) Mrs Humes **D:** Fr £18.00–£22.50 **S:** Fr £18.00 **Beds:** 2D 1T **Baths:** 2 En 1 Sh (3)

Broomshaw Hill Farm, *Willia Road, Haltwhistle, Northd, NE49 9NP.* C18th farmhouse, enlarged and modernised to very high standards. Set on the side of a wooded valley through which runs the Haltwhistle Burn. It stands on the conjunction of a footpath and bridleway, both leading to Hadrian's Wall. **Open:** Mar to Nov
01434 320866 Mrs Brown *stay@broomshaw.co.uk* www.broomshaw.co.uk **D:** Fr £23.00–£24.00 **Beds:** 1T 2D **Baths:** 2 En 1 Pr (6)

Riverway House, *4 Wydon Avenue, Haltwhistle, Northd, NE49 0AS.* Roman wall area. Free packed lunch. Spa bath facility. **Open:** All year (not Xmas/New Year)
01434 320378 Mrs Dawson **D:** Fr £15.00–£17.00 **S:** Fr £15.00–£17.00 **Beds:** 1D 1S **Baths:** 1 Sh (10) (1)

Manor House Hotel, *Main Street, Haltwhistle, Northd, NE49 0BS.* Small hotel with busy public bar serving good selection of real ales, wines & spirits. **Open:** All year
01434 322588 R Nicholson **D:** Fr £15.00–£22.00 **S:** Fr £20.00–£25.00 **Beds:** 1F 1D 4T **Baths:** 3 En 3 Sh (4) × **cc**

National Grid References given are for villages, towns and cities – not for individual houses

Oakey Knowe Farm, *Haltwhistle, Northd, NE49 0NB.* Oakey Knowe Farm/ Equitation smallholding of 18 acres is situated within walking distance of Haltwhistle and Roman Wall. Has panoramic views over the Tyne Valley, comfortable, friendly atmosphere for both yourself and horse if required. **Open:** All year
01434 320648 (also fax) Mrs Murray **D:** Fr £18.00–£20.00 **S:** Fr £20.00–£25.00 **Beds:** 1F 1T 1D **Baths:** 1 Pr 1 Sh (6)

Harbottle

NT9304

The Byre Vegetarian B&B, *Harbottle, Morpeth, Northumberland, NE65 7DG.* Central for coast and Cheviots. Beautiful Walks. Historic village. **Open:** All year
01669 650476 Mrs Srinivasan *rosemary@the-byre.co.uk* www.the-byre.co.uk **D:** Fr £18.00–£24.00 **S:** Fr £18.00–£29.00 **Beds:** 1T 1D **Baths:** 1 En 1 Pr (2)

Haydon Bridge

NY8464

Hadrain Lodge Country Hotel, *Hindshield Moss, North Road, Haydon Bridge, Hexham, Northumberland, NE47 6NF.* In tranquil rural location, set in open pasture near Hadrian's Wall. **Open:** All year
01434 688688 Mrs Murray **Fax: 01434 684867** *hadrianlodge@hadrianswall.co.uk* www.hadrianswall.co.uk **D:** Fr £22.50–£25.00 **S:** Fr £25.00–£29.50 **Beds:** 3F 4D 1T 1S **Baths:** 8 En 1 Pr cc

Hexham

NY9364

Topsy Turvy, *9 Leazes Lane, Hexham, Northd, NE46 3BA.* Situated in market town near Hadrian's Wall. Comfortable, colourful, friendly and peaceful. **Open:** All year **Grades:** ETC 4 Diamond
01434 603152 M McCormick *topsy.turvy@ukonline.co.uk* **D:** Fr £20.00 **Beds:** 2D **Baths:** 1 En 1 Pr

High Reins, *Leazes Lane, Hexham, Northd, NE46 3AT.* Quiet area, close to pleasant countryside and golf course. **Open:** All year **Grades:** ETC 4 Diamond
01434 603590 Mrs Walton *walton45@hotmail.com* **D:** Fr £25.00–£27.00 **S:** Fr £28.00–£30.00 **Beds:** 2D 1T 1S **Baths:** 4 En (6)

Dene House, *Juniper, Hexham, Hexham, Northd, NE46 1SJ.* Northumbria, near Hadrian's Wall. Former winners of best bed and breakfast. **Open:** All year (not Xmas/ New Year)
01434 673413 (also fax) Mrs Massey *margaret@dene-house.hexham.co.uk* www.denehouse-hexham.co.uk **D:** Fr £22.00 **S:** Fr £25.00 **Beds:** 1T 1D 1S **Baths:** 2 En (4) cc

Old Red House Farm, *Dipton Mill, Hexham, NE46 1XY.* Superbly appointed C19th private stone cottage in lovely rural location. **Open:** Feb to Oct
01434 604463 Mrs Bradley *susan.bradley@ukonline.co.uk* **D:** Fr £23.00–£25.00 **S:** Fr £30.00 **Beds:** 1T **Baths:** 1 Pr (2)

Woodley Field, *Allendale Road, Hexham, Northumberland, NE46 2NB.* Large stone-built Victorian family house situated south-western outskirts of Hexham. Set in 2 acres of mature gardens with ample off-road parking. The bedrooms have recently been upgraded to ensuites, but remain very spacious with delightful views. **Open:** All year (not Xmas/New Year)
01434 601600 Mrs Charlton **D:** Fr £27.50–£40.00 **S:** Fr £35.00–£45.00 **Beds:** 1F 1D **Baths:** 2 En (10)

Horsley (Newcastle-upon-Tyne)

NZ0965

Belvedere, *Harlow Hill, Horsley, Newcastle-upon-Tyne, NE15 0QD.* Stone built 1830s house on Hadrian's Wall, lovely rural views. **Open:** Easter to Nov **Grades:** ETC 4 Diamond
01661 853689 Mrs Carr *pat.carr@btinternet.com* www.belvederehouse.co.uk **D:** Fr £19.00 **S:** Fr £23.00 **Beds:** 1T 1D **Baths:** 2 En (3)

Juniper

NY9358

Peth Head Cottage, *Juniper, Hexham, Northd, NE47 0LA.* Pretty rose-covered cottage in very peaceful location. Ideal for Hadrian's Wall. **Open:** All year **Grades:** ETC 4 Diamond, Silver, AA 4 Diamond
01434 673286 Mrs Liddle **Fax: 01434 673038** *tedliddle@compuserve.com* www.peth-head-cottage.co.uk **D:** Fr £20.00 **S:** Fr £20.00 **Beds:** 2D **Baths:** 2 En (2) cc

Kirkwhelpington

NY9984

Cornhills, *Kirkwhelpington, Northumberland, NE19 2RE.* Large Victorian farmhouse. Working farm, outstanding views in peaceful surroundings. **Open:** All year (not Xmas)
01830 540232 Ms Thornton **Fax: 01830 540388** *cornhills@farming.co.uk* northumberlandfarmhouse.co.uk **D:** Fr £21.00–£23.00 **S:** Fr £25.00–£30.00 **Beds:** 1D 2T **Baths:** 2 En 1 Pr (10)

Lanehead

NY7985

Ivy Cottage, *Lanehead, Tarset, Hexham, Northumberland, NE48 1NT.* 200-year-old cottage with stunning views over open countryside. **Open:** All year
01434 240337 (also fax) Mrs Holland *john.holland@compaq.com* **D:** Fr £18.00–£20.00 **S:** Fr £18.00–£20.00 **Beds:** 1T 1D **Baths:** 1 En 1 Sh

Lesbury

NU2312 *Saddle Grill Hotel*

Hawkhill Farmhouse, *Lesbury, Alnwick, Northumberland, NE66 3PG.* Large traditional farmhouse set in extensive, secluded gardens, with magnificent views of the Aln valley mid way Alnwick/ Alnmouth. Ideal for beaches, castles and places of interest, walking, golf and bird watching. Warm welcome and very peaceful. **Open:** All year (not Xmas)
01665 830380 Mrs Vickers **Fax: 01665 830093** **D:** Fr £23.00–£25.00 **S:** Fr £25.00–£30.00 **Beds:** 2T 1D **Baths:** 3 En (10) (10)

Longframlington

NU1300

The Lee Farm, *Longframlington, Morpeth, Northd, NE65 8JQ.* Award-winning quality accommodation in beautiful peaceful location near Rothbury. **Open:** All year (not Xmas/New Year) **Grades:** ETC 4 Diamond, Gold
01665 570257 (also fax) S Aynsley *engs@leefarm.co.uk* www.leefarm.co.uk **D:** Fr £25.00 **S:** Fr £35.00 **Beds:** 1F 1T 1D **Baths:** 2 En 1 Pr (2) (4)

Longhirst

NZ2289

Barnacre, *Longhirst, Morpeth, Northumberland, NE61 3LX.* Beautiful barn conversion in village centre. Spacious rooms. **Open:** All year (not Xmas/New Year)
01670 790116 Mrs Rudd *linda@mrudd.fslife.co.uk* **D:** Fr £22.50–£25.00 **S:** Fr £25.00–£30.00 **Beds:** 3F 2T **Baths:** 2 En 1 Sh (4)

BEDROOMS
D = Double
T = Twin
S = Single
F = Family

Morpeth

NZ2085

Elder Cottage, *High Church, Morpeth, Northd, NE61 2QT.* C18th cottage with garden and sun room; easy access from A1. **Open:** All year (not Xmas) **Grades:** ETC 4 Diamond, Silver **01670 517664** Mrs Cook **Fax: 01670 517644** *cook@eldercot.freeserve.co.uk* www.eldercottage.co.uk **D:** Fr £17.50–£20.00 **S:** Fr £20.00–£25.00 **Beds:** 2D 1T **Baths:** 1 Sh (3)

Chestnut House, *2 Dacre Street, Morpeth, Northd, NE61 1HW.* A family run guesthouse set in the Heart of Morpeth. **Open:** All year **Grades:** ETC 3 Diamond **01670 518777 & 01670 515026** Mrs Lishman **Fax: 01670 514646** *chesnuthouse.guest@virgin.net* www.chestnuthouse.net **D:** Fr £19.00–£24.00 **S:** Fr £21.00–£35.00 **Beds:** 1F 4T 3D 5S **Baths:** 3 En 3 Pr 3 Sh (15)

Newton

NZ0364

Crookhill Farm, *Newton, Stocksfield, Northd, NE43 7UX.* Comfortable welcoming farmhouse ideal for exploring Hadrian's Wall, Beamish and NT Properties. **Open:** All year **Grades:** ETC 3 Diamond **01661 843117** Mrs Leech **Fax: 01661 844702** **D:** Fr £20.00–£22.50 **S:** Fr £20.00–£22.50 **Beds:** 1F 1T 1S **Baths:** 1 Sh (4)

Ninebanks

NY7853

Taylor Burn, *Ninebanks, Hexham, Northd, NE47 8DE.* Large, comfortable farmhouse, excellent food, warm welcome, wonderful scenery. **Open:** All year **01434 345343** Mrs Ostler *mavis@taylorburn.freeserve.co.uk* **D:** Fr £18.00 **S:** Fr £18.00 **Beds:** 1D 1S 1T **Baths:** 1 Pr (7) (5)

North Charlton

NU1623

North Charlton Farmhouse, *North Charlton, Chathill, Northumberland, NE76 5HP.* **Open:** All year **01665 579443** Ms Armstrong **Fax: 01665 579407** *ncharlton1@agricplus.net* www.northcharlton.com **D:** Fr £30.00 **S:** Fr £35.00–£40.00 **Beds:** 1T 2D **Baths:** 2 En 1 Pr (12) (10)
A warm welcome awaits you in our newly restored beautifully furnished farmhouse, offering modern comfort in elegant surroundings. Ideally located for enjoying coast, castles Holy Island. Chellingham only 10 mins' drive and a little further is Wooler, gateway to the Cheviot Hills.

Otterburn

NY8893

Dunns Houses, *Otterburn, Newcastle-upon-Tyne, NE19 1LB.* **Open:** All year **01830 520677 & 07808 592701 (M)** Ms Findlay *dunnshouses@hotmail.com* www.northumberlandfarmholidays.co.uk **D:** Fr £22.50–£30.00 **S:** Fr £25.00–£30.00 **Beds:** 1F 1D 1T **Baths:** 2 En 1 Pr (10)
Warm, friendly welcome to this Victorian farmhouse with spacious ensuite bedrooms, lounge, traditional English breakfast made from local produce. Magnificent countryside views, activities, onsite fishing, birdwatching and stables. Kielder, Hadrian's Wall and historical houses and towns. Expect serene tranquillity.

The Butterchurn Guest House, *Main Street, Otterburn, Newcastle-upon-Tyne, Northumberland, NE19 1NP.* **Open:** All year **Grades:** ETC 4 Diamond, RAC 4 Diamond **01830 520585** Val Anderson *keith@butterchurn.freeserve.co.uk* www.butterchurn.freeserve.co.uk **D:** Fr £22.50–£25.00 **S:** Fr £25.00–£30.00 **Beds:** 1F 2T 3D 1S **Baths:** 7 En (10) cc
Excellent ensuite quality accommodation in rural Northumberland. Ideally situated in Northumberland National Park to explore 'the Land of Far Horizons'. Jewels include Kielder Water and forest, Hadrian's Wall, the Cheviot Hills, castles and coastline.

Ponteland

NZ1673

Stone Cottage, *Prestwick Road, Ponteland, Newcastle-upon-Tyne, NE20 9BX.* **Open:** All year **01661 823957 (also fax)** *stay@stonecottageguesthouse.com* www.stonecottageguesthouse.com **D:** Fr £20.00–£22.50 **S:** Fr £25.00–£28.00 **Beds:** 1F 1T 1D **Baths:** 1 En 1 Sh (10)
160-year-old stone cottage, extensively modernised and upgraded. Large, well kept gardens with secure parking. Situated 8 miles from Newcastle City Centre on the edge of Ponteland Village with its historic inns and ancient church. 5 mins' walk Newcastle Airport.

Hazel Cottage, *Eachwick, Newcastle-upon-Tyne, NE18 0BE.* Peaceful Northumbrian farmhouse in own grounds. Warm welcome, lovely rooms. **Open:** All year **Grades:** ETC 4 Diamond, Silver **01661 852415** Mrs Charlton **Fax: 01661 854797** *hazelcottage@eachwick.fsbusiness.co.uk* www.hazel-cottage.co.uk **D:** Fr £22.00–£24.00 **S:** Fr £26.00 **Beds:** 2T 2D **Baths:** 4 En (4) cc

7 Collingwood Cottages, *Limestone Lane, Ponteland, Newcastle-upon-Tyne, NE20 0DD.* Open views over countryside fields. 2.5 miles from Newcastle airport. **Open:** All year (not Xmas/New Year) **01661 825967** Mrs Baxter **D:** Fr £18.00–£20.00 **S:** Fr £25.00 **Beds:** 1F 1D **Baths:** 1 Sh (4)

Riding Mill

NZ0161

Low Fotherley Farm, *Riding Mill, Northumberland, NE44 6BB.* **Open:** All year (not Xmas/New Year) **Grades:** ETC 4 Diamond **01434 682277 (also fax)** Mrs Adamson *hugh@lowfotherley.fsnet.co.uk* www.westfarm.freeserve.co.uk **D:** Fr £22.50 **S:** Fr £25.00–£28.00 **Beds:** 1T 1D **Baths:** 1 En 1 Pr
Low Fotherley is an impressive Victorian farmhouse built around 1895 in the beautiful Northumbrian countryside. Close to Hexham, Corbridge, Hadrian's Wall, Scottish Borders. Spacious accommodation with open fires and beams. Aga farmhouse breakfast with home-made marmalade and jams. Families welcome.

Broomley Fell Farm, *Riding Mill, Northumberland, NE44 6AY.* Warm welcome in cosy separate annexe, beams and log fire. **Open:** All year **01434 682682** Ms Davies **Fax: 01434 682728** *enquiries@broomleyfell.com* www.broomleyfell.co.uk **D:** Fr £20.00 **S:** Fr £20.00–£25.00 **Beds:** 1F 1S **Baths:** 1 En 1 Pr (6) cc

Rochester

NY8398

Redesdale Arms Hotel, *Rochester, Otterburn, Newcastle-upon-Tyne, NE19 1TA.* Friendly, comfortable country inn. Home cooking, ring for special bargain breaks. **Open:** All year **Grades:** ETC 4 Diamond **01830 520668** Mrs Wright **Fax: 01830 520063** *redesdalehotel@hotmail.com* www.redesdale-hotel.co.uk **D:** Fr £30.00–£35.00 **S:** Fr £38.00–£43.00 **Beds:** 3F 3T 4D **Baths:** 10 En (40) cc

Woolaw Farm, *Rochester, Newcastle-upon-Tyne, NE19 1TB.* Hill farm steeped in history with beautiful views and warm hospitality. **Open:** All year **01830 520686** Mrs Chapman *info@woolawfarm.co.uk* www.woolawfarm.co.uk **D:** Fr £17.50–£20.00 **S:** Fr £20.00–£25.00 **Beds:** 2T **Baths:** 2 En

Rothbury

NU0501

Katerina's Guest House, Sun Buildings, *High Street, Rothbury, Morpeth, Northumberland, NE65 7TQ.* **Open:** All year **01669 620691 & 07977 555692** *cath@katerinasguesthouse.co.uk* www.katerinasguesthouse.co.uk **D:** Fr £23.00–£25.00 **S:** Fr £40.00 **Beds:** 3D **Baths:** 3 En
Charming old building with beautiful 4-poster bedrooms, all ensuite, TV etc. Perfect situation close to all village amenities. Ideal central location for hills, coastline, castles, Hadrian's Wall, Scottish Borders. Extensive menus for breakfasts and (if required) evening meals. No smoking.

The Lee Farm, *Longframlington, Morpeth, Northd, NE65 8JQ.* Award-winning quality accommodation in beautiful peaceful location near Rothbury. **Open:** All year (not Xmas/New Year) **Grades:** ETC 4 Diamond, Gold **01665 570257 (also fax)** S Aynsley *enqs@leefarm.co.uk* www.leefarm.co.uk **D:** Fr £25.00 **S:** Fr £35.00 **Beds:** 1F 1T 1D **Baths:** 2 En 1 Pr (2) (4)

Orchard Guest House, *High Street, Rothbury, Morpeth, Northd, NE65 7TL.* A warm welcome and quality accommodation is offered in this comfortable Georgian home. Guest lounge with books and information. Excellent freshly cooked breakfasts. Rothbury is the ideal location for exploring beautiful Northumberland with its countryside, coast, castles, NT and Hadrian's Wall. **Open:** All year (not Xmas/New Year) **01669 620684** Mrs Pickard *email@orchardguesthouse.co.uk* www.orchardguesthouse.co.uk **D:** Fr £23.00–£25.00 **S:** Fr £25.00–£30.00 **Beds:** 1F 2T 3D **Baths:** 3 En 3 Pr

Wagtail Farm, *Rothbury, Morpeth, Northumberland, NE65 7PL.* Comfortable bedrooms, good breakfasts, in a beautiful location. **Open:** May to Oct **01669 620367** Mrs Taylor *wagtail@tinyworld.co.uk* **D:** Fr £19.00 **S:** Fr £24.50 **Beds:** 2D **Baths:** 1 En 1 Pr (12) (2)

Silverton House, *Rothbury, Morpeth, Northumberland, NE65 7RJ.* Built in 1901 as a work house, now a comfortable home. **Open:** All year (not Xmas) **01669 621395** Mrs Wallace *maggie.wallace1@virgin.net* **D:** Fr £18.00–£19.00 **S:** Fr £25.00–£38.00 **Beds:** 1D 1T (2)

Seahouses

NU2032 *Bamburgh Castle, Lodge Inn, Olde Ship*

Leeholme, *93 Main Street, Seahouses, Northd, NE68 7TS.* Perfectly situated for exploring Northumbria. Warm welcome. Hearty breakfast assured! **Open:** Mar to Oct **01665 720230** Mr & Mrs Wood **D:** Fr £18.00–£25.00 **S:** Fr £20.00–£25.00 **Beds:** 2T 1D **Baths:** 1 En 2 Sh (2)

Wyndgrove House, *156 Main Street, Seahouses, Northumberland, NE68 7HA.* Family-run guest house. Ideal base for countryside, coast and Farne Islands. **Open:** All year **01665 720658** Mr & Mrs Haile **D:** Fr £20.00–£25.00 **S:** Fr £20.00–£25.00 **Beds:** 4F 2T 1D **Baths:** 2 En 3 Sh cc

Seaton Sluice

NZ3376

The Waterford Arms, *Collywell Bay Road, Seaton Sluice, Whitley Bay, NE26 4QZ.* Very famous fish restaurant in a busy tourist area. **Open:** All year **0191 237 0450** **D:** Fr £22.95–£24.95 **S:** Fr £30.00 **Beds:** 1F 2T 2D **Baths:** 5 En 2 Pr (30) 2 cc

Slaley

NY9757

Rose & Crown Inn, *Slaley, Hexham, Northd, NE47 0AA.* Warm, friendly family-run inn, with good wholesome home cooking. Meals served daily. **Open:** All year **01434 673263** Mr & Mrs Pascoe **Fax: 01434 673305** *rosecrowninn@supanet.com* **D:** Fr £22.50–£25.00 **S:** Fr £27.50–£32.50 **Beds:** 2T 1S **Baths:** 3 En 3 Pr (5) (35) cc

Rye Hill Farm, *Slaley, Hexham, Northd, NE47 0AH.* Small livestock farm. Gorgeous views all round. Pretty ensuite rooms in converted barn. We are noted for tasty evening meals (home cooked), friendly atmosphere and large bath towels. 5 miles south of Hexham. **Open:** All year **01434 673259 (also fax)** Mrs Courage *enquiries@consult-courage.co.uk* www.ryehillfarm.co.uk **D:** Fr £22.50 **S:** Fr £28.00 **Beds:** 2F 3D 1T **Baths:** 6 En (6) cc

Stamfordham

NZ0771

Church House, *Stamfordham, Newcastle-upon-Tyne, NE18 0PB.* **Open:** All year **01661 886736 & 07889 312623 (M)** Mrs Fitzpatrick *bedandbreakfast@stamfordham.fsbusiness.co.uk* **D:** Fr £22.50 **S:** Fr £25.00 **Beds:** 3T **Baths:** 2 Sh (4)
Beautiful C17th listed stone house facing green in lovely rural village. Close to Hadrian's Wall, Corbridge/Hexham, Newcastle & on the new Reivers cycling route. An ideal base for exploring Northumberland's outstanding countryside, coastline & historic past. Welcoming hosts.

Please respect a B&B's wishes regarding children, animals and smoking

Steel

NY9363

Dukesfield Hall Farm, *Steel, Hexham, Northumberland, NE46 1SH.* Charming Grade II farmhouse. warm and friendly. Excellent facilities. **Open:** All year
01434 673634 Mrs Swallow *cath@dukesfield.supanet.com* **D:** Fr £20.00 **S:** Fr £20.00 **Beds:** 1T 2D **Baths:** 3 En (4)

Stocksfield

NZ0561

Old Ridley Hall, *Stocksfield, Northd, NE43 7RU.* Large private house. Listed. Quiet. Near Metro centre, Durham, Beamish. **Open:** All year (not Xmas)
01661 842816 Mrs Aldridge *oldridleyhall@talk21.com* **D:** Fr £23.00–£29.00 **S:** Fr £23.00–£29.00 **Beds:** 1F 2T 1S **Baths:** 1 Pr 2 Sh (14)

Swarland

NU1603 *Cook and Barker, Granby Inn, Anglers Arms*

Swarland Old Hall, *Swarland, Morpeth, Northumberland, NE65 9HU.* Grade 2 listed Georgian farmhouse, situated on the banks of the river Coquet, with breathtaking views over the Northumberland countryside. An ideal base for touring, walking and golfing and also to explore the magnificent coast, castles and countryside. Full colour brochure available on request. **Open:** All year (not Xmas/New Year)
01670 787642 & 07801 688153 (M) Mrs Proctor *proctor@swarlandoldhall.fsnet.co.uk* www.swarlandoldhall.com **D:** Fr £22.00 **S:** Fr £30.00 **Beds:** 1F 1T 1D **Baths:** 2 En 1 Pr (3) (8)

Thropton

NU0202

Farm Cottage Guest House, *Thropton, Morpeth, Northumberland, NE65 7NA.* Olde worlde cottage with pretty country gardens, exceptional evening meals. Table licence. **Open:** All year (not Xmas) **Grades:** ETC 4 Diamond, Silver
01669 620831 (also fax) Mrs Telford *joan@farmcottageguesthouse.co.uk* www.farmcottageguesthouse.co.uk **D:** Fr £21.00–£23.00 **S:** Fr £31.00–£33.00 **Beds:** 3D 1T **Baths:** 4 En (4) cc

Lorbottle, *West Steads, Thropton, Morpeth, Northd, NE65 7JT.* Spacious farmhouse overlooking the Simonside Hills, Coquet Valley, Cheviot Hills. Rothbury 5 miles. **Open:** All year
01665 574672 (also fax) Mrs Farr *helen.farr@farming.co.uk* www.visit-rothbury.co.uk/accom/bb_lorbottle.html **D:** Fr £20.00 **S:** Fr £20.00–£27.00 **Beds:** 1D 1T 1S **Baths:** 1 Sh (3)

Troughend

NY8692

Brown Rigg Cottage, *Troughend, Otterburn, Newcastle-upon-Tyne, NE19 1LG.* Wind and solar powered 200-year-old cottage. Excellent meals. **Open:** All year
01830 520541 A D Boon **Fax: 01830 520999** *davidn.boon@btinternet.com* **D:** Fr £25.00 **S:** Fr £25.00 **Beds:** 1T 1D **Baths:** 1 Sh (6)

Twice Brewed

NY7567

Saughy Rigg Farm, *Twice Brewed, Haltwhistle, Northumberland, NE49 9PT.* Near Hadrian's Wall, delicious food, comfortable accommodation, children & pets welcome. **Open:** All year
01434 344746 Ms McNulty *kathandbrad@aol.com* www.northumberlandaccommodation.co.uk **D:** Fr £15.00 **S:** Fr £15.00 **Beds:** 1F 1T **Baths:** 1 En 1 Pr

Wark (Bellingham)

NY8577

Woodpark Farm, *Wark, Hexham, Northd, NE48 3PZ.* Listed farmhouse. **Open:** May to Oct
01434 230259 Mrs Bell **D:** Fr £17.00 **S:** Fr £20.00 **Beds:** 1F 1D **Baths:** 1 Sh (3)

Warkworth

NU2405

Bide A While, *4 Beal Croft, Warkworth, Morpeth, Northd, NE65 0XL.* **Open:** All year **Grades:** ETC 3 Diamond
01665 711753 D M Graham **D:** Fr £18.00–£20.00 **S:** Fr £20.00–£24.00 **Beds:** 1F 2D **Baths:** 1 En 1 Sh (3)
Bungalow in historic village of Warkworth, which has a castle, ancient church and hermitage. Good base for touring Northumberland, birdwatching, etc. On cycle route, and within a mile of the beach and sea.

Please respect a B&B's wishes regarding children, animals and smoking

North Cottage, *Birling, Warkworth, Morpeth, Northd, NE65 0XS.* Centrally situated to explore Northumbria. Comfortable ensuite ground floor bedrooms. **Open:** All year (not Xmas/New Year)
01665 711263 Mrs Howliston *edithandjohn@another.com* www.accta.co.uk/north **D:** Fr £22.00–£24.00 **S:** Fr £25.00–£30.00 **Beds:** 1T 2D 1S **Baths:** 3 En 1 Sh (4)

Hermitage Inn, *23 Castle St, Warkworth, Morpeth, Northumberland, NE65 0UL.* Perfectly situated for exploring Northumberland coast. Warm welcome. Excellent food. **Open:** All year
01665 711258 **D:** Fr £20.00–£25.00 **S:** Fr £20.00–£25.00 **Beds:** 2F 2D 1S **Baths:** 3 En 2 Pr cc

West Woodburn

NY8887

Yellow House Farm, *West Woodburn, Hexham, Northumberland, NE48 2SB.* Old farmhouse with all modern conveniences, warm welcome & tranquillity awaits you. **Open:** All year
01434 270070 Mrs Walton www.yellowhousebandb.co.uk **D:** Fr £15.00–£20.00 **S:** Fr £15.00–£24.00 **Beds:** 1F 1T 1D **Baths:** 3 En (6)

Plevna House, *West Woodburn, Hexham, Northumberland, NE48 2RA.* Centre for Borders, Hadrian's Wall, Kielder and coast. Warm welcome. **Open:** All year (not Xmas/New Year)
01434 270369 Mr Pickford *plevnaho@aol.com* **D:** Fr £18.00–£20.00 **S:** Fr £25.00 **Beds:** 2D **Baths:** 2 En (4)

Whitton

NU0500

Whitton Farmhouse Hotel, *Whitton, Rothbury, Morpeth, Northd, NE65 7RL.* **Open:** Easter to Oct **Grades:** ETC 4 Diamond
01669 620811 (also fax) *whittonfarmhotel@supanet.com* www.smoothhound.co.uk/hotels/whitton **D:** Fr £25.00–£29.00 **S:** Fr £25.00–£29.00 **Beds:** 1F 1T 1D **Baths:** 3 En (10)
Charming unusual converted farmhouse and buildings on edge of National Park, overlooking Coquet Valley. Convenient for coast and country with many historic houses and castles nearby. Separate residents lounge with bar and delightful dining room. Excellent reputation for food.

Planning a longer stay? Always ask for any special rates

Wooler

NT9928

Winton House, *39 Glendale Road, Wooler, Northumberland, NE71 6DL.* Edwardian house, quiet position, comfortable, spacious rooms. Walkers/cyclists welcome. **Open:** Mar to Oct **Grades:** ETC 3 Diamond **01668 281362 (also fax)** Mr Gilbert *winton.house@virgin.net* www.wintonhouse.ntb.org.uk **D:** Fr £20.00–£23.00 **S:** Fr £27.00–£30.00 **Beds:** 1T 2D **Baths:** 2 En 1 Sh (4)

St Hilliers, *6 Church Street, Wooler, Northd, NE71 6DA.* Stone-built village house, quiet side of town. Homely, excellent breakfast **Open:** All year **01668 281340** Mrs Hugall **D:** Fr £18.00–£20.00 **S:** Fr £20.00–£25.00 **Beds:** 2T 1D **Baths:** 1 Sh

Wylam

NZ1164

Wormald House, *Main Street, Wylam, Northd, NE41 8DN.* Very welcoming, pleasant country home in attractive Tyne Valley village. **Open:** All year (not Xmas) **01661 852529 (also fax)** Mr & Mrs Craven *john.craven3@btinternet.com* **D:** Fr £20.00–£22.00 **S:** Fr £20.00–£22.00 **Beds:** 1D 1T **Baths:** 2 En (3) **cc**

Nottinghamshire

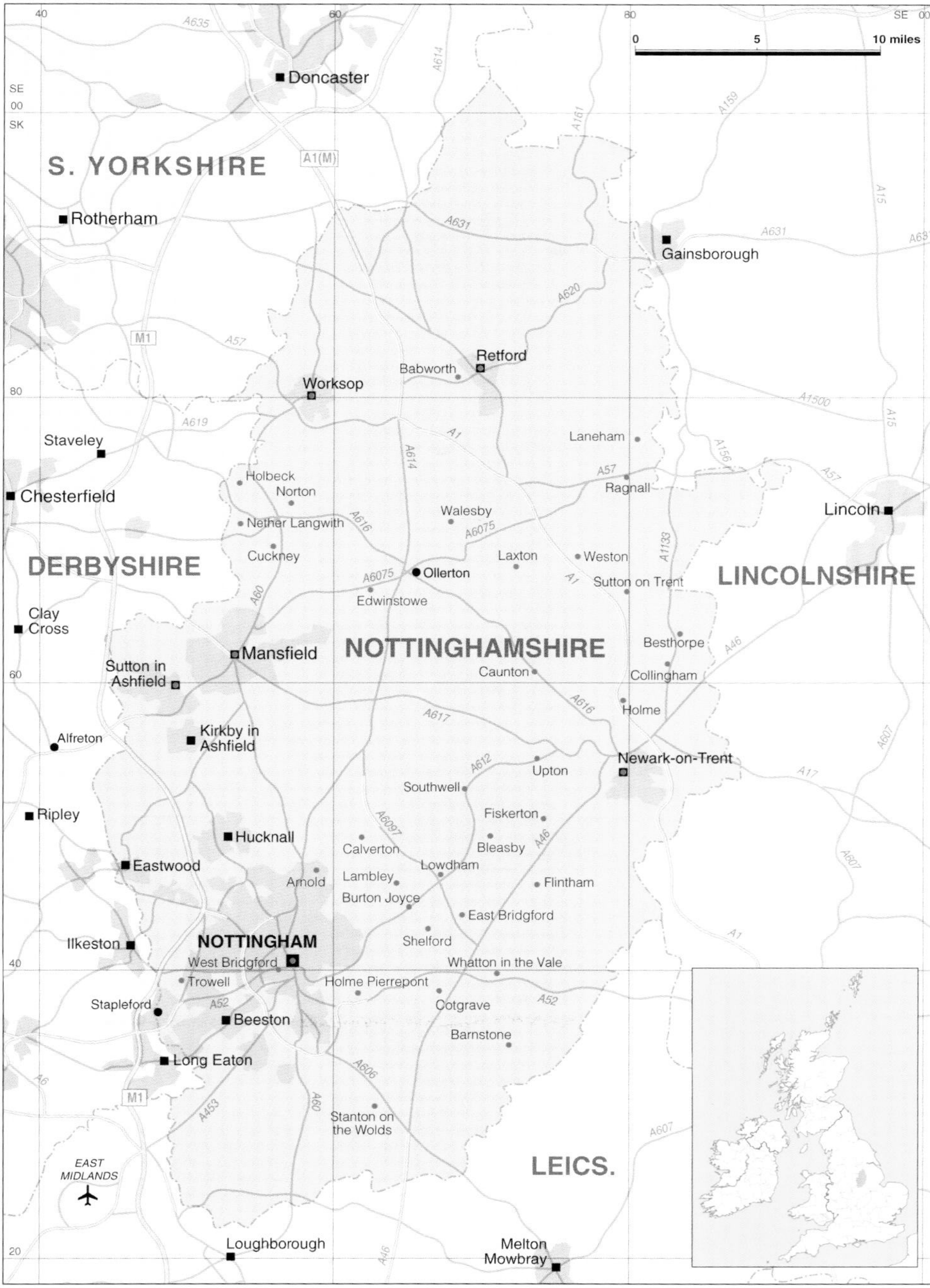

0
5
10 miles
Doncaster
S. YORKSHIRE
Rotherham
Gainsborough
Retford
Babworth
Worksop
Laneham
Staveley
Holbeck
Norton
Ragnall
Chesterfield
Walesby
Lincoln
Nether Langwith
Cuckney
Laxton
Weston
DERBYSHIRE
Ollerton
Sutton on Trent
LINCOLNSHIRE
Edwinstowe
Clay Cross
Besthorpe
Mansfield
NOTTINGHAMSHIRE
Sutton in Ashfield
Caunton
Collingham
Holme
Alfreton
Kirkby in Ashfield
Newark-on-Trent
Upton
Southwell
Ripley
Fiskerton
Hucknall
Calverton
Bleasby
Eastwood
Lowdham
Arnold
Lambley
Flintham
Burton Joyce
East Bridgford
Shelford
Ilkeston
NOTTINGHAM
West Bridgford
Whatton in the Vale
Trowell
Holme Pierrepont
Stapleford
Cotgrave
Beeston
Barnstone
Long Eaton
Stanton on the Wolds
EAST MIDLANDS
LEICS.
Loughborough
Melton Mowbray

Arnold
SK5845

Rufford House, *117 Redhill Road, Arnold, Nottingham, NG5 8GZ.* Convenient Nottingham city centre, Sherwood Forest & Robin Hood country. **Open:** All year **Grades:** ETC 4 Diamond **0115 926 1759 (also fax)** *ruffordhouse@hotmail.com* www.ruffordhouse.co.uk **D:** Fr £18.00–£20.00 **S:** Fr £19.00–£25.00 **Beds:** 1F 1T 1D 1S **Baths:** 2 En 1 Pr 1 Sh (5)

Babworth
SK6880

The Barns Country Guest House, *Morton Farm, Babworth, Retford, Notts, DN22 8HA.* Rural setting close to A1 on Pilgrim Fathers Trail. **Open:** All year (not Xmas) **01777 706336** H R R Kay **Fax: 01777 709773** *harry@thebarns.co.uk* www.thebarns.co.uk **D:** Fr £22.00–£26.00 **S:** Fr £30.00–£33.00 **Beds:** 1F 5D **Baths:** 6 En (6) cc

Barnstone
SK7335

Barnstone Olde House, *Barnstone, Nottingham, NG13 9JP.* Central for Newark, Grantham, Nottingham. Landscaped garden, rustic charm, beautiful view. **Open:** All year (not Xmas) **01949 860456 (also fax)** Mrs Baker **D:** Fr £20.00–£25.00 **S:** Fr £22.50–£30.00 **Beds:** 2D 1T **Baths:** 2 En (4)

Besthorpe
SK8265

Lord Nelson Inn, *Main Road, Besthorpe, Newark, Nottinghamshire, NG23 7HR.* C18th former coaching inn with excellent food reputation. **Open:** All year (not Xmas/New Year) **01636 892265** **D:** Fr £20.00 **S:** Fr £25.00 **Beds:** 2T 1D 1S **Baths:** 1 En 1 Sh (20) cc

Bleasby
SK7149

Little Rudsey Farm, *Bleasby, Nottingham, NG14 7FR.* Traditional farmhouse, rural setting. Robin Hood country. Newark/Nottingham/Lincoln/Southwell easy reach. **Open:** All year (not Xmas/New Year) **01636 830249** Mrs Norman **D:** Fr £16.00 **S:** Fr £16.00 **Beds:** 1F 1T **Baths:** 1 Sh (4) (3)

Burton Joyce
SK6443

Willow House, *12 Willow Wong, Burton Joyce, Nottingham, NG14 5FD.* 1850s house with Victorian charm. Beautiful riverbanks 2 mins' walk. **Open:** All year **0115 931 2070** Mrs Baker **D:** Fr £19.00 **S:** Fr £16.00–£25.00 **Beds:** 1F 1D 1T **Baths:** 2 Sh

Calverton
SK6149

Patchings Farm Arts Centre, *Oxton Road, Calverton, Nottingham, NG14 6NU.* Part of 60-acre art centre. Private garden. **Open:** All year **0115 965 3479** **Fax: 0115 9655308** *admin@patchingsartcentre.co.uk* www.patchingsartcentre.co.uk **D:** Fr £20.00 **S:** Fr £25.00 **Beds:** 3T **Baths:** 3 En cc

Caunton
SK7460

Knapthorpe Lodge, *Hockerton Road, Caunton, Newark, Notts, NG23 6AZ.* Large farmhouse overlooking beautiful countryside. Comfortable & friendly. **Open:** All year **01636 636262** **Fax: 01636 636415** **D:** Fr £20.00–£25.00 **S:** Fr £25.00–£30.00 **Beds:** 1F 1D **Baths:** 1 En 1 Pr (6)

Collingham
SK8361

Lime Tree Farm, *Lunn Lane, Collingham, Newark, Notts, NG23 7LP.* Attractive, converted barn in quiet conservation area of village. **Open:** All year **Grades:** ETC 4 Diamond **01636 892044** Mrs Glenny **D:** Fr £18.00–£20.00 **S:** Fr £20.00–£25.00 **Beds:** 1D 2T **Baths:** 2 En 1 Pr (6)

Cotgrave
SK6435

Marl Pit Cottage, *28 Main Road, Cotgrave, Nottingham, NG12 3HN.* Quality cottage accommodation, semi-rural location, very comfortable and friendly. **Open:** All year (not Xmas) **0115 989 4805 (also fax)** Mrs Prescott *mp1@nascr.net* **D:** Fr £20.00 **Beds:** 2D **Baths:** 1 Sh (2)

Cuckney
SK5670

The Greendale Oak, *High Croft, Cuckney, Mansfield, Notts, NG20 9NQ.* 300-year-old pub/restaurant near Sherwood Forest & the Dureries. **Open:** All year **01623 844441 & 01623 844237** **D:** Fr £37.00 **S:** Fr £18.50 **Beds:** 1F 1T 1D 2S **Baths:** 2 Sh (4) cc

East Bridgford
SK6943

Barn Farm Cottage, *Kneeton Road, East Bridgford, Nottingham, NG13 8PH.* Lovely cottage overlooking fields and Trent Valley. Delicious organic breakfast. **Open:** All year **01949 20196** Mrs Shouls **D:** Fr £20.00 **S:** Fr £20.00 **Beds:** 1F 2T 1S **Baths:** 1 En 2 Sh (6)

Edwinstowe
SK6266

Marion's Manor, *Ollerton Road, Edwinstowe, Mansfield, Nottinghamshire, NG21 9QG.* Enjoy a break in the heart of Sherwood Forest staying with a real Marion. **Open:** All year **01623 822135** **D:** Fr £18.00–£25.00 **S:** Fr £22.00–£25.00 **Beds:** 1F 1D 1T **Baths:** 3 En (4)

Robin Hood Farm, *Rufford Road, Edwinstowe, Mansfield, Notts, NG21 9HX.* Olde farmhouse in Robin Hood's village in Sherwood Forest. Close Clumber & Rufford Country Parks. **Open:** All year **01623 824367** *robinhoodfarm@aol.com* **D:** Fr £17.50–£20.00 **S:** Fr £17.50–£20.00 **Beds:** 1F 1D 1T **Baths:** 1 Sh (6)

Fiskerton
SK7351

The Three Firs, *21 Marlock Close, Fiskerton, Southwell, Notts, NG25 0UB.* Modern detached corner residence in quiet cul-de-sac with secluded garden. **Open:** All year (not Xmas) **01636 830060 & 07941 021484 (M)** Mr & Mrs Jakeman **Fax: 01636 830060** *enquiries@threefirs.co.uk* www.threefirs.co.uk **D:** Fr £19.00–£24.00 **S:** Fr £20.00–£26.00 **Beds:** 2D 2S **Baths:** 1 En 1 Pr 1 Sh (5) (4)

Flintham
SK7445

The Boot & Shoe Inn, *Main Street, Flintham, Newark, Notts, NG23 5LA.* Recently renovated family-run pub in quiet village. **Open:** All year (not Xmas/New Year) **Grades:** ETC 4 Diamond **01636 525246** K M Butler www.boot&shoeinn.net **D:** Fr £25.00 **S:** Fr £35.00 **Beds:** 1F 1T 2D 1S **Baths:** 5 En (5) cc

Holbeck

SK5473 *Greendale Oak, Elm Tree*

The Old Orchard Cottage, *Holbeck, Worksop, Notts, S80 3NF.* Winner of four tourism awards **Open:** All year (not Xmas/ New Year)
01909 720659 Mrs Brown **D:** Fr £23.00–£30.00 **S:** Fr £38.00–£40.00 **Beds:** 1T 2D **Baths:** 3 En (3)

Holme

SK8059

Gothic Farmhouse, *Main Street, Holme, Newark, Nottinghamshire, NG23 7RZ.* Old farmhouse near old church close to Trent River. **Open:** All year (not Xmas/New Year)
01636 640656 Mr & Mrs Oxford **D:** Fr £25.00–£50.00 **S:** Fr £25.00 **Beds:** 2T **Baths:** 1 En 1 Sh

Holme Pierrepont

SK6339

Holme Grange Cottage, *Adbolton Lane, Holme Pierrepont, Nottingham, NG12 2LU.* Victorian cottage, 3 miles city, close to National Water Sports Centre. **Open:** All year (not Xmas)
0115 981 0413 *jean.colinwightman@talk21.com*
D: Fr £18.00–£20.00 **S:** Fr £18.00–£20.00 **Beds:** 1F 1D 1T **Baths:** 1 En 1 Sh (6)

Lambley

SK6345

Magnolia Guest House, *22 Spring Lane, Lambley, Nottingham, NG4 4PH.* Close to Sherwood Forest, Robin Hood country and Nottingham Castle. **Open:** All year
Grades: ETC 4 Diamond
0115 931 4404 Fax: 0115 9314582
magnoliahouse@lineone.net **D:** Fr £20.00 **S:** Fr £22.00–£25.00 **Beds:** 1F 1T 1D 1S **Baths:** 3 En (6)

Laneham

SK8076

The Old Cottage, *Laneham, Retford, Notts, DN22 0NA.* Quiet location, close to River Trent, Sherwood Forest, Lincoln, Newark. **Open:** All year
01777 228555 Mrs Hardman **Fax: 01777 228900 D:** Fr £20.00 **S:** Fr £25.00 **Beds:** 1F 1T 2S **Baths:** 3 En 1 Pr (10) (6)

Laxton

SK7267

Manor Farm, *Moorhouse Road, Laxton, Newark, Notts, NG22 0NU.* Old comfortable farmhouse in medieval village near to Sherwood Forest. **Open:** All year (not Xmas)
01777 870417 Mrs Haigh **D:** Fr £18.00–£20.00 **S:** Fr £18.00–£20.00 **Beds:** 2F 1D **Baths:** 1 Sh (3)

Lilac Farm, *Laxton, Newark, Notts, NG22 0NX.* Laxton: last remaining open field village. Heritage museum adjacent to Lilac Farm. **Open:** All year (not Xmas/New Year)
01777 870376 (also fax) Mrs Rose **D:** Fr £18.00–£20.00 **S:** Fr £20.00 **Beds:** 1F 2D **Baths:** 1 Sh (6)

Lowdham

SK6746

Old School Mews, *64a Main Street, Lowdham, Nottingham, NG14 7BE.* Spacious, interesting, historic converted school house in Robin Hood country. **Open:** All year (not Xmas/ New Year)
0115 966 4838 & 07732 923187 & 07808 841013 (M) J A Turnell *robert@turnell75.freeserve.co.uk* **D:** Fr £22.50 **S:** Fr £30.00 **Beds:** 2T 1D **Baths:** 1 En 1 Pr

Mansfield

SK5361

Parkhurst Guest House, *28 Woodhouse Road, Mansfield, Notts, NG18 2AF.* Friendly family-run guest house, walking distance to Mansfield centre. Licensed bar. **Open:** All year
01623 627324 Fax: 01623 621855
philfletcher@parkhurst28.freeserve.co.uk
www.parkhurstguesthouse.co.uk **D:** Fr £19.00–£22.00 **S:** Fr £22.00–£27.00 **Beds:** 3F 4D 2T 3S **Baths:** 5 En 1 Sh (10)

Bridleways Guest House, *Newlands Farm Lane, Mansfield, Notts, NG19 0HU.* Bridgeways - originally 2 late-C18th farm cottages, retains many period features inside. **Open:** Jan to Dec
01623 635725 D: Fr £20.00–£25.00 **S:** Fr £22.50–£25.00 **Beds:** 1F 2D 2T 1S **Baths:** 6 En (20)

Nether Langwith

SK5370

Boon Hills Farm, *Nether Langwith, Mansfield, Notts, NG20 9JQ.* Comfortable stone farmhouse with large garden on working farm. **Open:** Mar to Oct
01623 743862 Mrs Palmer *michael.palmer3@virgin.net* **D:** Fr £18.00–£20.00 **S:** Fr £20.00 **Beds:** 2D 1T **Baths:** 1 En 1 Sh (4)

Newark

SK7953

Racecourse Farm, *Station Road, Rolleston, Newark, Notts, NG23 5SE.* 200-year-old cottage next to racecourse, golf course and 3 miles from both Southwell and Newark. **Open:** All year
01636 812176 Mr Smith *brian@bcsmith.fsnet.co.uk* **D:** Fr £22.00–£23.00 **S:** Fr £25.00 **Beds:** 1T 1D **Baths:** 1 En 1 Sh (4)

The Boot & Shoe Inn, *Main Street, Flintham, Newark, Notts, NG23 5LA.* Recently renovated family-run pub in quiet village. **Open:** All year (not Xmas/New Year)
Grades: ETC 4 Diamond
01636 525246 K M Butler
www.boot&shoeinn.net **D:** Fr £25.00 **S:** Fr £35.00 **Beds:** 1F 1T 2D 1S **Baths:** 5 En (5) **cc**

Rutland Arms, *13-15 Barnbygate, Newark, Nottinghamshire, NG24 1PX.* Central location. Old coaching inn. **Open:** All year
01636 703399 D: Fr £20.00 **S:** Fr £35.00 **Beds:** 2F 2T 2D 4S **Baths:** 10 En **cc**

Norton

SK5772

Norton Grange Farm, *Norton, Cuckney, Mansfield, Notts, NG20 9LP.* Situated in beautiful village on edge of Sherwood Forest. **Open:** All year (not Xmas)
01623 842666 Mr Palmer **D:** Fr £18.00–£20.00 **S:** Fr £20.00–£22.00 **Beds:** 1F 1D 1T **Baths:** 1 Sh (4)

B&B owners may vary rates – be sure to check when booking

Nottingham

SK5641

Orchard Cottage Superior B&B, *Moor Cottages, Trowell Moor, Trowell, Nottingham, NG9 3PQ.* **Open:** All year **Grades:** ETC 4 Diamond
0115 928 0933 & 07790 817597 (M) Mr Woodland **Fax: 0115 928 0933** *orchardcottage.bandb@virgin.net* www.orchardcottages.com **D:** Fr £22.50–£30.00 **S:** Fr £40.00–£48.00 **Beds:** 2T 1D **Baths:** 3 En (6) **cc**
Orchard Cottage is a totally refurbished wing of a workhouse built 1817 and situated in a tranquil greenbelt location, surrounded by open farmland and orchards. Close to M1 J25/26. Short distance from several pubs serving excellent evening meals.

Gallery Hotel, *8-10 Radcliffe Road, West Bridgford, Nottingham, NG2 5FW.* Old Victorian house family hotel, run for 13 years by Mr & Mrs Don Masson. **Open:** All year **Grades:** ETC 3 Diamond
0115 981 3651 Mr & Mrs Masson **Fax: 0115 981 3732** www.yell.com.uk/sites/gallery-hotel **D:** Fr £25.00 **S:** Fr £29.00–£35.00 **Beds:** 3F 5D 4T 3S **Baths:** 15 En (1) (50)

Adams' Castle View Guest House, *85 Castle Boulevard, Nottingham, NG7 1FE.* Comfortable city guest house, close to bus/railway stations, activities. **Open:** All year **Grades:** ETC 3 Diamond
0115 950 0022 Mr Adams **D:** Fr £22.50–£25.00 **S:** Fr £22.50–£25.00 **Beds:** 1D 1T 2S **Baths:** 4 En

Talbot House Hotel, *18-20 Bridgford Road, West Bridgford, Nottingham, NG2 6AB.* Central position. 1 mile Nottingham city centre, National Ice Centre. **Open:** All year
0115 981 1123 & 0115 982 1814 Mr Brown **Fax: 0115 981 3545** *jktalbot@onetel.net.uk* www.talbothousehotel.com **D:** Fr £25.00–£45.00 **S:** Fr £25.00–£45.00 **Beds:** 6F 6D 6T 5S **Baths:** 20 En 3 Sh (30) **cc**

B&B owners may vary rates – be sure to check when booking

Grantham Hotel, *24-26 Radcliffe Road, West Bridgford, Nottingham, NG2 5FW.* Ideally located within few mins' walk to Trent Bridge, double fronted house. **Open:** All year
0115 981 1373 Fax: 0115 981 8567 D: Fr £24.00 **S:** Fr £33.00 **Beds:** 3F 4T 2D 1S **Baths:** 15 En 2 Sh (8) **cc**

The Willows, Tophouse Farm, *Lamin's Lane, Arnold, Nottingham, NG5 8PH.* Working farm near Sherwood Forest. Excellent neighbouring bar and restaurant. **Open:** All year (not Xmas/New Year)
0115 967 0089 A Lamin *lamin.tophousefarm@btinternet.com* **D:** Fr £19.00–£20.00 **S:** Fr £22.00–£25.00 **Beds:** 1T **Baths:** 1 En (20)

Ragnall

SK8073

Ragnall House, *Ragnall, Newark, Notts, NG22 0UR.* Period residence in large grounds. Lincoln and Sherwood Forest nearby. **Open:** All year
01777 228575 (also fax) Mrs Hatfield *ragnallhouse@gofornet.co.uk* **D:** Fr £18.00–£20.00 **S:** Fr £18.00–£20.00 **Beds:** 1F 1D 2T 1S **Baths:** 2 En 2 Pr 1 Sh (7)

Shelford

SK6642

Fox Cottage, *Main Street, Shelford, Nottingham, NG12 1ED.* Beautiful cottage in delightful gardens with country views, quiet village **Open:** All year
0115 933 5741 & 07976 705066 (M) Mrs Lewis **Fax: 0115 933 5741 D:** Fr £20.00 **S:** Fr £25.00 **Beds:** 3D **Baths:** 3 En (8)

Southwell

SK7053

The Three Firs, *21 Marlock Close, Fiskerton, Southwell, Notts, NG25 0UB.* **Open:** All year (not Xmas)
01636 830060 & 07941 021484 (M) Mr & Mrs Jakeman **Fax: 01636 830060** *enquiries@threefirs.co.uk* www.threefirs.co.uk **D:** Fr £19.00–£24.00 **S:** Fr £20.00–£26.00 **Beds:** 2D 2S **Baths:** 1 En 1 Pr 1 Sh (5) (4)
Modern detached corner residence in quiet cul-de-sac with secluded garden. Patio, comfortable TV lounge, inglenook fire in winter, off road parking. Two quaint real ale pubs nearby. River/fishing 0.25 mile, race/golf course 0.75 mile, power boating 2 miles, dinghy sailing 4 miles.

Barn Lodge, *Duckers Cottage, Brinkley, Southwell, Notts, NG25 0TP.* Converted barn in open countryside. Railway station, racecourse, Southwell Minster nearby. **Open:** All year (not Xmas/New Year)
01636 813435 Mrs Hanbury *barnlodge@hotmail.com* **D:** Fr £22.50 **S:** Fr £25.00 **Beds:** 1F 1D 1T **Baths:** 3 En (3)

Church Street Bed & Breakfast, *56 Church Street, Southwell, Nottinghamshire, NG25 0HG.* Breakfast our speciality! Beautifully restored Georgian Grade II town house, friendly relaxed atmosphere. **Open:** All year
01636 812004 Mr Wright *ian.wright5@btinternet.com* www.southwell-online.co.uk **D:** Fr £25.00 **S:** Fr £30.00 **Beds:** 1T 2D **Baths:** 1 En 1 Sh (2)

Stanton-on-the-Wolds

SK6330

Laurel Farm, *Browns Lane, Stanton-on-the-Wolds, Keyworth, Nottingham, NG12 5BL.* Lovely old farmhouse in 3 acres. Spacious rooms, convenient attractions. **Open:** All year
0115 937 3488 Mrs Moffat **Fax: 0115 937 6490** *laurelfarm@yahoo.com* www.s-h-systems.co.uk/hotels/laurelfa.html **D:** Fr £22.50–£27.50 **S:** Fr £35.00–£40.00 **Beds:** 2D 1T **Baths:** 2 En 1 Pr (8) **cc**

Sutton in Ashfield

SK4958

Dalestorth Guest House, *Skegby Lane, Skegby, Sutton in Ashfield, Notts, NG17 3DH.* Grade II Georgian Listed building. Clean, friendly accommodation, hotel standards. **Open:** All year
01623 551110 Mr Jordan **Fax: 01623 442241 D:** Fr £15.00–£17.50 **S:** Fr £16.00–£18.00 **Beds:** 2F 3D 3T 5S **Baths:** 8 Sh (50)

Sutton on Trent

SK7965

Woodbine Farmhouse, *1 Church Street, Sutton on Trent, Newark, Notts, NG23 6PD.* Heavily beamed farmhouse. Quiet, yet near A1. Aga cooking. **Open:** All year (not Xmas)
01636 822549 Mrs Searle **Fax: 01636 821716** *woodbinefmhouse@aol.com* **D:** Fr £18.00–£21.00 **S:** Fr £20.00 **Beds:** 3D 1T 1S 1F **Baths:** 1 En 3 Sh (5)

All details shown are as supplied by B&B owners in Autumn 2002

Trowell

SK4839

Orchard Cottage Superior B&B, *Moor Cottages, Trowell Moor, Trowell, Nottingham, NG9 3PQ.* Orchard Cottage is a totally refurbished wing of a workhouse built 1817. **Open:** All year **Grades:** ETC 4 Diamond
0115 928 0933 & 07790 817597 (M) Mr Woodland **Fax: 0115 928 0933** *orchardcottage.bandb@virgin.net* www.orchardcottages.com **D:** Fr £22.50–£30.00 **S:** Fr £40.00–£48.00 **Beds:** 2T 1D **Baths:** 3 En (6) **cc**

Church Farm Guest House, *1 Nottingham Road, Trowell, Nottingham, NG9 3PA.* C17th former farmhouse. **Open:** All year (not Xmas)
0115 930 1637 Fax: 0115 930 6991 D: Fr £20.00–£22.50 **S:** Fr £20.00–£25.00 **Beds:** 1F 3D 2T 2S **Baths:** 2 Sh

Upton (Southwell)

SK7354

The Wheelhouse, *Mill Lane, Upton, Newark, Notts, NG23 5SZ.* Mill situated over river, views over all elevations, overlooks racecourse. **Open:** All year (not Xmas)
01636 813572 Mrs Scothern **D:** Fr £20.00 **S:** Fr £20.00 **Beds:** 1F 1D 1S **Baths:** 1 En (6)

Walesby

SK6870

13 New Hill, *Walesby, Newark, Notts, NG22 9PB.* 1950 semi-detached house with large garden in a small village. **Open:** All year (not Xmas)
01623 863834 Mrs Marsh **D:** Fr £15.00 **S:** Fr £15.00 **Beds:** 2D **Baths:** 1 Sh (0) (3)

RATES

D = Price range per person sharing in a double or twin room

S = Price range for a single room

West Bridgford

SK5836

Acorn Hotel, *4 Radcliffe Road, West Bridgford, Nottingham, NG2 5FW.* **Open:** All year
0115 981 1297 Mr Palley **Fax: 0115 981 7654** *reservations@acorn-hotel.co.uk* www.acorn-hotel.co.uk **D:** Fr £25.00–£32.00 **S:** Fr £35.00–£40.00 **Beds:** 2F 7T 2D 1S **Baths:** 12 En (12) **cc**
The Acorn Hotel is conveniently located 1.5 miles from Nottingham city centre & just 200 yards from Trent Bridge. All ensuite bedrooms are tastefully decorated with TV & tea & coffee making facilities. Rates include traditional full English breakfast.

Gallery Hotel, *8-10 Radcliffe Road, West Bridgford, Nottingham, NG2 5FW.* Old Victorian house family hotel, run for 13 years by Mr & Mrs Don Masson. **Open:** All year **Grades:** ETC 3 Diamond
0115 981 3651 Mr & Mrs Masson **Fax: 0115 981 3732** www.yell.com.uk/sites/gallery-hotel **D:** Fr £25.00 **S:** Fr £29.00–£35.00 **Beds:** 3F 5D 4T 3S **Baths:** 15 En (1) (50)

Grantham Hotel, *24-26 Radcliffe Road, West Bridgford, Nottingham, NG2 5FW.* Ideally located within few mins' walk to Trent Bridge, double fronted house. **Open:** All year
0115 981 1373 Fax: 0115 981 8567 D: Fr £24.00 **S:** Fr £33.00 **Beds:** 3F 4T 2D 1S **Baths:** 15 En 2 Sh (8) **cc**

Croft Hotel, *6-8 North Road, West Bridgford, Nottingham, NG2 7NH.* Charming, quiet Victorian B&B, 1.5 miles from Nottingham city centre. **Open:** All year (not Xmas/New Year)
0115 981 2744 (also fax) Kennedy *croft.hotel.wb@talk21.com* www.smoothhound.co.uk/hotels/crofth.html **D:** Fr £18.00–£20.00 **S:** Fr £20.00–£25.00 **Beds:** 2F 3T 2D 7S **Baths:** 5 Sh (12)

Weston

SK7767

The Boot and Shoe Hotel, *Great North Road, Weston, Newark, Notts, NG23 6SY.* Excellent food and beers. Off A1. Close to power stations. **Open:** All year
01636 821257 D: Fr £20.00 **S:** Fr £20.00 **Beds:** 2F 1D **Baths:** 1 Sh **cc**

Whatton in the Vale

SK7439

The Dell, *Church Street, Whatton in the Vale, Nottingham, Notts., NG13 9EL.* Conservation area residence. Guests private sitting rooms, swimming pool, snooker. **Open:** All year
01949 850832 Mrs Fraser **D:** Fr £17.50–£19.50 **S:** Fr £25.00–£27.50 **Beds:** 1F 1T 1D **Baths:** 1 En 1 Pr (3)

Worksop

SK5879

Dukeries Park Hotel, *29 Park Street, Worksop, Notts, S80 1HW.* **Open:** All year **Grades:** AA 4 Diamond
01909 476674 *dukeries@supanet.com* **D:** Fr £25.00–£27.00 **S:** Fr £30.00–£40.00 **Beds:** 2T 2D 2S **Baths:** 6 En **cc**
A warm welcome and friendly service is assured at this carefully restored Victorian building within easy walking distance of the town centre. Quality accommodation complemented by smart public rooms which include a well-appointed lounge, bar and attractive breakfast room.

Sherwood Guest House, *57 Carlton Road, Worksop, Notts, S80 1PP.* Comfortable/friendly accommodation near railway station, Clumber Park, A1/M1. **Open:** All year **Grades:** ETC 3 Diamond
01909 474209 Mr Wilkinson **Fax: 01909 476470** *cherwould@aol.com* **D:** Fr £21.00–£23.50 **S:** Fr £21.00–£26.00 **Beds:** 1F 1D 3T 1S **Baths:** 2 En 2 Sh (2)

Riseholme Guest House, *215 Carlton Road, Worksop, Nottinghamshire, S81 7HN.* Very comfortable,detached Victorian house. 10 minutes from town centre. **Open:** All year
01909 481506 *riseholme215@aol.com* **D:** Fr £20.00 **S:** Fr £21.00 **Beds:** 1T 2D **Baths:** 2 Sh (8) (3)

Oxfordshire

Abingdon

SU4997

Barrows End, *3 The Copse, Abingdon, Oxon, OX14 3YW.* Modern chalet bungalow, peaceful setting. Easy access Oxford/Abingdon. **Open:** All year (not Xmas)
01235 523541 Mrs Harmsworth *DSHarm@tesco.net* **D:** Fr £24.00–£25.00 **S:** Fr £26.00–£28.00 **Beds:** 3T **Baths:** 1 En 2 Pr (3)

Adderbury

SP4735

Le Restaurant Francais at Morgans Orchard, *9 Twyford Gardens, Adderbury, Banbury, Oxon, OX17 3JA.* North Oxfordshire's premier award-winning French restaurant with family hospitality. **Open:** All year **Grades:** ETC 3 Diamond
01295 812047 C Morgan **Fax: 01295 812341** *morgansorchard@aol.com* www.banbury-cross.co.uk/morgans **D:** Fr £20.00–£25.00 **S:** Fr £40.00 **Beds:** 2T 1D **Baths:** 3 En (4) **cc**

Ascott-under-Wychwood

SP3018

Meadowbank House, *Shipton Road, Ascott-under-Wychwood, Chipping Norton, Oxon, OX7 6AG.* Beautiful C17th house, peacefully situated in picturesque Cotswold countryside. **Open:** All year (not Xmas/New Year)
01993 830612 (also fax) Mrs Ridley *ingrid@meadowbank-ascott.co.uk* www.meadowbank-ascott.co.uk **D:** Fr £20.00–£22.50 **S:** Fr £25.00 **Beds:** 1T 1D **Baths:** 2 En (4)

Ashbury

SU2685

The Village Stores, *Ashbury, Swindon, Wiltshire, SN6 8NA.* Thatched cottage in pretty downland village, 5 mins from Ridgeway. **Open:** All year (not Xmas/New Year)
01793 710262 (also fax) Mr & Mrs Schiff **D:** Fr £20.00–£25.00 **S:** Fr £20.00–£25.00 **Beds:** 1F 1T 1D **Baths:** 1 Pr

Aston

SP3303 *The Trout*

Chimney Farmhouse, *Chimney-on-Thames, Aston, Bampton, Oxon, OX18 2EH.* Peaceful farmhouse offers warm welcome and comfortable accommodation. Ideal for exploring Oxfordshire and Cotswolds. **Open:** Feb to Nov
01367 870279 www.country-accom.co.uk/chimneyfarmhouse **D:** Fr £22.50–£30.00 **S:** Fr £25.00–£30.00 **Beds:** 1T 1D 1S **Baths:** 3 En (10) (6)

Aston Upthorpe

SU5585

Middle Fell, *Moreton Road, Aston Upthorpe, Didcot, Oxon, OX11 9ER.* Georgian village house, tastefully appointed. Secluded garden bordering Aston Stud. **Open:** All year (not Xmas)
01235 850207 (also fax) C Millin **D:** Fr £22.50–£25.00 **S:** Fr £27.00–£37.00 **Beds:** 1F 1D 1T **Baths:** 3 En (10) (4)

Benson

SU6191

Fyfield Manor, *Brook Street, Benson, Wallingford, Oxon, OX10 6HA.* Medieval dining room. Beautiful water gardens. Essentially a family house. **Open:** All year (not Xmas/New Year)
01491 835184 Mrs Brown **Fax: 01491 825635** **D:** Fr £25.00 **S:** Fr £30.00 **Beds:** 1D 1T **Baths:** 2 En 1 Pr (10) (6)

Bicester

SP5822

The Old School, *Stratton Audley, Bicester, Oxfordshire, OX27 9BJ.* **Open:** All year
01869 277371 Mrs Wertheimer *sawertheimer@euphony.net* www.old-school.co.uk **D:** Fr £30.00–£35.00 **S:** Fr £30.00–£35.00 **Beds:** 3T 1S **Baths:** 2 Sh (6)
Interesting C17th house in pretty village. Pleasant garden with lovely view. Tennis court. Guests' own drawing room. Tea and home-made cakes on arrival. Village has charming thatched pub serving excellent meals. Very comfortable beds. Everyone sleeps well - so peaceful.

Planning a longer stay? Always ask for any special rates

Home Farm House, *Middle Aston, Bicester, Oxon, OX25 5PX.* Peaceful C17th farmhouse with stunning views and lovely garden. **Open:** All year
01869 340666 Fax: 01869 347789 *cparsons@telinco.co.uk* **D:** Fr £25.00–£28.00 **S:** Fr £25.00–£35.00 **Beds:** 1T 1D **Baths:** 1 En 1 Pr (12) (4)

Blackthorn

SP6218

Lime Trees Farm, *Lower Road, Blackthorn, Bicester, Oxon, OX25 1TG.* Relaxed, comfortable accommodation providing a perfect springboard for Oxford and Cotswolds. **Open:** All year **Grades:** ETC 4 Diamond
01869 248435 Fax: 01869 325843 *keithcrampton@tiscali.co.uk* www.smoothhound.co.uk/hotels/limetrees.html **D:** Fr £25.00–£30.00 **S:** Fr £30.00–£40.00 **Beds:** 1T 1D **Baths:** 1 En 1 Pr

Bletchingdon

SP5018

Stonehouse Farm, *Weston Road, Bletchingdon, Kidlington, Oxon, OX5 3EA.* C17th farmhouse set in 560 acres, 15 mins from Oxford. **Open:** All year (not Xmas/New Year)
01869 350585 Mrs Hedges **D:** Fr £18.00–£22.00 **S:** Fr £20.00–£24.00 **Beds:** 1F 1D 1T 1S **Baths:** 2 Sh (12) (6)

Bloxham

SP4236

Brook Cottage, *Little Bridge Road, Bloxham, Banbury, Oxon, OX15 4PU.* Warm welcome to C17th thatched cottage. Personal management by owner. **Open:** All year
01295 721089 **D:** Fr £18.50 **S:** Fr £18.50 **Beds:** 1D 1T 1S **Baths:** 1 En 1 Pr (4)

Buscot

SU2397

Apple Tree House, *Buscot, Faringdon, Oxon, SN7 8DA.* Old property in National Trust village, 5 mins' walk River Thames, one acre garden. **Open:** All year (not Xmas)
01367 252592 Mrs Reay *emreay@aol.com* **D:** Fr £18.00–£22.00 **S:** Fr £23.00–£28.00 **Beds:** 2D 1T **Baths:** 1 En 2 Pr (10)

National Grid References given are for villages, towns and cities – not for individual houses

Chalgrove

SU6396

Cornerstones, *1 Cromwell Close, Chalgrove, Oxford, OX44 7SE.* Pretty detached bungalow, situated just off B480 in charming Oxfordshire village. **Open:** All year
01865 890298 D: Fr £14.50 **S:** Fr £23.00 **Beds:** 2T **Baths:** 1 Sh (5) (2)

Charlbury

SP3619

Cotswold View Caravan & Camping Site, *Banbury Hill Farm, Enstone Road, Charlbury, Chipping Norton, Oxon, OX7 3JH.* Situated on eastern edge of Cotswolds, overlooking the Evenlode Valley. **Open:** All year (not Xmas)
01608 810314 Mrs Widdows **Fax: 01608 811891 D:** Fr £18.00–£25.00 **S:** Fr £20.00–£35.00 **Beds:** 7F 2D 3T 1S **Baths:** 11 En 1 Sh (10) **cc**

Childrey

SU3587 *Star Inn*

Ridgeway House, *West Street, Childrey, Wantage, Oxon, OX12 9UL.* Award winning bed and breakfast. All ensuite, quiet and wonderful views. **Open:** All year
01235 751538 (also fax) Mrs Roberts *robertsfamily@compuserve.com* **D:** Fr £25.00–£29.00 **S:** Fr £29.00–£39.00 **Beds:** 2F 2T 2D 2S **Baths:** 2 En (5)

Chipping Norton

SP3126

1 Lower Barns, *Salford, Chipping Norton, Oxon, OX7 5YP.* Traditionally furnished, well situated for Cotswolds, Oxford, Stratford. Homely welcome. **Open:** All year (not Xmas/New Year)
01608 643276 Mrs Barnard **D:** Fr £18.00 **S:** Fr £18.00 **Beds:** 1T **Baths:** 1 En (2)

Cholsey

SU5886

The Well Cottage, *Caps Lane, Cholsey, Wallingford, Oxon, OX10 9HQ.* Delightful cottage with ensuite bedrooms in secluded garden flat. **Open:** All year
01491 651959 & 07887 958920 (M) J Alexander **Fax: 01491 651675** *thewellcottage@talk21.com* **D:** Fr £15.00–£25.00 **S:** Fr £20.00–£30.00 **Beds:** 2T 1D **Baths:** 2 En 1 Pr

Deddington

SP4631

Hill Barn, *Milton Gated Road, Deddington, Banbury, Oxon, OX15 0TS.* Peaceful countryside ground floor accommodation. Convenient Oxford, Cotswolds, Warwick, Stratford. **Open:** All year (not Xmas) **Grades:** ETC 2 Diamond
01869 338631 Mrs White *hillbarn-bb@supanet.com* **D:** Fr £20.00–£25.00 **S:** Fr £25.00–£30.00 **Beds:** 1F 1D 2T **Baths:** 1 En 1 Sh (6)

Stonecrop Guest House, *Hempton Road, Deddington, Banbury, Oxon, OX15 0QH.* Detached house close to places of interest. A warm welcome. **Open:** All year
01869 338335 Fax: 01869 338505 D: Fr £16.00–£19.00 **S:** Fr £16.00–£19.00 **Beds:** 1F 1D 1T 1S **Baths:** 2 Sh (10) (6)

Ducklington

SP3507

Newhouse Farm, *Aston Road, Ducklington, Witney, Oxon, OX29 7QY.* **Open:** All year (not Xmas/New Year)
01993 702411 (also fax) *r.hook@farmline.com* **D:** Fr £18.50–£22.50 **S:** Fr £19.50–£23.50 **Beds:** 1D 1S **Baths:** 1 Sh (4)
A warm welcome awaits you at our comfortable farmhouse on working mixed/livery farm situated in a quiet countryside location between Ducklington & Aston. Ideal for visiting local pottery, the Cotswolds, Witney, Blenheim Palace, Oxford and its colleges.

East End

SP3914

Forge Cottage, *East End, North Leigh, Witney, Oxon, OX8 6PZ.* Old cottage. Organic home grown food. Hot toast available. **Open:** May to Nov
01993 881120 Mrs French *jill.french@talk21.com* **D:** Fr £22.00–£25.00 **Beds:** 1D **Baths:** 1 En (2)

Epwell

SP3441

Yarnhill Farm, *Shenington Road, Epwell, Banbury, Oxon, OX15 6JA.* Peaceful farmhouse; ideally situated for Cotswolds, Stratford-upon-Avon, Oxford. **Open:** All year (not Xmas)
01295 780250 D: Fr £18.00–£25.00 **S:** Fr £18.00–£25.00 **Beds:** 1D 1T 1S **Baths:** 1 Pr 1 Sh (8) (6)

Ewelme

SU6491

Fords Farm, *Ewelme, Wallingford, Oxon, OX10 6HU.* Picturesque setting in historic village. Warm, friendly atmosphere. Good views. **Open:** All year
01491 839272 Miss Edwards **D:** Fr £24.00–£25.00 **S:** Fr £30.00–£35.00 **Beds:** 1D 2T **Baths:** 1 Pr 1 Sh (8)

May's Farm, *Turner's Court, Ewelme, Wallingford, Oxon, OX10 6QF.* Friendly farmhouse and bungalow - wonderful views. Working stock farm, peaceful. **Open:** All year
01491 641294 & 01491 642056 Mrs Passmore **Fax: 01491 641697** *apister.v@virgin.net* **D:** Fr £20.00–£25.00 **S:** Fr £22.50–£35.00 **Beds:** 1F 1T 1S **Baths:** 1 En 1 Sh (6)

Faringdon

SU2895

Faringdon Hotel, *1 Market Place, Faringdon, Oxon, SN7 7HL.* **Open:** All year
01367 240536 Fax: 01367 243250 D: Fr £30.00–£35.00 **S:** Fr £45.00–£60.00 **Beds:** 3F 14D 1T 3S **Baths:** 20 En **cc**
Situated on the edge of the Cotswolds, the Faringdon Hotel is the ideal touring base for Oxford, Blenheim Palace, and the Thames Valley. Offering comfort and relaxation in the peaceful surroundings, plus authentic Thai restaurant. Telephone for brochure.

Portwell House Hotel, *Market Place, Faringdon, Oxon, SN7 7HU.* Relax in the ancient market town of Faringdon within reach of the Cotswolds. **Open:** All year
01367 240197 Mr Pakeman **Fax: 01367 244330 D:** Fr £25.00 **S:** Fr £40.00 **Beds:** 2F 3D 2T 1S **Baths:** 8 En (2) (4) **cc**

Fifield

SP2319

Merryfield, *High Street, Fifield, Chipping Norton, Oxon, OX7 6HL.* Quiet and peaceful, an ideal centre for touring the Cotswolds. **Open:** All year (not Xmas) **Grades:** ETC 3 Diamond
01993 830517 Mrs Palmer *jpmgtd@freeuk.com* merryfieldbandb.co.uk **D:** Fr £25.00–£30.00 **S:** Fr £28.00–£30.00 **Beds:** 2T **Baths:** 1 En 1 Pr (4)

B&B owners may vary rates – be sure to check when booking

Freeland

SP4112

Shepherds Hall Inn, *Witney Road, Freeland, Witney, Oxon, OX29 8HQ.* **Open:** All year **Grades:** ETC 3 Diamond
01993 881256 Mr Fyson **Fax: 01993 883455** **D:** Fr £25.00–£27.50 **S:** Fr £25.00–£35.00 **Beds:** 1F 1D 2T 1S **Baths:** 5 En (50) **cc**
Attractive inn with excellent well-appointed accommodation. Wide selection of appetising meals available lunch times and evenings. Ideally situated for Oxford, Woodstock - Blenheim Palace - and Cotswolds. On A4095 Woodstock-Witney road.

Garsington

SP5801

Hill Copse Cottage, *Wheatley Road, Garsington, Oxford, Oxfordshire, OX44 9DT.*
Detached house surrounded by farmland with lovely views. Secure parking. **Open:** All year (not Xmas/New Year) **Grades:** ETC 3 Diamond
01865 361478 & 07778 776209 (M) Mrs Winstone **Fax: 01865 361478** **D:** Fr £30.00 **S:** Fr £30.00–£40.00 **Beds:** 1F 2D 1S **Baths:** 4 En (5)

Goring

SU6081 *Catherine Wheel, John Barleycorn*

The Catherine Wheel, *Station Road, Goring, Reading, Berks, RG8 9HB.* Accommodation in a Victorian cottage in riverside village. **Open:** All year
01491 872379 Mrs Kerr **D:** Fr £20.00 **S:** Fr £25.00 **Beds:** 2D 1T **Baths:** 2 Sh **cc**

Northview House, *Farm Road, Goring-on-Thames, Reading, Oxon, RG8 0AA.* Five minutes from Ridgeway. Close to pubs, river and stations. **Open:** All year (not Xmas/New Year)
01491 872184 Mr & Mrs Sheppard *hi@goring-on-thames.freeserve.co.uk* **D:** Fr £18.00 **Beds:** 2D 1T **Baths:** 1 Sh (3)

Please respect a B&B's wishes regarding children, animals and smoking

Great Milton

SP6302

Colletts View, *Great Milton, Oxford, Oxfordshire, OX44 7NY.* Set in lovely gardens, ground floor rooms, Oxford, Chilterns close. **Open:** All year (not Xmas/New Year)
01844 278824 Mrs Hayes *sputnik@ukgateway.net* **D:** Fr £18.00–£20.00 **S:** Fr £20.00–£22.00 **Beds:** 2F 2T **Baths:** 1 Sh (15) (2)

Hanwell

SP4344

The Coach House, *Hanwell Castle, Hanwell, Banbury, Oxon, OX17 1HN.* Part of C15th castle in 20 acre garden undergoing restoration. **Open:** Apr to Oct
01295 730764 Mrs Taylor **D:** Fr £18.00–£25.00 **S:** Fr £18.00–£25.00 **Beds:** 1F 1D 1T **Baths:** 3 En (1) (6)

Headington

SP5407

Sandfield House, *19 London Road, Headington, Oxford, OX3 7RE.* Fine period house. Direct coaches to London, Heathrow & Gatwick. **Open:** All year (not Xmas)
01865 762406 (also fax) Mrs Anderson *stay@sandfield-guesthouse.co.uk* www.sandfield-guesthouse.co.uk **D:** Fr £29.00–£34.00 **S:** Fr £30.00–£34.00 **Beds:** 2D 2S **Baths:** 3 En 1 Pr (6) (5) **cc**

Henley-on-Thames

SU7682

Orchard Dene Cottage, *Lower Assenden, Henley-on-Thames, Oxon, RG9 6AG.* **Open:** All year **Grades:** ETC 4 Diamond
01491 575490 (also fax) Mrs Batchelor Smith *orcharddene@freeuk.com* www.orcharddene.freeuk.com **D:** Fr £20.00–£25.00 **S:** Fr £25.00 **Beds:** 1D 1S **Baths:** 1 Sh
Two miles from Henley, in beautiful walking country (Chilterns, Thames Path, Oxfordshire Way) and within easy reach of the Cotswolds, Oxford and Windsor by rail or road. Enjoy an interesting garden, comfortable rooms, relaxed atmosphere and a full English breakfast.

Lenwade, *3 Western Road, Henley-on-Thames, Oxon, RG9 1JL.* Beautiful Victorian family home, convenient river, restaurants, public transport. **Open:** All year (not Xmas)
01491 573468 (also fax) Mrs Williams *lenwadeuk@compuserve.com* www.w3b-ink.com/lenwade **D:** Fr £30.00–£32.50 **S:** Fr £45.00–£50.00 **Beds:** 2D 1T **Baths:** 2 En 1 Pr (2)

Pennyford House, *Peppard, Henley-on-Thames, Oxon, RG9 5JE.* Family home with dogs. Happy atmosphere. Nice garden. Local interests. **Open:** All year
01491 628272 Mrs Howden-Ferme **Fax: 01491 628779** **D:** Fr £25.00–£35.00 **S:** Fr £30.00–£35.00 **Beds:** 1T 3D 1S **Baths:** 4 En 1 Pr (10)

Alexander House, *21 Upton Close, Henley-on-Thames, Oxon, RG9 1BT.* Modern town house. 2 mins' walk river, town centre, station. **Open:** All year
01491 575331 Mrs Inglis **Fax: 01491 412421** *alexanderhouse@tesco.net* **D:** Fr £40.00–£50.00 **S:** Fr £20.00–£25.00 **Beds:** 1T 1D **Baths:** 1 En 1 Pr

The Old Wood, *197 Greys Road, Henley-on-Thames, Oxfordshire, RG9 1SP.* Quiet location close town centre. Ground floor rooms, wooded garden. **Open:** All year (not Xmas/New Year)
01491 573930 Janice Jones **Fax: 01491 576285** *janice@janicejones.co.uk* **D:** Fr £22.50–£25.00 **S:** Fr £28.00–£30.00 **Beds:** 1F 1D **Baths:** 1 Sh (3)

New Lodge, *Henley Park, Henley-on-Thames, Oxon, RG9 6HU.* Victorian lodge in tranquil park settings. Minimum two nights stay. **Open:** All year
01491 576340 (also fax) Mrs Warner *newlodge@mail.com* **D:** Fr £23.00–£25.00 **S:** Fr £30.00–£32.00 **Beds:** 1F 2D **Baths:** 1 En 1 Pr (4)

The Laurels, *107 St Marks Road, Henley-on-Thames, Oxon, RG9 1LP.* Walking distance to town, river and station. Quiet, clean, comfortable. **Open:** All year
01491 572982 Mrs Bridekirk **D:** Fr £28.00–£30.00 **S:** Fr £38.00–£48.00 **Beds:** 1T 1D 1S **Baths:** 2 En 1 Pr (10) (3)

Ledard, *Rotherfield Road, Henley-on-Thames, Oxon, RG9 1NN.* Elegant Victorian house and garden within easy reach of Henley. **Open:** All year (not Xmas)
01491 575611 Mrs Howard *alan.howard@iee.org* **D:** Fr £20.00 **S:** Fr £20.00 **Beds:** 1F 1D 1T **Baths:** 2 Pr (4)

Alftrudis, *8 Norman Avenue, Henley-on-Thames, Oxon, RG9 1SG.* Victorian home, quiet cul-de-sac two minutes town centre station, river. **Open:** All year
01491 573099 & 07802 408643 (M) Mrs Lambert **Fax: 01491 411747** *b&b@alftrudis.fsnet.co.uk* **D:** Fr £27.50–£30.00 **S:** Fr £45.00–£50.00 **Beds:** 2D 1T **Baths:** 2 En 1 Pr (8) (2)

Hethe

SP5829

Manor Farm, *Hethe, Bicester, Oxfordshire, OX6 9ES.* Between Oxford and Stratford. Charming stone manor house in lovely village. **Open:** All year
01869 277602 Mrs Reynolds **Fax: 01869 278376 D:** Fr £25.00–£30.00 **S:** Fr £30.00–£35.00 **Beds:** 2D **Baths:** 1 En 1 Pr (2)

Kirtlington

SP4919

Two Turnpike Cottages, *Kirtlington, Oxford, OX5 3HB.* Cotswold stone cottage with pretty gardens in village setting. **Open:** All year
01869 350706 Mrs Jones *margarethjones@hotmail.com* **D:** Fr £25.00–£30.00 **S:** Fr £35.00 **Beds:** 2D **Baths:** 1 Sh (2)

Leafield

SP3115

Langley Farm, *Leafield, Witney, Oxon, OX8 5QD.* Working farm set in open country 3 miles from Burford. **Open:** May to Oct
01993 878686 Mrs Greves *gwengreves@farmline.com* **D:** Fr £17.50–£20.00 **Beds:** 2D 1T **Baths:** 1 Pr 2 Sh (8)

Letcombe Regis

SU3886

Quince Cottage, *Letcombe Regis, Wantage, Oxon, OX12 9JP.* Large thatched cottage, exposed beams, near Ridgeway, warm family atmosphere. **Open:** All year
01235 763652 Mrs Boden **D:** Fr £21.00–£25.00 **S:** Fr £25.00 **Beds:** 1T 1S **Baths:** 1 Pr (1) (2)

National Grid References given are for villages, towns and cities – not for individual houses

Planning a longer stay? Always ask for any special rates

Lewknor

SU7197

Moorcourt Cottage, *Weston Road, Lewknor, Watlington, Oxfordshire, OX49 5RU.* **Open:** All year (not Xmas/New Year) **Grades:** ETC 4 Diamond
01844 351419 (also fax) Mrs Hodgson *p.hodgson@freeuk.com* **D:** Fr £25.00 **S:** Fr £35.00 **Beds:** 1T 1D **Baths:** 1 En 1 Pr (4)
Beautiful C15th cottage. Views of Chiltern Hills and farmland. Quiet, friendly and very comfortable. Traditional English breakfast. Ideal touring centre for Oxford, Henley on Thames, Cotswolds. Frequent bus service to London from Lewknor. Many walks, cycleways, public golf courses nearby.

Lockinge

SU4287

Lockinge Kiln Farm, *The Ridgeway, Lockinge, Wantage, Oxon, OX12 8PA.* Quiet comfortable farmhouse, working farm. Ideal walking, riding, cycling country. **Open:** All year (not Xmas)
01235 763308 (also fax) Mrs Cowan *stellacowan@hotmail.com* **D:** Fr £20.00 **S:** Fr £25.00 **Beds:** 1D 2T **Baths:** 3 Sh (10) (3)

Long Hanborough

SP4114

Gorselands Hall, *Boddington Lane, North Leigh, Witney, Oxon, OX29 6PU.* Lovely old country house. Convenient for Blenheim Palace, Oxford, Cotswolds. **Open:** All year **Grades:** ETC 4 Diamond
01993 882292 Mr & Mrs Hamilton **Fax: 01993 883629** *hamilton@gorselandshall.com* www.gorselandshall.com **D:** Fr £22.50–£25.00 **S:** Fr £35.00 **Beds:** 4D 1T 1F **Baths:** 6 En (6) cc

Wynford House, *79 Main Road, Long Hanborough, Near Woodstock, Oxon, OX8 8BX.* Comfortable warm family house in village. Good walks, local pubs. **Open:** All year (not Xmas)
01993 881402 Mrs Ellis **Fax: 01993 883661 D:** Fr £22.00–£24.00 **S:** Fr £30.00–£40.00 **Beds:** 1F 1D 1T **Baths:** 1 En 1 Sh

Long Wittenham

SU5493

The Machine Man Inn, *Fieldside, Long Wittenham, Abingdon, Oxon, OX14 4QP.* **Open:** All year
01865 407835 Mr Evans *crispinevans@aol.com* www.machinemaninn.com **D:** Fr £22.50–£27.50 **S:** Fr £35.00–£45.00 **Beds:** 1F 1T 2D 3S **Baths:** 5 En 1 Pr (10) cc
Peacefully situated in attractive Thamesside village, roughly equal distance to Abingdon, Didcot, Wallingford, close to Thames Path, Pendon Museum, Wittenham Clumps. Residents lounge, licensed bar, evening meals, packed lunches. Special rates for cyclists, walkers & business people.

Milton Common

SP6503

Byways, *Old London Road, Milton Common, Thame, Oxon, OX9 2JR.* A spacious bungalow, comfortable and cosy, good views, with large garden. **Open:** All year
01844 279386 D: Fr £23.00 **S:** Fr £25.00 **Beds:** 2T **Baths:** 1 En 1 Pr (3)

Nether Westcote

SP2220

Cotswold View Guest House, *Nether Westcote, Chipping Norton, Oxon, OX7 6SD.* Cotswold view guest house, built on site of my family's farmyard. **Open:** All year (not Xmas/New Year)
01993 830699 Mr Gibson *info@cotswoldview-guesthouse.co.uk* www.cotswoldview-guesthouse.co.uk **D:** Fr £20.00–£25.00 **S:** Fr £25.00–£30.00 **Beds:** 2D 2T 1S 2F **Baths:** 5 En 2 Pr (8) cc

Nettlebed

SU6986

Park Corner Farm House, *Nettlebed, Henley-on-Thames, Oxon, RG9 6DX.* Queen Anne farmhouse in AONB between Henley-on-Thames and Oxford. **Open:** All year (not Xmas/New Year)
01491 641450 Mrs Rutter **D:** Fr £22.50 **S:** Fr £25.00 **Beds:** 2T 1S **Baths:** 1 Sh 1 Pr (6)

BATHROOMS
En = Ensuite
Pr = Private
Sh = Shared

National Grid References given are for villages, towns and cities – not for individual houses

North Leigh

SP3812

Elbie House, *East End, North Leigh, Witney, Oxon, OX8 6PZ.* Beautifully restored C16th home. High priority to cleanliness & quality. **Open:** All year **Grades:** ETC 4 Diamond, Silver
01993 880166 Mrs Buck *mandy@cotswoldbreak.co.uk* www.cotswoldbreak.co.uk
D: Fr £25.00–£27.50 **S:** Fr £35.00–£38.00
Beds: 3F **Baths:** 3 En (7) (10)

North Leigh Guest House, *28 Common Road, North Leigh, Witney, Oxon, OX8 6RA.* Clean friendly family home, guest own suite. Evening meal available.
Open: All year
01993 881622 Mrs Perry **D:** Fr £22.50 **S:** Fr £22.50 **Beds:** 1F 1T **Baths:** 2 En (5)

North Moreton

SU5689

Stapleton's Chantry, *Long Wittenham Road, North Moreton, Didcot, Oxfordshire, OX11 9AX.* **Open:** All year (not Xmas/New Year)
01235 818900 & 07876 654388 (M) Fax: 01235 818555 *stapletonchantry@aol.com* www.smoothhound.co.uk/hotels/stapletonschantry.html **D:** Fr £25.00–£37.50 **S:** Fr £30.00–£50.00 **Beds:** 1T 4D **Baths:** 2 En 1 Pr 2 Sh (6)
Welcoming friendly B&B in lovely C16th family home, beautiful gardens surrounded by excellent walking country. Seriously comfortable rooms with flowers from garden, luxury ensuite self contained B&B cottage in garden. Delicious local produce breakfasts, genuinely kind helpful family. Convenient Oxford, London, Henley, Cotswolds, Chilterns, M4, M40, Heathrow.

RATES
D = Price range per person sharing in a double or twin room
S = Price range for a single room

North Newington

SP4239

Broughton Grounds Farm, *North Newington, Banbury, Oxon, OX15 6AW.*
Open: All year (not Xmas)
01295 730315 Margaret Taylor
broughtongrounds@hotmail.com
www.broughtongrounds.co.uk **D:** Fr £20.00–£25.00 **S:** Fr £20.00–£25.00 **Beds:** 1D 1T 1S
Baths: 1 Sh (2) (3)
Enjoy warm hospitality and peaceful surroundings at our C17th stone farmhouse. A working family farm situated on the Broughton Castle estate with beautiful views and walks. Very comfortable spacious accommodation, log fire, delicious breakfast with home produce. M40 6m.

North Stoke

SU6186

Footpath Cottage, *The Street, North Stoke, Wallingford, Oxon, OX10 6BJ.* Lovely old cottage, peaceful river village. Warm welcome, excellent food. **Open:** All year
01491 839763 Mrs Tanner **D:** Fr £20.00–£25.00 **S:** Fr £20.00 **Beds:** 1D 1S **Baths:** 1 Sh 1 En

Nuneham Courtenay

SU5598

The Old Bakery, *Nuneham Courtenay, Oxford, OX44 9NX.* C18th country cottage, ideally situated for Oxford centre. Healthy, hearty breakfasts.
Open: All year
01865 343585 Fax: 01865 341336 *addisonjill@hotmail.com* **D:** Fr £32.50–£45.00 **S:** Fr £45.00–£55.00 **Beds:** 1F 1T 1D **Baths:** 3 En (10) cc

Oxford

SP5106

Green Gables, *326 Abingdon Road, Oxford, OX1 4TE.* **Open:** All year (not Xmas/New Year)
01865 725870 Mr & Mrs Bhella **Fax: 01865 723115** *green.gables@virgin.net* www.greengables.uk.com **D:** Fr £29.00–£35.00 **S:** Fr £45.00–£55.00 **Beds:** 4F 5D 1T 1S **Baths:** 11 En (9) cc
Characterful detached Edwardian house set back from the road. Bright spacious rooms with TV and beverage facilities. Ensuite rooms. 1.25 miles to city centre, on bus routes. Ample off-street parking. Direct line phones in rooms and disabled room available.

Sportsview Guest House, *106-110 Abingdon Road, Oxford, OX1 4PX.* **Open:** All year (not Xmas) **Grades:** ETC 3 Diamond
01865 244268 Mrs Saini **Fax: 01865 249270** *stay@sportsview-guest-house.freeserve.co.uk* www.smoothhound.co.uk/hotelssportsvi.html **D:** Fr £27.00–£33.00 **S:** Fr £30.00–£50.00 **Beds:** 5F 6T 3D 6S **Baths:** 12 En 12 Pr 2 Sh (4) (11) cc
Friendly family-run Victorian house, overlooking Queens sports ground and boat house. Situated in South, half mile from city centre. Few mins' walk towpath for very pleasant walk to city. Few hundred yards from open-air swimming pool.

Eurobar Hotel, *48 George Street, Oxford, OX1 2AQ.* **Open:** All year (not Xmas/New Year)
01865 725087 Fax: 01865 243367 *eurobarox@aol.com* www.oxfordcity.co.uk/accom/eurobar **D:** Fr £29.50–£40.00 **S:** Fr £45.00–£65.00 **Beds:** 2F 2T 5D 4S **Baths:** 7 En 1 Pr 2 Sh cc
City centre location. Minutes' walk to university colleges, theatres, shops, restaurants, museums, bus & train stations, etc. Ideal for business & tourist travellers.

The Bungalow, *Cherwell Farm, Mill Lane, Old Marston, Oxford, OX3 0QF.* Delightful small, family-run modern bungalow in 5 acres open countryside, no bus route. 3 miles to city centre. Excellent location. Non-smoking. **Open:** Mar to Oct **Grades:** ETC 3 Diamond
01865 557171 Mrs Burdon *sheilamundy1@btopenworld.com* **D:** Fr £25.00–£28.00 **S:** Fr £25.00–£35.00 **Beds:** 2D 2T **Baths:** 2 En 1 Sh (7) (6)

Arden Lodge, *34 Sunderland Avenue, Oxford, OX2 8DX.* Perfectly situated for Oxford city centre, touring Cotswolds, Stratford, London. **Open:** All year (not Xmas/New Year)
01865 552076 Mr Price **D:** Fr £23.00–£25.00 **S:** Fr £28.00–£35.00 **Beds:** 1F 1D 1S **Baths:** 1 En 2 Pr (5) (4)

Highfield West, *188 Cumnor Hill, Oxford, OX2 9PJ.* Comfortable home in residential area, heated outdoor pool in season. **Open:** All year (not Xmas/New Year)
01865 863007 Mr & Mrs Mitchell *highfieldwest@email.msn.com* www.oxfordcity.co.uk/accom/highfieldwest **D:** Fr £26.00–£29.00 **S:** Fr £29.00–£33.00 **Beds:** 1F 1D 1T 2S **Baths:** 3 En 1 Sh (5)

Bronte Guest House, *282 Iffley Road, Oxford, OX4 4AA.* One mile from the city centre, friendly guest house. **Open:** All year
01865 244594 **D:** Fr £22.00–£30.00 **S:** Fr £22.00–£30.00 **Beds:** 2F 2T 2D 1S **Baths:** 5 En 1 Pr 1 Sh (5)

All Seasons Guest House, *63 Windmill Road, Headington, Oxford, Oxfordshire, OX3 7BP.* Comfortable guest house, non-smoking, parking, convenient airports and Brookes University. **Open:** All year
Grades: AA 3 Diamond
01865 742215 Mr & Mrs Melbye **Fax: 01865 432691** *admin@allseasonsguesthouse.com* www.allseasonsguesthouse.com **D:** Fr £25.00–£34.00 **S:** Fr £30.00–£50.00 **Beds:** 1T 3D 2S **Baths:** 4 En 1 Sh (6) (6) cc

58 St John Street, *Oxford, OX1 2QR.* Tall Victorian house central to all colleges, museums and theatres. **Open:** All year
01865 515454 Mrs Old **D:** Fr £20.00 **S:** Fr £18.00–£20.00 **Beds:** 1F 1T 1S **Baths:** 2 En (1)

Homelea Guest House, *356 Abingdon Road, Oxford, OX1 4TE.* A family-run guest house, 1m from Oxford city centre.
Open: All year **Grades:** ETC 4 Diamond
01865 245150 *homelea@talk21.com* www.guesthouseoxford.com **D:** Fr £32.00–£35.00 **S:** Fr £50.00–£70.00 **Beds:** 3T 3D
Baths: 6 En 1 Pr (3) (7) cc

Pine Castle Hotel, *290 Iffley Road, Oxford, OX4 4AE.* Close to shops, launderette, post office. Frequent buses. River walks nearby. **Open:** All year (not Xmas)
01865 241497 & 01865 728887 Mrs Trkulja **Fax: 01685 727230** *stay@pinecastle.co.uk* **D:** Fr £32.50–£37.00 **S:** Fr £55.00–£60.00 **Beds:** 1F 5D 2T **Baths:** 8 En (4)

Gables Guest House, *6 Cumnor Hill, Oxford, Oxfordshire, OX2 9HA.* Award winning detached house with beautiful garden. Close to city. **Open:** All year (not Xmas)
01865 862153 Mrs Tompkins **Fax: 01865 864054** *stay@gables-oxford.co.uk* www.oxfordcity.co.uk/accom/gables **D:** Fr £22.00 **S:** Fr £26.00 **Beds:** 2S 2D 2T **Baths:** 6 En (6)

Acorn Guest House, *260 Iffley Road, Oxford, Oxfordshire, OX4 1SE.* Modern comfort in Victorian house convenient for all local attractions. **Open:** All year (not Xmas/New Year)
01865 247998 Mrs Lewis **D:** Fr £24.00–£26.00 **S:** Fr £29.00 **Beds:** 2F 4D 2T 4S **Baths:** 1 En 4 Sh (9) (11) cc

Peppard

SU7081

Pennyford House, *Peppard, Henley-on-Thames, Oxon, RG9 5JE.* Family home with dogs. Happy atmosphere. Nice garden. Local interests. **Open:** All year
01491 628272 Mrs Howden-Ferme **Fax: 01491 628779** **D:** Fr £25.00–£35.00 **S:** Fr £30.00–£35.00 **Beds:** 1T 3D 1S **Baths:** 4 En 1 Pr (10)

Slaters Farm, *Peppard, Henley-on-Thames, Oxon, RG9 5JL.* Quiet, friendly country house with lovely garden and tennis court. **Open:** All year (not Xmas)
Grades: ETC 3 Diamond
01491 628675 (also fax) Mrs Howden **D:** Fr £25.00 **S:** Fr £30.00 **Beds:** 1D 2T **Baths:** 1 Pr 1 Sh (6)

Pishill

SU7289

Bank Farm, *Pishill, Henley-on-Thames, Oxon, RG9 6HS.* Quiet comfortable farmhouse, beautiful countryside. Convenient Oxford, London, Windsor. **Open:** All year (not Xmas) **Grades:** ETC 2 Diamond
01491 638601 Mrs Lakey *bankfarm@btinternet.com* **D:** Fr £25.00 **S:** Fr £21.00–£25.00 **Beds:** 1F 1D **Baths:** 1 En 1 Sh (5)

Radley

SU5298

Hollies, *8 New Road, Radley, Abingdon, Oxon, OX14 3AP.* Rural small and friendly family B&B, convenient for all attractions.
Open: All year
01235 529552 *brianholl@tinyworld.co.uk* **D:** Fr £25.00 **S:** Fr £25.00 **Beds:** 2T **Baths:** 1 Sh

Ramsden

SP3515

Ann's Cottage, *Ramsden, Chipping Norton, Oxon, OX7 3AZ.* Charming period cottage in pretty Cotswold village. Excellent pub/restaurant nearby. **Open:** All year (not Xmas/New Year) **Grades:** ETC 3 Diamond
01993 868592 Mrs Foxwood *foxwoodfamily@lineone.net* **D:** Fr £20.00 **S:** Fr £20.00–£25.00
Beds: 1T 1S **Baths:** 1 Sh (10) (2)

Please respect a B&B's wishes regarding children, animals and smoking

Salford

SP2828

1 Lower Barns, *Salford, Chipping Norton, Oxon, OX7 5YP.* Traditionally furnished, well situated for Cotswolds, Oxford, Stratford. Homely welcome. **Open:** All year (not Xmas/New Year)
01608 643276 Mrs Barnard **D:** Fr £18.00 **S:** Fr £18.00 **Beds:** 1T **Baths:** 1 En (2)

Shenington

SP3742

Top Farm House, *Shenington, Banbury, Oxfordshire, OX15 6LZ.* C17th Hornton stone farmhouse set on the edge of village green. **Open:** All year (not Xmas/New Year) **Grades:** ETC 3 Diamond
01295 670226 **Fax: 01295 678170** *info@topfarmhouse.co.uk* www.topfarmhouse.co.uk
D: Fr £20.00–£25.00 **S:** Fr £25.00–£30.00
Beds: 1T 2D **Baths:** 1 En 1 Sh (4)

Shipton-under-Wychwood

SP2717

Garden Cottage, *Fiddlers Hill, Shipton-under-Wychwood, Chipping Norton, Oxon, OX7 6DR.* Attractive stone cottage, country views, quiet, ideal for exploring Cotswolds.
Open: All year (not Xmas)
01993 830640 C Worker **D:** Fr £15.00–£25.00
S: Fr £25.00–£35.00 **Beds:** 1D 1T **Baths:** 2 En (8) (2)

Souldern

SP5231 *Fox Inn*

Towerfields, *Tusmore Road, Souldern, Bicester, Oxon, OX6 9HY.* Comfortable ensuite rooms, easy access to Oxford and Stratford. Beautiful views. **Open:** All year
01869 346554 C Hamilton Gould **Fax: 01869 345157** *hgould@souldern.powernet.co.uk* **D:** Fr £26.00–£28.00 **S:** Fr £30.00–£32.00 **Beds:** 1F 1T 1D 1S **Baths:** 4 En (10) (20)

The Fox Inn, *Souldern, Bicester, Oxon, OX6 9JN.* Stone inn, beautiful village convenient for Oxford, Woodstock, Stratford and Warwick. Bar/restaurant.
Open: All year (not Xmas)
01869 345284 Mr MacKay **Fax: 01869 345667**
D: Fr £22.50–£27.50 **S:** Fr £32.00–£38.00
Beds: 3D 1T **Baths:** 2 En 1 Sh (6) cc

Planning a longer stay? Always ask for any special rates

Southcoombe

SP3327 *Blue Boar*

Southcoombe Lodge Guest House, *Southcoombe, Chipping Norton, Oxon, OX7 5QH.* Southcombe Lodge - next door to Chipping Norton golf club **Open:** All year **01608 643068** Mrs Findlay **D:** Fr £23.00–£26.00 **S:** Fr £26.00–£35.00 **Beds:** 1F 2T 3D **Baths:** 4 En 2 Sh (10)

Sparsholt

SU3487 *The Star Inn*

Westcot Lodge, *Westcot, Sparsholt, Wantage, Oxon, OX12 9QA.* Comfortable country house. Peaceful hamlet. Magnificent views to Ridgeway, one mile. **Open:** All year (not Xmas/New Year) **01235 751251** Mrs Upton **D:** Fr £30.00 **S:** Fr £30.00 **Beds:** 1T 1D 1S **Baths:** 1 Pr 1 Sh (2)

Steventon

SU4691

Tethers End, *Abingdon Road, Steventon, Abingdon, Oxon, OX13 6RW.* **Open:** All year **Grades:** ETC 3 Diamond **01235 834015** Mrs Miller **Fax: 01235 862990** *peterdmiller@btinternet.com* www.millerbandb.co.uk **D:** Fr £23.00–£25.00 **S:** Fr £30.00–£32.00 **Beds:** 1F 1D **Baths:** 2 En

Comfortable ground floor accommodation, situated on the edge of a peaceful village green. Ideally placed for visiting Oxford, Abingdon, Wantage, historic Ridgeway, Blenheim Palace and Didcot Railway Centre. Caroline and Peter Miller offer you a warm welcome.

Stratton Audley

SP6026

West Farm, *Stratton Audley, Bicester, Oxfordshire, OX6 9BW.* C17th farmhouse offering a high standard of accommodation situated in an attractive peaceful village. **Open:** All year **01869 278344 (also fax)** Ms Howson *richardsarahowson@hotmail.com* www.westfarmbb.co.uk **D:** Fr £30.00 **S:** Fr £30.00–£35.00 **Beds:** 2T **Baths:** 2 Pr (7)

The Old School, *Stratton Audley, Bicester, Oxfordshire, OX27 9BJ.* Interesting C17th house in pretty village. Pleasant garden with lovely view. **Open:** All year **01869 277371** Mrs Wertheimer *sawertheimer@euphony.net* www.old-school.co.uk **D:** Fr £30.00–£35.00 **S:** Fr £30.00–£35.00 **Beds:** 3T 1S **Baths:** 2 Sh (6)

Sutton Courtenay

SU5093

Bekynton House, *7 The Green, Sutton Courtenay, Abingdon, Oxon, OX14 4AE.* Courthouse overlooking village green, Thames and 3 pubs - 5 minutes. **Open:** All year (not Xmas) **01235 848630 & 01235 848888** Ms Cornwall **Fax: 01235 848436** *suecornwall@aol.com* **D:** Fr £30.00 **S:** Fr £30.00 **Beds:** 1D 2T 1S **Baths:** 2 Sh

Tetsworth

SP6802

Little Acre, *4 High Street, Tetsworth, Thame, Oxon, OX9 7AT.* Warm welcome- every comfort. Near Chilterns, Oxford, Cotswolds, Heathrow Airport. **Open:** All year **Grades:** ETC 4 Diamond **01844 281423 (also fax)** Ms Tanner **D:** Fr £18.00–£22.50 **S:** Fr £25.00–£35.00 **Beds:** 1F 2D 2T **Baths:** 3 En 2 Sh (5)

Thame

SP7005

Vine Cottage, *Moreton, Thame, Oxon, OX9 2HX.* Novelist's enchanting thatched cottage in tranquil hamlet. Perfect touring base. **Open:** All year (not Xmas/New Year) **01844 216910** Ms Blumenthal **D:** Fr £23.00–£26.00 **S:** Fr £26.00 **Beds:** 1D 1S **Baths:** 1 Sh (10) (4)

Oakfield, *Thame Park Road, Thame, Oxon, OX9 3PL.* Lovely farmhouse home, 25 acres grounds - part of larger 400-acre mixed farm. **Open:** All year (not Xmas) **01844 213709 & 07785 764447 (M)** **D:** Fr £20.00–£25.00 **S:** Fr £27.50 **Beds:** 1D 2T **Baths:** 1 En 1 Sh (8) (6)

Tiddington

SP6504

Albury Farm, *Draycott, Tiddington, Thame, Oxon, OX9 2LX.* Peaceful open views in quiet location, clean, tidy, friendly. **Open:** All year **01844 339740 (also fax)** Mrs Ilbery **D:** Fr £20.00 **S:** Fr £20.00 **Beds:** 1D 1T **Baths:** 1 Pr 1 Sh (4)

Uffington

SU3089

Norton House, *Broad Street, Uffington, Faringdon, Oxon, SN7 7RA.* Friendly C18th family home in centre of quiet, pretty village. **Open:** All year (not Xmas) **01367 820230 (also fax)** Mrs Oberman *carloberman@aol.com* **D:** Fr £20.00–£21.00 **S:** Fr £23.00–£26.00 **Beds:** 1F 1D 1S **Baths:** 2 Pr (3)

Wallingford

SU6089

Little Gables, *166 Crowmarsh Hill, Wallingford, Oxford, OX10 8BG.* Delightfully large private house where a warm welcome awaits you. **Open:** All year **Grades:** ETC 3 Diamond **01491 837834** Mrs Reeves **Fax: 01491 834426** *jill@stayingaway.com* www.stayingaway.com **D:** Fr £25.00–£35.00 **S:** Fr £35.00–£45.00 **Beds:** 2F 2D 3T 1S **Baths:** 2 En 1 Pr

52 Blackstone Road, *Wallingford, Oxon, OX10 8JL.* Small friendly house, half mile from R Thames. 10-min walk from town. **Open:** All year (not Xmas/New Year) **01491 201917** Mrs Barnard *enid.barnard@ebarnard.fsnet.co.uk* **D:** Fr £20.00–£35.00 **S:** Fr £17.50 **Beds:** 1D 1S (1)

North Farm, *Shillingford Hill, Wallingford, Oxon, OX10 8NB.* Generous farmhouse breakfast after a peaceful night. Explore Oxfordshire countryside. **Open:** All year (not Xmas/New Year) **01865 858406** Mrs Warburton **Fax: 01865 858519** *northfarm@compuserve.com* www.country-accom.co.uk/north-farm **D:** Fr £25.00–£30.00 **S:** Fr £30.00–£45.00 **Beds:** 1T 2D **Baths:** 1 En 2 Pr (10) (6)

Wantage

SU4087

The Bell Inn, *38 Market Place, Wantage, Oxon, OX12 8AH.* C16th market town inn serving good food in a warm and friendly atmosphere. **Open:** All year **01235 763718 (also fax)** Mrs Williams **D:** Fr £25.00–£35.00 **S:** Fr £45.00–£55.00 **Beds:** 7F 2T 2D 5S **Baths:** 10 En

Waterperry

SP6205

Holbeach, *Worminghall Road, Waterperry, Oxford, OX33 1LF.* Private country home, good food, comfortable beds and friendly service. **Open:** All year (not Xmas) **01844 339623** **D:** Fr £20.00 **S:** Fr £20.00–£25.00 **Beds:** 1F 2D 1S **Baths:** 1 En 1 Pr 1 Sh (6)

Watlington

SU6894

Woodgate Orchard Cottage, *Howe Road, Watlington, Oxon, OX9 5EL.* Warm welcome, countryside location, comfortable rooms, home-cooking, restful gardens, red kites gliding above. **Open:** All year
01491 612675 (also fax) R Roberts *mailbox@wochr.freeserve.co.uk* **D:** Fr £25.00–£35.00 **S:** Fr £30.00 **Beds:** 1F 1T 1D **Baths:** 1 En 1 Pr (8)

Witney

SP3509

The Witney Hotel, *7 Church Green, Witney, Oxon, OX8 6AZ.* Family-run B&B, Listed building overlooking historic Church Green, few mins' walk local amenities. **Open:** All year (not Xmas/New Year) **Grades:** ETC 3 Diamond
01993 702137 Mrs McDermott **Fax: 01993 705337** *reservations@thewitneyhotel.co.uk* **D:** Fr £54.00 **S:** Fr £37.00 **Beds:** 2F 5D 2T 1S **Baths:** 10 En **cc**

Springhill Farm, *Cogges, Witney, Oxon, OX29 6UL.* Lovely views, warm welcome, comfortable rooms in our old farmhouse. **Open:** All year (not Xmas/New Year) **Grades:** ETC 3 Diamond
01993 704919 & 07808 229569 (M) Mrs Strainge **D:** Fr £22.50–£25.00 **S:** Fr £22.50–£28.00 **Beds:** 1F 1D 1T **Baths:** 3 En (4) **1**

Ann's Cottage, *Ramsden, Chipping Norton, Oxon, OX7 3AZ.* Charming period cottage in pretty Cotswold village. Excellent pub/restaurant nearby. **Open:** All year (not Xmas/New Year) **Grades:** ETC 3 Diamond
01993 868592 Mrs Foxwood *foxwoodfamily@lineone.net* **D:** Fr £20.00 **S:** Fr £20.00–£25.00 **Beds:** 1T 1S **Baths:** 1 Sh (10) (2)

Quarrydene, *Dene Rise, Witney, Oxon, OX8 5LU.* Friendly B&B, quiet location, only a few minutes walk from town centre. **Open:** All year (not Xmas/New Year)
01993 772152 & 07850 054786 (M) Mrs Marshall **Fax: 01993 772152** *jeanniemarshall@quarrydene.fsworld.co.uk* www.fsworld.co.uk **D:** Fr £25.00 **S:** Fr £25.00–£30.00 **Beds:** 1T 1D 2S **Baths:** 1 En 2 Sh (2)

Woodcote

SU6481

The Hedges, *South Stoke Road, Woodcote, Reading, Berks, RG8 0PL.* Peaceful, rural situation, historic Area of Outstanding Natural Beauty. **Open:** All year (not Xmas) **Grades:** ETC 3 Diamond
01491 680461 Mrs Howard-Allen *Howard-Allen@hedgeswoodcote.freeserve.co.uk* **D:** Fr £18.00–£20.00 **S:** Fr £18.00–£20.00 **Beds:** 2T 2S **Baths:** 1 Pr 1 Sh (4)

Woodstock

SP4416

The Lawns, *2 Flemings Road, Woodstock, Oxon, OX20 1NA.* **Open:** All year **Grades:** ETC 2 Diamond
01993 812599 (also fax) Mr & Mrs Farrant *thelawns@amserve.net* www.thelawns.co.uk **D:** Fr £19.00–£20.00 **S:** Fr £25.00–£30.00 **Beds:** 1F 1T 1D 1S **Baths:** 1 Pr 1 Sh **cc**
Lovely homely accommodation. Attractive garden surroundings, real old English (eccentric) welcome. Just see the garden items (unusual). 5 mins' walk to town centre and Blenheim Palace Gates - probably among the best (value for money) B&B accommodation in England. Free taxi-cab collection service.

Plane Tree House B&B, *48 Oxford Street, Woodstock, Oxon, OX20 1TT.* **Open:** All year (not Xmas) **Grades:** ETC 4 Diamond, Silver
01993 813075 Mrs Clark **D:** Fr £25.00–£37.50 **S:** Fr £45.00–£70.00 **Beds:** 2D 1T **Baths:** 2 En 1 Pr
A recently renovated Listed Cotswold stone house with exposed beams and open fires in Woodstock's historic town centre. Only minutes' walk from Blenheim Palace and excellent shops and restaurants. An ideal base for touring Oxford and the Cotswolds.

Planning a longer stay? Always ask for any special rates

BEDROOMS
D = Double
T = Twin
S = Single
F = Family

Elbie House, *East End, North Leigh, Witney, Oxon, OX8 6PZ.* **Open:** All year **Grades:** ETC 4 Diamond, Silver **01993 880166**
Mrs Buck *mandy@cotswoldbreak.co.uk* www.cotswoldbreak.co.uk **D:** Fr £25.00–£27.50 **S:** Fr £35.00–£38.00 **Beds:** 3F **Baths:** 3 En (7) (10)
Beautifully restored C16th home. High priority to cleanliness & quality. Large ensuite rooms. Banquet breakfast using fresh produce, home-made jams & bread. Many super walks including Roman Villa. Close to Blenheim Palace, all Cotswolds towns/villages & Oxford.

Hamilton House, *43 Hill Rise, Old Woodstock, Woodstock, Oxon, OX20 1AB.* **Open:** All year
01993 812206 & 07778 705568 Mrs Bradford **Fax: 01993 812206** www.smoothhound.co.uk/hotels/hamiltonh.html **D:** Fr £22.00–£25.00 **S:** Fr £30.00–£40.00 **Beds:** 1T 2D **Baths:** 3 En **cc**
Very widely acclaimed B&B. Offering unbeatable standards of cleanliness, service and hospitality. Almost every amenity available. Excellent location for beginning and ending your tour. Constantly revisited due unquestionably to the helpfulness and friendliness of Kay - your hostess.

Gorselands Hall, *Boddington Lane, North Leigh, Witney, Oxon, OX29 6PU.* Lovely old country house. Convenient for Blenheim Palace, Oxford, Cotswolds. **Open:** All year **Grades:** ETC 4 Diamond
01993 882292 Mr & Mrs Hamilton **Fax: 01993 883629** *hamilton@gorselandshall.com* www.gorselandshall.com **D:** Fr £22.50–£25.00 **S:** Fr £35.00 **Beds:** 4D 1T 1F **Baths:** 6 En (6) **cc**

The Townhouse, *16 High Street, Woodstock, Oxon, OX20 1TE.* Listed building, centrally located. Ideal for Blenheim Palace, Oxford, Cotswolds. **Open:** All year
01993 810843 (also fax) Ms Edsor *info@woodstock-townhouse.com* www.woodstock-townhouse.com **D:** Fr £32.50–£37.50 **S:** Fr £45.00–£50.00 **Beds:** 1F 1T 3D **Baths:** 5 En **cc**

Woolstone

SU2988

Hickory House, *Woolstone, Faringdon, Oxon, SN7 7QL.* **Open:** All year (not Xmas) **01367 820303** Mrs Grist **Fax: 01367 820958** *rlg@hickoryhouse.freeserve.co.uk* **D:** Fr £19.00–£25.00 **S:** Fr £21.00–£25.00 **Beds:** 2T **Baths:** 2 En (2)
Situated in a delightful village beneath the White Horse Hill near the Ridgeway, Hickory House offers comfortable, spacious accommodation in a recently built self-contained extension. Pub serving food is a minute's walk. Oxford, Bath and the Cotswolds are within easy driving distance.

Wootton (Woodstock)

SP4319 *Killingworth Castle*

8 Manor Court, *Wootton, Woodstock, Oxon, OX20 1EU.* Ideal centre for exploring Cotswolds and Oxford. Friendly village home. **Open:** All year (not Xmas/New Year) **01993 811186** Mrs Fletcher **D:** Fr £20.00 **S:** Fr £20.00 **Beds:** 1T 1S (12) (2)

Yarnton

SP4712

Kings Bridge Guest House, *Woodstock Road, Yarnton, Kidlington, Oxon, OX5 1PH.* Ideally situated for Oxford and Blenheim Palace in Woodstock. **Open:** All year (not Xmas/New Year) **01865 841748** Ms Shaw **Fax: 01865 370215** *kings.bridge@talk21.com* **D:** Fr £22.50–£30.00 **S:** Fr £35.00–£50.00 **Beds:** 1F 2D 1T **Baths:** 4 En (6) **cc**

Rutland

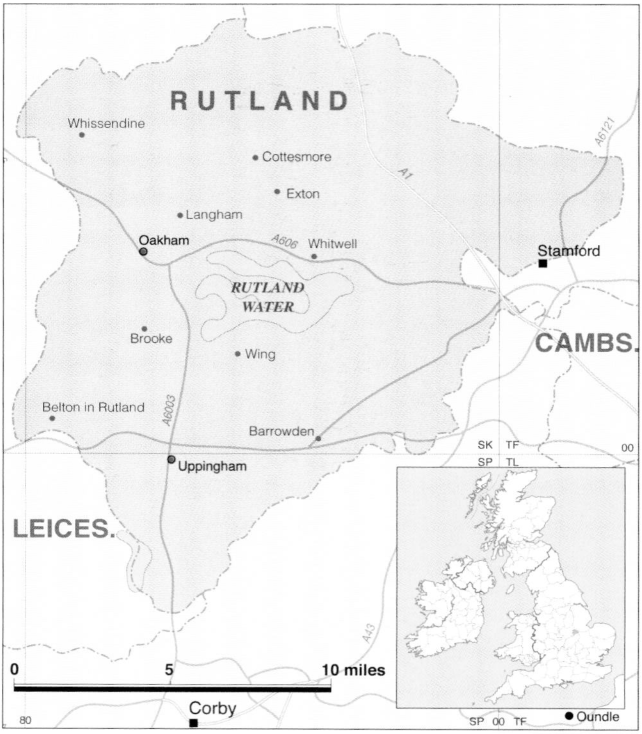

Barrowden

SK9500

Exeter Arms, *Barrowden, Oakham, Rutland, LE15 8EQ.* C17th village inn with C21st accommodation, overlooking Welland Valley. **Open:** All year (not Xmas/ New Year)
01572 747247 Mr & Mrs Blencowe **Fax: info@exeterarms.co.uk** www.exeterarms.co.uk **D:** Fr £25.00–£35.00 **S:** Fr £30.00–£35.00 **Beds:** 2T 1D **Baths:** 3 En cc

Ashleigh House, *2 Wakerley Road, Barrowden, Oakham, Rutland, LE15 8EP.* Stunning views of Welland Valley, Rockingham Forest. Barrowden is a beautiful Rutland village. **Open:** All year (not Xmas/New Year)
01572 747398 Mrs Kennedy **Fax: 01572 747117** *ashleighhouse@cwcom.net* **D:** Fr £18.50–£25.00 **S:** Fr £20.00–£35.00 **Beds:** 1T 2D **Baths:** 1 En 1 Pr 1 Sh (4)

31 Wakerley Road, *Barrowden, Oakham, Rutland, LE15 8EP.* Rutland Water, Welland Valley. Bungalow, garden, attractive conservation village. **Open:** All year (not Xmas/New Year)
01572 747455 Mr & Mrs Hennessy **D:** Fr £18.00–£20.00 **S:** Fr £18.00–£28.00 **Beds:** 1F 1T 1D 1S **Baths:** 1 En 1 Sh (8)

RATES
D = Price range per person sharing in a double or twin room
S = Price range for a single room

Belton in Rutland

SK8101

The Old Rectory, *4 New Road, Belton in Rutland, Oakham, Rutland, LE15 9LE.* **Open:** All year
01572 717279 Mr Peach *bb@iepuk.com* www.rutnet.co.uk/orb **D:** Fr £20.00–£28.00 **S:** Fr £25.00–£35.00 **Beds:** 1F 2D 3T 1S **Baths:** 4 En 1 Sh (10) cc
Large country house and guest annexe in conservation village overlooking Eyebrook valley and rolling Rutland countryside. Comfortable/ varied selection of rooms, mostly ensuite, direct outside access. Real farmhouse or continental breakfast. Public house 100 yds. 10 minutes Rutland Water.

Brooke

SK8505

The Old Rectory, *Brooke, Oakham, Rutland, LE15 8DE.* Stone thatched cottage in quiet hamlet. Large garden, good walking area. **Open:** All year
01572 770558 (also fax) Mrs Clemence **D:** Fr £20.00–£25.00 **S:** Fr £20.00–£25.00 **Beds:** 1F 1T 1S **Baths:** 3 En (6)

Cottesmore

SK9013

The Tithe Barn, *Clatterpot Lane, Cottesmore, Oakham, Rutland, LE15 7DW.* Comfortable, spacious, ensuite rooms with a wealth of original features. **Open:** All year
01572 813591 **D:** Fr £18.00–£24.00 **S:** Fr £20.00–£35.00 **Beds:** 2F 1D 1T **Baths:** 3 En 1 Pr (1) (6) cc

Exton

SK9211

Fox & Hounds, *Exton, Oakham, Rutland, LE15 8AP.* Country inn overlooking village green. 2 miles Rutland Water, half mile Bransdale Gardens. **Open:** All year (not Xmas/New Year)
01572 812403 D Hillier **D:** Fr £20.00–£22.00 **S:** Fr £22.00–£24.00 **Beds:** 1D 1T 1S (20)

Hall Farm, *Cottesmore Road, Exton, Oakham, Rutland, LE15 8AN.* Close to Rutland Water and Geoff Hamilton's Barnsdale TV gardens. **Open:** All year (not Xmas)
01572 812271 Mr & Mrs Williamson **D:** Fr £17.50–£22.00 **S:** Fr £20.00–£24.50 **Beds:** 1F 1D 1T **Baths:** 1 En 2 Sh (6)

Langham

SK8410

Keighwood House, *The Range, Langham, Oakham, Rutland, LE15 7EB.* Large, modern, detached house. 0.33 acre nature and gardens, picturesque village. **Open:** All year (not Xmas)
01572 755924 Mr McMorran **D:** Fr £25.00 **S:** Fr £25.00 **Beds:** 1D 1T 2S **Baths:** 1 Sh
(3)

Oakham

SK8508

Westgate Lodge, *9 Westgate, Oakham, Rutland, LE15 6BH.* Town centre, all rooms ensuite and ground floor off-road parking. **Open:** All year (not Xmas/New Year)
01572 757370 (also fax) Mr & Mrs Garwood *westgatelodge@amserve.com* **D:** Fr £22.50–£25.00 **S:** Fr £35.00–£50.00 **Beds:** 1F 1T 1D **Baths:** 3 En

Kirkee House, *35 Welland Way, Oakham, Rutland, LE15 6SL.* In quiet residential area close to town centre. Warm welcome is guaranteed. **Open:** All year (not Xmas/New Year)
01572 757401 Mrs Beech **Fax: 01572 757301** *carolbeech@kirkeehouse.demon.co.uk* **D:** Fr £22.00 **S:** Fr £22.00 **Beds:** 1T 1D 1S **Baths:** 3 En

Angel House, *20 Northgate, Oakham, Rutland, LE15 6QS.* Unique Victorian house. Converted outbuildings. Secluded courtyard. Lounge, patio, fridge/freezer, microwave. **Open:** All year
01572 756153 Mrs Weight **D:** Fr £11.00–£17.00 **S:** Fr £22.00–£34.00 **Beds:** 1D 2T **Baths:** 3 En

Dial House, *18 Uppingham Road, Oakham, Rutland, LE15 6JD.* Traditional English home, within walking distance of attractive and historic town centre. Rutland Water is nearby, offering bird watching, cycling, fishing and woodland walks, short drives take you to beautiful stately homes and gardens. Good local pubs and restaurants. **Open:** All year (not Xmas/New Year)
01572 771685 Mrs Davis *virginia@oakham2000.freeserve.co.uk* **D:** Fr £22.50–£25.00 **S:** Fr £25.00–£35.00 **Beds:** 2T 1D 1S **Baths:** 4 En (4)

Uppingham

SP8699

Beaumont Chase Farm, *Stockerston Road, Uppingham, Oakham, Rutland, LE15 9HJ.* Old farmhouse in beautiful countryside. Good walking, birdwatching and cycling. **Open:** All year (not Xmas/New Year)
01572 823677 & 07980 567237 (M) Mrs Nourish *beaumontchase@farming.co.uk* **D:** Fr £21.00–£24.00 **S:** Fr £25.00–£30.00 **Beds:** 1F 1D **Baths:** 2 En (2) (4)

Boundary Farm B&B, *Glaston Road, Uppingham, Oakham, Rutland, LE15 9PX.* Modern farmhouse in countryside. 5 mins easy walk into Uppingham. **Open:** Easter to Dec
01572 822354 (also fax) Mrs Scott **D:** Fr £21.00 **S:** Fr £22.00 **Beds:** 1T 1D **Baths:** 2 En
(3)

Whitwell

SK9208

The Cottage, *9 Main Road, Whitwell, Oakham, Rutland, LE15 8BW.* Perfect for Rutland Water. Comfortable accommodation, warm welcome, good breakfast. **Open:** All year (not Xmas/New Year)
01780 460793 Mrs Maher **D:** Fr £20.00 **S:** Fr £25.00 **Beds:** 1D 1D/T **Baths:** 2 En (10)
(6)

Wing

SK8903

The Kings Arms Inn, *Top Street, Wing, Oakham, Rutland, LE15 8SE.* Central Rutland, traditional village inn, ensuite accommodation, home-cooked food. **Open:** All year
01572 737634 Mr Hornsey **Fax: 01572 737255** *enquiries@thekingsarms-wing.co.uk* www.thekingsarms-wing.co.uk **D:** Fr £30.00–£35.00 **S:** Fr £40.00–£50.00 **Beds:** 4F 4D **Baths:** 8 En (40) **cc**

Shropshire

Winsford
A51
A41
A533
A50
Congleton
Sandbach
60
A34
CHESHIRE
Crewe
A534
Biddulph
A483
A534
Kidsgrove
Nantwich
Wrexham
A500
A49
A530
A529
STOKE-ON-TRENT
Newcastle-under-Lyme
A525
A525
WREXHAM
Whitchurch
40
A5
A495
A51
A53
A41
A529
STAFFORDSHIRE
Ellesmere
Whixall
Stone
Craignant
Market Drayton
A5
Weston-under-Redcastle
A519
Oswestry
Hordley
A528
Wem
Llanforda
A5013
A41
Trefonen
Maesbury
Burlton
Preston Brockhurst
A442
Llynclys
A5
A49
A53
Sambrook
Pant
Knockin
Ruyton XI Towns
A519
Chetwynd
Rowton (Telford)
20
POWYS
A518
Leaton
High Ercall
Newport
Melverley
A495
Walcot (Shrewsbury)
Longdon upon Tern
A41
A490
Ford
A442
A458
Shrewsbury
Withington
Wellington
Oakengates
A5
Halfway House
Wrockwardine
A5
St George's
Nobold
A458
Welshpool
Telford
Little Wenlock
Shifnal
M54
A458
Minsterley
Leighton
A483
A488
Ironbridge
Pulverbatch
SHROPSHIRE
Coalport
A41
SJ
00
SO
Snailbeach
Frodesley
Harley
A49
A442
Montgomery
All Stretton
Cardington
Nordley
A454
Church Stretton
Bridgnorth
A489
Norbury
Brockton (Much Wenlock)
Rushbury
Bishop's Castle
Acton Scott
A458
Upper Affcot
Abdon
Mainstone
Strefford
Alveley
Stourbridge
A488
Aston on Clun
Stottesdon
Clun
Clunton
Norton
Cleedownton
A442
80
Clungunford
A49
Middleton (Ludlow)
Kidderminster
Llanfair Waterdine
A4117
Cleobury Mortimer
Ludlow
Bewdley
Hope Bagot
Knighton
A4113
Stourport-on-Severn
A488
A456
Woofferton
A449
A442
WORCESTERSHIRE
A443
0
5
10 miles
Droitwich
20
40
60
80

Abdon

SO5786

Earnstrey Hill House, *Abdon, Craven Arms, Shropshire, SY7 9HU.* Comfortable, warm, spacious family house 1200ft up Brown Clee Hill. Wonderful walking. **Open:** All year (not Xmas)
01746 712579 Mrs Scurfield **Fax: 01746 712631 D:** Fr £25.00 **S:** Fr £30.00 **Beds:** 1D 2T **Baths:** 1 En 2 Sh

Acton Scott

SO4589 *Station Inn, Plough Inn*

Acton Scott Farm, *Acton Scott, Church Stretton, Shropshire, SY6 6QN.* Lovely C17th farmhouse in peaceful hamlet. Good walking area. **Open:** Mar to Oct
01694 781260 Mrs Jones **D:** Fr £19.00–£22.00 **S:** Fr £20.00–£40.00 **Beds:** 1F 1T 1D **Baths:** 2 En 1 Pr (6)

All Stretton

SO4595

Inwood Farm, *All Stretton, Church Stretton, Shropshire, SY6 6LA.* Comfortable old manor house on Long Mynd. Ideal walking/riding. **Open:** All year
01694 724781 Mrs Traill *pauline.traill@btopenworld.com* www.inwoodfarm.co.uk **D:** Fr £20.00–£25.00 **S:** Fr £20.00–£25.00 **Beds:** 1F 1T 2D 1S **Baths:** 3 En 1 Sh (8)

Stretton Hall Hotel, *All Stretton, Church Stretton, Shropshire, SY6 6HG.* Outstanding country manor hotel. Warm, comfortable and excellent value. **Open:** All year
01694 723224 Mr & Mrs Parry *enquiries@strettonhall.co.uk* www.strettonhall.co.uk **D:** Fr £30.00–£55.00 **S:** Fr £40.00–£65.00 **Beds:** 1F 1T 9D 1S **Baths:** 12 En (50) **cc**

RATES
D = Price range per person sharing in a double or twin room
S = Price range for a single room

Alveley

SO7684 *Red Lion, Royal Oak*

Arnside, *Kidderminster Road, Alveley, Bridgnorth, Shropshire, WV15 6LL.* Luxurious bungalow in acre of lawned gardens. Beautifully furnished ensuite rooms. Pubs/shops in walking distance. Perfectly situated for visiting historic Bridgnorth, Ironbridge, Shrewsbury and exploring rural delights of Shropshire and Worcestershire. Convenient for Kidderminster, Worcester and Black Country. **Open:** All year (not Xmas)
01746 780007 (also fax) Mr Haynes *arnside@ptah.freeserve.co.uk* www.virtual-shropshire.co.uk/arnside **D:** Fr £20.00–£35.00 **S:** Fr £30.00–£35.00 **Beds:** 1F 1T 1D **Baths:** 3 En (6)

Aston on Clun

SO3881

Millstream Cottage, *Aston on Clun, Craven Arms, Shropshire, SY7 8EP.* Grade II Listed cottage, 6 acres private fields/woodland. Comfortable beds, good breakfast. AONB. **Open:** All year
01588 660699 & 07977 922572 (M) Miss Reeves **D:** Fr £24.00–£26.00 **S:** Fr £24.00–£26.00 **Beds:** 1D 1T **Baths:** 1 Sh (2)

Bishop's Castle

SO3288

Broughton Farm, *Bishop's Castle, Shropshire, SY15 6SZ.* Originally a medieval hall house, now a spacious and comfortable farmhouse. **Open:** Feb to Dec
01588 638393 Mr & Mrs Bason **Fax: 01588 638153 D:** Fr £18.00–£22.00 **S:** Fr £20.00–£25.00 **Beds:** 1T 2D **Baths:** 1 En 1 Sh (6)

Old Brick Guest House, *7 Church Street, Bishop's Castle, Shropshire, SY9 5AA.* C17th house in conservation area. Log fires. Beautiful garden. **Open:** All year (not Xmas/New Year)
01588 638471 P Hutton *oldbrick@beeb.net* www.oldbrick.co.uk **D:** Fr £25.00 **S:** Fr £29.00 **Beds:** 1F 1T 2D **Baths:** 4 En **cc**

Bridgnorth

SO7193

Bearwood Lodge, *10 Kidderminster Road, Bridgnorth, Shropshire, WV15 6BW.* Family guest house. Large private car park. Conservatory gardens. **Open:** All year
01746 762159 Mr Lloyd **D:** Fr £20.00–£23.00 **S:** Fr £30.00–£35.00 **Beds:** 3T 2D 1S **Baths:** 5 En (5) (9)

Wyndene Guest House, *57 Innage Lane, Bridgnorth, Shropshire, WV16 4HS.* Near to Severn Valley Railway, Ironbridge and Much Wenlock. **Open:** All year
01746 764369 & 07977 943074 (M) Mrs Morse *wyndene@bridgnorth2000.freeserve.co.uk* **D:** Fr £20.00–£22.00 **S:** Fr £20.00–£21.00 **Beds:** 1D 1T 2S **Baths:** 1 En 1 Sh (3)

St Leonards Gate, *6 Church Street, Bridgnorth, Shropshire, WV16 4EQ.* Grade II Listed family home, located in picturesque church cul-de-sac. **Open:** All year
01746 766647 Mr & Mrs Buchanan **D:** Fr £36.00–£46.00 **S:** Fr £20.00–£26.00 **Beds:** 1F 1T 1D 1S **Baths:** 1 En

Pen-Y-Ghent, *7 Sabrina Road, Bridgnorth, Shropshire, WV15 6DQ.* Riverside family house within walking distance of Bridgnorth. **Open:** All year (not Xmas/New Year)
01746 762880 Mrs Firman **D:** Fr £19.00 **S:** Fr £25.00 **Beds:** 2D 2S **Baths:** 2 En 1 Pr 1 Sh (8)

Brockton (Much Wenlock)

SO5793

Old Quarry Cottage, *Brockton, Much Wenlock, Shropshire, TF13 6JR.* Lovely stone cottage set in the countryside. Close to Ironbridge, Wenlock Edge and Ludlow. **Open:** All year (not Xmas/New Year)
01746 785596 Mrs Thorpe *nan@brockton.fsbusiness.co.uk* **D:** Fr £20.00–£21.00 **S:** Fr £30.00 **Beds:** 1T 1D **Baths:** 2 En (2)

Burlton

SJ4526

The Grove, *Burlton, Shrewsbury, SY4 5SZ.* Tucked away in Brother Cadfael country 9m north of Shrewsbury. Imposing 'foursquare' sandstone farmhouse. **Open:** All year
01939 270310 Mrs Martin **D:** Fr £17.00–£19.00 **S:** Fr £20.00 **Beds:** 1T 1D **Baths:** 2 En (4)

Cardington

SO5095

Grove Farm, *Cardington, Church Stretton, Shropshire, SY6 7JZ.* Central to many places of interest, good home cooking. Recommended. **Open:** All year
01694 771451 Mrs Pennington **D:** Fr £16.00–£18.00 **S:** Fr £18.00–£20.00 **Beds:** 1F 1T **Baths:** 1 Sh (10)

Please respect a B&B's wishes regarding children, animals and smoking

Chetwynd

SJ7321

Lane End Farm, *Chester Road, Chetwynd, Newport, Shropshire, TF10 8BN.* Friendly farmhouse in wonderful countryside. Large comfortable rooms. Delicious breakfasts. **Open:** All year **Grades:** ETC 4 Diamond, Silver **01952 550337 (also fax)** Mrs Park www.virtual-shropshire.co.uk/lef **D:** Fr £20.00–£25.00 **S:** Fr £25.00–£30.00 **Beds:** 2D 1T **Baths:** 2 En 1 Pr (5)

Church Stretton

SO4593

Malt House Farm, *Lower Wood, Church Stretton, Shropshire, SY6 6LF.* **Open:** All year (not Xmas/New Year) **01694 751379** Mrs Bloor **D:** Fr £18.50–£20.00 **S:** Fr £20.00–£25.00 **Beds:** 1T 2D **Baths:** 3 En (3)
'The Malthouse' is a working farm quietly situated amidst stunning scenery on the lower slopes of the magnificent Long Mynd Hills. A superb walking country, lots of local interest. Good farmhouse food, comfortable rooms, warm welcome. Phone for brochure.

Belvedere Guest House, *Burway Road, Church Stretton, Shropshire, SY6 6DP.* Beautiful rural surroundings, on the edge of 6,000 acres of National Trust hill country. **Open:** All year (not Xmas) **01694 722232 (also fax)** Mr Rogers *belv@bigfoot.com* www.s-h-systems.co.uk/hotels/belveder **D:** Fr £25.00–£27.00 **S:** Fr £25.00–£30.00 **Beds:** 3F 4D 2T 3S **Baths:** 6 En 3 Sh (8) **cc**

Woolston Farm, *Brereton, Church Stretton, Shropshire, SY6 6QD.* Victorian farmhouse, outstanding views and very peaceful location. Large bedrooms. **Open:** Mar to Nov **01694 781201** Mrs Brereton *joanna@breretonhouse.f9.co.uk* **D:** Fr £21.00 **S:** Fr £26.00 **Beds:** 1T 2D **Baths:** 3 En

Old Rectory House, *Burway Road, Church Stretton, Shropshire, SY6 6DW.* Georgian house-lovely garden - great view - convenient town and hills. **Open:** All year **01694 724462** Mr Smith **Fax: 01694 724799** *Smamos@btinternet.com* www.oldrectoryhouse.co.uk **D:** Fr £18.00–£25.00 **S:** Fr £20.00–£25.00 **Beds:** 2D 1T **Baths:** 1 En 1 Sh (4)

Cleedownton

SO5880

Lower House Farm, *Cleedownton, Ludlow, Shropshire, SY8 3EH.* Come and be pampered in perfect peace and quiet in our medieval farmhouse. **Open:** All year **Grades:** ETC 4 Diamond, Gold **01584 823648** Mr Black *gsblack@talk21.com* www.ludlow.org.uk/lowerhousefarm **D:** Fr £28.50–£35.00 **S:** Fr £38.50–£45.00 **Beds:** 2D 1T **Baths:** 3 En (12) (6)

Cleobury Mortimer

SO6775

The Old Cider House, *1 Lion Lane, Cleobury Mortimer, Kidderminster, Worcestershire, DY14 8BT.* **Open:** All year (not Xmas/New Year) **Grades:** ETC 4 Diamond **01299 270304 (also fax)** Mrs Lennox *lennox@old-cider-house.fsnet.co.uk* **D:** Fr £25.00 **S:** Fr £25.00 **Beds:** 2D **Baths:** 2 En (5)
Delightful old cottage with prize winning garden, in the old market town of Cleobury Mortimer. One downstairs bedroom. Good pub food within easy walking distance. Ideal centre for walking, and exploring such places as Bridgnorth, Severn Valley Railway and Ludlow.

Clun

SO3080

The Old Stables And Saddlery, Crown House, *Church Street, Clun, Craven Arms, Shropshire, SY7 8JW.* Superb self-contained Georgian stable conversion in lovely courtyard garden. **Open:** All year (not Xmas) **Grades:** ETC 4 Diamond **01588 640780** Mrs Bailey & Mr R Maund *crownhouseclun@talk21.com* **D:** Fr £20.00–£23.00 **S:** Fr £22.00–£25.00 **Beds:** 1D 1T 1S **Baths:** 1 En 1 Pr 1 Sh (8) (2)

Llanhedric Farm, *Clun, Craven Arms, Shropshire, SY7 8NG.* Tranquil country retreat - rooms overlooking beautiful views of Clun Valley. **Open:** Easter to Nov **01588 640203 (also fax)** M Jones *llanhedric@talk21.com* **D:** Fr £19.00–£22.00 **S:** Fr £20.00–£25.00 **Beds:** 1F 1T 1D **Baths:** 1 En 1 Sh

Clungunford

SO3978 *Engine & Tender, Hundred House*

North Barn, *Abcott Manor, Clungunford, Craven Arms, Shropshire, SY7 0PX.* Peacefully situated in south Shropshire Hills. Ideal for walking, touring. **Open:** All year (not Xmas/New Year) **01588 660596** P Mattison **D:** Fr £19.00–£20.00 **S:** Fr £21.00–£22.00 **Beds:** 1D 1S **Baths:** 1 Sh (5) (4)

Clunton

SO3381 *Sun Inn*

Hurst Mill Farm, *Clunton, Craven Arms, Shropshire, SY7 0JA.* Riverside farm in beautiful Clun Valley. Winner of 'Breakfast Challenge'. **Open:** All year (not Xmas) **01588 640224 (also fax)** Mrs Williams **D:** Fr £23.00 **S:** Fr £25.00 **Beds:** 2T 1D **Baths:** 1 En 1 Sh (2) (6)

Coalport

SJ6902

Thorpe House, *Coalport, Telford, Shropshire, TF8 7HP.* Riverside country house in beautiful Ironbridge Gorge, close to museums. **Open:** All year **Grades:** ETC 3 Diamond **01952 586789 (also fax)** Mr Richards *thorpehouse@tiscali.co.uk* **D:** Fr £18.00–£25.00 **S:** Fr £18.00–£35.00 **Beds:** 1F 2D 1S **Baths:** 2 En 1 Sh (6)

Craignant

SJ2535

The Quarry, *Craignant, Selattyn, Oswestry, Shropshire, SY11 4LT.* Attractive farmhouse. Offa's Dyke path 0.1 miles. **Open:** Easter to Oct **01691 658674** Mrs Tomley **D:** Fr £16.00 **S:** Fr £16.00 **Beds:** 1D 2S 3F **Baths:** 1 Sh

Ellesmere

SJ3934

The Grange, *Grange Road, Ellesmere, Shropshire, SY12 9DE.* Peaceful Georgian country house in 10 acres. Characterful and spacious. **Open:** All year (not Xmas) **01691 623495** Mrs Ward-Allen **Fax: 01691 623227** *rosie@thegrange.uk.com* www.thegrange.uk.com **D:** Fr £29.00–£33.00 **S:** Fr £30.00 **Beds:** 2F 4D 3T 5S **Baths:** 11 En 3 Sh (15)

Hordley Hall, *Hordley, Ellesmere, Shropshire, SY12 9BB.* Georgian house, large garden, very peaceful, rural location, home cooking. **Open:** All year
01691 622772 Mrs Rodenhurst **D:** Fr £20.00–£25.00 **S:** Fr £20.00–£25.00 **Beds:** 2D 1T 1S **Baths:** 2 En 1 Sh (6)

Mereside Farm, *Ellesmere, Shropshire, SY12 0PA.* Happy friendly atmosphere in C18th farmhouse situated between the mere and canal. **Open:** All year (not Xmas)
01691 622404 (also fax) Mrs Stokes *nicky@mereside.free-online.co.uk* www.ellesmere.co.uk/mereside **D:** Fr £20.00 **S:** Fr £20.00–£25.00 **Beds:** 1D 1T **Baths:** 1 En 1 Pr (7)

Ford

SJ4113

Cardeston Park Farm, *Ford, Shrewsbury, Shropshire, SY5 9NH.* Large farm house set in peaceful countryside close to Welsh border. **Open:** All year (not Xmas)
01743 884265 (also fax) Mrs Edwards **D:** Fr £20.00–£40.00 **S:** Fr £20.00–£40.00 **Beds:** 2D 1T **Baths:** 2 En 1 Pr (4)

Frodesley

SJ5101

Meadow-lands, *Lodge Lane, Frodesley, Dorrington, Shrewsbury, Shropshire, SY5 7HD.*
Open: All year **Grades:** ETC 3 Diamond
01694 731350 (also fax) Ron & Jennie Repath *meadowlands@talk21.com* www.meadowlands.co.uk **D:** Fr £20.00–£25.00 **S:** Fr £20.00–£27.50 **Beds:** 2D 1T **Baths:** 2 En 1 Pr (4)
Comfortable modern house set in eight acres of accessible gardens, woodland and paddocks. Quiet location in delightful hamlet with panoramic views of Stretton Hills. Large residents' lounge, silent fridge in guest rooms, brochure available, maps and guides for loan.

Halfway House

SJ3411

Brambleberry, *Halfway House, Shrewsbury, Shropshire, SY5 9DD.* Tastefully furnished house, lovely garden, rooms overlooking beautiful Shropshire countryside. **Open:** All year (not Xmas)
01743 884762 Mrs Astbury **D:** Fr £15.00–£25.00 **S:** Fr £17.00–£25.00 **Beds:** 1D 1T 1S **Baths:** 1 Sh (8) (6)

Harley

SJ5901 *Plume of Feathers*

Rowley Farm, *Harley, Shrewsbury, Shropshire, SY5 6LX.* Clean comfortable Georgian farm house. **Open:** Easter to Oct
01952 727348 Ms Munslow **D:** Fr £18.00–£20.00 **S:** Fr £22.00–£25.00 (2)

High Ercall

SJ5917

The Mill House, *Shrewsbury Road, High Ercall, Telford, Shropshire, TF6 6BE.* Grade II converted watermill on working small holding and family home. **Open:** All year (not Xmas/New Year) **Grades:** ETC 4 Diamond
01952 770394 Mrs Yates *mill-house@talk21.com* www.virtual-shropshire.co.uk/millhouse **D:** Fr £15.00–£20.00 **S:** Fr £25.00–£30.00 **Beds:** 1F 1T 1S **Baths:** 2 En 1 Pr (4)

Hope Bagot

SO5874

Croft Cottage, *Cumberley Lane, Hope Bagot, Ludlow, Shropshire, SY8 3LJ.* Peace and quiet - brook, gardens, badgers, honey, dogs and ducks! **Open:** All year (not Xmas)
01584 890664 Mrs Hatchell **Fax: 0870 1299897** *croft.cottage@virgin.net* www.croftcottage.org.uk **D:** Fr £21.00–£25.00 **S:** Fr £25.00–£27.00 **Beds:** 1D 1T **Baths:** 1 En 1 Pr (4)

Hordley

SJ3830

Hordley Hall, *Hordley, Ellesmere, Shropshire, SY12 9BB.* Georgian house, large garden, very peaceful, rural location, home cooking. **Open:** All year
01691 622772 Mrs Rodenhurst **D:** Fr £20.00–£25.00 **S:** Fr £20.00–£25.00 **Beds:** 2D 1T 1S **Baths:** 2 En 1 Sh (6)

Ironbridge

SJ6703

Golden Ball Inn, *1 Newbridge Road, Ironbridge, Telford, Shropshire, TF8 7BA.* Ironbridge's oldest and finest inn and restaurant. Relaxed atmosphere. **Open:** All year (not Xmas/New Year) **Grades:** ETC 4 Diamond
01952 432179 Fax: 01952 433123 *matrowland@hotmail.com* www.goldenballinn.com **D:** Fr £29.00–£65.00 **S:** Fr £45.00 **Beds:** 1T 2D **Baths:** 3 En (40) **cc**

Post Office House, *6 The Square, Ironbridge, Telford, Shropshire, TF8 7AQ.* **Open:** All year
Grades: ETC 3 Diamond
01952 433201 Mrs Hunter **Fax: 01952 433582** *hunter@pohouse-ironbridge.fsnet.co.uk* www.pohouse-ironbridge.fsnet.co.uk **D:** Fr £24.00–£29.00 **S:** Fr £38.00–£40.00 **Beds:** 1F/T 1D/T 1D **Baths:** 2 En 1 Pr
Comfortable C18th house. Grade II Listed. In the square overlooking Iron Bridge and beautiful wooded Ironbridge Gorge, whilst centrally located for museums. Within easy reach of Bridgnorth, Much Wenlock, Shrewsbury, Weston Park, Cosford Aerospace Museum and Telford International Centre.

The Library House, *11 Severn Bank, Ironbridge, Telford, Shropshire, TF8 7AN.*
Open: All year (not Xmas) **Grades:** ETC 5 Diamond, Gold, AA 5 Diamond
01952 432299 Mr Maddocks **Fax: 01952 433967** *info@libraryhouse.com* www.libraryhouse.com **D:** Fr £30.00 **S:** Fr £50.00 **Beds:** 1F 3D 1T **Baths:** 3 En (10)
Grade II Listed building situated in the World Heritage Site of the Ironbridge Gorge, and 60 metres from the famous Iron Bridge itself. Central for all the museums, Telford Town Centre, Telford Business Park and the Exhibition Centre.

Woodlands Farm Guesthouse, *Beech Road, Ironbridge, Telford, Shropshire, TF8 7PA.* Excellent quality & value. Set in 4 acres of grounds. 2 mins Ironbridge. **Open:** All year (not Xmas/New Year) **Grades:** AA 3 Diamond
01952 432741 Mr & Mrs Allen *woodlandsfarm@ironbridge68.fsnet.co.uk* www.woodlandsfarmguesthouse.co.uk **D:** Fr £22.50–£25.00 **S:** Fr £20.00–£45.00 **Beds:** 1F 1T 1D 1S **Baths:** 3 En 1 Pr (5) (8) **cc**

BATHROOMS
En = Ensuite
Pr = Private
Sh = Shared

Planning a longer stay? Always ask for any special rates

Knockin

SJ3222

Top Farm House, *Knockin, Oswestry, Shropshire, SY10 8HN.* Lovely half timbered C16th house in attractive village. Comfortable and pretty ensuite bedrooms. **Open:** All year
01691 682582 P Morrissey **Fax: 01691 682070** *p.a.m@knockin.freeserve.co.uk* **D:** Fr £22.50–£25.00 **S:** Fr £27.50–£30.00 **Beds:** 1F 1T 1D **Baths:** 3 En (12) (6)

Leaton

SJ4618

The Old Vicarage, *Leaton, Shrewsbury, Shropshire, SY4 3AP.* Set in acres of grounds in beautiful open countryside 4 miles from medieval Shrewsbury. **Open:** All year
01939 290989 (also fax) Ms Mansell Jones *m-j@oldvicleaton.freeserve.co.uk* **D:** Fr £20.00 **S:** Fr £25.00 **Beds:** 1T 1D **Baths:** 2 En (6)

Leighton

SJ6105

Eye Manor, *Leighton, Ironbridge, Shrewsbury, SY5 6SQ.* Manor house listed in Domesday Book, close to Ironbridge. **Open:** All year (not Xmas/New Year)
01952 510066 Mrs Chillcott **Fax: 01952 610066 D:** Fr £20.00–£25.00 **S:** Fr £20.00–£30.00 **Beds:** 1T **Baths:** 1 Pr

Little Wenlock

SJ6406

Wenboro Cottage, *Church Lane, Little Wenlock, Telford, Shrops, TF6 5BB.* Pretty cottage set in peaceful village near Ironbridge and Telford centre. **Open:** All year (not Xmas)
01952 505573 Mrs Carter *rcarter@wenboro.freeserve.co.uk* **D:** Fr £20.00–£22.50 **S:** Fr £25.00 **Beds:** 1D 1T **Baths:** 1 En 1 Pr (2)

Llanfair Waterdine

SO2476

The Mill, *Lloyney, Llanfair Waterdine, Knighton, Powys, LD7 1RG.* Wonderful countryside in the Teme Valley, home cooking. **Open:** All year (not Xmas/New Year)
01547 528049 (also fax) Mr & Mrs Davies www.smoothhound.co.uk/hotels/mill1.html **D:** Fr £20.00 **S:** Fr £20.00 **Beds:** 2D 2T 1S **Baths:** 1 En 2 Pr 2 Sh (6) 2

Llanforda

SJ2528

The Old Mill Inn, *Candy, Llanforda, Oswestry, Shropshire, SY10 9AZ.* On Offa's Dyke path. Excellent, superb food and welcome. **Open:** All year
01691 657058 (also fax) Mrs Atkinson *theoldmill.inn@virgin.net* **D:** Fr £20.00 **S:** Fr £20.00–£35.00 **Beds:** 2T 1D 2S **Baths:** 2 Sh (50) **cc**

Llynclys

SJ2823

Bridge House, *Llynclys, Oswestry, SY10 8AE.* Lovely rooms. Beautiful views. Superb breakfasts. Comfort, quality and value. **Open:** All year (not Xmas/New Year)
01691 830496 (also fax) Mr & Mrs Taylor *jenny@llynclys.freeserve.co.uk* **D:** Fr £18.50–£22.00 **S:** Fr £20.00–£25.00 **Beds:** 1T 1D **Baths:** 2 En (5) (4)

Longdon upon Tern

SJ6215

Red House Farm, *Longdon upon Tern, Wellington, Telford, Shropshire, TF6 6LE.* Late Victorian farmhouse with comfortable well furnished rooms. Excellent breakfasts. **Open:** All year
01952 770245 Mrs Jones *rhf@virtual-shropshire.co.uk* www.virtual-shropshire.co.uk/redhouse-farm **D:** Fr £18.00–£25.00 **S:** Fr £20.00–£25.00 **Beds:** 1F 1T 1D 1S **Baths:** 2 En 1 Sh (4)

Ludlow

SO5174

Henwick House, *Gravel Hill, Ludlow, Shropshire, SY8 1QU.* **Open:** Jan to Dec
01584 873338 Mrs Cecil-Jones **D:** Fr £22.00 **S:** Fr £22.00–£35.00 **Beds:** 1D 2T 1S **Baths:** 2 En (3)
Warm, comfortable Georgian coach house with private parking. Friendly, informal atmosphere, good traditional English breakfast. Ensuite bedrooms, comfortable beds, TV, tea/coffee facilities and much more. Easy walking distances from town centre and local inns.

National Grid References given are for villages, towns and cities – not for individual houses

All details shown are as supplied by B&B owners in Autumn 2002

Lower House Farm, *Cleedownton, Ludlow, Shropshire, SY8 3EH.* **Open:** All year **Grades:** ETC 4 Diamond, Gold
01584 823648 Mr Black *gsblack@talk21.com* www.ludlow.org.uk/lowerhousefarm **D:** Fr £28.50–£35.00 **S:** Fr £38.50–£45.00 **Beds:** 2D 1T **Baths:** 3 En (12) (6)
Come and be pampered in perfect peace and quiet in our medieval farmhouse. Beams, inglenooks and flagstones. Magnificent views, delicious food. Terrific walking country. Recommended by 'Homes and Gardens', praised by the Telegraph's Paddy Burt.

Arran House, *42 Gravel Hill, Ludlow, Shropshire, SY8 1QR.* Comfortable Victorian house. 5 minutes walk town centre, railway station. **Open:** All year
01584 873764 Mrs Bowen **D:** Fr £17.00–£19.00 **S:** Fr £17.00–£19.00 **Beds:** 1T 1D 2S **Baths:** 1 Sh (5) (4)

Maesbury

SJ3026

Ashfield Farmhouse, *Maesbury, Oswestry, Shropshire, SY10 8JH.* Charming C16th coaching/farmhouse. 1 mile Oswestry, A5/A483. Stylish. Comfort with beautiful surroundings. **Open:** All year
01691 653589 & 07989 477414 (M) Mrs Jones **Fax: 01691 653589** *marg@ashfieldfarmhouse.co.uk* www.ashfieldfarmhouse.co.uk **D:** Fr £22.00–£28.00 **S:** Fr £25.00–£35.00 **Beds:** 1F 1T 1D **Baths:** 2 En 1 Pr (8) **cc**

Mainstone

SO2787 *Castle Hotel*

New House Farm, *Mainstone, Clun, Craven Arms, Shropshire, SY7 8NJ.* Peaceful C18th farmhouse. Set high - Clun Hills. Ring for brochure. **Open:** Easter to Oct
01588 638314 Mrs Ellison *sarah@bishopscastle.co.uk* www.new-house-clun.co.uk **D:** Fr £25.00–£27.50 **S:** Fr £27.50–£30.00 **Beds:** 1F 1T **Baths:** 1 En 1 Pr (10) (6)

Market Drayton

SJ6734

80 Rowan Road, *Market Drayton, Shropshire, TF9 1RR.* Peaceful, hospitable. Home form home. Short walk to town centre. **Open:** All year (not Xmas/New Year)
01630 655484 (also fax) Mrs Russell **D:** Fr £19.00–£21.00 **S:** Fr £20.00–£22.00 **Beds:** 1T **Baths:** 1 Pr (1)

Melverley

SJ3316

Church House, *Melverley, Oswestry, Shropshire, SY10 8PJ.* Beautiful setting next to River Vyrnwy by historic Melverley church. **Open:** All year (not Xmas) **01691 682754** Mr & Mrs Sprackling *melverley@aol.com* members.aol.com/melverley **D:** Fr £17.00–£20.00 **S:** Fr £20.00 **Beds:** 1F 1D 1T **Baths:** 2 Pr (3)

Middleton (Ludlow)

SO5377 *The Unicorn*

Middleton Court, *Middleton, Ludlow, Shropshire, SY8 2DZ.* Only 2 miles from Ludlow. Gourmet breakfast. Stunning 1864. **Open:** All year (not Xmas/New Year) **01584 872842** Miss O'Meara **D:** Fr £25.00–£27.50 **S:** Fr £30.00 **Beds:** 2D **Baths:** 1 Pr 1 Sh (10)

Minsterley

SJ3705

Cricklewood Cottage, *Plox Green, Minsterley, Shrewsbury, Shropshire, SY5 0HT.* Delightful C18th cottage in unspoilt Shropshire countryside. Beautiful cottage garden. **Open:** All year (not Xmas) **01743 791229** Costello *paul.crickcott@bushinternet.com* www.smoothhound.co.uk/hotels/crickle.html **D:** Fr £23.50–£26.00 **S:** Fr £23.50–£35.00 **Beds:** 1T 2D **Baths:** 3 En (8) (3)

Newport

SJ7418

Lane End Farm, *Chester Road, Chetwynd, Newport, Shropshire, TF10 8BN.* Friendly farmhouse in wonderful countryside. Large comfortable rooms. Delicious breakfasts. **Open:** All year **Grades:** ETC 4 Diamond, Silver **01952 550337 (also fax)** Mrs Park www.virtual-shropshire.co.uk/lef **D:** Fr £20.00–£25.00 **S:** Fr £25.00–£30.00 **Beds:** 2D 1T **Baths:** 2 En 1 Pr (5)

Sambrook Manor, *Sambrook, Newport, Shropshire, TF10 8AL.* 200-acre mixed farm. Old manor farmhouse built in 1702. Beautiful gardens. **Open:** All year (not Xmas) **01952 550256 & 07811 915535 (M)** Mrs Mitchell **D:** Fr £18.00–£25.00 **S:** Fr £18.00–£25.00 **Beds:** 2D 1T **Baths:** 3 En (5)

The Three Fishes Hotel, *Pave Lane, Newport, Shropshire, TF10 9LQ.* Traditional family-run pub, set in heart of Shropshire countryside. **Open:** All year **01952 825580 (also fax)** *threefishnewport@aol.com* **D:** Fr £20.00–£30.00 **S:** Fr £32.50–£40.00 **Beds:** 3F 4T 1D **Baths:** 6 En 1 Sh (70) **cc**

Nobold

SJ4710

The Day House, *Nobold, Shrewsbury, Shropshire, SY5 8NL.* Delightful period farmhouse, extensive gardens, abundant wildlife, easy access Shrewsbury. **Open:** All year (not Xmas/New Year) **01743 860212 (also fax)** Mrs Roberts **D:** Fr £23.00–£26.00 **S:** Fr £25.00–£27.00 **Beds:** 1F 1T 1D **Baths:** 3 En

Norbury

SO3592

Suttocks Wood, *Norbury, Bishops Castle, Shropshire, SY9 5EA.* Scandinavian house in a woodland setting near Long Mynd and Stiperstones. **Open:** All year **01588 650433** Mrs Williams **Fax: 01588 650492** *shuttockswood@baclays.net* www.go2.co.uk/suttockswood/index.html **D:** Fr £23.00–£26.00 **S:** Fr £25.00–£28.00 **Beds:** 1D 2T **Baths:** 3 En (12) (8) **cc**

Nordley

SO6996

The Albynes, *Nordley, Bridgnorth, Shropshire, WV16 4SX.* Beautiful country house peacefully set in Parkland. Guest rooms overlook gardens. **Open:** All year (not Xmas/New Year) **01746 762261** Mrs Woolley **D:** Fr £20.00–£25.00 **S:** Fr £25.00–£30.00 **Beds:** 1D 1T 1S **Baths:** 2 En 1 Pr (10)

Norton (Craven Arms)

SO4581

The Firs, *Norton, Craven Arms, Shropshire, SY7 9LS.* **Open:** All year **Grades:** ETC 4 Diamond, AA 4 Diamond **01588 672511 (also fax)** Mrs Bebbington *thefirs@go2.co.uk* www.go2.co.uk/firs **D:** Fr £22.50–£25.00 **S:** Fr £27.00–£32.50 **Beds:** 1F 2D **Baths:** 2 En 1 Pr (5) Victorian stone farmhouse standing in large garden with ample parking, magnificent views in Area of Outstanding Natural Beauty. Walking distance of Stokesay Castle, 6 miles to historic Ludlow, with its abundance of Michelin star restaurants. Horse and pony stabling available.

Oakengates

SJ7011

Sunnymede Guest House, *Leonard Street, Oakengates, Telford, Shropshire, TF2 6EU.* Close to Telford amenities, 5 mins from M54, junction 5. **Open:** All year (not Xmas/New Year) **01952 612980** Mrs Hume **D:** Fr £20.00 **S:** Fr £20.00 **Beds:** 1T 1D 2S **Baths:** 2 Sh (6) **cc**

Oswestry

SJ2929

Ashfield Farmhouse, *Maesbury, Oswestry, Shropshire, SY10 8JH.* Charming C16th coaching/farmhouse. 1 mile Oswestry, A5/A483. Stylish. Comfort with beautiful surroundings. **Open:** All year **01691 653589 & 07989 477414 (M)** Mrs Jones **Fax: 01691 653589** *marg@ashfieldfarmhouse.co.uk* www.ashfieldfarmhouse.co.uk **D:** Fr £22.00–£28.00 **S:** Fr £25.00–£35.00 **Beds:** 1F 1T 1D **Baths:** 2 En 1 Pr (8) **cc**

Pant

SJ2722

Three Firs, *Pant, Oswestry, Shropshire, SY10 8LB.* Quiet homely countryside accommodation adjoining golf course, Welsh/English border. **Open:** All year **01691 831375** *three.firs@lineone.net* **D:** Fr £18.00–£25.00 **S:** Fr £18.00–£25.00 **Beds:** 2F 1D **Baths:** 2 En 1 Sh (6)

Pulverbatch

SJ4202

Lane Farm, *Wilderley, Pulverbatch, Shrewsbury, SY5 8DF.* C17th farmhouse on Shropshire Way. Excellent views, food & welcome! **Open:** All year **01743 718935** S Greig *sarahgreig2002@yahoo.com* www.homepages.enterprise.net/bgreig **D:** Fr £20.00–£25.00 **S:** Fr £26.00–£30.00 **Beds:** 1T 1D **Baths:** 1 En 1 Pr (4)

Rowton (Telford)

SJ6119 *Seven Stars*

Church Farm, *Rowton (Wellington), Wellington, Telford, Shropshire, TF6 6QY.* Superb breakfast. Spacious rooms. Relaxing spa bath. **Open:** All year (not Xmas/New Year) **01952 770381** Mrs Evans *church.farm@pipemedia.co.uk* **D:** Fr £20.00–£22.00 **S:** Fr £25.00–£35.00 **Beds:** 3F 1T 2D **Baths:** 2 En (10)

Rushbury
SO5191

The Coates, *Rushbury, Church Stretton, Shropshire, SY6 7DZ.* C15th family farmhouse with tennis court, in beautiful peaceful countryside. **Open:** Feb to Nov
01694 771330 (also fax) Mrs Madeley **D:** Fr £19.00–£22.00 **S:** Fr £22.00–£25.00 **Beds:** 2T **Baths:** 1 En 1 Sh

Ruyton-XI-Towns
SJ3922

Brownhill House, *Brownhill, Ruyton-XI-Towns, Shrewsbury, SY4 1LR.* Old world standards, modern facilities and relaxed atmosphere. All rooms ensuite. **Open:** All year
01939 261121 Yoland & Roger Brown **Fax: 01939 260626** *brownhill@eleventowns.co.uk* www.eleventowns.co.uk **D:** Fr £17.50–£23.00 **S:** Fr £20.50–£26.00 **Beds:** 1D 1T 1S **Baths:** 3 En (5) cc

Sambrook
SJ7024

Sambrook Manor, *Sambrook, Newport, Shropshire, TF10 8AL.* 200-acre mixed farm. Old manor farmhouse built in 1702. Beautiful gardens. **Open:** All year (not Xmas)
01952 550256 & 07811 915535 (M) Mrs Mitchell **D:** Fr £18.00–£25.00 **S:** Fr £18.00–£25.00 **Beds:** 2D 1T **Baths:** 3 En (5)

Shifnal
SJ7407

Treetops, *The Hem, Shifnal, Shropshire, TF11 9PS.* C18th cottage with friendly atmosphere, near Ironbridge, Cosford, Weston Park. **Open:** All year
01952 460566 Mrs Bell *julia@treetops.enta.net* **D:** Fr £22.50–£25.00 **S:** Fr £22.00–£25.00 **Beds:** 1D 1T 1S **Baths:** 1 Pr 1 Sh (3)

Shrewsbury
SJ4912

Abbey Court House, *134 Abbey Foregate, Shrewsbury, Shropshire, SY2 6AU.* Quality accommodation, close to town centre & abbey. Off-road parking. **Open:** All year **Grades:** AA 4 Diamond
01743 364416 Mrs Macleod **Fax: 01743 358559** *info@abbeycourt.org* www.abbeycourt.org **D:** Fr £20.00–£25.00 **S:** Fr £23.00–£35.00 **Beds:** 2F 3D 3T 2S **Baths:** 4 En 2 Sh (10) cc

Merevale House, *66 Ellesmere Road, Shrewsbury, SY1 2QP.* **Open:** All year (not Xmas)
01743 243677 J Spooner **D:** Fr £18.00 **Beds:** 3D **Baths:** 1 Sh (3)
Lovely Victorian house with private parking and pretty garden. 10 minutes' walk to town and railway and bus stations. Very attractive bedrooms with drinks, biscuits, television and many extra home comforts. Good breakfasts with vegetarians also catered for.

Brownhill House, *Brownhill, Ruyton-XI-Towns, Shrewsbury, SY4 1LR.* **Open:** All year
01939 261121 Yoland & Roger Brown **Fax: 01939 260626** *brownhill@eleventowns.co.uk* www.eleventowns.co.uk **D:** Fr £17.50–£23.00 **S:** Fr £20.50–£26.00 **Beds:** 1D 1T 1S **Baths:** 3 En (5) cc
Old world standards, modern facilities and relaxed atmosphere. All rooms ensuite. Local/home-grown produce. Ground floor room. Computers, fax, email. Easy access, Chester to Ludlow, Snowdonia to Ironbridge. Unique 2-acre garden the icing on the cake!

Severn Cottage, *Coton Hill, Shrewsbury, Shropshire, SY1 2DZ.* Spectacular views of river and countryside. Town centre 500 metres. **Open:** Mar to Nov
01743 358467 Mr Tudor **Fax: 01743 289920** *david.tudor@virgin.net* www.shrewsburynet.com **D:** Fr £25.00–£27.50 **S:** Fr £30.00–£35.00 **Beds:** 2D **Baths:** 2 Pr (10) (3)

Castlecote Guest House, *77 Monkmoor Road, Shrewsbury, Shropshire, SY2 5AT.* Family-run, comfortable Victorian house, close to all amenities. **Open:** All year (not Xmas) **Grades:** ETC 3 Diamond
01743 245473 Mrs Tench *btench@castlecote.fsbusiness.co.uk* **D:** Fr £21.00–£26.00 **S:** Fr £21.00–£26.00 **Beds:** 2F 3D 2T **Baths:** 1 En 2 Sh (4)

Avonlea, *33 Coton Crescent, Coton Hill, Shrewsbury, Shropshire, SY1 2NZ.* Comfortable, attractive Edwardian town house. 10-minute walk from town centre. **Open:** Jan to Dec **Grades:** ETC 2 Diamond
01743 359398 Mrs O'Keefe **D:** Fr £17.00–£19.00 **S:** Fr £18.00–£20.00 **Beds:** 2T 1S **Baths:** 1 En 1 Sh (11)

Lythwood Hall Bed & Breakfast, *2 Lythwood Hall, Bayston Hill, Shrewsbury, Shropshire, SY3 0AD.* Quality accommodation, beautiful grounds, peaceful location, excellent food, vehicle storage. **Open:** All year
07074 874747 & 01743 874747 Mr & Mrs Bottomley **Fax: 01743 874747** *lythwoodhall@amserve.net* **D:** Fr £20.00–£22.00 **S:** Fr £20.00–£25.00 **Beds:** 1D 1T **Baths:** 1 Pr 1 Sh (2)

The Stiperstones, *18 Coton Crescent, Coton Hill, Shrewsbury, SY1 2NZ.* Very comfortable, quality accommodation. High standard of cleanliness. Extensive facilities. **Open:** All year
01743 246720 & 01743 350303 Judy MacLeod **Fax: 01743 350303** *thestiperstones@aol.com* www.thestiperstones.com **D:** Fr £19.00–£21.00 **S:** Fr £22.50 **Beds:** 1F 2D 2T 1S **Baths:** 4 Sh (6)

Sandford House Hotel, *St. Julians Friars, Shrewsbury, SY1 1XL.* Georgian town house close to river. **Open:** All year
01743 343829 (also fax) *sandfordhouse@lineone.net* **D:** Fr £25.00–£27.00 **S:** Fr £40.00 **Beds:** 4F 2T 2D 2S **Baths:** 10 En cc

Meole Brace Hall, *Meole Brace , Shrewsbury, Shropshire, SY3 9HF.* Beautiful house set in 3 acres yet close to town. **Open:** All year (not Xmas/New Year)
01743 235566 & 07710 644696 (M) Mrs Hathaway **Fax: 01743 236886** *enquiries@meolebracehall.co.uk* **D:** Fr £24.50–£28.00 **S:** Fr £39.00–£46.00 **Beds:** 1T 2D **Baths:** 2 En 1 Pr (12) (12)

Snailbeach
SJ3702

Sycamore Cottage, *5 Perkins Beach, Snailbeach, Stiperstones, Shrewsbury, Shropshire, SY5 0PE.* Perfect location on Stiperstones Hills for exploring beautiful South Shropshire. Very comfortable accommodation. **Open:** All year (not Xmas/New Year)
01743 790914 Mrs Barrett **D:** Fr £21.00 **S:** Fr £25.00 **Beds:** 1T **Baths:** 1 En (2)

St George's
SJ7010

Grove House, *1 Stafford Street, St Georges, Telford, Shropshire, TF2 9JW.* Ideally situated for all of Shropshire attractions. Home from home. **Open:** All year (not Xmas/New Year) **Grades:** ETC 4 Diamond
01952 616140 (also fax) Mr & Mrs Woodhall **D:** Fr £19.00 **S:** Fr £22.00–£28.00 **Beds:** 1F 2T 3D 2S **Baths:** 7 En 1 Pr (5) (8)

Stottesdon

SO6682

Cox's Barn, *Bagginswood, Stottesdon, Kidderminster, Worcs, DY14 8LS.* Rural setting, perfectly situated for exploring Ludlow, Bridgnorth, Bewdley, Worcester. **Open:** All year
01746 718415 Mr & Mrs Thompson **D:** Fr £20.00–£25.00 **Beds:** 3D **Baths:** 3 En (4)

Strefford

SO4385

Strefford Hall, *Strefford, Craven Arms, Shropshire, SY7 8DE.* Spacious farmhouse in peaceful setting with panoramic views of Wenlock Edge. **Open:** All year (not Xmas/ New Year)
01588 672383 Mrs Morgan **Fax: 01588 673855** *strefford@orange.net* **D:** Fr £23.00 **S:** Fr £25.00–£28.00 **Beds:** 1T 2D **Baths:** 3 En

Telford

SJ6909

The Old Rectory, *Stirchley Village, Telford, Shropshire, TF3 1DY.* Quiet location, secluded garden, convenient Telford town centre and Ironbridge. **Open:** All year (not Xmas/New Year)
01952 596308 (also fax) Mrs Miller *hazelmiller@waitrose.com* **D:** Fr £21.00–£22.50 **S:** Fr £28.00 **Beds:** 1F 2T 1D 2S **Baths:** 4 En 2 Pr (6) 1

Church Farm, *Wrockwardine, Wellington, Telford, Shropshire, TF6 5DG.* Down a lime-tree avenue lies our superbly situated C18th village farmhouse. **Open:** All year
01952 244917 (also fax) J Savage *jo@churchfarm.freeserve.co.uk* www.churchfarmshropshire.co.uk **D:** Fr £24.00–£28.00 **S:** Fr £26.00–£36.00 **Beds:** 3T 3D **Baths:** 3 Pr 1 Sh cc

Wenboro Cottage, *Church Lane, Little Wenlock, Telford, Shrops, TF6 5BB.* Pretty cottage set in peaceful village near Ironbridge and Telford centre. **Open:** All year (not Xmas)
01952 505573 Mrs Carter *rcarter@wenboro.freeserve.co.uk* **D:** Fr £20.00–£22.50 **S:** Fr £25.00 **Beds:** 1D 1T **Baths:** 1 En 1 Pr (2)

Stone House, *Shifnal Road, Priorslee, Telford, Shropshire, TF2 9NN.* A warm, friendly guest house with a large walled garden. **Open:** All year
01952 290119 (also fax) Mrs Silcock *dave@stonehouseguesthouse.freeserve.co.uk* www.smoothhound.co.uk/hotels/stonehou.html **D:** Fr £20.00–£21.00 **S:** Fr £26.00–£27.00 **Beds:** 1F 2D 2T **Baths:** 5 En (4)

Trefonen

SJ2526

The Pentre, *Trefonen, Oswestry, Shropshire, SY10 9EE.* Rural bliss, C16th farmhouse, stunning views, dinner specialities. **Open:** All year (not Xmas/New Year)
01691 653952 Mr Gilbert *thepentre@micro-plus-web.net* **D:** Fr £21.00 **S:** Fr £29.00 **Beds:** 2F **Baths:** 2 En (10)

Upper Affcot

SO4486

Travellers Rest Inn, *Upper Affcot, Church Stretton, Shropshire, SY6 6RL.* Traditional inn with good food, real ale, good company. **Open:** All year (not Xmas)
01694 781275 Mr Allison **Fax: 01694 781555** *reception@travellersrestinn.co.uk* www.travellersrestinn.co.uk **D:** Fr £25.00 **S:** Fr £30.00 **Beds:** 5D 2T 1S **Baths:** 8 En (30) cc

Walcot (Shrewsbury)

SJ5911

Alscott Inn, *Walcot, Wellington, Telford, Shropshire, TF6 5EQ.* Friendly, family run country inn. Home cooking, Beer garden. **Open:** All year (not Xmas/New Year)
01952 248484 Ms Young *alscottinn@yahoo.co.uk* **D:** Fr £16.00–£20.00 **S:** Fr £20.00–£25.00 **Beds:** 2D 2T **Baths:** 2 En 1 Sh (40) cc

Wellington

SJ6411

Lord Nelson Hotel, *11-13 Park Street, Wellington, Telford, Shropshire, TF1 3AE.* Relaxed atmosphere in comfortable surroundings. Central to Shropshire's tourist attractions. **Open:** All year
01952 223498 **D:** Fr £18.50–£25.00 **S:** Fr £45.00 **Beds:** 2D 2T 8F **Baths:** 12 En cc

Wem

SJ5129

Forncet, *Soulton Road, Wem, Shrewsbury, Shropshire, SY4 5HR.* Warm welcome at spacious Victorian house. Ideal for touring, good home cooking. **Open:** All year (not Xmas)
01939 232996 Mr & Mrs James **D:** Fr £19.00 **S:** Fr £20.00 **Beds:** 1D 1T 1S **Baths:** 2 Sh (6)

Foxleigh House, *Foxleigh Drive, Wem, Shrewsbury, Shropshire, SY4 5BP.* Comfort assured in Georgian/Victorian home near Shropshire Way. **Open:** All year (not Xmas/ New Year)
01939 233528 (also fax) B L Barnes *foxleigh01@aol.com* **D:** Fr £20.00–£24.00 **S:** Fr £24.00–£25.00 **Beds:** 4T **Baths:** 1 Pr 1 Sh (8) (6)

Greenfields, *55 Roden Grove, Wem, Shrewsbury, SY4 5HJ.* Comfortable, relaxing atmosphere within 10 minutes walk of town centre. **Open:** All year
01939 232850 Mrs Johnson **D:** Fr £18.00 **S:** Fr £18.50 **Beds:** 2D 1S **Baths:** 1 Sh (2)

Weston-under-Redcastle

SJ5628

Windmill Cottage Guest House, *Weston-under-Redcastle, Shrewsbury, Shropshire, SY4 5UX.* Next to Hawkstone golf follies. Ideal walkers, golfers, countryside lovers. **Open:** Feb to Dec
01939 200219 (also fax) Mr & Mrs Trasatti *glt@windmillcottage.co.uk* www.windmillcottage.co.uk **D:** Fr £20.00 **S:** Fr £30.00 **Beds:** 4T **Baths:** 4 En (9) (8)

Whitchurch

SJ5441

Roden View, *Dobson's Bridge, Whixall, Whitchurch, Shropshire, SY13 2QL.* Make yourselves at home and enjoy the comfort of our C17th country cottage. **Open:** Feb to Dec
01948 710320 (also fax) J James *gary@rodenview.com* **D:** Fr £20.00 **S:** Fr £20.00 **Beds:** 1D/F 1D 2T **Baths:** 4 En (8)

Stoneleigh, *16 Sedgeford, Whitchurch, Shropshire, SY13 1EX.* Home from home, comfortable beds, good breakfast, beautiful garden. **Open:** All year (not Xmas)
01948 664618 Mrs Gibson **D:** Fr £15.00 **S:** Fr £15.00 **Beds:** 1D 1T 1S **Baths:** 2 Sh (3)

Hamner Arms Village Hotel, *Hamner, Whitchurch, Shropshire, SY13 3DE.* A return to the values of yesteryear. Service and hospitality. **Open:** All year
01948 830532 Fax: 01948 830740
enquiries@thehamnerarms.freeserve.co.uk
www.thehamnersarms.freeserve.co.uk **D:** Fr £25.00–£37.50 **S:** Fr £35.00–£47.50 **Beds:** 4F 24D **Baths:** 28 En (80) **cc**

Whixall

SJ5134

Roden View, *Dobson's Bridge, Whixall, Whitchurch, Shropshire, SY13 2QL.* Make yourselves at home and enjoy the comfort of our C17th country cottage. **Open:** Feb to Dec
01948 710320 (also fax) J James *gary@rodenview.com* **D:** Fr £20.00 **S:** Fr £20.00 **Beds:** 1D/F 1D 2T **Baths:** 4 En (8)

Withington

SJ5712

Garden Cottage, *Withington, Shrewsbury, Shropshire, SY4 4QA.* Delightful Grade II Listed country house, great charm and character, quiet village setting.
Open: All year (not Xmas)
01743 709511 (also fax) Mrs Hopper
silvia.hopper@garden-cottage.fsnet.co.uk **D:** Fr £20.00–£22.00 **S:** Fr £19.00–£30.00 **Beds:** 1D 1T 1S **Baths:** 1 En 1 Sh (6)

Woofferton

SO5268 *The Boot*

Ravenscourt Manor, *Woofferton, Ludlow, Shropshire, SY8 4AL.* Ancient manor close to Ludlow, superb ensuite rooms.
Open: Mar to Jan
01584 711905 & 07855 797845 (M)
Mrs Purnell **Fax: 01584 711905 D:** Fr £27.50–£30.00 **S:** Fr £35.00–£40.00 **Beds:** 1F 1T 1D **Baths:** 3 En

Wrockwardine

SJ6211

Church Farm, *Wrockwardine, Wellington, Telford, Shropshire, TF6 5DG.* Down a lime-tree avenue lies our superbly situated C18th village farmhouse. **Open:** All year
01952 244917 (also fax) J Savage
jo@churchfarm.freeserve.co.uk
www.churchfarmshropshire.co.uk **D:** Fr £24.00–£28.00 **S:** Fr £26.00–£36.00 **Beds:** 3T 3D **Baths:** 3 Pr 1 Sh **cc**

RATES
D = Price range per person sharing in a double or twin room
S = Price range for a single room

Somerset

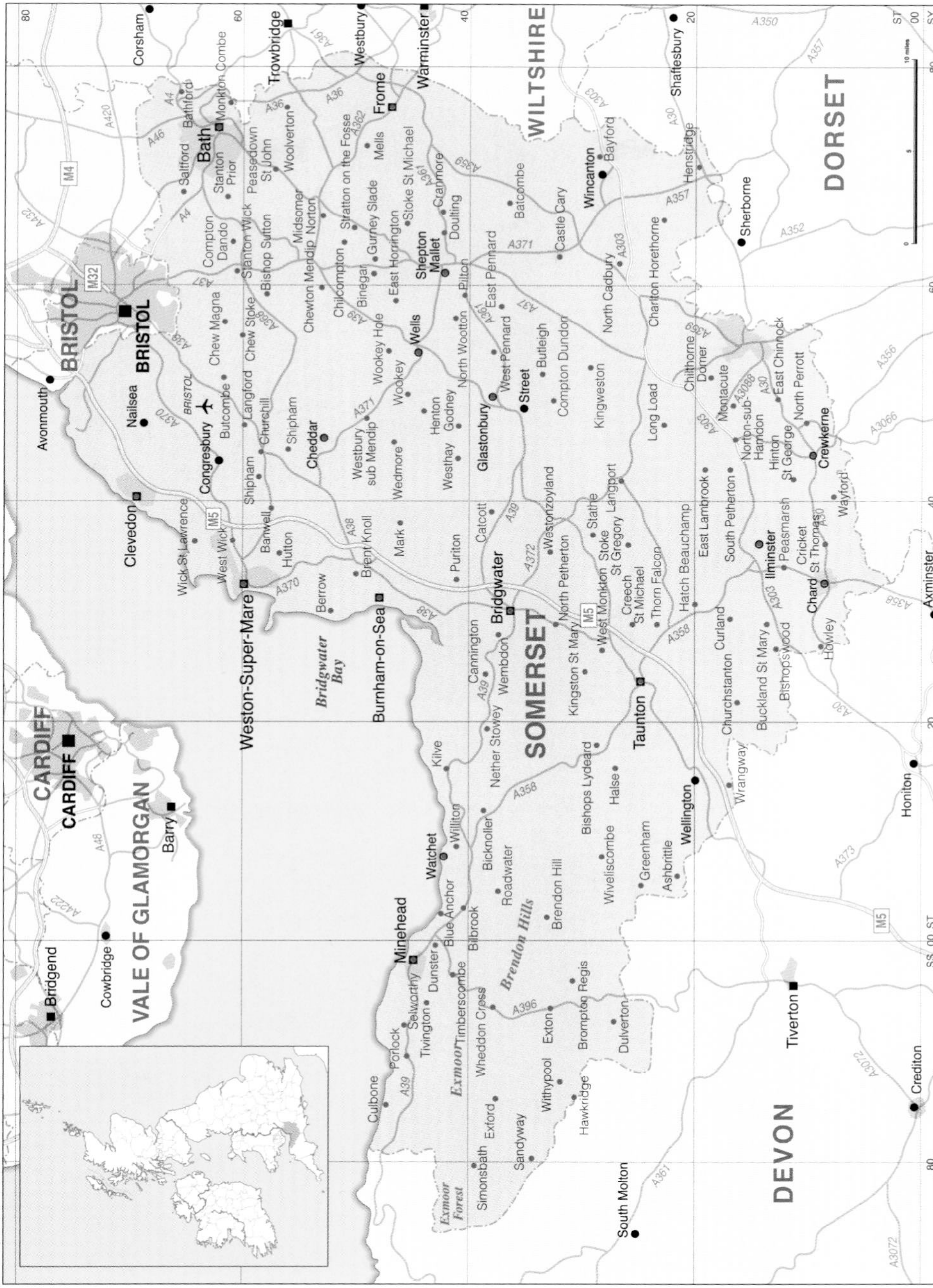
WILTSHIRE
DORSET
DEVON
SOMERSET
VALE OF GLAMORGAN
CARDIFF
BRISTOL
Bridgwater Bay
Brendon Hills
Exmoor
Exmoor Forest
Bath
Frome
Trowbridge
Westbury
Warminster
Corsham
Shaftesbury
Wincanton
Sherborne
Shepton Mallet
Wells
Cheddar
Glastonbury
Street
Bridgwater
Taunton
Wellington
Minehead
Watchet
Burnham-on-Sea
Weston-Super-Mare
Clevedon
Nailsea
Congresbury
Avonmouth
Yeovil
Crewkerne
Ilminster
Chard
Axminster
Honiton
Tiverton
Crediton
South Molton
Dulverton
Porlock
Dunster
Barry
Cowbridge
Bridgend
Castle Cary
Langport
Somerton
Bruton
Keynsham
Midsomer Norton
Wiveliscombe
Williton
Cannington

Ashbrittle

ST0521

Lower Westcott Farm, *Ashbrittle, Wellington, Somerset, TA21 0HZ.* Devon/Somerset borders family farm, ideal Moors/Coasts. Picturesque countryside. **Open:** All year (not Xmas)
01398 361296 Mrs Heard **D:** Fr £18.00–£20.00 **S:** Fr £18.00–£20.00 **Beds:** 1F 1T **Baths:** 1 En 1 Pr (4)

Banwell

ST3959

Banwell Castle, *Banwell, Weston-super-Mare, Somerset, BS29 6NX.* Victorian castle, outstanding views, still a family home. **Open:** All year
01934 822263 Mr Parsons **Fax: 01934 823946** *BanwellCastle@supanet.com* www.BanwellCastle.co.uk **D:** Fr £25.00 **S:** Fr £25.00 **Beds:** 4D **Baths:** 4 En (40) cc

Batcombe

ST6837

Batcombe Vale, *Batcombe, Shepton Mallet, Somerset, BA4 6BW.* Own secluded valley of lakes and wild gardens. Wells-Longleat. **Open:** Mar to Nov
01749 830246 (also fax) Mrs Sage *donaldsage@compuserve.com* **D:** Fr £18.00–£20.00 **S:** Fr £20.00–£22.00 **Beds:** 1F 1T 1D (6)

Valley View Farm, *Batcombe, Shepton Mallet, Somerset, BA4 6AJ.* Bungalow residence, extensive gardens, secluded, overlooking a picturesque valley. **Open:** All year (not Xmas/New Year)
01749 850302 & 07813 679020 (M) Mrs Mead **Fax: 01749 850302** *valleyviewfarm@lineone.net* **D:** Fr £20.00 **S:** Fr £22.00–£25.00 **Beds:** 1T 1D **Baths:** 1 En 1 Sh

Bath

ST7464

Dorset Villa, *14 Newbridge Road, Bath, BA1 3JZ.* Walking distance from centre and amenities. Quality surroundings. Cooked breakfast. **Open:** All year (not Xmas/New Year)
01225 425975 (also fax) *reception@dorsetvilla-bath.activehotels.com* www.dorsetvilla.co.uk **D:** Fr £19.00–£30.00 **S:** Fr £20.00–£34.00 **Beds:** 2F 2T 4D 1S **Baths:** 8 En 1 Sh (9) cc

Bailbrook Lodge, *35-37 London Road West, Bath, BA1 7HZ.* **Open:** All year
01225 859090 Mrs Sexton **Fax: 01225 852299** *hotel@bailbrooklodge.co.uk* www.bailbrooklodge.co.uk **D:** Fr £30.00–£45.00 **S:** Fr £39.00–£50.00 **Beds:** 4F 4D 4T **Baths:** 12 En (14) cc
Bailbrook Lodge is an imposing Georgian House set it its own gardens. The elegant period bedrooms (some four posters) offer ensuite facilities, TV and hospitality trays, bar and restaurant overlook gardens. Private parking. 1.5 miles from Bath centre. Close to M4.

Wentworth House Hotel, *106 Bloomfield Road, Bath, BA2 2AP.* **Open:** All year
01225 339193 Mrs Boyle **Fax: 01225 310460** *stay@wentworthhouse.co.uk* www.wentworthhouse.co.uk **D:** Fr £26.00–£50.00 **S:** Fr £40.00–£70.00 **Beds:** 2F 12D 2T 2S **Baths:** 17 En 1 Pr (5) (20) cc
A Victorian mansion 15 minutes' walk from the city. Quiet location with large garden and car park. Heated swimming pool, licensed restaurant and cocktail bar. Golf and walks nearby. Lovely rooms, some with four-poster beds and conservatories.

Wellsway Guest House, *51 Wellsway, Bath, BA2 4RS.* Edwardian house near Alexandra Park. Easy walks to city centre. **Open:** All year
01225 423434 Mrs Strong **D:** Fr £18.00–£20.00 **S:** Fr £20.00–£25.00 **Beds:** 1F 1D 1T 1S **Baths:** 4 Sh (4)

Planning a longer stay? Always ask for any special rates

Cranleigh, *159 Newbridge Hill, Bath, BA1 3PX.* **Open:** All year (not Xmas)
Grades: AA 4 Diamond
01225 310197 Mr Poole **Fax: 01225 423143** *cranleigh@btinternet.com* www.cranleighguesthouse.com **D:** Fr £33.00–£48.00 **S:** Fr £45.00–£55.00 **Beds:** 2F 2T 4D **Baths:** 8 En (5) (5) cc
Charming Victorian house a short distance from the city centre. Spacious bedrooms, most with country views, offer comfort and quality. Imaginative breakfasts served in elegant dining room include fresh fruit salad and scrambled eggs with smoked salmon.

The Ayrlington, *24/25 Pulteney Road, Bath, BA2 4EZ.* **Open:** All year (not Xmas/New Year)
01225 425495 Fax: 01225 469029 *mail@ayrlington.com* www.ayrlington.com **D:** Fr £37.50–£77.50 **S:** Fr £37.50–£77.50 **Beds:** 3F 1T 8D **Baths:** 12 En cc
Located within an easy 5-minute level walk of Bath city centre, the Ayrlington is a small, tranquil, non-smoking luxury hotel. Its 12 elegantly appointed rooms boast every modern amenity, and some feature four-poster beds and spa baths. Private parking.

Flaxley Villa, *9 Newbridge Hill, Bath, BA1 3PW.* Comfortable Victorian house near Royal Crescent. 15-minute walk to centre. **Open:** All year
01225 313237 Mrs Cooper **D:** Fr £20.00–£30.00 **S:** Fr £18.00–£36.00 **Beds:** 3D 1T 1S **Baths:** 3 En (5)

The Albany Guest House, *24 Crescent Gardens, Bath, BA1 2NB.* **Open:** All year (not Xmas/New Year) **Grades:** ETC 4 Diamond, Silver
01225 313339 Mrs Wotley *the_albany@lineone.net* www.bath.org/hotel/albany.htm **D:** Fr £18.00–£27.50 **S:** Fr £30.00–£40.00 **Beds:** 2D 2T **Baths:** 2 En (5) (3)
Jan and Bryan assure you of a warm welcome to their non-smoking Victorian home. 5 minutes' walk to the city centre - Roman Baths, Abbey, Royal Crescent etc. Delicious English or vegetarian breakfast. Imaginatively decorated rooms and first-class service.

Marlborough House, *1 Marlborough Lane, Bath, BA1 2NQ.* **Open:** All year **01225 318175** L Dunlop **Fax: 01225 466127** *mars@manque.dircon.co.uk* www.marlborough-house.net **D:** Fr £32.50–£47.50 **S:** Fr £45.00–£75.00 **Beds:** 2F 1T 3D 1S **Baths:** 7 En cc
Enchanting small hotel in the heart of Bath, exquisitely furnished, but run in friendly and informal style. Specialising in organic vegetarian cuisine. Our central location, gorgeous rooms, and unique menu make us truly special. Base for Cotswolds Way & Limestone Link walks.

Crofton Cottage, *Bath Road, Swineford, Bitton, Bristol, BS30 6LW.* **Open:** All year **0117 932 3671** Mr and Mrs Marsh *crofton.cott@virgin.net* www.smoothhound.co.uk/croftoncottage **D:** Fr £20.00–£25.00 **S:** Fr £30.00–£35.00 **Beds:** 1T 1D **Baths:** 2 En (6)
4 miles from Bath and 6 miles from Bristol on the A431. This pretty 1800s cottage, recently refurbished, on the banks of the River Avon, with private fishing and moorings. Offering bed and breakfast to a high standard.

14 Raby Place, *Bathwick Hill, Bath, Somerset, BA2 4EH.* Charming Georgian terraced house with beautiful interior rooms. **Open:** All year **Grades:** ETC 4 Diamond
01225 465120 Mrs Guy **Fax: 01225 465283** **D:** Fr £25.00–£28.00 **S:** Fr £25.00–£35.00 **Beds:** 1F 2D 1T 1S **Baths:** 3 En 2 Pr

The Old Chapel, *Compton Dando, BS39 4JZ.* **Open:** All year **Grades:** ETC 4 Diamond **01761 490903 (also fax)** Mr Graham *info@the-old-chapel.com* www.the-old-chapel.com **D:** Fr £26.00–£27.50 **S:** Fr £35.00 **Beds:** 1T 2D **Baths:** 3 En (5) (4) cc
Former chapel in unspoilt Somerset village 15 mins' drive from Bath. Spacious ensuite accommodation offering excellent value without compromising standards. Superb breakfast with vegetarian option. Courtesy daytime transport to Bath. Ideal base for touring. Special rates for three nights.

Dene Villa, *5 Newbridge Hill, Bath, BA1 3PW.* Victorian family-run guest house, a warm welcome is assured.**Open:** All year
01225 427676 Mrs Surry **Fax: 01225 482684** *denevilla@yahoo.co.uk* **D:** Fr £23.00–£25.00 **S:** Fr £23.00–£25.00 **Beds:** 1F 1D 1T 1S **Baths:** 3 En (3) (4)

Cherry Tree Villa, *7 Newbridge Hill, Bath, Somerset, BA1 3PW.* Small friendly Victorian home 1 mile from city centre. **Open:** All year (not Xmas/New Year) **Grades:** ETC 3 Diamond
01225 331671 Ms Goddard **D:** Fr £18.00–£24.00 **S:** Fr £20.00–£30.00 **Beds:** 1F/T 1D 1S **Baths:** 1 Sh (4)

Royal Park Guest House, *16 Crescent Gardens, Bath, Somerset, BA1 2NA.* Close to Bath's centre - Roman Baths, Royal Crescent and Circus. **Open:** All year (not Xmas) **Grades:** ETC 2 Diamond
01225 317651 Fax: 01225 483950 *royal@parkb-b.freeserve.co.uk* **D:** Fr £21.00–£25.00 **S:** Fr £25.00–£30.00 **Beds:** 1F 1T 1D 1S **Baths:** 3 En 1 Pr (5) (3)

Glan y Dwr, *14 Newbridge Hill, Bath, BA1 3PU.* Personal attention to ensure you have a comfortable stay in Bath. **Open:** All year
01225 317521 (also fax) Mr Jones *glanydwr@hotmail.com* **D:** Fr £18.00–£26.00 **S:** Fr £20.00–£35.00 **Beds:** 2D 1T 3S **Baths:** 1 En 1 Pr 1 Sh (3) 2

RATES

D = Price range per person sharing in a double or twin room

S = Price range for a single room

The Old Red House, *37 Newbridge Road, Bath, BA1 3HE.* A romantic Victorian gingerbread house with stained glass windows, comfortable bedrooms, superbly cooked breakfasts. **Open:** Feb to Dec
01225 330464 Fax: 01225 331661 *oldredhouse@amserve.net* www.oldredhouse.co.uk **D:** Fr £24.00–£35.00 **S:** Fr £30.00–£45.00 **Beds:** 1F 4D 1T 1S **Baths:** 3 En 1 Pr 1 Sh (4) (4) cc

Hotel St Clair, *1 Crescent Gardens, Bath, BA1 2NA.* Friendly B&B serving great breakfasts, 5 mins' walk from city. **Open:** All year **Grades:** AA 3 Diamond
01225 425543 (also fax) *hotel-st-clair@ukonline.co.uk* www.web.ukonline.co.uk/hotel-st-clair **D:** Fr £20.00–£37.50 **S:** Fr £26.00–£65.00 **Beds:** 4F 4T 8D 2S **Baths:** 16 En 2 Sh (2) cc

No 2 Crescent Gardens, *Upper Bristol Road, Bath, BA1 2NA.* Beautiful B&B in the heart of Bath. Warm welcome. **Open:** All year (not Xmas/New Year)
01225 331186 Mr Bez **D:** Fr £19.00–£25.00 **S:** Fr £19.00–£25.00 **Beds:** 1F 3T 3D **Baths:** 3 En 1 Sh

Koryu B&B, *7 Pulteney Gardens, Bath, Somerset, BA2 4HG.* Completely renovated Victorian home, extremely clean, beautiful linens. Delicious breakfasts with wide menu. **Open:** All year
01225 337642 (also fax) Mrs Shimizu **D:** Fr £24.00–£25.00 **S:** Fr £28.00–£30.00 **Beds:** 1F 2D 2T 2S **Baths:** 5 En 2 Sh (2)

Lindisfarne, *41a Warminster Road, Bath, Somerset, BA2.* Friendly and comfortable with great breakfasts. Handy for historic Bath. **Open:** All year
01225 466342 *lindisfarne-bath@talk21.com* **D:** Fr £20.00–£30.00 **S:** Fr £35.00–£38.00 **Beds:** 1F 1T 2D **Baths:** 4 En (8) (6) cc

Membland Guest House, *7 Pulteney Terrace Pulteney Road, Bath, BA2 4HJ.* Comfortable Victorian guest house close to Roman Baths, Abbey, train/coach stations. **Open:** All year (not Xmas)
01225 336712 & 07958 599572 (M) Mr Moore *prmoore@wimpey.co.uk* www.accommodation-bath.com **D:** Fr £20.00–£24.00 **S:** Fr £30.00–£35.00 **Beds:** 1F 1T 1D

Forres House, *172 Newbridge Road, Bath, BA1 3LE.* A warm welcome, comfortable bed and big breakfast awaits you. **Open:** All year
01225 427698 J Jones *clive.sampson@eke.co.uk* **D:** Fr £20.00–£25.00 **S:** Fr £30.00–£35.00 **Beds:** 2F 1T 2D **Baths:** 5 En (5) cc

National Grid References given are for villages, towns and cities – not for individual houses

Georgian Guest House, *34 Henrietta Street, Bath, BA2 6LR.* Situated just 2 mins walk to city centre in a peaceful location. **Open:** All year (not Xmas)
01225 424103 Mr Kingwell **Fax: 01225 425279** *georgian@georgian-house.co.uk* www.georgian-house.co.uk **D:** Fr £30.00–£35.00 **S:** Fr £30.00–£50.00 **Beds:** 7D 2T 2S **Baths:** 7 En 1 Sh cc

Grove Lodge, *11 Lambridge, Bath, BA1 6BJ.* Grade II listed Georgian villa, large rooms with views. **Open:** All year (not Xmas/New Year)
01225 310860 I Miles **Fax: 01225 429630** *grovelodge@bath24.fsnet.co.uk* **D:** Fr £25.00–£32.50 **S:** Fr £30.00–£45.00 **Beds:** 1F 2T 3D **Baths:** 3 En 2 Pr (6)

Blairgowrie House, *55 Wellsway, Bath, BA2 4RT.* Fine late Victorian residence operating as a privately owned family-run guest house. **Open:** All year
01225 332266 Mr Roberts **Fax: 01225 484535** *blairgowrie.bath@ukgateway.net* **D:** Fr £27.50–£30.00 **Beds:** 1T 2D **Baths:** 2 En 1 Pr

3 Thomas Street, *Walcot, Bath, Somerset, BA1 5NW.* Charming Georgian house convenient to all city amenities and shops. **Open:** All year (not Xmas)
01225 789540 Ms Saunders **D:** Fr £20.00–£22.50 **S:** Fr £20.00–£22.50 **Beds:** 2T **Baths:** 1 En 1 Sh

The Glade, *Shaft Road, Combe Down, Bath, Somerset, BA2 7HP.* Secluded sylvan retreat. Comfortable, spacious accommodation in half acre natural woodland garden. **Open:** All year
01225 833172 L Markham *theglade@uk2.net* www.thegladebath.co.uk **D:** Fr £18.00–£27.50 **S:** Fr £20.00–£30.00 **Beds:** 1F 1D **Baths:** 2 En (4)

Brookfields, *29 London Road West, Bath, Somerset, BA1 7HZ.* One mile from Bath centre. Easy from M4. Parking. All facilities **Open:** All year
01225 859090 **D:** Fr £20.00–£27.50 **S:** Fr £25.00–£40.00 **Beds:** 3D **Baths:** 2 En 1 Pr (14) cc

Bathford

ST7966 *Crown Inn, Swan Inn, Avondale*

Bridge Cottage, *Northfield End, Ashley Road, Bathford, Bath, BA1 7TT.* Idyllic cottage in award-winning gardens, village location adjoining Bath. **Open:** Easter to Oct
01225 852399 Mrs Mackay *daphne@bridge-cottages.co.uk* **D:** Fr £25.00–£27.50 **S:** Fr £35.00–£37.50 **Beds:** 1T 2D **Baths:** 3 En (2)

Garston Cottage, *Ashley Road, Bathford, Bath, N E Somerset, BA1 7TT.* 3 miles from Bath, walled garden, spa pool, pool room. **Open:** All year
01225 852510 Ms Smart **Fax: 01225 852793** *garstoncot@aol.com* **D:** Fr £25.00–£30.00 **S:** Fr £25.00–£35.00 **Beds:** 1F 1T 1D **Baths:** 3 En 1 Sh (1) cc

Bayford

ST7228

The Unicorn Inn, *Bayford, Wincanton, Somerset, BA9 9NL.* Bordering three counties, warm welcome, excellent food-real ale. **Open:** All year
01963 32324 Mrs Waite **D:** Fr £22.00–£26.00 **S:** Fr £30.00 **Beds:** 1T 2D 1S **Baths:** 4 En (20) cc

Berrow

ST2952

Martins Hill Farmhouse, *Red Road, Berrow, Burnham-on-Sea, Somerset, TA8 2RW.* Quiet farmhouse overlooking countryside. Golf course, sandy beach 1 mile. **Open:** Mar to Oct
01278 751726 Mrs Davies **Fax: 01278 751230** **D:** Fr £20.00–£22.50 **Beds:** 1F 1D 1T **Baths:** 1 En 1 Pr 1 Sh (6) cc

Bicknoller

ST1139

Quantock Moor Farm Cottage, *Bicknoller, Taunton, Somerset, TA4 4ER.* Peaceful surroundings, on Greenway path around Quantock Hills - ideal touring. **Open:** All year (not Xmas)
01984 656626 Mrs Seamons *quantock@operamail.com* **D:** Fr £17.00 **S:** Fr £17.00 **Beds:** 1D 1T 1S **Baths:** 1 Pr (3)

Bilbrook

ST0240

Steps Farmhouse, *Bilbrook, Minehead, Somerset, TA24 6HE.* **Open:** Feb to Nov **Grades:** ETC 4 Diamond
01984 640974 Mr & Mrs James *info@stepsfarmhouse.co.uk* www.stepsfarmhouse.co.uk **D:** Fr £22.00–£25.00 **S:** Fr £25.00–£30.00 **Beds:** 1F 1D 1T **Baths:** 3 En (6)
Traditional C16th former farmhouse situated near Dunster offering ensuite B&B accommodation, in barn conversions located in beautiful secluded gardens with views towards Exmoor; breakfasts are served in our cosy dining room with oak beams and inglenook fireplace.

Planning a longer stay? Always ask for any special rates

Binegar

ST6149

Mansefield House, *Old Rectory Garden, Binegar, Bath, Somerset, BA3 4UG.* Spacious detached house, edge of Mendip Hills. Quiet village location. Good food local inns. **Open:** All year (not Xmas/New Year)
01749 840568 Ms Anstey **Fax: 01749 840572** *mansfieldhouse@aol.com* **D:** Fr £25.00 **S:** Fr £30.00 **Beds:** 2T 1D **Baths:** 2 En 1 Pr (4)

Bishop Sutton

ST5859

Centaur, *Ham Lane, Bishop Sutton, Bristol, BS39 5TZ.* Comfortable house, peaceful location, within easy reach Bath, Bristol, Wells, Cheddar. **Open:** Mar to Oct **Grades:** ETC 3 Diamond
01275 332321 Mrs Warden **D:** Fr £19.00–£21.00 **S:** Fr £17.50–£25.00 **Beds:** 1F 1T 1S **Baths:** 1 En 2 Sh (4)

Bishops Lydeard

ST1629

West View, *Minehead Road, Bishops Lydeard, Taunton, Somerset, TA4 3BS.* Delightful listed Victorian house in village near the West Somerset Steam Railway. **Open:** All year
01823 432223 (also fax) Mrs Pattemore *westview@pattemore.freeserve.co.uk* **D:** Fr £20.00–£25.00 **S:** Fr £20.00–£30.00 **Beds:** 2T 1D **Baths:** 2 En (10)

The Mount, *32 Mount Street, Bishops Lydeard, Taunton, Somerset, TA4 3AN.* Comfortable Georgian period residence in picturesque village at foot of Quantock Hills. **Open:** All year (not Xmas)
01823 432208 Mr & Mrs Hinton *d.hinton@talk21.com* **D:** Fr £20.00 **S:** Fr £20.00–£25.00 **Beds:** 1D 3T **Baths:** 2 Sh (2) (4)

Bishopswood

ST2512 *Candelight Inn*

Hawthorne House, *Bishopswood, Chard, Somerset, TA20 3RS.* Comfortable C19th house situated in the Blackdown Hills (AONB) 1 mile off the A303. **Open:** All year
01460 234482 & 07710 255059 (M) R & S Newman-Coburn **Fax: 01460 234482** *info@roger-sarah.co.uk* www.roger-sarh.co.uk **D:** Fr £22.00 **S:** Fr £30.00 **Beds:** 1T 2D **Baths:** 2 En 1 Pr (12)

Blagdon

ST4958

Butcombe Farm, *Aldwick Lane, Butcombe, Bristol, BS40 7UW.* Converted C14th manor house with character accommodation nestled at foot of Mendip Hills. Glorious countryside. ideal for walking cycling, horse riding,golf, clay pigeon and fishing nearby at Blagdon Lake. Close to Bristol, Bath, Cheddar, Wells, Glastonbury and Exmoor. **Open:** All year (not Xmas/New Year) **01761 462380** Mr Harvey **Fax: 01761 462300** *info@butcombe-farm.demon.co.uk* www.butcombe-farm.demon.co.uk **D:** Fr £20.00–£27.00 **S:** Fr £30.00–£39.00 **Beds:** 2T 3D **Baths:** 5 En cc

Blue Anchor

ST0343

Langbury Hotel, *Blue Anchor, Minehead, Somerset, TA24 6LB.* Small hotel. Sea views. 4 miles Minehead, in quiet village. **Open:** All year **Grades:** ETC 3 Diamond, AA 3 Diamond **01643 821375** Paula Smythe **Fax: 01643 822012** *enquiries@langbury.co.uk* www.langbury.co.uk **D:** Fr £22.00–£25.00 **S:** Fr £25.00–£30.00 **Beds:** 1F 2D 2T **Baths:** 5 En (5) cc

Brendon Hill

ST0234

Ralegh's Cross Inn, *Brendon Hill, Watchet, Somerset, TA23 0LN.* **Open:** All year **01984 640343 (also fax)** Mrs Brinkley www.raleghscross.co.uk **D:** Fr £20.00–£35.00 **S:** Fr £30.00–£45.00 **Beds:** 4F 5T 8D **Baths:** 17 En cc Reputedly a C16th coaching inn, situated in the beautiful Brendon Hills. All food is freshly prepared and home cooked. Daily and weekend specials. We're famous locally for our farmer's carvery. 'An ideal base for discovering Exmoor, the Quantocks and the varied and interesting coastline'.

BATHROOMS
En = Ensuite
Pr = Private
Sh = Shared

Brent Knoll

ST3250

Woodlands Country House Hotel, *Hill Lane, Brent Knoll, Highbridge, Somerset, TA9 4DF.* Quiet rural setting, lovely views, 5 minutes M5 J22. Warm welcome, comfortable accommodation. **Open:** All year **Grades:** AA 2 Star **01278 760232 Fax: 01278 769090** *info@woodlands-hotel.co.uk* www.woodlands-hotel.co.uk **D:** Fr £30.00 **S:** Fr £30.00 **Beds:** 1F 1T 6D **Baths:** 8 En (16) cc

Bridgwater

ST3037

Ash-Wembdon Farm, *Hollow Lane, Wembdon, Bridgwater, Somerset, TA5 2BD.* Enjoy a refreshing and memorable stay at our elegant yet homely farmhouse. **Open:** All year (not Xmas) **Grades:** ETC 4 Diamond, Silver **01278 453097** Mrs Rowe **Fax: 01278 445856** *mary.rowe@btinternet.com* www.farmaccommodation.co.uk **D:** Fr £22.00–£25.00 **S:** Fr £25.00–£30.00 **Beds:** 2D 1T **Baths:** 2 En 1 Pr (10) (4) cc

The Acorns, *61 Taunton Road, Bridgwater, Somerset, TA6 3LP.* Jill & Ken offer welcoming and friendly hospitality with modern facilities, good breakfast, guest lounge. **Open:** All year (not Xmas) **01278 445577 & 07767 892703 (M)** *jillgraham@theacorns.fsbusiness.co.uk* **D:** Fr £17.50–£20.00 **S:** Fr £17.50–£20.00 **Beds:** 3F 2D 5T 3S **Baths:** 5 En 3 Sh (15)

RATES
D = Price range per person sharing in a double or twin room
S = Price range for a single room

Brompton Regis

SS9431

Bruneton House, *Brompton Regis, Dulverton, Somerset, TA22 9NN.* **Open:** All year (not Xmas) **Grades:** AA 3 Diamond **01398 371224** J Stringer *brunetonhouse@hotmail.com* **D:** Fr £20.00–£25.00 **S:** Fr £22.50–£25.00 **Beds:** 2D 1T **Baths:** 1 En 2 Pr (3) Spacious C17th house with beautiful garden overlooking the Pulham Valley. Exmoor village location, only 1 mile from Wimbleball Lake, ideally situated for North Devon and Somerset coastline. Relaxed accommodation in comfortable sunny rooms with easy access to country pursuits amid stunning scenery.

Buckland St Mary

ST2613

Hillside Guest Accommodation & Self-catering Apartment, *Buckland St Mary, Chard, Somerset, TA20 3TQ.* Quality accommodation with views, ideal base for Somerset, Devon, Dorset. **Open:** All year (not Xmas/New Year) **01460 234599 & 07703 633770 (M)** Mr Harkness **Fax: 01460 234599** *royandmarge@hillsidebsm.freeserve.co.uk* www.theAA.com/hotels/103591.html **D:** Fr £22.50–£25.00 **S:** Fr £22.50–£38.00 **Beds:** 1T 1D 1S **Baths:** 1 En 1 Sh (4)

Burnham-on-Sea

ST3049

Priorsmead, *23 Rectory Road, Burnham-on-Sea, Somerset, TA8 2BZ.* Edwardian family home, peaceful gardens, swimming, quality accommodation. Reduction three nights. **Open:** All year (not Xmas) **01278 782116 & 07990 595585 (M)** Mrs Alexander **Fax: 01278 782116** *PriorsMead@aol.com* www.priorsmead.co.uk **D:** Fr £17.00–£20.00 **S:** Fr £20.00–£25.00 **Beds:** 1D 2T **Baths:** 2 En 1 Pr (12) (3)

B&B owners may vary rates – be sure to check when booking

Planning a longer stay? Always ask for any special rates

Somewhere House, *68 Berrow Road, Burnham-on-Sea, Somerset, TA8 2EZ.* Victorian property within easy reach of town centre, near golf course. **Open:** All year (not Xmas/New Year) **Grades:** ETC 3 Diamond
01278 795236 Mr & Mrs Fellingham *di@somewherehouse.com* www.somewherehouse.com **D:** Fr £20.00 **S:** Fr £26.00 **Beds:** 2F 2T 1D **Baths:** 5 En (6)

Butleigh

ST5233

Court Lodge, *Butleigh, Glastonbury, Somerset, BA6 8SA.* Attractive modernised 1850 lodge. In picturesque garden, edge of Butleigh. 3m Glastonbury, Street. **Open:** All year (not Xmas)
01458 850575 Mrs Atkinson **D:** Fr £16.50 **S:** Fr £16.50 **Beds:** 1D 1S **Baths:** 2 En

Cannington

ST2539

Gurney Manor Mill, *Gurney Street, Cannington, Bridgwater, Somerset, TA5 2HW.*
Open: All year
01278 653582 Mr & Mrs Sutton **Fax: 01278 653993** *gurneymill@yahoo.co.uk* www.gurneymill.freeserve.co.uk **D:** Fr £20.00–£30.00 **S:** Fr £25.00–£35.00 **Beds:** 2F 1T 1D **Baths:** 4 En (15) **cc**
Old watermill and barn conversion with waterfall and wildlife in picturesque Cannington, with pubs, restaurants and shops. Private fishing, golf course and heritage gardens within walking distance. Ideal location for touring West Country. Gateway to the Quantock Hills.

Castle Cary

ST6332 *Pilgrim's Rest, George Hotel, Manor Inn*

Clanville Manor, *Castle Cary, Somerset, BA7 7PJ.* C18th elegance. C21st comfort.
Open: All year (not Xmas/New Year)
01963 350124 & 07966 512732 (M) Mrs Snook **Fax: 01963 350313** *info@clanvillemanor.co.uk* www.clanvillemanor.co.uk **D:** Fr £25.00–£30.00 **S:** Fr £25.00–£45.00 **Beds:** 1F 1T 1D 1S **Baths:** 3 En (6) **cc**

Catcott

ST3939

Honeysuckle, *King William Road, Catcott, Bridgwater, Somerset, TA7 9HV.* Pretty village location, close to Glastonbury, Wells, Cheddar Gorge. Pubs in village. **Open:** All Year (Not Xmas) **Grades:** AA 4 Diamond
01278 722890 Mr & Mrs Scott **D:** Fr £19.00–£25.00 **S:** Fr £17.00–£25.00 **Beds:** 1D 1T **Baths:** 1 En 1 Sh (6) (3)

Chard

ST3208

The Firs, *Crewkerne Road, Cricket St Thomas, Chard, Somerset, TA20 4BU.* Warm and friendly 'home from home' with beautiful countryside views. **Open:** All year
01460 65646 (also fax) S Bright **D:** Fr £20.00 **S:** Fr £25.00 **Beds:** 1T 2D **Baths:** 1 En 2 Pr

Yew Tree Cottage, *Hornsbury Hill, Chard, Somerset, TA20 3DB.* Equipped to a high standard with large ensuite bathrooms, large mature gardens, excellent position. **Open:** All year (not Xmas/New Year)
01460 64735 Viv & Phillip Hopkins **Fax: 01460 66163** *ytcottage@aol.com* yewtreecottage.org.uk **D:** Fr £22.50 **S:** Fr £30.00–£35.00 **Beds:** 1T 2D **Baths:** 3 En (10) (4)

Charlton Horethorne

ST6623

Beech Farm, *Sigwells, Charlton Horethorne, Sherborne, Dorset, DT9 4LN.*
Open: All year (not Xmas/New Year)
01963 220524 (also fax) Mrs Stretton **D:** Fr £17.00 **S:** Fr £17.00 **Beds:** 1T 1D 1F **Baths:** 1 En 1 Sh (6)
Comfortable, spacious farmhouse with relaxed atmosphere on dairy farm with horses. Wonderful views from Corton Beacon. 4 miles from historic abbey town of Sherborne, 6 miles from Wincanton. Just 2 miles off A303. Less 10% for 2 nights or more.

Ashclose Farm, *Charlton Horethorne, Sherborne, Dorset, DT9 4PG.* Comfortable farmhouse, peaceful countryside, friendly welcome and relaxed atmosphere.
Open: All year (not Xmas)
01963 220360 Mr & Mrs Gooding *gooding@ashclosefarm.freeserve.co.uk* **D:** Fr £18.00–£22.00 **S:** Fr £18.00–£22.00 **Beds:** 1D 1T 1S **Baths:** 1 En 1 Sh (5)

Cheddar

ST4553

Tor Farm Guest House, *Nyland, Cheddar, Somerset, BS27 3UD.* **Open:** All year (not Xmas) **Grades:** ETC 4 Diamond, AA 4 Diamond
01934 743710 Mrs Ladd *bcjbkj@aol.com* **D:** Fr £25.00–£30.00 **S:** Fr £30.00 **Beds:** 2F 3D 2T **Baths:** 7 En (10) **cc**
High quality farmhouse accommodation close to Bath, Wells, Glastonbury and Cheddar.

Southland House, *Upper New Road, Cheddar, Somerset, BS27 3DW.* Excellent ensuite accommodation, outskirts of Cheddar Village, ideal touring centre.
Open: All year (not Xmas)
01934 742189 Mrs Biggin *bb@southlandhouse.freeserve.co.uk* **D:** Fr £20.00–£23.00 **S:** Fr £25.00–£30.00 **Beds:** 1F 1T **Baths:** 2 En (1) (4)

Constantine, *Lower New Road, Cheddar, Somerset, BS27 3DY.* Beautiful views of Cheddar Gorge and Mendips. Good breakfast.
Open: All year (not Xmas) **Grades:** ETC 3 Diamond
01934 741339 Mr & Mrs Mitchell **D:** Fr £18.00–£20.00 **S:** Fr £18.00–£20.00 **Beds:** 1F 2D 1S **Baths:** 1 Sh (5)

Chew Magna

ST5763

North Elm Farm, *Norton Lane, Chew Magna, Bristol, BS40 8RW.* Old farmhouse near village. Ideal for touring Bath, Bristol Wells. Guests' kitchen, lounge & front door.
Open: All year (not Xmas/New Year)
01275 333595 (also fax) **D:** Fr £20.00 **S:** Fr £17.50 **Beds:** 1D 1T 2S **Baths:** 2 En 1 Sh

Chew Stoke

ST5561

Orchard House, *Bristol Road, Chew Stoke, Bristol, BS40 8UB.* Family-run 'home from home'. **Open:** All year **01275 333143** Mrs Hollomon **Fax: 01275 333754** *orchardhse@ukgateway.net* www.orchardhse.ukgateway.net **D:** Fr £20.00–£25.00 **S:** Fr £22.00–£27.00 **Beds:** 1F 1D 2T 1S **Baths:** 4 En 1 Pr (8) cc

Chewton Mendip

ST5953

Franklyns Farm, *Chewton Mendip, Bath, Somerset, BA3 4NB.* Cosy farmhouse in heart of Mendip Hills. Superb views, peaceful setting. Large garden, tennis. **Open:** All year **Grades:** ETC 3 Diamond **01761 241372 (also fax)** Mrs Clothier **D:** Fr £20.00 **S:** Fr £22.50 **Beds:** 2T 1D **Baths:** 2 En 1 Pr

Chilcompton

ST6452

Pipers Pool, *Wells Road, Chilcompton, Bath, Somerset, BA3 4ET.* Friendly welcome, indoor pool, great food, near Bath, Cheddar, Wells. **Open:** All year (not Xmas/New Year) **01761 233803** Mrs Sawyer **D:** Fr £20.00–£25.00 **S:** Fr £25.00–£30.00 **Beds:** 1T 2D **Baths:** 1 En (6)

Chilthorne Domer

ST5219

Jessops, *Vagg Lane, Chilthorne Domer, Yeovil, BA22 8RY.* New bungalow, Jessops, with panoramic views, set in open countryside, one ensuite with four-poster. **Open:** All year (not Xmas/New Year) **01935 841097 (also fax)** Mr & Mrs White **D:** Fr £40.00–£48.00 **S:** Fr £20.00–£25.00 **Beds:** 1T 1D 1S **Baths:** 1 En 1 Sh

Churchill

ST4359

Clumber Lodge, *New Road, Churchill, Winscombe, Somerset, BS25 5NW.* Bungalow with pretty garden, situated at the foot of Mendip Hills (AONB). **Open:** All year **01934 852078 (also fax) D:** Fr £15.00–£17.00 **S:** Fr £16.00–£18.00 **Beds:** 2T **Baths:** 1 Sh (3)

Churchstanton

ST1914

Thatched Country Cottage & Garden, *Stapley, Churchstanton, Taunton, Somerset, TA3 7QA.* **Open:** All year **Grades:** ETC 3 Diamond **01823 601224 (also fax)** Mrs Parry *colvin.parry@virgin.net* **D:** Fr £16.50–£20.00 **S:** Fr £24.00 **Beds:** 1F 1D 1S **Baths:** 1 En 1 Pr (4)
Picturesque thatched cottage. Traditional garden, croquet lawn plus 2.5 acres arboretum. Idyllic tranquillity in beautiful AONB countryside. Central for touring north/south coasts, Exmoor, Dartmoor, Bath, Wells, Cheddar etc. Encircled by many famous private/National Trust gardens. Stress-free paradise.

Compton Dando

ST6464

The Old Chapel, *Compton Dando, BS39 4JZ.* Former chapel in unspoilt Somerset village 15 mins' drive from Bath. **Open:** All year **Grades:** ETC 4 Diamond **01761 490903 (also fax)** Mr Graham *info@the-old-chapel.com* www.the-old-chapel.com **D:** Fr £26.00–£27.50 **S:** Fr £35.00 **Beds:** 1T 2D **Baths:** 3 En (5) (4) cc

Compton Dundon

ST4933

Rickham House, *Compton Dundon, Somerton, Somerset, TA11 6QA.* Fantastic views, filling farmhouse breakfasts. Close to Clarks village/Glastonbury. **Open:** All year **Grades:** ETC 4 Diamond **01458 445056 & 07884 498400 (M)** Ms Rood *rickham.house@talk21.com* **D:** Fr £25.00–£30.00 **S:** Fr £30.00 **Beds:** 2D **Baths:** 2 En

Planning a longer stay? Always ask for any special rates

Cranmore

ST6643

Burnt House Farm, *Waterlip, Cranmore, Shepton Mallet, Somerset, BA4 4RN.* Amazing breakfasts in happy cottage-style period farmhouse. Tea/cake on arrival. Wine for multiple night stays. TVs in bedrooms. Full-sized snooker table. Hot hydro garden spa tub. Summerhouse. Organic farm. Organic home-made bread/jam. Great mid-Somerset location. ETC 4 Diamond Silver Award. **Open:** All year **01749 880280** Mr Hoddinott **Fax: 01749 880004 D:** Fr £22.00–£25.00 **S:** Fr £25.00–£30.00 **Beds:** 1F 1D 1T **Baths:** 1 En 2 Pr (4) (10)

Creech St Michael

ST2625

Creechbarn, *Vicarage Lane, Creech St Michael, Taunton, TA3 5PP.* Converted longbarn in rural location. Quiet. 3 mins M5 J25. **Open:** All year (not Xmas/New Year) **01823 443955** H M Humphreys **Fax: 01823 443509** *mick@somersite.co.uk* www.somersite.co.uk **D:** Fr £20.00–£22.00 **S:** Fr £27.00–£29.00 **Beds:** 1T 2D **Baths:** 1 En (4)

Crewkerne

ST4409

Manor Farm, *Wayford, Crewkerne, Somerset, TA18 8QL.* Beautiful Victorian home in a peaceful location with undulating views. **Open:** All year **Grades:** AA 4 Diamond **01460 78865 & 07767 620031 (M)** Mr Emery www.manorfarm.com **D:** Fr £22.00–£25.00 **S:** Fr £22.00–£25.00 **Beds:** 3F 1T **Baths:** 4 En (50)

Cricket St Thomas

ST3708

The Firs, *Crewkerne Road, Cricket St Thomas, Chard, Somerset, TA20 4BU.* Warm and friendly 'home from home' with beautiful countryside views. **Open:** All year **01460 65646 (also fax)** S Bright **D:** Fr £20.00 **S:** Fr £25.00 **Beds:** 1T 2D **Baths:** 1 En 2 Pr

Culbone

SS8448

Silcombe Farm, *Culbone, Porlock, Minehead, Somerset, TA24 8JN.* Comfortable secluded Exmoor farmhouse overlooking sea in beautiful walking country. **Open:** All year (not Xmas) **01643 862248** Mrs Richards **D:** Fr £20.00–£22.00 **S:** Fr £20.00 **Beds:** 1D 2T 1S **Baths:** 1 En 1 Sh (4) (6)

Curland
ST2717

The Spinney, *Curland, Taunton, Somerset, TA3 5SE.* Quality ensuite B&B with excellent evening meals (recommended). Convenient from M5 and A303. **Open:** All year
01460 234362 (also fax) Mr & Mrs Bartlett *bartlett.spinney@zetnet.co.uk* www.somerweb.co.uk/spinney-bb **D:** Fr £22.00–£24.00 **S:** Fr £30.00 **Beds:** 1F 1D 1T **Baths:** 3 En (6)

Doulting
ST6443

Temple House Farm, *Doulting, Shepton Mallet, Somerset, BA4 4RQ.* Listed farmhouse, warm welcome, close to East Somerset Railway and many other attractions. **Open:** All year
01749 880294 Mrs Reakes **D:** Fr £42.00 **S:** Fr £25.00 **Beds:** 1T 1D (5) (4)

Dulverton
SS9128

Springfield Farm, *Ashwick Lane, Dulverton, Somerset, TA22 9QD.* Ensuite accommodation with delicious meals. Ideal location for walking/touring Exmoor and North Devon. **Open:** Easter to Nov **Grades:** ETC 4 Diamond
01398 323722 (also fax) Mrs Vellacott *info@springfieldfarms.co.uk* www.springfieldfarms.co.uk **D:** Fr £22.50–£25.00 **S:** Fr £25.00–£35.00 **Beds:** 2D 1T/F **Baths:** 2 En 1 Pr (3) (3)

Winsbere House, *64 Battleton, Dulverton, Somerset, TA22 9HU.* Delightful private house. Lovely country views. Excellent location touring Exmoor. **Open:** All year (not Xmas/New Year) **Grades:** ETC 3 Diamond
01398 323278 Mrs Rawle *winsbere@btopenworld.com* www.exmoor.tv/winsberehouse.htm **D:** Fr £17.00–£22.50 **S:** Fr £20.00 **Beds:** 1T 2D **Baths:** 2 En 1 Sh (8) (3)

Paper Mill House, *32 Lady Street, Dulverton, Somerset, TA22 9DB.* 'Step back in time'. Historic house overlooking mill-leat, Barle Valley. **Open:** All year (not Xmas/New Year)
01398 323651 Mr Latchem **D:** Fr £20.00–£25.00 **S:** Fr £20.00–£25.00 **Beds:** 1T 2D 1S **Baths:** 2 Pr

Town Mills, *Dulverton, Somerset, TA22 9HB.* Enjoy English breakfast served in your spacious comfortable bedroom. Relax. **Open:** All year
01398 323124 J Buckingham *townmills@onetel.co.uk* **D:** Fr £20.00–£27.00 **S:** Fr £25.00–£42.00 **Beds:** 1T 4D **Baths:** 3 En 2 Sh (5)

Highercombe Farm, *Dulverton, Somerset, TA22 9PT.* On the very edge of expansive moorland, you will find our welcoming farmhouse home. **Open:** Mar to Nov
01398 323616 (also fax) Mrs Humphrey *abigail@highercombe.demon.co.uk* www.highercombe.demon.co.uk **D:** Fr £20.00 **S:** Fr £28.00 **Beds:** 2D 1T **Baths:** 3 En (6)

Dunster
SS9943

Spears Cross Hotel, *1 West Street, Dunster, Minehead, Somerset, TA24 6SN.* Family-run C15th hotel in picturesque medieval village of Dunster. **Open:** All year **Grades:** ETC 4 Diamond, Silver
01643 821439 Mr & Mrs Capel *mjcapel@aol.com* www.smoothhound.co.uk/hotels/spearsx.html **D:** Fr £24.00–£27.50 **S:** Fr £30.00–£35.00 **Beds:** 2F 1T 1D **Baths:** 4 En (5) cc

Buttercross, *St Georges Street, Dunster, Minehead, Somerset, TA24 6RS.* Quiet location, close to village centre. Spacious period home. **Open:** All year (not Xmas/New Year)
01643 821413 S M Buck *megabucks@buttercross39.freeserve.co.uk* **D:** Fr £20.00–£25.00 **S:** Fr £20.00–£25.00 **Beds:** 1F 1D **Baths:** 1 En 1 Sh (10)

East Chinnock
ST4913

The Gables Guest House, *High Street, East Chinnock, Yeovil, Somerset, BA22 9DR.* 300-year-old cottage on A30 between Yeovil and Crewkerne. Cream teas and home cooking. **Open:** All year (not Xmas/New Year)
01935 862237 (also fax) L W J Jones **D:** Fr £18.00–£20.00 **S:** Fr £18.00–£20.00 **Beds:** 1F 2T 2D **Baths:** 3 En (6)

East Horrington
ST5746

Manor Farm, *Old Frome Road, East Horrington, Wells, BA5 3DP.* Guaranteed warm welcome to our stunning C15th Listed farmhouse. Abundant period features. **Open:** All year
01749 679832 & 07774 733702 (M) Mrs Fridd **Fax: 01749 679849** *fridd@fridd-wells.freeserve.co.uk* **D:** Fr £25.00 **S:** Fr £30.00 **Beds:** 2T **Baths:** 1 En 1 Pr (3)

East Lambrook
ST4318

East Lambrook Farm, *East Lambrook, South Petherton, Somerset, TA13 5HH.* C17th thatched farmhouse. Quiet, comfortable, excellent breakfasts, large garden, tennis. **Open:** All year (not Xmas)
01460 240064 Mrs Eeles **D:** Fr £24.00–£26.00 **S:** Fr £24.00–£26.00 **Beds:** 2D 1T **Baths:** 2 Pr (3) (3)

East Pennard
ST5937

Pennard Hill Farm, *Stickleball Hill, East Pennard, Shepton Mallet, Somerset, BA4 6UG.* Total luxury and tranquillity. Breathtaking views. Ravishing outdoor pool. **Open:** All year
01749 890221 Mrs Judah **Fax: 01749 890665** *phebejudah@aol.com* **D:** Fr £50.00–£80.00 **S:** Fr £70.00–£140.00 **Beds:** 1T 4D 3S **Baths:** 3 En 2 Pr 3 Sh

Exford
SS8538

Stockleigh Lodge, *Exford, Minehead, Somerset, TA24 7PZ.* **Open:** All year **Grades:** RAC 3 Diamond
01643 831500 Fax: 01643 831595 *myra@stockleighexford.freeserve.co.uk* www.stockleighexford.freeserve.co.uk **D:** Fr £20.00–£25.00 **S:** Fr £25.00–£35.00 **Beds:** 2F 2T 3D 2S **Baths:** 9 En (12) cc
A large country house set in its own wooded grounds. Being in the centre of Exmoor National Park, ideally located for exploring on foot, horseback or car. Stabling available for riders to bring their own horse on holiday.

Court Farm, *Exford, Minehead, Somerset, TA24 7LY.* In the heart of Exmoor. **Open:** All year (not Xmas/New Year)
01643 831207 (also fax) Mr & Mrs Horstmann *beth@courtfarm.co.uk* www.courtfarm.co.uk **D:** Fr £18.00 **S:** Fr £18.00 **Beds:** 1T 1D **Baths:** 1 Sh (15) cc

Planning a longer stay? Always ask for any special rates

Edgcott House, *Exford, Minehead, Somerset, TA24 7QG.* Old country house, peacefully situated in heart of Exmoor National Park. **Open:** All year (not Xmas/New Year)
01643 831495 (also fax) G Lamble **D:** Fr £20.00–£23.00 **S:** Fr £20.00–£23.00 **Beds:** 1T 2D **Baths:** 1 En 2 Pr (6)

Exton

SS9233

Exton House Hotel, *Exton, Dulverton, Somerset, TA22 9JT.* A small family-run hotel set amidst wonderful scenery on the side of Exton valley. **Open:** All year
01643 851365 Mr & Mrs Glaister **Fax: 01643 851213 D:** Fr £25.00–£32.50 **S:** Fr £32.50 **Beds:** 3F 4D 1T 1S **Baths:** 8 En 1 Pr (9) cc

Frome

ST7747

Wadbury House, *Mells, Frome, Somerset, BA11 3PA.* Historic house, quiet surroundings, outdoor heated pool & winter log fires. **Open:** All year **Grades:** ETC 3 Diamond
01373 812359 Mrs Brinkmann *sbrinkman@btinternet.com* **D:** Fr £28.00–£36.00 **S:** Fr £28.00–£36.00 **Beds:** 1F 2T 2D **Baths:** 3 En 1 Pr (10)

Kensington Lodge Hotel, *The Butts, Frome, Somerset, BA11 4AA.* Comfortable hotel fitness and leisure facilities near Bath, Longleat, Cheddar Caves. **Open:** All year
01373 463935 Mr Aryan **Fax: 01373 303570** *irajaryan@aol.com* **D:** Fr £25.00 **S:** Fr £30.00–£40.00 **Beds:** 1F 2D 3T 1S **Baths:** 6 En (40)

Glastonbury

ST5039

Meadow Barn, *Middlewick Holiday Cottages, Wick Lane, Glastonbury, Somerset, BA6 8JW.* **Open:** All year (not Xmas)
01458 832351 & 07855 120580 (M)
Mrs Shirley Kavanagh **Fax: 01458 832351** *info@middlewickholidaycottages.co.uk* www.s.-h-systems.co.uk/212436 **D:** Fr £24.00–£26.00 **S:** Fr £30.00–£32.00 **Beds:** 1F/T 1D **Baths:** 2 En
Tastefully converted barn, ground floor ensuite accommodation. Set in 8 acres of orchards and gardens, with far reaching views over the Mendips. Complemented by an indoor heated swimming pool. Within walking distance of the famed Glastonbury Tor.

Lottisham Manor, *Glastonbury, Somerset, BA6 8PF.* C16th manor house. Lovely garden. Hard tennis court. Perfect peace and comfort. **Open:** All year
01458 850205 Mrs Barker-Harland **D:** Fr £17.50–£20.00 **S:** Fr £17.50–£20.00 **Beds:** 1D 1T 1S **Baths:** 2 Sh (8)

Pippin, *4 Ridgeway Gardens, Glastonbury, Somerset, BA6 8ER.* Every comfort in peaceful home opposite Chalice Hill. Short walk Tor/town. **Open:** All year **Grades:** ETC 3 Diamond
01458 834262 Mrs Slater *daphneslater@talk21.com* www.smoothhound.co.uk/hotels/pippin.html **D:** Fr £17.50–£19.00 **S:** Fr £20.00–£22.00 **Beds:** 1D 1T **Baths:** 1 Sh (2)

Hillclose, *Street Road, Glastonbury, Somerset, BA6 9EG.* Warm friendly atmosphere, clean rooms, comfortable beds, full English breakfast. **Open:** All year (not Xmas)
01458 831040 (also fax) Mr & Mrs Riddle *hillclose@talk21.com* **D:** Fr £18.00–£25.00 **S:** Fr £25.00–£40.00 **Beds:** 1F 2D 1T **Baths:** 2 Sh (4)

Court Lodge, *Butleigh, Glastonbury, Somerset, BA6 8SA.* Attractive modernised 1850 lodge. In picturesque garden, edge of Butleigh. 3m Glastonbury, Street. **Open:** All year (not Xmas)
01458 850575 Mrs Atkinson **D:** Fr £16.50 **S:** Fr £16.50 **Beds:** 1D 1S **Baths:** 2 En

Shambhala Healing Centre, *Coursing Batch, Glastonbury, Somerset, BA6 8BH.* Beautiful house, sacred site on side of the Tor. Healing, massage, great vegetarian food. **Open:** All year
01458 833081 & 01458 831797 Mrs Nixon **Fax: 01458 831797** *isisandargon@shambhala.co.uk* **D:** Fr £64.00 **S:** Fr £35.00 **Beds:** 2T 2D 1S **Baths:** 2 En 2 Sh cc

Little Orchard, *Ashwell Lane, Glastonbury, Somerset, BA6 8BG.* Glastonbury, famous for historic Tor, King Arthur, abbey ruins and alternative centre. **Open:** All year
01458 831620 Mrs Gifford www.smoothhound.co.uk/hotels/orchard.html **D:** Fr £16.50–£21.00 **S:** Fr £17.00–£22.00 **Beds:** 1F 1D 1T 2S **Baths:** 2 Sh

National Grid References given are for villages, towns and cities – not for individual houses

Blake House, *3 Bove Town, Glastonbury, Somerset, BA6 8JE.* Listed stone house, close to town centre and all attractions. **Open:** All year (not Xmas/New Year)
01458 831680 S Hankins *dshankins@ukonline.co.uk* www.blake-house.co.uk **D:** Fr £20.00–£22.00 **S:** Fr £25.00–£30.00 **Beds:** 1T 2D **Baths:** 3 En (2)

1 The Gables, *Street Road, Glastonbury, Somerset, BA6 9EG.* One minute from town centre. Good English breakfast. **Open:** All year (not Xmas/New Year)
01458 832519 Mrs Stott **D:** Fr £17.00 **S:** Fr £17.00 **Beds:** 1F 1T 2D **Baths:** 1 Sh

Divine Light, *16a Magdelene Street, Glastonbury, Somerset, BA6 9EH.* Central. Listed. Guest kitchen, lounge, terraced garden. Healing and massage. **Open:** All year
01458 835909 Mr & Mrs Flanagan *info@glastonburyrose.co.uk* www.divinelightcentre.co.uk **D:** Fr £20.00–£25.00 **S:** Fr £30.00–£35.00 **Beds:** 1T 1D **Baths:** 1 Sh

Godney

ST4842

Double Gate Farm, *Godney, Wells, Somerset, BA5 1RX.* Comfortable, friendly, award-winning accommodation. Delicious breakfasts. **Open:** All year (not Xmas/New Year)
01458 832217 Mrs Millard **Fax: 01458 835612** *doublegatefarm@aol.com* www.doublegatefarm.com **D:** Fr £27.50 **S:** Fr £35.00 **Beds:** 1F 3D 2T **Baths:** 6 En (8)

Greenham

ST0720

Greenham Hall, *Greenham, Wellington, Somerset, TA21 0JJ.* Impressive Victorian turreted house with an informal friendly atmosphere. **Open:** All year
01823 672603 Mrs Ayre **Fax: 01823 672307** *greenhamhall@btopenworld.com* www.greenhamhall.co.uk **D:** Fr £22.50–£25.00 **S:** Fr £30.00–£35.00 **Beds:** 1F 3D 2T 1S **Baths:** 4 En 1 Pr 2 Sh

Gurney Slade

ST6249

Lilac Cottage, *Gurney Slade, Bath, BA3 4TT.* Charming C18th house in village location between Bath and Wells. **Open:** All year **Grades:** AA 2 Diamond
01749 840469 Mrs Anderson *lilaccotbandb@aol.com* **D:** Fr £20.00–£25.00 **S:** Fr £20.00–£25.00 **Beds:** 1F 2D 1T **Baths:** 1 En 1 Sh

Halse

ST1327

New Inn, *Halse, Taunton, Somerset, TA4 3AF.* Typical village inn, friendly atmosphere, relax and enjoy excellent home cooked fayre. **Open:** All year
01823 432352 Ms Hayes **D:** Fr £18.00–£21.00 **S:** Fr £20.00–£35.00 **Beds:** 2T 3D 5S **Baths:** 6 En 4 Sh P ⊬ TV ✕ ▥ ☕ **cc**

Hatch Beauchamp

ST2920

The Hatch Inn, *Hatch Beauchamp, Taunton, Somerset, TA3 6SG.* Situated in heart of village, we've been offering 'inn' hospitality for over 200 years. **Open:** All year
01823 480245 Fax: 01823 481104 *nicole@thehatchinn.co.uk* www.thehatchinn.co.uk **D:** Fr £30.00 **S:** Fr £30.00 **Beds:** 2F 6D **Baths:** 8 En P (26) ⊬ TV ✕ V ▥ ✻ ☕ **cc**

Hawkridge

SS8530

East Hollowcombe Farm, *Hawkridge, Dulverton, Somerset, TA22 9QL.* Ideal Two Moors Way, views open moorland. Home cooked meals, fresh veg from garden. **Open:** All year (not Xmas/New Year)
01398 341622 H Floyd **D:** Fr £14.00 **S:** Fr £17.50 **Beds:** 1F 1T 1D 1S **Baths:** 1 Sh ♨ P (8) TV ♞ ✕ V ▥ ☕

Henstridge

ST7219

Quiet Corner Farm, *Henstridge, Somerset, BA8 0RA.* Country house atmosphere with lovely garden; imaginative breakfasts. Recommended by 'Which?'. **Open:** All year **Grades:** ETC 4 Diamond
01963 363045 (also fax) Mrs Thompson *quietcorner.thompson@virgin.net* **D:** Fr £22.00–£25.00 **S:** Fr £28.00–£30.00 **Beds:** 1F 2D **Baths:** 1 En 1 Sh ♨ P (8) ⊬ TV V ▥ ☕

Fountain Inn Motel, *High Street, Henstridge, Templecombe, Somerset, BA8 0RA.* Friendly village inn with modern ensuite accommodation, ideal touring base. Discounts for 3+ nights. **Open:** All year **Grades:** ETC 2 Diamond
01963 362722 Sue Petts *sue@fountaininnmotel.com* **D:** Fr £22.50–£25.00 **S:** Fr £27.50–£30.00 **Beds:** 5D 1T **Baths:** 6 En ♨ P (30) TV ♞ ✕ V ▥ ♿ ☕

Henton

ST4945 *The Pheasant, Panborough Inn, Burcott Inn*

Rose Farm, *Henton, Wells, Somerset, BA5 1PD.* You will be well looked after at our lovely Georgian farmhouse, overlooking the Mendip Hills. Just outside the beautiful city of Wells. Cheddar, Glastonbury, Street and coast are all nearby. Delicious breakfasts served by Inglenook fireplace. Attractive, stylish accommodation. **Open:** All year (not Xmas/New Year)
01749 672908 Mrs Doherty *rosefarm5@yahoo.co.uk* **D:** Fr £23.00–£25.50 **Beds:** 1D **Baths:** 1 En P (2) ⊬ V ▥ ☕

Hinton St George

ST4212

Rookwood, *West Street, Hinton St George, Somerset, TA17 8SA.* Comfortable accommodation in tranquil setting, Listed NGS Garden. **Open:** All year (not Xmas/New Year)
01460 73450 Mrs Hudspith *betty.hudspith@virgin.net* **D:** Fr £19.00–£20.00 **S:** Fr £20.00 **Beds:** 2T **Baths:** 1 En 1 Pr ♨ (10) P (2) ⊬ TV ▥ ☕

Ludneymead, *Hinton St George, Somerset, TA17 8TD.* Family run farm close to many attractions. Secluded, peaceful, open views. **Open:** Easter to Oct
01460 57145 Mrs Chapman **D:** Fr £19.00–£21.00 **Beds:** 1D **Baths:** 1 Pr TV ✕ V ☕

Howley

ST2609

Howley Tavern, *Howley, Chard, Somerset, TA20 3DX.* C16th free house. Idyllic setting overlooking the beautiful Yarty Valley. **Open:** All year
01460 62157 K Leaf **D:** Fr £25.00 **S:** Fr £29.50 **Beds:** 1F 1T 1D 1S **Baths:** 3 En ♨ P TV ♞ ✕ V ▥ ☕ **cc**

Hutton

ST3458

Moorlands Country Guest House, *Hutton, Weston-super-Mare, Somerset, BS24 9QH.* Fine Georgian house, extensive landscaped gardens, village pub serves meals. **Open:** All year **Grades:** ETC 3 Diamond
01934 812283 (also fax) Mrs Holt *margaret_holt@email.com* www.guestaccom.co.uk **D:** Fr £20.00–£26.00 **S:** Fr £20.00–£31.00 **Beds:** 3F 2D 1T 1S **Baths:** 5 En 1 Sh ♨ P (7) TV ♞ V ▥ ♿3 ☕ **cc**

Ilminster

ST3614

Hermitage, *29 Station Road, Ilminster, Somerset, TA19 9BE.* Friendly Listed C17th house. Beams, inglenooks, four-posters. 2 acres delightful garden. **Open:** All year (not Xmas) **Grades:** ETC 3 Diamond
01460 53028 G Phillips www.smoothhound.co.uk/hotels/hermitagebb.html **D:** Fr £19.00–£22.00 **S:** Fr £22.00–£36.00 **Beds:** 1T 1D **Baths:** 1 En P (2) TV V ☕

Hylands, *22 New Road, Ilminster, Somerset, TA19 9AF.* Attractive Edwardian end-of-terrace. Small country town. Family home **Open:** All year (not Xmas/New Year)
01460 52560 Mrs Hayter *hayterbandb@talk21.com* **D:** Fr £12.50–£15.00 **S:** Fr £15.00 **Beds:** 1F 1D **Baths:** 2 Sh ♨ P (2) ⊬ TV V ▥

Kilve

ST1443

The Old Rectory, *Kilve, Bridgwater, Somerset, TA5 1DZ.* Foot of Quantocks; scenic walking/touring, local beach, pub, comfortable. **Open:** All year (not Xmas)
01278 741520 Chris & Jan Alder *oldrectorykilve@yahoo.co.uk* **D:** Fr £22.00–£25.00 **S:** Fr £20.00–£25.00 **Beds:** 1F 1D 1T **Baths:** 3 En P (4) TV ▥ ☕

Kingston St Mary

ST2229

Lower Marsh Farm, *Kingston St Mary, Taunton, Somerset, TA2 8AB.* Warm welcome is assured at our tastefully refurbished. **Open:** All year
01823 451331 (also fax) Mr & Mrs Gothard *mail@lowermarshfarm.co.uk* www.lowermarshfarm.co.uk **D:** Fr £22.50–£25.00 **S:** Fr £25.00–£28.00 **Beds:** 1F 1T 1D **Baths:** 2 En 1 Pr ♨ P ⊬ TV ✕ ▥ ☕

Kingweston

ST5230

Lower Farm, *Kingweston, Somerton, Somerset, TA11 6BA.* Comfortable well-equipped rooms, excellent Aga breakfasts, friendly helpful hosts. **Open:** All year (not Xmas/New Year)
01458 223237 Mr & Mrs Sedgman **Fax: 01458 223276** *lowerfarm@kingweston.demon.co.uk* lowerfarm.net **D:** Fr £25.00–£30.00 **S:** Fr £27.50–£45.00 **Beds:** 1D 1T 1F **Baths:** 2 En 1 Pr ♨ P ⊬ TV V ▥ ☕

Planning a longer stay? Always ask for any special rates

Langport

ST4126

Amberley, *Long Load, Langport, Somerset, TA10 9LD.* Quality accommodation with far-reaching views on edge of Somerset Levels. **Open:** All year (not Xmas) **01458 241542** Ms Jarvis *jeanatamberley@talk21.com* **D:** Fr £17.00–£18.00 **S:** Fr £17.00–£18.00 **Beds:** 1F 1T 1D **Baths:** 1 En 1 Sh (4)

Long Load

ST4623

Fairlight, *Martock Road, Long Load, Langport, Somerset, TA10 9LG.* Detached bungalow, magnificent views. 2.5 acre garden, orchard & plantation. **Open:** All year (not Xmas/New Year) **01458 241323** Mrs Hook **D:** Fr £17.50–£18.50 **S:** Fr £18.50–£19.00 **Beds:** 1D 1T **Baths:** 1 En 1 Pr (10) (6)

Mark

ST3747

Laurel Farm, *The Causeway, Mark, Highbridge, Somerset, TA9 4PZ.* Farmhouse over 300 years old. Ideal for touring or overnight stops. **Open:** All year **Grades:** ETC 3 Diamond **01278 641216 Fax: 01278 641447 D:** Fr £18.00–£22.00 **S:** Fr £19.00–£22.00 **Beds:** 1F 1T 1D **Baths:** 3 En

Martock

ST4619 *Nag's Head*

Madey Mills, *Martock, Somerset, TA12 6NN.* Peaceful accommodation on working dairy farm, country views, riverside walk. **Open:** All year **01935 823268** Ms Clarke **D:** Fr £18.00 **S:** Fr £18.00 **Beds:** 1D 1S

The Nags Head, *East Street, Martock, Somerset, TA12 6NF.* The Nags Head is a charming village pub which dates back over 150 years. **Open:** All year **01935 823432 Fax: 01935 824265 D:** Fr £25.00 **S:** Fr £30.00 **Beds:** 1F **Baths:** 1 En (24) **cc**

Mells

ST7249

Wadbury House, *Mells, Frome, Somerset, BA11 3PA.* Historic house, quiet surroundings, outdoor heated pool & winter log fires. **Open:** All year **Grades:** ETC 3 Diamond **01373 812359** Mrs Brinkmann *sbrinkman@btinternet.com* **D:** Fr £28.00–£36.00 **S:** Fr £28.00–£36.00 **Beds:** 1F 2T 2D **Baths:** 3 En 1 Pr (10)

The Talbot 15th Cenury Coaching Inn, *Mells, Frome, Somerset, BA11 3PN.* Beautiful coaching inn with ensuite and 4-poster bedrooms, tythe barn bar, award-winning oak-beamed restaurant and private cobbled courtyard. Located just south of Bath on the Mendip Hills, ideal for tourists, weddings, meetings and functions. **Open:** All year **01373 812254 Fax: 01373 813599** *roger@talbotinn.com* www.talbotinn.com **D:** Fr £35.00–£37.50 **S:** Fr £39.50–£45.00 **Beds:** 1F 3T 4D **Baths:** 7 En 1 Pr (10) **cc**

Midsomer Norton

ST6554

Ellsworth, *Fosseway, Midsomer Norton, Bath, Somerset, BA3 4AU.* Situated on the A367 on Somerset border 9 miles from city of Bath. **Open:** All year **01761 412305 (also fax)** Mrs Gentle *accommodation@ellsworth.fsbusiness.co.uk* www.ellsworth.fsbusiness.co.uk **D:** Fr £25.00–£30.00 **S:** Fr £25.00–£35.00 **Beds:** 2F 2T 3D **Baths:** 7 En (2) (4)

Minehead

SS9646

Hindon Organic Farm, *Minehead, Exmoor, Somerset, TA24 8SH.* Stay in farm style & comfort. Organic hospitality & shop. **Open:** All year (not Xmas/New Year) **01643 705244 (also fax)** Mrs Webber *info@hindonfarm.co.uk* www.hindonfarm.co.uk **D:** Fr £28.50–£30.00 **S:** Fr £28.50–£30.00 **Beds:** 1T 2D **Baths:** 1 Pr (6)

Old Ship Aground, *The Quay, Minehead, Somerset, TA24 5UL.* Located on the harbour, well-placed for Exmoor and coast. **Open:** All year **01643 702087** A Phillips **Fax: 01643 709066** *enquiries@oldshipaground.co.uk* oldshipaground.co.uk **D:** Fr £20.00–£25.00 **S:** Fr £25.00–£30.00 **Beds:** 3F 3T 4D 2S **Baths:** 12 En (3) **cc**

Beaconwood Hotel, *Church Road, North Hill, Minehead, Somerset, TA24 5SB.* Edwardian country house hotel, set in 2 acres of terraced gardens with panoramic views. **Open:** All year **01643 702032 (also fax)** Mr Roberts *beaconwood@madasafish.com* www.beaconwoodhotel.co.uk **D:** Fr £30.00–£35.00 **S:** Fr £33.00–£40.00 **Beds:** 2F 6D 6T **Baths:** 14 En (25) * **cc**

Planning a longer stay? Always ask for any special rates

Wyndcott Hotel, *Martlet Road, Minehead, Somerset, TA24 5QE.* A superb country house hotel adjacent to beach and Exmoor. **Open:** All year (not Xmas/New Year) **01643 704522 Fax: 01634 707577** *mineheadhotel@msn.com* **D:** Fr £35.00–£55.00 **S:** Fr £30.00–£40.00 **Beds:** 2F 4T 4D 1S **Baths:** 11 En (8) **cc**

Moorlands BandB, *Moor Road, Minehead, Somerset, TA24 5RT.* Elevated position, panoramic views. Warm welcome. Wonderful Exmoor touring base. **Open:** All year (not Xmas/New Year) **01643 703453** Mrs Beakes *moorlands@amserve.net* **D:** Fr £17.50 **Beds:** 1T 2D **Baths:** 1 Sh (12) (3)

1 Glenmore Road, *Minehead, Somerset, TA24 5BQ.* Superior Victorian family-run guest house, excellent range of breakfasts including vegetarian. **Open:** All year **01643 706225** Mrs Sanders **D:** Fr £17.00–£19.00 **S:** Fr £17.00 **Beds:** 1F 1D 1T 1S **Baths:** 2 En 1 Sh (6) (2)

St Audries Bay Holiday Park, *West Quantockhead, Minehead, Somerset, TA4 4DY.* Family holiday centre overlooking sea. Indoor pool. Entertainment. Licensed restaurant. **Open:** May to Oct **01984 632515 Fax: 01984 632785** *mrandle@staudriesbay.co.uk* www.staudriesbay.co.uk **D:** Fr £22.00–£34.00 **Beds:** 20F 20T 20D 20S **Baths:** 80 En **cc**

Monkton Combe

ST7762

The Manor House, *Monkton Combe, Bath, BA2 7HD.* Restful rambling medieval manor by millstream in Area of Outstanding Natural Beauty. **Open:** All year **01225 723128** Mrs Hartley **Fax: 01225 722972** *beth@manorhousebath.co.uk* www.manorhousebath.co.uk **D:** Fr £22.50–£35.00 **S:** Fr £30.00–£35.00 **Beds:** 2F 5D 1T **Baths:** 8 En (12) 2

Montacute

ST4916

Mad Hatters Tea Rooms, *1 South Street, Montacute, Somerset, TA15 6XD.* Listed Georgian property in picturesque village. Idyllic walks, Near NT properties. **Open:** All year **01935 823024** Mrs Hicken **D:** Fr £17.50–£21.00 **S:** Fr £23.00–£29.00 **Beds:** 1D 1T 1S **Baths:** 1 Pr 2 En

National Grid References given are for villages, towns and cities – not for individual houses

Nether Stowey

ST1839

Apple Tree Hotel, *Keenthorne, Nether Stowey, Bridgwater, TA5 1HZ.* Quiet country hotel, offering quality accommodation & cuisine. Fully licensed. **Open:** All year (not Xmas/New Year) **Grades:** AA 2 Star **01278 733238 Fax: 01278 732693** *appletreehotel@hotmail.com* www.appletreehotel.com **D:** Fr £30.00–£35.00 **S:** Fr £40.00–£50.00 **Beds:** 2F 2T 6D 4S **Baths:** 14 En (30) cc

North Cadbury

ST6327

Ashlea House, *High Street, North Cadbury, Yeovil, Somerset, BA22 7DP.* 1 km A303, centre village, highly commended service, accommodation, home cooking. **Open:** All year (not Xmas/New Year) **01963 440891** Mr & Mrs Wade *ashlea@btinternet.com* www.ashlea.btinternet.co.uk **D:** Fr £22.00–£25.00 **S:** Fr £25.00–£27.00 **Beds:** 1T 1D **Baths:** 1 En 1 Pr (2)

North Perrott

ST4709

The Manor Arms, *North Perrott, Crewkerne, TA18 7SG.* Lovely C16th Listed inn overlooking village green, high standard of ensuite accommodation. **Open:** All year **01460 72901 (also fax)** Mr Gilmore *info@manorarmshotel.co.uk* www.manorarmshotel.co.uk **D:** Fr £19.00–£24.00 **S:** Fr £35.00–£38.00 **Beds:** 1F 5D 3T **Baths:** 9 En (24) cc

North Petherton

ST2832

Quantock View House, *Bridgwater Road, North Petherton, Bridgwater, Somerset, TA6 6PR.* Central for Cheddar, Wells, Glastonbury, the Quantocks and the sea. **Open:** All year **01278 663309** Mrs Howlett & Mrs Terry *irene@quantockview.freeserve.co.uk* www.quantock view.freeserve.co.uk **D:** Fr £19.00–£23.00 **S:** Fr £23.00–£27.00 **Beds:** 2F 1D 1T **Baths:** 4 En (8) cc

The Walnut Tree Hotel, *North Petherton, Bridgwater, TA6 6QA.* Set in heart of Somerset; fully modernised coaching inn, 2 restaurants; ideal touring location. **Open:** All year (not Xmas) **01278 662255** Mr Goulden **Fax: 01278 663946** *info@walnuttreehotel.com* www.walnuttreehotel.com **D:** Fr £37.50–£42.50 **S:** Fr £62.00–£75.00 **Beds:** 5F 21D 5T **Baths:** 32 En (72) 2 cc

North Wootton

ST5641

Riverside Grange, *Tanyard Lane, North Wootton, Wells, Somerset, BA4 4AE.* A charming converted tannery, quietly situated on the River edge. **Open:** All year **01749 890761** Mrs English **D:** Fr £19.50–£22.00 **S:** Fr £25.00–£29.00 **Beds:** 1D 1T **Baths:** 2 Pr (6)

Norton-sub-Hamdon

ST4715

Courtfield, *Norton-sub-Hamdon, Stoke-sub-Hamdon, Somerset, TA14 6SG.* Comfortable, relaxed, peaceful. Breakfast in conservatory. Special accommodation, beautiful gardens. **Open:** All year (not Xmas) **01935 881246** Mrs Constable *courtfield@hotmail.com* **D:** Fr £25.00–£28.00 **S:** Fr £38.00 **Beds:** 1D 1T **Baths:** 2 Pr (8) (4)

Brook House, *Norton-sub-Hamdon, Stoke-sub-Hamdon, Somerset, TA14 6SR.* Gracious Georgian family home in unspoilt quiet Hamstone village with pub providing good food. **Open:** Easter to Nov **01935 881789 (also fax)** Mr & Mrs Fisher **D:** Fr £25.00 **S:** Fr £35.00 **Beds:** 1D 1T **Baths:** 2 Pr (10) (2)

Peasedown St John

ST7057 *Prince of Wales*

Eastfield Farm and Guest House, *Dunkerton Hill, Peasedown St John, Bath, Somerset, BA2 8PF.* Peaceful, sturdy house set in 3 acres. Beautiful views. **Open:** Easter to Oct **01761 432161** Mrs Newland **D:** Fr £17.00–£20.00 **S:** Fr £24.00–£30.00 **Beds:** 1F 1T 1D **Baths:** 3 Sh (4)

Peasmarsh

ST3412

Graden, *Peasmarsh, Donyatt, Ilminster, Somerset, TA19 0SG.* Comfortable house in rural situation, close to Somerset, Devon & Dorset border. **Open:** All year **01460 52371** G E Bond **D:** Fr £16.00–£34.00 **S:** Fr £17.00–£18.00 **Beds:** 1F 1T 2D **Baths:** 2 En

Pilton

ST5940

The Long House, *Pylle Road, Pilton, Shepton Mallet, Somerset, BA4 4BP.* Picturesque, quiet village. Friendly, comfortable, unpretentious. **Open:** All year (not Xmas/New Year) **01749 890701** Mr & Mrs Case **D:** Fr £40.00–£65.00 **S:** Fr £27.00–£35.00 **Beds:** 1F 1D 1T **Baths:** 3 En (10) (7)

Porlock

SS8846

West Porlock House, *Country House Hotel, West Porlock, Porlock, Minehead, Somerset, TA24 8NX.* Superbly set in beautiful woodland garden with magnificent sea views. **Open:** Feb to Nov **Grades:** ETC 4 Diamond **01643 862880** Mrs Dyer **D:** Fr £26.00–£28.00 **S:** Fr £30.00 **Beds:** 1F 2D 2T **Baths:** 2 En 3 Pr (6) (8) cc

Sparkhayes Farm House, *Sparkhayes Lane, Porlock, Minehead, Somerset, TA24 8NE.* Character farmhouse accommodation in the captivating Exmoor village of Porlock. **Open:** All year (not Xmas/New Year) **01643 862765 (also fax)** Mr Weaver *dlatham123@aol.com* www.sparkhayesfarmhouse.co.uk **D:** Fr £22.00–£23.00 **Beds:** 1F 1D **Baths:** 2 En (8) (3)

Silcombe Farm, *Culbone, Porlock, Minehead, Somerset, TA24 8JN.* Comfortable secluded Exmoor farmhouse overlooking sea in beautiful walking country. **Open:** All year (not Xmas) **01643 862248** Mrs Richards **D:** Fr £20.00–£22.00 **S:** Fr £20.00 **Beds:** 1D 2T 1S **Baths:** 1 En 1 Sh (4) (6)

Hurlstone, *Sparkhayes Lane, Porlock, Minehead, Somerset, TA24 8NE.* Quiet house near village centre sea and moorland views. **Open:** All year (not Xmas) **01643 862650** Mrs Coombs **D:** Fr £18.00 **S:** Fr £18.00 **Beds:** 1D 1T **Baths:** 1 Sh

Overstream Hotel, *Parsons Street, Porlock, Minehead, Somerset, TA24 8QJ.* Situated in the centre of Porlock, between Exmoor and the sea. **Open:** Easter to Nov **01643 862421 (also fax) D:** Fr £21.00–£30.00 **S:** Fr £30.00 **Beds:** 1F 2T 4D 2S **Baths:** 9 En

Leys, *The Ridge, Bossington Lane, Porlock, Minehead, Somerset, TA24 8HA.* Beautiful family home, delightful garden, with magnificent views. **Open:** All year (not Xmas) **01643 862477 (also fax)** Mrs Stiles-Cox **D:** Fr £19.00 **S:** Fr £19.00 **Beds:** 1D/T 2S **Baths:** 1 Sh (4)

Puriton

ST3241

Rockfield House, *Puriton Hill, Puriton, Bridgwater, Somerset, TA7 8AG.* Just off M5 (J23). Good food and friendly atmosphere. **Open:** All year (not Xmas)
01278 683561 (also fax) Mrs Pipkin *rockfieldhouse@talk21.com* **D:** Fr £16.00–£20.00 **S:** Fr £16.00 **Beds:** 1F 1D 1T 1S **Baths:** 2 En 1 Sh (5)

Roadwater

ST0338

Wood Advent Farm, *Roadwater, Watchet, Somerset, TA23 0RR.* **Open:** All year (not Xmas/New Year)
01984 640920 (also fax) *info@woodadventfarm.co.uk* www.woodadventfarm.co.uk **D:** Fr £22.50–£25.50 **S:** Fr £25.00–£35.00 **Beds:** 2T 3D **Baths:** 3 En 2 Pr (10) (10) cc
Relax in peaceful Exmoor, enjoy the tranquillity of our beautiful home in acres of open countryside. Explore Dunster Castle, Selworthy, the steam train, take walks from the farm, returning for tea and a swim. Indulge at night in our licensed dining room.

Saltford

ST6866

Long Reach House Hotel, *321 Bath Road, Saltford, Bristol, BS31 1TJ.* Gracious house standing in 2 acres midway between Bath and Bristol. **Open:** All year
01225 400500 Fax: 01225 400700 *lrhouse@aol.com* bath.co.uk.visitbritain.co.uk **D:** Fr £22.50–£45.00 **S:** Fr £45.00–£50.00 **Beds:** 2F 7T 7D 2S **Baths:** 18 En cc

Sandyway

SS7933

Barkham, *Sandy, Exmoor, Devon, EX36 3LU.* Tucked away in hidden valley in the heart of Exmoor. **Open:** All year (not Xmas)
01643 831370 (also fax) Mrs Adie *adie.exmoor@btinternet.com* holidays.exmoor.com **D:** Fr £28.00–£32.00 **Beds:** 2D 1S **Baths:** 2 En 1 Pr (12) (6)

Selworthy

SS9146

Selworthy Farm, *Selworthy, Minehead, Somerset, TA24 8TL.* Comfortable farmhouse, peaceful, ideal for exploring Exmoor. Walkers paradise. **Open:** Jan to Nov
01643 862577 Mrs Leeves **D:** Fr £20.00–£25.00 **S:** Fr £25.00 **Beds:** 1T 1D 1S **Baths:** 2 En (11) (3)

Shepton Mallet

ST6143

Park Farm House, *Forum Lane, Bowlish, Shepton Mallet, Somerset, BA4 5JL.* Comfortable C17th house with peaceful garden and private off-road parking. **Open:** All year
01749 343673 Fax: 01749 345279 *john.majorie@ukonline.co.uk* **D:** Fr £18.50 **Beds:** 2T 1D **Baths:** 1 En 2 Pr (3)

Belfield House, *34 Charlton Road, Shepton Mallet, Somerset, BA4 5PA.* Impressive Georgian house. Ideally situated for Mendips, Cheddar, Longleat and Bath **Open:** All year (not Xmas/New Year)
01749 344353 Mr & Mrs Smith *reservations@belfield-house.co.uk* www.belfield-house.co.uk **D:** Fr £20.00–£24.00 **S:** Fr £25.00–£30.00 **Beds:** 1F 2T 1D 2S **Baths:** 4 En 1 Sh (6) cc

Shipham

ST4457

Herongates, *Horseleaze Lane, Shipham, Winscombe, Somerset, BS25 1UQ.* Noted for quality, peaceful location. **Open:** All year (not Xmas/New Year)
01934 843280 Mrs Stickland **D:** Fr £15.50–£18.50 **S:** Fr £15.50–£18.50 **Beds:** 2D 1T **Baths:** 2 En 1 Pr (3)

Simonsbath

SS7739 *Poltimore Arms, Sportsman, Exmoor Forest Hotel*

Emmett's Grange Farm, *Simonsbath, Minehead, Somerset, TA24 7LD.* Emmett's Grange provides and oasis of friendly civilisation within its own 900 acres amidst the stunning wild and rugged Exmoor National Park. Luxurious B&B with moorland views. Guests own elegant drawing room. Gourmet food available and many local pubs. Fully licensed. **Open:** All year (not Xmas/New Year)
01643 831138 & 01643 831093 T Barlow **Fax: 01643 831138** *emmetts.grange@virgin.net* **D:** Fr £29.00–£38.00 **S:** Fr £34.00–£43.00 **Beds:** 1T 2D cc

South Petherton

ST4316

Watergore House, *Watergore, South Petherton, Somerset, TA13 5JG.* Picturesque old hamstone house with large garden just off A303. **Open:** All year (not Xmas)
01460 240677 (also fax) Mr & Mrs Gordon **D:** Fr £20.00 **S:** Fr £20.00 **Beds:** 2D 1T **Baths:** 2 Sh (6) (4)

Stanton Prior

ST6762

Poplar Farm, *Stanton Prior, Bath, BA2 9HX.* Spacious C17th farmhouse. Family-run farm. Idyllic village setting. **Open:** All year (not Xmas)
Grades: ETC 3 Diamond, AA 3 Diamond
01761 470382 (also fax) Mrs Hardwick *poplarfarm@talk21.com* www.poplarfarmbath.co.uk **D:** Fr £20.00–£30.00 **S:** Fr £20.00–£30.00 **Beds:** 1F 1D 1T **Baths:** 2 En (4) (6)

Stanton Wick

ST6061 *Carpenters' Arms*

Greenacres Guest House, *Stanton Wick, Pensford, Bristol, BS39 4BX.* Comfortable family home in rural hamlet. Convenient towns and touring. **Open:** All year
01761 490397 Mrs Bond **D:** Fr £20.00–£25.00 **S:** Fr £20.00–£25.00 **Beds:** 1F 1T 1D 2S **Baths:** 1 En 2 Sh (1)

Stathe

ST3728

Black Smock Inn, *Stathe, Bridgwater, Somerset, TA7 0JN.* Overlooking River Parrett. Panoramic views Somerset Levels. Home-made food speciality. **Open:** All year
01823 698352 Mr Horsham **Fax: 01823 690138** *blacksmock@aol.co.uk* www.blacksmock.co.uk **D:** Fr £17.50–£22.00 **S:** Fr £21.00–£26.00 **Beds:** 3D/T 1 S **Baths:** 2 En 1 Sh (30) cc

Stoke St Gregory

ST3427

Parsonage Farm, *Stoke St Gregory, Taunton, Somerset, TA3 6ET.* Georgian farmhouse situated on the Somerset Levels. Working dairy farm. **Open:** All year (not Xmas/New Year)
01823 698205 Mrs House **D:** Fr £17.00–£20.00 **S:** Fr £19.00–£23.00 **Beds:** 1F **Baths:** 1 Sh (2)

Stoke St Michael

ST6646

Stoke Bottom Farm, *Stoke St Michael, Bath, BA3 5HW.* Modern farm house, situated in beautiful valley. Half mile off A367 Bath-Exeter road. **Open:** All year (not Xmas/New Year)
01761 232273 **D:** Fr £17.50–£20.00 **S:** Fr £20.00–£25.00 **Beds:** 1F 1T **Baths:** 1 En 1 Pr (5) (2)

Stratton-on-the-Fosse

ST6650 *Ring O'Roses*

Oval House, *Stratton-on-the-Fosse, Bath, Somerset, BA3 4RB.* Charming, friendly C17th home, ideal for visiting Bath, etc. **Open:** All year (not Xmas/New Year)
01761 232183 (also fax) Mrs Mellotte *mellotte@clara.co.uk* www.mellotte.clara.co.uk **D:** Fr £19.00–£20.00 **S:** Fr £20.00 **Beds:** 1T 1S **Baths:** 2 Sh (10) cc

Taunton

ST2324

The Old Mill, *Bishops Hull, Taunton, Somerset, TA1 5AB.* **Open:** All year (not Xmas) **Grades:** ETC 5 Diamond, Silver
01823 289732 (also fax) Mr & Mrs Slipper **D:** Fr £24.00–£27.00 **S:** Fr £35.00 **Beds:** 2D **Baths:** 1 En 1 Pr
Grade II Listed former corn mill in lovely riverside setting, retaining many original workings. Two delightful bedrooms overlooking the river. Enjoy breakfast from our extensive menu amidst the wheels and cogs of a bygone era. Enjoyed by all who stay.

Yallands Farmhouse, *Staplegrove, Taunton, Somerset, TA2 6PZ.* **Open:** All year **Grades:** ETC 4 Diamond, Silver, AA 4 Diamond
01823 278979 Mr & Mrs Kirk *mail@yallands.co.uk* www.yallands.co.uk **D:** Fr £25.00–£29.00 **S:** Fr £32.00–£35.00 **Beds:** 1F 3D 1T 2S **Baths:** 7 En (6) cc
A warm welcome is assured at our beautiful C16th house. An oasis of 'Old England' close to town centre yet unexpectedly peaceful and secluded. Comfortable, attractive ensuite rooms with ground floor room available. Out of season discounts. Phone for brochure.

Lower Marsh Farm, *Kingston St Mary, Taunton, Somerset, TA2 8AB.* **Open:** All year **01823 451331 (also fax)** Mr & Mrs Gothard *mail@lowermarshfarm.co.uk* www.lowermarshfarm.co.uk **D:** Fr £22.50–£25.00 **S:** Fr £25.00–£28.00 **Beds:** 1F 1T 1D **Baths:** 2 En 1 Pr
Only 10 mins M5 J25. A warm welcome is assured at our tastefully refurbished farmhouse on a working farm overlooking the vale of Taunton, nestling at the foot of the Quantock Hills. Attractive ensuite rooms, dining room and gardens, with traditional home-cooked breakfast.

Yallands Farmhouse, *Staplegrove, Taunton, Somerset, TA2 6PZ.* Beautiful C16th house. An oasis of 'Old England'. **Open:** All year **Grades:** ETC 4 Diamond, Silver, AA 4 Diamond
01823 278979 Mr & Mrs Kirk *mail@yallands.co.uk* www.yallands.co.uk **D:** Fr £25.00–£29.00 **S:** Fr £32.00–£35.00 **Beds:** 1F 3D 1T 2S **Baths:** 7 En (6) cc

Blorenge Guest House, *57 Staplegrove Road, Taunton, Somerset, TA1 1DG.* We are situated within 10 minutes of all Taunton's amenities. **Open:** All year
01823 283005 (also fax) Mr Painter *enquiries@blorengehouse.co.uk* www.blorengehouse.co.uk **D:** Fr £23.00–£40.00 **S:** Fr £28.00–£42.00 **Beds:** 3F 5T 9D 7S **Baths:** 17 En 2 Sh (18) cc

Hillview Guest House, *Bishop's Hull, Taunton, Somerset, TA1 5EG.* Spacious accommodation, warm and friendly atmosphere in attractive village near Taunton. **Open:** All year
01823 275510 (also fax) Mr Morgan **D:** Fr £17.50–£22.50 **S:** Fr £17.50–£25.00 **Beds:** 2F 1D 1T 1S **Baths:** 2 En 3 Sh (6) cc

Thorn Falcon

ST2723

Lower Farm, *Thorn Falcon, Taunton, Somerset, TA3 5NR.* Picturesque C15th thatched farmhouse, log fires, peaceful location, 3 miles Taunton. **Open:** All year (not Xmas)
01823 443549 (also fax) Mrs Titman *lowerfarm@talk21.com* www.somersite.co.uk/lowerfarm.htm **D:** Fr £23.00–£25.00 **S:** Fr £30.00 **Beds:** 1F 1D 1T **Baths:** 1 En 1 Pr (10)

Timberscombe

SS9542

Wellum, *Brook Street, Timberscombe, Minehead, Somerset, TA24 7TG.* Lovely, spacious old house situated in Avil Valley, spectacular views. **Open:** Mar to Nov
01643 841234 Mrs Kelsey **D:** Fr £16.00–£20.00 **S:** Fr £16.00–£20.00 **Beds:** 1D 1T **Baths:** 1 Pr 1 Sh

Tivington

SS9345

Clements Cottage, *Tivington, Minehead, Somerset, TA24 8SU.* C16th cross-passage house with spectacular views of the Bristol Channel. **Open:** All year
01643 703970 *clementscottage@exmoorbandb.co.uk* **D:** Fr £18.50–£20.00 **S:** Fr £18.50–£20.00 **Beds:** 1F 1T 1D **Baths:** 1 En 1 Sh (3)

Watchet

ST0643

Esplanade House, *Watchet, Somerset, TA23 0AJ.* Comfortable Georgian farmhouse, with pretty garden, in historic harbour/marina setting. **Open:** All year (not Xmas/New Year)
01984 633444 Mrs Fawcus **D:** Fr £20.00–£25.00 **S:** Fr £23.50–£27.00 **Beds:** 1T 2D **Baths:** 2 En 1 Pr (8) (3)

Downfield House, *16 St Decuman's Road, Watchet, Somerset, TA23 0HR.* Spacious Victorian country house with converted and modernised coach house within a large garden in an elevated location. Views over the town and harbour from some rooms, comfortable lounge with open fire, chandeliered dining rooms, residents licence. Self-catering flat also available. **Open:** All year
01984 631267 **Fax: 01984 634369** **D:** Fr £24.00–£29.00 **S:** Fr £36.00–£41.00 **Beds:** 5D 2T **Baths:** 7 En (12) (15) cc

Wayford

ST4006

Manor Farm, *Wayford, Crewkerne, Somerset, TA18 8QL.* Beautiful Victorian home in a peaceful location with undulating views. **Open:** All year **Grades:** AA 4 Diamond
01460 78865 & 07767 620031 (M) Mr Emery www.manorfarm.com **D:** Fr £22.00–£25.00 **S:** Fr £22.00–£25.00 **Beds:** 3F 1T **Baths:** 4 En (50)

Wedmore

ST4347

The George Hotel, *Church Street, Wedmore, Somerset, BS28 4AB.* C16th coaching inn set in centre of village in heart of the Somerset Levels. **Open:** All year
01934 712124 Mr Hodge **Fax: 01934 712251** *reception@thegeorgewedmore.co.uk* www.thegeorgewedmore.co.uk **D:** Fr £17.50–£25.00 **S:** Fr £20.00–£25.00 **Beds:** 2F 3D 3T **Baths:** 3 En 1 Sh (30) cc

B&B owners may vary rates – be sure to check when booking

Wells

ST5445

Double Gate Farm, *Godney, Wells, Somerset, BA5 1RX.* **Open:** All year (not Xmas/New Year)
01458 832217 Mrs Millard **Fax: 01458 835612** *doublegatefarm@aol.com* www.doublegatefarm.com **D:** Fr £27.50 **S:** Fr £35.00 **Beds:** 1F 3D 2T **Baths:** 6 En (8)
Comfortable, friendly, award-winning accommodation. Delicious breakfasts with home-made bread and local produce, taken in our farmhouse dining room or the garden. Games room with snooker, table-tennis and darts. Two golden retrievers and two moggies, central for touring. Cyclists/walkers welcome.

White Hart Hotel, *Sadler Street, Wells, Somerset, BA5 2RR.* **Open:** All year **Grades:** ETC 2 Star, AA 2 Star, RAC 2 Star
01749 672056 Mr Rossi **Fax: 01749 671074** *info@whitehart-wells.co.uk* www.whitehart-wells.co.uk **D:** Fr £43.00–£48.00 **S:** Fr £65.00–£70.00 **Beds:** 2F 4T 8D 1S **Baths:** 15 Pr cc
C15th coaching hotel which occupies a very desirable position in the heart of the medieval city of Wells. Located opposite Wells Cathedral, the hotel is ideal for exploring historic Wells & the Mendips, close to West & East Mendip Way.

17 Priory Road, *Wells, Somerset, BA5 1SU.* Large Victorian house. Home-made bread and preserves. Few mins' walk shops, cathedral, bus station. **Open:** All year (not Xmas)
01749 677300 Mrs Winter www.smoothhound.co.uk/hotels/brian.html **D:** Fr £20.00 **S:** Fr £20.00–£25.00 **Beds:** 3F 3S **Baths:** 2 Sh (5)

The Crown at Wells, *Market Place, Wells, Somerset, BA5 2RP.* C15th inn offering affordable accommodation, fabulous food and fine wine, in relaxed and comfortable surroundings. **Open:** All year
01749 673457 Adrian & Sarah Lawrence **Fax: 01749 679792** *reception@crownatwells.co.uk* www.crownatwells.co.uk **D:** Fr £30.00–£50.00 **S:** Fr £45.00–£75.00 **Beds:** 4F 5D 4T 2S **Baths:** 15 En (15) cc

Lilac Cottage, *Gurney Slade, Bath, BA3 4TT.* Charming C18th house in village location between Bath and Wells. **Open:** All year **Grades:** AA 2 Diamond
01749 840469 Mrs Anderson *lilaccotbandb@aol.com* **D:** Fr £20.00–£25.00 **S:** Fr £20.00–£25.00 **Beds:** 1F 2D 1T **Baths:** 1 En 1 Sh

30 Mary Road, *Wells, Somerset, BA5 2NF.* Small, friendly family home, 10 mins' walk city centre, bright modern rooms, breakfast choice. **Open:** Feb to Nov
01749 674031 (also fax) Mrs Bailey *triciabailey30@hotmail.com* www.travelengland.org.uk **D:** Fr £18.00 **S:** Fr £18.00 **Beds:** 2D 2S **Baths:** 1 Sh (3) (5)

Cadgwith House, *Hawkers Lane, Wells, Somerset, BA5 3JH.* Delightfully furnished spacious family house, backing onto field. Beautiful bathrooms. **Open:** All year **Grades:** ETC 4 Diamond
01749 677799 Mr & Mrs Pletts *rplettscadgwith@aol.com* **D:** Fr £19.00–£22.00 **S:** Fr £18.00–£25.00 **Beds:** 1F 1D 1T 1S **Baths:** 3 En 1 Pr (3)

Carmen B&B, *Bath Road, Wells, Somerset, BA5 3LQ.* Delightfully furnished rooms, 0.75 mile easy walk to city centre. **Open:** All year (not Xmas)
01749 677331 Mrs Parker *linda@carmenbandb.fsnet.co.uk* **D:** Fr £20.00–£22.00 **S:** Fr £25.00–£30.00 **Beds:** 1T 1D **Baths:** 2 En (2)

The Limes, *29 Chamberlain Street, Wells, Somerset, BA5 2PQ.* Beautifully restored Victorian town house in the centre of historic Wells. **Open:** All year (not Xmas)
01749 675716 Fax: 01749 674874 *accommodation@thelimes.uk.com* www.thelimes.uk.com **D:** Fr £21.00–£24.00 **S:** Fr £32.00 **Beds:** 1D 1T (2) cc

All details shown are as supplied by B&B owners in Autumn 2002

Broadleys, *21 Wells Road, Wookey Hole, Wells, Somerset, BA5 1DN.* Large detached house situated between Wells and Wookey Hole with panoramic countryside views. **Open:** All year (not Xmas)
01749 674746 (also fax) Mrs Milton *broadleys.wells@btopenworld.com* **D:** Fr £22.50–£25.00 **S:** Fr £30.00–£35.00 **Beds:** 3D **Baths:** 2 En 1 Pr (10) (4)

Number One Portway, *1 Portway, Wells, Somerset, BA5 2BA.* Comfortable Victorian house in comfortable setting. **Open:** All year
01749 678864 & 07970 969354 (M) D: Fr £18.00–£25.00 **S:** Fr £20.00–£25.00 **Beds:** 1F 1D **Baths:** 1 En 1 Pr

Wembdon

ST2837

Ash-Wembdon Farm, *Hollow Lane, Wembdon, Bridgwater, Somerset, TA5 2BD.* Enjoy a refreshing and memorable stay at our elegant yet homely farmhouse. **Open:** All year (not Xmas) **Grades:** ETC 4 Diamond, Silver
01278 453097 Mrs Rowe **Fax: 01278 445856** *mary.rowe@btinternet.com* www.farmaccommodation.co.uk **D:** Fr £22.00–£25.00 **S:** Fr £25.00–£30.00 **Beds:** 2D 1T **Baths:** 2 En 1 Pr (10) (4) cc

Model Farm, *Perry Green, Wembdon, Bridgwater, Somerset, TA5 2BA.* Between Quantocks and Levels. Comfortable Victorian farmhouse in peaceful rural setting. **Open:** All year (not Xmas/New Year)
01278 433999 Mr & Mrs Wright *rmodelfarm@aol.com* **D:** Fr £25.00–£30.00 **S:** Fr £35.00 **Beds:** 1F 1D 1T **Baths:** 3 En cc

West Monkton

ST2628

Prockters Farm, *West Monkton, Taunton, Somerset, TA2 8QN.* Beautiful C17th beamed farmhouse, large garden, 2 pubs easy walking. **Open:** All year
01823 412269 (also fax) Mrs Besley *info@scoot.co.uk* www.scoot.co.uk **D:** Fr £21.00–£23.00 **S:** Fr £21.00–£30.00 **Beds:** 2D 2T 2S 6F **Baths:** 2 En 2 Pr 2 Sh (6) cc

West Pennard

ST5438

The Lion at Pennard, *Glastonbury Road, West Pennard, Glastonbury, Somerset, BA6 8NH.* C15th coaching inn offering excellent ales, fine food and friendly atmosphere. **Open:** All year
01458 832 941 Mr Moore **Fax: 01458 830 660** *thelion@pennardfsbusiness.co.uk* **D:** Fr £25.00–£35.00 **S:** Fr £45.00–£50.00 **Beds:** 1F 2T 4D **Baths:** 7 En cc

West Wick

ST3661

Orchard House, *Summer Lane, West Wick, Weston-super-Mare, Somerset, BS24 7TF.* A luxury guest house close to M5 (J21). **Open:** All year
01934 520948 (also fax) D: Fr £21.00–£27.00 **S:** Fr £36.00–£49.00 **Beds:** 2D **Baths:** 2 En (4)

Westbury-sub-Mendip

ST5048

Lana, Hollow Farm, *The Hollow, Westbury-sub-Mendip, Wells, Somerset, BA5 1HH.* **Open:** All year (not Xmas/New Year)
01749 870635 S M Stott **D:** Fr £20.00–£22.00 **S:** Fr £23.00–£26.00 **Beds:** 1T 2D **Baths:** 3 En (3)
Modern farmhouse on working farm. Comfortable family home, in beautiful gardens, with views over the Somerset Levels and Mendips. Quiet location. Breakfast room for sole use of guests. Full English breakfast. Meals available at local pub, five mins' walk away.

Westhay

ST4342

New House Farm, *Burtle Road, Westhay, Glastonbury, Somerset, BA6 9TT.* Large Victorian farmhouse on working dairy farm on Somerset Levels, ideally situated for touring Wells Cheddar, Bath etc. Enjoy our large farmhouse breakfasts, 4 course evening meals on request own or local produce used. A warm welcome is assured. **Open:** All year
01458 860238 Mrs Bell **Fax: 01458 860568** *newhousefarm@farmersweekly.net* **D:** Fr £23.00–£24.00 **S:** Fr £26.00–£27.00 **Beds:** 1F 2D **Baths:** 3 En cc

Weston-super-Mare

ST3261

Arilas, *78 Clevedon Road, Weston-super-Mare, Somerset, BS23 1DF.* Family guest house close to beach, parks and local shops. **Open:** All year
01934 628283 Mrs Watkins **D:** Fr £16.00–£20.00 **S:** Fr £16.00–£20.00 **Beds:** 1F 1D 1T 1S **Baths:** 1 En 2 Sh

The Weston Rose, *2 Osborne Road, Weston-super-Mare, BS23 3EL.* **Open:** All year
01934 412690 Mrs Trueman *westonrose@beeb.net* **D:** Fr £14.00–£19.00 **S:** Fr £15.00–£23.00 **Beds:** 4F 3D 2T **Baths:** 4 En 2 Sh (5)
Hearty traditional breakfasts - a feast for the eye and stomach. Our own prize winning preserves, yoghurts and fresh fruits always available. All rooms have fridges and hair dryers - most have ceiling fans. Our motto is 'Comfort is our concern' - let us prove it!

Braeside Hotel, *2 Victoria Park, Weston-super-Mare, Somerset, BS23 2HZ.* **Open:** All year (not Xmas/New Year) **Grades:** ETC 4 Diamond
01934 626642 (also fax) Mr & Mrs Wallington *braeside@tesco.net* www.braesidehotel.co.uk **D:** Fr £26.00 **S:** Fr £26.00 **Beds:** 1F 5D 1T 2S **Baths:** 9 En
Fabulous views over Weston Bay; two minutes' walk from sandy beach. Quiet location. Directions: with sea on left, take first right after Winter Gardens, then first left into Lower Church Road. Victoria Park is on the right after the left-hand bend.

Moorlands Country Guest House, *Hutton, Weston-super-Mare, Somerset, BS24 9QH.* Fine Georgian house, extensive landscaped gardens, village pub serves meals. **Open:** All year **Grades:** ETC 3 Diamond
01934 812283 (also fax) Mrs Holt *margaret_holt@email.com* www.guestaccom.co.uk **D:** Fr £20.00–£26.00 **S:** Fr £20.00–£31.00 **Beds:** 3F 2D 1T 1S **Baths:** 5 En 1 Sh (7) 3 cc

Courtland Guest House, *41 Severn Road, Weston-super-Mare, Somerset, BS23 1DP.* Friendly family-run guest house, close to sea front and town. **Open:** All year
01934 621117 M & G Woods *gillandmick@btopenworld.com* **D:** Fr £18.00–£22.00 **S:** Fr £18.00–£22.00 **Beds:** 1F 1T 4D 2S **Baths:** 2 En 2 Sh (5) (6)

Kenilworth B&B, *115 Locking Road, Weston-super-Mare, Somerset, BS23 3ER.* Free tea/coffee making, Sky TV, English breakfast, central heating, car space. **Open:** All year (not Xmas)
01934 629398 Mrs Searle **D:** Fr £14.00–£16.00 **S:** Fr £20.00–£25.00 **Beds:** 1F 3D 2T 1S **Baths:** 2 Sh

Clifton Villa B&B, *11 Clifton Road, Weston-super-Mare, Somerset, BS23 1BJ.* Bed and breakfast in family home, near town and beach. **Open:** All year (not Xmas)
01934 413243 Mr Weeks **D:** Fr £13.00–£17.00 **S:** Fr £15.00–£20.00 **Beds:** 1F 1D 1T **Baths:** 2 En 1 Sh

Everley Villa, *35 Clevedon Road, Weston-Super-Mare, Somerset, BS23 1DB.* Your comfort, our pleasure. Spacious accommodation, short walk beach, station. **Open:** All year
01934 643856 Mr & Mrs Howes **D:** Fr £20.00–£25.00 **S:** Fr £20.00–£35.00 **Beds:** 2F 3D **Baths:** 2 En 1 Pr

Westonzoyland

ST3434

Staddlestones, *3 Standards Road, Westonzoyland, Bridgwater, Somerset, TA7 0EL.* **Open:** All year (not Xmas/New Year) **Grades:** ETC 5 Diamond, Silver
01278 691179 Mrs Eldridge **Fax: 01278 691333** *staddlestones@euphony.net* www.staddlestonesguesthouse.co.uk **D:** Fr £27.00 **S:** Fr £32.00 **Beds:** 1T 2D **Baths:** 2 En 1 Pr cc
Spacious, comfortable Georgian home in village close to M5 offering warm welcome, quality hospitality and a good base for exploring Somerset. The area offers a wide range of natural, historical and tourist attractions. Good walking, fishing and cycling and excellent golf courses.

Phoenicia, *31 Liney Road, Westonzoyland, Bridgwater, Somerset, TA7 0EU.* Private suite in modern detached house, village location. Comfortable beds. **Open:** All year (not Xmas/New Year) **Grades:** AA 3 Diamond
01278 691385 Mr & Mrs Pumfrey **D:** Fr £21.00–£22.50 **S:** Fr £21.00–£22.50 **Beds:** 2S 1D **Baths:** 1 Pr (10)

Wheddon Cross

SS9238 *Rest & Be Thankful, Royal Oak*

Little Quarme Farm, *Wheddon Cross, Minehead, Exmoor, Somerset, TA24 7EA.* Old farmhouse, beautifully furnished and decorated. Outstanding, peaceful location, superb views. **Open:** Mar to Nov
01643 841249 (also fax) Mrs Cody-Boutcher *106425.743@compuserve.com* www.littlequarme.co.uk **D:** Fr £20.00–£25.00 **S:** Fr £25.00–£30.00 **Beds:** 2D 1T **Baths:** 3 En (6)

Planning a longer stay? Always ask for any special rates

Rest & Be Thankful Inn, *Wheddon Cross, Exmoor, Minehead, Somerset, TA24 7DR.* Old coaching inn, ideal Exmoor location for walking and touring. **Open:** All year (not Xmas)
01643 841222 (also fax) Mr Weaver *enquiries@restandbethankful.co.uk* www.restandbethankful.co.uk **D:** Fr £27.00–£30.00 **S:** Fr £27.00–£30.00 **Beds:** 3D 1T 1S **Baths:** 5 En 1 Sh (11) (30) cc

Cutthorne Farm, *Luckwell Bridge, Wheddon Cross, Minehead, Somerset, TA24 7EW.* Tucked away in the heart of Exmoor, hidden in its own private valley, Cutthorne is a country house which is truly 'off the beaten track'. Log fires. Ensuite bathrooms. Four poster bedroom. Candlelit dinners. Licensed. No smoking. Fly-fishing. Dogs welcome. **Open:** All year (not Xmas/New Year)
01643 831255 (also fax) Mrs Durbin *durbin@cutthorne.co.uk* www.cutthorne.co.uk **D:** Fr £25.00–£34.00 **S:** Fr £35.00–£40.00 **Beds:** 1T 2D **Baths:** 3 En (12) (6)

Triscombe Farm, *Wheddon Cross, Minehead, Somerset, TA24 7HA.* Nestling in its own secluded valley with a stream cascading through the garden. **Open:** All year (not Xmas/New Year)
01643 851227 (also fax) Mrs Brinkley **D:** Fr £20.00–£30.00 **S:** Fr £25.00–£40.00 **Beds:** 1T 2D **Baths:** 1 En 2 Pr

Sundial Guest House, *Wheddon Cross, Minehead, Somerset, TA24 7DP.* All ensuite, residents' lounge, log fires, cosy and welcoming. **Open:** Mar to Nov
01643 841188 Fax: 01643 841870 *admin@sundialguesthouse.co.uk* sundialguesthouse.co.uk **D:** Fr £18.00–£23.00 **S:** Fr £20.00–£26.00 **Beds:** 2T 1D 1S **Baths:** 4 En (5)

Wick St Lawrence

ST3665

Icleton Farm, *Wick St Lawrence, Weston-super-Mare, BS22 7YJ.* C15th farmhouse 5 mins from M5 J21, ideal for touring West Country. **Open:** All year (not Xmas)
01934 515704 Mrs Parsons **D:** Fr £17.00–£20.00 **S:** Fr £17.00–£20.00 **Beds:** 1F 1D **Baths:** 1 Pr (2) (2)

Williton

ST0741

Foresters Arms Hotel, *55 Long Street, Williton, Taunton, Somerset, TA4 4QY.* C17th coaching inn on A39 between Quantock and Brendon Hills. **Open:** All year
01984 632508 Mr Goble **D:** Fr £17.50–£21.00 **S:** Fr £18.50–£22.00 **Beds:** 2F2T 4D 1S **Baths:** 6 En 1 Sh (20) cc

Withypool

SS8435

The Old Rectory, *Withypool, Minehead, Somerset, TA24 7QP.* Pleasant view, comfortable beds and a good, hearty English breakfast. **Open:** Easter to Oct
01643 831553 Mr Clatworthy **D:** Fr £16.00 **S:** Fr £16.00 **Beds:** 1D 1T 1S **Baths:** 1 Sh (4)

Wiveliscombe

ST0827

Clerkspool, *1 Ford Road, Wiveliscombe, Taunton, Somerset, TA4 2NJ.* Rambling family house, large garden. Exmoor and Quantock Hills nearby. **Open:** All year (not Xmas)
01984 623364 Mr & Mrs Pearce **D:** Fr £20.00–£24.00 **Beds:** 1F 1T **Baths:** 1 En 1 Sh (8)

Wookey

ST5145

Highgate Cottage, *Worth, Wookey, Wells, Somerset, BA5 1LW.* Pretty, country location, 5 mins cathedral city of Wells. Local inns nearby. **Open:** All year (not Xmas/New Year)
01749 674201 D: Fr £22.00 **S:** Fr £25.00 **Beds:** 1F 1T 1S **Baths:** 2 En (4)

Wookey Hole

ST5347

Broadleys, *21 Wells Road, Wookey Hole, Wells, Somerset, BA5 1DN.* Large detached house situated between Wells and Wookey Hole with panoramic countryside views. **Open:** All year (not Xmas)
01749 674746 (also fax) Mrs Milton *broadleys.wells@btopenworld.com* **D:** Fr £22.50–£25.00 **S:** Fr £30.00–£35.00 **Beds:** 3D **Baths:** 2 En 1 Pr (10) (4)

Woolverton

ST7854

The Old School House, *Woolverton, Bath, Somerset, BA3 6RH.* Homely accommodation. Converted Victorian school, 10 minutes south of Bath. **Open:** All year (not Xmas/New Year)
01373 830200 (also fax) Peter & Mary Thornton **D:** Fr £20.00–£25.00 **S:** Fr £25.00–£30.00 **Beds:** 1F 1T 2D **Baths:** 1 Sh

Wrangway

ST1217

Hangeridge Farm, *Wrangway, Wellington, TA21 9QG.* **Open:** ALl year (not Xmas/New Year)
01823 662339 Mrs Chave **D:** Fr £18.00 **Beds:** 1T 1D **Baths:** 1 Pr
Set in 1 acre gardens with herbaceous borders, flowering shrubs, in the shadow of the Wellington Monument, lovely walks, Devon coasts, situated between junction 26 & 27, 5 mins drive from Wellington.

RATES
D = Price range per person sharing in a double or twin room
S = Price range for a single room

Staffordshire

National Grid References given are for villages, towns and cities – not for individual houses

Haughton

SJ8620

The Old School, *Newport Road, Haughton, Stafford, Staffordshire, ST18 9JH.* Listed building (1841) in centre of attractive village close to Stafford. **Open:** All year **Grades:** AA 3 Diamond
01785 780358 (also fax) Mrs Jenks *info@theoldsc.co.uk* www.theoldsc.co.uk **D:** Fr £20.00 **S:** Fr £20.00–£25.00 **Beds:** 1D 1T 1S **Baths:** 2 Sh

Hednesford

SK0012

York House Guest House, *34 Anglesey Street, Hednesford, Cannock, Staffs, WS12 5AA.* Quiet, comfortable, spacious Edwardian house to accommodate worker or player. **Open:** All year
01543 422502 Ms Brown **D:** Fr £18.00 **S:** Fr £26.00 **Beds:** 1F 4T 1D **Baths:** 2 En 1 Sh (8)

Ilam

SK1350

Throwley Hall Farm, *Ilam, Ashbourne, Derbyshire, DE6 2BB.* Comfortable large, rural Georgian farmhouse with delicious full breakfasts. **Open:** All year (not Xmas) **Grades:** ETC 4 Diamond
01538 308202 Mrs Richardson **Fax: 01538 308243** *throwleyhall@talk21.com* www.throwleyhallfarm.co.uk **D:** Fr £25.00–£30.00 **S:** Fr £30.00–£40.00 **Beds:** 2F 1T 1D **Baths:** 3 En 1 Pr

King's Bromley

SK1216

5 Manor Road, *King's Bromley, Burton-on-Trent, Staffs, DE13 7HZ.* Early C19th manor cottage. **Open:** All year (not Xmas)
01543 472769 Mr Hodges *patandjohn@btinternet.com* **D:** Fr £16.50 **S:** Fr £16.50 **Beds:** 1D 1T **Baths:** 1 Sh (1)

Leek

SJ9856

Beechfields, *Park Road, Leek, Staffordshire, ST13 8JS.* Large Victorian house in spacious gardens. Delicious breakfast. Warm and relaxing. **Open:** All year (not Xmas)
01538 372825 Mrs Rider *judith@beech-fields.fsnet.co.uk* **D:** Fr £20.00 **S:** Fr £25.00 **Beds:** 1F 2D **Baths:** 3 En (4)

Marchington

SK1330

Forest Hills, *Moisty Lane, Marchington, Uttoxeter, Staffs, ST14 8JY.* **Open:** All year **Grades:** ETC 4 Diamond
01283 820447 Mrs Brassington **D:** Fr £24.00 **S:** Fr £28.00 **Beds:** 3D 2T **Baths:** 5 En (5) (6)
Quiet Edwardian house enjoying views across River Dove Valley. Situated in a rural village with two pubs and a post office, good connection A50/M1. Easy access to Peak District and Alton Towers. Comfortable bedrooms, generous breakfasts and friendly atmosphere.

Mayfield

SK1546

Dove House, *Bridge Hill, Mayfield, Ashbourne, Derbyshire, DE6 2HN.* Large detached Victorian house close to Peak District and Alton Towers. **Open:** All year (not Xmas/New Year)
01335 343329 Mrs Green **D:** Fr £20.00 **S:** Fr £28.00 **Beds:** 1D **Baths:** 1 En (1)

Newcastle-under-Lyme

SJ8546

Durlston Guest House, *Kimberley Road 'off A34, Newcastle under Lyme, Staffs, ST5 9EG.* 10 mins' walk from town centre, convenient for Alton Towers and Potteries. **Open:** All year (not Xmas)
01782 611708 Mr & Mrs Stott **Fax: 01782 639770** *durlston.guesthouse3@ntlworld.com* **D:** Fr £17.50–£18.00 **S:** Fr £20.00–£21.00 **Beds:** 2F 1D 1T 3S **Baths:** 2 Sh cc

All details shown are as supplied by B&B owners in Autumn 2002

Newchapel

SJ8654

The Old Vicarage, *Birchenwood Road, Newchapel, Stoke-on-Trent, Staffordshire, ST7 4QT.* Built 1848 in tranquil gardens. 10 mins M6. Rural retreat. **Open:** All year
01782 785270 Mrs Kent-Baguley *oldvicarageb&b@birchenwood.freeserve.co.uk* **D:** Fr £20.00–£25.00 **S:** Fr £20.00–£25.00 **Beds:** 1F 1D 1S **Baths:** 2 En 1 Pr (8) (6)

Norbury

SJ7823

Oulton House Farm, *Norbury, Stafford, ST20 0PG.* Visit our warm, comfortable Victorian farmhouse with marvellous countryside views. **Open:** All year (not Xmas) **Grades:** ETC 4 Diamond
01785 284264 (also fax) Mrs Palmer *judy@oultonhousefarm.co.uk* www.oultonhousefarm.co.uk **D:** Fr £25.00 **S:** Fr £35.00 **Beds:** 2D 1T **Baths:** 3 En (3) cc

Oakamoor

SK0544

Admirals House, *Mill Road, Oakamoor, Stoke on Trent, Staffs, ST10 3AG.* **Open:** All year (not Xmas/New Year) **Grades:** ETC 3 Diamond
01538 702187 Mr Winfield *admiralshouse@btinternet.com* www.admiralshouse.co.uk **D:** Fr £25.00 **S:** Fr £35.00 **Beds:** 3F 2T 2D **Baths:** 7 En (12) cc
Tranquil location in the picturesque Churnet Valley opposite riverside picnic site, woodland walks & cycle trail. Elegant, fully licensed 'Á la carte' restaurant. Central to market towns of Leek, Ashbourne & Uttoxeter. Ideal for Peak District & Potteries. Alton Towers 1.5 miles.

Ribden Farm, *Oakamoor, Stoke on Trent, Staffs, ST10 3BW.* Listed stone farmhouse (1748). Some rooms with four poster beds, all ensuite with TVs. **Open:** All year (not Xmas)
01538 702830 Mrs Shaw **D:** Fr £20.00–£24.00 **S:** Fr £30.00–£35.00 **Beds:** 5F 2D 1T **Baths:** 7 En 1 Pr (10) cc

Slindon
SJ8232

Slindon House Farm, *Slindon, Eccleshall, Stafford, Staffordshire, ST21 6LX.* Farmhouse accommodation 10 mins from M6 J14/15. **Open:** All year (not Xmas) **01782 791237** Mrs Bonsall *bonsallslindonhouse@supanet.com* www.slindonhousefarm.co.uk **D:** Fr £22.50 **S:** Fr £27.00 **Beds:** 1T 1D **Baths:** 1 En 1 Pr (4)

Stafford
SJ9223

Littywood House, *Bradley, Stafford, Staffordshire, ST18 9DW.* **Open:** All year (not Xmas) **Grades:** ETC 4 Diamond **01785 780234** Mrs Busby **Fax: 01785 780770** *sue@littywood.co.uk* www.littywood.co.uk **D:** Fr £21.00–£25.00 **S:** Fr £25.00–£35.00 **Beds:** 1D 1T **Baths:** 1 En 1 Pr (10)
Littywood is a beautiful double moated C14th manor house, set in its own grounds.

Cedarwood, *46 Weeping Cross, Stafford, Staffordshire, ST17 0DS.* Unusual detached bungalow in own grounds, excellent accommodation and hospitality. **Open:** All year **Grades:** ETC 4 Diamond, Silver **01785 662981** Mrs Welsby **D:** Fr £18.00–£20.00 **S:** Fr £18.00–£20.00 **Beds:** 1D 1T 1S **Baths:** 3 Pr (3)

Bailey Hotel, *63 Lichfield Road, Stafford, Staffordshire, ST17 4LL.* Modern detached hotel, comfortably furnished, parking in own grounds. **Open:** All year (not Xmas) **01785 214133** Mr & Mrs Ayres **Fax: 01785 227920** **D:** Fr £18.00–£23.00 **S:** Fr £21.50–£30.00 **Beds:** 1F 5D 3T 2S **Baths:** 4 En 2 Sh (11)

RATES
D = Price range per person sharing in a double or twin room
S = Price range for a single room

Stanshope
SK1254

Stanshope Hall, *Stanshope, Ashbourne, Derbyshire, DE6 2AD.* **Open:** All year (not Xmas) **01335 310278** Miss Chambers **Fax: 01335 310127** *naomi@stanshope.demon.co.uk* www.stanshope.net **D:** Fr £30.00–£40.00 **S:** Fr £30.00–£50.00 **Beds:** 2D 1T **Baths:** 3 En (3) **cc**
Peace and quiet and lovely views over Peak District hills. C17th hall with theatrical touches providing comfortable accommodation, home cooking, vegetables from the garden & interesting wine list. 20 mins Alton Towers, 40 mins Chatsworth, walks from the door.

Stoke-on-Trent
SJ8747

The Hollies, *Clay Lake, Endon, Stoke on Trent, Staffs, ST9 9DD.* Beautiful Victorian house, set in lovely garden, with country view. **Open:** All year (not Xmas) **01782 503252** Mrs Hodgson **D:** Fr £20.00–£22.00 **S:** Fr £22.00–£35.00 **Beds:** 1F 2D 2T **Baths:** 5 En (2) (5)

Reynolds Hey, *Park Lane, Endon, Stoke-on-Trent, Staffordshire, ST9 9JB.* Built 1640, modernised farmhouse. Superb views, close to Doultons, Alton Towers. **Open:** All year (not Xmas) **01782 502717** Mrs Weaver **D:** Fr £20.00 **S:** Fr £25.00 **Beds:** 1F 1D 1T **Baths:** 3 En (3)

The Corrie Guest House, *13 Newton Street, Stoke-on-Trent, Staffs, ST4 6JN.* Victorian house, quiet central location. **Open:** All year **01782 614838 (also fax)** Burton *the.corrie@talk21.com* **D:** Fr £19.00–£22.00 **S:** Fr £22.00–£31.00 **Beds:** 3T 3D 2S **Baths:** 3 En 3 Sh (5) (9)

Stone
SJ9034

Field House, *Stafford Road, Stone, Staffs, ST15 0HE.* **Open:** All year **Grades:** AA 3 Diamond **01785 605712** Mrs Busfield **D:** Fr £17.50–£19.50 **S:** Fr £25.00–£29.00 **Beds:** 1F 1D 1T **Baths:** 1 En 1 Sh (4)
Listed Georgian house offering charming spacious accommodation in warm, relaxed atmosphere, situated in beautiful grounds close to canal, town centre and excellent choice of restaurants. Ideal for Wedgwood Potteries, Shugborough, Alton Towers and the Peak District. Non-smoking bedrooms.

Stubwood
SK0939

Rowan Lodge, *Stubwood, Denstone, Ulloxeter, Staffordshire, ST14 5HU.* A short drive to Alton Towers/Peak District. **Open:** All year (not Xmas/New Year) **01889 590913** Mrs Warren **D:** Fr £17.00–£20.00 **S:** Fr £18.00–£22.00 **Beds:** 1F 1D **Baths:** 2 En (2)

Swynnerton
SJ8535

Home Farm, *Swynnerton, Stone, Staffs, ST15 0RA.* Elizabethan farmhouse, easy access to Alton towers and potteries. **Open:** All year **01782 796241** Mrs Cope *homefarm@cope32.fsnet.co.uk* **D:** Fr £17.50–£20.00 **S:** Fr £17.50 **Beds:** 1F 3D 3T 3S **Baths:** 2 En 2 Pr 2 Sh (10)

Tamworth
SK2203

Victoria Court Hotel, *42 Victoria Road, Tamworth, Staffs, B79 7HU.* Minutes from railway station and town centre. In-house Italian restaurant. **Open:** All year **01827 64698** Mrs Morlini **Fax: 01827 312368** *victoriacourthotel@btinternet.com* **D:** Fr £21.50–£26.50 **S:** Fr £23.00–£43.00 **Beds:** 2F 1T 2D 4S **Baths:** 5 En 1 Sh (20) **cc**

Uttoxeter
SK0933

White Hart Hotel, *Carter Street, Uttoxeter, Staffs, ST14 8EU.* Friendly C16th coaching inn, close to Alton towers. **Open:** All year **01889 562437** Mr Wood **Fax: 01889 565099** *white.hart.hotel.104111@punchgroupe.co.uk* **D:** Fr £31.50–£63.00 **S:** Fr £56.00 **Beds:** 3F 5T 11D 2S **Baths:** 21 En (40) **cc**

Warslow
SK0858

The Greyhound Inn, *Warslow, Buxton, Derbyshire, SK17 0JN.* Cosy village pub, open fires, good home cooking, exceptionally friendly. **Open:** All year
01298 84249 Mr Mullarkey **D:** Fr £17.50
Beds: 2D 2S **Baths:** 1 Sh (20) cc

Waterhouses
SK0850

Lee House Farm, *Waterhouses, Stoke On Trent, Staffordshire, ST10 3HW.* Lovely Georgian farmhouse, village setting, close to the Manifold Valley. **Open:** All year
01538 308439 Ms Little **D:** Fr £20.00–£25.00
S: Fr £25.00–£30.00 **Beds:** 2D 1T **Baths:** 3 En (4)

Whitgreave
SJ8928 *Greyhound*

Whitgreave Manor, *Whitgreave, Stafford, ST18 9SP.* Beautiful Victorian manor house in own mature grounds. Peaceful setting. **Open:** All year
01785 251767 (also fax) Mrs Challinor
whitgreave.uk@virgin.net **D:** Fr £27.50–£35.00
S: Fr £30.00–£40.00 **Beds:** 1F 3T 2D 5S
Baths: 5 En

Whittington (Lichfield)
SK1608

Hawthorns House, *44a Church Street, Whittington, Lichfield, Staffs, WS14 9JX.* Old Victorian house. 15 minutes Belfry and most motorways. **Open:** All year (not Xmas/ New Year)
01543 432613 Mrs Christie **D:** Fr £38.00–£40.00 **S:** Fr £19.00–£20.00 **Beds:** 2T 1D
Baths: 1 Sh

Winshill
SK2623

Meadow View, *203 Newton Road, Winshill, Burton-upon-Trent, Staffs, DE15 0TU.* Double-fronted house overlooking River Trent in attractive wooded garden.
Open: All year (not Xmas)
01283 564046 Mrs Hancox **D:** Fr £17.00 **S:** Fr £17.00 **Beds:** 1T 1S **Baths:** 1 Pr (10) (3)

Wombourne
SO8792

24 Dinkinson Road, *Wombourne, Wolverhampton, W Mids, WV5 0NH.* Central to many Midland attractions. **Open:** All year
01902 895614 Mrs Whitmore **D:** Fr £13.50
S: Fr £13.50 **Beds:** 1T

Suffolk

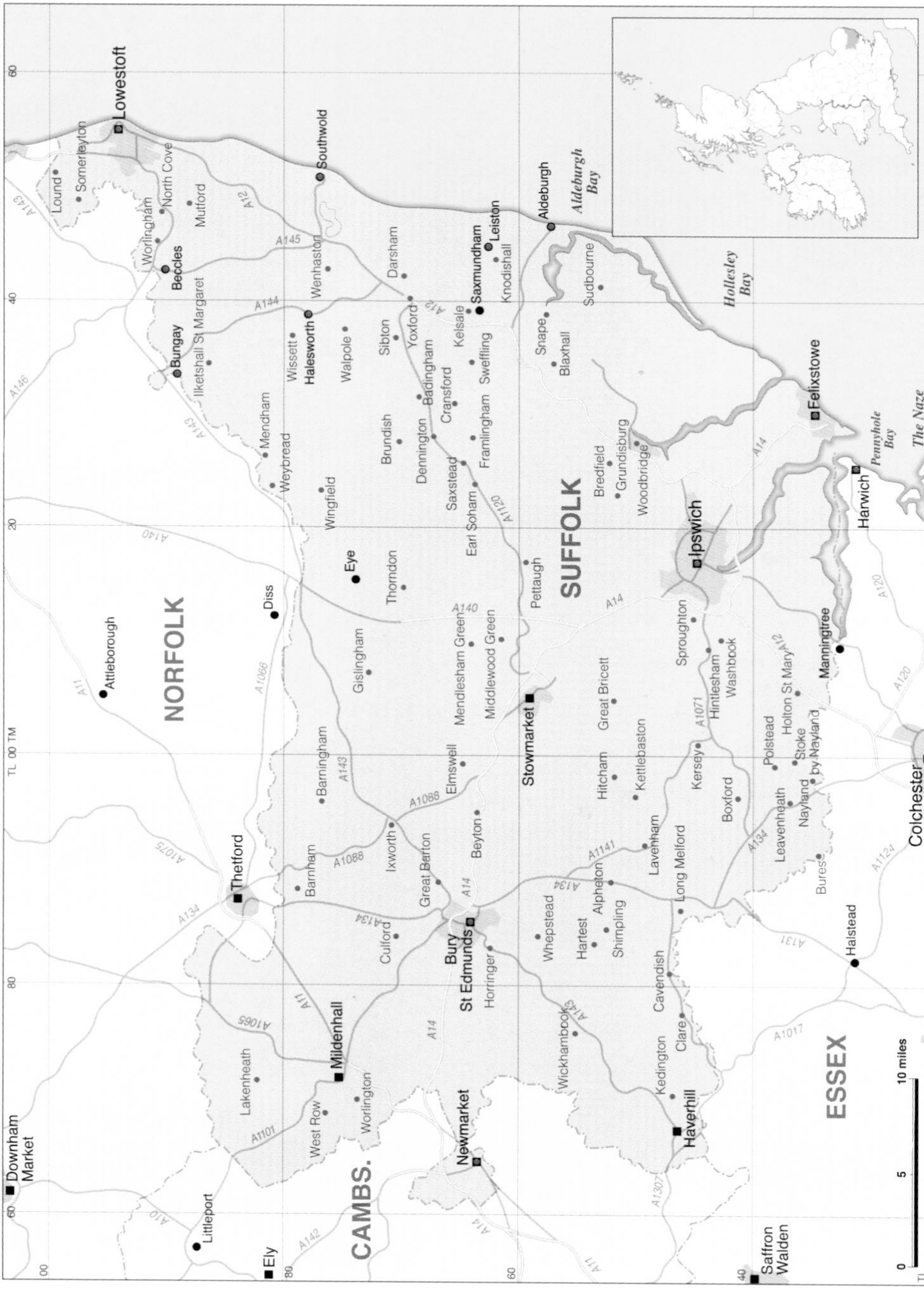

NORFOLK
SUFFOLK
ESSEX
CAMBS.
Lowestoft
Somerleyton
Lound
North Cove
Mutford
Worlingham
Beccles
Southwold
Wenhaston
Darsham
Aldeburgh
Aldeburgh Bay
Leiston
Knodishall
Saxmundham
Kelsale
Yoxford
Sibton
Walpole
Halesworth
Wissett
Bungay
Ilketshall St Margaret
Mendham
Weybread
Wingfield
Brundish
Dennington
Badingham
Cransford
Sweffling
Framlingham
Saxstead
Earl Soham
Snape
Blaxhall
Sudbourne
Hollesley Bay
Felixstowe
Pennyhole Bay
The Naze
Harwich
Bredfield
Grundisburg
Woodbridge
Ipswich
Pettaugh
Eye
Thorndon
Diss
Attleborough
Gislingham
Mendlesham Green
Middlewood Green
Stowmarket
Sproughton
Hintlesham
Washbook
Manningtree
Great Bricett
Kettlebaston
Hitcham
Kersey
Polstead
Holton St Mary
Stoke by Nayland
Nayland
Boxford
Leavenheath
Colchester
Bures
Lavenham
Long Melford
Alpheton
Shimpling
Hartest
Whepstead
Cavendish
Clare
Kedington
Haverhill
Wickhambrook
Halstead
Thetford
Barnham
Barningham
Ixworth
Elmswell
Beyton
Great Barton
Bury St Edmunds
Culford
Horringer
Mildenhall
Lakenheath
West Row
Worlington
Newmarket
Downham Market
Littleport
Ely
Saffron Walden
10 miles

Aldeburgh

TM4656 *Mill Inn, Cross Keys, The Victoria, Railway Inn*

Faraway, *28 Linden Close, Aldeburgh, Suffolk, IP15 5JL.* Quiet, being off main road. Garden, car parking, dogs welcome. **Open:** Easter to Nov
01728 452571 Mrs Burrell **D:** Fr £18.00–£20.00 **S:** Fr £18.00–£20.00 **Beds:** 1F 1T 1S **Baths:** 2 Sh

Alpheton

TL8850

Amicus, *Old Bury Road, Alpheton, Sudbury, Suffolk, CO10 9BT.* Just off A134 amid peaceful surroundings, ideal for garden lovers. **Open:** All year (not Xmas)
01284 828579 & 07779 076519 (M) Mrs Burcham **D:** Fr £17.50–£20.00 **S:** Fr £20.00–£25.00 **Beds:** 1D 1T **Baths:** 2 Pr (2)

Badingham

TM3068 *Queens Head (Dennington), Queens Head (Bramfield)*

Colston Hall, *Badingham, Woodbridge, Suffolk, IP13 8LB.* Antique 4 poster bed. Excellent breakfasts. Surrounded by peaceful countryside. **Open:** All year
01728 638375 Mrs Bellefontaine **Fax: 01728 638084** *lizjohn@colstonhall.com* www.colstonhall.com **D:** Fr £25.00–£35.00 **S:** Fr £30.00–£50.00 **Beds:** 2T 4D **Baths:** 6 En cc

Barnham

TL8779

East Farm, *Barnham, Thetford, Norfolk, IP24 2PB.* Come and stay in large welcoming farmhouse and enjoy the farm countryside. **Open:** All year (not Xmas) **Grades:** ETC 4 Diamond
01842 890231 Mrs Heading **Fax: 01842 890457 D:** Fr £22.00–£23.50 **S:** Fr £24.00–£27.00 **Beds:** 1D 1T **Baths:** 2 En (6)

Barningham

TL9676 *Royal George*

College House Farm, *Bardwell Road, Barningham, Bury St Edmunds, Suffolk, IP31 1DF.* Self-catering cottages. **Open:** All year (not Xmas/New Year)
01359 221512 (also fax) Mrs Brightwell www.abreakwithtradition.co.uk **D:** Fr £25.00–£28.00 **S:** Fr £25.00–£28.00 **Beds:** 1F 1T 1D 1S **Baths:** 1 En 1 Pr 1 Sh (5) (8)

Beccles

TM4289

Ashtree Cottage, *School Lane, Worlingham, Beccles, Suffolk, NR34 7RH.* C18th farmhouse set in rural surroundings with spacious accommodation. **Open:** All year **Grades:** ETC 4 Diamond
01502 715206 Fax: 01502 711745 *helen@dhswilcock.freeserve.co.uk* **D:** Fr £20.00–£27.00 **S:** Fr £20.00–£27.00 **Beds:** 1F 1D **Baths:** 1 Sh

Catherine House, *2 Ringsfield Road, Beccles, Suffolk, NR34 9PQ.* Well furnished family home, excellent facilities, view over Waveney Valley. **Open:** All year
01502 716428 (also fax) Mrs Renilson **D:** Fr £22.00 **S:** Fr £22.00 **Beds:** 3D **Baths:** 2 En 1 Pr (4)

Beyton

TL9363

Manorhouse, *The Green, Beyton, Bury St Edmunds, Suffolk, IP30 9AF.* **Open:** All year (not Xmas)
01359 270960 Mrs Dewsbury *manorhouse@beyton.com* www.beyton.com **D:** Fr £25.00–£30.00 **S:** Fr £38.00–£45.00 **Beds:** 2D 2T **Baths:** 4 En (6)
This C15th timbered longhouse overlooks the Green in centre of pretty village with local hostelries. This is a place to relax and unwind. Large luxurious rooms, king-size beds. Excellent breakfasts at individual tables. 4 miles east of Bury St Edmunds.

Blaxhall

TM3656

The Ship Inn, *Blaxhall, Woodbridge, Suffolk, IP12 2DY.* Quiet rooms in stables of C17th village inn. Cask ales and home-cooked food. **Open:** All year
01728 688316 *shipinnblaxhall@aol.com* www.shipinnblaxhall.co.uk **D:** Fr £20.00–£22.50 **S:** Fr £25.00–£32.00 **Beds:** 4T **Baths:** 4 En cc

National Grid References given are for villages, towns and cities – not for individual houses

Boxford

TL9640

Hurrels Farm, *Boxford Lane, Boxford, Sudbury, Suffolk, CO10 5JY.* An attractive Grade II Tudor farmhouse, ideal for visiting Suffolk/Essex border. **Open:** All year (not Xmas/New Year)
01787 210215 Dr Alok **Fax: 01787 211806** *hurrells@aol.com* **D:** Fr £20.00 **S:** Fr £25.00 **Beds:** 2D 1S **Baths:** 2 Sh (10) (6)

Bredfield

TM2652

Moat Farmhouse, *Dallinghoo Road, Bredfield, Woodbridge, Suffolk, IP13 6BD.* Ideal family home accommodation. Reductions for children. Self contained on ground floor. **Open:** Mar to Oct
01473 737475 Mrs Downing **D:** Fr £17.00 **S:** Fr £17.00 **Beds:** 1D 1T **Baths:** 1 Sh (1) (4)

Brundish

TM2669

Woodlands Farm, *Brundish, Woodbridge, Suffolk, IP13 8BP.* **Open:** All year (not Xmas/New Year)
01379 384444 Mrs Graham *woodlandsfarm@hotmail.com* www.smoothhound.co.uk/hotels/woodlandsfarm.html **D:** Fr £21.00–£25.00 **S:** Fr £25.00–£27.50 **Beds:** 2D 1T **Baths:** 3 En (10) (6)
A warm friendly welcome awaits at our comfortable cottage-style farmhouse. Perfectly situated among orchards near Framlingham. Ideal for exploring coast/countryside by foot, cycle or car. Excellent breakfasts using fresh local produce and our own free-range eggs.

Bungay

TM3389

36, Fairfield Road, *Bungay, Suffolk, NR35 1RY.* Comfortable family home overlooking open countryside. 10 minute walk to public indoor pool and to Bungay with its ancient castle, fine Georgian buildings, market place, butter cross and antiques. The River Waveney, Otter Trust, Aviation Museum, a short journey away. **Open:** All year
01986 893897 Mr & Mrs Tate *heather.tate@talk21.com* **D:** Fr £20.00–£22.00 **S:** Fr £30.00–£35.00 **Beds:** 1D 1T **Baths:** 1 En 1 Pr (2)

Planning a longer stay? Always ask for any special rates

Bures

TL9034

Queens House Guest House, *Church Square, Bures, Suffolk, CO8 5AB.* C17th coaching inn. Set in Stone Valley. Ideal for walks and cycling. **Open:** All year
01787 227760 Mr Arnold **Fax: 01787 227082** *rogerarnold@cs.com* **D:** Fr £26.00 **S:** Fr £33.00 **Beds:** 1F 2T 2D **Baths:** 4 En 1 Pr (6) **cc**

Bury St Edmunds

TL8564

Oak Cottage, *54 Guildhall Street, Bury St Edmunds, Suffolk, IP33 1QF.* Listed Tudor cottage, 2 mins from theatre, museums, shops, restaurants, cathedral, abbey gardens. **Open:** All year
01284 762745 & 07887 638553 Sheila Keeley **Fax: 01284 762745** *sheekee@talk21.com* **D:** Fr £18.00–£27.50 **S:** Fr £18.00–£31.00 **Beds:** 1F 1D 1T 1S **Baths:** 1 En 1 Pr 1 Sh (1)

16 Cannon Street, *Bury St Edmunds, Suffolk, IP33 1JY.* Good English breakfast near railway station, bus station. **Open:** All year (not Xmas/New Year)
01284 761776 Mrs Norton **D:** Fr £16.00–£18.00 **S:** Fr £18.00–£20.00 **Beds:** 1T 1S **Baths:** 1 Sh (8)

Hilltop, *22 Bronyon Close, Bury St Edmunds, Suffolk, IP33 3XB.* Home from Home. Quiet area. Ground floor bedroom, ensuite. **Open:** All year
01284 767066 & 07719 660142 (M) Mrs Hanson *bandb@hilltop22br.freeserve.co.uk* www.hilltop22br.freeserve.co.uk **D:** Fr £16.00–£20.00 **S:** Fr £16.00–£25.00 **Beds:** 1F 1T 1S **Baths:** 1 Pr 1 Sh (2)

Cavendish

TL8046 *The Bull*

The Red House, *Stour Street, Cavendish, Sudbury, Suffolk, CO10 8BH.* C16th house in delightful garden. Homely atmosphere. Delicious breakfasts. **Open:** All year (not Xmas/New Year)
01787 280611 (also fax) M P Theaker *bg.theaker@btinternet.com* **D:** Fr £24.00–£26.50 **Beds:** 2T **Baths:** 1 En 1 Pr (2)

The Grape Vine, *The Green, Cavendish, Sudbury, Suffolk, CO10 8BB.* Tudor house facing village green in Upper Stour Valley. **Open:** All year
01787 280423 Morley *peterj_morley@hotmail.com* **D:** Fr £14.25–£18.50 **S:** Fr £24.00 **Beds:** 1T 1D **Baths:** 2 En

Clare

TL7645

Ship Stores, *22 Callis Street, Clare, Sudbury, Suffolk, CO10 8PX.* Set in the beautiful small town of Clare, all rooms ensuite, breakfast to remember. **Open:** All year
01787 277834 Mrs Bowles *shipclare@aol.co.uk* www.ship-stores.co.uk **D:** Fr £20.50–£23.00 **S:** Fr £25.00–£41.00 **Beds:** 1F 3D 1T **Baths:** 5 En (3) **cc**

Cransford

TM3164

High House Farm, *Cransford, Framlingham, Woodbridge, Suffolk, IP13 9PD.* Beautiful oak-beamed C15th farmhouse on family farm. Spacious and comfortable accommodation. **Open:** All year
01728 663461 Mrs Kindred **Fax: 01728 663409** *bb@highhousefarm.co.uk* www.highhousefarm.co.uk **D:** Fr £20.00 **S:** Fr £25.00–£30.00 **Beds:** 1F 1D **Baths:** 1 En 1 Pr (4)

Culford

TL8369

47 Benyon Gardens, *Culford, Bury St Edmunds, Suffolk, IP28 6EA.* A modern bungalow overlooking fields and quietly situated. **Open:** All year (not Xmas/New Year)
01284 728763 Mrs Townsend **D:** Fr £16.00–£32.00 **S:** Fr £18.00 (4)

Darsham

TM4169

White House Farm, *Main Road, Darsham, Saxmundham, Suffolk, IP17 3PP.* Period farmhouse. Extensive gardens. Close Minsmere/Dunwich/Southwold. All facilities. **Open:** All year **Grades:** ETC 3 Diamond
01728 668632 & 07810 511804 (M) Mrs Newman **D:** Fr £20.00–£27.50 **S:** Fr £25.00–£35.00 **Beds:** 1T 2D **Baths:** 1 En 1 Sh (5) (20)

Priory Farm, *Priory Lane, Darsham, Saxmundham, Suffolk, IP17 3QD.* B&B in comfortable C17th farmhouse, peaceful countryside. Ideal base for exploring Suffolk coast. **Open:** Mar to Oct
01728 668459 Mrs Bloomfield **Fax: 01728 668744** www.prioryfarm.ision.co.uk **D:** Fr £25.00–£30.00 **S:** Fr £35.00–£40.00 **Beds:** 1D 1T **Baths:** 2 Pr (12) (2)

National Grid References given are for villages, towns and cities – not for individual houses

Please respect a B&B's wishes regarding children, animals and smoking

Dennington

TM2867

Fieldway, *Saxtead Road, Dennington, Woodbridge, Suffolk, IP13 8AP.* Stylish house in quiet location facing village green. All rooms overlook beautiful garden. **Open:** All year (not Xmas)
01728 638456 (also fax) Mrs Turan **D:** Fr £20.00 **S:** Fr £22.00 **Beds:** 1D 1T **Baths:** 1 Pr 1 Sh (5) (4)

Earl Soham

TM2363

Bridge House, *Earl Soham, Woodbridge, Suffolk, IP13 7RT.* Beautiful C16th house. Warm welcome, good food, varied menu. **Open:** All year
01728 685473/685289 J A Baker *bridgehouse46@hotmail.com* **D:** Fr £25.00–£27.50 **S:** Fr £28.00 **Beds:** 1T 2D **Baths:** 3 En (5)

Elmswell

TL9863

Elmswell Hall, *Elmswell, Bury St Edmunds, IP30 9EN.* Ideally situated for exploring East Anglia. Warm welcome, hearty breakfast. **Open:** All year (not Xmas/New Year) **Grades:** ETC 4 Diamond
01359 240215 (also fax) K Over *kate@elmswellhall.freeserve.co.uk* www.elmswellhall.co.uk **D:** Fr £30.00 **S:** Fr £30.00 **Beds:** 1T 1D **Baths:** 1 En 1 Pr (6)

Kiln Farm, *Kiln Lane, Elmswell, Bury St Edmunds, Suffolk, IP30 9QR.* Situated in the heart of Suffolk. Self-catering also Available. **Open:** All year
01359 240442 Mrs Knights *barry-sue@kilnfarm.fsnet.co.uk* **D:** Fr £20.00–£25.00 **S:** Fr £25.00–£35.00 **Beds:** 1F 1D 1T 1S **Baths:** 4 En (10)

Felixstowe

TM3034

Iddesleigh Private Guest House, *11 Constable Road, Felixstowe, IP11 7HL.* We offer a cordial welcome in a friendly atmosphere. **Open:** All year
01394 670546 & 01394 270167 Fax: 01394 273214 D: Fr £16.50–£21.00 **S:** Fr £17.50–£21.00 **Beds:** 2F 2T 2D 2S **Baths:** 1 En 1 Pr 2 Sh (3)

All details shown are as supplied by B&B owners in Autumn 2002

Framlingham

TM2863

Boundary Farm, *off Saxmundham Road, Framlingham, Woodbridge, Suffolk, IP13 9NU.* C17th farmhouse, open countryside, ideal touring base. Brochure on request. **Open:** All year (not Xmas)
01728 723401 Mrs Cook **Fax: 01728 723877** *bf@fish.co.uk* **D:** Fr £18.00–£25.00 **S:** Fr £20.00–£25.00 **Beds:** 2D 1T **Baths:** 1 En 1 Sh (4)

Shimmens Pightle, *Dennington Road, Framlingham, Woodbridge, Suffolk, IP13 9JT.* Comfortable home, beautiful garden. Home-made preserves, locally cured bacon. Ground-floor rooms. **Open:** Easter to Oct
01728 724036 Mrs Collett **D:** Fr £23.50–£25.00 **S:** Fr £26.00 **Beds:** 1D 2T **Baths:** 1 Sh (8) (10)

Gislingham

TM0771

West View House, *High Street, Gislingham, Eye, Suffolk, IP23 8HS.* **Open:** All year (not Xmas/New Year) **Grades:** ETC 3 Star, AA 3 Diamond
01379 783975 Ms England *reesengland@clara.net* **D:** Fr £20.00 **S:** Fr £30.00 **Beds:** 1T 2D **Baths:** 1 Pr (2) (4)
C16th, comfortably furnished, heavily beamed former village beer house, in attractive gardens. Free range chickens provide breakfast eggs! Ideal location for walking, cycling or exploring Bury St Edmunds, Lavenham, the Norfolk Broads or the delightful Suffolk coastal area.

Great Barton

TL8866

Cherry Trees, *Mount Road, Cattishall, Great Barton, Bury St Edmunds, Suffolk, IP31 2QU.* Surrounded by lovely garden with fields beyond, yet only 2 miles from the centre of historic Bury St Edmunds. Comfortable beds and full English breakfast. Pub nearby for good meals. **Open:** All year (not Xmas)
01284 787501 Mrs Salmon **D:** Fr £19.00–£20.00 **S:** Fr £24.00–£26.00 (4) (5)

Great Bricett

TM0350

Riverside Cottage, *The Street, Great Bricett, Ipswich, IP7 7DH.* Charming and extremely comfortable ensuite rooms overlooking half-acre garden. **Open:** All year (not Xmas)
01473 658266 & 07811 837728 (M) Mr Horne *chasmhorne@aol.com* **D:** Fr £23.00–£27.50 **S:** Fr £25.00–£30.00 **Beds:** 1D 1T **Baths:** 2 En (1) (3)

Grundisburgh

TM2250 *The Dog, The Green*

Hawthorn Cottage, *Lower Road, Grundisburgh, Woodbridge, Suffolk, IP13 6UQ.* Super detached barn conversion in quiet village. **Open:** All year
01473 738199 Lady Hutchison **D:** Fr £22.00–£25.00 **Beds:** 2T **Baths:** 1 Pr (6)

Halesworth

TM3877

Rumburgh Farm, *Halesworth, Suffolk, IP19 0RU.* Attractive C17th timber framed farmhouse on a mixed enterprise farm. **Open:** Jan to Oct **Grades:** ETC 4 Diamond
01986 781351 (also fax) Mr & Mrs Binder *binder@rumburghfarm.freeserve.co.uk* www.rumburghfarm.freeserve.co.uk **D:** Fr £19.00–£25.00 **S:** Fr £25.00–£30.00 **Beds:** 1F 1D **Baths:** 2 En

Hartest

TL8352

Giffords Hall, *Hartest, Bury St Edmunds, Suffolk, IP29 4EX.* Lovely Georgian house set among vineyards, flower meadows and animals. **Open:** All year (not Xmas)
01284 830464 Mr Kemp *inquiries@giffords.co.uk* www.giffordshall.co.uk **D:** Fr £22.00–£25.00 **S:** Fr £22.00–£25.00 **Beds:** 2T **Baths:** 3 En (5) **cc**

Hintlesham

TM0843

College Farm, *Hintlesham, Ipswich, Suffolk, IP8 3NT.* Peaceful C15th farmhouse near Constable Country & Ipswich. Spacious rooms with country views. **Open:** All year (not Xmas) **Grades:** ETC 4 Diamond
01473 652253 (also fax) Mrs Bryce *bryce1@agripro.co.uk* **D:** Fr £20.00–£25.00 **S:** Fr £20.00–£30.00 **Beds:** 1T 2D 1S **Baths:** 2 En 1 Sh (12) (5)

Birch Farm, *Hintlesham, Ipswich, Suffolk, IP8 3NJ.* Ideal for touring Suffolk or for businessmen working in Ipswich/Hadleigh **Open:** All year
01473 652249 Mrs Bryce **Fax: 01473 652825** *birchfarm@lineone.net* **D:** Fr £45.00–£50.00 **S:** Fr £25.00–£30.00 **Beds:** 2D **Baths:** 2 En

Hitcham

TL9750

Pansy Cottage, *The Causeway, Hitcham, Ipswich, Suffolk, IP7 7NE.* Pansy Cottage is set in the heart of rolling countryside. **Open:** All year (not Xmas/New Year)
01449 740858 R Edden **D:** Fr £18.00 **S:** Fr £20.00 **Beds:** 1D 1S

Holton St Mary

TM0636

Stratford House, *Holton St Mary, Colchester, Essex, CO7 6NT.* A warm welcome in a very comfortable family home in Constable country. Easy access to A12, A14 and Harwich. Traditional breakfast. Good pubs and restaurants locally. **Open:** All year (not Xmas)
01206 298246 (also fax) Mrs Selleck **D:** Fr £20.00–£25.00 **S:** Fr £20.00–£25.00 **Beds:** 1D 1T 1S **Baths:** 1 Sh (10) (10)

Horringer

TL8261

12 The Elms, *Horringer, Bury St Edmunds, Suffolk, IP29 5SE.* Friendly modern house close to Ickworth NT House and Gardens. **Open:** All year
01284 735400 Ms Pemberton **D:** Fr £18.00–£20.00 **S:** Fr £25.00–£40.00 **Beds:** 1D 1T 1S **Baths:** 1 Sh (3)

Ilketshall St Margaret

TM3585

Shoo-Devil Farmhouse, *Ilketshall St Margaret, Bungay, Suffolk, NR35 1QU.* Enchanting thatched C16th farm house in secluded garden near St Peters Brewery. **Open:** All year (not Xmas)
01986 781303 (also fax) Mrs Lewis **D:** Fr £25.00 **S:** Fr £25.00 **Beds:** 1D 1T **Baths:** 2 En (4)

B&B owners may vary rates – be sure to check when booking

Ipswich

TM1644

Maple House, *114 Westerfield Road, Ipswich, Suffolk, IP4 2XW.* Attractive house one mile from town centre; close to park. **Open:** All year (not Xmas)
01473 253797 Mrs Seal **D:** Fr £15.00–£17.50 **S:** Fr £18.00–£20.00 **Beds:** 1D 3S **Baths:** 4 En (3)

Redholme, *52 Ivry Street, Ipswich, IP1 3QP.* Victorian house, ensuite bathrooms, quiet central area, friendly and helpful. **Open:** All year
01473 250018 Mr & Mrs McNeil **Fax: 01473 233174** *john@redholmeipswich.co.uk* www.redholmeipswich.co.uk **D:** Fr £23.00–£26.00 **S:** Fr £30.00–£36.00 **Beds:** 1F 2T 1S **Baths:** 4 En (5)

Craigerne, *Cauldwell Avenue, Ipswich, Suffolk, IP4 4DZ.* Large Victorian house, 3/4 acre pretty gardens. Friendly welcome. **Open:** All year (not Xmas)
01473 714061 Mrs Krotunas **D:** Fr £18.00 **S:** Fr £18.00–£26.00 **Beds:** 1D 1T 2S **Baths:** 2 En 2 Sh (6)

Cliffden Guest House, *21 London Road, Ipswich, Suffolk, IP1 2EZ.* Close to town centre. Full Sky TV. Family run. **Open:** All year
01473 252689 Mrs Staples **Fax: 01473 252685** *cliffden.hotel@virgin.net* **D:** Fr £21.00–£32.00 **S:** Fr £25.00–£35.00 **Beds:** 3F 1D 3T 8S **Baths:** 7 Pr 3 Sh (5) **cc**

Ixworth

TL9270

Robert Peel House, *Ixworth, Bury St Edmunds, Suffolk, IP31 2HH.* Grade II Listed building in village setting. Central to all East Anglia. **Open:** May to Oct
01359 230555 Mr Dew **Fax: 01359 232553** **D:** Fr £18.00–£22.00 **S:** Fr £25.00–£29.00 **Beds:** 1F 5T **Baths:** 6 En (6) (6)

Kedington

TL7046

Orchard House, *Mill Road, Kedington, Suffolk, CB9 7NN.* Comfortable, friendly accommodation. Clare, Bury St Edmunds, Cambridge, Newmarket Triangle. **Open:** All year (not Xmas/New Year)
01440 713113 (also fax) Mrs Osborne **D:** Fr £20.00–£25.00 **S:** Fr £18.00–£25.00 **Beds:** 2D 2S **Baths:** 1 En 1 Sh 1 Pr (5) (6)

Kelsale

TM3865

Mile Hill Barn, *Main Road, North Green, Kelsale, Saxmundham, Suffolk, IP17 2RG.* Luxury ensuite accommodation, converted barn, centrally located-Minsmere Heritage Coast. **Open:** All year
01728 668519 Mr Covington *b&b@milehillbarn.freeserve.co.uk* www.abreakwithtradition.co.uk/prop_8.html **D:** Fr £30.00–£38.00 **Beds:** 2D 1T **Baths:** 3 En (20)

Touch Wood, *Main Road, Kelsale, Saxmundham, Suffolk, IP17 2NS.* Quiet positioned house, convenient for Aldeburgh, Heritage Coast and countryside. **Open:** All year (not Xmas/New Year)
01728 603214 & 07976 223378 (M) Mrs Craddock **D:** Fr £18.50 **S:** Fr £20.50 **Beds:** 2D **Baths:** 2 En (2)

Kersey

TM0044 *The Bell, White Hart*

Red House Farm, *Kersey, Ipswich, Suffolk, IP7 6EY.* Comfortable Listed farmhouse between Kersey and Boxford. Central for Constable country. **Open:** All year
01787 210245 Mrs Alleston **D:** Fr £20.00–£22.00 **S:** Fr £25.00–£28.00 **Beds:** 1T 1S **Baths:** 1 Pr 1 Sh (4)

Kettlebaston

TL9649

Box Tree Farm, *Kettlebaston, Lavenham, Suffolk, IP7 7PZ.* **Open:** All year **Grades:** ETC 3 Diamond
01449 741318 Mrs Carpenter **Fax: 01449 740195** *junecarpenter@hotmail.com* **D:** Fr £20.00 **S:** Fr £25.00–£30.00 **Beds:** 1T 1D 1S **Baths:** 2 En 1 Pr
A warm welcome awaits you at our family-run farmhouse, situated in a peaceful rural location. Comfortable accommodation with magnificent views & farmhouse breakfast. Excellent local pubs and restaurants.

Knodishall

TM4261

Sun Cottage, *Snape Road, Knodishall, Saxmundham, Suffolk, IP17 1UT.* Warm, friendly welcome in pink washed cottage adjoining village common. **Open:** Easter to Oct
01728 833892 (also fax) J Gadsby *suncottage@supanet.com* **D:** Fr £20.00–£22.00 **S:** Fr £24.00 **Beds:** 1T 1D **Baths:** 1 En (3)

Lakenheath

TL7182

Bell Inn, *20 High Street, Lakenheath, Brandon, Suffolk, IP27 9DS.* Old coaching house. **Open:** All year
01842 860308 (also fax) C F Guy **D:** Fr £20.00–£45.00 **S:** Fr £20.00–£30.00 **Beds:** 2F 1T 2D 1S **Baths:** 6 En (20) **cc**

Lavenham

TL9149

The Red House, *29 Bolton Street, Lavenham, Suffolk, CO10 9RG.* **Open:** Feb to Dec **Grades:** ETC 4 Diamond
01787 248074 D Schofield www.lavenham.co.uk/redhouse **D:** Fr £30.00 **S:** Fr £40.00–£50.00 **Beds:** 1T 2D **Baths:** 3 En (5)
In the heart of medieval Lavenham, the Red House is a comfortable friendly home. Attractively decorated bedrooms, pretty sitting room, sunny country garden to relax in. The town has a wealth of timber-framed houses and a magnificent church.

Brett Farm, *The Common, Lavenham, Sudbury, Suffolk, CO10 9PG.* Riverside bungalow in picturesque countryside. 5 mins' walk from historic village of Lavenham. **Open:** All year (not Xmas/New Year) **Grades:** ETC 4 Diamond
01787 248533 M Hussey *brettfarmbandb@aol.com* **D:** Fr £25.00 **S:** Fr £30.00 **Beds:** 1T 2D **Baths:** 2 En 1 Pr

Woolcombers Cottage, *38 Prentice Street, Lavenham, Sudbury, Suffolk, CO10 9RD.* Warm welcome, quality accommodation. C15th cottage. Excellent food walking distance. **Open:** All year (not Xmas/New Year)
01787 247237 (also fax) *anroy@lineone.net* **D:** Fr £25.00–£28.00 **S:** Fr £28.00–£32.00 **Beds:** 1T **Baths:** 1 Pr

Leiston

TM4462

White Horse Hotel, *Station Road, Leiston, Suffolk, IP16 4HD.* Ideally located to enjoy many delights of region including bird sanctuaries at Minsmere, Havergate. **Open:** All year
01728 830694 Fax: 01728 833105 *whihorse@globalnet.co.uk* www.whitehorsehotel.co.uk
D: Fr £28.00 **S:** Fr £35.00 **Beds:** 2F 5D 3T 3S **Baths:** 13 En (14) **cc**

Long Melford

TL8645

High Street Farm House, *Long Melford, Sudbury, Suffolk, CO10 9BD.* Warm welcome. C15th beamed farmhouse. Pretty garden. Good food. **Open:** All year (not Xmas)
01787 375765 & 07950 269955 (M) Mrs Taylor *mail@gallopingchef.co.uk* **D:** Fr £25.00–£27.00 **S:** Fr £27.00–£35.00 **Beds:** 2D 1T 1S **Baths:** 2 En 2 Pr (5)

1 Westropps, *Long Melford, Sudbury, Suffolk, CO10 9HW.* This comfortable modern house situated in Long Melford is an ideal base for touring Suffolk with its many pretty villages, old churches, antique shops and pubs. Audrey Fisher, born in nearby Lavenham, is happy to share her local knowledge. **Open:** All year (not Xmas/New Year)
01787 373660 (also fax) Mrs Fisher *audgrabase@tesco.net* **D:** Fr £22.50–£25.00 **S:** Fr £25.00–£27.00 **Beds:** 1T 1D 1S **Baths:** 1 En 1 Sh (3)

Lound

TM5099

Hall Farm, *Jay Lane/Church Lane, Lound, Lowestoft, Norfolk, NR32 5LJ.* Peaceful, traditional Suffolk farmhouse - spacious rooms, field views, huge breakfast.
Open: Easter to Oct
01502 730415 Ms Ashley *josephashley@compuserve.com* **D:** Fr £18.00–£22.00 **S:** Fr £18.00–£25.00 **Beds:** 1F 1D 2S **Baths:** 2 En 2 Sh (6)

Lowestoft

TM5493

The Albany Hotel, *400 London Road, Lowestoft, Suffolk, NR33 0QB.* Comfortable, homely accommodation guaranteed with our attention focused on your requirements. **Open:** All year
Grades: ETC 4 Diamond
01502 574394 Fax: 01502 581198 *geoffry.ward@btclick.com* www.albanyhotel-lowestoft.co.uk **D:** Fr £22.00–£27.00 **S:** Fr £20.00–£30.00 **Beds:** 1F 2T 2D 3S **Baths:** 6 En 1 Sh **cc**

The Jays Guest House, *14 Kirkley Cliff, Lowestoft, Suffolk, NR33 0BY.* Licensed seafront guest house - for sensible rate, just phone for details. **Open:** All year
01502 561124 B Smith **D:** Fr £15.00–£20.00 **S:** Fr £15.00–£20.00 **Beds:** 1F 2D 1T 2S **Baths:** 2 En 2 Sh (6) **cc**

Royal Court Hotel, *146 London Road South, Lowestoft, Suffolk, NR33 0AZ.* The hotel at bed and breakfast prices; central position. **Open:** All year
01502 568901 (also fax) D: Fr £18.00–£20.00 **S:** Fr £20.00–£25.00 **Beds:** 6F 1D 9T 2S **Baths:** 18 En (12) **2** **cc**

Mendham

TM2782

Weston House Farm, *Mendham, Harleston, Norfolk, IP20 0PB.* Attractive farmhouse, comfortably furnished, with large garden in peaceful rural setting.
Open: Mar to Nov
01986 782206 Mrs Holden **Fax: 01986 782414** *holden@farmline.com* **D:** Fr £20.00–£25.00 **S:** Fr £25.00–£30.00 **Beds:** 2D 1T **Baths:** 3 En (6)

Mendlesham Green

TM0963

Cherry Tree Farm, *Mendlesham Green, Mendlesham Green, Suffolk, IP14 5RQ.* Quality home cooking, garden fresh vegetables, wine from the Suffolk Vineyards. **Open:** All year (not Xmas/New Year)
01449 766376 Mr Ridsdale **D:** Fr £25.00–£30.00 **S:** Fr £35.00–£40.00 **Beds:** 3D **Baths:** 3 En (3)

Middlewood Green

TM0961

Three Bears Cottage, *Mulberrytree Farm, Blacksmiths Lane, Middlewood Green, Stowmarket, Suffolk, IP14 5EU.* Self-contained converted barn B&B, sleeps 6. Indoor swimming pool. **Open:** All year
Grades: ETC 3 Diamond
01449 711707 (also fax) Mr Beckett **D:** Fr £24.00 (5)

Mutford

TM4888

Ash Farm, *Dairy Lane, Mutford, Beccles, Suffolk, NR34 7QJ.* C16th farmhouse, quiet countryside, close to seaside (5 miles), warm welcome. **Open:** All year
01502 476892 Mrs Warnes *jdwarnes@aol.com* **D:** Fr £20.00 **S:** Fr £20.00 **Beds:** 1F **Baths:** 1 En (2)

Nayland

TL9734 *The Angel*

Gladwins Farm, *Harpers Hill, Nayland, Colchester, Essex, CO6 4NU.* Traditional Suffolk farmhouse B&B, ensuite rooms, 22 acres beautiful rolling Constable country.
Open: All year (not Xmas)
01206 262261 Mrs Dossor **Fax: 01206 263001** *gladwinsfarm@compuserve.com* www.gladwinsfarm.co.uk **D:** Fr £28.00–£30.00 **S:** Fr £25.00–£30.00 **Beds:** 2D 1S **Baths:** 2 En 1 Pr (8) (14) **cc**

Hill House, *Gravel Hill, Nayland, Colchester, Essex, CO6 4JB.* C15th beamed house on edge of village overlooking valley.
Open: All year (not Xmas/New Year)
01206 262782 Mrs Heigham **D:** Fr £24.00–£25.00 **S:** Fr £25.00–£30.00 **Beds:** 1T 1D 1S **Baths:** 1 En 1 Pr (10) (6)

Newmarket

TL6463

14 Cardigan Street, *Newmarket, CB8 8HZ.*
Open: All year
01638 667483 Mr & Mrs Crighton *crighton@rousnewmarket.freeserve.co.uk* **D:** Fr £22.00–£25.00 **S:** Fr £22.00–£25.00 **Beds:** 2T 2S **Baths:** 1 Pr
We are a family home offering good basic accommodation, comfortable rooms and full English breakfasts. Centrally situated in town, ideal for racing enthusiasts and tourists alike. Midway between Cambridge and Bury St Edmunds. Connections to Ely and London.

29 Manderston Road, *Newmarket, Suffolk, CB8 0NL.* B&B in historic Newmarket.
Open: All year
01638 603245 J Marshall **D:** Fr £20.00 **Beds:** 1T **Baths:** 1 Sh

North Cove

TM4689

Fairfields Guest House, *Old Lowestoft Road, North Cove, Beccles, NR34 7PD.* Within easy reach of Norfolk Broads. Private car park, walking distance local pub. **Open:** All year
01502 476261 Mrs Charalambous **D:** Fr £17.50–£19.00 **S:** Fr £25.00 **Beds:** 2F 1T 2D **Baths:** 3 En 1 Sh (6)

RATES
D = Price range per person sharing in a double or twin room
S = Price range for a single room

All details shown are as supplied by B&B owners in Autumn 2002

Polstead

TL9938

Polstead Lodge, *Mill Street, Polstead, Colchester, Essex, CO6 5AD.* Village of outstanding beauty. Perfectly situated for exploring South Suffolk and Constable Country. **Open:** All year (not Xmas/New Year) **Grades:** ETC 4 Diamond
01206 262196 (also fax) Mrs Howard *howards@polsteadlodge.freeserve.co.uk* www.polsteadlodge.com **D:** Fr £25.00–£30.00 **S:** Fr £25.00–£50.00 **Beds:** 1F 1T 1D **Baths:** 1 En 1 Sh (9)

Saxtead

TM2565 *Queen's Head*

Bantry, *Chapel Road, Saxtead, Woodbridge, Suffolk, IP13 9RB.* B&B in self-contained ensuite private apartments separate from house. **Open:** All year
01728 685578 Mrs Jones *cheryl.jones@sleepysuffolk.co.uk* www.sleepysuffolk.co.uk **D:** Fr £20.00–£25.00 **S:** Fr £30.00–£40.00 **Beds:** 1T 2D **Baths:** 3 En (9) (3)

Shimpling

TL8551

Gannocks House, *Old Rectory Lane, Shimpling, Bury St Edmunds, Suffolk, IP29 4HG.* Country house in quiet setting, rooms with luxury ensuite facilities/ fine furnishings. **Open:** All year
01284 830499 (also fax) *gannocks-house@lineone.net* www.countrybreak.co.uk **D:** Fr £22.50–£25.00 **S:** Fr £25.00–£45.00 **Beds:** 1F 1D 1T **Baths:** 3 En (8) (5)

Sibton

TM3669

Park Farm, *Sibton, Saxmundham, Suffolk, IP17 2LZ.* Enjoy a friendly farmhouse welcome with your every comfort assured. **Open:** All year (not Xmas) **Grades:** ETC 4 Diamond
01728 668324 Mrs Gray *margaret.gray@btinternet.com* www.farmstayanglia.co.uk/parkfarm **D:** Fr £23.00–£27.00 **S:** Fr £28.00–£32.00 **Beds:** 1D 2T **Baths:** 2 En 1 Pr (6)

Snape

TM3959

Flemings Lodge, *Gromford Lane, Snape, Saxmundham, Suffolk, IP17 1RG.* Very quiet lane, friendly welcome, hearty breakfasts in quality accommodation. **Open:** All year (not Xmas)
01728 688502 (also fax) Mrs Edwards **D:** Fr £20.00–£22.00 **S:** Fr £28.00–£35.00 **Beds:** 1D 1T **Baths:** 1 Sh (4)

Somerleyton

TM4897

Dove Wood Cottage, *5 Station Cottages, Somerleyton, Lowestoft, Norfolk, NR32 5QN.* Charming Edwardian cottage. Peaceful garden. Woodland walks, beautiful Broadland views. **Open:** All year (not Xmas/New Year)
01502 732627 Ms Spencer **D:** Fr £20.00 **S:** Fr £22.00 **Beds:** 1F 1D **Baths:** 1 Pr 1 Sh (4)

Southwold

TM5076

Victoria House, *9 Dunwich Road, Southwold, Suffolk, IP18 6LJ.* **Open:** All year
01502 722317
Mr & Mrs Henshaw *victoria@southwold.info* www.victoria.southwold.info **D:** Fr £25.00–£35.00 **S:** Fr £28.00–£35.00 **Beds:** 1D 1T 1S **Baths:** 2 En 1 Pr
Situated close to beach and town centre of charming unique Southwold. Double room has half tester bed and balcony, with sea views. We pride ourselves in providing high standard comfortable accommodation with a hearty English breakfast to start your day.

Acton Lodge, *18 South Green, Southwold, Suffolk, IP18 6HB.* Victorian merchant's mansion; superb location on Green 50 yards from beach **Open:** All year
01502 723217 Mrs Smith **D:** Fr £25.00–£35.00 **S:** Fr £30.00–£50.00 **Beds:** 1T 3D **Baths:** 2 En 1 Pr (6)

Northcliffe Guest House, *20 North Parade, Southwold, Suffolk, IP18 6LT.* Charming Victorian terrace. Panoramic sea view, relaxed atmosphere, individually designed rooms, licensed. **Open:** All year
01502 724074 Mrs Henshaw **Fax: 01502 722218** www.s-h-systems.co.uk/hotels/northcli.html **D:** Fr £20.00–£30.00 **S:** Fr £25.00–£45.00 **Beds:** 5D 1T 1S **Baths:** 5 En 1 Sh

Planning a longer stay? Always ask for any special rates

Amber House, *North Parade, Southwold, Suffolk, IP18 6LT.* Victorian seafront house, with magnificent views, comfortable and homely atmosphere. **Open:** All year (not Xmas)
01502 723303 (also fax) Mrs Spring *spring@amberhouse.fsnet.co.uk* www.southwold.blythweb.co.uk/amber_house/index.htm **D:** Fr £27.50–£30.00 **S:** Fr £35.00–£50.00 **Beds:** 1F 3D 1T **Baths:** 5 En (5)

No 21 North Parade, *21 North Parade, Southwold, Suffolk, IP18 6LT.* Peace, tranquillity and stunning sea views overlooking Blue Flag beach. **Open:** All year (not Xmas/New Year)
01502 722573 *richard.comrie@cw.com.net* **D:** Fr £50.00–£65.00 **S:** Fr £35.00 **Beds:** 1T 2D

Prospect Guest House, *33 Station Road, Southwold, Suffolk, IP18 6AX.* Situated in the heart of Southwold, fine food and accommodation, car park. **Open:** All year (not Xmas/New Year)
01502 722757 Mr Whyman *sally@prospect-place.demon.co.uk* **D:** Fr £20.00–£25.00 **S:** Fr £25.00–£30.00 **Beds:** 5D **Baths:** 5 En (5)

Sproughton

TM1244

Finjaro Guest House, *Valley Farm Drive, Hadleigh Road, Sproughton, Ipswich, Suffolk, IP8 3EL.* Deluxe accommodation 10 minutes from Ipswich, surrounded by open fields. **Open:** All year (not Xmas)
01473 652581 & 07050 065465 (M) Mrs Finbow **Fax: 01473 652139** *jan@finjaro.freeserve.co.uk* www.s-h-systems.co.uk/hotels/finjaro.html **D:** Fr £20.00–£25.00 **S:** Fr £23.00–£25.00 **Beds:** 1D 2S 1T **Baths:** 2 Sh (3) (5)

Stoke-by-Nayland

TL9836

Thorington Hall, *Stoke-by-Nayland, Colchester, Essex, CO6 4SS.* Beautiful C17th house belonging to the National Trust. **Open:** Easter to Sep
01206 337329 Mrs Wollaston **D:** Fr £24.00 **S:** Fr £32.00 **Beds:** 1F 1D 1T 1S **Baths:** 1 Sh (4)

BATHROOMS
En = Ensuite
Pr = Private
Sh = Shared

Nether Hall, *Thorington Street, Stoke-by-Nayland, Colchester, Essex, CO6 4ST.* Nether Hall is a C15th gem. The bedrooms are extremely comfortable and spacious. The River Box borders the 3-acre garden and old roses cascade over the house, barn and walls. A spectacle during the summer. Hard tennis court. Excellent local pubs. **Open:** All year
01206 337373 Mr & Mrs Jackson **Fax: 01206 337496** *patrick.jackson@talk21.com* **D:** Fr £30.00 **S:** Fr £30.00 **Beds:** 1T 1D 1S **Baths:** 2 En 1 Pr (6)

Sudbourne

TM4153

Long Meadow, *Gorse Lane, Sudbourne, Woodbridge, Suffolk, IP12 2BD.* Comfortable, friendly home from home, lovely garden, quiet rural location. **Open:** All year (not Xmas) **Grades:** ETC 3 Diamond
01394 450269 Mrs Wood **D:** Fr £21.00–£23.00 **S:** Fr £20.00–£22.00 **Beds:** 1D 1T 1S **Baths:** 1 Pr 1 Sh (12) (6)

Sweffling

TM3463

Wayside, *Glemham Road, Sweffling, Saxmundham, Suffolk, IP17 2QB.* Comfortable accommodation on edge of village near Heritage Coast attractions. **Open:** All year (not Xmas/New Year)
01728 663256 M Wilkinson **D:** Fr £20.00–£22.00 **S:** Fr £22.00–£25.00 **Beds:** 1T 1D **Baths:** 2 En (5) (4)

Thorndon

TM1369

Moat Farm, *Thorndon, Eye, Suffolk, IP23 7LX.* Moat Farm is an old Suffolk house in peaceful village. **Open:** All year (not Xmas/New Year)
01379 678437 (also fax) J & G Edgecombe *gerolde@clara.co.uk* **D:** Fr £20.00–£23.00 **S:** Fr £24.00–£28.00 **Beds:** 1F 2T 2D **Baths:** 2 En 1 Pr 1 Sh

Walpole

TM3674

The Old Vicarage, *Walpole, Halesworth, Suffolk, IP19 9AR.* Spacious bedrooms, lovely views from every room. **Open:** All year
01986 784295 Mr Calver **D:** Fr £20.00–£25.00 **S:** Fr £25.00–£30.00 **Beds:** 1T 1D **Baths:** 2 Pr (6)

Washbrook

TM1142

Stebbings, *Back Lane, Washbrook, Ipswich, IP8 3JA.* **Open:** All year (not Xmas) **Grades:** ETC 4 Diamond
01473 730216 & 07989 061088 (M) Mrs Fox *caroline@foxworld.fsnet.co.uk* **D:** Fr £20.00 **S:** Fr £20.00 **Beds:** 2T 1S (2)
Detached Georgian cottage, quiet village location, secure parking, mature pretty gardens and outbuildings. Full English breakfast with local produce. 3 miles Ipswich town centre. Ideally situated, Suffolk countryside and Constable Country. Easy access A12, A14. Pets and children welcome. No smoking.

High View, *Back Lane, Washbrook, Ipswich, Suffolk, IP8 3JA.* Comfortable Edwardian house set in secluded garden. Quiet village location. **Open:** All year (not Xmas/New Year) **Grades:** ETC 4 Diamond
01473 730494 Mrs Steward *rosanna.steward@virgin.net* **D:** Fr £21.00–£23.00 **S:** Fr £21.00–£23.00 **Beds:** 1T 1D 1S **Baths:** 1 Sh (12) (5)

Wenhaston

TM4175

The Old Vicarage, *Wenhaton, Halesworth, Suffolk, IP19 9EG.* Period house in large grounds. Very peaceful, warm welcome assured. **Open:** All year
01502 478339 Mr & Mrs Heycock **Fax: 01502 478068** *theycock@aol.com* **D:** Fr £25.00–£30.00 **S:** Fr £28.00–£33.00 **Beds:** 1T 2D **Baths:** 1 Pr 1 Sh (12) (3)

West Row

TL6775 *Red Lion*

Pear Tree House, *Chapel Road, West Row, Mildenhall, Bury St Edmunds, Suffolk, IP28 8PA.* C1750 former village inn, handy for touring East Anglia. **Open:** All year
01638 711112 (also fax) Mr Knight *peartree@12stay.co.uk* www.peartree.12stay.co.uk **D:** Fr £20.00–£25.00 **S:** Fr £25.00–£35.00 **Beds:** 1T 2D **Baths:** 2 En 1 Pr (2) **cc**

All details shown are as supplied by B&B owners in Autumn 2002

Weybread

TM2480

The Crown Inn, *The Street, Weybread, Diss, Norfolk, IP21 5TL.* Traditional English pub. Excellent fishing. Countryside walks. Coastline driving distance. **Open:** All year
01379 586710 L Rice **D:** Fr £30.00–£45.00 **S:** Fr £30.00 **Beds:** 1T 1D 1F **Baths:** 3 En (15)

Whepstead

TL8357

Folly House B&B, *Folly Lane, Whepstead, Bury St Edmunds, IP29 4TJ.* Bed & Breakfast in the country, indoor pool. Excellent breakfasts. **Open:** All year (not Xmas)
01284 735207 L Lower **D:** Fr £20.00–£25.00 **S:** Fr £25.00–£35.00 **Beds:** 1F 1D 1T **Baths:** 1 En 1 Sh (10)

Wickhambrook

TL7554

The Old Bakery, *Off Mill Lane, Farley Green, Wickhambrook, Newmarket, Suffolk, CB8 8PX.* C17th house, quiet countryside, large rooms, comfortable beds, quality breakfasts. **Open:** All year (not Xmas)
01440 820852 (also fax) L Lambert *info@theoldbakery.freeserve.co.uk* www.theoldbakery.freeserve.co.uk **D:** Fr £20.00–£22.50 **S:** Fr £30.00–£35.00 **Beds:** 2D 1T **Baths:** 3 En (4)

Wingfield

TM2276

Gables Farm, *Wingfield, Diss, Norfolk, IP21 5RH.* Timbered C16th moated farmhouse, all rooms furnished to highest standards. Well-kept gardens for guests. **Open:** Jan to Dec
01379 586355 Sue Harvey **Fax: 01379 588058** *gables-farm@ntlworld.com* www.gablesfarm.co.uk **D:** Fr £25.00–£27.50 **S:** Fr £30.00–£32.00 **Beds:** 1T 2D **Baths:** 3 En (6)

Wissett

TM3579

Wissett Lodge, *Wissett, Halesworth, Suffolk, IP19 0JQ.* C16th farmhouse set in lovely countryside. Home to the Bloomsburys in 1916. **Open:** All year
01986 873173 (also fax) G M & C E Kiddy *geoffrey.kiddy@farmersweekly.net* **D:** Fr £18.00 **Beds:** 1T **Baths:** 1 Pr

Woodbridge

TM2649

Deben House, *29 Ipswich Road, Woodbridge, Suffolk, IP12 4BS.* Relaxed family home, large garden, river views, historic market town. **Open:** All year
01394 386644 John & Tamsin Passmore *info@debenhouse.co.uk* www.debenhouse.co.uk
D: Fr £20.00–£25.00 **S:** Fr £20.00–£25.00
Beds: 1F 1D 1S **Baths:** 1 Pr (3)

Worlingham

TM4490

Ashtree Cottage, *School Lane, Worlingham, Beccles, Suffolk, NR34 7RH.* C18th farmhouse set in rural surroundings with spacious accommodation. **Open:** All year **Grades:** ETC 4 Diamond
01502 715206 Fax: 01502 711745 *helen@dhswilcock.freeserve.co.uk* **D:** Fr £20.00–£27.00
S: Fr £20.00–£27.00 **Beds:** 1F 1D **Baths:** 1 Sh

Colville Arms Motel, *Lowestoft Road, Worligham , Beccles, Suffolk, NR34 7EF.* Village location close to Lowestoft, Norwich, Yarmouth, Broads, golf and fishing. **Open:** All year
01502 712571 (also fax) P & N Brooks *pat@thecolvillearms.freeserve.co.uk* **D:** Fr £22.50–£27.50 **S:** Fr £32.50–£40.00 **Beds:** 4T 5D 2S
Baths: 11 En cc

Worlington

TL6973

The Old Forge, *Newmarket Road, Worlington, Bury St Edmunds, Suffolk, IP28 8RZ.* An attractive C18th cottage across road from pub near golf course. **Open:** All year (not Xmas/New Year)
01638 718014 Mrs Wilson **Fax: 01638 711616**
D: Fr £28.00–£40.00 **S:** Fr £28.00 **Beds:** 1T
Baths: 1 Pr (2)

RATES
D = Price range per person sharing in a double or twin room
S = Price range for a single room

Yoxford

TM3968

The Griffin, *High Street, Yoxford, Saxmundham, Suffolk, IP17 3EP.* **Open:** All year
Grades: ETC 3 Diamond
01728 668229 Fax: 01728 667040 *i.terry@virgin.net* www.thegriffin.co.uk **D:** Fr £27.50–£30.00 **S:** Fr £35.00 **Beds:** 1F 1T 1D **Baths:** 1 En 2 Pr (20) cc
A friendly & welcoming C14th half-timbered inn, serving restaurant and bar meals including medieval dishes, real ale, good wine & log fires. Situated in the centre of picturesque Yoxford, 'the Garden of Suffolk'. Close to coast, Southwold, Dunwich, Minsmere, Snape & Aldeburgh.

The Old Mill House, *Main Road, Yoxford, Saxmundham, Suffolk, IP17 3HE.* Comfortable secluded Regency house. Peaceful grounds. Good food. Warm welcome. **Open:** All year
01728 668536 R J Draper **D:** Fr £20.00–£25.00
S: Fr £23.00 **Beds:** 1F 1D **Baths:** 1 Pr (6)

Surrey

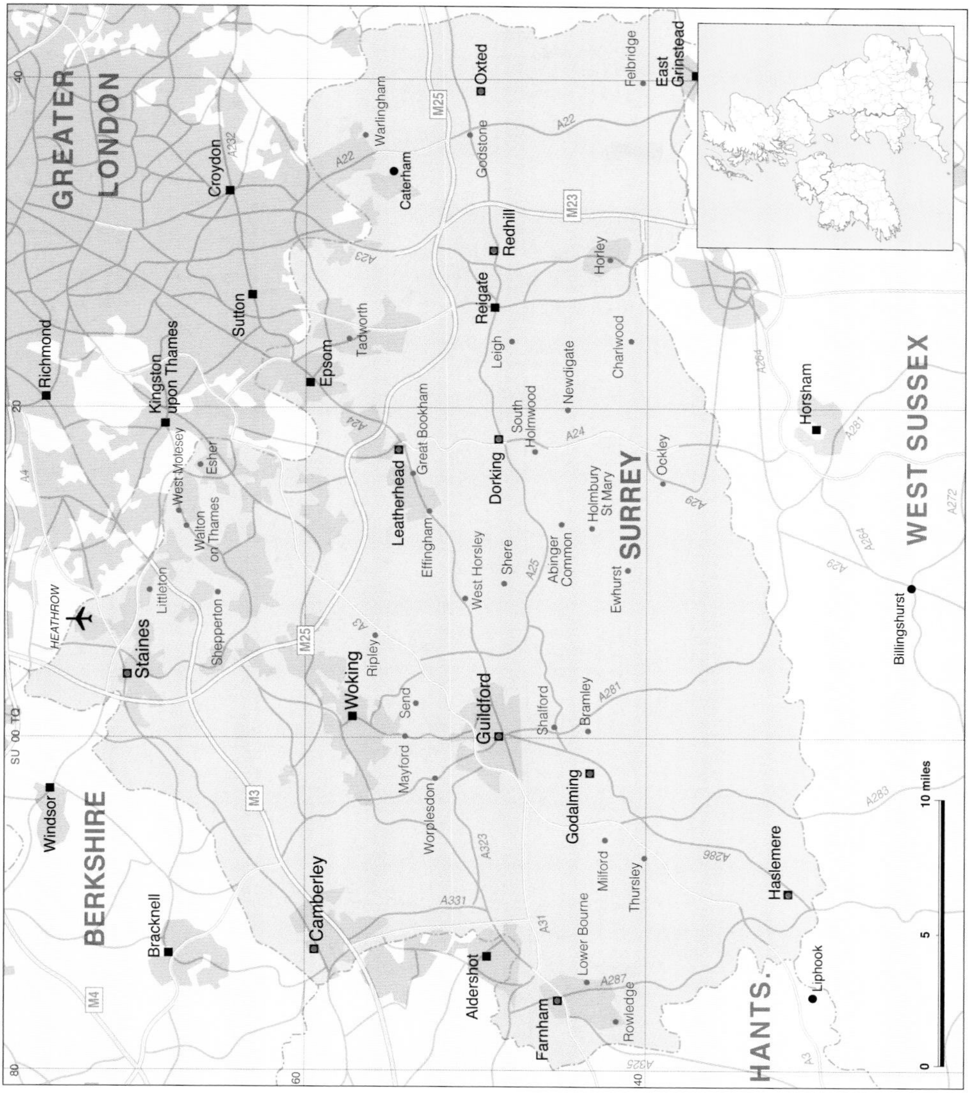

GREATER LONDON
BERKSHIRE
SURREY
WEST SUSSEX
HANTS.
HEATHROW
Richmond
Kingston upon Thames
Sutton
Croydon
Epsom
Tadworth
Caterham
Warlingham
Oxted
Godstone
Redhill
Reigate
Horley
Felbridge
East Grinstead
Windsor
Bracknell
Staines
Littleton
Shepperton
Walton on Thames
West Molesey
Esher
Woking
Ripley
Send
Mayford
Worplesdon
Guildford
Shalford
Bramley
Leatherhead
Great Bookham
Effingham
West Horsley
Shere
Dorking
South Holmwood
Leigh
Newdigate
Charlwood
Abinger Common
Holmbury St Mary
Ewhurst
Ockley
Camberley
Aldershot
Farnham
Lower Bourne
Rowledge
Godalming
Milford
Thursley
Haslemere
Liphook
Horsham
Billingshurst
M25
M23
M3
M4
A22
A23
A24
A25
A29
A3
A31
A281
A283
A286
A287
A323
A325
A331
A232
A264
A272
A4
SU 00 TQ
20
40
60
80
0
5
10 miles

Abinger Common

TQ1145

Park House Farm, *Leith Hill Road, Abinger Common, Dorking, Surrey, RH5 6LW.* Spacious home with bright, tastefully decorated rooms, all with excellent views. **Open:** All year (not Xmas/New Year) **01306 730101** Mr & Mrs Wallis **Fax: 01306 730643** *peterwallis@msn.com* www.smoothhound.co.uk/hotels/parkhous.html **D:** Fr £20.00–£30.00 **S:** Fr £30.00–£50.00 **Beds:** 1T 2D **Baths:** 3 En (12) (10)

Bramley

TQ0044

Beevers Farm, *Chinthurst Lane, Bramley, Guildford, Surrey, GU5 0DR.* Peaceful surroundings, friendly atmosphere. Own preserves, honey, eggs. Nearby villages. **Open:** Feb to Dec **01483 898764 (also fax)** Mr Cook *beevers@onetel.net.uk* **D:** Fr £18.00–£25.00 **S:** Fr £30.00 **Beds:** 1F 2T **Baths:** 1 Pr 1 Sh (10)

Camberley

SU8860

Youlden Lodge, *12 Youlden Drive, Camberley, Surrey, GU15 1AL.* Spacious Tudor style house, ample parking, convenient M3. Continental breakfast. **Open:** All year **01276 61793** Mrs Bennie **D:** Fr £25.00 **S:** Fr £25.00 **Beds:** 1D 1T 2S **Baths:** 2 Sh (5)

Charlwood

TQ2441

Swan Cottage, *Swan Lane, Charlwood, Horley, Surrey, RH6 0DB.* Studio apartment in garden of C15th cottage. 3m Gatwick Airport. **Open:** All year **01293 863429 (also fax)** Mrs Peskett *thepesketts@thepesketts.free-online.co.uk* **D:** Fr £21.00–£23.00 **S:** Fr £25.00 **Beds:** 2T **Baths:** 1 Sh (2)

Dorking

TQ1649

Steyning Cottage, *Horsham Road, South Holmwood, Dorking, Surrey, RH5 4NE.* Special rates for long term, including dinner. French spoken. **Open:** All year (not Xmas) **01306 888481** Mrs Treays **D:** Fr £20.00–£22.00 **S:** Fr £20.00–£22.50 **Beds:** 1T 1S **Baths:** 1 Sh (4)

Shrub Hill, *3 Calvert Road, Dorking, Surrey, RH4 1LT.* Quiet comfortable family home with excellent views. **Open:** All year (not Xmas) **01306 885229** Mrs Scott Kerr *jackiesk@ntlworld.com* **D:** Fr £25.00–£26.00 **S:** Fr £30.00–£35.00 **Beds:** 1T 1S 1D **Baths:** 1 Sh 1 En (8) (2)

The Waltons, *5 Rose Hill, Dorking, Surrey, RH4 2EG.* Listed house in conservation area. Beautiful views and friendly atmosphere. **Open:** All year **01306 883127 & 07802 469953 (M)** Mrs Walton **Fax: 01306 883127** *thewaltons@rosehill5.demon.co.uk* **D:** Fr £17.50–£20.00 **S:** Fr £20.00–£32.50 **Beds:** 1F 1D 1T 1S **Baths:** 3 Sh (3)

Effingham

TQ1153

Chalklands, *Beech Avenue, Effingham, Surrey, KT24 5PJ.* Large detached house overlooking golf course. Good pub food nearby. **Open:** All year (not Xmas) **Grades:** ETC 3 Diamond **01372 454936** Mrs Reilly **Fax: 01372 459569** *rreilly@onetel.net.uk* **D:** Fr £23.00–£25.00 **S:** Fr £30.00–£35.00 **Beds:** 1F 1D 1T **Baths:** 2 En 1 Pr (8)

Crosslands Guest House, *Guildford Road, Effingham, Surrey, KT24 5PE.* Date of house 1280, 1775 & 1904 - pub for 400 years. **Open:** All year (not Xmas/New Year) **01372 453479** J Gifford **D:** Fr £22.00–£25.00 **S:** Fr £22.00–£25.00 **Beds:** 1T 1D 1S **Baths:** 1 En 1 Sh

Esher

TQ1464

Lilac Cottage, *14 Greenways, Hinchley Wood, Esher, Surrey, KT10 0QD.* Luxury friendly family home convenient London, Hampton Court, Wisley, Sandown. **Open:** All year (not Xmas) **020 8398 7546 (also fax)** Mrs Evans *evans@greenways.demon.co.uk* **D:** Fr £30.00 **S:** Fr £35.00 **Beds:** 1D 1T **Baths:** 2 En cc

Ewhurst

TQ0940

Malricks, *The Street, Ewhurst, Cranleigh, Surrey, GU6 7RH.* Modern detached house, village location. Large attractive garden overlooking fields. **Open:** All year **Grades:** ETC 3 Diamond **01483 277575** Mrs Budgen **D:** Fr £20.00 **S:** Fr £20.00 **Beds:** 1F 1T **Baths:** 1 En 1 Sh (3)

High Edser, *Shere Road, Ewhurst, Cranleigh, Surrey, GU6 7PQ.* C16th farmhouse in Area of Outstanding Natural Beauty - a beautiful setting. **Open:** All year (not Xmas) **01483 278214 & 07775 865125 (M)** Mrs Franklin-Adams **Fax: 01483 278200** *franklinadams@highedser.demon.co.uk* **D:** Fr £25.00–£27.50 **S:** Fr £25.00–£35.00 **Beds:** 2D 1T **Baths:** 1 Sh (6)

Farnham

SU8446

Pittersfield, *Hole Lane, Bentley, Farnham, Surrey, GU10 5LT.* **Open:** All year **01420 22414 (also fax)** Mrs Coulton **D:** Fr £25.00–£30.00 **S:** Fr £30.00–£40.00 **Beds:** 1T 1D 1S **Baths:** 2 Pr (3) Mews style accommodation in converted stables. Separate from main house. Set in peaceful surroundings, large garden, in rural location. Many attractions to visit. M3, M4 & A3 in easy reach.

Orchard House, *13 Applelands Close, Farnham, Surrey, GU10 4TL.* Visitors warmly welcomed at our quietly located home overlooking countryside. **Open:** All year (not Xmas/New Year) **01252 793813** D C Warburton **D:** Fr £22.50–£25.00 **S:** Fr £22.50–£25.00 **Beds:** 1T 1S **Baths:** 1 Sh (3)

Hawkridge, *20 Upper Old Park Lane, Farnham, Surrey, GU9 0AT.* Large family home in beautiful countryside. One mile from town. **Open:** All year (not Xmas/New Year) **01252 722068** Mr & Mrs Ackland *chris.ackland@tesco.net* **D:** Fr £22.00–£27.00 **S:** Fr £27.00–£35.00 **Beds:** 1T 1D 1S **Baths:** 1 Sh (10) (4)

Felbridge

TQ3639

Toads Croak House, *30 Copthorne Road, Felbridge, East Grinstead, W Sussex, RH19 2NS.* Beautiful Sussex cottage-style house, gardens. Gatwick parking. 18th independent year. **Open:** All year **01342 328524 (also fax)** *toadscroakhouse@aol.com* **D:** Fr £19.00–£24.00 **S:** Fr £25.00–£33.00 **Beds:** 1F 1D 2T **Baths:** 2 En 1 Sh (7)

National Grid References given are for villages, towns and cities – not for individual houses

All details shown are as supplied by B&B owners in Autumn 2002

Gatwick (Surrey side)

TQ2843

Southbourne Guest House, *34 Massetts Road, Horley, Surrey, RH6 7DS.* **Open:** All year (not Xmas/New Year) **Grades:** ETC 2 Diamond **01293 771991 & 01293 820112** Breda & Tony Breen **Fax: 01293 820112** *reservations@southbournegatwick.com* www.southbournegatwick.com **D:** Fr £22.50–£27.50 **S:** Fr £30.00–£40.00 **Beds:** 2F 3T 2D 2S **Baths:** 2 En 2 Sh (20) cc A warm welcome awaits you in our family-run guest house. 5 mins drive Gatwick in our courtesy car from 9.30am to 9.30pm. 5 minutes walk from local pubs, restaurants and shops. 30 minutes by train from London.

Melville Lodge Guest House, *15 Brighton Road, Gatwick, Horley, Surrey, RH6 7HH.* Friendly house, airport 5 minutes drive, train to London/Brighton. Cooked breakfast. **Open:** All year **01293 784951** Mr & Mrs Brooks **Fax: 01293 785669** *melvillelodge.guesthouse@tesco.net* www.melville.portland.co.uk **D:** Fr £19.00–£22.50 **S:** Fr £25.00–£35.00 **Beds:** 1F 3D 2T 1S **Baths:** 3 En 2 Sh

Swan Cottage, *Swan Lane, Charlwood, Horley, Surrey, RH6 0DB.* Studio apartment in garden of C15th cottage. 3m Gatwick Airport. **Open:** All year **01293 863429 (also fax)** Mrs Peskett *thepesketts@thepesketts.free-online.co.uk* **D:** Fr £21.00–£23.00 **S:** Fr £25.00 **Beds:** 2T **Baths:** 1 Sh (2)

BEDROOMS
D = Double
T = Twin
S = Single
F = Family

Godalming

SU9643

52 Twycross Road, *Godalming, GU7 2HJ.* **Open:** All year (not Xmas/New Year) **01483 422055 (also fax)** Mrs Greenwood *hazeldickgreenwood@btinternet.com* **D:** Fr £20.00–£25.00 **S:** Fr £20.00–£25.00 **Beds:** 1D 1S **Baths:** 2 Sh (12) (2) Detached family house on outskirts of town in a pleasant area, convenient for A3, mainline station to London, local shops & pubs. Historic Guildford 4 miles away. Easy access to beautiful surrounding countryside. Double room with ensuite shower facility.

Sherwood, *Ashstead Lane, Godalming, Surrey, GU7 1SY.* We have 4 cats and one Cavalier King Charles Spaniel - we welcome animal lovers. **Open:** All year **01483 427545 (also fax)** Mr & Mrs Harrison *amandauk43@hotmail.com* **D:** Fr £27.00 **S:** Fr £27.00 **Beds:** 1T 2S **Baths:** 1 Sh (5)

Godstone

TQ3551

Godstone Hotel, *The Green, Godstone, Surrey, RH9 8DT.* C16th coaching house, original features, inglenook fireplaces. Our restaurant is renowned in the vicinity. **Open:** All year **01883 742461 (also fax)** Mr Howe **D:** Fr £27.50 **S:** Fr £39.00 **Beds:** 6D 2T **Baths:** 8 Pr

Great Bookham

TQ1354

Selworthy, *310 Lower Road, Great Bookham, Leatherhead, Surrey, KT23 4DW.* Attractive location overlooking green belt. Convenient M25, Gatwick and Heathrow airports. **Open:** All year (not Xmas) **Grades:** ETC 3 Diamond **01372 453952 (also fax)** Mrs Kent *bnb@selworthy.fslife.co.uk* **D:** Fr £21.00–£24.00 **S:** Fr £26.00–£29.00 **Beds:** 1D 1T **Baths:** 1 Sh (10) (4)

Guildford

SU9949

Westbury Cottage, *Waterden Road, Guildford, Surrey, GU1 2AN.* Cottage-style house in large secluded garden, 5 mins town centre, 2 mins station. **Open:** All year (not Xmas) **01483 822602 (also fax)** Mrs Smythe *smythe.smythe@ntlworld.com* **D:** Fr £25.00 **S:** Fr £35.00–£40.00 **Beds:** 1D 2T **Baths:** 1 Sh (6) (3)

Quietways, *29 Liddington Hall Drive, Guildford, Surrey, GU3 3AE.* **Open:** Jan to Nov **Grades:** ETC 3 Diamond **01483 232347 & 07799 626198 (M)** Mr White *bill.white@amserve.net* **D:** Fr £20.00 **S:** Fr £25.00 **Beds:** 1D 1T **Baths:** 1 En 1 Pr (2) Off A323, quiet cottage, end of cul-de-sac. Lounge, conservatory, pleasant garden.

The Old Malt House, *Worplesdon, Guildford, Surrey, GU3 3PT.* Old country house with spacious, comfortable rooms in extensive grounds. **Open:** All year **Grades:** ETC 3 Diamond **01483 232152** Mrs Millar **D:** Fr £18.00–£20.00 **S:** Fr £20.00–£25.00 **Beds:** 1S 2T **Baths:** 2 Sh (6) cc

Atkinsons Guest House, *129 Stoke Road, Guildford, Surrey, GU1 1ET.* Clean, friendly, close to all amenities. 10 mins walk to town centre. **Open:** All year **01483 538260** Mrs Atkinson **D:** Fr £47.00 **S:** Fr £30.00 **Beds:** 1D 1T 2S **Baths:** 2 En 1 Sh (6) (2)

Hampton B&B, *38 Poltimore Road, Guildford, GU2 7PN.* Panoramic views. Walking distance of station and town centre. Quality accommodation. **Open:** All year (not Xmas/New Year) **01483 572012 & 07973 343495 (M)** Mrs Morris *vgmorris@aol.com* www.hampton-bedandbreakfast.co.uk **D:** Fr £24.00–£28.00 **S:** Fr £32.00–£50.00 **Beds:** 1T 2D **Baths:** 1 En 1 Sh (1)

Beevers Farm, *Chinthurst Lane, Bramley, Guildford, Surrey, GU5 0DR.* Peaceful surroundings, friendly atmosphere. Own preserves, honey, eggs. Nearby villages. **Open:** Feb to Dec **01483 898764 (also fax)** Mr Cook *beevers@onetel.net.uk* **D:** Fr £18.00–£25.00 **S:** Fr £30.00 **Beds:** 1F 2T **Baths:** 1 Pr 1 Sh (10)

B&B owners may vary rates – be sure to check when booking

2 Wodeland Avenue, *Guildford, GU2 4JX.* Centrally located rooms with panorama. Friendly and modernised family home. **Open:** All year (not Xmas)
01483 451142 Mrs Hay **Fax: 01483 572980** *rozanne.hay@talk21.com* **D:** Fr £20.00–£22.00 **S:** Fr £20.00–£25.00 **Beds:** 1D 1T **Baths:** 1 Pr 1 Sh (3) (3)

Haslemere

SU8932

Deerfell, *Fernden Lane, Haslemere, Surrey, GU27 3LA.* Wonderfully peaceful and scenic, Deerfell offers comfortable ensuite rooms, bath/shower, tea/coffee, TV, lounge with open fire. Breakfast served in handsome dining room. Many places of interest. London accessible from Haslemere train station: 4 miles. **Open:** Feb to Dec
01428 653409 Mrs Carmichael *deerfell@tesco.net* **D:** Fr £24.00 **S:** Fr £29.00 **Beds:** 2T 1S **Baths:** 2 En (6) (3)

Holmbury St Mary

TQ1144

Woodhill Cottage, *Holmbury St Mary, Dorking, Surrey, RH5 6NL.* Comfortable family home on outskirts of lovely rural village. **Open:** All year
01306 730498 Mrs McCann *woodhillcottage@amserve.net* **D:** Fr £21.00–£25.00 **S:** Fr £26.00–£32.00 **Beds:** 1T 2D **Baths:** 1 En 1 Sh (5) (3)

Bulmer Farm, *Holmbury St Mary, Dorking, Surrey, RH5 6LG.* Quiet, modernised C17th farmhouse/barn, large garden, picturesque village, self-catering. **Open:** All year
01306 730210 Mrs Hill **D:** Fr £23.00–£25.00 **S:** Fr £23.00–£37.00 **Beds:** 3D 5T **Baths:** 5 En 2 Sh (12) (12) 3

Horley

TQ2843

Vulcan Lodge Guest House, *27 Massetts Road, Horley, Surrey, RH6 7DQ.* Our warm hospitality compliments the highest quality of facilities and services. **Open:** All year
01293 771522 *karen@vulcan-lodge.com* www.vulcan-lodge.com **D:** Fr £27.50–£30.00 **S:** Fr £36.00–£40.00 **Beds:** 1F 1T 1D 2S **Baths:** 4 En 1 Sh (15) cc

Southbourne Guest House, *34 Massetts Road, Horley, Surrey, RH6 7DS.* Warm welcome awaits in our family-run guest house. 5 mins' drive Gatwick. **Open:** All year (not Xmas/New Year) **Grades:** ETC 2 Diamond
01293 771991 & 01293 820112 Breda & Tony Breen **Fax: 01293 820112** *reservations@southbournegatwick.com* www.southbournegatwick.com **D:** Fr £22.50–£27.50 **S:** Fr £30.00–£40.00 **Beds:** 2F 3T 2D 2S **Baths:** 2 En 2 Sh (20) cc

Prinsted Guest House, *Oldfield Road, Horley, Surrey, RH6 7EP.* Spacious Victorian house in quiet situation, ideal for Gatwick Airport. **Open:** All year (not Xmas) **Grades:** ETC 3 Diamond, AA 3 Diamond
01293 785233 Mrs Kendall **Fax: 01293 820624** *kendall@prinstedguesthouse.co.uk* www.prinstedguesthouse.co.uk **D:** Fr £19.00–£24.00 **S:** Fr £32.00–£33.00 **Beds:** 2D 3T 2S **Baths:** 6 En 1 Pr (10) cc

Yew Tree, *31 Massetts Road, Horley, Surrey, RH6 7DQ.* Tudor-style house, ½ acre gardens, close Gatwick Airport, near town centre. **Open:** All year
01293 785855 (also fax) Mr Stroud **D:** Fr £15.00–£20.00 **S:** Fr £20.00–£25.00 **Beds:** 1F 2D 1T 2S **Baths:** 1 En 1 Sh (2) (10) cc

Victoria Lodge Guest House, *161 Victoria Road, Horley, Surrey, RH6 7AS.* 5 mins from Gatwick Airport and Horley town. Families welcome. **Open:** All year
01293 432040 Mr & Mrs Robson **Fax: 01293 432042** *prnrjr@globalnet.co.uk* www.gatwicklodge.co.uk **D:** Fr £19.00–£25.00 **S:** Fr £30.00–£48.00 **Beds:** 2F 2D 2S **Baths:** 2 En 2 Sh (14) cc

Gorse Cottage, *66 Balcombe Road, Horley, Surrey, RH6 9AY.* Friendly, family run. 2 miles Gatwick Airport. Five mins station, serving London/South Coast. **Open:** All year (not Xmas/New Year)
01293 784402 (also fax) **D:** Fr £18.00–£20.00 **S:** Fr £25.00–£28.00 **Beds:** 1T 2S **Baths:** 1 En 1 Sh (2) (3)

The Gables, *50 Bonehurst Road, Horley, Surrey, RH6 8QG.* Family run guest house, near Gatwick Airport. Local pubs nearby. **Open:** All year (not Xmas/New Year)
01293 774553 & 01293 453345 Mr Hinojosa **Fax: 01243 430006** *enquiries@thegablesguesthouse.co.uk* www.thegablesguesthouse.co.uk **D:** Fr £18.00–£21.00 **S:** Fr £30.00–£33.00 **Beds:** 2F 9T 4D 2S **Baths:** 3 En 3 Sh cc

BEDROOMS
D = Double
T = Twin
S = Single
F = Family

Leatherhead

TQ1656

Selworthy, *310 Lower Road, Great Bookham, Leatherhead, Surrey, KT23 4DW.* Attractive location overlooking green belt. Convenient M25, Gatwick and Heathrow airports. **Open:** All year (not Xmas) **Grades:** ETC 3 Diamond
01372 453952 (also fax) Mrs Kent *bnb@selworthy.fslife.co.uk* **D:** Fr £21.00–£24.00 **S:** Fr £26.00–£29.00 **Beds:** 1D 1T **Baths:** 1 Sh (10) (4)

Leigh

TQ2246

Barn Cottage, *Church Road, Leigh, Reigate, Surrey, RH2 8RF.* Converted C17th barn, gardens with swimming pool, 100 yards from pub, 0.25 hr Gatwick. **Open:** All year
01306 611347 Mrs Comer **D:** Fr £25.00–£30.00 **S:** Fr £40.00–£45.00 **Beds:** 1D 1T **Baths:** 1 Sh (3)

Littleton

TQ0668

Old Manor House, *Squires Bridge Road, Littleton, Shepperton, Middx, TW17 0QG.* Listed building dating from reign of Henry VII, set in 5 acres of garden. **Open:** All year(not Xmas)
01932 571293 Mrs Bouwens *victor@oldmanorhouse.demon.co.uk* www.oldmanorhouse.demon.co.uk **D:** Fr £25.00–£27.50 **S:** Fr £30.00 **Beds:** 1D 1T 1S **Baths:** 1 En 1 Sh (10) (6)

Lower Bourne

SU8444

49 Burnt Hill Road, *Lower Bourne, Farnham, Surrey, GU10 3NA.* 300 year old cottage, overlooking paddocks. London 45 mins train. **Open:** All year
01252 715058 Mrs Sendall *diana@sendall.screaming.net* **D:** Fr £25.00 **S:** Fr £28.00–£35.00 **Beds:** 1T 1D 2S **Baths:** 2 En 1 Sh (10) (6)

Mayford

SU9956

East House, *Beech Hill, Mayford, Woking, Surrey, GU22 0SB.* Charming, quiet, Old English-style house, beautiful garden. **Open:** All year
01483 763218 (also fax) A Moss *vladmoss@aol.com* **D:** Fr £20.00 **S:** Fr £22.00 **Beds:** 1T 1D 1S **Baths:** 1 Sh (5) (2)

National Grid References given are for villages, towns and cities – not for individual houses

Milford
SU9442

Coturnix House, *Rake Lane, Milford, Godalming, Surrey, GU8 5AB.* Modern house, family atmosphere, countryside position, easy access road/rail. **Open:** All year
01483 416897 Mr Bell *100523.1037@compuserve.com* www.coturnix.freeserve.co.uk
D: Fr £25.00 **S:** Fr £25.00 **Beds:** 1D 1T 1S
Baths: 1 Pr 1 Sh (1) (6)

Newdigate
TQ1942

Sturtwood Farm, *Partridge Lane, Newdigate, Dorking, Surrey, RH5 5EE.* Comfortable welcoming farmhouse in beautiful wooded countryside. Many historic properties nearby. **Open:** All year (not Xmas/New Year)
01306 631308 Mrs MacKinnon **Fax: 01306 631908 D:** Fr £22.50–£25.00 **S:** Fr £30.00–£35.00 **Beds:** 1T 1S 1D **Baths:** 1 En 1 Sh (6)

Oxted
TQ3852

Meads, *23 Granville Road, Oxted, Surrey, RH8 0BX.* Tudor-style house on Kent/Surrey border. Station to London.
Open: All year
01883 730115 Mrs Holgate *Holgate@meads9.fsnet.co.uk* **D:** Fr £30.00–£35.00 **S:** Fr £35.00 **Beds:** 1T 1D 1S **Baths:** 1 En 1 Pr

Old Forge House, *Merle Common, Oxted, Surrey, RH8 0JB.* Welcoming family home in rural surroundings. Ten minutes from M25. **Open:** All year (not Xmas)
01883 715969 Mrs Mills **D:** Fr £24.00–£28.00 **S:** Fr £25.00–£30.00 **Beds:** 1D 1T 1S **Baths:** 1 Sh (4)

Pinehurst Grange Guest House, *East Hill (Part of A25), Oxted, Surrey, RH8 9AE.* Comfortable Victorian ex-farmhouse with traditional service and relaxed friendly atmosphere. **Open:** All year (not Xmas/New Year)
01883 716413 & 07790 607658 (M)
Mr Rodgers **D:** Fr £22.50 **S:** Fr £30.00
Beds: 1D 1T 1S **Baths:** 1 Sh (5) (3)

Redhill
TQ2750

Lynwood Guest House, *50 London Road, Redhill, Surrey, RH1 1LN.* Adjacent to a lovely park, within 6 minutes walk from railway station, town centre. **Open:** All year
01737 766894 Mrs Trozado **Fax: 01737 778253** *lynwoodguesthouse@yahoo.co.uk* www.lynwoodguesthouse.co.uk **D:** Fr £26.00–£28.00 **S:** Fr £35.00 **Beds:** 4F 2D 1T 2S
Baths: 3 En 6 Pr 1 Sh (8) **cc**

Ripley
TQ0456

The Half Moon, *High Street, Ripley, Woking, GU23 6AN.* Old world inn, all rooms colour TV, washbasins, tea/coffee.
Open: All year
01483 224380 (also fax) Mr Beale **D:** Fr £20.00–£22.50 **S:** Fr £40.00–£45.00 **Beds:** 1D 6T **Baths:** 4 Pr 1 Sh (7) (20)

Rowledge
SU8243

Hope Cottage, *15 Lickfolds Road, Rowledge, Farnham, Surrey, GU10 4AF.* Quiet location with large garden and conservatory. Friendly and welcoming.
Open: All year (not Xmas/New Year)
01252 792942 Mrs Turnbull *jane@turnbull.uk.net* **D:** Fr £25.00–£30.00 **S:** Fr £25.00–£30.00 **Beds:** 2D 1S **Baths:** 1 Sh

Send
TQ0255

Grant-chester, *Boughton Hall Avenue, Send, Woking, Surrey, GU23 7DF.*
Open: All year (not Xmas/New Year)
01483 225383 Mrs Winterbourne *gary@hotmail.com* **D:** Fr £24.00 **S:** Fr £30.00
Beds: 3T 2S **Baths:** 3 Sh (9)
Attractive family house with large garden. 4 miles from Guildford, Woking and close to M25 and A3. Wisley Gardens, Clandon Park and golf courses nearby. Own transport recommended. Parking available. Long term stays very welcome.

Shalford
TQ0046

The Laurels, *23 Dagden Road, Shalford, Guildford, Surrey, GU4 8DD.* Quiet detached house. Direct access to footpaths. Near Guildford centre. **Open:** All year
01483 565753 Mrs Deeks **D:** Fr £20.00–£23.00 **S:** Fr £22.00 **Beds:** 1T 1D (6) (5)

Shepperton
TQ0767

Splash Cottage, *91 Watersplash Road, Shepperton, TW17 0EE.* Olde worlde cottage with pretty bedrooms and old fashioned hospitality. **Open:** All year **Grades:** ETC 3 Diamond
01932 229987 (also fax) Mr Shaw *info@lazy-river.co.uk* www.lazy-river.co.uk **D:** Fr £22.50–£27.50 **S:** Fr £30.00–£35.00 **Beds:** 2D 1T

The Bull Inn, *152 Laleham Road, Shepperton, TW17 0DB.* Perfect for visiting all main attractions in Surrey. Friendly Atmosphere. **Open:** All year
01932 221667 D: Fr £21.00 **S:** Fr £16.00
Beds: 3T 1S **Baths:** 3 En 1 Sh (20)
cc

Shere
TQ0747

Cherry Trees, *Gomshall Lane, Shere, Guildford, Surrey, GU5 9HE.* Quiet comfortable house, lovely garden, village at foot of North Downs. **Open:** All year (not Xmas/New Year)
01483 202288 Mrs Warren **D:** Fr £25.00 **S:** Fr £25.00–£30.00 **Beds:** 2D 3F 1S **Baths:** 2 En 1 Sh (4)

Lockhurst Hatch Farm, *Lockhurst Hatch Lane, Shere, Guildford, Surrey, GU5 9JN.* Farmhouse dating from C15th. Area of Outstanding Natural Beauty.
Open: All year
01483 202689 G Gellatly **D:** Fr £25.00 **S:** Fr £30.00 **Beds:** 1F **Baths:** 1 En (2)

South Holmwood
TQ1745

Steyning Cottage, *Horsham Road, South Holmwood, Dorking, Surrey, RH5 4NE.* Special rates for long term, including dinner. French spoken. **Open:** All year (not Xmas)
01306 888481 Mrs Treays **D:** Fr £20.00–£22.00 **S:** Fr £20.00–£22.50 **Beds:** 1T 1S
Baths: 1 Sh (4)

Staines
TQ0471

The Penton, *39 Penton Road, Staines, TW18 2JL.* Homely character cottage close to River Thames, access to scenic walks and historic surroundings. **Open:** All year
01784 458787 D: Fr £20.00–£25.00 **S:** Fr £20.00–£26.00 **Beds:** 4F 1D 1T 1S **Baths:** 2 En 1 Sh (2)

Thursley

SU9039

Little Cowdray Farm, *Thursley, Godalming, Surrey, GU8 6QJ.* Farmhouse built early 50's with excellent views. 1.5 miles from A3. **Open:** All year (not Xmas/ New Year)
01428 605016 Mrs Goble **D:** Fr £36.00 **S:** Fr £18.00 **Beds:** 1T **Baths:** 1 Sh

Hindhead Hill Farm, *Portsmouth Road, Thursley, Godalming, Surrey, GU8 6NN.* Small Christian family farm. Our own free-range eggs for breakfast. **Open:** All year (not Xmas)
01428 684727 Mrs Roe **Fax: 01428 685004** *cproe@supanet.com* **D:** Fr £20.00–£21.00 **S:** Fr £21.00 **Beds:** 1F 1T **Baths:** 1 En 1 Pr (4)

Walton-on-Thames

TQ1066

Beech Tree Lodge, *7 Rydens Avenue, Walton-on-Thames, Surrey, KT12 3JB.* 10 mins station to London and Surrey countryside. Quiet location. **Open:** All year **Grades:** ETC 3 Diamond
01932 886667 & 01932 242738 Mrs Spiteri *joanspiteri@aol.com* **D:** Fr £20.00–£21.00 **S:** Fr £30.00–£38.00 **Beds:** 1F 1T 1S **Baths:** 2 Sh (8)

Warlingham

TQ3558

Glenmore, *Southview Road, Warlingham, Surrey, CR6 9JE.* Victorian House in the large grounds close to the countryside and London. **Open:** All year
01883 624530 Fax: 01883 624199 D: Fr £17.50 **S:** Fr £22.00 **Beds:** 2F 1T 2D **Baths:** 1 En 2 Sh (6)

West Horsley

TQ0752

Brinford, *Windmill Hill, Off Shere Road, West Horsley, Surrey, KT24 6EJ.* Modern house in peaceful rural location in Surrey Hills. Easy reach Guildford NT properties, Hampton Court, Windsor, London. Good walking area. **Open:** All year **Grades:** ETC 3 Diamond
01483 283636 Mrs Wiltshire **D:** Fr £24.00–£28.00 **S:** Fr £30.00–£38.00 **Beds:** 1D 1T 1S **Baths:** 1 En 1 Sh (4)

West Molesey

TQ1268

Pilgrim's Retreat, *43 Grange Road, West Molesey, Surrey, KT8 2PR.* Friendly, family home, one mile from Hampton Court. Continental breakfast. **Open:** All year (not Xmas/New Year)
020 8224 2460 Ms Vaughan-Spruce *vaughan_spruce@hotmail.com* **D:** Fr £16.50 **S:** Fr £22.00 **Beds:** 1T 1S **Baths:** 1 Sh (1)

Worplesdon

SU9753

The Old Malt House, *Worplesdon, Guildford, Surrey, GU3 3PT.* Old country house with spacious, comfortable rooms in extensive grounds. **Open:** All year **Grades:** ETC 3 Diamond
01483 232152 Mrs Millar **D:** Fr £18.00–£20.00 **S:** Fr £20.00–£25.00 **Beds:** 1S 2T **Baths:** 2 Sh (6) cc

East Sussex

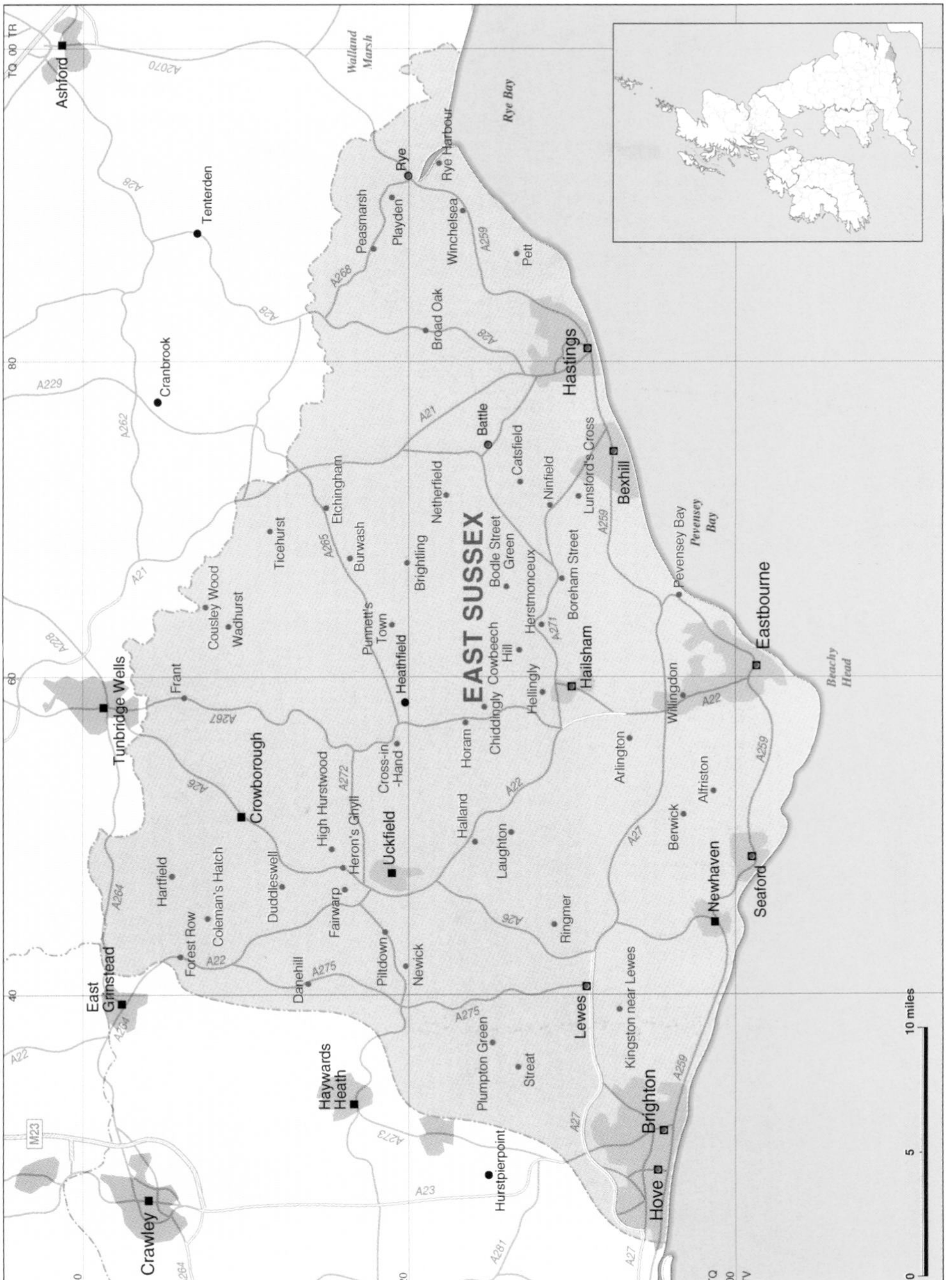
EAST SUSSEX
Ashford
Tenterden
Cranbrook
Tunbridge Wells
Crowborough
East Grinstead
Crawley
Haywards Heath
Hurstpierpoint
Walland Marsh
Rye Bay
Pevensey Bay
Beachy Head
Rye
Rye Harbour
Playden
Peasmarsh
Winchelsea
Pett
Broad Oak
Hastings
Battle
Catsfield
Lunsford's Cross
Bexhill
Ninfield
Netherfield
Etchingham
Ticehurst
Burwash
Brightling
Bodle Street Green
Herstmonceux
Boreham Street
Pevensey Bay
Eastbourne
Cousley Wood
Wadhurst
Punnett's Town
Heathfield
Cowbeech Hill
Hailsham
Hellingly
Chiddingly
Frant
Willingdon
Horam
Cross-in-Hand
High Hurstwood
Arlington
Alfriston
Halland
Laughton
Berwick
Uckfield
Heron's Ghyll
Hartfield
Coleman's Hatch
Duddleswell
Fairwarp
Seaford
Newhaven
Ringmer
Forest Row
Piltdown
Newick
Danehill
Lewes
Kingston near Lewes
Plumpton Green
Streat
Brighton
Hove
A21
A22
A23
A26
A27
A28
A229
A259
A262
A264
A265
A267
A268
A271
A272
A273
A275
A281
A2070
M23
TQ
TV
0
5
10 miles

Planning a longer stay? Always ask for any special rates

Alfriston

TQ5103

Dacres, *Alfriston, Polegate, East Sussex, BN26 5TP.* Studio apartment in pretty cottage. Beautiful gardens. Organic breakfasts. **Open:** All year
01323 870447 Mrs Embry **D:** Fr £25.00 **S:** Fr £40.00 **Beds:** 1T **Baths:** 1 Pr (1)

Meadowbank, *Sloe Lane, Alfriston, East Sussex, BN26 5UR.* Lovely tranquil accommodation. Close village centre. Superb breakfasts. **Open:** All year (not Xmas/New Year)
01323 870742 Mrs Petch **D:** Fr £20.00–£25.00 **S:** Fr £30.00–£35.00 **Beds:** 1T 2D **Baths:** 1 En 2 Sh (4)

Arlington

TQ5407 *Old Oak, Rose Cottage, Yew Tree*

Bates Green, *Arlington, Polegate, E. Sussex, BN26 6SH.* Peaceful location. Tranquil garden. Close Sussex towns. **Open:** All year (not Xmas/New Year)
01323 482039 (also fax) C McCutchan **D:** Fr £30.00–£35.00 **Beds:** 2T 2D **Baths:** 3 En (3)

Battle

TQ7515

Bell Cottage, *Vinehall Road, Robertsbridge, Battle, E Sussex, TN32 5JN.* C17th converted inn, beamed throughout. Delightful gardens. Warm welcome assured. **Open:** All year (not Xmas)
01580 881164 Mrs Lowe **Fax: 01580 880519**
patricia.lowe@tesco.net www.bellcottage.co.uk
D: Fr £20.00–£25.00 **S:** Fr £25.00–£30.00
Beds: 1D 2T **Baths:** 1 En 1 Pr 1 Sh (3) cc

Bell Cottage, *Vinehall Road, Robertsbridge, Battle, E Sussex, TN32 5JN.* C17th converted inn, beamed throughout. Delightful gardens. Warm welcome assured. **Open:** All year (not Xmas)
01580 881164 Mrs Lowe **Fax: 01580 880519**
patricia.lowe@tesco.net www.bellcottage.co.uk
D: Fr £20.00–£25.00 **S:** Fr £25.00–£30.00
Beds: 1D 2T **Baths:** 1 En 1 Pr 1 Sh (3) cc

Fox Hole Farm, *Kane Hythe Road, Battle, E Sussex, TN33 9QU.* A restored country cottage. Perfect place to relax and unwind. **Open:** All year
01424 772053 Mr Collins **Fax: 01424 773771**
D: Fr £24.50–£27.50 **S:** Fr £29.00–£39.00
Beds: 3D **Baths:** 3 En (6) cc

Kelklands, *Off Chain Lane, Battle, East Sussex, TN33 0HG.* Peaceful situation, short walk into town. No smoking, easy parking. **Open:** All year
01424 773013 M Burgess **D:** Fr £20.00 **S:** Fr £20.00 **Beds:** 1F 1T 1S **Baths:** 2 En 1 Sh (2) (5)

Berwick

TQ5104

Dawes House, *Berwick, Polegate, E Sussex, BN26 5QS.* Delightful period country home near Alfriston in scenic Cuckmere Valley. **Open:** Feb to Nov
01323 871276 (also fax) Mrs Wardroper
D: Fr £22.50–£27.50 **S:** Fr £25.00–£30.00
Beds: 1D 1T **Baths:** 1 En 1 Pr (4)

Bexhill-on-Sea

TQ7308

Buenos Aires, *24 Albany Road, Bexhill-on-Sea, E Sussex, TN40 1BZ.* **Open:** All year
Grades: ETC 4 Diamond
01424 212269 (also fax) Mr & Mrs Robson
buenosairesguesthouse@hotmail.com **D:** Fr £17.50–£22.50 **S:** Fr £20.00–£30.00 **Beds:** 1F 1D 1T 1S **Baths:** 1 En 2 Sh (5)
Well-established guest house offering a high standard of comfortable accommodation in a warm and friendly atmosphere. Situated close to seafront, town centre and De La Warr Pavilion, offering both ensuite and standard rooms.

Wakeford House, *Potmans Lane, Lunsford's Cross, Bexhill-on-Sea, E. Sussex, TN39 5JL.* Edwardian-style house in country setting with peaceful one acre garden. **Open:** All year
01424 892013 Mrs Skinner **Fax: 01424 893978** *wakeford@wakefordhouse.com*
www.wakefordhouse.com **D:** Fr £25.00–£30.00 **S:** Fr £30.00 **Beds:** 3F 1D 1S 1T
Baths: 1 En 1 Sh (5)

Planning a longer stay? Always ask for any special rates

Manor Barn, *Lunsford's Cross, Bexhill on Sea, E. Sussex, TN39 5JJ.* Ensuite chalets, semi-rural setting on A269, 3 miles sea. **Open:** All year
01424 893018 (also fax) Mrs Gillingham
D: Fr £18.00–£19.50 **S:** Fr £25.00–£26.50
Beds: 1F 1D 1T 1S **Baths:** 4 En (6)

Marabou Bed & Breakfast, *60 Devonshire Road, Bexhill-on-Sea, E Sussex, TN40 1AX.* Comfortable seaside B&B. **Open:** All year
01424 215052 (also fax) **D:** Fr £17.00–£22.00
S: Fr £17.00–£22.00 **Beds:** 3F 3T 10D
Baths: 16 En cc

16 Magdalen Road, *Bexhill-on-Sea, E. Sussex, TN40 1SB.* Large, friendly, family house close to station, shops and sea front. **Open:** All year (not Xmas/New Year)
01424 218969 Barker **D:** Fr £15.00–£20.00
S: Fr £15.00–£30.00 **Beds:** 1F 1T 1D **Baths:** 2 Sh

Bodle Street Green

TQ6514

The Stud Farm, *Bodle Street Green, Hailsham, E. Sussex, BN27 4RJ.* Comfortable farmhouse on working farm. Situated between Heathfield, Hailsham, Battle. **Open:** All year (not Xmas/New Year)
01323 833201 (also fax) Mr & Mrs Gentry
D: Fr £20.00–£21.00 **S:** Fr £22.00–£25.00
Beds: 1D 2T **Baths:** 1 Pr 1 Sh (3)

Boreham Street

TQ6611

Baldocks, *Boreham Street, Hailsham, E Sussex, BN27 4SQ.* **Open:** All year (not Xmas)
01323 832107
D: Fr £20.00 **S:** Fr £20.00–£30.00 **Beds:** 1D 1T **Baths:** 1 Sh (2)
A warm welcome awaits you at this part C16th cottage in 1066 country, with many local walks. Situated 2 miles from beautiful Herstmonceux Castle and grounds and 5 miles from Pevensey Castle - a good bird watching area, especially around the marshes.

BEDROOMS
D = Double
T = Twin
S = Single
F = Family

Brightling

TQ6821

Swallowfield Farm, *Brightling, Robertsbridge, East Sussex, TN32 5HB.* Elizabethan farmhouse and self-contained cottage in thirty acres of outstanding beauty. **Open:** All year
01424 838225 Mrs Page **Fax: 01424 838885**
jssp@swallowfieldfarm.freeserve.co.uk
www.swallowfieldfarm.com **D:** Fr £23.00–£25.00 **S:** Fr £25.00–£30.00 **Beds:** 1F 2T
Baths: 2 En (20)

Brighton

TQ3106

Claremont House Hotel, *Second Avenue, Hove, E Sussex, BN3 2LL.* **Open:** All year **Grades:** ETC 4 Diamond
01273 735161 (also fax) Mr Brewerton
claremonthove@aol.com
www.claremonthousehotel.co.uk **D:** Fr £37.50–£60.00 **S:** Fr £40.00–£65.00 **Beds:** 2F 6D/T 4S **Baths:** 12 En **cc**
Claremont House is an elegantly presented Victorian villa, situated just a few hundred yards from the seafront and minutes from the centre of Brighton. The individually decorated rooms are very comfortably furnished, all benefiting from ensuite facilities. Bar available.

Arlanda Hotel, *20 New Steine, Brighton, E. Sussex, BN2 1PD.* **Open:** All year **Grades:** ETC 4 Diamond, Silver, AA 4 Diamond, RAC 4 Diamond
01273 699300 Mr Mathews **Fax: 01273 600930** *arlanda@brighton.co.uk*
www.arlandahotel.co.uk **D:** Fr £30.00–£60.00 **S:** Fr £30.00–£60.00 **Beds:** 1T 9D 6S
Baths: 16 En **cc**
A charming Grade II Regency townhouse, situated in a garden square adjacent to the seafront. The hotel provides a peaceful and relaxing base for exploring historic yet vibrant Brighton. You are assured a warm welcome and a clean and comfortable stay.

Avalon House, *7 Upper Rock Gardens, Brighton, East Sussex, BN2 1QE.* **Open:** All year (not Xmas)
01273 692344
avalonbrighton@aol.com **D:** Fr £22.50–£30.00 **S:** Fr £25.00–£30.00 **Beds:** 1F 2T 5D 1S
Baths: 8 En (12) **cc**
A Grade II listed building, being two minutes from seafront and ten minutes walk from town centre, Royal Pavilion and the famous 'Lanes'. All rooms tastefully decorated, most equipped with CD players and fridges. A friendly welcome awaits you.

Brighton Marina House Hotel, *8 Charlotte Street, Brighton, E. Sussex, BN2 1AG.*
Open: All year
01273 605349 Mr Jung **Fax: 01273 679484**
rooms@jungs.co.uk www.brighton-mh-hotel.co.uk **D:** Fr £25.00–£99.00 **S:** Fr £25.00–£55.00 **Beds:** 3F 7D 4T 3S **Baths:** 7 Pr 1 Sh
Ideal location, 2 mins walk to the beach. Unique and innovative experience in today's B&B. Rooms only offer (without breakfast). Most rooms non-smoking. Free Internet and e-mail facility. We cater for vegans, vegetarians, English and Continental.

Ambassador Hotel, *23 New Steine, Brighton, E. Sussex, BN2 1PD.* **Open:** All year (not Xmas) **Grades:** ETC 4 Diamond
01273 676869 Mr Koullas **Fax: 01273 689988**
D: Fr £28.00–£40.00 **S:** Fr £28.00–£40.00
Beds: 5F 5D 4T 6S **Baths:** 20 En **cc**
Situated in a seafront garden square - excellent location from where you can explore the sights, shops and entertainment that Brighton has to offer. Overlooking the sea and Palace Pier. You'll enjoy our freshly cooked English or vegetarian breakfast in our spacious dining room.

Fyfield House, *26 New Steine, Brighton, E. Sussex, BN2 1PD.* Welcoming, clean home from home with superb views of sea. **Open:** All year (not Xmas)
01273 602770 (also fax) Mr & Mrs Culpeck
fyfield@aol.com www.brighton.co.uk/hotels/fyfield **D:** Fr £27.50–£45.00 **S:** Fr £27.50–£45.00 **Beds:** 2F 7D 1T 4S **Baths:** 9 En 2 Sh **cc**

Ainsley House Hotel, *28 New Steine, Brighton, E. Sussex, BN2 1PQ.* Regency town house. Comfortable rooms. Excellent breakfasts, warm welcome, sea views. **Open:** All year (not Xmas)
01273 605310 Mrs King **Fax: 01273 688604**
ahhotel@fastnet.co.uk www.ainsleyhotel.com
D: Fr £25.00–£45.00 **S:** Fr £28.00–£36.00
Beds: 2F 4D 2T 3S **Baths:** 9 En 2 Sh **cc**

Dudley House, *10 Madeira Place, Brighton, E. Sussex, BN2 1TN.* Grade 2 listed Victorian town house, centrally located, near seafront. **Open:** All year
01273 676794 Mr & Mrs Lacey *office@dudleyhousebrighton.com*
www.dudleyhousebrighton.com **D:** Fr £20.00–£35.00 **S:** Fr £20.00–£50.00 **Beds:** 6D
Baths: 3 En 3 Sh (10) **cc**

Market Inn, *1 Market Street, Brighton, East Sussex, BN1 1HH.* Traditional inn, in the centre of Brighton's famous 'Lanes' area, close to sea front. **Open:** All year
01273 329483 Fax: 01273 777227 *ac.tull@reallondonpubs.com* **D:** Fr £25.00–£30.00 **S:** Fr £45.00 **Beds:** 2D **Baths:** 2 En **cc**

14 Roedean Way, *Brighton, East Sussex, BN2 5RJ.* Situated above Brighton Marina. Stunning sea views. Quiet. Lovely garden. **Open:** All year (not Xmas/New Year)
01273 605369 Mrs Shepherd *rube@rshepherd.freeserve.co.uk* **D:** Fr £25.00–£28.00
S: Fr £27.50–£30.00 **Beds:** 1T 1D **Baths:** 2 Pr (2)

Trouville Hotel, *11 New Steine, Brighton, E. Sussex, BN2 1PB.* Listed Regency townhouse restored to high standard and situated in a seafront square. **Open:** Feb to Dec
01273 697384 Mr Hansell **D:** Fr £29.50–£32.50 **S:** Fr £29.00–£45.00 **Beds:** 2F 3D 1T 2S **Baths:** 6 Pr 1 Sh **cc**

B&B owners may vary rates – be sure to check when booking

Oriental Hotel, *9 Oriental Place, Brighton, E. Sussex, BN1 2LJ.* Stylish, friendly and relaxed hotel with contemporary decor, centrally located. **Open:** All year (not Xmas/ New Year) **Grades:** ETC 3 Diamond
01273 205050 Fax: 01273 821096 *info@orientalhotel.co.uk* www.orientalhotel.co.uk **D:** Fr £42.50–£57.50 **S:** Fr £40.00–£50.00 **Beds:** 1F 6D 2S **Baths:** 7 En 2 Sh cc

Brighton Royal Hotel, *76 Grand Parade, Brighton, E. Sussex, BN2 2JA.* Opposite Brighton's Royal Pavilion. Close to bars, clubs, shops, seafront, and theatres. **Open:** All year
01273 604182 (also fax) D: Fr £27.50–£40.00 **S:** Fr £27.50–£35.00 **Beds:** 1F 1T 7D 1S **Baths:** 1 En 1 Pr 1 Sh (10) cc

Diana House, *25 St Georges Terrace, Brighton, E. Sussex, BN2 1JJ.* Friendly run guest house. Close to seafront and town centre. **Open:** All year
01273 605797 Mrs Burgess *diana@enterprise.net* www.dianahouse.co.uk **D:** Fr £25.00–£27.00 **S:** Fr £50.00–£54.00 **Beds:** 5F 5D 1S **Baths:** 9 En 2 Sh cc

Regency Hotel, *28 Regency Square, Brighton, East Sussex, BN1 2FH.* Regency townhouse in prestigious square. Delightful, direct sea views, family managed. **Open:** All year
01273 202690 Fax: 01273 220438 *enquiries@regencybrighton.co.uk* www.regencybrighton.co.uk **D:** Fr £40.00–£70.00 **S:** Fr £55.00–£65.00 **Beds:** 1F 2T 6D 4S **Baths:** 9 Pr 2 Sh (3) (500) cc

New Steine Hotel, *12a New Steine, Brighton, E. Sussex, BN2 1PB.* With 4 Diamonds, New Steine Hotel offers high standard of service with personal touch. **Open:** All year
01273 681546 Mr Guyat **Fax: 01273 679118 D:** Fr £20.00–£41.00 **S:** Fr £25.00–£35.00 **Beds:** 2T 7D 2S **Baths:** 7 En 3 Sh (12) cc

Paskins Hotel, *19 Charlotte Street, Brighton, E. Sussex, BN2 1AG.* Organic and natural food. Delicious traditional and vegetarian breakfasts. Stylish. **Open:** All year
01273 601203 Fax: 01273 621973 *Welcome@paskins.co.uk* www.paskins.co.uk **D:** Fr £22.50–£45.00 **S:** Fr £22.50–£35.00 **Beds:** 2F 10D 2T 6S **Baths:** 17 En 3 Sh

Broad Oak (Rye)

TQ8220

Layces Bed & Breakfast, *Chitcombe Road, Broad Oak, Rye, E. Sussex, TN31 6EU.* Luxury accommodation. Beautiful countryside, convenient for historic sites and gardens. **Open:** All year **Grades:** ETC 4 Diamond, Silver
01424 882836 Mr Stephens **Fax: 01424 882281** *stephens@layces.fsnet.co.uk* www.layces.co.uk **D:** Fr £20.00 **S:** Fr £27.00 **Beds:** 1T 2D **Baths:** 3 En (5) cc

Furnace Lane Oast, *Broad Oak (Rye), Rye, E. Sussex, TN31 6ET.* Double oasthouse in peaceful rural setting. Ideal for local touring. **Open:** All year
01424 882407 (also fax) Mr Sevastopulo *furnacelane@pavilion.co.uk* www.seetb.org.uk/furnace-lane-oast **D:** Fr £25.50–£30.00 **S:** Fr £30.00–£40.00 **Beds:** 1F 1T 1D **Baths:** 3 En (5)

Burwash

TQ6724

Woodlands Farm, *Heathfield Road, Burwash, Etchingham, E. Sussex, TN19 7LA.* Comfortable, quiet, friendly C16th farmhouse, 0.25 mile off road. **Open:** All year
01435 882794 (also fax) Mrs Sirrell *liz.sir@lineone.net* www.smoothhound.co.uk/hotels/woodlands.html **D:** Fr £20.00–£23.00 **S:** Fr £20.00–£26.00 **Beds:** 2D 2T **Baths:** 1 En 2 Sh (6)

Catsfield

TQ7214

Farthings Farm, *Catsfield, Battle, East Sussex, TN33 9BA.* Edwardian house on a 70-acre farm set half mile off the road. **Open:** All year (not Xmas)
01424 773107 Mrs Rodgers www.farthingsfarm.co.uk **D:** Fr £25.00 **S:** Fr £30.00 **Beds:** 2D 1T **Baths:** 2 Pr (3)

Chiddingly

TQ5414

Hale Farm House, *Chiddingly, Lewes, E Sussex, BN8 6HQ.* C14th Listed beamed farmhouse, spacious rooms, situated on Wealdway overlooking South Downs. **Open:** All year
01825 872619 (also fax) Mrs Burrough *s.burrough@virgin.net* www.cuckmere-valley.co.uk/hale **D:** Fr £18.00–£25.00 **S:** Fr £18.00–£25.00 **Beds:** 1F 2T **Baths:** 1 En 1 Sh (3)

Coleman's Hatch

TQ4533 The Hatch

Gospel Oak, *Sandy Lane, Coleman's Hatch, Hartfield, E. Sussex, TN7 4ER.* A charming county cottage in heart of Ashdown Forest. **Open:** All year
01342 823840 Mrs Hawker **D:** Fr £22.50–£50.00 **S:** Fr £25.00–£28.00 **Beds:** 1T 1D **Baths:** 2 En (4)

B&B owners may vary rates – be sure to check when booking

Cousley Wood

TQ6533 Old Vine

Cheviots, *Cousley Wood, Wadhurst, E. Sussex, TN5 6HD.* Country house in beautiful Weald, good base for many NT properties. **Open:** Easter to Oct
01892 782952 Mr Field *cheviots.guesthouse@dial.pipex.com* **D:** Fr £22.50–£27.50 **S:** Fr £22.00–£27.00 **Beds:** 1T 1D 2S **Baths:** 2 En 1 Sh (4) cc

Cowbeech Hill

TQ6113

Batchelors, *Cowbeech Hill, Hailsham, E Sussex, BN27 4JB.* Situated perfectly for exploring East Sussex, warm welcome, farmhouse breakfast. **Open:** All year
01323 832215 Mrs Barrow **D:** Fr £22.50–£25.00 **S:** Fr £30.00 **Beds:** 1D 2T **Baths:** 1 En 1 Pr 2 Sh (10) (3)

Cross-in-Hand

TQ5521

Old Corner Cottage, *Little London Road, Cross-in-Hand, Heathfield, E. Sussex, TN21 0LT.* High quality accommodation situated conveniently for many National Trust properties and gardens. **Open:** All year **Grades:** AA 5 Diamond
01435 863787 (also fax) Mrs Brown *hamishcjbrown@aol.com* **D:** Fr £22.00–£26.00 **S:** Fr £25.00–£30.00 **Beds:** 2D 1T **Baths:** 3 En (10)

Danehill

TQ4027 Coach & Horses, The Sloop, The Griffin

Sliders Farmhouse, *Furners Green, Danehill, Uckfield, E. Sussex, TN22 3RT.* Picturesque C16th country house, peacefully situated down a country lane. **Open:** All year (not Xmas)
01825 790258 (also fax) Mr Salmon *jean&davidsalmon@freeserve.co.uk* **D:** Fr £22.00–£30.00 **S:** Fr £34.00–£40.00 **Beds:** 1F 1D 1T **Baths:** 3 En (10)

New Glenmore, *Sliders Lane, Furners Green, Danehill, East Sussex, TN22 3RU.* Spacious bungalow set in 6 acres near Bluebell Railway and Sheffield Park. **Open:** All year (not Xmas/New Year)
01825 790783 (also fax) Mr Robinson *alan.robinson@bigfoot.com* **D:** Fr £20.00 **S:** Fr £35.00 **Beds:** 1F 1T 1D **Baths:** 1 En 1 Sh

Duddleswell

TQ4628

Toll Platt, *Duddleswell, Nutley, Uckfield, E. Sussex, TN22 3JB.* Self-contained wing of country cottage upon the Ashdown Forest. Prior arrangement only. **Open:** All year (not Xmas/New Year)
01825 712683 D Bradbury **Fax: 01825 713120 D:** Fr £25.00 **S:** Fr £25.00 **Beds:** 1D **Baths:** 1 En (2)

Eastbourne

TQ5900

Ambleside Private Hotel, *24 Elms Avenue, Eastbourne, E. Sussex, BN21 3DN.* **Open:** All year **01323 724991** Mr Pattenden **D:** Fr £18.00–£22.00 **S:** Fr £18.00–£22.00 **Beds:** 4D 4T 2S **Baths:** 2 Sh 3 En
Situated on quiet avenue adjacent to seafront, pier, town centre, theatres. Convenient for railway and coach stations. Short distance from South Downs Way, Weald way. Colour TV in bedrooms. Compliant with environmental and fire regulations.

Camberley Hotel, *27-29 Elms Avenue, Eastbourne, E. Sussex, BN21 3DN.* **Open:** Mar to Oct
01323 723789 D: Fr £19.00–£23.00 **S:** Fr £19.00–£23.00 **Beds:** 4F 3D 3T 2S **Baths:** 7 En 2 Sh (3)
Situated in a pleasant avenue close to town centre, sea front and all amenities. Licensed, ensuite, tea-making, colour TV in bedrooms. English breakfast. Bedrooms non-smoking.

Cherry Tree Hotel, *15 Silverdale Road, Eastbourne, E. Sussex, BN20 7AJ.* Award-winning family-run hotel, close to sea front, downlands and theatres. **Open:** All year **Grades:** ETC 2 Star, Silver
01323 722406 Mr Henley **Fax: 01323 648838** *anncherrytree@aol.com* www.eastbourne.org/cherrytree-hotel **D:** Fr £28.00–£38.00 **S:** Fr £28.00–£38.00 **Beds:** 1F 4D 3T 2S **Baths:** 10 En (7) cc

Meridale Guest House, *91 Royal Parade, Eastbourne, East Sussex, BN22 7AE.* Quality B&B, sea front, quiet end of town, excellent value. **Open:** All year **01323 729686 Fax: 01323 419042** *crcmeridale@talk21.com* **D:** Fr £19.50 **S:** Fr £22.50 **Beds:** 2F 1T 3D **Baths:** 6 En cc

Southcroft, *15 South Cliff Avenue, Eastbourne, E. Sussex, BN20 7AH.* Non-smoking, friendly and family-run. Close to Downs, theatres, town centre. **Open:** All year
01323 729071 Mrs Skriczka *southcroft@eastbourne34.freeserve.co.uk* www.southcrofthotel.co.uk **D:** Fr £27.00–£34.00 **S:** Fr £27.00–£35.00 **Beds:** 2D 1T **Baths:** 3 En

Alfriston Hotel, *16 Lushington Road, Eastbourne, E. Sussex, BN21 4LL.* Victorian townhouse hotel, town centre conservation area, near station/sea. **Open:** All year (not Xmas/New Year)
01323 725640 *alfristonhotel@fsbdial.co.uk* **D:** Fr £25.00–£28.00 **S:** Fr £25.00–£28.00 **Beds:** 3D 2T 5S **Baths:** 8 En 1 Sh (12)

Camelot Lodge Hotel, *35 Lewes Road, Eastbourne, East Sussex, BN21 2BU.* High quality, friendly, family-run hotel in ideal location. **Open:** All year **Grades:** AA 3 Diamond
01323 725207 Fax: 01323 722799 *info@camelotlodgehotel.com* www.camelotlodgehotel.com **D:** Fr £25.00 **S:** Fr £25.00–£30.00 **Beds:** 3F 1T 3D **Baths:** 7 En

Edelweiss Hotel, *10-12 Elms Avenue, Eastbourne, E. Sussex, BN21 3DN.* Central family-run hotel just off sea front. Comfortable and welcoming. **Open:** All year
01323 732071 (also fax) Mr & Mrs Butler *peterbutler@fsbdial.co.uk* www.smoothhound.co.uk/hotels/edelweis.html **D:** Fr £16.00–£20.00 **S:** Fr £16.00–£25.00 **Beds:** 1F 6D 5T 2S **Baths:** 3 En 4 Sh cc

Heatherdene Hotel, *26-28 Elms Avenue, Eastbourne, E. Sussex, BN21 3DN.* Good food and comfortable rooms. Train and coach stations nearby. **Open:** All year
01323 723598 (also fax) Mrs Mockford **D:** Fr £17.00–£45.00 **S:** Fr £16.00–£25.00 **Beds:** 1F 4D 8T 3S **Baths:** 6 En 3 Sh 3

The Manse, *7 Dittons Road, Eastbourne, East Sussex, BN21 1DW.* Character house located in quiet area yet within 5 mins' walk of town centre. **Open:** All year (not Xmas)
01323 737851 Mrs Walker **D:** Fr £15.00–£20.00 **S:** Fr £20.00–£25.00 **Beds:** 1F 2T **Baths:** 2 En 1 Pr (8) (1)

Sheldon Hotel, *9-11 Burlington Place, Eastbourne, East Sussex, BN21 4AS.* Situated within a few minutes walk of sea front, theatres. Licensed. **Open:** All year
01323 724120 Fax: 01323 430406 *gmeyer@sheldonhotel.fsbusiness.co.uk* www.smoothhound.co.uk/hotels/sheldon.html **D:** Fr £25.00–£31.00 **S:** Fr £25.00–£31.00 **Beds:** 4F 6T 8D 6S **Baths:** 24 En cc

Etchingham

TQ7126 *The Bull, Rose & Crown*

King Johns Lodge, *Sheepstreet Lane, Etchingham, East Sussex, TN19 7AZ.* Historic Listed house in 7 acres of gardens. Exceptional furnishings and settings. **Open:** All year (not Xmas/New Year)
01580 819232 Fax: 01580 819562 D: Fr £35.00–£40.00 **S:** Fr £50.00–£55.00 **Beds:** 1F 1T 2D **Baths:** 2 En 2 Pr (7) (12)

Fairwarp

TQ4626

Broom Cottage, *Browns Brook, Fairwarp, Uckfield, E Sussex, TN22 3BY.* Victorian cottage in lovely garden on Ashdown Forest. Very peaceful. **Open:** All year
01825 712942 D: Fr £24.00–£30.00 **S:** Fr £30.00 **Beds:** 1D 1T **Baths:** 1 Sh

Forest Row

TQ4234

Woodcote, *Park Road, Forest Row, RH18 5BX.* Friendly family home in private road adjacent to Ashdown Forest. **Open:** All year (not Xmas/New Year)
01342 822170 S Hillen **Fax: 01342 823134** *shhillen@hotmail.com* **D:** Fr £30.00–£60.00 **S:** Fr £30.00–£60.00 **Beds:** 1T 1D **Baths:** 1 En (2)

Frant

TQ5935

Melling, *The Green, Frant, Tunbridge Wells, E Sussex, TN3 9ED.* Pretty house overlooks village green. Walkers welcome. **Open:** All year (not Xmas)
01892 750380 D: Fr £20.00 **S:** Fr £20.00 **Beds:** 1T **Baths:** 1 Sh

Hailsham

TQ5809

Longleys Farm Cottage, *Harebeating Lane, Hailsham, E Sussex, BN27 1ER.* Quiet country location near prime tourist attractions. Informal and friendly. **Open:** All year **Grades:** ETC 3 Diamond
01323 841227 (also fax) J Hook **D:** Fr £19.00 **S:** Fr £22.00–£25.00 **Beds:** 1F 1D 1T **Baths:** 2 En 1 Pr (4)

RATES
D = Price range per person sharing in a double or twin room
S = Price range for a single room

Halland

TQ5016

Shortgate Manor Farm, *Halland, Lewes, E Sussex, BN8 6PJ.* **Open:** All year **Grades:** ETC 4 Diamond, Silver
01825 840320 (also fax) *ewalt@shortgate.co.uk* www.shortgate.co.uk **D:** Fr £27.50–£35.00 **S:** Fr £35.00–£40.00 **Beds:** 1T 2D **Baths:** 3 En (10) (6)
Enchanting C18th farmhouse set in 8 acres, with 2 acres of landscaped gardens which are open under the NGS every June. The 3 charming bedrooms all offer ensuite facilities with TVs, courtesy trays and bathrobes. Glyndebourne 4 miles. 2 nights preferred.

Tamberry Hall, *Eastbourne Road, Halland, Lewes, East Sussex, BN8 6PS.* Enjoy the warm and friendly surroundings of this delightful country house, savour your sumptuous breakfast overlooking secluded gardens. Relax in the comfort of your beautiful room with every amenity. Truly a stay to remember. Glyndebourne 10 minutes. Golf 2 minutes. **Open:** All year (not Xmas/New Year)
01825 880090 (also fax) Ms Baynham *bedandbreakfast@tamberryhall.fsbusiness.co.uk* www.fsbusiness.co.uk **D:** Fr £22.50–£30.00 **S:** Fr £35.00–£45.00 **Beds:** 1F 2D **Baths:** 3 En (4)

Hartfield

TQ4735

The Paddocks, *Chuck Hatch, Hartfield, East Sussex, TN7 4EX.* In the Ashdown Forest, 0.25 mile from Pooh Sticks Bridge. Walkers and children welcome. **Open:** All year (not Xmas)
01892 770623 Ms McAll **D:** Fr £22.00 **S:** Fr £22.00 **Beds:** 1D 1T 1S **Baths:** 1 Pr 1 Sh

Hastings

TQ8110

Westwood Farm, *Stonestile Lane, Hastings, E. Sussex, TN35 4PG.* Working sheep farm, peaceful, rural. Outstanding views over Brede Valley. **Open:** All year (not Xmas)
01424 751038 (also fax) Mr York *york@westwood-farm.fsnet.co.uk* **D:** Fr £19.00–£27.00 **S:** Fr £23.00–£30.00 **Beds:** 1F 1D 1T **Baths:** 2 En 1 Pr (5) (8)

Emerydale, *6 King Edward Avenue, Hastings, E. Sussex, TN34 2NQ.* Warm welcome. Perfectly situated for exploring 1066 country. Off A21. **Open:** All year (not Xmas) **Grades:** ETC 4 Diamond
01424 437915 Mrs Emery **Fax: 01424 444124** *jan@emerydale.co.uk* **D:** Fr £20.00–£22.50 **S:** Fr £20.00–£25.00 **Beds:** 1D 1T 1S **Baths:** 1 En 1 Sh (12)

White Cottage, *Battery Hill, Hastings, E. Sussex, TN35 4AP.* Friendly family-run B&B on outskirts of peaceful Fairlight, beautiful gardens, far-reaching channel views. **Open:** Feb to Oct
01424 812528 Fax: 01424 812285 *juneandjohn@whitecottagebb.fsnet.co.uk* **D:** Fr £22.50–£25.00 **S:** Fr £30.00 **Beds:** 1T 3D **Baths:** 3 En 1 Pr (7) (4)

Pendragon Lodge, *Watermill Lane, Pett, Hastings, E Sussex, TN35 4HY.* Rye (near) luxury accommodation amidst Sussex countryside. Home-made bread, preserves. **Open:** All year **Grades:** ETC 5 Diamond, SIlver, AA 5 Diamond, Premier
01424 814051 *pendragon_lodge@hotmail.com* www.pendragonlodge.co.uk **D:** Fr £28.50–£32.00 **S:** Fr £30.00–£35.00 **Beds:** 1T 2D **Baths:** 3 En (5) (5) cc

Grand Hotel, *Grand Parade, St Leonards On Sea, Hastings, E. Sussex, TN38 ODD.* Seafront family hotel in heart of 1066 country. Unrestricted parking. **Open:** All year **Grades:** ETC 3 Diamond
01424 428510 & 08702 257025 Mr & Mrs Mann **Fax: 01424 428510 D:** Fr £18.00–£35.00 **S:** Fr £24.00–£45.00 **Beds:** 3F 6D 4T 4S **Baths:** 3 En 4 Pr 12 Sh 2

Millifont Guest House, *8/9 Cambridge Gardens, Hastings, E. Sussex, TN34 1EH.* Centrally situated 15 bedroom guest house, lounge/games room. **Open:** All year (not Xmas)
01424 425645 (also fax) Mr Main **D:** Fr £18.00–£22.50 **S:** Fr £18.00–£20.00 **Beds:** 2F 5D 4T 4S **Baths:** 2 En 1 Pr 4 Sh

B&B owners may vary rates – be sure to check when booking

Lavender and Lace, *106 All Saints Street, Old Town, Hastings, E. Sussex, TN34 3BE.* Situated in heart of historic Old Town of Hastings, charming period house just 400 yards from the fishing harbour. The area contains a wealth of interest for the visitor who is able to browse amongst the many antique shops, wine bars, bistros and restaurants. **Open:** Mar to Dec (not New Year)
01424 716290 (also fax) Ms Gould **D:** Fr £20.00–£25.00 **Beds:** 1T 2D **Baths:** 1 En 1 Pr (10)

Lansdowne Hotel, *1 Robertson Terrace, Hastings, E. Sussex, TN34 1JE.* Family run for 25 years; great value for money and very high standards. **Open:** All year
01424 429605 Mr Rumble *lansdowne.hotel@btinternet.com* **D:** Fr £23.50–£28.50 **S:** Fr £24.50–£31.00 **Beds:** 6F 15D 3T 4S **Baths:** 28 En 2 Sh cc

Cambridge Guest House, *18 Cambridge Gardens, Hastings, E. Sussex, TN34 1EH.* Friendly, clean, family guest house. 3 minutes walk to town centre **Open:** All year
01424 712995 D: Fr £16.00–£22.00 **S:** Fr £14.00–£20.00 **Beds:** 1F 4T 1D 3S **Baths:** 3 En 2 Sh

Heathfield

TQ5821

Old Corner Cottage, *Little London Road, Cross-in-Hand, Heathfield, E. Sussex, TN21 0LT.* **Open:** All year **Grades:** AA 5 Diamond
01435 863787 (also fax) Mrs Brown *hamishcjbrown@aol.com* **D:** Fr £22.00–£26.00 **S:** Fr £25.00–£30.00 **Beds:** 2D 1T **Baths:** 3 En (10)
High quality accommodation situated conveniently for many National Trust properties and gardens. The lovely Sussex coast is only a short drive, within a short distance from the Cuckoo Trail cycle track running from Heathfield to Pole Gate. Comfortable guest sitting room.

Spicers B&B, *21 Cade Street, Heathfield, E Sussex, TN21 9BS.* Old beamed cottage on the high Weald of East Sussex. **Open:** All year **Grades:** ETC 4 Diamond
01435 866363 Mr Gumbrell **Fax: 01435 868171** *sleep@spicersbb.co.uk* www.spicersbb.co.uk **D:** Fr £21.00–£22.50 **S:** Fr £22.00–£25.00 **Beds:** 1D 1T 1S **Baths:** 1 En 2 Pr 3 cc

Please respect a B&B's wishes regarding children, animals and smoking

Iwood, *Mutton Hall Lane, Heathfield, E Sussex, TN21 8NR.* Secluded chalet bungalow in lovely gardens with distant views South Downs and sea. Situated within coastal towns including 1066 attractions around Hastings and historic towns of battle, Lewes and Royal Tunbridge Wells. Be prepared for an excellent breakfast! **Open:** All year (not Xmas/New Year)
01435 863918 Fax: 01435 868575 *iwoodbb@aol.com* www.iwoodbb.co.uk **D:** Fr £21.00–£23.00 **S:** Fr £20.00–£25.00 **Beds:** 1F 1D 1S **Baths:** 1 En 2 Pr (2) 3

Hellingly

TQ5812

Grove Hill House, *Hellingly, Hailsham, E Sussex, BN27 4HG.* Period farmhouse in beautiful quiet setting in over 2 acres of grounds. **Open:** All year
01435 812440 (also fax) Mrs Berthon **D:** Fr £19.00–£22.00 **S:** Fr £25.00–£30.00 **Beds:** 1D 1T **Baths:** 1 En 1 Pr (4)

Heron's Ghyll

TQ4826

Tanglewood, *Oldlands Hall, Heron's Ghyll, Uckfield, E Sussex, TN22 3DA.* Peaceful setting on Ashdown Forest. Large pretty garden, warm welcome. **Open:** All year (not Xmas)
01825 712757 Mrs Clarke **D:** Fr £24.00 **S:** Fr £25.00–£30.00 **Beds:** 2D 1T **Baths:** 1 Pr 1 Sh (6)

Herstmonceux

TQ6312

Sandhurst, *Church Road, Herstmonceux, Hailsham, E Sussex, BN27 1RG.* Large bungalow in countryside. Easy access to village and coast. **Open:** All year (not Xmas)
01323 833088 *junerussell@compuserve.com* **D:** Fr £20.00–£25.00 **S:** Fr £20.00–£30.00 **Beds:** 2F 2D **Baths:** 3 En 1 Pr (4)

High Hurstwood

TQ4926

Huckleberry, *Perryman's Lane, High Hurstwood, Uckfield, E Sussex, TN22 4AG.* Pretty country house, prize winning garden. Near Ashdown Forest and many country houses. **Open:** All year (not Xmas/New Year)
01825 733170 Ms White **D:** Fr £22.50–£27.50 **S:** Fr £22.50–£30.00 **Beds:** 1F 1T 1D 1S **Baths:** 3 En 1 Pr 1 Sh

Horam

TQ5717

Oak Mead Nursery, *Cowden Hall Lane, Horam, Heathfield, E. Sussex, TN21 9ED.* Set in beautiful, quiet countryside, off road parking, good breakfasts. **Open:** Jan to Dec
01435 812962 Mrs Curtis **D:** Fr £19.00 **S:** Fr £19.00–£24.00 **Beds:** 1D 1T 1S **Baths:** 2 En 1 Pr (4)

Hove

TQ2805

Claremont House Hotel, *Second Avenue, Hove, E Sussex, BN3 2LL.* Claremont House is an elegantly presented Victorian villa, few hundred yards from seafront. **Open:** All year **Grades:** ETC 4 Diamond
01273 735161 (also fax) Mr Brewerton *claremonthove@aol.com* www.claremonthousehotel.co.uk **D:** Fr £37.50–£60.00 **S:** Fr £40.00–£65.00 **Beds:** 2F 6D/T 4S **Baths:** 12 En **cc**

Adastral Hotel, *8 Westbourne Villas, Hove, E. Sussex, BN3 4GQ.* Large Victorian villa near seafront, leisure centre & Brighton nightlife. **Open:** All year
01273 888800 Mrs Orford **Fax: 01273 883839** *info@adastralhotel.co.uk* **D:** Fr £45.00–£52.50 **S:** Fr £66.00–£82.00 **Beds:** 2D 5S 11F **Baths:** 18 En (2) **cc**

Lichfield House, *30 Waterloo Street, Hove, E. Sussex, BN3 1AN.* Town centre location, close to sea and night life. **Open:** All year
01273 777740 Mr Byrne *feelgood@lichfieldhouse.freeserve.co.uk* www.lichfieldhouse.freeserve.co.uk **D:** Fr £16.00–£35.00 **S:** Fr £32.00–£80.00 **Beds:** 2F 5D 2T 1S **Baths:** 4 En 1 Pr 1 Sh (2)

Kingston near Lewes

TQ3908

Settlands, *Wellgreen Lane, Kingston near Lewes, Lewes, E Sussex, BN7 3NP.* Delightful, spacious accommodation. Close to Lewes, Brighton, Glyndebourne and Downland walks. **Open:** All year (not Xmas)
01273 472295 Mrs Arlett *diana-a@solutions-inc.co.uk* **D:** Fr £22.50–£27.50 **S:** Fr £25.00–£30.00 **Beds:** 1D 1T **Baths:** 2 Sh (3)

B&B owners may vary rates – be sure to check when booking

Laughton

TQ5013

Holly Cottage, *Lewes Road, Laughton, Lewes, E. Sussex, BN8 6BL.* Charming C18th Listed country cottage. **Open:** All year
01323 811309 Mrs Clarke **Fax: 01323 811106** **D:** Fr £23.00–£25.00 **S:** Fr £30.00–£35.00 **Beds:** 1F 1T 1D **Baths:** 3 En (3)

Lewes

TQ4110

Castle Banks Cottage, *4 Castle Banks, Lewes, E. Sussex, BN7 1UZ.* Beamed cottage, pretty garden, quiet lane, close to castle, shops, restaurants. **Open:** All year (not Xmas)
01273 476291 Mrs Wigglesworth *aswigglesworth@aol.com* **D:** Fr £25.00 **S:** Fr £25.00–£35.00 **Beds:** 1T 1S **Baths:** 1 Sh

Millers, *134 High Street, Lewes, E. Sussex, BN7 1XS.* Enjoy a warm welcome in an attractive C16th townhouse. **Open:** All year (not Xmas/New Year)
01273 475631 Mrs Tammar **Fax: 01273 486226** *millers134@aol.com* www.hometown.aol.com/millers134 **D:** Fr £31.50 **S:** Fr £56.00 **Beds:** 2D **Baths:** 2 En

Crown Inn, *191 High Street, Lewes, East Sussex, BN7 2NA.* Welcoming C17th inn, centrally located. Meeting room available. **Open:** All year
01273 480670 Fax: 01273 480679 *sales@crowninn-lewes.co.uk* www.crowninn-lewes.co.uk **D:** Fr £25.00–£35.00 **S:** Fr £37.50–£48.00 **Beds:** 1F 3T 4D **Baths:** 6 En 1 Sh **cc**

Phoenix House, *23 Gundreda Road, Lewes, E Sussex, BN7 1PT.* Comfortable family home, quiet road, 5 minutes to town centre. **Open:** All year (not Xmas/New Year)
01273 473250 Mrs Greene *charg55@yahoo.com* **D:** Fr £17.50–£22.50 **S:** Fr £25.00 **Beds:** 1T 1D 1S **Baths:** 1 Pr 1 Sh (2)

Lunsford's Cross

TQ7210

Wakeford House, *Potmans Lane, Lunsford's Cross, Bexhill-on-Sea, E. Sussex, TN39 5JL.* Edwardian-style house in country setting with peaceful one acre garden. **Open:** All year
01424 892013 Mrs Skinner **Fax: 01424 893978** *wakeford@wakefordhouse.com* www.wakefordhouse.com **D:** Fr £25.00–£30.00 **S:** Fr £30.00 **Beds:** 3F 1D 1S 1T **Baths:** 1 En 1 Sh (5)

B&B owners may vary rates – be sure to check when booking

Manor Barn, *Lunsford's Cross, Bexhill on Sea, E. Sussex, TN39 5JJ.* Ensuite chalets, semi-rural setting on A269, 3 miles sea. **Open:** All year
01424 893018 (also fax) Mrs Gillingham **D:** Fr £18.00–£19.50 **S:** Fr £25.00–£26.50 **Beds:** 1F 1D 1T 1S **Baths:** 4 En (6)

Netherfield
TQ7118

Roseneath, *Netherfield Road, Netherfield, Battle, E Sussex, TN33 9PY.* Situated in an area of outstanding natural beauty - 1066 country. **Open:** All year
01424 772953 Mrs Vane *roseneath00@mircosoft.com* **D:** Fr £40.00–£60.00 **S:** Fr £25.00–£30.00 **Beds:** 1T 2D **Baths:** 1 En 1 Sh

Newick
TQ4121

Holly Lodge, *Oxbottom Lane, Newick, Lewes, E Sussex, BN8 4RA.* Georgian family house in pretty garden on outskirts of village. **Open:** All year (not Xmas)
01825 722738 Fax: 01825 723624 D: Fr £22.50–£24.50 **S:** Fr £25.00 **Beds:** 1F 2D 1T **Baths:** 1 En 1 Pr (6)

Pinecroft, *Allington Road, Newick, Lewes, E Sussex, BN8 4NA.* Easy reach of Lewes, Brighton, National Trust gardens and Gatwick. **Open:** All year
01825 723824 (also fax) Mrs Thomas *diane.pinecroft@ic24.net* **D:** Fr £36.00 **S:** Fr £20.00 **Beds:** 1F 1T **Baths:** 1 Sh (2)

Ninfield
TQ7012

Moonshill Farm, *The Green, Ninfield, Battle, E. Sussex, TN33 9LH.* **Open:** All year (not Xmas/New Year)
01424 892645 (also fax) Mrs Ive *june@ive13.fsnet.co.uk* **D:** Fr £20.00–£25.00 **Beds:** 1F 1T 1D **Baths:** 3 En (4)
In the heart of the '1066' country, in the centre of the village Ninfield. Farmhouse in 10 acres of garden, orchard stables. Enjoy beautiful walks, horse riding. Every comfort in own safe, quiet and peaceful home. Large car park.

Peasmarsh
TQ8723

Kimbley Cottage, *Main Street, Peasmarsh, Rye, E. Sussex, TN31 6UL.* Friendly country house. 5 minutes' drive to historic Rye, beaches 15 minutes. **Open:** All year (not Xmas)
01797 230514 Mrs Richards **D:** Fr £21.00–£22.00 **S:** Fr £27.00 **Beds:** 3D **Baths:** 3 En (4)

Pett
TQ8714

Pendragon Lodge, *Watermill Lane, Pett, Hastings, E Sussex, TN35 4HY.* Rye (near) luxury accommodation amidst Sussex countryside. Home-made bread, preserves. **Open:** All year **Grades:** ETC 5 Diamond, Silver, AA 5 Diamond, Premier
01424 814051 *pendragon_lodge@hotmail.com* www.pendragonlodge.co.uk **D:** Fr £28.50–£32.00 **S:** Fr £30.00–£35.00 **Beds:** 1T 2D **Baths:** 3 En (5) (5) **cc**

Pevensey Bay
TQ6504 *The Moorings*

Napier House, *The Promenade, Pevensey Bay, E. Sussex, BN24 6HD.* An enviable location. Glorious sea views. Rooms with balconies. **Open:** All year
01323 766242 Mrs Gregory **D:** Fr £20.00–£25.00 **S:** Fr £25.00–£30.00 **Beds:** 1F 2T 2D **Baths:** 2 En 2 Sh (5) (8)

Piltdown
TQ4422

Holly Farm, *Piltdown, Uckfield, E. Sussex, TN22 3XB.* Comfortable Victorian house, near Bluebell Railway, Sheffield Park, Fletching, Buxted. **Open:** All year
01825 722592 (also fax) Ms Mayes **D:** Fr £25.00 **S:** Fr £25.00 **Beds:** 1F 2D **Baths:** 1 Pr 1 Sh

Playden
TQ9221

The Corner House, *Peasmarsh Road, Playden, Rye, E. Sussex, TN31 7UL.* A warm welcome awaits. Friendly country house. Excellent accommodation, hearty breakfast. **Open:** All year
01797 280439 *richardturner5@virgin.net* www.smoothhound.co.uk/hotels/corner2.html **D:** Fr £18.00–£25.00 **S:** Fr £20.00–£25.00 **Beds:** 1F 1D 1T **Baths:** 1 Sh (3)

Planning a longer stay? Always ask for any special rates

Plumpton Green
TQ3616

Farthings, *Station Road, Plumpton Green, Lewes, E. Sussex, BN7 3BY.* Relaxed friendly atmosphere in village setting under South Downs **Open:** All year (not Xmas)
01273 890415 M Baker **D:** Fr £20.00–£25.00 **S:** Fr £25.00–£30.00 **Beds:** 1T 2D **Baths:** 1 En 1 Sh

Punnett's Town
TQ6320

Ringwood, *Forest Lane, Punnetts Town, Heathfield, E Sussex, TN21 9JA.* Detached Victorian annexe situated in beautiful countryside. Ideal walking, cycling. **Open:** Apr to Oct
01435 830630 Mrs Batehup **D:** Fr £22.50 **S:** Fr £30.00 **Beds:** 1T **Baths:** 1 En (2)

Ringmer
TQ4412

Gote Farm, *Gote Lane, Ringmer, Lewes, E. Sussex, BN8 5HX.* Traditional Sussex farmhouse near Glyndebourne, Newhaven, Brighton and South Downs Way. **Open:** All year (not Xmas) **Grades:** ETC 4 Diamond
01273 812303 (also fax) Mrs Craig *janecraig@ukgateway.net* **D:** Fr £22.50 **S:** Fr £25.00–£30.00 **Beds:** 1D 1T 1S **Baths:** 2 Sh (4)

Rye
TQ9120

Culpeppers, *15 Love Lane, Rye, E. Sussex, TN31 7NE.* Quiet, peaceful, few minutes walk central Rye/public transport/restaurants/pubs. Designated walks/cycle paths nearby. Parking. **Open:** All year (not Xmas) **Grades:** ETC 4 Diamond, Silver
01797 224411 (also fax) P Ciccone *peppersrye@aol.com* www.culpeppers-rye.com **D:** Fr £25.00–£27.00 **S:** Fr £25.00–£26.00 **Beds:** 1T 2S **Baths:** 1 En 2 Sh

The Old Vicarage, *66 Church Square, Rye, E. Sussex, TN31 7HF.* Splendid Georgian house, peaceful and picturesque setting. Superb breakfast. Award hotel. **Open:** All year (not Xmas) **Grades:** AA 5 Diamond, Premier
01797 222119 Mr Masters **Fax: 01797 227466** *oldvicarageryе@tesco.net* www.oldvicarageryе.co.uk **D:** Fr £30.00–£45.00 **S:** Fr £45.00–£65.00 **Beds:** 1F 2D 1T **Baths:** 4 En (8) (4)

Little Saltcote, *22 Military Road, Rye, East Sussex, TN31 7NY.* Genuine welcome in Edwardian family home, generous English/vegetarian breakfasts. **Open:** All year (not Xmas) **Grades:** AA 3 Diamond
01797 223210 D Martin **Fax: 01797 224474** *littlesaltcote.rye@virgin.net* **D:** Fr £20.00–£25.00 **S:** Fr £28.00–£35.00 **Beds:** 3F 2D **Baths:** 3 En 1 Sh (3)

Aviemore Guest House, *28/30 Fishmarket Road, Rye, E. Sussex, TN31 7LP.* Imposing Tudor-style Victorian house. Town centre 2 minute walk, situated on the A259. **Open:** All year **Grades:** ETC 3 Diamond
01797 223052 (also fax) Mr & Mrs Cogan *aviemore@lineone.net* www.smoothhound.co.uk/hotels/aviemore.html **D:** Fr £20.00–£23.00 **S:** Fr £25.00 **Beds:** 3D 4T 1S **Baths:** 4 En 2 Sh cc

Cinque Ports Hotel, *Cinque Ports Street, Rye, E. Sussex, TN31 7AN.* Family-run centralised inn for picturesque Rye. **Open:** All year **Grades:** ETC 3 Diamond
01797 222319 (also fax) *elaine@wickhamrobinson.freeserve.co.uk* **D:** Fr £25.00–£30.00 **S:** Fr £40.00 **Beds:** 1F 1T 1D **Baths:** 3 En (20)

Western House, *113 Winchelsea Road, Rye, E. Sussex, TN31 7EL.* Charming C18th Listed house few minutes walk from town centre. **Open:** All year (not Xmas/New Year)
01797 223419 M Dellar **D:** Fr £22.50–£25.00 **S:** Fr £25.00–£30.00 **Beds:** 1F 1T 1T **Baths:** 3 En (10) (3)

Jeakes House, *Mermaid Street, Rye, E Sussex, TN31 7ET.* Award-winning C16th B&B hotel in cobbled old town-centre. Traditional elegance with modern amenities. **Open:** All year
01797 222828 (also fax) Mrs Hadfield *jeakeshouse@btinternet.com* www.jeakeshouse.com **D:** Fr £28.50–£48.50 **S:** Fr £29.50–£63.00 **Beds:** 2F 8D 1T 1S **Baths:** 9 En 1 Pr 2 Sh (12) (20) cc

Four Seasons, *96 Udimore Road, Rye, East Sussex, TN31 7DY.* Situated on Cadborough Cliffs, we have glorious views across Brede Valley to the sea. Ideal spot for touring, walking, cycling, 6 minutes walk from medieval heart of Rye. Breakfast on local organic, free-range produce. Convenient for Dover-Hastings cycle path. **Open:** All year
01797 224305 Fax: 01797 229450 *coxsam@btinternet.com* **D:** Fr £18.00–£22.00 **S:** Fr £23.00–£25.00 **Beds:** 1T 2D **Baths:** 2 En 1 Pr (10) (3)

Planning a longer stay? Always ask for any special rates

National Grid References given are for villages, towns and cities – not for individual houses

The Rise, *82 Udimore Road, Rye, E Sussex, TN31 7DY.* Pleasant comfortable house, terraced gardens, all bedrooms facing green fields to distant sea. **Open:** All year (not Xmas/New Year)
01797 222285 T E Francis *therise@bb-rye.freeserve.co.uk* **D:** Fr £25.00–£30.00 **S:** Fr £30.00–£35.00 **Beds:** 1T 3D (1) (4)

Magnolia House, *15 Udimore Road, Rye, E Sussex, TN31 7DS.* Situated within a few minutes' walk to Rye. **Open:** All year
01797 222561 www.magnoliaguesthouse.co.uk **D:** Fr £22.50–£25.00 **S:** Fr £22.50–£25.00 **Beds:** 2F 1T 2D 1S **Baths:** 6 En cc

Vine Cottage, *25a Udimore Road, Rye, E Sussex, TN31 7DS.* Situated in pretty gardens opposite 1066 Walk. 7 min walk town centre and station. **Open:** Apr to Oct
01797 222822 (also fax) Mrs Thomson **D:** Fr £17.00–£18.00 **S:** Fr £22.00–£25.00 **Beds:** 1T 1S (2) (2)

Rye Harbour

TQ9319

The Old Vicarage, *Rye Harbour, Rye, E. Sussex, TN31 7TT.* Victorian former vicarage, quietly situated, antique furniture, open fires, sumptuous breakfasts, near sea. **Open:** All year
01797 222088 Mr Bosher **D:** Fr £19.50 **S:** Fr £22.50 **Beds:** 1D 1T **Baths:** 1 Sh (2)

Seaford

TV4898

Holmes Lodge, *72 Claremont Road, Seaford, East Sussex, BN25 2BJ.* **Open:** All year **Grades:** ETC 3 Diamond
01323 898331 M D Parr **Fax: 01323 491346** *holmes.lodge@freemail.co.uk* www.seaford.co.uk/holmes/holmes.htm **D:** Fr £20.00–£28.00 **S:** Fr £25.00–£35.00 **Beds:** 2F 1D 3S **Baths:** 1 Pr 2 Sh (10)
Sherlock Holmes theme. Convenient for Downs, walks/cycling, Cuckmere Haven, Seven Sisters, Beachy Head, Newhaven Ferry. Beach/town/trains 300 metres, bus-stop outside, singles/groups welcome all year. Bar/restaurant adjacent. Tea/coffee in rooms. Conservatory, large garden, sea views.

Silverdale, *21 Sutton Park Road, Seaford, E. Sussex, BN25 1RH.* Family run, town centre house hotel. Excellent value for money. **Open:** All year **Grades:** ETC 4 Diamond, AA 4 Diamond
01323 491849 Mr Cowdrey **Fax: 01323 891131** *silverdale@mistral.co.uk* www.mistral.co.uk/silverdale/silver.htm **D:** Fr £13.00–£33.00 **S:** Fr £25.00–£45.00 **Beds:** 2F 6D **Baths:** 6 En 2 Sh (5) 1 cc

Streat

TQ3515

North Acres, *Streat, Hassocks, E. Sussex, BN6 8RX.* Unique Victorian country house in tiny hamlet near South Downs. **Open:** All year (not Xmas)
01273 890278 (also fax) J & V Eastwood *eastwood_streat@yahoo.com* **D:** Fr £20.00 **S:** Fr £20.00–£25.00 **Beds:** 2F 2T 1S **Baths:** 3 Sh (20)

Ticehurst

TQ6930

Pashley Farm, *Pashley Road, Ticehurst, Wadhurst, East Sussex, TN5 7HE.* Peaceful Victorian farmhouse with glorious views of the Sussex Weald. **Open:** All year (not Xmas/New Year)
01580 200362 Mrs Humphrey **Fax: 01580 200832** *colina@pashleyfarm.co.uk* www.pashleyfarm.co.uk **D:** Fr £40.00 **S:** Fr £30.00 **Beds:** 1T 1D **Baths:** 1 Sh (4)

Wadhurst

TQ6431

Kirkstone, *Mayfield Lane, Wadhurst, E. Sussex, TN5 6HX.* Large Victorian house with fine views in rural East Sussex. **Open:** All year (not Xmas)
01892 783204 Mr & Mrs Inman *colininman@onetel.net.uk* **D:** Fr £20.00–£22.00 **S:** Fr £22.00–£25.00 **Beds:** 1F 1T **Baths:** 2 Sh (4)

Spring Cottage, *Best Beech Hill, Wadhurst, E. Sussex, TN5 6JH.* Modern family house, split level. Close National Trust Properties - views! **Open:** All year (not Xmas)
01892 783896 Ms Bones **Fax: 01892 784866** **D:** Fr £18.00–£25.00 **S:** Fr £25.00–£35.00 **Beds:** 1F 1D **Baths:** 1 En 1 Sh (4)

All details shown are as supplied by B&B owners in Autumn 2002

Willingdon

TQ5802

Butlers Gate, *24 Wish Hill, Willingdon, Eastbourne, BN20 9EX.* Attractive room, quiet family home, Victorian brass bed, sea views. **Open:** All year (not Xmas)
01323 509897 **D:** Fr £20.00 **S:** Fr £25.00
Beds: 1F **Baths:** 1 En (6) (2)

Winchelsea

TQ9017

Strand House, *Tanyards Lane, Winchelsea, Rye, E. Sussex, TN36 4JT.* Charming C15th house, beams, inglenooks, pretty gardens, lounge, licensed, four-poster. **Open:** All year (not Xmas)
01797 226276 Mr & Mrs Woods **Fax: 01797 224806** *strandhouse@winchelsea98.fsnet.co.uk*
D: Fr £24.00–£36.00 **S:** Fr £30.00–£38.00
Beds: 2F 7D 1T **Baths:** 9 En 1 Pr (4) (10)
cc

West Sussex

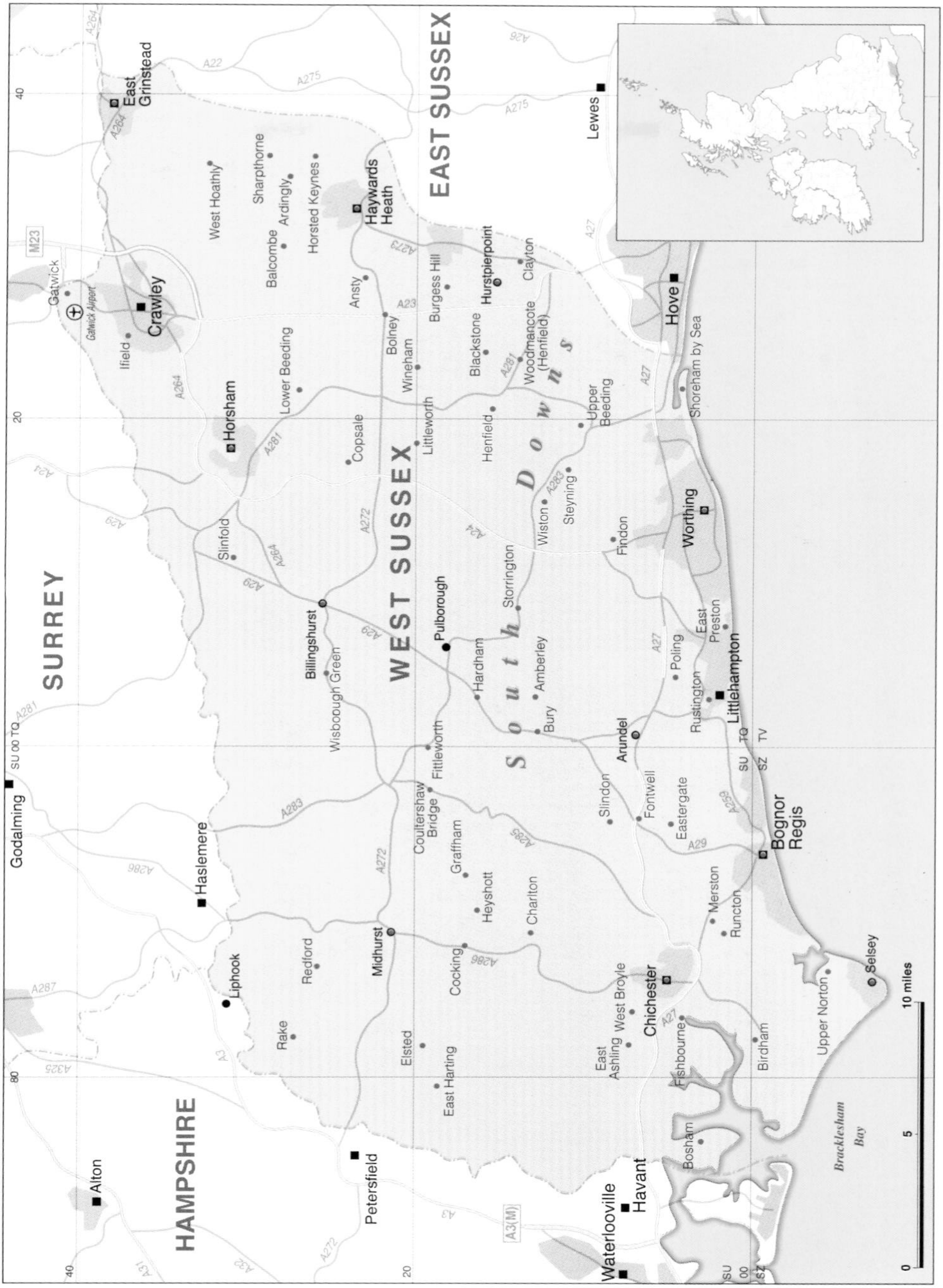

SURREY
HAMPSHIRE
WEST SUSSEX
EAST SUSSEX
South Downs
East Grinstead
Crawley
Gatwick
Gatwick Airport
Ifield
Horsham
Lower Beeding
West Hoathly
Sharpthorne
Ardingly
Balcombe
Horsted Keynes
Haywards Heath
Ansty
Bolney
Burgess Hill
Hurstpierpoint
Clayton
Blackstone
Woodmancote (Henfield)
Wineham
Henfield
Upper Beeding
Copsale
Littleworth
Lewes
Hove
Shoreham by Sea
Steyning
Wiston
Worthing
Findon
Slinfold
Billingshurst
Wisbough Green
Pulborough
Storrington
Hardham
Amberley
Bury
Arundel
Poling
East Preston
Rustington
Littlehampton
Fittleworth
Coultershaw Bridge
Graffham
Heyshott
Charlton
Slindon
Fontwell
Eastergate
Bognor Regis
Merston
Runcton
Selsey
Upper Norton
Birdham
Chichester
West Broyle
East Ashling
Fishbourne
Bosham
Bracklesham Bay
Midhurst
Cocking
Redford
Rake
Elsted
East Harting
Liphook
Haslemere
Godalming
Alton
Petersfield
Havant
Waterlooville
10 miles

Amberley
TQ0313

Bacons, *Amberley, Arundel, W. Sussex, BN18 9NJ.* Pretty, old cottage in the heart of the village. **Open:** All year (not Xmas)
01798 831234 Mrs Jollands **D:** Fr £20.00 **S:** Fr £20.00 **Beds:** 2T **Baths:** 1 Sh

Woodybanks, *Crossgates, Amberley, Arundel, W. Sussex, BN18 9NR.* Beautiful views, guest sitting room, discount for 2 nights plus. **Open:** All year (not Xmas/New Year) **Grades:** AA 4 Diamond
01798 831295 Mr & Mrs Hardy
www.woodybanks.co.uk **D:** Fr £20.00–£25.00 **S:** Fr £25.00 **Beds:** 1T 1D **Baths:** 2 Sh (3)

Ansty
TQ2823

Netherby, *Bolney Road, Ansty, Haywards Heath, W Sussex, RH17 5AW.* **Open:** All year **Grades:** ETC 4 Diamond
01444 455888 (also fax) Mr & Mrs Gilbert *susan@gilbert58.freeserve.co.uk* **D:** Fr £20.00 **S:** Fr £25.00 **Beds:** 2D 1T **Baths:** 1 Sh (4)
Cosy Victorian detached country cottage on A272. 1.25 miles from A23, convenient for Gatwick Airport, Hickstead, Ardingly Showground, Brighton, Glyndebourne Opera, Bluebell Railway and National Trust Gardens. Firm beds, full English breakfast, sinks in all rooms, warm welcome.

Ardingly
TQ3429

Stonelands West Lodge, *Ardingly Road, West Hoathly, East Grinstead, West Sussex, RH19 4RA.* Victorian lodge on B2028 between Turners Hill and Ardingly. Close Wakehurst Place. **Open:** All year **Grades:** ETC 3 Diamond
01342 715372 & 07759 295200 (M)
Mrs Hutchings **D:** Fr £25.00–£35.00 **S:** Fr £25.00–£30.00 **Beds:** 1T 1D 1S **Baths:** 1 En 1 Sh (2)

The Mount, *Little London, Ardingly, Haywards Heath, West Sussex, RH17 6TJ.* Wakehurst Place, Bluebell Railway, Ardingly Showground, South Downs, Sheffield Park. **Open:** All year (not Xmas/New Year)
01444 892252 Dr Dale **Fax: 01444 892974**
jwdale@ardingly.demon.co.uk **D:** Fr £20.00 **S:** Fr £20.00 **Beds:** 2D 2S

Arundel
TQ0106

Woodacre, *Arundel Road, Fontwell, Arundel, W Sussex, BN18 0SD.* Set in beautiful garden surrounded by woodland. Everyone made welcome.
Open: All year
01243 814301 Ms Richards **Fax: 01243 814344** *wacrebb@aol.com* www.woodacre.co.uk **D:** Fr £22.50–£30.00 **S:** Fr £30.00–£35.00 **Beds:** 1F 2T 1D **Baths:** 1 En 1 Pr 2 Sh (20) cc

Portreeves Acre, *The Causeway, Arundel, W. Sussex, BN18 9JL.* 3 minute from station, castle and town centre. **Open:** All year (not Xmas/New Year)
01903 883277 Mr Rogers **D:** Fr £21.00–£23.00 **S:** Fr £30.00–£35.00 **Beds:** 1F 1D 1T **Baths:** 2 En 1 Pr (12) (6)

Balcombe
TQ3130 *Half Moon*

Rocks Lane Cottage, *Rowhill Lane, Balcombe, Haywards Heath, W. Sussex, RH17 6JG.* Stone cottage with spectacular views and private, comfortable accommodation. **Open:** All year
01444 811245 Mrs Parry **Fax: 01444 811986**
kpa@fsbdial.co.uk **D:** Fr £25.00 **S:** Fr £30.00–£35.00 **Beds:** 1D **Baths:** 1 En (1)

Billingshurst
TQ0825

Groom Cottage, *Station Road, Billingshurst, W Sussex, RH14 9RF.* Comfortable rooms. Five minutes from station and village. English breakfast. **Open:** All year (not Xmas/New Year)
01403 782285 Ms Gander **D:** Fr £20.00–£22.50 **S:** Fr £25.00–£30.00 **Beds:** 2T **Baths:** 2 En (2)

Birdham
SU8200

Seldens, *Bell Lane, Birdham, Chichester, W. Sussex, PO20 7HY.* Lovely, spacious, secluded bungalow, large attractive gardens. 2 miles beach. **Open:** All year (not Xmas)
01243 512358 Mrs Hepburn **D:** Fr £22.50 **S:** Fr £25.00 **Beds:** 2D **Baths:** 1 En 1P (3)

B&B owners may vary rates – be sure to check when booking

National Grid References given are for villages, towns and cities – not for individual houses

The Red House, *Lock Lane, Birdham Pool, Birdham, Chichester, W Sussex, PO20 7BB.* Listed Georgian property with stunning views over Birdham Pool. Warm welcome, quiet location. **Open:** All year
01243 512488 Mrs Groom **Fax: 01243 514563**
susie.redhouse@ukonline.co.uk
www.redhousehideaway.co.uk **D:** Fr £30.00–£35.00 **S:** Fr £35.00–£40.00 **Beds:** 1T 1D **Baths:** 2 En

Blackstone
TQ2416

Yeomans Hall, *Blackstone, Henfield, W Sussex, BN5 5TB.* Medieval house with cottage garden. Conservation area in rural hamlet. **Open:** All year (not Xmas)
01273 494224 (also fax) Mr Kerridge *stay@yeomanshall.fsnet.co.uk* **D:** Fr £24.00–£27.50 **S:** Fr £38.00–£40.00 **Beds:** 2D 1S **Baths:** 2 En (2)

Bognor Regis
SZ9398

Jubilee Guest House, *Gloucester Road, Bognor Regis, W Sussex, PO21 1NU.* Family-run business 75 yds seafront, beach. Easy reach Brighton, Arundel, Chichester, Portsmouth. **Open:** All year (not Xmas/New Year)
01243 863016 **Fax: 01243 868017**
jubileeguesthouse@breathemail.net
www.jubileeguesthouse.com **D:** Fr £20.00–£35.00 **S:** Fr £20.00–£35.00 **Beds:** 3F 1D 2S **Baths:** 2 En 1 Sh (4) cc

Selwood Lodge, *93 Victoria Drive, Bognor Regis, W. Sussex, PO21 2DZ.* Friendly family hotel. Licensed bar. Games room. Garden. No restrictions. **Open:** All year
01243 865071 (also fax) Mrs Bodle *doreen@selwoodlodge.fsnet.co.uk* **D:** Fr £18.00–£20.00 **S:** Fr £25.00 **Beds:** 2F 2D 1T **Baths:** 1 En 2 Sh (3)

Regis Lodge, *Gloucester Road, Bognor Regis, W. Sussex, PO21 1NU.* Attractive seaside guest house, comfortable and clean throughout. Ideal base. **Open:** Apr to Sep
01243 827110 (also fax) Mr Rider *frank@regislodge.fsbusiness.co.uk* www.regislodge.co.uk **D:** Fr £20.00–£30.00 **S:** Fr £20.00–£30.00 **Beds:** 3F 3D 2T **Baths:** 8 En (5) (9)

All details shown are as supplied by B&B owners in Autumn 2002

Bolney

TQ2623

Butchers, *Ryecroft Road, Bolney, Haywards Heath, W Sussex, RH17 5PS.* Comfortable bedroom with ensuite bathroom. Breakfast room overlooking landscaped gardens. **Open:** All year (not Xmas)
01444 881503 Mrs Darby **D:** Fr £25.00–£27.50 **S:** Fr £30.00–£35.00 **Beds:** 1D (1)

Bosham

SU8004

Good Hope, *Delling Lane, Old Bosham, Chichester, W. Sussex, PO18 8NR.* Friendly comfortable ground floor accommodation in beautiful historic harbour village. **Open:** All year (not Xmas) **Grades:** ETC 4 Diamond
01243 572487 Mrs Jones **Fax: 01243 530760** **D:** Fr £25.00–£28.00 **S:** Fr £30.00–£45.00 **Beds:** 1T **Baths:** 1 En (2)

Barford, *Bosham Lane, Bosham, Chichester, W Sussex, PO18 8HL.* Cottage-style bungalow near Saxon church and quay, cycle hire. **Open:** All year
01243 573393 (also fax) Mr & Mrs Flanagan *Tony@aflanagan.freeserve.co.uk* **D:** Fr £22.00 **S:** Fr £27.00 **Beds:** 2D 1T **Baths:** 1 Sh (1)

Burgess Hill

TQ3119

The Homestead, *Homestead Lane, Valebridge Road, Burgess Hill, West Sussex, RH15 0RQ.* Peaceful home in 7.5 acres. Ground floor bedrooms with wheelchair access. **Open:** All year
08000 640015 & 01444 246899 **Fax: 01444 241407** *homestead@burgess-hill.co.uk* www.burgess-hill.co.uk **D:** Fr £25.00–£30.00 **S:** Fr £25.00–£30.00 **Beds:** 1S 1D 1T 1F **Baths:** 4 En (12) cc

Bury

TQ0113

Harkaway, *8 Houghton Lane, Bury, Pulborough, W. Sussex, RH20 1PD.* Quiet location beneath South Downs. Full English and vegetarian breakfast. **Open:** All year **Grades:** AA 3 Diamond
01798 831843 Mrs Clarke *carol@harkaway.org.uk* **D:** Fr £20.00–£22.50 **S:** Fr £20.00 **Beds:** 1D 1T 2S **Baths:** 1 En 1 Sh (6) (3)

Pulborough Eedes Cottage, *Bignor Park Road, Bury Gate, Bury, Pulborough, W Sussex, RH20 1EZ.* Quiet country house surrounded by farmland, very warm personal welcome. **Open:** All year (not Xmas) **Grades:** ETC 4 Diamond
01798 831438 **Fax: 01798 831942** *eedes.bandb.hare@amserve.com* **D:** Fr £25.00–£27.50 **S:** Fr £30.00 **Beds:** 2D 2T **Baths:** 2 En 1 Sh (10)

Tanglewood, *Houghton Lane, Bury, Pulborough, W Sussex, RH20 1PD.* Warm welcome in our comfortable home, with beautiful views of South Downs. **Open:** All year
01798 831606 (also fax) Mrs House **D:** Fr £22.00–£25.00 **S:** Fr £18.00–£20.00 **Beds:** 1D 1S **Baths:** 1 Sh (3)

Charlton

SU8812

Woodstock House Hotel, *Charlton, Chichester, West Sussex, PO18 0HU.* **Open:** All year **Grades:** ETC 4 Diamond, AA 4 Diamond
01243 811666 (also fax) A F Nugent *info@woodstockhousehotel.co.uk* www.woodstockhousehotel.co.uk **D:** Fr £32.00–£48.00 **S:** Fr £45.00–£55.00 **Beds:** 4T 6D 2S **Baths:** 12 En (10) cc
Converted from an old farmhouse, our licensed bed and breakfast hotel is set in the heart of the magnificent South Downs. A comfortable, peaceful base to explore the numerous attractions of Goodwood, West Dean, Chichester and for walking the Downs.

Chichester

SU8604

Strudwick House, *4 The Lane, Chichester, W Sussex, PO19 5PY.* Quiet, spacious residence, convenient for city centre, theatre & Goodwood. **Open:** All year
01243 527293 Mrs Davenport *polly.davenport@btinternet.com* **D:** Fr £25.00–£35.00 **S:** Fr £30.00–£40.00 **Beds:** 1T 2D **Baths:** 2 En 1 Pr (2)

Cedar House, *8 Westmead Road, Chichester, W Sussex, PO19 3JD.* Beautiful accommodation, close to city centre and many local attractions. **Open:** All year **Grades:** ETC 4 Diamond, AA 4 Diamond
01243 787771 Mr & Mrs Woodcock *mel.judi@talk21.com* **D:** Fr £22.50–£25.00 **S:** Fr £20.00–£25.00 **Beds:** 2D 1T 1S **Baths:** 2 En 1 Sh (5)

Draymans, *112 St Pancras, Chichester, W Sussex, PO19 4LH.* Listed Georgian town house, part converted brewery. Central Chichester. **Open:** All year
01243 789872 Mrs Jaeger **Fax: 01243 785474** *liz@jaegerl.freeserve.co.uk* www.jaegerl.freeserve.co.uk **D:** Fr £23.00–£25.00 **S:** Fr £25.00–£30.00 **Beds:** 2D 1S **Baths:** 1 En 1 Sh

Abelands Barn, *Merston, Chichester, West Sussex, PO20 1DY.* Traditional Sussex stone barn and annexe converted into a spacious family home. **Open:** All year
01243 533826 Mr Ayling **Fax: 01243 784474** **D:** Fr £30.00–£40.00 **Beds:** 1F 1D 1T **Baths:** 3 En (5)

Riverside Lodge, *7 Market Avenue, Chichester, W. Sussex, PO19 1JU.* Traditional brick and flint house near city centre. **Open:** All year (not Xmas) **Grades:** ETC 3 Diamond
01243 783164 Mrs Tregear *tregeardavid@hotmail.com* www.riverside-lodge-chichester.co.uk **D:** Fr £24.00–£27.00 **S:** Fr £25.00–£27.00 **Beds:** 2D **Baths:** 2 En (2)

5 Willowbed Avenue, *Chichester, W Sussex, PO19 2JD.* Friendly house. Walking distance to city centre. Continental breakfast. **Open:** All year
01243 786366 Mrs Pring **D:** Fr £20.00–£22.50 **S:** Fr £22.50–£25.00 **Beds:** 1T 2S **Baths:** 1 Pr 1 Sh (10) (2)

Litten House, *148 St Pancras, Chichester, W. Sussex, PO19 7SH.* Unexpectedly quiet Georgian house with garden, king-sized bed. City centre. **Open:** All year **Grades:** ETC 4 Diamond
01243 774503 Mrs Steward **Fax: 01243 539187** *victoria@littenho.demon.co.uk* www.littenho.demon.co.uk **D:** Fr £22.00–£30.00 **S:** Fr £27.00–£35.00 **Beds:** 1D 2T **Baths:** 3 Sh

17 Grenville Gardens, *Donnington, Chichester, W. Sussex, PO19 2XB.* Petite modern accommodation quietly situated near historic Chichester. Goodwood nearby. **Open:** All year
01243 775825 (also fax) D Johnson **D:** Fr £20.00–£30.00 **S:** Fr £20.00 **Beds:** 1D/T **Baths:** 1 Pr (5)

Friary Close, Friary Lane, *Chichester, W Sussex, PO19 1UF.* Grade II Listed Georgian house built astride the ancient city wall in central Chichester. **Open:** All year
01243 527294 Mr & Mrs Taylor **Fax: 01243 533876** *friaryclose@argonet.co.uk* **D:** Fr £25.00–£35.00 **S:** Fr £35.00 **Beds:** 3T **Baths:** 3 En (3) cc

Clayton

TQ3014

Dower Cottage, *Underhill Lane, Clayton, Hassocks, W. Sussex, BN6 9PL.* **Open:** All year (not Xmas)
01273 843363 Mrs Bailey **Fax: 01273 846503** *andy@dowerbailey.freeserve.co.uk* www.dowercottage.co.uk **D:** Fr £27.50–£32.50 **S:** Fr £35.00–£50.00 **Beds:** 2F 2D 1T 1S **Baths:** 2 En 1 Sh (8)
Large country house in beautiful location overlooking the Sussex Weald. Ideal for walking, cycling, riding the South Downs Way yet only 15 mins from Brighton for nightlife. Library for guest use and colour TVs in all rooms. Peace and quiet away from city stress!

Cocking

SU8717

Moonlight Cottage Tea Rooms, *Chichester Road, Cocking, Midhurst, W. Sussex, GU29 0HN.* Warm welcome, pretty tea rooms/ garden, comfortable bed, excellent breakfast. **Open:** All year
01730 813336 Mrs Longland *bedtime@moonlightcottage.net* www.moonlightcottage.net **D:** Fr £20.00–£23.00 **S:** Fr £20.00–£23.00 **Beds:** 2D 1T **Baths:** 1 Sh (5)

Copsale

TQ1724

Copsale Farm, *Copsale, Horsham, W. Sussex, RH13 6QU.* **Open:** All year
01403 732237 Mrs Churcher **D:** Fr £20.00 **S:** Fr £20.00 **Beds:** 1F 2D **Baths:** 1 En 1 Sh (7)
Spacious C14th beamed farmhouse amid 37 acres. Rurally situated, easy access to Horsham and main routes. Next to Downs Link, Bridle Path. Walkers and cyclists welcomed. Traditional English breakfast (vegetarians welcome). Local pub for evening meals. 45 mins airport/seaport.

Birchwood, *Broadwater Lane, Copsale, Horsham, W Sussex, RH13 6QW.* Enjoy a relaxing stay in our chalet bungalow set in 7 acres. **Open:** All year (not Xmas/New Year)
01403 731313 Mrs Deane *wendy@copsale.fsnet.co.uk* **D:** Fr £22.50 **S:** Fr £26.00–£30.00 **Beds:** 1F 1T **Baths:** 1 Sh (12) (4)

Coultershaw Bridge

SU9618

The Old Railway Station, *Coultershaw Bridge, Petworth, W Sussex, GU28 0JF.* Without a doubt the most beautiful railway station in Britain. **Open:** All year
01798 342346 (also fax) Mrs Rapley *mlr@old-station.co.uk* www.old-station.co.uk **D:** Fr £32.00–£47.00 **S:** Fr £40.00–£65.00 **Beds:** 1T 5D **Baths:** 6 En (12) (20) cc

East Ashling

SU8207

Englewood, *East Ashling, Chichester, W. Sussex, PO18 9AS.* Chichester 6 mins, easy access Bosham, theatres, Goodwood, Fishbourne, Singleton, Westdean. **Open:** All year (not Xmas)
01243 575407 (also fax) Ms Jones *sjenglewood@tinyworld.co.uk* **D:** Fr £23.50–£28.00 **S:** Fr £34.00–£37.00 **Beds:** 2D **Baths:** 2 En (4)

East Grinstead

TQ3938

Cranston House, *Cranston Road, East Grinstead, W. Sussex, RH19 3HW.* Hotel style accommodation in residential area. Gatwick 15 minutes. **Open:** All year (not Xmas)
01342 323609 (also fax) Mr Linacre *stay@cranstonhouse.screaming.net* www.cranstonhouse.co.uk **D:** Fr £18.00–£25.00 **S:** Fr £28.00–£35.00 **Beds:** 1F 2D 4T **Baths:** 7 En (6) (6)

Grinstead Lodge Guest House, *London Road, East Grinstead, W Sussex, RH19 1QE.* Friendly family run with ample parking. Open all year round. **Open:** All year
01342 317222 (also fax) **D:** Fr £22.00–£28.00 **S:** Fr £20.00–£33.00 **Beds:** 1F 4T 2D 2S **Baths:** 7 En 1 Sh (8) cc

Please respect a B&B's wishes regarding children, animals and smoking

East Harting

SU7919

Oakwood, *Eastfield Lane, East Harting, Petersfield, Hampshire, GU31 5NF.* Foot of South Downs, beautiful countryside, Chichester, Portsmouth easy reach. **Open:** All year
01730 825245 Mrs Brightwell **D:** Fr £20.00–£22.50 **S:** Fr £20.00–£25.00 **Beds:** 2T **Baths:** 2 Pr

East Preston

TQ0602 *Spotted Cow*

Roselea Cottage, *2 Elm Avenue, East Preston, Littlehampton, West Sussex, BN16 1HJ.* Near Goodwood, Arundel, Worthing and beach. Warm welcome, home-made bread. **Open:** All year
01903 786787 Mrs Bartram **Fax: 01903 770220** *roselea.cottage@tesco.net* **D:** Fr £20.00–£25.00 **S:** Fr £25.00–£35.00 **Beds:** 1T 1D **Baths:** 1 En 1 Pr (12) (3)

Eastergate

SU9404

Downfields, *Level Mare Lane, Eastergate, Chichester, W Sussex, PO20 6SB.* Country house near Chichester, Arundel, Goodwood, Bognor Regis. 6m from coast, large garden. **Open:** All year (not Xmas)
01243 542012 & 01243 542306 Mrs Cane **D:** Fr £18.00–£25.00 **S:** Fr £20.00–£27.00 **Beds:** 1T **Baths:** 1 Pr (4)

Elsted

SU8119

Three, *Elsted, Midhurst, W Sussex, GU29 0JY.* Oldest house in village (1520). Pub, cricket ground, church nearby. Warm welcome. **Open:** Mar to Nov
01730 825065 Mrs Hill **Fax: 01730 825496** *rh@rhill.ftech.co.uk* **D:** Fr £30.00 **S:** Fr £30.00 **Beds:** 1D 1T 1S **Baths:** 1 Pr 1 Sh

Findon

TQ1208

The Coach House, *41 High Street, Findon, Worthing, West Sussex, BN14 0SU.* Village location in South Downs. Excellent walks/cycling. Close to coast. **Open:** All year
01903 873924 A Goble **D:** Fr £20.00–£24.00 **S:** Fr £25.00–£29.00 **Beds:** 1F 1T 1D **Baths:** 3 En (3)

Racehorse Cottage, *Nepcote, Findon, Worthing, W Sussex, BN14 0SN.* Cottage sheltering under Cissbury Rine. Breakfast provided. **Open:** All year (not Xmas)
01903 873783 Mr Lloyd **D:** Fr £20.00 **S:** Fr £25.00 **Beds:** 2T **Baths:** 1 Sh (5) (2) cc

Fishbourne
SU8304

Wilbury House, *Main Road, Fishbourne, Chichester, W Sussex, PO18 8AT.* Attractive home near Fishbourne Roman Palace, overlooking farmland and Bosham's picturesque harbour, 1.5 miles. **Open:** All year (not Xmas)
01243 572953 (also fax) Mrs Penfold *jackie.penfold@talk21.com* **D:** Fr £25.00–£30.00 **S:** Fr £25.00–£35.00 **Beds:** 1F 2D 1T 1S **Baths:** 4 En 1 Pr (5) (4)

Fittleworth
TQ0019

The Swan Inn, *Lower Street, Fittleworth, Pulborough, W Sussex, RH20 1EN.* **Open:** All year **Grades:** ETC 4 Diamond, Silver
01798 865429 C Ridley **Fax: 01798 865721** *hotel@swaninn.com* www.swaninn.com **D:** Fr £30.00–£37.00 **S:** Fr £35.00–£75.00 **Beds:** 4T 8D 3S **Baths:** 15 En (15) **cc**
Traditional C14th coaching inn steeped in history. Well placed for visiting many historic houses, Petworth, Arundel, Chichester & other places of interest. Cask ales, excellent home cooked cuisine served in a rustic setting, with log fires in the winter.

Fontwell
SU9506

Woodacre, *Arundel Road, Fontwell, Arundel, W Sussex, BN18 0SD.* Set in beautiful garden surrounded by woodland. Everyone made welcome. **Open:** All year
01243 814301 Ms Richards **Fax: 01243 814344** *wacrebb@aol.com* www.woodacre.co.uk **D:** Fr £22.50–£30.00 **S:** Fr £30.00–£35.00 **Beds:** 1F 2T 1D **Baths:** 1 En 1 Pr 2 Sh (20) **cc**

Gatwick
TQ2740

April Cottage, *10 Langley Lane, Ifield, Crawley, West Sussex, RH11 0NA.* Warm and friendly 200-year-old house in quiet lane. Near pubs, shops. **Open:** All year
01293 546222 Mrs Pedlow **Fax: 01293 518712** *aprilcottage.guesthouse@tesco.net* www.aprilcottageguesthouse.co.uk **D:** Fr £22.50–£30.00 **Beds:** 1F 1D 2T **Baths:** 2 En 2 Sh (8)

Graffham
SU9217

Brook Barn, *Selham Road, Graffham, Petworth, W Sussex, GU28 0PU.* High quality accommodation with own conservatory. Ideal touring/walking area. **Open:** All year (not Xmas) **Grades:** ETC 5 Diamond, Silver
01798 867356 Mr & Mrs Jollands **D:** Fr £30.00–£37.50 **S:** Fr £40.00–£60.00 **Beds:** 1D **Baths:** 1 En (2)

Hardham
TQ0417

Moseley's Barn, *London Road, Hardham, Pulborough, West Sussex, RH20 1LB.* Converted C17th barn with galleried beamed hall with panoramic views of South Downs. **Open:** All year
01798 872912 (also fax) Mrs Newton **D:** Fr £22.50–£27.50 **S:** Fr £30.00–£40.00 **Beds:** 1T 2D **Baths:** 2 En 1 Pr (10)

Haywards Heath
TQ3324

Birch House, *Lewes Road, Haywards Heath, W Sussex, RH17 7SP.* Within travelling distance of National Trust gardens and town centre. **Open:** All year (not Xmas/New Year)
01444 457020 Mrs Wheeler **Fax: 01444 457054** **D:** Fr £22.50 **S:** Fr £35.00–£45.00 **Beds:** 2D **Baths:** 2 En (3)

12 Petlands Road, *Haywards Heath, W Sussex, RH16 4HH.* Homely cottage atmosphere. **Open:** All year
01444 454473 Mrs Hartley **D:** Fr £25.00 **S:** Fr £25.00 **Beds:** 1D 1T 1S **Baths:** 1 Sh (1)

Pinehurst, *Tylers Green, Haywards Heath, W. Sussex, RH16 4BW.* Beautiful oak-beamed country house set in mature gardens backing onto nature reserve. **Open:** All year
01444 456578 Mrs O'Riordan **D:** Fr £25.00–£35.00 **S:** Fr £35.00–£40.00 **Beds:** 1D 2T **Baths:** 4 En (8) (4)

Henfield
TQ2116

Lyndhurst, *38 Broomfield Road, Henfield, West Sussex, BN5 9UA.* Elegant Victorian house on edge of village. Ideal touring base. **Open:** All year
01273 494054 Mrs Slingsby **Fax: 01273 491334** *linda.Slingsby@ukgateway.net* www.smoothhound.co.uk/hotels/lyndhurst.html **D:** Fr £22.50–£27.50 **S:** Fr £30.00–£37.50 **Beds:** 1F 1D 1T **Baths:** 3 En (6)

1 The Laurels, *Martyns Close, Henfield, West Sussex, BN5 9RQ.* Quiet village location. Easy access to Brighton, Gatwick and many places of interest. **Open:** All year
01273 493518 & 07788 713864 (M) Mr Harrington *malc.harrington@lineone.net* www.no1thelaurels.co.uk **D:** Fr £25.00–£30.00 **S:** Fr £20.00–£30.00 **Beds:** 2D 1S **Baths:** 2 En 1 Sh (3)

Leeches, *West End Lane, Henfield, W Sussex, BN5 9RG.* Rural Tudor farmhouse. River and country walks. Heated swimming pool. **Open:** All year
01273 492495 Mrs Abbott **Fax: 01273 493000** **D:** Fr £22.50–£25.00 **S:** Fr £25.00 **Beds:** 1D 2T 2S **Baths:** 2 Pr 2 Sh (5) (6)

Heyshott
SU8917

Little Hoyle, *Hoyle Lane, Heyshott, Midhurst, W Sussex, GU29 0DX.* Comfortable, welcoming, peaceful, large garden, splendid views to South Downs, near Petworth, Goodwood, Chichester. **Open:** All year (not Xmas)
01798 867359 (also fax) Mr & Mrs Ralph **D:** Fr £23.00–£26.00 **S:** Fr £35.00 **Beds:** 1D **Baths:** 1 En (2)

Horsham
TQ1731

Birchwood, *Broadwater Lane, Copsale, Horsham, W Sussex, RH13 6QW.* **Open:** All year (not Xmas/New Year)
01403 731313 Mrs Deane *wendy@copsale.fsnet.co.uk* **D:** Fr £22.50 **S:** Fr £26.00–£30.00 **Beds:** 1F 1T **Baths:** 1 Sh (12) (4)
Enjoy a relaxing stay in our chalet bungalow set in 7 acres. Quiet rural location with village pub. Near to coastal resorts & good walks. Breakfast in our lovely conservatory with picturesque fish pool. Both rooms/bathroom on ground floor.

The Larches, *28 Rusper Road, Horsham, West Sussex, RH12 4BD.* Friendly family house close to stations and attractive town centre. Separate visitor's entrance. **Open:** All year
01403 263392 Mrs Lane **Fax: 01403 249980** **D:** Fr £23.00–£25.00 **S:** Fr £20.00–£25.00 **Beds:** 1F 2T 2S **Baths:** 2 En (3)

Planning a longer stay? Always ask for any special rates

The Wirrals, *1 Downsview Road, Horsham, W Sussex, RH12 4PF.* Attractive detached home with a welcoming atmosphere and comfortable accommodation. **Open:** All year (not Xmas) **Grades:** ETC 3 Diamond
01403 269400 (also fax) Mrs Archibald *p.archibald@lineone.net* website.lineone.net/~p.archibald/webba.htm **D:** Fr £20.00–£23.00 **S:** Fr £23.00–£25.00 **Beds:** 1D 1S **Baths:** 1 Sh (2)

Alton House, *29 Rusper Road, Horsham, W Sussex, RH12 4BA.* 15 mins Gatwick Airport, Leonardslee and Nymans Gardens, 35 minutes Worthing, Brighton. **Open:** All year
01403 211825 Mrs Ashton **D:** Fr £22.50–£25.00 **S:** Fr £35.00 **Beds:** 3D 1T **Baths:** 3 Pr 1 Sh (1) (4)

The Studio at The Hermitage, *Tower Hill, Horsham, West Sussex, RH13 7JS.* Private, self-contained, semi-rural location. 1 mile Horsham town. **Open:** All year
01403 270808 *hermitagejem@netscapeonline.co.uk* **D:** Fr £22.50–£27.50 **S:** Fr £30.00–£35.00 **Beds:** 1T **Baths:** 1 En (2)

Horsted Keynes
TQ3827

The Croft, *Lewes Road, Horsted Keynes, Haywards Heath, W Sussex, RH17 7DP.* Warm welcome assured in comfortable family house situated in a quiet village location. **Open:** All year
01825 790546 Mrs Ollif **D:** Fr £22.50–£25.00 **S:** Fr £25.00–£30.00 **Beds:** 1T 1D **Baths:** 1 Sh (4)

Hurstpierpoint
TQ2816 *White Horse, New Inn*

Bankyfield, *21 Hassocks Road, Hurstpierpoint, W. Sussex, BN6 9QH.* Georgian house in Downland village. Brighton 5 miles. **Open:** All year (not Xmas/New Year)
01273 833217 Mrs Norris **D:** Fr £23.00–£25.00 **S:** Fr £25.00 **Beds:** 1T **Baths:** 1 Pr (1)

Ifield
TQ2537

Waterhall Country House, *Prestwood Lane, Ifield Wood, Ifield, Crawley, W Sussex, RH11 0LA.* Attractive country house set in 28 acres - ideal for Gatwick bed & breakfast. **Open:** All year (not Xmas)
01293 520002 Mrs Dawson **Fax: 01293 539905** *info@waterhall.co.uk* www.smoothhound.co.uk/hotels/waterhall.html **D:** Fr £22.50 **S:** Fr £35.00 **Beds:** 4D 3T 1S 2F **Baths:** 10 En (25) cc

Littlehampton
TQ0202

Victoria Hotel, *59 New Road, Littlehampton, W. Sussex, BN17 5AU.* Comfortable accommodation. Warm welcome. Full English breakfast and seaside walks. **Open:** All year (not Xmas/New Year)
01903 717175 **D:** Fr £20.00–£25.00 **S:** Fr £20.00–£30.00 **Beds:** 2F 3D 1S **Baths:** 2 Sh (5) (5)

Littleworth
TQ1920

Pound Cottage, *Mill Lane, Littleworth, Partridge Green, W. Sussex, RH13 8JU.* Comfortable detached country house, warm welcome and good English breakfasts. **Open:** All year **Grades:** ETC 3 Diamond
01403 710218 Mrs Brown **Fax: 01403 711337** *poundcottagebb@amserve.net* **D:** Fr £22.00 **S:** Fr £22.00 **Beds:** 1D 1T 1S **Baths:** 1 Sh (8)

Lower Beeding
TQ2128

The Old Posthouse, *Plummers Plain, Lower Beeding, Horsham, W. Sussex, RH13 6NU.* Victorian house, beautiful garden, close to Leonardslee, Nymans, Bluebell Railway, Horsham, Brighton. **Open:** All year (not Xmas)
01403 891776 (also fax) Dr Crisp *russell@oldposthouse.com* www.oldposthouse.com **D:** Fr £22.50 **S:** Fr £28.00 **Beds:** 2D 2T 2S **Baths:** 6 En (6) cc

Village Pantry, *Handcross Road, Plummers Plain, Lower Beeding, Horsham, W Sussex, RH13 6NU.* Superb comfortable rooms, lovely garden. Close Gatwick, Horsham, Brighton, Crawley. Warm welcome. **Open:** All year (not Xmas)
01403 891319 (also fax) Mrs Jays **D:** Fr £20.00–£25.00 **S:** Fr £26.00–£40.00 **Beds:** 1F 2D 1T 1S **Baths:** 3 En 1 Sh (6)

Merston
SU8902

Abelands Barn, *Merston, Chichester, West Sussex, PO20 1DY.* Traditional Sussex stone barn and annexe converted into a spacious family home. **Open:** All year
01243 533826 Mr Ayling **Fax: 01243 784474** **D:** Fr £30.00–£40.00 **Beds:** 1F 1D 1T **Baths:** 3 En (5)

Midhurst
SU8821

Three, *Elsted, Midhurst, W Sussex, GU29 0JY.* Oldest house in village (1520). Pub, cricket ground, church nearby. Warm welcome. **Open:** Mar to Nov
01730 825065 Mrs Hill **Fax: 01730 825496** *rh@rhill.ftech.co.uk* **D:** Fr £30.00 **S:** Fr £30.00 **Beds:** 1D 1T 1S **Baths:** 1 Pr 1 Sh

Oakhurst Cottage, *Carron Lane, Midhurst, W. Sussex, GU29 9LF.* Beautiful cottage in lovely surroundings within easy reach of Midhurst amenities. **Open:** All year
01730 813523 Mrs Whitmore Jones **D:** Fr £25.00–£30.00 **S:** Fr £25.00–£30.00 **Beds:** 1D 1T 1S **Baths:** 1 En 1 Sh (4) (2)

Poling
TQ0404

Medlar Cottage, *Poling, Arundel, W. Sussex, BN18 9PT.* Attractive country home in quiet village location. Restful and relaxing. **Open:** All year (not Xmas)
01903 883106 (also fax) Mr & Mrs Mercer **D:** Fr £20.00–£22.50 **S:** Fr £20.00–£25.00 **Beds:** 2D 1T 1S **Baths:** 1 En 2 Sh (2) (3)

Rake
SU8027

Glendale, *Hatch Lane, Rake, Liss, Hampshire, GU33 7NJ.* Large family house in 4.5 acres, garden with tennis court set in country woodland. **Open:** All year (not Xmas)
01730 893451 Mrs Browse **Fax: 01730 892626** *carol@cbrowse.fsnet.co.uk* **D:** Fr £22.50–£25.00 **S:** Fr £25.00–£30.00 **Beds:** 1D 1T 1S **Baths:** 1 En 1 Pr

Redford
SU8625

Redford Cottage, *Redford, Midhurst, W Sussex, GU29 0QF.* Warm welcome in old beamed cottage in quiet country location. **Open:** All year (not Xmas)
01428 741242 (also fax) C Angela **D:** Fr £30.00–£35.00 **S:** Fr £35.00–£40.00 **Beds:** 1T 2D **Baths:** 3 En (10)

Runcton
SU8801

Springdale Cottage, *Runcton, Chichester, W Sussex, PO20 6PS.* Beautiful C18th cottage in delightful gardens down country lane. **Open:** All year
01243 783912 Mr & Mrs Davey **D:** Fr £20.00–£25.00 **S:** Fr £20.00–£25.00 **Beds:** 1F 1T 1D 1S **Baths:** 1 En 1 Pr 1 Sh (6)

Rustington

TQ0502

Kenmore Guest House, *Claigmar Road, Rustington, Littlehampton, W. Sussex, BN16 2NL.* Secluded Edwardian house in the heart of the village close to the sea. **Open:** All year
01903 784634 (also fax) Mrs Dobbs *kenmoreguesthouse@amserve.net* **D:** Fr £23.50–£26.00 **S:** Fr £23.50–£26.00 **Beds:** 3F 3D 1T 1S **Baths:** 8 En (8) cc

Selsey

SZ8593

St Andrews Lodge, *Chichester Road, Selsey, Chichester, W. Sussex, PO20 0LX.* Friendly family-run small hotel, 7 miles south of Chichester. **Open:** All year (not Xmas/New Year) **Grades:** ETC 4 Diamond, AA 4 Diamond
01243 606899 Mr & Mrs Humphery **Fax: 01243 607826** *info@standrewslodge.co.uk* **D:** Fr £30.00–£45.00 **S:** Fr £30.00–£50.00 **Beds:** 2F 3T 4D 1S **Baths:** 10 En (15) cc

Sharpthorne

TQ3732

Saxons, *Horsted Lane, Sharpthorne, East Grinstead, W. Sussex, RH19 4HY.* Detached country house, beautiful countryside. Near National Trust properties. **Open:** All year **Grades:** ETC 4 Diamond
01342 810821 Mrs Smith *aliexcol@aol.com* **D:** Fr £20.00–£25.00 **S:** Fr £25.00–£35.00 **Beds:** 2D 1T **Baths:** 1 Sh 1 En (6)

Shoreham-by-Sea

TQ2205

The Crabtree, *6 Buckingham Road, Shoreham-by-Sea, W. Sussex, BN43 5UA.* All rooms comfortably decorated. Close to sea front, station, local attractions. **Open:** All year
01273 463508 L B Dove **D:** Fr £17.50–£20.00 **S:** Fr £20.00–£25.00 **Beds:** 2F 1T 1D **Baths:** 1 Sh (10)

Slindon

SU9608

Mill Lane House, *Mill Lane, Slindon, Arundel, W. Sussex, BN18 0RP.* In peaceful village on South Downs, views to coast. **Open:** All year
01243 814440 Mrs Fuente **Fax: 01243 814436** **D:** Fr £22.50 **S:** Fr £28.50 **Beds:** 2D 1T **Baths:** 3 En (7)

Slinfold

TQ1131

Wendys Cottage, *Five Oaks Road, Slinfold, Horsham, West Sussex, RH13 7RQ.* Farmhouse 3 miles from Horsham. Ample parking. English breakfast. **Open:** All year
01403 782326 (also fax) **D:** Fr £20.00–£22.50 **S:** Fr £25.00–£30.00 **Beds:** 1F 1T **Baths:** 2 En

Steyning

TQ1711

Buncton Manor Farm, *Steyning Road, Wiston, Steyning, W. Sussex, BN44 3DD.* C15th partly moated farmhouse close to the South Downs Way. **Open:** All year **Grades:** ETC 4 Diamond
01903 812736 C Rowland **Fax: 01903 814838** *bunctonmanor@onetel.net.uk* www.bunctonmanor.supanet.com **D:** Fr £20.00–£22.00 **S:** Fr £36.00–£38.00 **Beds:** 1T 1D **Baths:** 1 Sh (5)

Storrington

TQ0814

Chardonnay, *Hampers Lane, Storrington, Pulborough, W Sussex, RH20 3HZ.* Warm welcome in quiet South Downs location. Excellent home-cooked breakfast. **Open:** All year **Grades:** ETC 4 Diamond
01903 746688 Mrs Searancke *annsearancke@bigfoot.com* **D:** Fr £23.50–£25.00 **S:** Fr £23.50–£25.00 **Beds:** 1T 2D **Baths:** 3 En (5)

Upper Beeding

TQ1910

The Rising Sun, *Upper Beeding, Steyning, W. Sussex, BN44 3TQ.* **Open:** All year (not Xmas)
01903 814424 Mr & Mrs Taylor-Mason *the_rising_sun@btopenworld.com* www.risingsun.tk **D:** Fr £15.00 **S:** Fr £18.00 **Beds:** 2D 1T 2S **Baths:** 1 Sh (20) cc
A delightful Georgian country inn, set amidst the South Downs. Tony and Sue offer a warm welcome, fine selection of real ales and traditional home-cooked food lunchtime and evenings. Comfortable rooms, all with wash basin. Renowned full English breakfast.

National Grid References given are for villages, towns and cities – not for individual houses

West Broyle

SU8406

Primrose Cottage, *Old Broyle Road, West Broyle, Chichester, W. Sussex, PO19 3PR.* Victorian house 1.75 miles Chichester, close to theatre, Goodwood, countryside. **Open:** All year
01243 788873 Mrs Brooks **D:** Fr £22.00–£28.00 **S:** Fr £25.00–£44.00 **Beds:** 1T 1D 1S **Baths:** 2 Sh (4)

West Hoathly

TQ3632

Stonelands West Lodge, *Ardingly Road, West Hoathly, East Grinstead, West Sussex, RH19 4RA.* Victorian lodge on B2028 between Turners Hill and Ardingly. Close Wakehurst Place. **Open:** All year **Grades:** ETC 3 Diamond
01342 715372 & 07759 295200 (M) Mrs Hutchings **D:** Fr £25.00–£35.00 **S:** Fr £25.00–£30.00 **Beds:** 1T 1D 1S **Baths:** 1 En 1 Sh (2)

Wineham

TQ2320

Frylands Farm, *Wineham, Henfield, W. Sussex, BN5 9BP.* Tudor farmhouse, large garden, swimming pool. Fishing available. **Open:** All year
01403 710214 Mr & Mrs Fowler www.frylands.co.uk **D:** Fr £20.00–£23.00 **S:** Fr £25.00 **Beds:** 1F 1T 1D **Baths:** 1 Pr 1 Sh (6)

Wisborough Green

TQ0425

Lower Sparr Farm, *Skiff Lane, Wisborough Green, W Sussex, RH14 0AA.* Farmhouse set in quiet surroundings overlooking large garden and pastureland. **Open:** All year (not Xmas) **Grades:** ETC 4 Diamond
01403 820465 Mrs Sclater **Fax: 01403 820678** *sclater@lowersparrbb.f9.co.uk* www.lowersparrbb.f9.co.uk **D:** Fr £26.00 **S:** Fr £26.00 **Beds:** 1D 1T 1S **Baths:** 2 Pr (4)

Wiston

TQ1414

Buncton Manor Farm, *Steyning Road, Wiston, Steyning, W. Sussex, BN44 3DD.* C15th partly moated farmhouse close to the South Downs Way. **Open:** All year **Grades:** ETC 4 Diamond
01903 812736 C Rowland **Fax: 01903 814838** *bunctonmanor@onetel.net.uk* www.bunctonmanor.supanet.com **D:** Fr £20.00–£22.00 **S:** Fr £36.00–£38.00 **Beds:** 1T 1D **Baths:** 1 Sh (5)

Woodmancote (Henfield)

TQ2314

Eaton Thorne House, *Woodmancote, Henfield, E. Sussex, BN5 9BD.* **Open:** All year (not Xmas/New Year)
01273 492591 Mrs Langthorne *eatonthorne@amserve.com* homepage.virgin.net/eaton.thorne **D:** Fr £25.00 **S:** Fr £27.50 **Beds:** 1F 1T 1D **Baths:** 3 En (6)
Award-winning C15th cottage set in lovely gardens and paddocks. Beautifully furnished with antiques and open fires. Close to National Trust properties, many stately houses and gardens. South Down walks are close, also Brighton 8 miles and Gatwick Airport.

The Tithe Barn, *Brighton Road, Woodmancote, Henfield, West Sussex, BN5 9ST.* Woodmancote - West Sussex. Converted flint barn with views of South Downs. **Open:** All year
01273 492986 (also fax) Mrs Warren *chriswarren@breathemail.net* **D:** Fr £18.00–£25.00 **S:** Fr £18.00–£25.00 **Beds:** 2T 1S **Baths:** 1 Sh (3)

Worthing

TQ1303

Rosedale House, *12 Bath Road, Worthing, W. Sussex, BN11 3NU.* Delightful Victorian house run by friendly Nightingale. Nestling by a delightful seaside town. **Open:** All year
01903 233181 Mrs Nightingale *rosedale@amserve.net* **D:** Fr £25.00–£28.50 **S:** Fr £25.00–£33.00 **Beds:** 1T 2D 1S **Baths:** 2 En 1 Sh

Tudor Lodge, *25 Oxford Road, Worthing, W. Sussex, BN11 1XQ.* Victorian house near amenities for warm welcome and excellent breakfast. **Open:** All year (not Xmas)
01903 234401 Mrs Colbourn **D:** Fr £18.00–£20.00 **S:** Fr £18.00–£20.00 **Beds:** 1D 1T 1S **Baths:** 1 Sh (2)

B&B owners may vary rates – be sure to check when booking

Merton Guest House, *96 Broadwater Road, Worthing, W Sussex, BN14 8AW.* Friendly and attentive service with high standard accommodation. **Open:** All year **Grades:** ETC 4 Diamond
01903 238222 (also fax) Mr Smith *stay@mertonhouse.freeserve.co.uk* www.mertonhouse.co.uk **D:** Fr £26.00–£28.50 **S:** Fr £30.00–£40.00 **Beds:** 3D 1T 1S **Baths:** 5 En (8) (5) cc

Manor Guest House, *100 Broadwater Road, Worthing, West Sussex, BN14 8AN.* Detached cottage-style house. Ideally situated for business and pleasure. **Open:** All year
01903 236028 Mr Emms **Fax: 01903 230404** *stay@manorworthing.com* www.manorworthing.com **D:** Fr £20.00–£30.00 **S:** Fr £20.00–£35.00 **Beds:** 2F 3D 1S **Baths:** 3 En 1 Sh (8) cc

Marina, *191 Brighton Road, Worthing, W Sussex, BN11 2EX.* Charming Victorian house offering comfortable accommodation set in seafront location. **Open:** All year (not Xmas/New Year)
01903 207844 *marinaworthing@aol.com* **D:** Fr £22.50–£26.00 **S:** Fr £22.50–£40.00 **Beds:** 1F 1T 1D 2S **Baths:** 1 En 4 Sh cc

Teesside

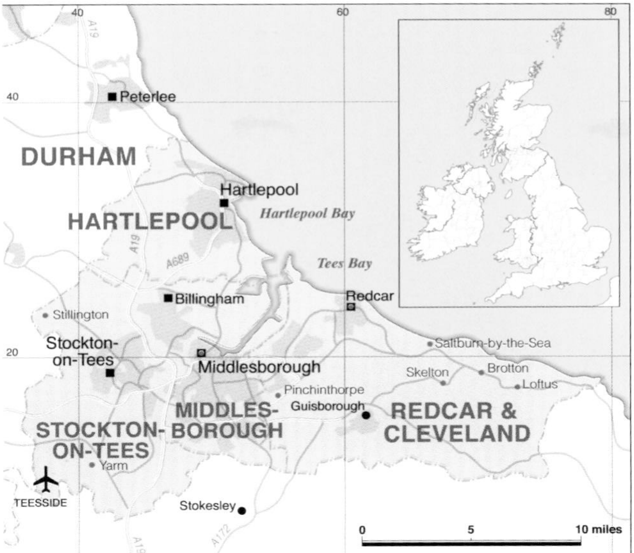

Brotton

NZ6820

Hunley Hall Golf Club and Hotel, *Brotton, Saltburn-by-the-Sea, TS12 2QQ.* **Open:** All year **01287 676216** E Lillie **Fax: 01287 678250** *enquiries@hunleyhall.co.uk* www.hunleyhall.co.uk **D:** Fr £30.00–£33.00 **S:** Fr £30.00–£35.00 **Beds:** 1F 4T 3D **Baths:** 8 En (80) cc

Occupying a peaceful country location with unrivalled panoramic views of the golf course and dramatic coastline. Family owned and run hotel with professional, yet informal friendly service. Well-equipped bedrooms and a wide selection of quality meals and beverages.

The Arches Hotel, *Birkbeck Low Farm, Brotton, Saltburn-by-the-Sea, TS12 2QX.* Beautiful coastal and golf course views. Special terms for long stays. **Open:** All year **01287 677512 Fax: 01287 677150** *birkralysc@aol.com* www.gorally.co.uk **D:** Fr £20.00–£30.00 **S:** Fr £30.00–£35.00 **Beds:** 11F 5T 6D **Baths:** 22 Pr (20) cc

Loftus

NZ7118

White Horse Inn, *73 High Street, Loftus, Saltburn-by-the-Sea, TS13 4HG.* Friendly village pub near to Yorkshire moors and seaside. **Open:** All year (not Xmas) **01287 640758** C Rowe **D:** Fr £18.00–£21.00 **S:** Fr £18.00–£21.00 **Beds:** 2F 1T **Baths:** 1 En 1 Sh (5)

Middlesbrough

NZ5118

White House Hotel, *311 Marton Road, Middlesbrough, TS4 2HG.* Family run, close to centre, good English breakfast, car parking. **Open:** All year **01642 244531 D:** Fr £15.00–£17.50 **S:** Fr £18.50–£22.00 **Beds:** 2F 2D 6T 5S **Baths:** 4 En 3 Sh

Pinchinthorpe (Middlesbrough)

NZ5418

Pinchinthorpe Hotel, *Pinchinthorpe, Guisborough, TS14 8HG.* In N Yorks National Park close to Heartbeat & Herriot country **Open:** All year **01287 630200 (also fax)** G Tinsley **D:** Fr £45.00–£65.00 **S:** Fr £65.00–£85.00 **Beds:** 6D **Baths:** 6 En

Redcar

NZ6124

Central Private Hotel, *44 Queen Street, Redcar, TS10 1BD.* Centre of town, near race course, station golf club, pubs, beach. **Open:** All year **01642 482309 D:** Fr £16.00–£24.00 **S:** Fr £18.00–£27.00 **Beds:** 5F 10T 5D 5S **Baths:** 9 En 5 Pr 5 Sh

Saltburn-by-the-Sea

NZ6722

Westerlands Guest House, *27 East Parade, Skelton, Saltburn-by-the-Sea, TS12 2BJ.* Large modern detached house, beautiful views sea/countryside, alongside way long-distance path. **Open:** All year **Grades:** ETC 4 Diamond **01287 650690** Mr Bull **D:** Fr £16.00 **S:** Fr £16.00 **Beds:** 6F 3D 3S **Baths:** 3 Pr (5)

Runswick Bay Hotel, *Runswick Bay, Saltburn-by-the-Sea, TS13 5HR.* In well-known village of Runswick Bay and within North York Moors National Park. **Open:** All year (not Xmas/New Year) **01947 840997 D:** Fr £22.50–£25.00 **S:** Fr £25.00–£28.00 **Beds:** 1F 1T 4D **Baths:** 6 En cc

Merhba, *11 Dundas Street, Saltburn-by-the-Sea, TS12 1BL.* Warm welcome. Full English breakfast. Ideal centre for touring area. **Open:** Feb to Dec **01287 622566** *pcookmerhba@ntlworld.co.uk* **D:** Fr £14.00–£16.00 **S:** Fr £15.00–£17.00 **Beds:** 1F 1T 1D 1S **Baths:** 4 Sh

Skelton (Saltburn)

NZ6518

Westerlands Guest House, *27 East Parade, Skelton, Saltburn-by-the-Sea, TS12 2BJ.* Large modern detached house, beautiful views sea/countryside, alongside Cleveland way long-distance path. **Open:** All year **Grades:** ETC 4 Diamond **01287 650690** Mr Bull **D:** Fr £16.00 **S:** Fr £16.00 **Beds:** 6F 3D 3S **Baths:** 3 Pr (5)

Wharton Arms Hotel, *High Street, Skelton, Saltburn-by-the-Sea, TS12 2DY.* Friendly pub 3 miles from North York moors. 2 miles from Saltburn. **Open:** All year (not Xmas/New Year)
01287 650618 Ms Cummings **D:** Fr £20.00 **S:** Fr £20.00 **Beds:** 1F 2T 1D 1S **Baths:** 5 En (15)

Stillington

NZ3724

Post Office House, *Redmarshall Street, Stillington, Stockton-on-Tees, TS21 1JS.* Spacious modern rooms. Private entrance with own keys. **Open:** All year
01740 630301 (also fax) *harewood@tesco.net* **D:** Fr £20.00 **S:** Fr £25.00 **Beds:** 2D **Baths:** 2 En

Yarm

NZ4112

Squirrel Wood, *2 Valley Close, Yarm, TS15 9SE.* Friendly, comfortable, modern, detached house in peaceful wooded surroundings. **Open:** All year (not Xmas)
01642 780633 Mr & Mrs Bond *bonds@squirrelwood.fsnet.co.uk* **D:** Fr £23.00–£30.00 **S:** Fr £23.00–£30.00 **Beds:** 1T 2S 1D **Baths:** 1 En 1 Sh (5) (2)

Tyne & Wear

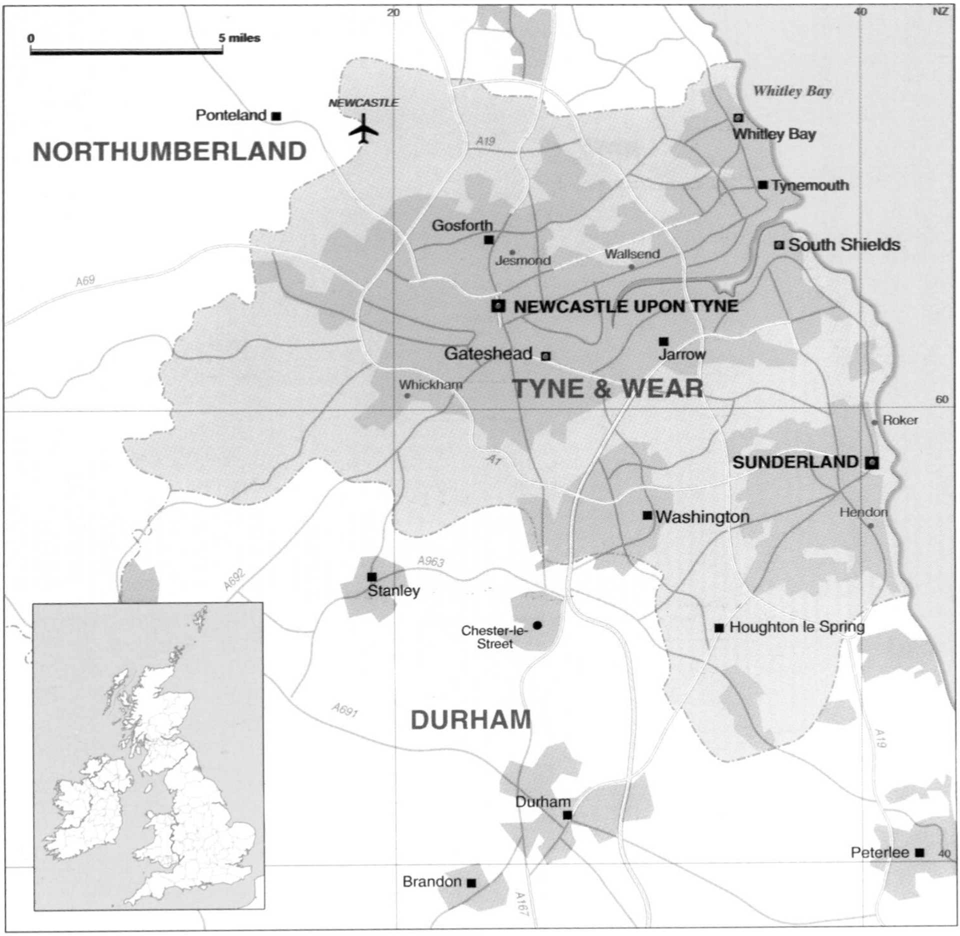

Gateshead

NZ2561

Shaftesbury Guest House, *245 Prince Consort Road, Gateshead, Tyne & Wear, NE8 4DT.* Good quality accommodation, mins from Quayside, arena and metro centre. **Open:** All year **Grades:** ETC 3 Diamond **0191 4782544 (also fax) D:** Fr £20.00–£25.00 **S:** Fr £25.00–£35.00 **Beds:** 2F 8T 3D 2S **Baths:** 2 En 3 Sh

Bellevue Guest House, *31-33 Belle Vue Bank, Low Fell, Gateshead, NE9 6BQ.* Victorian terrace, centrally located for Metro Centre, Newcastle stadium, Beamish Museum. **Open:** All year **0191 487 8805** Mr Wallace **D:** Fr £18.00–£20.00 **S:** Fr £18.00–£28.00 **Beds:** 1F 1D 2T 2S **Baths:** 2 En 1 Sh

B&B owners may vary rates – be sure to check when booking

Cox Close House, *Ravensworth, Gateshead, NE11 0HQ.* Unique C16th building. Secluded yet near city and tourist attractions. **Open:** All year **0191 488 7827** *johnpat@grayravensworth.freeserve.co.uk* **D:** Fr £18.00–£22.00 **S:** Fr £18.00–£22.00 **Beds:** 1F 1D 1T **Baths:** 1 En 1 Sh

All details shown are as supplied by B&B owners in Autumn 2002

Hendon

NZ3956

Acorn Guest House, *10 Mowbray Road, Hendon, Sunderland, SR2 8EN.* Situated near town centre, Mowbray Park and all local amenities. **Open:** All year
0191 514 2170 A Morrison
theacornguesthouse@hotmail.com **D:** Fr £15.00 **S:** Fr £16.00 **Beds:** 3F 5T 1D (9)

Jesmond

NZ2566

Jesmond Park Hotel, *74-76 Queens Road, Jesmond, Newcastle-upon-Tyne, NE2 2PR.* Very clean, quiet, comfortable hotel, offering good full English breakfast. **Open:** All year
0191 281 2821 Fax: 0191 281 0515 *stay@jesmondpark.com* **D:** Fr £22.00–£26.00 **S:** Fr £25.00–£36.00 **Beds:** 5F 5D 3T 5S **Baths:** 13 En 3 Sh

Grosvenor Hotel, *24-28 Grosvenor Road, Jesmond, Newcastle-upon-Tyne, NE2 2RR.* Ideally situated to explore Newcastle-upon-Tyne and experience its legendary nightlife. **Open:** All year
0191 281 0543 Fax: 0191 281 9217 D: Fr £35.00–£45.00 **S:** Fr £35.00–£45.00 **Beds:** 3F 25T 11D 14S **Baths:** 53 En (7) cc

Roker

NZ4059 *Queen Vic*

8 St Georges Terrace, *Roker, Sunderland, SR6 9LX.* Friendly, family run guest house near seafront and city centre. **Open:** All year
0191 567 2438 R L Dawson
belmontguesthouse@hotmail.com
www.belmontguesthouse.com **D:** Fr £17.00–£19.00 **S:** Fr £20.00–£28.00 **Beds:** 2F 2T 2D 1S **Baths:** 3 En 2 Sh cc

South Shields

NZ3666

Marina Guest House, *32 Seaview Terrace, South Shields, Tyne & Wear, NE33 2NW.* Three storey Victorian house overlooking the park, with panoramic sea views. **Open:** All year (not Xmas/New Year) **Grades:** ETC 3 Diamond
0191 456 1998 (also fax) Mr & Mrs Mercer *austin@marina32.fsnet.co.uk* **D:** Fr £19.00–£20.00 **S:** Fr £25.00–£26.00 **Beds:** 2F 2T 2S **Baths:** 4 Pr 1 Sh

Saraville Guest House, *103 Ocean Road, South Shields, NE33 2JL.* Family-run & centrally located. Close to Metro. **Open:** All year
0191 454 1169 (also fax) Mrs Taylor *emma@saraville.freeserve.co.uk* **D:** Fr £20.00 **S:** Fr £25.00–£28.00 **Beds:** 1F 1D 1T 2S **Baths:** 3 En (6)

Sunderland

NZ3957

Braeside Guest House, *26 Western Hill, Beside University, Sunderland, SR2 7PH.* Experience our unique theme rooms, hearty northern breakfasts, Northumbria's beautiful countryside. **Open:** Jan to Nov
0191 565 4801 Fax: 0191 552 4198 *george@the20thhole.co.uk* www.the20thhole.co.uk **D:** Fr £15.00–£17.50 **S:** Fr £18.00–£23.00 **Beds:** 2T 1D **Baths:** 1 En 1 Sh (12)

Wallsend

NZ3066 *Anson Pub, Hadrian Lodge Hotel*

Imperial Guest House, *194 Station Road, Wallsend, Newcastle-upon-Tyne, NE28 8RD.* Behind the unassuming terraced frontage lies a guest house with a difference. **Open:** All year
0191 236 9808 (also fax) Mr Brownlee *enquiries@imperialguesthouse.co.uk*
www.imperialguesthouse.co.uk **D:** Fr £20.00–£25.00 **S:** Fr £20.00–£35.00 **Beds:** 1T 1D **Baths:** 1 En 1 Sh (12)

Whickham

NZ2161

East Byermoor Guest House, *Fellside Road, Whickham, Newcastle upon Tyne, NE16 5BD.* Formal farmhouse. Rural location. Convenient for cities and coast. **Open:** All year
01207 262687 *eastbyermoor-gh.arbon@virgin.net* **D:** Fr £22.00–£25.00 **S:** Fr £22.00–£25.00 **Beds:** 2T 4D **Baths:** 5 En 1 Pr (13) cc

Whitley Bay

NZ3572

Buncrana Guest House, *50 North Parade, Whitley Bay, Tyne & Wear, NE26 1PB.* Family-run. Twenty metres to Promenade, beach, pubs and restaurants. **Open:** All year (not Xmas/New Year)
0191 252 5715 D: Fr £15.00–£20.00 **S:** Fr £17.50–£25.00 **Beds:** 2F 1T

Cherrytree House, *35 Brook Street, Whitley Bay, NE26 1AF.* Edwardian town house near sea front in a quiet street. **Open:** All year
0191 251 4306 (also fax) Mr Coleman *cherrytreehouse@cherrytreehouse.free-online.co.uk*
D: Fr £16.00–£25.00 **S:** Fr £20.00–£35.00 **Beds:** 1F 2T 2D 2S **Baths:** 1 En 3 Pr

Marlborough Hotel, *20-21 East Parade, Whitley Bay, NE26 1AP.* Traditional family hotel on sea front overlooking the beach, 5 mins' walk town centre. **Open:** All year (not Xmas)
0191 251 3628 J A Thompson **Fax: 0191 252 5033** *reception@marlborough-hotel.com*
www.marlborough-hotel.com **D:** Fr £28.00–£32.00 **S:** Fr £22.00–£38.00 **Beds:** 4F 5D 3T 5S **Baths:** 14 En 1 Pr 2 Sh (3) (5) 3 cc

The Lindsay Guest House, *50 Victoria Avenue, Whitley Bay, NE26 2BA.* Small family-run guest house, overlooking tennis courts and bowling green. **Open:** All year
0191 252 7341 A Ward **Fax: 0191 252 7505**
info@lindsayguesthouse.co.uk
www.lindsayguesthouse.co.uk **D:** Fr £20.00–£25.00 **S:** Fr £25.00–£30.00 **Beds:** 4F 2D **Baths:** 4 En 2 Sh (3)

Metro Guest House, *26 Percy Road, Whitley Bay, NE26 2AX.* A comfortable and friendly guest house in the centre of Whitley Bay. **Open:** All year
0191 253 0123 E Douglas **D:** Fr £14.00–£15.00 **S:** Fr £14.00–£15.00 **Beds:** 2F 1T 2S **Baths:** 2 Sh (3)

Park Lodge Hotel, *160-164 Park Avenue, Whitley Bay, NE26 1AU.* You are assured a warm welcome in friendly, relaxed accommodation. An excellent location for business and pleasure. Close to Newcastle and surrounding business districts. Discover the delights of Northumbria's plentiful castles, beaches and Roman ruins. Sea views from some rooms. **Open:** All year (not Xmas/New Year)
0191 253 0288 *parklodgehotel@hotmail.com*
www.the-parklodgehotel.co.uk **D:** Fr £25.00–£30.00 **S:** Fr £50.00–£55.00 **Beds:** 3F 4T 5D 4S **Baths:** 16 En (8) cc

BATHROOMS
En = Ensuite
Pr = Private
Sh = Shared

Warwickshire

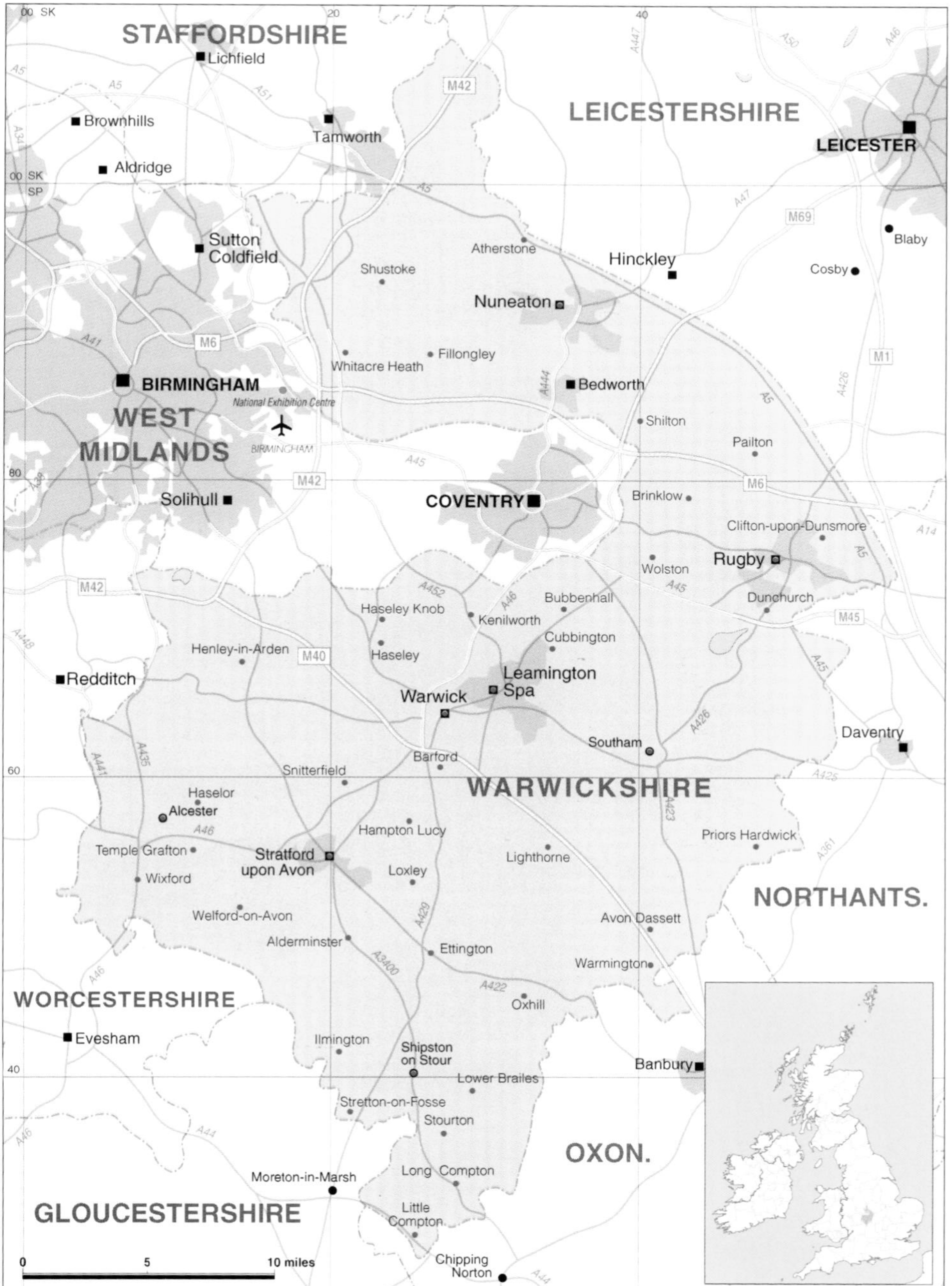
STAFFORDSHIRE
Lichfield
Brownhills
Aldridge
Tamworth
LEICESTERSHIRE
LEICESTER
Sutton Coldfield
Atherstone
Shustoke
Hinckley
Blaby
Cosby
Nuneaton
Whitacre Heath
Fillongley
BIRMINGHAM
National Exhibition Centre
WEST MIDLANDS
BIRMINGHAM
Bedworth
Shilton
Pailton
Solihull
COVENTRY
Brinklow
Clifton-upon-Dunsmore
Wolston
Rugby
Bubbenhall
Dunchurch
Haseley Knob
Kenilworth
Cubbington
Henley-in-Arden
Haseley
Redditch
Leamington Spa
Warwick
Southam
Daventry
Barford
Snitterfield
WARWICKSHIRE
Haselor
Alcester
Hampton Lucy
Priors Hardwick
Temple Grafton
Stratford upon Avon
Lighthorne
Wixford
Loxley
NORTHANTS.
Welford-on-Avon
Avon Dassett
Alderminster
Ettington
Warmington
WORCESTERSHIRE
Oxhill
Evesham
Ilmington
Shipston on Stour
Banbury
Lower Brailes
Stretton-on-Fosse
Stourton
OXON.
Long Compton
Moreton-in-Marsh
GLOUCESTERSHIRE
Little Compton
0 5 10 miles
Chipping Norton

Alcester

SP0857

The Globe Hotel, *54 Birmingham Road, Alcester, Warks, B49 5EG.* **Open:** All year **Grades:** ETC 4 Diamond
01789 763287 (also fax) Mr Machin
www.theglobehotel.com **D:** Fr £22.50–£32.50 **S:** Fr £35.00–£55.00 **Beds:** 1F 9D 1S **Baths:** 9 En 1 Sh (11) cc
A warm & friendly small hotel in the historic market town of Alcester, 7 miles from Stratford-upon-Avon. Stylish & comfortable, well appointed, ensuite rooms, totally refurbished 2000. Elegant dining room, non-smoking lounge, lounge/bar, private parking.

Roebuck Inn, *Birmingham Road, Alcester, Warks, B49 5QA.* Traditional country inn, non-smoking, restaurants, excellent food, beer, beds.
Open: All year
01789 762410 Fax: 01789 765794
www.theroebuckinn.co.uk **D:** Fr £25.00–£30.00 **S:** Fr £35.00–£45.00 **Beds:** 1F 6D 4T **Baths:** 11 En

Orchard Lawns, *Wixford, Alcester, Warks, B49 6DA.* Delightful house and grounds in small village, ideal touring centre. **Open:** All year (not Xmas) **Grades:** ETC 4 Diamond, Silver
01789 772668 Mrs Kember
margaret.orchardlawns@farmersweekly.net **D:** Fr £22.00–£25.00 **S:** Fr £22.00–£25.00 **Beds:** 1D 1T 1S **Baths:** 1 En 1 Sh (6)

Alderminster

SP2248 *The Bell*

Stour View, *Alderminster, Stratford-upon-Avon, Warwickshire, CV37 8NY.* Country bungalow, quiet, private accommodation. Central for Warwick, Cotswolds and Stratford-upon-Avon. **Open:** All year (not Xmas/New Year)
01789 450593 (also fax) Mrs Moody
moody.stourview@btinternet.com **D:** Fr £17.50–£19.50 **S:** Fr £25.00–£30.00 **Beds:** 1T **Baths:** 1 En (3)

Planning a longer stay? Always ask for any special rates

Atherstone

SP3197

Abbey Farm, *Merevale Lane, Atherstone, Warks, CV9 2LA.* **Open:** All year (not Xmas)
01827 715091 & 07956 421675 (M) Mr & Mrs Jones **Fax: 01827 715091** *tim_ali_jones@yahoo.com* **D:** Fr £27.50–£32.50 **S:** Fr £55.00–£65.00 **Beds:** 2D **Baths:** 2 En (10) cc
Period farmhouse overlooking lake surrounded by beautiful, unspoilt parkland. C12th Cistercian Merevale Abbey ruins in grounds. Under 15 mins to NEC, 12 miles to Belfry, 1/2 hour to East Midlands & Birmingham International Airport, NAC Stoneleigh & Birmingham city centre.

Manor Farm, *Ratcliffe Culey, Atherstone, Warks, CV9 3NY.* Victorian house located in small quiet friendly village in beautiful countryside. **Open:** All year
01827 712269 Mrs Trivett *jane@trivetts.com*
D: Fr £17.00–£18.00 **S:** Fr £20.00–£25.00 **Beds:** 3D **Baths:** 2 Sh (3) cc

Avon Dassett

SP4150

Crandon House, *Avon Dassett, Leamington Spa, Warks, CV33 0AA.* **Open:** All year (not Xmas) **Grades:** ETC 5 Diamond, Silver
01295 770652 Miss Lea **Fax: 01295 770632**
crandonhouse@talk21.com www.crandonhouse.co.uk **D:** Fr £22.00–£27.00 **S:** Fr £32.00–£35.00 **Beds:** 3D 2T **Baths:** 4 En 1 Pr (8) (8) cc
Luxury farmhouse accommodation with beautiful views. Situated between three lovely villages. Small working farm with rare breeds of cattle and sheep. Attractive non-smoking bedrooms. Choice of delicious breakfasts from our extensive menu. Large garden. Located 4 miles from M40 Junction 12. 'Welcome Host' award.

Barford

SP2760

Avonside Cottage, *1 High Street, Barford, Warwick, CV35 8BU.* C17th riverside cottage. Luxurious and spacious guest rooms. Delightful garden. **Open:** All year (not Xmas)
01926 624779 D: Fr £23.00–£27.00 **Beds:** 1D 1T **Baths:** 2 En (4)

Brinklow

SP4379

The White Lion, *Broad Street, Brinklow, Rugby, Warks, CV23 0LN.* A warm welcome awaits you at our traditional country inn. **Open:** All year (not Xmas)
01788 832579 Mr Yeend *brinklowlion@aol.com* www.thewhitelion-inn.co.uk **D:** Fr £20.00 **S:** Fr £25.00 **Beds:** 1D 3T **Baths:** 4 En

Bubbenhall

SP3572

Bubbenhall House, *Paget's Lane, Bubbenhall, Coventry, CV8 3BJ.* High quality accommodation in 5 acres of woodland, excellent breakfast. **Open:** All year **Grades:** AA 4 Red Diamond
024 7630 2409 (also fax) *wharrison@bubbenhallhouse.freeserve.co.uk* www.bubbenhallhouse.com **D:** Fr £30.00–£35.00 **S:** Fr £35.00–£45.00 **Beds:** 1T 2D **Baths:** 3 En (12)

Clifton-upon-Dunsmore

SP5376

Dunsmore Home Farm, *Watling Street, Clifton-upon-Dunsmore, Rugby, Warks, CV23 0AQ.* Victorian farmhouse in Warwickshire countryside. Rugby and motorways 3 miles. **Open:** All year (not Xmas/New Year)
01788 860168 (also fax) Ms Yates **D:** Fr £20.00–£22.00 **S:** Fr £24.00–£25.00 **Beds:** 1F 1T 1D **Baths:** 3 En 1 Sh

Cubbington

SP3468

Bakers Cottage, *52/54 Queen Street, Cubbington, Leamington Spa, CV32 7NA.* C17th cottage. Ideal sightseeing base for Leamington Spa, Warwick, Stratford. **Open:** All year **Grades:** ETC 4 Diamond
01926 772146 E Soden **D:** Fr £22.50–£25.00 **S:** Fr £25.00–£30.00 **Beds:** 1D 2T **Baths:** 2 En 1 Pr (4)

Dunchurch

SP4871

Toft Hill, *Dunchurch, Rugby, Warks, CV22 6NR.* Country house situated on outskirts of picturesque village of Dunchurch. **Open:** All year
01788 810342 Mary Wells **D:** Fr £22.50 **S:** Fr £22.50 **Beds:** 1F 1D 1S **Baths:** 1 Pr 1 Sh

Ettington

SP2648

The Leys, *64 Banbury Road, Ettington, Stratford-upon-Avon, Warks, CV37 7SU.* Comfortable stylish family village home tastefully decorated. Excellent full English breakfast. **Open:** All year (not Xmas/New Year)
01789 740365 & 07836 366615 (M) Mrs Brewer **Fax: 01789 740365** *bobbrewer@beeb.net* **D:** Fr £18.00–£20.00 **S:** Fr £20.00–£25.00 **Beds:** 1D 1T **Baths:** 2 Pr (10) (2)

Fillongley

SP2887

Bourne Brooke Lodge, *Mill Lane, Fillongley, Coventry, W Mids, CV7 8EE.* Peace and tranquillity, high standards of comfort and cleanliness, no smoking. **Open:** All year
01676 541898 (also fax) Mrs Chamberlain *bournebrookelodge@care4free.net* **D:** Fr £25.00 **S:** Fr £25.00–£35.00 **Beds:** 1D 2T 1S **Baths:** 3 En (6)

Hampton Lucy

SP2557

Hill House, *Hampton Lucy, Warwick, CV35 8AU.* **Open:** All year (not Xmas/New Year)
Grades: ETC 4 Diamond
01789 840329 Mrs Hunter *eliz_hunter@hotmail.com* www.stratford-upon-avon.co.uk/hillhouse.htm **D:** Fr £22.50–£25.00 **S:** Fr £30.00–£35.00 **Beds:** 1D/S/F 1T/F **Baths:** 2 Pr (6)
This charming Georgian country house, traditionally furnished to the highest standard, offers a wonderfully peaceful stay and superb rural views. Only eight minutes by car from Stratford and Warwick. Ideal base for touring Cotswolds and NEC. A warm welcome awaits.

Haseley

SP2268

Shrewley Pools Farm, *Haseley, Warwick, CV35 7HB.* Glorious early C17th Listed farmhouse, beautiful 1 acre gardens. Working farm. **Open:** All year (not Xmas)
01926 484315 Mrs Dodd **D:** Fr £22.50–£30.00 **S:** Fr £30.00–£35.00 **Beds:** 1F 1T **Baths:** 2 En (6)

Haseley Knob

SP2371

Croft Guest House, *The Croft, Haseley Knob, Warwick, CV35 7NL.* Friendly family country guest house. Near Warwick, Coventry, Stratford, NEC/NAC. **Open:** All year (not Xmas)
01926 484447 (also fax) Mr & Mrs Clapp *david@croftguesthouse.co.uk* www.croftguesthouse.co.uk **D:** Fr £24.00–£26.00 **S:** Fr £35.00–£36.00 **Beds:** 2F 3D 3T 1S **Baths:** 7 En 2 Pr (8) **cc**

Haselor

SP1257

Walcote Farm, *Walcote, Haselor, Alcester, Warks, B49 6LY.* **Open:** All year
Grades: ETC 4 Diamond
01789 488264 Mr & Mrs Finnemore *john@walcotefarm.co.uk* www.walcotefarm.co.uk
D: Fr £21.00–£24.00 **S:** Fr £28.00–£35.00 **Beds:** 1T 2D **Baths:** 3 En (6)
Easy to find our beautiful C16th oak-beamed farmhouse, in a tranquil picturesque hamlet. Ideal location for walking, cycling and visiting Shakespeare and National Trust properties, Warwick Castle, Cotswolds, NEC, and many more places of interest. Our website shows room availability.

Henley-in-Arden

SP1566

Holland Park Farm, *Buckley Green, Henley-in-Arden, Solihull, W Mids, B95 5QF.* **Open:** All year
01564 792625 (also fax) Mrs Connolly **D:** Fr £25.00 **S:** Fr £30.00 **Beds:** 2F **Baths:** 2 En (4)
A Georgian-style house set in centre of peaceful farmland including the historic grounds of the mount and other interesting walks. Ideally situated in Shakespeare country. Convenient to airport, NEC, NAC and Cotswolds. Closed on Christmas day. H of E 3 stars.

Ilmington

SP2143

Folly Farm Cottage, *Back Street, Ilmington, Warwickshire, CV36 4LJ.* Large country cottage surrounded by pretty cottage gardens, situated in delightful Cotswold village. **Open:** All year (not Xmas/New Year) **Grades:** ETC 4 Diamond, Gold
01608 682425 (also fax) *slowe@follyfarm.co.uk* www.follyfarm.co.uk **D:** Fr £26.00–£41.00 **S:** Fr £39.00–£45.00 **Beds:** 3D (7)

Kenilworth

SP2872

The Cottage Inn, *36 Stoneleigh Road, Kenilworth, Warks, CV8 2GD.* Friendly family-run free house - great traditional ales and fine wines. Real home-cooked specials. **Open:** All year
01926 853900 Mr Jones **Fax: 01926 748167**
D: Fr £20.00–£22.50 **S:** Fr £30.00–£35.00 **Beds:** 4D 2T **Baths:** 6 En (20) **cc**

Enderley Guest House, *20 Queens Road, Kenilworth, Warwickshire, CV8 1JQ.* Friendly, comfortable Victorian house close to town centre. NEC, Warwick University nearby. **Open:** All year
01926 855388 Fax: 01926 850450 D: Fr £22.50–£30.00 **S:** Fr £27.00–£30.00 **Beds:** 1F 1T 2D 1S **Baths:** 5 En (2)

Hollyhurst Guest House, *47 Priory Road, Kenilworth, Warks, CV8 1LL.* Friendly, relaxed atmosphere in comfortable Victorian town house near centre. **Open:** All year (not Xmas) **Grades:** AA 3 Diamond
01926 853882 Mr & Mrs Wheat **Fax: 01926 855211** *admin@hollyhurstguesthouse.co.uk* www.hollyhurstguesthouse.co.uk **D:** Fr £22.00–£23.50 **S:** Fr £27.00–£32.00 **Beds:** 1F 2D 4T 1S **Baths:** 3 Pr 2 Sh (7)

Banner Hill Farm, *Rouncil Lane, Kenilworth, Warks, CV8 1NN.* Homely Georgian farmhouse. Middle of nowhere. No distance from anywhere. **Open:** All year (not Xmas)
01926 852850 Mr Snelson **D:** Fr £16.00–£20.00 **S:** Fr £16.00–£25.00 **Beds:** 1F 1D 2T 2S **Baths:** 3 En 1 Pr 2 Sh (8)

Victoria Lodge Hotel, *180 Warwick Road, Kenilworth, CV8 1HU.* Built in 1850, completely refurbished luxury accommodation, beautiful Victorian walled garden. **Open:** All year (not Xmas)
01926 512020 Mr Woolcock **Fax: 01926 858703** *info@victorialodgehotel.co.uk* www.victorialodgehotel.co.uk **D:** Fr £32.00 **S:** Fr £42.00–£52.00 **Beds:** 6D 2T 1S **Baths:** 9 En (10) **cc**

Howden House, *170 Warwick Road, Kenilworth, CV8 1HS.* Comfortable home conveniently located for Warwick University, NAC, NEC, Airports. **Open:** All year (not Xmas)
01926 850310 Mrs Allen **D:** Fr £19.00–£20.00 **S:** Fr £21.00–£24.00 **Beds:** 1D 1T 2S

Abbey Guest House, *41 Station Road, Kenilworth, Warks, CV8 1JD.* Comfortable Victorian house, well-equipped bedrooms, close to town centre. **Open:** All year (not Xmas)
01926 512707 Mrs Jefferies *the-abbey@virgin.net* **D:** Fr £22.50 **S:** Fr £26.00 **Beds:** 3D 2T 2S **Baths:** 6 En 1 Pr (2)

Planning a longer stay? Always ask for any special rates

Castle Laurels Hotel, *22 Castle Road, Kenilworth, CV8 1NG.* Beautiful Victorian house opposite the castle in Kenilworth old town. **Open:** All year (not Xmas)
01926 856179 N C Moore **Fax: 01926 854954** *moores22@aol.com* www.castlelaurelshotel.co.uk **D:** Fr £28.50 **S:** Fr £36.00–£45.00 **Beds:** 5D 3T 3S **Baths:** 11 En (12) **cc**

Leamington Spa

SP3165

St Andrew's B&B, *11 St Andrews Road, Leamington Spa, Warks, CV32 7EU.* Relax and enjoy our peaceful home. Special welcome. Delicious food. **Open:** All year (not Xmas)
01926 428864 Mrs Poultney *standrews11@btinternet.com* www.snapandstay.co.uk **D:** Fr £20.00–£24.00 **S:** Fr £23.00–£25.00 **Beds:** 1D 1T **Baths:** 1 En 1 Sh (1)

Victoria Park Hotel, *12 Adelaide Road, Royal Leamington Spa, Warwickshire, CV31 3PW.* A cosy, comfortable establishment in a quiet, yet convenient location. **Open:** All year (not Xmas/New Year)
01926 424195 Fax: 01926 421521 *info@victoriaparkhotelleamingtonspa.co.uk* www.victoriaparkhotelleamingtonspa.co.uk **D:** Fr £30.00–£37.50 **S:** Fr £39.50 **Beds:** 7F 1T 6D 6S **Baths:** 20 En (15) **cc**

Almond House, *8 Parklands Avenue, Lillington, Leamington Spa, Warwickshire, CV32 7BA.* Quietly located, convenient for NEC, M40, NAC five minutes away. **Open:** All year (not Xmas/New Year)
01926 424052 Mrs Mewett **D:** Fr £20.00–£22.50 **S:** Fr £25.00 **Beds:** 1T 1D **Baths:** 2 Pr (4)

Charnwood Guest House, *47 Avenue Road, Leamington Spa, Warks, CV31 3PF.* Comfortable, informal atmosphere, close to town centre, also Warwick Castle. **Open:** All year (not Xmas)
01926 831074 (also fax) Mr Booth **D:** Fr £18.00–£20.00 **S:** Fr £18.00–£30.00 **Beds:** 1F 2D 2T 1S **Baths:** 2 En 2 Sh (6) **cc**

Hedley Villa Guest House, *31 Russell Terrace, Leamington Spa, Warks, CV31 1EZ.* Friendly house within walking distance of railway station and town. **Open:** All year
01926 424504 Mr Tocker & Mrs P Ashfield **Fax: 01926 745801 D:** Fr £19.00–£25.00 **S:** Fr £25.00–£30.00 **Beds:** 2F 1T 1D 3S **Baths:** 1 En 4 Sh

Lighthorne

SP3456

Redlands Farm, *Banbury Road, Lighthorne, Warwick, Warks, CV35 0AH.* **Open:** All year (not Xmas/New Year)
01926 651241 (also fax) D: Fr £22.50–£27.50 **S:** Fr £22.50–£35.00 **Beds:** 1F 1D 1S **Baths:** 1 En 2 Sh (8)
This carefully renovated C16th stone farmhouse with spacious bedrooms & comfortable sitting room is set in 2 acres of garden with a swimming pool. 10 National Trust properties, Gaydon Motor Museum, Stratford, Warwick & Cotswolds are all within easy reach.

Little Compton

SP2630

Rigside, *Little Compton, Moreton-in-Marsh, Glos, GL56 0RR.* Lovely landscaped gardens backing onto farmland. **Open:** All year
01608 674128 (also fax) Ms Cox *rigside@lineone.net* **D:** Fr £22.00–£23.00 **S:** Fr £20.00–£22.00 **Beds:** 2D 1S 1T **Baths:** 2 En 1 Sh (9) (6)

Long Compton

SP2832

Tallet Barn, *Yerdley Farm, Long Compton, Shipston-on-Stour, Warks, CV36 5LH.* Comfortable annexed rooms, a warm welcome and a quiet village location. **Open:** All year
01608 684248 Mrs Richardson **Fax: 01068 684248 D:** Fr £20.00–£21.00 **S:** Fr £25.00 **Beds:** 1D 1T **Baths:** 2 En (6) (2)

Lower Brailes

SP3139

The George Hotel, *High Street, Lower Brailes, Banbury, Oxon, OX15 5NU.* A C12th inn, good, friendly public bar, large gardens with undercover outside eating area. In Cotswolds near Stratford-upon-Avon (14 miles). Well-kept local, off-road foot ways. Good centre to visit entire Cotswold area. **Open:** All year
01608 685223 Fax: 01608 685916 D: Fr £25.00–£60.00 **S:** Fr £25.00–£60.00 **Beds:** 1F 8T 1D 1S **Baths:** 1 En 9 Pr 1 Sh (1) (80) **cc**

Loxley

SP2552

Elm Cottage, *Stratford Road, Loxley, Warks, CV35 9JW.* Private house in open countryside. Stratford-upon-Avon 3 miles. **Open:** All year (not Xmas) **Grades:** ETC 4 Diamond
01789 840609 Mrs Brocklehurst **D:** Fr £23.00 **S:** Fr £26.00 **Beds:** 1D 1T 1S **Baths:** 1 Sh (6)

Nuneaton

SP3691

La Tavola Calda, *68 & 70 Midland Road, Nuneaton, Warks, CV11 5DY.* A family-run Italian restaurant and hotel. Handy for M69 - M6. **Open:** All year (not Xmas/New Year) **Grades:** ETC 2 Diamond
07747 010702 (M) Mr Emanuele **D:** Fr £32.00–£35.00 **S:** Fr £20.00–£25.00 **Beds:** 2F 5T 1S **Baths:** 8 En (5) **cc**

Oxhill

SP3145

Nolands Farm & Country Restaurant, *Oxhill, Warwick, CV35 0RJ.* **Open:** All year **01926 640309** Mrs Hutsby **Fax: 01926 641662** *inthecountry@nolandsfarm.co.uk* www.nolandsfarm.co.uk **D:** Fr £23.00–£27.00 **S:** Fr £35.00–£45.00 **Beds:** 1F 6D 2T 1S **Baths:** 10 En (7) (10) **cc**
Situated in tranquil valley. All bedrooms annexed, some overlooking the old stable yard, garden or fields. All ensuite. Romantic four poster bedrooms, doubles/twins/singles. Licensed bar, dinner. Facilities include lake for fishing, clay pigeon shooting, own hot air balloon and cycling.

Pailton

SP4781

White Lion Inn, *Coventry Road, Pailton, Rugby, Warks, CV23 0QD.* C17th coaching inn recently modernised retaining all the olde worlde atmosphere. **Open:** All year
01788 832359 (also fax) Mr Brindley **D:** Fr £19.50–£24.50 **S:** Fr £21.00–£31.00 **Beds:** 9D **Baths:** 5 En 2 Sh (60) **cc**

BEDROOMS
D = Double
T = Twin
S = Single
F = Family

Priors Hardwick

SP4756

Hill Farm, *Priors Hardwick, Southam, Warwickshire, CV23 8SP.* Outstanding Westerly views over peaceful countryside. A real rural retreat! **Open:** All year (not Xmas/New Year)
01327 260338 Ms Darbishire *hillfarmbandb@farming.co.uk* www.warwicksfarmhols.co.uk
D: Fr £20.00 **S:** Fr £25.00 **Beds:** 1T 1D
Baths: 1 Sh (10)

Rugby

SP5075

Dunsmore Home Farm, *Watling Street, Clifton-upon-Dunsmore, Rugby, Warks, CV23 0AQ.* Victorian farmhouse in Warwickshire countryside. Rugby and motorways 3 miles.
Open: All year (not Xmas/New Year)
01788 860168 (also fax) Ms Yates **D:** Fr £20.00–£22.00 **S:** Fr £24.00–£25.00 **Beds:** 1F 1T 1D **Baths:** 3 En 1 Sh

Lawford Hill Farm, *Lawford Heath Lane, Rugby, Warks, CV23 9HG.* Enjoy a stay at our farmhouse set in beautiful gardens.
Open: All year (not Xmas/New Year)
01788 542001 Mr & Mrs Moses **Fax: 01788 537880** *lawford.hill@talk.com* www.lawfordhill.co.uk **D:** Fr £22.00–£24.00 **S:** Fr £26.00–£30.00 **Beds:** 3T 3D **Baths:** 6 En

Shilton

SP4085

Barnacle Hall, *Shilton Lane, Shilton, Coventry, CV7 9LH.* C16th farmhouse; excellent spacious accommodation. Attractive gardens. Warm welcome.
Open: All year (not Xmas/New Year)
024 7661 2629 (also fax) Mrs Grindal **D:** Fr £23.50–£26.00 **S:** Fr £30.00–£33.00 **Beds:** 1T 2D **Baths:** 2 En 1 Pr

Shipston on Stour

SP2540

Shipston Guest House, *42 Church Street, Shipston on Stour, Warks, CV36 4AS.* Charming C17th cottage in delightful country town of Shipston-on-Stour.
Open: All year (not Xmas)
01608 661002 Mrs Roberts **Fax: 01608 664008** *petelain@aol.com* **D:** Fr £21.00–£25.00 **S:** Fr £30.00 **Beds:** 1F 1D 1T **Baths:** 2 En 1 Pr

Shustoke

SP2290

The Old Vicarage, *Shawbury Lane, Shustoke, Coleshill, Birmingham, Warks, B46 2LA.* **Open:** All year (not Xmas)
Grades: AA 3 Diamond
01675 481331 (also fax) R A Hawkins *jbhawk@doctors.org.uk* **D:** Fr £20.00–£25.00 **S:** Fr £22.00–£30.00 **Beds:** 3D **Baths:** 1 En 2 Sh (6)
This friendly old house set in a large leafy garden is by the village church. Comfort and country hospitality in the peace of rural Warwickshire, within easy reach of NEC, Belfry and Forest of Arden golf courses, Birmingham International airport and Midlands motorways.

Snitterfield

SP2159

The Hill Cottage, *Kings Lane, Snitterfield, Stratford upon Avon, Warks, CV37 0QA.* Character house in 1.5 acres with bluebell wood. Stratford 3 miles. **Open:** All year (not Xmas)
01789 731830 Mrs Waldron **Fax: 01789 730288** *thehillcottagesbb@hotmail.com* **D:** Fr £26.00–£32.00 **S:** Fr £40.00–£45.00 **Beds:** 1D 1T 1S **Baths:** 1 En 1 Sh (4)

Southam

SP4162

Briarwood, *34 Warwick Road, Southam, Leamington Spa, Warwickshire, CV47 0HN.* Edwardian house on the outskirts of a small market town. **Open:** All year (not Xmas)
01926 814756 Mrs Bishop **D:** Fr £20.00–£25.00 **S:** Fr £20.00–£30.00 **Beds:** 1D 1S **Baths:** 2 En (1)

Stourton

SP2937

Brook House, *Stourton, Shipston-on-Stour, Warwickshire, CV36 5HQ.* Lovely old house, edge pretty Cotswold village. Ideal touring Stratford, Oxford, Cotswolds.
Open: All year (not Xmas/New Year)
01608 686281 Mrs McDonald *graemedonald@msn.com* **D:** Fr £22.00–£23.00 **S:** Fr £27.00–£30.00 **Beds:** 1F 1D **Baths:** 1 En 1 Pr (7) (4)

Stratford-upon-Avon

SP1955

Stretton House, *38 Grove Road, Stratford-upon-Avon, Warks, CV37 6PB.*
Open: All year (not Xmas) **Grades:** ETC 3 Diamond, AA 3 Diamond
01789 268647 (also fax) Mr Machin *skyblues@strettonhouse.co.uk* **D:** Fr £15.00–£28.00 **S:** Fr £20.00–£40.00 **Beds:** 1F 2D 3T 1S **Baths:** 4 En (8) (6)
We've got a home from home where a warm and friendly welcome awaits you. Comfortable accommodation at reasonable prices. Ensuite and standard rooms. Best B&B recommended, Stratford in Bloom Guest House 1997/98 & 2001. Town centre 3 mins' walk.

Blue Boar Inn, *Temple Grafton, Alcester, Warks, B49 6NR.* **Open:** All year
01789 750010 Mr Brew **D:** Fr £35.50–£40.00 **S:** Fr £45.00–£60.00 **cc**
Old English Inn located near Stratford-upon-Avon. High quality family-run accommodation. Renowned for fine food and real ales. Ideal for golfing, fishing, walking, touring. Close to NEC, Cotswolds, Worcester, Cheltenham, Birmingham, Coventry. Winter bargains available. Telephone for brochure.

B&B owners may vary rates – be sure to check when booking

Travellers Rest Guest House, *146 Alcester Road, Stratford-upon-Avon, Warwickshire, CV37 9DR.* **Open:** All year (not Xmas/New Year) **Grades:** AA 3 Diamond **01789 266589 (also fax)** *travellersrest146@hotmail.com* **D:** Fr £20.00–£28.00 **S:** Fr £25.00–£35.00 **Beds:** 1F 1T 1D **Baths:** 3 En (2)
Traditional luxury ensuite accommodation with home comforts. Hearty English breakfast, vegetarian or continental. Payphone and private parking. Easy walk to railway station, town centre, Ann Hathaway's cottage, theatre, riverside walks and restaurants. Good location for Warwick Castle and Cotswold villages.

Penshurst, *34 Evesham Place, Stratford-upon-Avon, Warks, CV37 6HT.* **Open:** All year **Grades:** ETC 3 Diamond **01789 550197** Mrs Cauvin **Fax: 01789 295322** *karen@penshurst.net* www.penshurst.net **D:** Fr £16.00–£24.00 **S:** Fr £18.00–£24.00 **Beds:** 2F 3D 1T 1S **Baths:** 4 En 1 Pr 2 Sh 2
A prettily refurbished Victorian town house 5 minutes walk from centre. Totally non-smoking. Delicious breakfasts, either English or Continental, served from 7.00 am right up until 10.30 am. Excellent value for money. Visit our website for more details and photos.

Heron Lodge, *260 Alcester Road, Stratford-upon-Avon, Warks, CV37 9JQ.* **Open:** All year (not Xmas/New Year) **Grades:** ETC 4 Diamond **01789 299169 Fax: 01789 204463** *chrisandbob@heronlodge.com* www.heronlodge.com **D:** Fr £19.00–£27.00 **S:** Fr £26.00–£30.00 **Beds:** 1F 1T 2D **Baths:** 4 En (5) (7) cc
Friendly, high quality accommodation within walking distance of Anne Hathaway's Cottage. Guest conservatory overlooking pretty garden. Breakfasts include fruit platters, full English and Bob's popular syrup pancakes. Guestbook comments: 'very high standard of accommodation', 'fantastic pancakes!', 'superb breakfast', 'what hospitality'.

The Hill Cottage, *Kings Lane, Snitterfield, Stratford upon Avon, Warks, CV37 0QA.* Character house in 1.5 acres with bluebell wood. Glorious views to Stratford (3 miles). 5 minutes junction 15/M40. **Open:** All year (not Xmas) **01789 731830** Mrs Waldron **Fax: 01789 730288** *thehillcottagesbb@hotmail.com* **D:** Fr £26.00–£32.00 **S:** Fr £40.00–£45.00 **Beds:** 1D 1T 1S **Baths:** 1 En 1 Sh (4)

Cymbeline House, *24 Evesham Place, Stratford-upon-Avon, Warks, CV37 6HT.* Clean, comfortable, convenient Victorian house. 5 mins theatre, town, river. **Open:** All year (not Xmas) **01789 292958 (also fax)** *cymbelinebb@btopenworld.com* **D:** Fr £18.00–£30.00 **S:** Fr £18.00–£30.00 **Beds:** 1F 1T 3D 2S **Baths:** 7 En (4)

Hunters Moon Guest House, *150 Alcester Road, Stratford-upon-Avon, Warks, CV37 9DR.* Rosemary & David will make your stay in Stratford enjoyable. **Open:** All year (not Xmas) **01789 292888** Mrs Austin **Fax: 01789 204101** *thehuntersmoon@ntlworld.com* www.huntersmoonguesthouse.com **D:** Fr £23.00–£28.00 **S:** Fr £28.00–£32.00 **Beds:** 2F 2D 1T 2S **Baths:** 7 Pr (2) (6)

Minola Guest House, *25 Evesham Place, Stratford-upon-Avon, Warks, CV37 6HT.* Minola's is situated in the old town of Stratford. Theatres within walking distance. **Open:** All year (not Xmas) **01789 293573** Mr & Mrs Castelli **Fax: 01789 551625 D:** Fr £22.00–£25.00 **S:** Fr £23.00–£35.00 **Beds:** 2D 1T 2S **Baths:** 4 Pr 1 Sh (2)

BATHROOMS
En = Ensuite
Pr = Private
Sh = Shared

Parkfield Guest House, *3 Broad Walk, Stratford-upon-Avon, Warks, CV37 6HS.* Lovely Victorian house in quiet side street, 5 mins walk from town centre. **Open:** All year **Grades:** ETC 3 Diamond, AA 3 Diamond **01789 293313** R Pettitt *parkfield@btinternet.com* www.parkfieldbandb.co.uk **D:** Fr £23.00–£24.00 **S:** Fr £25.00–£35.00 **Beds:** 3F 1T 2D 1S **Baths:** 6 En 1 Pr (7) cc

Green Haven, *217 Evesham Road, Stratford-upon-Avon, Warks, CV37 9AS.* First class accommodation within walking distance of the town centre. **Open:** All year (not Xmas) **Grades:** ETC 4 Diamond **01789 297874 (also fax)** Mr & Mrs Learmount *susanlearmount@green-haven.co.uk* **D:** Fr £20.00–£25.00 **S:** Fr £25.00–£45.00 **Beds:** 1F 2D 2T **Baths:** 5 En (6)

Faviere, *127 Shipston Road, Stratford-upon-Avon, Warks, CV37 7LW.* A ten minute walk will bring you to the theatres and town centre. **Open:** All year **Grades:** ETC 4 Diamond **01789 293764** Mr & Mrs Martinez **Fax: 01789 269365** *reservations@faviere.com* www.faviere.com **D:** Fr £18.00–£26.00 **S:** Fr £25.00–£40.00 **Beds:** 3F 4D/T **Baths:** 7 En (7)

Eastnor House Hotel, *33 Shipston Road, Stratford-upon-Avon, Warks, CV37 7LN.* High quality accommodation, located near the RSC and town centre. **Open:** All year **01789 268115 Fax: 01789 551133** *enquiries@eastnorhouse.com* www.eastnorhouse.com **D:** Fr £35.00–£40.00 **S:** Fr £49.00–£55.00 **Beds:** 2F 5T 3D **Baths:** 10 En (10) cc

BEDROOMS
D = Double
T = Twin
S = Single
F = Family

Curtain Call, *142 Alcester Road, Stratford-upon-Avon, Warwickshire, CV37 9DR.* Romantic four-poster beds for that special night away. **Open:** All year
01789 267734 (also fax) J Purlan *curtaincall@btinternet.com* www.curtaincallguesthouse.co.uk **D:** Fr £20.00–£30.00 **S:** Fr £30.00–£45.00 **Beds:** 1F 2D 1T 2S **Baths:** 4 En 1 Sh (6) **cc**

Linhill Guest House, *35 Evesham Place, Stratford-upon-Avon, Warks, CV37 6HT.* Family-run Victorian guest house, 5 mins town centre. Choice of breakfasts, home-cooked evening meals. **Open:** All year
01789 292879 Ms Tallis **Fax: 01789 299691** *linhill@bigwig.net* **D:** Fr £15.00–£25.00 **S:** Fr £15.00–£25.00 **Beds:** 2F 4D 4T 1S **Baths:** 3 En

Arrandale Guest House, *208 Evesham Road, Stratford-upon-Avon, Warks, CV37 9AS.* Comfortable, double-glazed, family run. 15 min walk Shakespearean properties.
Open: All year (not Xmas)
01789 267112 Mrs Mellor **D:** Fr £16.50–£19.00 **S:** Fr £26.50–£29.00 **Beds:** 2D 1T **Baths:** 2 En 1 Sh (3) **cc**

Broadlands Guest House, *23 Evesham Place, Stratford-upon-Avon, Warks, CV37 6HT.* Relaxed and friendly atmosphere five minutes to town centre. **Open:** All year (not Xmas) **Grades:** ETC 3 Diamond
01789 299181 Mr P Gray & Mr J L Worboys **Fax: 01789 551382** *broadlands.com@virgin.net* www.stratford-upon-avon.co.uk/broadlands.htm **D:** Fr £25.00–£35.00 **S:** Fr £30.00–£50.00 **Beds:** 3D 1T 2S **Baths:** 5 En (12)

Acer House, *44 Albany Road, Stratford-upon-Avon, Warks, CV37 6PQ.* Quality accommodation, quiet, near town centre. Rooms overlook pleasant garden. **Open:** All year (not Xmas/New Year)
01789 204962 Mrs Hall **D:** Fr £18.00–£19.00 **S:** Fr £18.00–£20.00 **Beds:** 1T 1S **Baths:** 1 Sh

Moonlight Guest House, *144 Alcester Road, Stratford-upon-Avon, Warks, CV37 9DR.* Most bedrooms have coffee-making facilities, hairdryers most bedrooms.
Open: All year
01789 298213 E Dionisi **D:** Fr £16.00–£19.00 **S:** Fr £16.00–£19.00 **Beds:** 5F 2T 2D 2S **Baths:** 3 En 3 Pr 1 Sh (1)

Newlands, *7 Broad Walk, Stratford-upon-Avon, Warks, CV37 6HS.* Elegant Victorian townhouse, quiet cul-de-sac, close to centre and theatres. **Open:** All year
01789 298449 Mrs Walter **Fax: 01789 267806** *newlandslynwalter@hotmail.com* **D:** Fr £23.00–£25.00 **S:** Fr £25.00 **Beds:** 2F 1D/T 1S **Baths:** 4 En 1 Pr (5) (2) **cc**

The Dylan Guest House, *10 Evesham Place, Stratford-upon-Avon, Warks, CV37 6HT.* Charming Victorian house, 5 minutes town centre, theatre and river. **Open:** All year (not Xmas)
01789 204819 Mr Elmy *elmy@lineone.net* **D:** Fr £23.00–£25.00 **S:** Fr £24.00–£26.00 **Beds:** 1F 3D 1T 1S **Baths:** 5 En (5) (5)

Clomendy, *10 Broad Walk, Stratford-upon-Avon, Warwickshire, CV37 6HS.* Small Victorian house, central, rail/coach guests met, non smoking. **Open:** All year (not Xmas/New Year)
01789 266957 Mr Jones **D:** Fr £20.00–£23.00 **S:** Fr £30.00 **Beds:** 1T 1D 1S **Baths:** 2 En 1 Pr (5) (1)

Stretton-on-Fosse

SP2238

Jasmine Cottage, *Stretton-on-Fosse, Moreton-in-Marsh, Glos, GL56 9SA.* Warm welcome awaits in cosy country cottage in peaceful village. **Open:** All year (not Xmas)
01608 661972 Mrs Campbell Smith **D:** Fr £20.00 **S:** Fr £25.00 **Beds:** 1D 1T **Baths:** 1 Sh

Temple Grafton

SP1254

Blue Boar Inn, *Temple Grafton, Alcester, Warks, B49 6NR.* Old English Inn located near Stratford-upon-Avon. High quality family-run accommodation. **Open:** All year
01789 750010 Mr Brew **D:** Fr £35.50–£40.00 **S:** Fr £45.00–£60.00 **cc**

Warmington

SP4147

Pond Cottage, *The Green, Warmington, Banbury, Oxon, OX17 1BU.* Picturesque cottage (listed). Village pub. Warwick Castle (14m), Banbury (5m). **Open:** Feb to Nov
01295 690682 V G Viljoen **D:** Fr £23.00 **S:** Fr £25.00–£33.50 **Beds:** 1D 1S **Baths:** 1 En 1 Pr (2)

The Old Rectory, *Warmington, Banbury, Oxfordshire, OX17 1BU.* Beautiful C18th house with lovely garden on the green in idyllic peaceful village. **Open:** All year (not Xmas)
01295 690531 Mrs Cockcroft **Fax: 01295 690526** *sirwhcockcroft@clara.co.uk* **D:** Fr £25.00–£30.00 **S:** Fr £35.00 **Beds:** 2T 1D **Baths:** 3 En (3)

Planning a longer stay? Always ask for any special rates

Warwick

SP2865

Chesterfields, *84 Emscote Road, Warwick, CV34 5QJ.* The ideal location for Warwick Castle, Stratford and the Cotswolds. **Open:** All year (not Xmas) **Grades:** RAC 3 Diamond
01926 774864 & 07710 223456 (M) Mr & Mrs Chapman *chapman@chesterfields.freeserve.co.uk* **D:** Fr £20.00–£22.00 **S:** Fr £20.00–£27.00 **Beds:** 2F 2D 1T 2S **Baths:** 1 Sh (8)

Austin Guest House, *96 Emscote Road, Warwick, CV34 5QJ.* Black and white Victorian house, one mile from town centre and castle.
Open: All year (not Xmas)
01926 493583 Mr & Mrs Winter **Fax: 01926 493679** *mike.austinhouse96@ntlworld.com* www.austinhousewarwick.co.uk **D:** Fr £19.00–£23.00 **S:** Fr £20.00–£46.00 **Beds:** 2F 2D 2T 1S **Baths:** 5 En 1 Sh (6) **cc**

Ashburton Guest House, *74 Emscote Road, Warwick, CV34 5QG.* Extremely high standard of accommodation and close to town centre. **Open:** All year (not Xmas) **Grades:** ETC 3 Diamond
01926 401082 Mrs Whitelaw **Fax: 01926 774642** *ashburtongh@aol.com* **D:** Fr £22.00 **S:** Fr £20.00–£27.00 **Beds:** 2F 1T 4S **Baths:** 4 En 1 Pr 2 Sh (3) **cc**

Croft Guest House, *The Croft, Haseley Knob, Warwick, CV35 7NL.* Friendly family country guest house. Near Warwick, Coventry, Stratford, NEC/NAC. **Open:** All year (not Xmas)
01926 484447 (also fax) Mr & Mrs Clapp *david@croftguesthouse.co.uk* www.croftguesthouse.co.uk **D:** Fr £24.00–£26.00 **S:** Fr £35.00–£36.00 **Beds:** 2F 3D 3T 1S **Baths:** 7 En 2 Pr (8) **cc**

The Seven Stars, *Friars Street, Warwick, CV34 6HD.* Quality Bed/Breakfast. Large beamed rooms. Town centre. Car park.
Open: All year
01926 492658 A Flynn **Fax: 01926 411747** *7stars-warwick@gofornet.co.uk* **D:** Fr £25.00–£30.00 **S:** Fr £38.00–£45.00 **Beds:** 1D **Baths:** 1 En (11) **cc**

Agincourt Lodge Hotel, *36 Coten End, Warwick, CV34 4NP.* Walking distance to castle & all amenities. Four-poster beds. Non-smoking bedrooms. **Open:** All year (not Xmas/New Year)
01926 499399 (also fax) A & M Black-Band **D:** Fr £26.50–£35.00 **S:** Fr £37.50–£47.00 **Beds:** 1F 1T 4D **Baths:** 5 En **cc**

Welford-on-Avon

SP1451

One Acre Guest House, *Barton Road, Welford-on-Avon, Stratford upon Avon, Warks, CV37 8EZ.* Pretty Shakespearean village 4 miles Stratford-upon-Avon, 6 miles Cotswolds. **Open:** Mar to Nov
01789 750477 Ms Clifton **D:** Fr £20.00 **S:** Fr £30.00 **Beds:** 3D (12) (3)

Springfields Farm, *Welford Road, Welford-on-Avon, Stratford upon Avon, Warks, CV37 8RA.* Farmhouse - walk in Shakespeare's paths. **Open:** All year
01789 720361 & 01789 720361 Mrs Reid **Fax: 01789 720885** *enquiries@reidgroup.co.uk* www.reidgroup.co.uk **D:** Fr £16.00–£20.00 **S:** Fr £16.00 **Beds:** 1F 1D 2T 1S **Baths:** 1 En 1 Sh (12)

B&B owners may vary rates – be sure to check when booking

Whitacre Heath

SP2192

Heathland Farm, *Birmingham Road, Whitacre Heath, Coleshill, W Mids, B46 2ER.* Comfortable, quiet secluded farmhouse, outskirts of village, courtyard parking. **Open:** All year
01675 462129 & 07970 754521 (M) Mr Barnes **D:** Fr £21.00–£22.00 **S:** Fr £25.00–£28.00 **Beds:** 3T 2S **Baths:** 5 En 1 Pr (10)

Wixford

SP0854

Orchard Lawns, *Wixford, Alcester, Warks, B49 6DA.* Delightful house and grounds in small village, ideal touring centre. **Open:** All year (not Xmas) **Grades:** ETC 4 Diamond, Silver
01789 772668 Mrs Kember *margaret.orchardlawns@farmersweekly.net* **D:** Fr £22.00–£25.00 **S:** Fr £22.00–£25.00 **Beds:** 1D 1T 1S **Baths:** 1 En 1 Sh (6)

Wolston

SP4175

The Byre, *Lords Hill Farm, Wolston, Coventry, Warks, CV8 3GB.* Homely hospitality, situated in a country lane. Near Ryton Gardens. **Open:** All year (not Xmas) **Grades:** ETC 4 Diamond, Silver
024 7654 2098 Mrs Gibbs **D:** Fr £23.00–£39.00 **S:** Fr £23.00–£39.00 **Beds:** 2D 1T **Baths:** 1 En 1 Sh (5) (4)

Lords Hill Farm, *Coalpit Lane, Wolston, Coventry, Warks, CV8 3GB.* Lovely views, peaceful, private. Convenient motorway, ground floor, Ryton Gardens. **Open:** All year (not Xmas/New Year)
024 7654 4430 Mrs Gibbs **D:** Fr £27.00 **S:** Fr £27.00 **Beds:** 1D **Baths:** 1 Pr (2)

Please respect a B&B's wishes regarding children, animals and smoking

West Midlands

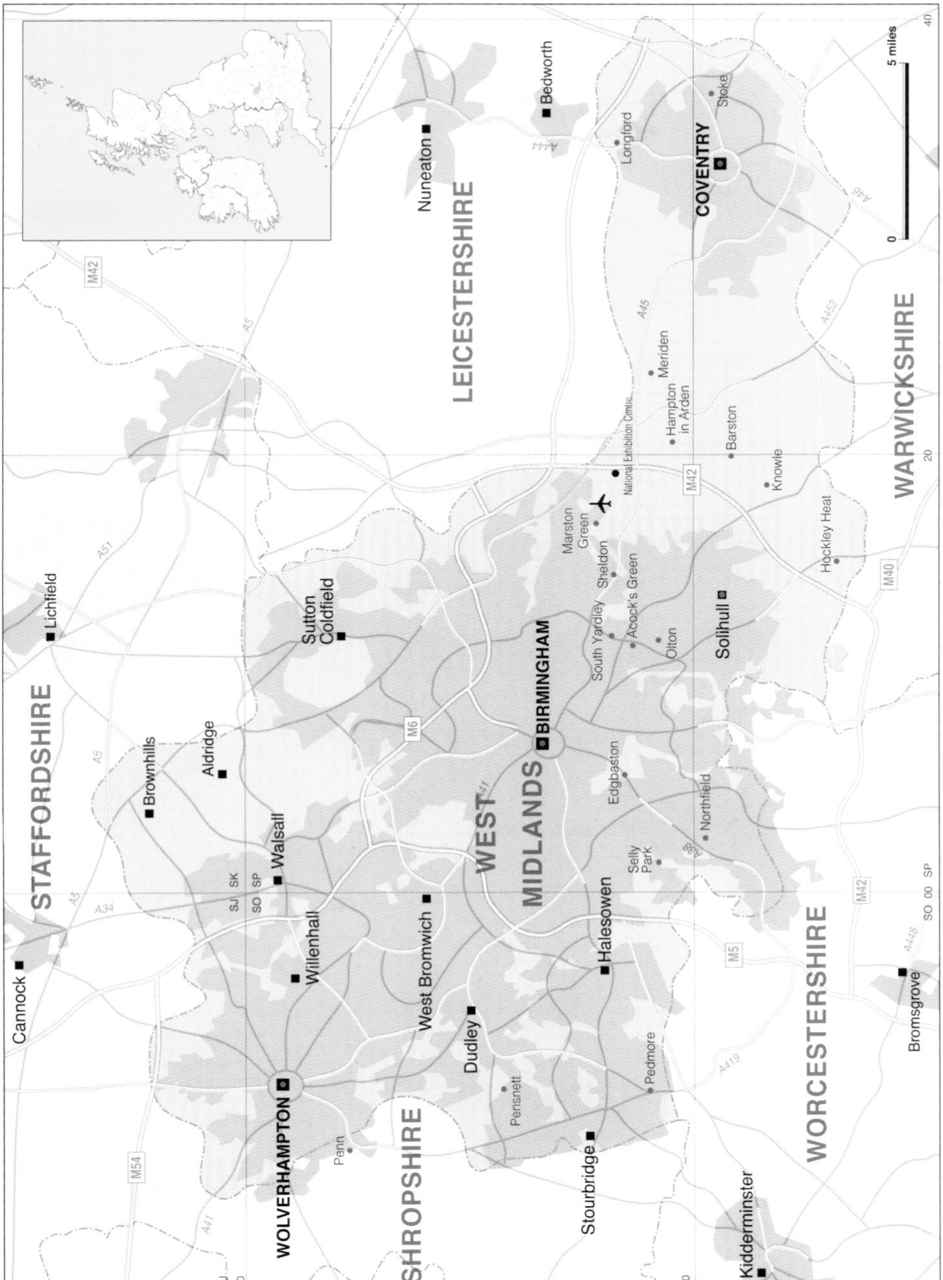

Barston

SP2078

The Gatehouse, *Barston Lane, Barston, Solihull, W Mids, B92 0JN.* Large Victorian house - close to Junction 5 M42. **Open:** All year (not Xmas/New Year)
01675 443274 (also fax) Mr Emmett **D:** Fr £20.00–£30.00 **S:** Fr £20.00–£30.00 **Beds:** 1D 2T 3S **Baths:** 2 En 1 Sh (20)

BIRMINGHAM Acock's Green

SP1183

Greenway House Hotel, *978 Warwick Road, Acock's Green, Birmingham, B27 6QG.* Small, privately run hotel, friendly service, very close to motorway network. **Open:** All year (not Xmas) **Grades:** ETC 2 Diamond
0121 706 1361 & 0121 624 8356 Fax: 0121 706 1361 D: Fr £17.00–£19.00 **S:** Fr £18.00–£26.00 **Beds:** 3F 3D 2T 6S **Baths:** 8 En 6 Sh (18)

Atholl Lodge, *16 Elmdon Road, Acock's Green, Birmingham, B27 6LH.* Friendly guest house, convenient for NEC, airport, Birmingham, Solihull centres. **Open:** All year (not Xmas)
0121 707 4417 (also fax) Mrs Davey **D:** Fr £18.00–£23.00 **S:** Fr £23.00–£27.00 **Beds:** 1F 1D 1T 5S **Baths:** 2 En 4 Sh (10)

Ashdale House Hotel, *39 Broad Road, Acock's Green, Birmingham, B27 7UX.* Victorian house overlooking park, near to airport, station, NEC and city centre. **Open:** All year
0121 706 3598 Mrs Read **Fax: 0121 707 2324 D:** Fr £20.00–£23.00 **S:** Fr £22.00–£28.00 **Beds:** 2F 1D 6S **Baths:** 4 En 1 Pr 4 Sh (1) (4) cc

BIRMINGHAM Edgbaston

SP0584

Woodville House, *39 Portland Road, Edgbaston, Birmingham, B16 9HN.* First class accommodation, 1m city centre. All rooms colour TV, tea/coffee making facilities. **Open:** All year (not Xmas)
0121 454 0274 Mr Desousa **Fax: 0121 454 5965 D:** Fr £17.00 **S:** Fr £17.00 **Beds:** 2F 3D 5T 6S **Baths:** 4 En 3 Pr (12)

BIRMINGHAM Marston Green

SP1785

Alden, *7 Elmdon Road, Marston Green, Birmingham, B37 7BS.* Home from home, family run village guesthouse, near NEC, airport. **Open:** All year (not Xmas/New Year)
0121 684 2851 (also fax) *powellalden@aol.com* **D:** Fr £22.50–£25.00 **S:** Fr £30.00–£35.00 **Beds:** 4T 1S **Baths:** 5 En (5)

BIRMINGHAM Northfield

SP0279

Clay Towers B&B, *51 Frankley Beeches Road, Northfield, Birmingham, B31 5AB.* Very comfortable, warm welcome, easy access, near Birmingham centre, M5/M42. **Open:** All year (not Xmas/New Year) **Grades:** ETC 4 Diamond
0121 628 0053 (also fax) Mr Clay **D:** Fr £22.50–£27.00 **S:** Fr £30.00–£35.00 **Beds:** 1T 2D **Baths:** 2 En 1 Pr (4)

BIRMINGHAM Selly Park

SP0582

Awentsbury Hotel, *21 Serpentine Road, Selly Park, Birmingham, B29 7HU.* Victorian country house set in own gardens, close to Birmingham University. **Open:** All year
0121 472 1258 (also fax) Mr Kerr *ian@awentsbury.co.uk* www.awentsbury.com **D:** Fr £27.00–£30.00 **S:** Fr £38.00–£48.00 **Beds:** 1F 2D 8T 5S **Baths:** 6 Pr 2 Sh (12)

BIRMINGHAM Sheldon

SP1584

Elmdon Guest House, *2369 Coventry Road, Sheldon, Birmingham, B26 3PN.* Situated close to NEC, NIA, airport, railway, restaurants, pubs and town centre. **Open:** All year (not Xmas/New Year)
0121 742 1626 & 0121 688 1720 Mr Gardner **Fax: 0121 742 1626 D:** Fr £22.50–£27.50 **S:** Fr £32.00–£42.00 **Beds:** 1F 4T 2D **Baths:** 7 Pr (7) cc

BIRMINGHAM South Yardley

SP1284

Gables Nest, *1639 Coventry Road, South Yardley, Birmingham, B26 1DD.* Friendly family-run guest house situated near to the National Exhibition Centre. **Open:** All year
0121 708 2712 M A Page **Fax: 0121 707 3396 D:** Fr £20.00–£25.00 **S:** Fr £20.00–£30.00 **Beds:** 1F 3T 1S **Baths:** 4 En1 Pr

Coventry

SP3378

Abigail Guest House, *39 St Patricks Road, Coventry, W Mids, CV1 2LP.* Small, comfortable, convenient, city-centre, near NEC, NAC and universities. **Open:** All year (not Xmas)
024 7622 1378 (also fax) Mrs Ford *ag002a@netgates.co.uk* www.abigailuk.com **D:** Fr £19.00–£22.00 **S:** Fr £20.00–£25.00 **Beds:** 1F 1D 1T 3S **Baths:** 2 Sh

Croft On The Green, *23 Stoke Green, Coventry, CV3 1FP.* Friendly, family-run guest house in a quiet conservation area. **Open:** All year
024 7645 7846 (also fax) Mr & Mrs Barnby *croftonthegreen@aol.com* www.croftonthegreen.co.uk **D:** Fr £22.50–£25.00 **S:** Fr £22.50–£30.00 **Beds:** 2F 3T 4D 6S **Baths:** 9 En 1 Pr 2 Sh (10) cc

Gilcrist Guest House, *106 St James Lane, Coventry, W Mids, CV3 3GS.* Excellent accommodation near all Midland motorways, Jaguar, NEC and Peugeot. **Open:** All year (not Xmas)
024 7630 2001 Mrs Howes **D:** Fr £20.00–£22.00 **S:** Fr £20.00–£22.00 **Beds:** 1T 1S **Baths:** 1 Sh (3)

Vardre, *68 Spencer Avenue, Coventry, W Mids, CV5 6NP.* In parkland, but near cathedral, shops, sports centres. NEC & NAC. **Open:** All year
024 7671 5154 Mrs Smith *valvardre@aol.com* **D:** Fr £17.00 **S:** Fr £17.00–£25.00 **Beds:** 1D 1T 1S **Baths:** 1 Sh (5) (2)

Brookfields, *134 Butt Lane, Allesley, Coventry, W Mids, CV5 9FE.* Well appointed, friendly. 6 mile NEC, 3 miles Coventry. Local amenities, semi-rural location. **Open:** All year (not New Year)
024 7640 4866 Mrs Marson **Fax: 024 7640 2022 D:** Fr £27.50 **S:** Fr £30.00 **Beds:** 1D 1T 2S **Baths:** 4 En (4)

Almar Lodge, *37 Mount Nod Way, Coventry, W Mids, CV5 7GY.* Homely accommodation, quiet location, near NEC/NAC, A45, transport available. **Open:** All year (not Xmas)
024 7646 8841 Mrs Bastock **D:** Fr £16.00–£20.00 **S:** Fr £16.00–£20.00 **Beds:** 1T 1S **Baths:** 1 En 1 Sh (2)

Albany Guest House, *121 Holyhead Road, Coventry, W Mids, CV1 3AD.* Located near city centre, NEC, NAC. Skating, cinema close by. **Open:** All year
024 7622 3601 (also fax) Mr Jones **D:** Fr £17.00–£18.00 **S:** Fr £18.00–£20.00 **Beds:** 1F 3T 1S **Baths:** 2 Sh (5)

Chester House, *3 Chester Street, Coventry, W Mids, CV1 4DH.* Large white building in Chester Street, ten minute walk to town. **Open:** All year
024 7622 3857 Mrs Saunders **D:** Fr £17.00–£22.50 **S:** Fr £17.00–£22.50 **Beds:** 1F 2D 1T 1S **Baths:** 1 En 1 Sh

BATHROOMS
En = Ensuite
Pr = Private
Sh = Shared

Hampton in Arden

SP2081

The Hollies Guest House, *Kenilworth Road, Hampton in Arden, Solihull, W Mids, B92 0LW.* The Hollies offers excellent accommodation, just 2.5 miles from NEC. **Open:** All year (not Xmas)
01675 442681 & 01675 442941 Mrs Hardwick **Fax: 01675 442941** *thehollies@hotmail.com* www.theholliesguesthouse.co.uk **D:** Fr £22.50–£30.00 **S:** Fr £30.00–£45.00 **Beds:** 1F 5D 3T 1S **Baths:** 10 En (12)

The Cottage, *Kenilworth Road, Hampton in Arden, Solihull, W Mids, B92 0LW.* Excellent accommodation in a charming cosy cottage close to the NEC. **Open:** All year (not Xmas)
Grades: ETC 3 Diamond, AA 3 Diamond, RAC 3 Diamond
01675 442323 Mr Howles **Fax: 01675 443323** **D:** Fr £20.00–£28.00 **S:** Fr £30.00 **Beds:** 2F 2D 1T 4S **Baths:** 8 En 1 Pr (10)

Hockley Heath

SP1573

Illshaw Heath Farm, *Kineton Lane, Hockley Heath, Solihull, B94 6RX.* Working farm close to NEC, Birmingham airport and Shakespeare country. **Open:** All year (not Xmas) **Grades:** ETC 4 Diamond
01564 782214 Ms Garner **D:** Fr £20.00–£22.50 **S:** Fr £25.00–£30.00 **Beds:** 1D 4T **Baths:** 4 En 1 Pr (8)

Knowle

SP1876 *Wilsons Arms*

Achill House, *35 Hampton Road, Knowle, Solihull, W. Mids, B93 0NR.* High standard affordable family run guest house. 100 yards Knowle High Street. **Open:** All year
01564 774090 (also fax) Mrs Liszewski *achill5@aol.com* **D:** Fr £35.00–£45.00 **S:** Fr £20.00–£35.00 **Beds:** 2F 2T 1D **Baths:** 4 En 2 Sh (6) cc

Longford

SP3584

Chogan Bed & Breakfast, *33 Longford Road, Longford, Coventry, Warwickshire, CV6 6DY.* Old cottage-style building, very modern accommodation, sky digital lounge. **Open:** All year
024 7666 1861 Fax: 024 7668 9733 D: Fr £18.00–£25.00 **S:** Fr £18.00–£25.00 **Beds:** 1F 3T 3S **Baths:** 2 En 2 Sh cc

Meriden

SP2482 *Bull's Head*

Grange Farm, *Fillongley Road, Meriden, Coventry, W Mids, CV7 7HU.* NEC, Airport, 8 mins. Countryside setting. Annexe accommodation. Farmhouse breakfast. **Open:** All year (not Xmas/New Year)
01676 22312 Ms Byrne **D:** Fr £20.00 **S:** Fr £25.00 **Beds:** 1T 1D **Baths:** 2 En (10)

Olton

SP1382

Abberose, *18 Victoria Road, Olton, Birmingham, B27 7YA.* Comfortable, private, detached home guest house. Convenient to Airport, NEC, ICC, NIA. **Open:** All year (not Xmas/New Year)
0121 708 0867 D: Fr £40.00–£46.00 **S:** Fr £21.00–£28.00 **Beds:** 1F 2T 1D 2S **Baths:** 2 En 1 Pr 1 Sh (4)

Pedmore

SO9182

The Limes Hotel, *260 Hagley Road, Pedmore, Stourbridge, W Mids, DY9 0RW.* Quiet comfortable Victorian property serving excellent food. **Open:** All year
01562 882689 E Rix **D:** Fr £28.00–£32.50 **S:** Fr £40.00–£49.00 **Beds:** 3T 4D 1S **Baths:** 8 En (12) cc

Penn

SO8996 *Mount Tavern*

Pencroft Guest House, *100 Coalway Road, Penn, Wolverhampton, W Mids, WV3 7NB.* Warm welcome friendly guest house. Homely with private parking. **Open:** All year (not Xmas/New Year)
01902 340906 & 07961 810420 (M) Ms Hall **D:** Fr £34.00 **S:** Fr £19.00 **Beds:** 2T 2D 2S **Baths:** 1 Sh (1) (3)

Pensnett

SO9089

107 Chapel Street, *Pensett, Brierley Hill, West Midlands, DY5 4EG.* Cosy semi, home from home. Central for local towns & Merryhill Centre. **Open:** All year
01384 481708 & 07751 392489 (M) B Simmonds **D:** Fr £20.00 **S:** Fr £20.00 **Beds:** 1D **Baths:** 1 Sh (3)

Solihull

SP1579

Ammonds, *11 Clifton Crescent, Solihull, W Mids, B91 3LG.* Friendly, quiet, 5 mins Solihull, M42. Near NEC, Stratford, Warwick. Weekday let. **Open:** All year (not Xmas/New Year)
0121 704 9399 Mrs Hammond **S:** Fr £19.00 **Beds:** 3S **Baths:** 1 Sh (8) (3)

Ravenhurst Guest House, *56 Lode Lane, Solihull, W Mids, B91 2AW.* Solihull centre, railways, airports, pubs, restaurants, motorway access on doorstep. **Open:** All year **Grades:** ETC 3 Diamond
0121 705 5754 Mr Keppy **Fax: 0121 704 0717** *ravenhurstaccom@aol.com* www.ravenhurst-guesthouse.co.uk **D:** Fr £20.00–£25.00 **S:** Fr £25.00–£40.00 **Beds:** 1F 2D 2T **Baths:** 2 En 3 Sh (6) cc

Acorn Guest House, *29 Links Drive, Solihull, W Mids, B91 2DJ.* Homely service in a quiet family house overlooking golf course. **Open:** All year (not Xmas) **Grades:** ETC 4 Diamond, Silver
0121 705 5241 Mrs Wood *acorn.wood@btinternet.com* **D:** Fr £20.00–£25.00 **S:** Fr £20.00–£25.00 **Beds:** 1D 2T 2S **Baths:** 1 En 1 Pr 1 Sh (5)

Bibury House, *Kenilworth Road, Solihull, West Midlands, B92 0LR.* Imposing refurbished country house 5 mins NEC and airport. **Open:** All year
01675 443518 (also fax) A Hardwick *biburyhouse@aol.com* **D:** Fr £22.00–£24.00 **S:** Fr £28.00 **Beds:** 2F 3T 2D **Baths:** 7 En (9)

Cedarwood Guest House, *347 Lyndon Road, Solihull, W Mids, B92 7QT.* Family-run guest house providing comfort away from home. **Open:** All year
0121 743 5844 (also fax) *bookings@cedarwoodguesthouse.co.uk* www.cedarwoodguesthouse.co.uk **D:** Fr £50.00–£60.00 **S:** Fr £35.00–£45.00 **Beds:** 2D 2S **Baths:** 4 En (8) cc

Michaelmas House, *1159 Warwick Road, Solihull, West Midlands, B91 3HQ.* An elegant Georgian-style house with mature gardens. 1m Solihull town centre. **Open:** All year (not Xmas/New Year)
0121 705 1414 (also fax) Mrs Horton **D:** Fr £25.00 **S:** Fr £25.00–£30.00 **Beds:** 3F 1T 1D 1S **Baths:** 2 En 1 Pr 1 Sh (6)

Stoke

SP3679

Avon Gables, *33 Avon Street, Stoke , Coventry, West Midlands, CV2 3GJ.* Elegant Edwardian house, comfortable airy rooms. **Open:** All year (not Xmas/New Year)
024 7644 9521 Mrs Lewis *avongables_marion@yahoo.co.uk* **D:** Fr £20.00–£25.00 **Beds:** 2T 1D **Baths:** 1 En 2 Sh (2) (3)

RATES

D = Price range per person sharing in a double or twin room

S = Price range for a single room

Wolverhampton

SO9198

The New Inns, *Salop Street, Wolverhampton, West Midlands, WV3 0SR.* Town centre. Contractors welcome. Evening meal £2.50 extra. **Open:** All year
01902 423779 **D:** Fr £17.50 **S:** Fr £17.50 **Beds:** 1F 2T 2D 2S **Baths:** 3 Sh

Haven Hotel and Restaurant, *15 Claremont Street, Wolverhampton, W Mids, WV14 6BA.* Public bar and restaurants, home-cooked food. Family run hotel. **Open:** All year
01902 491661 (also fax) Mr Foster **D:** Fr £17.00 **S:** Fr £18.00–£30.00 **Beds:** 3F 7T 6S **Baths:** 9 En 3 Sh **cc**

Wiltshire

GLOUCESTERSHIRE
OXFORDSHIRE
BERKSHIRE
SOMERSET
WILTSHIRE
HAMPSHIRE
DORSET
Stroud
Cirencester
Carterton
Nailsworth
Faringdon
Tetbury
Oaksey
Leigh
Cricklade
Charlton
Sevenhampton
Willesley
Sopworth
Sherston
Malmesbury
Wantage
Little Somerford
Dauntsey
Swindon
Lower Wanborough
Bishopstone
Wanborough
Wootton Bassett
Lambourn Downs
Christian Malford
Chiseldon
LYNEHAM
Kington St Michael
Kington Langley
Yatton Keynell
Hilmarton
Chippenham
Ogbourne St George
Biddestone
Bremhill
Winterbourne Monkton
Hartham Park
Calne
Gastard
Corsham
Box
Lacock
Avebury
Marlborough
Hungerford
Manton
Calstone Wellington
West Overton
Lockeridge
Newbury
Atworth
Melksham
Bromham
Bath
Easton Royal
Bradford-on-Avon
Semington
Seend Cleeve
Winsley
Devizes
Pewsey
Hilperton
Woodborough
Manningford Abbots
Poulshot
Trowbridge
Potterne
Steeple Ashton
Easterton
Rushall
Collingbourne Ducis
West Ashton
Littleton Panell
Westbury
Bratton
West Lavington
Salisbury Plain
Enford
Netheravon
Chapmanslade
Frome
Corsley
Andover
Warminster
Shrewton
Crockerton
Codford St Peter
Amesbury
Winterbourne Stoke
Codford St Mary
Netton
Stapleford
Kilmington
Little Langford
Stoford
Mere
Hindon
Laverstock
Wilton
East Knoyle
Salisbury
Wincanton
Coombe Bissett
Whaddon
Ludwell
Alvediston
Whitsbury Down
Shaftesbury
Charlton
Landford
Nomansland
Blandford Forum
Ringwood
New Forest
Brockenhurst
0
5
10 miles
M4
A4
A30
A303
A338
A345
A350
A36

Alvediston

ST9723

The Crown Inn, *Alvediston, Salisbury, SP5 5JY.* Thatched pub, delicious food, central for great walks, cycle rides.
Open: All year
01722 780335 Fax: 01722 780836 D: Fr £23.75 **S:** Fr £25.00 **Beds:** 1T 2D **Baths:** 3 En (30) cc

Amesbury

SU1541

Westavon, *76 Countess Road, Amesbury, Salisbury, SP4 7AT.* **Open:** All year
01980 623698 (also fax) Mrs Walker **D:** Fr £20.00 **S:** Fr £30.00 **Beds:** 1T 2D **Baths:** 2 En 1 Pr (4)
Well-appointed detached house set in attractive landscaped gardens, with ample safe parking. Just 2 miles from Stonehenge, with the lovely south Wiltshire countryside all around us. Winter breaks 3 nights - 4th night free. A warm and friendly reception assured.

Catkin Lodge, *93 Countess Road, Amesbury, Salisbury, SP4 7AT.* The nearest B&B to Stonehenge. Friendly, comfortable and good value. **Open:** All year **Grades:** AA 3 Diamond
01980 624810 Mr Grace **Fax: 01980622139** *info@catkinlodge.fsnet.co.uk* www.catkinlodge.fsnet.co.uk **D:** Fr £22.00–£30.00 **S:** Fr £25.00–£40.00 **Beds:** 2F 1D 1T **Baths:** 1 En 1 Sh (5) (5)

Atworth

ST8665 *Golden Fleece*

Church Farm, *Atworth, Melksham, Wilts, SN12 8JA.* Working dairy farm. Large garden/patio area. Walking distance to pubs.
Open: Easter to Nov
01225 702215 Mrs Hole *churchfarm@tinyonline.co.uk* www.churchfarm-atworth.freeserve.co.uk **D:** Fr £20.00–£25.00 **S:** Fr £25.00–£35.00 **Beds:** 1F 1T 1D **Baths:** 1 En 1 Sh

Kings Stile Cottage, *153 Bath Road, Atworth, Melksham, Wiltshire, SN12 8JR.* Cottage in village location. Convenient for Bath, Bradford-on-Avon, NT properties. Delicious breakfasts. **Open:** All year
01225 706202 (also fax) Mr & Mrs Hughes *sean@kingstile.freeserve.co.uk* **D:** Fr £18.00–£20.00 **S:** Fr £20.00–£25.00 **Beds:** 1T 1D (2)

Avebury

SU1069

6 Beckhampton Road, *Avebury, Marlborough, Wilts, SN8 1QT.* Nearby Avebury Stone Circle, Ridgeway Walk, Silbury Hill, bus route. **Open:** Mar to Oct
01672 539588 Mrs Dixon **D:** Fr £20.00 **S:** Fr £25.00–£30.00 **Beds:** 1D 1T **Baths:** 1 Sh (6)

Biddestone

ST8673 *White Horse*

Home Farm, *Biddestone, Chippenham, Wilts, SN14 7DQ.* C17th Cotswold stone farmhouse in village centre. Visit Bath and Stonehenge. **Open:** All year (not Xmas/New Year)
01249 714475 I Smith **Fax: 01249 701488** *audrey.smith@homefarmbandb.co.uk* www.homefarmbandb.co.uk **D:** Fr £22.50–£25.00 **S:** Fr £27.00–£32.00 **Beds:** 2F 1D 1S **Baths:** 3 En 1 Pr (4) cc

Home Place, *Biddestone, Chippenham, Wiltshire, SN14 7DG.* End of farmhouse, on village green. Opposite duck pond.
Open: All year
01249 712928 Ms Hall **D:** Fr £15.00–£17.50 **S:** Fr £15.00–£17.50 **Beds:** 1F 1T 1S **Baths:** 1 Sh (2)

Bishopstone (Swindon)

SU2483

Prebendal Farm, *Bishopstone, Swindon, Wilts, SN6 8PT.* Farmhouse serving local organic produce, short walk to excellent pubs. TVs in all rooms. **Open:** All year (not Xmas/New Year)
01793 790485 Mrs Selbourne **Fax: 01793 791487** *prebendal@aol.com* www.prebendal.com **D:** Fr £30.00–£35.00 **S:** Fr £30.00–£40.00 **Beds:** 3D 1T **Baths:** 2 En 1 Sh (12)

Box

ST8268

Lorne House, *London Road, Box, Corsham, Wiltshire, SN13 8NA.* Offers some of the best hospitality and comfort.
Open: All year (not Xmas/New Year)
Grades: ETC 4 Diamond, AA 4 Diamond
01225 742597 *lornehousebandb@aol.com* www.lornehouse.net **D:** Fr £22.50–£25.00 **S:** Fr £30.00–£35.00 **Beds:** 1F 1T 2D **Baths:** 4 En (6) cc

Norbin Farmhouse, *Bradford Road, Box, Corsham, Wiltshire, SN13 8JJ.* 'What a beautiful spot you have here', guests have repeatedly said.
Open: All year **Grades:** ETC 4 Diamond
01225 866907 Mrs Hiller **Fax: 01225 309205** *gillhillier@yahoo.co.uk* www.norbin-farm.co.uk
D: Fr £25.00–£30.00 **S:** Fr £30.00–£40.00
Beds: 2F 1D **Baths:** 3 En (10)

Saltbox Farm, *Drewetts Mill Lane, Box, Corsham, Wilts, SN13 8PT.* C18th farmhouse set in conservation area of the Box Valley.
Open: Feb to Nov
01225 742608 (also fax) M M Gregory **D:** Fr £21.00–£23.00 **Beds:** 1F 1D **Baths:** 1 En 1 Pr (3)

Bradford-on-Avon

ST8261

Chard's Barn, *Leigh Grove, Bradford-on-Avon, Wilts, BA15 2RF.*
Open: All year (not Xmas)
01225 863461 Mr & Mrs Stickney *stickney@chardsbarn.freeserve.co.uk* **D:** Fr £23.00–£25.00 **S:** Fr £25.00–£35.00 **Beds:** 1D 1T 1S **Baths:** 2 En 1 Pr (4)
Quiet C17th barn in unspoilt countryside with lovely gardens, view and walks. All ground floor, individually styled bedrooms, choice of breakfasts. Historic town and golf course, one mile. Close - Bath, Castle Combe, Longleat. Easy for Salisbury Plain and Stonehenge.

The Locks, *265 Trowbridge Road, Bradford-on-Avon, Wilts, BA15 1UA.* Adjoining canal tow path. Ideal walking/cycling 1m town centre. **Open:** All year
01225 863358 Mrs Benjamin **D:** Fr £17.50–£20.00 **S:** Fr £25.00–£35.00 **Beds:** 1F 2T **Baths:** 1 En 1 Pr 1 Sh (3) (6)

Great Ashley Farm, *Ashley Lane, Bradford-on-Avon, Wilts, BA15 2PP.* Delightful rooms. Great hospitality. Delicious breakfast. Colour brochure. Sliver Award.
Open: All year (not Xmas)
01225 864563 (also fax) Mrs Rawlings *greatashleyfarm@farmersweekly.net* **D:** Fr £20.00–£24.00 **S:** Fr £25.00–£45.00 **Beds:** 1F 2D **Baths:** 3 En

Springfields, *182a Great Ashley, Bradford on Avon, Wilts, BA15 2PP.* Unique ground-level ensuite double room with adjoining dining room/lounge. Peaceful countryside setting. **Open:** All year
01225 866125 Ms Rawlings **D:** Fr £20.00–£22.50 **S:** Fr £30.00–£35.00 **Beds:** 1D **Baths:** 1En

Bratton
ST9152

The Duke Inn, *Melbourne Street, Bratton, Westbury, Wilts, BA13 4RW.* Traditional oak-beamed village inn serving good fresh food, real ale. **Open:** All year **01380 830242** Mr Overend **Fax: 01380 831239 D:** Fr £25.00 **S:** Fr £30.00 **Beds:** 2D 1T **Baths:** 2 Sh (14) (30) cc

Bremhill
ST9773

Lowbridge Farm, *Bremhill, Calne, Wilts, SN11 9HE.* Peace and scenic views. Visit interesting places, jacuzzi for guests. **Open:** All year **01249 815889** Miss Sinden **D:** Fr £25.00 **S:** Fr £25.00 **Beds:** 1F 1D 1T **Baths:** 1 Sh (8)

Bromham
ST9665

Wayside, *Chittoe Heath, Bromham, Chippenham, Wilts, SN15 2EH.* **Open:** All year **01380 850695** Mr & Mrs Seed **Fax: 01380 850696** *mail@jandlseed.co.uk* **D:** Fr £22.50–£27.50 **S:** Fr £30.00 **Beds:** 1F 1D 1T **Baths:** 3 En (6)
Wayside is a family home, situated in the heart of North Wiltshire countryside. It has easy road access and is close to Bath, Chippenham, Calne and Melksham. Also nearby are the NT village of Lacock and Bowood Park. High quality accommodation.

Calne
ST9971

Lower Sands Farm, *Low Lane, Calne, Wilts, SN11 8TR.* Old farmhouse, very quiet, homely and friendly. Good breakfast, large garden. **Open:** All year (not Xmas) **01249 812402** Mrs Henly **D:** Fr £20.00 **S:** Fr £20.00 **Beds:** 1D 1T 1S **Baths:** 1 Sh (10)

Calstone Wellington
SU0268

Manor Farmhouse, *Calstone Wellington, Calne, Wiltshire, SN11 8PY.* Unique, secluded downland location. Interesting house with genuine history and Victorian 4 poster. **Open:** All year **01249 816804** Mrs Maundell **Fax: 01249 817966** *calstonebandb@farmersweekly.net* www.calstone.co.uk **D:** Fr £27.50–£32.50 **S:** Fr £30.00–£40.00 **Beds:** 2D **Baths:** 2 En (12) (2)

National Grid References given are for villages, towns and cities – not for individual houses

Chapmanslade
ST8348

Spinney Farm, *Thoulstone, Chapmanslade, Westbury, Wilts, BA13 4AQ.* In heart of Wiltshire countryside. Easy reach of Bath, Longleat. **Open:** All year **01373 832412** Mrs Hoskins **D:** Fr £20.00 **S:** Fr £22.00 **Beds:** 1F 1D 1T **Baths:** 2 Sh (8)

Charlton (Malmesbury)
ST9588

Stonehill Farm, *Charlton, Malmesbury, Wilts, SN16 9DY.* C15th farmhouse on family-run dairy farm, lush rolling countryside. **Open:** All year **01666 823310 (also fax)** Mr & Mrs Edwards *johnedna@stonehillfarm.fsnet.co.uk* **D:** Fr £23.00–£25.00 **S:** Fr £24.00–£30.00 **Beds:** 2D 1T **Baths:** 1 En 1 Sh (3)

Charlton (Shaftesbury)
ST9022

Charnwood Cottage, *Charlton, Shaftesbury, Dorset, SP7 9LZ.* C17th thatched cottage with lovely garden. Good base for touring. **Open:** All year (not Xmas/New Year) **01747 828310 (also fax)** Mr & Mrs Morgan **D:** Fr £19.00–£20.00 **Beds:** 1T 1D **Baths:** 1 Sh (2)

Chippenham
ST9173

Bramleys, *73 Marshfield Road, Chippenham, Wilts, SN15 1JR.* Large Victorian house, Grade II Listed. **Open:** All year **01249 653770** Mrs Swatton **D:** Fr £18.00–£20.00 **S:** Fr £17.00–£19.00 **Beds:** 1F 3T 1S **Baths:** 1 Pr 1 Sh (4)

Chiseldon
SU1879

Courtleigh House, *40 Draycott Road, Chiseldon, Swindon, Wilts, SN4 0LS.* Large well-appointed country home; large garden with downland views. **Open:** All year (not Xmas) **Grades:** ETC 4 Diamond **01793 740246** Ms Hibberd *rhib494369@aol.com* **D:** Fr £22.50–£25.00 **S:** Fr £25.00–£27.00 **Beds:** 2T 1S **Baths:** 1 En 1 Sh (3)

Christian Malford
ST9678

The Ferns, *Church Road, Christian Malford, Chippenham, Wiltshire, SN15 4BW.* Quiet quality accommodation, 3 miles J17 M4. Convenient Bath/Heritage Sites. **Open:** All year (not Xmas/New Year) **01249 720371** Mrs Ault *susan.ault@btopenworld.com* **D:** Fr £20.00 **S:** Fr £20.00 **Beds:** 1T 1D 1S **Baths:** 1 Sh (4)

Beanhill Farm, *Main Road, Christian Malford, Chippenham, Wiltshire, SN15 4BS.* Beautiful Cotswold stone farmhouse on working livestock farm, offering a warm welcome for the business person and tourist alike. Generous quality breakfasts. Convenient for M4 (J17 3m). Excellent base for exploring the Cotswolds, Bath, Chippenham and Avebury. Also for visiting the racing at Castle Combe Circuit. **Open:** All year **01249 720672 & 07775 660000 (M)** Mrs Kimber **Fax: 01249 720672** *bb@beanhillfarm.fsbusiness.co.uk* **D:** Fr £20.00–£25.00 **S:** Fr £20.00–£25.00 **Beds:** 1F 1D 1S **Baths:** 1 Sh (9)

Codford St Mary
ST9739

Glebe Cottage, *Church Lane, Codford St. Mary, Warminster, Wiltshire, BA12 0PJ.* 250-year-old former home of the Sexton, situated in attractive Wylye Valley. **Open:** All year (not Xmas/New Year) **01985 850565 & 01985 850666** Mrs Richardson-Aitken **Fax: 01985 850666** *bobr-a@care4free.net* **D:** Fr £25.00–£27.00 **S:** Fr £25.00–£27.00 **Beds:** 1F 1T **Baths:** 2 Pr (3) (3)

Codford St Peter
ST9640

The George Hotel, *Codford St Peter, Warminster, Wilts, BA12 0NG.* Friendly village, family pub. **Open:** All year **01985 850270 (also fax)** *thegeorgecodford@hotmail.com* **D:** Fr £19.00–£21.00 **S:** Fr £25.50–£28.50 **Beds:** 3F 1T **Baths:** 2 En 1 Sh cc

BEDROOMS
D = Double
T = Twin
S = Single
F = Family

Collingbourne Ducis
SU2453

Manor Farm, *Collingbourne Kingston, Marlborough, Wilts, SN8 3SD.* **Open:** All year **01264 850859 (also fax)** Jackie & James Macbeth *stay@manorfm.com* www.manorfm.com **D:** Fr £25.00–£35.00 **S:** Fr £25.00–£35.00 **Beds:** 1D 1T 1S **Baths:** 1 En 1 Sh (6) **cc**
Attractive period farmhouse with comfortable and spacious rooms on working family farm. Private airstrip. Pleasure flights by aeroplane and helicopter can be arranged. Unusual activities available from reflexology to hot-air ballooning. Sumptuous traditional, vegetarian, vegan and other special diet breakfasts.

Coombe Bissett
SU1026

Swaynes Firs Farm, *Grimsdyke, Coombe Bissett, Salisbury, Wilts, SP5 5RF.* Spacious farmhouse on working farm with horses, cattle, poultry, geese and duck ponds. **Open:** All year (not Xmas) **01725 519240** Mr Shering *swaynes.firs@virgin.net* www.swaynesfirs.co.uk **D:** Fr £20.00–£22.50 **S:** Fr £25.00–£30.00 **Beds:** 1F 2T **Baths:** 3 En (6)

Cross Farm, *Coombe Bissett, Salisbury, Wilts, SP5 4LY.* Farmhouse in peaceful setting. Attractive village. Good walking. Many places to visit. **Open:** All year **01722 718293** Mrs Kittermaster **Fax: 01722 718665** *s.j.kittermaster@talk21.com* **D:** Fr £20.00 **S:** Fr £20.00 **Beds:** 1F 1T 1S **Baths:** 2 Sh (4)

RATES
D = Price range per person sharing in a double or twin room
S = Price range for a single room

Corsham
ST8670

Park Farm Barn, *Westrop, Corsham, Wiltshire, SN13 9QF.* **Open:** All year **01249 715911** Mrs Waldron **Fax: 01249 701107** *thewaldrons@lineone.net* www.parkfarm.co.uk **D:** Fr £22.50–£25.00 **S:** Fr £30.00–£35.00 **Beds:** 1T 2D **Baths:** 3 En (4)
Situated in the delightful hamlet of Westrop, one mile from Corsham. Our converted C18th tithe barn offers superb B&B in recently rebuilt farm buildings adjacent to our barn. Corsham Court, Bath, Lacock, Castle Combe and Bradford-on-Avon are within easy reach.

Corsley
ST8246

Sturford Mead Farm, *Corsley, Warminster, Wilts, BA12 7QU.* Farmhouse in Area of Outstanding Natural Beauty close to Longleat. **Open:** All year **01373 832213 (also fax)** Mrs Corp *lynn_sturford.bed@virgin.net* **D:** Fr £22.00 **S:** Fr £30.00 **Beds:** 1D 2T **Baths:** 2 En 1 Pr (6)

Crockerton
ST8642

Stoneyside, *PottersHill, Crockerton, Warminster, Wiltshire, BA12 8AS.* Quiet bungalow, easy access, peaceful garden, fine views of valley, close to Longleat. **Open:** All year (not Xmas) **Grades:** ETC 4 Diamond **01985 218149 (also fax)** Mrs Elkins **D:** Fr £21.00–£23.00 **S:** Fr £27.00–£32.00 **Beds:** 1D 1T **Baths:** 1 En 1 Pr (2)

Tanhouse Cottage, *Crockerton, Warminster, Wilts, BA12 8AU.* C16th farmhouse, log fires, beams. **Open:** All year (not Xmas/New Year) **01985 214816** S J Dickinson **D:** Fr £20.00 **S:** Fr £20.00 **Beds:** 1T 1D 2S **Baths:** 2 Sh (6)

Dauntsey
ST9982

Olivemead Farm, *Olivemead Lane, Dauntsey, Chippenham, Wilts, SN15 4JQ.* Delightful C18th farmhouse, convenient M4, Bath, Cotswolds, Stonehenge. **Open:** All year (not Xmas) **01666 510205 (also fax)** Mrs Candy *olivemead@farming.co.uk* **D:** Fr £20.00 **S:** Fr £20.00–£22.00 **Beds:** 1F 1D 1T **Baths:** 1 Sh (6)

Devizes
SU0061

Eastcott Manor, *Easterton, Devizes, Wilts, SN10 4PL.* **Open:** All year (not Xmas) **01380 813313** Mrs Firth **D:** Fr £24.00–£27.00 **S:** Fr £24.00–£27.00 **Beds:** 1D 1T 2S **Baths:** 2 En 2 Pr (6)
Elizabethan manor house in own grounds. Tranquil location.

Littleton Lodge, *Littleton Panell, Devizes, Wilts, SN10 4ES.* Charming Victorian house in conservation village, large garden, overlooking vineyard, good pubs nearby. **Open:** All year **Grades:** AA 4 Diamond **01380 813131** Mr & Mrs Linton **Fax: 01380 816969** *stay@littletonlodge.co.uk* www.littletonlodge.co.uk **D:** Fr £27.50–£30.00 **S:** Fr £35.00–£40.00 **Beds:** 2D 1T **Baths:** 3 En (5) **cc**

Craven House, *Station Road, Devizes, Wilts, SN10 1BZ.* Victorian house 50 yds from centre for restaurants and pubs. **Open:** All year **Grades:** AA 2 Diamond **01380 723514 (also fax)** Mrs Shaw *shawg640@aol.com* visitwiltshire.co.uk/cravenhouse **D:** Fr £20.00 **S:** Fr £25.00 **Beds:** 1T 1D 2T **Baths:** 2 En 1 Pr 1 Sh

Asta, *66 Downlands Road, Devizes, Wilts, SN10 5EF.* One mile from town centre. Detached house in quiet area. **Open:** All year **01380 722546** R Milne-Day **D:** Fr £17.00 **S:** Fr £17.00 **Beds:** 1D 1S **Baths:** 1 Sh (1)

Glenholme Guest House, *77 Nursteed Road, Devizes, Wilts, SN10 3AJ.* Friendly, comfortable house. Warm welcome. Lovely historic town. **Open:** All year **01380 723187** Mrs Bishop **D:** Fr £36.00 **S:** Fr £20.00 **Beds:** 1F 1T **Baths:** 1 Sh

Lower Foxhangers Farm, *Rowde, Devizes, Wilts, SN10 1SS.* Relax with pleasant dreams in our rural retreat amid the Wiltshire countryside. **Open:** May to Oct **01380 828254 (also fax)** Mr & Mrs Fletcher *sales@foxhangers.co.uk* www.foxhangers.co.uk **D:** Fr £20.00–£22.00 **S:** Fr £22.00–£25.00 **Beds:** 2D 1T **Baths:** 1 Pr 2 En (4)

Gate House, *Wick Lane, Devizes, Wilts, SN10 5DW.* Spacious, comfortable, peaceful, in quiet road. A few minutes from Devizes. **Open:** All year (not Xmas/New Year) **01380 725283** Mrs Stratton **Fax: 01380 722382** *laura@gatehouse-b-and-b.freeserve.co.uk* **D:** Fr £20.00–£22.50 **S:** Fr £25.00 **Beds:** 1T 1D 1S **Baths:** 1 En 1 Sh (8)

Eastleigh House, *3 Eastleigh Road, Devizes, Wilts, SN10 3EE.* Relaxed atmosphere in comfortable accommodation, centrally located for Bath, Salisbury and Avebury. **Open:** All year (not Xmas/New Year)
01380 726918 (also fax) Mrs Davis **D:** Fr £22.50–£23.50 **S:** Fr £25.00–£30.00 **Beds:** 1T 1S **Baths:** 2 En (3)

East Knoyle

ST8830 *Fox & Hounds*

Moors Farmhouse, *East Knoyle, Salisbury, Wilts, SP3 6BU.* A perfect countryside retreat. Beautiful and interesting area. **Open:** All year (not Xmas/New Year)
01747 830385 Mrs Reading **Fax: 01747 830877** *romreading@moorsfarm.demon.co.uk*
D: Fr £27.00 **S:** Fr £35.00 **Beds:** 1F 1T (6)

Easterton

SU0255

Eastcott Manor, *Easterton, Devizes, Wilts, SN10 4PL.* Elizabethan manor house in own grounds. Tranquil location. **Open:** All year (not Xmas)
01380 813313 Mrs Firth **D:** Fr £24.00–£27.00 **S:** Fr £24.00–£27.00 **Beds:** 1D 1T 2S **Baths:** 2 En 2 Pr (6)

Easton Royal

SU2060

Follets, *Easton Royal, Pewsey, Wilts, SN9 5LZ.* Convenient for Kennet & Avon canal. Stonehenge and Avebury. **Open:** All year (not Xmas/New Year)
01672 810619 (also fax) Mrs Landless *margaretlandless@talk21.com* **D:** Fr £22.50–£25.00 **S:** Fr £30.00–£35.00 **Beds:** 2D 1T **Baths:** 3 En (6)

Enford

SU1351

Enford House, *Enford, Pewsey, Wilts, SN9 6DJ.* Salisbury Plain. River village, old rectory, good local pub with food. **Open:** All year (not Xmas)
01980 670414 Mr Campbell **D:** Fr £18.00–£20.00 **S:** Fr £20.00–£25.00 **Beds:** 1D 2T **Baths:** 3 Sh (5)

Gastard

ST8868

Heatherly Cottage, *Ladbrook Lane, Gastard, Corsham, Wilts, SN13 9PE.* C17th cottage set in quiet location with large garden. Guests have separate wing. **Open:** All year (not Xmas/New Year)
01249 701402 Mrs Daniel **Fax: 01249 701412** *ladbrook1@aol.com* www.smoothhound.co.uk/hotels/heather3.html **D:** Fr £23.00–£25.00 **S:** Fr £27.00–£30.00 **Beds:** 1T 2D **Baths:** 3 En (10) (8)

Planning a longer stay? Always ask for any special rates

Hartham Park

ST8672

Church Farm, *Hartham Park, Corsham, Wiltshire, SN13 0PU.* Cotswold farmhouse in rural location, stunning views, quiet and peaceful. **Open:** All year (not Xmas/New Year)
01249 715180 Mrs Jones **Fax: 01249 715572** *kmjbandb@aol.com* www.churchfarm.cjb.net
D: Fr £22.50–£25.00 **S:** Fr £25.00–£32.00 **Beds:** 1F 1D 1S **Baths:** 2 En 1 Pr (1) (6)

Hilmarton

SU0275 *White Horse*

Burfoots, *1 The Close, Hilmarton, Calne, Wilts, SN11 8TQ.* Situated between Bath/Swindon, Lacock Castle Combe, Avebury. M4 nearby. **Open:** All year (not Xmas/New Year)
01249 760492 Mr & Mrs Cooke **Fax: 01249 760609** *cookeburfoots@aol.com* www.burfoots.co.uk **D:** Fr £20.00–£25.00 **S:** Fr £27.00 **Beds:** 1T 1D 1S **Baths:** 3 En (10) (5)

Hilperton

ST8759

62b Paxcroft Cottages, *Devizes Road, Hilperton, Trowbridge, Wiltshire, BA14 6JB.* Small friendly house on the outskirts of Trowbridge. Far-reaching views. **Open:** All year **Grades:** ETC 4 Diamond
01225 765838 S J Styles *paxcroftcottages@hotmail.com* **D:** Fr £22.00 **S:** Fr £22.00–£25.00 **Beds:** 1F 1T 1D **Baths:** 2 En 1 Pr (6)

Hindon

ST9132

Chicklade Lodge, *Chicklade, Hindon, Salisbury, Wilts, SP3 5SU.* Charming Victorian cottage. Under 2 hours' drive from Heathrow. **Open:** All year
01747 820389 Mrs Jerram *aud.jerram@virgin.net* **D:** Fr £20.00 **S:** Fr £25.00 **Beds:** 2T 1D **Baths:** 1 Sh (5) (4)

Kilmington

ST7736

The Red Lion Inn, *On B3092 (Mere to Frome road), Kilmington, Warminster, Wilts, BA12 6RP.* Unspoilt C15th traditional inn. Stourhead 1 mile. Comfortable beds, good breakfasts. **Open:** All year (not Xmas/New Year)
01985 844263 Mr Gibbs **D:** Fr £17.50 **S:** Fr £25.00 **Beds:** 1D 1T **Baths:** 1 Sh (4) (25)

Kington Langley

ST9277

Finnygook, *Days Lane, Kington Langley, Chippenham, Wilts, SN15 5PA.* Secluded house and garden overlooking countryside, ideal touring base, Cotswolds, Mendips, Wiltshire Downs M4 J17 1 mile. **Open:** All year (not Xmas/New Year)
01249 750411 (also fax) Mrs Weston *accommodation@finnygook.fsnet.co.uk* **D:** Fr £18.50–£25.00 **S:** Fr £18.50–£30.00 **Beds:** 2T 2D 1S **Baths:** 1 Pr 1 Sh (4)

Kington St Michael

ST8977

The Jolly Huntsman Inn, *Kington St Michael, Chippenham, Wilts, SN14 6JB.* Very friendly country pub, lots of local amenities. Easily accessible. **Open:** All year
01249 750305 Mr Lawrence **Fax: 01249 750182** **D:** Fr £30.00 **S:** Fr £45.00 **Beds:** 3F 3D **Baths:** 6 En (15) cc

Lacock

ST9168

The Old Rectory, *Lacock, Chippenham, Wilts, SN15 2JZ.* **Open:** All year **01249 730335** Mrs Sexton **Fax: 01249 730166** *elaine@oldrectorylacock.co.uk*
D: Fr £22.50–£27.50 **S:** Fr £25.00–£45.00 **Beds:** 2F 3D 1T **Baths:** 4 En (6)
Superb Gothic Victorian architecture, in 8 acres of grounds and gardens, many original features, 4-poster beds. Excellent pubs a stroll away in medieval Lacock. Good location for tourists and business people, M4 J17 close by. Bath 12m, London 2 hrs.

Lacock Pottery, *The Tanyard, Lacock, Chippenham, Wilts, SN15 2LB.* Stay at Lacock's working pottery. Rooms overlooking beautiful medieval church. **Open:** All year (not Xmas/New Year)
01249 730266 Mrs McDowell **Fax: 01249 730948** *simone@lacockbedandbreakfast.com* www.lacockbedandbreakfast.com **D:** Fr £35.00–£45.00 **S:** Fr £39.00–£59.00 **Beds:** 1T 2D **Baths:** 2 En 1 Pr (6) cc

B&B owners may vary rates – be sure to check when booking

Landford

SU2619

Springfields, *Lyndhurst Road, Landford, Salisbury, Wilts, SP5 2AS.* Friendly hospitality close to New Forest, Salisbury, Southampton. Lovely rooms. **Open:** All year **01794 390093 (also fax)** Mrs Westlake *springfields_bb@libertysurf.co.uk* web.libertysurf.co.uk/springfieldsbandb **D:** Fr £17.00–£20.00 **S:** Fr £25.00 **Beds:** 2D 1S **Baths:** 2 Sh (6)

Laverstock

SU1530

The Twitterings, *73 Church Road, Laverstock, Salisbury, Wiltshire, SP11QZ.* Quiet location. Comfortable self contained rooms. English breakfast, friendly hospitality. **Open:** All year (not Xmas/New Year) **Grades:** ETC 3 Diamond **01722 321760** Mrs Henly **D:** Fr £21.00 **S:** Fr £25.00–£30.00 **Beds:** 1T 1D **Baths:** 2 En (4)

Leigh

SU0692

Waterhay Farm, *Leigh, Cricklade, Swindon, Wilts, SN6 6QY.* Working farm. Cotswold stone beamed farmhouse set in peaceful surroundings. **Open:** All year (not Xmas/New Year) **Grades:** ETC 4 Diamond **01285 861253** Mrs Rumming **D:** Fr £21.00–£25.00 **S:** Fr £23.00–£30.00 **Beds:** 1T 1D **Baths:** 2 En (2)

Little Langford

SU0436

Little Langford Farmhouse, *Little Langford, Salisbury, Wilts, SP3 4NR.* Elegant Victorian farmhouse. Beautiful countryside. Excellent sightseeing area. **Open:** Feb to Nov **01722 790205** Mrs Helyer **Fax: 01722 790086** *bandb@littlelangford.co.uk* www.dmac.co.uk/llf **D:** Fr £26.00–£28.00 **S:** Fr £40.00–£45.00 **Beds:** 1F 1T 1D **Baths:** 1 En 2 Pr (5)

Little Somerford

ST9684

Lovett Farm, *Little Somerford, Chippenham, Wilts, SN15 5BP.* Delightful farmhouse on working farm with beautiful views from the attractive ensuite bedrooms. **Open:** All year **01666 823268 (also fax)** Mrs Barnes *lovetts_farm@hotmail.com* **D:** Fr £23.00–£25.00 **S:** Fr £25.00–£30.00 **Beds:** 1D 1T **Baths:** 2 En (3) (5)

Littleton Panell

ST9954

Littleton Lodge, *Littleton Panell, Devizes, Wilts, SN10 4ES.* Charming Victorian house in conservation village, large garden, overlooking vineyard, good pubs nearby. **Open:** All year **Grades:** AA 4 Diamond **01380 813131** Mr & Mrs Linton **Fax: 01380 816969** *stay@littletonlodge.co.uk* www.littletonlodge.co.uk **D:** Fr £27.50–£30.00 **S:** Fr £35.00–£40.00 **Beds:** 2D 1T **Baths:** 3 En (5) cc

Lockeridge

SU1467

The Taffrail, *Back Lane, Lockeridge, Marlborough, Wilts, SN8 4ED.* Great welcome, comfort, tranquillity. Delightful modern home and lovely garden. **Open:** Jan to Nov **01672 861266 (also fax)** Mrs Spencer *spencer_taffrail@onetel.net.uk* **D:** Fr £17.50 **S:** Fr £20.00 **Beds:** 1D 1T 1S **Baths:** 1 Sh (8) (3)

Lower Wanborough

SU2083

Iris Cottage, *Bury Croft, Lower Wanborough, Swindon, Wilts, SN4 0AP.* Very comfortable village cottage. Swindon 4 miles. Near Ridgeway Path. **Open:** All year (not Xmas) **01793 790591** Mrs Rosier **D:** Fr £19.00 **S:** Fr £20.00 **Beds:** 2S **Baths:** 1 Sh (2)

Ludwell

ST9122

Ye Olde Wheelwrights, *Birdbush, Ludwell, Shaftesbury, Dorset, SP7 9NH.* Accommodation in separate annexe. Children and families welcome. Hearty breakfast. **Open:** All year (not Xmas) **Grades:** RAC 3 Diamond, Sparkling **01747 828955** C Dieppe *chris@cdieppe.freeserve.co.uk* **D:** Fr £19.00–£22.00 **S:** Fr £22.00–£25.00 **Beds:** 1T 1D **Baths:** 1 Sh

Malmesbury

ST9387

Stonehill Farm, *Charlton, Malmesbury, Wilts, SN16 9DY.* **Open:** All year **01666 823310 (also fax)** Mr & Mrs Edwards *johnedna@stonehillfarm.fsnet.co.uk* **D:** Fr £23.00–£25.00 **S:** Fr £24.00–£30.00 **Beds:** 2D 1T **Baths:** 1 En 1 Sh (3)
C15th farmhouse on family run dairy farm, in lush rolling countryside on Wilts/Glos border, 3.5 miles from Malmesbury's Abbey Church & Market Cross. Wonderfully situated for Bath, Cotswolds, pretty villages & Malmesbury garden. Warm Welcome. Delicious breakfasts.

Bremilham House, *Bremilham Road, Malmesbury, Wilts, SN16 0DQ.* **Open:** All year (not Xmas) **Grades:** ETC 3 Diamond **01666 822680** Mrs Ball **D:** Fr £19.00 **S:** Fr £22.50 **Beds:** 2D 1T **Baths:** 2 Sh (3)
Delightful Edwardian cottage set in a mature walled garden in a quiet location on the edge of historic Malmesbury, England's oldest borough. The town, dominated by a stunning Norman Abbey, is central for Bath, Cheltenham, Salisbury and the glorious Cotswolds.

Kings Arms Hotel, *High Street, Malmesbury, Wilts, SN16 9AA.* Warm welcome. Meals served using fresh produce. Excellent restaurant. **Open:** All year **01666 823383** Mr Timms www.malmesburywilts.freeserve.co.uk **D:** Fr £27.00–£33.00 **S:** Fr £35.00–£45.00 **Beds:** 1F 1T 5D 1S **Baths:** 8 En (20) cc

Manningford Abbots

SU1459

Huntlys Farm, *Manningford Abbotts, Pewsey, Wilts, SN9 6HZ.* Thatched farmhouse in Vale of Pewsey. Comfortable, peaceful, wonderful breakfasts. **Open:** All year **Grades:** ETC 3 Diamond **01672 563663 & 07900 211789 (M)** Mrs Andrews **Fax: 01672 563663** *meg@gimspike.fsnet.co.uk* **D:** Fr £22.00–£23.00 **S:** Fr £22.00–£28.00 **Beds:** 1T/F 1D **Baths:** 1 En 1 Pr (6) (2)

Manton

SU1768

Sunrise Farm, *Manton, Marlborough, Wilts, SN8 4HL.* Peacefully located approximately 1 mile from Marlborough. Friendly, comfortable, relaxing atmosphere. **Open:** Mar to Oct **01672 512878 (also fax)** Mrs Couzens **D:** Fr £19.00–£20.00 **S:** Fr £19.00–£25.00 **Beds:** 1D 2T **Baths:** 2 Pr (14) (3)

Marlborough

SU1869

Browns Farm, *Marlborough, Wilts, SN8 4ND.* Peaceful farmhouse on edge of Savernake Forest. Overlooking open farmland. **Open:** All year **01672 515129** Mrs Crockford *crockford@farming.co.uk* **D:** Fr £16.00–£20.00 **S:** Fr £20.00–£25.00 **Beds:** 1F 1T 2D **Baths:** 1 En 1 Sh (6)

Cartref, *63 George Lane, Marlborough, Wilts, SN8 4BY.* Friendly family home near town centre. Ideal for Avebury, Wiltshire Downs. **Open:** All year (not Xmas/New Year) **Grades:** ETC 3 Diamond
01672 512771 S Harrison **D:** Fr £19.00 **S:** Fr £25.00–£27.00 **Beds:** 1T 2D 1F **Baths:** 1 Sh (6) (2)

13 Hyde Lane, *Marlborough, Wiltshire, SN8 1JL.* Comfortable home in town centre and near lovely walking country.
Open: Easter to Oct
01672 514415 Mrs Luxton **D:** Fr £19.00 **S:** Fr £20.00–£25.00 **Beds:** 2T **Baths:** 1 Pr (5)

Melksham
ST9063

Longhope Guest House, *9 Beanacre Road, Melksham, Wilts, SN12 8AG.* Victorian house in it's own grounds. City of Bath nearby. **Open:** All year **Grades:** ETC 3 Diamond
01225 706737 (also fax) Mrs Hyatt *longhope@aol.com* **D:** Fr £22.50–£25.00 **S:** Fr £28.00–£30.00 **Beds:** 2F 2D 1T 1S **Baths:** 6 En (10)

The Old Manor, *48 Spa Road, Melksham, Wiltshire, SN12 7NY.* Old manor house in 0.75 acre. Splendid breakfast. **Open:** All year
01225 793803 *theoldmanor@yahoo.co.uk* **D:** Fr £20.00–£23.00 **S:** Fr £25.00–£35.00 **Beds:** 1F 2T 1D **Baths:** 1 En 2 Sh (8)

Springfield BandB, *403 The Spa, Melksham, Wiltshire, SN12 6QL.* Charming 'historic' family home. Lovely gardens. Quiet location. Returning clients. **Open:** All year
01225 703694 (also fax) J & P Jory **D:** Fr £23.00–£26.00 **S:** Fr £25.00–£36.00 **Beds:** 1F 1T 1D **Baths:** 1 En 1 Pr (3)

Mere
ST8132

The Beeches, *Chetcombe Road, Mere, Warminster, Wilts, BA12 6AU.* High quality accommodation. Central for walking & touring, ideal stopover. **Open:** All year
01747 860687 Mrs Smith **D:** Fr £19.00–£23.00 **S:** Fr £25.00–£27.00 **Beds:** 1F 1D 2S **Baths:** 1 En 1 Sh (6)

Downleaze, *North Street, Mere, Warminster, Wilts, BA12 6HH.* Comfortable red brick house, quiet, close to town centre. Warm welcome. Stourhead - 2 miles.
Open: All year (not Xmas/New Year)
01747 860876 Mrs Lampard **D:** Fr £16.00–£18.00 **S:** Fr £17.50–£20.00 **Beds:** 1D 1T **Baths:** 1 Sh (5) (6)

Netheravon
SU1549

Paddock House, *High Street, Netheravon, Salisbury, Wiltshire, SP4 9QP.* Comfortable village house in Netheravon. Close to Stonehenge and Avebury.
Open: All year (not Xmas/New Year)
01980 670401 (also fax) Mrs Davis **D:** Fr £18.00–£20.00 **S:** Fr £18.00–£20.00 **Beds:** 1T 1D **Baths:** 1 En 1 Sh (3) (2)

Netton
SU1336

The Old Bakery, *Netton, Salisbury, Wilts, SP4 6AW.* The Old Bakery is a pleasantly modernised former village bakery in the Woodford Valley. **Open:** All year (not Xmas)
01722 782351 Mrs Dunlop *valahen@aol.com* www.members.aol.com/valahen **D:** Fr £18.00–£22.00 **S:** Fr £25.00–£30.00 **Beds:** 1D 1T 1S **Baths:** 3 En (5) (3)

Thorntons, *Netton, Salisbury, Wilts, SP4 6AW.* Tranquil village convenient for Salisbury and Stonehenge. Home cooking a speciality. **Open:** All year (not Xmas)
01722 782535 (also fax) Mrs Bridger **D:** Fr £19.00–£25.50 **S:** Fr £20.00–£27.00 **Beds:** 1F 1D 1S **Baths:** 2 Sh (5)

Avonbank, *Netton, Salisbury, Wilts, SP4 6AW.* Comfortable modern house with very pretty garden overlooking water meadow and River Avon. **Open:** All year (not Xmas)
01722 782331 Mrs Vincent *vincent@netton.freeserve.co.uk* **D:** Fr £16.00–£20.00 **S:** Fr £20.00–£25.00 **Beds:** 3F 2T 1D **Baths:** 1 En 1 Sh (3)

Nomansland
SU2517

Clovenway House, *Forest Road, Nomansland, Sailsbury, Wiltshire, SP5 2BN.* Country house, garden overlook New Forest, close village pub, restaurant.
Open: All year
01794 390620 (also fax) Mrs Fryer **D:** Fr £18.00–£22.00 **S:** Fr £20.00–£30.00 **Beds:** 1F 1T 1D **Baths:** 1 En 2 Pr (5) (4)

BATHROOMS
En = Ensuite
Pr = Private
Sh = Shared

Oaksey
ST9993

Manby's Farm, *Oaksey, Malmesbury, Wiltshire, SN16 9SA.*
Open: All year **Grades:** ETC 4 Diamond
01666 577399 Mr Shewry-Fitzgerald *manbys@oaksey.junglelink.co.uk* www.cotswoldbandb.com **D:** Fr £25.00–£30.00 **S:** Fr £30.00–£35.00 **Beds:** 1F 1T 1D **Baths:** 3 En (3) **cc**
A warm welcome awaits guests at our farmhouse, situation on the Wilts/Glos border. Bright, cheerful rooms, ground and first floor, adaptable accommodation, heated indoor swimming pool. Relax over breakfast in our elegant dining room. Ideal location for visiting Bath, Cotswolds, Oxford. Wheelchair friendly.

Ogbourne St George
SU1974

The Inn With The Well, *Marlborough Road, Ogbourne St George, Marlborough, Wilts, SN8 1SQ.* Explore the Marlborough Downs. Friendly, good food and excellent rooms. **Open:** All year (not Xmas/New Year)
01672 841445 Mr & Mrs Shaw **Fax: 01672 841056** *theinnwiththewell@compuserve.com* www.theinnwiththewell.com **D:** Fr £25.00–£30.00 **S:** Fr £40.00–£45.00 **Beds:** 3T 2D 1F **Baths:** 6 Pr (15) **cc**

Foxlynch, *Bytham Road, Ogbourne St George, Marlborough, Wilts, SN8 1TD.* Bunkroom - 2 bunks make up double bed, TV, central heating, ensuite, camping - 4 tents. **Open:** All year
01672 841307 Mr Edwins **D:** Fr £15.00 **S:** Fr £15.00 **Beds:** 1F **Baths:** 1 En (4)

Pewsey
SU1660

Old Dairy House, *Sharcott, Pewsey, Wilts, SN9 5PA.* Thatched dairy house in four acres. Pewsey 1 mile. **Open:** All year
01672 562287 Mr & Mrs Stone *old.dairy@virgin.net* business.virgin.net/neville.burrell/sharcott **D:** Fr £30.00 **S:** Fr £35.00

Please respect a B&B's wishes regarding children, animals and smoking

Potterne

ST9958

Blounts Court Farm, *Coxhill Lane, Potterne, Devizes, Wiltshire, SN10 5NQ.* Traditional farmhouse set in 150 acres; beautiful rooms, homely atmosphere. **Open:** All year
01380 727180 Mr & Mrs Cary **D:** Fr £25.00 **S:** Fr £32.00–£37.00 **Beds:** 1D 1T **Baths:** 2 En (8)

Poulshot

ST9659

Townsend Farmhouse, *Poulshot, Devizes, Wilts, SN10 1SD.* Large, comfortable farmhouse on outskirts of village in central Wiltshire. **Open:** All year
01380 828221 (also fax) Mrs Young *mg.boo@virgin.net* **D:** Fr £20.00–£45.00 **S:** Fr £20.00 **Beds:** 2D 1T **Baths:** 1 Sh (4) (3)

Poulshot Lodge Farm, *Poulshot, Devizes, Wilts, SN10 1RQ.* Picturesque farmhouse in Poulshot; centrally situated for exploring historic Wiltshire. **Open:** All year (not Xmas)
01380 828255 Mr & Mrs Hues **D:** Fr £19.00–£20.00 **S:** Fr £20.00–£22.00 **Beds:** 2T **Baths:** 1 Sh (5) (2)

Rushall

SU1256

Little Thatch, *Rushall, Pewsey, Wilts, SN9 6EN.* A picturesque thatched house with a beautiful garden in the heart of Wiltshire countryside. **Open:** All year **Grades:** ETC 3 Diamond
01980 635282 (also fax) Mrs Newton **D:** Fr £21.50–£25.00 **S:** Fr £25.00–£29.00 **Beds:** 2T **Baths:** 1 En 1 Sh (3)

Salisbury

SU1430

Swaynes Firs Farm, *Grimsdyke, Coombe Bissett, Salisbury, Wilts, SP5 5RF.* **Open:** All year (not Xmas)
01725 519240 Mr Shering *swaynes.firs@virgin.net* www.swaynesfirs.co.uk **D:** Fr £20.00–£22.50 **S:** Fr £25.00–£30.00 **Beds:** 1F 2T **Baths:** 3 En (6)
Spacious farmhouse on working farm with horses, cattle, poultry, geese and duck ponds. All rooms ensuite with colour TV and nice views. Ideal for visiting historic sites in area, with a Bronze Age Celtic ditch on the farm.

Griffin Cottage, *10 St Edmunds Church Street, Salisbury, Wilts, SP1 1EF.* **Open:** All year (not Xmas/New Year)
01722 328259 & 07968 225442 (M) Mrs Brandon **Fax: 01722 416928** *mark@brandonasoc.demon.co.uk* www.smoothhound.co.uk/hotels/griffinc.html **D:** Fr £20.00–£22.00 **S:** Fr £40.00–£44.00 **Beds:** 2D **Baths:** 1 Sh
400-year old cottage 3 mins walk from Salisbury's Market Square. Ideal for visiting Cathedral and Stonehenge. Inglenook log-fire, lavender-scented beds and home-baked bread. Organic ingredients where possible and breakfasts healthily grilled not fried. Vegetarian and coeliac diets a speciality.

The Old Rectory B&B, *75 Belle Vue Road, Salisbury, Wiltshire, SP1 3YE.* **Open:** All year **Grades:** ETC 4 Diamond
01722 502702 Ms Smith **Fax: 01722 501135** *stay@theoldrectory-bb.co.uk* www.theoldrectory-bb.co.uk **D:** Fr £23.00–£30.00 **S:** Fr £30.00–£45.00 **Beds:** 2T 1D **Baths:** 2 En 1 Pr (10) (1)
Welcoming Victorian home, nestled in rich green English garden on a quiet street. Offering warm hospitality, bright airy bedrooms, quiet breakfast/sitting room with picture window and open fire. 5 minute walk to city centre. Perfect for a quiet comfortable stay.

Byways House, *31 Fowlers Road, Salisbury, Wilts, SP1 2QP.* Attractive Victorian house, quiet, parking. Fowlers Road opposite youth hostel. **Open:** All year (not Xmas/New Year)
01722 328364 Mr & Mrs Arthey **Fax: 01722 322146** *byways@bed-breakfast-salisbury.co.uk* www.stonehenge-uk.com **D:** Fr £25.00–£39.00 **S:** Fr £35.00–£60.00 **Beds:** 3F 7T 7D 4S **Baths:** 19 En 1 Sh (15) **cc**

Hayburn Wyke Guest House, *72 Castle Road, Salisbury, Wilts, SP1 3RL.* **Open:** All year **Grades:** AA 3 Diamond, RAC 3 Diamond
01722 412627 Mrs Curnow **Fax: 01722 412 627** *hayburn.wyke@tinyonline.co.uk* www.hayburnwykeguesthouse.co.uk **D:** Fr £22.00–£28.00 **S:** Fr £30.00–£50.00 **Beds:** 2F 3D 2T **Baths:** 4 En 3 Sh (7) **cc**
A family-run friendly guest house, Hayburn Wyke is a fine Victorian house, situated by Victoria Park, half a mile riverside walk from Salisbury Cathedral and city centre. Many places to visit locally, including Stonehenge, Wilton House and Old Sarum.

Highbank, *299A Castle Road, Salisbury, Wiltshire, SP1 3SB.* **Open:** All year (not Xmas/New Year)
01722 337819 Mr & Mrs Wilcox **D:** Fr £21.00–£23.50 **S:** Fr £30.00–£35.00 **Beds:** 1F 2T **Baths:** 1 En 1 Sh (5)
Purpose built, quiet accommodation, situated 1.5 miles north of city centre in elevated position overlooking Old Sarum and Avon Valley. 8 miles from Stonehenge and New Forest. Excellent base for sightseeing. Warm welcome assured. Comfortable rooms. Full English breakfast.

Farthings, *9 Swaynes Close, Salisbury, Wilts, SP1 3AE.* Peaceful Victorian house in quiet street near city centre. **Open:** All year
01722 330749 (also fax) Mrs Rodwell *enquiries@farthingsbandb.co.uk* www.farthingsbandb.co.uk **D:** Fr £20.00–£30.00 **S:** Fr £20.00–£30.00 **Beds:** 1D 1T 2S **Baths:** 2 En 1 Sh (1)

Tamar House, *237 Castle Road, Salisbury, Wiltshire, SP1 3RY.* Attractive friendly home, convenient for city centre and Stonehenge. **Open:** All year
01722 324809 Mrs Rampton **D:** Fr £20.00–£22.50 **S:** Fr £23.00–£25.00 **Beds:** 1F 1T 1S **Baths:** 1 Sh (3) (3)

The Retreat Inn, *33 Milford Street, Salisbury, Wilts, SP1 2AP.* C18th coaching inn, relaxed, friendly atmosphere. Ideal for touring South West. **Open:** All year **Grades:** ETC 3 Diamond
01722 338686 Fax: 01722 414496 *admin@theretreatinn.co.uk* www.theretreatinn.co.uk **D:** Fr £50.00–£60.00 **S:** Fr £40.00 **Beds:** 1F 4T 3D 4S **Baths:** 12 En **cc**

Malvern Guest House, *31 Hulse Road, Salisbury, Wilts, SP1 3LU.* Friendly guest house, but non-smoking. **Open:** All year
01722 327995 (also fax) Mrs Elkins *malvern_gh@madasafish.com* **D:** Fr £45.00–£50.00 **S:** Fr £30.00–£45.00 **Beds:** 2T 1D **Baths:** 2 En 1 Sh

Planning a longer stay? Always ask for any special rates

Wyndham Park Lodge, *51 Wyndham Road, Salisbury, Wilts, SP1 3AB.* Large Victorian house, close to city centre. Friendly family-run establishment. **Open:** All year
01722 416517 P Legg & S Coppen **Fax: 01722 328851** *wyndham@wyndham51.freeserve.co.uk*
D: Fr £19.00–£21.00 **S:** Fr £26.00–£32.00
Beds: 1F 1T 1D 1S **Baths:** 4 En (3) cc

Holly Tree House, *53 Wyndham Road, Salisbury, Wilts, SP1 3AH.* Detached family home close to city centre - parking, No Smoking. **Open:** All year
01722 322955 Mrs Middleton **D:** Fr £18.00–£20.00 **Beds:** 1T 1D **Baths:** 1 Sh (2)

Cricket Field House Hotel, *Wilton Road, Salisbury, Wilts, SP2 7NS.* All rooms ensuite. Ample car parking, Beautiful garden. **Open:** All year (not Xmas)
01722 322595 (also fax) Mrs James www.cricketfieldhousehotel.com **D:** Fr £30.00–£35.00 **S:** Fr £40.00–£45.00 **Beds:** 1F 7D 3T 3S **Baths:** 14 En (14)

Websters, *11 Hartington Road, Salisbury, Wilts, SP2 7LG.* Set on the end of a delightfully colourful terrace with sumptuous choices for breakfast. **Open:** All year
01722 339779 (also fax) Mrs Webb *websters.salis@eclipse.co.uk* www.smoothhound.co.uk/hotels/websters.html **D:** Fr £19.00–£21.00 **S:** Fr £30.00–£34.00 **Beds:** 1D 2T 2S **Baths:** 5 En (12) (5) 1 cc

The White Horse Hotel, *38 Castle Street, Salisbury, SP1 1BN.* Traditional pub/inn offering a beautiful Cathedral view and only 10 mins' walk. **Open:** All year
01722 327844 Fax: 01722 336226 D: Fr £35.00–£50.00 **S:** Fr £27.00–£35.00 **Beds:** 2F 3T 4D **Baths:** 1 En 2 Sh (9) cc

Weaver's Cottage, *37 Bedwin Street, Salisbury, Wilts, SP1 3UT.* C15th city centre cottage, cosy, oak-beamed, 2 mins market square and bus station. **Open:** All year (not Xmas)
01722 341812 Mrs Bunce **D:** Fr £15.00–£20.00 **S:** Fr £23.00–£25.00 **Beds:** 1F 1D **Baths:** 1 Sh

Seend Cleeve

ST9261

Rew Farm, *Seend Cleeve, Melksham, Wiltshire, SN12 6PS.* Working dairy farm. Few mins' walk to Kennet and Avon Canal. **Open:** All year (not Xmas/New Year)
01380 828289 & 07967 894328 (M) A Newman **D:** Fr £20.00 **S:** Fr £25.00 **Beds:** 1T (2)

Semington

ST8960

New House Farm, *Littleton, Semington, Trowbridge, Wilts, BA14 6LF.* Victorian former farmhouse, open countryside, lovely gardens, good touring centre. **Open:** All year **Grades:** ETC 4 Diamond
01380 870349 Mrs Ball **D:** Fr £23.00–£25.00 **S:** Fr £27.00–£30.00 **Beds:** 2D 1T **Baths:** 3 En (10)

Sevenhampton

SU2090

Roves Farm, *Sevenhampton, Swindon, Wilts, SN6 7QG.* Spacious comfortable quiet accommodation surrounded by beautiful countryside on a working farm. **Open:** All year
01793 763939 (also fax) *joanna@rovesfarm.co.uk* www.rovesfarm.co.uk **D:** Fr £20.00–£22.00 **S:** Fr £26.00–£27.00 **Beds:** 1F 1T **Baths:** 2 En (4)

Sherston

ST8586

Widleys Farm, *Sherston, Malmesbury, Wilts, SN16 0PY.* 200-year-old farmhouse. Peaceful and quiet. Log fires in season. Working farm. **Open:** All year (not Xmas)
01666 840213 Mrs Hibbard **Fax: 01666 840156 D:** Fr £22.00–£25.00 **S:** Fr £24.00–£27.00 **Beds:** 1F 1D 1T **Baths:** 1 En 1 Sh (6)

Shrewton

SU0644 *George Inn*

Maddington House, *Shrewton, Salisbury, Wilts, SP3 4JD.* Listed house, 3 miles from Stonehenge in pretty village. **Open:** All year (not Xmas/New Year)
01980 620406 (also fax) J Robothan *rsrobathan@freenet.co.uk* **D:** Fr £22.50–£25.00 **S:** Fr £30.00 **Beds:** 1F 1T 1D **Baths:** 2 En 1 Pr (7) (4)

Sopworth

ST8286 *The Rattlebone*

Manor Farm, *Sopworth, Chippenham, Wilts, SN14 6PR.* Quiet, working farm in beautiful countryside. Spacious rooms. Warm welcome. **Open:** Easter to Oct
01454 238676 (also fax) Mrs Barker *manor.farm@virgin.net* **D:** Fr £19.00–£22.00 **S:** Fr £25.00–£30.00 **Beds:** 2F **Baths:** 1 En 1 Sh (4)

Stapleford

SU0737

Elm Tree Cottage, *Stapleford, Salisbury, Wilts, SP3 4LH.* Light airy rooms with conservatory or large garden for relaxation. **Open:** Easter to Oct
01722 790507 Mrs Sykes *jan.sykes@virgin.net* **D:** Fr £22.50–£25.00 **S:** Fr £22.00 **Beds:** 1F 2D **Baths:** 3 Pr (3)

Steeple Ashton

ST9056

Ashton Mill Farm, *Steeple Ashton, Trowbridge, Wilts, BA14 6HQ.* **Open:** All year
01380 870083 Mrs Langley *ashtonmillfarm@tiscali.co.uk* **D:** Fr £20.00–£25.00 **S:** Fr £25.00–£30.00 **Beds:** 1D 1F 1T **Baths:** 2 Sh (4)
Get away from bustle and stress to a warm welcome at a unique, extremely peaceful farmhouse retreat in West Wiltshire. Conveniently located for Bath, Salisbury, and many National Trust properties including Stourhead, Lacock and Avebury. Ideal for walking, cycling, gliding.

Stoford

SU0835

The Swan Inn, *A36 Warminster Road, Stoford, Salisbury, Wilts, SP2 0PR.* Family-run coaching inn set in the picturesque Wylye Valley. **Open:** All year
01722 790236 Mr Ringwood **Fax: 01722 790115** *info@theswanatstoford.co.uk* www.theswanatstoford.co.uk **D:** Fr £22.50–£30.00 **S:** Fr £35.00–£65.00 **Beds:** 2F 4T 3D **Baths:** 9 En (90) cc

Swindon

SU1685

Bradford Guest House, *40 Devizes Road, Old Town, Swindon, Wilts, SN1 4BG.* Small friendly guest house. **Open:** All year (not Xmas/New Year)
01793 642427 Ms McCalla **Fax: 01793 430381** *sam@smccalla.freeserve.co.uk* www.zednet.co.uk/bradfordshire **D:** Fr £21.00–£24.00 **S:** Fr £27.00–£33.00 **Beds:** 2T 4D 2S **Baths:** 8 En cc

Trowbridge

ST8557

44 Wingfield Road, *Trowbridge, Wilts, BA14 9ED.* Fine Victorian house. 'Home from home'. **Open:** All year
01225 761455 Mr & Mrs Dobbin **D:** Fr £20.00 **Beds:** 1F 1D 1T 1S

62b Paxcroft Cottages, *Devizes Road, Hilperton, Trowbridge, Wiltshire, BA14 6JB.* **Open:** All year
Grades: ETC 4 Diamond
01225 765838 S J Styles *paxcroftcottages@hotmail.com* **D:** Fr £22.00 **S:** Fr £22.00–£25.00 **Beds:** 1F 1T 1D **Baths:** 2 En 1 Pr (6)
Small friendly house on the outskirts of Trowbridge. Far-reaching views overlooking the Wiltshire Downs. Lovely gardens. Tastefully furnished throughout. Centrally situated for Bath, Salisbury, Bristol. Many attractions in easy reach. Visitors lounge with cable tv.

Wanborough
SU2082

Ducksbridge, *Bury Croft, Wanborough, Swindon, Wilts, SN4 0AP.* Large house, lawns & lake. **Open:** All year (not Xmas)
01793 790338 Mr & Mrs Sadler **D:** Fr £18.00–£20.00 **S:** Fr £20.00–£25.00 **Beds:** 1D 2T 2S **Baths:** 1 En 1 Sh

Hard Crag, *Foxhill, Wanborough, Swindon, Wilts, SN4 0DR.* Comfortable B&B situated 100 metres from Ridgeway Trail. **Open:** All year (not Xmas/New Year)
01793 790058 Ms Osborne **D:** Fr £20.00–£25.00 **S:** Fr £20.00–£25.00 **Beds:** 2D 2S **Baths:** 2 En 1 Pr 1 Sh (7)

Warminster
ST8745

Belmont, *9 Boreham Road, Warminster, BA12 9JP.* Well-situated for town, spacious rooms, friendly welcome, good facilities. **Open:** All year
01985 212799 (also fax) Mrs Monkcom *monkcom@freeuk.com* **D:** Fr £17.00–£20.00 **S:** Fr £16.00–£25.00 **Beds:** 2D **Baths:** 1 Sh (5) (6)

West Ashton
ST8755

Water Gardens, *131 Yarnbrook Road, West Ashton, Trowbridge, Wiltshire, BA14 6AF.* Detached bungalow, large gardens ideally situated for Bath and area. **Open:** All year (not Xmas)
01225 752045 Mrs Heard *lucy@heard28.freeserve.co.uk* www.s-h-systems.co.uk/hotels/water2html **D:** Fr £18.00 **Beds:** 1F 1D 1T **Baths:** 3 En (3)

Planning a longer stay? Always ask for any special rates

West Lavington
SU0052

Parsonage House, *West Lavington, Devizes, Wilts, SN10 4LT.* Welcoming relaxed family home in peaceful surroundings overlooking the church. **Open:** All year (not Xmas/New Year)
01380 813345 Mrs West **D:** Fr £20.00–£25.00 **S:** Fr £25.00–£30.00 **Beds:** 1D 1T **Baths:** 1 Sh (3)

West Overton
SU1268

Cairncot, *West Overton, Marlborough, Wilts, SN8 4ER.* Situated between Avebury and Marlborough, Cairncot offers comfortable accommodation with superb country views. **Open:** All year
01672 861617 Mrs Leigh *aaw@comms-audit.co.uk* **D:** Fr £20.00–£25.00 **S:** Fr £20.00 **Beds:** 1D 1S **Baths:** 1 Sh (6)

Westbury
ST8650

Brokerswood House, *Brokerswood, Westbury, Wilts, BA13 4EH.* Situated in front of 80 acres of woodland, open to the public. **Open:** All year (not Xmas)
01373 823428 Mrs Phillips **D:** Fr £15.00–£18.00 **S:** Fr £15.00–£18.00 **Beds:** 3F 1D 1T 1S **Baths:** 1 En 1 Pr 1 Sh (1) (6)

Whaddon
SU1926

Three Crows Inn, *Old Southampton Road, Whaddon, Salisbury, Wiltshire, SP5 3HB.* Quiet country inn, oak beams, home cooked food, country walks. **Open:** All year (not Xmas/New Year)
01722 710211 (also fax) Ms Sutton *lsu4210600@aol.com* www.threecrowns.co.uk **D:** Fr £36.00–£48.50 **S:** Fr £18.00–£25.00 **Beds:** 2T 2D **Baths:** 2 En 2 Sh **cc**

Willesley
ST8488

Tavern House, *Willesley, Tetbury, Glos, GL8 8QU.* Luxury Bed & Breakfast ideally situated for Westonbirt Arboretum, Bath, Bristol, Gloucester & Cheltenham. **Open:** All year
01666 880444 Mrs Robertson *robertson@tavernhouse.co.uk* **D:** Fr £32.50–£42.50 **S:** Fr £50.00–£70.00 **Beds:** 1T 3D **Baths:** 4 En (20)

Winsley
ST7961

Conifers, *4 King Alfred Way, Winsley, Bradford-on-Avon, Wilts, BA15 2NG.* Quiet area, pleasant outlook, friendly atmosphere, convenient Bath, lovely walks. **Open:** All year
01225 722482 Mrs Kettlety **D:** Fr £17.00–£18.00 **S:** Fr £18.00–£20.00 **Beds:** 1T 1D **Baths:** 1 Sh

3 Corners, *Cottles Lane, Winsley, Bradford-on-Avon, Wilts, BA15 2HJ.* House in quiet village edge location, attractive rooms and gardens. **Open:** All year (not Xmas)
01225 865380 Mrs Cole *sandra@turleigh.freeserve.co.uk* **D:** Fr £22.50–£25.00 **S:** Fr £26.00–£30.00 **Beds:** 1F 1D **Baths:** 1 En 1 Pr (4)

Winterbourne Monkton
SU1072

The New Inn, *Winterbourne Monkton, Swindon, Wilts, SN4 9NW.* Friendly 200-year-old Inn within 1 mile of Avebury Stone Circle. **Open:** All year
01672 539240 Fax: 01672 539150 *mick@folliard.fsnet.co.uk* **D:** Fr £25.00–£30.00 **S:** Fr £45.00–£50.00 **Beds:** 1F 2T 2D **Baths:** 5 En (20) **cc**

Winterbourne Stoke
SU0741

Scotland Lodge, *Winterbourne Stoke, Salisbury, SP3 4TF.* Spacious comfortable rooms, easy access. Good touring centre. Personal service. **Open:** All year
01980 620943 Mrs Singleton **Fax: 01980 621403** *scotland.lodge@virgin.net.co.uk* www.scotland-lodge.co.uk **D:** Fr £17.50–£27.50 **S:** Fr £25.00–£30.00 **Beds:** 1F 2T 1D **Baths:** 4 En

Woodborough
SU1159

St Cross, *Woodborough, Pewsey, Wilts, SN9 5PL.* Pewsey Vale - heart of crop circles, beautiful countryside, Kennet & Avon Canal 8 mins' walk. **Open:** All year
01672 851346 (also fax) Mrs Gore **D:** Fr £25.00–£35.00 **Beds:** 1D 1T **Baths:** 1 Sh (6) (1)

National Grid References given are for villages, towns and cities – not for individual houses

Wootton Bassett

SU0683

The Hollies, *Greenhill Hook, Wootton Bassett, Swindon, SN4 8EH.* Ideal for business or touring. Beautiful views, peaceful attractive gardens. **Open:** All year (not Xmas/New Year) **Grades:** ETC 3 Diamonds
01793 770795 (also fax) D: Fr £19.00–£22.50 **S:** Fr £22.00–£38.00 **Beds:** 2D 2S **Baths:** 1 En 2 Sh (12) (5)

Yatton Keynell

ST8676

Oakfield Farm, *Easton Piercy Lane, Yatton Keynell, Chippenham, Wilts, SN14 6JU.* Cotswold stone farmhouse in open countryside. Ideal for Cotswolds, Bath, Stonehenge. **Open:** Mar to Oct
01249 782355 Mrs Read **Fax: 01249 783458**
D: Fr £20.00–£22.50 **S:** Fr £25.00–£30.00
Beds: 2D 1T **Baths:** 1 En 1 Sh (8)

Worcestershire

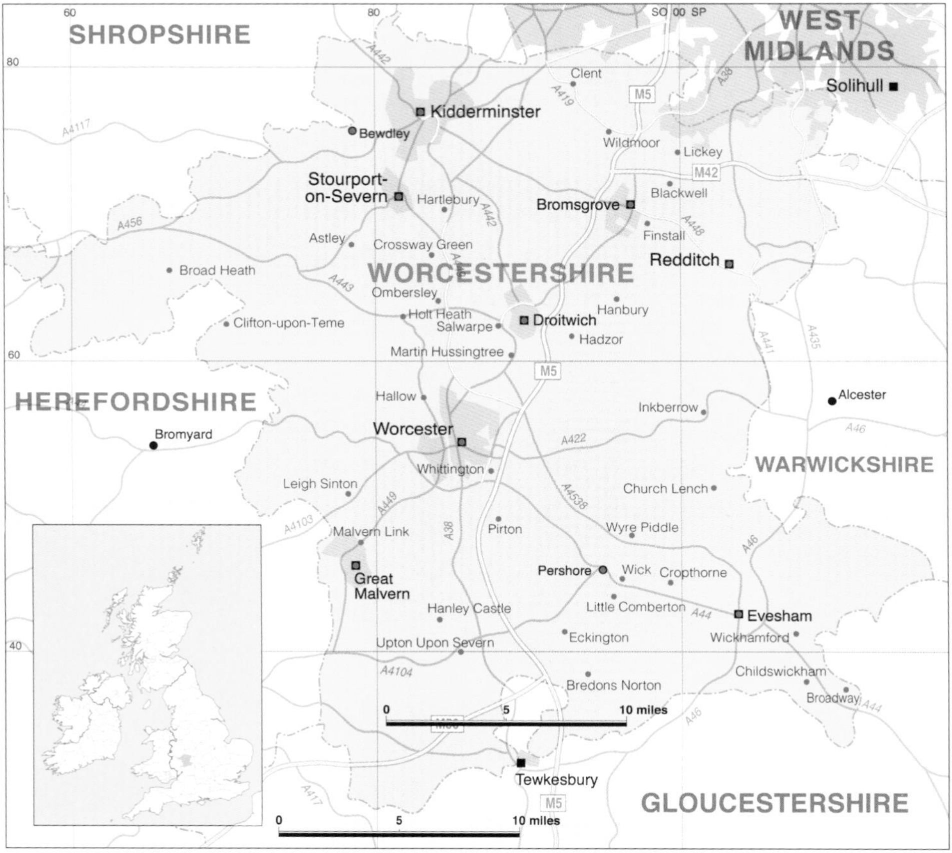

Astley

SO7868

Woodhampton House, *Weather Lane, Astley, Stourport-on-Severn, Worcestershire,* DY13 0SF. Set in rural Worcestershire, delightful coach house. Always warm welcome. **Open:** All year (not Xmas/New Year)

01299 826510 Mrs Knight **Fax: 01299 827059** *pete-a@sally-a.freeserve.co.uk* **D:** Fr £22.50–£25.00 **S:** Fr £25.00–£30.00 **Beds:** 1F 1T 1D 1S **Baths:** 2 En (3)

Bewdley

SO7875

Bank House, *14 Lower Park, Bewdley, Worcs,* DY12 2DP. Warm family atmosphere, superb breakfasts, close to town centre/countryside/river. **Open:** All year (not Xmas) **Grades:** AA 3 Diamond

01299 402652 (also fax) Mrs Nightingale *fleur.nightingale@virgin.net* **D:** Fr £22.00 **S:** Fr £22.00 **Beds:** 1F 1T 1S **Baths:** 2 Sh (2)

Planning a longer stay? Always ask for any special rates

Lightmarsh Farm, *Crundalls Lane, Bewdley, Worcs,* DY12 1NE. Elevated position, outstanding views, peaceful location. Comfortable accommodation, quality breakfasts. **Open:** All year (not Xmas/New Year)

01299 404027 Mrs Grainger **D:** Fr £22.50 **S:** Fr £30.00 **Beds:** 1D 1T **Baths:** 1 En 1 Pr (10) (6)

BEDROOMS
D = Double
T = Twin
S = Single
F = Family

All details shown are as supplied by B&B owners in Autumn 2002

Blackwell

SO9972

Rosa Lodge, *38 Station Road, Blackwell, Bromsgrove, B60 1PZ.* Country village house in Blackwell, near Bromsgrove. Superb food in Edwardian-style dining room. **Open:** All year
0121 445 5440 (also fax) *sandra@rosalodge.co.uk* www.rosalodge.co.uk **D:** Fr £25.00 **S:** Fr £30.00 **Beds:** 2D 1T 1S **Baths:** 3 En 1 Pr (15) (6) cc

Bredons Norton

SO9339

Round Bank House, *Lampitt Lane, Bredons Norton, Tewkesbury, Glos, GL20 7HB.* Beautiful views and countryside, very peaceful, homely and comfortable. **Open:** All year (not Xmas/New Year)
01684 772983 & 01684 772142 Mr & Mrs Thornton **Fax: 01684 773035 D:** Fr £23.00–£27.00 **S:** Fr £28.00–£30.00 **Beds:** 1T 1D **Baths:** 1 En

Broad Heath

SO6665 *Tally Ho Inn, Fox Inn, Lion Inn*

Court Farm, *Hanley Childe, Broad Heath, Tenbury Wells, Worcs, WR15 8QY.* Court farm is a C15th oak-beamed and very spacious farmhouse. **Open:** All year (not Xmas/New Year)
01885 410265 Mrs Yarnold **D:** Fr £22.50 **S:** Fr £25.00–£30.00 **Beds:** 1T 1D **Baths:** 1 En 1 Pr (10)

Broadway

SP0937

Crown & Trumpet Inn, *Church Street, Broadway, Worcs, WR12 7AE.* **Open:** All year **01386 853202 & 08700 750500** Mr Scott *ascott@cotswoldholidays.co.uk* www.cotswoldholidays.co.uk **D:** Fr £23.00–£25.00 **S:** Fr £45.00–£55.00 **Beds:** 3D 1T **Baths:** 4 En (6)
C17th Cotswold stone inn with log fire. Seasonal homemade local dishes with own beer brewed for us. 'Cotteswold Gold' for summer and 'Lords-A-Leaping' for winter. Also at Christmas with our mulled wine. Situated behind the village green.

Milestone House, *122 High Street, Broadway, Worcs, WR12 7AJ.* **Open:** All year **Grades:** AA 4 Diamond
01386 853432 *milestone.house@talk21.com* www.milestone-broadway.co.uk **D:** Fr £28.00–£34.00 **S:** Fr £45.00–£60.00 **Beds:** 1T 3D **Baths:** 4 En cc
Milestone House is situated in the Upper High Street, just a short walk from the centre of the village of Broadway. Built in the early part of C17th, the house, a Grade II Listed building, has a wealth of period charm and character.

Brook House, *Station Road, Broadway, Worcs, WR12 7DE.* Traditional Victorian house with large rooms, overlooking fields, hills and gardens. **Open:** All year (not Xmas)
01386 852313 Mr & Mrs Thomas **D:** Fr £22.00–£26.00 **S:** Fr £22.50–£40.00 **Beds:** 2F 2D 1T 1S **Baths:** 3 En 1 Pr 1 Sh (6)

Bowers Hill Farm, *Bowers Hill, Willersey, Evesham, Worcs, WR11 7HG.* Peaceful Cotswold location, offering high quality facilities and spectacular views. **Open:** All year **Grades:** ETC 4 Diamond, AA 4 Diamond
01386 834585 Ms Bent **Fax: 01386 830234** *sarah@bowershillfarm.com* www.bowershillfarm.com **D:** Fr £22.50–£25.00 **S:** Fr £30.00–£35.00 **Beds:** 1F 1T 1D **Baths:** 3 En cc

Southwold House, *Station Road, Broadway, Worcs, WR12 7DE.* Spacious tastefully decorated Edwardian house in picturesque Cotswold village. 4 mins' walk pubs, restaurants. **Open:** All year
01386 853681 Mrs Smiles **Fax: 01386 854610 D:** Fr £24.00–£25.00 **S:** Fr £25.00–£27.00 **Beds:** 1F 4D 2T 1S **Baths:** 7 En (8) cc

Windrush House, *Station Road, Broadway, Worcs, WR12 7DE.* Elegant Edwardian detached house located near Broadway village green. **Open:** All year
01386 853577 Susan & Richard Pinder **Fax: 01386 853790** *richard@broadway-windrush.co.uk* www.broadway-windrush.co.uk **D:** Fr £25.00–£30.00 **S:** Fr £25.00–£40.00 **Beds:** 3D 2T **Baths:** 5 En (6)

Quantocks, *Evesham Road, Broadway, Worcs, WR12 7PA.* Large detached house in 3 acres with superb views of Cleeve/Bredon/Malvern Hills. **Open:** Mar to Nov
01386 853378 Mr & Mrs Stephens *quantocks_broadway@yahoo.co.uk* **D:** Fr £22.50–£25.00 **S:** Fr £30.00–£35.00 **Beds:** 1F 1T **Baths:** 2 En

Bromsgrove

SO9570

Woodcote Farm, *Kidderminster Road, Bromsgrove, Worcs, B61 9EA.* Attractive C18th farmhouse with moated garden on organic working farm. **Open:** All year
01562 777795 & 07767 617968 Mrs Prichard **Fax: 01562 777024** *woodcotefarm@btinternet.com* www.woodcotefarm.com **D:** Fr £22.50–£25.00 **S:** Fr £25.00–£30.00 **Beds:** 1F 1D 1T **Baths:** 2 En 1 Sh (10)

Avoncroft Guest House, *77 Redditch Road, Bromsgrove, Worcs, B60 4JP.* Quality accommodation located on A38. M5/M42 5 mins away. **Open:** All year
01527 832819 Mr Carter **D:** Fr £25.00 **S:** Fr £30.00–£37.50 **Beds:** 2T 1D 1S **Baths:** 4 En (9)

Bea's Lodge, *245 Pennine Road, Bromsgrove, Worcs, B61 0TG.* Modern house in quiet area, convenient for M5, M6, M40, M42. **Open:** All year
01527 877613 Mrs Lodge **D:** Fr £20.00 **S:** Fr £20.00 **Beds:** 1T 1S **Baths:** 1 Sh (3) (2)

Childswickham

SP0738

Mount Pleasant Farm, *Childswickham, Broadway, Worcs, WR12 7HZ.* Working farm 3 miles from Broadway. Very quiet accommodation, excellent views. **Open:** All year
01386 853424 Mrs Perry *helen@mount_pleasant.fslife.co.uk* **D:** Fr £25.00 **S:** Fr £30.00 **Beds:** 2D 1T 1S **Baths:** 4 Pr (5) (10)

Church Lench

SP0251

Hill Barn Orchard, *Evesham Road, Church Lench, Evesham, Worcs, WR11 4UB.* Stylish house and garden, trout lakes all in 50 acres. **Open:** Easter to Oct
01386 871035 (also fax) Mr & Mrs Badger **D:** Fr £25.00 **S:** Fr £40.00 **Beds:** 2T **Baths:** 2 En (6) (6)

BEDROOMS
D = Double
T = Twin
S = Single
F = Family

Clent

SO9279

St Elisabeths Cottage, *Woodman Lane, Clent, Stourbridge, W Mids, DY9 9PX.* Large country cottage close to motorway links. Excellent pubs nearby. **Open:** All year **Grades:** ETC 4 Diamond
01562 883883 Mrs Blankstone **Fax: 01562 885034** *st_elizabeth_cot@btconnect.com* **D:** Fr £28.00–£30.00 **S:** Fr £28.00–£30.00 **Beds:** 2D 1T **Baths:** 3 En (6)

Clifton upon Teme

SO7161 *Lion Inn, Talbot*

Pitlands Farm, *Clifton upon Teme, Worcester, WR6 6DX.* C15th beamed farmhouse. Ideally situated for exploring Heart of England/Welsh Marshes. **Open:** Feb to Nov
01886 812220 (also fax) Mrs Mann **D:** Fr £20.00–£23.00 **S:** Fr £23.00–£25.00 **Beds:** 1F 2T **Baths:** 2 En 1 Pr (3) (10)

Cropthorne

SO9944

Cedars Guest House, *Evesham Road, Cropthorne, Pershore, Worcs, WR10 3JU.* Ideal for touring Cotswolds, Malverns, Stratford-upon-Avon & Cheltenham. **Open:** All year
01386 860219 Mrs Ward *cedarsguesthouse@ukonline.co.uk* **D:** Fr £18.00–£22.00 **S:** Fr £18.00–£25.00 **Beds:** 1F 2D 2T **Baths:** 3 En 2 Sh (6)

Crossway Green

SO8468

Garden Cottages, *Crossway Green, Hartlebury, Stourport-on-Severn, Worcs, DY13 9SJ.* Oak-beamed cottage in rural position close to main roads. **Open:** All year (not Xmas/New Year) **Grades:** ETC 4 Diamond, Gold
01299 250626 (also fax) Mr & Mrs Terry *accommodation@mamod.co.uk* www.gardencottages.co.uk **D:** Fr £25.00–£30.00 **S:** Fr £25.00–£30.00 **Beds:** 1F 1T 1D 1S **Baths:** 3 En 1 Pr

B&B owners may vary rates – be sure to check when booking

Yew Tree House, *Norchard, Crossway Green, Stourport on Severn, DY13 9SN.* **Open:** All year **Grades:** ETC 4 Diamond, Silver
01299 250921 & 07971 112621 (M) Mrs Knight **Fax: 01299 253472** *paul@knightp.swinternet.co.uk* www.yewtreeworcester.co.uk **D:** Fr £27.50–£30.00 **S:** Fr £35.00 **Beds:** 1F 2T 2D **Baths:** 5 En
Built in 1754, stepping over the threshold is a fascinating mix of elegance and atmosphere. Peacefully tucked away but convenient to all motorway systems and sightseeing. Splendid breakfasts provided, weather permitting served in beautiful gardens. Tennis court on site by arrangement.

Droitwich

SO8963

Merrivale, *216 Worcester Road, Droitwich, Worcs, WR9 8AY.* Four-poster beds. Friendly welcome. 3 miles M5 J5/6. **Open:** All year
01905 778213 **D:** Fr £15.00–£17.50 **S:** Fr £20.00–£30.00 **Beds:** 1T 2D **Baths:** 1 En 1 Sh (3)

Temple Broughton Farm, *Broughton Green, Droitwich, WR9 7EF.* Listed manor house, elegantly furnished, spectacular views with tennis court. **Open:** All year (not Xmas/New Year)
01905 391456 Mrs Lawson **Fax: 01905 391515** **D:** Fr £25.00–£27.50 **S:** Fr £30.00–£35.00 **Beds:** 1T 3D **Baths:** 3 En 1 Sh (6)

RATES
D = Price range per person sharing in a double or twin room
S = Price range for a single room

Eckington

SO9241

The Anchor Inn & Restaurant, *Catheridge Lane, Eckington, Pershore, Worcs, WR10 3BA.* **Open:** All year
01386 750356 (also fax) Mr Kelly *anchoreck@aol.com* www.anchoreckington.co.uk **D:** Fr £22.50–£30.00 **S:** Fr £25.00–£40.00 **Beds:** 3T 2D **Baths:** 5 Pr (25) **cc**
Traditional village inn off the main road, comfortable lounge, separate restaurant. Chef-prepared cuisine. Central for Worcester, Evesham, Cheltenham and Tewkesbury. Situated between the Cotswolds and the Malvern Hills.

Evesham

SP0343

Pevensey Lodge, *2 Croft Road, Evesham, Worcs, WR11 4NE.* **Open:** All year
01386 442077 Mrs Oldham **Fax: 01386 40564** *june@pevenseylodge.com* www.pevenseylodge.com **D:** Fr £25.00–£30.00 **S:** Fr £40.00–£50.00 **Beds:** 2D 2S **Baths:** 2 En 1 Sh (4)
Warm welcome in early C20th house in own grounds. Quiet location, 5 mins walk to town centre/railway station. Full English breakfast of your choice. Short drive to Stratford, Cheltenham and Cotswolds. A real comfortable home from home.

6 Fountain Gardens, *Waterside, Evesham, Worcs, WR11 1JY.* Evesham town house, non-smoking, friendly, comfortable beds, good food. **Open:** All year
01386 47384 (also fax) Mrs Roberts *sheila.roberts@care4free.net* **D:** Fr £15.00–£17.00 **S:** Fr £15.00–£17.00 **Beds:** 1D 1S **Baths:** 1 Sh (4)

Planning a longer stay? Always ask for any special rates

Bowers Hill Farm, *Bowers Hill, Willersey, Evesham, Worcs, WR11 7HG.* Peaceful Cotswold location, offering high quality facilities and spectacular views. **Open:** All year **Grades:** ETC 4 Diamond, AA 4 Diamond
01386 834585 Ms Bent **Fax: 01386 830234** *sarah@bowershillfarm.com* www.bowershillfarm.com **D:** Fr £22.50–£25.00 **S:** Fr £30.00–£35.00 **Beds:** 1F 1T 1D **Baths:** 3 En cc

Anglers View, *90 Albert Road, Evesham, Worcs, WR11 4LA.* 5 minutes form town/bus stations and River Avon. **Open:** All year
01386 442141 S Tomkotwicz *sarahbandb2000@yahoo.co.uk* **D:** Fr £17.50–£30.00 **S:** Fr £20.00–£35.00 **Beds:** 1F 3T **Baths:** 1 Pr 2 Sh (2)

Finstall

SO9770

Stoke Cross Farm, *Dusthouse Lane, Finstall, Bromsgrove, Worcs, B60 3AE.* Quiet rural setting on outskirts of town, convenient for motorways. **Open:** All year (not Xmas/New Year)
01527 876676 J Orford **Fax: 01527 874729** **D:** Fr £16.00–£17.00 **S:** Fr £20.00–£22.00 **Beds:** 1F 1T 1D **Baths:** 2 Sh (2) (6)

Hadzor

SO9162

Hadzor Court, *Hadzor, Droitwich, Worcs, WR9 7DR.* **Open:** All year (not Xmas) **01905 794401 & 01905 794424** Mrs Brooks **Fax: 01905 794636** *hadzorcourt_droitwichspa@hotmail.com* **D:** Fr £20.00 **S:** Fr £30.00 **Beds:** 1D 1T **Baths:** 2 En
Listed farmhouse in historic hamlet. Wonderful character, antiques, countryside, sun-terrace, business and meeting facilities, cellar bar, country weddings. 40 mins Stratford-upon-Avon, 25 mins Worcester, 40 mins Birmingham Airport, NEC.

Hallow

SO8258

Ivy Cottage, *Sinton Green, Hallow, Worcester, WR2 6NP.* Charming cottage in quiet village, 4m from Worcester centre. **Open:** Mar to Oct
01905 641123 Mrs Rendle **D:** Fr £21.00 **S:** Fr £25.00–£30.00 **Beds:** 1D 1T 1S **Baths:** 1 En 1 Pr (4)

Hanbury

SO9663 *Eagle & Sun, Red Lion*

Upper Hollowfields Farm, *Hollowfields Road, Hanbury, Redditch, Worcs, B96 6RJ.* Country house. Beautifully appointed rooms. Convenient for motorways and towns. **Open:** All year
01527 821461 (also fax) Mrs Terry **D:** Fr £18.00–£21.00 **S:** Fr £23.00–£30.00 **Beds:** 1T 1D 1S **Baths:** 3 En

Hanley Castle

SO8341

Four Hedges, *The Rhydd, Hanley Castle, Malvern, Worcester, WR8 0AD.* Friendly family house, spacious garden. Three Counties showground 4 miles. **Open:** All year (not Xmas)
01684 310405 (also fax) Mrs Cooper *fredgies@aol.com* **D:** Fr £20.00 **S:** Fr £17.00–£20.00 **Beds:** 1D 1T 2S **Baths:** 1 En 1 Sh (5)

The Chestnuts, *Gilberts End, Hanley Castle, Worcester, Worcs, WR8 0AS.* Delightful family home with a relaxed welcoming atmosphere in a tranquil setting. **Open:** All year
01684 311219 Ms Parker **D:** Fr £20.00–£25.00 **S:** Fr £20.00–£30.00 **Beds:** 1F 1T 1D **Baths:** 3 En

Hartlebury

SO8370

Garden Cottages, *Crossway Green, Hartlebury, Stourport-on-Severn, Worcs, DY13 9SJ.* Oak-beamed cottage in rural position close to main roads. **Open:** All year (not Xmas/New Year) **Grades:** ETC 4 Diamond, Gold
01299 250626 (also fax) Mr & Mrs Terry *accommodation@mamod.co.uk* www.gardencottages.co.uk **D:** Fr £25.00–£30.00 **S:** Fr £25.00–£30.00 **Beds:** 1F 1T 1D 1S **Baths:** 3 En 1 Pr

Holt Heath

SO8163 *Red Lion*

Heathwood, *Holt Heath, Worcester, Worcs, WR6 6NA.* Large Victorian family house. Perfectly placed for touring and business. **Open:** All year
01905 621771 (also fax) Ms Beare-Wolfenden **D:** Fr £25.00–£35.00 **Beds:** 1D **Baths:** 1 En (2)

Planning a longer stay? Always ask for any special rates

Inkberrow

SP0057

Perrymill Farm, *Little Inkberrow, Inkberrow, Worcester, WR7 4JQ.* Attractive Georgian farmhouse set in rural Worcestershire - family run. **Open:** All year
01386 792177 Mrs Alexander **Fax: 01386 793449** *alexander@estatesgazette.net* **D:** Fr £25.00 **S:** Fr £25.00 **Beds:** 1T 1D 1S **Baths:** 1 Sh (8)

Kidderminster

SO8276

Hollies Farm Cottage, *Franche, Kidderminster, Worcestershire, DY11 5RW.* Country cottage. Just off the beaten track. Wonderful views. Farmhouse breakfast. **Open:** All year (not Xmas/New Year) **Grades:** ETC 4 Diamond
01562 745677 Mrs Glover **Fax: 01562 824580** *pete@top-floor.fsbusiness.co.uk* **D:** Fr £22.00–£24.00 **S:** Fr £25.00 **Beds:** 1T 1D **Baths:** 2 En

Leigh Sinton

SO7750

Chirkenhill, *Leigh Sinton, Malvern, Worcs, WR13 5DE.* Regency farmhouse situated in some of Worcestershire's most beautiful countryside. **Open:** All year
01886 832205 Mrs Wenden *wenden@eidosnet.co.uk* **D:** Fr £22.00–£25.00 **S:** Fr £25.00–£30.00 **Beds:** 2D 1T **Baths:** 3 Pr (6)

Lickey

SO9975

Honeypot, *305 Old Birmingham Road, Lickey, Bromsgrove, Worcs, B60 1HQ.* Attractive detached house, large garden and comfortable guests lounge. **Open:** All year
0121 445 2580 E Stanworth **D:** Fr £21.00–£22.00 **S:** Fr £21.00–£22.00 **Beds:** 1D 1T **Baths:** 1 Sh

Merrivale, *309 Old Birmingham Road, Lickey, Bromsgrove, Worcs., B60 1HQ.* Attractive bungalow in 5 acres of woodland and pastures. **Open:** All year (not Xmas/New Year)
0121 445 1694 (also fax) Mr Smith *alincolnsmith@bushinternet.com* **D:** Fr £20.00 **Beds:** 1T 1D **Baths:** 2 En (5)

National Grid References given are for villages, towns and cities – not for individual houses

B&B owners may vary rates – be sure to check when booking

Little Comberton

SO9643

Byeways, *Pershore Road, Little Comberton, Pershore, WR10 3EW.* Countryside location centrally situated for visiting Stratford, Broadway, Cheltenham, Oxford. **Open:** Jan to Nov
01386 710203 (also fax) G Wright **D:** Fr £16.00–£20.00 **S:** Fr £18.00–£20.00 **Beds:** 1F

Malvern

SO7846

Chirkenhill, *Leigh Sinton, Malvern, Worcs, WR13 5DE.* Regency farmhouse situated in some of Worcestershire's most beautiful countryside. **Open:** All year
01886 832205 Mrs Wenden *wenden@eidosnet.co.uk* **D:** Fr £22.00–£25.00 **S:** Fr £25.00–£30.00 **Beds:** 2D 1T **Baths:** 3 Pr (6)

Nether Green Farm, *Ridge Way Cross, Malvern, Worcs, WR13 5JS.* 5 Miles to spa town of Malvern and Malvern Hills for great walking. **Open:** All year (not Xmas)
01886 880387 Mrs Orford **D:** Fr £17.50–£20.00 **S:** Fr £16.00 **Beds:** 1D 1T 1S **Baths:** 1 Sh (3)

Mellor Heights, *46a West Malvern Road, Malvern, Worcestershire, WR14 4NA.* Modern, comfortable family home high in the Malvern Hills. **Open:** All year (not Xmas/New Year) **Grades:** ETC 3 Diamond
01684 565105 Ms Mellor *mellorheights@onetel.net.uk* **D:** Fr £20.00 **S:** Fr £20.00–£25.00 **Beds:** 1T 1D **Baths:** 1 Sh (10)

The Elms, *52 Guarlford Road, Malvern, Worcs, WR14 3QP.* Queen Anne farmhouse, relaxed friendly atmosphere. Close to Malvern/showground. **Open:** All year (not Xmas/New Year)
01684 573466 Mrs Holland *jili_holland@yahoo.co.uk* **D:** Fr £25.00 **S:** Fr £25.00 **Beds:** 1T 1D **Baths:** 1 Sh (10) (2)

Cowleigh Park Farm, *Cowleigh Road, Malvern, Worcs, WR13 5HJ.* Peacefully situated C17th timbered farmhouse at foot of Malvern Hills. **Open:** All year (not Xmas/New Year)
01684 566750 (also fax) Mrs Stringer *cowleighparkfarm@talk21.com* **D:** Fr £27.00–£28.00 **S:** Fr £38.00–£40.00 **Beds:** 2T 1D **Baths:** 3 En (7) (8)

Malvern Link

SO7847

Edgeworth, *4 Carlton Road, Malvern Link, Worcs, WR14 1HH.* Edwardian family home near station and access to hill walks. **Open:** All year
01684 572565 Mrs Garland *susan.garland@talk21.com* **D:** Fr £18.00–£20.00 **S:** Fr £19.00–£22.00 **Beds:** 1D 2S **Baths:** 1 Sh (2)

Rathlin, *1 Carlton Road, Malvern Link, Worcs, WR14 1HH.* A private family home offering friendly B&B accommodation. **Open:** All year
01684 572491 Mrs Guiver **D:** Fr £18.00–£22.00 **S:** Fr £18.00–£22.00 **Beds:** 1T 2D **Baths:** 1 En 2 Sh (1)

Martin Hussingtree

SO8860

Knoll Farm, *Ladywood Road, Martin Hussingtree, Worcester, Worcs., WR3 7SY.* **Open:** All year
01905 455565 Mrs Griggs *knollfarmwr3@hotmail.com* **D:** Fr £25.00 **S:** Fr £25.00–£30.00 **Beds:** 1T 2D **Baths:** 2 En 1 Sh (10)
The house is set in a rural location with wonderful views towards Abberley and Malvern Hills. Comfortable rooms, full English breakfast and a warm welcome. Between the historic towns of Worcester and Droitwich. Close to M5, off-road parking.

Ombersley

SO8463

The Old Farmhouse, *Hadley Heath, Ombersley, Droitwich, Worcs, WR9 0AR.* Beautiful country house, peaceful location. Tennis. 5 mins M5 J6. Warm welcome. **Open:** All year **Grades:** ETC 5 Diamond, Silver
01905 620837 J M Lambe **Fax: 01905 621722** *judylambe@ombersley.demon.co.uk* www.the-old-farmhouse.com **D:** Fr £27.50–£30.00 **S:** Fr £30.00–£35.00 **Beds:** 2T 2D 1S **Baths:** 3 En 1 Sh

Greenlands, *Uphampton, Ombersley, Droitwich, Worcs, WR9 0JP.* C16th picturesque house. Peaceful conservation hamlet. Character bedrooms. Every comfort. **Open:** All year
01905 620873 Mrs Crossland *xlandgreenlands@onetel.net.uk* **D:** Fr £18.00–£25.00 **S:** Fr £20.00–£40.00 **Beds:** 2D 1T 1S **Baths:** 1 En 2 Sh (6)

Pershore

SO9445

Aldbury House, *George Lane, Wyre Piddle, Pershore, Worcs, WR10 2HX.* **Open:** All year
01386 553754 (also fax) *aldbury@onetel.net.uk* **D:** Fr £22.00–£25.00 **S:** Fr £30.00–£35.00 **Beds:** 2T 1D **Baths:** 3 En (4)
A warm welcome is guaranteed in our quietly located, spacious modern home. All rooms are comfortably furnished and we serve generous breakfasts. With easy access to the M5, an ideal base for visiting Worcester, Evesham, Stratford, The Malverns & Cotswolds.

The Barn, *Pensham Hill House, Pensham Hill, Pershore, Worcs, WR10 3HA.* Superior ground floor accommodation in a C17th barn conversion. **Open:** All year **Grades:** ETC 5 Diamond, Gold
01386 555270 Mrs Horton **Fax: 01386 552894** **D:** Fr £30.00–£32.50 **S:** Fr £37.50–£40.00 **Beds:** 2D 2T **Baths:** 3 En (6)

Besford Bridge House, *Besford Bridge, Pershore, Worcs, WR10 2AD.* Georgian farmhouse in rural location just 2 miles from Pershore. **Open:** All year (not Xmas/New Year)
01386 553117 Mrs Dodwell *sallydodwell@classicfm.net* **D:** Fr £18.00–£24.00 **S:** Fr £20.00–£24.00 **Beds:** 2D **Baths:** 1 Sh (2)

Pirton

SO8747

The Old Smithy, *Pirton, Worcester, WR8 9EJ.* C17th black and white country house, quiet location near M5. **Open:** All year (not Xmas) **Grades:** ETC 4 Diamond
01905 820482 Mrs Wynn *welcome@TheOldSmithy.co.uk* www.smoothhound.co.uk/hotels/oldsmith.html **D:** Fr £20.00–£25.00 **S:** Fr £25.00–£27.00 **Beds:** 1D 1T **Baths:** 1 Pr 1 Sh (6) **cc**

Redditch

SP0368

Walcote, *Dagnell End Road, Bordesley, Redditch, Worcs, B98 9BH.* Comfortable country home, 3m to M42, opposite golf course. **Open:** All year (not Xmas/New Year)
01527 68784 Mrs Smith **D:** Fr £17.50 **S:** Fr £17.50 **Beds:** 2T 1S **Baths:** 1 Sh (1) (7)

Oakland, *64 Ledbury Close, Matchborough East, Redditch, Worcs, B98 0BS.* Detached family home with easy access to Warwick, Stratford, motorway network. **Open:** All year
01527 524764 Mr & Mrs Lewis **D:** Fr £20.00–£25.00 **Beds:** 1D **Baths:** 1 En (3)

Salwarpe

SO8762

Middleton Grange, *Ladywood Road, Salwarpe, Droitwich Spa, Worcestershire, WR9 5PA.* C18th farmhouse set in picturesque gardens in rural location. **Open:** All year **Grades:** ETC 4 Diamond, Silver
01905 451678 S Harrison **Fax: 01905 453978** *salli@middletongrange.com* www.middletongrange.com **D:** Fr £25.00–£30.00 **S:** Fr £30.00 **Beds:** 2T 3D **Baths:** 4 En 1 Pr (8)

Stoulton

SO9050

Caldewell, *Stoulton, Worcester, WR7 4RL.* Georgian mansion in parkland setting with animals and miniature railway. **Open:** All year (not Xmas)
01905 840894 (also fax) Mrs Booth *sheila@caldewell.demon.co.uk* www.caldewell.demon.co.uk **D:** Fr £20.00–£22.50 **S:** Fr £23.00–£27.00 **Beds:** 3D 1T **Baths:** 2 En 2 Sh (6)

Stourport-on-Severn

SO8171

Baldwin House, *8 Lichfield Street, Stourport-on-Severn, Worcs, DY13 9EU.* Grade II Listed Georgian town house, close to historic canal basins. **Open:** All year
01299 877221 & 07966 365541 (M) Mrs Barclay **Fax: 01299 877221** *balwinhousebb@aol.com* **D:** Fr £20.00–£25.00 **S:** Fr £22.50–£30.00 **Beds:** 2F 4D 2T 2S **Baths:** 7 En 1 Sh

Upton-upon-Severn

SO8540

Four Hedges, *The Rhydd, Hanley Castle, Malvern, Worcester, WR8 0AD.* Friendly family house, spacious garden. Three Counties showground 4 miles. **Open:** All year (not Xmas)
01684 310405 (also fax) Mrs Cooper *fredgies@aol.com* **D:** Fr £20.00 **S:** Fr £17.00–£20.00 **Beds:** 1D 1T 2S **Baths:** 1 En 1 Sh (5)

Lockeridge Farm, *Upton-upon-Severn, Worcester, WR8 0RP.* **Open:** All year (not Xmas)
01684 592193 Mrs Albert *frank@albert85.freeserve.co.uk* **D:** Fr £16.00–£18.00 **S:** Fr £21.00–£23.00 **Beds:** 2F 1T **Baths:** 1 Sh (4)
C16th farmhouse in quiet location, central to Worcester, Hereford, Gloucester, Cheltenham, Stratford on Avon. Off-road parking for larger vehicles. Ideally situated for 3 counties. Showground site of various events, comfortable accommodation all rooms showers ensuite. Friendly service, visitor satisfaction.

Tiltridge Farm & Vineyard, *Upper Hook Road, Upton-upon-Severn, Worcester, WR8 0SA.* Pretty farmhouse with vineyards between River Severn and Malvern Hills. **Open:** All year (not Xmas/New Year) **Grades:** ETC 4 Diamond, Silver
01684 592906 Fax: 01684 594142 *sandy@tiltridge.com* **D:** Fr £25.00 **S:** Fr £30.00 **Beds:** 1T 2D **Baths:** 3 En (10)

Jasmin, *21 School Lane, Upton-upon-Severn, Worcester, WR8 0LD.* Comfortable modern bungalow in quiet road and near town centre. **Open:** All year
01684 593569 D Leighton **D:** Fr £20.00–£25.00 **S:** Fr £25.00–£27.50 **Beds:** 1T 1D **Baths:** 1 Sh

Whittington

SO8753

Woodview, *High Park, Whittington, Worcester, WR5 2RS.* Comfortable friendly accommodation set in 10 acres garden, donkey paddocks. **Open:** All year (not Xmas)
01905 351893 Mrs Wheeler *betty.wheeler@talk21.com* **D:** Fr £19.00–£22.00 **S:** Fr £20.00–£25.00 **Beds:** 2D 2T **Baths:** 1 En 2 Sh (4)

Wick

SO9545

6 Hopney Cottage, *Wick, Pershore, Worcs, WR10 3JT.* Spacious cottage providing a friendly atmosphere, comfortable bedrooms with views. **Open:** All year (not Xmas)
01386 556341 (also fax) Mrs Shakespeare *hopneycottage@hotmail.com* **D:** Fr £18.00–£25.00 **S:** Fr £18.00 **Beds:** 2D 2T 1S **Baths:** 1 En 1 Sh (10)

Wickhamford

SP0642

Avonwood, *30 Pitchers Hill, Wickhamford, Evesham, Worcestershire, WR11 6RT.* High standard of furnishings and decor. 3 miles from Broadway. **Open:** All year (not Xmas/New Year)
01386 834271 (also fax) Ms Morgan **D:** Fr £19.50 **S:** Fr £19.50–£26.00 **Beds:** 1T 2D **Baths:** 3 En (12) (8)

Wildmoor

SO9575 *Wildmoor Oak*

Home Farm, *Mill Lane, Wildmoor, Bromsgrove, Worcs, B61 0BX.* Modern comfortable extension of farmhouse. **Open:** All year
01527 874964 Mr Lees **D:** Fr £20.00 **S:** Fr £20.00–£25.00 **Beds:** 3T 2S **Baths:** 3 Sh (5)

Worcester

SO8555

Five Ways Hotel, *Angel Place, Worcester, Worcs., WR1 3QN.* **Open:** All year
01905 616980 Fax: 01905 616344 D: Fr £20.00–£25.00 **S:** Fr £30.00–£35.00 **Beds:** 3F 3T 3D 1S **Baths:** 10 Pr (12) (6) **cc**
Small family run city centre hotel. Within walking distance of train & bus stations, racecourse, river, cathedral, Worcester Porcelain Works & county cricket ground. Stratford Upon Avon 25 miles, Cotswolds 15 miles, Malvern Hills 8 miles & Rugby Club 4 miles.

Oaklands B&B, *Grange Lane, Claines, Worcester, WR3 7RR.* Peaceful, rural outlook, yet easy access Worcester city, Stratford, Cotswolds. **Open:** All year (not Xmas) **Grades:** ETC 4 Diamond
01905 458871 Mrs Gadd **Fax: 01905 759362** *barbaragadd@hotmail.com* **D:** Fr £25.00–£30.00 **S:** Fr £30.00 **Beds:** 1F 1D 1T 1S **Baths:** 4 En (6)

The Old Smithy, *Pirton, Worcester, WR8 9EJ.* C17th black and white country house, quiet location near M5. **Open:** All year (not Xmas) **Grades:** ETC 4 Diamond
01905 820482 Mrs Wynn *welcome@TheOldSmithy.co.uk* www.smoothhound.co.uk/hotels/oldsmith.html **D:** Fr £20.00–£25.00 **S:** Fr £25.00–£27.00 **Beds:** 1D 1T **Baths:** 1 Pr 1 Sh (6) **cc**

Burgage House, *4 College Precincts, Worcester, WR1 2LG.* Georgian house in perfect location next to Worcester Cathedral. **Open:** All year (not Xmas/New Year)
01905 25396 (also fax) Mrs Ratcliffe www.burgagehouse.co.uk **D:** Fr £25.00–£27.50 **S:** Fr £30.00 **Beds:** 1F 1T 2D **Baths:** 4 En

Planning a longer stay? Always ask for any special rates

Wyre Piddle

SO9647

Aldbury House, *George Lane, Wyre Piddle, Pershore, Worcs, WR10 2HX.* A warm welcome is guaranteed in our quietly located, spacious modern home. **Open:** All year
01386 553754 (also fax) *aldbury@onetel.net.uk* **D:** Fr £22.00–£25.00 **S:** Fr £30.00–£35.00 **Beds:** 2T 1D **Baths:** 3 En (4)

East Yorkshire

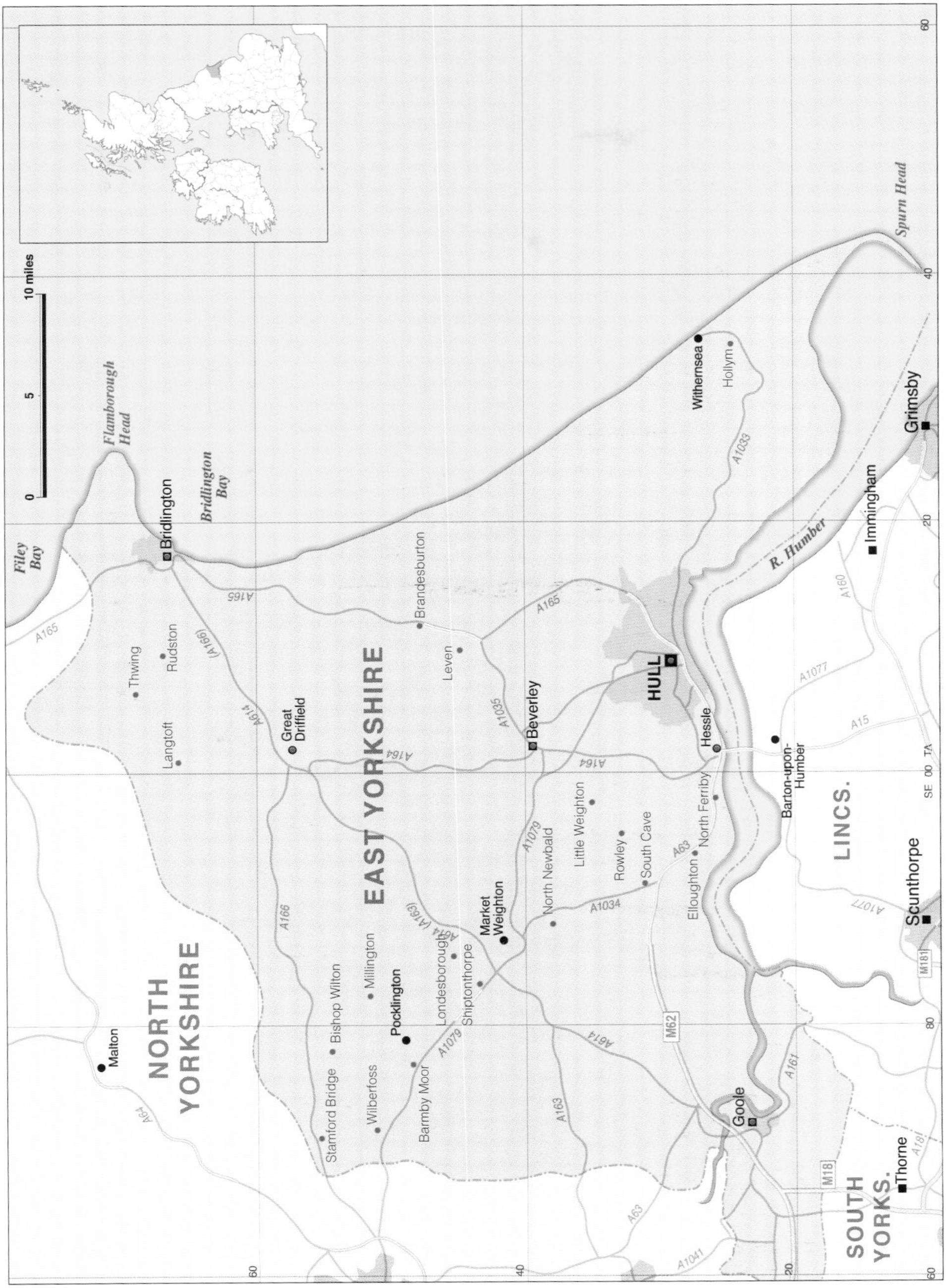

Barmby Moor

SE7748

Alder Carr House, *York Road, Barmby Moor, York, YO42 4HU.* Country house with spacious comfortable rooms. Ideal for York/The Moors. **Open:** All year (not Xmas)
01759 380566 Mrs Steel **D:** Fr £22.50 **S:** Fr £30.00 **Beds:** 1F 2D **Baths:** 2 En 1 Pr (10)

Beverley

TA0440

Number One, *1 Woodlands, Beverley, E. Yorks, HU17 8BT.* Victorian house, home cooking, open fires, library, lovely gardens. **Open:** All year
01482 862752 Mrs King *neilandsarah@mansle.karoo.co.uk* **D:** Fr £19.00–£22.50 **S:** Fr £23.00–£29.00 **Beds:** 1D 1T 1S **Baths:** 1 En 1 Sh (1)

Bishop Wilton

SE7955

High Belthorpe, *Bishop Wilton, York, YO42 1SB.* Large comfortable farmhouse in peaceful setting with wonderful views, private fishing. **Open:** All year (not Xmas)
01759 368238 M Hamdan *keebyah@netscapeonline.co.uk* **D:** Fr £17.63 **S:** Fr £20.00 **Beds:** 1F 1D

Brandesburton

TA1247

Burton Lodge Hotel, *Brandesburton, Driffield, E. Yorks, YO25 8RU.* Charming country hotel, set in 2 acres of grounds adjoining golf course. **Open:** All year (not New Year) **Grades:** ETC 2 Star, AA 2 Star
01964 542847 Fax: 01964 544771 *email@burtonlodge.fsnet.co.uk* www.burtonlodge.fsnet.co.uk **D:** Fr £25.00–£28.00 **S:** Fr £36.00–£40.00 **Beds:** 2F 4T 2D 1S **Baths:** 9 En (15) cc

Bridlington

TA1867

Aire Valley Guest House, *50 New Burlington Road, Bridlington, E. Yorks, YO15 3HS.* Friendly welcome, relaxed atmosphere. Ideal location, traditional meals, weekly discounts. **Open:** All year (not Xmas/New Year)
01262 608786 S Dawson *airevalley@newburlingtonrd.fsnet.co.uk* **D:** Fr £14.00–£17.00 **S:** Fr £14.00–£17.00 **Beds:** 2F 1T 2D 2S **Baths:** 2 Sh (2)

Edelweiss, *86/88 Windsor Crecent, Bridlington, E Yorks, YO15 3JA.* **Open:** All year (not Xmas/New Year) **Grades:** ETC 3 Diamond
01262 673822 Fax: 01262 604622 *edelweiss1st@amserve.com* www.hometown.aol.co.uk/edelweiss1st/index.html **D:** Fr £16.00–£20.00 **S:** Fr £21.00–£25.00 **Beds:** 4F 4T 3D 2S **Baths:** 1 En 8 Pr 3 Sh
Only a 2 min walk to the beach, harbour, town centre, bus and rail stations. Discounts for OAPs & parties of six or more. Free colour brochure on request. First class accommodation, food & service at an affordable price.

Winston House Hotel, *5/6 South Street, Bridlington, E. Yorks, YO15 3BY.* **Open:** All year **Grades:** ETC 3 Diamond
01262 670216 (also fax) Mrs Otto *bob.liz@winstonhouse.fsnet.co.uk* **D:** Fr £19.00–£23.00 **S:** Fr £20.00 **Beds:** 1F 6D 1T 3S **Baths:** 9 En 2 Pr cc
Always a warm welcome and friendly atmosphere. Quietly situated minutes from beach, harbour and town. Four poster for that special occasion. Enjoy a varied, generous home-cooked menu. Ideal for touring the Moors. York an hour away. Short breaks available.

Grantlea Guest House, *2 South Street, Bridlington, E Yorks, YO15 3BY.* **Open:** All year (not Xmas) **Grades:** ETC 3 Diamond
01262 400190 M J & S B Odey www.bridlington.net/accommodation/hotels/grantlea/ **D:** Fr £19.00 **S:** Fr £19.00 **Beds:** 2D 2T 1S **Baths:** 4 En 1 Pr
Situated on south side of Bridlington, 1 min from beach & Spa Theatre. 2 mins from harbour and town centre. Ideal for walking, fishing and golf as well as beach holidays. All rooms have colour TVs and tea/coffee making facilities.

Planning a longer stay? Always ask for any special rates

The Bay Court Hotel, *35A Sands Lane, Bridlington, E Yorks, YO15 2JG.* **Open:** Mar to Nov **Grades:** ETC 4 Diamond
01262 676288 *bay.court@virgin.net* www.baycourt.co.uk **D:** Fr £25.00–£32.00 **S:** Fr £25.00–£28.00 **Beds:** 2T 3D 2S **Baths:** 5 En 2 Pr (4) cc
Perfectly situated opposite Bridlington's quiet North Bay promenade, also giving easy access to harbour and nearby cliffs. You will receive a warm friendly welcome, be assured of both tasteful and comfortable accommodation as well as delicious food. Licensed bar with wide selection of wines.

Seawind's Guest House, *48 Horsforth Avenue, Bridlington, E Yorks, YO15 3DF.* **Open:** All year **Grades:** ETC 3 Diamond
01262 676330 M J Chambers *seawinds@btinternet.com* **D:** Fr £17.50–£21.00 **S:** Fr £17.50 **Beds:** 1T 4D 1S **Baths:** 3 En 2 Sh (4)
Small, comfortable, adults only guest house. 10 mins stroll from town centre, 2 mins from Spa Theatre & magnificent south beach. Ideal base to tour East Yorkshire. Off street parking for 4 cars. Reduced rates for 3 or more nights.

Victoria Hotel, *25 Victoria Road, Bridlington, E. Yorks, YO15 2AT.* Small, friendly, family-run hotel. Ideal for beach, town centre, harbour. **Open:** All year
01262 673871 Fax: 01262 609431 *victoria.hotel@virgin.net* www.victoriahotelbridlington.co.uk **D:** Fr £22.00 **S:** Fr £27.00 **Beds:** 6F 2T 2D 2S **Baths:** 12 En (6) cc

Stonmar Guest House, *15 Flamborough Road, Bridlington, E. Yorks, YO15 2HU.* An excellent family run guest house with traditional home-cooked meals. **Open:** All year
01262 674580 (also fax) Mrs Laverick **D:** Fr £18.50–£24.00 **S:** Fr £18.50–£24.00 **Beds:** 3F 5D 1S **Baths:** 2 En 2 Sh (4)

Longleigh B&B, *12 Swanland Avenue, Bridlington, E. Yorks, YO15 2HH.* Quiet location, 4 minutes from town and sea front. **Open:** All year
01262 676234 D: Fr £16.00–£18.00 **S:** Fr £16.00–£17.00 **Beds:** 2D 1S

Gables Private Hotel, *16 Landsdowne Road, Bridlington, YO15 2QS.* Prime location, 50 yds from promenade, close to all amenities. **Open:** Easter to Oct
01262 672516 D: Fr £15.00–£16.00 **S:** Fr £15.00–£16.00 **Beds:** 1F 1T 1D 1S **Baths:** 2 Sh (3)

B&B owners may vary rates – be sure to check when booking

Richmond Guest House, *9 The Crescent, Bridlington, E Yorks, YO15 2NX.* Welcoming B&B looking out over the sea **Open:** All year (not Xmas)
01262 674366 J Brewer **D:** Fr £19.00–£24.00 **S:** Fr £20.00–£22.00 **Beds:** 5F 2T 3D 1S **Baths:** 2 En 2 Sh (4)

Elloughton

SE9428 *Red Hawk, Buccaneer, Half Moon*

Chat Moss, *16 Larchmont Close, Elloughton, Brough, E. Yorks, HU15 1AW.* Modern, quiet, 0.75m from Brough station, buses and shops. **Open:** All year (not Xmas/ New Year)
01482 666514 Mrs Dixon **D:** Fr £18.00–£18.50 **S:** Fr £18.00 **Beds:** 1T 1D **Baths:** 1 Sh (10) (3)

Goole

SE7423

Briarcroft Hotel, *49-51 Clifton Gardens, Goole, East Yorkshire, DN14 6AR.* Comfortable, friendly, licensed, ideally situated for touring Yorkshire. **Open:** All year
01405 763024 Mr Ramsdale **Fax: 01405 767317** *briarcrofthotel@aol.com* www.briarcroft.co.uk **D:** Fr £20.00–£24.00 **S:** Fr £26.00–£39.00 **Beds:** 2F 6D 4T 5S **Baths:** 10 Pr 6 Sh (6)

Great Driffield

TA0257

The Wold Cottage, *Wold Newton, Driffield, E Yorks, YO25 0HL.* Award-winning spacious C18th farmhouse away from roads. Ideal for Bampton cliffs and historic house. **Open:** All year
01262 470696 (also fax) Mrs Gray *woldcott@wold-newton.freeserve.co.uk* **D:** Fr £24.00–£30.00 **S:** Fr £25.00–£30.00 **Beds:** 2D 1T **Baths:** 3 En (10) **cc**

Hessle

TA0326

Redcliffe House, *Redcliffe Road, Hessle, E Yorks, HU13 0HA.* Elegant spacious rooms. Friendly service. Idyllic secluded gardens. Close Hull. **Open:** All year
01482 648655 S Skiba **D:** Fr £25.00–£30.00 **S:** Fr £30.00–£40.00 **Beds:** 2D 2T 2F 1S **Baths:** 4 En 1 Sh (6)

Hollym

TA3425

Plough Inn, *Northside Road, Hollym, Withernsea, E Yorks, HU19 2RS.* Relaxed friendly atmosphere, open coal fires, large beer garden. **Open:** All year
01964 612049 Mr Robinson **D:** Fr £16.00–£20.00 **S:** Fr £20.00 **Beds:** 1F 4T **Baths:** 3 En (20)

Hull

TA0929

Beck House, *628 Beverley High Road, Hull, HU6 7LL.* Traditional town house, B&B, fine accommodation, close to university etc. **Open:** All year
01482 445468 Mrs Aylwin **D:** Fr £19.00–£22.00 **S:** Fr £19.00–£22.00 **Beds:** 3D 2S **Baths:** 5 En (4) **cc**

Marlborough Hotel, *232 Spring Bank, Hull, HU3 1LU.* Family run. Near to city centre. Victorian building. **Open:** All year
01482 224479 (also fax) Mr Norman **D:** Fr £18.00 **S:** Fr £18.00 **Beds:** 3F 7T 3D 14S **Baths:** 5 Sh

Anry Hotel, *68 Louis Street, Spring Bank, Hull, HU3 1LZ.* Good quality accommodation. Ideally located for the city centre. **Open:** All year
01482 326292 **D:** Fr £19.00 **S:** Fr £34.00 **Beds:** 3T 8S **Baths:** 2 En 3 Sh (8)

The Earlsmere Hotel, *76-78 Sunnybank, Hull, HU3 1LQ.* Comfortable, quiet home. One mile from city centre. **Open:** All year **Grades:** AA 3 Diamond, RAC 3 Diamond
01482 41977 *su@earlsmerehotel.karro.co.uk* **D:** Fr £17.00–£20.00 **S:** Fr £19.00–£30.00 **Beds:** 4F 4T 7D 3S **Baths:** 7 En 1 Sh **cc**

Roseberry Guest House, *86 Marlborough Avenue, Hull, HU5 3JT.* Warm, clean Victorian B&B on tree-lined avenue. **Open:** All year
01482 445256 **D:** Fr £17.00–£21.00 **S:** Fr £19.00–£30.00 **Beds:** 1F 1T 2D 2S **Baths:** 1 En 3 Pr 1 Sh **cc**

Allandra Hotel, *5 Park Avenue, Hull, HU5 3EN.* Charming Victorian town house hotel, family run, close all amenities, convenient universities/town centre. **Open:** All year
01482 493349 **Fax: 01482 492680** **D:** Fr £19.50 **S:** Fr £26.00 **Beds:** 2F 1T 7D **Baths:** 10 En (5) **cc**

Langtoft

TA0166

The Ship Inn, *Scarborough Road, Langtoft, Driffield, East Yorks, YO25 3TH.* C17th coaching inn, guest rooms overlooking rolling Wolds countryside. **Open:** All year
01377 267243 **D:** Fr £20.00–£22.00 **S:** Fr £29.50–£31.50 **Beds:** 2T 2D 2S **cc**

National Grid References given are for villages, towns and cities – not for individual houses

Leven

TA1144

New Inn, *44 South Street, Leven, Beverley, HU17 5NZ.* Old Georgian coaching house adjacent to rural canal - fishing allowed. **Open:** All year
01964 542223 P T Oliver **D:** Fr £17.50 **S:** Fr £23.00 **Beds:** 1F 3D 1T 1S **Baths:** 6 En (50) **cc**

Little Weighton

SE9933

Rosedale B&b, *9 Skidby Road, Little Weighton, Cottingham, E Yorks, HU20 3UY.* Bungalow accommodation set in large beautiful garden at the foot of the Yorkshire Wolds. **Open:** All year
01482 846074 I Wilkinson **D:** Fr £15.00 **S:** Fr £20.00 **Beds:** 1F 2T **Baths:** 1 En 1 Sh (6)

Londesborough

SE8645

Towthorpe Grange, *Towthorpe, Market Weighton, York, YO43 3LB.* On Wolds Way Link Route and near Cycle Route 66. **Open:** All year (not Xmas/New Year) **Grades:** ETC 2 Diamond
01430 873814 Mrs Rowlands **D:** Fr £17.00 **S:** Fr £17.00 **Beds:** 1T 1D 1S **Baths:** 2 Sh (6) (2)

Millington

SE8351

Laburnum Cottage, *Millington, York, YO42 1TX.* Ensuite bedrooms, guest lounge, picturesque village, touring/walking, pub near. **Open:** Mar to Oct
01759 303055 Mrs Dykes *roger&maureen@labcott.fslife.co.uk* **D:** Fr £20.00–£24.00 **S:** Fr £22.00–£24.00 **Beds:** 1F 1D **Baths:** 2 En (2)

North Ferriby

SE9826

B&B at 103, *103 Ferriby High Road, North Ferriby, East Yorks, HU14 3LA.* Comfortable house, large garden, overlooking river near Humber Bridge and Hull. **Open:** All year **Grades:** ETC 3 Diamond
01482 633637 & 07808 387651 (M) Mrs Simpson *info@bnb103.co.uk* www.bnb103.co.uk **D:** Fr £15.00 **S:** Fr £15.00 **Beds:** 1D 1T 1S **Baths:** 1 Sh (7) (2)

North Newbald

SE9136

The Gnu Inn, *The Green, North Newbald, York, YO43 4SA.* Traditional country inn in picturesque surroundings; good for walkers and cyclists. **Open:** All year
01430 827799 **D:** Fr £20.00–£30.00 **S:** Fr £20.00–£30.00 **Beds:** 1F 1D 1T **Baths:** 3 En (25) cc

Rowley

SE9832

Rowley Manor Hotel, *Rowley, Little Weighton, Cottingham, E. Yorks, HU20 3XR.* Situated in 35 acres of gardens & lawns, farmland. **Open:** All year
01482 848248 **Fax: 01482 849900** *info@rowleymanir.com* **D:** Fr £55.00–£95.00 **S:** Fr £55.00–£70.00 **Beds:** 3T 10D 3S **Baths:** 16 En (50) cc

Rudston

TA0966

Bosville Arms, *High Street, Rudston, Driffield, East Yorkshire, YO25 4UB.* Quality country retreat in historic Yorkshire village near east coast. **Open:** All year
01262 420259 (also fax) *hogan@bosville.freeserve.co.uk* www.bosville.freeserve.co.uk **D:** Fr £24.95–£28.75 **S:** Fr £29.95–£34.95 **Beds:** 3T 3D (40) cc

BEDROOMS
D = Double
T = Twin
S = Single
F = Family

Shiptonthorpe

SE8543

Robeanne House Farm & Stables, *Driffield Lane, Shiptonthorpe, York, YO43 3PW.* Comfortable family house, large spacious rooms, countryside views. **Open:** All year
Grades: AA 3 Diamond
01430 873312 (also fax) Mrs Wilson *robert@robeannefreeserve.co.uk* **D:** Fr £20.00–£25.00 **S:** Fr £20.00–£25.00 **Beds:** 3F 2D 1T **Baths:** 6 En (10) cc

South Cave

SE9231

Rudstone Walk, *South Cave, Nr Beverley, Brough, E. Yorks, HU15 2AH.* Superb courtyard ensuite rooms. Renowned farmhouse breakfasts. Telephone/e-mail for brochure. **Open:** All year (not Xmas/New Year) **Grades:** ETC 4 Diamond, AA 4 Diamond, RAC 4 Diamond
01430 422230 Mrs Greenwood **Fax: 01430 424552** *office@rudstone-walk.co.uk* www.rudstone-walk.co.uk **D:** Fr £27.50–£29.50 **S:** Fr £40.00–£47.00 **Beds:** 2F 5D 7S **Baths:** 14 En 3 Sh cc

Stamford Bridge

SE7155

High Catton Grange, *Stamford Bridge, York, YO41 1EP.* A warm welcome awaits you at this C18th farmhouse in peaceful rural location. **Open:** All year (not Xmas/New Year)
01759 371374 (also fax) Ms Foster **D:** Fr £19.00–£23.00 **S:** Fr £28.00–£35.00 **Beds:** 1F 1D **Baths:** 1 En 1 Pr (6)

Thwing

TA0569 *Rampant Horse, Boswell Arms, Burton Arms*

Garth House, *Main Street, Thwing, Driffield, E Yorks, YO25 3DY.* Thwing is a quiet Yorkshire Wolds village off the beaten track. We offer a warm welcome, privacy and the choice to relax or explore the coast, Yorkshire Wolds, North York Moors and places of historic interest at your own pace. **Open:** All year (not Xmas)
01262 470843 (also fax) Mr Dell *plasdell@thwing.freeserve.co.uk.* **D:** Fr £20.00 **S:** Fr £20.00 **Beds:** 2D **Baths:** 1 En 1 Pr (1)

Wilberfoss

SE7351

Cuckoo Nest Farm, *Wilberfoss, York, YO41 5NL.* Red brick traditional house, Park and Ride nearby for York. **Open:** All year (not Xmas)
01759 380365 J M Liversidge **D:** Fr £20.00–£25.00 **S:** Fr £23.00 **Beds:** 1T 1D **Baths:** 1 Pr

Withernsea

TA3427

Vista Mar Guest House, *48 Promenade, Withernsea, E. Yorks, HU19 2DW.* Seafront location, residents lounge, central for all amenities. **Open:** All year
01964 612858 Mr & Mrs Hirst **D:** Fr £13.00–£16.00 **S:** Fr £15.00–£20.00 **Beds:** 1F 1D 2T 3S **Baths:** 2 En 2 Sh

Please respect a B&B's wishes regarding children, animals and smoking

North Yorkshire

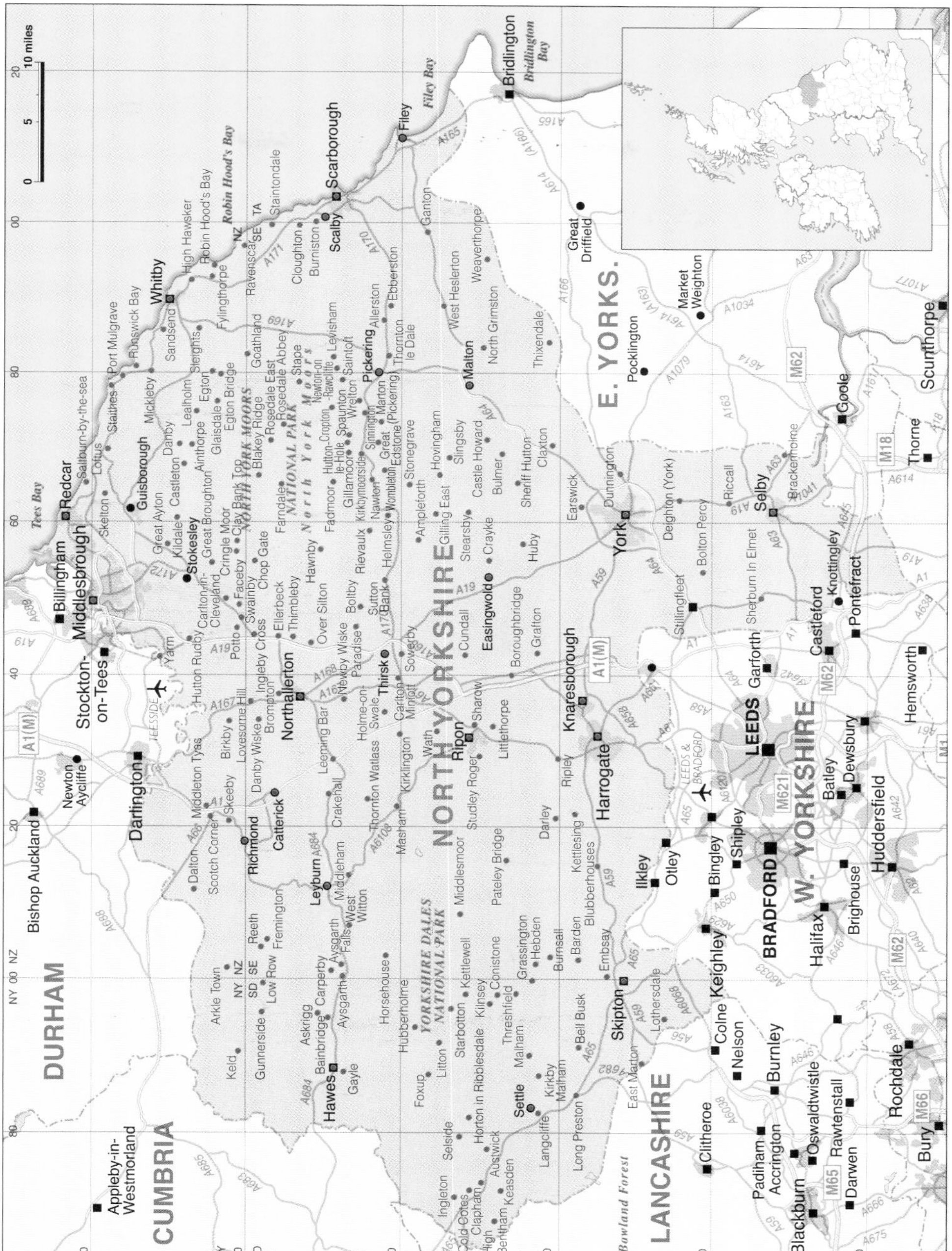

B&B owners may vary rates – be sure to check when booking

Ainthorpe

NZ7008

Rowantree Farm, *Ainthorpe, Danby, Whitby, N. Yorks, YO21 2LE.* Situated in the heart of the North York Moors, with panoramic moorland views. **Open:** All year (not Xmas/New Year) **Grades:** ETC 3 Diamond
01287 660396 Mrs Tindall *krbsatindall@aol.com* **D:** Fr £17.00–£18.00 **S:** Fr £17.00–£18.00 **Beds:** 1F 1T **Baths:** 2 Pr P (4) TV V

Ampleforth

SE5878 *White Horse, White Swan*

Carr House Farm, *Shallowdale, Ampleforth, York, YO62 4ED.* Idyllic C16th farmhouse, romantic 4-poster bedrooms, internationally recommended, Heartbeat countryside. **Open:** All year (not Xmas)
01347 868526 & 07977 113197 (M) Mrs Lupton *ampleforth@hotmail.com* www.guestaccom.co.uk/912.htm **D:** Fr £20.00 **S:** Fr £20.00 **Beds:** 3D **Baths:** 3 En (7) P (5) TV V

Arkle Town

NZ0002

The Ghyll, *Arkle Town, Arkengarthdale, Richmond, DL11 6EU.* Perfectly situated for exploring Yorkshire Dales. Warm welcome, farmhouse breakfast. **Open:** All year (not Xmas) **Grades:** ETC 3 Diamond
01748 884353 Mr & Mrs Good **Fax: 01748 884015** *bookings@theghyll.co.uk* www.theghyll.co.uk **D:** Fr £20.00 **S:** Fr £20.00–£30.00 **Beds:** 1T 2D **Baths:** 3 En P (6) TV V **cc**

Askrigg

SD9491 *King's Arms, The Crown*

Milton House, *Askrigg, Leyburn, N. Yorks, DL8 3HJ.* Lovely old Dales family home situated in Askrigg village in beautiful countryside. Warm welcome. **Open:** All year (not Xmas)
01969 650217 Mrs Percival **D:** Fr £20.00–£22.00 **S:** Fr £25.00–£30.00 **Beds:** 3D **Baths:** 3 En (10) P (3) TV V

The Apothecary's House, *Market Place, Askrigg, Leyburn, DL8 3HT.* **Open:** All year (not Xmas/New Year) **Grades:** ETC 4 Diamond, Silver
01969 650626 D: Fr £23.00–£25.00 **S:** Fr £30.00–£32.00 **Beds:** 1T 2D **Baths:** 2 En 1 Pr P (3) TV V
Charming Georgian house built around 1756 by James Lightfoot, the apothecary. Unlike him, we don't claim to cure your ills, but we can provide comfortable , individually styled accommodation ensuring you get the most from your stay in the Yorkshire Dales.

Austwick

SD7668

Dalesbridge House, *Austwick, Settle, N Yorks, LA2 8AZ.* Friendly relaxing ensuite B&B. Outstanding views and a great atmosphere. **Open:** All year
015242 51021 Mr Beavan **Fax: 015242 51051** *info@dalesbridge.co.uk* www.dalesbridge.co.uk **D:** Fr £25.00 **S:** Fr £29.00 **Beds:** 1F 2T 2D 1S **Baths:** 4 En 1 Sh P (60) TV V **cc**

Aysgarth

SE0088 *George & Dragon, Fox and Hound*

Cornlee, *Aysgarth, Leyburn, North Yorks, DL8 3AE.* Yorkshire Dales B&B overlooking village green. **Open:** All year
01969 663779 (also fax) *cornlee@tesco.net* www.cornlee.co.uk **D:** Fr £18.00–£22.00 **S:** Fr £25.00 **Beds:** 1T 2D **Baths:** 2 En 1 Pr (10) TV V

RATES
D = Price range per person sharing in a double or twin room
S = Price range for a single room

Field House, *Aysgarth, Leyburn, DL8 3AB.* **Open:** All year (not Xmas/New Year) **Grades:** ETC 4 Diamond
01969 663556 Mr & Mrs Evans *ros@voidalimage.com* www.wensleydale.org **D:** Fr £25.00 **S:** Fr £25.00 **Beds:** 2D **Baths:** 1 En 1 Pr P (4) TV V
Secluded Georgian style house away from the main road and close to Aysgarth Falls. Quiet and peaceful with beautiful views. Excellent base for walking, touring or just unwinding. Come and stay - where the magic of the Dales is on the doorstep.

Aysgarth Falls

SE0188

Wensleydale Farmhouse, *Aysgarth Falls, Leyburn, N. Yorks, DL8 3SR.* Local to Aysgath Falls. Superb views, friendly, comfortable. Walkers welcome. **Open:** All year (not Xmas) **Grades:** ETC 3 Diamond
01969 663534 (also fax) Mr & Mrs Wykes *wykesarego@aol.com* **D:** Fr £22.00–£24.00 **S:** Fr £25.00–£27.00 **Beds:** 2D 1T **Baths:** 3 En (6) P (4) TV

Barden (Skipton)

SE0557

Little Gate Farm, *Drebley, Barden, Skipton, N Yorks, BD23 6AU.* Beautiful Grade I Listed C15th Dales farmhouse; all rooms look down to River Wharfe. **Open:** Easter to Nov
01756 720200 D: Fr £19.00 **S:** Fr £19.00 **Beds:** 1F 1D 1T **Baths:** 1 Pr 1 Sh P TV V

Howgill Lodge, *Barden, Skipton, N. Yorks, BD23 6DJ.* Uninterrupted views over beautiful Wharfedale. Once experienced, you will return. **Open:** All year (not Xmas) **Grades:** ETC 5 Star
01756 720655 Mrs Foster *info@howgill-lodge.co.uk* www.howgill-lodge.co.uk **D:** Fr £30.00 **S:** Fr £35.00 **Beds:** 1F 2D 1T **Baths:** 4 En P (10) TV V **cc**

Planning a longer stay? Always ask for any special rates

Bedale
SE2688

Green Dragon, *16 Market Place, Bedale, N Yorks, DL8 1EQ.* Good quality accommodation close to Yorkshire Dales. Golf course nearby. **Open:** All year (not Xmas/New Year)
01677 425246 Mr Wanless **D:** Fr £22.50–£25.00 **S:** Fr £30.00 **Beds:** 2T 2D 2S **Baths:** 6 En (1) cc

Waggon And Horses, *20 Market Place, Bedale, N. Yorks, DL8 1EQ.* Traditional cosy pub c1680 in attractive market town, selection of real ales, large bedrooms. **Open:** All year
01677 422747 Mr Young **D:** Fr £22.50–£25.00 **S:** Fr £25.00–£30.00 **Beds:** 3F **Baths:** 3 En (10)

Bell Busk
SD9056

Tudor House, *Bell Busk, Skipton, N Yorks, BD23 4DT.* Formerly a Victorian railway station retaining its character and charm yet with modern amenities. **Open:** Feb to Dec
01729 830301 (also fax) Mr Hitchen *bellbusk.hitch@virgin.net* www.tudorbellbusk.co.uk **D:** Fr £25.00 **S:** Fr £21.00–£35.00 **Beds:** 1T 3D 1S **Baths:** 4 En 1 Sh (10) cc

Birkby
NZ3202 *Cavalry Arms, Black Bull*

Woods End, *46 Inglewood Avenue, Birkby, Huddersfield, West Yorkshire, HD2 2DS.* Easy access to the Dales and West Yorkshire's commercial centres. **Open:** All year
01484 513580 & 07710 691151 (M) Ms Smith-Moorhouse *smithmoorehouse@ntlworld.com* **D:** Fr £25.00 **S:** Fr £25.00 **Beds:** 1D 1S **Baths:** 1 Pr 1 Sh

Blakey Ridge
SE6897

The Lion Inn, *Blakey Ridge, Kirkbymoorside, York, YO62 6LQ.* C16th family run freehouse. Highest point of North Yorkshire Moors. **Open:** All year
Grades: ETC 3 Diamond
01751 417320 Mr Croosland *dkc@lionblakey.freeserve.co.uk* www.lionblakey.co.uk **D:** Fr £17.50–£32.00 **S:** Fr £17.50–£36.50 **Beds:** 3F 6D 1T **Baths:** 8 Pr 2 Sh (150)

Blubberhouses
SE1655

Scaife Hall Farm, *Blubberhouses, Otley, N. Yorks, LS21 2PL.* Working farm in picturesque rural location. Ideal base for touring/walking. **Open:** All year (not Xmas) **Grades:** ETC 4 Diamond, Silver
01943 880354 Mrs Ryder *christine.a.ryder@btinternet.com* www.yorkshirebandb.com **D:** Fr £24.00–£27.00 **S:** Fr £35.00 **Beds:** 2D 1T **Baths:** 3 En

Boltby
SE4986

Town Pasture Farm, *Boltby, Thirsk, N. Yorks, YO7 2DY.* Comfortable farmhouse in beautiful village, central for Yorkshire Dales. **Open:** All year (not Xmas)
Grades: ETC 3 Diamond
01845 537298 Mrs Fountain **D:** Fr £19.50–£22.00 **S:** Fr £20.00–£23.00 **Beds:** 1F 1T **Baths:** 2 En (3)

Low Paradise Farm, *Boltby, Thirsk, N. Yorks, YO7 2HS.* Warm welcome. Hill walking, cycling and Herriot Museum nearby. **Open:** Mar to Nov
01845 537253 Mrs Todd **D:** Fr £17.00–£18.00 **S:** Fr £20.00 **Beds:** 1D 2T **Baths:** 1 Sh (6) (7)

Willow Tree Cottage, *Boltby, Thirsk, North Yorkshire, YO7 2DY.* Large luxurious room with kitchenette. Quiet hillside village, spectacular views. **Open:** All year (not Xmas) **Grades:** ETC 4 Diamond
01845 537406 S C E Townsend **Fax: 01845 537073** *townsend.sce@virgin.net* **D:** Fr £25.00–£30.00 **S:** Fr £30.00–£35.00 **Beds:** 1F **Baths:** 1 En (5) (2)

Bolton Percy
SE5341

Beckside House, *Main Street, Bolton Percy, York, YO23 7AQ.* Self contained ground floor accommodation in very peaceful village near York. **Open:** All year (not Xmas)
01904 744246 Mrs Rhodes *peter.rhodes@tesco.net* **D:** Fr £17.50 **S:** Fr £20.00 **Beds:** 1D **Baths:** 1 En (1)

Boroughbridge
SE3966 *Punch Bowl*

Heaton House, *York Road, Boroughbridge, York, YO51 9HE.* Elegant Georgian farmhouse - landscaped gardens. **Open:** All year (not Xmas/New Year)
01423 323777 Mr & Mrs Rhodes www.heatonhouse.co.uk **D:** Fr £45.00 **S:** Fr £30.00 **Beds:** 1F 1T 2D **Baths:** 1 En 2 Pr 1 Sh (12) (20)

Primrose Cottage, *Marton-cum-Grafton, York, North Yorkshire, YO51 9QJ.* Warm hospitality in country cottage in picturesque village 1 mile east of A1(M). **Open:** All year
Grades: ETC 4 Diamond
01423 322835 & 01423 322711 P M Styan **Fax: 01423 322835 & 01423 323985** *primrosecottage@btinternet.com* www.primrosecottagegrafton.co.uk **D:** Fr £20.00 **S:** Fr £27.50 **Beds:** 2T 1D **Baths:** 1 Pr 1 Sh (8)

Brackenholme
SE7030

Hagthorpe House, *Selby Road, Brackenholme, Selby, N. Yorks, YO8 6EL.* Beautiful country house, large garden, tennis, golf, fishing nearby. **Open:** All year (not Xmas)
01757 638867 Mrs Jackson *hagthorpe@supanet.com* **D:** Fr £17.00–£20.00 **S:** Fr £18.00–£22.00 **Beds:** 1D 1T **Baths:** 1 Sh (3)

Brawby
SE7378 *Golden Lion*

Brawby Grange, *Brawby, Malton, N. Yorks, YO17 6PZ.* Comfortable farmhouse quiet location, central heating, wash basins all rooms, TV in lounge. **Open:** All year (not Xmas/New Year)
01653 668245 N Fairweather **D:** Fr £17.00–£18.00 **Beds:** 1T 2D **Baths:** 1 Pr

Brompton
SE3796 *Green Tree, Village Inn*

Hallikeld House, *Brompton, Northallerton, N. Yorks, DL6 2UE.* Comfortable country setting. **Open:** Easter to Nov
01609 773613 Mrs Saxby **Fax: 01607 770262** **D:** Fr £16.00–£18.00 **S:** Fr £16.00–£18.00 (2)

Bulmer
SE6967

Lower Barn, *Bulmer, Castle Howard, York, YO60 7ES.* 200 year old converted barn. Recommended by Which? magazine and B&B guide. **Open:** All year (not Xmas/New Year)
01653 618575 (also fax) Mrs Nolan *isabelhall@lowerbarn.fsnet.co.uk* www.lowerbarn.fsnet.co.uk **D:** Fr £18.00–£20.00 **Beds:** 1T 1D **Baths:** 2 Sh (5)

Burniston

TA0192

Harmony Country Lodge, *Limestone Road, Burniston, Scarborough, N Yorks, YO13 0DG.* Octagonal peaceful retreat with superb sea views and 360 degree panorama. Aromatherapy massage available. **Open:** All year
0800 2985841 Mr & Mrs Hewitt *tony@harmonylodge.net* www.harmonylodge.net
D: Fr £22.50–£30.00 **S:** Fr £22.50–£32.50
Beds: 1F 5D 1T 1S **Baths:** 5 En 3 Sh (7) (12)

Burnsall

SE0361

Holly Tree Farm, *Thorpe, Burnsall, Skipton, N. Yorks, BD23 6BJ.* Relax in a quiet, homely Dales sheep farm. **Open:** All year (not Xmas)
01756 720604 A Hall *hollytreefarm@amserve.net*
D: Fr £18.00–£20.00 **S:** Fr £18.00–£20.00
Beds: 1D 1S **Baths:** 1 Sh (5) (2)

Burnsall Manor House Hotel, *Burnsall, Skipton, N. Yorks, BD23 6BW.* Comfortable, friendly, relaxed. Good food. Ideal walking and cycling base. **Open:** All year **Grades:** AA 3 Diamond
01756 720231 (also fax) Mr Lodge *joe@manorhouseuk.co.uk* manorhouseuk.co.uk
D: Fr £24.50–£28.50 **S:** Fr £24.50–£28.50
Beds: 5D 3T **Baths:** 5 En 1 Pr 2 Sh (9)

Carlton Miniott

SE3981

Carlton House Farm, *Carlton Miniott, Thirsk, N. Yorks, YO7 4NJ.* Warm Yorkshire welcome awaits in comfortable home. Lovely gardens and lanes to walk. **Open:** All year
01845 524139 Mrs Lee **D:** Fr £15.00–£20.00
S: Fr £15.00 **Beds:** 2D **Baths:** 1 Sh (10) (4)

Grove Dene, *Carlton Miniott, Thirsk, N. Yorks, YO7 4NJ.* Very homely bungalow 2 miles west of Thirsk, friendly B&B.
Open: All year
01845 524257 Mrs Corner **D:** Fr £16.00 **S:** Fr £20.00 **Beds:** 1D **Baths:** 1 Sh (3)

Carlton-in-Coverdale

SE0684

Abbots Thorn, *Carlton-in-Coverdale, Leyburn, N. Yorks, DL8 4AY.* **Open:** Jan to Dec
Grades: ETC 4 Diamond
01969 640620 Mrs Lashmar *abbots.thorn@virgin.net* www.abbotsthorn.co.uk **D:** Fr £20.00–£27.00 **S:** Fr £25.00–£40.00 **Beds:** 2D 1T **Baths:** 2 En 1 Pr (12)
Relax and unwind at our comfortable traditional Yorkshire Dales home. Oak-beamed guest lounge with woodburner for those chilly evenings. Indulge yourself in our fabulous dinners. Superb scenery, terrific touring, wonderful walking. All bedrooms have beautiful views over glorious Coverdale.

Carperby

SE0089

Cross House, *Carperby, Leyburn, N Yorks, DL8 4DQ.* Modernised farmhouse, near Aysgarth Falls, excellent walking centre. Quiet. **Open:** All year (not Xmas/New Year)
Grades: ETC 3 Diamond
01969 663457 Mrs Mason **D:** Fr £16.00–£20.00 **S:** Fr £16.00–£20.00 **Beds:** 1T 1D
Baths: 1 En 1 Pr

Castle Howard

SE7170

Lower Barn, *Bulmer, Castle Howard, York, YO60 7ES.* 200 year old converted barn. Recommended by Which? magazine and B&B guide. **Open:** All year (not Xmas/New Year)
01653 618575 (also fax) Mrs Nolan *isabelhall@lowerbarn.fsnet.co.uk* www.lowerbarn.fsnet.co.uk **D:** Fr £18.00–£20.00 **Beds:** 1T 1D **Baths:** 2 Sh (5)

High Gaterley Farm, *Castle Howard, York, YO60 7HT.* Within the parkland of the estate with magnificent views over the Howardian Hills. **Open:** All year **Grades:** ETC 4 Diamond
01653 694636 (also fax) Mrs Turner *relax@highgaterley.com* www.highgaterley.com **D:** Fr £21.00–£27.50 **S:** Fr £35.00 **Beds:** 2D 1T
Baths: 1 En 2 Sh (10)

Castleton

NZ6808

Greystones Bed & Breakfast, *30 High Street, Castleton, Whitby, N. Yorks, YO21 2DA.* Betwixt sea and moors, Greystones makes the perfect resting place. **Open:** All year
Grades: ETC 3 Diamond
01287 660744 D Wedgwood *thewedgwood@aol.com* **D:** Fr £17.00 **S:** Fr £17.00 **Beds:** 3D
Baths: 1 Pr 1 Sh

Catterick

SE2497

Rose Cottage Guest House, *26 High Street, Catterick, Richmond, N. Yorks, DL10 7LJ.* Small cosy stone-built guest house, midway London-Edinburgh. **Open:** All year (not Xmas)
01748 811164 Mrs Archer **D:** Fr £19.50–£22.50 **S:** Fr £24.00–£29.00 **Beds:** 1D 2T 1S
Baths: 2 En 1 Sh (4)

Chop Gate

SE5599

Hill End Farm, *Chop Gate, Middlesbrough, TS9 7JR.* Beautiful views down the valley of Bilsdale, midway between Helmsley and Stokesley.
Open: Easter to Nov
01439 798278 Mrs Johnson **D:** Fr £21.00 **S:** Fr £25.00 **Beds:** 1F 1T **Baths:** 2 En (5) (3)

Clapham

SD7469

Arbutus Guest House, *Riverside, Clapham, Lancaster, LA2 8DS.* Situated in heart of village, overlooking river. Excellent food and parking. **Open:** All year
015242 51240 Mrs Cass **Fax: 015242 51197** *info@arbutus.co.uk* www.arbutus.co.uk **D:** Fr £20.00–£26.00 **S:** Fr £20.00–£36.00 **Beds:** 2F 1D 2T 1S **Baths:** 5 En 1 Pr (6)

Claxton

SE6960

Claxton Hall Cottage, *Malton Road, Claxton, York, YO60 7RE.* Peaceful cottage, beams and log fires. Home baked cake on arrival. **Open:** All year
01904 468697 (also fax) Mrs Brough *claxcott@aol.com* members.aol.com/claxcott
D: Fr £20.00–£27.50 **S:** Fr £20.00–£27.50
Beds: 1T 2D **Baths:** 1 En 2 Sh (10) **cc**

B&B owners may vary rates – be sure to check when booking

Clay Bank Top

NZ5701

Maltkiln House, *Clay Bank Top, Bilsdale, Middlesbrough, TS9 7HZ.* Warm welcome. Home cooking. Wonderful views. Licensed. Convenient footpaths/bridleways. **Open:** All year (not Xmas/New Year)
01642 778216 (also fax) G D Broad *stay@maltkiln.co.uk* www.maltkiln.co.uk **D:** Fr £18.50–£22.00 **S:** Fr £20.00–£25.00 **Beds:** 1T 1D 1S **Baths:** 1 En 1 Sh (10) (2) cc

Cloughton

TA0094

Gowland Farm, *Gowland Lane, Cloughton, Scarborough, N. Yorks, YO13 0DU.* Warm, friendly, peaceful, beautiful views, quiet, convenient Whitby/Scarborough/coast. **Open:** Easter to Sept
01723 870924 Mr Martin www.gowlandfarm.co.uk **D:** Fr £16.50–£18.00 **S:** Fr £16.50–£18.00 **Beds:** 1D 1T 1S **Baths:** 1 Sh (3) (6)

Cold Cotes

SD7171 *Goat Gap*

Moor View, *Cold Cotes, Clapham, N Yorks, LA2 8JA.* Beautiful detached home peacefully situated just off the A65 at the foot of Ingleborough in the Dales National Park. Stunning views (and sunsets if you're lucky!) Ideally situated for walking, cycling, touring, or just simply relaxing. A warm welcome awaits. **Open:** All year (not Xmas)
015242 42085 Mrs Woodhead *Garynjenny@hotmail.com* **D:** Fr £25.00 **S:** Fr £30.00 **Beds:** 1T 1D **Baths:** 1 En 1 Pr (2)

Conistone

SD9867 *Tennants Arms*

Ebony House, *Conistone, Skipton, N Yorks, BD23 5HS.* Peaceful, picturesque hamlet. Excellent walking. Spectacular views. **Open:** Mar to Oct
01756 753139 Mrs Robinson **D:** Fr £22.00–£25.00 **S:** Fr £30.00 **Beds:** 2D **Baths:** 2 En (4)

Crakehall

SE2489

Waterside, *Glenaire, Great Crakehall, Bedale, N. Yorks, DL8 1HS.* Country house in 1-acre garden, trout stream. Bedrooms overlook garden to water's edge. **Open:** All year (not Xmas)
01677 422908 Mrs Smith **Fax: 01677 422280 D:** Fr £19.00–£22.00 **S:** Fr £25.00 **Beds:** 1D 2T **Baths:** 2 En 1 Pr (5) (4)

Crayke

SE5670

The Hermitage, *Crayke, York, YO61 4TB.* Stone-built house set in large garden, located on edge of small pretty village. **Open:** All year
01347 821635 Mr Moverley **D:** Fr £26.00–£27.00 **S:** Fr £26.00–£27.00 **Beds:** 1D 2T **Baths:** 1 En 1 Sh (4)

Cringle Moor

NZ5503

Beakhills Farm, *Cold Moor, Cringle Moor, Chop Gate, Stokesley, Middlesbrough, TS9 7JJ.* Cosy farmhouse on working farm. **Open:** All year
01642 778371 Mrs Cook **D:** Fr £16.00 **S:** Fr £16.00 **Beds:** 1F 1T 1D

Cropton

SE7589

High Farm, *Cropton, Pickering, N. Yorks, YO18 8HL.* **Open:** All year
01751 417461 Mrs Feaster **Fax: 01751 417807** *highfarmcropton@aol.com* www.hhml.com/bb/highfarmcropton.htm **D:** Fr £23.00 **S:** Fr £28.00 **Beds:** 3D **Baths:** 3 En (10) (10) cc
Relax and unwind in the homely atmosphere of this lovely Victorian farmhouse, situated on edge of quiet village and offering fine views over open countryside. Beautiful two acre garden, home-made teas and private parking. Stroll to local inn and brewery.

Burr Bank Cottage, *Cropton, Pickering, N. Yorks, YO18 8HL.* Walks, rides, drives to coast, Moors, Dales, Wolds, York less than 45 mins away. **Open:** All year
01751 417777 Ms Richardson **Fax: 01751 417789** *bandb@burrbank.com* www.burrbank.com **D:** Fr £27.00 **S:** Fr £27.00 **Beds:** 1D 1T **Baths:** 2 En (12) (10)

BATHROOMS
En = Ensuite
Pr = Private
Sh = Shared

Cundall

SE4272 *Farmers Inn, Angel Inn*

Lodge Farm, *Cundall, York, YO61 2RN.* Warm welcome. Peaceful, quiet, panoramic views, explore North Yorkshire. **Open:** Mar to Dec
01423 360203 (also fax) Mrs Barker **D:** Fr £20.00–£25.00 **S:** Fr £30.00–£35.00 **Beds:** 1F 1T 1D 1S **Baths:** 1 En 1 Pr (6)

Dalton (Richmond)

NZ1108

Holmedale, *Dalton, Richmond, N. Yorks, DL11 7HX.* Georgian House in quiet village midway Richmond and Barnard Castle. **Open:** All year (not Xmas)
01833 621236 (also fax) Mrs Brooks **D:** Fr £19.00 **S:** Fr £19.00 **Beds:** 1D 1T **Baths:** 2 En

Stonesthrow, *Dalton, Richmond, North Yorkshire, DL11 7HS.* Quiet village between Richmond and Barnard Castle. Close to Yorkshire Dales. **Open:** All year
01833 621493 & 07970 655726 (M) Mrs Lawson **D:** Fr £18.00 **S:** Fr £20.00 **Beds:** 2D **Baths:** 1 Sh (8) (3)

Broaches Farm, *Dalton, Richmond, North Yorkshire, DL11 7HW.* Idyllic situation between historic towns of Richmond and Barnard Castle. **Open:** All year (not Xmas/New Year)
01833 621369 Mrs Hutchinson **Fax: 01833 621560** *jude1@farmersweekly.net* **D:** Fr £20.00–£25.00 **S:** Fr £20.00–£25.00 **Beds:** 1F 1D **Baths:** 1 Pr 1 Sh (4)

Danby

NZ7008

Sycamore House, *Danby, Whitby, N. Yorks, YO21 2NW.* C17th farmhouse with stunning views. Ideal area for walking/touring. **Open:** All year (not Xmas)
Grades: ETC 3 Diamond
01287 660125 Mr Lowson **Fax: 01287 669122** *sycamore.danby@btinternet.com* **D:** Fr £22.50–£25.00 **S:** Fr £22.50–£25.00 **Beds:** 1F 1D 1T 1S **Baths:** 1 En 1 Sh (6)

Planning a longer stay? Always ask for any special rates

Holly Lodge Farm, *Danby Head, Danby, Whitby, N Yorks, YO21 2NW.* Beautiful views over Danby Dale near to Heartbeat and Herriot country, Whitby, York. **Open:** Easter to Oct
01287 660469 Mrs Shirley **D:** Fr £18.00–£19.00 **S:** Fr £18.00–£20.00 **Beds:** 1D 1T 1S **Baths:** 1 Pr (4)

Danby Wiske

SE3398 *White Swan*

The Manor House, *Danby Wiske, Northallerton, N. Yorks, DL7 0LZ.* C16th house built of hand-made brick. **Open:** All year (not Xmas/New Year)
01609 774662 Mrs Sanders **D:** Fr £17.00 **S:** Fr £17.00 **Beds:** 1T 1D 2S **Baths:** 2 Sh (4)

Darley

SE2059

Brimham Guest House, *Silverdale Close, Darley, Harrogate, N. Yorks, HG3 2PQ.* Family-run guest house, set in beautiful gardens. Winner of 1999 'Yorkshire In Bloom' competition. **Open:** All year (not Xmas)
01423 780948 Mrs Barker **D:** Fr £15.00 **S:** Fr £20.00 **Beds:** 2D 1T **Baths:** 3 En (1) (4)

Deighton (York)

SE6244

Rush Farm, *York Road, Deighton, York, YO19 6HQ.* **Open:** Mar to Oct **Grades:** ETC 3 Diamond
01904 728459 Mr Newsholme *david@rushfarm.fsnet.co.uk* www.rushfarm.fsnet.co.uk **D:** Fr £20.00 **S:** Fr £25.00 **Beds:** 2F 3D **Baths:** 5 En (8) cc
Family farmhouse standing in open countryside with pleasant views. Ideally situated for visiting the city of York, the moors, the Dales and coast. Quality accommodation offering family care. Situated approximately 4 miles south of York.

Grimston House, *Deighton, York, YO19 6HB.* **Open:** All year **01904 728328 Fax: 01904720093** *grimstonhouse@talk21.com* www.grimstonhouse.com **D:** Fr £48.00–£52.00 **S:** Fr £33.00–£39.00 **Beds:** 1F 1T 5D **Baths:** 5 En
Attractive spacious 1930's country house set in Deighton village, 5 miles from York centre. Ample parking, on bus route, 50 yds from local pub which supplies bar meals. Situated on main A19 York, Selby Road.

Dunnington

SE6652

Brookland House, *Hull Road, Dunnington, York, YO19 5LW.* Private detached house, country area. Wholesome breakfast, home-made preserves. **Open:** Mar to Dec
01904 489548 & 07801 496248 (M) Mrs Foster **D:** Fr £18.00–£22.00 **S:** Fr £20.00–£25.00 **Beds:** 1D 1T 1S **Baths:** 1 Sh (3)

Earswick

SE6257

Fairthorne, *356 Strenshall Road, Earswick, York, YO32 9SW.* Peaceful country setting, dormer bungalow. 3 miles from York, easy reach North York Moors. **Open:** Dec to Dec
01904 768609 (also fax) J W Harrison **D:** Fr £18.00–£20.00 **S:** Fr £25.00 **Beds:** 1F 1D **Baths:** 1 En (2)

The Lodge, *302 Strensall Rd, Earswick, York, YO32 9SW.* Comfortable Christian house in countryside, 3.5 miles north of York. **Open:** All year
01904 761387 (also fax) Mrs Edmondson *the.lodge@talk21.com* thelodgebandb.co.uk **D:** Fr £20.00 **S:** Fr £25.00 **Beds:** 1F 1D 1T **Baths:** 2 En 1 Sh (3)

Easingwold

SE5369

Garbutts Ghyll, *Thornton Hill, Easingwold, York, YO61 3PZ.* Traditional farm within own wooded valley. Period furnishings, organic cooking. **Open:** Easter to Nov
01347 868644 Mrs Glaister **Fax: 01347 868133 D:** Fr £18.00–£22.00 **S:** Fr £16.00–£18.00 **Beds:** 1T 1D **Baths:** 1 En

Yeoman's Course House, *Thornton Hill, Easingwold, York, YO61 3PY.* Set in an elevated position overlooking the beautiful Vale of York. **Open:** Easter to Oct **Grades:** ETC 3 Diamond
01347 868126 Mr & Mrs Addy **Fax: 01347 868129** *chris@yeomanscourse.fsnet.co.uk* **D:** Fr £20.00 **S:** Fr £20.00–£21.00 **Beds:** 1T 2D (12) (8)

The George, *Market Place, Easingwold, York, YO61 3AD.* Friendly inn offering warm welcome, good food, cask ales. **Open:** All year **Grades:** ETC 2 Star, AA 2 Star
01347 821698 Mr Riley **Fax: 01347 823448** *info@the-george-hotel.co.uk* www.the-george-hotel.co.uk **D:** Fr £30.00–£40.00 **S:** Fr £52.50 **Beds:** 2F 5T 8D **Baths:** 15 En (10) cc

East Marton

SD9050

Sawley House, *East Marton, Skipton, N. Yorks, BD23 3LP.* C12th farmhouse - stables, restaurant by canal on Pennine Way. **Open:** All year (not Xmas)
01282 843207 Mrs Pilling *sawleyhouse@pilling23.freeserve.co.uk* www.pilling23.freeserve.co.uk **D:** Fr £22.00 **S:** Fr £25.00 **Beds:** 1T 1D **Baths:** 2 Sh (12)

Drumlins, *Heber Drive, East Marton, Skipton, North Yorkshire, BD23 3LS.* In quiet cul-de-sac off A59. Open views, easy access Dales, Pennine Way, Skipton. **Open:** All year
01282 843521 Ms Moran www.yorkshirenet.co.uk/stayat/drumlins/index.htm **D:** Fr £22.00 **S:** Fr £26.00 **Beds:** 1F 1T 1D **Baths:** 3 En

Ebberston

SE8982

Givendale Head Farm, *Ebberston, Scarborough, N. Yorks, YO13 9PU.* Beautiful views in a quiet location. Warm welcome. Farmhouse breakfast. **Open:** All year (not Xmas/New Year) **Grades:** ETC 3 Diamond
01723 859383 Mrs Gwilliam *sue.gwillam@talk21.com* www.givendaleheadfarm.co.uk **D:** Fr £20.00–£23.00 **S:** Fr £23.00–£25.00 **Beds:** 1T 2D **Baths:** 3 En (3)

B&B owners may vary rates – be sure to check when booking

Foxholm Hotel, *Ebberston, Scarborough, N. Yorks, YO13 9NJ.* Peaceful, licensed ground floor rooms. Country inn in quiet picturesque village. **Open:** All year (not Xmas)
01723 859550 (also fax) Mrs Clyde *kay@foxholm.freeserve.co.uk* www.foxholm.freeserve.co.uk **D:** Fr £23.00–£25.00 **S:** Fr £28.00–£30.00 **Beds:** 2D 2T **Baths:** 4 En (20) cc

Egton

NZ8006

Flushing Meadow, *Egton, Whitby, N Yorks, YO21 1UA.* Superb moorland views. Convenient for Esk Valley, steam railway and Whitby. **Open:** All year (not Xmas/New Year) **Grades:** ETC 3 Diamond
01947 895395 Mrs Johnson *flushing_meadow_egton@yahoo.co.uk* **D:** Fr £17.50–£20.00 **S:** Fr £15.00–£17.50 **Beds:** 1D 1T 1S **Baths:** 1 En 1 Sh (3)

Egton Bridge

NZ8005 *Horseshoe Hotel*

Broom House, *Broom House Lane, Egton Bridge, Whitby, N Yorks, YO21 1XD.* Perfect location, accommodation, food, welcome etc. Visit website for details. **Open:** All Year (not Xmas)
01947 895279 Mr & Mrs White **Fax: 01947 895657** *welcome@broomhouseegtonbridge.freeserve.co.uk* www.egton-bridge.co.uk **D:** Fr £21.50–£23.50 **S:** Fr £26.00 **Beds:** 1F 1T 4D **Baths:** 6 En (7)

Ellerbeck

SE4397

Old Mill House, *Ellerbeck, Osmotherley, Northallerton, N. Yorks, DL6 2RY.* Delightful C17th mill set central for walking touring North Yorkshire. **Open:** Easter to Nov
01609 883466 Mrs Shepherd **D:** Fr £20.00–£25.00 **S:** Fr £20.00–£25.00 **Beds:** 1T 2D **Baths:** 1 En 1 Sh (4)

Embsay

SE0053

Bondcroft Farm, *Embsay, Skipton, N Yorks, BD23 6SF.* Sheep and beef farm, well known for training and breeding sheep dogs. **Open:** All year
01756 793371 Ms Clarkson *bondcroftfarm@bondcroftfarm.yorks.net* **D:** Fr £20.00–£22.50 **Beds:** 1T 2D **Baths:** 3 En (6) cc

Faceby

NZ4903

Four Wynds, *Whorl Hill, Faceby, Middlesbrough, TS9 7BZ.* Small holding in beautiful countryside. Located off A172 between Swainby/Faceby. **Open:** All year
01642 701315 Mr Barnfather **D:** Fr £18.00–£20.00 **S:** Fr £18.00–£20.00 **Beds:** 1F 1D 1T **Baths:** 1 En 1 Sh (8)

Fadmoor

SE6789

Mount Pleasant, *Rudland, Fadmoor, York, YO62 7JJ.* Friendly welcome. Ideal for walking, touring from moors. Brochure available. **Open:** All year (not Xmas)
01751 431579 Mary Clarke *info@mountpleasantbedandbreakfast.co.uk* www.mountpleasantbedandbreakfast.co.uk **D:** Fr £15.00–£17.00 **S:** Fr £15.00–£17.00 **Beds:** 1F 1T **Baths:** 1 Sh (4) (6)

Farndale

SE6697

Olive House Farm, *Farndale, Kirkbymoorside, York, YO60 7JY.* Homely farmhouse B&B on a working farm. Beautiful views. **Open:** Easter to Oct
01751 433207 Mrs Blacklock **D:** Fr £14.00 **Beds:** 2F **Baths:** 1 Sh (4)

Filey

TA1180

The Gables, *2a Rutland Street, Filey, N Yorks, YO14 9JB.* Characteristic Edwardian guest house. Friendly accommodation, comfortable ensuite rooms, colour TV. Central all amenities. **Open:** All year **Grades:** ETC 4 Diamond, AA 4 Diamond
01723 514750 R & K Broome *kate_gables@talk21.com* **D:** Fr £18.00–£20.00 **S:** Fr £24.00–£25.00 **Beds:** 1F 2T 2D **Baths:** 5 En

Abbots Leigh Guest House, *7 Rutland Street, Filey, N. Yorks, YO14 9JA.* Close to the beach, gardens and town centre amenities. **Open:** All year
01723 513334 B E Illinworth and Miss C. Cullen **D:** Fr £19.00–£20.00 **S:** Fr £24.00–£25.00 **Beds:** 1F 2T 3D **Baths:** 6 En (3) (4) cc

Foxup

SD8676

Bridge Farm, *Foxup, Arncliffe, Skipton, N. Yorks, BD23 5QP.* Working Dales farm situated in Littondale (the forgotten valley). **Open:** Easter to Oct
01756 770249 Mrs Lund **D:** Fr £15.00 **S:** Fr £18.00 **Beds:** 1T 2D **Baths:** 1 Sh (4)

Fremington

SE0499

Broadlands, *Fremington, Richmond, DL11 6AW.* Peaceful village setting 5 mins from Reeth, spectacular views, comfortable accommodation. **Open:** All year
01748 884297 (also fax) Mrs Rudez **D:** Fr £19.00 **S:** Fr £27.00 **Beds:** 1D 1T 1S **Baths:** 1 Sh (12) (4)

Fylingthorpe

NZ9404

South View, *Sledgates, Fylingthorpe, Robin Hood's Bay, Whitby, N. Yorks, YO22 4TZ.* Comfortable detached house. Sea and country views. Ideal touring/walking area. **Open:** Easter to Oct
01947 880025 Mrs Reynolds **D:** Fr £17.00–£19.00 **Beds:** 2D **Baths:** 1 Sh (5) (2)

Red House, *Thorpe Lane, Fylingthorpe, Whitby, North Yorkshire, YO22 4TH.* Large Victorian house and garden. Panelled staircase and gallery. Beautiful views. **Open:** Easter to Oct
01947 880079 Mrs Collinson **D:** Fr £18.00–£22.50 **S:** Fr £20.00–£25.00 **Beds:** 1T 2D **Baths:** 1 En 1 Sh (3)

Low Farm, *Fylingthorpe, Whitby, N Yorks, YO22 4QF.* Imposing Georgian farmhouse built from local stone, set in beautiful countryside on working farm. **Open:** May to Nov
01947 880366 (also fax) Mrs Hodgson **D:** Fr £18.00–£21.00 **Beds:** 1F **Baths:** 1 En (1)

Ganton

SE9977

The Ganton Greyhound, *Main Street, Ganton, Scarborough, N Yorks, YO12 4NX.* Family and country inn/hotel, 9 miles from coast. **Open:** All year (not Xmas)
01944 710116 T Bennet **Fax: 01944 710738** *gantongreyhound@supanet.com* **D:** Fr £27.50 **S:** Fr £45.00 **Beds:** 6F 4D 6T 2S **Baths:** 16 En (20) cc

National Grid References given are for villages, towns and cities – not for individual houses

Please respect a B&B's wishes regarding children, animals and smoking

Gayle

SD8789

Dalesview, *East Marry, Gayle, Hawes, N. Yorks,* DL8 3RZ. Modern, comfortable, bungalow. Ideal for touring, cycling and walking. **Open:** Easter to Nov
01969 667397 Mrs McGregor **D:** Fr £20.00 **S:** Fr £25.00 **Beds:** 1D 1T 1S **Baths:** 3 En (2)

East House, *Gayle, Hawes, N. Yorks,* DL8 3RZ. Delightful house. Superb views, ideal centre for touring the Dales.
Open: Feb to Nov **Grades:** ETC 4 Diamond
01969 667405 & 07866 108148 (M) Mrs Ward *lornaward@lineone.net* dalesaccommodation.com/easthouse **D:** Fr £21.00–£24.00 **S:** Fr £21.00 **Beds:** 1T 1D 1S **Baths:** 2 En 1 Pr

Gillamoor

SE6889

The Royal Oak Inn, *Gillamoor, Kirkbymoorside, York,* YO62 6HX. C17th Inn, excellent accommodation and cuisine. Log fires, centrally located.
Open: All year **Grades:** ETC 3 Diamond
01751 431414 (also fax) Mr & Mrs McGill **D:** Fr £26.00–£30.00 **S:** Fr £30.00–£37.50 **Beds:** 1T 5D **Baths:** 6 En (12) (6) cc

Gilling East

SE6177

Hall Farm, *Gilling East, York,* YO62 4JW. Warm family welcome, fantastic views, close to Moors, Helmsley, York. **Open:** All year (not Xmas)
01439 788314 Virginia Collinson *virginia@collinson2.fsnet.co.uk* **D:** Fr £18.00–£20.00 **S:** Fr £15.00–£20.00 **Beds:** 1D **Baths:** 1 En 3

Glaisdale

NZ7603 *Moon & Sixpence, Horseshoe Inn*

Postgate Farm, *Glaisdale, Whitby, N Yorks,* YO21 2PZ. C17th Listed farmhouse in beautiful Esk Valley, a walkers' paradise. Whitby 10 miles. **Open:** All year (not Xmas)
01947 897353 (also fax) Mrs Thompson *j-m.thompson.bandb@talk21.com* **D:** Fr £16.00–£21.00 **S:** Fr £20.00–£30.00 **Beds:** 2D 1T **Baths:** 3 En (4)

Red House Farm, *Glaisdale, Whitby, N. Yorks,* YO21 2PZ. **Open:** All year
01947 897242 (also fax) T J Spashett *spashettredhouse@aol.com* www.redhousefarm.net **D:** Fr £25.00 **S:** Fr £25.00–£35.00 **Beds:** 1F 1T 2D 1S **Baths:** 3 En 1 Pr (4)
Listed Georgian farmhouse featured in 'Houses of the North York Moors'. Refurbished to highest standards but retaining original features. Excellent walks, bridleways from doorstep. 400 yds Coast to Coast Walk. Friendly animals, stabling, billiards room, middle of NP just 8m coast & Whitby.

Arncliffe Arms Hotel, *Glaisdale, Whitby, N. Yorks,* YO21 2QL. Very friendly & comfortable accommodation. Romantic area along River Esk, close Beggars' Bridge. **Open:** All year
01947 897209 (also fax) Mr Westwood **D:** Fr £15.00 **S:** Fr £15.00 **Beds:** 2D 2T 1S **Baths:** 1 Sh

Hollins Farm, *Glaisdale, Whitby, N. Yorks,* YO21 2PZ. Comfortable C16th farmhouse near moors, 8 miles coast, wonderful scenery. **Open:** All year (not Xmas)
01947 897516 Mrs Mortimer **D:** Fr £15.00 **Beds:** 3F 1D 2T **Baths:** 2 Sh (6)

Goathland

NZ8301 *Goathland Hotel, Inn on the Moor*

The Beacon Country House, *Goathland, Whitby, N Yorks,* YO22 5AN. Late Victorian country house in 1 acre grounds.
Open: All year
01947 896409 Mrs Katz **Fax: 01947 896431** *stewartkatz@compuserve.com* www.beacongoathland.co.uk **D:** Fr £22.50–£25.00 **S:** Fr £22.50 **Beds:** 1F 2T 2D **Baths:** 4 En 1 Pr cc

Fairhaven Country Hotel, *The Common, Goathland, Whitby, N. Yorks,* YO22 5AN. Edwardian country house, superb moorland views in centre of village.
Open: All year
01947 896361 Mr Ellis **Fax: 01947 896099** *royellis@thefairhavenhotel.co.uk* www.thefairhavenhotel.co.uk **D:** Fr £27.00–£35.00 **S:** Fr £22.00–£35.00 **Beds:** 3F 2T 2D 2S **Baths:** 5 En 2 Sh (9) cc

Prudom House, *Goathland, Whitby, N. Yorks,* YO22 5AN. **Open:** Feb to Dec
Grades: ETC 4 Diamond, Silver
01947 896368 Fax: 01947 896030 *info@prudomhouse.co.uk* www.prudomhouse.co.uk **D:** Fr £28.50–£32.50 **S:** Fr £38.50 **Beds:** 2T 3D 1S **Baths:** 6 En (12)
Cosy C18th farmhouse in the village of Goathland, just opposite the church. Excellent accommodation and quality food. Magnificent cottage gardens and moorland views. A perfect location for exploring the North York Moors and Heritage Coast.

Grafton

SE4163

Primrose Cottage, *Marton-cum-Grafton, York, North Yorkshire,* YO51 9QJ. Warm hospitality in country cottage in picturesque village 1 mile east of A1(M).
Open: All year **Grades:** ETC 4 Diamond
01423 322835 & 01423 322711 P M Styan **Fax: 01423 322835 & 01423 323985** *primrosecottage@btinternet.com* www.primrosecottagegrafton.co.uk **D:** Fr £20.00 **S:** Fr £27.50 **Beds:** 2T 1D **Baths:** 1 Pr 1 Sh (8)

Grassington

SE0064

Raines Close, *13 Station Road, Grassington, Skipton, N. Yorks,* BD23 5LS. Close to village amenities. Lovely views. Ideal touring or walking base.
Open: All year (not Xmas/New Year)
Grades: ETC 4 Diamond
01756 752678 Mr Benson *rainesclose@yorks.net* www.rainesclose.co.uk **D:** Fr £24.00–£30.00 **S:** Fr £30.00 **Beds:** 1T 3D **Baths:** 3 En 1 Pr (10) (4) cc

Lythe End, *Wood Lane, Grassington, Skipton, N. Yorks,* BD23 5DF. Comfortable accommodation, views, quiet village location, ideal walking/touring base.
Open: All year (not Xmas)
01756 753196 Mrs Colley *aandccolley@freeuk.com* **D:** Fr £23.00–£25.00 **S:** Fr £30.00–£33.00 **Beds:** 1F 1D **Baths:** 1 En 1 Pr (12) (2)

Planning a longer stay? Always ask for any special rates

Mayfield Bed & Breakfast, *Low Mill Lane, Grassington, Skipton, N. Yorks, BD23 5BX.* Beautiful Dales longhouse. Guest rooms overlook fells and river. **Open:** All year
01756 753052 Mr & Mrs Trewartha *suzanneatmayfield@talk21.com* www.mayfield_grassington.co.uk **D:** Fr £22.00–£25.00 **S:** Fr £28.00 **Beds:** 1F 1D 1T **Baths:** 1 En 1 Sh (5)

Grove House, *1 Moor Lane, Grassington, Skipton, N Yorks, BD23 5BD.* C18th private home. Peaceful village location on Dales Way.
Open: All year (not Xmas/New Year
01756 753364 Lynn Whyte **Fax: 01756 753603** *lynn@grovehousegrassington.net* www.grovehousegrassington.net **D:** Fr £25.00–£30.00 **S:** Fr £40.00–£60.00 **Beds:** 1T 2D **Baths:** 2 En 1 Pr

Craiglands, *1 Brooklyn, Threshfield, Grassington, Skipton, BD23 5ER.* Elegant Edwardian house offering quality accommodation and superb breakfasts. **Open:** All year (not Xmas)
Grades: ETC 4 Diamond
01756 752093 Mrs Wallace *craiglands@talk21.com* www.craiglands.com **D:** Fr £23.00–£30.00 **S:** Fr £21.00–£28.00 **Beds:** 2D 1T 1S **Baths:** 3 En 1 Pr (3) cc

Town Head Guest House, *1 Low Lane, Grassington, Skipton, N. Yorks, BD23 5AU.* Friendly guest house at the head of the village between cobbled streets and moors. **Open:** All year (not Xmas)
01756 752811 Mrs Lister **D:** Fr £25.00 **S:** Fr £30.00 **Beds:** 3D 1T **Baths:** 4 En (3)

Ashfield House Hotel, *Grassington, Skipton, N. Yorks, BD23 5AE.* Quality food and accommodation in spectacular Yorkshire Dales National Park. **Open:** All year (not Xmas)
01756 752584 (also fax) Harrison *info@ashfieldhouse.co.uk* www.ashfieldhouse.co.uk **D:** Fr £30.00–£34.00 **S:** Fr £30.00–£54.00 **Beds:** 3T 4D **Baths:** 6 En 1 Pr (5) (8) cc

Great Ayton

NZ5611 *Dudley Arms*

Eskdale Cottage, *31 Newton Road, Great Ayton, Middlesbrough, TS9 6DT.* Victorian cottage in Picturesque village with River Lever running through it. Warm welcome. **Open:** All year (not Xmas)
01642 724306 Mrs Houghton *info@mhoughton.co.uk* **D:** Fr £18.00–£20.00 **S:** Fr £20.00–£22.00 **Beds:** 2T **Baths:** 1 Pr (0) (2)

The Wheelhouse, *Langbaurgh Grange, Great Ayton, Middlesbrough, Cleveland, TS9 6QQ.* Converted barn/mill in half acre gardens with open views to Cleveland Hills. **Open:** All year
01642 724523 **D:** Fr £17.00 **S:** Fr £19.00 **Beds:** 1F 1D **Baths:** 2 Pr (3)

Great Broughton

NZ5406

Ingle Hill, *Ingleby Road, Great Broughton, North Yorks, TS9 7ER.* Spectacular views North York Moors, warm welcome, transport to walks. **Open:** All year (not Xmas)
01642 712449 Mrs Sutcliffe www.spotlight osmotherley **D:** Fr £17.50 **S:** Fr £18.50 **Beds:** 1F 1D 2T **Baths:** 2 En 2 Sh (4) cc

Great Edstone

SE7084

Cowldyke Farm, *Great Edstone, Kirkbymoorside, York, YO62 6PE.* Family-run working farm set in idyllic peaceful Yorkshire countryside. **Open:** All year (not Xmas)
01751 431242 Mrs Benton www.cowldyke-farm.co.uk **D:** Fr £20.00 **S:** Fr £20.00 **Beds:** 1F 1D **Baths:** 2 En (3) (10)

Gunnerside

SD9598 *Kings Head*

Dalegarth House, *Gunnerside, Richmond, DL11 6LD.* Traditional breakfast. Home-made bread and preserves. Warm welcome. **Open:** Feb to Nov
01748 886275 Mrs Calvert **D:** Fr £18.00–£20.00 **S:** Fr £20.00 **Beds:** 1T **Baths:** 1 En (4)

Harrogate

SE3055

Alamah, *88 Kings Road, Harrogate, N. Yorks, HG1 5JX.* Delightful Victorian guest house, 100 yds Exhibition Centre, 5 mins walk town centre. **Open:** All year
Grades: ETC 4 Diamond
01423 502187 Mr Wilkinson **Fax: 01423 566175** **D:** Fr £26.00–£30.00 **S:** Fr £27.00–£33.00 **Beds:** 1F 2T 2D 2S **Baths:** 6 En 1 Pr (10)

Sherwood, *7 Studley Road, Harrogate, N. Yorks, HG1 5JU.* Centrally located near Harrogate town centre, in a quiet tree-lined street. **Open:** All year
01423 503033 C Grant **Fax: 01423 564659** *sherwood@hotels.harrogate.com* www.sherwood-hotel.com **D:** Fr £20.00–£25.00 **S:** Fr £30.00–£50.00 **Beds:** 1T 4D 1S **Baths:** 4 En 1 Sh cc

Oakbrae Guest House, *3 Springfield Avenue, Harrogate, N. Yorks, HG1 2HR.* Centrally situated for all amenities, warm and friendly. **Open:** All year
01423 567682 (also fax) **D:** Fr £25.00 **S:** Fr £30.00 **Beds:** 2T 3D 3S **Baths:** 7 En 1 Pr (12) (6)

Hollins House, *17 Hollins Road, Harrogate, N. Yorks, HG1 2JF.* Clean, quiet spacious accommodation in a warm and friendly family-run Victorian house.
Open: All year
01423 503646 (also fax) Mr Hamblin **D:** Fr £21.00–£24.00 **S:** Fr £28.00–£30.00 **Beds:** 3T 2D 1S **Baths:** 3 En 3 Sh (5) cc

Geminian House, *13 Franklin Road, Harrogate, N. Yorks, HG1 5ED.* Family-run guest house close to town centre. **Open:** All year
01423 523347 & 01423 561768 **Fax: 01423 523347** *geminian@talk21.com* www.geminian.org.uk **D:** Fr £20.00–£25.00 **S:** Fr £25.00–£30.00 **Beds:** 1F 2T 3D 2S **Baths:** 8 En

The Alexander, *88 Franklin Road, Harrogate, N. Yorks, HG1 5EN.* Elegant friendly fully restored Victorian residence close to the town centre. **Open:** All year
01423 503348 Mrs Toole **Fax: 01423 540230** **D:** Fr £24.00–£25.00 **S:** Fr £24.00–£25.00 **Beds:** 3F 2D 2S **Baths:** 5 En 1 Sh

Staveleigh, *20 Ripon Road, Harrogate, HG1 2JJ.* Luxury award-winning accommodation. Large rooms, excellent breakfasts. Walking distance town and conference centre. **Open:** All year
Grades: ETC 4 Diamond, SIlver
01423 524175 Ms Sutton **Fax: 01423 524178** *enquiries@staveleigh.co.uk* www.staveleigh.co.uk **D:** Fr £25.00–£34.00 **S:** Fr £35.00–£55.00 **Beds:** 1F 1D 1T **Baths:** 2 En 1 Pr (3)

Knabbs Ash, *Skipton Road, Kettlesing, Felliscliffe, Harrogate, N. Yorks, HG3 2LT.* Peaceful country farm house six miles west of Harrogate. **Open:** All year (not Xmas/New Year)
01423 771040 S Smith **Fax: 01423 771515** *colin+sheila@knabbsash.freeserve.co.uk* www.yorkshirenet.co.uk/stayat/knabbsash **D:** Fr £25.00 **S:** Fr £35.00 (10)

The Gables Hotel, *2 West Grove Road, Harrogate, N. Yorks, HG1 2AD.* Comfortable accommodation, excellent food, friendly service. Ideal business/pleasure. **Open:** All year (not Xmas/New Year) **Grades:** ETC 3 Diamond
01423 505625 Fax: 01423 561312 *gableshotel@quista.net* www.harrogategables.co.uk **D:** Fr £27.50–£30.00 **S:** Fr £35.00–£48.00 **Beds:** 2F 1T 2D 4S **Baths:** 9 En (5) **cc**

Shannon Court Hotel, *65 Dragon Avenue, Harrogate, N. Yorks, HG1 5DS.* Family-run licensed hotel close to town centre & Conference Centre.
Open: All year
01423 509858 R S Evans **Fax: 01423 530606** *shannon@courthotel.freeserve.co.uk* www.courthotel.freeserve.co.uk **D:** Fr £27.50–£35.00 **S:** Fr £35.00–£45.00 **Beds:** 2F 1T 3D 2S **Baths:** 8 En (5) (3) **cc**

Parnas Hotel, *98 Franklin Road, Harrogate, N. Yorks, HG1 5EN.* Warm welcome to family-run licensed hotel in pleasant garden. Easy walk to town centre, conference centre, Valley Gardens. Great touring base. York half hour. Close to Emmerdale, Heartbeat country and Dales. Stop over on your way to Scotland.
Open: All year
01423 564493 Mr & Mrs Naylor **Fax: 01423 563554** *info@parnashotel.co.uk* www.parnashotel.co.uk **D:** Fr £27.50 **S:** Fr £40.00 **Beds:** 2F 3D 2T 2S **Baths:** 9 En (8) **cc**

Ashley House Hotel, *36-40 Franklin Road, Harrogate, N. Yorks, HG1 5EE.* **Open:** All year
01423 507474 Mr & Mrs Thomas **Fax: 01423 560858** *ashleyhousehotel@btinternet.com* www.ashleyhousehotel.com **D:** Fr £32.50–£45.00 **S:** Fr £45.00–£55.00 **Beds:** 1F 6D 6T 5S **Baths:** 18 En (4) **cc**
High standard of accommodation at reasonable prices. Friendly hotel aiming to give you a memorable stay and value for money. Delightful bar with extensive collection of whiskies. Excellent restaurants within walking distance. Tour Dales and Moors from convenient location in this lovely spa town.

The Belmont Hotel, *86 Kings Road, Harrogate, N. Yorks, HG1 5JX.* **Open:** All year (not Xmas/New Year) **Grades:** ETC 4 Diamond
01423 528086 Mrs Buchanan *marilyn@thebelmont86.fsnet.co.uk* www.smoothhound.co.uk/hotels/belmonthotel.html **D:** Fr £27.50–£30.00 **S:** Fr £33.00–£50.00 **Beds:** 2T 3D 2S **Baths:** 7 En (6) **cc**
We are about 200 yards from the Conference Centre/Exhibition Halls and five minutes walk into town - wonderful restaurants, cosmopolitan cafe-bars and very special shops. Returning to this mellow, comfortable house is a delight. Superb breakfasts. A warm welcome assured.

Alexa House, *26 Ripon Road, Harrogate, N. Yorks, HG1 2JJ.* **Open:** All year **01423 501988** Mr Landalt **Fax: 01423 504086** *alexahouse@msn.com* www.alexa-house.co.uk **D:** Fr £32.50–£40.00 **S:** Fr £40.00–£50.00 **Beds:** 2F 2T 6D 3S **Baths:** 13 En (10) **cc**
Elegant detached Georgian residence, 4 minutes walk from town centre and exhibition halls. Discerning ensuite accommodation with friendly and personal service assured. Exceptional breakfasts, light meals served at all times, honesty bar, private floodlit car park.

The Coppice, *9 Studley Road, Harrogate, N. Yorks, HG1 5JU.* **Open:** All year
01423 569626 Mr & Mrs Richardson **Fax: 01423 569005** *coppice@harrogate.com* www.harrogate.com/coppice **D:** Fr £25.00–£29.00 **S:** Fr £30.00–£40.00 **Beds:** 1F 1T 2D 1S **Baths:** 5 En (5) **cc**
A high standard of comfortable, clean accommodation, excellent food and warm friendly welcome awaits you. Our beautiful Victorian guest house is quietly situated yet close to the elegant town centre. Ideal for exploring the Dales. Halfway stop London to Edinburgh.

Spring Lodge, *22 Spring Mount, Harrogate, N. Yorks, HG1 2HX.* Centrally situated Edwardian town house in a quiet cul-de-sac. Non-smoking. **Open:** All year (not Xmas) **Grades:** ETC 3 Diamond
01423 506036 Mr Vinter **Fax: 01423 506066** *dv22harrogate@aol.com* www.yorkshirenet.co.uk **D:** Fr £19.00–£23.00 **S:** Fr £22.00–£40.00 **Beds:** 1F 3D 1S **Baths:** 2 En 1 Sh (1)

Hawes

SD8789

East House, *Gayle, Hawes, N. Yorks, DL8 3RZ.* Delightful house. Superb views, ideal centre for touring the Dales. **Open:** Feb to Nov **Grades:** ETC 4 Diamond
01969 667405 & 07866 108148 (M) Mrs Ward *lornaward@lineone.net* dalesaccommodation.com/easthouse **D:** Fr £21.00–£24.00 **S:** Fr £21.00 **Beds:** 1T 1D 1S **Baths:** 2 En 1 Pr

The Bungalow, *Springbank, Hawes, N. Yorks, DL8 3NW.* Large bungalow, excellent views, quiet, off-road parking. **Open:** Easter to Oct
01969 667209 Mrs Garnett **D:** Fr £18.00–£20.00 **Beds:** 2D 1T **Baths:** 2 En 1 Sh (4)

Overdales View, *Simonstone, Hawes, N Yorks, DL8 3LY.* Friendly welcome. Lovely views, rural surroundings, comfortable beds good food. **Open:** Easter to Oct
01969 667186 Mrs Sunter *irene.sunter@tiscali.co.uk* **D:** Fr £18.00–£19.00 **S:** Fr £20.00 **Beds:** 1F/T 1D 1S **Baths:** 1 Sh (5)

Ebor House, *Burtersett Road, Hawes, N. Yorks, DL8 3NT.* Family-run friendly and central. Off road parking and cycle store. **Open:** All year (not Xmas) **Grades:** ETC 3 Diamond
01969 667337 (also fax) Mrs Clark *gwen@eborhouse.freeserve.co.uk* **D:** Fr £18.00–£22.00 **S:** Fr £19.00–£25.00 **Beds:** 2D 1T **Baths:** 2 En 1 Sh (4)

Dalesview, *East Marry, Gayle, Hawes, N. Yorks, DL8 3RZ.* Modern, comfortable, bungalow. Ideal for touring, cycling and walking.
Open: Easter to Nov
01969 667397 Mrs McGregor **D:** Fr £20.00 **S:** Fr £25.00 **Beds:** 1D 1T 1S **Baths:** 3 En (2)

Fairview House, *Burtersett Road, Hawes, N Yorks, DL8 3NP.* **Open:** Feb to Dec **Grades:** ETC 4 Diamond **01969 667348 & 07890 916425 (M)** Mr & Mrs Rice **Fax: 01969 667348** *fairview.hawes@virgin.net* **D:** Fr £27.50–£30.00 **S:** Fr £23.00–£35.00 **Beds:** 1F 1T 2D 2S **Baths:** 4 En 2 Sh (5)
Situated on the edge of town, Fairview House is an immaculate mid-Victorian house. Standing in well tended gardens, offering luxury accommodation with superb views of Fells/Dales. Near to countryside museum and ropemakers. Ideal for touring/walking. Phone for brochure.

Overdales View, *Simonstone, Hawes, N Yorks, DL8 3LY.* Friendly welcome. Lovely views, rural surroundings, comfortable beds good food. **Open:** Easter to Oct **01969 667186** Mrs Sunter *irene.sunter@tiscali.co.uk* **D:** Fr £18.00–£19.00 **S:** Fr £20.00 **Beds:** 1F/T 1D 1S **Baths:** 1 Sh (5)

Hawnby

SE5489

Laskill Grange, *Hawnby, Helmsley, York, YO62 5NB.* Built on a medieval site once belonging to Rievaulx Abbey. Stunning scenery. **Open:** All year **01439 798268** Mrs Smith **Fax: 01439 798498** *suesmith@laskillfarm.fsnet.co.uk* www.laskillfarm.co.uk **D:** Fr £27.50–£30.00 **S:** Fr £27.50–£30.00 **Beds:** 3D 2T 1S **Baths:** 5 En 1 Pr (20) **cc**

Hebden

SE0263

Court Croft, *Church Lane, Hebden, Skipton, BD23 5DX.* Family farmhouse in quiet village close to the Dales Way. **Open:** All year **01756 753406** Mrs Kitching **D:** Fr £17.50 **S:** Fr £17.50–£20.00 **Beds:** 2T **Baths:** 1 Sh (4)

B&B owners may vary rates – be sure to check when booking

Helmsley

SE6184 Crown, Feathers, Black Swan, Royal Oak, Feversham Arms

Ashberry, *41 Ashdale Road, Helmsley, York, YO62 5DE.* Warm welcome in comfortable home, start of Cleveland Way. **Open:** All year **01439 770488** Mrs *oneil@ashberry.co.uk* **D:** Fr £17.50 **S:** Fr £17.50–£21.00 **Beds:** 1T 1D 1S **Baths:** 1 Sh (4) (2)

Laskill Grange, *Hawnby, Helmsley, York, YO62 5NB.* **Open:** All year **01439 798268** Mrs Smith **Fax: 01439 798498** *suesmith@laskillfarm.fsnet.co.uk* www.laskillfarm.co.uk **D:** Fr £27.50–£30.00 **S:** Fr £27.50–£30.00 **Beds:** 3D 2T 1S **Baths:** 5 En 1 Pr (20) **cc**
Built on a medieval site once belonging to Rievaulx Abbey. Stunning scenery offering impressive accommodation divided between main house & luxurious converted barns. Charming C19th property, situated in England's finest National Park. Haven of peace and tranquillity. All bedrooms ensuite and charmingly decorated.

The Carlton Lodge, *53 Bondgate, Helmsley, York, YO62 5EY.* Ideal touring, walking, national park, moors, dales, coast and York. **Open:** All year **Grades:** ETC 4 Diamond, AA 4 Diamond **01439 770557 Fax: 01439 770623** *stwls@carlton-lodge.com* www.carlton-lodge.com **D:** Fr £25.00–£35.00 **S:** Fr £27.50–£35.00 **Beds:** 2T 6D **Baths:** 6 En 2 Sh (35) **cc**

4 Ashdale Road, *Helmsley, York, YO62 5DD.* Quiet private house 5 mins from Market Square and shops. **Open:** All year (not Xmas) **01439 770375** Mrs Barton **D:** Fr £15.00–£16.00 **S:** Fr £16.00 **Beds:** 1D 1T **Baths:** 1 Sh (2)

Stilworth House, *1 Church Street, Helmsley, York, YO62 5AD.* Elegant rooms, beautiful location overlooking castle, hearty breakfast, warm welcome. **Open:** All year (not Xmas) **01439 771072** Mrs Swift www.stilworth.co.uk **D:** Fr £22.00–£30.00 **S:** Fr £30.00–£50.00 **Beds:** 1F 2D 1T **Baths:** 3 Pr 1 Sh (4)

14 Elmslac Road, *Helmsley, York, YO62 5AP.* Quiet house 4 mins walk from market square. Pleasant situation. **Open:** All year **01439 770287** Mrs Holding **D:** Fr £13.50–£14.50 **S:** Fr £14.00 **Beds:** 1D **Baths:** 1 Pr (12)

High Bentham

SD6669

Fowgill Park Farm, *High Bentham, Lancaster, LA2 7AH.* Beamed farmhouse enjoying panoramic views, close to caves and waterfalls. **Open:** Easter to Oct **015242 61630** Mrs Metcalfe **D:** Fr £19.00–£22.00 **Beds:** 1D 1T **Baths:** 2 En (4)

High Hawsker

NZ9207

Old Blacksmiths Arms, *High Hawsker, Whitby, N. Yorks, YO22 4LH.* Originally first pub in village. Large garden with pond. **Open:** Easter to Oct **01947 880800** Mrs Stubbs **D:** Fr £18.00–£19.00 **S:** Fr £21.00–£24.00 **Beds:** 1T 2D **Baths:** 2 Sh (12) (3)

Holme-on-Swale

SE3582

Glen Free, *Holme-on-Swale, Thirsk, N Yorks, YO7 4JE.* Secluded cottage, one mile from A1. Ideal for Herriot country and Dales. **Open:** All year (not Xmas) **01845 567331** Mrs Bailes **D:** Fr £16.00–£18.00 **S:** Fr £16.00–£18.00 **Beds:** 1F 1D **Baths:** 1 Sh (4)

Horsehouse

SE0481

The Thwaite Arms, *Horsehouse, Leyburn, N. Yorks, DL8 4TS.* Warm and cosy traditional Dales inn set in beautiful tranquil Coverdale. **Open:** All year (not Xmas/New Year) **01969 640206** Mrs Powell **D:** Fr £23.00 **S:** Fr £40.00 **Beds:** 1T 1D **Baths:** 1 Pr (10)

Horton-in-Ribblesdale

SD8072

Studfold House, *Horton-in-Ribblesdale, Settle, N. Yorks, BD24 0ER.* Georgian house in beautiful grounds with panoramic views. **Open:** All year (not Xmas/New Year) **01729 860200** Mr & Mrs Horsfall *info@studfoldhouse.co.uk* www.studfoldhouse.co.uk **D:** Fr £17.00–£21.00 **S:** Fr £21.00 **Beds:** 1F 1T 1D 1S **Baths:** 2 En 1 Pr 1 Sh (8)

The Golden Lion Hotel, *Horton-in-Ribblesdale, Settle, N. Yorks, BD24 0HB.* Friendly, comfortable village hotel. **Open:** All year
01729 860206 Mrs Johnson **D:** Fr £18.00–£21.00 **Beds:** 2T 2D 1S **Baths:** 1 En 1 Sh cc

The Willows, *Horton-in-Ribblesdale, Settle, N. Yorks, BD24 0HT.* Large detached house, luxurious bedrooms in lovely Yorkshire Dales. **Open:** Easter to Sept
01729 860373 (also fax) Mrs Barker **D:** Fr £20.00–£24.00 **S:** Fr £20.00–£25.00 **Beds:** 1F 1D 1T **Baths:** 1 En 1 Pr 1 Sh (5)

Hovingham

SE6675 *Malt Shovel, Worsley Arms*

Sedgwick Country Guest House, *Park Street, Hovingham, York, YO62 4JZ.* North from York A64. Left Castle Howard. Left (2 miles) Hovington. **Open:** All year
01653 628740 (also fax) F J Smurthwaite *sedgwick.ges-ho@amserve.net* www.sedgwickcountryguest.co.uk **D:** Fr £21.00–£25.00 **S:** Fr £21.00–£30.00 **Beds:** 2F 2T 2D 1S **Baths:** 8 En cc

Hubberholme

SD9278

Church Farm, *Hubberholme, Skipton, N. Yorks, BD23 5JE.* Traditional C16th Dales farmhouse on working hill farm. Ideal for walking/touring. **Open:** All year
01756 760240 Mrs Huck **D:** Fr £20.00 **S:** Fr £20.00 **Beds:** 2D 2T **Baths:** 1 En 1 Pr

Huby (Easingwold)

SE5665

New Inn Motel, *Main Street, Huby, York, YO61 1HQ.* Huby, 'twixt York and Easingwold, for coast, Moors, Dales, Herriot/Heartbeat country. **Open:** All year
01347 810219 Mrs Birkinshaw **D:** Fr £24.00–£25.00 **S:** Fr £28.00–£35.00 **Beds:** 3F 2D 2T 1S **Baths:** 8 En (8)

Hutton Rudby

NZ4606

Greenview, *13 Eastside, Hutton Rudby, Yarm, N Yorks, TS15 0DB.* Overlooking the village green at Hutton Rudby, Greenview offers you a delightful stay bordering the National Park in North Yorkshire. Rooms have showers, comfortable beds, with a hearty breakfast. Ideal for Coast to Coast, Cleveland Way and new cycle route. **Open:** All year
01642 701739 Mrs Ashton **D:** Fr £18.00 **S:** Fr £18.00 **Beds:** 1D 1T **Baths:** 2 En (3)

Hutton-le-Hole

SE7089

Moorlands of Hutton-le-Hole, *Hutton-le-Hole, York, YO62 6UA.* **Open:** All year **Grades:** ETC 4 Diamond, Silver, AA 4 Diamond
01751 417548 Kate Seekings & Barry Jenkinson **Fax: 01751 417760** *guest@moorlandshouse.com* www.moorlandshouse.com **D:** Fr £32.50–£35.00 **S:** Fr £40.00–£45.00 **Beds:** 1T 2D **Baths:** 3 En (6) cc
Award winning Georgian home in beautiful English village. Within the National Park, ideal for exploring Yorkshire's Moors, coast & history. Relax by log fires or in our stream side garden. Sumptuous breakfasts, deep armchairs, tea, cake, croquet, tennis & memorable dinners.

Ingleby Cross

NZ4500

North York Moors Adventure Ctr, *Park House, Ingleby Cross, Northallerton, N. Yorks, DL6 3PE.* Park House, traditional sandstone farmhouse set in the National Park. **Open:** Easter to Oct
01609 882571 (also fax) Mr Bennett www.coast-to-coast.org.uk **D:** Fr £15.00 **S:** Fr £15.00 **Beds:** 3F 1D 3T **Baths:** 2 Sh (1) (20)

Ingleton

SD6973

The Dales Guest House, *Main Street, Ingleton, Carnforth, North Yorkshire, LA6 3HH.* **Open:** All year
015242 41401 Penny & Paul Weaire *dalesgh@hotmail.com* www.ingleton.yorks.net **D:** Fr £21.00–£23.00 **S:** Fr £21.00–£23.00 **Beds:** 1T 3D 1S **Baths:** 5 En cc
A friendly welcome, cosy rooms with views and substantial home cooked meals await you. An ideal base for exploring the Dales, Forest of Bowland and Lakes. Special price breaks are available and various activities can be arranged for small groups.

BATHROOMS
En = Ensuite
Pr = Private
Sh = Shared

B&B owners may vary rates – be sure to check when booking

Springfield Country House Hotel, *26 Main Street, Ingleton, Carnforth, Lancs, LA63HJ.* **Open:** All year (not Xmas)
015242 41280 (also fax) Mr Thornton **D:** Fr £23.00–£25.00 **S:** Fr £25.00–£28.00 **Beds:** 1F 3D 1T **Baths:** 5 En 1 Pr (12) cc
Detached Victorian villa; large garden at rear running down to River Greta. Patio, small pond and waterfall. Home-grown vegetables in season. Front garden with patio, conservatory and fountain.

Riverside Lodge, *24 Main Street, Ingleton, Carnforth, LA63HJ.* **Open:** All year **Grades:** ETC 3 Diamond
015242 41359 Mr & Mrs Foley *info@riversideingleton.co.uk* www.riversideingleton.co.uk **D:** Fr £40.00–£48.00 **S:** Fr £32.00 **Beds:** 7D 1T **Baths:** 8 En (8) cc
This delightful Victorian house stands above terraced gardens and enjoys splendid views of Ingleborough and the wooded riverbank of the Greta. Nearby waterfalls walk and caves. Ideal base for walking/touring Yorkshire Dales and Lake District.

Seed Hill Guest House, *Ingleton, Carnforth, LA6 3AB.* A wonderful old Listed guest house in the centre of Ingleton. **Open:** All year
015242 41799 Mr & Mrs Brown *adrianseedhill@hotmail.com* www.come2ingleton.com **D:** Fr £19.00–£22.00 **S:** Fr £25.00–£29.00 **Beds:** 1F 1T 2D 1S **Baths:** 5 En (5) cc

Inglenook Guest House, *20 Main Street, Ingleton, Carnforth, North Yorkshire, LA6 3HJ.* Quality accommodation offering superb views. Delightful setting. Patio overlooking river. **Open:** All year (not Xmas) **Grades:** ETC 3 Diamond, AA 3 Diamond
015242 41270 C & P Smith *inglenook20@hotmail.com* www.nebsweb.co.uk/inglenook **D:** Fr £22.00 **S:** Fr £22.00–£44.00 **Beds:** 1F 2T 2D **Baths:** 4 En 1 Pr (5) cc

Ingleborough View Guest House, *Main Street, Ingleton, Carnforth, Lancashire, LA6 3HH.* Picturesque riverside location. Ideal for local walks/touring Dales.
Open: All year
015242 41523 Mrs Brown *anne@ingleboroughview.co.uk* www.ingleboroughview.co.uk **D:** Fr £19.00–£21.00 **S:** Fr £25.00–£28.00 **Beds:** 1F 2T 2D **Baths:** 2 En 3 Pr (5)

Gatehouse Farm, *Far West House, Ingleton, Carnforth, Lancs, LA6 3NR.* Working farm, home cooking, in Yorkshire Dales National Park. **Open:** All year (not Xmas/New Year)
015242 41458 & 015242 41307 Mrs Lund **D:** Fr £21.00–£22.00 **S:** Fr £21.00–£22.00 **Beds:** 1T 2D **Baths:** 2 En 1 Pr (3)

Nutstile Farm, *Ingleton, Carnforth, Lancs, LA6 3DT.* Secluded working Dales farm with outstanding views. **Open:** All year
015242 41752 Mrs Brennand **D:** Fr £20.00 **Beds:** 1F 1T 2D **Baths:** 2 En 1 Pr (3)

Bridge End Guest House, *Mill Lane, Ingleton, Carnforth, Lancs, LA6 3EP.* Georgian Listed building, riverside location adjacent to Waterfalls Walk entrance. **Open:** All year
015242 41413 Mrs Garner *garner01@tinyworld.co.uk* **D:** Fr £19.00–£22.00 **S:** Fr £25.00 **Beds:** 3D **Baths:** 3 En (8) (8) **cc**

Keasden
SD7266

Lythe Birks, *Keasden, Lancaster, LA2 8EZ.* Converted barn in its own grounds overlooking three peaks. **Open:** All year
015242 51688 Mrs Phinn **D:** Fr £19.50 **S:** Fr £25.00 **Beds:** 2D 1T

Keld
NY8901

Greenlands, *Keld, Richmond, DL11 6DY.* Refurbished farmhouse amidst the peace and beauty of upper Swaledale. **Open:** All year
01748 886576 Mrs Thompson **D:** Fr £19.50 **Beds:** 2D **Baths:** 2 En (2)

Kettlesing
SE2256

Knabbs Ash, *Skipton Road, Kettlesing, Felliscliffe, Harrogate, N. Yorks, HG3 2LT.* Peaceful country farm house six miles west of Harrogate. **Open:** All year (not Xmas/New Year)
01423 771040 S Smith **Fax: 01423 771515** *colin+sheila@knabbsash.freeserve.co.uk* www.yorkshirenet.co.uk/stayat/knabbsash **D:** Fr £25.00 **S:** Fr £35.00 (10)

Kettlewell
SD9772

Greta House, *Middle Lane, Kettlewell, Skipton, N Yorks, BD23 5QX.* **Open:** All year **01756 760268** Mrs Light *sue@gretahouse.com* www.gretahouse.com **D:** Fr £25.00–£30.00 **S:** Fr £35.00–£40.00 **Beds:** 1T 1D **Baths:** 2 En
Greta House built circa 1680, a quality B&B offering organic & free range produce. We are ideally situated in an area of outstanding natural & historic beauty. Perfect for walking, cycling, touring or just relaxing.

Chestnut Cottage, *Kettlewell, Skipton, N. Yorks, BD23 5RL.* Delightful country cottage. Beautiful gardens, leading down to village stream. **Open:** All year **Grades:** ETC 3 Diamond
01756 760804 Mrs Lofthouse **D:** Fr £20.00–£25.00 **S:** Fr £25.00–£30.00 **Beds:** 1D 2T **Baths:** 2 Sh (3)

Market House, *Middle Lane, Kettlewell, Skipton, N Yorks, BD23 5QX.* High quality accommodation with beautiful views. Ideal touring/walking area. **Open:** All year
01756 761188 Mrs Whiteley **D:** Fr £25.00 **S:** Fr £30.00–£35.00 **Beds:** 1T 1D **Baths:** 1 Sh

Lynburn, *Kettlewell, Skipton, N. Yorks, BD23 5RF.* Beautiful Dales cottage, close proximity to Herriot, Bronte and Emmerdale. **Open:** All year **Grades:** ETC 3 Diamond
01756 760803 Mrs Thornborrow *lorna@lthornborrow.fsnet.co.uk* **D:** Fr £19.00–£25.00 **S:** Fr £25.00–£30.00 **Beds:** 1D 1T **Baths:** 1 Sh (12) (2)

Kildale
NZ6009

Bankside Cottage, *Kildale, Whitby, North Yorkshire, YO21 2RT.* Homely country cottage, beautiful views. Taxi service available. **Open:** All year (not Xmas/New Year)
01642 723259 Mrs Addison **D:** Fr £19.00 **S:** Fr £19.00 **Beds:** 1F 1T 1D **Baths:** 1 Sh (4)

Kilnsey
SD9767

Skirfare Bridge Dales Barn, *Kilnsey, Skipton, N. Yorks, BD23 5PT.* Converted stone barn in beautiful limestone countryside of upper Wharfedale. **Open:** All year
01756 752465 (also fax) Mrs Foster www.yorkshirenet.co.uk/ydales/bunkbarns/kilnsey **D:** Fr £8.00 **S:** Fr £8.00 **Beds:** 5F 1T **Baths:** 3 Sh (8)

Kirkby Malham
SD8961 *Buck Inn*

Yeoman's Barn, *Kirkby Malham, Skipton, North Yorks, BD23 4BL.* Converted C17th barn, large oak beams, newly decorated bedrooms. Warm welcome, tea tray on arrival, open fire. Market towns of Skipton, Settle and Hawes all nearby. Malham Cove, Janets Foss and Gordale Scar - all suitable for the weekend walker.
Open: All year (not Xmas/New Year)
01729 830639 Mrs Turner **D:** Fr £20.00–£25.00 **S:** Fr £25.00–£35.00 **Beds:** 2D **Baths:** 2 En (5)

Kirkbymoorside
SE6987 *George & Dragon, King's Head*

Red Lion House, *Crown Square, Kirkbymoorside, York, YO62 6AY.* Lovely Georgian house, situated in quiet square in centre of small market town. **Open:** All year (not Xmas)
01751 431815 S & A Thompson *angela.thomson@red-lion-house.freeserve.co.uk* **D:** Fr £20.00–£22.50 **S:** Fr £25.00 **Beds:** 2D 1T **Baths:** 1 En 1 Sh

Sinnington Common Farm, *Kirkbymoorside, York, YO62 6NX.* Spacious ground floor. Panoramic views, family farm.
Open: All year
01751 431719 (also fax) Mrs Wiles *felicity@scfarm.demon.co.uk* **D:** Fr £18.00–£22.00 **S:** Fr £23.00–£27.00

Kirklington
SE3181 *The Bull*

Morar House, *Kirklington, Bedale, N Yorks, DL8 2NE.* Charming C17th cottage in picturesque village in heart of North Yorkshire. Traditional breakfast in farmhouse kitchen, stone-flagged floors, acre of garden. Two miles from A1, perfectly situated for York, Harrogate, Dales, Moors, East Coast and local places of interest.
Open: All year (not Xmas/New Year)
01845 567293 Mrs Webb **D:** Fr £19.00–£25.00 **S:** Fr £19.00–£25.00 **Beds:** 1T 1D **Baths:** 2 En (4)

B&B owners may vary rates – be sure to check when booking

Knaresborough

SE3557

Newton House Hotel, *5/7 York Place, Knaresborough, N Yorks, HG5 0AD.* Situated in picturesque Knaresborough, a C17th former coaching inn. **Open:** All year (not Xmas)
01423 863539 Mr & Mrs Elliott **Fax: 01423 869748** *newtonhouse@btinternet.com* www.newtonhousehotel.com **D:** Fr £27.50–£32.50 **S:** Fr £35.00–£45.00 **Beds:** 2F 7D 2T 1S **Baths:** 11 En 1 Pr (12) cc

Kirkgate House, *17 Kirkgate, Knaresborough, N Yorks, HG5 8AD.* Friendly non-smoking accommodation near the market place, bus and train station. **Open:** All year
01423 862704 (also fax) S F Giesen **D:** Fr £22.00 **S:** Fr £26.00–£32.00 **Beds:** 2D 1T **Baths:** 3 En (2)

Watergate Haven, *Ripley Road, Knaresborough, N Yorks, HG5 9BU.* B&B/Self-catering accommodation. Close to main attractions. **Open:** All year
01423 864627 Fax: 01423 861087 *watergate.haven@virgin.net* **D:** Fr £25.00–£27.00 **S:** Fr £30.00–£35.00 **Beds:** 1F 1T 1D 1S **Baths:** 4 En (12) cc

Holly Corner, *3 Coverdale Drive, Knaresborough, N Yorks, HG5 9BW.* **Open:** All year **01423 864204 & 07713 135713 (M)** Mrs MacLellan **Fax: 01423 864204** www.hotelmaster.co.uk/knaresborough/hollycorner **D:** Fr £25.00–£27.00 **S:** Fr £28.00–£35.00 **Beds:** 1T 1D 1S **Baths:** 2 Pr (2)
Large, private, Tudor-style family home in quiet private drive. Guaranteed friendly and personal service. Easy access Dales, York, Harrogate, Ripon, A1(M). Town centre/riverside, walking distance 8 minutes. Plants and preserves for sale. No smoking. Proprietor: Mrs Jan MacLellan.

Langcliffe

SD8264

Bowerley Hotel & Conference Centre, *Langcliffe, Settle, BD24 9LY.* Country house hotel in 3 acres, bar, restaurant, warm welcome. **Open:** All year
01729 823811 G Ralph **Fax: 01729 822317** *bowerleyhotel@aol.com* **D:** Fr £25.00–£29.00 **S:** Fr £32.00–£39.00 **Beds:** 2F 8T 6D 2S **Baths:** 18 En (50) cc

Lealholm

NZ7607 *Ye Old Horse Shoe*

High Park Farm, *Lealholm, Whitby, YO21 2AQ.* Peaceful location. 15 minutes from the coast many attractions close by. **Open:** Easter to Oct
01947 897416 Mrs Welford **D:** Fr £18.50 **S:** Fr £23.50 **Beds:** 1D **Baths:** 1 En (5) (1)

Leeming Bar

SE2890

Little Holtby, *Leeming Bar, Northallerton, N. Yorks, DL7 9LH.* **Open:** All year (not Xmas) **01609 748762** Mrs Hodgson *littleholtby@yahoo.co.uk* www.littleholtby.co.uk **D:** Fr £25.00–£30.00 **S:** Fr £30.00–£35.00 **Beds:** 3D 1T **Baths:** 2 En 1 Pr 1 Sh (10) (10)
Today's discerning traveller is looking for somewhere special, where the warmth of welcome will remain a treasured memory. All guest rooms have wonderful views - treat yourself to a really memorable stay.

Levisham

SE8390

Rectory Farmhouse, *Levisham, Pickering, N. Yorks, YO18 7NL.* Picturesque village surrounded by beautiful scenery; excellent walking, horseriding or just relaxing. **Open:** All year
01751 460304 Mrs Holt *rectoryfarmhouse@barclays.net* www.levisham.com **D:** Fr £20.00–£25.00 **S:** Fr £24.00 **Beds:** 2D 1T **Baths:** 3 En (8)

Leyburn

SE1190 *Sandpiper Inn, Boulton Arms, Golden Lion*

Secret Garden House, *Grove Square, Leyburn, N. Yorks, DL8 5AE.* Georgian house, acre-walled garden. Central Leyburn. Off-street parking. **Open:** All year (not Xmas/New Year)
01969 623589 Mr Digges *njdigges@yahoo.co.uk* **D:** Fr £22.00–£28.00 **S:** Fr £22.00–£28.00 **Beds:** 1T 2D 1S **Baths:** 3 En (12) (10)

Littlethorpe

SE3269

Moor End Farm, *Knaresborough Road, Littlethorpe, Ripon, N. Yorks, HG4 3LU.* Friendly, non-smoking first-class accommodation. Pleasantly situated. Ideal for touring. **Open:** All year (not Xmas)
01765 677419 Mrs Spensley *pspensley@ukonline.co.uk* yorkshirebandb.co.uk **D:** Fr £23.00–£26.00 **S:** Fr £30.00–£40.00 **Beds:** 2D 1T **Baths:** 2 En 1 Pr (5)

Litton

SD9074

Park Bottom, *Litton, Skipton, BD23 5QJ.* Peaceful setting, wonderful views, ideal for walking, Which? recommended. **Open:** All year (not Xmas)
01756 770235 Lyn & Bryan Morgan *bryan@parkbottomlitton.freeserve.co.uk* **D:** Fr £25.00–£28.00 **S:** Fr £32.00–£35.00 **Beds:** 1F 2D 1T **Baths:** 4 En (5)

Long Preston

SD8358

Inglenook, *22 Main Street, Long Preston, Skipton, BD23 4PH.* Traditional mullion-windowed cottage, village setting, ideal for Dales exploration. **Open:** All year
01729 840511 Mrs Parton **D:** Fr £18.00–£20.00 **S:** Fr £25.00–£30.00 **Beds:** 1F **Baths:** 1 Pr (4)

Lothersdale

SD9645

Lynmouth, *Dale End, Lothersdale, Skipton, N Yorks, BD20 8EH.* On path, pretty bungalow set in lovely grounds. **Open:** All year (not Xmas)
01535 632744 (also fax) Mrs Pearson **D:** Fr £17.50 **S:** Fr £17.50 **Beds:** 1F 1D 1T **Baths:** 3 En (4)

Burlington House, *Lothersdale, Keighley, W. Yorks, BD20 8EL.* Between Howarth and Dales, friendly old house on Pennine Way. **Open:** All year
01535 634635 Mrs Wood **D:** Fr £17.00 **S:** Fr £17.00 **Beds:** 1T 1D **Baths:** 1 Sh (3)

Lovesome Hill

SE3599

Lovesome Hill Farm, *(off A167), Lovesome Hill, Northallerton, N. Yorks, DL6 2PB.* Ideal situation for exploring Herriot's Dales and Moors. Traditional working farm and welcome. **Open:** All year (not Xmas/New Year)
01609 772311 M Pearson **Fax: 01609 774715** **D:** Fr £42.00–£60.00 **S:** Fr £26.00–£35.00 **Beds:** 1F 1T 3D 1S **Baths:** 6 En

Please respect a B&B's wishes regarding children, animals and smoking

Low Row

SD9897 *Farmers Arms, Punch Bowl*

Summer Lodge, *Low Row, Richmond, North Yorks, DL11 6NP.* Set in a valley of its own in beautiful Swaledale. **Open:** Mar to Oct
01748 886504 Mr Porter **D:** Fr £23.00–£26.00 **S:** Fr £23.00–£26.00 **Beds:** 1F **Baths:** 1 En

Malham

SD9062

Beck Hall, *Malham, Skipton, N. Yorks, BD23 4DJ.* Set in large streamside. Family run. Garden. **Open:** All year (not Xmas/New Year)
01729 830332 Mr & Mrs Boatwright **D:** Fr £19.00–£28.00 **S:** Fr £22.00–£35.00 **Beds:** 2F 3T 7D 2S **Baths:** 11 En 2 Sh (30) cc

Eastwood Guest House, *Malham, Skipton, North Yorkshire, BD23 4DA.* High quality B&B in central village location. **Open:** All year
01729 830409 Mrs McIntyre *eastwood_house@hotmail.com* **D:** Fr £20.00–£25.00 **S:** Fr £18.00–£30.00 **Beds:** 1F 1T 1D **Baths:** 3 En

Malton

SE7871

Suddabys Crown Hotel, *Wheelgate, Malton, N. Yorks, YO17 0HP.* **Open:** All year (not Xmas) **01653 692038** Mr & Mrs Suddaby **Fax: 01653 691812** *suddaby@crownhotel.plus.com* www.suddabyscrown.co.uk **D:** Fr £18.00–£32.00 **S:** Fr £18.00–£42.00 **Beds:** 2F 2D 4T **Baths:** 2 En 2 Sh (10)
Former Georgian coaching inn, located in historic market town close by all the attractions of Ryedale and the North Yorkshire Moors. Seven Real Ales always available in the Public Bar. Malton Brewery to the rear of the hotel - visits arranged.

The Brow, *York Road, Malton, N. Yorks, YO17 0AX.* Georgian House, garden, fantastic riverside views, private parking. **Open:** All year (not Xmas)
01653 693402 Mrs Hopkinson **D:** Fr £18.00–£30.00 **S:** Fr £18.00–£30.00 **Beds:** 1F 2D 1T 1S **Baths:** 3 En 1 Sh (6)

Marton (Pickering)

SE7383

Wildsmith House, *Marton, Sinnington, York, YO62 6RD.* Former farmhouse in pretty village. Ideally situated for exploring N Yorks. **Open:** Mar to Nov **Grades:** ETC 4 Diamond, Silver
01751 432702 Mr & Mrs Steele *wildsmithhouse@talk21.com* www.pb-design.com/swiftlink/bb/1102.htm **D:** Fr £22.00–£28.00 **S:** Fr £27.00–£33.00 **Beds:** 2T **Baths:** 2 En (12)

Masham

SE2280 *Blue Lion, Black Sheep*

Haregill Lodge, *Ellingstring, Masham, Ripon, North Yorkshire, HG4 4PW.* C18th farmhouse. Excellent views, superb cooking. Ideal base for Dales/Moors. **Open:** All year (not Xmas)
01677 460272 (also fax) Ms Greensit *haregilllodge@freenet.co.uk* **D:** Fr £20.00–£23.00 **S:** Fr £21.00–£23.00 **Beds:** 2T 1D **Baths:** 2 En 1 Pr (4)

Bank Villa, *Masham, Ripon, North Yorks, HG4 4DB.* Welcoming Grade II Listed home in half-acre terraced gardens, 2 mins' walk from Masham's unique market place, refurbished to a high standard with individually decorated ensuite bedrooms, 2 delightful lounges, ideal base for exploring the Dales and Herriot country. **Open:** All year (not Xmas)
01765 689605 (also fax) Lucy & Bobby Thomson **D:** Fr £20.00–£27.50 **S:** Fr £30.00–£40.00 **Beds:** 1F 3D 2T **Baths:** 3 En 1 Pr (5)

Mickleby

NZ8012

Northfield Farm, *Mickleby, Saltburn-by-the-Sea, N Yorks, TS13 5NE.* Quiet, friendly, comfortable farmhouse. Open views, ideal situation for walking. **Open:** Easter to Oct
01947 840343 Mrs Prudom **D:** Fr £15.00–£20.00 **S:** Fr £18.00 **Beds:** 1F 1D 1T **Baths:** 1 En 1 Sh

Middleham

SE1287

Yore View, *Leyburn Road, Middleham, Leyburn, DL8 4PL.* Former 1921 picture house situated 200 yards from Middleham centre. **Open:** All year
01969 622987 Mrs Roper **D:** Fr £20.00–£25.00 **S:** Fr £25.00–£30.00 **Beds:** 1F 2D **Baths:** 2 En 1 Pr (5) cc

Planning a longer stay? Always ask for any special rates

BATHROOMS
En = Ensuite
Pr = Private
Sh = Shared

Middlesmoor

SE0874

Dovenor House, *Middlesmoor, Harrogate, HG3 5ST.* Beautiful stone house on edge of village with unsurpassed views. **Open:** All year
01423 755697 (also fax) Mrs Thurland www.nidderdale.co.uk **D:** Fr £18.00 **S:** Fr £18.00–£20.00 **Beds:** 2F 1T **Baths:** 1 Sh (3)

Middleton Tyas

NZ2206

Greencroft, *Middleton Tyas, Richmond, DL10 6PE.* Friendly family home ideal for Dales, York and east coast. **Open:** All year
01325 377392 Mrs Alsop **Fax: 01833 621423** *greecroft@madasafish.com* **D:** Fr £18.00–£20.00 **S:** Fr £25.00 **Beds:** 1F 1T **Baths:** 2 En (4)

Nawton

SE6584

Little Manor Farm, *Highfield Lane, Nawton, York, YO62 7TU.* **Open:** Easter to Oct **01439 771672** Ms Avison **D:** Fr £18.50–£25.00 **S:** Fr £20.00–£28.00 **Beds:** 2D **Baths:** 1 Sh (5) (10)
Very comfortable Yorkshire Victorian family farmhouse. Idyllic situation set in own grounds of 25 acres. Superb panoramic views overlooking hills on the edge of two moors. 150 yds from Cleveland Link walk. Delicious continental and full traditional English breakfast.

Newby Wiske

SE3688

Well House, *Newby Wiske, Northallerton, N. Yorks, DL7 9EX.* A perfect location between Northallerton & Thirsk, with beautiful gardens. **Open:** All year
01609 772253 (also fax) Mrs Smith **D:** Fr £20.00–£25.00 **S:** Fr £25.00–£30.00 **Beds:** 2D **Baths:** 2 En (6)

Newton-on-Rawcliffe

SE8190

Rawcliffe House Farm, *Stape, Pickering, N Yorks, YO18 8JA.* Luxury, ensuite ground floor room with open-beamed ceilings, every convenience & comfort.
Open: All year (not Xmas/New Year)
Grades: ETC 4 Diamond
01751 473292 Mr Allsopp **Fax: 01751 473766** *office@yorkshireaccommodation.com* www.yorkshireaccommodation.com **D:** Fr £26.50–£28.50 **S:** Fr £32.00–£35.50 **Beds:** 2D 1T **Baths:** 3 En (8) (10)

Swan Cottage, *Newton-on-Rawcliffe, Pickering, N. Yorks, YO18 8QA.* Picturesque tranquil village, Quiet pub next door, wide breakfast choice. **Open:** All year
01751 472502 Mrs Heaton **D:** Fr £15.50–£16.50 **S:** Fr £15.50–£16.50 **Beds:** 1D 1T 1S **Baths:** 1 Sh (2)

North Grimston

SE8467

Middleton Arms, *North Grimston, Malton, N. Yorks, YO17 8AX.* Friendly country pub with excellent reputation for quality food and homely accommodation.
Open: All year (not Xmas)
01944 768255 Mrs Grayston **Fax: 01944 768389** **D:** Fr £20.00 **S:** Fr £27.50 **Beds:** 2D 1T **Baths:** 1 Pr 1 Sh

Northallerton

SE3794

Honeypots, *4 Pennine View, Northallerton, DL7 8HP.* Well-recommended guest house (visitors love it!) decorated to extremely high standard. **Open:** All year (not Xmas/New Year)
01609 777264 *val@lougnu.demon.co.uk* **D:** Fr £18.00–£20.00 **S:** Fr £18.00–£20.00 **Beds:** 1T **Baths:** 1 Pr (12) (1)

Porch House, *68 High Street, Northallerton, N. Yorks, DL7 8EG.* Built 1584 original fireplaces and beams between Yorkshire Dales and Moors. **Open:** All year (not Xmas)
01609 779831 J A Barrow **Fax: 01609 778603** **D:** Fr £24.50–£26.00 **S:** Fr £33.00–£35.00 **Beds:** 4D 2T **Baths:** 6 En (12) (6)

Alverton Guest House, *26 South Parade, Northallerton, N. Yorks, DL7 8SG.* Modernised Victorian town house convenient for all the county town facilities.
Open: All year (not Xmas)
01609 776207 (also fax) Mr Longley *alverton.26@talk21.com* **D:** Fr £22.00–£23.00 **S:** Fr £22.00–£27.00 **Beds:** 1F 1D 1T 2S **Baths:** 3 En 1 Sh (4)

Over Silton

SE4593

Moorfields Farm, *Over Silton, Thirsk, N. Yorks, YO7 2LJ.* Yorkshire stone farmhouse, close to North Yorkshire Moors. **Open:** All year
01609 883351 Mrs Goodwin *goodwins80@fsnet.co.uk* **D:** Fr £15.00 **S:** Fr £15.00 **Beds:** 1D 1S **Baths:** 1 Sh (2) (4) cc

Paradise

SE4687

High Paradise Farm, *Boltby, Thirsk, N Yorks, YO7 2HT.* Set between the forest and the moors in Herriot country. **Open:** All year
01845 537235 Mr & Mrs Skilbeck **Fax: 01845 537033** *info@highparadise.co.uk* www.highparadise.co.uk **D:** Fr £20.00 **S:** Fr £23.00 **Beds:** 1F 1T 1D **Baths:** 3 En cc

Pateley Bridge

SE1565 *Birch Tree, Crown, Harefield, Grassfields, Miner's Arms, Sportsman's Arms, Talbot*

Dale View, *Old Church Lane, Pateley Bridge, Harrogate, N. Yorks, HG3 5LY.* Comfortable ensuite rooms, Beautiful views over Yorkshire Dales. Private parking.
Open: All year
01423 711506 Mrs Simpson **Fax: 01423 711892** *bandb@daleview.com* **D:** Fr £19.00–£25.00 **S:** Fr £25.00–£30.00 **Beds:** 1F 2D **Baths:** 3 En (5)

Greengarth, *Greenwood Road, Pateley Bridge, Harrogate, N. Yorks, HG3 5LR.* Central detached bungalow in lovely Dales town. Ground floor rooms. **Open:** All year (not Xmas/New Year)
01423 711688 Mrs Ravilious **D:** Fr £18.00–£20.00 **S:** Fr £18.00–£30.00 **Beds:** 1T 2D 1S **Baths:** 2 En 1 Sh (5) (4)

Pickering

SE7984

Rawcliffe House Farm, *Stape, Pickering, N Yorks, YO18 8JA.* **Open:** All year (not Xmas/New Year) **Grades:** ETC 4 Diamond
01751 473292 Mr Allsopp **Fax: 01751 473766** *office@yorkshireaccommodation.com* www.yorkshireaccommodation.com **D:** Fr £26.50–£28.50 **S:** Fr £32.00–£35.50 **Beds:** 2D 1T **Baths:** 3 En (8) (10)
Luxury, ensuite ground floor room with open-beamed ceilings, every convenience & comfort. Own key in annexed room situated around a south-facing courtyard. set in 42 acres of North Yorkshire Moors. Aga cooked breakfast, using local produce taken in adjacent farmhouse.

Vivers Mill, *Mill Lane, Pickering, N. Yorks, YO18 8DJ.* **Open:** All year **Grades:** ETC 3 Diamond
01751 473640 Mr Saul & Mrs S Baxter *viversmill@talk21.com* www.viversmill.com **D:** Fr £22.00–£27.00 **S:** Fr £25.00–£27.00 **Beds:** 1F 5D 2T **Baths:** 7 En 1 Pr (5) (10)
Ancient watermill set in peaceful surroundings, sympathetically restored with working waterwheel and milling machinery retained. Original millstone centrepiece of large comfortable lounge. Ideal base for Moors, railway, Heartbeat, coast, York. Non-smoking.

Barker Stakes Farm, *Lendales Lane, Pickering, N Yorks, YO18 8EE.* Superb location, excellent food, comfortable rooms. Homemade bread & preserves. **Open:** All year (not Xmas/New Year) **Grades:** ETC 3 Diamond
01751 476759 Mrs Hardy **D:** Fr £20.00–£23.00 **S:** Fr £25.00–£30.00 **Beds:** 1T 2D **Baths:** 1 Pr 1 Sh (5) (6)

Kirkham Garth, *Whitby Road, Pickering, N. Yorks, YO18 7AT.* Quiet, private, homely residence. Ideal for York, forests, Moors and coast. **Open:** All year (not Xmas)
01751 474931 Mrs Rayner **D:** Fr £20.00–£22.00 **Beds:** 1F 1D 1T **Baths:** 1 Sh (3)

Heathcote Guest House, *100 Eastgate, Pickering, N. Yorks, YO18 7DW.* Our beautiful Victorian house is ideally situated for exploring the North Yorkshire Moors, visiting historic Whitby or the fascinating city of York. We provide superb breakfasts and delicious evening meals in a lovely setting; an ideal place to relax. **Open:** All year (not Xmas/New Year)
01751 476991 (also fax) Mrs Lovejoy *joanlovejoy@lineone.net* **D:** Fr £21.00–£24.00 **S:** Fr £21.00 **Beds:** 3D 2T **Baths:** 5 En (5) cc

Clent House, *15 Burgate, Pickering, North Yorkshire, YO18 7AU.* Late C18th house, comfortable ensuite bedrooms, close to town centre, castle, Moors railway.
Open: All year (not Xmas)
01751 477928 K & I Loveday *swiftlink-bb-1315@pb-design.com* www.pb-design.com/swiftlink/bb/1315.htm **D:** Fr £20.00 **S:** Fr £20.00–£25.00 **Beds:** 1F 1T 1D **Baths:** 3 En (3)

Potto

NZ4703

Dog & Gun Country Inn, *Potto, Northallerton, DL6 3HQ.* Traditional country inn situated beside North York Moors NP. Warm friendly welcome. **Open:** All year
01642 700232 D: Fr £20.00–£25.00 **S:** Fr £25.00–£30.00 **Beds:** 2F 2T 2D **Baths:** 5 En (30) cc

Ravenscar

NZ9801

Smugglers Rock Country House, *Ravenscar, Scarborough, N. Yorks, YO13 0ER.* Panoramic views over National Park and sea. Self catering cottages also available. **Open:** Mar to Oct **Grades:** ETC 4 Diamond
01723 870044 Mr & Mrs Gregson *info@smugglersrock.co.uk* www.smugglersrock.co.uk **D:** Fr £24.00–£27.00 **S:** Fr £27.00–£31.00 **Beds:** 1F 4D 2T 1S **Baths:** 8 En (12)

Dunelm, *Raven Hall Road, Ravenscar, Scarborough, N. Yorks, YO13 0NA.* Friendly, flexible B&B. Heather moors, dramatic cliffs, splendid bay view. **Open:** All year (not Xmas)
01723 870430 Jenny Bartlet **D:** Fr £16.00–£18.00 **S:** Fr £16.00–£18.00 **Beds:** 1D 1T 1S **Baths:** 2 Sh

Reeth

SE0399 *King's Arms, Buck Inn, Black Bull, Bridge Hotel*

2 Bridge Terrace, *Reeth, Richmond, N. Yorks, DL11 6TP.* Dry - cured Gloucester Old Spot bacon, local bread, fresh fruit, yoghurt. **Open:** Easter to Nov
01748 884572 Mrs Davies *davidsizer@freenetname.co.uk* **D:** Fr £16.50–£17.50 **S:** Fr £20.00–£22.00 **Beds:** 1D 1T **Baths:** 1 Sh

Elder Peak, *Arkengarthdale Road, Reeth, Richmond, N Yorks, DL11 6QX.* Friendly welcome. Good food. Peaceful, beautiful views. Ideal walking, touring. **Open:** Easter to Oct
01748 884770 Mrs Peacock **D:** Fr £17.00 **S:** Fr £17.00–£20.00 **Beds:** 1D 1T **Baths:** 1 Sh (5) (2)

Arkle House, *Mill Lane, Reeth, Richmond, North Yorks, DL11 6SJ.* Quietly located alongside the Arkle Beck, Reeth, Swaledale. A beautiful old Georgian house full of character. Picturesque village full of beautiful rolling countryside. Excellent base for walking and touring the Dales. Family room available as double or twin. Friendly welcome. **Open:** All year
01748 884815 (also fax) *info@arklehouse.com* www.arklehouse.com **D:** Fr £22.00–£27.00 **S:** Fr £30.00–£40.00 **Beds:** 1F 1D **Baths:** 2 En (2)

Riccall

SE6237

South Newlands Farm, *Selby Road, Riccall, York, YO19 6QR.* Friendly, comfortable, easy access to York. Dales & Moors short drive away. **Open:** All year
01757 248203 Mrs Swann **Fax: 01757 249450** *pswann3059@aol.com* **D:** Fr £18.00–£22.00 **S:** Fr £20.00–£25.00 **Beds:** 1F 1D 1T **Baths:** 2 En (3) cc

Dairymans of Riccall, *14 Kelfield Road, Riccall, York, YO19 6PG.* High quality accommodation. Ideal base for exploring Yorkshire's many treasures. **Open:** All year (not Xmas/New Year)
01757 248532 *bookings@dairymansriccall.co.uk* www.dairymansriccall.co.uk **D:** Fr £20.00–£22.50 **S:** Fr £18.00–£20.00 **Beds:** 1F 1T 1D 1S **Baths:** 2 En 1 Pr 1 Sh (6) (3) cc

Richmond

NZ1701

Emmanuel Guest House, *41 Maison Dieu, Richmond, N. Yorks, DL10 7AU.* Friendly family run guest house. Tea/coffee on arrival. **Open:** All year (not Xmas/New Year)
01748 823584 Mrs Simpson **Fax: 01748 821554** *emmanuelguesthouse@netscapeonline.co.uk* **D:** Fr £20.00–£21.00 **S:** Fr £18.00–£19.00 **Beds:** 1F 2T 2S **Baths:** 1 En 1 Sh (2)

Channel House, *8 Frenchgate, Richmond, N. Yorks, DL10 4JG.* Georgian town house near castle, shops, restaurants. Warm friendly welcome. **Open:** All year
01748 823844 K Eagle-Moore *channelhousekerri@hotmail.com* **D:** Fr £20.00–£22.50 **Beds:** 2D **Baths:** 1 En 1 Pr

Nuns Cottage, *5 Hurgill Road, Richmond, N Yorks, DL10 4AR.* Close to Richmond's centre, Grade II Listed, surrounded by stone walls and gardens. Decorated in period style and furnished with antiques. Beams, open fire and guests sitting-room. Bedrooms with all facilities / private bathrooms. Excellent meals. Welcoming and comfortable. **Open:** All year
01748 822809 Mrs Parks *alan.parks@btinternet.com* www.richmond.org.uk/business/nunscottge **D:** Fr £22.00–£25.00 **S:** Fr £30.00–£39.00 **Beds:** 1T 2D **Baths:** 3 Pr (10) (270)

66 Frenchgate, *Richmond, DL10 7AG.* Comfortable rooms in beautiful old house. Stunning views of Richmond. **Open:** All year (not Xmas)
01748 823421 Mrs Woodward *paul@66french.freeserve.co.uk* **D:** Fr £20.00–£21.00 **S:** Fr £25.00–£26.00 **Beds:** 2D 1T **Baths:** 2 En 1 Pr

The Buck Inn, *27 Newbiggin, Richmond, N. Yorks, DL10 4DX.* Elevated beer garden with magnificent views overlooking River Swale Valley, Castle and views of Colloden Tower all from a pub with character and old world charm, excellent accommodation of the highest standard, and breakfasts to satisfy the keenest appetite. **Open:** All year
01748 822259 E Fluen **D:** Fr £22.00–£25.00 **S:** Fr £25.00 **Beds:** 3F 1T 1D 1S **Baths:** 6 En

Caldwell Lodge, *Gilling West, Richmond, N. Yorks, DL10 5JB.* Friendly welcome. Pretty village. 1 mile Scotch Corner. Great breakfast. **Open:** Easter to Oct
01748 825468 Mrs Bolton **D:** Fr £20.00–£25.00 **S:** Fr £25.00–£27.00 **Beds:** 1F 1D **Baths:** 1 Sh (4)

The Restaurant On The Green, *5-7 Bridge Street, Richmond, N. Yorks, DL10 4RW.* Gateway to Dales. Good food and fine wines in historic house. **Open:** All year **Grades:** ETC 3 Diamond
01748 826229 (also fax) Bennett *accom.bennett@talk21.com* www.coast2coast.co.uk/restaraurantonthegreen **D:** Fr £22.00 **S:** Fr £27.00 **Beds:** 1T 1D **Baths:** 2 En (10)

West End Guest House, *45 Reeth Road, Richmond, N. Yorks, DL10 4EX.* Beautifully appointed ensuite accommodation, close to town & river. **Open:** All year (not Xmas/New Year)
01748 824783 Mr Teeley *westend@richmond.org* www.stayatwestend.com **D:** Fr £25.00 **S:** Fr £25.00–£35.00 **Beds:** 1T 3D 1S **Baths:** 4 En 1 Pr

National Grid References given are for villages, towns and cities – not for individual houses

Pottergate Guest House, *4 Pottergate, Richmond, N Yorks, DL10 4AB.* Comfortable guest house, friendly service, excellent value for money. **Open:** All year
01748 823826 Mrs Firby **D:** Fr £19.00 **S:** Fr £20.00–£23.00 **Beds:** 1F 3D 1T 2S **Baths:** 3 Sh (3)

27 Hurgill Road, *Richmond, N. Yorks, DL10 4AR.* Small, friendly guest house. **Open:** All year (not Xmas) **Grades:** ETC 2 Diamond
01748 824092 (also fax) Mrs Lee **D:** Fr £19.00–£20.00 **S:** Fr £20.00–£21.00 **Beds:** 1D 2T 1S **Baths:** 1 Sh

Rievaulx

SE5785

Barn Close Farm, *Rievaulx, Helmsley, York, YO62 5LH.* Barn close. Hill farm in valley of Rievaulx. Recommended in Telegraph. **Open:** All year
01439 798321 Mrs Milburn **D:** Fr £20.00–£25.00 **Beds:** 1F 1D **Baths:** 1 En 1 Pr (6)

Ripley

SE2860

Newton Hall, *Ripley, Harrogate, N. Yorks, HG3 3DZ.* Close to Harrogate, Fountains Abbey, the Dales, Skipton, Bolton Abbey, York. **Open:** All year
01423 770166 Mrs Iveson **D:** Fr £20.00–£25.00 **S:** Fr £30.00 **Beds:** 2D 1T **Baths:** 1 Sh

Slate Rigg Farm, *Birthwaite Lane, Ripley, Harrogate, N. Yorks, HG3 3JQ.* Secluded working family farm with beautiful views of Lower Nidderdale. **Open:** All year (not Xmas/New Year) **Grades:** ETC 3 Diamond
01423 770135 Mrs Bowes *slaterigffarm@hotmail.com* **D:** Fr £20.00–£25.00 **S:** Fr £25.00–£30.00 **Beds:** 1F 1T **Baths:** 2 Sh (4)

Ripon

SE3171

Bishopton Grove House, *Ripon, N. Yorks, HG4 2QL.* Large comfortable Georgian house near Fountains Abbey and River Laver. **Open:** All year
01765 600888 Mrs Wimpress *wimpress@bronco.co.uk* **D:** Fr £27.50 **S:** Fr £20.00–£30.00 **Beds:** 1F 1D 1T **Baths:** 3 En (3)

Middle Ridge, *42 Mallorie Park Drive, Ripon, HG4 2QF.* Traditional,family owned, tastefully furnished, quiet, garden, conservatory, city outskirts. **Open:** Easter to Sept
01765 690558 Mrs Parker *john@midrig.demon.co.uk* **D:** Fr £18.00–£20.00 **S:** Fr £25.00–£30.00 **Beds:** 1D 1T **Baths:** 1 Sh (3)

Moor End Farm, *Knaresborough Road, Littlethorpe, Ripon, N. Yorks, HG4 3LU.* Friendly, non-smoking first-class accommodation. Pleasantly situated. Ideal for touring. **Open:** All year (not Xmas)
01765 677419 Mrs Spensley *pspensley@ukonline.co.uk* yorkshirebandb.co.uk **D:** Fr £23.00–£26.00 **S:** Fr £30.00–£40.00 **Beds:** 2D 1T **Baths:** 2 En 1 Pr (5)

The George Country Inn, *Main Street, Wath, Ripon, N. Yorks, HG4 5EN.* **Open:** All year **01765 640202 & 01765 640635 Fax: 01765 640632** *georgecountryinn.wath@btopenworld.com* **D:** Fr £24.00 **S:** Fr £29.50 **Beds:** 2F 2D **Baths:** 4 En **cc**
Friendly and cosy family-run inn in picturesque village. Public bar and lounge with fire places, featuring 'The Thai House at Wath', an authentic Thai restaurant. Ideal touring area for Yorkshire Dales. Close to Ripon, Thirsk and Harrogate.

Robin Hood's Bay

NZ9504 *The Dolphin, The Falcon, Bay Hotel, Victoria Hotel, Fylingdales Inn, Laurel Inn, Flask Inn*

Meadowfield, *Mount Pleasant North, Robin Hood's Bay, Whitby, N. Yorks, YO22 4RE.* Refurbished Victorian house. Friendly, comfortable, plenty of food. Non-smoking. **Open:** All year (not Xmas)
01947 880564 Mrs Luker **D:** Fr £17.00–£19.50 **S:** Fr £20.00–£24.00 **Beds:** 2D 1T 2S **Baths:** 1 En 1 Sh

Rosegarth, *Thorpe Lane, Robin Hood's Bay, Whitby, N. Yorks, YO22 4RN* Friendly, comfortable accommodation. **Open:** Easter to Nov
01947 880578 Mr Stubbs **D:** Fr £19.00 **Beds:** 1T 1D (9) **cc**

Muir Lea Stores, *Robin Hood's Bay, Whitby, N. Yorks, YO22 4SF.* C18th smugglers' retreat. **Open:** All year
01947 880316 Mrs Leaf **D:** Fr £17.00 **S:** Fr £20.00 **Beds:** 3D 1S **cc**

BATHROOMS
En = Ensuite
Pr = Private
Sh = Shared

Devon House, *Station Road, Robin Hood's Bay, Whitby, N. Yorks, YO22 4RL.* Devon House is a family-run B&B offering guests clean and comfortable accommodation. **Open:** All year (not Xmas/New Year)
01947 880197 D H Duncalfe *duncalfe@devonhouserhb.freeserve.co.uk* devonhouserhb.freeserve.co.uk **D:** Fr £21.00–£22.00 **S:** Fr £42.00–£44.00 **Beds:** 1F 1T 2D **Baths:** 4 En (10) (4)

Glen-lyn, *Station Road, Robin Hood's Bay, Whitby, N Yorks, YO22 4RA.* Come and sample the delights of Robin Hood's Bay and stay in a tastefully decorated, well appointed detached bungalow. You can relax in the large, well-maintained mature gardens with seating area around a pond with water feature. **Open:** All year
01947 880391 Mrs Price *jmpglenlyn@aol.com* **D:** Fr £21.00–£22.00 **Beds:** 1T 1D **Baths:** 2 En

Clarence Dene, *Station Road, Robin Hood's Bay, Whitby, North Yorks, YO22 4RH.* Situated above this historic village. Clarence Dene retains many original Art Nouveau features. The spacious bedrooms have been sympathetically decorated and furnished, all are clean. comfortable and well appointed with ensuite facilities. **Open:** All year
01947 880272 Mrs Howard *dhcdene@aol.com* www.robinhoodsbay.net **D:** Fr £20.00 **Beds:** 1F 1T 3D **Baths:** 5 En

The White Owl, *Station Road, Robin Hood's Bay, Whitby, N Yorks, YO22 4RL.* Interesting house, Centre of village. Accommodation in self-contained apartments. **Open:** All year
01947 880879 Mr & Mrs Higgins *higgins@whiteowlrhb.co.uk* **D:** Fr £22.00–£23.00 **Beds:** 1F 2D 1T **Baths:** 4 En (4)

RATES
D = Price range per person sharing in a double or twin room
S = Price range for a single room

Rosedale Abbey

SE7295

Sevenford House, *Rosedale Abbey, Pickering, N. Yorks, YO18 8SE.* **Open:** All year (not Xmas)
01751 417283 Ms Sugars **Fax: 01751 417505** *sevenford@aol.com* www.sevenford.com **D:** Fr £22.50–£25.00 **S:** Fr £30.00–£35.00 **Beds:** 1F 1D 1T **Baths:** 3 En (9)
In the heart of the North Yorkshire Moors lies the picturesque village of Rosedale Abbey and nestling half way up the valley side is Sevenford House, which sits in four acres of grounds offers charming ensuite accommodation with outstanding views.

Rosedale East

SE7197

The Orange Tree, *Dale Head, Rosedale East, Pickering, N. Yorks, YO18 8RH.* In the heart of National Park. Spectacular views. Ideal touring, walking, cycling. **Open:** All year (not Xmas)
01751 417219 Mr Davies **D:** Fr £21.00–£23.00 **S:** Fr £26.00–£28.00 **Beds:** 1F 2T 2D (6)

Runswick Bay

NZ8016

Cockpit House, *The Old Village, Runswick Bay, Saltburn-by-the-Sea, N Yorks, TS13 5HU.* Seafront position, near pub, beach, cafe, all sea views. **Open:** All year **Grades:** ETC 2 Diamond
01947 840504 Mrs Smith **D:** Fr £17.50 **S:** Fr £17.50–£21.00 **Beds:** 1D 2T **Baths:** 1 Sh

Saintoft

SE7989

Beech Cottage, *Saintoft, Pickering, North Yorkshire, YO18 8QQ.* Large garden property nestled amongst trees, a particularly beautiful area. **Open:** All year
01751 417625 P & E Bramley **D:** Fr £16.00–£18.00 **S:** Fr £20.00–£24.00 **Beds:** 1F 1T **Baths:** 2 En (2)

Sandsend

NZ8612

Estbek House, *Sandsend, Whitby, N. Yorks, YO21 3SU.* Fully equipped designer bedrooms. Fresh food, licensed restaurant. **Open:** All year
01947 893424 (also fax) Mr Cooper *R.C.Hill@Onyxnet.co.uk* www.fastfix.co.uk/estbek **D:** Fr £29.50 **S:** Fr £27.50–£39.50 **Beds:** 1F 2D 2T **Baths:** 4 En 1 Pr cc

Scarborough

TA0388

Leeway Hotel, *71 Queens Parade, Scarborough, YO12 7HT.* A family-run licensed hotel overlooking the North Bay and Castle. **Open:** Easter to Nov
01723 374371 Mr Saville *leeway@supanet.com* **D:** Fr £17.00–£20.00 **S:** Fr £17.00–£18.00 **Beds:** 2F 5D 2S **Baths:** 6 En (6)

Fixton, *Scarborough, N Yorks, YO11 3UD.* Rural location near coast, Moors, Wolds, warm welcome, secure parking. **Open:** All year (not Xmas)
01723 890272 (also fax) Mrs Wheater **D:** Fr £18.00–£20.00 **S:** Fr £18.00 **Beds:** 2F 2D 1S **Baths:** 2 En 1 Sh

Red Lea Hotel, *Prince Of Wales Terrace, Scarborough, N. Yorks, YO11 2AJ.* Traditional hotel with good facilities and expansive sea views. **Open:** All year
01723 362431 Mr & Mrs Lee **Fax: 01723 371230** *redlea@globalnet.co.uk* www.redleahotel.co.uk **D:** Fr £27.00–£38.00 **S:** Fr £27.00–£38.00 **Beds:** 7F 16D 23T 22S **Baths:** 68 En cc

Richmond Private Hotel, *135 Columbus Ravine, Scarborough, N. Yorks, YO12 7QZ.* Small, comfortable, family-run hotel. Friendly atmosphere, good home cooking. **Open:** All year
01723 362934 Mr & Mrs Shaw **D:** Fr £15.00–£18.00 **S:** Fr £15.00–£18.00 **Beds:** 2F 4D 1T 1S **Baths:** 3 En 1 Sh

Gordon Hotel, *24 Ryndleside, Scarborough, N. Yorks, YO12 6AD.* Detached private hotel, warm welcome, good food, free off-road parking. **Open:** All year
01723 362177 Mr Strickland *sales@gordonhotels.co.uk* www.gordonhotel.co.uk. or www.scarborough-hotels.com **D:** Fr £20.00–£25.00 **S:** Fr £25.00–£30.00 **Beds:** 3F 1T 5D 1S **Baths:** 7 En 3 Pr (8) cc

Clog and Garland, *26 Eastborough, Scarborough, N. Yorks, YO11 1NW.* 100 yards from beach and town centre, close to all attractions. **Open:** All year
01723 362865 M Walker www.clogandgarland.freeserve.com **D:** Fr £18.00–£22.00 **S:** Fr £18.00–£25.00 **Beds:** 2F 1T 2D **Baths:** 5 En

Villa Marina Hotel, *59 Northstead Manor Drive, Scarborough, N. Yorks, YO12 6AF.* Detached, quiet location overlooking Peasholm Park, close to north side attractions. **Open:** Easter to Oct
01723 361088 Mr & Mrs Pearson **D:** Fr £22.00–£25.00 **Beds:** 2F 6D 2T **Baths:** 10 En (5) (9) cc

Blands Clliff Lodge and Restaurant, *Blands Cliff, Scarborough, N. Yorks, YO11 1NR.* Town centre located. Licensed family hotel. 100m from beach. **Open:** Easter to Oct
01723 351423 Fax: 01723 353211 *flats@scarborough.co.uk* www.scarborough-flats.co.uk **D:** Fr £15.00–£20.00 **S:** Fr £15.00–£20.00 **Beds:** 5F 2T 5D 4S **Baths:** 6 En 10 Sh cc

Brambles Lodge, *156 Filey Road, Scarborough, N. Yorks, YO11 3AA.* **Open:** Feb to Nov
01723 374613 Lynne & Bill Nightingale *nightingales22@aol.com* www.smoothhound.co.uk/hotels/brambleslodge.html **D:** Fr £22.00–£24.00 **S:** Fr £22.00–£24.00 **Beds:** 2F 3D 1T 1S **Baths:** 7 En (6) (10)
Seeking excellent standard of hospitality, cleanliness and ample private parking? Welcome to Bramble Lodge. All rooms ensuite. 100% non-smoking. Only 1.5m from town centre, but far from the hustle and bustle of the high season. Ideal touring base for National Park.

Wharncliffe Hotel, *26 Blenheim Terrace, Scarborough, N Yorks, YO12 7HD.* Overlooking beautiful North Bay. Central, licensed bar. Clean and comfortable. **Open:** All year **Grades:** ETC 4 Diamond
01723 374635 Mr & Mrs Trigg *dandawharncliffe@aol.com* **D:** Fr £22.00–£28.00 **S:** Fr £27.00–£30.00 **Beds:** 3F 8D 1T **Baths:** 12 En (8) cc

Dene Lea Hotel, *7 Rutland Terrace, Scarborough, N. Yorks, YO12 7JB.* Victorian hotel overlooking North Bay. Friendly family-run hotel, central to all amenities. **Open:** All year
01723 361495 Mr & Mrs Stevens **D:** Fr £16.50–£22.50 **S:** Fr £20.00–£25.00 **Beds:** 2F 7D 2T 1 **Baths:** 5 En 3Sh (2) (2)

Russell Hotel, *22 Ryndleside, Scarborough, N Yorks, YO12 6AD.* Detached 10-bedroom hotel, licensed, overlooking Peasholm Glen. Convenient all North Bay attractions. **Open:** All year **Grades:** ETC 3 Diamond
01723 365453 Lyn Stanley & Glen Martin **Fax: 01723 369029** *info@russellhotel.net* www.russellhotel.net **D:** Fr £20.00–£30.00 **S:** Fr £22.00–£33.00 **Beds:** 7F 2D 1T **Baths:** 7 En (6) 2

Howdale Hotel, *121 Queens Parade, Scarborough, N. Yorks, YO12 7HU.* Comfortable hotel, panoramic sea views, memorable breakfasts, 10 mins town. **Open:** Easter to Nov
01723 372696 (also fax) Mr & Mrs Abbott *maria_keith_howdalehotel@yahoo.co.uk* www.howdalehotel.moonfruit.com **D:** Fr £19.00–£24.00 **S:** Fr £25.00–£28.00 **Beds:** 2F 10D 2T 1S **Baths:** 13 En 2 Sh (9) **cc**

Outlook Hotel, *18 Ryndleside, Scarborough, N. Yorks, YO12 6AD.* Select location overlooking park. Ideal for coast and Yorkshire Moors. **Open:** All year (not Xmas/New Year) **Grades:** RAC 3 Diamond
01723 364900 *info@outlookhotel.co.uk* www.outlookhotel.co.uk **D:** Fr £20.00–£25.00 **S:** Fr £20.00–£30.00 **Beds:** 2F 2T 6D **Baths:** 10 En (6) (8)

Acacia Private Hotel, *37 Esplanade Road, Scarborough, N. Yorks, YO11 2AT.* Small Victorian Hotel offering quality accommodation. Close to town/spa complex. **Open:** Feb to Nov
01723 373270 Annette & Margery Allcock **D:** Fr £20.00 **S:** Fr £25.00 **Beds:** 3T 2D 2F **Baths:** 7 En (5) (8)

The Anchor Hotel, *61 Northstead Manor Drive, Scarborough, N. Yorks, YO12 6AF.* Attractive detached hotel overlooking Peasholm Park & lake. Customer care awards. **Open:** All year **Grades:** ETC 1 Star
01723 364518 Mrs Hurrell **Fax: 01723 376311 D:** Fr £20.00–£25.00 **S:** Fr £20.00–£35.00 **Beds:** 4F 2D 4T 2S **Baths:** 12 En (10) **cc**

Princess Court, *11 Princess Royal Terrace, Scarborough, N. Yorks, YO11 2RP.* Spotless rooms with warm friendly service and home cooking. **Open:** All year
01723 501922 Rose *andy@princesscourt.co.uk* www.princesscourt.co.uk **D:** Fr £20.00–£21.00 **S:** Fr £30.00–£31.00 **Beds:** 1F 2T 2D 2S **Baths:** 6 En 1 Pr

Ryndle Court Hotel, *47 Northstead Manor Drive, Scarborough, N. Yorks, YO12 6AF.* Delightfully situated overlooking Peasholm Park and near the sea. **Open:** Feb to Nov **Grades:** ETC 2 Star, RAC 2 Star
01723 375188 (also fax) Mr & Mrs Davies *enquiries@ryndlecourt.co.uk* www.ryndlecourt.co.uk **D:** Fr £29.00–£31.00 **S:** Fr £29.00–£39.00 **Beds:** 1F 6D 5T 2S **Baths:** 14 En (10) **cc**

Dolphin Hotel, *151 Columbus Ravine, Scarborough, N. Yorks, YO12 7QZ.* **Open:** All year (not Xmas/New Year)
01723 374217 Mrs Robinson *thedolphin@breathe.com* www.thedolphin.info **D:** Fr £16.00–£20.00 **S:** Fr £26.00–£30.00 **Beds:** 2F 1T 3D **Baths:** 5 En 1 Pr
The Dolphin offers comfortable accommodation, friendly welcome with a high degree of service. Ideally situated for a relaxing weekend, traditional seaside holiday, or as a base to explore the beautifully rugged NE coast and North Yorkshire Dales.

Scotch Corner

NZ2105

Vintage Hotel, *Scotch Corner, Richmond, N. Yorks, DL10 6NP.* Conveniently situated roadside inn on A66, only quarter mile from A1 at Scotch Corner. **Open:** All year (not Xmas/New Year) **Grades:** ETC 3 Diamonds, RAC 3 Diamonds
01748 824424 Mr & Mrs Fothergill **Fax: 01748 826272 D:** Fr £19.00–£27.00 **S:** Fr £27.50–£42.50 **Beds:** 3D 2T 3S **Baths:** 5 En 1 Sh (7) (40) **cc**

Selby

SE6132

Hazeldene Guest House, *32-34 Brook Street, Selby, N. Yorks, YO8 4AR.* Attractive period house, featuring spacious ensuite rooms, market town location. **Open:** All year (not Xmas)
01757 704809 Mr Leake **Fax: 01757 709300** *selbystay@breathe.com* www.hazeldene-selby.co.uk **D:** Fr £22.00–£24.00 **S:** Fr £25.00–£33.00 **Beds:** 3D 3T 2S **Baths:** 5 En 2 Sh (6) **cc**

Selside

SD7875

South House Farm, *Selside, Settle, N. Yorks, BD24 0HU.* Comfortable farmhouse accommodation set in the centre of the Peaks. **Open:** Easter to Oct
01729 860271 Ms Kenyon **D:** Fr £20.00 **S:** Fr £20.00 **Beds:** 1F 2D 1T **Baths:** 1 En (1) (6)

Settle

SD8163

Liverpool House, *Chapel Square, Settle, N. Yorks, BD24 9HR.* Situated in quiet area yet within 3 mins walk town square. **Open:** All year **Grades:** AA 4 Diamond
01729 822247 Mr & Mrs Duerden **D:** Fr £19.00–£24.00 **S:** Fr £20.00–£22.00 **Beds:** 4D 1T 2S **Baths:** 2 En 2 Sh (8) **cc**

Sharow

SE3271

Half Moon Inn, *Sharow Lane, Sharow, Ripon, N. Yorks, HG4 5BP.* Quiet C18th country inn on outskirts of historic Ripon. **Open:** All year (not Xmas/New Year)
01765 600291 D: Fr £20.00 **S:** Fr £24.50 **Beds:** 1T 2D **Baths:** 3 En 1 Sh (10) **cc**

Sherburn in Elmet

SE4933

Church Hill Guest House, *3 Church Hill, Sherburn in Elmet, Leeds, LS25 6AX.* **Open:** All year
01977 681000 A Beattie **Fax: 01977 683030 D:** Fr £17.50–£20.00 **S:** Fr £18.50–£25.00 **Beds:** 1D 2T 1S **Baths:** 2 En 1 Sh (8) **cc**
The accommodation is a purpose-built annexe joined to owners' house, all recently refurbished to high standard. Our register has many glowing testimonials. Very easy to find and extremely convenient for York, Dales, Moors, Pennines. Relaxed, easygoing and friendly.

Wheelgate Guest House, *7 Kirkgate, Sherburn in Elmet, Leeds, West Yorkshire, LS25 6BH.* Olde worlde cottage-style house, convenient for Leeds, York, Selby. **Open:** All year (not Xmas)
01977 682231 Mrs Tomlinson **Fax: 01977 685287 D:** Fr £18.00–£23.00 **S:** Fr £25.00–£29.00 **Beds:** 1D 3T **Baths:** 1 En 2 Sh (4) (7)

National Grid References given are for villages, towns and cities – not for individual houses

Sheriff Hutton

SE6466 *Blacksmith's Arms*

Hall Farm, *High Stittenham, Sheriff Hutton, York, YO60 7TW.* Perfectly situated for visiting York, Castle Howard and the North York Moors. **Open:** All year
01347 878461 Mrs Hemingway *hallfarm@btinternet.com* www.hallfarm.btinternet.co.uk
D: Fr £20.00–£23.00 **S:** Fr £25.00–£30.00
Beds: 1F 1T 1D **Baths:** 3 En (0) (20)

Sinnington

SE7486

Green Lea, *Sinnington, York, YO62 6SH.* Large converted bungalow in lovely pretty village off A170. Lovely garden to relax in. **Open:** Mar to Oct
01751 432008 Mr & Mrs Turnbull **D:** Fr £18.00–£22.50 **S:** Fr £18.00–£22.50 **Beds:** 1F 1T 1D **Baths:** 2 En 1 Sh (5) (4)

Skeeby

NZ1903

The Old Chapel, *Richmond Road, Skeeby, Richmond, North Yorks, DL10 5DR.* Beautifully converted Victorian chapel situated in small village near Richmond. **Open:** All year (not Xmas/New Year)
01748 824170 & 07803 103871 (M) H Allan *hazel@theoldchapel.fsnet.co.uk* **D:** Fr £20.00 **S:** Fr £25.00 **Beds:** 2D **Baths:** 2 En (2)

Skipton

SD9851 *Bull, Elm Tree, Sailor, Craven Heifer, Devonshire Arms, Albion, White Swan, Bay Horse, Angel*

Bourne House, *22 Upper Sackville Street, Skipton, N Yorks, BD23 2EB.* Edwardian townhouse, quiet location, close to town centre, easy parking. **Open:** All year (not Xmas/New Year)
01756 792633 Mr & Mrs Barton **Fax: 01756 701609** *bournehouse@totalise.co.uk* www.bournehouseguesthouse.co.uk **D:** Fr £16.00–£18.00 **S:** Fr £17.00–£25.00 **Beds:** 1T 2D 1S **Baths:** 1 En 2 Sh (3) **cc**

Dalesgate Lodge, *69 Gargrave Road, Skipton, N. Yorks, BD23 1QN.* Comfortable rooms, friendly welcome. Special winter breaks available. **Open:** All year
01756 790672 Mr & Mrs Mason **D:** Fr £17.50–£20.00 **S:** Fr £20.00–£25.00 **Beds:** 2D/T 2S **Baths:** 4 En (2)

Spring Gardens Cottage, *20 Queens Street, Skipton, BD23 1HE.* **Open:** All year (not Xmas/New Year)
01756 790739 **D:** Fr £20.00 **Beds:** 1D **Baths:** 1 En (2)
Cottage-style building featuring luxury double room ensuite. Private Sky TV lounge. Within 10 mins walk of Skipton town centre with its historic castle and markets, yet situated in a tranquil area, for a peaceful break. Gateway to the Dales.

Low Skibeden Farmhouse, *Harrogate Road, Skipton, N. Yorks, BD23 6AB.* C16th farmhouse with little luxuries and fireside treats at no extra charge. **Open:** All year
01756 793849 & 07050 207787 Mrs Simpson **Fax: 01756 793804** *skibhols.yorksdales@talk21.com* www.yorkshirenet.uk/accgde/lowskibeden **D:** Fr £22.00–£26.00 **S:** Fr £30.00–£40.00 **Beds:** 3F 1D 1T **Baths:** 4 En 1 Sh (12) (5) **cc**

Sleights

NZ8607

Ryedale House, *154-8 Coach Road, Sleights, Whitby, N. Yorks, YO22 5EQ.* National Park country. Magnificent moor/dale/coastal scenery. Relaxing house for non-smokers. **Open:** Apr to Oct **Grades:** ETC 4 Diamond
01947 810534 (also fax) Mrs Beale **D:** Fr £21.50–£22.50 **S:** Fr £19.00–£24.00 **Beds:** 2D 2S **Baths:** 2 En 1 Pr (3) **cc**

Slingsby

SE6975

Beech Tree House Farm, *South Holme, Slingsby, York, YO62 4BA.* Working farm. Beautiful area between York and Scarborough. Children welcome. **Open:** All year (not Xmas)
01653 628257 **D:** Fr £18.00 **S:** Fr £18.00
Beds: 2F 1D 1T **Baths:** 3 Pr (6)

Planning a longer stay? Always ask for any special rates

Sowerby

SE4281

The Old Manor House, *27 Front Street, Sowerby, Thirsk, N. Yorks, YO7 1JQ.* Charming C16th Manor house overlooking village Green Herriot Museum town. **Open:** Mar to Oct
01845 526642 Mr Jackson **Fax: 01845 526568**
D: Fr £20.00–£30.00 **S:** Fr £35.00–£40.00
Beds: 3D **Baths:** 3 En (5) **cc**

Spaunton

SE7289

Holywell House, *Spaunton Bank Foot, Spaunton, Appleton Le Moors, York, YO62 6TR.* C18th beamed cottage with large garden. **Open:** All year (not Xmas/New Year)
01751 417624 Mrs Makepeace **D:** Fr £36.00 **S:** Fr £18.00 **Beds:** 1D 1T 1S (5) (4)

Staintondale

SE9998

Island House, *Island Farm, Staintondale, Scarborough, N Yorks, YO13 0EB.* Space, tranquillity, relaxation, tennis, snooker, on organic farm. Beautiful countryside. **Open:** Easter to Nov
01723 870249 M Clarke *roryc@tinyworld.co.uk* www.islandhousefarm.co.uk **D:** Fr £20.00–£25.00 **S:** Fr £25.00–£27.00 **Beds:** 1T 2D **Baths:** 3 En (6)

Staithes

NZ7718

Brooklyn, *Brown's Terrace, Staithes, Saltburn-by-the-Sea, TS13 5BG.* Sea captain's house, central, but quiet, in picturesque fishing village. **Open:** All year (not Xmas)
01947 841396 Ms Heald **D:** Fr £20.00 **S:** Fr £20.00 **Beds:** 1T 2D **Baths:** 2 Sh

Springfields, *42 Staithes Lane, Staithes, Saltburn-by-the-Sea, N Yorks, TS13 5AD.* Victorian house with countryside views. Lounge available. In National Park. **Open:** All year
01947 841011 Mrs Verrill **D:** Fr £15.00 **S:** Fr £15.00 **Beds:** 1D 1S **Baths:** 1 En 1 Sh (1)

Stape

SE7993

Seavy Slack Farm, *Stape, Pickering, N. Yorks, YO18 8HZ.* Comfortable farmhouse on a working farm serving good food. **Open:** All year (not Xmas)
01751 473131 Mrs Barrett **D:** Fr £20.00–£25.00 **S:** Fr £25.00 **Beds:** 1T 2D **Baths:** 3 En (5) (6)

Starbotton

SD9574

Fox & Hounds Inn, *Starbotton, Skipton, N. Yorks, BD23 5HY.* Traditional cosy Dales inn. **Open:** Mar to Dec
01756 760269 Mr & Mrs McFadyen **Fax: 01756 760862** *hilarymcfadyen@supanet.com*
D: Fr £27.50 **S:** Fr £35.00 **Beds:** 1D 1T (12) cc

Stearsby

SE6172

The Granary, *Stearsby, Brandsby, York, YO61 4SA.* Converted C18th granary set in beautiful 1-acre garden located in quiet Yorkshire hamlet. **Open:** All year (not Xmas/New Year)
01347 888652 (also fax) Mr & Mrs Turl *roberttturl@thegranary.org.uk* **D:** Fr £22.00–£25.00 **S:** Fr £25.00–£30.00 **Beds:** 3D **Baths:** 3 En (6)

Stonegrave

SE6578

Manor Cottage, *Stonegrave , York, YO62 4LJ.* Quiet friendly home offering comfortable spacious accommodation and peaceful garden. **Open:** All year (not Xmas/New Year)
01653 628599 Trudy Visser *gideon.v@virgin.net* business.virgin.net/gideon.v/index.html **D:** Fr £17.50–£20.00 **S:** Fr £20.00–£25.00 **Beds:** 2T **Baths:** 2 En (4)

Studley Roger

SE2870

The Wheelhouse, *2 Parklands, Studley Roger, Ripon, HG4 3AY.* Renovated mill next to Studley Royal Oak Park and Fountains Abbey. **Open:** All year (not Xmas)
01765 604508 J Burton *itis@itis.slv.co.uk* **D:** Fr £23.00–£25.00 **Beds:** 1D **Baths:** 1 En (8) (4)

Sutton Bank

SE5182

Cote Faw, *Hambleton Cottages, Sutton Bank, Thirsk, N. Yorks, YO7 2EZ.* Comfortable cottage in National Park, central for visiting North Yorkshire. **Open:** All year (not Xmas)
Grades: ETC 2 Diamond
01845 597363 Mrs Jeffray **D:** Fr £17.00–£18.00 **S:** Fr £17.00–£18.00 **Beds:** 1F 1D 1S **Baths:** 1 Sh (3)

Swainby

NZ4702

Churchview House, *72 High Street, Swainby, Northallerton, N Yorks, DL6 3DG.* Stunning accommodation, breakfast & views. Peaceful. Walking, cycling & sightseeing. **Open:** All year **Grades:** ETC 5 Diamond, Gold
01642 706058 (also fax) Clare Nevin *churchviewhouse@aol.com* www.churchviewhouse.co.uk **D:** Fr £29.00 **S:** Fr £35.00 **Beds:** 1T 1D **Baths:** 2 En (8)

Thimbleby

SE4495

Stonehaven, *Thimbleby, Osmotherly, Northallerton, DL6 3PY.* Comfortable farmhouse, super view, lovely walks, good beds and good food. **Open:** Mar to Nov
01609 883689 Mrs Shepherd **D:** Fr £24.00 **S:** Fr £20.00–£22.00 **Beds:** 1D 1T **Baths:** 1 En 1 Pr (1) (3) cc

Thirsk

SE4282

Laburnham House, *31 Topcliff Rd, Thirsk, N. Yorks, YO7 1RX.* Spacious detached house, tastefully furnished with antiques and in the traditional manner. **Open:** Mar to Nov **Grades:** ETC 4 Diamond, Silver
01845 524120 Mrs Ogleby www.smoothhound.co.uk/hotels/laburnhamhse.html **D:** Fr £21.50–£22.50 **Beds:** 1F 1D 1T **Baths:** 2 En 1 Pr (5) (3)

Town Pasture Farm, *Boltby, Thirsk, N. Yorks, YO7 2DY.* Comfortable farmhouse in beautiful village, central for Yorkshire Dales. **Open:** All year (not Xmas)
Grades: ETC 3 Diamond
01845 537298 Mrs Fountain **D:** Fr £19.50–£22.00 **S:** Fr £20.00–£23.00 **Beds:** 1F 1T **Baths:** 2 En (3)

Fourways Guest House, *Town End, Thirsk, N. Yorks, YO7 1PY.* Ideal holiday base for touring the North York Moors/Dales.
Open: All year
01845 522601 Mrs Baukar *fourways@nyorks.fsbusiness.co.uk* **D:** Fr £19.00–£21.00 **S:** Fr £21.00–£24.00 **Beds:** 1F 2T 2D 3S **Baths:** 7 En 1 Pr 1 Sh (6) cc

St James' House, *36 The Green, Thirsk, N Yorks, YO7 1AQ.* Two minutes' walk from market place. **Open:** All year
01845 526565 Mr Ogleby **D:** Fr £20.00 **S:** Fr £30.00 **Beds:** 3D **Baths:** 2 En (1) (3)

Thixendale

SE8461

Manor Farm, *Thixendale, Malton, N. Yorks, YO17 9TG.* Working farm. Private spacious accommodation, overlooking pretty garden. Substantial breakfasts.
Open: All year (not Xmas/New Year)
01377 288315 (also fax) Mrs Brader **D:** Fr £20.00 **S:** Fr £20.00 **Beds:** 2F 1D 1T 1S **Baths:** 1 Pr

Thornton le Dale

SE8382

Banavie, *Roxby Road, Thornton le Dale, Pickering, N. Yorks, YO18 7SX.* **Open:** All year (not Xmas)
Grades: ETC 4 Diamond
01751 474616 Mrs Bowes *ella@banavie.fsbusiness.co.uk* www.banavie.uk.com
D: Fr £20.00–£23.00 **S:** Fr £25.00–£27.00 **Beds:** 1F 2D **Baths:** 3 En (4)

Very warm welcome awaits all guests at Banavie. Tastefully furnished accommodation in quiet part of this picturesque village. Ideal for a quiet relaxing night. Yorkshire breakfast, tea tray on arrival, own keys. Ideal for York, coast, moors, steam railway & walking.

Tangalwood, *Roxby Road, Thornton le Dale, Pickering, N. Yorks, YO18 7SX.* Friendly comfortable accommodation, quietly situated. Ideal for York, Moors, coast. **Open:** Easter to Oct
Grades: ETC 4 Diamond
01751 474688 Mrs Wardell **D:** Fr £19.00–£20.00 **S:** Fr £22.00–£25.00 **Beds:** 1D 1T 1S **Baths:** 2 En 1 Pr (7) (2)

Nabgate, *Wilton Road, Thornton le Dale, Pickering, N. Yorks, YO18 7QP.* **Open:** All year **Grades:** ETC 4 Diamond
01751 474279 & 07703 804859 (M)
Mrs Pickering **D:** Fr £20.00–£25.00 **S:** Fr £22.00–£25.00 **Beds:** 2D 1T **Baths:** 3 En (4)

Situated on the edge of beautiful Thornton le Dale, in TV's Heartbeat country, this clean and friendly home offers excellent Yorkshire breakfasts. Central for Moors, Coast, Steam Railway, York, Castle Howard and Dalby Forest. Garden for guest to relax in. Own keys.

Thornton Watlass

SE2385

Buck Inn, *Thornton Watlass, Ripon, N. Yorks, HG4 4AH.* Delightful country inn overlooking the cricket green in a quiet village just 5 mins from the A1. Relax in our comfortable bedrooms, enjoy our superb home-cooked food and drink from our selection of five real ales. Large secluded garden with children's playground.
Open: All year (not Xmas)
01677 422461 Mr & Mrs Fox **Fax: 01677 422447** *buckwatlass@btinternet.com* www.smoothhound.co.uk/hotels/buckinn.html **D:** Fr £27.50–£32.00 **S:** Fr £38.00–£42.00 **Beds:** 1F 3D 2T 1S **Baths:** 5 En 1 Sh (20) cc

Threshfield

SD9863

Grisedale Farm, *Threshfield, Skipton, N Yorks, BD23 5NT.* Friendly traditional Dales farmhouse near Grassington with beautiful rural location. **Open:** All year (not Xmas/New Year)
01756 752516 Mrs Kitching *janette.kitching@tesco.net* **D:** Fr £15.00–£18.00 **S:** Fr £20.00 **Beds:** 1T 1D **Baths:** 1 Sh (2)

Wath

SE3277

The George Country Inn, *Main Street, Wath, Ripon, N. Yorks, HG4 5EN.* Family-run inn in picturesque village. Public bar and lounge with fireplaces. **Open:** All year
01765 640202 & 01765 640635 Fax: 01765 640632 *georgecountryinn.wath@btopenworld.com* **D:** Fr £24.00 **S:** Fr £29.50 **Beds:** 2F 2D **Baths:** 4 En cc

Weaverthorpe

SE9670

The Star Inn, *Weaverthorpe, Malton, N. Yorks, YO17 8EY.* Country inn, quiet locality, fine food, traditional ales and open log fires.
Open: All year
01944 738273 Mr Richardson *starinn@quista.net* www.starinn.net **D:** Fr £20.00–£26.00 **S:** Fr £20.00–£26.00 **Beds:** 1F 1D 1T **Baths:** 3 En (5) (30) cc

West Heslerton

SE9176

The Old Rectory, *West Heslerton, Malton, North Yorkshire, YO17 8RE.* B&B in fine Georgian house set in 2 acres of garden. **Open:** All year (not Xmas/New Year)
01944 728285 Mr & Mrs Hillas *bhillas@supanet.com* www.theoldrectoryny.co.uk **D:** Fr £19.00–£21.00 **S:** Fr £19.00–£21.00 **Beds:** 1F 1T 1D **Baths:** 3 En (10) cc

West Witton

SE0688

The Old Star, *West Witton, Leyburn, N. Yorks, DL8 4LU.* **Open:** All year (not Xmas) **Grades:** ETC 3 Diamond
01969 622949 Mr & Mrs Martin *theoldstar@amserve.com* **D:** Fr £17.00–£21.00 **S:** Fr £17.00–£21.00 **Beds:** 1F 2T 4D **Baths:** 5 En (12)
Former C17th coaching inn now a family-run guest house. Oak beams, log fire and informal relaxing atmosphere. Situated in the Yorkshire Dales National Park, the Old Star is an ideal base for touring, walking or cycling.

Whitby

NZ8910

Haven Guest House, *4 East Crescent, Whitby, N. Yorks, YO21 3HD.* Comfortable friendly guest house with sea views. Full English breakfast. **Open:** All year (not Xmas/New Year)
01947 603842 Chris & Stevie Connell **Fax: 01947 605934** *info@thehavenwhitby.co.uk* thehavenwhitby.co.uk **D:** Fr £21.00–£24.00 **S:** Fr £20.00 **Beds:** 1F 5D 2S **Baths:** 5 En 3 Sh (5)

White Horse and Griffin, *Church Street, Whitby, YO22 4BH.* Historic inn with echoes of Captain Cook, Scorsby, Stephenson and Dickens. **Open:** All year
01947 604857 Mr Perkins **D:** Fr £24.00–£35.00 **S:** Fr £24.00–£35.00 **Beds:** 3F 2T 6D 1S **Baths:** 12 En cc

Havelock Guest House, *30 Hudson Street, Whitby, YO21 3ED.* Conveniently situated for the spa, beach, harbour and shops. Sauna available. **Open:** All year (not Xmas)
01947 602295 (also fax) M J Ryder **D:** Fr £17.00–£19.50 **S:** Fr £17.00 **Beds:** 2F 5D 1T 5S **Baths:** 7 En 2 Sh

Seaview Guest House, *5 East Crescent, Whitby, N Yorks, YO21 3HD.* Family-run guest house with high standard of cleanliness. Close to beach and town.
Open: All year (not Xmas/New Year)
01947 604462 L Boettger *cview@supanet.com* **D:** Fr £19.00–£22.00 **S:** Fr £19.00–£21.00 **Beds:** 1F 5D 2S **Baths:** 6 En 1 Sh

Falcon Guest House, *29 Falcon Terrace, Whitby, N. Yorks, YO21 1EH.* Quiet private house near centre. Sunny breakfast room, organic produce. **Open:** All year
01947 603507 Mr Lyth **D:** Fr £18.00 **S:** Fr £20.00 **Beds:** 2F **Baths:** 1 Sh

The Yorkshire House, *Moorlands, North Promenade, Whitby, N. Yorks, YO21 3JX.* Fine sea views. Warm Christian welcome. Special interest breaks available. **Open:** All year
01947 603584 L Atkinson **Fax: 01947 821668** **D:** Fr £20.60–£32.60 **S:** Fr £20.60–£32.60 **Beds:** 2F 10T 8D 10S **Baths:** 14 En 7 Sh (20) cc

Ryedale House, *154-8 Coach Road, Sleights, Whitby, N. Yorks, YO22 5EQ.* **Open:** Apr to Oct **Grades:** ETC 4 Diamond
01947 810534 (also fax) Mrs Beale **D:** Fr £21.50–£22.50 **S:** Fr £19.00–£24.00 **Beds:** 2D 2S **Baths:** 2 En 1 Pr (3) cc
National Park country. Magnificent moor/dale/coastal scenery. Relaxing house for non-smokers, high standard private facilities with many extras. Lovely gardens, valley views, extensive traditional wholefood/vegetarian breakfasts. Regret no pets or children. Minimum 2 nights.

Serendipity, *17 Abbey Terrace, Whitby, North Yorkshire, YO21 3HQ.* **Open:** All year
01947 603868 Mr King & Jane Robinson **Fax: 01947 602025** *enquiries@serendipityhotel.co.uk* www.serendipityhotel.co.uk **D:** Fr £22.00–£25.00 **S:** Fr £32.00–£35.00 **Beds:** 6F 1T 2D **Baths:** 6 En 3 Pr
Serendipity is family-run, close to sea & town. Comfortable rooms are all ensuite or have private bathrooms, TV, coffee and tea facilities. Excellent breakfast. Easy access to the North York Moors and villages & other major tourist attractions.

Rosslyn Guest House, *11 Abbey Terrace, Whitby, YO21 3HQ.* **Open:** All year (not Xmas) **Grades:** ETC 3 Diamond
0800 2985254 A Briers **Fax: 01947 604086** *rosslynhouse@bushinternet.com* www.guesthousewhitby.co.uk **D:** Fr £19.50–£21.00 **S:** Fr £20.00–£25.00 **Beds:** 2F 2D 1T 2S **Baths:** 6 En 1 Pr (2)
Quality accommodation at affordable prices, close to harbourside and moorlands. Rosslyn is a fine Victorian home, retaining many original features, with all modern requirements needed to make your stay comfortable & enjoyable. 'Midweek winter special stay 3 nights, pay for only 2'.

Wheeldale Hotel, *North Promenade, Whitby, YO21 3JX.* **Open:** Feb to Nov **Grades:** ETC 4 Diamond
01947 602365 Mr & Mrs Bouttell *wheeldale_hotel@lineone.net* www.wheeldale-hotel.co.uk **D:** Fr £26.00–£32.00 **Beds:** 1T 8D **Baths:** 9 En (9) cc
Set in a quiet peaceful location overlooking Whitby's West Cliff. The harbour and town are only minutes walk away. Owned and run by Liz and Ian who guarantee a warm welcome and a comfortable and relaxing stay.

BATHROOMS
En = Ensuite
Pr = Private
Sh = Shared

Arches Guesthouse, *8 Havelock Place, Hudson Street, Whitby, N Yorkshire, YO21 3ER.* **Open:** All year **Grades:** ETC 4 Diamond
01947 601880 Mr Brew *archeswhitby@freeola.com* www.whitbyguesthouses.co.uk
D: Fr £20.00–£24.00 **S:** Fr £20.00–£30.00 **Beds:** 2F 1T 4D 2S **Baths:** 6 En 1 Pr 2 Sh cc
Friendly family-run guest house, where a warm welcome and a large breakfast is always assured. The ideal base for experiencing the old world charms of this historic seaside town, exploring the beautiful North Yorkshire Moors or simply relaxing.

Arundel House Hotel, *Bagdale, Whitby, North Yorkshire, YO21 1QJ.* Manor house near town centre, private parking, restaurant & bar. **Open:** All year **Grades:** RAC 3 Diamond
01947 603645 Fax: 0870 165 6214 *arundel_house@hotmail.com* www.arundelhousehotel.co.uk **D:** Fr £25.00–£27.00 **S:** Fr £30.00–£35.00 **Beds:** 3F 5D 2T 1S **Baths:** 11 En (7) cc

Wombleton

SE6684

Rockery Cottage, *Main Street, Wombleton, York, YO62 7RX.* Quiet village location, ideally placed for touring Moors/coast. **Open:** All year
01751 432257 & 07771 657222 (M) Mrs Sleight *enquiries@rockerycottage.co.uk* www.rockerycottage.co.uk **D:** Fr £22.50–£28.00 **S:** Fr £25.00–£28.00 **Beds:** 1D 1S 1T **Baths:** 3 En (12) (3)

RATES
D = Price range per person sharing in a double or twin room
S = Price range for a single room

Wrelton

SE7686 *New Inn, Apple Tree*

The Huntsman Restaurant and Guest House, *Main Street, Wrelton, Pickering, N. Yorks, YO18 8PG.* Quiet village location, 2 miles Pickering, leading to Rosedale and Moors. Converted stone-built farmhouse, rustic character beamed ceilings, garden, patio, private parking. Comfortable ensuite beds, licensed bar, Carol's home cooking. Special offer 3 for 2. Short breaks - brochure. **Open:** All year
01751 472530 Mr Lower *howard@thehuntsman.freeserve.co.uk* www.europage.co.uk/huntsman **D:** Fr £16.00–£24.00 **S:** Fr £18.00–£26.00 **Beds:** 1T 2D **Baths:** 3 En (10) cc

York

SE5951 *Nag's Head*

Bowen House, *4 Gladstone Street, Huntington Road, York, YO31 8RF.* Small, family-run, Victorian guest house with period furnishings throughout. **Open:** All year (not Xmas)
01904 636881 Mrs Wood **Fax: 01904 338700** *info@bowenhouse.co.uk* www.bowenhouse.co.uk **D:** Fr £18.50–£24.00 **S:** Fr £23.00–£28.00 **Beds:** 1F 2D 1T 1S **Baths:** 2 En 1 Sh (4) cc

Avenue Guest House, *6 The Avenue, Clifton, York, YO30 6AS.* This family-run charming Victorian guest house is quietly situated in a beautiful tree-lined avenue. The city centre is a ten minute riverside walk. Some rooms are ensuite. Families are welcome. Non-smoking throughout. Free, easy permit parking always available. **Open:** All year (not Xmas/New Year)
01904 620575 *allen@avenuegh.fsnet.co.uk* www.avenuegh.fsnet.co.uk **D:** Fr £17.00–£22.00 **S:** Fr £20.00–£25.00 **Beds:** 4F 3D **Baths:** 4 En 3 Sh (4)

Grange Lodge, *52 Bootham Crescent, Bootham, York, YO30 7AH.* Lovely family-run guest house. **Open:** All year
01904 621137 Mrs Robinson *grangeldg@aol.com* **D:** Fr £20.00–£25.00 **S:** Fr £25.00 **Beds:** 2F 3D 1T 1S **Baths:** 1 En 5 Pr 2 Sh

Park View Guest House, *34 Grosvenor Terrace, Bootham, York, YO30 7AG.* Victorian town house close to centre. Front rooms have views of Minster. **Open:** All year (not Xmas)
01904 620437 (also fax) Mrs Harding *park_view@talk21.com* **D:** Fr £24.00–£27.50 **S:** Fr £27.50–£35.00 **Beds:** 1F 2D 2T 1S **Baths:** 5 En 1 Pr

Coppers Lodge, *15 Alma Terrace, York, YO10 4DQ.* Homely, comfortable, full English breakfast. **Open:** All year
01904 639871 Mrs Grima **D:** Fr £20.00 **S:** Fr £20.00 **Beds:** 5F 2D 1S **Baths:** 1 Pr 3 Sh (5)

Turnberry House, *143 Fulford Road, York, YO10 4HG.* Edwardian, high quality accommodation, excellent breakfast, close to city centre. **Open:** All year **Grades:** ETC 3 Diamond
01904 658435 Mrs Manders **Fax: 01904 630263** *turnberry.house@virgin.net* **D:** Fr £25.00–£30.00 **S:** Fr £30.00–£35.00 **Beds:** 2F 2T 2D 1S **Baths:** 5 En (6)

Cornmill Lodge, *120 Haxby Road, York, YO31 8JP.* Vegetarian/vegan guest house. 15 mins' walk to York Minster. **Open:** All year
01904 620566 (also fax) Mrs Williams *cornmillyork@aol.com* www.cornmillyork.co.uk **D:** Fr £20.00–£28.00 **S:** Fr £20.00–£28.00 **Beds:** 2D 1T/F 1S **Baths:** 3 En 1 Pr (4) cc

Avimore House Hotel, *78 Stockton Lane, York, YO31 1BS.* Small friendly family-run B&B. 15 mins' walk to city. **Open:** All year (not Xmas/New Year)
01904 425556 Mrs Lewis **Fax: 01904 426264** *aviemore.house@tinyonline.co.uk* **D:** Fr £23.00–£25.00 **S:** Fr £24.00–£26.00 **Beds:** 1F 1T 1D 2S **Baths:** 5 En (3)

Georgian House Hotel, *35 Bootham, York, YO30 7BT.* Quality city centre accommodation with car park. **Open:** All year (not Xmas)
01904 622874 Mr Semple **Fax: 01904 635379** *georgian.house@virgin.net* www.georgianhouse.co.uk **D:** Fr £22.00–£30.00 **S:** Fr £25.00–£45.00 **Beds:** 3F 9D 1T 1S **Baths:** 11 En 2 Sh (5) (8) cc

Wold View House Hotel, *171-175 Haxby Road, York, YO31 8JL.* Turn-of-the-20th-Century hotel, tea and coffee facilities, clock radio alarms, all ensuite. **Open:** All year (not Xmas/New Year)
01904 632061 (also fax) Mr & Mrs Wheeldon www.woldviewhousehotel.co.uk **D:** Fr £19.00–£26.00 **S:** Fr £19.00–£26.00 **Beds:** 2F 2T 10D 3S **Baths:** 17 En (1)

Bank House, *9 Southlands Road, York, YO23 1NP.* Privately-owned guest house in quiet position adjacent to the Racecourse. **Open:** All year
01904 627803 & 07713 639596 (M) Mr Farrell **D:** Fr £16.00–£25.00 **S:** Fr £20.00–£25.00 **Beds:** 2F 1T 3D 1S **Baths:** 7 En

Crescent Guest House, *77 Bootham, York, YO30 7DQ.* Georgian building built in 1770. 5 mins walk to Minster and town centre. **Open:** All year **Grades:** ETC 2 Diamond
01904 623216 (also fax) E H Whitelegg www.guesthousesyork.net **D:** Fr £18.00–£25.00 **S:** Fr £20.00–£30.00 **Beds:** 4F 3T 5D 1S **Baths:** 8 En 2 Pr cc

Planning a longer stay? Always ask for any special rates

St Raphael Guest House, *44 Queen Annes Road, Bootham, York, YO30 7AF.* Family-run mock Tudor guest house, tastefully decorated. **Open:** All year **01904 645028** Mrs Foster **Fax: 01904 658788** *straphael2000@yahoo.co.uk* **D:** Fr £20.00–£25.00 **S:** Fr £21.00–£28.00 **Beds:** 3F 2D 1T 2S **Baths:** 8 En (2) cc

The Bentley Hotel, *25 Grosvenor Terrace, Bootham, York, YO30 7AG.* Victorian town house overlooking York Minster & offering premier quality accommodation. **Open:** Feb to Dec **Grades:** ETC 4 Diamond **01904 644313 & 07860 199440 (M)** Mr Lefebve **Fax: 01904 644313** *bentley.ofyork@btinternet.com* www.bentleyofyork.co.uk **D:** Fr £22.00–£30.00 **S:** Fr £28.00–£32.00 **Beds:** 3D 1T 2S **Baths:** 4 En 1 Sh (1)

Bay Tree Guest House, *92 Bishopthorpe Road, York, YO23 1JS.* Tastefully decorated Victorian town house, 10 mins' walk from attractions. **Open:** All year (not Xmas) **01904 659462 (also fax)** Mr Ridley *d.ridley.baytree@ondigital.co.uk* **D:** Fr £25.00 **S:** Fr £25.00 **Beds:** 1F 1D 1T 2S **Baths:** 2 En 1 Sh (1)

The Limes, *135 Fulford Road, York, YO10 4HE.* Perfectly situated for City, University and golf club. Warm welcome. **Open:** All year (not Xmas) **01904 624548 Fax: 01904 624944** *queries@limeshotel.co.uk* www.limeshotel.co.uk **D:** Fr £25.00–£35.00 **S:** Fr £35.00–£60.00 **Beds:** 5F 3D **Baths:** 8 En (8) cc

Sagar B&B The Bungalow, *Kexby, York, YO41 5LA.* A modern bungalow, four miles east of York on A1079. **Open:** All year (not Xmas) **01759 380247** Mrs Sagar *lynnesagar@btinternet.com* www.sagarsbed-breakfast.ukf.net **D:** Fr £18.00 **S:** Fr £20.00–£22.00 **Beds:** 1D 1T **Baths:** 2 En (2)

Ashbourne House, *139 Fulford Road, York, YO10 4HG.* Friendly family-run Victorian establishment. Providing the highest of standards. **Open:** All year (not Xmas/New Year) **01904 639912** Mr & Mrs Minns **Fax: 01904 631332** *ashbourneh@aol.com* **D:** Fr £20.00–£30.00 **S:** Fr £34.00–£40.00 **Beds:** 2F 2T 3D **Baths:** 6 En 1 Pr (6) cc

Heworth Court Hotel, *76 Heworth Green, York, YO31 7TQ.* Established recommended hotel. Ample parking, York Minster within 1 mile. **Open:** All year **01904 425156** Mr Smith *hotel@heworth.co.uk* **D:** Fr £30.00–£52.50 **S:** Fr £46.00–£65.00 **Beds:** 2F 5T 10D 8S **Baths:** 25 En (25) cc

Bronte Guesthouse, *22 Grosvenor Terrace, Bootham, York, YO30 7AG.* Award-winning Victorian guest house. 5 mins' walk from city centre. **Open:** All year (not Xmas/New Year) **01904 621066 Fax: 01904 653434** *100754.300@compuserve.com* **D:** Fr £26.00–£30.00 **S:** Fr £30.00–£40.00 **Beds:** 1F 1T 2D 2S **Baths:** 6 En (1) cc

Newton Guest House, *Neville Street, Haxby Road, York, YO31 8NP.* **Open:** All year (not Xmas) **Grades:** ETC 3 Diamond **01904 635627** Mrs Tindall **D:** Fr £25.00–£30.00 **Beds:** 2D 1T **Baths:** 3 En (3)
Lovely accommodation offered a short stroll from the beautiful city of York and all it's historic attractions. We have 20 years experience looking after visitors in our home to the city, ensuite rooms with hospitality tray. Great Yorkshire welcome assured.

Kismet Guest House, *147 Haxby Road, York, YO31 8JW.* Close to city centre, friendly welcome, substantial breakfast. Cleanliness foremost. **Open:** All year **01904 621056** B Chamberlain & N Summers *kismetguesthouse@yahoo.com* **D:** Fr £25.00–£30.00 **S:** Fr £20.00–£25.00 **Beds:** 1F 1T 4D **Baths:** 1 Sh (6)

Ascot House, *80 East Parade, York, YO31 7YH.* **Open:** All year (not Xmas) **Grades:** AA 4 Diamond **01904 426826** Mrs Wood **Fax: 01904 431077** *J&K@ascot-house-york.demon.co.uk* www.ascothouseyork.com **D:** Fr £22.00–£30.00 **S:** Fr £22.00–£52.00 **Beds:** 3F 8D 3T 1S **Baths:** 12 En 1 Pr 1 Sh (14) cc
A family-run Victorian villa, built in 1869, with rooms of character and many four-poster or canopy beds. Superb English breakfasts. Fifteen minutes walk to Jorvik Viking Centre, Castle Museum or York Minster. Residential licence, sauna, private enclosed car park.

Ivy House Farm, *Kexby, York, YO41 5LQ.* C19th farmhouse, central for York, East Coast, Dales, Herriot country. **Open:** All year (not Xmas) **Grades:** RAC 3 Diamond **01904 489368 (also fax)** Mrs Daniel *kevin-jayne-daniel@supanet.com* **D:** Fr £16.00–£20.00 **S:** Fr £20.00–£22.00 **Beds:** 1F 1D 1T 1S **Baths:** 2 En 1 Sh (10)

The Hazelwood, *24-25 Portland Street, Gillygate, York, YO31 7EH.* **Open:** All year **Grades:** ETC 4 Diamond, Silver, AA 4 Diamond, RAC 4 Diamond, Sparkling **01904 626548 Fax: 01904 628032** www.thehazelwoodyork.com **D:** Fr £37.50–£50.00 **S:** Fr £35.00–£95.00 **Beds:** 2F 8D 3T 1S **Baths:** 14 En (8) (8) cc
High quality B&B in the very heart of York, only 400 yards from York Minster. Elegant Victorian townhouse in quiet residential area with own car park. Individually styled ensuite bedrooms. Wide choice of quality breakfasts including vegetarian. Non smoking.

Holly Lodge, *206 Fulford Road, York, YO10 4DD.* **Open:** All year **01904 646005** Mr Gallagher www.thehollylodge.co.uk **D:** Fr £29.00–£39.00 **S:** Fr £58.00–£68.00 **Beds:** 1F 3D 1T **Baths:** 5 En 5 Pr (7) cc
Ideally located 10 mins riverside walk from the centre, convenient for all York's amenities. This fine Georgian building, with comfortable rooms, walled garden and car park, offers a warm welcome. Booking recommended. Located on A19,1.5 miles towards the city from A19/A64 intersection.

George Hotel, *6 St Georges Place, York, YO24 1DR.* Family run Victorian residence. 10 min walk to 'Walls'. Parking. **Open:** All year (not Xmas/New Year) **01904 625056 Fax: 01904 625009** *sixstgeorg@aol.com* members.aol.com/sixstgeorg **D:** Fr £25.00–£27.50 **S:** Fr £35.00–£50.00 **Beds:** 5F 5D **Baths:** 10 En (6) cc

Blakeney Hotel, *180 Stockton Lane, York, YO31 1ES.* **Open:** All year (not Xmas) **Grades:** ETC 3 Diamond **01904 422786 (also fax)** Mr Whiteford *reception@blakeneyhotel-york.co.uk* www.blakeneyhotel-york.co.uk **D:** Fr £25.00–£30.00 **S:** Fr £30.00–£40.00 **Beds:** 11F 2T 2D 2S **Baths:** 9 En 1 Pr 2 Sh (12) cc
Superb location for visiting York city centre and exploring the Yorkshire Dales, Moors and coast. Friendly, family-run hotel offering a warm welcome, comfortable accommodation, excellent cuisine, fine wines and guaranteed personal service. Our aim is to persuade you to return!

Acer Hotel, *52 Scarcroft Hill, York, YO24 1DE.* **Open:** All year (not Xmas/New Year)
01904 653839 & 01904 677017 & 07941 542443 (M) Fax: 01904 677017 *info@acerhotel.co.uk* www.acerhotel.co.uk **D:** Fr £30.00–£40.00 **S:** Fr £45.00 **Beds:** 1F 3D **Baths:** 4 En cc
WINNER GUEST ACCOMMODATION OF THE YEAR AWARD 2001 - York Tourism Awards. Elegant licensed hotel, offering superior ensuite accommodation in a friendly atmosphere. Non-smoking, acclaimed breakfasts, luxurious Four Poster Room. Short walk from attractions, railway station and racecourse. Quietly situated.

All details shown are as supplied by B&B owners in Autumn 2002

Barrington House, *15 Nunthorpe Avenue, Scarcroft Road, York, YO23 1PF.* **Open:** All year (not Xmas/New Year) **01904 634539** Mr Bell *alan.bell@btinternet.com* **D:** Fr £18.00–£26.00 **S:** Fr £20.00–£28.00 **Beds:** 2F 1T 3D 1S **Baths:** 7 En cc
Beautiful Edwardian guest-house in quiet cul-de-sac. Ten minutes walk from city centre and all York's attractions. Near station, racecourse and theatres. All ensuite and hearty breakfasts. Spotlessly clean. Unrestricted parking. A perfect base for exploring Dales, Moors and coast.

Nunmill House, *85 Bishopthorpe Road, York, YO23 1NX.* **Open:** Feb to Nov **Grades:** ETC 4 Diamond, Silver, AA 4 Diamond **01904 634047** Mr & Mrs Whitbourn-Hammond **Fax: 01904 655879** *info@nunmill.co.uk* www.nunmill.co.uk **D:** Fr £26.00–£32.00 **S:** Fr £45.00 **Beds:** 1F 6D 1T **Baths:** 7 En 1 Pr (6)
Splendid Victorian house, lovingly furnished and smoke-free, for those looking for comfortable yet affordable accommodation. Easy walk to all attractions. SAE for brochure. Please visit our website.

Cumbria House, *2 Vyner Street, Haxby Road, York, YO31 8HS.* Lovely family-run guest house. Private car park. Ideal for city centre. **Open:** All year **01904 636817** Mrs Clark *reservation@cumbriahouse.freeserve.co.uk* www.cumbriahouse.com **D:** Fr £21.00–£25.00 **S:** Fr £23.00–£30.00 **Beds:** 2F 2D 1T 1S **Baths:** 2 En 4 Sh (5) cc

The Beckett, *58 Bootham Crescent, York, YO30 7AH.* City centre, Victorian, magnificent breakfast, warm welcome, elegant, comfortable, friendly. **Open:** All year (not Xmas/New Year) **01904 644728** M Sloan **Fax: 01904 639915** *nova@woko.freeserve.co.uk* www.mywebsite.net/thebeckett **D:** Fr £25.00–£35.00 **S:** Fr £25.00–£45.00 **Beds:** 1T 4D 1S 1F **Baths:** 7 En cc

Foss Bank Guest House, *16 Huntington Road, York, YO31 8RB.* Overlooking the River Foss. 10-minute stroll to city centre. **Open:** All year (not Xmas/New Year) **Grades:** ETC 3 Diamond **01904 635548** www.fossbank.co.uk **D:** Fr £21.00–£26.00 **S:** Fr £23.00–£25.00 **Beds:** 1T 3D 1S **Baths:** 3 En (7) (4)

Briar Lea Guest House, *8 Longfield Terrace, Bootham, York, YO30 7DJ.* Small friendly guest house 5 mins walk from city centre. **Open:** All year **01904 635061** Mr & Mrs Barlow **Fax: 01904 330356** *briarleahouse@msn.com* www.briarlea.co.uk **D:** Fr £24.00–£25.00 **S:** Fr £25.00–£40.00 **Beds:** 2F 2T 2D **Baths:** 6 En (2) cc

Bishopgarth Guest House, *3 Southlands Road, Bishopthorpe Road, York, YO23 1NP.* Quiet, near central location. Highest standards of cuisine, comfort, cleanliness, care. **Open:** All year (not Xmas/New Year) **Grades:** ETC 3 Diamond **01904 635220** Mrs Spreckley *megspreckley@aol.com* **D:** Fr £19.00–£24.00 **S:** Fr £20.00–£45.00 **Beds:** 2F 2D 1T **Baths:** 5 En 2 Sh cc

Northolme Guest House, *114 Shipton Road, York, YO30 5RN.* Warm welcome, comfortable accommodation, hearty breakfast. Handy for city centre. **Open:** All year (not Xmas/New Year) **Grades:** ETC 3 Diamond **01904 639132** J L Liddle *g.liddle@tesco.net* www.northolmeguesthouse.co.uk **D:** Fr £17.50–£24.00 **S:** Fr £19.00–£28.00 **Beds:** 1F 1D 2T 1S **Baths:** 3 En 1 Sh (4)

Ivy House Farm, *Kexby, York, YO41 5LQ.* C19th farmhouse, central for York, East Coast, Dales, Herriot country. **Open:** All year (not Xmas) **Grades:** RAC 3 Diamond **01904 489368 (also fax)** Mrs Daniel *kevin-jayne-daniel@supanet.com* **D:** Fr £16.00–£20.00 **S:** Fr £20.00–£22.00 **Beds:** 1F 1D 1T 1S **Baths:** 2 En 1 Sh (10)

Fairthorne, *356 Strenshall Road, Earswick, York, YO32 9SW.* Peaceful country setting, dormer bungalow. 3 miles from York, easy reach North York Moors. **Open:** Dec to Dec **01904 768609 (also fax)** J W Harrison **D:** Fr £18.00–£20.00 **S:** Fr £25.00 **Beds:** 1F 1D **Baths:** 1 En (2)

BATHROOMS
En = Ensuite
Pr = Private
Sh = Shared

Warrens Guest House, *30 Scarcroft Road, York, YO23 1NF.* **Open:** All year (not Xmas/New Year) **Grades:** ETC 3 Diamond **01904 643139** Mr & Mrs Warren **Fax: 01904 658297** *warrensgh@btinternet.com* www.warrens.ndo.co.uk **D:** Fr £25.00–£30.00 **S:** Fr £35.00–£50.00 **Beds:** 2F 2T 2D **Baths:** 6 En (6) **cc** Quality accommodation in Victorian townhouse, 350 yards from medieval city walls. Close to racecourse, train station, city attractions. High quality, great value. 4-poster and ground-floor rooms available. Quality breakfast (including vegetarian) served in conservatory. Special deals available for midweek breaks.

South Yorkshire

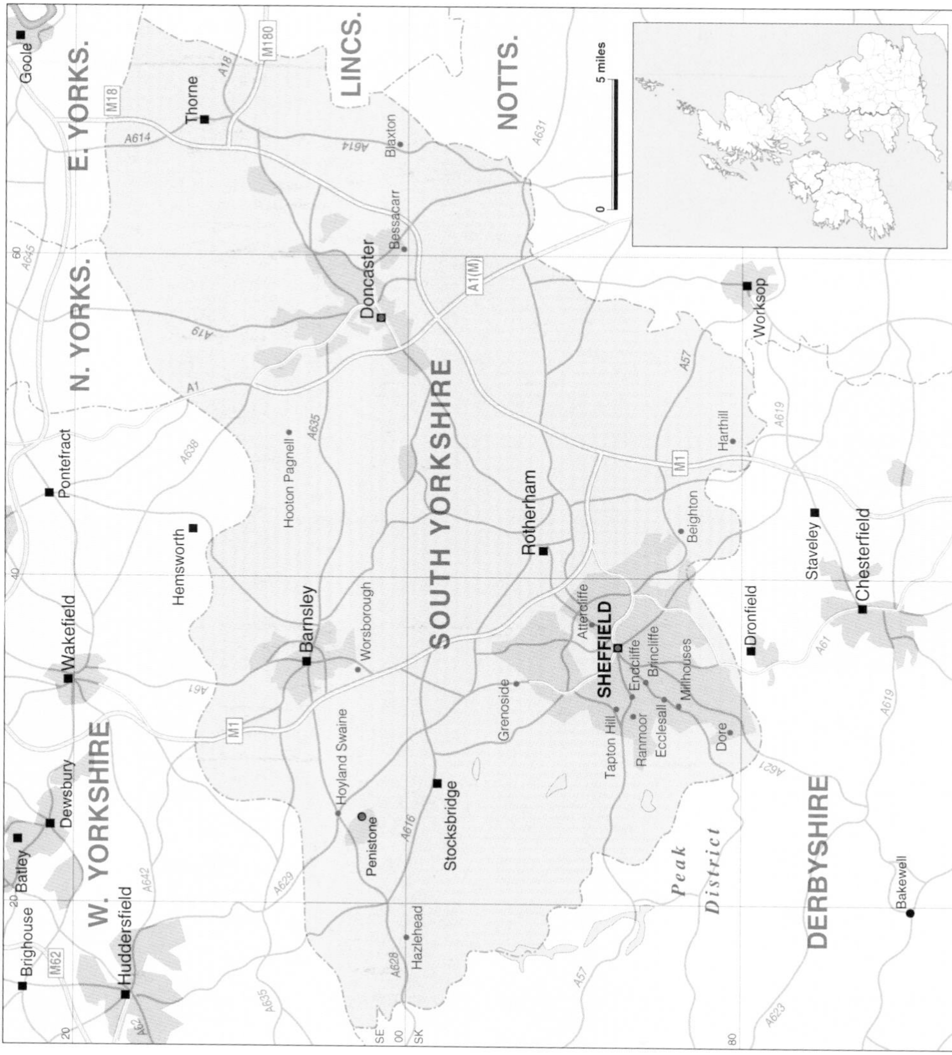

Beighton

SK4483

Beighton Bed and Breakfast, *50 High Street, Beighton, Sheffield, S20 1EA.* Within easy reach for arena, Don Valley, Meadowhall, Chatsworth and Rother Valley. **Open:** All year
0114 269 2004 Fax: 0114 2692004 D: Fr £16.00–£18.00 **S:** Fr £17.00–£28.00 **Beds:** 1F 1T 1D 3S **Baths:** 6 En

Bessacarr

SE6101

10 Saxton Avenue, *Bessacarr, Doncaster, South Yorkshire, DN4 7AX.* Friendly 1930 house, quiet, leafy residential area. Near Dome, racecourse. **Open:** All year
01302 535578 & 07773 912437 (M) A Gibbs **D:** Fr £22.00 **S:** Fr £22.50–£27.50 **Beds:** 2T 1D 1S **Baths:** 1 En 1 Sh (2)

BEDROOMS
D = Double
T = Twin
S = Single
F = Family

Blaxton

SE6700

Station Hotel, *Stationroad, Blaxton, Doncaster, DN9 3AA.* **Open:** All year
01302 770218 *station@globalnet.co.uk* **D:** Fr £22.00–£26.00 **S:** Fr £24.00–£28.00 **Beds:** 2F 5T **Baths:** 4 En 3 Sh (8) cc
Situated close to the new proposed international Finningley Airport, Doncaster Racecourse, 6 miles East of Doncaster. Easy access to all major motorway networks. Close drive to the market town of Bawtry.

Doncaster

SE5702

Rockingham Arms Hotel, *Bennetthorpe, Doncaster, DN2 6AA.* Not far from Doncaster centre, racecourse, railway station and Doncaster Dome. **Open:** All year
01302 360980 **D:** Fr £25.00 **S:** Fr £30.00–£35.00 **Beds:** 5F 9T 2D 2S **Baths:** 9 En 4 Pr 6 Sh cc

The Wheatley Hotel, *Thorne Road, Doncaster, DN2 5DR.* Ideally situated just 1 mile from Doncaster Racecourse and Exhibition Centre.
Open: All year (not Xmas/New Year)
01302 364092 **Fax: 01302 328176** *info@thewheatleyhotel.co.uk* **D:** Fr £27.50–£55.00 **S:** Fr £35.00–£49.50 **Beds:** 13F 11T 2S **Baths:** 2 En 11 Pr (3) (1) cc

Dore

SK3181

Critchleys, *6 Causeway Head Road, Dore, Sheffield, S17 3DJ.* A modern guest house near city and country. Friendly, clean, excellent food. **Open:** All year
0114 236 4328 (also fax) M L Critchleys **D:** Fr £17.50–£22.50 **S:** Fr £25.00–£35.00 **Beds:** 1F 3D 3T 2S **Baths:** 5 En 3 Sh (9) (4)

Grenoside

SK3393 *Red Lion*

Middleton Green Farm, *Cinder Hill Lane, Grenoside, Sheffield, S35 8NH.* C17th farmhouse. Sauna and jacuzzi available.
Open: All year
0114 245 3279 (also fax) Ms Mennell **D:** Fr £25.00 **S:** Fr £30.00 **Beds:** 1F 2T 1D **Baths:** 3 En (10)

Harthill

SK4980 *Bee Hive*

57 Firvale, *Harthill, Sheffield, S26 7XP.* Delightful cottage, warm conservatory.
Open: All year
01909 773605 D Stevens **D:** Fr £20.00 **S:** Fr £20.00 **Beds:** 1T 1D **Baths:** 2 En

Hazlehead

SE1800

Delmont Grange, *Flouch, Hazlehead, Sheffield, S36 4HH.* Moorland views near 'Summer Wine' country. Penistone market town. **Open:** All year
01226 767279 Mrs Cuss *nancuss@lineone.net* **D:** Fr £22.50 **S:** Fr £22.50 **Beds:** 1F 1T 1D **Baths:** 2 En (8)

Hooton Pagnell

SE4808

Rock Farm, *Hooton Pagnell, Doncaster, S. Yorks, DN5 7BT.* Traditional stone farmhouse in picturesque village 2m NW of A1. **Open:** All year
01977 642200 (also fax) Mrs Harrison **D:** Fr £20.00 **S:** Fr £18.00–£20.00 **Beds:** 1F 1D 1S **Baths:** 1 En 1 Sh (6)

Hoyland Swaine

SE2604

Fell House, *354 Barnsley Road, Hoylandswaine, Sheffield, S36 7HD.* 1830s cottage. Beautiful views, private suite to relax in comfort. **Open:** All year (not Xmas)
01226 790937 & 07808 355 329 (M) Ms Sykes **D:** Fr £18.00 **S:** Fr £23.00 **Beds:** 1F **Baths:** 1 En (2)

Penistone

SE2403

Carr House, *Royd Lane, Penistone, Sheffield, S36 9NY.* Converted barn and cottage in Summer Wine country. Uninterrupted views. **Open:** All year (not Xmas)
01226 762917 Mr Worboys *mgc@wworboys.freeserve.co.uk* **D:** Fr £12.50–£20.00 **S:** Fr £15.00–£25.00 **Beds:** 1F 4D 1T **Baths:** 3 En 2 Sh (6)

Old Vicarage Guest House & Tea Rooms, *Shrewsbury Road, Penistone, Sheffield, S36 6DY.* Situated in centre of Penistone, close to Pennine Way trail.
Open: All year
01226 370607 Mr Storer **Fax: 01226 766521** *enquires@old vicarage.co.uk* **D:** Fr £25.00–£55.00 **S:** Fr £25.00–£35.00 **Beds:** 2F 4D 4S **Baths:** 5 En 5 Sh (10) cc

SHEFFIELD Attercliffe

SK3788

Swan Hotel, *756 Attercliffe Road, Sheffield, S9 3RQ.* Family-run hotel, close Sheffield city centre, next to Don Valley Stadium and Sheffield Arena. **Open:** All year
0114 244 7978 Fax: 0114 242 4928
swansheffield@btinternet.com
www.swansheffield.co.uk **D:** Fr £17.50–£24.00 **S:** Fr £25.00–£35.00 **Beds:** 4F 4D 4T 1S **Baths:** 10 En 3 Sh (15) cc

SHEFFIELD Brincliffe

SK3385

Peace Guest House, *92 Brocco Bank, Hunters Bar, Sheffield, S11 8RS.* B&B close to centre, university, hospitals. Friendly, comfortable, family run. **Open:** All year
0114 268 5110 & 0114 267 0760 Mr Manavi **D:** Fr £18.00–£40.00 **S:** Fr £22.00–£27.00 **Beds:** 1F 2D 2T 3S **Baths:** 2 En 1 Pr 1 Sh (6) cc

SHEFFIELD Central

SK3586

Beech House, *44 Broomgrove Road, Sheffield, S10 2NA.* Large homely Victorian house, close to universities, hospitals, Peak District. **Open:** All year (not Xmas)
0114 266 2537 Miss Boler **D:** Fr £20.00 **S:** Fr £22.00 **Beds:** 1F 3D 3T 1S **Baths:** 2 Sh (12) (4)

SHEFFIELD Ecclesall

SK3284

Hillside, *28 Sunningdale Mount, Ecclesall, Sheffield, S11 9HA.* Your comfort is our interest. Quiet, modern, welcoming, close buses and town (2.5 miles). **Open:** All year
0114 262 0833 Mrs Whitehead **D:** Fr £19.00 **S:** Fr £19.00 **Beds:** 1T 1S **Baths:** 1 Sh (1) (2)

SHEFFIELD Endcliffe

SK3286

Nini's Guest House, *41 Endcliffe Rise Road, Sheffield, S11 8RU.* Family-run, offering a friendly and welcoming atmosphere.
Open: All year
0114 266 9114 A Kocura **D:** Fr £20.00 **S:** Fr £22.00 **Beds:** 1D 2T 1S (3)

SHEFFIELD Millhouses

SK3283

Tyndale, *164 Millhouses Lane, Sheffield, S7 2HE.* Quiet, comfortable family accommodation. Convenient for city and Peak District. **Open:** All year **Grades:** ETC 3 Diamond
0114 236 1660 (also fax) Mr & Mrs Wilmshurst **D:** Fr £20.00 **S:** Fr £20.00 **Beds:** 1F 1D 1S **Baths:** 1 Sh (3)

SHEFFIELD Ranmoor

SK3186 *Bull's Head, Rising Sun*

Martins Guest House, *397 Fulwood Road, Sheffield, S10 3GE.* Victorian mansion on bus route. **Open:** All year
0114 230 8588 Martins **D:** Fr £22.00–£25.00 **S:** Fr £25.00–£30.00 **Beds:** 3F 2T **Baths:** 2 En 2 Pr 1 Sh (10)

B&B owners may vary rates – be sure to check when booking

SHEFFIELD Tapton Hill

SK3286

St Pellegrino Hotel, *2 Oak Park, Sheffield, S10 5SD.* Friendly family-run hotel. Situated near to the centre of Sheffield. **Open:** All year
0114 268 1953 A Lawera **Fax: 0114 266 0151** **D:** Fr £25.00–£35.00 **S:** Fr £24.00–£35.00 **Beds:** 5F 2D 3T 4S **Baths:** 1 En 5 Pr 3 Sh (20)

Planning a longer stay? Always ask for any special rates

Worsbrough

SE3503 *Burton Inn*

The Button Mill Inn, *Park Road, Worsbrough, Barnsley, South Yorkshire, S70 5LJ.* Olde worlde inn opposite Worsborough Country Park and Mill. Fishing reservoir and public walkways in walking distance. Comfortable rooms with televisions. Good food cooked fresh. Large menu to choose from. Vegetarian meals. Large wine list. Good selection of cask beers. **Open:** All year (not Xmas)
01226 282639 (also fax) Mr Loftus **D:** Fr £22.50 **S:** Fr £25.00 **Beds:** 1F 1D 3T 2S **Baths:** 7 Pr (14) (60) **cc**

West Yorkshire

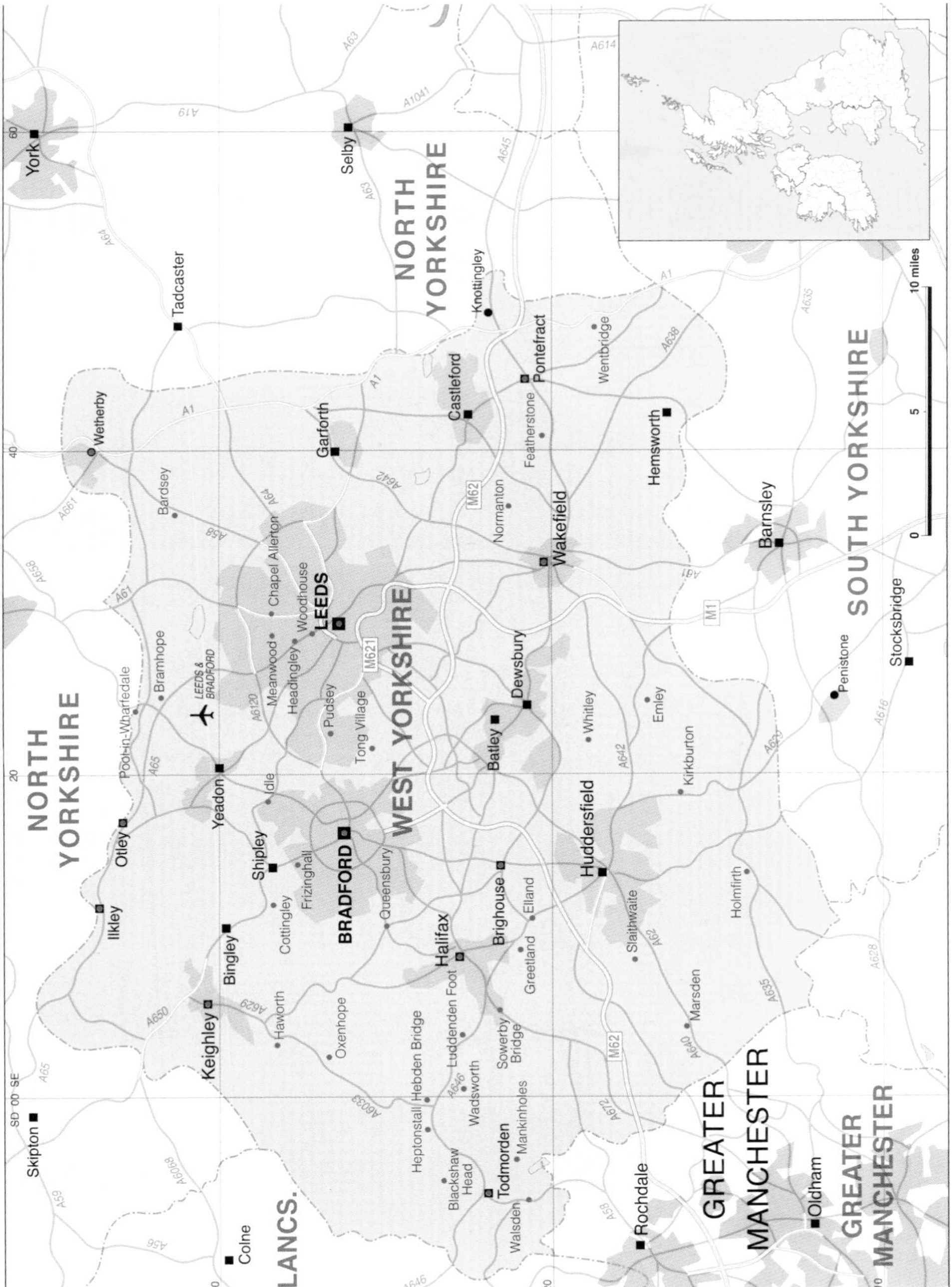

BATHROOMS
En = Ensuite
Pr = Private
Sh = Shared

Bardsey

SE3643

Gables B&B, *Mill Lane, Bardsey, Leeds, West Yorkshire, LS17 9AN.* **Open:** All year (not Xmas)
01937 574163 Mr & Mrs Gregory **D:** Fr £20.00–£24.00 **S:** Fr £22.00–£27.00 **Beds:** 3D 1T 2S **Baths:** 2 En 2 Sh (6)
Distinctive detached family home, in half acre gardens, offers friendly hospitality for any visitors to North Leeds, immediately adjacent extensive nature reserve, country walks. 4 miles Harewood House. Approx. 2.5m from A1, 5m from Leeds. Several premier W Yorks golf courses close by.

Bingley

SE1139

Ashley End, *22 Ashley Road, off Ashfield Crescent, Bingley, W. Yorks, BD16 1DZ.* Quiet, private house 5 miles Bradford, near main bus routes. **Open:** All year (not Xmas)
Grades: ETC 3 Diamond
01274 569679 Mrs Robertson **D:** Fr £19.00–£20.00 **S:** Fr £18.00–£20.00 **Beds:** 1T 2S **Baths:** 1 Sh

Blackshaw Head

SD9527

Higher Earnshaw Water, *Blackshaw Head, Hebden Bridge, W. Yorks, HX7 7JB.* Family smallholding, comfortable old farmhouse in lovely countryside. Warm welcome. **Open:** All year (not Xmas/New Year)
01422 844117 Mr & Mrs Redmond **D:** Fr £22.00 **S:** Fr £23.00 **Beds:** 1F 1D 1S **Baths:** 1 Sh (4)

Badger Fields Farm, *Badger Lane, Blackshaw Head, Hebden Bridge, W. Yorks, HX7 7JX.* Amidst beautiful gardens, spectacular views, 2 miles from Hebden Bridge. **Open:** All year
01422 845161 Mrs Whitaker **D:** Fr £19.00–£20.00 **S:** Fr £20.00–£22.00 **Beds:** 1F 1D **Baths:** 1 Sh (3)

Bradford

SE1632

Westleigh Hotel, *30 Easby Road, Bradford, W. Yorks, BD7 1QX.* **Open:** All year
01274 727089 Mr Kerwick **Fax: 01274 394658** *tony@thewestleighhotel.com* www.thewestleighhotel.com **D:** Fr £23.00–£26.00 **S:** Fr £29.00–£35.00 **Beds:** 5F 10T 4D 9S **Baths:** 11 En 4 Sh (22) **cc**
High quality accommodation only a few mins walk from the city centre. Close by are the university, Alhambra Theatre, National Photographic Museum, ice rink, nightclubs, cinema, bowling alley and main shopping centre. M62 3 miles. Airport 12 miles.

Carnoustie, *8 Park Grove, Bradford, W. Yorks, BD9 4JY.* Detached Victorian house near Lister Park and University Management School. **Open:** All year
Grades: ETC 3 Diamond
01274 490561 (also fax) Mr Sugden *carnoustie1@activemail.co.uk* **D:** Fr £20.00–£22.00 **S:** Fr £26.00–£28.00 **Beds:** 1D 1T 1S **Baths:** 3 En (3)

New Beehive Inn, *Westgate, Bradford, W. Yorks, BD1 3AA.* Renowned gaslit inn. Centrally situated. Characterful and spacious bedrooms. **Open:** All year
01274 721784 Mr Wagstaff **Fax: 01274 735092 D:** Fr £19.00–£23.00 **S:** Fr £24.00–£30.00 **Beds:** 2F 6T 4D 1S **Baths:** 10 En 2 Pr (20) **cc**

Prince of Wales, *91 Harrogate Road, Eccleshill, Bradford, West Yorkshire, BD2 3ES.* Warm friendly pub 10 mins from Bradford, 15 mins Leeds, 10 mins Leeds-Bradford Airport. **Open:** All year
01274 638729 Mr Peat **D:** Fr £15.00–£25.00 **S:** Fr £15.00–£25.00 **Beds:** 1F 3D 3T 1S **Baths:** 4 En 4 Sh (1) (30) **cc**

Bramhope

SE2543

The Cottages, *Moor Road, Bramhope, Leeds, LS16 9HH.* Old cottages, furnished to a high standard, fringe of village. **Open:** All year (not Xmas) **Grades:** ETC 4 Diamond, Silver
0113 284 2754 Mrs Adams **D:** Fr £25.00 **S:** Fr £38.00 **Beds:** 4D 1T **Baths:** 5 En (5)

Brighouse

SE1423

Lane Head Hotel, *2 Brighouse Wood Lane, Brighouse, Huddersfield, HD6 2AL.* A renovated C17th coaching inn retaining many original features. **Open:** All year
01484 714108 Mr & Mrs Mccue **Fax: 01484 380540 D:** Fr £20.00–£23.50 **S:** Fr £29.38–£35.25 **Beds:** 10D 4T **Baths:** 14 En **cc**

Cottingley

SE1137

March Cote Farm, *Woodside Avenue, Cottingley, Bingley, W. Yorks, BD16 1UB.* A friendly welcome awaits you in our fully modernised farmhouse. **Open:** All year
01274 487433 Mrs Warin **Fax: 01274 488153** *jeanwarin@nevisuk.net* www.yorkshire.co.uk/accgde/marchcote **D:** Fr £20.00–£25.00 **S:** Fr £22.00–£25.00 **Beds:** 1F 2D **Baths:** 2 En 1 Pr (6)

Elland

SE1121

Pinfold Guest House, *Dewsbury Road, Elland, West Yorkshire, HX5 9JU.* Recently refurbished Victorian coaching inn. Warm and homely atmosphere. **Open:** All year
01422 372645 Mr & Mrs Parr *debbie@dlsbusiness.fsnet.co.uk* **D:** Fr £19.00 **S:** Fr £26.00 **Beds:** 1F 1D 2T 3S **Baths:** 7 En (10)

China Palace Hotel and Restaurant, *Park Road, Elland, W. Yorks, Hx5 9HP.* High quality English run rural house and Chinese restaurant. All rooms fully ensuite. **Open:** All year (not Xmas/New Year)
01422 310408 Fax: 01422 377232 D: Fr £19.95 **S:** Fr £29.50 **Beds:** 1F 4T 5D 4S **Baths:** 14 En (90) **cc**

Emley

SE2413

Thorncliffe Farmhouse, *Thorncliffe Lane, Emley, Huddersfield, West Yorkshire, HD8 9RS.* Rural C18th stone farmhouse on Kirklees Way. Close M1 J38. **Open:** All year (not Xmas)
01924 848277 Mrs Judd **D:** Fr £17.50–£20.00 **S:** Fr £19.50–£25.00 **Beds:** 2T **Baths:** 2 En 1 Pr (4)

BEDROOMS
D = Double
T = Twin
S = Single
F = Family

Featherstone

SE4219

Rolands Croft Guest House, *Rolands Croft, Featherstone, Pontefract, W Yorks, WF7 6ED.* A barn conversion overlooking fields and next to pub with meals at great prices. **Open:** All year
01977 790802 Mr Sutton **D:** Fr £39.00–£44.00 **S:** Fr £27.00 **Beds:** 1F 2T 1D 1S cc

Frizinghall

SE1435

Park Grove Hotel, *28 Park Grove, Frizinghall, Bradford, BD9 4JY.* Quietly positioned, Victorian style, situated 2 mins from city centre. **Open:** All year
01274 543444 Mr Singh **Fax: 01274 495619** *enquiry@parkgrovehotel.co.uk* www.parkgrovehotel.co.uk **D:** Fr £25.00–£30.00 **S:** Fr £40.00–£47.00 **Beds:** 2F 9D 2T 2S **Baths:** 15 En (9) cc

Greetland

SE0821

Crawstone Knowl Farm, *Rochdale Road, Greetland, Halifax, W. Yorks, HX4 8PX.* Large comfortable Pennine farmhouse, convenient for Halifax, Huddersfield and Dales. **Open:** All year
01422 370470 Mrs Shackleton **D:** Fr £16.00–£20.00 **S:** Fr £16.00–£20.00 **Beds:** 1F 1D 1T **Baths:** 3 En (7)

Halifax

SE0925

Heathleigh Guest House, *124 Skircoat Road, Halifax, West Yorkshire, HX1 2RE.* A beautiful Victorian house offering a warm welcome, comfortable beds and a delicious breakfast. **Open:** All year
01422 323957 Ms Eccles **D:** Fr £20.00–£22.50 **S:** Fr £20.00–£25.00 **Beds:** 1F 1D 2S **Baths:** 2 En 1 Pr 1 Sh (2)

Tower House Hotel, *Master Lane, Halifax, HX2 7EW.* This country-style hotel is situated at the foot of 'Wainhouse Tower' (the famous folly). The older part of the hotel lays claim to 'ghostly goings on'! The family restaurant 'La Terraza' opens every day from 4.00pm. **Open:** All year
01422 345000 Fax: 01422 320875 www.towerhousehotel.co.uk **D:** Fr £27.50–£30.00 **S:** Fr £39.50–£60.00 **Beds:** 3F 2T 10D 1S **Baths:** 16 En (65) cc

Mozart House, *34 Prescott Street, Halifax, West Yorkshire, HX1 2QW.* Large Victorian terrace house, 3-minute walk from town centre. **Open:** All year
01422 340319 D: Fr £18.00 **S:** Fr £20.00–£25.00 **Beds:** 5T 1D **Baths:** 5 En 1 Pr (4) cc

Haworth

SE0337

Park Top House, *1 Rawdon Road, Haworth, Keighley, West Yorkshire, BD22 8DX.*
Open: All year (not Xmas/New Year)
Grades: ETC 4 Diamond
01535 646102 Mr & Mrs Milnes *gmilnes@parktophouse.fsnet.co.uk* **D:** Fr £18.00–£20.00 **S:** Fr £18.00–£20.00 **Beds:** 1T 1D 1S **Baths:** 2 En 1 Pr (3)
A high standard and a warm welcome awaits you at Park Top House. Conveniently situated close to Haworth's cobbled Main Street, Bronte Parsonage Museum & Worth Valley Steam Railway. Splendid views over Haworth Park and Bronte Country. Good walking area.

Bronte Cottage, *4 Park Top Row, Main Street, Haworth, Keighley, W. Yorks, BD22 8DN.* Modern cottage with view, situated on Haworth's cobbled main street. **Open:** All year
01535 647012 Mrs Gray **D:** Fr £17.50–£25.00 **S:** Fr £25.00–£35.00 **Beds:** 1F 1D 1T **Baths:** 2 En 1 Pr (10) (3)

Kershaw House, *90 West Lane, Haworth, Keighley, West Yorkshire, BD22 8EN.* Situated on the edge of the Moors, in the heart of Bronte country. **Open:** All year (not Xmas)
01535 642074 & 07973 734758 *jbrosnan@whsmithnet.co.uk* **D:** Fr £45.00 **S:** Fr £27.50–£30.00 **Beds:** 1T 2D 1S **Baths:** 3 En 1 Pr (4)

Aitches Guest House, *West Lane, Haworth, Keighley, West Yorkshire, BD22 8DU.* Large Victorian house, tastefully furnished, nestling on the cobbled street of Haworth. **Open:** All year
01535 642501 *Aitches@talk21.com* www.aitches.co.uk **D:** Fr £20.00–£30.00 **S:** Fr £25.00–£30.00 **Beds:** 1T 3D **Baths:** 4 En cc

Hole Farm, *Dimples Lane, Haworth, Keighley, W. Yorks, BD22 8QS.* Perfectly situated for Bronte museum and Moors. Warm welcome. **Open:** All year (not Xmas/New Year)
01535 644755 (also fax) Mrs Milner *janet@bronteholidays.co.uk* www.bronteholidays.co.uk **D:** Fr £20.00 **S:** Fr £30.00 **Beds:** 1D **Baths:** 1 En

Woodlands Drive Private Hotel, *Woodlands Grange, Haworth, Keighley, W. Yorks, BD22 8PB.* 4-bedroom detached house, quiet location, 1 mile town centre. Near woods/nature trails. **Open:** All year
01535 646814 Ms Harker *woodlandsgrange@hotmail.com* **D:** Fr £17.00 **S:** Fr £17.00 **Beds:** 1D 1S **Baths:** 1 Sh (1)

Weavers Restaurant And Bar, *15 West Lane, Haworth, Keighley, W. Yorks, BD22 8DU.* Set on the cobbles in the heart of the village. **Open:** All year (not Xmas/New Year)
01535 643822 Mr & Mrs Rushworth *weavers@amserve.net* www.weaversmallhote.co.uk **D:** Fr £35.00 **S:** Fr £50.00 **Beds:** 1T 2D 1S (10) cc

The Old Registry, *4 Main Street, Haworth, Keighley, West Yorkshire, BD22 8DA.* Victorian guest house, where courtesy and charm extend, 4-poster beds, ensuite rooms. **Open:** All year
01535 646503 Mrs Herdman www.oldregistry.co.uk **D:** Fr £18.00–£25.00 **S:** Fr £18.00–£30.00 **Beds:** 1F 3T 5D 1S **Baths:** 9 En 1 Pr cc

Hebden Bridge

SD9927

Higher Earnshaw Water, *Blackshaw Head, Hebden Bridge, W. Yorks, HX7 7JB.* Family smallholding, comfortable old farmhouse in lovely countryside. Warm welcome. **Open:** All year (not Xmas/New Year)
01422 844117 Mr & Mrs Redmond **D:** Fr £22.00 **S:** Fr £23.00 **Beds:** 1F 1D 1S **Baths:** 1 Sh (4)

Prospect End, *8 Prospect Terrace, Hebden Bridge, West Yorkshire, HX7 6NA.* Town edge location. Very private guest rooms. Extensive breakfast menu. **Open:** All year
01422 843586 (also fax) Ann Anthon **D:** Fr £17.00–£19.00 **S:** Fr £21.00–£25.00 **Beds:** 1T 1D **Baths:** 2 En

Heptonstall

SD9728

Poppyfields House, *29 Slack Top, Heptonstall, Hebden Bridge, West Yorkshire, HX7 7HA.* Pennine House set amidst the dramatic hills of Calderdale. Wooded valleys, tumbling streams. **Open:** All year
01422 843636 Mrs Simpson **Fax: 01422 845621 D:** Fr £19.00–£22.00 **S:** Fr £22.00–£25.00 **Beds:** 1F 1D **Baths:** 2 En (4)

B&B owners may vary rates – be sure to check when booking

Holmfirth

SE1408

Holme Castle Country Hotel, *Holme Village, Holmfirth, Huddersfield, W. Yorks, HD7 1QG.* **Open:** All year
01484 680680 Ms Hayfield **Fax: 01484 686764** *jill.hayfield@virgin.net* www.holmecastle.com **D:** Fr £27.00–£40.00 **S:** Fr £35.00–£60.00 **Beds:** 1F 2T 3D 1S **Baths:** 5 Pr 1 Sh (12) **cc**
Unusual mill house in Peak Park. 7 unique bedrooms, splendid views. Oak panelling, antiques, open fires. Hospitality, delicious fresh food, world wines. Established 1983. Meetings, celebrations, textile/felt making courses. 'Room With a View' contemporary art gallery. A6024 2.5 miles SW Holmfirth.

Idle

SE1737

Glengarry Guest House, *175 Albion Road, Idle, Bradford, W. Yorks, BD10 9QP.* Within easy reach of Bronte land/Moors/ industrial heritage/TVs 'Emmerdale'. **Open:** All year
01274 613781 Mr Swain **D:** Fr £14.50–£15.00 **S:** Fr £16.00–£16.50 **Beds:** 2T 1S **Baths:** 2 Sh (5)

Ilkley

SE1147

Archway Cottage, *24 Skipton Road, Ilkley, W. Yorks, LS29 9EP.* Beautiful Victorian cottage in central Ilkley with outstanding moorland views. **Open:** All year (not Xmas)
01943 603399 Mrs Green *thegreen@archcottage.fsnet.co.uk* **D:** Fr £35.00–£40.00 **S:** Fr £20.00–£25.00 **Beds:** 1F 2D 1T **Baths:** 2 En 2 Sh (2)

RATES
D = Price range per person sharing in a double or twin room
S = Price range for a single room

Keighley

SE0541

Currer Laithe Farm, *Moss Carr Road, Long Lee, Keighley, W. Yorks, BD21 4SL.* **Open:** All year (not Xmas)
01535 604387 Miss Brown www.edgey8843.free-online.co.uk/currer/index.htm **D:** Fr £16.00 **S:** Fr £15.00 **Beds:** 2F 1D 3T **Baths:** 3 En 3 Pr 1 Sh (10)
C16th working Pennine hill farm in Bronte Country. Splendid views of Airedale, Ilkley Moor, Ingleborough. Traditional fare. Guests returning for twenty years. Groups welcome. Excellent base for Haworth, Dales, museums, abbeys, markets, mill shops. Inglenook fireplace, beams and mullions.

Kirkburton

SE1912

Manor Mill Cottage, *21 Linfit Lane, Kirkburton, Huddersfield, West Yorkshire, HD8 0TY.* Warm welcoming cottage twixt Huddersfield and Wakefield in rural peaceful countryside. **Open:** All year
01484 604109 Ms Askham *manormill@paskham.freeserve.co.uk* **D:** Fr £20.00 **S:** Fr £20.00 **Beds:** 1D 1T **Baths:** 2 En (3)

LEEDS Chapel Allerton

SE3037

Highbank Hotel & Restaurant, *83 Harehills Lane, Leeds, LS7 4HA.* Convenient, affordable, comfortable traditional hotel with modern facilities and secure car park. **Open:** All year **Grades:** AA 2 Diamond
0870 7456744 & 0113 262 2164 Mr Thomas **Fax: 0870 7456734** *info@highbankhotel.co.uk* www.highbankhotel.co.uk **D:** Fr £18.00–£25.00 **S:** Fr £20.00–£39.50 **Beds:** 4F 4D 5T 8S **Baths:** 8 En 3 Sh (30) **cc**

Please respect a B&B's wishes regarding children, animals and smoking

LEEDS Headingley

SE2836

49 St Chad's Drive, *Headingley, Leeds, West Yorkshire, LS6 3PZ.* Pleasant, comfortable semi-detached family home near park and universities. **Open:** All year
0113 275 0703 Mrs Ballantine **D:** Fr £20.00–£22.00 **S:** Fr £23.00–£25.00 (1)

Number 23, *23 St Chad's Rise, Far Headingley, Leeds, West Yorkshire, LS6 3QE.* Quiet cul-de-sac overlooking church grounds. Easy access to public transport. **Open:** All year (not Xmas/New Year)
0113 275 7825 Mr & Mrs Sheldrake **D:** Fr £18.00 **S:** Fr £17.00–£18.00 **Beds:** 1T 4S **Baths:** 1 Sh (2)

LEEDS Meanwood

SE2837

Aragon Hotel, *250 Stainbeck Lane, Leeds, LS7 2PS.* Large Victorian house set in large gardens, quiet and non-smoking. **Open:** All year (not Xmas)
0113 275 9306 R & D Woodward **Fax: 0113 275 7166** www.aragonhotel.co.uk **D:** Fr £24.90–£26.50 **S:** Fr £39.90–£43.90 **Beds:** 2F 6D 2T 2S **Baths:** 12 En (20) **cc**

LEEDS Woodhouse

SE2835

Moorlea Hotel, *146 Woodsley Road, Leeds, LS2 9LZ.* **Open:** All year **Grades:** ETC 3 Diamond
0113 243 2653 Fax: 0113 246 5393 *themoorleahotel@aol.com* **D:** Fr £20.00–£26.50 **S:** Fr £27.00–£40.00 **Beds:** 2F 2T 3D 5S **Baths:** 7 En 2 Sh
Warm, friendly, relaxed. Ideally situated for business or pleasure. 5 mins to University, Headingley CC. 10 mins to LGI, city centre, theatres, night clubs. High quality English breakfast or varied continental buffet. Comfortable restaurant, residents bar with draught ale & lager.

Luddenden Foot

SE0424

Rockcliffe West, *Burnley Road, Luddenden Foot, Halifax, W. Yorks, HX2 6HL.* Spacious, friendly Victorian home with delightful gardens and hillside views. **Open:** All year (not Xmas/New Year)
01422 882151 (also fax) Mrs Hodgeson *rockcliffe.b.b@virgin.net* **D:** Fr £19.00 **S:** Fr £24.00 **Beds:** 1T 1D **Baths:** 1 En 1 Pr (2)

National Grid References given are for villages, towns and cities – not for individual houses

Mankinholes

SD9623

Cross Farm, *Mankinholes, Todmorden, West Yorkshire, OL14 7JQ.* 400-year-old stone Pennine farmhouse and barn with hillside views. **Open:** All year
01706 813481 Mrs Hancock **D:** Fr £19.50 **S:** Fr £19.50 **Beds:** 2T 2D **Baths:** 3 Pr (4)

Marsden

SE0411

Forest Farm, *Mount Road, Marsden, Huddersfield, W. Yorks, HD7 6NN.* Come as a guest, leave as a friend. **Open:** All year (not Xmas)
01484 842687 (also fax) Mr & Mrs Fussey *mayandted@aol.com* **D:** Fr £18.00 **S:** Fr £20.00 **Beds:** 2D 1T **Baths:** 2 Sh (6) **cc**

Pear Tree Cottage, *18 Grange Avenue, Marsden, Huddersfield, West Yorkshire, HD7 6AQ.* Cosy former mill workers' cottage amid dramatic South Pennine scenery. Convenient transport, village amenities, canal. **Open:** All year (not Xmas)
01484 847518 & 07833 112981 (M) Mr & Mrs Goodall **Fax: 01484 847518** *john@jgoodall.fsnet.co.uk* mysite.freeserve.com/pear_tree_cottage **D:** Fr £15.00–£17.50 **S:** Fr £15.00–£17.50 **Beds:** 1F 1S **Baths:** 2 Sh

Throstle Nest Cottage, *3 Old Mount Road, Marsden, Huddersfield, West Yorkshire, HD7 6DU.* Olde worlde C17th country cottage in beautiful Colne Valley. Close to all amenities. **Open:** All year (not Xmas)
01484 846371 (also fax) Ms Hayes *throstle-nest@faxvia.net* **D:** Fr £15.00–£20.00 **S:** Fr £18.00–£20.00 **Beds:** 1F 1T **Baths:** 1 Sh (3)

Normanton

SE3822

Station Lodge Guesthouse, *21-27 Lower Station Road, Normanton, W. Yorks, WF6 2BE.* Excellent central communication links; 100 metres railway station, M62/M1 0.75 mile. **Open:** All year
01924 223741 D & S Walker *suewalker@themanse49.freeserve.co.uk* **D:** Fr £18.00–£20.00 **S:** Fr £18.00–£20.00 **Beds:** 4T 1D 5S **Baths:** 8 En

Otley

SE2045

18 Harecroft Road, *Otley, W. Yorks, LS21 2BQ.* Quiet, friendly, private residence near River Wharfe and all amenities. **Open:** All year
01943 463643 Mrs Mandy **D:** Fr £18.00 **S:** Fr £18.00 **Beds:** 1T 2S **Baths:** 2 Sh (2)

Oxenhope

SE0335

Springfield Guest House, *Shaw Lane, Oxenhope, Keighley, W. Yorks, BD22 9QL.* Large Victorian residence set in large well-kept grounds. **Open:** All year
01535 643951 Mrs Hargreaves **Fax: 01535 644672** *best_bb_uk@msm.com* www.s-h-systems.co.uk/hotels/sprungfi.html **D:** Fr £20.00 **S:** Fr £22.50–£25.00 **Beds:** 1F 3D 1T 3S **Baths:** 2 En 2 Sh (6)

Pontefract

SE4521

Tudor Guest House, *18 Tudor Close, Pontefract, W. Yorks, WF8 4NJ.* Private house, residential area, near to town centre and racecourse. **Open:** All year (not Xmas)
01977 701007 Mrs Kilby **D:** Fr £17.50–£18.00 **S:** Fr £25.00–£27.00 **Beds:** 2D **Baths:** 2 En 2 Pr (2)

Pool-in-Wharfedale

SE2445

Rawson Garth, *Pool Bank Farm, Pool-in-Wharfedale, Otley, W. Yorks, LS21 1EU.* Attractively converted coach house, open country views in heart of Emmerdale country. **Open:** All year (not Xmas)
0113 284 3221 Mrs Waterhouse **D:** Fr £20.00 **S:** Fr £30.00 **Beds:** 2D 1T **Baths:** 2 En 1 Pr (12) (4) **cc**

Pudsey

SE2233

Heatherlea House, *105 Littlemoor Road, Pudsey, Leeds, West Yorkshire, LS28 8AP.* Tastefully furnished, friendly, award-winning gardens. Near motorways, airport, Dales. **Open:** All year **Grades:** ETC 3 Diamond
0113 257 4397 Mr & Mrs Barton **D:** Fr £19.00 **S:** Fr £20.00–£25.00 **Beds:** 1T 1S **Baths:** 1 Sh (2)

Planning a longer stay? Always ask for any special rates

Planning a longer stay? Always ask for any special rates

Queensbury

SE1030

Mountain Hall, *Brighouse & Denholme Road, Queensbury, Bradford, W. Yorks, BD13 1LH.* Situated at 1200ft with panoramic views of Bradford-dale. Quiet rural area. **Open:** All year (not Xmas)
01274 816258 Mrs Ledgard **Fax: 01274 884001** **D:** Fr £20.00–£25.00 **S:** Fr £20.00–£25.00 **Beds:** 3T 5D 5S **Baths:** 9 En 1 Sh (10) **cc**

Sowerby Bridge

SE0523

The Dene, *Triangle, Sowerby Bridge, W Yorks, HX6 3EA.* Georgian stone house in walled garden with wooded valley views. **Open:** All year (not Xmas) **Grades:** ETC 4 Diamond
01422 823562 Mr & Mrs Noble *knoble@uk2.net* **D:** Fr £22.50 **S:** Fr £25.00 **Beds:** 1F 1T 1D **Baths:** 3 En (4)

Stanbury

SE0137

Wuthering Heights Inn, *26 Main Street, Stanbury, Keighley, W. Yorks, BD22 0HB.* Warm & friendly country pub, excellent food and traditional ales. **Open:** All year
01535 643332 Mrs Mitchell **D:** Fr £17.00 **S:** Fr £17.00 **Beds:** 1F 1D 1T 1S **Baths:** 2 Sh (20)

Todmorden

SD9424

Cherry Tree Cottage, *Woodhouse Road, Todmorden, W. Yorks, OL14 5RJ.* C17th detached country cottage nestling amidst lovely Pennine countryside. **Open:** All year (not Xmas)
01706 817492 Mrs Butterworth **D:** Fr £16.00–£24.50 **S:** Fr £16.00 **Beds:** 1F 1D 1T 1S **Baths:** 3 En 1 Pr 1 Sh

The Berghof Hotel, *Cross Stone Road, Todmorden, W. Yorks, OL14 8RQ.* Authentic Austrian hotel and restaurant, function suite and conference facilities. **Open:** All year
01706 812966 (also fax) Mrs Brandstatter *berghof@tinyworld.co.uk* www.berghof.co.uk **D:** Fr £27.50–£35.00 **S:** Fr £42.50–£55.00 **Beds:** 5D 2T **Baths:** 7 En (40) **cc**

Wadsworth

SE0126

Hare & Hounds, *Wadsworth, Hebden Bridge, HX7 8TN.* A family-run country pub, ensuite bedrooms, Good Beer Guide.
Open: All year
01422 842671 (also fax) S Greenwood
www.hare.and.hounds.connectfree.co.uk
D: Fr £22.50–£25.00 **S:** Fr £35.00–£40.00
Beds: 4D **Baths:** 4 En (25) cc

Wakefield

SE3220

Savile Guest House, *78 Savile Street, Wakefield, W. Yorks, WF1 3LN.* Saville Guest House is a small, friendly place to stay.
Open: All year
01924 374761 Fax: 01924 382740 D: Fr £18.00–£20.00 **S:** Fr £20.00–£25.00 **Beds:** 2F 4T 2D 2S **Baths:** 8 En 8 Pr 2 Sh (10) cc

Stanley View Guesthouse, *226/228 Stanley Road, Wakefield, W. Yorks, WF1 4AE.* Close to city centre and motorway network M1/M62. **Open:** All year
01924 376803 Mr Heppinstall **Fax: 01924 369123** *enquiries@stanleyviewguesthouse.co.uk*
www.stanleyviewguesthouse.co.uk **D:** Fr £21.00–£31.00 **S:** Fr £22.00–£42.00 **Beds:** 4F 10T 5D 2S **Baths:** 17 En 2 Pr (10) cc

Walsden

SD9322

Highstones Guest House, *Lane Bottom, Walsden, Todmorden, W. Yorks, OL14 6TY.* Large house set in half an acre with lovely views over open countryside.
Open: All year
01706 816534 Mrs Pegg **D:** Fr £18.00 **S:** Fr £18.00 **Beds:** 2D 1S **Baths:** 2 Sh 1 Pr (3)

Wentbridge

SE4817

Bridge Guest House, *Wentbridge, Pontefract, W. Yorks, WF8 3JJ.* Picturesque village close A1 & M62 with a friendly welcome. **Open:** All year
01977 620314 D: Fr £21.00–£25.00 **S:** Fr £21.00–£25.00 **Beds:** 4T 2D 1S **Baths:** 2 En 2 Sh (8)

Wetherby

SE4048

14 Woodhill View, *Wetherby, W. Yorks, LS22 4PP.* Quiet residential area near to town centre. **Open:** All year
01937 581200 & 07967 152091 Mr Green **D:** Fr £19.00 **S:** Fr £29.00 **Beds:** 1D 1T **Baths:** 1 Sh (3) cc

National Grid References given are for villages, towns and cities – not for individual houses

Whitley

SE2217

The Woolpack Country Inn, *Whitley Road, Whitley, Dewsbury, West Yorkshire, WF12 0LZ.* Charming country inn equidistant from Huddersfield, Wakefield & Dewsbury.
Open: All year
01924 499999 (also fax) V Barraclough
enquiries@woolpackhotel.co.uk
www.woolpackhotel.co.uk **D:** Fr £27.50 **S:** Fr £44.50 **Beds:** 5T 6D **Baths:** 11 En (80) cc

RATES
D = Price range per person sharing in a double or twin room
S = Price range for a single room

Aberdeenshire & Moray

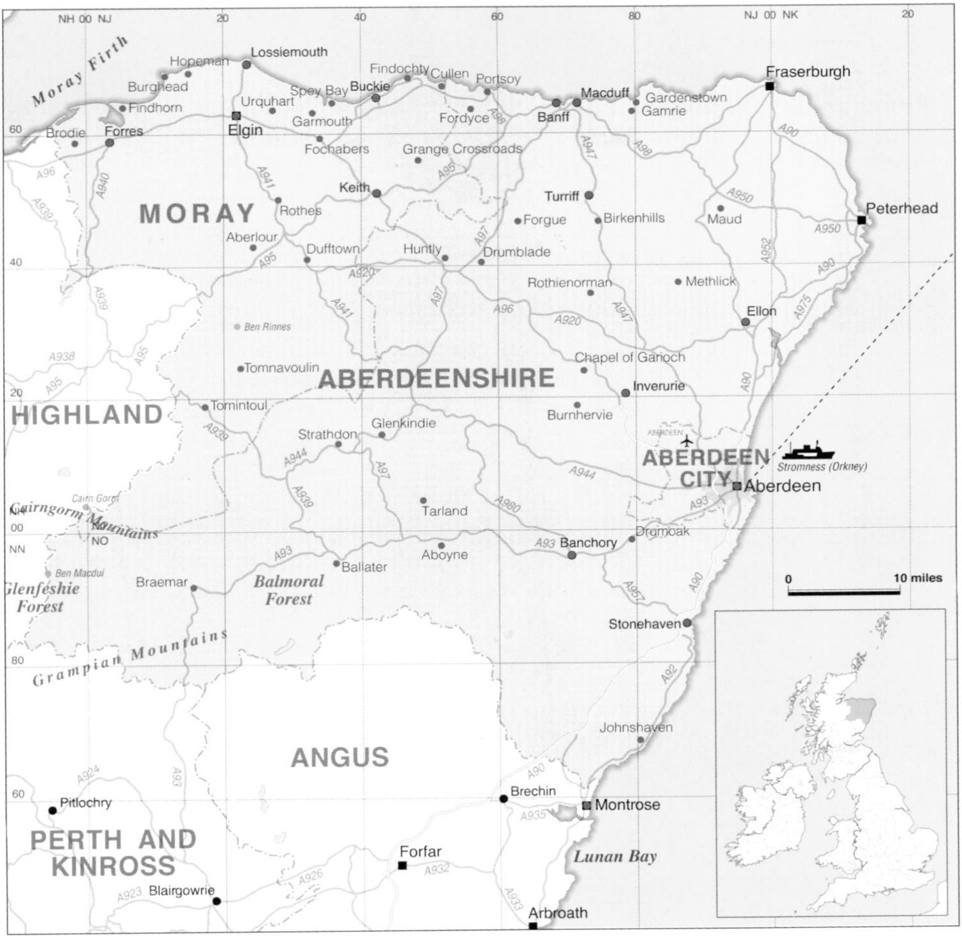

Aberdeen

NJ9306

Dunrovin Guest House, *168 Bon Accord Street, Aberdeen, AB11 6TX.* **Open:** All year
01224 586081 Mrs Dellanzo *dellanzo@hotmail.com* www.dunrovin.freeservers.com
D: Fr £18.50–£40.00 **S:** Fr £25.00–£40.00
Beds: 1F 2D 1T 4S **Baths:** 4 En 2 Sh
Family-run C19th guest house set in a tree-lined street approximately 1000 yards to city centre and also park and river. Rail and bus stations are both only a 10-minute walk and there is easy parking. Surgery across road. Satellite TV throughout.

Roselea Private Hotel, *12 Springbank Terrace, Aberdeen, AB11 6LS.* Friendly family-run city centre hotel situated close to bus/rail links & ferry terminal. **Open:** All year
01224 583060 (also fax) *candfmoore@roseleahotel.demon.co.uk* www.roseleahotel.demon.co.uk **D:** Fr £17.00–£21.00 **S:** Fr £24.00–£30.00 **Beds:** 1F 3D 2T **Baths:** 2 En 2 Sh cc

Aberdeen Springbank Guest House, *6 Springbank Terrace, Aberdeen, AB11 6LS.*
Comfortable family-run Victorian terraced house, non-smoking, 5 minutes from city centre. **Open:** All year
01224 592048 (also fax) Mr & Mrs Robertson *betty@springbank6.fsnet.co.uk* www.aberdeenspringbankguesthouse.co.uk
D: Fr £16.00–£20.00 **S:** Fr £21.00–£26.00
Beds: 3F 4D 3T 4S **Baths:** 12 En 4 Sh

Beeches Private Hotel, *193 Great Western Road, Aberdeen, AB10 6PS.* Victorian detached property, residential area close to the city centre. **Open:** All year (not Xmas)
01224 586413 & 07801 182210 Mr Sandison **Fax: 01224 596919** *beeches-hotel@talk21.com* www.beeches-hotel.com **D:** Fr £20.00–£22.50 **S:** Fr £30.00–£35.00 **Beds:** 2F 2D 2T 3S **Baths:** 9 En (13) cc

Roselynd House, *27 Kings Gate, Aberdeen, AB15 4EL.* Friendly, family-run, smoke-free accommodation in beautiful Victorian townhouse. **Open:** All year
01224 640942 Mrs Neyedli **Fax: 01224 636435** *roselynd27@aol.com* www.roselyndguesthouse.co.uk **D:** Fr £20.00–£28.00 **S:** Fr £25.00–£38.00 **Beds:** 1F 2D 1T 1S **Baths:** 3 En 1 Sh (3)

Lonicera Guest House, *261 Great Western Road, Aberdeen, AB10 6PP.* Family-run, smart comfortable guest house. Excellent location for all attractions. City centre 5 mins, airport 20 mins. **Open:** All year **Grades:** STB 3 Star
01224 583200 (also fax) *lonicerab&b@jeancp.freeserve.co.uk* www.accommodation.uk.net/loniceraguesthouse.html **D:** Fr £18.00–£22.00 **S:** Fr £22.00–£30.00 **Beds:** 1F 2T 1S **Baths:** 2 En 1 Sh (4) cc

Roselodge Guest House, *3 Springbank Terrace, Aberdeen, AB11 6LS.* Quiet city centre location, convenient for all amenities. Private parking. **Open:** All year (not Xmas) **Grades:** STB 2 Star
01224 586794 (also fax) Mrs Wink *marywink@onetel.net.uk* **D:** Fr £17.00–£20.00 **S:** Fr £20.00–£22.00 **Beds:** 3F 2T 1S **Baths:** 2 Sh (3)

Crown Private Hotel, *10 Spring Bank Terrace, Aberdeen, AB1 2LS.* Small, family-run central 3 Star guest house. Recommended by AA. **Open:** All year **Grades:** STB 3 Star
01224 586842 Mr Buthlay **Fax: 01224 573787** *crown_hotel@yahoo.co.uk* crownprivatehotel.ourfamily.com **D:** Fr £19.00–£22.00 **S:** Fr £28.00–£32.00 **Beds:** 2F 2D 2T 3S **Baths:** 7 En 1 Sh

St Elmo, *64 Hilton Drive, Aberdeen, AB24 4NP.* Traditional granite family home, near historic university and city centre. **Open:** All year
01224 483065 Mrs Watt *stelmobandb@aol.com* www.home.aol.com/stelmobandb **D:** Fr £16.00–£17.00 **S:** Fr £20.00–£24.00 **Beds:** 1D 2T **Baths:** 1 Sh (1) (2)

Butler's Islander Guest House, *122 Crown Street, Aberdeen, AB11 6HJ.* City centre location near rail, bus and ferry links. **Open:** All year (not Xmas/New Year)
01224 212411 A Butler **Fax: 01224 586448** *bookings@butlerigh.demon.co.uk* www.butlerigh.demon.co.uk **D:** Fr £13.50–£22.00 **S:** Fr £22.00–£35.00 **Beds:** 3T 3D 1S **Baths:** 2 En 2 Sh cc

Maclean's BandB, *8 Boyd Orr Avenue, Aberdeen, AB12 5RG.* Perfectly situated for fishing, golf, bowling, walks, flower gardens, swimming. **Open:** All year
01224 248726 (also fax) *j.maclean@abdn.ac.uk* www.cableol.net/jonathan **D:** Fr £16.00–£20.00 **S:** Fr £18.00–£20.00 **Beds:** 2T 1D (3)

Aberlour

NJ2642

83 High Street, *Aberlour, Banffshire, AB38 9QB.* The heart of a village famous for whisky and shortbread. **Open:** All year
01340 871000 Miss Gammack *ruth@resolute.fsnet.co.uk* www.resolute.fsnet.co.uk **D:** Fr £15.00–£16.00 **S:** Fr £15.00–£16.00 **Beds:** 1T 2D **Baths:** 2 Sh cc

Aboyne

NO5298

Newton of Drumgesk, *Dess, Aboyne, Aberdeenshire, AB34 5BL.* **Open:** All year (not Xmas)
013398 86203 & 013398 87453 & 07703 203177 (M) Mrs Selwyn Bailey **Fax: 013398 86203** *crogerbailey@aol.com* www.drumgesk.co.uk **D:** Fr £22.50 **S:** Fr £22.50 **Beds:** 1T 2D **Baths:** 2 En (6)
Comfortable, quiet, typical Scottish farmhouse in own acreage. Newly modernised. Cot/high chair available. Beautiful views of hills and woods. Nice walks. Horse-riding by appointment only. Castle & Whisky Trails nearby.

Struan Hall, *Ballater Road, Aboyne, Aberdeenshire, AB34 5HY.* We are quietly situated in 2 acres of woodland garden. **Open:** Mar to Oct
013398 87241 (also fax) Mrs Ingham *struanhall@zetnet.co.uk* www.accomodata.co.uk/struanhall.htm **D:** Fr £26.00–£28.50 **S:** Fr £26.00–£34.00 **Beds:** 1D 2T 1S **Baths:** 3 En 1 Pr (7) (6) cc

Birse Lodge House, *Charleston road, Aboyne, Aberdeenshire, AB34 5EL.* Friendly Victorian family home in the heart of Royal Deeside. **Open:** All year (not Xmas/New Year)
013398 86253 **Fax: 013398 87796** *birselodgehouse@btinternet.com* **D:** Fr £27.00 **S:** Fr £32.00 **Beds:** 1T 2D **Baths:** 3 En (3)

Ballater

NO3695

Morven Lodge, *29 Braemar Road, Ballater, Aberdeenshire, AB35 5RQ.* Fine Victorian house in renowned village, close to all amenities. **Open:** May to Sep **Grades:** STB 2 Star
013397 55373 Mrs Henchie **D:** Fr £18.00–£19.00 **S:** Fr £25.00–£30.00 **Beds:** 1F 1D 1T **Baths:** 1 Pr 1 Sh (2) (5)

Deeside Hotel, *Braemar Road, Ballater, Aberdeenshire, AB35 5RQ.* Quiet location. Informal dining. Good touring base. Two ground floor bedrooms. **Open:** Feb to Dec
013397 55420 Mr Brooker **Fax: 013397 55357** *deesidehotel@btconnect.com* www.deesidehotel.co.uk **D:** Fr £23.00–£28.00 **S:** Fr £28.00–£31.50 **Beds:** 1F 4D 4T **Baths:** 9 Pr (15) cc

Morvada Guest House, *Braemar Road, Ballater, Aberdeenshire, AB35 5RL.* **Open:** All year (not Xmas)
013397 56334 (also fax) Mr Campbell *morvada@aol.com* www.morvada.com **D:** Fr £21.00–£24.00 **S:** Fr £26.00–£30.00 **Beds:** 5D 1T **Baths:** 6 En (6) cc
Allan and Thea Campbell welcome you to this lovely Victorian villa set in the beautiful village of Ballater. Excellent rooms, quality breakfasts, and a prime location for fine restaurants, Balmoral Castle, the Cairngorm Mountains, the Whisky and Castle Trails.

Celicall, *3 Braemar Road, Ballater, Aberdeenshire, AB35 5RL.* **Open:** Easter to Oct
013397 55699 Mrs Cowie *celicall@euphony.net* **D:** Fr £19.00–£22.00 **S:** Fr £25.00–£28.00 **Beds:** 2T 2D **Baths:** 4 En (4)
Small family-run guest house in centre of Royal Deeside village of Ballater with its Royal Warrant shops. Close to bars and restaurants. Short drive from Glen Muck and on the Castle and Whisky Trail. Secure overnight off-road parking.

Darrochlee, *5a Monaltrie Road, Ballater, Aberdeenshire, AB35 5QE.* Centrally-located in beautiful highland village. Balmoral Castle 7m away. **Open:** Apr to Oct
013397 55287 Mrs Wilkie **Fax: 013397 56006** *lyn.wilkie@fsbdial.co.uk* **D:** Fr £17.50 **S:** Fr £20.00 **Beds:** 1T 2D **Baths:** 1 Sh

Findochty

NJ4668 Harbour Bar, The Admiral

15 Station Road, *Findochty, Buckie, Banffshire, AB56 2PJ.* Between Inverness and Aberdeen. Home cooking, good breakfast. Ideal dolphin watching. **Open:** Easter to Nov
01542 834992 Mrs Loades **D:** Fr £16.00 **S:** Fr £16.00 **Beds:** 1F 1T 1D **Baths:** 1 Sh

Fochabers

NJ3458

Castlehill Farm, *Blackdam, Fochabers, Moray, IV32 7LJ.* Ideally situated for exploring the area. Panoramic views of Ben Aigen. **Open:** All year (not Xmas/New Year) **Grades:** STB 3 Star, AA 3 Diamond
01343 820351 A Shand **Fax: 01343 821856 D:** Fr £16.00–£20.00 **S:** Fr £17.00–£22.00 **Beds:** 2D **Baths:** 1 En 1 Sh (5)

Fordyce

NJ5563

Academy House, *School Road, Fordyce, Portsoy, Banffshire, AB45 2SJ.* Tastefully decorated and furnished country house. Paintings and pottery throughout. **Open:** All year
01261 842743 Mrs Leith *academy_house@hotmail.com* www.fordyceaccommodation.com **D:** Fr £20.00–£24.00 **S:** Fr £25.00–£27.00 **Beds:** 1D 1T **Baths:** 1 En 1 Sh (5)

Forgue

NJ6145 Bognie Arms Hotel, Rothie Inn

Yonder Bognie, *Forgue, Huntly, Aberdeenshire, AB54 6BR.* Comfortable accommodation near Huntly, on Castle and Whisky trails. Central heating throughout, residents lounge with colour TV. En-suite bedrooms have electric blankets, colour TV, tea/coffee making facilities and hairdryers. Food hygiene certificate held. French and Italian spoken. Warm welcome assured. **Open:** All year
01466 730375 Mrs Ross **D:** Fr £16.00–£18.00 **S:** Fr £20.00 **Beds:** 2D **Baths:** 2 En (6)

Forres

NJ0358

Morven, *Caroline Street, Forres, Moray, IV36 0AN.* Beautiful house, town centre location. Warm, friendly atmosphere. Private parking. Brochure available. **Open:** All year
01309 673788 (also fax) Mrs MacDonald *morven2@globalnet.co.uk* www.golfgreenfees.com/morven **D:** Fr £17.00–£19.00 **S:** Fr £18.00–£25.00 **Beds:** 3T **Baths:** 2 En 1 Pr (5)

Mayfield Guest House, *Victoria Road, Forres, Moray, IV36 3BN.* Mayfield is centrally located with spacious rooms and a quiet, relaxed ambience. **Open:** All year (not Xmas) **Grades:** STB 4 Star
01309 676931 W Hercus *bill-hercus@mayfieldghouse.freeserve.co.uk* www.mayfieldghouse.freeserve.co.uk **D:** Fr £18.00–£25.00 **S:** Fr £25.00–£30.00 **Beds:** 1D 2T **Baths:** 2 En 1 Pr (4) cc

Heather Lodge, *Tytler Street, Forres, Moray, IV36 0EL.* Situated in quiet area near town. **Open:** All year
01309 672377 Mr Ross **D:** Fr £18.00–£20.00 **S:** Fr £18.00–£20.00 **Beds:** 2T 3S **Baths:** 7 En (12)

Gamrie

NJ7965

The Palace Farm, *Gamrie, Banff, AB45 3HS.* Late C18th farmhouse. Hearty Scottish breakfasts. Scenic clifftop villages close by. **Open:** All year (not Xmas/New Year)
01261 851261 P Duncan **Fax: 01261 851 401** *robbie@palace-farm.freeserve.co.uk* **D:** Fr £19.00–£20.00 **S:** Fr £20.00–£25.00 **Beds:** 1F 1T 1D **Baths:** 3 En (6)

Gardenstown

NJ8064

Bankhead Croft, *Gamrie, Banff, Aberdeenshire & Moray, AB45 3HN.* Modern country cottage, offering high standards of comfort in tranquil surroundings. **Open:** All year
01261 851584 (also fax) Mrs Smith *lucinda@bankheadcroft.freeserve.co.uk* www.destination.scotland.com/bankhead **D:** Fr £15.00–£18.00 **S:** Fr £18.00–£20.00 **Beds:** 1F 1D 1T **Baths:** 1 Pr (6)

Garmouth

NJ3364

Rowan Cottage, *Station Road, Garmouth, Fochabers, Moray, IV32 7LZ.* C18th cottage with garden in rural village at Spey estuary. **Open:** Jan to Nov
01343 870267 Mrs Bingham **Fax: 01343 870621** *patricia@pbingham.fsnet.co.uk* **D:** Fr £17.00 **S:** Fr £17.00 **Beds:** 1D 1T 1S **Baths:** 1 Sh (4)

National Grid References given are for villages, towns and cities – not for individual houses

Glenkindie

NJ4313

Glenkindie Arms Hotel, *Glenkindie, Alford, AB33 8SX.* 400 year old Drovers' (Cattlemen's) Inn, with log fire in winter. **Open:** All year
019756 41288 Fax: 019756 41319 *johnhowie@tinyworld.co.uk* www.glekindiearms.co.uk **D:** Fr £17.50 **S:** Fr £17.50 **Beds:** 1F 1T 1D 2S **Baths:** 2 Sh cc

Grange Crossroads

NJ4754

Chapelhill Croft, *Grange Crossroads, Keith, Banffshire, AB55 3LQ.* Warm welcome, rural location. Ideal for Whisky and Castle Trails. **Open:** All year (not Xmas/New Year)
01542 870302 Mrs Fleming *chapelhill@btinternet.com* www.scottishholidays.net/chapelhill **D:** Fr £14.00–£17.00 **S:** Fr £17.00–£20.00 **Beds:** 1T 1D **Baths:** 1 En 1 Sh

Hopeman

NJ1469 Station Hotel, Duffus Inn

Ardent House, *43 Forsyth Street, Hopeman, Elgin, Moray, IV30 2SY.* Traditional stone built house with conservatory overlooking secluded rose garden. **Open:** All year (not Xmas/New Year)
01343 830694 (also fax) N McPherson *normaardent@aol.com* www.ardenthouse.fsnet.co.uk **D:** Fr £16.00–£22.00 **S:** Fr £18.00–£30.00 **Beds:** 1T 2D **Baths:** 1 En 1 Sh (6) (4)

Huntly

NJ5240

Hillview, *Provost Street, Huntly, Aberdeenshire, AB54 8BB.* Peaceful, quality accommodation. Touring, Whisky Trail, castles, hill view, off-street parking. **Open:** All year **Grades:** STB 3 Star
01466 794870 Mrs Florence **D:** Fr £16.00–£17.00 **S:** Fr £18.00–£20.00 **Beds:** 2D 1T/F **Baths:** 1 En 1 Sh

Dunedin Guest House, *17 Bogie Street, Huntly, Aberdeenshire, AB54 5DX.* Dunedin Guest House. A few minutes walk from town centre. All rooms ensuite. **Open:** All year
01466 794162 Mrs Keith *dorothykeith@btinternet.com* **D:** Fr £16.00–£18.50 **S:** Fr £18.50–£23.00 **Beds:** 1F 1D 4T **Baths:** 6 En (8)

Greenmount, *43 Gordon Street, Huntly, Aberdeenshire, AB54 8EQ.* Family-run Georgian house. Excellent base for touring NE Scotland. **Open:** All year (not Xmas) **Grades:** STB 3 Star
01466 792482 Mr Manson **D:** Fr £17.00–£20.00 **S:** Fr £17.00–£25.00 **Beds:** 2F 4T 2S **Baths:** 4 En 1 Pr 1 Sh

Inverurie

NJ7721

Kingsgait, *3 St. Andrews Gardens, Inverurie, Aberdeenshire, AB51 3XT.* Friendly family run establishment close to town centre. **Open:** All year
01467 620431 (also fax) Mrs Christie *muriel@mchrstie25.freeserve.co.uk* **D:** Fr £18.00–£23.00 **S:** Fr £18.00–£23.00 **Beds:** 2T 1S **Baths:** 1 En 1 Sh

Johnshaven

NO7966

Ellington, *Station Place, Johnshaven, Montrose, DD10 0JD.* Comfortable modern family home in old fishing village. Ground-floor twin room. **Open:** All year (not Xmas)
01561 362756 Mrs Gibson *ellington13@supanet.com* **D:** Fr £18.00–£20.00 **S:** Fr £20.00 **Beds:** 1T 1D **Baths:** 2 En

Keith

NJ4250

The Haughs, *Keith, Banffshire, AB55 6QN.* Large comfortable farmhouse. Lovely view from dining room over rolling countryside. **Open:** Easter to Oct
01542 882238 (also fax) Mrs Jackson *jiwjackson@aol.com* www.haughsfarmbedandbreakfast.net **D:** Fr £19.00–£21.00 **S:** Fr £22.00–£27.00 **Beds:** 1F 2D 1T **Baths:** 3 En 1 Pr

Lossiemouth

NJ2370

Laburnum, *54 Queen Street, Lossiemouth, Moray, IV31 6PR.* Family-run home close to all amenities, including beaches. **Open:** All year
01343 813482 (also fax) Mrs Stephen *bsteph@tiscali.co.uk* **D:** Fr £16.00–£20.00 **S:** Fr £17.00–£20.00 **Beds:** 1F 1S 1D **Baths:** 1 En 1 Pr 1 Sh

Skerryhill, *63 Dunbar Street, Lossiemouth, Moray, IV31 6AN.* Near beaches and golf course. Convenient for Castle and Whisky Trails. **Open:** All year
01343 813035 Mrs Stewart **D:** Fr £16.00–£18.00 **S:** Fr £17.00 **Beds:** 1F 2D 1T **Baths:** 1 Sh

Maud

NJ9248

Pond View, *Brucklay, Maud, Peterhead, AB42 4QN.* Quiet house with panoramic view close to the National Cycle Route. **Open:** All year
01771 613675 & 07929 594168 (M) J & M Hepburn *mhepburn@lineone.net* **D:** Fr £20.00 **S:** Fr £22.00–£25.00 **Beds:** 1T 1D

Methlick

NJ8537

Sunnybrae Farm, *Gight, Methlick, Ellon, Aberdeenshire, AB41 7JA.* Traditional farmhouse; comfort in a peaceful location with lovely views. **Open:** All year **Grades:** STB 2 Star
01651 806456 (also fax) Mrs Staff *sunnybrae-farm@talk21.com* **D:** Fr £18.00–£20.00 **S:** Fr £18.00–£20.00 **Beds:** 1T 1D 1S **Baths:** 2 En

Portsoy

NJ5866

The Boyne Hotel, *2 North High Street, Portsoy, Banff, Aberdeenshire & Moray, AB45 2PA.* Family run hotel situated 100 yards from C17th harbour. **Open:** All year
01261 842242 Mr Christie *enquiries@boynehotel.co.uk* www.boynehotel.co.uk **D:** Fr £20.00–£25.00 **S:** Fr £20.00–£25.00 **Beds:** 4D 4T 4S **Baths:** 12 En **cc**

Rothes

NJ2749

Eastbank Hotel, *15/17 High Street, Rothes, Banffshire, AB38 7AU.* Speyside family-run Whisky Trail Hotel. Friendly atmosphere. Excellent food. **Open:** All year
01340 831564 (also fax) Mrs Humphreys **D:** Fr £17.50–£25.00 **S:** Fr £20.00–£28.00 **Beds:** 2F 3D 3T 3S **Baths:** 4 Pr 3 Sh

Rothienorman

NJ7235

Rothie Inn, *Main Street, Rothienorman, Inverurie, Aberdeenshire, AB51 8UD.* Family-run village inn in the heart of castle country. **Open:** All year (not Xmas) **Grades:** STB 3 Star
01651 821206 (also fax) Miss Thomson *rothieinn@accom90.freeserve.co.uk* **D:** Fr £20.00–£25.00 **S:** Fr £25.00–£30.00 **Beds:** 1F 1T **Baths:** 2 En **cc**

Spey Bay

NJ3565

31 The Muir, Bogmoor, *Spey Bay, Fochabers, IV32 7PN.* 1/4 Mile from Speyside Way. Dolphins, salmon, osprey at estuary. **Open:** All year
01343 820196 J Philpott **D:** Fr £15.00–£16.00 **S:** Fr £15.00–£16.00 **Beds:** 2D

Stonehaven

NO8786

Glencairn, *9 Dunnottar Avenue, Stonehaven, AB39 2JD.* Coastal location close to open-air swimming pool and picturesque fishing harbour. **Open:** All year **Grades:** STB 3 Star
01569 762612 & 07766 305437 (M) M Sangster **Fax: 01569 764065** *msangster@amserve.net* www.theglencairn.co.uk **D:** Fr £20.00 **S:** Fr £20.00–£22.00 **Beds:** 1T 1D 1S **Baths:** 2 En 1 Pr

Tewel Farm, *Stonehaven, Kincardineshire, AB39 3UU.* Traditional farmhouse on outskirts of Stonehaven, situated on Auchenblae Road. Scenic. **Open:** All year **Grades:** STB 2 Star
01569 762306 & 07815 167404 (M) Mrs Farquhar **Fax: 01569 760386 D:** Fr £18.00–£20.00 **S:** Fr £21.00–£23.00 **Beds:** 1D 1T **Baths:** 2 En

Alexander Guest House, *36 Arduthie Road, Stonehaven, Kincardineshire, AB39 2DP.* Friendly, comfortable. Convenient for town centre, harbour, train. Superb breakfast. **Open:** All year (not Xmas) **Grades:** STB 3 Star
01569 762265 Mrs Henderson **Fax: 08701 391045** *marion@alexanderguesthouse.com* www.alexanderguesthouse.com **D:** Fr £22.00–£30.00 **S:** Fr £20.00–£30.00 **Beds:** 3F 1T 1D 2S **Baths:** 5 En 2 Sh **cc**

The Grahams, *71 Cameron Street, Stonehaven, Kincardineshire, AB39 2HE.* Traditional Scottish home. Town centre/harbour within ten minutes' walk. **Open:** Mar to Dec **Grades:** STB 2 Star
01569 763517 *arthur@grahams71.fsnet.co.uk* **D:** Fr £18.50 **S:** Fr £21.00 **Beds:** 1F 1T 1S **Baths:** 2 Sh **cc**

Arduthie House, *Ann Street, Stonehaven, Kincardineshire, AB3 2DA.* Elegant detached Victorian guest house with attractive garden, central Stonehaven. **Open:** All year (not Xmas)
01569 762381 Mrs Marr **Fax: 01569 766366** *arduthie@talk21.com* **D:** Fr £24.00–£26.00 **S:** Fr £18.00 **Beds:** 1F 2D 2T 1S **Baths:** 5 En 1 Pr

44 Evan Street, *Stonehaven, Aberdeenshire, AB39 2ET.* Victorian town house. Near sea. Handy for Dunnottar Castle. **Open:** All year (not Xmas/New Year)
01569 763494 Mrs Horne *lorrainehorne@tinyworld.co.uk* **D:** Fr £18.00 **S:** Fr £25.00 **Beds:** 2D **Baths:** 2 Sh

Strathdon

NJ3512

Buchaam Farm, *Strathdon, Aberdeenshire, AB36 8TN.* Enjoy Scottish hospitality on 600-acre family-run farm in an area of unspoilt beauty. **Open:** Apr to Oct
019756 51238 (also fax) Mrs Ogg *e.ogg@talk21.com* **D:** Fr £17.00 **S:** Fr £17.00 **Beds:** 1F 1D 1T **Baths:** 2 Sh (3)

Tarland

NJ4704 *Aberdeen Arms, Loch Kinnord, Boat Inn*

Kirklands of Cromar, *Bridge Street, Tarland, Aboyne, Aberdeenshire, AB34 4YN.* By same architect as Balmoral Castle. Visit castles and Whisky Trail. **Open:** All year
013398 81082 Ms Stewart *morna@kirkland.u-net.com* kirklandsofcromar.co.uk **D:** Fr £17.00–£18.00 **S:** Fr £17.00–£30.00 **Beds:** 2F 1T 1D **Baths:** 1 En

All details shown are as supplied by B&B owners in Autumn 2002

Tomintoul

NJ1618

Findron Farm, *Braemar Road, Tomintoul, Ballindalloch, Banffshire, AB37 9ER.* Situated in the Castle, Distillery area. Warm welcome. Farmhouse breakfast. **Open:** All year (not Xmas/New Year)
01807 580382 (also fax) Mrs Turner *elmaturner@talk21.com* www.cometo/findronfarmhouse **D:** Fr £15.00–£17.00 **S:** Fr £15.00–£17.00 **Beds:** 1F 1D 1T **Baths:** 2 En 1 Pr

Croughly Farm, *Tomintoul, Ballindalloch, Banffshire, AB37 9EN.* Farmhouse with breathtaking views of Cairngorm mountains.Overlooking River Conglas. **Open:** May to Oct
01807 580476 (also fax) Mrs Shearer *johnannecroughly@tinyworld.co.uk* **D:** Fr £16.00–£18.00 **S:** Fr £18.00–£20.00 **Beds:** 1F 1D **Baths:** 1 Pr 1 En (3)

Tomnavoulin

NJ2126

Roadside Cottage, *Tomnavoulin, Glenlivet, Ballindalloch, Banffshire, AB37 9JL.* Warm welcome, cool prices. Total customer care in glorious countryside. **Open:** All year (not Xmas)
01807 590486 (also fax) Mrs Marks **D:** Fr £16.00–£18.00 **S:** Fr £16.00–£18.00 **Beds:** 1F 1D 1S **Baths:** 2 Sh (4)

Turriff

NJ7250

Lower Plaidy, *Turriff, Aberdeenshire, AB53 5RJ.* Traditional farmhouse. On castle trail, golf, fishing, sporting activities locally. **Open:** All year (not Xmas/New Year)
01888 551679 Mr & Mrs Daley *lowplaidy@aol.com* www.lowerplaidy.co.uk **D:** Fr £18.00–£22.00 **S:** Fr £18.00–£22.00 **Beds:** 1T 1D 1S **Baths:** 1 Sh (5)

Urquhart

NJ2862

The Old Church of Urquhart, *Parrandier, Meft Road, Urquhart, Elgin, IV30 8NH.* Distinctly different place to explore Malt Whisky Country, sea and Highlands. **Open:** All year
01343 843063 (also fax) A Peter *parrandier@freeuk.com* www.oldkirk.co.uk **D:** Fr £20.00–£26.50 **S:** Fr £27.00–£29.00 **Beds:** 1F 2T 1D **Baths:** 2 En 1 Pr (5) **cc**

BATHROOMS
En = Ensuite
Pr = Private
Sh = Shared

Angus

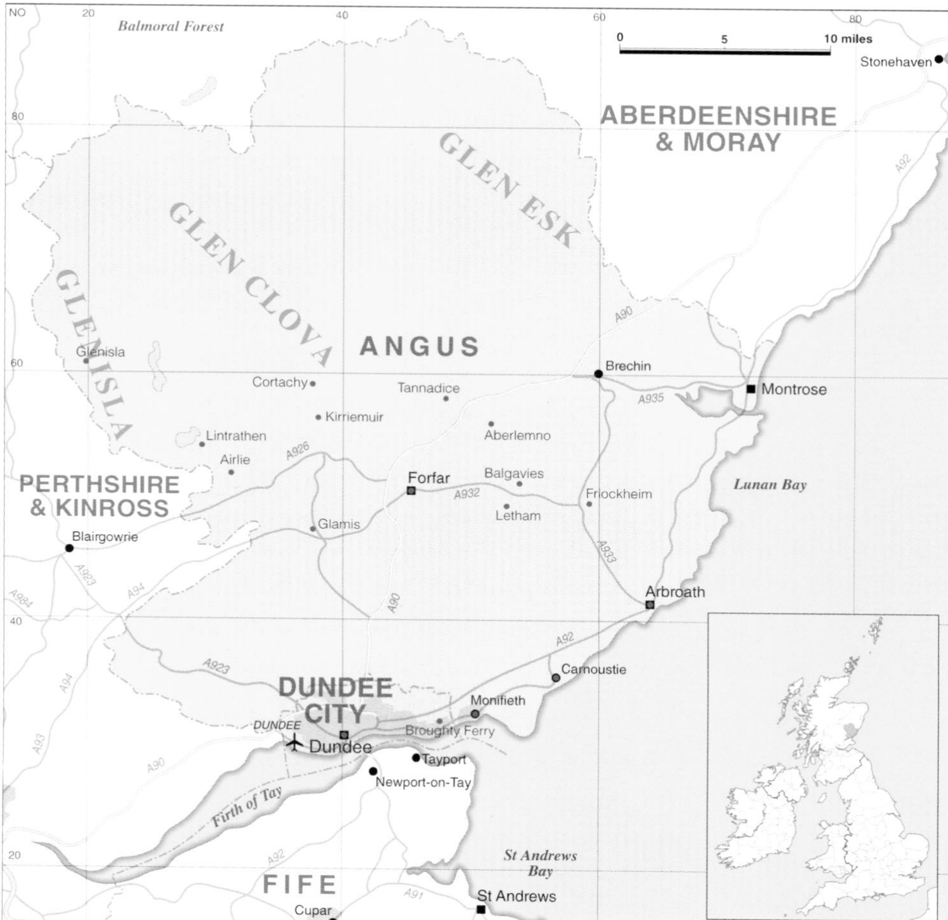

Aberlemno

NO5255

Blibberhill Farmhouse, *Aberlemno, Brechin, Angus, DD9 6TH.* Glamis nearby. Perth (1 hr), St. Andrews (40 mins), Aberdeen (50 mins). **Open:** All year
01307 830323 Mrs Stewart
www.farmhouse-holidays.co.uk **D:** Fr £17.00–£20.00 **S:** Fr £18.00 **Beds:** 1F 1T 1D **Baths:** 3 En 2 Sh (5) **cc**

RATES
D = Price range per person sharing in a double or twin room
S = Price range for a single room

BEDROOMS
D = Double
T = Twin
S = Single
F = Family

Airlie

NO3150

The Brae Of Airlie Farmhouse, *The Kirkton of Airlie, Airlie, Kirriemuir, Angus, DD8 5NJ.* Hillwalking, cycling, birdwatching, historic castles, music festivals, rugged scenery. **Open:** All year
01575 530293 (also fax) M Gardyne *mamie.gardyne@tesco.net* www.angusglens.co.uk **D:** Fr £25.00 **S:** Fr £25.00 **Beds:** 2T **Baths:** 1 En 1 Sh (4)

Arbroath

NO6441 *Old Brewhouse, Letham Grange Hotel, Colliston Inn*

Fairway View B and B, *2 Fairway View, Letham Grange, Arbroath, DD11 4XE.* Rural setting. Warm welcome. Hearty breakfast. Golf courses of Angus. **Open:** All year
01241 890762 Mrs Mackie **Fax: 01241 890213** *chris_mackie1952@hotmail.com* **D:** Fr £25.00 **S:** Fr £25.00 **Beds:** 1T 1D 1S **Baths:** 1 En 1 Sh (3)

Balgavies

NO5350

Redroofs, *Balgavies, Guthrie, Forfar, Angus, DD8 2TN.* Warm welcome in house set in large wooded area. All rooms on ground floor. TVs and refrigerators in all rooms. Ideal base for touring and activities, golf, fishing, walks, glens and seaside. Private secluded parking off B9113 Forfar-Montrose road. Discount on five or more days stay. **Open:** All year
01307 830268 (also fax) Mr & Mrs Milne *redroofs.forfar@virgin.net* **D:** Fr £20.00 **S:** Fr £22.50 **Beds:** 1F 1T 1D **Baths:** 3 En (10) 3

Broughty Ferry

NO4630 *Tay Cregan Hotel*

Homebank, *9 Ellislea Road, Broughty Ferry, Dundee, DD5 1JH.* Splendid Victorian mansion house. Charming ambience, elegant gardens and decor. **Open:** All year
01382 477481 (also fax) Mrs Moore *pat.moore.homebank@bushinternet.com* **D:** Fr £25.00–£30.00 **S:** Fr £25.00–£40.00 **Beds:** 1F 1T 1D 1S **Baths:** 2 En 1 Pr 1 Sh (7)

All details shown are as supplied by B&B owners in Autumn 2002

Carnoustie

NO5634

16 Links Parade, *Carnoustie, Angus, DD7 7JE.* Stone-built villa overlooking 18th fairway of championship golf course. **Open:** All year
01241 852381 (also fax) Bill & Mary Brand *billbrand@dechmont16.freeserve.co.uk* www.dechmont16.freeserve.co.uk **D:** Fr £18.00 **S:** Fr £18.00 **Beds:** 1D 1T 1S **Baths:** 1 Sh

Park House, *Park Avenue, Carnoustie, Angus, DD7 7JA.* Victorian house, three minutes from championship golf course, sea views. **Open:** All year (not Xmas)
01241 852101 (also fax) R Reyner *parkhouse@bbcarnoustie.fsnet.co.uk* www.bbcarnoustie.fsnet.co.uk **D:** Fr £25.00 **S:** Fr £25.00 **Beds:** 1D 1T 2S (3) cc

Cortachy

NO3959

Muirhouses Farm, *Cortachy, Kirriemuir, Angus, DD8 4QG.* Beautiful farmhouse in extensive mature garden on busy farm. **Open:** All year (not Xmas/New Year) **Grades:** STB 3 Star
01575 573128 (also fax) Mrs McLaren *muirhousesfarm@farming.co.uk* www.muirhousesfarm.co.uk **D:** Fr £20.00–£25.00 **S:** Fr £22.50–£25.00 **Beds:** 1F 1D 1S **Baths:** 1 Pr 1 Sh (4)

Dundee

NO3632

Aberlaw Guest House, *230 Broughty Ferry Road, Dundee, Angus, DD4 7JP.* Victorian house overlooking River Tay. Warm welcome from Brian and Aileen. **Open:** All year **Grades:** STB 3 Star
01382 456929 (also fax) Mr Tyrie *aberlawguesthouse@btinternet.com* www.aberlawguesthouse.btinternet.co.uk **D:** Fr £25.00–£30.00 **S:** Fr £20.00–£25.00 **Beds:** 2T 2D 2S **Baths:** 2 En 1 Sh (12) (6)

Ardmoy, *359 Arbroath Road, Dundee, Angus, DD4 7SQ.* Ardmoy is a family-run lovely house, overlooking the River Tay. **Open:** All year **Grades:** STB 3 Star
01382 453249 Mrs Taylor *ardmoy@btopenworld.com* **D:** Fr £18.00–£26.00 **S:** Fr £18.00–£26.00 **Beds:** 1F 1D 1T 1S **Baths:** 2 En 1 Sh (5) (4)

Elm Lodge, *49 Seafield Road, Dundee, Angus, DD1 4NW.* Large Victorian Listed family home. Rooms with river view. **Open:** Jan to Dec
01382 228402 Mrs McDowall **D:** Fr £20.00–£25.00 **S:** Fr £20.00–£25.00 **Beds:** 1D 1T 1S **Baths:** 1 Sh (4)

Ash Villa, *216 Arbroath Road, Dundee, Angus, DD4 7RZ.* Friendly family guest house. Nearby sea, river, mountains. Ideal walking, exploring, castles, wildlife. **Open:** All year
01382 450831 & 07811 989621 (M) J M Hill **Fax: 01382 450831** *ashvilla_guesthouse@talk21.com* **D:** Fr £18.00–£22.00 **S:** Fr £18.00–£26.00 **Beds:** 1F 1T 1S **Baths:** 1 En 2 Sh (4)

Forfar

NO4550

Wemyss Farm, *Montrose Road, Forfar, Angus, DD8 2TB.* 190-acre mixed farm situated 2.5 miles along B9113. **Open:** All year
01307 462887 (also fax) Mrs Lindsay *wemyssfarm@hotmail.com* **D:** Fr £18.00 **S:** Fr £22.00 **Beds:** 1F 1D **Baths:** 2 Sh (6) cc

Friockheim

NO5849

Balmoral Hotel, *30 Gardyne Streel, Friockheim, Arbroath, Angus, DD11 4SQ.* Relaxed friendly atmosphere, comfortable accommodation. Central for golfing/shooting/fishing. **Open:** All year
01241 828224 **D:** Fr £17.50–£22.50 **S:** Fr £20.00–£25.00 **Beds:** 1F 2T 1D **Baths:** 3 Sh (3)

Glamis

NO3846

Arndean, *Linross, Glamis, Forfar, Angus, DD8 1QN.* Close to Glamis Castle and in ideal walking country. **Open:** All year (not Xmas)
01307 840535 Mrs Rufflead *arndean@btinternet.com* www.arnbog.btinternet.co.uk **D:** Fr £16.00 **S:** Fr £16.00–£20.00 **Beds:** 2T **Baths:** 1 Sh (3)

Glenisla

NO2160

The Kirkside House Hotel, *11 Conigre Close, Glenisla, Blairgowrie, Perthshire, PH11 8PH.* Overlooking upper River Isla; peace, tranquillity, good food, friendly service. Ideal for touring. **Open:** All year
01575 582313 Janice Appleby & Tony Willis **D:** Fr £22.50 **S:** Fr £22.50 **Beds:** 1F 3D 1S **Baths:** 3 En 1 Sh (50) cc

Kirriemuir

NO3853

Crepto, *Kinnordy Place, Kirriemuir, Forfar, Angus, DD8 4JW.* 10 minutes walk from town centre. Friendly, warm welcome. Comfortable. **Open:** All year
01575 572746 Mrs Lindsay *davendjessma@bun.com* **D:** Fr £22.00–£25.00 **S:** Fr £22.00–£25.00 **Beds:** 1D 1T 1S **Baths:** 2 Sh (3)

Muirhouses Farm, *Cortachy, Kirriemuir, Angus, DD8 4QG.* Beautiful farmhouse in extensive mature garden on busy farm. **Open:** All year (not Xmas/New Year) **Grades:** STB 3 Star
01575 573128 (also fax) Mrs McLaren *muirhousesfarm@farming.co.uk* www.muirhousesfarm.co.uk **D:** Fr £20.00–£25.00 **S:** Fr £22.50–£25.00 **Beds:** 1F 1D 1S **Baths:** 1 Pr 1 Sh (4)

Letham

NO5248

Whinney-Knowe, *8 Dundee Street, Letham, Forfar, DD8 2PQ.* Large semi-detached villa in friendly rural surroundings. Guests lounge. **Open:** All year **Grades:** STB 3 Star
01307 818288 E Mann *whinneyknowe@btinternet.com* **D:** Fr £18.00–£20.00 **S:** Fr £20.00–£25.00 **Beds:** 1T 2D **Baths:** 1 En 1 Sh (4)

RATES
D = Price range per person sharing in a double or twin room
S = Price range for a single room

Lintrathen

NO2853

Lochside Lodge, *Bridgend of Lintrathen, Lintrathen, Kirriemuir, Angus, DD8 5JJ.* In Angus glens, a picturesque converted farm steading alongside Lintrathen Loch. **Open:** All year **Grades:** STB 4 Star
01575 560340 Fax: 01575 560202 *enquiries@lochsidelodge.com* www.lochsidelodge.com **D:** Fr £30.00–£35.00 **S:** Fr £35.00–£40.00 **Beds:** 1F 2T 1D **Baths:** 4 Pr (20) **cc**

Tannadice

NO4758 *Finavon Hotel, Drovers Arms*

Glencoul House, *Tannadice, Forfar, Angus, DD8 3SF.* Near Glamis Castle, Angus Glens, beaches. Golf courses, St. Andrews, fishing. **Open:** All year (not Xmas/New Year)
01307 860248 (also fax) Mrs Kirby *glencoul@waitrose.com* **D:** Fr £19.00–£20.00 **S:** Fr £20.00 **Beds:** 1F 1T **Baths:** 2 Sh (3)

Argyll & Bute

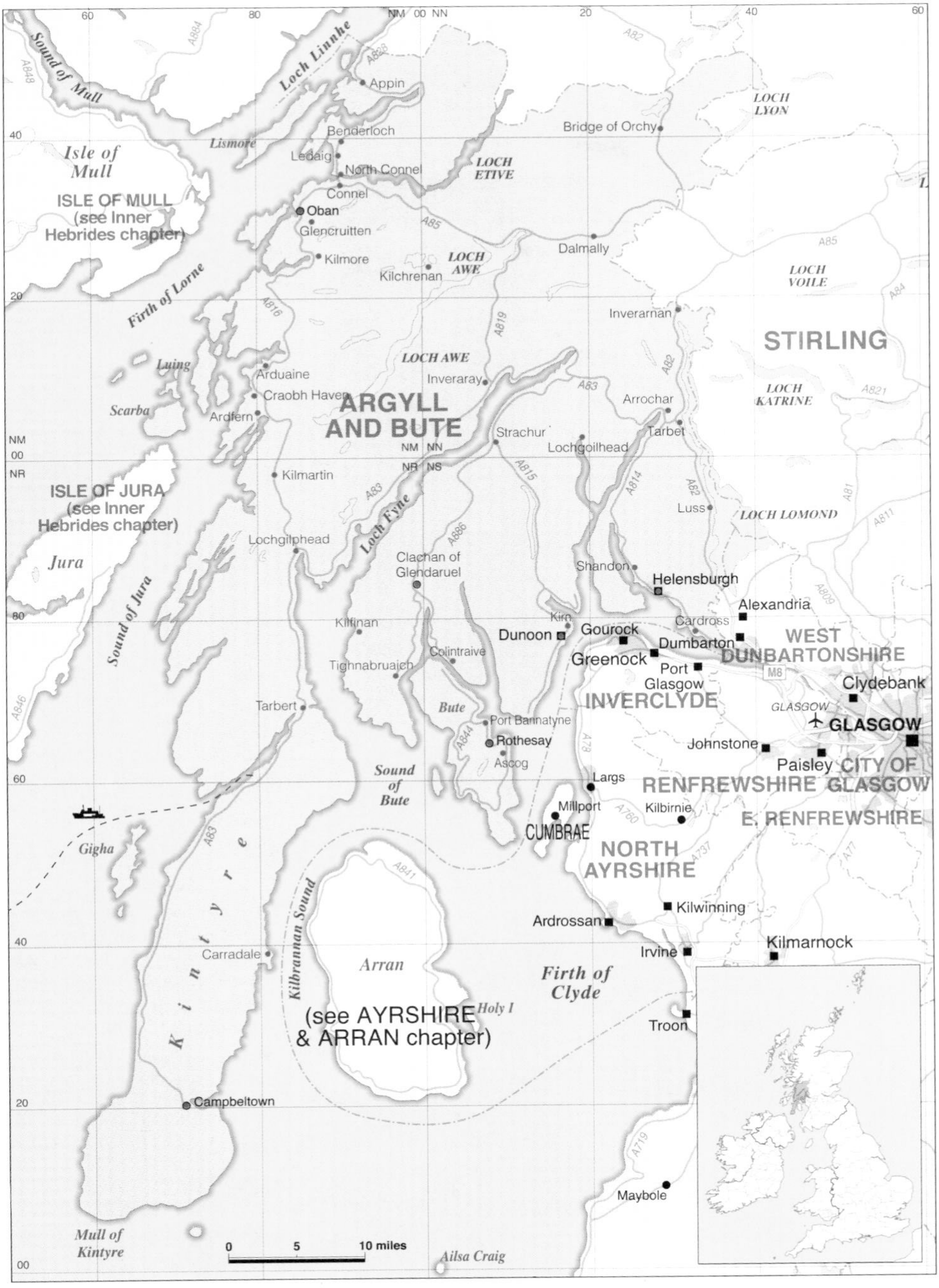

Sound of Mull
Loch Linnhe
Appin
Lismore
Benderloch
Ledaig
North Connel
Connel
LOCH ETIVE
Isle of Mull
ISLE OF MULL (see Inner Hebrides chapter)
Oban
Glencruitten
Kilmore
Kilchrenan
LOCH AWE
Dalmally
Bridge of Orchy
LOCH LYON
LOCH VOILE
Firth of Lorne
Inverarnan
STIRLING
Luing
Arduaine
Craobh Haven
Ardfern
Scarba
LOCH AWE
Inveraray
ARGYLL AND BUTE
Arrochar
LOCH KATRINE
Tarbet
Strachur
Lochgoilhead
Kilmartin
ISLE OF JURA (see Inner Hebrides chapter)
Jura
Luss
LOCH LOMOND
Loch Fyne
Lochgilphead
Clachan of Glendaruel
Shandon
Helensburgh
Alexandria
Sound of Jura
Kilfinan
Kirn
Cardross
Dunoon
Gourock
Dumbarton
WEST DUNBARTONSHIRE
Colintraive
Greenock
Port Glasgow
Tighnabruaich
Clydebank
INVERCLYDE
Tarbert
Bute
Port Bannatyne
GLASGOW
Rothesay
Johnstone
Ascog
Paisley
CITY OF GLASGOW
Sound of Bute
Largs
RENFREWSHIRE
Millport
Kilbirnie
E. RENFREWSHIRE
CUMBRAE
NORTH AYRSHIRE
Gigha
Kintyre
Kilbrannan Sound
Kilwinning
Ardrossan
Carradale
Irvine
Kilmarnock
Arran
Firth of Clyde
(see AYRSHIRE & ARRAN chapter)
Holy I
Troon
Campbeltown
Maybole
Mull of Kintyre
0 5 10 miles
Ailsa Craig

Appin

NM9346 *Creggan Inn, Pier House*

Lurignish Farm, *Appin, Argyll, PA38 4BN.* Traditional lochside hill farm, good home-cooking, golf, boating, riding nearby. **Open:** May to Sept
01631 730365 Mrs Macleod *lurignish@amserve.net* **D:** Fr £18.00–£21.00 **S:** Fr £20.00–£23.00 **Beds:** 1F 1D **Baths:** 1 Sh (4)

Ardfern

NM8004

Lunga, *Ardfern, Lochgilphead, Argyll, PA31 8QR.* C17th estate mansion overlooks islands & Firth of Lorne. 3,000 acre private coastal estate. **Open:** All year **Grades:** STB 1 Star
01852 500237 Mr Lindsay-MacDougall **Fax: 01852 500639** *colin@lunga.demon.co.uk* www.lunga.com **D:** Fr £19.00–£24.00 **S:** Fr £19.00–£24.00 **Beds:** 1F 2D 1T 1S **Baths:** 4 Pr 1 Sh

Tigh An Innis, *Ardlarach Road, Ardfern, Lochgilphead, Argyll, PA31 8QN.* Peaceful high-quality accommodation with panoramic view towards Loch Craignish. **Open:** All year (not Xmas)
01852 500682 Mrs Wylie *joan.wylie@tesco.net* **D:** Fr £20.00–£23.00 **S:** Fr £25.00–£28.00 **Beds:** 1T 2D **Baths:** 3 En (3)

Arduaine

NM8010

Asknish Cottage, *Arduaine, Oban, Argyll, PA34 4XQ.* **Open:** All year **01852 200247** Miss Campbell *elsbeth@arduaine.org.uk* **D:** Fr £17.00–£18.00 **S:** Fr £17.00–£22.00 **Beds:** 1D 1T **Baths:** 1 Sh (3)
Halfway between Oban & Lochgilphead. Warm welcome in hillside cottage overlooking islands Jura to Luing, ideal base for island hopping, Arduaine Gardens, 0.5 miles. Boat trips, birds, castles, walking, etc. nearby. Wild garden, tame owner.

RATES
D = Price range per person sharing in a double or twin room
S = Price range for a single room

Arrochar

NN2904

Lochside Guest House, *Arrochar, Dunbartonshire, G83 7AA.* Located on Loch Long, great for walking, ornithology, touring, sailing. **Open:** All year
01301 702467 Maria & Iain Gourlay *lochsidegh7@aol.com* **D:** Fr £19.00–£27.00 **S:** Fr £25.00–£30.00 **Beds:** 1F 3D 1T 1S **Baths:** 4 En 2 Pr (10) cc

Ferry Cottage, *Ardmay, Arrochar, Dunbartonshire, G83 7AH.* **Open:** All year (not Xmas/New Year) **Grades:** STB 2 Star
01301 702428 Mrs Bennetton **Fax: 01301 702729** *caroleferrycott@aol.com* www.ferrycottage.com **D:** Fr £18.50–£25.00 **S:** Fr £22.00–£35.00 **Beds:** 1F 2D 1T **Baths:** 3 En 1 Sh (2) (6) cc
Quietly situated 1 mile south of Arrochar (A814) 5 minutes drive from Loch Lomond. All ensuite rooms have breathtaking views overlooking Loch Long towards the 'Cobbler'. Major credit cards, private parking. Excellent base for touring the surrounding area. 'Non Smoking establishment'.

Burnbrae, *Shore Road, Arrochar, G83 7AG.* Charming lochside location. Stunning views overlooking Arrochar Alps. Mooring available. **Open:** All year
01301 702988 & 07919 083754 (M) Mrs Mathieson **D:** Fr £25.00–£30.00 **S:** Fr £35.00–£40.00 **Beds:** 1T 1D **Baths:** 2 En (3)

Seabank, *Main Road, Arrochar, G83 7AG.* Lovely old house, beautiful views Loch and Arrochar Alps. Great base hill-walking, touring, fishing. Loch Lomond 2 miles, Glasgow 40 miles, historic Stirling 50 miles. 200 metres walking distance village pub. Great food, reasonably priced, warm welcome from Sam and Kathleen. **Open:** All year
01301 702555 (also fax) S Smillie *sam@seabankarrochar.fsnet.co.uk* **D:** Fr £16.00–£20.00 **S:** Fr £20.00–£28.00 **Beds:** 1F 1D 1T **Baths:** 1 Sh (8) (6)

Fascadail, *Shore Road, Arrochar, G83 7AB.* Magnificent loch and mountain views. Ideal base touring and walking. **Open:** All year
01301 702344 *fascadail@easynet.co.uk* www.fascadail.com **D:** Fr £20.00–£27.50 **S:** Fr £30.00–£45.00 **Beds:** 2T 5D **Baths:** 6 En 1 Pr (8) cc

BATHROOMS
En = Ensuite
Pr = Private
Sh = Shared

Benderloch

NM9038

Hawthorn, *Benderloch, Oban, Argyll, PA37 1QS.* High-quality peaceful accommodation, beautiful views. Ideal touring/walking base. **Open:** All year **Grades:** STB 4 Star
01631 720452 Mrs Currie *janecurrie@hotmail.com* www.hawthorn-cottages.co.uk **D:** Fr £18.00–£24.00 **S:** Fr £18.00–£24.00 **Beds:** 1F 1D 1T **Baths:** 2 En 1 Pr (5) cc

Bridge of Orchy

NN2939

Glen Orchy Farm, *Glen Orchy, Bridge of Orchy, Argyll, PA33 1BD.* Remote sheep farm. Enjoy wildlife, birdwatching, walking, climbing amongst beautiful scenery. **Open:** Mar to Nov
01838 200221 Mrs MacLennan **Fax: 01838 200231** **D:** Fr £16.00–£18.00 **S:** Fr £16.00–£18.00 **Beds:** 2F **Baths:** 1 Sh

BUTE Ascog

NS1062

Ascog Farm, *Ascog, Rothesay, Isle of Bute, PA20 9LL.* Features on BBC TV's 'Holidays Out' - come and be spoilt. **Open:** All year (not Xmas/New Year)
01700 503372 I Watson **D:** Fr £20.00 **S:** Fr £20.00 **Beds:** 1D 3S **Baths:** 2 Sh (8) (4)

National Grid References given are for villages, towns and cities – not for individual houses

BEDROOMS
D = Double
T = Twin
S = Single
F = Family

BUTE Port Bannatyne

NS0867

Port Royal Hotel, *37 Marine Road, Port Bannatyne, Isle of Bute, PA20 0LW.* **Open:** All year
01700 505073 *stay@butehotel.com* www.butehotel.com **D:** Fr £22.00–£26.00 **S:** Fr £22.00–£35.00 **Beds:** 1F 4T **Baths:** 2 En 1 Pr 1 Sh (5)
A traditional village inn, the Port Royal Hotel looks across Kames Bay to the stunning Argyll mountains. Sparking cottage rooms, real ale, fine wine and fresh local produce, blessed by a dedicated Russian chef, await nature lovers, yachtsmen and travellers.

BUTE Rothesay

NS0864

Battery Lodge, *25 Battery Place, Rothesay, Isle of Bute, PA20 9DU.* **Open:** All year
01700 502169 M Leyden **D:** Fr £20.00–£22.00 **S:** Fr £18.00–£20.00 **Beds:** 2F 1T 4D 1S **Baths:** 4 En 2 Pr 1 Sh (7)
Built in 1865, Battery Lodge is a splendid mid-Victorian enjoying spectacular views across Rothesay Bay to the Argyllshire Hills. Your hosts Martin and Lorraine offer attractive bedrooms, most with ensuite facilities, plus warm Scottish hospitality with beautiful home cooking.

BEDROOMS
D = Double
T = Twin
S = Single
F = Family

The Moorings, *7 Mount Stewart Road, Rothesay, Isle of Bute, PA20 9DY.* **Open:** Mar to Dec **Grades:** STB 3 Star
01700 502277 (also fax) Mr & Mrs Hill *fjhbute@aol.com* www.visitbute.com **D:** Fr £22.50–£27.50 **S:** Fr £27.50–£30.00 **Beds:** 3D 1T 1S **Baths:** 4 En **cc**
Upgraded charming Victorian lodge (1850). Located overlooking the moorings in quiet conservation seafront location, spectacular views. Close to all amenities & a selection of excellent restaurants. Walkers & Cyclists Welcome Scheme, ideal for the West Island Way.

Alamein House Hotel, *28 Battery Place, Rothesay, Isle of Bute, PA20 9DU.* Magnificent seafront location. Yachting, fishing, riding, cycling and golf closeby. **Open:** All year
01700 502395 J F Hutchings **D:** Fr £19.00–£21.00 **S:** Fr £20.00–£22.00 **Beds:** 1F 3T 3D **Baths:** 3 En 1 Pr 2 Sh (5)

Campbeltown

NR7220

White Hart Hotel, *Main Street, Campbeltown, Argyll, PA28 6AN.* **Open:** All year (not Xmas/New Year)
01586 552440 Fax: 01586 554972 *whitehartho tel@amserve.net* www.whiteh.com **D:** Fr £25.00–£30.00 **S:** Fr £27.50–£45.00 **Beds:** 3F 6T 6D 4S **Baths:** 19 En **cc**
Attractive white painted hotel is a landmark in this west coast fishing port. Ideally situated for the new Campbeltown - Ballycastle Irish ferry, Machrinanish golf course, walking in the Mull of Kintyre, birdwatching, fishing or relaxing. Bargain breaks available midweek & weekend.

Homestone Farm, *Campbeltown, Argyll, PA28 6RL.* Wonderfully, peaceful location on working farm/riding centre. Excellent food. **Open:** Easter to Oct
01586 552437 L McArthur *lorna@relaxscotland.com* **D:** Fr £18.00 **S:** Fr £18.00 **Beds:** 3D 2S **Baths:** 3 En 1 Sh (10)

Glen Mhairi, *Craigown Road, Campbeltown, Argyll, PA28 6HQ.* Superb location overlooking town and loch. Modern bungalow, warm welcome. **Open:** Easter to Oct
01586 552952 Mrs Craig **D:** Fr £18.50–£20.00 **S:** Fr £20.00–£22.50 **Beds:** 1T 1D **Baths:** 1 Pr 1 Sh (2)

Cardross

NS3477

Kirkton House, *Darleith Road, Cardross, Dumbarton, G82 5EZ.* Old farmstead hotel. Tranquil setting. Clyde views. Wine and dine. **Open:** Feb to Nov
01389 841951 Fax: 01389 841868 *stil@kirktonhouse.co.uk* www.kirktonhouse.co.uk **D:** Fr £30.50–£35.00 **S:** Fr £40.50–£45.00 **Beds:** 4F 2T **Baths:** 6 En (12) **cc**

Glengate Cottage, *Main Road, Cardross, Dumbarton, G82 5NZ.* Picturesque village. Minutes from Helensburgh seaside town. NTS properties and golf nearby. **Open:** All year
01389 841737 Miss Mackie **D:** Fr £19.00–£21.00 **S:** Fr £17.00 **Beds:** 2D 1S **Baths:** 1 Pr 1 Sh (2)

Carradale

NR8138

The Mains Farm, *Carradale, Campbeltown, Argyll, PA28 6QG.* Traditional, comfortable farmhouse near beach, forest walks, fishing, golf, wildlife. **Open:** Easter to Oct
01583 431216 Mrs MacCormick *maccormick@mainsfarm.freeserve.co.uk* **D:** Fr £17.50 **S:** Fr £17.50 **Beds:** 1F 1D 1S **Baths:** 1 Sh (3)

Kiloran Guest House, *Carradale, Campbeltown, Argyll, PA28 6QG.* Lovely Victorian house. Warm welcome. Good home cooking. Sandy beaches. **Open:** All year
01583 431795 J A Nicholson **D:** Fr £18.50–£25.00 **S:** Fr £22.00–£28.00 **Beds:** 1F 3T 1D **Baths:** 2 En 1 Pr 1 Sh (6)

Clachan of Glendaruel

NS0083

Glendaruel Hotel, *Clachan of Glendaruel, Colintraive, Argyll, PA22 3AA.* Charming family run hotel. Ideal for fishing, touring, walking etc. **Open:** All year (not Xmas)
01369 820274 Fax: 01369 820317 *info@glendaruel-hotel.com* www.glendaruel-hotel.com **D:** Fr £30.00–£35.00 **S:** Fr £35.00–£40.00 **Beds:** 3T 2D 1S **Baths:** 6 En (10) **cc**

Colintraive

NS0374

Colintraive Hotel, *Colintraive, Argyll, PA22 3AS.* Former Victorian hunting lodge. Comfortable and informal family run hotel. **Open:** All year
01700 841207 Mr Williamson *kyleshotel@aol.com* **D:** Fr £22.00–£28.00 **S:** Fr £26.00–£30.00 **Beds:** 1F 1D 1T **Baths:** 4 Pr

Connel

NM9133 *Lcoknell Arms, Dunstaffanage Arms, Falls of Lora*

Rosebank, *Connel, Oban, Argyll, PA37 1PA.* Family house in quiet situation in Connel village overlooking Loch Etive, 5 miles from Oban. Excellent touring centre, large garden at rear. Home made preserves a speciality. Hand-knitted articles for sale. A warm welcome to home and overseas visitors. **Open:** May to Sept
01631 710316 R L MacKechnie **D:** Fr £14.00–£16.00 **S:** Fr £15.00–£17.00 **Beds:** 1D 1T 1S **Baths:** 1 Sh

Craobh Haven

NM7907

Lunga, *Ardfern, Lochgilphead, Argyll, PA31 8QR.* C17th estate mansion overlooks islands & Firth of Lorne. 3,000 acre private coastal estate. **Open:** All year **Grades:** STB 1 Star
01852 500237 Mr Lindsay-MacDougall **Fax: 01852 500639** *colin@lunga.demon.co.uk* www.lunga.com **D:** Fr £19.00–£24.00 **S:** Fr £19.00–£24.00 **Beds:** 1F 2D 1T 1S **Baths:** 4 Pr 1 Sh

Buidhe Lodge, *Craobh Haven, Lochgilphead, Argyll, PA31 8UA.* Swiss-style lodge located on shores of Loch Shuna. Near NTS Arduaine Gardens. **Open:** All year (not Xmas)
01852 500291 Mr & Mrs Twinn www.buidhelodge.com **D:** Fr £23.00–£26.00 **S:** Fr £33.00 **Beds:** 2D 4T **Baths:** 6 Pr (8)

Dalmally

NN1626

Orchy Bank Guest House, *Dalmally, Argyll, PA33 1AS.* Victorian house on the bank of the River Orchy. **Open:** All year **Grades:** STB 2 Star
01838 200370 Mr Burke *aj.burke@talk21.com* **D:** Fr £18.00–£20.00 **S:** Fr £20.00–£25.00 **Beds:** 2F 2D 2T 2S **Baths:** 4 Sh (8)

Dunoon

NS1776

Abbots Brae Hotel, *Bullwood Road, Dunoon, Argyll, PA23 7QJ.* **Open:** All year
01369 705021 Fax: 01369 701191 *info@abbotsbrae.co.uk* www.abbotsbrae.co.uk **D:** Fr £25.00–£50.00 **S:** Fr £30.00–£45.00 **Beds:** 1F 1T 6D **Baths:** 8 En (8) **cc**
Award-winning small country house set in its own woodland garden with breathtaking views of the sea & hills. Very spacious bedrooms including four-poster and king size beds. Situated at the gateway to the New Loch Lomond National Park.

Craigieburn Hotel, *Alexandra Parade, East Bay, Dunoon, Argyll, PA23 8AN.* Friendly, family-run private hotel with superb sea views. **Open:** All year (not Xmas) **Grades:** STB 2 Star
01369 702048 Mrs Hutchinson *emma.hutchinson@btinternet.com* www.btinternet.com/~emma.hutchinson **D:** Fr £17.00–£20.00 **S:** Fr £17.00–£20.00 **Beds:** 3F 2D 2T 2S **Baths:** 3 Sh (5)

Lyall Cliff Hotel, *Alexandra Parade, East Bay, Dunoon, Argyll, PA23 8AW.* Beautifully situated family-run seafront hotel. 3 ground floor rooms. **Open:** Jan to Oct **Grades:** STB 3 Star, AA 3 Diamond
01369 702041 (also fax) Mr & Mrs Norris *lyallcliff@talk21.com* www.lyallcliff.co.uk **D:** Fr £21.00–£26.00 **S:** Fr £25.00–£32.00 **Beds:** 2F 4D 4T **Baths:** 10 En (4) (10) **cc**

BATHROOMS
En = Ensuite
Pr = Private
Sh = Shared

Glencruitten

NM8729

Barranrioch Farm, *Glencruitten, Oban, Argyll, PA34 4QD.* Peaceful working farm close to Oban. Enclosed play area. **Open:** All year
01631 770223 Mrs Nicholson *barranrioch@crosswinds.net* **D:** Fr £15.00–£20.00 **S:** Fr £15.00–£20.00 **Beds:** 1F 1D **Baths:** 1 En 1 Pr (10)

Helensburgh

NS2982

Sinclair House, *91/93 Sinclair Street, Helensburgh, G848TR.* **Open:** All year
01436 676301 *bookings@sinclairhouse.com* www.sinclairhouse.com **D:** Fr £18.00–£25.00 **S:** Fr £20.00–£50.00 **Beds:** 1F 2T 2D 1S **Baths:** 4 En 1 Sh (7) **cc**
Located in Helensburgh on the Clyde Estuary, Sinclair House is at the gateway to Loch Lomond and the Trossachs National Park. We make an ideal touring base with Stirling, Edinburgh, Ayr, Glasgow and Fort William all within a 90 min drive.

Yetholm, *103 East Princes Street, Helensburgh, Dunbartonshire, G84 7DN.* Near Hill House - Rennie Mackintosh. 10 mins Loch Lomond. Good base golf, sailing, Trossachs. **Open:** All year (not Xmas) **Grades:** STB 3 Star
01436 673271 Mrs Mackenzie **D:** Fr £18.00–£22.00 **S:** Fr £20.00–£22.00 **Beds:** 1D 1T **Baths:** 1 Pr 1 En (5) (3)

Eastbank, *10 Hanover Street, Helensburgh, Argyll, G84 7AW.* Upper flat of Victorian house 30 minutes from Glasgow airport. **Open:** All year (not Xmas) **Grades:** STB 3 Star
01436 673665 (also fax) Mrs Ross *enquiries@eastbankscotland.com* **D:** Fr £18.00–£25.00 **S:** Fr £18.00–£22.00 **Beds:** 1F 1T 1S **Baths:** 1 En 1 Sh (3) (4) **cc**

Arran View, *32 Barclay Drive, Helensburgh, Dunbartonshire, G84 9RA.* Convenient NT Hill House, Loch Lomond, golf, Faslane Naval Base. **Open:** All year **Grades:** STB 4 Star
01436 673713 Mr & Mrs Sanders **Fax: 01436 672595** *arranview@btinternet.com* www.btinternet.com/~arranview **D:** Fr £20.00–£22.00 **S:** Fr £20.00–£25.00 **Beds:** 1D 1T 2S **Baths:** 2 En 1 Pr 1 Sh (5)

Ravenswood, *32 Suffolk Street, Helensburgh, Dunbartonshire, G84 9PA.* Member walkers and cyclists scheme - Sliver Green Tourism award. **Open:** All year
01436 672112 (also fax) Mrs Richards *ravenswood@breathemail.net* **D:** Fr £25.00–£40.00 **S:** Fr £25.00–£50.00 **Beds:** 2D 1T 1S **Baths:** 2 En 1 Pr 1 Sh (4)

County Lodge Hotel, *Old Luss Road, Helensburgh, Dunbartonshire, G84 7BH.* Travel Lodge style accommodation. Twin/Double rooms ensuite at £39.95. **Open:** All year
01436 672034 Fax: 01436 672033 D: Fr £22.95 **S:** Fr £22.95 **Beds:** 7T/D **Baths:** 7 En cc

Maybank, *185 East Clyde Street, Helensburgh, Dunbartonshire, G84 7AG.* Attractive early Victorian home in a level location. **Open:** All year
01436 672865 Mrs Barella **D:** Fr £18.00 **S:** Fr £22.00 **Beds:** 2D/T 1S **Baths:** 2 Sh

28 Macleod Drive, *Helensburgh, Dunbartonshire, G84 9QS.* Stunning views near Loch Lomond, golf, walking and the Highlands. **Open:** June to Sept
01436 675206 Mr & Mrs Calder *g.calder@talk21.com* **D:** Fr £17.00–£19.00 **S:** Fr £18.00–£20.00 **Beds:** 1F 1T 1S **Baths:** 2 Sh (3)

4 Redclyffe Gardens, *Helensburgh, Dunbartonshire, G84 9JJ.* Modern family home; sea views, quiet cul-de-sac, adjacent Mackintosh Hill House. **Open:** All year (not Xmas)
01436 677688 (also fax) Mrs Weston *dweston440@aol.com* www.stayatlochlomond.com/bweston **D:** Fr £21.00–£24.00 **S:** Fr £25.00–£30.00 **Beds:** 1D 1T **Baths:** 1 Pr 1 En (3)

Drumfork Farm, *Helensburgh, G84 7JY.* Working farm with friendly family, 20 minutes from Loch Lomond. **Open:** All year (not Xmas/New Year)
01436 672329 (also fax) Mrs Howie *drumforkfm@aol.com* **D:** Fr £20.00–£25.00 **S:** Fr £30.00–£40.00 **Beds:** 2T 1D **Baths:** 3 En (4) cc

Inveraray

NN0908

Minard Castle, *Minard, Inveraray, Argyll, PA32 8YB.* Warm welcome in our C19th castle beside Loch Fyne. **Open:** Apr to Oct **Grades:** STB 4 Star
01546 886272 (also fax) Mr Gayre *reinoldgayre@minardcastle.com* www.minardcastle.com **D:** Fr £35.00–£45.00 **S:** Fr £35.00–£45.00 **Beds:** 2F 1T **Baths:** 3 En (6) cc

The Old Rectory, *Inveraray, Argyll, PA32 8UH.* Family-run Georgian house overlooking Loch Fyne. **Open:** All year (not Xmas)
01499 302280 Mrs Maclaren **D:** Fr £15.00–£20.00 **S:** Fr £15.00–£20.00 **Beds:** 4F 3D 1T 1S **Baths:** 3 Sh (3) (9)

Creag Dhubh, *Inveraray, Argyll, PA32 8XF.* Family run B&B. Unrestricted views across Loch Fyne. **Open:** All year (not Xmas/New Year)
01499 302430 J MacLugash *creagdhubh@freeuk.com* **D:** Fr £20.00–£25.00 **S:** Fr £25.00–£30.00 **Beds:** 2F 3D **Baths:** 5 En (2) (6) cc

Claonairigh House, *Bridge of Douglas, Inveraray, Argyll, PA32 8XT.* Historic country house ideally situated for Argyll countryside and coast. Excellent breakfasts, beautiful rooms. **Open:** All year (not Xmas)
01499 302160 Fax: 01499 302774 *fiona@argyll-scotland.demon.co.uk* **D:** Fr £16.00–£25.00 **S:** Fr £16.00–£25.00 **Beds:** 1D 2T **Baths:** 3 En (8)

Inverarnan

NN3118 *Drovers Inn*

Rose Cottage, *Inverarnan, Glen Falloch, Arrochar, Dunbartonshire, G83 7DX.* Renovated C18th cottage on West Highland Way, Loch Lomond. **Open:** All year (not Xmas/New Year)
01301 704255 Mr & Mrs Fletcher *fletcher.j3@talk21.com* **D:** Fr £19.00–£25.00 **Beds:** 2D **Baths:** 2 En (4)

Kilchrenan

NN0322 *Lcoknell Arms, Dunstaffnage Arms, Falls of Lora, Kilchrenan Inn*

Innisfree, *Kilchrenan, Taynuilt, Argyll, PA35 1HG.* Wonderful scenery, modern croft house, quiet. Oban 19 miles, popular destination. **Open:** Easter to Sept
01866 833352 Mrs Wright **D:** Fr £18.00 **S:** Fr £18.00 **Beds:** 1D 1T **Baths:** 2 Sh (4)

Kilfinan

NR9378

Auchnaskeoch Farm House, *Kilfinan, Tighnabruaich, Argyll, PA21 2ER.* Enjoy unspoiled countryside and magnificent scenery; a warm Scottish welcome awaits you. **Open:** All year (not Xmas)
01700 811397 Mrs Mackay **Fax: 01700 811799 D:** Fr £17.50–£20.00 **S:** Fr £18.00–£21.00 **Beds:** 1D **Baths:** 1 En (1)

Planning a longer stay? Always ask for any special rates

Kilmartin

NR8398

Burndale, *Kilmartin, Lochgilphead, Argyll, PA31 8RQ.* C19th stone built ex-manse in the village of Kilmartin. **Open:** Easter to Nov
01546 510235 Mr & Mrs Friel *alan-hawkins@burndale-kilmartin.freeserve.co.uk* **D:** Fr £23.00 **S:** Fr £26.00 **Beds:** 2T 1D 1S **Baths:** 2 En 1 Pr (6)

Kilmore

NM8825

Invercairn, *Musdale Road, Kilmore, Oban, Argyll, PA34 4XX.* Beautiful spot. 10-minute drive Oban town centre. Wonderful base for splendours of Argyll. **Open:** Easter to Oct
01631 770301 (also fax) Mrs MacPherson *invercairn.kilmore@virgin.net* www.bandboban.com **D:** Fr £20.00–£25.00 **S:** Fr £25.00–£30.00 **Beds:** 2D 1T **Baths:** 3 En (4)

Kirn

NS1877

Rosscairn Hotel, *51 Hunter Street, Kirn, Dunoon, Argyll, PA23 8JR.* Quiet, friendly atmosphere, excellent food. Ideal base to explore Argyll. **Open:** All year (not Xmas/New Year)
01369 704344 (also fax) Mr & Mrs Jones *rosscairn@kirn.fsnet.co.uk* rosscairn.freeserve.co.uk **D:** Fr £22.00–£26.00 **S:** Fr £25.00–£30.00 **Beds:** 3F 2T 2D 1S **Baths:** 7 En 1 Pr (10) cc

Ledaig

NM9037

An Struan, *Ledaig, Oban, Argyll, PA37 1QS.* Large modern bungalow in the picturesque village of Benderloch, 7 miles north of Oban. **Open:** All year (not Xmas)
01631 720301 Mrs Knowles **Fax: 01631 720734** *frankwop@btinternet.com* www.oban.org.uk/accommodation/anstruan.index.html **D:** Fr £18.00–£22.00 **S:** Fr £20.00–£25.00 **Beds:** 2D 1T **Baths:** 1 En 1 Sh

Lochgilphead

NR8687

Kilmory House, *Paterson Street, Lochgilphead, Argyll, PA31 8JP.* Lovely house and gardens situated lochside. Most rooms with loch views. **Open:** Mar to Oct
01546 603658 Mr Moore **D:** Fr £16.50–£20.00 **S:** Fr £20.00–£25.00 **Beds:** 2D 3T **Baths:** 3 En 2 Pr (10) (16) cc

Planning a longer stay? Always ask for any special rates

Empire Travel Lodge, *Union Street, Lochgilphead, Argyll, PA31 8JS.* Former cinema converted to create quality travel lodge. **Open:** All year (not Xmas) **01546 602381** Mr Haysom **Fax: 01546 606606** **D:** Fr £23.00 **S:** Fr £23.00 **Beds:** 2F 5D 2T **Baths:** 9 En (9) 1 cc

Corbiere, *Achnabreac, Lochgilphead, Argyll, PA31 8SG.* Bedrooms are spacious, comfortable, thoughtfully equipped. Peaceful, rural location. **Open:** All year (not Xmas/New Year) **01546 602764** Mrs Sinclair **D:** Fr £16.50–£17.50 **S:** Fr £20.00 **Beds:** 1T 1D **Baths:** 2 Sh

Luss

NS3592

Doune of Glen Douglas Farm, *Luss, Loch Lomond, Alexandria, Argyll & Bute, G83 8PD.* Remote working hill sheep farm set in 6000 acres hills above Loch Lomond. **Open:** Easter to Oct **01301 702312** Mrs Robertson **Fax: 01301 702916** *pjrobertson@glendouglas.u-net.com* **D:** Fr £22.00–£30.00 **S:** Fr £25.00–£35.00 **Beds:** 2D 1T **Baths:** 1 En 2 Sh cc

Shantron Farm, *Shantron Cottage, Luss, Alexandria, Dunbartonshire, G83 8RH.* 5000-acre farm with spectacular views of loch and surrounding area. **Open:** Mar to Nov **01389 850231 (also fax)** Mrs Lennox *rjlennox@shantron.u-net.com* www.staylochlomond.com **D:** Fr £22.00–£25.00 **S:** Fr £25.00–£30.00 **Beds:** 1F 1D 1T **Baths:** 3 En (3) cc

North Connel

NM9134 *Lochnell Arms, Dunstaff Nage Arms, Falls of Lora Hotel*

Santana Lodge, *Bonawe Road, North Connel, Oban, PA37 1RA.* Beautiful bungalow. Quiet area. Perfect for touring West Highlands Islands. **Open:** Easter to Sept **01631 710380** Mrs Scott **D:** Fr £16.00–£20.00 **S:** Fr £20.00–£25.00 **Beds:** 1FN 2T 1D 1S **Baths:** 2 Sh (5) (6)

Oban

NM8630

Harbour View Guest House, *Shore Street, Oban, Argyll, PA34 4LQ.* Centrally-situated town house. **Open:** All year (not Xmas) **01631 563462** Mrs McDougall *dilysmcdougall@aol.com* **D:** Fr £15.00–£17.00 **S:** Fr £15.00–£17.00 **Beds:** 2F 1D 1T **Baths:** 2 Sh

Glenara Guest House, *Rockfield Road, Oban, Argyll, PA34 5DQ.* **Open:** All year **Grades:** STB 4 Star **01631 563172** Mrs Bingham **Fax: 01631 571125** *glenara_oban@hotmail.com* www.smoothhound.co.uk/hotels/glenara.html **D:** Fr £21.00–£27.00 **S:** Fr £25.00–£35.00 **Beds:** 1F/T 3D **Baths:** 4 En (12) (5)

We offer to our guests a quality of room, breakfast and welcome which will ensure your return. Centrally-situated, sea views, off-street parking. Individually furnished rooms with king-sized beds reflecting Dorothy's commitment to quality. Glenara is a no-smoking guest house.

Feorlin, *Longsdale Road, Oban, Argyll, PA34 5DZ.* **Open:** Mar to Nov **Grades:** STB 3 Star **01631 562930 & 07990 790953 (M)** Mrs Campbell *feorlin@btinternet.com* www.feorlin-oban.co.uk **D:** Fr £18.00–£20.00 **Beds:** 1F **Baths:** 1 En (2)

A warm welcome and traditional Scottish hospitality awaits you at Feorlin, a charming bungalow less than 8 mins walk from town and leisure sports complex. Great breakfasts with fresh produce, free-range eggs, home-made jams and marmalade.

Dana Villa, *Dunollie Road, Oban, Argyll, PA34 5PJ.* Scottish hospitality, family-run. Close to all amenities and waterfront. **Open:** All year **01631 564063** Mrs Payne *edna.payne@btopenworld.com* www.danavilla.com **D:** Fr £15.00 **S:** Fr £20.00 **Beds:** 2F 2D 3T 1S **Baths:** 3 En 1 Pr 2 Sh

Ardenlee, *Pulpit Hill, Oban, Argyll, PA34.* Comfortable bungalow, rural area near Viewpoint, ten mins from town. **Open:** Easter to Oct **01631 564255** Mrs Campbell **D:** Fr £16.00–£19.00 **Beds:** 2D 1T **Baths:** 3 En (3)

Greencourt, *Benvoulin Lane, Oban, Argyll, PA34 5EF.* Great hospitality. Immaculate rooms, delicious breakfast, peaceful location. **Open:** All year (not Xmas/New Year) **01631 563987** Mr & Mrs Cook *relax@greencourt-oban.fsnet.co.uk* **D:** Fr £22.00–£28.00 **S:** Fr £35.00–£45.00 **Beds:** 2T 5D 1S (8) cc

Roseneath Guest House, *Dalriach Road, Oban, Argyll, PA34 5EQ.* Quiet yet conveniently located for all terminals, towns and amenities. **Open:** Feb to Nov **01631 562929 Fax: 01631 567218** *quirkers@aol.com* www.oban.org.uk/accommodation.roseneath **D:** Fr £20.00–£27.00 **S:** Fr £26.00 **Beds:** 2T 6D **Baths:** 8 En (6) (8) cc

Corriemar House, *Esplanade, Oban, Argyll, PA34 5AQ.* Large Victorian house in prime location on Oban's seafront. Ideal for use as a base for touring local islands and loch or just relax and watch the sun setting over Oban Bay. **Open:** All year **01631 562476** A Russell **Fax: 01631 564339** *corriemar@tinyworld.co.uk* **D:** Fr £24.00–£40.00 **S:** Fr £24.00–£45.00 **Beds:** 2F 6D 4T 2S **Baths:** 12 En 2 Pr (10) cc

The Torrans, *Drummore Road, Oban, Argyll, PA34 4JL.* Detached bungalow overlooking Oban in pleasant peaceful residential area. Private parking. **Open:** All year **01631 565342** Mrs Calderwood **D:** Fr £16.00 **S:** Fr £20.00 **Beds:** 1T 2D **Baths:** 2 En 1 Pr (3)

Alltavona, *Corran Esplanade, Oban, Argyll, PA34 5AQ.* Victorian villa lying on Oban's esplanade. Outstanding views of Oban Bay and surrounding islands. **Open:** Feb to Nov **01631 565067 (also fax)** Ms Harris *carol@alltavona.co.uk* **D:** Fr £20.00–£33.00 **S:** Fr £20.00–£55.00 **Beds:** 1F 5D 2T (5)

Thelwillows, *Glenslellgh Road, Oban, Argyll, PA34 4PP.* Large garden, private road, idyllic wooded country hillside, overlooking pleasant mile walk to town. **Open:** All year (not Xmas/New Year) **01631 566240 & 07833 504094 (M)** D F Coates **Fax: 01631 566783** *enquiries@obanaccommodation.com* **D:** Fr £20.00–£25.00 **S:** Fr £20.00–£25.00 **Beds:** 1T 1D **Baths:** 2 En (4)

Shandon

NS2586

Garemount Lodge, *Shandon, Helensburgh, G84 8NP.* Delightful lochside home, large garden, convenient Loch Lomond, Glasgow, Highlands. **Open:** All year (not Xmas) **01436 820780 (also fax)** Mrs Cowie *nickcowie@compuserve.com* www.stayatlochlomond.com/garemount **D:** Fr £20.00–£23.00 **S:** Fr £28.00–£36.00 **Beds:** 1F 1D **Baths:** 1 En 1 Pr (4)

All details shown are as supplied by B&B owners in Autumn 2002

Strachur

NN1001

Barnacarry, *Strathlachlan, Strachur, Cairndow, Argyll, PA27 8BU.* Comfortable cottage circa 1658, set on Loch Fyne shore. **Open:** Mar to Oct **Grades:** STB 3 Star
01369 860212 Mrs Somerville **D:** Fr £22.00–£24.00 **S:** Fr £23.00–£25.00 **Beds:** 2T **Baths:** 1 Sh (3) (2)

Tarbert (Kintyre)

NR8668 *Anchor Hotel, Columba Hotel, Victoria Hotel, Tarbert, Islay Frigate, Stonefield Hotel*

Tarbert Hotel, *Harbour Street, Tarbert, Argyll, PA29 6UB.* The hub of the local community - a lively meeting place, giving a true reflection of Scottish hospitality. Our food is famous and its value unsurpassed. Ideal base for touring or relaxing overlooking the bustling fishing and sailing harbour of Tarbert. **Open:** All year
01880 820264 Fax: 01880 820847 *iain.robertson@tarberthotel.com* **D:** Fr £25.00–£27.50 **S:** Fr £27.50–£30.00 **Beds:** 1F 5D 10T 4S **Baths:** 18 En 1 Sh cc

Tarbet

NN3104

Lochview, *Tarbet, Arrochar, Dunbartonshire, G83 7DD.* Clean, comfortable, friendly welcome in 200-year-old Georgian house. **Open:** All year (not Xmas)
01301 702200 Mrs Fairfield *efairfield@lineone.net* **D:** Fr £16.00–£18.00 **S:** Fr £20.00 **Beds:** 1F 1T 1D **Baths:** 1 Sh 1 En

Bon-Etive, *Tarbet, Arrochar, Dunbartonshire, G83 7DF.* Private home, quiet location, view of Loch and Ben Lomond. **Open:** Easter to Oct **Grades:** STB 3 Star
01301 702219 Mrs Kelly *bonetive@talk21.com* **D:** Fr £17.50–£18.50 **Beds:** 1D 1T **Baths:** 1 Sh

Aye Servus, *Tyneloan Road, Tarbet Loch Lomond, Arrochar, Argyll & Bute, G83 7DD.* Elevated position with magnificent views over Ben and Loch Lomond. **Open:** All year **Grades:** STB 3 Star
01301 702819 Mrs McDonald *ayeservus@talk21.com* www.accomodata.co.uk/ayeservus.htm **D:** Fr £17.00–£19.00 **S:** Fr £22.00–£25.00 **Beds:** 1T 1D **Baths:** 1 Sh (6) (2)

Tighnabruaich

NR9773

The Kyles Hotel, *Shore Road, Tighnabruaich, Argyll, PA21 2BE.* **Open:** All year
01700 811674 Fax: 01700 811721 *thekyleshotel@netscape.net* **D:** Fr £25.00–£30.00 **S:** Fr £45.00–£50.00 **Beds:** 2T 3D **Baths:** 5 En (30) cc
Cosy family-run hotel, with renowned hospitality, offering regular entertainment and an extensive home-made bar menu. Ideally situated in the beautiful 'Kyles of Bute' where walking, fishing, golfing and sailing are all minutes away. Function suite available for bookings.

Ayrshire & Arran

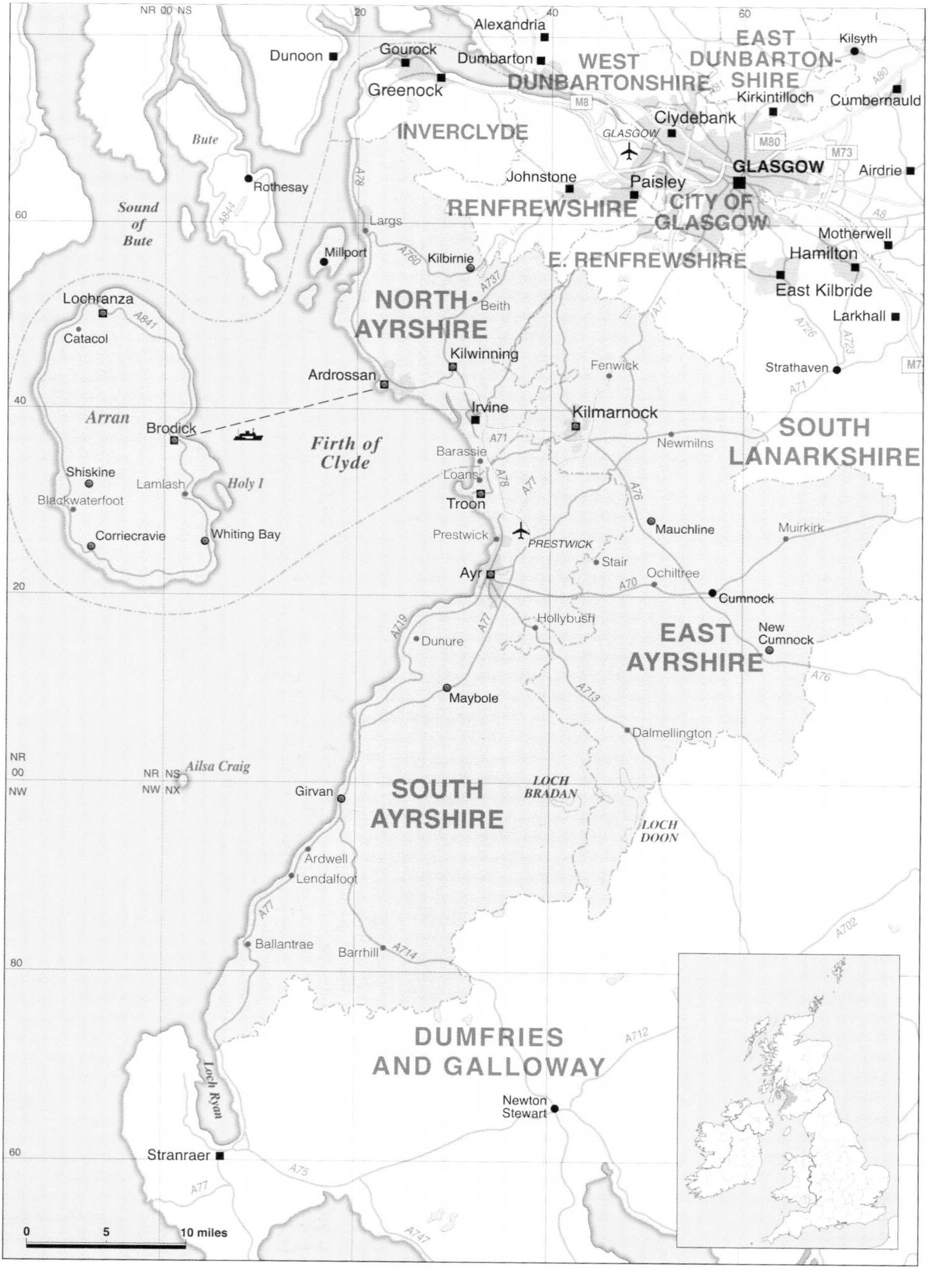

Ardrossan

NS2342

Hazelhurst B&B, *13 Barony Court, Ardrossan, KA22 8DZ.* High-quality accommodation at seafront. Ideal touring/long stay area. **Open:** All year
01294 463942 Mr Hamilton **D:** Fr £18.00–£20.00 **S:** Fr £18.00–£20.00 **Beds:** 1D 2S **Baths:** 1 Sh (10)

Ardwell

NX1693

Ardwell Farm, *Ardwell, Girvan, Ayrshire, KA26 0HP.* Picturesque farmhouse with rooms overlooking the Firth of Clyde. **Open:** All year
01465 713389 Mrs Melville **D:** Fr £14.00–£15.00 **S:** Fr £14.00–£16.00 **Beds:** 2T 1D **Baths:** 1 Sh (3)

ARRAN Blackwaterfoot

NR8928

Blackwaterfoot Hotel, *Blackwaterfoot, Brodick, Isle of Arran, KA27 8EU.* Good food, real ale and creature comforts for outdoor people. **Open:** Easter to Oct
01770 860202 *info@blackwaterfoot-lodge.co.uk* www.blackwaterfoot-lodge.co.uk **D:** Fr £25.00–£30.00 **S:** Fr £25.00–£45.00 **Beds:** 2F 3T 2D 1S **Baths:** 6 En 1 Sh (6) cc

Tsalta, *Blackwaterfoot, Brodick, Isle of Arran, KA27 8HB.* Traditional Scottish hospitality in newly built bungalow - locally owned. **Open:** All year (not Xmas/New Year)
01770 860405 **D:** Fr £20.00–£22.00 **S:** Fr £22.00 **Beds:** 1T 1D 1S **Baths:** 2 En 1 Sh cc

ARRAN Brodick

NS0136

Strathwhillan House, *Brodick, Isle of Arran, KA27 8BQ.* **Open:** All year (not Xmas)
Grades: STB 3 Star
01770 302331 Mrs Williams *strathwhillan@talk21.com* www.strathwhillan.co.uk **D:** Fr £16.00–£28.00 **S:** Fr £18.00–£24.00 **Beds:** 1F 2T 2D 3S **Baths:** 2 En 3 Sh 1 cc
Beautifully-situated, award-winning guest house with sea and mountain views, convenient for ferry (150m) and local amenities, with a fine reputation for hospitality, value, and superb breakfasts, Strathwhillan is an ideal holiday base. Ground floor accommodation. Totally non-smoking.

Dunvegan Guest House, *Brodick, Isle of Arran, KA27 8AJ.* Dunvegan House, situated 500 yds from pier, overlooking Bay. Brochure available. **Open:** All year
01770 302811 (also fax) **D:** Fr £30.00–£35.00 **S:** Fr £35.00 **Beds:** 3T 7D **Baths:** 9 En 1 Pr (10)

Kingsley Hotel, *Brodick, Isle of Arran, KA27 8AJ.* Well-known Arran hotel, reputation for warm welcome, good food, relaxing friendly atmosphere. **Open:** Easter to Sept
01770 302226 *kingsleyhotel@connectfree.co.uk* **D:** Fr £29.00–£29.50 **S:** Fr £29.00–£29.50 **Beds:** 2F 6D 11T 8S **Baths:** 27 En (30) cc

Rosaburn Lodge, *Brodick, Isle of Arran, KA27 8DP.* On beautiful banks of River Rosa within 2 acres of private landscaped gardens. **Open:** All year
01770 302383 **D:** Fr £24.00–£27.50 **S:** Fr £24.00–£27.50 **Beds:** 1T 2D **Baths:** 3 En

Sunnyside, *Kings Cross, Brodick, Isle of Arran, KA27 8RG.* Welcome to Sunnyside - a warm, comfortably furnished modern bungalow with superb views across The Clyde, and secluded suntrap garden. A full wholesome breakfast is assured. Private parking, and separate entrance for guests. Kings Cross: a picturesque hamlet 8 miles SE of Brodick. **Open:** All year (not Xmas)
01770 700422 **D:** Fr £17.50–£19.50 **S:** Fr £17.50–£19.50 **Beds:** 1T 1S **Baths:** 1 En 1 Sh

ARRAN Catacol

NR9149

Catacol Bay Hotel, *Catacol, Brodick, Isle of Arran, KA27 8HN.* Small friendly fully licensed hotel nestling in hills at picturesque north end of Arran. **Open:** All year (not Xmas)
01770 830231 Mr Ashcroft **Fax: 01770 830350** *davecatbay@lineone.net* www.catacol.co.uk **D:** Fr £20.00–£25.00 **S:** Fr £20.00–£25.00 **Beds:** 3F 1D 1T 1S **Baths:** 2 Sh (30) cc

ARRAN Lochranza

NR9349

Croftbank Cottage, *Lochranza, Brodick, Isle of Arran, KA27 8HL.* Cottage centre village - magnificent castle views all rooms. Shower/basin both rooms. **Open:** All year
01770 830201 (also fax) Mrs Evans **D:** Fr £20.00–£22.00 **Beds:** 2T **Baths:** 1 Sh (2)

Butt Lodge Country House Hotel, *Lochranza, Brodick, Isle of Arran, KA27 8JF.* Beautiful family-run hotel, residential licence. 2 acres of gardens with an abundance of wildlife. **Open:** Feb to Jan
01770 830240 **Fax: 01770 830211** *butt.lodge@virgin.net* **D:** Fr £25.00–£40.00 **S:** Fr £25.00–£48.00 **Beds:** 5F 1D 1T 3S **Baths:** 1 Pr cc

ARRAN Shiskine

NR9129

Croftlea, *Shiskine, Brodick, Isle of Arran, KA27 8EN.* Comfortable house with garden. Quiet location 2 miles beach/golf course. **Open:** Easter to Oct
01770 860259 Mrs Henderson **D:** Fr £18.00–£20.00 **S:** Fr £25.00 **Beds:** 2D 3T **Baths:** 3 En 1 Sh (5)

Ayr

NS3422

Belmont Guest House, *15 Park Circus, Ayr, KA7 2DJ.* **Open:** All year (not Xmas)
Grades: STB 2 Star, AA 3 Diamond
01292 265588 Mr Hillhouse **Fax: 01292 290303** *belmontguesthouse@btinternet.com* www.belmontguesthouse.co.uk **D:** Fr £20.00–£22.00 **S:** Fr £22.00–£24.00 **Beds:** 2F 2D 1T **Baths:** 5 En cc
Try a breath of fresh 'Ayr'. Warm, comfortable hospitality assured in this Victorian town house, situated in a quiet residential area within easy walking distance of the town centre and beach. Ground floor bedrooms available. Glasgow (Prestwick) airport 6 miles. Green Tourism Silver Award.

Inverlea Guest House, *42 Carrick Road, Ayr, KA7 2RB.* **Open:** All year
01292 266756 (also fax) Mr & Mrs Bryson *jcb@inverlea42fsnet.co.uk* **D:** Fr £16.00–£21.00 **S:** Fr £20.00–£25.00 **Beds:** 3F 2D 2T 1S **Baths:** 3 En 2 Pr 3 Sh (5)
Family-run Victorian guest house which has ensured personal attention for 17 years. Few minutes walk from beach and town centre. Burns Cottage and 7 golf courses nearby. Large enclosed car park at rear of house.

The Dunn Thing Guest House, *13 Park Circus, Ayr, KA7 2DJ.* **Open:** All year **01292 284531** Mrs Dunn **Fax: 01292 262944** *sheiladunn13@aol.com* www.thedunnthing.co.uk **D:** Fr £18.00–£22.00 **S:** Fr £20.00–£24.00 **Beds:** 1F 1T 1D **Baths:** 3 En Warm welcome at this Victorian house, close to town centre.

Failte, *9 Prestwick Road, Ayr, KA8 8LD.* Small friendly B&B, near to beach, shops, airport & racecourse. **Open:** All year (not Xmas/New Year) **Grades:** STB 2 Star **01292 265282 & 07986 025541 (M)** Mrs Thomson *jenniferfailte@btinternet.com* www.jenniferfailte.co.uk **D:** Fr £17.00–£20.00 **S:** Fr £17.00–£20.00 **Beds:** 1D 1T **Baths:** 1 En 1 Pr

Sunnyside, *26 Dunure Road, Doonfoot, Ayr, KA7 4HR.* Close to Burns Cottage, Brig O'Doon, spacious rooms, family welcome. **Open:** All year (not Xmas) **Grades:** STB 3 Star **01292 441234 (also fax)** Mrs Malcolm *sunnysideayr@aol.com* **D:** Fr £20.00–£22.00 **S:** Fr £26.00–£28.00 **Beds:** 2F **Baths:** 2 En (4)

Kilkerran, *15 Prestwick Road, Ayr, KA8 8LD.* Friendly family-run guest house on main A79 Ayr-Prestwick route. **Open:** All year **01292 266477** Ms Ferguson *margaret@kilkerran-gh.demon.co.uk* **D:** Fr £16.00–£20.00 **S:** Fr £16.00–£20.00 **Beds:** 3F 2D 2T 2S **Baths:** 2 En 1 Pr 3 Sh (10)

23 Dalblair Road, *Ayr, KA7 1UF.* Central town, five minutes from beach. Golf courses nearby. Friendly. **Open:** All year (not Xmas/New Year) **01292 264798** Mr & Mrs Gambles *jacmar23@aol.com* **D:** Fr £22.00–£30.00 **S:** Fr £25.00–£30.00 **Beds:** 4F 1T 1D 2S **Baths:** 3 En 1 Pr (4)

Lochinver, *32 Park Circus, Ayr, KA7 2DL.* Town centre B&B establishment with reasonable rates. **Open:** All year **01292 265086 (also fax)** Mr Young *young.lochinver@talk21.com* www.smoothhound.co.uk/hotels **D:** Fr £18.00–£25.00 **S:** Fr £18.00–£25.00 **Beds:** 1F 1T 1D 1S **Baths:** 3 En 1 Pr

Deanbank, *44 Ashgrove Street, Ayr, KA7 3BG.* Convenient for town centre, station, golf and Burns Country. **Open:** All year (not Xmas) **01292 263745** Ms Wilson **D:** Fr £18.00–£20.00 **S:** Fr £20.00–£25.00 **Beds:** 1F 1T **Baths:** 1 Sh (1)

Finlayson Arms Hotel, *Coylton, Ayr, KA6 6JT.* Superbly located for golfing holidays - over 30 courses nearby including Turnberry and Royal Troon. **Open:** All year (not Xmas/New Year) **01292 570298 (also fax) D:** Fr £22.50–£27.50 **S:** Fr £25.00–£35.00 **Beds:** 1F 7T **Baths:** 8 En (12) cc

Ballantrae

NX0982

The Haven, *75 Main Street, Ballantrae, Girvan, Ayrshire, KA26 0NA.* Delightful coastal village bungalow. Superb breakfasts. Ferries nearby. Panoramic views. **Open:** All year **Grades:** STB 3 Star **01465 831306** Mrs Sloan **Fax: 01465 831526 D:** Fr £19.00 **S:** Fr £23.00–£26.00 **Beds:** 1F 1T **Baths:** 2 Pr (3) (2)

Orchard Lea, *14 Main Street, Ballantrae, Girvan, Ayrshire, KA26 0NB.* Comfortable house offers superb breakfast. Quiet coastal village, ferries nearby. **Open:** All year (not Xmas) **01465 831509** Mr & Mrs Ward **D:** Fr £17.00 **S:** Fr £17.00 **Beds:** 2D 1T **Baths:** 1 Sh (12)

Ardstinchar Cottage, *81 Main Street, Ballantrae, Girvan, Ayrshire, KA26 0NA.* Beautiful cottage in magnificent countryside. **Open:** All year (not Xmas/New Year) **01465 831343** Mrs Drummond **D:** Fr £16.00–£20.00 **S:** Fr £20.00–£25.00 **Beds:** 2D 1T **Baths:** 1 Sh (3)

Barassie

NS3232

Fordell, *43 Beach Road, Barassie, Troon, KA10 6SU.* Ideal spot for many reasons. Quiet, comfortable accommodation overlooking sea. **Open:** All year (not Xmas/New Year) **01292 313224** Mrs Mathieson **Fax: 01292 312141** *morag@fordell-troon.co.uk* www.fordell-troon.co.uk **D:** Fr £20.00–£25.00 **S:** Fr £25.00–£30.00 **Beds:** 2T **Baths:** 2 Sh

Barrhill

NX2382

14 Main Street, *Barrhill, Girvan, Ayrshire, KA26 0PQ.* Comfortable, homely, in small village. Central for local beauty spots. **Open:** All year **01465 821344** Mrs Hegarty **D:** Fr £15.00–£18.00 **S:** Fr £18.00 **Beds:** 1F **Baths:** 1 Pr 1 Sh

Blair Farm, *Barrhill, Girvan, Ayrshire, KA26 0RD.* Beautiful farmhouse, lovely views. Enjoy peace, comfort & friendly hospitality. **Open:** Easter to Nov **01465 821247** Mrs Hughes www.dalbeattie.com/farmholidays/qblfb.htm **D:** Fr £20.00–£22.00 **S:** Fr £25.00 **Beds:** 1D 1T **Baths:** 1 En 1 Pr

Beith

NS3553

Shotts Farm, *Barmill, Beith, Ayrshire, KA15 1LB.* Ideal for exploring south-west Scotland, located between A736/737. **Open:** All year **01505 502273 & 07890 037766 (M)** Mrs Gillan **Fax: 01505 502273** *gurlston@hotmail.com* **D:** Fr £15.00–£20.00 **S:** Fr £17.00–£20.00 **Beds:** 1F 2D **Baths:** 1 En 1 Sh (4)

Townend of Shuterflat Farm, *Beith, Ayrshire, KA15 2LW.* Comfortable farmhouse, warm welcome, 15 minutes Glasgow Airport and city centre. **Open:** All year **01505 502342** Mrs Lamont **D:** Fr £17.50 **S:** Fr £17.50 **Beds:** 1T 2D **Baths:** 1 Sh (4)

Dalmellington

NS4805

Bellsbank House, *Bellsbank Road, Dalmellington, Ayr, KA6 7PR.* Deep in Burns country. Dating from 1700's, a warm and friendly experience is assured. Sited high on a hill with panoramic views of Doon valley, fishing, shooting and championship golf courses. Forest parks, trails and walks all on your doorstep. **Open:** All year **01292 550248 (also fax)** *enquiries@bellsbankhouse.fsnet.co.uk* **D:** Fr £20.00–£40.00 **S:** Fr £25.00–£40.00 **Beds:** 1F 2D 1S **Baths:** 2 En 1 Pr (30) cc

Dunure

NS2515

Cruachan, *38 Station Road, Dunure, Ayr, KA7 4LL.* Magnificent views to Arran. Close to harbour and castle park. **Open:** Apr to Oct **01292 500494** Mr Evans **Fax: 01292 500266** *dnevans@lineone.net* **D:** Fr £20.00–£25.00 **S:** Fr £20.00–£30.00 **Beds:** 1D 1T **Baths:** 1 En 1 Pr (4)

National Grid References given are for villages, towns and cities – not for individual houses

BEDROOMS
D = Double
T = Twin
S = Single
F = Family

Fisherton Farm, *Dunure, Ayr, KA7 4LF.* Delightful traditional Scottish farmhouse. Coastal location on working farm. **Open:** All year (not Xmas/New Year)
01292 500223 (also fax) Mrs Wilcox *lesleywilcox@hotmail.com* **D:** Fr £20.00–£25.00 **S:** Fr £20.00–£25.00 **Beds:** 1D 1S **Baths:** 2 Pr (6)

Fenwick
NS4643

West Tannacrieff, *Fenwick, Kilmarnock, Ayrshire, KA3 6AZ.* High quality spacious rooms. Good food, easily accessible from A77. **Open:** All year
01560 600258 & 07773 226332 (M) Mrs Cuthbertson **Fax: 01560 600914** *westtannacrieff@btopenworld.com* www.smoothhound.co.uk/hotels/westtannacrieff.html **D:** Fr £20.00 **S:** Fr £22.50 **Beds:** 1F 2T **Baths:** 3 En

Girvan
NX1897

Hotel Westcliffe, *15-16 Louisa Drive, Girvan, Ayrshire, KA26 9AH.* Family-run hotel for 38 years on sea front, all rooms ensuite. Spa/steam room. **Open:** All year (not Xmas/New Year)
01465 712128 (also fax) Mrs Jardine **D:** Fr £26.00 **S:** Fr £28.00 **Beds:** 6F 5D 8T 5S **Baths:** 24 En (6) cc

Hollybush
NS3914

Malcolmston Farm, *Hollybush, Ayr, KA6 6EZ.* Farmhouse on A713 near Ayr, (near Turnberry and Troon). **Open:** Easter to Nov
01292 560238 Mrs Drummond **D:** Fr £16.00–£18.00 **S:** Fr £16.00–£18.00 **Beds:** 1F 2D **Baths:** 1 En 2 Sh (4)

Kilbirnie
NS3154 *Mossend Hotel*

Alpenrose, *113 Herriot Avenue, Kilbirnie, Ayrshire, KA25 7JB.* Ideal for tour cycle coast. Wonderful home cooked breakfast. **Open:** All year
01505 683122 E Cameron **D:** Fr £11.00–£15.00 **S:** Fr £11.00–£15.00 **Beds:** 1F 1T 1D 1S **Baths:** 1 Sh (1) (2)

Kilmarnock
NS4238

Hillhouse Farm, *Grassyards Road, Kilmarnock, Ayrshire, KA3 6HG.* **Open:** All year **Grades:** STB 4 Star
01563 523370 (also fax) Mrs Howie www.smoothhound.co.uk/hotels/hillhouse.html **D:** Fr £18.00–£21.00 **S:** Fr £20.00–£22.00 **Beds:** 3F 1T **Baths:** 3 En 1 Pr (8)
The Howie family extend a warm welcome to their working dairy farm. Large bedrooms with superb views over garden and Ayrshire countryside. Central location for coast, golf, fishing, Glasgow and Prestwick Airports. Real farmhouse breakfast, home-baking for supper in lounge.

Tamarind, *24 Arran Avenue, Kilmarnock, Ayrshire, KA3 1TP.* Scottish hospitality. Seasonal indoor pool. Golf easy reach. Ideal touring. **Open:** All year **Grades:** STB 3 Star
01563 571788 Mrs Turner **Fax: 01563 533515** *james@tamarind25.freeserve.co.uk* **D:** Fr £17.50–£20.00 **S:** Fr £25.00–£30.00 **Beds:** 1F 2T 1S **Baths:** 4 En (4) cc

West Tannacrieff, *Fenwick, Kilmarnock, Ayrshire, KA3 6AZ.* High quality spacious rooms. Good food, easily accessible from A77. **Open:** All year
01560 600258 & 07773 226332 (M) Mrs Cuthbertson **Fax: 01560 600914** *westtannacrieff@btopenworld.com* www.smoothhound.co.uk/hotels/westtannacrieff.html **D:** Fr £20.00 **S:** Fr £22.50 **Beds:** 1F 2T **Baths:** 3 En

BATHROOMS
En = Ensuite
Pr = Private
Sh = Shared

Kilwinning
NS3043

Claremont Guest House, *27 Howgate, Kilwinning, Ayrshire, KA13 6EW.* Friendly family B&B close to town centre and public transport. **Open:** All year (not Xmas)
01294 553905 Mrs Filby **D:** Fr £18.00–£20.00 **S:** Fr £18.00–£20.00 **Beds:** 1F 1S **Baths:** 2 Sh (10)

Largs
NS2059

Stonehaven Guest House, *8 Netherpark Crescent, Largs, KA30 8QB.* **Open:** All year (not Xmas) **Grades:** STB 4 Star
01475 673319 Mr Martin *stonehaven.martin@virgin.net* **D:** Fr £20.00–£26.00 **S:** Fr £18.00–£26.00 **Beds:** 1D 1T 1S **Baths:** 1 En 1 Sh
Enjoy magnificent views over Largs Bay, the Isles of Cumbrae, Arran and Bute with Routenburn Golf Course behind. All bedrooms are furnished to a high standard and a traditional Scottish breakfast can be enjoyed while watching the ferry crossing to the Island.

South Whittleburn Farm, *Brisbane Glen, Largs, Ayrshire, KA30 8SN.* Superb farmhouse accommodation. Enormous, delicious breakfasts. Warm, friendly hospitality, highly recommended. **Open:** All year (not Xmas)
01475 675881 Mrs Watson **Fax: 01475 675080** *largsbandb@southwhittlieburnfarm.freeserve.co.uk* www.smoothhound.co.uk/hotels/whittlie.html **D:** Fr £20.50–£25.00 **S:** Fr £20.50–£25.50 **Beds:** 1F 1D 1T **Baths:** 3 En (10)

Rutland Guest House, *22 Charles Street, Largs, Ayrshire, KA30 8HJ.* Ideal base for diving, golfing, walking and visiting islands. **Open:** All year
01475 675642 Mrs Russell **Fax: 01475 672422** *rutlandhouse@btinternet.com* **D:** Fr £17.00–£18.00 **S:** Fr £18.00–£20.00 **Beds:** 3F 1D 1T **Baths:** 1 En 1 Pr 2 Sh

Haven House, *18 Charles Street, Largs, Ayrshire, KA30 8HJ.* Excellent base for sailing, diving, golfing, climbing & all watersports. **Open:** All year
01475 676389 Mrs McQueen **Fax: 01475 672422** *m.l.mcqueen@btinternet.com* **D:** Fr £16.00–£32.00 **S:** Fr £17.00–£20.00 **Beds:** 1F 1T 1D 1S **Baths:** 2 Pr 2 Sh (4)

BEDROOMS
D = Double
T = Twin
S = Single
F = Family

Belmont House, *2 Broomfield Place, Largs, Ayrshire, KA30 8DR.* Interesting old waterfront house. Spacious rooms. Views of islands and highlands. **Open:** All year
01475 676264 Mr & Mrs Clarke
belmont.house@i12.com www.belmont.i12.com
D: Fr £20.00–£25.00 **S:** Fr £20.00–£25.00
Beds: 2D 1T **Baths:** 1 En 2 Pr (4) (2)

Lendalfoot

NX1389

The Smiddy, *Lendalfoot, Girvan, KA26 0JF.* Friendly, comfortable, marvellous views overlooking sea. Ideal touring/walking area. **Open:** May to Sep
01465 891204 Mrs Bell **D:** Fr £15.00–£17.00
S: Fr £18.00 **Beds:** 1D 1T **Baths:** 1 Sh

Loans

NS3431 *Old Loans Inn*

Craikslamd Cottage, *Loans, Troon, Ayrshire, KA10 7HN.* Attractive rural situation. Easy reach of golf courses and beach. **Open:** All year (not Xmas/New Year)
01292 314924 Mrs Webster *tomwebster@supanet.com* **D:** Fr £20.00–£22.00 **S:** Fr £22.00–£25.00 **Beds:** 1F **Baths:** 1 En

Mauchline

NS4927

Dykefield Farm & Treborane Cottage, *Mauchline, KA5 6EY.* Farmhouse B&B with friendly, family atmosphere. Private lounge for guests. **Open:** All year
01290 553170 & 01290 550328 Mrs Smith
D: Fr £15.00 **S:** Fr £15.00 **Beds:** 4F **Baths:** 1 En (3)

Ardwell, *103 Loudoun Street, Mauchline, KA5 5BH.* Beautiful rooms, near centre of historic village. Great golf locally. **Open:** All year
01290 552987 Mrs Houston **D:** Fr £15.00–£17.00 **S:** Fr £17.00–£19.00 **Beds:** 2F
Baths: 2 En (2)

Maybole

NS2909

Homelea, *62 Culzean Road, Maybole, Ayrshire, KA19 8AH.* Attractive Victorian family home near Culzean Castle, Burns Country and Turnberry Golf. **Open:** Easter to Oct
Grades: STB 3 Star
01655 882736 Mrs McKellar **Fax: 01655 883557** *gilmour_mck@msn.com* **D:** Fr £19.00
S: Fr £23.00 **Beds:** 1F 1T 1S **Baths:** 2 Sh (3)

Muirkirk

NS6927 *Dumfries Arms*

La Orilla, *29 Garronhill, Muirkirk, Cumnock, Ayrshire, KA18 3RY.* Central for Ayrshire/Lanarkshire. Warm welcome. Relaxed atmosphere. Good breakfast.
Open: All year (not Xmas/New Year)
01290 661335 (also fax) Mrs Kirk **D:** Fr £15.00 **S:** Fr £15.00 **Beds:** 2T **Baths:** 1 Sh (2)

New Cumnock

NS6113

Low Polquheys Farm, *New Cumnock, Cumnock, Ayrshire, KA18 4NX.* Warm welcome in modern farmhouse. Situated near Dumfriesshire/Ayrshire border.
Open: Feb to Dec
01290 338307 Mrs Caldwell *marjorie@low-polquheys.freeserve.co.uk* **D:** Fr £15.00–£18.00 **S:** Fr £15.00–£18.00 **Beds:** 1F 1T 1S
Baths: 1 Sh (2)

Newmilns

NS5237

Whatriggs Farm, *Newmilns, Ayrshire, KA16 9LJ.* Family-run 700-acre farm, with golf and family attractions nearby. **Open:** All year (not Xmas)
01560 700279 Mrs Mitchell *info@whatriggs.co.uk* www.whatriggs.co.uk **D:** Fr £15.00–£17.50 **S:** Fr £15.00–£17.50 **Beds:** 2F
Baths: 1 Sh (6)

Ochiltree

NS5121

Laigh Tarbeg Farm, *Ochiltree, Cymnock, KA18 2RL.* Modern working dairy farm traditional farmhouse of great character with a warm family welcome.
Open: Easter to Oct
01290 700242 (also fax) Mrs Watson **D:** Fr £18.00–£20.00 **S:** Fr £18.00–£22.00 **Beds:** 2F
Baths: 1 Pr 1 Sh (1)

Prestwick

NS3425

Golf View Hotel, *17 Links Road, Prestwick, KA9 1QG.* **Open:** All year
Grades: STB 4 Star, AA 4 Diamond
01292 671234 & 01292 470396
Elizabeth Martinez **Fax: 01292 671244**
welcome@golfviewhotel.com golfviewhotel.com
D: Fr £36.00 **S:** Fr £45.00 **Beds:** 1F 3T 1D 1S
Baths: 6 En (3) (8) cc
Enjoy stunning golf course and beach views. Burns Country easily accessible. Close Prestwick Airport, station, Troon ferries, major roads and on cycle route 7. Family-run Victorian house retaining traditional features and offering a true Ayrshire welcome, with full Scottish breakfast.

Stair

NS4423

Stair Inn, *Stair, Mauchline, KA5 5HW.* Conservation area. Guest rooms of a very high standard. **Open:** All year
01292 591562 Mr Boyd **Fax: 01292 591650**
D: Fr £22.50–£25.00 **S:** Fr £35.00–£39.00
Beds: 2F 3T 1D **Baths:** 6 En cc

Troon

NS3230

The Cherries, *50 Ottoline Drive, Troon, Ayrshire, KA10 7AW.* Beautiful quiet home on golf course near beaches and restaurants. **Open:** All year
01292 313312 Mrs Tweedie **Fax: 01292 319007** *thecherries50@hotmail.com*
www.smoothhound.co.uk/hotels/cherries
D: Fr £20.00–£25.00 **S:** Fr £20.00–£25.00
Beds: 1F 1T 1S **Baths:** 1 En 1 Pr 1 Sh (5)

The Beeches, *63 Ottoline Drive, Troon, KA10 7AN.* Bright spacious house, gardens. Every amenity, beaches, golf, marina, castle. **Open:** All year **Grades:** STB 3 Star
01292 314180 & 07946 775513 (M)
Mrs Sinclair **D:** Fr £18.00–£20.00 **S:** Fr £20.00–£22.00 **Beds:** 1D 1T 1S **Baths:** 2 Pr (4)

Rosedale Guest House, *9 Firth Road, Barassie, Troon, KA10 6TF.* Quiet seafront location - ideal for Sea Cat ferry to Ireland.
Open: All year (not Xmas)
01292 314371 Mrs Risk *hmrisk@hotmail.com*
D: Fr £20.00–£25.00 **S:** Fr £20.00–£25.00
Beds: 1D 1T 1S (5)

Sunnybrae, *160 Magdala Terrace, Galashiels, Selkirkshire, TD1 2HZ.* Comfortable, friendly family-run home. Convenient for touring Borders and Edinburgh. **Open:** All year (not Xmas/New Year) **Grades:** STB 3 Star
01896 758042 Mrs Anderson *bandb@sunnybrae.co.uk* www.sunnybrae.co.uk **D:** Fr £18.00–£20.00 **S:** Fr £18.00–£20.00 **Beds:** 1T 2D **Baths:** 2 En 1 Pr (3)

Gattonside

NT5435

Fauhope House, *Fauhope, Gattonside, Melrose, Roxburghshire, TD6 9LU.* An Edwardian house looking over the River Tweed to Melrose Abbey. **Open:** All year
01896 823184 & 01896 822245 Mrs Robson **Fax: 01896 823184 D:** Fr £25.00 **S:** Fr £32.00 **Beds:** 2T 1D **Baths:** 3 En **cc**

Hawick

NT5015

Wiltonburn Farm, *Hawick, Roxburghshire, TD9 7LL.* Delightful setting on hill farm with designer cashmere knitwear shop. **Open:** All year (not Xmas) **Grades:** STB 3 Star
01450 372414 & 07711 321226 Mrs Shell **Fax: 01450 378098** *shell@wiltonburnfarm.u-net.com* www.wiltonburnfarm.co.uk **D:** Fr £20.00–£22.50 **S:** Fr £20.00–£25.00 **Beds:** 1F 1D 1T **Baths:** 1 En 1 Pr 1 Sh (6) **cc**

The Laurels Guest House, *8 Princes Street, Hawick, Roxburghshire, TD9 7AY.* Friendly welcome, few mins from town centre and leisure facilities. **Open:** All year **Grades:** STB 2 Star
01450 370002 D: Fr £18.00–£19.00 **S:** Fr £19.00–£20.00 **Beds:** 2T 1D 1S **Baths:** 3 En 1 Pr

Ellistrin, *6 Fenwick Park, Hawick, Roxburghshire, TD9 9PA.* Welcoming family home in quiet area, close to all amenities. **Open:** Easter to Oct
01450 374216 Mrs Smith **Fax: 01450 373619** *ellistrin@compuserve.com* www.ellistrin.co.uk **D:** Fr £18.00 **S:** Fr £18.00 **Beds:** 2D 1T **Baths:** 3 En (3)

Kirkton Farmhouse, *Hawick, Roxburghshire, TD9 8QJ.* Welcome to our spacious farmhouse - we look forward to looking after you. **Open:** All year
01450 372421 (also fax) Mrs Bell *bell.kirton@virgin.net* **D:** Fr £16.00 **S:** Fr £22.00 **Beds:** 1T 2D **Baths:** 1 Sh

Heiton

NT7130

Goldilands, *Roxburgh Road, Heiton, Kelso, TD5 8TP.* New bungalow, 2 miles from Kelso, adjacent to golf course. **Open:** All year
01573 450671 (also fax) Mrs Brotherston *jimbroth@aol.com* www.smoothhound.co.uk/hotels/goldilands.html **D:** Fr £20.00 **S:** Fr £25.00 **Beds:** 2T 1D **Baths:** 3 En (2) (3)

Innerleithen

NT3336

Caddon View Hotel, *14 Pirn Road, Innerleithen, Peebles-shire, EH44 6HH.* **Open:** All year (not Xmas) **Grades:** STB 4 Star
01896 830208 Mr & Mrs Djellil *caddonview@aol.com* www.caddonview.co.uk **D:** Fr £28.00–£35.00 **S:** Fr £38.00–£55.00 **Beds:** 2F 3D 3T **Baths:** 8 En (6) **cc**
Charming Victorian family house by the River Tweed, ideally situated for walking, fishing, touring or just relaxing. All rooms individually designed and equipped to make you feel at home. Fine dining experience at reasonable price in the French restaurant. 30 miles from Edinburgh.

St Ronan's Hotel, *High Street, Innerleithen, Peebles-shire, EH44 6HF.* **Open:** All year
01896 831487 *catherine.ross@lineone.net* **D:** Fr £23.00–£28.00 **S:** Fr £35.00–£45.00 **Beds:** 2F 2D 2T **Baths:** 5 En 1 Pr (25) **cc**
A small family-owned/run hotel concentrating on flexible friendly service, ensuring every guest is comfortable, whether walkers, cyclists, fishermen, businessmen or tourists just enjoying the beauty of our scenic countryside. Ideally situated within easy travelling distance to Edinburgh & Glasgow.

BATHROOMS
En = Ensuite
Pr = Private
Sh = Shared

Jedburgh

NT6520

Edgerston Rink Smithy, *Jedburgh, Roxburghshire, TD8 6PP.* **Open:** All year
01835 840328 Mr & Mrs Smart *royglen.rink@btinternet.com* **D:** Fr £18.00–£20.00 **S:** Fr £23.00–£25.00 **Beds:** 2D **Baths:** 2 Pr (12) (4)
Converted smithy overlooking the Cheviot Hills backing on to natural woodland, with walks from garden. Very private facilities of a superior standard. Warm welcome assured. Private visitors lounge with TV, music centre etc. Rural location, 7 miles south of Jedburgh.

Froylehurst, *The Friars, Jedburgh, Roxburghshire, TD8 6BN.* Detached Victorian house in large garden. Spacious guest rooms, 2 mins town centre. **Open:** Mar to Nov **Grades:** STB 4 Star
01835 862477 (also fax) Mrs Irvine **D:** Fr £18.00–£20.00 **S:** Fr £20.00–£25.00 **Beds:** 2F 1D 1T **Baths:** 2 Sh (5) (5)

Willow Court, *The Friars, Jedburgh, Roxburghshire, TD8 6BN.* First class accommodation, yet only two mins from town centre. **Open:** All year
01835 863702 Mr McGovern **Fax: 01835 864601** *mike@willowcourtjedburgh.co.uk* www.willowcourtjedburgh.co.uk **D:** Fr £18.00–£22.00 **S:** Fr £22.00–£30.00 **Beds:** 1F 1T 2D **Baths:** 3 En 1 Pr (5)

Hundalee House, *Jedburgh, Roxburghshire, TD8 6PA.* Large Victorian private house. **Open:** Mar to Nov
01835 863011 (also fax) Mrs Whittaker *sheila.whittaker@btinternet.com* **D:** Fr £20.00–£25.00 **S:** Fr £25.00–£35.00 **Beds:** 1F 3D 1T **Baths:** 4 En 1 Pr (5) (10)

Windyridge, *39 Dounehill, Jedburgh, Roxburghshire, TD8 6LJ.* Quiet location, stunning views, great food, warm hospitality, modern comfortable house. **Open:** All year
01835 864404 Mrs Lowe *jlowelowe6r@supanet.com* **D:** Fr £20.00–£22.00 **S:** Fr £20.00–£25.00 **Beds:** 1F 1T 1D 1S **Baths:** 2 En 1 Sh (3)

Ferniehirst Mill Lodge, *Jedburgh, Roxburghshire, TD8 6PQ.* Modern guest house in peaceful setting, country lovers' paradise. **Open:** All year
01835 863279 (also fax) Mr Swanston *ferniehirstmill@aol.com* **D:** Fr £23.00 **S:** Fr £23.00 **Beds:** 1F 3D 4T 1S **Baths:** 9 En 1 Sh (10) cc

Fernlea, *Allerton Place, Jedburgh, Roxburghshire, TD8 6LG.* Luxurious ground floor accommodation, with good food, 10 mins all amenities. **Open:** All year
01835 862318 (also fax) Mrs Ferguson **D:** Fr £18.00–£22.00 **S:** Fr £25.00–£27.00 **Beds:** 3F 2D 1S **Baths:** 3 En (2)

Riverview, *Newmill Farm, Jedburgh, Roxburghshire, TD8 6TH.* Spacious modern villa overlooking River Jed with country views. **Open:** Apr to Oct
01835 862145 & 01835 864607 Mrs Kinghorn **D:** Fr £18.00–£20.00 **S:** Fr £25.00 **Beds:** 1T 2D **Baths:** 3 En (4)

Meadhon House, *48 Castlegate, Jedburgh, Roxburghshire, TD8 6BB.* C17th stone-built house with views overlooking Jedburgh Abbey and Castle. Perfectly situated for exploring Scottish Borders, ancient monuments and historic buildings. You are assured a warm welcome and extremely comfortable accommodation just over 1 hour's drive from Edinburgh and Newcastle on A68. **Open:** All year (not Xmas/New Year)
01835 862504 (also fax) Mrs Poloczek *meadhon@aol.com* **D:** Fr £20.00–£22.00 **S:** Fr £30.00 **Beds:** 3F 2D **Baths:** 5 En (12) (3) cc

Kelso

NT7234

Craignethan House, *Jedburgh Road, Kelso, Roxburghshire, TD5 8AZ.* Comfortable welcoming family home in superb setting. Wonderful breakfasts anytime! **Open:** All year
01573 224818 Mrs McDonald **D:** Fr £20.00 **S:** Fr £20.00 **Beds:** 2D 1T **Baths:** 1 Pr 1 Sh (6) 3

Lochside, *Town Yetholm, Kelso, Roxburghshire, TD5 8PD.* **Open:** All year
01573 420455 & 07974 378911 (M) Mrs Hurst *yvonnehurst@hotmail.com* www.oldlochsidefarm.co.uk **D:** Fr £25.00 **S:** Fr £25.00 **Beds:** 1D 2T **Baths:** 3 En (2)
Experience Lochside, a magnificent Victorian mansion house nestled in the Cheviot hills, overlooking Yetholm Loch wildlife reserve. Stunning horses and white park cattle roam surrounding parkland. Enjoy a warm welcome, superb home-cooking, luxurious interiors, log fires & beautiful garden.

Bellevue House, *Bowmont Street, Kelso, Roxburghshire, TD5 7DZ.* Extremely comfortable accommodation. 5 mins walk to town centre, river. **Open:** All year (not Xmas/New Year) **Grades:** STB 3 Star
01573 224588 Mr & Mrs Thompson *bellevuekelso@aol.com* **D:** Fr £27.00–£29.00 **S:** Fr £35.00–£45.00 **Beds:** 3D 3T **Baths:** 6 En (7) cc

Duncan House, *Chalkheugh Terrace, Kelso, Roxburghshire, TD5 7DX.* Georgian riverside house, spectacular views river & castle. 2 mins to centre town. **Open:** All year (not Xmas)
01573 225682 Mrs Robertson **D:** Fr £18.00–£20.00 **S:** Fr £18.00–£20.00 **Beds:** 3F 1D **Baths:** 3 En 3 Pr 1 Sh (6)

The Central Guest House, *51 The Square, Kelso, Roxburghshire, TD5 7HF.* Grade II listed, self-catering guest house in town centre. All rooms ensuite. **Open:** All year
01890 883664 Mr Woodhead **D:** Fr £15.00–£18.00 **S:** Fr £15.00–£18.00 **Beds:** 1F 1D 3T **Baths:** 4 En

Kirk Yetholm

NT8228

Valleydene, *High Street, Kirk Yetholm, Kelso, Roxburghshire, TD5 8PH.* Traditional Scottish welcome. Log fire. Comfortable rooms with excellent views. **Open:** All year
01573 420286 Mrs Campbell **D:** Fr £22.00 **S:** Fr £25.00–£30.00 **Beds:** 2T 1D **Baths:** 2 En 1 Pr (12) (4)

B&B owners may vary rates – be sure to check when booking

Langlee

NT6417

The Spinney, *Langlee, Jedburgh, Roxburghshire, TD8 6PB.* Spacious house in main house and in nearby pine cabins. **Open:** Mar to Nov
01835 863525 Mrs Fry **Fax: 01835 864883** *thespinney@btinternet.com* **D:** Fr £21.00–£23.00 **Beds:** 2D 1T 3F **Baths:** 5 En 1 Pr (6) cc

Langshaw

NT5139

Over Langshaw Farm, *Langshaw, Galashiels, Selkirkshire, TD1 2PE.* Welcoming family farm superb location in unspoilt border countryside. **Open:** All year **Grades:** STB 3 Star
01896 860244 (also fax) Mrs Bergius *bergius@overlangshaw.fsnet.co.uk* **D:** Fr £20.00–£22.00 **S:** Fr £25.00 **Beds:** 1F 1D **Baths:** 1 En 1 Pr 1 Sh

Lauder

NT5247

The Grange, *6 Edinburgh Road, Lauder, Berwickshire, TD2 6TW.* **Open:** All year (not Xmas)
01578 722649 (also fax) Tricia and Peter Gilardi *trishnpete.lauder@amserve.net* **D:** Fr £18.00–£20.00 **S:** Fr £18.00–£21.00 **Beds:** 1D 2T **Baths:** 1 Sh (3)
A peaceful haven from which to explore the tranquil Scottish and English Borders, yet less than an hour's drive from Edinburgh. Overlooking the rolling Lammermuir Hills and on the Southern Upland Way, an ideal base for walking, cycling or relaxing.

Longformacus

NT6957

Eildon Cottage, *Longformacus, Duns, Berwickshire, TD11 3NX.* Leave crowds behind set in beautiful rolling Lammermuir Hill village. **Open:** All year (not Xmas/New Year)
01361 890230 Mrs Amos **D:** Fr £20.00–£25.00 **S:** Fr £20.00–£25.00 **Beds:** 1F 1T 1D **Baths:** 2 En 1 Pr (3)

Kintra Ha, *Gifford Road, Longformacus, Duns, Berwickshire, TD11 3NZ.* Recently converted, detached property. Edinburgh 50 mins. Access to rural pursuits. **Open:** All year
01361 890660 (also fax) Mrs Lamb *lamb@kintrastell.co.uk* **D:** Fr £20.00 **S:** Fr £25.00 **Beds:** 1D 1T **Baths:** 2 En

Melrose

NT5433

Torwood Lodge, *High Cross Avenue, Melrose, Roxburghshire, TD6 9SU.* High-quality accommodation with beautiful views. Ideal touring/walking area. **Open:** All year (not Xmas/New Year)
01896 822220 Mrs Young *torwoodlodge@beeb.net* www.torwoodlodge.co.uk **D:** Fr £23.50 **Beds:** 2T 1D **Baths:** 3 En (3)

Old Abbey School House, *Waverley Road, Melrose, Roxburghshire, TD6 9SH.* Charming old school house with character. Large bedrooms, restful atmosphere. **Open:** Mar to Nov
01896 823432 Mrs O'Neill *oneill@abbeyschool.fsnet.co.uk* **D:** Fr £18.00–£22.00 **S:** Fr £25.00 **Beds:** 1T 2D **Baths:** 1 Pr 1 Sh (5)

Priory View, *15 Priors Walk, Melrose, Roxburghshire, TD6 9RB.* Friendly, hospitable B&B for a wide variety of guests. **Open:** All year **Grades:** STB 3 Star
01896 822087 Mrs Haldane *ellen.haldane@ukonline.co.uk* **D:** Fr £18.00 **S:** Fr £30.00–£36.00 **Beds:** 1T 2D **Baths:** 1 Sh (8)

Mountain Cross

NT1547

Rowallan, *Mountain Cross, West Linton, Peebles-shire, EH46 7DF.* Bungalow with beautiful rural views. Easy access to Edinburgh & touring Borders. **Open:** Apr to Oct
01968 660329 C Cottam *carolinecottam@aol.com* **D:** Fr £18.00 **Beds:** 1F 1D **Baths:** 2 Sh (10) (3)

Newcastleton

NY4887

Cleughside Farm, *Bailey, Newcastleton, Roxburghshire, TD9 0TR.* Independent traveller? Venture off the beaten track to Cleughside Farm. **Open:** All year **Grades:** STB 3 Diamond
016977 48634 (also fax) *alicewhy@aol.com* www.cleughside.freeserve.co.uk **D:** Fr £20.00–£22.00 **S:** Fr £25.00–£30.00 **Beds:** 1F 1T/D 1D **Baths:** 1 En 1 Sh (3)

Bailey Mill, *Bailey, Newcastleton, Roxburghshire, TD9 0TR.* Courtyard apartments in converted C18th grain mill. Ideal retreat. Jacuzzi, pony trekking, meals & bar. **Open:** All year
016977 48074 & 016977 48057 Mrs Copeland **Fax: 016977 48674** *pam@baileymill.fsnet.co.uk* www.holidaycottagescumbria.co.uk **D:** Fr £20.00–£22.00 **S:** Fr £22.00–£28.00 **Beds:** 4F 6T 3D 4S **Baths:** 6 En 4 Pr 6 Sh cc

Peebles

NT2540

Lyne Farmhouse, *Lyne Farm, Peebles, EH45 8NR.* **Open:** All year (not Xmas)
01721 740255 (also fax) Mrs Waddell *awaddell@farming.co.uk* www.lynefarm.co.uk **D:** Fr £18.00–£20.00 **S:** Fr £20.00–£22.00 **Beds:** 2D 1T **Baths:** 2 Sh
Beautiful Georgian farmhouse, with tastefully decorated rooms overlooking scenic Stobo Valley. Walled garden plus hill-walking, picnic areas and major Roman fort all on farm. Ideally placed for Edinburgh and picturesque town of Peebles, plus Border towns and historic houses.

Selkirk

NT4728

Ivy Bank, *Hillside Terrace, Selkirk, TD7 4LT.* Superior detached accommodation with panoramic views of local hills. **Open:** Easter to Dec
01750 21470 Mrs MacKenzie *nettamackenzie@ivybankselkirk.freeserve.co.uk* **D:** Fr £20.00 **S:** Fr £20.00 **Beds:** 1D 1T 1S **Baths:** 2 En 1 Pr 1 Sh (4) cc

Hillholm, *36 Hillside Terrace, Selkirk, TD7 4ND.* Victorian house, warm welcome, 5 mins walk to centre or golf. **Open:** Mar to Oct
01750 21293 Mrs Hannah **D:** Fr £20.00–£25.00 **S:** Fr £25.00–£27.00 **Beds:** 1T 2D **Baths:** 2 En 1 Pr (10)

Ettrickshaws Hotel, *Ettrickbridge, Selkirk, TD7 5HW.* This splendid Victorian country house nestling in 12 acres of woodland, boasts private salmon and trout fishing. 12 golf courses within half an hour and the opportunity to enjoy riding and walking in the Scottish Borders. Excellent home cooking and service. **Open:** All year
01750 52229 (also fax) J Oldhead *jenny@ettrickshaws.co.uk* www.ettrickshaws.co.uk **D:** Fr £45.00–£60.00 **S:** Fr £55.00–£70.00 **Beds:** 1T 4D **Baths:** 5 En (12) (10) cc

St Abbs

NT9167

Castle Rock Guest House, *Murrayfield, St Abbs, Eyemouth, Berwickshire, TD14 5PP.* Victorian house with superb views over sea and rocks. **Open:** Feb to Nov
018907 71715 Mrs Wood **Fax: 018907 71520** *boowood@compuserve.com* **D:** Fr £23.00–£25.00 **S:** Fr £23.00–£25.00 **Beds:** 1F 1D 1T 1S **Baths:** 4 En (4) cc

St Boswells

NT5930

Whitehouse Farmhouse, *St Boswells, Melrose, Roxburghshire, TD6 0ED.* Large welcoming country house, log fires, home-cooked dinners. Spectacular views. **Open:** All year
01573 460343 Mrs Tyrer **Fax: 01573 460361** *tyrer.whitehouse@lineone.net* **D:** Fr £28.00–£35.00 **S:** Fr £32.00–£45.00 **Beds:** 2T 1D **Baths:** 3 En (10) cc

Town Yetholm

NT8127

Lochside, *Town Yetholm, Kelso, Roxburghshire, TD5 8PD.* Experience Lochside, a magnificent Victorian mansion house nestled in the Cheviot Hills. **Open:** All year
01573 420455 & 07974 378911 (M) Mrs Hurst *yvonnekhurst@hotmail.com* www.oldlochsidefarm.co.uk **D:** Fr £25.00 **S:** Fr £25.00 **Beds:** 1D 2T **Baths:** 3 En (2)

Blunty's Mill, *Kirk Yetholm, Kelso, Roxburghshire, TD5 6PG.* Fabulous rural location set in 6 acres. Friendly welcome guaranteed. **Open:** All year
01573 420288 Mrs Brooker *gail_rowan@hotmail.com* **D:** Fr £22.00–£30.00 **Beds:** 2T **Baths:** 1 Sh (10)

BATHROOMS
En = Ensuite
Pr = Private
Sh = Shared

West Linton

NT1551

The Gordon Arms Hotel, *Dolphinton Road, West Linton, Peebles-shire, EH46 7DR.* Small, friendly country inn, award winning food, traditional bar. **Open:** All year
01968 660208 **D:** Fr £24.00 **S:** Fr £28.00 **Beds:** 1F 1T 2D 1S **Baths:** 1 Sh cc

Yarrow Feus

NT3426

Ladhope Farm, *Yarrow Feus, Yarrow Valley, Selkirk, TD7 5NE.* Beautiful farmhouse, log fires, very peaceful. Ideal for hunting, touring. **Open:** Easter to Oct
01750 82216 Mrs Turnbull *anne@scottish.borders.com* **D:** Fr £18.00–£20.00 **S:** Fr £20.00–£22.00 **Beds:** 1F 1D **Baths:** 1 Sh (4)

Meadow View, *Watch Hill Road, Canonbie, DG14 0TF.* A warm Scottish welcome assured in this friendly home. **Open:** Easter to Oct
013873 71786 Mrs Bell **D:** Fr £17.50 **S:** Fr £20.00 **Beds:** 1F 1D **Baths:** 2 En (3)

Carsluith

NX4855

Cairnholy Farmhouse, *Carsluith, Newton Stewart, DG8 7EA.* **Open:** All year **Grades:** STB 3 Star
01557 840249 Mr & Mrs Moorhouse *cairnholy@aol.com* www.cairnholy.co.uk **D:** Fr £18.00–£20.00 **S:** Fr £22.00 **Beds:** 1T 2D **Baths:** 1 En 1 Sh
6000 years ago the ancients came here to worship their gods and bury their kings; we'll just rest and feed you. Scented gardens in the summer, log fires in the winter and a cuppa anytime.

Castle Douglas

NX7662

Smithy House, *The Buchan, Castle Douglas, Kirkcudbrightshire, DG7 1TH.* **Open:** All year (not Xmas/New Year) **Grades:** STB 4 Star
01556 503841 Mrs Carcas *enquiries@smithyhouse.co.uk* www.smithyhouse.co.uk
D: Fr £24.00–£27.00 **S:** Fr £40.00 **Beds:** 2D 1T **Baths:** 2 En 1 Pr (4) cc
Relax in the peaceful tranquillity of our home, enjoying the natural surroundings of the countryside, within convenient walking distance of the shops and restaurants in town, Varied breakfast menu concentrating on local produce. Children over 16. Member Scotland's Best B&Bs.

The Craig, *44 Abercromby Road, Castle Douglas, Kirkcudbrightshire, DG7 1BA.* Large sandstone villa next to golf course. Short walk into town. **Open:** All year **Grades:** STB 3 Star
01556 504840 Mrs Lawrie *mgtgordon@btinternet.com* **D:** Fr £18.00–£23.00 **S:** Fr £18.00–£23.00 **Beds:** 1T 1D 1S **Baths:** 1 Sh (4)

Albion House, *49 Ernespie Road, Castle Douglas, Kircudbrightshire, DG7 1LD.* Substantial Victorian house, set in attractive, large garden. Every comfort. **Open:** All year (not Xmas/New Year)
01556 502360 (also fax) Mrs Kirk **D:** Fr £20.00–£25.00 **S:** Fr £25.00–£35.00 **Beds:** 1F 1T 1D **Baths:** 2 En

Colvend

NX8654

Wilmar, *Colvend, Dalbeattie, Kirkcudbrightshire, DG5 4QW.* Comfortable rural family home near coast. Ideal walking, cycling, touring. **Open:** All year (not Xmas/New Year)
01556 620648 *turnbullwilmar@yahoo.co.uk*
D: Fr £18.00–£20.00 **Beds:** 1T 1D **Baths:** 2 En

Coxhill

NT0904

Coxhill Farm, *Old Carlisle Road, Coxhill, Moffat, Dumfriesshire, DG10 9QN.* Stylish farmhouse set in 70 acres, outstanding views, private parking. **Open:** All year (not Xmas/New Year)
01683 220471 Mrs Long **Fax: 01683 220871**
D: Fr £22.50 **S:** Fr £30.00 **Beds:** 1D 1T **Baths:** 2 En

Creetown

NX4758

Cherrytrees, *59 St John Street, Creetown, Newton Stewart, DG8 7JB.* **Open:** All year
01671 820229 (also fax) *cherryscone@supanet.com* www.cherrytrees-creetown.co.uk **D:** Fr £22.50–£25.00 **S:** Fr £22.50–£25.00 **Beds:** 1T 1D **Baths:** 2 En (2) cc
Situated in quiet village off A75, and on NR7 cycle route. Ideally located for touring, hills, forest or beaches. Cherrytrees is the 4 star quality accommodation in the area for your visit. Deluxe guest lounge with open fire.

Wal-d-mar, *Mill Street, Creetown, Newton Stewart, Wigtownshire, DG8 7JN.* **Open:** All year (not Xmas)
01671 820369 (also fax) M Lockett *howie@thebogue.freeserve.co.uk* **D:** Fr £16.50 **S:** Fr £16.50 **Beds:** 1D 1S **Baths:** 1 Sh (3)
Modern bungalow in quiet village location, ideal base for touring, walking, golf, etc. Comfortable beds, good breakfasts, private off-road parking, warm Scottish welcome assured. Situated between Dumfries and Stranraer on the Cree estuary.

B&B owners may vary rates – be sure to check when booking

National Grid References given are for villages, towns and cities – not for individual houses

The Haven, *23 Harbour Street, Creetown, Newton Stewart, DG8 7JJ.* Peaceful location in village; centrally placed for all holiday activities. **Open:** All year (not Xmas/New Year) **Grades:** STB 2 Star
01671 820546 G & E A Stott *creehaven@aol.com*
D: Fr £22.50 **S:** Fr £25.00 **Beds:** 2T 1D **Baths:** 3 En (3)

Crocketford

NX8372

Henderland Farm, *Crocketford Road, Crocketford or Ninemile Bar, Dumfries, DG2 8QD.* Substantial farmhouse, comfortably furnished with views of lovely open countryside. **Open:** All year (not Xmas)
01387 730270 Mrs Smyth **D:** Fr £18.00–£20.00 **S:** Fr £20.00 **Beds:** 1F 1D 1T **Baths:** 3 En (4)

Crossmichael

NX7366

Culgruff House Hotel, *Crossmichael, Castle Douglas, Kirkcudbrightshire, DG7 3BB.* Victorian baronial mansion, own grounds, overlooking loch, village, Galloway Hills. **Open:** All year
01556 670230 Mr Grayson **D:** Fr £18.50–£28.50 **S:** Fr £21.00–£28.50 **Beds:** 4F 4D 7T 2S **Baths:** 4 En 4 Sh (40) cc

Airds Farm, *Crossmichael, Castle Douglas, Kirkcudbrightshire, DG7 3BG.* Scenic views over Loch Ken and the Galloway Hills. **Open:** All year
01556 670418 (also fax) Mrs Keith *tricia@airds.com* www.airds.com **D:** Fr £18.00–£23.00 **S:** Fr £23.00–£27.00 **Beds:** 1F 1T 2D 1S **Baths:** 2 En 1 Sh (6)

Cummertrees

NY1466

Solway Sporting Breaks, *2 Queenberry Terrace, Cummertrees, Annan, Dumfriesshire, DG12 5QF.* Quality tourist accommodation, can arrange golf, salmon fishing, birdwatching, weddings. **Open:** All year
01461 700333 *solwaysb@aol.com* www.solwaysportingbreaks.co.uk **D:** Fr £17.50–£20.00 **S:** Fr £20.00–£25.00 **Beds:** 1F 2D 1S **Baths:** 2 Sh (3) cc

Dalbeattie

NX8361 *Pheasant, Anchor, Smugglers, Laurie Arms, Clonyard House*

13 Maxwell Park, *Dalbeattie, Kirkcudbrightshire, DG5 4LR.* Perfectly situated for walks, beaches, golf. Warm welcome. Farmhouse breakfast. **Open:** All year
01556 610830 & 07808 146505 (M) Mrs Tattersfield **D:** Fr £18.00–£22.00 **S:** Fr £26.00 **Beds:** 1T 2D **Baths:** 1 En 1 Sh (2)

Dumfries

NX9776

Southpark Country House, *Quarry Road, Locharbriggs, Dumfries, DG1 1QG.* **Open:** All year **Grades:** STB 3 Star, AA 4 Diamond
01387 711188 Mr Maxwell **Fax: 01387 711155** *info@southparkhouse.co.uk* www.southparkhouse.co.uk **D:** Fr £19.50–£23.00 **S:** Fr £23.00–£25.00 **Beds:** 1F 1T 2D 1S **Baths:** 3 En 2 Pr (10) cc
One of Southwest's finest establishments, situated on edge of town. Ample private parking, enjoying easy access from all major routes. yet only 5 minutes from Dumfries centre. Saver breaks Sept-April. Guests commented:- 'Excellent location, breathtaking views and the finest hospitality'.

Fernwood, *4 Casslands, Dumfries, DG2 7NS.* Victorian sandstone villa, close to golf course and town centre. **Open:** All year (not Xmas)
01387 253701 (also fax) Mrs Vaughan *pamelavaughan@yahoo.com* **D:** Fr £18.00–£20.00 **S:** Fr £18.00–£25.00 **Beds:** 1F 1D 2S **Baths:** 2 Sh (6)

Wallamhill House, *Kirkton, Dumfries, DG1 1SL.* Country house, beautiful views, spacious rooms, leisure suite, safe parking. **Open:** All year (not Xmas) **Grades:** STB 4 Star
01387 248249 (also fax) Mrs Hood *wallamhill@aol.com* www.wallamhill.co.uk **D:** Fr £22.00–£25.00 **S:** Fr £25.00–£28.00 **Beds:** 1F 2D 1T **Baths:** 4 En (8) cc

Waverley Guest House, *21 St Mary's Street, Dumfries, DG1 1HB.* 5 minutes from town centre, across from railway station. On main road. **Open:** All year
01387 254080 F Meikle-Latta **Fax: 01387 254848** *southwest.lumber@virgin.net* **D:** Fr £16.00–£20.00 **S:** Fr £18.50–£24.00 **Beds:** 5F 3T 1D 5S **Baths:** 6 En cc

30 Hardthorn Avenue, *Dumfries, DG2 9JA.* Non-smoking private house with car parking in quiet residential area. **Open:** Easter to Oct
01387 253502 (also fax) Ms Sloan *anniesbandb@aol.com* **D:** Fr £16.00–£18.00 **S:** Fr £23.00–£25.00 **Beds:** 1D 1T **Baths:** 1 Sh (2)

17 Rotchell Road, *Dumfries, DG2 7SE.* Small, friendly, family establishment, near town centre. **Open:** All year
01387 255615 Mrs Kempsell *joank@tinyworld.co.uk* **D:** Fr £20.00 **S:** Fr £20.00 **Beds:** 1F 1T 1D **Baths:** 3 En (4)

Brackenbridge, *67 New Abbey Road, Dumfries, DG2 7JY.* Brackenridge Bed & Breakfast, walking distance into the town centre and all local attractions. **Open:** All year
01387 263962 Mr & Mrs Thomson **D:** Fr £18.50–£25.00 **S:** Fr £20.00 **Beds:** 3F 3T 1D 1S **Baths:** 2 En 1 Pr

Dunscore

NX8684

Low Kirkbride Farmhouse, *Dunscore, Dumfries, DG2 0SP.* Warm comfortable farmhouse with beautiful views, superb breakfasts, tasty home-baking. **Open:** All year
01387 820258 (also fax) Mrs Kirk *lowkirkbride@btinternet.com* www.lowkirkbridefarm.com **D:** Fr £16.00–£18.00 **S:** Fr £16.00–£18.00 **Beds:** 1F 1T 1D **Baths:** 3 En (4)

Ecclefechan

NY1974

Carlyle House, *Ecclefechan, Lockerbie, Dumfriesshire, DG11 3DG.* C18th house in small village. Central to Dumfries & Galloway and Borders. **Open:** All year (not Xmas/New Year)
01576 300322 (also fax) Mrs Martin **D:** Fr £14.50 **S:** Fr £14.50 **Beds:** 1F 1T 1S **Baths:** 2 Sh (6)

Gelston

NX7658 *Smuggler's Inn, Crows Nest, Douglas Arms*

Rose Cottage Guest House, *Gelston, Castle Douglas, Kirkcudbrightshire, DG7 1SH.* Quiet country guest house in small village, 2.5 miles from Castle Douglas. **Open:** All year (not Xmas)
01556 502513 (also fax) Mr Steele **D:** Fr £18.00–£20.50 **S:** Fr £18.00 **Beds:** 2D 3T 1S **Baths:** 1 En 2 Sh (10)

Oakleaf Cottage, *Nether Linkins, Gelston, Castle Douglas, DG7 1SU.* Newly renovated cottage with woodland garden. Stunning views, hill and forest backdrop. Mild climate. The area beckons you to walk, paint, cycle and much more. We have bantams, ducks, dogs and abundant wildlife. Conservatory, guest kitchen for your added convenience. **Open:** All year
01556 680247 Mr Driver and Mrs D Cook **D:** Fr £21.00–£23.00 **S:** Fr £23.00–£25.00 **Beds:** 1T **Baths:** 1 En (2)

Glencaple

NX9968 *Nith Hotel*

Riverside, *Shore Park, Glencaple, Dumfries, DG1 4RF.* Detached house in small village, superb views over River Nith. **Open:** All year (not Xmas/New Year)
01387 770423 Mrs Anderson **D:** Fr £17.50 **S:** Fr £20.00 **Beds:** 1F **Baths:** 1 Pr (1)

Glenluce

NX1957

Bankfield Farm, *Glenluce, Newton Stewart, Wigtownshire, DG8 0JF.* Large spacious farmhouse on the outskirts of quiet country village. **Open:** All year
01581 300281 (also fax) Mrs Stewart **D:** Fr £18.00 **S:** Fr £20.00 **Beds:** 1F 1D 1T **Baths:** 2 En 1 Pr

High Auchenlarie

NX5353

High Auchenlarie Farmhouse, *High Auchenlarie, Gatehouse of Fleet, Castle Douglas, Kirkcudbrightshire, DG7 2HB.* Traditional farmhouse overlooking Fleet, Wigtown Bay, Isle of Man. Superb location. **Open:** Feb to Dec **Grades:** STB 3 Star
01557 840231 (also fax) Mrs Johnstone **D:** Fr £22.00–£26.00 **S:** Fr £30.00–£38.00 **Beds:** 1F 1T 1D **Baths:** 3 En (4)

Planning a longer stay? Always ask for any special rates

Please respect a B&B's wishes regarding children, animals and smoking

Morag, *19 Old Carlisle Road, Moffat, Dumfriesshire, DG10 9QJ.* Beautiful quiet location in charming town near Southern Upland Way. **Open:** All year **Grades:** STB 3 Star
01683 220690 Mr & Mrs Taylor *moragmoffat@tiscali.co.uk* **D:** Fr £18.00–£19.00 **S:** Fr £19.00–£21.00 **Beds:** 1D 1T 1S **Baths:** 1 Sh (10) (5)

Allanton Hotel, *21-22 High Street, Moffat, Dumfriesshire, DG10 9HL.* Small inn in the scenic town of Moffat. Home-cooking. **Open:** All year
01683 220343 & 01461 338330 Mr Kennedy **Fax: 01683 220914** *gordonkennedy439@msn.com* **D:** Fr £22.00–£30.00 **S:** Fr £24.00–£32.00 **Beds:** 1F 2T 3D 1S **Baths:** 2 En 6 Pr 1 Sh cc

Waterside, *Moffat, Dumfriesshire, DG10 9LF.* Large country house in 12 acres woodland garden with private stretch of river. **Open:** Easter to Oct
01683 220092 Mrs Edwards **D:** Fr £19.00–£21.00 **S:** Fr £21.00 **Beds:** 2D 2T **Baths:** 1 Pr 1 Sh (4)

Black Bull Hotel, *Churchgate, Moffat, Dumfriesshire, DG10 9EG.* Family run hotel, open all year. Accommodation and meals available. **Open:** All year
01683 220206 Miss Hughes **Fax: 01623 220403** *hotels@blackbullmoffat.co.uk* www.blackbullmoffat.co.uk **D:** Fr £26.50 **S:** Fr £35.00 **Beds:** 2F 4T 5D 1S **Baths:** 12 En cc

Morlich House, *Ballplay Road, Moffat, Dumfriesshire, DG10 9JU.* A superb Victorian country house set in quiet elevated grounds overlooking town. **Open:** Feb to Nov
01683 220589 Mrs Wells **Fax: 01683 221032** *morlich.house@ndirect.co.uk* www.morlich-house.ndirect.co.uk **D:** Fr £20.00–£23.00 **S:** Fr £20.00–£33.00 **Beds:** 2F 1D 1T 1S **Baths:** 4 En 1 Pr (6) cc

Hartfell House, *Hartfell Crescent, Moffat, Dumfriesshire, DG10 9AL.* Splendid Victorian manor house in peaceful location. **Open:** All year (not Xmas/New Year)
01683 220153 Mrs White *mary.whitsell@virgin.net* www.hartfellhouse.co.uk **D:** Fr £24.00 **S:** Fr £28.00 **Beds:** 2F 4D 1T 1S **Baths:** 7 En 1 Sh (8)

The Arden House Guest House, *High Street, Moffat, Dumfriesshire, DG10 9HG.* Former bank building off of town square with private car park. **Open:** Easter to Oct
01683 220220 I Standingford **D:** Fr £18.00–£20.00 **S:** Fr £18.00–£20.00 **Beds:** 2F 2T 2D 1S **Baths:** 4 En 1 Pr 2 Sh (7)

Annandale Arms Hotel, *High Street, Moffat, Dumfriesshire, DG10 9HF.* Gold Key Award Winner 2001. Attractive 240 year old Georgian Hotel standing in the centre of the tree-lined square of the beautiful town of Moffat. Private carpark. Only one mile off J15/A74 (M6) **Open:** All year (not Xmas)
01683 220013 *still@annandalearmshotel.co.uk* www.annandalearmshotel.co.uk **D:** Fr £35.00 **S:** Fr £45.00 **Beds:** 1F 4T 4D 1S **Baths:** 10 En (40) cc

Nethermill

NY0487

Lochrigghead Farmhouse, *Nethermill, Parkgate, Dumfries, DG1 3NG.* Farmhouse, picturesque surroundings. Good food, hospitality. Ideal for touring Scotland. **Open:** All year
01387 860381 Mrs Burgoyne *lochrigghead.burgo@talk21.co* **D:** Fr £17.00 **S:** Fr £17.00 **Beds:** 3F 1D 1T 1S **Baths:** 2 En 1 Pr 1 Sh (10)

New Abbey

NX9666

Abbey Arms Hotel, *No 1 The Square, New Abbey, Dumfries, DG2 8BX.* **Open:** All year **Grades:** STB 2 Star
01387 850489 Fax: 01387 850501 D: Fr £26.00 **S:** Fr £28.00 **Beds:** 2F 5T **Baths:** 6 En 1 Pr cc
Small family-run hotel in the picturesque village of New Abbey, renowned for home-cooking & a good bar. Ideally-located for golf, fishing, shooting, bird-watching, mountain-biking & walking. Within walking distance of Sweetheart Abbey.

New Galloway

NX6377 *Cross Keys*

Cross Keys Hotel, *High Street, New Galloway, Castle Douglas, Kirkcudbrightshire, DG7 3RN.* C18th olde worlde hotel. **Open:** All year (not Xmas/New Year)
01644 420494 (also fax) Mr Berriman www.crosskeys.com **D:** Fr £19.50–£23.50 **S:** Fr £25.00–£27.50 **Beds:** 2F 4T 3D 2S **Baths:** 3 En 2 Sh cc

Newton Stewart

NX4065

Eskdale, *Princess Avenue, Newton Stewart, DG8 6ES.* Attractive detached house, very quiet residential area, 5 mins' walk town centre. **Open:** All year **Grades:** STB 3 Star
01671 404195 Mrs Smith **D:** Fr £16.00–£18.00 **S:** Fr £20.00–£22.00 **Beds:** 1D 1T 1S **Baths:** 1 Pr 1 Sh (4)

Flowerbank Guest House, *Minnigaff, Newton Stewart, Wigtownshire, DG8 6PJ.* **Open:** All year (not Xmas) **Grades:** STB 3 Star
01671 402629 Mrs Inker *flowerbankgh@btopenworld.com* www.flowerbankgh.com **D:** Fr £20.00–£25.00 **S:** Fr £25.00–£35.00 **Beds:** 1F 2D 2T **Baths:** 4 En 1 Pr (7)
Geoff and Linda Inker welcome you to Flowerbank - a charming C18th detached house in an acre of stunning gardens on the banks of the River Cree, 1/2 mile from town. Delicious home-cooking. For happy holiday memories look no further!

Kiloran, *6 Auchendoon Road, Newton Stewart, Wigtownshire, DG8 6HD.* Detached bungalow with large maintained garden, views of Galloway Hills. **Open:** Apr to Oct **Grades:** STB 2 Star
01671 402818 Miss Wallace **D:** Fr £17.50–£18.00 **S:** Fr £17.50–£18.00 **Beds:** 1T 1D **Baths:** 1 Sh (3)

Ivy Bank Cottage, *Minnigaff, Newton Stewart, Dumfries & Galloway, DG8 6PQ.* 300 year old secluded riverside cottage, where breakfasts are legendary. **Open:** All year (not Xmas/New Year)
01671 403139 Mr Izod *chris@ivybank.fslife.co.uk* **D:** Fr £18.00–£21.00 **S:** Fr £18.00–£21.00 **Beds:** 1T 1D **Baths:** 1 Sh (2)

Newton Wamphray

NY1194

The Red House Hotel, *Newton Wamphray, Moffat, Dumfriesshire, DG10 9NF.* Small country hotel, close to M6 (M74) Motorway. **Open:** All year (not Xmas)
01576 470470 Mrs Wilson **D:** Fr £20.00–£25.00 **S:** Fr £20.00–£25.00 **Beds:** 1D 1T 1S **Baths:** 1 En 1 Sh (6)

Parkgate
NY0288

Lochrigghead Farmhouse, *Nethermill, Parkgate, Dumfries, DG1 3NG.* Farmhouse, picturesque surroundings. Good food, hospitality. Ideal for touring Scotland. **Open:** All year
01387 860381 Mrs Burgoyne *lochrigghead.burgo@talk21.co* **D:** Fr £17.00 **S:** Fr £17.00 **Beds:** 3F 1D 1T 1S **Baths:** 2 En 1 Pr 1 Sh (10)

Parton
NX6970

Drumrash Farm, *Parton, Castle Douglas, Kirkcudbrightshire, DG7 3NF.* Traditional farmhouse, 300 yards from working farm. Superb views over Loch Ken. **Open:** All year
01644 470274 & 07714 748509 (M) Mrs Cruikshank **D:** Fr £14.00–£16.00 **S:** Fr £15.00–£18.00 **Beds:** 2F 1D **Baths:** 1 En 2 Sh (6)

Portpatrick
NW9954

Melvin Lodge Guest House, *South Crescent, Portpatrick, Stranraer, Wigtownshire, DG9 8LE.* Very comfortable, friendly house starting Southern Upland Way. **Open:** All year
01776 810238 Mr & Mrs Pinder **D:** Fr £20.00–£23.00 **S:** Fr £20.00–£23.00 **Beds:** 4F 3D 1T 2S **Baths:** 5 En 1 Sh (8) cc

Rockcliffe
NX8453

The Cottage, *1 Barcloy Mill, Rockcliffe, Dalbeattie, Kirkcudbrightshire, DG5 4QL.* Quiet cottage in central village guest rooms overlooking garden and coast. **Open:** All year (not Xmas/New Year)
01556 630460 Mrs Bailey *elizabeth-bailey@rockcliffe-bandb.freeserve.co.uk* **D:** Fr £17.50–£18.50 **S:** Fr £23.00–£25.00 **Beds:** 1T 1D **Baths:** 1 En 1 Sh

Sandyhills
NX8855

Boreland of Southwick, *Southwick, Dumfries, DG2 8AN.* Warm and friendly welcome awaits you on the beautiful Solway Coast. **Open:** All year **Grades:** STB 4 Star
01387 780225 Mrs Dodd *boreland.southwick@virgin.net* www.borelandfarms.co.uk **D:** Fr £20.00–£25.00 **S:** Fr £20.00–£25.00 **Beds:** 1T 2D **Baths:** 3 En cc

Sanquhar
NS7809

4 Barons Court, *Sanquhar, Dumfriesshire, DG4 6EB.* Comfortable self-contained flat. Ideal for fishing, walking, golf and touring. **Open:** All year (not Xmas)
01659 50361 Mrs Clark **D:** Fr £17.00 **S:** Fr £17.00 **Beds:** 1F 1D **Baths:** 2 En

Stoneykirk
NX0853

Torrs Warren Hotel, *Stoneykirk, Portpatrick, Stranraer, Wigtownshire, DG9 9DH.* Delightful former manse set in peaceful countryside location. Warm welcome. **Open:** All year
01776 830298 Mrs Camlin **Fax: 01776 830204** *torrswarren@btinternet.com* **D:** Fr £24.00 **S:** Fr £28.00 **Beds:** 2F 2T 2D 2S **Baths:** 8 En (30) cc

Stranraer
NX0560

Ivy House, *London Road, Stranraer, DG9 8ER.* Lovely old town house, situated at the foot of Loch Ryan. **Open:** All year **Grades:** STB 2 Star
01776 704176 Mr & Mrs Mcmillan *ivyplace3@hotmail.com* www.ivyplace.worldonline.co.uk **D:** Fr £16.00–£19.00 **S:** Fr £18.00–£25.00 **Beds:** 1F 1D 1T **Baths:** 2 En 1 Pr (10)

Rankin's Close, *25/27 Dalrymple Street, Stranraer, Wigtownshire, DG9 7ET.* Friendly accommodation in central location. Ideal for castles/gardens/beaches. **Open:** All year
01776 702632 *dawnlongford@tinyworld.co.uk* **D:** Fr £16.00–£18.00 **S:** Fr £16.00 **Beds:** 1F 2T 1D 1S **Baths:** 1 En 2 Sh (2)

Lorenza, *2 Birnam Place, Station Street, Stranraer, Wigtownshire, DG9 7HN.* Central location, walking distance from town, train, bus and ferries. **Open:** All year (not Xmas/New Year)
01776 703935 Mrs Jameson **D:** Fr £18.00 **S:** Fr £20.00 **Beds:** 1T 2D **Baths:** 2 En 1 Pr (3)

Neptune's Rest, *25 Agnew Crescent, Stranraer, Wigtownshire, DG9 7JZ.* Neptune's Rest overlooks Agnew Park with its boating lake and miniature railway. **Open:** All year
01776 704729 Mr McClymont **D:** Fr £15.00–£20.00 **S:** Fr £16.00–£22.00 **Beds:** 2F 2D 1T 1S **Baths:** 3 En 2 Sh cc

Torthorwald
NY0378

Branetrigg Farm, *Torthorwald, Dumfries, DG1 3QB.* Farmhouse with panoramic views; ideal for touring, cycling, fishing and golfing. **Open:** Easter to Nov
01387 750650 Mrs Huston **D:** Fr £19.00–£21.00 **S:** Fr £25.00 **Beds:** 1F 1D **Baths:** 1 Sh

Whithorn
NX4440

Belmont, *St John Street, Whithorn, Newton Stewart, Wigtownshire, DG8 8PG.* Comfortable home in beautiful area. Warm welcome. **Open:** All year **Grades:** STB 3 Star
01988 500890 (also fax) B J Fleming *belmontbb@tiscali.co.uk* **D:** Fr £18.00–£20.00 **S:** Fr £18.00–£20.00 **Beds:** 2D 1S **Baths:** 1 Pr 1 Sh (8) (10)

The Steampacket Hotel, *Whithorn, Newton Stewart, Wigtownshire, DG8 8LA.* Family run harbourside inn. **Open:** All year (not Xmas/New Year)
01988 500334 *steampacketinn@btconnect.com* **D:** Fr £25.00–£35.00 **S:** Fr £25.00–£35.00 **Beds:** 1F 1T 5D **Baths:** 7 En cc

Wigtown
NX4355

Glaisnock House, *20 South Main Street, Wigtown, Newton Stewart, Wigtownshire, DG8 9EH.* Set in the heart of Scotland's book town, with licensed restaurant. **Open:** All year (not Xmas) **Grades:** STB 2 Star
01988 402249 (also fax) Mr & Mrs Cairns *cairns@glaisnock1.freeserve.co.uk* www.glaisnockhouse.co.uk **D:** Fr £18.50–£20.00 **S:** Fr £19.50–£21.50 **Beds:** 2F 1T 1S **Baths:** 2 En 1 Pr 1 Sh cc

Craigmount Guest House, *High Street, Wigtown, Wigtownshire, DG8 9EQ.* Welcoming, licensed family-run home with space to relax. Close to Stranraer for ferries to Ireland, walk the Galloway hills and forests, play golf, shoot, visit the beaches, stone circle and historic monuments, browse the shops in Scotland's book town. **Open:** All year
01988 402291 / 0800 980 4510 P Taylor *taylorpat1@talk21.com* **D:** Fr £18.00–£20.00 **S:** Fr £18.00–£25.00 **Beds:** 2F 2T 1S **Baths:** 2 En 1 Sh (10)

Edinburgh & Lothians

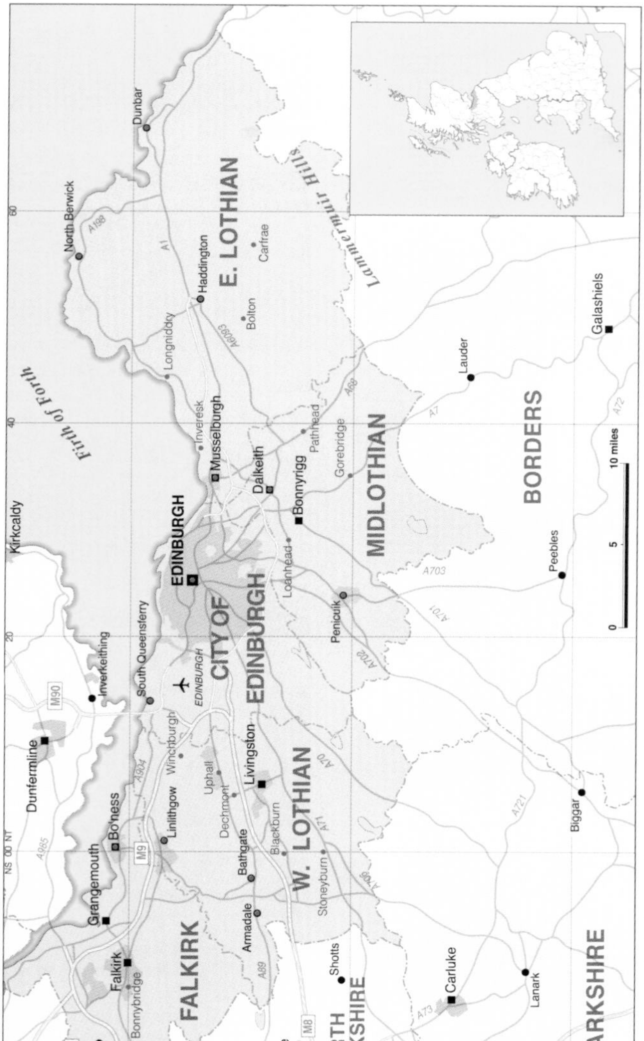

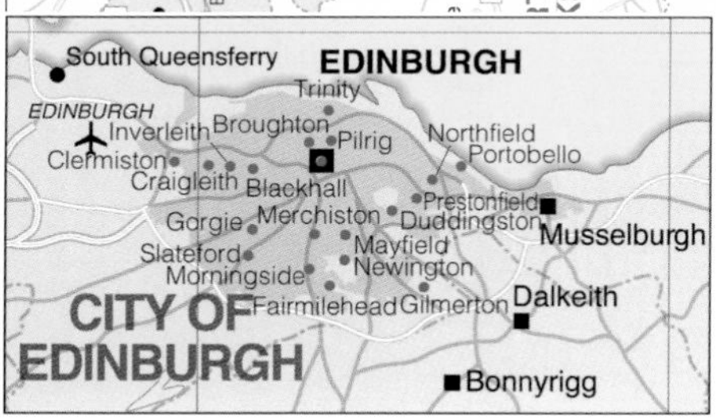

Armadale

NS9368

Tarrareoch Farm, *Armadale, Bathgate, W Lothian, EH48 3BJ.* C17th farmhouse all on one level. Midway Edinburgh/Glasgow. Beautiful countryside. **Open:** All year **01501 730404 (also fax)** Mrs Gibb **D:** Fr £16.00–£22.00 **S:** Fr £20.00–£26.00 **Beds:** 1F 2T **Baths:** 2 En 1 Sh (10)

Bathgate

NS9769

Hillview, *35 The Green, Bathgate, W Lothian, EH48 4DA.* Quality and friendly accommodation with spectacular views of West Lothian. **Open:** All year (not Xmas) **01506 654830 (also fax)** Mrs Connell *bigjdconnell@hotmail.com* **D:** Fr £15.00–£18.00 **S:** Fr £20.00–£24.00 **Beds:** 1F 1T **Baths:** 1 En 1 Sh

Blackburn

NS9865

Cruachan Guest House, *78 East Main Street, Blackburn, Bathgate, West Lothian, EH47 7QS.*
Open: All year (not Xmas) **01506 655221** Mr Harkins **Fax: 01506 652395** *cruachan.bb@virgin.net* www.cruachan.co.uk **D:** Fr £21.00–£24.00 **S:** Fr £28.00–£32.00 **Beds:** 1F 3D **Baths:** 3 En 1 Pr (5)

A relaxed & friendly base is provided at Cruachan from which to explore Central Scotland. Edinburgh only 30 mins by train. Kenneth and Jacqueline ensure you receive quality service, meticulously presented accommodation and of course a full Scottish breakfast.

BEDROOMS
D = Double
T = Twin
S = Single
F = Family

Bo'ness
NS9981

Haypark, *28 Grange Terrace, Bo'ness, EH51 9DS.* Attractive stone-built house overlooking the Forth, convenient for Edinburgh and Stirling. **Open:** May to Sep
01506 823193 (also fax) Mrs Croxford *peter_croxford@tesco.net* **D:** Fr £20.00–£25.00 **S:** Fr £25.00 **Beds:** 1T 1D **Baths:** 1 Sh

Bolton
NT5070 *The Goblin, Tweeddale Arms*

Fieldfare, *Upper Bolton Farm, Bolton, Haddington, E Lothian, EH41 4HL.* Quiet location on farm. Edinburgh, half a mile. Near hills and sea. **Open:** All year (not New Year)
01620 810346 Mrs Clark **D:** Fr £18.00–£22.00 **S:** Fr £20.00–£24.00 **Beds:** 1F 1T 1D **Baths:** 2 Pr

Bonnybridge
NS8380

Bandominie Farm, *Walton Road, Bonnybridge, Stirlingshire, FK4 2HP.* Farmhouse friendly atmosphere. 2 miles from A80, Castle Cary, B816. **Open:** All year (not Xmas/New Year)
01324 840284 Mrs Forrester **D:** Fr £17.00–£18.00 **S:** Fr £17.00–£18.00 **Beds:** 1D 1T 1S **Baths:** 1 Sh (3)

Carfrae
NT5769

Carfrae Farm, *Carfrae, Haddington, E Lothian, EH41 4LP.* Peaceful farmhouse overlooking lovely gardens. Edinburgh, The Borders, Golf nearby. **Open:** Apr to Oct
01620 830242 Mrs Gibson **Fax: 01620 830320** *dgcarfrae@aol.com* **D:** Fr £25.00–£27.00 **S:** Fr £35.00–£40.00 **Beds:** 2D 1T **Baths:** 2 En 1 Pr (10) (6)

Dalkeith
NT3467 *Justinlees Inn, Dalhousie Castle*

Rathan House, *45 Eskbank Road, Eskbank, Dalkeith, Midlothian, EH22 3BH.* Conservation area by Midlothian Cycleway, croquet lawn. Low fat breakfasts. **Open:** All year
0131 663 3291 (also fax) Mr & Mrs MacRae *bandb@edinvac.btinternet.co.uk* www.edinvac.btinternet.co.uk **D:** Fr £24.00–£32.00 **S:** Fr £28.00–£40.00 **Beds:** 1F 2T 1D **Baths:** 2 En 2 Pr (8) cc

Dechmont
NT0370

Bankhead Farm, *Dechmont, Broxburn, EH52 6NB.* Panoramic views of beautiful countryside yet easy access Edinburgh airport. **Open:** All year (not Xmas)
01506 811209 H Warnock **Fax: 01506 811815** *bankheadbb@aol.com* bankheadfarm.com **D:** Fr £22.00–£25.00 **S:** Fr £28.00–£35.00 **Beds:** 2F 2D 3S **Baths:** 7 En cc

Dunbar
NT6779

Overcliffe Guest House, *11 Bayswell Park, Dunbar, E Lothian, EH42 1AE.* Family-run, perfect for touring East Lothian's golf courses beaches. **Open:** All year
01368 864004 Mrs Bower **Fax: 01368 865995** *overcliffe@aol.com* **D:** Fr £20.00–£35.00 **S:** Fr £25.00–£35.00 **Beds:** 3F 2T **Baths:** 3 En 2 Sh (1) (2)

Goldenstones Hotel, *Queens Road, Dunbar, E Lothian, EH42 1LG.* The Goldenstones is a friendly, family-run hotel. **Open:** All year
01368 862356 Mr Currie **Fax: 01368 862344** **D:** Fr £30.00–£32.00 **S:** Fr £40.00–£45.00 **Beds:** 4F 15T **Baths:** 19 En cc

EDINBURGH Blackhall
NT2174

Sandilands House, *25 Queensferry Road, Edinburgh, EH4 3HB.* 1930s bungalow with many art deco features. Near Murrayfield Stadium. **Open:** All year
0131 332 2057 Mrs Sandilands **Fax: 0131 315 4476** **D:** Fr £20.00–£34.00 **S:** Fr £25.00–£45.00 **Beds:** 1F 1D 1T **Baths:** 3 En cc

EDINBURGH Broughton
NT2575

Ben Cruachan, *17 Mcdonald Road, Edinburgh, EH7 4LX.* Be assured of a very warm welcome at our family-run centrally situated guest house. **Open:** Apr to Oct
0131 556 3709 N Stark **D:** Fr £25.00–£35.00 **Beds:** 1F 1T 1D **Baths:** 3 En (10)

RATES
D = Price range per person sharing in a double or twin room
S = Price range for a single room

EDINBURGH Central
NT2573

6 Dean Park Crescent, *Edinburgh, EH4 1PN.* Warm friendly home. Large rooms. 10 mins walk to centre. **Open:** Easter to Oct **Grades:** STB 3 Star, RAC 4 Diamond
0131 332 5017 Mrs Kirkland *m.kirkland@blueyonder.co.uk* www.kirkland.pwp.blueyonder.co.uk **D:** Fr £22.00–£29.00 **S:** Fr £40.00–£55.00 **Beds:** 1F 1D 1T **Baths:** 1 En 1 Pr 1 Sh

17 Hope Park Terrace, *Edinburgh, EH8 9LZ.* Fifteen minutes' walk city centre. H&C in bedrooms. **Open:** All year
0131 667 7963 Mrs Frackelton **D:** Fr £25.00–£26.00 **S:** Fr £26.00–£28.00 **Beds:** 2D **Baths:** 1 Sh (10)

28 London Street, *Edinburgh, EH3 6NA.* Central Georgian 1st floor flat 5 minutes' walk from station. **Open:** Easter to Oct
0131 556 4641 Mr & Mrs Campbell **D:** Fr £18.00–£30.00 **S:** Fr £25.00–£50.00 **Beds:** 1F 1T 1D 1S **Baths:** 3 Sh (5) (1)

37 Howe Street, *Edinburgh, EH3 6TF.* Quiet Georgian garden flat, few minutes walk to Princes Street. **Open:** All year **Grades:** STB 2 Star
0131 557 3487 (also fax) Mrs Collie **D:** Fr £20.00–£25.00 **Beds:** 1D **Baths:** 1 Sh

Averon Guest House, *44 Gilmore Place, Edinburgh, EH3 9NQ.* Fully restored Georgian town house, built in 1770. Central Edinburgh with car park. **Open:** All year
0131 229 9932 Mr Cran **D:** Fr £18.00–£38.00 **S:** Fr £25.00–£38.00 **Beds:** 3F 2D 3T 1S **Baths:** 6 Pr (10) cc

Rothesay Hotel, *8 Rothesay Place, Edinburgh, EH3 7SL.* Heart of Edinburgh's Georgian New Town in the city centre, short walk Princes Street. **Open:** All year
0131 225 4125 Mr Borland *info@rothesay-hotel.demon.co.uk* **D:** Fr £25.00–£45.00 **S:** Fr £38.00–£65.00 **Beds:** 2F 4D 18T 12S **Baths:** 36 Pr

Glenora Hotel, *14 Rosebery Crescent, Edinburgh, EH12 5JY.* Small, city central hotel. Airport, bus stops nearby. **Open:** All year
0131 337 1186 www.glenorahotel.co.uk **D:** Fr £18.00–£55.00 **S:** Fr £25.00–£65.00 **Beds:** 1F 1T 5D 4S **Baths:** 11 En cc

Amaryllis Guest House, *21 Upper Gilmore Place, Edinburgh, EH3 9NL.* Warm, comfortable, friendly, central all attractions. Walkable but quietly situated. **Open:** All year (not Xmas)
0131 229 3293 (also fax) L Melrose *ghamaryllis@aol.com* **D:** Fr £18.00–£30.00 **S:** Fr £25.00–£40.00 **Beds:** 3F 1D 1T **Baths:** 4 En 1 Pr (10) (2) cc

BATHROOMS
En = Ensuite
Pr = Private
Sh = Shared

EDINBURGH Clermiston

NT1974 *The Old Inn*

Crannoch But and Ben, *467 Queensferry Road, Edinburgh, EH4 7ND.* Highly recommended. Airport and city centre situated three miles. **Open:** All year **0131 336 5688** *moiraconway@crannoch467.freeserve.co.uk* **D:** Fr £25.00–£28.00 **Beds:** 1F 1T 1D **Baths:** 2 En 1 Pr (5)

EDINBURGH Craigleith

NT2374

Six Marys Place Guest House, *Raeburn Place, Stockbridge, Edinburgh, EH4 1JN.* **Open:** All year **Grades:** STB 3 Star, AA 4 Diamond **0131 332 8965** The Manager **Fax: 0131 624 7060** *info@sixmarysplace.co.uk* www.sixmarysplace.co.uk **D:** Fr £30.00–£48.00 **S:** Fr £30.00–£48.00 **Beds:** 1F 2T 3D 2S **Baths:** 7 En 1 Pr **cc** Perfectly-located, 10 minutes from the city centre and 5 minutes from the celebrated Royal Botanic Gardens. This beautifully-restored Georgian townhouse, with its light, fresh decor, offers a warm, relaxed smoke-free atmosphere.

Galloway Guest House, *22 Dean Park Crescent, Edinburgh, EH4 6PH.* City centre location 10 minutes walk, Princes Street, free street parking. **Open:** All year **0131 332 3672 (also fax)** Mr Clark **D:** Fr £25.00–£30.00 **S:** Fr £30.00–£45.00 **Beds:** 3F 3T 3D 1S **Baths:** 6 En 1 Pr 2 Sh **cc**

St Bernards Guest House, *22 St Bernards Crescent, Edinburgh, EH4 1NS.* Victorian townhouse, 10-15 minute walk from city centre. **Open:** All year **0131 332 2339** Mr & Mrs Alsop **Fax: 0131 332 8842** *alexstbernards@aol.com* **D:** Fr £24.00–£30.00 **S:** Fr £25.00–£40.00 **Beds:** 4T 3D 1S **Baths:** 4 En 2 Sh **cc**

EDINBURGH Duddingston

NT2973

Sure & Steadfast, *76 Milton Road West, Duddingston, Edinburgh, EH15 1QV.* Small, family-run 3 star B&B situated about 2 miles from the city centre. **Open:** Easter to Sep **0131 657 1189** Mr & Mrs Taylor *a_t_taylor@ednet.co.uk* www.ednet.co.uk/~a_t_taylor **D:** Fr £16.50–£22.00 **S:** Fr £20.00–£44.00 **Beds:** 2D 1T **Baths:** 3 Sh (3) **cc**

EDINBURGH Fairmilehead

NT2468

Valhalla, *35 Comiston View, Edinburgh, EH10 6LP.* Modern detached property; quiet; golf, full breakfast. Warm welcome guaranteed. **Open:** All year **0131 445 5354** Mrs Stevenson-Renwick **D:** Fr £20.00–£32.00 **S:** Fr £25.00–£35.00 **Beds:** 1D 1T 1S **Baths:** 2 En 1 Pr (2)

EDINBURGH Gilmerton

NT2968

Emerald Guest House, *3 Drum Street, Gilmerton, Edinburgh, EH17 8QQ.* Victorian villa situated on bus route to city centre. **Open:** All year (not Xmas/New Year) **0131 664 5918** Mrs O'Connor **D:** Fr £20.00–£31.00 **S:** Fr £35.00 **Beds:** 1F 2T 2D **Baths:** 3 En 1 Sh (4) (5)

EDINBURGH Gorgie

NT2272

Invermark, *60 Polwarth Terrace, Edinburgh, EH11 1NJ.* On bus route into city, easy access from city bypass. **Open:** All year **0131 337 1066** Mrs Donaldson **D:** Fr £20.00 **S:** Fr £20.00 **Beds:** 1F 2T 1S **Baths:** 1 En 1 Pr (2)

RATES
D = Price range per person sharing in a double or twin room
S = Price range for a single room

EDINBURGH Inverleith

NT2475

The Inverleith Hotel, *5 Inverleith Terrace, Edinburgh, EH3 5NS.* Licensed Victorian Hotel, city centre, adjacent botanic gardens, groups accepted. **Open:** All year (not Xmas) **0131 556 2745** Mr & Mrs Case **Fax: 0131 557 0433** *hotel@inverleith.freeserve.co.uk* www.inverleith.freeserve.co.uk **D:** Fr £25.00–£50.00 **S:** Fr £30.00–£50.00 **Beds:** 2F 2D 2T 2S **Baths:** 8 En **cc**

EDINBURGH Mayfield

NT2672

Ivy Guest House, *7 Mayfield Gardens, Edinburgh, EH9 2AX.* **Open:** All year **0131 667 3411 & 01782 527692 (M)** Mr Green **Fax: 0131 620 1422** *don@ivyguesthouse.com* www.ivyguesthouse.com **D:** Fr £17.00–£35.00 **S:** Fr £17.00–£65.00 **Beds:** 2F 3D 2T 1S **Baths:** 6 En 2 Pr (7) Quiet, family-run Victorian villa guest house, many local restaurants, close to all Edinburgh's major cultural attractions, golf courses, Commonwealth swimming pool and university. A hearty Scottish breakfast and a warm welcome is assured.

Lauderville Guest House, *52 Mayfield Road, Edinburgh, EH9 2NH.* **Open:** All year **0131 667 7788** Mrs Marriott **Fax: 0131 667 2636** *res@laudervilleguesthouse.co.uk* www.laudervilleguesthouse.co.uk **D:** Fr £25.00–£45.00 **S:** Fr £30.00–£50.00 **Beds:** 1F 6D 2T 1S **Baths:** 10 En (6) **cc** Restored Victorian town house minutes from the city sights, Royal Mile, Castle, Princes Street. Elegant non-smoking bedrooms and excellent breakfast awaits, with varied menu including vegetarian. Secluded garden and secure car park. Traditional pubs and quality restaurants nearby.

Glenalmond Guest House, *25 Mayfield Gardens, Edinburgh, EH9 2BX.* **Open:** All year (not Xmas) **0131 668 2392 (also fax)** Mr & Mrs Fraser *glen@almond25.freeserve.co.uk* almond25.freeserve.co.uk **D:** Fr £25.00–£40.00 **S:** Fr £30.00–£40.00 **Beds:** 3F 4D 2T 1S **Baths:** 10 En (5)
Deb and Dave warmly welcome you to their superb accommodation. Ground, four-poster, ensuite rooms available. Close to Waverley Station. Varied breakfast served daily with home-made scones.

Hopetoun, *15 Mayfield Road, Edinburgh, EH9 2NG.* Completely non-smoking. Small family-run B&B, close Edinburgh University. Personal attention, relaxed, informal atmosphere. **Open:** All year (not Xmas) **0131 667 7691** Mrs Mitchell **Fax: 0131 466 1691** *hopetoun@aol.com* www.hopetoun.com **D:** Fr £20.00–£40.00 **S:** Fr £25.00–£40.00 **Beds:** 1F 1D 1T **Baths:** 1 En 1 Pr 1 Sh (6) (2) cc

The International, *37 Mayfield Gardens, Edinburgh, EH9 2BX.* Attractive stone-built Victorian house, 1.5m south of Princes Street. Magnificent views. **Open:** All year **0131 667 2511** Mrs Niven **Fax: 0131 667 1112** *intergh@easynet.co.uk* www.accommodation-edinburgh.com **D:** Fr £25.00–£45.00 **S:** Fr £30.00–£50.00 **Beds:** 2F 2D 2T 3S **Baths:** 9 Pr

Tania Guest House, *19 Minto Street, Edinburgh, EH9 1RQ.* Comfortable Georgian guest house, very good bus route, private parking available. Italian spoken. **Open:** All year (not Xmas) **0131 667 4144** Mrs Roscilli **D:** Fr £18.00–£25.00 **S:** Fr £20.00–£27.50 **Beds:** 3F 1D 1T 1S **Baths:** 2 En

Crion Guest House, *33 Minto Street, Edinburgh, EH9 2BT.* Family run guest house near city centre. Most tourist attractions. **Open:** All year **0131 667 2708 Fax: 0131 662 1946** *w.cheape@gilmourhouse.freeserve.co.uk* www.edinburghbedbreakfast.com **D:** Fr £20.00–£27.00 **S:** Fr £20.00–£27.00 **Beds:** 1D 2T 1S **Baths:** 1 Sh (2) cc

Sonas, *3 East Mayfield, Edinburgh, EH9 1SD.* Recommended by 'Which?' guide. Warm, friendly, comfortable, delicious breakfasts - Perfect! **Open:** All year (not Xmas) **0131 667 2781** Mrs Robins **Fax: 0131 667 0454** *sonas.guesthouse@virgin.net* **D:** Fr £19.00–£35.00 **S:** Fr £25.00–£35.00 **Beds:** 1F 2T 4D 1S **Baths:** 8 En

Ben Doran Guest House, *11 Mayfield Gardens, Edinburgh, EH9 2AX.* Beautiful refurbished Georgian house. Elegant, cosy, comfortable, central. Family run hotel. **Open:** All year **0131 667 8488** Dr Labaki **Fax: 0131 667 0076** *info@bendoran.com* www.bendoran.com **D:** Fr £25.00–£60.00 **S:** Fr £25.00–£60.00 **Beds:** 4F 3D 2T 1S **Baths:** 6 En 4 Sh (17) cc

Sylvern Guest House, *22 West Mayfield, Edinburgh, EH9 1TQ.* Detached Victorian villa one mile from Edinburgh City Centre, near Commonwealth Pool Festival Theatre, Edinburgh Castle, Royal Mile and University, good bus route, free private parking. TV in all rooms, full cooked breakfast. **Open:** All year **0131 667 1241 (also fax)** Mr & Mrs Livornese *sylvernguesthouse@amserve.net* **D:** Fr £17.00–£24.00 **S:** Fr £24.00–£32.00 **Beds:** 2F 2T 2D **Baths:** 4 En 2 Sh (8)

Lorne Villa Guest House, *9 East Mayfield, Edinburgh, EH9 1SD.* Festival city residence, serving fine Scottish cuisine with Scottish hospitality. **Open:** All year **0131 667 7159 (also fax)** Mr McCulloch *lornevilla@cableinet.co.uk* **D:** Fr £18.00–£32.00 **S:** Fr £18.00–£32.00 **Beds:** 1F 2D 3T 1S **Baths:** 3 En 1 Pr 3 Sh (6)

Parklands Guest House, *20 Mayfield Gardens, Edinburgh, EH9 2BZ.* Comfortable well maintained Victorian guest house near city centre. **Open:** All year **0131 667 7184** Mr Drummond **Fax: 0131 667 2011** *parklands_guesthouse@yahoo.com* **D:** Fr £22.00–£30.00 **S:** Fr £25.00–£40.00 **Beds:** 1F 2D 2T 1S **Baths:** 5 En 1 Pr (1)

EDINBURGH Merchiston

NT2472

Villa Nina Guest House, *39 Leamington Terrace, Edinburgh, EH10 4JS.* **Open:** All year (not Xmas/New Year) **0131 229 2644 (also fax)** Mr Cecco *villanina@amserve.net* **D:** Fr £18.00–£24.00 **Beds:** 1F 2D 2T **Baths:** 2 Sh
Good value Bed and Breakfast accommodation is offered in this comfortable Victorian town house in the centre of Edinburgh. Close to the Castle, Kings theatre, International Conference Centre and major attractions, 10 min walk to Princes Street.

Nova Hotel, *5 Bruntsfield Crescent, Edinburgh, EH10 4EZ.* Victorian, city centre, quiet area, free parking, fully licensed, all rooms ensuite. Lovely views. **Open:** All year **0131 447 6437 & 0131 447 7349** Mr McBride **Fax: 0131 452 8126 (preferred for bookings)** *jamie@scotland-hotels.demon.co.uk* www.novahotel.com **D:** Fr £25.00–£55.00 **S:** Fr £35.00–£70.00 **Beds:** 6F 2D 2T 2S **Baths:** 13 En 1 cc

Granville Guest House, *13 Granville Terrace, Edinburgh, EH10 4PQ.* Family-run guest house situated centrally in Edinburgh, all local amenities nearby. **Open:** All year **0131 229 1676 & 0131 229 4633** Mr Oussallem **Fax: 0131 229 4633** *granvilleguesthouse@tinyworld.co.uk* **D:** Fr £18.00–£30.00 **S:** Fr £18.00–£30.00 **Beds:** 3F 2T 3D 1S **Baths:** 6 En 1 Sh (2) cc

EDINBURGH Morningside

NT2471 Montpelier Bar, King's Bar

Sandeman House, *33 Colinton Road, Edinburgh, EH10 5DR.* Victorian family house centrally situated. Wonderful breakfasts. Street parking. **Open:** All year **0131 447 8080 (also fax)** Ms Sandeman *joycesandeman@freezone.co.uk* www.freeserve.co.uk/sandemanhouse **D:** Fr £30.00–£36.00 **S:** Fr £38.00–£45.00 **Beds:** 1T 1D 1S **Baths:** 3 En

EDINBURGH Newington

NT2671

Rowan Guest House, *13 Glenorchy Terrace, Edinburgh, EH9 2DQ.* **Open:** All year (not Xmas) **Grades:** STB 3 Star, AA 3 Diamond **0131 667 2463 (also fax)** Mr & Mrs Vidler *angela@rowan-house.co.uk* www.rowan-house.co.uk **D:** Fr £23.00–£35.00 **S:** Fr £24.00–£32.00 **Beds:** 1F 3D 2T 3S **Baths:** 3 En 3 Sh (2) (2) cc
Comfortable Victorian home in quiet, leafy, conservation area, a mile and a half from city centre, castle and Royal Mile. Delicious breakfast, including porridge and freshly-baked scones. A warm welcome and personal service from Alan and Angela. Free parking.

BEDROOMS
D = Double
T = Twin
S = Single
F = Family

BATHROOMS
En = Ensuite
Pr = Private
Sh = Shared

Kildonan Lodge Hotel, *27 Craigmillar Park, Edinburgh, EH16 5PE.* **Open:** All year (not Xmas) **0131 667 2793 Fax: 0131 667 9777** *info@kildonanlodgehotel.co.uk* www.kildonanlodgehotel.co.uk **D:** Fr £39.00–£65.00 **S:** Fr £55.00–£75.00 **Beds:** 2F 2T 6D 2S **Baths:** 12 En (16) cc
A warm welcome awaits you at Kildonan Lodge, situated close to city centre. Elegant Victorian lounge with open fire. Dine in our award-winning 'Potters' restaurant. Individually designed non-smoking bedrooms (some with four-posters & spa baths). Private car park.

Ben Craig House, *3 Craigmillar Park, Edinburgh, EH16 5PG.* Attractive Victorian villa. Conservatory breakfast room overlooking beautiful garden. Personally managed by owners. **Open:** All year (not Xmas)
0131 667 2593 Fax: 0131 667 1109 *bencraighouse@dial.pipex.com* www.bencraighouse.co.uk **D:** Fr £25.00–£40.00 **S:** Fr £30.00–£60.00 **Beds:** 1F 1T 3D **Baths:** 5 En cc

Kingsley Guest House, *30 Craigmillar Park, Edinburgh, EH16 5PS.* Friendly family run house on excellent bus route for sightseeing. **Open:** All year
0131 667 8439 (also fax) *accom.kingsley@virgin.net* **D:** Fr £20.00–£35.00 **S:** Fr £25.00–£40.00 **Beds:** 1F 2T 3D **Baths:** 3 En 2 Pr (3) (5)

EDINBURGH Northfield

NT2973

Brae Guest House, *119 Willowbrae Road, Edinburgh, EH8 7HN.* Friendly guest house. Meadowbank - Holyrood Palace, on main bus route. **Open:** All year
0131 661 0170 Mrs Walker *braeguesthouse@tinyworld.co.uk* **D:** Fr £18.00–£40.00 **S:** Fr £18.00–£40.00 **Beds:** 1F 1T 1D 1S **Baths:** 3 En 1 Pr

EDINBURGH Pilrig

NT2675

Glenburn Guest House, *22 Pilrig Street, Edinburgh, EH6 5AJ.* Clean, welcoming, budget accommodation. 15 minutes from the city centre. **Open:** All year (not Xmas)
0131 554 9818 (also fax) Mrs McVeigh *glenburn@lineone.net* www.candytape.com/glenburn **D:** Fr £18.00–£30.00 **S:** Fr £23.00–£30.00 **Beds:** 4F 5D 4T 2S **Baths:** 2 En 6 Sh cc

Sunnyside Guest House, *13 Pilrig Street, Edinburgh, EH6 5AN.* Beautiful Georgian family-run guest house. An easy atmosphere and ample breakfast. **Open:** All year (not Xmas)
0131 553 2084 Mr Wheelaghan *sunnyside.guesthouse@talk21.com* **D:** Fr £17.00–£30.00 **S:** Fr £17.00–£30.00 **Beds:** 2F 4D 2T 1S **Baths:** 4 En 1 Pr 1 Sh

EDINBURGH Portobello

NT3074

Hopebank, *33 Hope Lane North, Portobello, Edinburgh, EH15 2PZ.* **Open:** All year
0131 657 1149 Mrs Williamson **D:** Fr £22.00–£24.00 **S:** Fr £22.00–£24.00 **Beds:** 2D 1T **Baths:** 2 Pr 1 Sh
Victorian terraced villa, two minutes sea - beautiful promenade, 20 minutes city centre. Good food, Scottish hospitality, inexpensive bus service to centre. Non smoking, showers ensuite, TV in all rooms. Many golf courses nearby, good touring centre.

EDINBURGH Prestonfield

NT2771

Clashaidy, *21 Kilmaurs Road, Edinburgh, EH16 5DA.* Family-run B&B in quiet residential area. One mile from Princes Street. **Open:** All year
0131 667 2626 Fax: 0131 622 0942 *clashaidy@lineone.net* **D:** Fr £20.00–£25.00 **S:** Fr £30.00–£50.00 **Beds:** 1F 1T 1D (12) cc

Gifford House, *103 Dalkeith Road, Edinburgh, EH16 5AJ.* Elegant Victorian house. Superior rooms with Edinburgh's attractions within easy reach. **Open:** All year
0131 667 4688 (also fax) Mrs Dow *giffordhotel@btinternet.com* www.smoothhound.co.uk/hotels/gifford.html **D:** Fr £20.00–£38.00 **S:** Fr £23.00–£50.00 **Beds:** 2F 2D 2T 1S **Baths:** 7 En cc

Cameron Toll Guest House, *299 Dalkeith Road, Edinburgh, EH16 5JX.* Eco-friendly family guest house on A7, 10 minutes from city centre. **Open:** All year
0131 667 2950 M Deans **Fax: 0131 662 1987** *stil@edinburghguesthouse.co.uk* www.edinburghguesthouse.co.uk **D:** Fr £20.00–£35.00 **S:** Fr £25.00–£37.00 **Beds:** 3F 2T 3D 3S **Baths:** 10 En 1 Pr (4) cc

EDINBURGH Slateford

NT2271

13 Moat Street, *Edinburgh, EH14 1PE.* Comfortable accommodation 2 miles city centre. Unrestricted street parking. **Open:** Mar to Oct
0131 443 8266 David Hume **D:** Fr £18.00–£22.00 **S:** Fr £18.00–£25.00 **Beds:** 1D 1T

A'Bide'an'Abode Guest House, *18 Moat Place, Edinburgh, EH14 1PP.* Warm welcome at very well-appointed Victorian family home. **Open:** All year
0131 443 5668 (also fax) *bellshouse@also.co.uk* www.edinburghguesthouse.org.uk **D:** Fr £20.00–£35.00 **S:** Fr £30.00–£60.00 **Beds:** 2F 2T 2D **Baths:** 3 En 1 Pr 1 Sh cc

EDINBURGH Trinity

NT2476

Park View Villa Guest House, *254 Ferry Road, Edinburgh, EH5 3AN.* Charming Edwardian house, well-located for city breaks. Superb views. **Open:** All year **Grades:** STB 3 Star
0131 552 3456 *enquiries@parkviewvilla.com* www.parkviewvilla.com **D:** Fr £23.00–£40.00 **S:** Fr £25.00–£70.00 **Beds:** 8F 4T 4D **Baths:** 14 En 2 Pr cc

Fala

NT4361 *Juniper Lea Hotel*

Fala Hall Farm, *Fala, Pathhead, Midlothian, EH37 5SZ.* Secluded C16th farmhouse. 16m South East of Edinburgh. 0.5m from Fala (A 68). **Open:** All year (not Xmas/New Year)
01875 833249 (also fax) Lothian *H.Lothian@farming.co.uk* www.members.farmline.com/falahall_farm_BandB **D:** Fr £17.00–£22.00 **S:** Fr £22.00–£25.00 **Beds:** 1F 1T 1D **Baths:** 1 Sh

B&B owners may vary rates – be sure to check when booking

Falkirk

NS8680

Parkmore Guest House, *3 Park Street, Falkirk, FK1 1RE.* Situated in town centre, close to all local attractions. **Open:** All year **01324 633437** Colin & Diane Woodcock *parkmore@blueyonder.co.uk* **D:** Fr £20.00 **S:** Fr £20.00–£25.00 **Beds:** 1F 1T 2D 1S **Baths:** 2 En 1 Sh (2)

Benaiah, *11 Culmore Place, Falkirk, FK1 2RP.* Perfectly situated for exploring central Scotland. Near canal and Falkirk Wheel. **Open:** All year **Grades:** STB 2 Star **01324 621223 & 07718 300530 (M)** D Richardson *benaiah@onetel.net.uk* **D:** Fr £16.00–£19.00 **S:** Fr £22.00–£25.00 **Beds:** 2F 1T **Baths:** 1 Sh

Ashbank, *Main Street, Falkirk, FK2 9UQ.* Victorian cottage. Panoramic views. Near Grangemouth, M9 Motorway and trains. **Open:** All year **01770 860 202** Mr & Mrs Ward **Fax: 01770 860 570** *ashbank@guest-house.freeserve.co.uk* **D:** Fr £22.00–£25.00 **S:** Fr £25.00–£35.00 **Beds:** 2T 1D 1S **Baths:** 4 En

Gorebridge

NT3460

Carrington Barns, *Gorebridge, EH23 4LN.* **Open:** All year **01875 830200** Mrs Mann www.btinternet.com/~carringtonbarns **D:** Fr £22.00–£25.00 **S:** Fr £25.00–£30.00 **Beds:** 2T 1D **Baths:** 1 En 1 Pr 1 Sh (10) A beautiful farmhouse on a family-run, arable farm, with large gardens set in 300 acres of peaceful countryside. Only 10 miles from centre of Edinburgh. Generous breakfasts and a relaxed atmosphere. Half mile from National Cycle Route 1.

Ivory House, *14 Vogrie Road, Gorebridge, EH23 4HH.* Secluded Victorian house, 10 miles Edinburgh. Ideal base Borders/Coast. **Open:** All year **01875 820755** Mrs Maton *ivory.house@talk21.com* **D:** Fr £25.00–£35.00 **S:** Fr £27.50–£40.00 **Beds:** 1F 1D 1T **Baths:** 3 En (6) **cc**

Haddington

NT5173

Eaglescairnie Mains, *Haddington, E Lothian, EH41 4HN.* Superb farmhouse with wonderful views over conservation award-winning farm. **Open:** All year (not Xmas) **Grades:** STB 4 Star **01620 810491 (also fax)** Mrs Williams *williams.eagles@btinternet.com* **D:** Fr £25.00–£30.00 **S:** Fr £25.00–£35.00 **Beds:** 1D 1T 2S **Baths:** 2 En 1 Sh (6) **cc**

Inveresk

NT3572

Delta House, *16 Carberry Road, Inveresk, Musselburgh, E Lothian, EH21 7TN.* A beautiful Victorian house, 7 miles east of central Edinburgh overlooking fields. **Open:** All year (not Xmas) **0131 665 2107 (also fax)** **D:** Fr £20.00–£27.50 **S:** Fr £30.00–£50.00 **Beds:** 1F 3D **Baths:** 2 En 1 Pr (5) (3)

Lasswade

NT3266 *The Howgate, The Steading*

Gorton House, *Lasswade, Midlothian, EH18 1EH.* Historic house overlooking Roslin Glen including tennis court. Edinburgh centre only 8 miles away. **Open:** All year **0131 440 4332** Mr & Mrs Young **Fax: 0131 440 1779** *jquintinyoung@hotmail.com* www.gorton.plus.com **D:** Fr £20.00–£25.00 **S:** Fr £20.00–£25.00 **Beds:** 1F 2T **Baths:** 3 En (6)

Linlithgow

NS9977

Belsyde Farm, *Lanark Road, Linlithgow, W Lothian, EH49 6QE.* **Open:** Jan to Dec **Grades:** STB 3 Star, AA 3 Diamond **01506 842098 (also fax)** Mrs Hay *belsyde.guesthouse@vigin.net* www.belsydehouse.co.uk **D:** Fr £20.00–£25.00 **S:** Fr £20.00–£25.00 **Beds:** 1F 1D 2S **Baths:** 1 En 2 Sh (10) **cc** An C18th farmhouse in large, secluded gardens with panoramic views over the Forth estuary. Golfing & fishing available locally. All bedrooms have washbasin, tea/coffee making facilities, colour TV, central heating. Located close to M8, M9 & M90 & to Edinburgh Airport.

Thornton, *Edinburgh Road, Linlithgow, EH49 6AA.* **Open:** Feb to Nov **Grades:** STB 4 Star, AA 4 Diamond **01506 844 693** Mrs Inglis **Fax: 01506 844 876** *inglisthornton@aol.com* www.thornton-scotland.co.uk **D:** Fr £25.00–£30.00 **S:** Fr £28.00–£35.00 **Beds:** 1T 1D **Baths:** 2 En (12) (4) **cc** Victorian house near Union Canal, five minutes from station, town centre and Linlithgow Palace (Birthplace of Mary Queen of Scots). Easy road/rail access to Edinburgh, Stirling, Glasgow, Falkirk Wheel. Large garden. Winner AA 'Best Breakfast of the Year' Scotland.

Woodcockdale Farm, *Lanark Road, Linlithgow, W Lothian, EH49 6QE.* Look no further. Easy access to airport, Edinburgh, Stirling. Phone now. **Open:** All year **01506 842088 (also fax)** Mrs Erskine *arnhouse@hotmail.com* www.arnhouse.co.uk **D:** Fr £18.00–£25.00 **S:** Fr £18.00–£25.00 **Beds:** 3F 2D 1T 1S **Baths:** 4 En 1 Pr 2 Sh

Loanhead

NT2765

Inveravon House Hotel, *9 Inveravon Road, Loanhead, Midlothian, EH20 9EF.* Large Victorian house. **Open:** All year **0131 440 0124** Mr Potter **D:** Fr £20.00–£25.00 **S:** Fr £25.00 **Beds:** 5F 5D 1T 3S **Baths:** 13 En **cc**

Aaron Glen, *7 Nivensknowe Road, Loanhead, Edinburgh, EH20 9AU.* Hotel quality accommodation at B&B prices. **Open:** All year **0131 440 1293** Mrs Davidson **Fax: 0131 440 2155** *aaronglen1@aol.com* www.members.edinburgh.org/aaron **D:** Fr £20.00–£30.00 **S:** Fr £25.00–£60.00 **Beds:** 1F 3D 1T **Baths:** 5 En (8) 3 **cc**

Longniddry

NT4476

13 Glassel Park Road, *Longniddry, EH32 0NY.* 20 minutes by train to Edinburgh. Easy access to golf courses. **Open:** Easter to Sept **01875 852333** Mrs Morrison **D:** Fr £18.00–£20.00 **S:** Fr £25.00 **Beds:** 1D 1T **Baths:** 2 Pr (8) (2)

Please respect a B&B's wishes regarding children, animals and smoking

Musselburgh

NT3573

18 Woodside Gardens, *Musselburgh, Midlothian, EH21 7LJ.* Quiet bungalow, easy access Edinburgh, seaside, countryside and golf parking. **Open:** All year
Grades: STB 2 Star
0131 665 3170 & 0131 665 3344 Mrs Aitken
D: Fr £17.00–£20.00 **S:** Fr £17.00–£20.00
Beds: 1F 1D 1T **Baths:** 2 Sh (4)

Craigesk, *10 Albert Terrace, Musselburgh, Midlothian, EH21 7LR.* Terraced villa overlooking golf and racecourse. Bus/railway close by. **Open:** All year
Grades: STB 2 Star
0131 665 3344 & 0131 665 3170 Miss Mitchell
Fax: 0131 665 3344 *craigesk-b-b@talk21.com*
D: Fr £17.00–£19.00 **S:** Fr £18.00–£20.00
Beds: 2F 1D 1T 1S **Baths:** 2 Sh (4)

North Berwick

NT5585

Troon, *Dirleton Road, North Berwick, E Lothian, EH39 5DF.* Comfortable, spacious, pleasant bungalow outskirts seaside town, 35 minutes Edinburgh. **Open:** Apr to Oct
Grades: STB 3 Star
01620 893555 Mrs Dixon **D:** Fr £18.00–£25.00
Beds: 1D **Baths:** 1 En (1)

The Belhaven Hotel, *28 Westgate, North Berwick, E Lothian, EH39 4AH.* Overlooking golf course and sea; convenient for town centre and railway station. **Open:** Dec to Oct
01620 893009 M Free **D:** Fr £19.00–£26.00
S: Fr £20.00–£35.00 **Beds:** 2F 5T 2S **Baths:** 5 En 4 Sh (9)

Pathhead

NT3964

The Old Farm House, *47 Main Street, Pathhead, Midlothian, EH37 5PZ.* Comfortable B&B, 12 miles south of Edinburgh on the A68. **Open:** All year
01875 320100 Mr Reid **Fax: 01875 320501** *oldfarmhouse@tinyworld.co.uk* scotland2000.com/oldfarmhouse **D:** Fr £16.00–£18.00 **S:** Fr £20.00–£25.00 **Beds:** 1F 1T 1D **Baths:** 2 En 1 Pr (3) **cc**

Penicuik

NT2360

Loanstone House, *Loanstone, Penicuik, EH26 8PH.* A Victorian family house in peaceful country surroundings.
Open: Easter to Oct
01968 672449 Mrs Patch *the.patches@btinternet.com* **D:** Fr £17.50 **S:** Fr £20.00
Beds: 1D **Baths:** 1 Sh (2)

South Queensferry

NT1277

Priory Lodge, *8 The Loan, South Queensferry, EH30 9NS.* Beautiful guest house in a tranquil village, twenty minutes from Edinburgh. **Open:** All year (not Xmas)
Grades: STB 4 Star, AA 4 Diamond
0131 331 4345 (also fax) C C Lamb *calmyn@aol.com* www.queensferry.com **D:** Fr £27.00–£30.00 **S:** Fr £40.00–£56.00 **Beds:** 3F 1D 1T **Baths:** 5 En **cc**

Stoneyburn

NS9762

Eisenach, *1 Cannop Crescent, Stoneyburn, Bathgate, W Lothian, EH47 8EF.* Large detached countryside villa. **Open:** All year
01501 762659 Mrs Gray *cagray@eisenach.demon.co.uk* **D:** Fr £15.00 **S:** Fr £20.00
Beds: 1F 1D 1T 1S **Baths:** 1 Pr (3)

Uphall

NT0572

20 Houston Mains Holdings, *Uphall, Broxburn, EH52 6PA.* Charming guest house eleven miles from Edinburgh. Railway link nearby. **Open:** All year
01506 854044 Mr Fisher **Fax: 01506 855118** *michaelfisher@cmgh.freeserve.co.uk* www.coille-mhor.co.uk **D:** Fr £23.00–£25.00
S: Fr £35.00–£37.00 **Beds:** 1F 1T 4D **Baths:** 6 En **cc**

Winchburgh

NT0875

Turnlea, *123 Main Street, Winchburgh, Broxburn, EH52 6QP.* Central location. Edinburgh 12 miles, airport 6 miles and Linlithgow 6 miles. **Open:** All year (not Xmas/New Year) **Grades:** STB 3 Star
01506 890124 R W Redwood **Fax: 01506 891573** *roytumlea@hotmail.com* **D:** Fr £22.00–£25.00 **S:** Fr £25.00–£30.00 **Beds:** 1D 2T
Baths: 3 En (3) **cc**

Fife

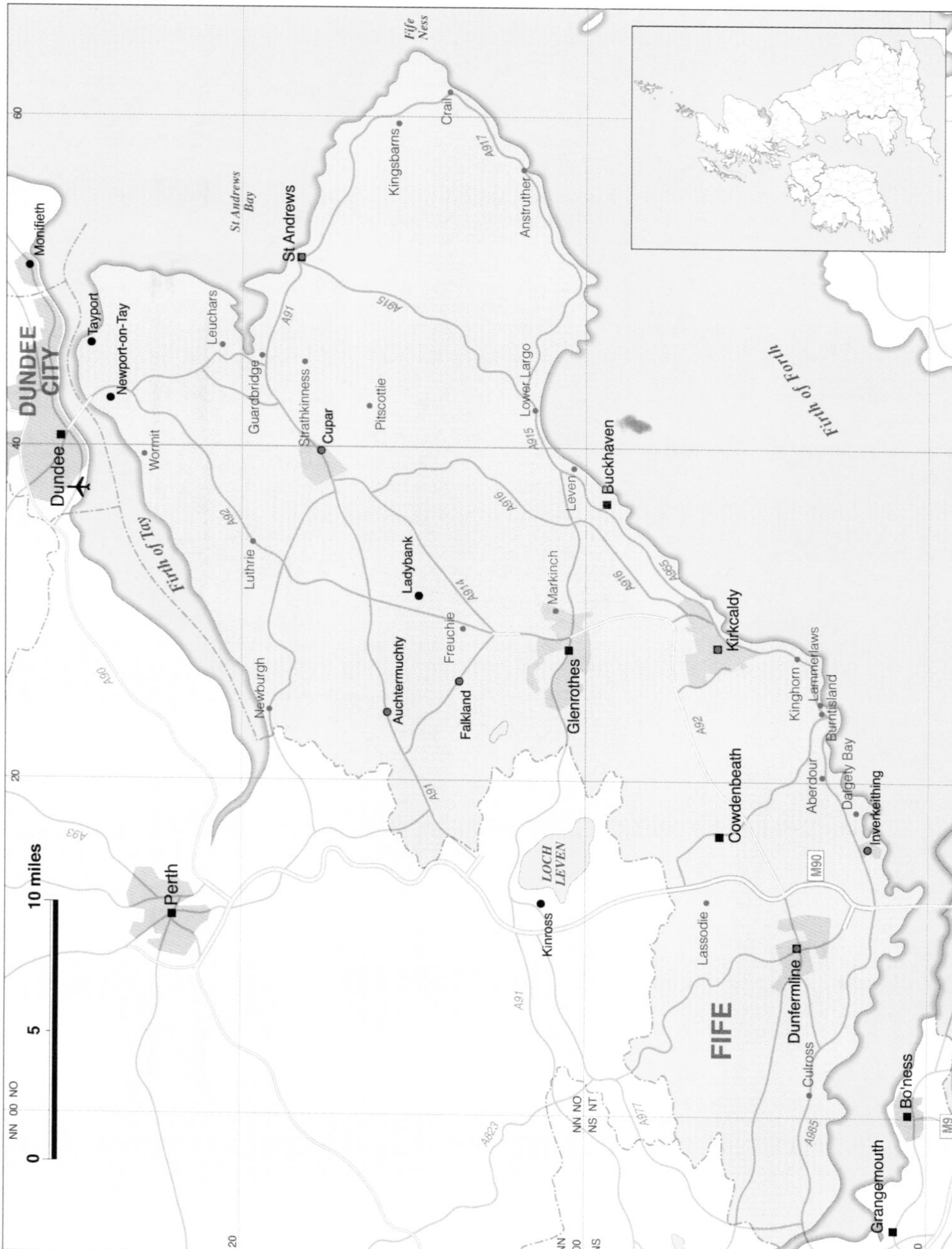

10 miles
5
0
NN 00 NO
NN NO
NS NT
NN
00
NS
20
40
60
80
Perth
Dundee
DUNDEE CITY
Monifieth
Tayport
Newport-on-Tay
Wormit
Firth of Tay
Leuchars
Guardbridge
St Andrews Bay
St Andrews
Strathkinness
Pitscottie
Cupar
Kingsbarns
Crail
Fife Ness
Anstruther
Lower Largo
Leven
Buckhaven
Luthrie
Ladybank
Markinch
Kirkcaldy
Newburgh
Auchtermuchty
Freuchie
Falkland
Glenrothes
Kinghorn
Lammerlaws
Burntisland
Aberdour
Dalgety Bay
Inverkeithing
Cowdenbeath
LOCH LEVEN
Kinross
Lassodie
Dunfermline
FIFE
Culross
Bo'ness
Grangemouth
Firth of Forth
A90
A93
A92
A91
A914
A915
A916
A917
A955
A977
A823
A985
M90
M9

Aberdour

NT1985

Aberdour Hotel, *38 High Street, Aberdour, Burntisland, Fife, KY3 0SW.* Friendly village inn, traditional cooking, real ales, Edinburgh half hour car/rail. **Open:** All year **Grades:** STB 3 Star, AA 2 Star
01383 860325 Mr Thomson **Fax: 01383 860808** *reception@aberdourhotel.co.uk* www.aberdourhotel.co.uk **D:** Fr £30.00–£32.50 **S:** Fr £45.00–£47.50 **Beds:** 4F 6D 6T **Baths:** 16 En (8) 1 **cc**

Anstruther

NO5603

Royal Hotel, *20 Rodger Street, Anstruther, Fife, KY10 3HU.* Family-run hotel, 100 yards seashore. Small harbour, sea trips to May Island Bird Sanctuary. **Open:** All year
01333 310581 Mr Cook **D:** Fr £18.00–£22.00 **S:** Fr £18.00–£25.00 **Beds:** 2F 4T 5D 2S **Baths:** 3 En

Mayview House, *Lands O'Barony, Ladywalk, Anstruther, Fife, KY10 3EX.* 10 miles from St. Andrews on the East coast, central to Fife. **Open:** All year
08707 407826 Mrs Paton *rpaton@totalise.co.uk* **D:** Fr £16.00–£24.00 **S:** Fr £16.00–£24.00 **Beds:** 1F 1D 1S **Baths:** 1 En 1 Pr 1 Sh (3)

The Sheiling, *32 Glenogil Gardens, Anstruther, Fife, KY10 3ET.* Pretty white bungalow, ground floor bedrooms overlook garden. Harbour 200m. **Open:** Easter to Sept
01333 310697 Mrs Ritchie **D:** Fr £16.00–£22.00 **S:** Fr £22.00 **Beds:** 2D **Baths:** 1 Sh 1 Pr (2)

Burntisland

NT2386 *Inchuen Hotel, Kingswood Hotel*

Gruinard, *148 Kinghorn Road, Burntisland, Fife, KY3 9JU.* Member of Scotland's best B&B. Coastal location. Spectacular views. **Open:** Mar to Nov
01592 873877 & 07798 738578 (M) Mrs Bowman *gruinard@dircon.co.uk* www.gruinardguesthouse.co.uk **D:** Fr £21.00–£26.00 **S:** Fr £30.00–£45.00 **Beds:** 1T 1D **Baths:** 2 En **cc**

148a Kinghorn Road, *Burntisland, Fife, KY3 9JU.* Panoramic views over River Forth, golf courses and water sports nearby. **Open:** All year
01592 872266 (also fax) Mrs Redford *c148m@aol.com* **D:** Fr £20.00–£25.00 **S:** Fr £25.00–£30.00 **Beds:** 1F 1D **Baths:** 2 En (2)

Crail

NO6107

The Honeypot Guesthouse & Tearoom, *6 High Street, Crail, Anstruther, Fife, KY10 3TD.* Centrally-located traditional guesthouse, offering comfortable B&B accommodation with evening meal. **Open:** All year
01333 450935 (also fax) *aileem@honeypotcrail.net* **D:** Fr £23.00 **S:** Fr £28.00 **Beds:** 1F 2D 2T **Baths:** 4 En 1 Pr (6)

Culross

NS9886

St Mungo's Cottage, *Low Causeway, Culross, Dunfermline, Fife, KY12 8HJ.* Historic village. Ideal for touring central Scotland. Edinburgh 40 min. Gardens. **Open:** All year (not Xmas/New Year) **Grades:** STB 3 Star
01383 882102 Mrs Jackson *martinpjackson@hotmail.com* www.milford.co.uk/scotland/accom/h-a-1763.html **D:** Fr £16.00–£22.00 **S:** Fr £20.00–£35.00 **Beds:** 1F 1T 1D **Baths:** 1 En 1 Sh (6) **cc**

Dundonald Arms Hotel, *Mid Causeway, Culross, Dunfermline, Fife, KY12 8HS.* C16th time warp riverside village; white cottages, cobbled causeways. **Open:** All year
01383 882443 Mrs Finlayson **Fax: 01383 881137 D:** Fr £20.00–£30.00 **S:** Fr £30.00–£40.00 **Beds:** 7F 3D 2T **Baths:** 7 En 7 Pr (30) **cc**

Cupar

NO3714 *Springfield Tavern, Pitscottie Inn, Meldrums Hotel, Ceres Inn*

Scotstarvit Farm, *Cupar, Fife, KY15 5PA.* Enviably located just off A916. Few minutes Cupar, 10 minutes St Andrews. **Open:** All year
01334 653591 (also fax) Mrs Chrisp **D:** Fr £16.00–£18.00 **S:** Fr £18.00–£24.00 **Beds:** 1T 1D **Baths:** 1 Pr 1 Sh (12)

Dalgety Bay

NT1583 *The Granary*

Wickers B and B, *5 Main Street West, Dalgety Bay, Dunfermline, KY11 9HJ.* Edinburgh 20 mins, rail halt 3 min walk. **Open:** All year
01383 415326 Ms Harper **D:** Fr £18.00–£25.00 **S:** Fr £5.00–£10.00 **Beds:** 1T 1D 1S **Baths:** 1 En 2 Sh (2)

Dunfermline

NT1087

Bowleys Farm, *Roscobie, Dunfermline, Fife, KY12 0SG.* Sample Scottish hospitality at its best! (30 minutes from Edinburgh). **Open:** Feb to Dec
01383 721056 Mrs Fotheringham *bowleysfarm@hotmail.com* **D:** Fr £18.00–£22.00 **S:** Fr £25.00 **Beds:** 2F **Baths:** 1 En 1 Sh (6)

Falkland

NO2507

The Hunting Lodge Hotel, *High Street, Falkland, Cupar, Fife, KY15 7BZ.* **Open:** All year
01337 857226 *timlees@huntinglodge.fsbusiness.co.uk* **D:** Fr £20.00–£30.00 **S:** Fr £25.00–£40.00 **Beds:** 2F 1T **Baths:** 1 En 1 Sh
Small family-run hotel, dating back to 1607, in the historic village of Falkland. The hotel is directly opposite Falkland Palace, the summer residence of the kings and queens of Scotland. Currently maintained by the National Trust for Scotland.

Templelands Farm, *Falkland, Cupar, Fife, KY15 7DE.* Panoramic views, National Trust properties nearby - abundance of golf courses. **Open:** Easter to Oct
01337 857383 Ms McGregor **D:** Fr £15.00 **S:** Fr £15.00–£18.00 **Beds:** 1F 1D 1S **Baths:** 2 Sh (3)

Freuchie

NO2806

Lomond Hills Hotel, *Parliament Square, Freuchie, Cupar, Fife, KY7 7EY.* Comfortable coaching inn, candlelit restaurant, bistro, comfortable lounges, leisure centre. **Open:** All year
01337 857329 (also fax) *lomondhillshotel@aol.com* **D:** Fr £30.00–£42.00 **S:** Fr £35.00–£50.00 **Beds:** 4F 11D 7T **Baths:** 24 En

Guardbridge

NO4519

Guardbridge Hotel, *Old St Andrews Road, Guardbridge, St Andrews, Fife, KY16 0UD.* C18th inn with railway memorabilia. **Open:** All year
01334 839337 Mrs Bayliss **Fax: 01334 839864 D:** Fr £23.00–£30.00 **S:** Fr £25.00–£30.00 **Beds:** 1D 1T 1S **Baths:** 1 Sh

Inverkeithing

NT1382 *The Granary*

The Roods, *16 Bannerman Avenue, Inverkeithing, Fife, KY11 1NG.* Award winning B&B set in quiet gardens close to coastal path. **Open:** All year
01383 415049 (also fax) Mrs Marley *bookings@theroods.com* www.theroods.com **D:** Fr £20.00–£25.00 **S:** Fr £20.00–£25.00 **Beds:** 1D 1T 1F **Baths:** 3 En cc

Kinghorn

NT2687

Craigo-Er, *45 Pettycur Road, Kinghorn, Fife, KY3 9RN.* Victorian house, panoramic sea views, direct regular Edinburgh rail links. **Open:** All year
01592 890527 Mrs Thomson **D:** Fr £19.00 **S:** Fr £19.00 **Beds:** 1D 2T **Baths:** 2 Sh (1)

Kingsbarns

NO5912

Kingsbarns Bed & Breakfast, *3 Main Street, Kingsbarns, St Andrews, Fife, KY16 8SL.* Warm, friendly, comfortable B&B in picturesque coastal village. Golf courses nearby. **Open:** Apr to Oct
01334 880234 Mrs Hay *farida@kingsbarns-bb.co.uk* www.kingsbarns-bb.co.uk **D:** Fr £22.00–£25.00 **S:** Fr £22.00–£28.00 **Beds:** 2D 1T **Baths:** 3 En (2)

Kirkcaldy

NT2791

Crawford Hall, *2 Kinghorn Road, Kirkcaldy, Fife, KY1 1SU.* **Open:** All year (not Xmas)
01592 262658 Mrs Crawford **D:** Fr £17.00–£19.00 **S:** Fr £17.00–£19.00 **Beds:** 1F 1T **Baths:** 1 Sh (4)
Large, rambling old C19th house, once local manse, set in lovely gardens. 2 minutes from beach, 10 minute walk to town centre, bus/railway stations. Comfortable rooms, hearty breakfast, handy for golfers, near St Andrews.

Cameron House, *44 Glebe Park, Kirkcaldy, Fife, KY1 1BL.* Friendly, welcome, good home-cooking, quiet, central location, mainline station. **Open:** All year (not Xmas)
01592 264531 Mrs Nicol **D:** Fr £16.00–£17.50 **S:** Fr £17.00–£20.00 **Beds:** 1F 1D **Baths:** 1 Sh (1)

Castleview, *17 Dysart Road, Kirkcaldy, Fife, KY1 2AY.* Situated on Fife coast near M90, within reach Edinburgh, Perth, Dundee. **Open:** All year (not Xmas)
01592 269275 Mrs Dick **D:** Fr £16.00–£17.00 **S:** Fr £17.00–£18.00 **Beds:** 1F 2T **Baths:** 1 Sh

North Hall Guest House, *143 Victoria Road, Kirkcaldy, Fife, KY1 1DQ.* Victorian manse with modern comforts. Two minutes from railway station. **Open:** All year (not Xmas/New Year)
01592 268864 Cairns *cairns@northall.freeserve.co.uk* www.smoothhound.co.uk/hotels/northall.html **D:** Fr £22.50–£26.00 **Beds:** 1T 2D **Baths:** 2 En 1 Pr (3)

Arboretum, *20 Southerton Road, Kirkcaldy, Fife, KY2 5NB.* Extended Bungalow overlooking large park close to all amenities. **Open:** All year
01592 643673 E Duncan **D:** Fr £19.00–£20.00 **S:** Fr £20.00–£22.00 **Beds:** 1T 1D **Baths:** 2 En (4)

Lammerlaws

NT2386

Inchcape Guest House, *1 South View, Lammerlaws, Burntisland, Fife, KY3 9BS.* 1 minute from beach. Centre view of river. **Open:** Apr to Oct
01592 873270 Mrs Sharp **D:** Fr £18.00 **S:** Fr £18.00

Lassodie

NT1292

Loch Fitty Cottage, *Lassodie, Dunfermline, Fife, KY12 0SP.* Enjoy the comfort of a family home, in rural setting. **Open:** All year
01383 831081 Mr Woolley *n.woolley@btinternet.com* www.lochfittybandb.btinternet.co.uk **D:** Fr £18.00–£20.00 **S:** Fr £18.00–£20.00 **Beds:** 1F 1D **Baths:** 1 En 1 Pr (4)

B&B owners may vary rates – be sure to check when booking

All details shown are as supplied by B&B owners in Autumn 2002

Leuchars

NO4521

Pitlethie Farm, *Leuchars, St Andrews, Fife, KY16 0DP.* Comfortable farmhouse base for golf and the St Andrews area. **Open:** All year
01334 838649 Mrs Black **Fax: 01334 839281** www.aboutscotland.com/fife/pitlethie.html **D:** Fr £25.00–£30.00 **S:** Fr £30.00–£35.00 **Beds:** 2D **Baths:** 1 Sh (10) cc

Pinewood Country House, *Tayport Road, St Michaels, Leuchars, St Andrews, Fife, KY16 0DU.* A quiet wooded area, ideal setting for short breaks or golfing holidays. **Open:** All year (not Xmas/New Year)
01334 839860 Mr Bedwell **Fax: 01334 839868** *accommodation@pinewoodhouse.com* www.pinewoodhouse.com **D:** Fr £22.00–£25.00 **S:** Fr £32.00–£44.00 **Beds:** 2T 3D **Baths:** 4 En 1 Pr cc

Leven

NO3800

Duniface Farm, *Windygates, Leven, Fife, KY8 5RH.* Charming C19th farmhouse - comfortable & welcoming, hearty breakfasts, ideal touring base. **Open:** All year
01333 350272 (also fax) Mrs Hamilton *audreymhamilton@tinyworld.co.uk* **D:** Fr £15.00–£17.00 **S:** Fr £15.00–£20.00 **Beds:** 1D 1F **Baths:** 1 Sh

Lower Largo

NO4102

Crusoe Hotel, *2 Main Street, Lower Largo, Leven, Fife, KY8 6BT.* Friendly family-run hotel. Harbour location, à la carte restaurant, bar meals. **Open:** All year
01333 320759 D & P Ferries **Fax: 01333 320865** *info@crusoe-hotel.co.uk* www.crusoehotel.co.uk. **D:** Fr £25.00–£45.00 **S:** Fr £45.00–£65.00 **Beds:** 2F 10T 2S **Baths:** 17 En cc

Luthrie

NO3319

Easter Kinsleith, *Luthrie, Cupar, Fife, KY15 4NR.* Gaplair is ideally situated for touring east and central Scotland. **Open:** Feb to Nov
01337 870363 Mr Rieu-Clarke *gapplair@compuserve.com* gapplairguesthouse.co.uk **D:** Fr £18.00–£20.00 **S:** Fr £18.00–£20.00 **Beds:** 1F 1D **Baths:** 2 En (6) (2) cc

Markinch

NO2901

Shythrum Farm, *Markinch, Glenrothes, Fife, KY7 6HB.* Peaceful farmhouse. Markinch 1 mile golfers haven, excellent touring base. **Open:** Mar to Oct
01592 758372 Mrs Craig **D:** Fr £18.00 **S:** Fr £18.00 **Beds:** 1F 1T **Baths:** 1 En 1 Pr (3)

Wester Markinch Cottage, *Balbirnie Estate, Markinch, Glenrothes, Fife, KY7 6JN.* Extended Victorian cottage, convenient for Edinburgh, Glasgow and St. Andrews. **Open:** All year (not Xmas/New Year)
01592 756719 & 07774 622497 (M) Ms Tjeransen **Fax: 01592 756719 D:** Fr £18.00–£25.00 **S:** Fr £16.00 **Beds:** 1D 2S 1T **Baths:** 1 En 1 Sh (4)

Newburgh

NO2318 *Abbey Inn, Baigwe Inn, Cree's Inn*

Ninewells Farm, *Woodriffe Road, Newburgh, Cupar, Fife, KY14 6EY.* Quiet and comfortable with magnificent views. Well-furnished. Warm welcome, excellent breakfast. **Open:** Apr to Oct
01337 840307 (also fax) B Baird *barbara@ninewellsfarm.co.uk* www.ninewells.co.uk **D:** Fr £19.00–£24.00 **S:** Fr £25.00–£34.00 **Beds:** 1F 1T 1D **Baths:** 1 En 2 Pr (14) (4)

Pitscottie

NO4113

Rockmount Cottage, *Dura Den Road, Pitscottie, Cupar, Fife, KY15 5TG.* Lovely C19th cottage tastefully modernised to a high standard just 7m from St. Andrews. **Open:** All year (not Xmas/New Year)
01334 828164 Mrs Reid *annmreid@rockmount1.freeserve.co.uk* **D:** Fr £18.00–£25.00 **S:** Fr £18.00–£25.00 **Beds:** 1F 1D 1S **Baths:** 1 Pr 2 Sh (3) 3

St Andrews

NO5116

Whitecroft Guest Lodges, *33 Strathkinness High Road, St Andrews, Fife, KY16 9UA.*
Open: All year
01334 474448 Mr & Mrs Horn *whitecroft@tesco.net* www.whitecroft-lodges.co.uk **D:** Fr £22.00–£28.00 **S:** Fr £30.00–£50.00 **Beds:** 3F 1T 1D **Baths:** 5 En (5) cc
Whitecroft is a converted 1890s farm croft set in 0.33 acre on Western edge of town. All rooms are ensuite with car parking and private entrances. Lovely views of Sidlaws and Eden Estuary, only 3 minutes by car to St Andrews.

The Paddock, *Sunnyside, Strathkinness, St Andrews, KY16 9XP.* **Open:** All year (not Xmas/New Year) **Grades:** STB 4 Star
01334 850888 Mrs Taylor **Fax: 01334 850870** *thepaddock@btinternet.com* www.thepadd.co.uk **D:** Fr £20.00–£26.00 **S:** Fr £25.00–£40.00 **Beds:** 1T 2D (8) cc
Quality ensuite accommodation in a modern residence with outstanding country views. Positioned in a secluded spot. Ample private parking. Guests may use the conservatory overlooking the gardens. St. Andrews 2 miles.

Edenside House, *Edenside, St Andrews, Fife, KY16 9SQ.* Pre-1775 farmhouse, 2.5 miles from St Andrews. Parking guaranteed. **Open:** All year
01334 838108 Douglas & Yvonne Reid **Fax: 01334 838493** *yvonne@edensidehouse.com* www.edensidehouse.com **D:** Fr £22.00–£32.00 **S:** Fr £30.00–£38.00 **Beds:** 1F 2D 5T **Baths:** 8 En (10) cc

Spinkstown Farmhouse, *St Andrews, Fife, KY16 8PN.* Superior accommodation in relaxing peaceful surroundings convenient to St Andrews. **Open:** All year (not Xmas)
01334 473475 (also fax) Mrs Duncan *anne@spinkstown.com* www.spinkstown.com **D:** Fr £23.00–£25.00 **S:** Fr £25.00–£30.00 **Beds:** 2D 1T **Baths:** 3 En (4) cc

Cairnsden B&B, *2 King Street, St Andrews, Fife, KY16 8JQ.* Comfortable family house, 7 mins town centre, early breakfasts for golfers. **Open:** All year (not Xmas)
01334 476326 Mrs Allan **Fax: 01334 840355 D:** Fr £16.00–£20.00 **S:** Fr £22.00–£25.00 **Beds:** 2D **Baths:** 1 Sh (1)

BEDROOMS
D = Double
T = Twin
S = Single
F = Family

Glenderran Guest House, *9 Murray Park, St Andrews, Fife, KY16 9AW.* 250 yards from the first tee of the Old Course and St Andrews Bay. Glenderran is a smartly presented Guest House with thoughtful amenities throughout. A warm welcome awaits you from your host Patrick Wood. **Open:** All year
01334 477951 Mr Wood **Fax: 01334 477908** *glenderran@telinco.com* www.glenderran.com **D:** Fr £30.00 **S:** Fr £30.00 **Beds:** 1T 2D 2S **Baths:** 3 En 2 Pr (12) cc

23 Kilrymont Road, *St Andrews, Fife, KY16 8DE.* Detached home, harbour area, East Sands, 10 mins famous golf course. **Open:** Apr to Dec
01334 477946 Mrs Kier *mkier@talk21.com* **D:** Fr £17.00–£19.00 **S:** Fr £17.00–£20.00 **Beds:** 1D 1S (7) (1)

Arden House, *2 Kilrymont Place, St Andrews, Fife, KY16 8DH.* Family run B&B. Convenient for golf, town centre, East Neuk. **Open:** All year (not Xmas/New Year)
01334 475478 Mrs Finlay **D:** Fr £20.00–£22.00 **S:** Fr £25.00–£27.00

Acorn BandB, *16 Priestden Road, St Andrews, Fife, KY16 8DJ.* Excellent accommodation, ideally placed for golfing, touring, walking or relaxing. **Open:** All year
01334 476009 (also fax) Mrs Cameron *acorn@homeofgolf.fsnet.co.uk* www.acorn.standrews.btinternet.co.uk **D:** Fr £20.00–£24.00 **Beds:** 1T 2D **Baths:** 3 En (4)

Coppercantie, *8 Lawhead Road West, St Andrews, Fife, KY16 9NE.* High standard of decor and breakfast, only minutes drive from centre. **Open:** All year (not Xmas)
01334 476544 Mrs Dobson *f.dobson@btinternet.com* www.coppercantie.co.uk **D:** Fr £20.00–£26.00 **S:** Fr £34.00–£40.00 **Beds:** 1F 1D 1T **Baths:** 1 En 2 Sh cc

Strathkinness

NO4616

Brig-A-Doon, *6 High Road, Strathkinness, St Andrews, Fife, KY16 9XY.* Brig-A-Doon was one time a Toll House. Panoramic views St Andrews Bay/Tay Estuary. **Open:** Easter to Oct
01334 850268 Mrs Watson **D:** Fr £20.00–£25.00 **S:** Fr £25.00 **Beds:** 1T 1D **Baths:** 1 En 1 Pr (5) (2)

Wormit

NO3925

Newton Farm, *Wormit, Newport-on-Tay, Fife, DD6 8RL.* Traditional farmhouse overlooking our own trout loch, fly fishing, quad biking. **Open:** Easter to Oct
01382 540125 K Crawford **Fax: 01382 542513** *ghcrawford@ukonline.co.uk* **D:** Fr £17.00 **Beds:** 1F 2T **Baths:** 1 Sh (8)

Glasgow & District

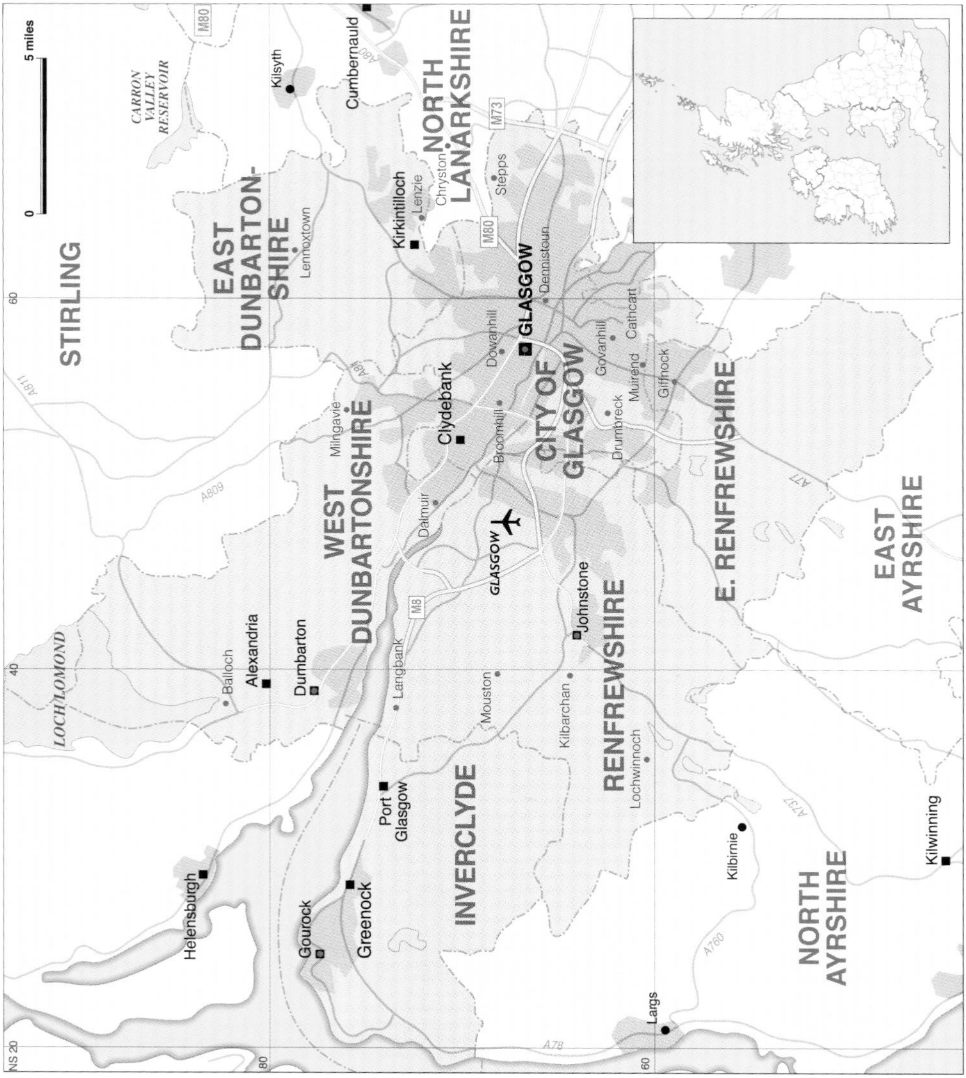

Balloch

NS3982

7 Carrochan Crescent, *Balloch, Alexandria, Dunbartonshire, G83 8PX.* A warm welcome awaits you, ideally situated for touring, etc. **Open:** Easter to Oct
Grades: STB 3 Star
01389 750078 Mrs Campbell **D:** Fr £16.00 **S:** Fr £18.00 **Beds:** 2D **Baths:** 1 Sh (2)

Glyndale, *6 McKenzie Drive, Lomond Road Estate, Balloch, Alexandria, Dunbartonshire, G83 8HL.* Easy access to Loch Lomond, Glasgow Airport, public transport. **Open:** All year (not Xmas)
01389 758238 Mrs Ross *glyndale_b_and_b@tinyworld.co.uk* **D:** Fr £16.50–£17.50 **S:** Fr £20.00 **Beds:** 1D 1T **Baths:** 1 Sh (2)

Heathpete, *24 Balloch Road, Balloch, Alexandria, Dunbartonshire, G83 8LE.* Superb hospitality offered in luxurious accommodation central to all amenities.
Open: All year
01389 752195 Mrs Hamill *sheathpete@aol.com*
D: Fr £12.00–£25.00 **S:** Fr £18.00–£25.00
Beds: 2F 2D **Baths:** 4 En (5)

Westville, *Riverside Lane, Balloch, Alexandria, Dunbartonshire, G83 8LF.* Bungalow overlooking River Leven at southern end of Loch Lomond. **Open:** All year (not Xmas) **Grades:** STB 2 Star
01389 752307 Mrs Oultram **D:** Fr £18.00–£20.00 **S:** Fr £19.00–£21.00 **Beds:** 1F 1D **Baths:** 1 Sh (5) (2)

Aird House, *1 Ben-Lomond Walk, Balloch, G83 8RJ.* A warm welcome awaits you, attention to detail throughout, idyllic setting. **Open:** All year (not Xmas/New Year) **Grades:** STB 3 Star
01389 754464 & 07814 730176 (M) Mrs MacDonald **D:** Fr £20.00–£25.00 **S:** Fr £25.00–£30.00 **Beds:** 1T 1D **Baths:** 1 En 1 Pr (2)

Argyll Lodge, *16 Luss Road, Balloch, Alexandria, Dunbartonshire, G83 0RH.* Clean comfortable friendly atmosphere, close to Loch Lomond National Park. **Open:** All year (not Xmas/New Year) **Grades:** STB 3 Star
01389 759020 Mrs McBride *argyll16@btopenworld.com* **D:** Fr £20.00 **S:** Fr £20.00–£30.00 **Beds:** 1F 1T 1D **Baths:** 2 En 1 Pr (4)

Braeburn Cottage, *West Auchencarroch Farm, Balloch, Alexandria, G83 9LU.* Peaceful location, magnificent views, set in beautiful gardens. Farmhouse breakfast served. **Open:** All year
01389 710998 Mrs Kay *braeburn@bigfoot.com* www.braeburn.telinco.co.uk **D:** Fr £16.00–£22.00 **S:** Fr £20.00–£30.00 **Beds:** 1F 1D **Baths:** 2 En (3)

Anchorage Guest House, *Balloch Road, Balloch, Alexandria, Dunbartonshire, G83 8SS.* Situated on the banks of Loch Lomond. Ideal base for touring, fishing, sailing & walking. **Open:** All year
01389 753336 Mr Bowman *anchorage_gh@hotmail.com* **D:** Fr £18.00–£25.00 **S:** Fr £20.00–£25.00 **Beds:** 1F 2D 4T **Baths:** 5 En 2 Sh (1) (6) 3

Dumbain Farm, *Balloch, Alexandria, Dunbartonshire, G83 8DS.* Converted byre on farm. Aga-cooked breakfast. Homemade raspberry jam. **Open:** All year **Grades:** STB 3 Star
01389 752263 Mrs Watson **D:** Fr £20.00–£25.00 **S:** Fr £25.00–£35.00 **Beds:** 1F 1T 1D **Baths:** 3 En (5)

Gowanlea Guest House, *Drymen Road, Balloch, Alexandria, Dunbartonshire, G83 8HS.* Award-winning family-run guest house B&B. Superior accommodation, excellent hospitality. Ideal touring base. **Open:** All year (not Xmas/New Year)
01389 752456 Mrs Campbell **Fax: 01389 710543** *gowanlea@aol.com* members.aol.com/gowanlea/gowanlea.htm **D:** Fr £19.00–£23.00 **S:** Fr £22.00–£30.00 **Beds:** 1T 3D **Baths:** 4 En (4) cc

Chryston

NS6870

Woodhead Farm, *Woodhead Road, Chryston, Glasgow, G69 9HY.* **Open:** All year (not Xmas/New Year)
0141 779 4913 (also fax) Mr Cook *ckrbrt2@aol.com* **D:** Fr £17.50–£20.00 **S:** Fr £20.00–£25.00 **Beds:** 1F 3T 2D **Baths:** 6 En (20)
Hikers, bikers, workers, all welcome in our fully-renovated farmhouse. We have bunkhouses & outbuilding accommodation. All are ensuite, our residents' lounge has pool table, Sky TV, & massive log fire for cosy nights in. Glasgow 5 mins, Loch Lomond 30 mins. Large gardens & surrounded by fields.

Dumbarton

NS4075 *Abbotsford Hotel*

Kilmalid House, *17 Glen Path, Dumbarton, G82 2QL.* Large manse overlooking castle and Clyde, 15 minutes from airport and Loch Lomond. **Open:** All year
01389 732030 Muirhead *kilmalid@ecossetel.com* **D:** Fr £18.00–£25.00 **S:** Fr £25.00–£40.00 **Beds:** 1F 1T 1D **Baths:** 1 Sh (8)

Giffnock

NS5658

Forres Guest House, *10 Forres Avenue, Giffnock, Glasgow, G46 6LJ.* Located in quiet south side suburbs. 5 minutes from city centre. **Open:** All year (not Xmas)
0141 638 5554 & 07710 864151 (M) Mrs Davies **Fax: 0141 571 9301** *june@10forres.freeserve.co.uk* www.junesdavies.com **D:** Fr £18.00–£20.00 **S:** Fr £18.00–£20.00 **Beds:** 2D (4)

Planning a longer stay? Always ask for any special rates

GLASGOW Broomhill

NS5467

Barrisdale Guest House, *115 Randolph Road, Glasgow, G11 7DS.* Delightful Victorian townhouse, perfectly situated for exploring Glasgow's many highlights. **Open:** All year
0141 339 7589 (also fax) Mr Phillips *barrisdale@btinternet.com* www.barrisdale-bnb.co.uk **D:** Fr £22.50–£30.00 **S:** Fr £30.00–£40.00 **Beds:** 1F 2T 1D **Baths:** 3 En 1 Pr

Lochgilvie House, *117 Randolph Road, Broomhill, Glasgow, G11 7DS.* Luxurious Victorian town house situated in Glasgow's prestigious West End, adjacent to rail station. **Open:** All year
0141 357 1593 Mrs Ogilvie **Fax: 0141 334 5828** *reservations@lochgilvie.demon.co.uk* www.lochgilvie.demon.co.uk **D:** Fr £25.00–£30.00 **S:** Fr £25.00–£35.00 **Beds:** 1F 2D 3T **Baths:** 4 En (10)

GLASGOW Cathcart

NS5860

24 Greenock Avenue, *Glasgow, G44 5TS.* Modern architect designed villa, 12 minutes from city centre. **Open:** Easter to Oct
0141 637 0608 Mrs Bruce **D:** Fr £20.00–£22.50 **S:** Fr £25.00 **Beds:** 2T 1D 1S **Baths:** 2 En 1 Pr 1 Sh

GLASGOW Central

NS5865

Kelvingrove Hotel, *944 Sauchiehall Street, Glasgow, G3 7TH.* Centrally located family-run hotel, set in Glasgow's fashionable West End. **Open:** All year (not Xmas)
0141 339 5011 & 0141 569 1121 Mr Wills **Fax: 0141 339 6566** *kelvingrove.hotel@business.ntl.com* www.kelvingrove-hotel.co.uk **D:** Fr £24.00–£29.00 **S:** Fr £33.00–£38.00 **Beds:** 8D 4T 7F **Baths:** 10 En (20) cc

Kirkland House, *42 St Vincent Crescent, Glasgow, G3 8NG.* City centre guest house with excellent rooms on beautiful Victorian Crescent in Finnieston. **Open:** All year
0141 248 3458 Mrs Divers **Fax: 0141 221 5174** *info@kirkland.net43.co.uk* www.kirkland.net43.co.uk **D:** Fr £27.00–£30.00 **S:** Fr £27.00–£30.00 **Beds:** 3D 2T 2S **Baths:** 6 En 2 Sh (1)

Hampton Court Hotel, *230 Renfrew Street, Glasgow, G3 6ST.* City centre location. Complimentary tea/coffee, full breakfast. Best prices guaranteed. family-run business. **Open:** All year **Grades:** STB 2 Star
0141 332 6623 Fax: 0141 332 5885 *reception@hamptoncourt.activehotels.com* www.hamptoncourt.activehotels.com **D:** Fr £20.00–£22.00 **S:** Fr £24.00–£32.00 **Beds:** 3F 5T 6D 4S **Baths:** 12 En 3 Sh cc

Adelaide's, *209 Bath Street, Glasgow, G2 4HZ.* Central location, close to all major attractions of revitalised city. **Open:** All year (not Xmas/New Year)
0141 248 4970 A R Meiklejohn **Fax: 0141 226 4247** *info@adelaides.freeserve.co.uk* www.adelaides.co.uk **D:** Fr £25.00–£28.00 **S:** Fr £30.00–£45.00 **Beds:** 2F 2T 2D 2S **Baths:** 6 En 2 Sh cc

GLASGOW Dalmuir

NS4970

13 Southview, *Dalmuir, Clydebank, Dunbartonshire, G81 3LA.* Semi-villa. Near Station/Glasgow Airport. Tourist Board Highly Commended. **Open:** All year
0141 952 7007 Mrs McCay **D:** Fr £15.00–£18.00 **S:** Fr £18.00–£20.00 **Beds:** 1T 1D 1S **Baths:** 1 En 1 Sh (1)

GLASGOW Dennistoun

NS6065

Seton Guest House, *6 Seton Terrace, Glasgow, G31 2HU.* Warm and friendly welcome assured. Five minutes from city centre. **Open:** All year (not Xmas)
0141 556 7654 Mr Passway **Fax: 0141 402 3655** *passway@seton.prestel.co.uk* www.vacations-scotland.co.uk/seton.html **D:** Fr £17.00–£18.00 **S:** Fr £24.00 **Beds:** 4F 2D 2T 1S **Baths:** 3 Sh

GLASGOW Dowanhill

NS5667

Belgrave Guest House, *2 Belgrave Terrace, Glasgow, G12 8JD.* Perfectly situated in the popular bustling West End of Glasgow. Within walking distance of many local attractions, pubs and restaurants. Underground station and city centre minutes away. Full Scottish breakfast. **Open:** All year
0141 337 1850 Fax: 0141 337 1741 *belgraveguesthse@hotmail.com* **D:** Fr £18.00–£25.00 **S:** Fr £20.00–£25.00 **Beds:** 2F 2T 3D 4S **Baths:** 2 En 9 Sh (8) cc

GLASGOW Drumbreck

NS5663

Glasgow Guest House, *56 Dumbreck Road, Glasgow, G41 5NP.* Turn-of-the-20th-Century red sandstone house, antique decoration, friendly welcome. **Open:** All year
0141 427 0129 Mr Bristow *brian.muir@ukonline.co.uk* **D:** Fr £20.00 **S:** Fr £25.00 **Beds:** 3D 3T 1S 1F **Baths:** 8 En (2) cc

GLASGOW Govanhill

NS5862

Dunkeld Hotel, *10-12 Queens Drive, Glasgow, G42 8BS.* Set in one of Glasgow's premier conservation streets overlooking Queen's Park. **Open:** All year
0141 424 0160 P Martin **Fax: 0141 423 4437** *dunkeldhot@aol.com* www.dunkeld-hotel.co.uk **D:** Fr £22.00–£29.95 **S:** Fr £30.00–£44.95 **Beds:** 4F 8T 11D 4S **Baths:** 21 En 6 Sh (10) cc

GLASGOW Muirend

NS5760

16 Bogton Avenue, *Muirend, Glasgow, G44 3JJ.* Quiet area, 12 mins city centre, restaurants/shops nearby. Parking available. **Open:** All year (not Xmas) **Grades:** STB 2 Star
0141 637 4402 (also fax) Mrs Paterson *amp@bogton.freeserve.co.uk* **D:** Fr £20.00 **S:** Fr £22.00 **Beds:** 1D 1S **Baths:** 2 Sh (2)

Johnstone

NS4362 *Lynnhurst Hotel*

Northview Guest House, *11 North Road, Johnstone, PA5 8NE.* Situated near to Glasgow airport. **Open:** All year
01505 336690 *mail@northview.fsbusiness.co.uk* www.northview.fsbusiness.co.uk **D:** Fr £20.00–£25.00 **S:** Fr £20.00–£30.00 **Beds:** 1F 1T 1D 2S **Baths:** 5 En (5) cc

Kilbarchan

NS4063

Gladstone Farmhouse, *Burntshields Road, Kilbarchan, Johnstone, Renfrewshire, PA10 2PB.* Quiet countryside, 10 minutes Glasgow airport on direct route. **Open:** All year
01505 702579 (also fax) Mrs Douglas **D:** Fr £18.00 **S:** Fr £20.00 **Beds:** 1F 1D 1T **Baths:** 1 Sh (6)

Planning a longer stay? Always ask for any special rates

BATHROOMS
En = Ensuite
Pr = Private
Sh = Shared

Langbank

NS3872

The Croft, *Houston Road, Langbank, Port Glasgow, PA14 6XT.* Overlooking River Clyde, unique plantsperson's garden. 10 minutes Glasgow Airport. **Open:** All year **Grades:** STB 3 Star
01475 540079 *info@croft-by-the-clyde.co.uk* www.croft-by-the-clyde.co.uk **D:** Fr £25.00–£30.00 **S:** Fr £30.00–£35.00 **Beds:** 1F 1T 1D **Baths:** 3 En (3)

Lennoxtown

NS6277

Eilean, *2 Whitefield Lodge, Service Street, Lennoxtown, Glasgow, G66 7JW.* **Open:** All year **Grades:** STB 4 Star
01360 312123 (also fax) Mr & Mrs White *ian.white@eilean.freeserve.co.uk* www.scotlandsbestbandbs.co.uk/eilean.html **D:** Fr £25.00 **S:** Fr £30.00 **Beds:** 1T 2D **Baths:** 3 En (3) cc
In an idyllic situation below the Campsie Hills, 'Eilean' is conveniently placed in central Scotland for a tranquil country holiday, yet within easy reach of Glasgow, Edinburgh, Stirling, Loch Lomond & The Trossachs. Enjoy a warm welcome & good Scottish hospitality.

Lenzie

NS6572

16 Laurel Avenue, *Lenzie, Glasgow, G66 4RU.* Detached bungalow. Ideally situated for exploring central Scotland, Glasgow and Edinburgh. **Open:** All year
0141 776 1634 D Martyn **Fax: 0141 578 6418** *davidmartyn@ntlworld.com* **D:** Fr £18.00 **S:** Fr £24.00 **Beds:** 1T 1D **Baths:** 1 En 1 Pr (2)

Lochwinnoch

NS3559

Garnock Lodge, *Lochwinnoch, Renfrewshire, PA12 4JT.* Warm welcome 10 miles to Glasgow Airport. Private parking. **Open:** All year

01505 503680 (also fax) Mr & Mrs McMeechan *enquiries@garnocklodge.co.uk* **D:** Fr £19.00–£22.00 **S:** Fr £25.00–£30.00 **Beds:** 1D 2T 1S **Baths:** 2 En 1 Sh (4) **cc**

Milngavie

NS5574

13 Craigdhu Avenue, *Milngavie, Glasgow, G62 6DX.* Very comfortable family house where a warm welcome is assured.

Open: Mar to Oct

0141 956 3439 Mrs Ogilvie **D:** Fr £18.00 **S:** Fr £20.00–£25.00 **Beds:** 1F 1T (4)

BATHROOMS

En = Ensuite

Pr = Private

Sh = Shared

Stepps

NS6668

Avenue End B&B, *21 West Avenue, Stepps, Glasgow, G33 6ES.* Self-built family home situated down quiet tree-lined lane, on main route to Stirling.

Open: All year

0141 779 1990 Mrs Wells **Fax: 0141 779 1990 & 0141 779 1951** *avenueend@aol.com* **D:** Fr £22.00–£23.00 **S:** Fr £25.00–£30.00 **Beds:** 1F 1D 1S **Baths:** 2 En 1 Pr (2)

Highland

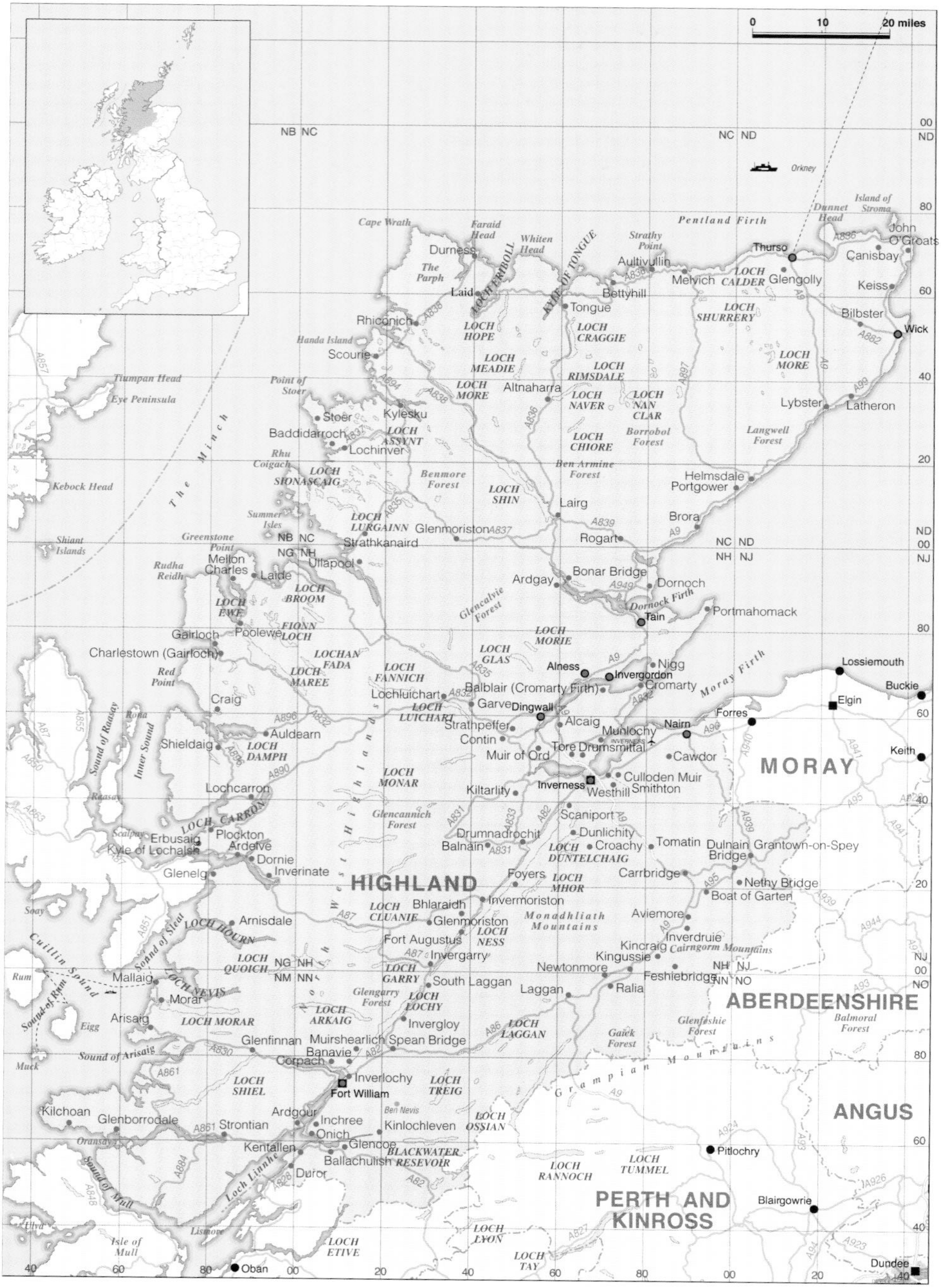

0
10
20 miles
Orkney
Pentland Firth
Cape Wrath
Faraid Head
Whiten Head
Strathy Point
Dunnet Head
Island of Stroma
John O'Groats
Thurso
Canisbay
Durness
The Parph
Aultivullin
Melvich
Glengolly
Keiss
Laid
LOCH ERIBOLL
KYLE OF TONGUE
Bettyhill
LOCH CALDER
Tongue
LOCH SHURRERY
Bilbster
Wick
Rhiconich
LOCH HOPE
LOCH CRAGGIE
Handa Island
Scourie
LOCH MEADIE
LOCH RIMSDALE
LOCH MORE
Tiumpan Head
Eye Peninsula
Point of Stoer
LOCH MORE
Altnaharra
LOCH NAVER
LOCH NAN CLAR
Lybster
Latheron
Stoer
Kylesku
Baddidarroch
LOCH ASSYNT
LOCH CHIORE
Borrobol Forest
Langwell Forest
Lochinver
The Minch
Rhu Coigach
LOCH SIONASCAIG
Benmore Forest
Ben Armine Forest
Kebock Head
LOCH SHIN
Helmsdale
Portgower
Lairg
Brora
Summer Isles
LOCH LURGAINN
Glenmoriston
Shiant Islands
Greenstone Point
Strathkanaird
Rogart
Ullapool
Mellon Charles
Rudha Reidh
Laide
Bonar Bridge
Ardgay
Dornoch
LOCH BROOM
LOCH EWE
Glencalvie Forest
Dornoch Firth
Tain
Portmahomack
Gairloch
Poolewe
FIONN LOCH
LOCH MORIE
Charlestown (Gairloch)
LOCHAN FADA
LOCH GLAS
Alness
Nigg
Red Point
LOCH MAREE
LOCH FANNICH
Invergordon
Lossiemouth
Balblair (Cromarty Firth)
Cromarty
Moray Firth
Buckie
Craig
Lochluichart
Garve
LOCH LUICHART
Dingwall
Elgin
Forres
Alcaig
Nairn
Strathpeffer
Munlochy
Sound of Raasay
Inner Sound
Rona
Auldearn
Contin
Shieldaig
LOCH DAMPH
Tore
Drumsmittal
Muir of Ord
Cawdor
Keith
MORAY
LOCH MONAR
Lochcarron
Inverness
Culloden Muir
Kiltarlity
Westhill
Smithton
Raasay
LOCH CARRON
Glencannich Forest
Scaniport
Scalpay
Erbusaig
Plockton
Drumnadrochit
Dunlichity
Kyle of Lochalsh
Ardelve
Balnain
LOCH DUNTELCHAIG
Croachy
Tomatin
Dulnain Bridge
Grantown-on-Spey
Dornie
Inverinate
Glenelg
HIGHLAND
Foyers
LOCH MHOR
Carrbridge
Nethy Bridge
Boat of Garten
West Highlands
Soay
LOCH CLUANIE
Bhlaraidh
Invermoriston
Monadhliath Mountains
Aviemore
Arnisdale
Glenmoriston
LOCH HOURN
Sound of Sleat
Fort Augustus
LOCH NESS
Inverdruie
Cairngorm Mountains
Kincraig
Kingussie
Cuillin Sound
LOCH QUOICH
Invergarry
Rum
Mallaig
LOCH GARRY
Newtonmore
Feshiebridge
South Laggan
Ralia
LOCH NEVIS
Glengarry Forest
LOCH LOCHY
Laggan
ABERDEENSHIRE
Morar
Sound of Rum
Arisaig
LOCH MORAR
LOCH ARKAIG
Invergloy
Glenfeshie Forest
Balmoral Forest
Eigg
LOCH LAGGAN
Gaick Forest
Glenfinnan
Muirshearlich
Spean Bridge
Sound of Arisaig
Banavie
Grampian Mountains
Muck
Corpach
LOCH SHIEL
Inverlochy
LOCH TREIG
Fort William
Ben Nevis
ANGUS
Kilchoan
Ardgour
Glenborrodale
Strontian
Inchree
Kinlochleven
LOCH OSSIAN
Onich
Oransay
Kentallen
Glencoe
BLACKWATER RESERVOIR
Pitlochry
Ballachulish
Sound of Mull
Loch Linnhe
Duror
LOCH RANNOCH
LOCH TUMMEL
PERTH AND KINROSS
Blairgowrie
Ulva
Lismore
LOCH LYON
Isle of Mull
LOCH ETIVE
LOCH TAY
Oban
Dundee

B&B owners may vary rates – be sure to check when booking

Alcaig

NH5657

Dun Eistein, *Alcaig, Conon Bridge, Dingwall, Ross-shire, IV7 8HS.* Highland country cottage. **Open:** May to Oct **01349 862210** Mrs Morrison *www.host.co.uk* **D:** Fr £18.50–£19.50 **S:** Fr £24.00 **Beds:** 1F 1D **Baths:** 1 En 1 Pr (3)

Alness

NH6569

An Laimhrig, *82 Obsdale Park, Alness, IV17 0TR.* Modern detached house, ideal touring centre, cyclists' stopover for John O'Groats. **Open:** All year **01349 882016 (also fax)** Ms MacDonald *m.mac4388@faxvia.net* **D:** Fr £18.00–£25.00 **S:** Fr £20.00–£30.00 **Beds:** 1F 2T 1D **Baths:** 2 En 1 Sh

Altnaharra

NC5635

1 Macleod Crescent, *Altnaharra, Lairg, Sutherland, IV27 4UG.* **Open:** All year **01549 411258** Mrs Barrie **D:** Fr £18.00 **S:** Fr £23.00 **Beds:** 1F 2T **Baths:** 3 En (3) Hamlet (pop. 31) nestling between 2 Munros, Ben Klebrig and Ben Hope, ideal base hill-walking. Cyclists welcome (CTC member), dry secure shelter for cycles, on direct inland route for End to End. Only B&B in Altnaharra, so early booking is advisable.

Ardelve

NG8727 *The Duich*

Loch Duich Hotel, *Ardelve, Kyle of Lochalsh, IV40 8DY.* On the road to Skye and Kyle, facing Eilean Donan Castle. **Open:** All year (not Xmas/New Year) **01599 555213 Fax: 01599 555214** *sales@lochduich.fg.co.uk* www.lochduich.fg.co.uk **D:** Fr £25.00–£35.00 **S:** Fr £30.00–£35.00 **Beds:** 1F 4T 4D 2S **Baths:** 9 En 2 Pr (40) cc

Caberfeidh House, *Ardelve, Kyle of Lochalsh, IV40 8DY.* Beautiful lochside house with superb views of Eilean Donan Castle. **Open:** All year (not Xmas/New Year) **01599 555293** Mr Newton **D:** Fr £18.00–£22.00 **S:** Fr £25.00–£30.00 **Beds:** 2T 3D 1S **Baths:** 2 En 1 Sh (6) cc

Ardgay

NH5990

Corvost, *Ardgay, Sutherland, IV24 3BP.* Homely, spectacular views, birds, walks, central touring, peaceful crofting area. **Open:** All year (not Xmas/New Year) **01863 755317 (also fax)** Mrs Munro **D:** Fr £16.00 **S:** Fr £18.00 **Beds:** 1T 1D **Baths:** 2 Sh

Ardgour

NN0163

The Inn at Ardgour, *Ardgour, Fort William, Inverness-shire, PH33 7AA.* Unique. Fabulous views of Loch Linnhe. A very special location. **Open:** Feb to Nov **Grades:** STB 4 Star **01855 841225 Fax: 01855 841214** *theinn@ardgour.biz* www.ardgour.biz **D:** Fr £30.00–£49.00 **S:** Fr £55.00 **Beds:** 2F 4T 4D **Baths:** 10 En (26) cc

Arisaig

NM6586 *Cnoc-na-Faire Hotel, Arisaig Hotel*

Leven House, *Borrodale, Arisaig, PH39 4NR.* Ideal for walking, touring, sails to Skye, Rhum, Eigg, Muck. **Open:** All year (not Xmas/New Year) **01687 450238** Mrs MacMillan *ejmacmillan@aol.com* www.hexhome.fsnet.co.uk/thehouse.html **D:** Fr £22.00 **S:** Fr £30.00 **Beds:** 2F **Baths:** 2 En

Arnisdale

NG8410

Corran, *Arnisdale, Kyle of Lochalsh, Ross-shire, IV40 8JJ.* House is situated in small village surrounded by massive mountains overlooking Loch Hourn. **Open:** All year **01599 522336** Mrs Nash **D:** Fr £13.00–£16.00 **S:** Fr £13.00–£16.00 **Beds:** 1F 1S **Baths:** 1 Sh

Auldearn

NH9155

Covenanters Inn, *Auldearn, Nairn, Inverness-shire, IV12 5TG.* Friendly family run inn. Excellent location for exploring Highlands. **Open:** All year **01667 452456** Mr Harrison *covenanters@aol.com* www.covenantes-inn.co.uk **D:** Fr £22.00–£35.00 **S:** Fr £35.00–£48.00 **Beds:** 2F 6T 6D **Baths:** 14 En (30) cc

Planning a longer stay? Always ask for any special rates

Aultivullin

NC8167

Catalina Guest House, *Aultivullin, Strathy Point, Thurso, Caithness, KW14 7RY.* On the far North Coast, private suite for just two. **Open:** All year **01641 541279** J Salisbury **Fax: 0870 1247960** *petesalisbury@catalina72.freeserve.co.uk* **D:** Fr £17.00–£20.00 **S:** Fr £20.00–£30.00 **Beds:** 1T **Baths:** 1 En (1)

Aviemore

NH8912

Ravenscraig Guest House, *Aviemore, Inverness-shire, PH22 1RP.* **Open:** All year **Grades:** STB 2 Star, AA 3 Diamond **01479 810278** Mr & Mrs Gatenby **Fax: 01479 810210** *ravenscrg@aol.com* www.aviemoreonline.com **D:** Fr £20.00–£25.00 **S:** Fr £20.00–£25.00 **Beds:** 2F 5D 4T 1S **Baths:** 12 En (16) cc Family-run guest house, central village location. Rooms recently refurbished, some with views over the Cairngorm Mountains. Perfect base for exploring the Highlands or just discovering the delights of our local area. Our aim is to make your stay an enjoyable one.

Cairngorm Guest House, *Grampian Road, Aviemore, Inverness-shire, PH22 1RP.* Clean, comfortable, cosy, rooms. Home-made cake and hearty breakfast. **Open:** All year **Grades:** STB 2 Star, AA 3 Diamond **01479 810630 (also fax)** Mrs Conn *conns@lineone.net* www.aviemore.co.uk **D:** Fr £20.00–£25.00 **S:** Fr £20.00–£30.00 **Beds:** 1F 5D 3T **Baths:** 9 En (2) (10) cc

Ardlogie Guest House, *Dalfaber Road, Aviemore, Inverness-shire, PH22 1PU.* Lovely, Speyside location. Superb Cairngorm views. Free swim, golf, fishing. **Open:** All year **01479 810747** Mr Willies *ardlogie.aviemore@btopenworld.com* www.aviemore.co.uk/ardlogie **D:** Fr £20.00 **S:** Fr £25.00 **Beds:** 4D 1T **Baths:** 5 En (3) cc

Rowan Tree Country Hotel, *Loch Alvie, Aviemore, Inverness-shire, PH22 1QB.* C17th coaching inn. Characterful bedrooms. Comfortable lounges. A warm welcome. **Open:** All year **01479 810207 (also fax)** *enquires@rowantreehotel.com* www.rowantreehotel.com **D:** Fr £26.50–£31.50 **S:** Fr £36.50–£41.50 **Beds:** 2F 3T 4D 1S **Baths:** 10 En 1 Sh (12) cc

Badachro

NG7773

Lochside, *Aird Road, Badachro, Gairloch, Wester Ross, IV21 2AB.* All rooms face south across beautiful sheltered Badachro Bay with its many boats. **Open:** All year
01445 741295 Mrs Foster www.host.co.uk
D: Fr £21.00–£22.00 **Beds:** 1F 1D **Baths:** 2 En

Baddidarroch

NC0822

Veyatie, *66 Baddidarroch, Lochinver, Lairg, Sutherland, IV27 4LP.* Peaceful, relaxing location. Magnificent mountain views, walkers paradise. Fantastic breakfasts. **Open:** All year (not Xmas)
01571 844424 (also fax) Mrs Chapman *veyatie@baddid.freeserve.co.uk* www.host.co.uk
D: Fr £20.00–£25.00 **S:** Fr £25.00–£38.00 **Beds:** 2D 1T **Baths:** 2 En 1 Pr (3)

Balblair (Cromarty Firth)

NH7066

Braelangwell House, *Balblair, Dingwall, Ross-shire, IV7 8LQ.* Beautiful Georgian mansion. Ideal for touring Scottish Highlands. Four-poster bed. **Open:** Apr to Oct **Grades:** STB 4 Star
01381 610353 Fax: 01381 610467 *braelangwell@btinternet.com* www.btinternet.com/~braelangwell **D:** Fr £25.00–£40.00 **S:** Fr £35.00–£50.00 **Beds:** 1T 2D **Baths:** 1 En 2 Pr (40)

Ballachulish

NN0858

Fern Villa Guest House, *Loanfern, Ballachulish, Argyll, PH49 4JE.* **Open:** All year **Grades:** STB 3 Star, AA 4 Diamond
01855 811393 Mr Chandler **Fax: 01855 811727** *stil@fernvilla.com* www.fernvilla.com
D: Fr £21.00–£23.00 **S:** Fr £26.00–£28.00 **Beds:** 3D 2T **Baths:** 5 En (5)
A warm welcome awaits you in this beautifully-upgraded Victorian house. The village is surrounded by the spectacular lochs and mountains of Glencoe. Natural cooking of Scotland forms the basis of our home-made dinner menus. Non-smoking.

B&B owners may vary rates – be sure to check when booking

Lyn Leven Guest House, *West Laroch, Ballachulish, Argyll, PA39 4JP.* **Open:** All year **Grades:** STB 4 Star, AA 4 Diamond, RAC 4 Diamond
01855 811392 Mrs Macleod **Fax: 01855 811600** www.lynleven.co.uk **D:** Fr £20.00–£25.00 **S:** Fr £25.00–£30.00 **Beds:** 4F 4D 4T **Baths:** 12 En (10) cc
Very warm Highland welcome in modern comfortable family-run award-winning guest house. Facing lovely Loch Leven. Private car parking.

Ardno House, *Lettermore, Ballachulish, Argyll, PH49 4JD.* Beautifully-appointed luxury villa nestling on the shores of Loch Linnhe. **Open:** Mar to Oct **Grades:** STB 4 Star
01855 811830 Mrs Weir *pamweir@globalnet.co.uk* www.users.globalnet.co.uk/~pamweir/index.html **D:** Fr £21.00–£26.00 **Beds:** 1F 2D **Baths:** 3 En (6)

Tigh Ard, *Brecklet, Ballachulish, Argyll, PH49 4JG.* Lovely family bungalow, panoramic view, private parking. **Open:** Easter to Sep
01855 811328 Mrs Dow **D:** Fr £17.00 **Beds:** 1D 1T **Baths:** 2 Sh (2)

Riverside House, *Ballachulish, Argyll, PH49 4JE.* Spacious rooms in modern house overlooking river mountains and loch. **Open:** Easter to Oct **Grades:** STB 3 Star
01855 811473 Mrs Watt *robwatt9@aol.com*
D: Fr £18.00–£23.00 **Beds:** 2D 1T **Baths:** 2 En 1 Pr (2) (4)

Inverlaroch, *Albert Road, Ballachulish, Argyll, PH49 4JR.* Modern, comfortable, spacious, homely bungalow. Excellent for walking and climbing. **Open:** All year (not Xmas)
01855 811726 Mrs Castles *inverlaroch@talk21.com* **D:** Fr £17.00–£21.00 **S:** Fr £34.00–£42.00 **Beds:** 1F 1D 1T **Baths:** 3 En (3) (5)

Balnain

NH4430

Glenurquhart House Hotel, *Balnain, Drumnadrochit, Inverness, IV63 6TJ.* **Open:** Mar to Dec **Grades:** STB 3 Star
01456 476234 C Hughes *carol@glenurquartlodges.co.uk* **D:** Fr £20.00–£35.00 **S:** Fr £20.00–£40.00 **Beds:** 2F 2D 1T 2S **Baths:** 5 En 1 Sh (8) cc
Set in 6 acres of wooded grounds with fantastic views of Loch Meiklie. This small family-run hotel offers the perfect place to relax and unwind. Ideally situated for exploring the scenic highlands of Scotland and nearby Loch Ness.

Banavie

NN1177 *Moorings Hotel*

Fordon, *Badabrie, Banavie, Fort William, Inverness-shire, PH33 7LX.* Modern house with beautiful views **Open:** All year (not Xmas/New Year)
01397 772737 P Wilkinson *fordon@supanet.com* **D:** Fr £17.00–£21.00 **S:** Fr £17.00–£25.00 **Beds:** 3F 1D **Baths:** 1 En 1 Sh

Bettyhill

NC7061 *Betty Hill Hotel*

Dunveaden House, *Bettyhill, Thurso, Caithness, KW14 7SP.* On A836 Thurso/Tongue Road. Picturesque scenery, golden beaches, highland. **Open:** All year
01641 521273 Mr & Mrs MacKenzie **D:** Fr £16.00–£17.00 **S:** Fr £16.00–£17.00 **Beds:** 3T 2D 1S **Baths:** 2 Sh (8)

Bhlaraidh

NH3816

Burnside Guest House, *Bhlaraidh, Glenmoriston, Inverness, IV63 7YH.* Comfortable family home situated in a forested mountain area of Glenmoriston. **Open:** Mar to Nov
01320 351269 (also fax) Mr & Mrs Lowe **D:** Fr £16.00–£17.50 **S:** Fr £16.00–£17.50 **Beds:** 2D 1T 1S **Baths:** 2 Sh (5)

Bilbster

ND2852

Bilbster House, *Bilbster, Wick, Caithness, KW1 5TB.* Traditionally furnished C17th house. Central for the many attractions of Caithness. **Open:** All year (not Xmas/New Year) **Grades:** STB 3 Star
01955 621212 (also fax) Mr Stewart *ianstewart@bilbster.freeserve.co.uk* www.accommodationbilbster.com **D:** Fr £18.00–£19.50 **S:** Fr £18.00–£19.50 **Beds:** 1T 1D **Baths:** 2 En 1 Sh (10)

Boat of Garten

NH9418 *Boat Hotel, Craigard Hotel, Old Bridge Inn, Heatherbrae, Skye of Curr Hotel, Strathspey Hotel*

Avingormack Guest House, *Boat of Garten, Inverness-shire, PH24 3BT.* Breathtaking views of the mountains, award-winning food - just perfect. **Open:** All year
01479 831614 Mrs Ferguson *avin.gormack@ukgateway.net* www.smoothhound.co.uk/hotels/avingormack.html **D:** Fr £19.00–£22.00 **S:** Fr £19.50 **Beds:** 1F 2D 1T **Baths:** 2 En 1 Sh (6) cc

Heathbank - The Victorian House, *Drumuillie Road, Boat of Garten, Inverness-shire, PH24 3BD.* **Open:** All year
Grades: STB 3 Star
01479 831234 Mr Lawton *heathbankhotel@aol.com* www.heathbankhotel.co.uk **D:** Fr £25.00–£35.00 **S:** Fr £35.00 **Beds:** 2T 5D **Baths:** 6 En 1 Pr (8) cc
Beautiful, large Victorian House, Licensed, home-cooking, some four-poster beds. Conveniently situated for golf, fishing, cycling, walking, climbing, bird-watching, snow sports, Strathspey Steam Railway & Cairngorm Mountains. An ideal base for touring the Highlands, Castles, Distilleries, Loch Ness.

The Old Ferryman's House, *Boat of Garten, Inverness-shire, PH24 3BY.* **Open:** All year
01479 831370 (also fax) Ms Matthews **D:** Fr £21.00–£22.00 **S:** Fr £21.00–£22.00 **Beds:** 1T 1D 2S **Baths:** 2 Sh (4)
'Which?' recommended former ferryman's house, just across River Spey from village, welcoming, homely, comfortable. Sitting room with wood stove, many books, no TV. No set breakfast times, home-cooked meals with Highland specialities. Numerous walks, beautiful Strathspey countryside and Cairngorm mountains, castles, distilleries.

Chapelton Steading, *Boat Of Garten, Inverness-shire, PH24 3BU.* Spacious rural retreat. Charming garden with views of Cairngorm Mountains. **Open:** Mar to Nov
01479 831327 Mrs Smyth *chapelton@btinternet.com* boatofgarten.com/chapelton **D:** Fr £22.00–£23.00 **S:** Fr £25.00–£26.00 **Beds:** 1T 2D **Baths:** 3 En (10) (4)

Bonar Bridge

NH6191

Kyle House, *Dornoch Road, Bonar Bridge, Argday, Sutherland, IV24 3EB.* Superb old Scottish house offering excellent accommodation. Ideal touring base. **Open:** Feb to Nov
01863 766360 (also fax) Mrs Thomson *thomsonsheila@msn.com* **D:** Fr £20.00–£23.00 **S:** Fr £24.00 **Beds:** 2F 1D 2T 1S **Baths:** 3 En 1 Sh (4) (6)

Planning a longer stay? Always ask for any special rates

Brora

NC9004

Clynelish Farm, *Brora, Sutherland, KW9 6LR.* Spacious, peaceful farmhouse with caring, friendly hosts. **Open:** Easter to Oct
01408 621265 (also fax) J Ballantyne *info@scotland2000.com* www.scotland2000.com **D:** Fr £20.00 **S:** Fr £20.00 **Beds:** 1F 1T 1D **Baths:** 2 En 1 Pr cc

Non Smokers Haven, *Tigh Fada, 18 Golf Road, Brora, Sutherland, KW9 6QS.* Top quality welcoming home. Also self-catering, prime seaside location. **Open:** All year (not Xmas/New Year)
01408 621332 (also fax) Mr & Mrs Clarkson **D:** Fr £18.00 **S:** Fr £20.00 **Beds:** 1D 2T **Baths:** 1 En 2 Pr (5) (6)

Glenaveron, *Golf Road, Brora, Sutherland, KW9 6QS.* A luxurious Edwardian house in mature gardens close to Brora golf club and beaches. **Open:** All year
01408 621601 (also fax) Mr Fortune *glenaveron@hotmail.com* **D:** Fr £24.00–£28.00 **S:** Fr £28.00–£34.00 **Beds:** 1F 1D 1T **Baths:** 3 En (3) 2 cc

Canisbay

ND3472

Bencorragh House, *Upper Gills, Canisbay, John o' Groats, Wick, Caithness, KW1 4YB.* Working croft. Panoramic views across Pentland Firth near Orkney ferries. **Open:** All year
01955 611449 (also fax) Mrs Barton *bartonsandy@hotmail.com* www.bencorraghhouse.com **D:** Fr £21.00–£22.00 **S:** Fr £25.00–£30.00 **Beds:** 1F 2D 1T **Baths:** 4 En (5) (6) cc

Carrbridge

NH9022

Cairn Hotel, *Main Road, Carrbridge, Inverness-shire, PH23 3AS.* **Open:** All year (not Xmas)
Grades: STB 3 Star
01479 841212 Mr Kirk **Fax: 01479 841362** *cairn.carrbridge@lineone.net* www.host.co.uk **D:** Fr £20.00–£25.00 **S:** Fr £19.00–£28.00 **Beds:** 2F 2D 1T 2S **Baths:** 4 En 1 Sh (15) cc
Enjoy the country pub atmosphere; log fire, malt whiskies, real ales and affordable food in this family owned village centre hotel close to the historic bridge. A perfect base for touring Cairngorms, Loch Ness, Whisky Trail and beyond.

Carrmoor Guest House, *Carr Road, Carrbridge, Inverness-shire, PH23 3AD.* Licensed, family-run, warm welcome. Popular restaurant, chef proprietor. **Open:** All year
Grades: STB 3 Star, AA 4 Diamond
01479 841244 (also fax) Mrs Stitt *christine@carrmoorguesthouse.co.uk* www.carrmoorguesthouse.co.uk **D:** Fr £20.00–£22.00 **S:** Fr £22.50–£27.00 **Beds:** 1F 3D 2T **Baths:** 6 En (6) cc

Craigellachie House, *Main Street, Carrbridge, Inverness-shire, PH23 3AS.* Perfectly situated for exploring the Cairngorms and Loch Ness. Close to historic bridge. **Open:** All year
01479 841641 (also fax) Mrs Pedersen *e.pedersen@talk21.com* www.host.co.uk **D:** Fr £16.00–£20.00 **S:** Fr £17.00–£26.00 **Beds:** 2F 2D 2T 1S **Baths:** 3 En 2 Sh (8) cc

Cruachan, *Carrbridge, Inverness-shire, PH23 3AA.* Modern bungalow **Open:** Easter to Nov
01479 841609 Mrs Campbell **Fax: 01479 841776** *ianccc@tesco.net* **D:** Fr £15.00–£18.00 **S:** Fr £16.00–£18.00 **Beds:** 1T 1D 1S **Baths:** 1 En 1 Pr 1 Sh (4)

Pine Ridge, *Carrbridge, Inverness-shire, PH23 3AA.* Pine Ridge is a beautiful 100-year-old home. **Open:** All year
01479 841646 Mrs Weston *jane.weston@tesco.net* **D:** Fr £16.00–£20.00 **S:** Fr £20.00–£25.00 **Beds:** 1F 1D 1T **Baths:** 1 En 1 Sh (6)

Cawdor

NH8449

Colonsay, *Piperhill Cawdor, Cawdor, Nairn, IV12 5SD.* **Open:** All year (not Xmas/New Year)
01667 404305 Mrs Murray *murray@micro-central.co.uk* **D:** Fr £18.00 **S:** Fr £22.00 **Beds:** 1F 1D **Baths:** 2 Sh (3)
Beautiful new traditionally-built detached house set in rural area close to Inverness, Nairn, Cawdor Castle and Culloden Battlefield, golf and fishing close by. Comfortable beds, tastefully-decorated rooms and good Scottish breakfasts and evening tea, private off-road parking.

Please respect a B&B's wishes regarding children, animals and smoking

Charlestown (Gairloch)

NG8175

Heatherdale, *Charlestown, Gairloch, Ross-shire, IV21 2AH.* 4 star S.T.B, peacefully situated on hillside, close to harbour, beach, hotels & restaurants. **Open:** Mar to Nov **Grades:** STB 4 Star
01445 712388 (also fax) Mrs MacIver *BrochoD1@aol.com* **D:** Fr £20.00–£24.00 **S:** Fr £28.00–£30.00 **Beds:** 1T 2D **Baths:** 3 En 1 Sh (1) (3)

Contin

NH4555

Millbrae, *Contin, Strathpeffer, Ross-shire, IV14 9EB.* Ideal walking, touring, cycling. Homely, peaceful, welcoming. Large, comfortable rooms. Big breakfast!
Open: All year
01997 421368 Mrs Redfern www.millbrae.inthehighlands.co.uk **D:** Fr £15.00 **S:** Fr £20.00 **Beds:** 1F 1D **Baths:** 1 Sh (4)

Hideaway B&B, *Craigdarroch Drive, Contin, Strathpeffer, Ross-shire, IV14 9EL.* Modern bungalow at gateway to Northwest Highlands. Consistent high standards.
Open: All year (not Xmas/New Year)
Grades: STB 3 Star
01997 421127 (also fax) *hideaway@bushinternet.com* www.visithideaway.co.uk
D: Fr £15.00–£16.00 **S:** Fr £16.00–£18.00 **Beds:** 1T 2D **Baths:** 3 En (4) 3

Corpach

NN0976

Heston, *Corpach, Fort William, Inverness-shire, PH33 7LT.* Comfortable house with excellent views on road to the Isles.
Open: Mar to Nov
01397 772425 Mrs Wynne **D:** Fr £18.00–£20.00 **S:** Fr £22.00 **Beds:** 1F 1D 1T **Baths:** 2 En (3) (3)

Ben Nevis View, *Corpach, Fort William, Inverness-shire, PH33 7JH.* Modern, comfortable house, 5 minutes by car from Fort William. **Open:** Feb to Oct
01397 772131 Mrs Mooney *bennevisview@amserve.net* www.bennevisview.co.uk **D:** Fr £18.00–£22.00 **S:** Fr £20.00–£25.00 **Beds:** 1F 1D **Baths:** 2 En (4)

The Neuk, *Corpach, Fort William, Inverness-shire, PH33 7LR.* Modern, privately-run, home cooking. Views over Ben Nevis. Private garden. **Open:** All year (not Xmas)
01397 772244 Mrs McCallum *norma.mccallum@theneuk10.fsinverness.co.uk*
D: Fr £18.00–£24.00 **S:** Fr £27.00–£36.00 **Beds:** 2F 1D 1T **Baths:** 4 En (6)

Croachy

NH6427

The Old Parsonage, *Croachy, Inverness, IV2 6UE.* 'Spacious, comfortable, welcoming-a good place to be'. Guest commendations! **Open:** All year
Grades: STB 4 Star
01808 521441 (also fax) Isabell Steel *oldparsonage@btinternet.com* **D:** Fr £20.00–£25.00 **S:** Fr £20.00–£25.00 **Beds:** 3D **Baths:** 2 En 1 Pr (6) cc

Cromarty

NH7867

Braelangwell House, *Balblair, Dingwall, Ross-shire, IV7 8LQ.* Beautiful Georgian mansion. Ideal for touring Scottish Highlands. Four-poster bed. **Open:** Apr to Oct **Grades:** STB 4 Star
01381 610353 Fax: 01381 610467 *braelangwell@btinternet.com* www.btinternet.com/~braelangwell **D:** Fr £25.00–£40.00 **S:** Fr £35.00–£50.00 **Beds:** 1T 2D **Baths:** 1 En 2 Pr (40)

7 Church Street, *Cromarty, Ross-shire, IV11 8XA.* 300-year-old house with warm welcome. **Open:** All year
01381 600488 Mrs Robertson **D:** Fr £16.00 **S:** Fr £16.00

Culloden Moor

NH7345

Bayview, *Westhill, Culloden Moor, Inverness, IV2 5BP.* Modern 2-storey house situated in half-acre landscaped garden. Beautiful views.
Open: Easter to Oct **Grades:** STB 3 Star
01463 790386 (also fax) Mrs Campbell *bayview.guest@lineone.net* www.bayviewguest.com **D:** Fr £18.00–£22.00 **S:** Fr £25.00–£30.00 **Beds:** 1T 2D **Baths:** 2 En 1 Pr (3)

Westhill House, *Westhill, Inverness, IV1 5BP.* Spacious, comfortable family home in lovely garden. Close to Culloden and Inverness. **Open:** Easter to Oct
01463 793225 Mrs Honnor **Fax: 01463 792503** *janethon@piccolopress.demon.co.uk* www.scotland-info.co.uk/westhill.htm **D:** Fr £18.00–£20.00 **S:** Fr £18.00–£20.00 **Beds:** 1F 1T 1S **Baths:** 2 En 1 Sh (4)

Culdoich Farm, *Culloden Muir, Inverness, IV2 5EL.* Old farmhouse in peaceful surroundings. Good farmhouse breakfast. **Open:** May to Oct
01463 790268 Mrs Alexander **D:** Fr £17.00 **S:** Fr £34.00 **Beds:** 1F 1T/D **Baths:** 1 Sh

Diabaig

NG7960

Ben Bhraggie, *Diabaig, Torridon, Achnasheen, Ross-shire, IV22 2HE.* Comfortable homely cottage - fishing and hill walkers' paradise. **Open:** Easter to Nov
01445 790268 Mrs Ross www.host.co.uk **D:** Fr £14.00 **S:** Fr £14.00 **Beds:** 1D 1T (3) (4)

Dornie

NG8826

Tigh Tasqaidh, *Dornie, Kyle of Lochalsh, Ross-shire, IV40 8EH.* Historic house on Sealoch. 1/4 mile Eilean Dowan Castle. Luxurious accommodation with stunning views. Outstanding walking/touring, 8 miles Isle of Skye. **Open:** All year
01599 555242 *igordoncan@aol.com* www.milford.co.uk **D:** Fr £23.00–£25.00 **S:** Fr £23.00–£25.00 **Beds:** 1T 2D **Baths:** 3 En (2) cc

Dornoch

NH8089 *Eagle Hotel, Dornoch Bridge Inn, Trentham Hotel, Burgh Field Hotel, Sutherland House, Castle Hotel, Mallin House Hotel*

Amalfi, *River Street, Dornoch, Sutherland, IV25 3LY.* Modern comfortable house alongside golf course. Award winning beach 300m. Friendly Highland hospitality.
Open: All year (not Xmas/New Year)
01862 810015 Mrs MacKay *mackay.amalfi@talk21.com* **D:** Fr £18.00–£21.00 **S:** Fr £20.00–£33.00 **Beds:** 1F 1T **Baths:** 2 En (2) (2)

Achandean Bungalow, *The Meadows, Dornoch, Sutherland, IV25 3SF.* **Open:** Easter to Oct **Grades:** AA 3 Diamond
01862 810413 (also fax) Mrs Hellier *basilhellier@amserve.net* **D:** Fr £18.00–£24.00 **S:** Fr £30.00 **Beds:** 2D 1T **Baths:** 2 En 1 Pr (3)
Audrey assures guests of a warm Highland welcome. Quiet, central, opposite fire station. Spacious comfortable ensuite bedrooms. Nearby golf course and cathedral. Perfect base for exploring Highlands. OAP's, disabled appreciated! Short breaks. Weekly rates. Lovely seaside town. Bird-watching and relaxation!

Tordarroch, *Castle Street, Dornoch, Sutherland, IV25 3SN.* Traditional stone-built house set within walled gardens, ensuring peace & quiet. **Open:** Easter to Oct
01862 810855 Mrs Matherson **D:** Fr £19.00–£21.00 **S:** Fr £19.00–£21.00 **Beds:** 1D 1T 1S **Baths:** 1 En 1 Pr 1 Sh (3)

Drumnadrochit

NH5030

The Loch Ness Lodge Hotel, *Drumnadrochit, Inverness, IV63 6TU.* **Open:** Easter to Oct **Grades:** STB 3 Star
01456 450342 Fax: 01456 450429 *info@lochness-hotel.com* www.lochness-hotel.com **D:** Fr £35.00–£50.00 **S:** Fr £45.00–£60.00 **Beds:** 2F 21T 4D **Baths:** 27 En cc
This picturesque Highland Hotel stands in delightful grounds and offers elegant ensuite accommodation and outstanding cuisine. Linked to the Visitor's Centre, with its unique exhibition, which attracts people from all around the world. Ideal base for walkers. Warm welcome awaits.

Twin Birches, *Milton, Drumnadrochit, IV63 6UA.* Friendly, good breakfast, comfortable room. Loch Ness, Urquhart Castle nearby. **Open:** All year (not Xmas/New Year)
01456 450359 Mrs Seeburg **D:** Fr £17.00 **S:** Fr £17.00 **Beds:** 1D **Baths:** 1 Pr (3)

Glen Rowan House, *West Lewiston, Drumnadrochit, Inverness, IV63 6UW.* Tasteful, comfortable accommodation in tranquil riverside setting. Ideal base for touring, walking, cycling. Close to Urquhart Castle and Loch Ness attractions. **Open:** All year
01456 450235 Mr & Mrs McConnell **Fax: 01456 450817** *info@glenrowan.co.uk* www.glenrowan.co.uk **D:** Fr £16.00–£26.00 **S:** Fr £25.00–£34.00 **Beds:** 1D 2T **Baths:** 3 En (12) (5) cc

Westwood, *Lower Balmacaan, Drumnadrochit, Inverness, IV63 6WU.* Comfortable bungalow near Loch Ness. Ideal walking and touring base. **Open:** All year **Grades:** STB 3 Star
01456 450826 (also fax) S Silke *sandra@westwoodbb.freeserve.co.uk* www.westwoodbb.freeserve.co.uk **D:** Fr £18.00–£22.00 **S:** Fr £18.00–£22.00 **Beds:** 1D 1T 1S **Baths:** 2 En 1 Sh (8) (4) cc

Bridgend House, *The Green, Drumnadrochit, Inverness, IV63 6TX.* Comfortable highland home overlooking village green. Ideal walking/touring area. **Open:** Feb to Dec
01456 450865 (also fax) Mrs Luffman www.host.co.uk **D:** Fr £18.00–£26.00 **S:** Fr £18.00–£30.00 **Beds:** 1F/T 1D 1S **Baths:** 1 En 1 Sh (10) (5)

Ferness Cottage, *Lewiston, Drumnadrochit, Inverness, IV3 6UW.* 200-year-old cottage within walking distance of Loch Ness. **Open:** Easter to Oct
01456 450564 Mrs Campbell *morag@glenferness.com* www.host.co.uk **D:** Fr £18.00–£23.00 **S:** Fr £20.00–£30.00 **Beds:** 1F 1T 2D **Baths:** 4 En

Drumsmittal

NH6449

Culbin Drumsmittal Croft, *Drumsmittal, North Kessock, Inverness, IV1 3XF.* Situated on a Highland working croft. Set in beautiful countryside, ideal touring base. **Open:** All year (not Xmas)
01463 731455 (also fax) Mrs Ross *info@rossculbin.co.uk* www.rossculbin.co.uk **D:** Fr £18.00–£20.00 **Beds:** 1F 1T 1D **Baths:** 1 Pr 1 Sh (4)

Dulnain Bridge

NH9924

Broomlands, *Dulnain Bridge, Grantown-on-Spey, Moray, PH26 3LT.* A traditional Scottish house in a quiet village. Ideal centre for touring the Highlands.
Open: Easter to Sept
01479 851255 Mrs Noble *ernest@noble56.fsnet.co.uk* **D:** Fr £16.00–£17.00 **S:** Fr £16.00–£20.00 **Beds:** 1F 1D 1S **Baths:** 1 Sh (4)

Dunlichity

NH6533

Dunlichity House, *Tordarroch, Inverness, IV2 6XF.* **Open:** All year **Grades:** STB 4 Star
01808 521442 Mrs Jeans *dunlichityhouse@talk21.com* www.dunlichityhouse.com **D:** Fr £30.00 **S:** Fr £35.00 **Beds:** 1F 2D **Baths:** 3 Pr (8)
Grounds have own well-stocked lochans. Accommodation in the East Wing with guests having their own private entrance. All rooms have beautiful water views. 15 minutes from the city of Inverness. Close to Loch Ness. Ideal touring/walking area.

Durness

NC4067

Port Na Con House, *Loch Eriboll, Lairg, Sutherland, IV27 4UN.* **Open:** All year **Grades:** AA 4 Diamond
01971 511367 (also fax) Mrs Black *portnacon70@hotmail.com* www.smoothhound.co.uk /hotels/portnaco.html **D:** Fr £19.00–£20.00 **S:** Fr £27.00–£28.00 **Beds:** 1F 2D 1T **Baths:** 1 En 1 Pr 1 Sh (4) cc
Former Customs House, sited on the shore of Loch Eriboll. All rooms overlook the sea and our raised conservatory offers magnificent views to Ben Hope (the northernmost Munro) and Ben Loyal. We have a restricted licence.

Glengolly House, *Durine, Durness, Lairg, Sutherland, IV27 4PN.* **Open:** All year **01971 511255 (also fax)** Mr Mackay *martin@glengolly.com* www.glengolly.com **D:** Fr £18.00–£22.00 **S:** Fr £20.00–£25.00 **Beds:** 1F 1T 1D **Baths:** 2 En 1 Pr (4)
Prepare to be enchanted by spectacular sunsets and breathtaking scenery. Come and stay at a traditional croft where you can watch Border Collies at work or listen to the corncrake. Visit Mackay Country - an area steeped in history.

Planning a longer stay? Always ask for any special rates

Caberfeidh Guest House, *Durness, Lairg, Sutherland, IV27 4QA.* Central village, caves, beaches and suited for exploring North Coast. **Open:** Easter to Sep
01971 511215 J Marsham **Fax: 01971 511339** *rispond@aol.com* **D:** Fr £15.00–£20.00 **S:** Fr £15.00–£20.00 **Beds:** 2F 1T 1D 1S **Baths:** 1 Sh (10)

Rowan House, *90 Laid, Loch Eriboll, Lairg, Sutherland, IV27 4UN.* Set in a spectacular setting with uninterrupted views across Loch Eriboll to Ben Hope. **Open:** All year
01971 511347 (also fax) Mr MacLellan *h.maclellan@btinternet.com* drive.to/laid **D:** Fr £15.00–£25.00 **S:** Fr £15.00–£25.00 **Beds:** 1F/T 2D **Baths:** 3 En (6)

Duror

NM9955

Lagnaha Farm, *Duror, Appin, Argyll, PA38 4BS.* Farmhouse, quality, comfort, modern en suite facilities in magnificent surroundings. **Open:** Easter to Oct
01631 740207 (also fax) Mrs Worthington *worthington@lagnaha.fsnet.co.uk* **D:** Fr £18.50–£25.00 **S:** Fr £20.00–£25.00 **Beds:** 2D 1S **Baths:** 1 En 1 Sh (4)

Erbusaig

NG7629

Old Schoolhouse, *Tigh Fasgaidh, Erbusaig, Kyle of Lochalsh, Ross-shire, IV40 8BB.* A house of special charm where the mood is mellow! **Open:** All year (not Xmas/New Year) **Grades:** STB 4 Star, AA 4 Diamond
01599 534369 (also fax) Mr & Mrs Cumine *cuminecandj@lineone.net* www.highland.plus.com/schoolhouse **D:** Fr £28.00 **S:** Fr £35.00–£40.00 **Beds:** 1T 2D **Baths:** 3 En (15) **cc**

Feshiebridge

NH8504

Balcraggan House, *Feshiebridge, Kincraig, Kingussie, Inverness-shire, PH21 1NG.* Wonderful setting where wildlife, walks and cycle routes abound. **Open:** All year
01540 651488 Mrs Gillies **D:** Fr £25.00 **S:** Fr £30.00–£35.00 **Beds:** 1D 1T **Baths:** 2 En (10) (3)

Fort Augustus

NH3709

Tigh Na Mairi, *Canalside, Fort Augustus, Inverness-shire, PH32 4BA.* **Open:** Easter to Oct **Grades:** STB 2 Star
01320 366766 & 07714 337089 (M) S V Callcutt **Fax: 01320 366766** *suecallcutt@talk21.com* www.host.co.uk **D:** Fr £18.00–£22.00 **S:** Fr £20.00–£30.00 **Beds:** 2D 1T **Baths:** 2 Sh (8) (2)
Within easy strolling distance of Loch Ness, this ex-ghillie's cottage offers breathtaking views. Ideal base for walking, cycling, touring or Nessie-hunting! Situated on the Caledonian Canal, the less energetic can just sit and watch the boats and swans glide by!

Old Pier House, *Fort Augustus, Inverness-shire, PH32 4BX.* Loch Ness farmhouse with panoramic views, boats, riding, highland cattle. **Open:** Apr to Nov
01320 366418 Mrs MacKenzie **Fax: 01320 366770** *old.pier@talk21.com* **D:** Fr £20.00–£30.00 **S:** Fr £25.00–£35.00 **Beds:** 1F 1T 1D **Baths:** 3 En (7) (10)

Sonas, *Inverness Road, Fort Augustus, Inverness-shire, PH32 4DH.* Modern bungalow in very attractive Highland village. Ideal touring centre. **Open:** All year
01320 366291 L H Service **D:** Fr £15.00 **S:** Fr £22.00 **Beds:** 1F 1T 1D **Baths:** 3 En (3)

Lorien House, *Station Road, Fort Augustus, Inverness-shire, PH32 4AY.* Luxurious family home overlooking Loch Ness and the Caledonian Canal. Excellent breakfasts- traditional, continental, fresh fruits, smoked fish. Very central for pubs, shops and restaurants, 10% discount at The Bothy. Less than an hour from Skye, Inverness and Ben Nevis. **Open:** All year
01320 366736 E Dickie **Fax: 01320 366263** *lorienhouse@aol.com* www.ipw.com/lorienhouse **D:** Fr £20.00–£25.00 **S:** Fr £35.00–£40.00 **Beds:** 2D 1F **Baths:** 3 En (2)

BATHROOMS
En = Ensuite
Pr = Private
Sh = Shared

Caledonian Cottage, *Station Road, Fort Augustus, Inverness-shire, PH32 4AY.* Warm, friendly and comfortable, the cottage has beautiful views and situated just minutes from the village with the Caledonian Canal Locks which flow down into Loch Ness. Perfect for walking, fishing, boating, cycling. No need to take the car. **Open:** All year
01320 366401 Ms Graham *cal@ipw.com* www.ipw.com/cal **D:** Fr £18.00–£25.00 **S:** Fr £15.00–£25.00 **Beds:** 1F 1T 1D **Baths:** 2 En 1 Pr (5)

Fort William

NN1073

Glenlochy Guest House, *Nevis Bridge, Fort William, Inverness-shire, PH33 6PF.* **Open:** All year **Grades:** STB 3 Star
01397 702909 A MacPherson *glenlochy1@aol.com* **D:** Fr £17.00–£29.00 **S:** Fr £17.00–£29.00 **Beds:** 2F 4D 3T 1S **Baths:** 8 En 2 Sh (14)
Situated in our extensive grounds overlooking River Nevis, 1/2 mile North of town and within easy walking distance of Ben Nevis. The famous West Highland Way Walk officially ends in the grounds. Private car park. Very comfortable B&B & self-catering accommodation.

Lawriestone Guest House, *Achintore Road, Fort William, PH33 6RQ.* **Open:** All year (not Xmas/New Year) **Grades:** STB 4 Star
01397 700777 (also fax) Mrs Smith *susan@lawriestone.co.uk* www.lawriestone.co.uk **D:** Fr £20.00–£30.00 **Beds:** 1T 3D **Baths:** 4 En (6)
Superb location overlooking Loch Linnhe and surrounding hills. Beautiful Victorian town house providing elegant, comfortable accommodation, warm Scottish hospitality, excellent breakfasts. Town centre 5 minutes walk. Ideal base for touring the Western Highlands. Beautiful gardens. Private parking. No smoking.

Planning a longer stay? Always ask for any special rates

Distillery House, *Nevis Bridge, North Road, Fort William, Inverness-shire, PH33 6LR.*
Open: All year **Grades:** STB 4 Star, AA 4 Diamond, RAC 4 Diamond
01397 700103 Mandy & Stuart McLean **Fax: 01397 702980** *disthouse@aol.com* www.fort-william.net/distillery-house **D:** Fr £20.00–£36.00 **S:** Fr £22.00–£38.00 **Beds:** 1F 3D 2T 1S **Baths:** 7 En (12) cc
Well-run guest house, ideally situated at end of Glen Nevis and West Highland Way.

Balcarres, *Seafield Gardens, Fort William, Inverness-shire, PH33 6RJ.*
Open: All year
01397 702377 Mrs Cameron **Fax: 01397 702232** *balcarres@btinternet.com* www.scotland2000.com/balcarres **D:** Fr £21.00–£25.00 **Beds:** 1F 1D 1T **Baths:** 3 En (5) cc
Executive villa in tranquil, elevated position with panoramic views overlooking Loch Linnie. Tastefully decorated throughout, full menu for breakfast. Fort William is an excellent touring base and an all-year-round holiday destination. 4 star self-catering also available.

11 Castle Drive, *Lochyside, Fort William, PH33 7NR.*
Open: All year
01397 702659 Mrs Grant *grantmoy@aol.com* **D:** Fr £16.00–£18.00 **S:** Fr £20.00–£24.00 **Beds:** 1T 1D **Baths:** 1 Sh (2)
Quiet residential area near castle. Views to Ben Nevis. Ideal base for walking, climbing, skiing. Intimate family home with cosy log fire in lounge where you can be assured of a warm and friendly welcome. Breakfast is the best in the West.

24 Henderson Row, *Fort William, Inverness-shire, PH33 6HT.* Quiet cul-de-sac 10 mins from town, lovely view of hills. Good Scottish hospitality. **Open:** All year **Grades:** STB 3 Star
01397 702711 Mrs Brady **D:** Fr £16.00–£18.00 **S:** Fr £18.00–£20.00 **Beds:** 2T **Baths:** 1 Sh

Alltonside Guest House, *Achintore Road, Fort William, Inverness-shire, PH33 6RW.* Alltonside Guest House commands magnificent views over Loch Linnhe to the hills beyond. **Open:** All year **Grades:** STB 3 Star
01397 703542 (also fax) Mrs Allton *alltonside@aol.com* **D:** Fr £16.00–£25.00 **S:** Fr £20.00–£30.00 **Beds:** 1F 3D 2T **Baths:** 6 Pr (8)

Stronchreggan View Guest House, *Achintore Road, Fort William, Inverness-shire, PH33 6RW.* Our house overlooks Loch Linnhe with views to Ardgour Hills. **Open:** Mar to Nov **Grades:** STB 3 Star
01397 704644 & 01397 704707 Fax: 01397 704644 *patricia@apmac.freeserve.co.uk* www.stronchreggan.co.uk **D:** Fr £19.00–£24.00 **S:** Fr £25.00–£38.00 **Beds:** 5D/F 2T **Baths:** 5 En 2 Pr (8) (7)

Stobahn, *Fassifern Road, Fort William, Inverness-shire, PH33 6BD.* Guest rooms overlooking Loch Linnhe. Just off High Street. **Open:** All year **Grades:** STB 2 Star
01397 702790 (also fax) *boggi@supanet.com* **D:** Fr £15.00–£20.00 **S:** Fr £18.00–£23.00 **Beds:** 1F 1T 2D **Baths:** 2 En 2 Sh cc

Blythedale, *Seafield Gardens, Fort William, PH33 6RJ.* Detached villa with beautiful Loch views. Ideal touring/walking areas. **Open:** All year **Grades:** STB 4 Star
01397 705523 D: Fr £23.00–£28.00 **S:** Fr £30.00–£45.00 **Beds:** 1F 1T 2D 1S **Baths:** 5 En (6)

Hillview Guest House, *Achintore Road, Fort William, Inverness-shire, PH33 6RW.*
Lochside location, magnificent views, home-cooked food. Warm welcome assured. **Open:** All year
01397 704349 Mrs McLindon *hillview.fortwilliam@care4free.net* www.hillview.fortwilliam.care4free.net **D:** Fr £16.00–£23.00 **S:** Fr £16.00–£23.00 **Beds:** 2F 3T 3D 1S **Baths:** 4 En 1 Pr 1 Sh (9) cc

Ben Nevis View, *Corpach, Fort William, Inverness-shire, PH33 7JH.* Modern, comfortable house, 5 minutes by car from Fort William.
Open: Feb to Oct
01397 772131 Mrs Mooney *bennevisview@amserve.net* www.bennevisview.co.uk **D:** Fr £18.00–£22.00 **S:** Fr £20.00–£25.00 **Beds:** 1F 1D **Baths:** 2 En (4)

Melantee, *Achintore Road, Fort William, Inverness-shire, PH33 6RW.* Comfortable bungalow overlooking Loch Linnhe and the Ardgour hills. **Open:** All year (not Xmas) **Grades:** STB 2 Star
01397 705329 Mrs Cook **Fax: 01397 700453** *floracookmelantee@yahoo.co.uk* **D:** Fr £16.50–£17.00 **S:** Fr £16.50–£17.00 **Beds:** 1F 1D 1T 1S **Baths:** 2 Sh (5) (6)

Rhu Mhor Guest House, *Alma Road, Fort William, Inverness-shire, PH33 6BP.* Old-fashioned in acre of wild and enchanting garden. **Open:** Easter to Oct
01397 702213 Mr MacPherson *ian@rhumhor.co.uk* www.rhumhor.co.uk **D:** Fr £16.00–£25.00 **S:** Fr £17.00–£44.00 **Beds:** 4F 1D 1T 1S **Baths:** 2 Sh 4 En (1) (7) cc

Ossian's Hotel, *High Street, Fort William, Inverness-shire, PH33 6DH.* Accommodation, food and drink for the budget traveller. Ideal town centre location. **Open:** All year
01397 700857 J Wallace **Fax: 01397 701030** *ossiansfw@aol.com* **D:** Fr £18.00–£25.00 **S:** Fr £20.00–£32.00 **Beds:** 10F 10D 10T 5S **Baths:** 32 En 3 Sh

Voringfoss, *5 Stirling Place, Fort William, Inverness-shire, PH33 6UW.* Experience the best of the Highland hospitality in a quiet situation. **Open:** All year
01397 704062 Mr & Mrs Fraser **D:** Fr £20.00–£26.00 **S:** Fr £20.00–£26.00 **Beds:** 2D 1T **Baths:** 3 En (4) cc

Abrach, *4 Caithness Place, Fort William, Inverness-shire, PH33 6JP.* Modern house in elevated position overlooking Loch Linnhe. **Open:** All year (not Xmas)
01397 702535 Mr & Mrs Moore **Fax: 01397 705629** *cmoore3050@aol.com* www.net-trak.com/~ecs/guest/abrach/ **D:** Fr £17.50–£23.00 **S:** Fr £20.00–£30.00 **Beds:** 1F 1D 1T 1S **Baths:** 2 En 1 Pr 1 Sh (6) cc

Glen Shiel Guest House, *Achintore Road, Fort William, Inverness-shire, PH33 6RW.* Lochside location, panoramic views. Large car park. Tea makers, colour TV in all rooms. **Open:** Easter to Oct
01397 702271 D: Fr £17.00–£21.00 **Beds:** 3D 1T **Baths:** 3 En 1 Pr 1 Sh (8) (7)

B&B owners may vary rates – be sure to check when booking

Ferndale, *Tomacharrich, Torlundy, Fort William, PH33 6SP.* Large bungalow in beautiful country setting, with wonderful views of Ben Nevis and Nevis Range Ski Slope. Ideal base for walking, cycling, skiing and touring. Pony trekking, trout fishing and golfing all nearby. Breakfast served in conservatory. Nearest B&B to skiing. **Open:** All year
01397 703593 Mrs Riley *ferndalebandb@aol.com* **D:** Fr £15.00–£20.00 **Beds:** 1F 2D **Baths:** 2 En 1 Pr (6)

Foyers

NH4920

Intake House, *Foyers, Inverness, IV2 6YA.* Overlooking the River Foyers near the famous Falls of Foyers. **Open:** Easter to Nov
01456 486258 (also fax) Mrs Grant **D:** Fr £15.00–£18.00 **S:** Fr £20.00–£25.00 **Beds:** 1T 2D **Baths:** 1 En 1 Sh (14) (5)

Gairloch

NG8076

13 Strath, *Gairloch, Ross-shire, IV21 2BX.* Good views, good varied breakfast, quiet, friendly cats. **Open:** Easter to Oct
01445 712085 Mrs Gibson *douglasg@ecosse.net* **D:** Fr £15.00 **S:** Fr £15.00 **Beds:** 1D 1S **Baths:** 1 Sh (3)

The Mountain Restaurant and Lodge, *Strath Square, Gairloch, Ross-shire, IV21 2BX.* Mountain hospitality and informal atmosphere, lochside in Gairloch's Village Square. Themed ensuite bedrooms, most with ocean/mountain views. Four-poster bedroom also available. On-site, the unique 'Mountain Coffee Company' featuring cappuccino and mountain latte drinks with real mountain home-baking! Plus adventure travel bookstore and nature shop. **Open:** All year
01445 712316 (also fax) Mr Rudge **D:** Fr £19.95–£27.95 **S:** Fr £27.00 **Beds:** 1T 2D **Baths:** 3 En cc

Whindley Guest House, *Auchtercairn Brae, Gairloch, Ross-shire, IV21 2BN.* Modern detached bungalow. Fantastic views. Warm welcome. Home cooking. **Open:** All year (not Xmas/New Year)
01445 712340 (also fax) Mrs Nichols *pam@whindley.co.uk* www.whindley.co.uk **D:** Fr £19.00–£21.00 **S:** Fr £19.00–£31.00 **Beds:** 1F 1T 1D **Baths:** 3 En

Garve

NH3961

The Old Manse, *Garve, Ross-shire, IV23 2PX.* Former manse, c.1860, set in quiet location amidst beautiful scenery. **Open:** All year (not Xmas)
01997 414201 (also fax) Mr & Mrs Hollingdale *peteholllingdale@supanet.com* **D:** Fr £16.00–£18.00 **S:** Fr £16.00–£18.00 **Beds:** 2D 1T **Baths:** 1 En 1 Sh (10) (6)

Glenborrodale

NM6160

Cala Darach, *Glenmore, Acharacle, Argyll, PH36 4JG.* Beautiful lochside house. Stunning views. Ideal walking/wildlife. Relaxing, peaceful. **Open:** Easter to Nov **Grades:** STB 4 Star
01972 500204 Mrs Kershaw **D:** Fr £22.00–£24.00 **S:** Fr £28.00 **Beds:** 1T 2D **Baths:** 2 En 1 Pr (4)

Glencoe

NN1058

Ardno House, *Lettermore, Ballachulish, Argyll, PH49 4JD.* **Open:** Mar to Oct **Grades:** STB 4 Star
01855 811830 Mrs Weir *pamweir@globalnet.co.uk* www.users.globalnet.co.uk/~pamweir/index.html **D:** Fr £21.00–£26.00 **Beds:** 1F 2D **Baths:** 3 En (6)
Beautifully-appointed luxury villa nestling on the shores of Loch Linnhe. Magnificent loch and mountain views. Each superior, spacious bedroom has an excellent private ensuite. Perfect base for touring scenic splendour of the Scottish Highlands. Near Glencoe and Ben Nevis. Wonderful walks. Warm welcome.

Planning a longer stay? Always ask for any special rates

Dunire Guest House, *Glencoe, Ballachulish, Argyll, PA39 4HS.* Family-run guest house. Great base for touring and walking. **Open:** All year (not Xmas/New Year)
01855 811305 Mrs Cameron **D:** Fr £17.00–£23.00 **S:** Fr £17.00–£23.00 **Beds:** 2T 4D **Baths:** 5 En 1 Pr (8)

Glencoe Hotel, *Glencoe, Ballachulish, Argyll, PA49 4HW.* A family-run Highland hotel in Glencoe village where a warm welcome, comfortable rooms and very good food are standard. All rooms have private facilities. Local and long distance buses stop at our door. Ask for Bargain Break details. **Open:** All year (not Xmas)
01855 811245 Mr MacConnacher **Fax: 01855 811687** *glencoehotel@hotmail.com* www.glencoehotel-scotland.com **D:** Fr £20.00–£36.00 **S:** Fr £32.00–£48.00 **Beds:** 3F 5T 6D 1S **Baths:** 15 En (40) cc

Glenelg

NG8118

Tigh Na Ros, *Kirkton, Glenelg, Kyle of Lochalsh, Ross-shire, IV40 8JR.* Peacefully-situated comfortable accommodation near Skye Ferry. French spoken, Continental cuisine. Lounge, log fire. **Open:** All year
01599 530015 (also fax) Dr Rawnsley *rosalindrawnsley@aol.com* **D:** Fr £20.00 **S:** Fr £20.00 **Beds:** 2T **Baths:** 1 En 1 Sh (4)

Marabhaig, *7 Coullindune, Glenelg, Kyle of Lochalsh, Ross-shire, IV40 8JU.* Marabhaig - situated on the shore of Glenelg Bay. Fantastic views. **Open:** All year
01599 522327 Mrs Cameron **D:** Fr £19.00–£21.00 **S:** Fr £21.00–£23.00 **Beds:** 2T 3D **Baths:** 3 En 2 Sh (6) 1

Glenfinnan

NM8980

Craigag Lodge Guest House, *Glenfinnan, Inverness-shire, PH37 4LT.* Victorian shooting lodge among superb mountain scenery. Ideal walking/wildlife. **Open:** Easter to Oct
01397 722240 Mr & Mrs Scott **D:** Fr £15.00–£20.00 **S:** Fr £18.00 **Beds:** 1F 1D 1T **Baths:** 1 Sh (9) (4)

Glengolly

ND1066

Shinval, *Glengolly, Thurso, Caithness, KW14 7XN.* Modern house with large garden. Four miles from Orkney ferry. **Open:** Jan to Dec
01847 894306 Mrs Sinclair **Fax: 01847 890711** *mary@shinval.swinternet.co.uk* **D:** Fr £15.00 **S:** Fr £15.00 **Beds:** 1F 1D 1T **Baths:** 1 En 2 Sh (4)

Grantown-on-Spey

NJ0327

Brooklynn, *Grant Road, Grantown-on-Spey, Moray, PH26 3LA.* **Open:** All year **Grades:** STB 4 Star
01479 873113 Alan &Silvia Woodier *brooklynn@woodier.com* www.woodier.com
D: Fr £20.00–£25.00 **S:** Fr £18.00–£30.00 **Beds:** 2T 3D 2S **Baths:** 5 En 1 Sh (5)
In our beautiful Victorian home enjoy a delicious home-cooked dinner with herbs and vegetables from the garden, relax with a malt in the lounge before retiring to your spacious, comfortable room. Tomorrow's for fishing, golf, birdwatching, Whisky Trail, walking, castles and so much more!

An Cala, *Woodlands Terrace, Grantown-on-Spey, Moray, PH26 3JU.* **Open:** All year
01479 873293 Val Dickinson **Fax: 01479 870297** *ancala@globalnet.co.uk* www.ancalahouse.co.uk **D:** Fr £23.00–£25.00 **S:** Fr £30.00–£35.00 **Beds:** 1F 1T 1D **Baths:** 3 En (7)
Ideally situated for Speyside walks, also of surrounding scenic countryside/forests. Breathe in clean, fresh air. A warm welcome; very comfortable rooms and beds. Homemade food, including marmalades and jams. Visit Grantown's museum, churches, tennis/golf clubs and surrounding castles.

Gaich Farm, *Grantown-on-Spey, Moray, PH26 3NT.* Beautiful working farmhouse overlooking Cairngorms, comfortable beds, good breakfast. **Open:** May to Sept
01479 851381 Mrs Laing **Fax: 01479 851 381** *gaich@tinyworld.co.uk* **D:** Fr £16.00–£17.00 **S:** Fr £16.00–£17.00 **Beds:** 1T 1D **Baths:** 1 Sh

Rossmor Guest House, *Woodlands Terrace, Grantown-on-Spey, Moray, PH26 3JU.*
Open: All year **Grades:** STB 4 Star, AA 4 Diamond
01479 872201 & 01479 872247 Mrs Steward **Fax: 01479 872201** *johnsteward.rossmor@lineone.net* www.rossmor.co.uk **D:** Fr £23.00–£25.00 **S:** Fr £25.00–£28.00 **Beds:** 2F 2T 2D **Baths:** 6 En (6) cc
Built in 1887 Rossmor is a beautiful Victorian house with original staircase etched glass and brass fittings, ideally located to explore the Highlands, to fish in the river Spey, or play golf at the many surrounding courses. Full Scottish breakfast.

Ardconnel, *Woodlands Terrace, Grantown-on-Spey, Moray, PH26 3JU.* A charming Victorian house. All rooms ensuite & beautifully-appointed. **Open:** All year (not Xmas) **Grades:** AA 5 Diamond, RAC 5 Diamond
01479 872104 (also fax) *ian.hallam2@btinternet.com* www.ardconnel.com **D:** Fr £30.00–£45.00 **S:** Fr £35.00–£60.00 **Beds:** 3D 2F 1S **Baths:** 6 En (8) (6)

Firhall Guest House, *Grant Road, Grantown-on-Spey, Moray, PH26 3LD.* Beautiful Victorian house set in the heart of Scottish Highlands. **Open:** All year (not Xmas)
01479 873097 (also fax) Mr Salmon *info@firhall.com* www.firhall.com **D:** Fr £18.00–£25.00 **S:** Fr £18.00–£30.00 **Beds:** 3F 1D 1T 1S **Baths:** 3 En 1 Pr 1 Sh (8)

Strathallan House, *Grant Road, Grantown-on-Spey, Moray, PH26 3LD.* Charming Victorian home, original features, first class accommodation, ensuite rooms. **Open:** All year **Grades:** STB 3 Star
01479 872165 (also fax) Mrs Butler *strathallanhouse@totalise.co.uk* strathallanhouse.co.uk **D:** Fr £19.00–£25.00 **S:** Fr £20.00–£25.00 **Beds:** 3D 1T 1F **Baths:** 4 En 1 Pr (7) (6) cc

Planning a longer stay? Always ask for any special rates

Kinross Guest House, *Woodside Avenue, Grantown-on-Spey, Moray, PH26 3JR.* Relaxing in a stunning part of Scotland. Sauna, gyms and cycles **Open:** All year
01479 872042 Mr Milne **Fax: 01479 873504** *milne@kinrosshouse.freeserve.co.uk* **D:** Fr £20.00–£28.00 **S:** Fr £20.00–£31.00 **Beds:** 2F 2T 1D 2S **Baths:** 5 En 2 Pr (13) (6) cc

Helmsdale

ND0215

The Old Manse, *Stittenham Road, Helmsdale, Sutherland, KW8 6JG.* Beautiful village settings, garden, access to salmon river, fishing arranged. **Open:** All year
01431 821597 Mrs Goodridge **D:** Fr £18.00–£20.00 **S:** Fr £18.00–£20.00 **Beds:** 1F 2T **Baths:** 1 En 1 Pr 1 Sh (4)

Inchree

NN0263

Glendevin, *Inchree, Onich, Fort William, Inverness-shire, PH33 6SE.* Superb accommodation, fabulous breakfasts, very peaceful location amidst magnificent scenery. **Open:** Easter to Oct
01855 821330 Ms Drever *info@glendevin.com* www.glendevin.com **D:** Fr £18.00–£23.00 **S:** Fr £20.00–£25.00 **Beds:** 1F 3D 1T **Baths:** 2 Pr 3 En (6)

Inverdruie

NH9011

Riverside Lodge, *Inverdruie, Aviemore, Inverness-shire, PH22 1QH.* Architect-designed house in own silver birch woodland with riverside location. **Open:** All year (not New Year)
01479 810153 Mrs Macintyre *riversidelodge@sol.co.uk* www.host.co.uk **D:** Fr £20.00–£25.00 **S:** Fr £25.00–£30.00 **Beds:** 1F 1T 1D **Baths:** 3 En (5)

Invergarry

NH3001

Ardgarry Farm, *Faichern, Invergarry, Inverness-shire, PH35 4HG.* Ideally situated for Great Glen Way, cycle track, Munros, touring. **Open:** All year
01809 501226 (also fax) J Fleming *ardgarry.farm@lineone.net* www.scottish-highlandholidays.co.uk **D:** Fr £14.00–£20.00 **S:** Fr £15.00–£20.00 **Beds:** 2T 2D **Baths:** 1 En 2 Sh (5) (8) cc

Lilac Cottage, *South Laggan, Invergarry, Inverness-shire, PH34 4EA.* Comfortable accommodation, warm welcome in the heart of the Great Glen. **Open:** All year
01809 501410 Mrs Jamieson *lilac.cottage@virgin.net* www.lilac-cottage-lochness.co.uk
D: Fr £14.00–£17.00 **S:** Fr £13.00–£20.00
Beds: 2D 1T **Baths:** 1 Sh (4)

Invergarry Hotel, *Invergarry, Inverness-shire, PH35 4HJ.* A wonderful base for touring the Highlands of Scotland. **Open:** All year (not Xmas/New Year)
01809 501206 R E MacCallum **Fax: 01809 501400** *hotel@invergarry.net* www.invergarry.net **D:** Fr £25.00–£35.00 **S:** Fr £30.00–£40.00
Beds: 1F 3T 5D **Baths:** 10 En (20) **cc**

Invergloy
NN2288

Riverside House, *Invergloy, Spean Bridge, Inverness-shire, PH34 4DY.*
Secluded, peaceful location, 12 acres woodland, gardens, Lochside beach/views, fishing. **Open:** Jan to Nov **Grades:** STB 4 Star
01397 712684 Mr & Mrs Dennis *enquiries@riversidelodge.org.uk* www.riversidelodge.org.uk **D:** Fr £25.00 **S:** Fr £25.00 **Beds:** 1F
Baths: 1 En (2)

Invergordon
NH7168

Craigaron, *17 Saltburn, Invergordon, Ross-shire, IV18 0JX.* Ground floor bedrooms (some seafront), good breakfast, friendly, value for money. **Open:** All year (not Xmas/New Year)
01349 853640 Mrs Brown **Fax: 01349 853619** *jobrown@craigaron.freeserve.co.uk* www.host.co.uk **D:** Fr £18.00–£22.00 **S:** Fr £20.00–£22.00
Beds: 4T 1S **Baths:** 2 En 1 Sh (6)

Inverinate
NG9221

Cruechan, *5 Glebe Road, Inverinate, Glenshiel, Kyle of Lochalsh, Ross-shire, IV40 8HD.* Seafront location, looking towards Mam Ratagan and Five Sisters of Kintail.
Open: All year
01599 511328 (also fax) Mrs Fraser **D:** Fr £17.00–£19.00 **S:** Fr £18.00–£20.00 **Beds:** 2F
Baths: 1 Sh

Foresters Bungalow, *Inverinate, Kyle of Lochalsh, Ross-shire, IV40 8HE.* Shores of Loch Duich on main A87, with superb views of the Kintail Mountains. **Open:** Easter to Oct
01599 511329 Mrs MacIntosh **Fax: 01599 511407** *Jean-MacIntosh@tesco.net* **D:** Fr £17.50–£20.00 **Beds:** 1D 1T **Baths:** 1 En 1 Pr (2) **cc**

Inverlochy
NN1174

19 Lundy Road, *Inverlochy, Fort William, Inverness-shire, PH33 6NY.* Family-run B&B. Views of Ben Nevis, passing steam trains.
Open: All year
01397 704918 Mrs Campbell *acampbell@talk21.com* **D:** Fr £13.00–£17.00 **S:** Fr £15.00–£20.00 **Beds:** 2F **Baths:** 1 Sh (2)

Invermoriston
NH4116

Georgeston, *Invermoriston, Inverness, IV3 6YA.* Bungalow situated near Loch Ness & ideal base for touring. **Open:** All year (not Xmas/New Year)
01320 351264 I Greig **D:** Fr £16.00–£20.00
S: Fr £25.00–£30.00 **Beds:** 1T 2D **Baths:** 1 En 1 Sh

Inverness
NH6645

Edenview, *26 Ness Bank, Inverness, IV2 4SF.* **Open:** Mar to Oct
01463 234397 Mrs Fraser **Fax: 01463 222742** *edenview@clara.co.uk* **D:** Fr £23.00–£30.00 **S:** Fr £22.00–£28.00 **Beds:** 1F 1D 1T **Baths:** 2 En 1 Pr (4)
Edenview Guest House occupies a beautiful situation overlooking the River Ness. Excellent touring centre for viewing the beautiful Scottish highlands, including Glen Affric, Loch Ness and the Black Isle. Castles, exhibitions, shopping, golf, dolphin-watching, monster-hunting.

Westbourne Guest House, *50 Huntly Street, Inverness, IV3 5HS.* **Open:** All year (not Xmas/New Year)
01463 220700 (also fax) Mr Paxton *richard@westbourne.org.uk* www.westbourne.org.uk **D:** Fr £25.00–£35.00
S: Fr £30.00–£40.00 **Beds:** 6F 2T 2D
Baths: 10 En (6) **cc**
Situated on the west bank overlooking the River Ness, five mins walk from city centre, train & bus stations. Rated AA & RAC 4 diamond. Rotary Club tourism award 2001/2002. Highly recommended for comfort & satisfaction. Highland hospitality assured.

B&B owners may vary rates – be sure to check when booking

Pitfaranne, *57 Crown Street, Inverness, IV2 3AY.* **Open:** All year **Grades:** STB 3 Star
01463 239338 Gwen & Jim Morrison **Fax: 01463 240356** *jims@pitfaranne.fsnet.co.uk* www.pitfaranne.co.uk **D:** Fr £16.00–£20.00
S: Fr £18.00–£26.00 **Beds:** 1F 2D 4T **Baths:** 1 En 1 Pr 2 Sh (5)
5 minutes from town centre/rail/bus stations. Find true Highland hospitality in friendly relaxed atmosphere of 100-year-old town house in quiet location. Private showers in all cosy guest rooms. Daily room service. Extensive varied menu. Self-contained 2 bedroom flat also available.

Eskdale Guest House, *41 Greig Street, Inverness, IV3 5PX.* Impeccably-run guest house offers all the comforts of home and a warm Highland welcome. **Open:** All year (not Xmas)
01463 240933 (also fax) Mrs Mazurek *eskdale.guesthouse@lineone.net* www.eskdaleguesthouse.co.uk **D:** Fr £16.00–£25.00 **S:** Fr £22.00–£25.00 **Beds:** 2F 2D 1T 1S **Baths:** 3 En 1 Sh (5)

11 Lovat Road, *Inverness, IV2 3NT.* Victorian house, central location, close to bus/trains. 'Crown Area'.
Open: All year (not Xmas/New Year)
01463 238300 Mrs Mccaffery *johnmccaffery@tesco.net* **D:** Fr £19.00 **S:** Fr £23.00 **Beds:** 1F 1T 1D 1S **Baths:** 2 Sh (12) (3)

Strathmhor Guest House, *99 Kenneth Street, Inverness, IV3 5QQ.* Warm welcome awaits at refurbished Victorian home. Comfortable bedrooms and good food. **Open:** All year
Grades: STB 3 Star
01463 235397 Mr & Mrs Reid *strathmhor@amserve.com* www.smoothhound.co.uk/hotels/strathmh.html **D:** Fr £18.00–£22.00 **S:** Fr £20.00–£25.00 **Beds:** 2F 2T 2D 1S **Baths:** 6 En 1 Pr (5)

Strathisla, *42 Charles Street, Inverness, IV2 3AH.* 2 mins walk to city centre. 1860 Victorian house.
Open: All year (not Xmas)
01463 235657 (also fax) Mr & Mrs Lewthwaite *strathislabb@talk21.com* www.strathisla-inverness.co.uk **D:** Fr £16.00–£18.00 **S:** Fr £18.00–£20.00 **Beds:** 1D 1T 1S
Baths: 1 Sh (2)

Merlewood House, *Merlewood Road, Inverness, IV2 4NL.* UK winner of 'Mansion & Manor of the Year' 1999 and 2000. **Open:** All year
01463 236060 Fax: 01463 711999 *merlewood@norcor.ltd.uk* www.merlewood.norcor.ltd.uk
D: Fr £25.00–£39.00 **S:** Fr £50.00–£68.00
Beds: 1T 3D **Baths:** 4 En (10) cc

Charden Villa, *11 Fairfield Road, Inverness, IV3 5QA.* Warm comfortable family-run house situated 10 mins' walk town centre.
Open: All year
01463 718058 Mrs Munro *liz@chardenvilla.fsnet.co.uk* **D:** Fr £18.00–£22.00
S: Fr £20.00–£25.00 **Beds:** 3F 1D **Baths:** 2 En 1 Sh

The Tilt, *26 Old Perth Road, Inverness, IV2 3UT.* Family home convenient for A9. Ideal touring base. **Open:** All year (not Xmas) **Grades:** STB 3 Star
01463 225352 (also fax) Mrs Fiddes *thetilt26@ukonline.co.uk* **D:** Fr £15.00–£17.00
S: Fr £17.00–£19.00 **Beds:** 1D 1T 1S **Baths:** 1 Sh (4)

Abb Cottage, *11 Douglas Row, Inverness, IV1 1RE.* Central, quiet, riverside historic Listed terraced cottage. Easy access transport. **Open:** Feb to Dec
01463 233486 Miss Storrar **D:** Fr £17.00–£20.00 **S:** Fr £20.00–£25.00 **Beds:** 3T
Baths: 1 Sh (12) (2)

Lyndon, *50 Telford Street, Inverness, IV3 5LE.* A warm and friendly welcome awaits you at the Lyndon. **Open:** All year (not Xmas/New Year) **Grades:** STB 3 Star
01463 232551 D Smith *lyndonguesthouse@btopenworld.com* www.lyndon-guest-house.co.uk **D:** Fr £18.00–£25.00 **S:** Fr £20.00–£30.00
Beds: 4F 1D 1T **Baths:** 6 En (6) cc

14 Glenburn Drive, *Inverness, IV2 4ND.* In residential area of city yet only 15 mins walk from centre. **Open:** May to Oct
01463 238832 (also fax) Mrs Macdonald *cairine@aol.com* **D:** Fr £17.00–£20.00 **S:** Fr £18.00–£21.00 **Beds:** 1T 1S (2)

East Dene, *6 Ballifeary Road, Inverness, IV3 5PJ.* Near Eden Court Theatre. **Open:** All year (not Xmas/New Year)
01463 232976 (also fax) J Greig *dgreig@nildram.co.uk* www.eastdene-inverness.co.uk
D: Fr £23.00–£30.00 **Beds:** 1T 2D **Baths:** 1 En 3 Pr cc

Planning a longer stay? Always ask for any special rates

Cambeth Lodge, *49 Fairfield Road, Inverness, IV3 5QP.* Victorian detached stone built house in quiet residential area.
Open: All year (not Xmas/New Year)
01463 231764 Mrs Carson-Duff *duffcambeth@tinyworld.co.uk* **D:** Fr £16.00–£19.50 **Beds:** 1T 2D **Baths:** 1 En 1 Pr 1 Sh (6)

30 Culduthel Road, *Inverness, IV2 4AP.* 1930s bungalow set in large garden, pleasant to relax in on summer evenings. Central heating. Lounge with open fire which you may have to share with a cat. Your hosts are both qualified local guides.
Open: All year
01463 717181 Mrs Dunnett **Fax: 01463 717188** *kathleensbnb@cs.com* www.puffinexpress.co.uk/bandb.htm **D:** Fr £12.50–£15.00 **S:** Fr £18.00–£22.00 **Beds:** 1D 1T **Baths:** 2 En (10) (2)

Loanfern Guest House, *4 Glenurquhart Road, Inverness, IV3 5NU.* Victorian house with character. 10 minutes walk from town centre. **Open:** All year (not Xmas/New Year)
01463 221660 (also fax) Mrs Campbell **D:** Fr £16.00–£22.00 **S:** Fr £18.00–£23.00 **Beds:** 1F 2T 2D **Baths:** 1 En 2 Sh (4)

Winmar House Hotel, *Kenneth Street, Inverness, IV3 5QG.* Full Scottish breakfast and friendly welcome. Ample parking.
Open: All year (not Xmas)
01463 239328 (also fax) Mrs Maclellan *winmarguesthouse@invernessll.freeserve.co.uk*
D: Fr £16.00–£22.00 **S:** Fr £16.00–£22.00
Beds: 1D 6T 3S **Baths:** 1 En 4 Pr 2 Sh (10) cc

MacGregor's, *36 Ardconnel Street, Inverness, IV2 3EX.* We are situated minutes from River Ness, shops and castle.
Open: All year (not Xmas/New Year)
01463 238357 Mrs MacGregor *james@seafieldorms.orknet.co.uk* www.seafieldorms.orknet.co.uk **D:** Fr £14.00–£18.00 **S:** Fr £15.00–£20.00 **Beds:** 1F 3D 1T 3S **Baths:** 2 En 3 Sh

Roseneath Guest House, *39 Greig Street, Inverness, IV3 5PX.* 100-year-old building in centre location 200 yards from River Ness. **Open:** All year
01463 220201 (also fax) Mr Morrison *roseneath@lineone.net* www.scottish-holiday.com **D:** Fr £15.00–£25.00 **Beds:** 3F 1T 2D
Baths: 5 En 1 Pr (7) (3) cc

Melness Guest House, *8 Old Edinburgh Road, Inverness, IV2 3HF.* Charming, award-winning guest house close to town centre. **Open:** All year
01463 220963 Fax: 01463 717037 *melness@joyce86.freeserve.co.uk* www.melnessie.co.uk
D: Fr £20.00–£26.00 **S:** Fr £25.00–£40.00
Beds: 1F 1T 1D **Baths:** 1 En 1 Sh (3) cc

101 Kenneth Street, *Inverness, IV3 5QQ.* Ideal base for day trips to North Highland and Islands. **Open:** All year
01463 237224 Mrs Reid **Fax: 01463 712249** *dalmoreguesthouse@amserve.net* **D:** Fr £16.00–£25.00 **S:** Fr £20.00–£25.00 **Beds:** 2F 2D 1T 1S **Baths:** 1 En 1 Pr 2 Sh (6) cc

Hazeldean House, *125 Lochalsh Road, Inverness, IV3 5QS.* Friendly Highland welcome. Only 10 mins' walk to town centre. **Open:** All year
01463 241338 Mr Stuart **Fax: 01463 236387** *mail@hazeldeanhouse.co.uk* www.hazeldenehouse.co.uk **D:** Fr £14.00–£18.00 **S:** Fr £16.00–£20.00 **Beds:** 2F 4D 3T 2S **Baths:** 3 En 2 Sh (6)

Macrae Guest House, *24 Ness Bank, Inverness, IV2 4SF.* Non-smoking house overlooking river. 5 mins from town.
Open: All year
01463 243658 *joycemacrae@hotmail.com* **D:** Fr £20.00–£24.00 **S:** Fr £30.00–£35.00 **Beds:** 1T 2D **Baths:** 2 En 1 Pr (5)

Alban House, *Bruce Gardens, Inverness, IV3 5EN.* Walking distance from town centre. Large garden, fish pond. Warm, relaxing ambience. **Open:** All year (not Xmas/New Year)
01463 714301 *enquiries@alban-house.freeserve.co.uk* **D:** Fr £25.00–£29.00
S: Fr £30.00–£38.00 **Beds:** 1F 3T 3D 2S
Baths: 9 En cc

Rotherwood Guest House, *7 Midmills Road, Inverness, IV2 3NZ.* Beautiful Victorian red sandstone villa, situated in a quiet side road, but only 3 mins walk from city centre. Central for restaurants, and ideal for touring all corners of the Highlands and Islands, including Isle of Skye and Loch Ness. **Open:** All year
01463 225732 *junejim.taylor@lineone.net* www.rotherwoodguesthouse.co.uk **D:** Fr £20.00–£25.00 **S:** Fr £25.00–£45.00 **Beds:** 1T 2D **Baths:** 3 En (11) (1) cc

Ardaroul, *3 Fairfield Road, Inverness, IV3 4QA.* Ideally situated near city centre and for exploring the beautiful scenery of the Scottish Highlands. You are assured a warm welcome and excellent accommodation. Choice of menu including full Scottish breakfast. Footbridge to city centre 5 mins away. **Open:** All year (not Xmas/New Year)
01463 237741 Mr & Mrs Murray *george.murray5@btopenworld.com* **D:** Fr £16.00–£20.00 **S:** Fr £16.00–£20.00 **Beds:** 1T 1D 2S
Baths: 2 Sh (2)

John O' Groats

ND3773

Seaview Hotel, *John o' Groats, Wick, Caithness, KW1 4YR.* Scenic seaside location. Family owned, five minutes from Orkney ferry. **Open:** All year
01955 611220 (also fax) Mr Mowat **D:** Fr £14.50–£25.00 **S:** Fr £20.00–£35.00 **Beds:** 3F 3D 2T 1S **Baths:** 5 En 2 Sh (20)

Please respect a B&B's wishes regarding children, animals and smoking

RATES

D = Price range per person sharing in a double or twin room

S = Price range for a single room

Keiss

ND3461 *Sinclair Bay*

Links View, *Keiss, Wick, Caithness, KW1 4XG.* Attractive location overlooking Sinclair Bay. 10 minutes from Orkney Ferry. **Open:** All year
01955 631376 Mrs Brooks **D:** Fr £16.00–£17.00 **S:** Fr £17.00 **Beds:** 1T 2D **Baths:** 1 Pr 1 Sh

Charnwood BandB, *Main Street, Keiss, Wick, Caithness, KW1 4UY.* Charnwood is located in the peaceful village of Keiss which overlooks Sinclair Bay with its miles of sandy beach and harbour. Both within walking distance. Keiss is just 15 minutes' drive to John O'Groats and the Orkney passenger ferry. **Open:** Easter to Oct
01955 631258 Mr & Mrs Hickman **D:** Fr £18.00–£20.00 **S:** Fr £20.00–£22.00 **Beds:** 1F 1D **Baths:** 1 Sh (3)

Kentallen

NN0157

Ardsheal House, *Kentallen, Appin, Argyll, PA38 4BX.* Spectacularly situated on shores of Loch Linnhe, in 800 acres of woodlands, fields, gardens. **Open:** All year
01631 740227 N V C Sutherland **Fax: 01631 740342** *info@ardsheal.co.uk* www.ardsheal.co.uk **D:** Fr £45.00 **S:** Fr £45.00 **Beds:** 1F 2T 4D 1S **Baths:** 8 En cc

Kilchoan

NM4963

Hill View, *Achnaha, Kilchoan, Acharacle, Argyll, PH36 4LW.* **Open:** Mar to Oct
01972 510322 Mrs Macphail **D:** Fr £15.00–£17.00 **S:** Fr £15.00–£17.00 **Beds:** 1T 1D 1S **Baths:** 1 Sh
Achnaha is situated in the centre of an extinct volcanic crater, 1 mile from the renowned Sanna Sands. The position is ideal for walking, geology & ornithology. Natural wildlife is in abundance in this remote part of the Peninsula. Enjoy the warm welcome in this traditional croft house.

Kiltarlity

NH5041 *Brockes Lodge, Priory Hotel*

Cherry Trees, *Kiltarlity, Beauly, Inverness-shire, IV4 7JD.* Come and visit this beautiful part of the Highlands of Scotland with excellent fishing, hill walking, golf. Visit the wonderful Glens of Affric and Strathfarrer, also Loch Ness. A warm welcome awaits you in this spacious, cosy, comfortable country house. **Open:** Feb to Nov
01463 741368 (also fax) Mrs Matheson *cherrytrees@mathesonJ.freeserve.co.uk* **D:** Fr £17.00–£21.00 **S:** Fr £19.00–£23.00 **Beds:** 2D **Baths:** 1Pr (3) (4)

Kincraig

NH8305

March House Guest House, *Feshiebridge, Kincraig, Kingussie, Inverness-shire, PH21 1NG.* Rustic, rural & really good 'home cooking', an ideal base. **Open:** Dec to Oct
01540 651388 (also fax) Caroline Hayes *caroline@marchhse01.freeserve.co.uk* www.kincraig.com/march **D:** Fr £20.00–£25.00 **S:** Fr £23.00 **Beds:** 1F 2D 3T **Baths:** 5 En 1 Pr

Ossian Hotel, *Kincraig, Kingussie, Inverness-shire, PH21 1QD.* Built in 1880s lochside village. Magnificent mountain views. **Open:** Feb to Dec
01540 651242 Mrs Rainbow **Fax: 01540 651633** *ossian@kincraig.com* www.kincraig.com/ossian.htm **D:** Fr £20.00–£31.00 **S:** Fr £20.00–£31.00 **Beds:** 2F 3D 2T 2S **Baths:** 8 En 1 Pr (20) cc

Insh House, *Kincraig, Kingussie, Inverness-shire, PH21 1NU.* Friendly family-run guest house in splendid rural location near loch and mountains. **Open:** All year
01540 651377 Nick & Patsy Thompson *inshhouse@btinternet.com* www.kincraig.com/inshhouse.htm **D:** Fr £19.00–£22.00 **S:** Fr £19.00–£25.00 **Beds:** 1F 1T 1D 2S **Baths:** 2 En 1 Sh

Balcraggan House, *Feshiebridge, Kincraig, Kingussie, Inverness-shire, PH21 1NG.* Wonderful setting where wildlife, walks and cycle routes abound. **Open:** All year
01540 651488 Mrs Gillies **D:** Fr £25.00 **S:** Fr £30.00–£35.00 **Beds:** 1D 1T **Baths:** 2 En (10) (3)

All details shown are as supplied by B&B owners in Autumn 2002

Kingussie

NH7500

The Osprey Hotel, *Kingussie, Inverness-shire, PH21 1EN.* **Open:** All year
Grades: STB 3 Star, AA 5 Diamond
01540 661510 (also fax) Mr & Mrs Burrow *aileen@ospreyhotel.co.uk* www.ospreyhotel.co.uk **D:** Fr £25.00–£32.00 **S:** Fr £25.00–£32.00 **Beds:** 3D 3T 2S **Baths:** 8 En cc
Small hotel in area of outstanding beauty, offering a warm welcome, ensuite accommodation and award-winning food. Aileen and Robert hold AA Food Rosettes and are members of the 'Taste of Scotland'. Ideal base for touring, walking, golf, fishing, etc.

The Scot House Hotel, *Kingussie, Inverness-shire, PH21 1HE.* **Open:** Feb to Dec
01540 661351 *enquiries@scothouse.com* www.scothouse.com **D:** Fr £28.50–£34.00 **S:** Fr £30.00–£40.00 **Beds:** 1F 5T 3D **Baths:** 9 En (30) cc
Award-winning family-run small hotel offering friendly service, excellent accommodation and wonderful food. Amid the magnificent scenery of The Cairngorms ('Monarch of The Glen' country). Nearby forest trails, hill walking, birdwatching, mountain railway, golf, skiing, distilleries, RSPB, wildlife park.

Greystones B&B, *Acres Road, Kingussie, Inverness-shire, PH21 1LA.* Victorian family house, pleasantly secluded, a five minute-walk from Kingussie. **Open:** All year (not Xmas)
01540 661052 Mark & Anne Johnstone **Fax: 01540 662162** *greystones@surf.to* www.surf.to/greystones **D:** Fr £22.00–£25.00 **S:** Fr £22.00–£25.00 **Beds:** 1F 1D 1T 1S **Baths:** 1 Pr 1 Sh (6) cc

Planning a longer stay? Always ask for any special rates

Dunmhor House, *67 High Street, Kingussie, Inverness-shire, PH21 1HX.* Centrally situated for numerous attractions in beautiful scenic Highland village.
Open: All year
01540 661809 & 07786 696384 (M) Fax: 01540 661809 *valeriedunmhor@aol.com* **D:** Fr £16.00–£20.00 **S:** Fr £16.00–£20.00 **Beds:** 2F 2D 1S **Baths:** 1 Sh 3 En (5)

The Hermitage, *Spey Street, Kingussie, Inverness-shire, PH21 1HN.* Warm Highland welcome in heart of Badenoch and Strathspey. Excellent touring base.
Open: All year (not Xmas)
01540 662137 Mr Taylor **Fax: 01540 662177** *thehermitage@clara.net* www.thehermitage-scotland.com **D:** Fr £21.00–£23.00 **S:** Fr £26.00–£28.00 **Beds:** 1F 1T 3D **Baths:** 5 En cc

Kinlochleven

NN1861

Edencoille, *Garbhien Road, Kinlochleven, Argyll, PA40 4SE.* Friendly, comfortable B&B. Home cooking our speciality. Family-run.
Open: All year **Grades:** STB 3 Star
01855 831358 (also fax) Mrs Robertson **D:** Fr £19.00–£23.00 **S:** Fr £30.00–£44.00 **Beds:** 2F 1D 2T **Baths:** 2 Sh 2 En (5)

Hermon, *Kinlochleven, Argyll, PH50 4RA.* Spacious bungalow in village surrounded by hills on West Highland Way.
Open: Easter to Sep
01855 831383 Miss MacAngus *h.macangus@tinyworld.co.uk* **D:** Fr £18.00–£20.00 **S:** Fr £25.00 **Beds:** 1D 2T **Baths:** 1 En 1 Sh (6)

Macdonald Hotel and Camp Site, *Fort William Road, Kinlochleven, Argyll, PH50 4QL.* Modern hotel in Highland style on shore of Loch Leven. Superb views.
Open: Mar to Dec
01855 831539 Mr & Mrs Reece **Fax: 01855 831416** *martin@macdonaldhotel.demon.co.uk* www.macdonaldhotel.demon.co.uk **D:** Fr £24.00–£32.00 **S:** Fr £24.00–£44.00 **Beds:** 1F 4D 5T **Baths:** 10 En (20) cc

BEDROOMS
D = Double
T = Twin
S = Single
F = Family

B&B owners may vary rates – be sure to check when booking

Kyle of Lochalsh

NG7627

Tigh-a-Cladach, *Badicaul, Kyle of Lochalsh, Ross-shire, IV40 8BB.* **Open:** Mar to Nov
01599 534891 (also fax) Mrs Matheson *murdomatheson120@hotmail.com* skyelochalsh.topcities.com/bed.html **D:** Fr £16.50 **S:** Fr £18.00–£20.00 **Beds:** 1T 2D 1S **Baths:** 2 Sh (5)
Situated between Kyle of Lochalsh and Plockton with superb views overlooking the Isle of Skye, all rooms with sea view. Guests can relax in the large garden or in the lounge and watch the seals play. Hotels and restaurants nearby for meals.

A'chomraich, *Main Street, Kyle of Lochalsh, Ross-shire, IV40 8DA.* Warm welcome near amenities. Quiet, great touring centre. **Open:** Easter to Oct
01599 534210 Mrs Murchison **D:** Fr £16.00–£18.00 **S:** Fr £20.00 **Beds:** 2D 1T **Baths:** 2 Sh (3) (3)

Ashgrove, *Balmacara Square, Kyle of Lochalsh, Ross-shire, IV40 8DJ.* Traditional cottage in National Trust village. Ideal base for walking/touring. **Open:** Mar to Nov
01599 566259 Mrs Gordon **D:** Fr £17.00–£20.00 **Beds:** 2D 1T **Baths:** 2 En 1 Pr (3)

3 Lochalsh Road, *Kyle of Lochalsh, IV40 8BP.* Waterfront, near railway, bus stations and Skye Bridge. Warm welcome.
Open: All year (nox Xmas/New Year)
Grades: STB 2 Star
01599 534429 Mrs MacQueen **D:** Fr £15.00–£18.00 **S:** Fr £16.00–£18.00 **Beds:** 1T 1D **Baths:** 1 En (5)

Kyle Hotel, *Main Street, Kyle of Lochalsh, Ross-shire, IV40 8AB.* Nestling in the village of Kyle of Lochalsh and ideally situated for exploring the Isle of Skye via the nearby bridge. Kyle Hotel offers extremely comfortable rooms and a fine restaurant specialising in fresh local foods including seafood and game. **Open:** All year
01599 534204 Fax: 01599 534932 *thekylehotel@btinternet.com* www.btinternet.com/~thekylehotel **D:** Fr £25.00–£47.00 **S:** Fr £25.00–£47.00 **Beds:** 14T 8D 9S **Baths:** 31 En cc

Kylesku

NC2233

Newton Lodge, *Kylesku, Lairg, Sutherland, IV27 4HW.* Highly recommended hotel overlooking small seal colony.
Open: Easter to Sept
01971 502070 (also fax) Mr & Mrs Brauer *newtonlge@aol.com* **D:** Fr £28.00–£30.00 **Beds:** 3T 4D **Baths:** 7 En (10) cc

Laggan (Newtonmore)

NN6194

Gaskmore House Hotel, *Laggan, Newtonmore, Inverness-shire, PH20 1BS.* Set in heart of the Highlands a wonderful place just to be. **Open:** Easter to Oct
01528 544250 (also fax) *gaskmorehouse@aol.com* **D:** Fr £25.00–£45.00 **S:** Fr £30.00–£50.00 **Beds:** 12T 12D 1S **Baths:** 25 En cc

Laid

NC4159

Rowan House, *90 Laid, Loch Eriboll, Lairg, Sutherland, IV27 4UN.* Set in a spectacular setting with uninterrupted views across Loch Eriboll to Ben Hope.
Open: All year
01971 511347 (also fax) Mr MacLellan *h.maclellan@btinternet.com* drive.to/laid **D:** Fr £15.00–£25.00 **S:** Fr £15.00–£25.00 **Beds:** 1F/T 2D **Baths:** 3 En (6)

Laide

NG8992 *Sand Hotel*

Cul Na Mara Guest House, *Catalina Slipway, Sand passage, Laide, Achnasheen, Ross-shire, IV22 2ND.* A stay at Cul Na Mara (Gaelic - Song of the Sea) is an enjoyable experience with superior bed and breakfast accommodation. Guest rooms fully ensuite complete with colour television - private dining room. **Open:** All year (not Xmas/New Year)
01445 731295 Bill Hart **Fax: 01445 731570** *billhart@dircon.co.uk* www.culnamara-guesthouse.co.uk **D:** Fr £22.00 **S:** Fr £33.00 **Beds:** 1F 1D **Baths:** 2 En (5) (4)

Lairg

NC5806

Muirness, *97 Lower Toroboll, Lairg, Sutherland, IV27 4DH.* Comfortable croft house, superb open views. Central for day trips, close to railway. **Open:** All year
01549 402489 Mrs Grey **D:** Fr £16.00–£18.00 **S:** Fr £18.00 **Beds:** 2D 1T **Baths:** 1 Pr 1 Sh (2)

Latheron
ND1933

Tacher, *Latheron, Caithness, KW5 6DX.* On A895 (Thurso). Modern, comfortable farmhouse. **Open:** May to Oct
01593 741313 Mrs Falconer www.host.co.uk **D:** Fr £16.00–£18.00 **S:** Fr £16.00–£20.00 **Beds:** 1F 1D 1T **Baths:** 1 En 1 Sh 1 Pr (8)

Lochcarron
NG8939

Aultsigh, *Croft Road, Lochcarron, Strathcarron, Ross-shire, IV54 8YA.* Spectacular views over Loch Carron. Ideal base for climbing or touring. **Open:** All year
01520 722558 Ms Innes *Moyra.Innes@btinternet.com* **D:** Fr £17.00–£18.00 **S:** Fr £18.00 **Beds:** 1F 1D 1T **Baths:** 2 Sh (6)

Lochinver
NC0922

Suilven, *Badnaban, Lochinver, Lairg, Sutherland, IV27 4LR.* 3 miles from Lochinver, off Achiltibuie Road. Sea angling available. **Open:** All year (not Xmas/New Year)
01571 844358 Mrs Brown **D:** Fr £17.00 **S:** Fr £22.00 **Beds:** 1T 1D **Baths:** 1 Sh (2)

Lochluichart
NH3263

4 Mossford Cottages, *Lochluichart, Garve, IV232QA.* Spectacular view across loch. Friendly informal atmosphere. Central touring position. **Open:** All year (not Xmas/New Year)
01997 414334 Mr & Mrs Doyle **D:** Fr £15.00–£18.00 **S:** Fr £15.00–£18.00 **Beds:** 1F 1T 1D 1S **Baths:** 2 En 1 Pr 1 Sh

Lybster (Wick)
ND2435

Hamnavoe, *Norland Road, Lybster, Caithness, KW3 6AT.* Comfortable bungalow overlooking beautiful countryside. Amenities nearby. Homely welcome. Excellent breakfast. **Open:** Easter to Oct
01593 721411 Mrs Barnie *janebarnie@hotmail.com* www.letsgonorth.com **D:** Fr £18.00–£20.00 **S:** Fr £18.00–£25.00 **Beds:** 1F 1T 1D **Baths:** 3 En (3)

Reisgill House, *Lybster, Caithness, KW3 6BT.* **Open:** All year (not Xmas/New Year)
01593 721212 (also fax) Ms Harper *helen@reisgill-house.com* www.reisgill-house.com **D:** Fr £20.00 **S:** Fr £20.00 **Beds:** 1F 2T 2D 1S **Baths:** 6 En (6)
Our C18th 7-bedroomed house stands in its own grounds one mile from Lybster. All the ensuite rooms have a sea view and we pride ourselves on home-baking and traditional food, salmon and venison being the two favourites.

Mallaig
NM6796

Spring Bank Guest House, *East Bay, Mallaig, Inverness-shire, PH41 4QF.* **Open:** All year (not Xmas/New Year) **Grades:** STB 1 Star
01687 462459 (also fax) Mr Smith **D:** Fr £17.00–£19.00 **S:** Fr £17.00–£19.00 **Beds:** 1F 2D 3T 2S **Baths:** 3 Sh
Spring Bank is a traditional Highland house, situated overlooking the harbour and ferry terminals to Skye, the Small Isles and Knoydart. Mallaig is at the end of the world-famous West Highland Line and is ideal for walking and touring.

Seaview, *Mallaig, Inverness-shire, PH41 4QS.* Family-run. Overlooking harbour, perfectly situated for ferry, train and bus. **Open:** All year (not Xmas/New Year) **Grades:** STB 3 Star
01687 462059 C King **Fax: 01687 462768** *seaviewmallaig@talk21.com* **D:** Fr £17.00–£24.00 **S:** Fr £18.00–£22.00 **Beds:** 2F 2D **Baths:** 3 En 1 Sh

Marine Hotel, *Mallaig, Inverness-shire, PH41 4PY.* Comfortable family run hotel in the fishing village of Mallaig, nearest to rail and ferry terminals. Experience Highland hospitality, our Scottish cuisine and fresh local seafood. Ideal base for day trips to Skye and Inner Hebrides. **Open:** All year (not Xmas/New Year)
01687 462217 E Ironside **Fax: 01687 462821** *marinehotel@btinternet.com* **D:** Fr £28.00–£32.00 **S:** Fr £30.00–£36.00 **Beds:** 2F 9T 5D 3S **Baths:** 18 En 1 Pr (4) **cc**

Rockcliffe, *East Bay, Mallaig, Inverness-shire, PH41 4QF.* Quality accommodation overlooking bay. Trains, ferries and restaurants very close. **Open:** Easter to Oct
01687 462484 Mrs Henderson **D:** Fr £16.00–£17.00 **S:** Fr £18.00 **Beds:** 2D 1S **Baths:** 2 Sh (2)

Planning a longer stay? Always ask for any special rates

Mellon Charles
NG8491

Tranquillity, *21 Mellon Charles, Aultbea, Achnasheen, Ross-shire, IV22 2JN.* Comfortable house in quiet lochside location with wonderful mountain views. **Open:** All year (not Xmas)
01445 731241 (also fax) Mr & Mrs Bond **D:** Fr £20.00 **S:** Fr £20.00–£30.00 **Beds:** 1F 1D 1S **Baths:** 2 En 1 Pr

Melvich
NC8865

Melvich Hotel, *Melvich, Thurso, Caithness, KW14 7YJ.* Stunning views. Brew pubs. 100 malts. Comfortable rooms. **Open:** All year (not Xmas/New Year)
01641 531206 Fax: 01641 531347 *melvichtl@aol.com* www.smoothhound.co.uk/hotels/melvichh.html **D:** Fr £20.00–£25.00 **S:** Fr £30.00–£35.00 **Beds:** 4T 6D 4S **Baths:** 14 En (8) **cc**

Tigh na Clash, *Melvich, Thurso, Caithness, KW14 7YJ.* Modern building. Country views. Ideally situated for touring North Coast. **Open:** Easter to Oct
01641 531262 (also fax) Mrs Ritchie *joan@tighnaclash.co.uk* www.tighnaclash.co.uk **D:** Fr £22.00–£23.00 **S:** Fr £22.00–£23.00 **Beds:** 1F 2T 3D 2S **Baths:** 7 En 1 Pr (8) **cc**

Morar
NM6793

Sunset, *Morar, Mallaig, Inverness-shire, PH40 4PA.* Family-run guest house, sea views, Thai food our speciality. **Open:** All year (not Xmas)
01687 462259 Mrs Clulow **Fax: 01687 460085** *sunsetgh@aol.com* www.sunsetguesthouse.co.uk **D:** Fr £14.00–£19.00 **S:** Fr £14.00–£19.00 **Beds:** 1F 1D 1T **Baths:** 1 En 1 Sh (2) (6)

Glengorm, *Morar, Mallaig, Inverness-shire, PH40 4PA.* In Morar Village. Silversand beaches nearby. Ferry to Skye 2 miles. **Open:** All year
01687 462165 Mrs Stewart *glengormmorar@talk21.com* **D:** Fr £15.00–£16.00 **Beds:** 1D 1T **Baths:** 1 Sh (4)

Muir of Ord
NH5250 *Priory Hotel*

Hillview Park, *Muir of Ord, Ross-shire, IV6 7XS.* Rural situation, adjacent to golf course. Ground floor bungalow. **Open:** Easter to Oct
01463 870787 Mrs Peterkin **D:** Fr £17.00–£19.00 **S:** Fr £18.00–£20.00 **Beds:** 1F 1D 1T **Baths:** 3 En (3)

Blairdhu Farmhouse, *Muir of Ord, Ross-shire, IV6 7RT.* **Open:** Easter to Oct **01463 870536 (also fax)** Mrs Morrison *donaldmorrison@amserve.net* **D:** Fr £15.00–£20.00 **S:** Fr £20.00 **Beds:** 1F 1D 1S **Baths:** 1 Pr 1 Sh (6)
Relax in renovated farmhouse surrounded by superb open views.

Birchgrove, *Arcan, Muir of Ord, Ross-shire, IV6 7UL.* Comfortable country house in quiet area. Guest rooms overlooking garden. **Open:** All year (not Xmas) **01997 433245** Mrs Bell **Fax: 01997 433304** **D:** Fr £15.00–£16.50 **S:** Fr £16.00–£17.00 **Beds:** 1F 1D 1T **Baths:** 1 En 1 Sh (3)

Muirshearlich

NN1380

Strone Farm, *Muirshearlich, Banavie, Fort William, Inverness-shire, PH33 7PB.* Rural setting, panoramic views Ben Nevis, Caledonian Canal. Traditional food. **Open:** Feb to Nov **01397 712773 (also fax)** Mrs Cameron **D:** Fr £18.00–£20.00 **S:** Fr £23.00–£25.00 **Beds:** 2D 1T (3)

Munlochy

NH6453

Craigiehowe, *3 Forestry House, Munlochy, Ross-shire, IV8 8NH.* Quiet cul-de-sac near to all services. **Open:** All year (not Xmas) **01463 811402** Mrs Munro **D:** Fr £15.00 **S:** Fr £16.00–£18.00 **Beds:** 2D

Nairn

NH8856

Aurora Hotel, *2 Academy Street, Nairn, Inverness-shire, IV12 4RJ.* **Open:** All year **01667 453551** M Sulgrani **Fax: 01667 456577** *aurorahotelnairn@aol.com* **D:** Fr £25.00–£35.00 **S:** Fr £34.50–£39.50 **Beds:** 1F 3T 3D 3S **Baths:** 7 En 1 Pr 2 Sh (8) cc
Ideally situated for touring the Highlands, the family-run Aurora Hotel provides comfortable accommodation within a relaxing environment. Our restaurant offers traditional Italian cuisine. Close to Nairn's town-centre, harbour, award-winning beach and two championship golf courses.

Durham House, *4 Academy Street, Nairn, IV12 4RJ.* Elegant Victorian villa near beaches, golf, castles and historic sites. **Open:** All year (not Xmas) **Grades:** STB 3 Star **01667 452345 (also fax)** P J Hudson *durhamhouse@nairn34.freeserve.co.uk* www.durhamhouse-nairn.co.uk **D:** Fr £18.00–£24.00 **S:** Fr £17.00–£20.00 **Beds:** 1F 1D 1T 1S **Baths:** 2 En 1 Pr 1 Sh (4) cc

Redburn, *Queen Street, Nairn, IV12 4AA.* Extremely attractive Victorian villa, quiet location, close to all amenities. **Open:** Easter to Oct **01667 452238 & 07747 090167 (M)** Mr & Mrs Clucas *clucas@redburnvilla.fsnet.co.uk* www.host.co.uk **D:** Fr £17.00–£20.00 **S:** Fr £17.00–£20.00 **Beds:** 1D 1T 1S **Baths:** 2 Sh (4)

Nethy Bridge

NJ0020

Aultmore House, *Nethy Bridge, Inverness-shire, PH25 3ED.* **Open:** All year **Grades:** STB 5 Star **01479 821473** Brian & Irene Taylor **Fax: 01479 821750** *taylor@aultmorehouse.co.uk* www.aultmorehouse.co.uk **D:** Fr £32.50–£40.00 **S:** Fr £35.00–£40.00 **Beds:** 8D 3T **Baths:** 5 En 2 Sh (20)
Aultmore House is a Grade A Listed Edwardian mansion set in 25 acres of formal gardens & mature wooded gardens on the outskirts of Nethybridge. Recently completely refurbished, it is an excellent base for exploring the Highlands & North East Scotland.

Aspen Lodge, *Nethy Bridge, Inverness-shire, PH25 3DA.* Warm welcome and memorable breakfast in heart of picturesque village. **Open:** All year (not Xmas) **01479 821042** Mrs Renton *linda@aspenlodge.fsnet.co.uk* www.nethybridge.com/aspenlodge.htm **D:** Fr £19.50 **S:** Fr £25.00 **Beds:** 1D 1T **Baths:** 1 En 1 Pr

Newtonmore

NN7199

The Pines, *Station Road, Newtonmore, Inverness-shire, PH20 1AR.* **Open:** All year (not Xmas) **01540 673271** Mr Walker **Fax: 01540 673882** www.smoothhound.co.uk/hotels/thepines **D:** Fr £20.00–£25.00 **S:** Fr £20.00–£25.00 **Beds:** 2D 2T 2S **Baths:** 6 En (12) (6) cc
Comfortable Edwardian home with river valley and mountain views. Large wooded garden rich in bird & wildlife. Traditional breakfasts freshly cooked using Scottish produce. Ideal base for RSPB reserves, walking, cycling, Munro bagging & touring the proposed Cairngorms National Park.

Glenquoich House, *Glen Road, Newtonmore, Inverness-shire, PH20 1EB.* High quality accommodation in village centre. Ideal touring/walking area. **Open:** All year **Grades:** STB 3 Star **01540 673461 (also fax)** C Watson *efb007@aol.com* **D:** Fr £18.50–£23.00 **S:** Fr £18.00–£25.00 **Beds:** 1F 2T 1D 1S **Baths:** 1 En 2 Sh (10) (5)

Alder Lodge Guest House, *Glen Road, Newtonmore, Inverness-shire, PH20 1EA.* Beautiful house, quiet situation, 0.25 mile from the shops and hotels. **Open:** All year **01540 673376** Mr Stewart **D:** Fr £15.00 **S:** Fr £15.00 **Beds:** 2 T 2D **Baths:** 1 Sh (6)

Nigg

NH8071

Nigg Ferry Hotel, *Nigg, Tain, Ross Shire, IV19 1QU.* Excellent views over water from lounge. Cruise ships are regular visitors in the Firth. Watch the dolphins at play from the lounge. Play golf at discount prices. Bird watching, shooting and fishing all available locally. **Open:** All year (not Xmas/New Year) **01862 851440 (also fax)** N F Kimber **D:** Fr £25.00 **Beds:** 8F 7T 1D **Baths:** 8 En (12) (20) cc

BEDROOMS
D = Double
T = Twin
S = Single
F = Family

BATHROOMS
En = Ensuite
Pr = Private
Sh = Shared

Onich

NN0261

Camus House, *Lochside Lodge, Onich, Fort William, Inverness-shire, PH33 6RY.* Beautiful Victorian country house in outstanding location between Fort William - Glencoe. **Open:** Feb to Nov
01855 821200 Fax: 01855 821 200 *young@camushouse.freeserve.co.uk* www.smoothhound.co.uk/hotels/camushouse.html **D:** Fr £23.50–£30.00 **S:** Fr £27.50–£35.00 **Beds:** 2F 2T 3D **Baths:** 6 En 1 Sh cc

Plockton

NG8033 *Plockton Hotel, Plockton Inn*

2 Frithard Road, *Plockton, Ross-shire, IV52 8TQ.* Modern, comfortable, 'home from home' accommodation **Open:** All year
01599 544226 (also fax) Mrs Cameron *ewen@frithard.freeserve.co.uk* **D:** Fr £15.00–£19.00 **S:** Fr £15.00–£20.00 **Beds:** 1T 2D

Poolewe

NG8580

Creagan, *Poolewe, Ross-shire, IV22 2LD.* Quiet country house in highland village. Private off-road parking, good breakfasts with home-baking. **Open:** Mar to Oct
01445 781424 (also fax) Mrs MacKenzie **D:** Fr £18.00–£20.00 **S:** Fr £25.00 **Beds:** 2D 1T **Baths:** 2 En 1 Pr (4)

Corriness Guest House, *Poolewe, Achnasheen, Ross-shire, IV22 2JU.* Cherished Edwardian villa by Inverewe Gardens and Loch Ewe. **Open:** Easter to Oct
01445 781262 Mrs Rowley **Fax: 01445 781263 D:** Fr £23.00–£25.00 **Beds:** 3T 2D **Baths:** 5 En (10) cc

Portgower

ND0013

Bayview BandB, *Portgower, Helmsdale, Sutherland, KW8 6HL.* A C19th cottage perfectly situated on the shore of the Moray Firth. Step through our garden gate and explore the beach and coastline which offer you peace, tranquillity and sea breezes. A warm welcome is offered by Alastair and Pat Leitch. **Open:** All year (not Xmas/New Year)
01431 821679 (also fax) Mr Leitch www.bayview-helmsdale.org.uk **D:** Fr £15.00 **S:** Fr £15.00 **Beds:** 2D (2)

Portmahomack

NH9184

Wentworth House, *Tarbatness Road, Portmahomack, Tain, Ross-shire, IV20 1YB.* Historic former manse beside golf course, overlooking Dornoch Firth, home of the bottle-nosed dolphins. **Open:** All year
01862 871897 Mrs Elliott *monicaelliott@wentworth39.demon.co.uk* **D:** Fr £20.00–£22.50 **S:** Fr £25.00 **Beds:** 3T **Baths:** 1 En 2 Sh (6)

Rhiconich

NC2552 *Fisherman's Mission*

Beachview BandB, *165 Drumnaguie, Rhiconich, Lairg, Sutherland, IV27 4RT.* Perfectly situated for exploring the delightful NW Highlands. Clean and comfortable accommodation overlooking sandy beach. Scottish breakfast. Near small fishing village. Ideal for walking, fishing, bird watching, golf, climbing and one mile from the famous Sandwood Bay Road End. **Open:** Easter to Oct
01971 521780 (also fax) Mrs Macdonald **D:** Fr £15.00–£18.00 **S:** Fr £18.00 **Beds:** 1F/T 2D **Baths:** 2 Sh (6)

Rogart

NC7303

Benview, *Lower Morness, Rogart, Sutherland, IV28 3XG.* Traditional country farmhouse offering peace and quiet, comfort, good food. **Open:** Easter to Oct
01408 641222 Mrs Corbett **D:** Fr £15.00–£15.50 **S:** Fr £16.00 **Beds:** 1T 1S 2D **Baths:** 2 Sh

Rothiemurchus

NH9308

Loiste View, *2 Dell Mhor, Rothiemurchus, Aviemore, Inverness-shire, PH22 1QW.* Aviemore semi-detached bungalow near tennis, canoeing. Ideal for walking **Open:** All year (not Xmas/New Year)
01479 810230 Mrs Bruce **D:** Fr £16.00 **S:** Fr £18.00 **Beds:** 1T 1D **Baths:** 1 Sh (2)

Scaniport

NH6239

Ballindarroch, *Aldourie, Inverness, IV2 6EL.* A warm, friendly country house, set in extensive woodland gardens. **Open:** All year
01463 751348 Mrs Parsons **Fax: 01463 751372** *BandB@ballindarroch.fsnet.co.uk* www.milford.co.uk/go/ballindarroch.html **D:** Fr £20.00–£30.00 **S:** Fr £20.00–£30.00 **Beds:** 1F 1D 1T 1S **Baths:** 1 Pr 2 Sh (8)

Scourie

NC1544

Badcall Stoerview, *Scourie, Lairg, Sutherland, IV27 4TH.* This house overlooks Eddrachillis Bay, the Mountains of Assynt, Badcall Islands. **Open:** May to Oct
01971 502411 (also fax) Mrs MacKay *badcall@supanet.com* www.badcall.supanet.com **D:** Fr £16.00–£17.00 **S:** Fr £25.00–£30.00 **Beds:** 1F 1D **Baths:** 1 Sh (5)

Minch View, *Scouriemore, Scourie, Lairg, Sutherland, IV27 4TG.* Modern comfortable croft house. Home-cooking. Outstanding views and hospitality. **Open:** Easter to Oct
01971 502010 Mrs MacDonald *aileen.macdonald@btinternet.com* **D:** Fr £19.00 **S:** Fr £19.00–£25.00 **Beds:** 2D 1T **Baths:** 2 Sh

Shieldaig (Loch Shieldaig)

NG8153

Tigh Fada, *117 Doireaonar, Shieldaig, Strathcarron, Ross-shire, IV54 8XH.* Family home on working croft, magnificent scenery. **Open:** Feb to Nov
01520 755248 (also fax) Mrs Calcott **D:** Fr £15.50 **S:** Fr £16.00–£18.00 **Beds:** 1F 1T **Baths:** 1 Sh (3) cc

Smithton

NH7145

3a Resaurie, *Smithton, Inverness, IV2 7NH.* **Open:** All year
01463 791714 Mrs Mansfield *mbmansfield@uk2.net* www.mansfieldhighlandholidays.f2s.com
D: Fr £17.00–£21.00 **S:** Fr £17.00–£30.00 **Beds:** 2D 1T **Baths:** 1 En 1 Sh (3) cc
Quiet residential area 3 miles east of Inverness. Public transport nearby. GB National Cycle Routes 1 & 7 passes door. Adjacent to farmland. Views to Moray Firth, Ben Wyvis and Ross-shire Hills. Home baking, high tea, Evening meals. A CHRISTIAN HOME.

BATHROOMS
En = Ensuite
Pr = Private
Sh = Shared

South Laggan

NN2996

Forest Lodge, *South Laggan, Invergarry, Inverness-shire, PH34 4EA.* Ian and Janet Shearer offer friendly hospitality, pleasant ensuite accommodation, and home cooking in their rurally set home close to the Great Glen Way. Walking or touring, Forest Lodge is the perfect stopover. **Open:** All year (not Xmas/New Year) **01809 501219** Mr & Mrs Shearer **Fax: 01809 501476** *info@flgh.co.uk* www.flgh.co.uk **D:** Fr £17.00–£22.00 **S:** Fr £24.00–£29.00 **Beds:** 2F 2T 3D **Baths:** 6 En 1 Pr (10) cc

Spean Bridge

NN2281

Coinachan Guest House, *Gairlochy Road, Spean Bridge, Inverness-shire, PH34 4EG.* **Open:** All year (not Xmas) **Grades:** STB 4 Star **01397 712417** H C Hoare **Fax: 01397 712528** *coinachan@supanet.com* **D:** Fr £20.00–£25.00 **S:** Fr £20.00–£35.00 **Beds:** 2D 1T **Baths:** 3 En
Enjoy a relaxing informal stay in a tastefully modernised C17th Highland home offering a high standard of comfort and attention to detail. Privately-situated overlooking mountains and moorland, carefully prepared 4 course dinner available. Perfect touring base, special 7 day rates.

Coire Glas Guest House, *Spean Bridge, Inverness-shire, PH34 4EU.* Spectacular views of Grey Corries. Ideal base for climbing / touring. **Open:** All year (not Xmas) **01397 712272 (also fax)** Mr & Mrs Shaw *enquiry@coireglas.co.uk* www.coireglas.co.uk **D:** Fr £14.50–£19.50 **S:** Fr £14.50–£25.00 **Beds:** 2F 4D 4T 1S **Baths:** 8 En 3 Sh (11) cc

Distant Hills Guest House, *Spean Bridge, Inverness-shire, PH34 4EU.* Perfectly situated for exploring Highlands. Panoramic views. **Open:** All year **01397 712452** *enquiry@distanthills.com* www.distanthills.com **D:** Fr £20.00–£24.00 **S:** Fr £30.00–£37.00 (12) cc

Mahaar, *Corrie Choillie Road, Spean Bridge, Inverness-Shire, PH34 4EP.* Ideal base for walking, cycling or touring, good highland hospitality. **Open:** All year **01397 712365 (also fax)** *alan@mahaar.co.uk* www.mahaar.co.uk **D:** Fr £16.50–£18.00 **S:** Fr £17.00–£18.50 **Beds:** 1F 1T 1D 2S **Baths:** 2 Sh cc

Dreamweavers, *Earendil, Mucomir, Spean Bridge, PH34 4EQ.* Traditional Scottish hospitality and cuisine amidst stunning Highland scenery. **Open:** All year **01397 712548** H Maclean *helen@dreamweavers.co.uk* www.dreamweavers.co.uk **D:** Fr £15.00–£20.00 **S:** Fr £15.00–£20.00 **Beds:** 1F 1T 1D **Baths:** 1 En 2 Pr (5) 3

Stoer

NC0328

Cruachan Guest House, *Stoer, Lochinver, Lairg, Sutherland, IV27 4JE.* Comfortable Highland home with log fires. Ideal walking/fishing area. **Open:** All year **01571 855303 (also fax)** Mrs Campbell *cruchan@rdplus.net* **D:** Fr £22.00 **S:** Fr £35.00–£44.00 **Beds:** 2T 2D **Baths:** 3 En 1 Pr (4)

Stoer Villa, *Stoer, Lairg, Sutherland, IV27 4JE.* Victorian villa near Atlantic, sandy beaches, hill walkers and anglers paradise. **Open:** All year (not Xmas/New Year) **01571 855305** Mrs Spykers **D:** Fr £15.00–£17.00 **S:** Fr £15.00–£17.00 **Beds:** 1D 1T **Baths:** 1 Sh (5)

Strathkanaird

NC1402

Loch Dubh House, *Strathkanaird, Ullapool, Wester Ross, IV26 2TW.* Out of town. Quiet and comfortable. Excellent breakfast. Ideal base **Open:** All year **01854 666224 Fax: 0870 0569379** *stay@lochdubhhouse.co.uk* www.lochdubhhouse.co.uk **D:** Fr £18.00–£28.00 **S:** Fr £20.00–£45.00 **Beds:** 1T 2D **Baths:** 1 En 1 Sh (4)

Strathpeffer

NH4858

Scoraig, *8 Kinnettas Square, Strathpeffer, Ross-shire, IV14 9BD.* Quiet location in Victorian village, ideal base for touring Highlands. **Open:** All year (not Xmas) **Grades:** STB 3 Star **01997 421847** Mrs MacDonald *macdonald@kinnettas.freeserve.co.uk* **D:** Fr £15.00–£17.00 **S:** Fr £15.00–£20.00 **Beds:** 1F 1D 1T 1S **Baths:** 1 En 1 Sh (6)

Burnhill, *Strathpeffer, Ross-shire, IV14 9DH.* Victorian house situated at entrance on former spa village. Excellent centre for touring. **Open:** Easter to Oct **01997 421292** Mrs Watt *jockwatt@icscotland.net* **D:** Fr £15.00–£18.00 **S:** Fr £18.00 **Beds:** 1F 1T 1D **Baths:** 1 En 1 Pr

Strathy Point

NC8167

Sharvedda, *Strathy Point, Thurso, Caithness, KW14 7RY.* Small working croft. Spectacular views to Orkney Islands. Spacious lounge. **Open:** All year **Grades:** STB 3 Star **01641 541311** Mrs Askhill *patsy@sharvedda.co.uk* www.sharvedda.co.uk **D:** Fr £22.00–£24.00 **S:** Fr £30.00–£35.00 **Beds:** 2T 1D **Baths:** 2 En 1 Pr

Strontian

NM8161

Carm Cottage, *Monument Park, Strontian, Acharacle, Argyll, PH36 4HZ.* Ideal stop for visiting Mull and smaller Isles, plus touring around Ardnamurchan. **Open:** Apr to Oct **01967 402268 & 01967 402112** Mrs Macnaughton **Fax: 01967 402095 D:** Fr £16.00–£19.00 **Beds:** 3F 1T 2D **Baths:** 1 En 1 Sh (3)

Tain (Dornoch Firth)

NH7881

Rosslyn, *4 Hartfield Gardens, Tain, Ross-shire, IV19 1DL.* **Open:** Mar to Nov **01862 892697** Mrs Anderson *agnes@anderson33.freeserve.co.uk* **D:** Fr £16.00–£18.00 **S:** Fr £17.00–£20.00 **Beds:** 1F 1T **Baths:** 2 Pr (4)
Tain has a first class golf course, Glenmorangie Distillery 2 miles away, Skibo Castle 5 miles away, Royal Dornoch Golf Course 10 miles away, Falls of Shin 20 miles away, local fishing. Stopover to Orkney ferries less than 2 hours away.

Golf View Guest House, *13 Knockbreck Road, Tain, Ross-shire, IV19 1BN.* Secluded Victorian house, overlooking Tain golf course and Dornoch Firth. **Open:** Feb to Nov **Grades:** STB 4 Star, AA 4 Diamond **01862 892856** Mrs Ross **Fax: 01862 892172** *booking@golf-view.co.uk* www.golf-view.co.uk **D:** Fr £20.00–£25.00 **S:** Fr £25.00–£40.00 **Beds:** 1F 1D 3T **Baths:** 3 En 1 Sh (5) (7) cc

Carringtons, *Morangie Road, Tain, Ross-shire, IV19 1PY.* Large Victorian house facing sea. Suitable stopover for Orkney Isles. **Open:** All year (not Xmas)
01862 892635 (also fax) Mrs Roberts *mollie1@btinternet.com* www.stelogic.com/carringtons **D:** Fr £16.00–£18.00 **S:** Fr £20.00–£25.00 **Beds:** 2F 1D **Baths:** 2 En

Thurso

ND1168

Ivordene, *Janetstown, Thurso, Caithness, KW14 7XF.* Peacefully situated modern farmhouse, near golf course, ferry to Orkney. **Open:** All year (not Xmas)
01847 894760 Mrs MacIvor **D:** Fr £16.00 **S:** Fr £16.00 **Beds:** 1F 1D 2T 1S **Baths:** 2 Sh

The St Clair Hotel, *Thurso, Caithness, KW14 7AJ.* Town centre, high standard, family run hotel. **Open:** All year
01847 896481 (also fax) Mrs Munro *stclairhotel@aol.com* www.stclairhotel.co.uk
D: Fr £25.00–£30.00 **S:** Fr £25.00–£32.00 **Beds:** 2F 12T 12D 6S **Baths:** 32 En cc

3 Ravenshill Road, *Thurso, Caithness, KW14 7PX.* Easy access to rail and ferry, spectacular Highland scenery. Warm welcome assured. **Open:** May to Sept
01847 894801 Mrs Milne **D:** Fr £16.00 **S:** Fr £17.00 **Beds:** 1D 1T **Baths:** 1 Sh

Tomatin

NH8029

Millcroft, *Old Mill Road, Tomatin, Inverness, IV13 7YN.* 1850 modernised crofthouse in quiet village. Ideal base for touring. **Open:** All year
01808 511405 Mrs Leitch *margaret_tomatin@hotmail.com* **D:** Fr £18.00 **S:** Fr £20.00–£25.00 **Beds:** 1D 1F **Baths:** 1 En 1 Pr

Tongue

NC5956

Strathtongue Old Manse, *Tongue, Lairg, Sutherland, IV27 4XR.* Attractive Victorian Highland manse. Woodland setting, lovely gardens, spectacular views, beautiful beach nearby. **Open:** All year (not Xmas/New Year)
01847 611252 Mrs MacKay *oldmanse@strathtongue.freeserve.co.uk* **D:** Fr £19.00–£21.00 **S:** Fr £20.00–£25.00 **Beds:** 2D 1T **Baths:** 1 En 2 Pr

BEDROOMS
D = Double
T = Twin
S = Single
F = Family

77 Dalcharn, *Tongue, Lairg, Sutherland, IV27 4XU.* Croft cottage set in quiet valley. Families welcome. Phone for brochure. **Open:** All year
01847 611251 Mrs MacIntosh **D:** Fr £13.00–£15.00 **S:** Fr £15.00 **Beds:** 1F 1D 1T 1S **Baths:** 1 En 1 Sh

Tore

NH6052

Fiveways Bed & Breakfast, *Tore, Muir of Ord, Ross-shire, IV6 7RY.* Large garden. Ideal touring & walking area. Dolphin- & bird-watching, golf. **Open:** All year (not Xmas/New Year)
01463 811408 Mrs MacKenzie **D:** Fr £15.00–£17.00 **S:** Fr £17.00 **Beds:** 1F 1D 1T **Baths:** 1 En 2 Sh

Ullapool

NH1294

3 Vyner Place, *Ullapool, Ross-shire, IV26 2XR.* Good base for touring Highlands & ferry to the Western Isles. **Open:** All year **Grades:** STB 4 Star
01854 612023 & 07766 182203 (M) Mrs MacRae **Fax: 01854 612023 D:** Fr £19.00–£22.00 **S:** Fr £25.00 **Beds:** 1D 1F/T **Baths:** 1 En 1 Pr

Broombank Bungalow, *Castle Terrace, Ullapool, IV26 2XD.* A warm welcome awaits. Panoramic views over Loch Broom and Summer Isles. **Open:** All year
01854 612247 Mrs Couper *shirley.couper@tesco.net* **D:** Fr £17.50–£20.00 **Beds:** 1T 2D **Baths:** 3 En

Westhill

NH7144 *Tomatin Inn, Cawdor Tavern*

Easter Muckovie Farm House, *Westhill, Inverness, IV2 5BN.* Original farmhouse modernised set in a rural location overlooking Inverness town, Moray Firth. **Open:** All year
01463 791556 J H MacLellan *dot.westhill@virgin.co.uk* **D:** Fr £18.00–£20.00 **S:** Fr £25.00 **Beds:** 2F **Baths:** 1 En 1 Pr

Planning a longer stay? Always ask for any special rates

Wick

ND3650

Bilbster House, *Bilbster, Wick, Caithness, KW1 5TB.* Traditionally furnished C17th house. Central for the many attractions of Caithness. **Open:** All year (not Xmas/New Year) **Grades:** STB 3 Star
01955 621212 (also fax) Mr Stewart *ianstewart@bilbster.freeserve.co.uk* www.accommodationbilbster.com **D:** Fr £18.00–£19.50 **S:** Fr £18.00–£19.50 **Beds:** 1T 1D **Baths:** 2 En 1 Sh

The Clachan, *13 Randolph Place, South Rd, Wick, Caithness, KW1 5NJ.* Family-run, perfect for exploring the North and Orkney Islands. **Open:** All year (not Xmas) **Grades:** STB 4 Star, AA 4 Diamond
01955 605384 Mrs Bremner *enquiry@theclachan.co.uk* www.theclachan.co.uk **D:** Fr £20.00–£22.00 **S:** Fr £25.00–£30.00 **Beds:** 2D 1T **Baths:** 3 En

9 Francis Street, *Wick, Caithness, KW1 5PZ.* 2 mins to railway & bus station, close to amenities. **Open:** All year (not Xmas/New Year)
01955 602136 & 07780 874477 (M) Mrs Carter *john.d.carter@talk21.com* **D:** Fr £16.00–£19.00 **S:** Fr £16.00–£19.00 **Beds:** 3F 1D **Baths:** 2 En 1 Sh

Quayside, *25 Harbour Quay, Wick, Caithness, KW1 5EP.* We provide comfortable accommodation within a relaxed atmosphere, overlooking a traditional harbour front. **Open:** All year
01955 603229 Mr Turner **Fax: 01955 604518** *quayside@quaysidewick.co.uk* www.quaysidewick.co.uk **D:** Fr £15.50–£19.50 **S:** Fr £18.00–£28.00 **Beds:** 2F 2D 1T 2S **Baths:** 2 En 2 Sh

Wellington Guest House, *41-43 High Street, Wick, Caithness, KW1 4BS.* Perfectly situated in the town centre close to railway station. **Open:** All year
01955 603287 **D:** Fr £22.50–£25.00 **S:** Fr £20.00–£25.00 **Beds:** 6T **Baths:** 6 En cc

RATES
D = Price range per person sharing in a double or twin room
S = Price range for a single room

Inner Hebrides

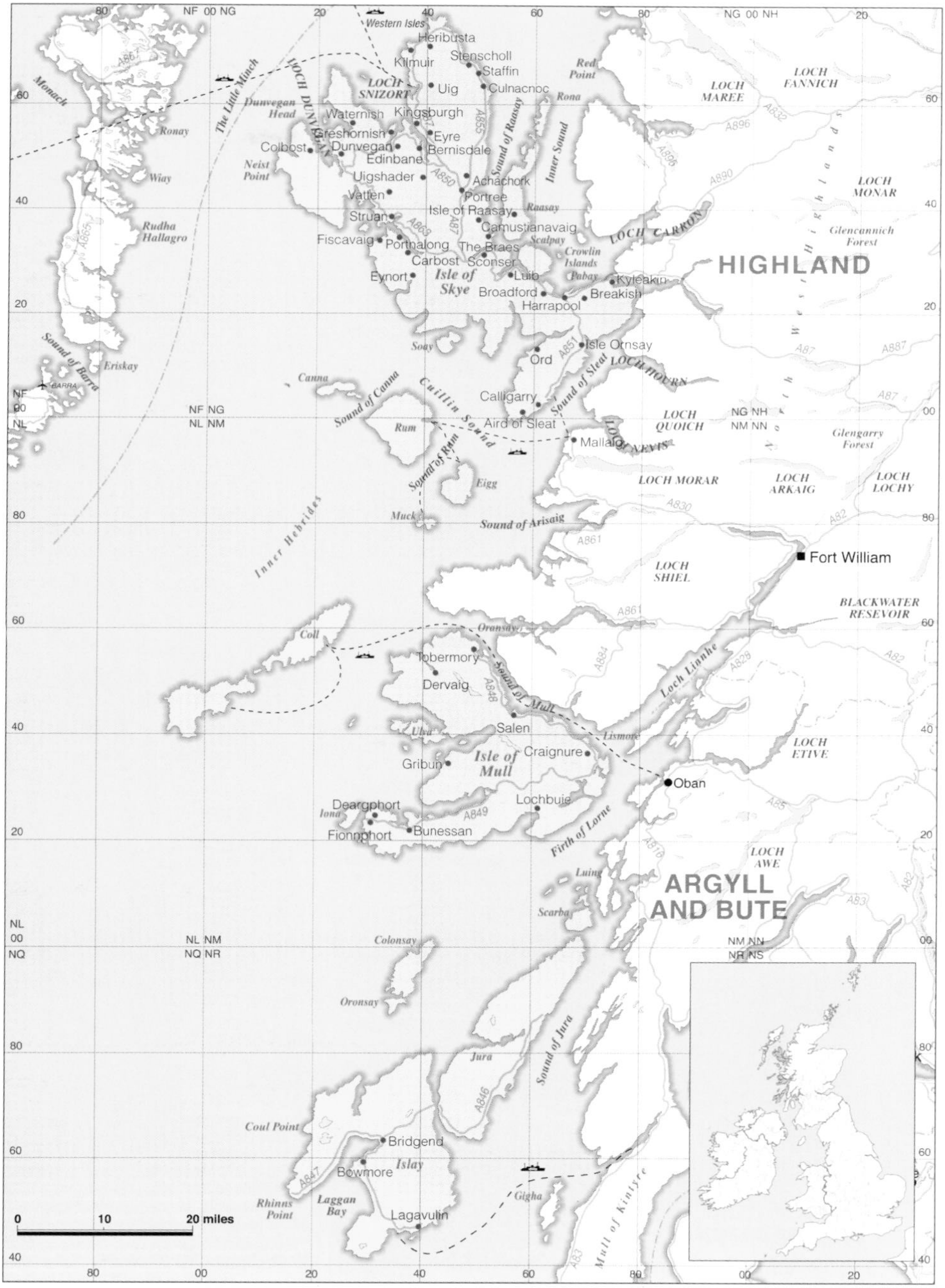

ISLAY Bowmore

NR3159

Lochside Hotel, *Shore Street, Bowmore, Isle of Islay, PA43 7LB.* Excellent value accommodation, food and whisky!
Open: All year
01496 810244 Mrs Birse *birse@lochsidehotel.co.uk* www.lochsidehotel.co.uk
D: Fr £20.00 **S:** Fr £20.00 **Beds:** 1F 1D 1T 5S **Baths:** 8 En

ISLAY Bridgend

NR3361

2 Mulindry Cottages, *Bridgend, Isle Of Islay, PA44 7PZ.* **Open:** All year **Grades:** STB 3 Star
01496 810397 Mrs Macfarlane **Fax: 01469 810397 D:** Fr £20.00 **S:** Fr £25.00 **Beds:** 1T **Baths:** 1 Sh 3
Comfortable accommodation in family home. All on ground floor. Good breakfast provided, quiet scenic area with views to surrounding hills and Iron Age fort. Ideal location for walking, bird-watching and fishing.

MULL Bunessan

NM3821

Tigh Na Lochan Guest House, *Assapol, Bunessan, Isle of Mull, PA67 6DW.*
Open: All year
01681 700247 Mrs Rothwell *libby@tighnalochan.fsnet.co.uk* **D:** Fr £20.00–£25.00 **S:** Fr £30.00–£35.00 **Beds:** 2T 2D **Baths:** 4 En (2) (6)
Situated on the south-west corner of the Isle of Mull, 5 miles from the Iona/Staffa ferries. You will find a warm friendly Scottish welcome. A picturesque Lochside setting with beautiful views, nearby are white sandy beaches. Perfect for a quiet break, walking, bird-watching and fishing, or generally relaxing. 2 doubles, 2 twins all ensuite with TV/video & tea/coffee-making facilities. Delicious evening meals served in conservatory overlooking the Loch using traditional Scottish fayre. Log fire in season, residents' lounge with widescreen TV, video, DVD & CD facilities.

Ardness House, *Tiraghoil, Bunessan, Isle of Mull, PA67 6DU.* Family-run B&B near Iona, Staffa, beaches, outstanding sea views.
Open: Easter to Oct
01681 700260 (also fax) Messrs MacNeill *ardness@supanet.com* www.isleofmullholidays.com **D:** Fr £18.00–£22.00 **Beds:** 2D 1T **Baths:** 3 En (3)

MULL Craignure

NM7136 *Craignure Inn, Ceildh Place*

Inverlussa, *Craignure, Isle of Mull, PA65 6BD.* Warm, spacious, elegant, relaxed home **Open:** Easter to Oct
01680 812436 Mrs Wilson **D:** Fr £18.00–£20.00 **S:** Fr £18.00–£20.00 **Beds:** 1F 2T 2D **Baths:** 1 En 1 Sh

Goldings, *Craignure, Isle of Mull, PA65 6AY.* Comfortable, newly built bungalow in quiet position, overlooking Loch Linnhe and Sound of Mull. 200 yards from buses and main ferry to Oban. You are assured, a warm welcome and relaxing stay. Ideal walking centre. Food, drink and shop nearby. **Open:** All year
01680 812427 (also fax) Mr & Mrs Roberts **D:** Fr £20.00–£25.00 **S:** Fr £20.00–£25.00 **Beds:** 1T 1D **Baths:** 1 Sh (3)

MULL Deargphort

NM3025

Red Bay Cottage, *Deargphort, Fionnphort, Isle of Mull, PA66 6BP.* Isolated, modernised home with restaurant. Ideal for Mull, Iona, Staffa. **Open:** All year (not New Year)
01681 700396 Mr Wagstaff **D:** Fr £16.50 **S:** Fr £16.50 **Beds:** 1D 2T **Baths:** 3 Sh (10)

MULL Dervaig

NM4352

Kengharair Farm, *Dervaig, Isle of Mull, PA75 6QR.* Victorian farmhouse on hillside, overlooking glen and river beautiful scenery. **Open:** All year
01688 400251 (also fax) Mrs Caskie **D:** Fr £16.00–£17.00 **S:** Fr £16.00–£18.00 **Beds:** 1F 2T **Baths:** 1 Sh (4)

MULL Fionnphort

NM3023

Bruach Mhor, *Fionnphort, Isle of Mull, PA66 6BL.* Near Iona/Staffa ferries. Beautiful coastline, walking, wildlife. Vegetarian cooking. **Open:** All year (not Xmas)
01681 700276 (also fax) Mrs Heald *heather@bruachmhor.ndo.co.uk* **D:** Fr £17.00 **S:** Fr £16.00–£20.00 **Beds:** 1F 1D 1T 1S **Baths:** 1 En 1 Sh (4)

Staffa House, *Fionnphort, Isle of Mull, PA66 6BL.* **Open:** Mar to Oct
01681 700677 (also fax) D: Fr £20.00–£25.00 **S:** Fr £25.00–£44.00 **Beds:** 2T 1D **Baths:** 3 En (5) cc
Full of antiques and individual touches which set Staffa House apart from similar establishments. 2 minutes walk Iona/Staffa (Fingal's Cave) ferries. Conservatory dining room full of floral extravaganza. Ideal for dinner watching Hebridean sunset and views of Iona and Abbey.

Caol-Ithe, *Fionnphort, Isle of Mull, PA66 6BL.* Warm, spacious bungalow. A highland hospitality awaits you. Private car parking. **Open:** All year (not Xmas/New Year)
01681 700375 (also fax) Mrs Dickson *mary@caol-ithe.demon.co.uk* **D:** Fr £20.00–£22.00 **S:** Fr £20.00–£22.00 **Beds:** 1T 2D **Baths:** 2 En 1 Sh

MULL Gribun

NM4534

Derryguaig, *Gribun, Isle of Mull, PA68 6EJ.* Situated bottom Ben More overlooking Loch na Keal. Ideal walking, cycling, wildlife. **Open:** All year
01680 300363 R & A MacKenzie www.derryguaig.freeserve.co.uk **D:** Fr £18.00–£20.00 **S:** Fr £18.00–£20.00 **Beds:** 1T 2D **Baths:** 2 Sh (4)

MULL Lochbuie

NM6124

Barrachandroman, *Kinlochspelve, Lochbuie, Isle of Mull, PA62 6AA.* Luxurious converted barn. Rural location, excellent walking, wildlife, birdwatching. **Open:** All year (not Xmas/New Year)
01680 814220 Mrs Railton Edwards **Fax: 01680 814247** *edwards@lochbuie.org.uk* **D:** Fr £25.00 **S:** Fr £25.00 **Beds:** 2D **Baths:** 1 En 1 Pr (6)

MULL Tobermory

NM5055

The Cedars, *Dervaig Road, Tobermory, Isle of Mull, PA75 6PY.* Detached bungalow, separate B&B facilities, set in wooded garden. **Open:** All year (not Xmas)
01688 302096 Mr Bettley *thecedars@talk21.com* www.tobermory.co.uk/thecedars **D:** Fr £15.00–£16.00 **S:** Fr £16.00–£20.00 **Beds:** 1D 1T **Baths:** 1 Sh (4)

National Grid References given are for villages, towns and cities – not for individual houses

2 Victoria Street, *Tobermory, Isle of Mull, PA75 6PH.* On-street parking, 5 minutes from shops and harbour. **Open:** All year (not Xmas/New Year)
01688 302263 (also fax) Mrs Harper *harper@victoriast2.fsnet.co.uk* **D:** Fr £14.00–£16.00 **S:** Fr £15.00–£18.00 **Beds:** 1D 1T **Baths:** 1 Sh

Harbour House, *Main Street, Tobermory, Isle of Mull, PA75 6NU.* Family-run guest house overlooking Tobermory Bay. **Open:** All year (not Xmas)
01688 302209 Mrs MacLean **Fax: 01688 302750** *harbourhou@aol.com* **D:** Fr £19.50–£22.00 **S:** Fr £19.50–£44.00 **Beds:** 2F 3D 2T 2S **Baths:** 5 En 2 Sh (10) cc

Tobermory Hotel, *53 Main Street, Tobermory, Isle of Mull, PA75 6NT.* Set on the waterfront of picturesque Tobermory Bay. Delicious meals and drinks. **Open:** All year (not Xmas)
01688 302091 Mr Stevens **Fax: 01688 302254** *tobhotel@tinyworld.co.uk* **D:** Fr £35.00–£45.00 **S:** Fr £39.00–£90.00 **Beds:** 2F 8D 4T 2S **Baths:** 15 En 1 Pr cc

Harbour Heights, *Western Road, Tobermory, Isle of Mull, PA75 6PR.* Recently refurbished with attention to comfort and style. Lounge themed in burgundy. **Open:** Easter to Oct
01688 302430 (also fax) Mr Stojak **D:** Fr £22.50–£25.00 **S:** Fr £25.00–£30.00 **Beds:** 2T 4D **Baths:** 6 En (12) (20)

RAASAY Isle of Raasay

NG5537

Isle Of Raasay Hotel, *Isle of Raasay, Kyle of Lochalsh, Ross-shire, IV40 8PB.* **Open:** All year **Grades:** STB 2 Star
01478 660222 (also fax) John & Rose Nicholson *johnandrose@isleofraasayhotel.freeserve.co.uk* www.isleofraasayhotel.co.uk **D:** Fr £29.00–£34.00 **S:** Fr £34.00 **Beds:** 2F 8T 1D 1S **Baths:** 12 En (10)
Hotel rooms have views 'overlooking the sea to Skye'. Raasay gives a rare glimpse of how the Highlands were 50 years ago, & is a rewarding experience for all who visit with wonderful walks & scenery.

6 Osgaig Park, *Isle of Raasay, Kyle of Lochalsh, Ross-shire, IV40 8PB.* Modern croft house, working croft, overlooking sea to Cuillins of Skye. **Open:** All year
01478 660207 Mrs MacKay *osgaig@lineone.net* **D:** Fr £15.50 **S:** Fr £20.00 **Beds:** 1T 1D **Baths:** 1 Sh (4)

SKYE Achachork

NG4745

Creag An Fhithich, *10 Achachork, Achachork, Portree, Isle of Skye, IV51 9HT.* Farm house with panoramic views, situated 2 miles north of Portree on A855. **Open:** Easter to Nov
01478 612213 (also fax) Mrs MacDonald *joanmacd@talk21.com* **D:** Fr £16.50 **S:** Fr £16.50 **Beds:** 1F 1D 1T 1S **Baths:** 1 En 2 Sh (6)

Myrtlebank, *Achachork, Portree, Isle of Skye, IV51 9HT.* Modern croft house overlooking Portree. Panoramic view towards Cuillin Mountains. **Open:** May to Aug
01478 612597 (also fax) Mrs Gilmour *skye.gilmour@lineone.net* **D:** Fr £16.00 **S:** Fr £16.00 **Beds:** 2F 1D 1S **Baths:** 2 En 1 Sh (5)

SKYE Aird of Sleat

NG5900

The Old School House, *Aird of Sleat, Ardvasar, Isle of Skye, IV45 8RN.* Old school house idyllically situated, 30 yards shore. Panoramic views of mountains across sea. **Open:** Mar to Oct
01471 844218 Mrs Newman ourworld.compuserve.com/homepages/ChrisBrady/newman.htm **D:** Fr £19.50–£24.00 **S:** Fr £19.50–£24.00 **Beds:** 1D 1T 1S **Baths:** 1 Sh (12) (6)

SKYE Bernisdale

NG4050

Lochview, *45 Park, Bernisdale, Portree, Isle of Skye, IV51 9NT.* High-quality accommodation and breakfast, with beautiful seaviews. Warm welcome assured. **Open:** Mar to Dec **Grades:** STB 4 Star
01470 532736 Mrs MacFarlane *margaret_lochview@yahoo.co.uk* **D:** Fr £21.00–£25.00 **S:** Fr £28.00–£35.00 **Beds:** 1F 1D **Baths:** 1 En 1 Pr

Rubislaw, *34 Bernisdale, Bernisdale, Skeabost Bridge, Portree, Isle of Skye, IV51 9NS.* Warm welcome to Highland hospitality, good food and comfortable accommodation. **Open:** Easter to Sept
01470 532212 (also fax) E M Macdonald *etta@rubislaw.u-net.com* **D:** Fr £16.00–£22.00 **Beds:** 1T 2D **Baths:** 2 En (4)

Planning a longer stay? Always ask for any special rates

SKYE Breakish

NG6623

Nethallan, *12 Lower Breakish, Breakish, Isle of Skye, IV42 8QA.* **Open:** All year (not Xmas/New Year)
01471 822771 (also fax) Mrs Hyndman *nethallanskye@aol.com* www.nethallan.co.uk **D:** Fr £20.00–£23.00 **S:** Fr £25.00–£30.00 **Beds:** 1F 1D **Baths:** 2 En
Warm, friendly welcome in spacious traditional Skye house. Set in a quiet water's edge location with stunning views and sunsets. Secluded sandy beach nearby. Local wildlife including otters, seals and many birds. Ideal touring/walking base. Every room faces the sea.

Hazelwood, *5 Lower Breakish, Breakish, Isle of Skye, IV42 8QA.* Peaceful location near sandy beach. Beautiful spot with beautiful views. **Open:** Easter to Oct
01471 822431 Mrs Munro **D:** Fr £14.00–£17.00 **S:** Fr £20.00 **Beds:** 1F 1T 1D **Baths:** 1 Sh

Ashfield, *Breakish, Isle of Skye, IV42 9PY.* Comfortable accommodation, overlooking sea and mountains. Short walk to beach. **Open:** Easter to Oct
01471 822301 Mrs Clarke **D:** Fr £16.00–£20.00 **S:** Fr £18.00–£20.00 **Beds:** 2D **Baths:** 1 En 1 Sh

SKYE Broadford

NG6423

The Sheiling, *2 Lower Harrapool, Broadford, Isle of Skye, IV49 9AQ.* **Open:** All year (not Xmas)
01471 822533 Mr & Mrs Shearer **D:** Fr £14.00–£22.00 **S:** Fr £14.00–£25.00 **Beds:** 1F 1T 1D 1S **Baths:** 1 En 1 Sh
A lovely old traditional Skye house with a friendly Scottish welcome and a good breakfast is always assured. An ideal base for touring Skye, close to Broadford village. The area has beautiful views over Broadford bay to the mountains beyond.

Caberfeidh, *1 Lower Harrapool, Broadford, Isle of Skye, IV49 9AQ.* Modern bungalow with spectacular views. Sea shore location. Warm welcome assured. **Open:** All year (not Xmas/New Year)
01471 822664 Mrs MacKenzie **D:** Fr £20.00–£23.00 **Beds:** 3D **Baths:** 3 En (4)

Millbrae House, *Broadford, Isle of Skye, IV49 9AE.* **Open:** Mar to Nov
01471 822310 (also fax) P & V Tordoff **D:** Fr £16.00–£22.00 **S:** Fr £16.00–£23.00 **Beds:** 2D 1T 1S **Baths:** 3 Pr 1 Sh
A refurbished croft house looking to the sea and hills. Bedrooms have private facilities with tea/coffee trays. Non-smoking. Antiques. Many foreign languages spoken. Packed lunches. Help with walking/driving tours gladly given. Very friendly.

Tigh Na Mara, *Lower Harrapool, Broadford, Isle of Skye, IV49 9AQ.* **Open:** May to Oct **Grades:** STB 2 Star
01471 822475 Mrs Scott *jackieconder@talk21.com* www.host.co.uk **D:** Fr £16.00–£20.00 **Beds:** 1F **Baths:** 1 Pr (1)
150-year-old traditional croft house in quiet position a few yards from the sea. Varied wildlife. Family room comprising double and single bed plus good sized bunks. Private sitting- and bathrooms. French and Italian spoken. TV and toys. Restaurants nearby.

Earsary, *7-8 Harrapool, Broadford, Isle of Skye, IV49 9AQ.* **Open:** All year **Grades:** STB 4 Star
01471 822697 Fax: 01471 822781 *earsary@isleofskye.net* www.isleofskye.net/earsary **D:** Fr £18.00–£24.00 **S:** Fr £25.00–£30.00 **Beds:** 1F 1T 1D **Baths:** 3 En (4)
Quiet family home on a working croft with highland cattle. Guests' lounge and patio overlooking the sea and Skye Mountains. 200 metres from the shoreline where birds and wildlife can be found. Pubs and shops five to ten mins walk.

BEDROOMS
D = Double
T = Twin
S = Single
F = Family

Lime Stone Cottage, *4 Lime Park, Broadford, Isle of Skye, IV49 9AG.* **Open:** All year **Grades:** STB 3 Star
01471 822142 (also fax) Mrs Mcloughin *kathielimepark@btinternet.com* www.limestonecottage.co.uk **D:** Fr £20.00–£26.00 **S:** Fr £35.00–£46.00 **Beds:** 1F 1T 1D **Baths:** 3 En (3)
This century-old crofter's cottage with panoramic views over bay/lochs/mountains. Combining romantic atmosphere with so many original features, makes for fond dreams to remember. Walking distance to many excellent restaurants and so much more.

SKYE Camustianavaig

NG5139

An Airigh Shamradh, *1/2 of 8 Camustianavaig, Camustianavaig, Portree, Isle of Skye, IV51 9LQ.* Outstanding sea views over Camustianavaig Bay to the Cuillin Hills. **Open:** All year
01478 650224 (also fax) Mrs Smith **D:** Fr £20.00 **Beds:** 1T 1D **Baths:** 2 En (4)

SKYE Culnacnoc

NG5162

Seaforth, *9 Lonfern, Culnacnoc, Portree, Isle of Skye, IV51 9JH.* Scenic, comfortable friendly croft house. Fishing available. Ideal hill walking. **Open:** Mar to Oct
01470 562245 Mr Mackenzie **D:** Fr £18.00 **S:** Fr £22.00 **Beds:** 2F **Baths:** 1 Sh (6)

SKYE Dunvegan

NG2547

An Cala, *1 Colbost, Dunvegan, Isle of Skye, IV55 8ZT.* Modern bungalow overlooking Loch Dunvegan. Lavish breakfast is our speciality. **Open:** All year (not Xmas)
01470 511393 Mrs Bohndorf *B&B@ancala.co.uk* www.ancala.co.uk **D:** Fr £20.00 **S:** Fr £22.00 **Beds:** 1T **Baths:** 1 Pr

Planning a longer stay? Always ask for any special rates

6 Castle Crescent, *Dunvegan, Isle of Skye, IV55 8WE.* Highland hospitality close to castle, shops and restaurants. **Open:** All year **Grades:** STB 3 Star
01470 521407 Mrs Stirling **D:** Fr £16.00–£18.00 **S:** Fr £18.00–£20.00 **Beds:** 1F 1T **Baths:** 1 Sh (1) (2)

6 Altavaid, *Harlosh, Dunvegan, Isle of Skye, IV55 8WA.* Modern house, small garden, open countryside. Loch Bracadale, MacLeods Tables, Dunvegan Castle. **Open:** Easter to Oct
01470 521704 Mrs Ewbank **D:** Fr £18.00–£20.00 **S:** Fr £18.00–£20.00 **Beds:** 1F 1T **Baths:** 2 En (2)

SKYE Edinbane

NG3451 *Edinbane Hotel, Stein Inn, Skeabost Lodge*

Shorefield House, *Edinbane, Portree, Isle of Skye, IV51 9PW.* Peaceful lochside village. Ideal for touring, quality accommodation and food. **Open:** All year
01470 582444 Mrs Prall **Fax: 01470 582414** *shorefieldhouse@aol.com* www.shorefield.com **D:** Fr £24.00–£30.00 **S:** Fr £26.00–£32.00 **Beds:** 2F 1T 1D 1S **Baths:** 5 En (5) 1 **cc**

SKYE Eynort

NG3826

The Blue Lobster, *Glen Eynort, Isle of Skye, IV47 8SG.* Walkers haven: Secluded, relaxed, in forest, by sea-loch and eagles! **Open:** All year
01478 640320 Mr Van der Vliet *bluelobster_grula@yahoo.com* **D:** Fr £18.00 **S:** Fr £23.00 **Beds:** 1D 2T (4)

SKYE Eyre

NG4153

Cruinn Bheinn, *4 Eyre, Snizort, Portree, Isle of Skye, IV51 9XB.* Large modern crofthouse situated ten minutes' drive from Portree. We offer true Highland hospitality. **Open:** Easter to Oct
01470 532459 Mrs Gordon **D:** Fr £17.00–£22.00 **Beds:** 2D 1T **Baths:** 3 En (3)

SKYE Fiscavaig

NG3334

Ivanhoe, *19 Fiscavaig, Fiscavaig, Carbost, Isle of Skye, IV47 8SN.* Modern bungalow in peaceful surroundings, situated above Fiscavaig Bay. Spectacular view over Loch Bracadale to 'Macleods Tables' in background. Ideal for exploring Skye, four miles from world famous 'Talisker Distillery'. Suitable for walkers and climbers, warm welcome awaits you. **Open:** All year (not Xmas/New Year)
01478 640360 P Wood **D:** Fr £16.00–£18.00 **S:** Fr £16.00–£18.00 **Beds:** 1T 1D **Baths:** 1 En 1 Sh (4)

Planning a longer stay? Always ask for any special rates

SKYE Greshornish

NG3454

Greshornish House Hotel, *Greshornish, Portree, Isle of Skye, IV51 9PN.* At the Isle of Skye B&B, pipers lead you into dinner **Open:** All year
01470 582266 C & J Dickson **Fax: 01470 582345** *jane@greshornishhotel.co.uk* www.greshornishhotel.co.uk **D:** Fr £25.00–£60.00 **S:** Fr £55.00–£75.00 **Beds:** 2F 2T 4D **Baths:** 8 En (20) cc

SKYE Heribusta

NG4070

1 Heribusta, *Kilmuir, Portree, Isle of Skye, IV51 9YX.* Panoramic sea views towards Outer Hebrides. Peaceful rural community, unrestricted views over unspoilt countryside. **Open:** Easter to Sept
01470 552341 Mrs Beaton *alanbeaton@yahoo.com* **D:** Fr £13.00–£15.00 **S:** Fr £14.00–£15.00 **Beds:** 2D 2S **Baths:** 2 Sh

SKYE Isle Ornsay

NG6912 *Isle Ornsay Hotel*

6 Duisdale Beag, *Isle Ornsay, Isle of Skye, IV43 8QU.* Beautiful, peaceful location just 10 minutes walk to pubs and restaurants. **Open:** All year (not Xmas/New Year)
01471 833230 MacDonald *macdonald@coillechalltainn.idps.co.uk* **D:** Fr £19.00 **S:** Fr £19.00–£24.00 **Beds:** 1T 2D **Baths:** 3 En (4)

SKYE Kilmuir (Uig)

NG3870

Whitewave - Skye's Outdoor Centre, *19 Lincro, Kilmuir, Portree, Isle of Skye, IV51 9YN.* Imagine a cross between an outdoor centre, an inn, and a ceilidh place. **Open:** All year
01470 542414 (also fax) J White *info@white-wave.co.uk* www.white-wave.co.uk **D:** Fr £16.00 **S:** Fr £16.00 **Beds:** 4F **Baths:** 1 En 2 Sh (8) 1 cc

SKYE Kingsburgh

NG3955

Iulan Dubh, *12 Kingsburgh, Kingsburgh, Snizort, Portree, Isle of Skye, IV51 9UT.* Panoramic views of Loch Snizort and Cuillins. **Open:** Apr to Sept
01470 532293 Mrs MacLean *r.campbell@iodhlann.fsnet.co.uk* **D:** Fr £17.00 **S:** Fr £17.00 **Beds:** 1D **Baths:** 1 En (3)

SKYE Kyleakin

NG7526

White Heather Hotel, *Kyleakin, Isle of Skye, IV41 8PL.* **Open:** Mar to Oct **Grades:** STB 3 Star
01599 534577 Fax: 01599 534427 *ian@whiteheatherhotel.co.uk* www.whiteheatherhotel.co.uk **D:** Fr £20.00–£28.00 **Beds:** 1F 3T 4D **Baths:** 8 En cc
Beautifully-situated overlooking the sea and mountains, the hotel is an ideal base for visiting Skye, Lochalsh and Plockton. Visitors Centre next door. Otter-spotting, seal cruises, castle walk. Large Scottish breakfast. Central for all road, rail and bus routes.

Blairdhu House, *Kyle Farm Rd, Kyleakin, Isle of Skye, IV41 8PR.* Beautifully situated house with panoramic views. Excellent spot for bird-watching. **Open:** All year
01599 534760 Ms Scott **Fax: 01599 534623** *blairdhu@aol.com* www.blairdhuhouse.co.uk **D:** Fr £20.00 **S:** Fr £25.00 **Beds:** 1F 4D 1T **Baths:** 6 En (6) cc

West Haven, *Kyleakin, Isle of Skye, IV41 8PH.* Friendly family guest house. Nearby sea, river, mountains. Ideal walking, castles, wildlife. **Open:** Easter to Oct
01599 534476 Mrs MacAskill **D:** Fr £18.00 **S:** Fr £18.00–£18.20 **Beds:** 1D 1T 1S **Baths:** 3 En (6)

SKYE Luib

NG5627

Luib House, *Luib, Broadford, Isle of Skye, IV49 9AN.* Our home is your home - and make full use of the guest lounge. **Open:** All year
01471 822724 Mrs Dobson **D:** Fr £18.00–£19.00 **S:** Fr £25.00 **Beds:** 2D 1T **Baths:** 2 En 1 Pr

SKYE Portree

NG4843

Cnoc Iain, *3 Sluggans, Portree, Isle of Skye, IV51 9LY.* Modern home with friendly atmosphere; good Scottish breakfast, panoramic views. **Open:** Mar to Oct **Grades:** STB 4 Star
01478 612143 Mrs MacSween *cnociain@tinyworld.co.uk* www.cnociain.com **D:** Fr £20.00–£28.00 **S:** Fr £30.00–£42.00 **Beds:** 2D 1T **Baths:** 3 En (3)

Jan & Jed's Cottage, *Lower Ollach, Braes, Portree, Isle of Skye, IV51 9LJ.* **Open:** Easter to Oct
01478 650301 Mrs Scott *jan.scott@amserve.net* **D:** Fr £20.00–£22.00 **Beds:** 1D **Baths:** 1 En (1)
Pretty little Skye crofter's cottage. Beautifully renovated in timeless country style, to provide a high standard of warmth and comfort for our two guests, who can enjoy their own sitting room overlooking our beautiful quiet, peaceful garden with wonderful sea views.

Creag An Fhithich, *10 Achachork, Achachork, Portree, Isle of Skye, IV51 9HT.* **Open:** Easter to Nov
01478 612213 (also fax) Mrs MacDonald *joanmacd@talk21.com* **D:** Fr £16.50 **S:** Fr £16.50 **Beds:** 1F 1D 1T 1S **Baths:** 1 En 2 Sh (6)
Farm house with panoramic views, situated 2 miles north of Portree on A855. Ideal for touring the north of the island plus the sights of the Old Man of Storr and Lealt Falls. A warm welcome awaits you with full Scottish breakfast.

Grenitote, *9 Martin Crescent, Portree, Isle of Skye, IV51 9DW.* Centrally-situated for viewing the beautiful scenery of Skye, Dunvegan Castle and museums. **Open:** All year **Grades:** STB 3 Star
01478 612808 Mrs Matheson **D:** Fr £18.00–£20.00 **Beds:** 1T 1D **Baths:** 2 En

An Traigh, *3 Heatherfield, Portree, Isle of Skye, IV51 9NE.* Seaside location, splendid views. 3 miles from town. Full breakfast. **Open:** Easter to Oct
01478 613236 Mrs McLeod *an_traigh@yahoo.co.uk* **D:** Fr £18.00–£20.00 **S:** Fr £18.00–£22.00 **Beds:** 1T 1D 1S **Baths:** 2 En 1 Pr (4)

Myrtlebank, *Achachork, Portree, Isle of Skye, IV51 9HT.* Modern croft house overlooking Portree. Panoramic view towards Cuillin Mountains. **Open:** May to Aug
01478 612597 (also fax) Mrs Gilmour *skye.gilmour@lineone.net* **D:** Fr £16.00 **S:** Fr £16.00 **Beds:** 2F 1D 1S **Baths:** 2 En 1 Sh (5)

Jacamar, *5 Achachork Road, Achacork, Portree, Isle of Skye, IV51 9HT.* Country bungalow overlooks Portree and Cuillins. Excellent cooking, Scottish breakfast. **Open:** All year
01478 612274 Mrs Thorpe **Fax: 01478 611191** *norman.pat@jacamar.idps.co.uk* **D:** Fr £15.00–£19.00 **S:** Fr £15.00–£19.00 **Beds:** 2F 1D 1S **Baths:** 2 En 1 Sh

25 Urquart Place, *Portree, Isle of Skye, IV51 9HJ.* Warm welcome, excellent accommodation and breakfasts. Special off-season deals available. **Open:** All year
01478 612374 Mrs Macdonald *elizabethmacdonald@talk21.com* **D:** Fr £15.00–£20.00 **S:** Fr £18.00–£25.00 **Beds:** 1F 1D 1S **Baths:** 1 En 1 Sh (2)

Easdale Bridge Road, *Portree, Isle of Skye, IV51 9ER.* Centrally-situated bungalow with view to Cuillin Hills. **Open:** All year (not Xmas/New Year)
01478 613244 & 07796 394678 (M) Mrs Matheson **D:** Fr £20.00–£25.00 **S:** Fr £25.00–£30.00 **Beds:** 2D **Baths:** 2 En (2)

Jacamar, *5 Achachork Road, Achacork, Portree, Isle of Skye, IV51 9HT.* Country bungalow overlooks Portree and Cuillins. Excellent cooking, Scottish breakfast. **Open:** All year
01478 612274 Mrs Thorpe **Fax: 01478 611191** *norman.pat@jacamar.idps.co.uk* **D:** Fr £15.00–£19.00 **S:** Fr £15.00–£19.00 **Beds:** 2F 1D 1S **Baths:** 2 En 1 Sh

12 Fraser Crescent, *Portree, Isle of Skye, IV51 9PH.* Family-run bed & breakfast, offering clean, comfortable accommodation, 5 mins from bus. **Open:** Apr to Oct
01478 612529 Mr Speed **D:** Fr £19.00–£20.00 **S:** Fr £19.00–£20.00 **Beds:** 1T 1D **Baths:** 1 Pr (2)

12 Stormyhill Road, *Portree, Isle of Skye, IV51 9DY.* Centrally located in Portree village, within five minutes walking distance to shop, restaurants. **Open:** All year
01478 613165 Mrs Nicolson *audrey-nicolson3@yahoo.co.uk* **D:** Fr £17.50–£20.00 **S:** Fr £20.00–£25.00 **Beds:** 1F 1T 2D **Baths:** 1 Pr 1 Sh (3)

SKYE Sconser

NG5131 *Sligachan Hotel*

Old Schoolhouse, *Sconser, Isle of Skye, IV48 8TD.* A warm friendly welcome waits you from a Gaelic-speaking family. On a working croft nestling at the foot of the Red Cuillin with magnificent frontal views overlooking Loch Sligachan, this is an ideal base for walking, touring Skye. **Open:** All year (not Xmas/New Year)
01478 650313 Mr & Mrs MacLeod *hectormcld@aol.com* **D:** Fr £13.00–£16.00 **Beds:** 1F 1T 1D **Baths:** 2 Sh

SKYE Staffin

NG4867

Quiraing Lodge, *Stenscholl, Staffin, Portree, Isle of Skye, IV51 9JS.* **Open:** All year
01470 562330 Mr Gardener *sam@quiraing-lodge.co.uk* www.quiraing-lodge.co.uk
D: Fr £24.00 **S:** Fr £24.00 **Beds:** 2F 2T 2D 1S **Baths:** 3 Sh (10)
Spacious family home, dramatically situated on Staffin Bay. Large walled garden leading to the sea. Our own home-made bread, and organic local produce whenever possible. Photography, arts and Crafts workshops (programme available). Boat/fishing trips locally. Gallery selling photography & crafts.

Gracelands, *5 Glasphein, Staffin, Portree, Isle of Skye, IV51 9LZ.* Fantastic sea and hill views. Boat/fishing trips. Hill walking. **Open:** Apr to Nov
01470 562313 Mrs Nicolson **D:** Fr £16.00–£18.00 **S:** Fr £18.00 **Beds:** 1F 2D 1T 1S **Baths:** 2 Sh (4) (3)

SKYE Stenscholl

NG4868

Quiraing Lodge, *Stenscholl, Staffin, Portree, Isle of Skye, IV51 9JS.* Spacious family home, dramatically situated on Staffin Bay. **Open:** All year
01470 562330 Mr Gardener *sam@quiraing-lodge.co.uk* www.quiraing-lodge.co.uk
D: Fr £24.00 **S:** Fr £24.00 **Beds:** 2F 2T 2D 1S **Baths:** 3 Sh (10)

SKYE Struan

NG3438

Ard-Bhealaidh, *Balgown, Struan, Isle of Skye, IV56 8FA.* Scenic lochside view, and a warm Highland welcome, await all who stay. **Open:** Easter to Oct
01470 572334 (also fax) Mr MacKay *ard-bhealaidh@uk-bedandbreakfasts.com* **D:** Fr £16.00–£18.00 **S:** Fr £16.00–£18.00 **Beds:** 1F 1D 1S **Baths:** 1 En 1 Sh (5)

The Anchorage, *9 Eabost West, Struan, Isle of Skye, IV56 8FE.* Modern comfortable bungalow with panoramic sea and mountain views. **Open:** All year
01470 572206 Mrs Campbell *eabost@aol.com* **D:** Fr £18.00–£20.00 **S:** Fr £20.00 **Beds:** 2D 1T **Baths:** 2 En 1 Pr (3) cc

Glenside, *4 Totarder , Struan, Isle of Skye, IV56 8FW.* Situated on working croft in lovely valley. Warm welcome assured. **Open:** Easter to Oct
01470 572253 Mrs MacCusbic **D:** Fr £17.00–£20.00 **S:** Fr £20.00–£22.00 **Beds:** 1D 1T **Baths:** 1 En 1 Pr (12) (3)

SKYE The Braes

NG5234

Tianavaig, *Camustianavaig, The Braes, Portree, Isle of Skye, IV51 9LQ.* A pretty rural seashore location magnificent sea and mountain views. **Open:** All year (not Xmas)
01478 650325 Mrs Corry www.host.co.uk
D: Fr £17.50–£20.00 **S:** Fr £17.50–£20.00 **Beds:** 2D **Baths:** 1 En 1 Pr (2)

SKYE Uig (Uig Bay)

NG3963

Ferry Inn Hotel, *Uig, Portree, Isle of Skye, IV51 9XP.* Family run hotel, close ferry terminal. Good food. Pets welcome. **Open:** All year
01470 542246 Fax: 01470 542377 D: Fr £25.00–£30.00 **S:** Fr £28.00–£35.00 **Beds:** 1F 2T 2D 1S **Baths:** 6 En (25) cc

SKYE Uigshader

NG4346

Torwood, *1 Peiness, Uigshader, Portree, Isle of Skye, IV51 9LW.* Modern home offering warm, comfortable accommodation, in countryside yet only 10 mins from Portree. **Open:** Easter to Oct
01470 532479 Mrs Gillies *anne@selma.co.uk*
D: Fr £16.00–£20.00 **Beds:** 1F 1D 1T **Baths:** 2 En 1 Pr (1) (4)

SKYE Vatten

NG2843

Sea View, *3 Herebost, Vatten, Dunvegan, Isle of Skye, IV55 8GZ.* Modern bungalow with sea views, near the famous Dunvegan castle. **Open:** Easter to Oct
01470 521705 Mrs Campbell **D:** Fr £16.00–£17.50 **Beds:** 1D 1T **Baths:** 1 En 1 Pr (2)

SKYE Waternish

NG2658

Lusta Cottage, *11-12 Lochbay, Waternish, Isle of Skye, IV55 8GD.* Modern cottage set in 18 acre croft with waterfalls to shore of Loch Bay. **Open:** May to Oct
01470 592263 Mrs Smith *lustacottage@supanet.com* www.isleofskyelustabandb.co.uk
D: Fr £20.00 **S:** Fr £20.00 **Beds:** 1D 1T **Baths:** 1 En 1 Pr (8)

Lanarkshire

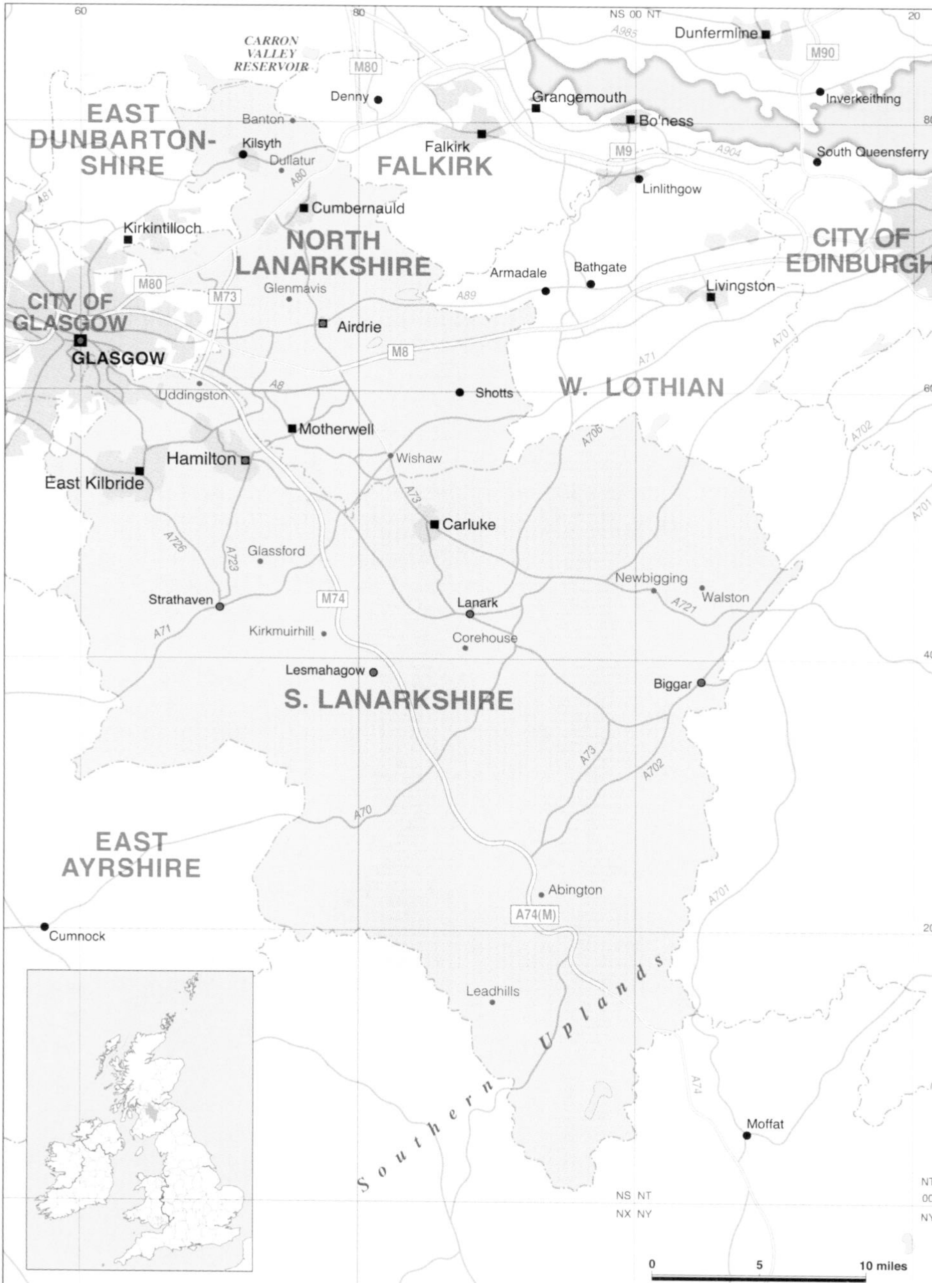

Airdrie

NS7665

Rosslee Guest House, *107 Forrest Street, Airdrie, Lanarkshire, ML6 7AR.* Central situation for Glasgow, Edinburgh, Stirling and Lanarkshire areas. **Open:** All year
01236 765865 Mr Smith **Fax: 01236 602809** *mikerosslee@blueyonder.co.uk* **D:** Fr £20.00–£25.00 **S:** Fr £20.00–£30.00 **Beds:** 1F 3T 2S **Baths:** 4 En 2 Pr (8)

Banton

NS7579

Auchenrivoch Farm, *Banton, Kilsyth, Glasgow, G65 0OZ.* Beautifully situated, south facing farmhouse. Large garden and views of Kelvin Valley. **Open:** All year
01236 822113 (also fax) Mrs Henderson **D:** Fr £20.00–£22.00 **S:** Fr £22.00–£24.00 **Beds:** 2T

Biggar

NT0437

Lindsaylands, *Biggar, Lanarkshire, ML12 6EQ.* Beautiful country house, peaceful setting, local touring, Edinburgh/Glasgow borders. **Open:** Easter to Nov
01899 220033 & 01899 221221 Mrs Stott **Fax: 01899 221009** *elspeth@lindsaylands.co.uk* www.lindsaylands.co.uk **D:** Fr £24.00–£28.00 **S:** Fr £28.00–£32.00 **Beds:** 2D 1T **Baths:** 2 En 1 Pr (8)

Walston Mansion Farmhouse, *Walston, Carnwath, Lanark, ML11 8NF.* A farmhouse that's 'home from home'. Good food, log fire. 5 miles north of Biggar. **Open:** All year **Grades:** STB 3 Star
01899 810338 (also fax) Mrs Kirby *kirby-walstonmansion@talk21.com* **D:** Fr £16.00–£18.00 **S:** Fr £18.00–£20.00 **Beds:** 1F 1T 1D 1S **Baths:** 2 En 1 Sh (6)

Woodgill, *12 Edinburgh Road, Biggar, Lanarkshire, ML12 6AX.* Friendly and welcoming family home in historic country town. **Open:** Easter to Oct
01899 220324 Mrs Brown **D:** Fr £18.00–£20.00 **S:** Fr £20.00–£22.00 **Beds:** 1D 1T **Baths:** 1 Sh (3)

Cultershogle, *12 Langvout Gate, Biggar, Lanarkshire, ML12 6UF.* Beautiful outlook from very comfortable bungalow; quiet location, home cooking. **Open:** All year (not Xmas)
01899 221702 Mr & Mrs Tennant **D:** Fr £18.00–£19.00 **S:** Fr £20.00 **Beds:** 2T **Baths:** 2 En (3)

Cormiston Cottage, *Cormiston Road, Biggar, ML12 6NS.* Delightful country cottage with beautiful views over the fields and hills beyond. **Open:** All year
01899 220 200 Mrs Wales **Fax: 0131 440 0272** *jwales4453@aol.com* **D:** Fr £20.00–£25.00 **S:** Fr £25.00–£30.00 **Beds:** 1F 1T **Baths:** 1 En (3) (2)

Corehouse

NS8841

Corehouse Home Farm, *Corehouse, Lanark, Lanarkshire, ML11 9TQ.* Working farm. Ground floor ensuite rooms. Near to spectacular waterfalls. **Open:** All year (not Xmas/New Year) **Grades:** STB 3 Star
01555 661377 Mrs Hamilton **Fax: 01555 660733** *corehouse@thegallop.com* thegallop.com/corehouse **D:** Fr £20.00–£22.00 **S:** Fr £24.00–£26.00 **Beds:** 2F 1D **Baths:** 3 En (6)

Dullatur

NS7476

Dullatur House, *Dullatur, Glasgow, G68 0AW.* Georgian mansion house circa 1740. **Open:** All year
01236 738855 (also fax) Mrs Moore *mooread@global.com* **D:** Fr £19.50–£23.50 **S:** Fr £21.50–£25.00 **Beds:** 1F 2T **Baths:** 2 En 1 Pr (4)

East Kilbride

NS6354

11 Markethill Road, *East Kilbride, Glasgow, G74 4AA.* 1920 sandstone villa, central location for Lanarkshire and 8 miles from Glasgow. **Open:** All year (not Xmas/New Year)
01355 231547 (also fax) Mrs Gibb *bb@ekgibb.freeserve.co.uk* www.ekgibb.freeserve.co.uk **D:** Fr £18.50 **S:** Fr £23.50 **Beds:** 5T **Baths:** 1 En 2 Sh (5)

National Grid References given are for villages, towns and cities – not for individual houses

Glassford

NS7247

Avonlea, *46 Millar Street, Glassford, Strathaven, Lanarkshire, ML10 6TD.* Comfortable homely accommodation. Country village near M74 J8. Rear garden. **Open:** Feb to Nov **Grades:** STB 3 Star, AA 2 Diamond
01357 521748 Miss Rankin **D:** Fr £18.00–£20.00 **S:** Fr £22.00–£25.00 **Beds:** 2T **Baths:** 1 Sh (7)

Glenmavis

NS7567

Braidenhill Farm, *Glenmavis, Airdrie, Lanarkshire, ML6 0PJ.* High-quality accommodation on small working farm in central area. **Open:** All year
01236 872319 Mrs Dunbar **D:** Fr £16.00–£20.00 **Beds:** 1F 1T 1D **Baths:** 1 En 1 Sh (3)

Rowan Lodge, *23 Condorrat Road, Glenmavis, Airdrie, Lanarkshire, ML6 0NS.* Excellent bungalow accommodation opposite village church. Ideal for touring. **Open:** All year
01236 753934 *june@rowanlodge.demon.co.uk* www.rowanlodge.demon.co.uk **D:** Fr £20.00–£30.00 **S:** Fr £20.00–£30.00 **Beds:** 1T 1D 1S **Baths:** 3 En (4) cc

Hamilton

NS7255

Glenmhor House, *6 Bent Road, Hamilton, Lanarkshire, ML3 6QB.* Minutes coach/rail station. Country park nearby. Hearty breakfast. **Open:** All year
01698 423293 (also fax) Ms McCabe **D:** Fr £17.00–£18.00 **S:** Fr £20.00 **Beds:** 1F 1T 1S **Baths:** 2 Sh

Kirkfieldbank

NS8643 *The Tavern*

Brig End BandB, *231 Riverside Road, Kirkfieldbank, Lanark, ML11 9JJ.* Between Two Bridges Garden down to River Clyde on walkway. **Open:** All year
01555 663855 Mrs Rankin **D:** Fr £19.00–£20.00 **S:** Fr £22.00–£25.00 **Beds:** 2T **Baths:** 1 En 1 Pr (3)

Kirkmuirhill

NS7943

Dykecroft Farm, *Kirkmuirhill, Lesmahagow, Lanark, ML11 0JQ.* Quality accommodation, lovely views. Ideal for touring all sports nearby. **Open:** All year
01555 892226 I H McInally *dykecroftbandb@talk21.com* **D:** Fr £20.00 **S:** Fr £22.00–£23.00 **Beds:** 1T 2D **Baths:** 2 Sh

Lanark

NS8843

Roselea, *9 Cleghorn Road, Lanark, ML11 7QT.* Edwardian House, original features. Close to New Lanark. Golf, fishing, riding and genealogy. **Open:** All year **01555 662540** Mrs Allen *margaretallen2@tesco.net* **D:** Fr £18.00–£20.00 **S:** Fr £17.00–£26.00 **Beds:** 1F 1D 1S **Baths:** 1 En 1 Sh (2)

Leadhills

NS8815

Meadowfoot Cottage, *Gowanbank, Leadhills, Biggar, Lanarkshire, ML12 6YB.* **Open:** All year (not Xmas) **Grades:** STB 3 Star **01659 74369** Mrs Ledger *stay@meadowfootcottage.co.uk* www.meadowfootcottage.co.uk **D:** Fr £20.00–£22.00 **S:** Fr £22.00–£37.00 **Beds:** 1F 1T **Baths:** 1 En 1 Sh (4) Blending history with modern amenities, the warmest welcome and delicious home-cooking makes your stay a real highlight. Ideal hill walking, Southern Upland Way, gold-panning, visiting Museum of Lead Mining, Edinburgh, Glasgow, coast. Peaceful stopover just six miles from M74.

Lesmahagow

NS8139

Auldtoun Farm, *Lesmahagow, Lanark, ML11 0JT.* **Open:** All year (not Xmas/New Year) **01555 892910 (also fax)** Mrs Muirhead **D:** Fr £17.50–£20.00 **S:** Fr £20.00–£25.00 **Beds:** 1F 1T 1D **Baths:** 1 En 1 Sh (6) Perfectly situated 1 mile off M74 J10, 22 miles south of Glasgow, 40 miles west of Edinburgh, good stopover on your way to the Highlands. You are assured of a warm welcome, comfortable accommodation and full Scottish breakfast.

Dykecroft Farm, *Kirkmuirhill, Lesmahagow, Lanark, ML11 0JQ.* Quality accommodation, lovely views. Ideal for touring all sports nearby. **Open:** All year **01555 892226** I H McInally *dykecroftbandb@talk21.com* **D:** Fr £20.00 **S:** Fr £22.00–£23.00 **Beds:** 1T 2D **Baths:** 2 Sh

Newbigging

NT0145

Nestlers Hotel, *Newbigging, Lanark, ML11 8NA.* Small intimate family run hotel in rural South Lanarkshire. **Open:** All year **01555 840680** Mr Anderson *nestlers@hotel98.freeserve.co.uk* **D:** Fr £23.50–£27.50 **S:** Fr £28.50–£35.00 **Beds:** 1F 2T 1D **Baths:** 4 En (9) **cc**

Strathaven

NS7044

Avonlea, *46 Millar Street, Glassford, Strathaven, Lanarkshire, ML10 6TD.* Comfortable homely accommodation. Country village near M74 J8. Rear garden. **Open:** Feb to Nov **Grades:** STB 3 Star, AA 2 Diamond **01357 521748** Miss Rankin **D:** Fr £18.00–£20.00 **S:** Fr £22.00–£25.00 **Beds:** 2T **Baths:** 1 Sh (7)

Kypemhor, *West Kype Farm, Strathaven, Lanarkshire, ML10 6PR.* Bungalow with scenic rural views, 3 miles from busy market town. **Open:** All year **01357 529831** Mrs Anderson **D:** Fr £17.00–£20.00 **S:** Fr £18.00–£22.00 **Beds:** 1D 1T **Baths:** 1 Sh (12)

Haroldslea, *3 Kirkhill Road, Strathaven, Lanarkshire, ML10 6HN.* Modern detached villa with garden in quiet residential area near village centre. **Open:** All year (not Xmas/New Year) **01357 520617** Mrs Goodwillie **D:** Fr £20.00 **S:** Fr £20.00 **Beds:** 1F 1D **Baths:** 2 Sh (2)

Uddingston

NS6960

Phoenix Lodge Guest House, *4 Girdons Way, Uddingston, Glasgow, G71 7ED.* Modern building, near motorways, station, tourist attractions locally, walks, pubs, restaurants. **Open:** All year **01698 815296 & 01698 811529** Mr Boyce **Fax: 01698 267567** **D:** Fr £19.00–£22.00 **S:** Fr £23.00–£25.00 **Beds:** 6F 1T 1D **Baths:** 3 En 2 Sh (8) **cc**

Walston

NT0545

Walston Mansion Farmhouse, *Walston, Carnwath, Lanark, ML11 8NF.* A farmhouse that's 'home from home'. Good food, log fire. **Open:** All year **Grades:** STB 3 Star **01899 810338 (also fax)** Mrs Kirby *kirby-walstonmansion@talk21.com* **D:** Fr £16.00–£18.00 **S:** Fr £18.00–£20.00 **Beds:** 1F 1T 1D 1S **Baths:** 2 En 1 Sh (6)

Wishaw

NS7954

The Mill House, *Garrion Bridge, Wishaw, Lanarkshire, ML2 0RR.* Mill House, built 1907 with delightful garden, comfortable warm home. **Open:** All year **01698 881166** Mrs Pinkerton **Fax: 01698 886874** *alanphotog@aol.com* **D:** Fr £15.00–£18.00 **S:** Fr £22.50–£27.50 **Beds:** 1F 1D 1T **Baths:** 1 En 1 Sh (6)

RATES

D = Price range per person sharing in a double or twin room

S = Price range for a single room

Orkney

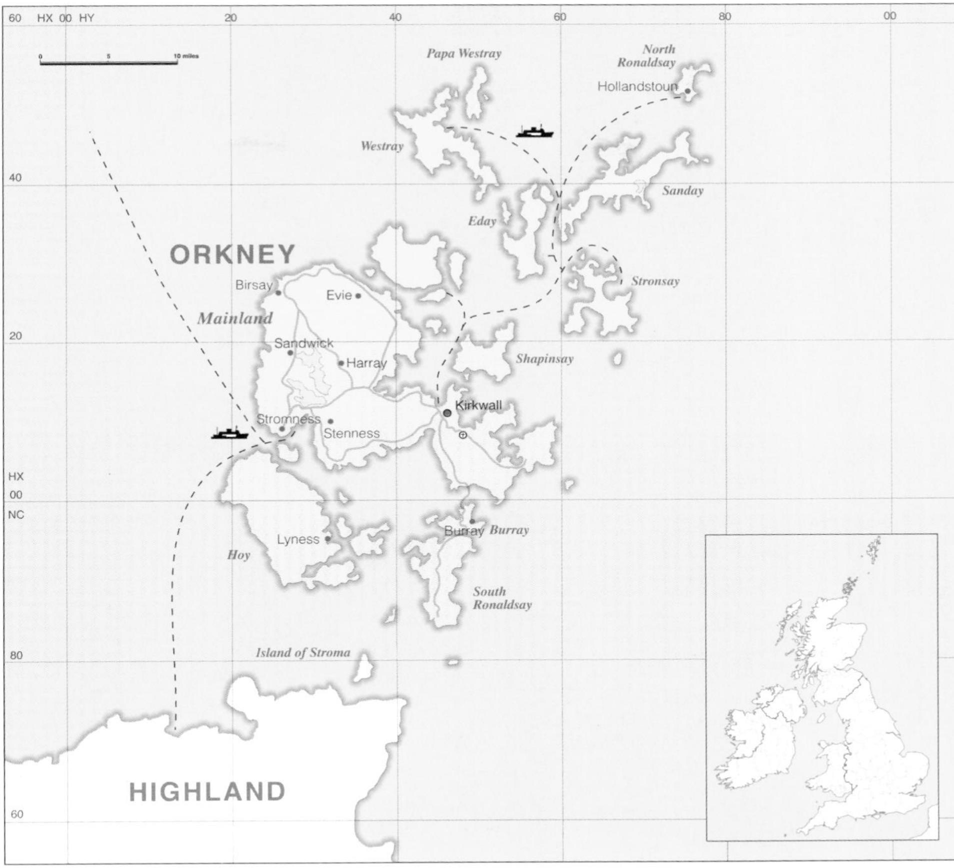

BURRAY — Burray

ND4795

Vestlay-banks, *Burray, Orkney, KW17 2SX.* Top quality accommodation overlooking Scapa Flow. Birdwatcher's paradise, peaceful haven.
Open: Mar to Oct **Grades:** STB 4 Star
01856 731305 Mrs Woodward **Fax: 01856 731400** *vestlaybanks@btinternet.com* www.vestlaybanks.co.uk **D:** Fr £22.00–£25.00 **S:** Fr £22.00–£25.00 **Beds:** 1T 1D **Baths:** 2 En

Planning a longer stay? Always ask for any special rates

Ankersted, *Burray, Orkney, KW17 2SS.* Purpose-built guest house, overlooking bay into Scapa Flow and Churchill Barrier.
Open: All year
01856 731217 (also fax) Mrs Watt *ankersted@tinyworld.co.uk* **D:** Fr £18.00–£20.00 **S:** Fr £18.00–£20.00 **Beds:** 2D 2S **Baths:** 4 En (6)

HOY — Lyness

ND3094

Stoneyquoy, *Lyness, Hoy, Orkney, KW16 3NY.* Orcadian/Dutch couple - 200 acre farm - leaflet available, guided tours.
Open: All year (not Xmas/New Year)
01856 791234 (also fax) Mrs Budge *arthurlouise@talk21.com* www.visithoy.com
D: Fr £17.00–£19.00 **S:** Fr £17.00–£19.00
Beds: 1T 1D 1S **Baths:** 2 En 1 Sh (6)

MAINLAND — Birsay

HY2527

Beachview, *Birsay, Orkney, KW17 2LX.* Seaside bungalow. Birdwatching, historic sites, fishing close by. TV in lounge.
Open: Easter to Oct
01856 721413 Ms Nieto *beachview@ecosse.net*
D: Fr £18.00–£20.00 **S:** Fr £18.00–£20.00
Beds: 1T 1D **Baths:** 1 Sh (3)

BEDROOMS
D = Double
T = Twin
S = Single
F = Family

MAINLAND Evie

HY3525

Woodwick House, *Evie, Orkney, KW17 2PQ.* Historic country house, bluebell Woodland, Burn secluded Bay, Open Fires. **Open:** All year
01856 751330 A Herdman **Fax: 01856 751383** *woodwickhouse@appleonline.net* www.orknet.co.uk/woodwick **D:** Fr £27.00–£38.00 **S:** Fr £30.00–£46.00 **Beds:** 3T 5D **Baths:** 4 En

MAINLAND Harray

HY3218

Merkister Hotel, *Harray, Orkney, KW17 2LF.* Situated on the shores of Loch Harray. Panoramic views. **Open:** All year (not Xmas/New Year)
01856 771336 L Munson **Fax: 01856 771515** **D:** Fr £25.00–£47.00 **S:** Fr £25.00–£55.00 **Beds:** 2F 3T 2D 2S **Baths:** 13 En 1 Pr cc

MAINLAND Kirkwall

HY4510

Royal Oak Guest House, *Holm Road, Kirkwall, Orkney, KW15 1PY.* **Open:** All year (not Xmas/New Year)
01856 877177 (also fax) *royal.oak@btinternet.com* www.royaloakhouse.co.uk **D:** Fr £22.00–£25.00 **S:** Fr £25.00–£30.00 **Beds:** 2F 3T 2D **Baths:** 7 En (10) cc
Royal Oak Guest House is a modern, purpose built guest house with views of Scapa Flow, close to Highland Park Distillery and walking distance from St Magnus Cathedral. Ideally situated for touring the many historical and archaeological sites on Orkney.

Please respect a B&B's wishes regarding children, animals and smoking

Elderwood, *4 Park Loan, Kirkwall, Orkney, KW15 1PU.* Modern bungalow in quiet cul-de-sac. **Open:** All year
01856 872657 Mrs Omand **D:** Fr £15.00 **S:** Fr £15.00 **Beds:** 1D 1T **Baths:** 2 Sh (2)

7 Matches Square, *Kirkwall, Orkney, KW15 1AU.* Personally-run neighbouring houses. Centrally-situated, shops, buses, ferries nearby. **Open:** All year
01856 872440 (also fax) Mrs Parkins **D:** Fr £16.00–£18.00 **S:** Fr £17.00–£20.00 **Beds:** 2T 1D 2S **Baths:** 1 En 2 Sh (2)

Polrudden Guest House, *Peerie Sea Loan, Kirkwall, Orkney, KW15 1UH.* Peaceful location, ten minutes walk from town centre. Stunning view. **Open:** All year (not Xmas)
01856 874761 Mrs Thornton **Fax: 01856 870950** *linda@polrudden.com* www.polrudden.com **D:** Fr £24.00 **S:** Fr £30.00 **Beds:** 2F 5T **Baths:** 7 En (7) cc

Shearwood, *Muddiesdale Road, off Pickaquoy Road, Kirkwall, Orkney, KW15 1RR.* Quiet country location, 10 mins walk town centre. Wonderful archaeology nearby. **Open:** All year
01856 873494 Mrs Braun **D:** Fr £16.00–£20.00 **S:** Fr £17.00 **Beds:** 2T 1D **Baths:** 2 Sh 1 En (12)

Lav'rockha Guest House, *Inganess Road, Kirkwall, Orkney, KW15 1SP.* Superior accommodation at an affordable price, Finalist - 1999 Orkney Food awards. **Open:** All year
01856 876103 (also fax) J Webster *lavrockha@orkney.com* www.norsecom.co.uk/lavrockha **D:** Fr £20.00–£24.00 **S:** Fr £24.00–£30.00 **Beds:** 1F 2T 2D **Baths:** 5 En cc

MAINLAND Sandwick

HY2519

Netherstove, *Sandwick, Stromness, Orkney, KW16 3LS.* Farmhouse B&B, overlooking the Bay of Skaill. Near Skara Brae. **Open:** Easter to Nov
01856 841625 (also fax) Mrs Poke *ann.poke@virgin.net* **D:** Fr £16.00–£18.50 **S:** Fr £16.00–£18.50 **Beds:** 1D 1T **Baths:** 2 Sh

MAINLAND Stenness

HY3010

Ramsquoy, *Stenness, Stromness, Orkney, KW16 3EZ.* Ramsquoy farmhouse views over Scapa Flow near Maeshowe & standing stones. **Open:** All year
01856 850316 (also fax) Mrs Swannie *info@Ramsquoy.com* www.Ramsquoy.com **D:** Fr £20.00–£25.00 **S:** Fr £18.00–£20.00 **Beds:** 1T 1D 2S **Baths:** 2 En 1 Sh

MAINLAND Stromness

HY2509

Lindisfarne, *Stromness, Orkney, KW16 3LL.* **Open:** Jan to Dec
01856 850828 Mrs Worthington **Fax: 01856 850805** *eprworthington@hotmail.com* www.geocities.com/tvworthington **D:** Fr £22.00 **S:** Fr £30.00 **Beds:** 1F 4T **Baths:** 5 En
Modern detached house, set in a elevated rural location, overlooking the town of Stromness views of Scapa Flow, the island of Gramsay, Hoy Hills and the island of Hoy, also Stromness harbour.

Orca Hotel, *76 Victoria Street, Stromness, Orkney, KW16 3BS.* Harbourside guest house in romantic fishing village. All amenities nearby, cellar bistro. **Open:** All year (not Xmas)
01856 850447 Ms Fischler *info@orcahotel.com* www.orcahotel.com **D:** Fr £18.00–£25.00 **S:** Fr £20.00–£25.00 **Beds:** 2F 1S 1D 2T **Baths:** 6 En (1)

NORTH RONALDSAY Hollandstoun

HY7553

North Ronaldsay Bird Observatory, *North Ronaldsay, Orkney, KW17 2BE.* Comfortable island guest accommodation. Solar and wind powered. **Open:** All year (not Xmas/New Year)
01857 633200 A E Duncan **Fax: 01857 633207** *alison@nrbo.prestel.co.uk* www.nrbo.f2s.com **D:** Fr £18.00 **S:** Fr £23.00 **Beds:** 2D 2T **Baths:** 4 En 2 cc

Perthshire & Kinross

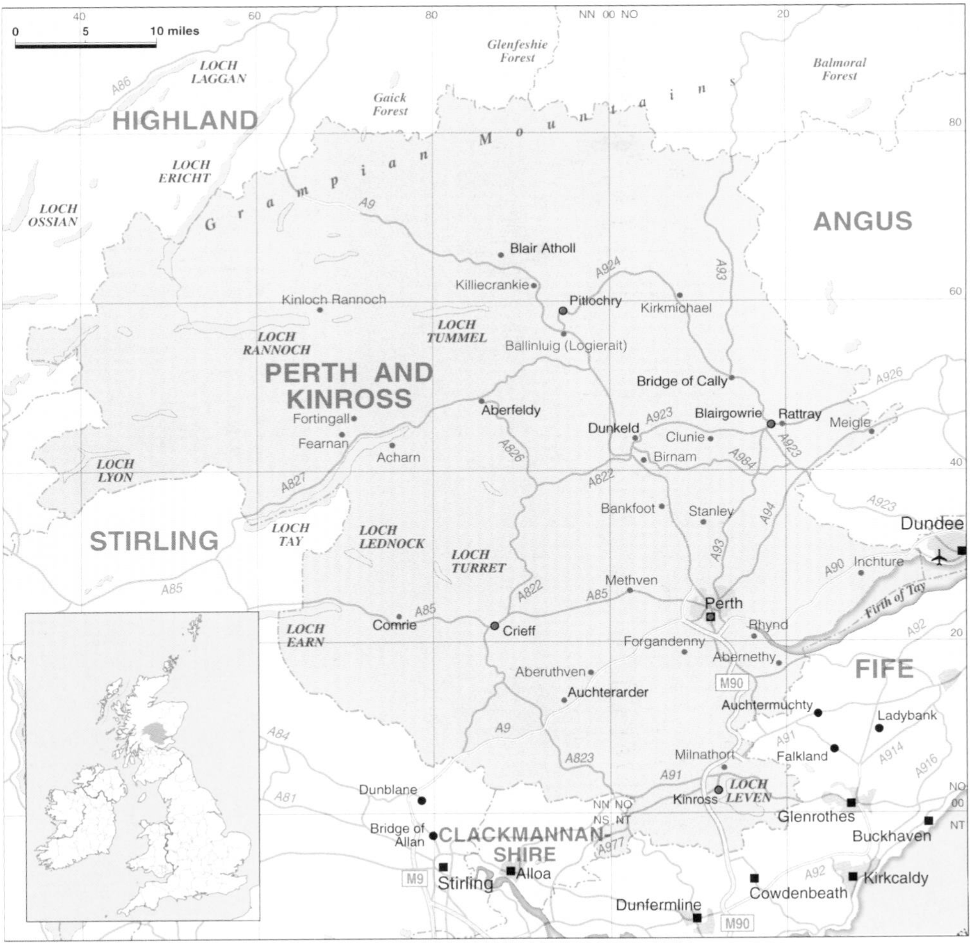

Aberfeldy

NN8549 *Black Watch Inn*

Tomvale, *Tom of Cluny Farm, Aberfeldy, Perthshire, PH15 2JT.* Modern farmhouse with outstanding views of Upper Tay Valley. **Open:** All year (not Xmas/New Year) **01887 820171 & 07808 515666 (M)** Mrs Kennedy **Fax: 01887 820171** *tomvale@aol.com* tomvale.co.uk **D:** Fr £18.00 **S:** Fr £20.00 **Beds:** 1F 1D **Baths:** 1 Sh

Handa, *Taybridge Road, Aberfeldy, PH15 2BH.* Pleasant views overlooking golf course and river. Quiet location. **Open:** All year (not Xmas/New Year) **01887 820334** Mrs Bassett-Smith **D:** Fr £18.00 **Beds:** 1T 1D **Baths:** 2 En

BATHROOMS
En = Ensuite
Pr = Private
Sh = Shared

Ardtornish, *Kenmore Street, Aberfeldy, PH15 2BL.* In beautiful friendly Highland Perthshire with walking, golf, cycling, water sports and more. **Open:** All year (not Xmas/New Year) **Grades:** STB 3 Star **01887 820629** Mrs Ross *ardtornish@talk21.com* **D:** Fr £16.00–£20.00 **S:** Fr £16.00–£20.00 **Beds:** 1D 1T 1D/T **Baths:** 1 En 1 Sh (3)

Abernethy
NO1816

Gattaway Farm, *Abernethy, Perth, Perthshire & Kinross, PH2 9LQ.* Large Georgian/ Victorian farmhouse; excellent views, excellent food. Recommended. **Open:** All year
01738 850746 Mrs Dawson **Fax: 01738 850925** *tarduff@aol.com* www.smoothhound.co.uk/hotels/gattaway.html **D:** Fr £22.00 **S:** Fr £27.00 **Beds:** 2D 1T **Baths:** 3 En (4) 1

Aberuthven
NN9815

Craiginver, *Aberuthven, Auchterarder, PH3 1HE.* Victorian former manse in large garden with views over Earn Valley. **Open:** Apr to Oct
01764 662411 J M Smith *jms@craiginver.freeserve.co.uk* **D:** Fr £18.50–£19.50 **S:** Fr £19.50–£20.50 **Beds:** 2T **Baths:** 1 En 1 Pr (8)

Acharn
NN7543 *Croft Na Caber, Kenmore Hotel*

12 Ballinlaggan, *Acharn, Aberfeldy, Perthshire, PH15 2HT.* Warm welcome, comfortable accommodation, hill walking, pony trekking, fishing, golf. **Open:** All year
01887 830409 Mrs Spiers *bandb.acharn@virgin.net* **D:** Fr £15.00 **S:** Fr £15.00 **Beds:** 1T 1S **Baths:** 1 Sh (1)

Auchterarder
NN9412

10 The Grove, Collearn, *Auchterarder, Perthshire, PH3 1PT.* Private house in quiet estate with off-street parking. **Open:** Jan to Dec
01764 662036 Mrs McFarlane **D:** Fr £17.50–£18.50 **S:** Fr £18.00–£20.00 **Beds:** 1T **Baths:** 1 Sh (1)

RATES
D = Price range per person sharing in a double or twin room
S = Price range for a single room

Ballinluig (Logierait)
NN9852

Cuil-An-Duin, *Ballinluig, Pitlochry, Perthshire, PH9 0NN.* **Open:** All year (not Xmas/New Year)
01796 482287 & 07773 004353 (M) Mrs McMillan **Fax: 01796 482659** *mcmillanjanet@aol.com* www.cottageguide.co.uk/redsquirrelcottages **D:** Fr £30.00–£35.00 **S:** Fr £30.00–£35.00 **Beds:** 1T 2D **Baths:** 2 En 1 Pr (6)
Quiet, delightfully secluded country house. Perfect location for overnight stop or touring base for scenic Highland Perthshire and beyond. Situated in 24 acres of mature woodland gardens. Very comfortably furnished. Extremely high standard. Private access to A9 and cycle route number 77. Also two cottage apartments.

Bankfoot
NO0635

Kayrene, *Cairneyhill Road, Bankfoot, Perth, PH1 4AD.* Gateway to Highlands. Ideal touring spot, golfing, fishing, castles, lochs etc. **Open:** All year
01738 787338 (also fax) Mrs McKay **D:** Fr £19.50–£21.00 **S:** Fr £25.00 **Beds:** 2D 1T **Baths:** 2 En 1 Pr (3)

Bankfoot Inn, *Main Street, Bankfoot, Perth, PH1 4AB.* Traditional C19th country inn. Comfortable rooms and good food. **Open:** All year
01738 787243 Mrs Rudden *bankfootinn@barbox.net* **D:** Fr £19.00 **S:** Fr £19.00 **Beds:** 2T 2D 2S **Baths:** 2 Sh

Birnam
NO0341

Birnam Bank Cottage, *Birnam Glen, Birnam, Dunkeld, Perthshire, PH8 0BW.* Detached cottage, quiet surroundings, outskirts of village. Warm welcome assured. **Open:** All year (not Xmas)
01350 727628 H M Stewart *elinorlynne@aol.com* **D:** Fr £18.00–£20.00 **S:** Fr £18.00–£20.00 **Beds:** 1F 1D **Baths:** 1 Sh (2)

Blair Atholl
NN8764

Dalgreine, *off St Andrews Crescent, Blair Atholl, Pitlochry, Perthshire, PH18 5SX.* Attractive comfortable guest house, set in beautiful surroundings near Blair Castle. **Open:** All year
Grades: STB 3 Star
01796 481276 Mr & Mrs Pywell & Mrs F Hardie *mail@dalgreine-guest-house.co.uk* **D:** Fr £18.00–£22.00 **S:** Fr £18.00 **Beds:** 1F 2D 2T 1S **Baths:** 2 En 1 Pr 1 Sh (6)

Blairgowrie
NO1745

The Laurels Guest House, *Golf Course Road, Rosemount, Blairgowrie, Perthshire, PH10 6LH.* **Open:** Jan to Dec
01250 874920 (also fax) Mr & Mrs McPherson **D:** Fr £19.50–£20.00 **S:** Fr £20.00–£30.00 **Beds:** 2D 3T 1S **Baths:** 4 En (8) **cc**
Converted C18th farmhouse. First class cooking, licensed. Our bedrooms are very well-equipped with power showers in ensuite rooms and bathroom.

Ridgeway, *Wester Essendy, Blairgowrie, Perthshire, PH10 6RA.* Bungalow overlooking loch and hills. Friendly, comfortable accommodation, large garden. **Open:** All year (not Xmas)
Grades: STB 3 Star
01250 884734 Mrs Mathews **Fax: 01250 884735** *pam.mathews@btinternet.com* www.ridgewayb-b.co.uk **D:** Fr £22.00 **S:** Fr £22.00 **Beds:** 1D 1T **Baths:** 2 En (8)

Garfield House, *Perth Road, Blairgowrie, Perthshire, PH10 6ED.* Attractive detached Victorian house. Quiet and comfortable with lovely homely atmosphere. **Open:** Jan to Dec
01250 872999 Mrs Safsaf **D:** Fr £17.00–£20.00 **S:** Fr £17.00–£20.00 **Beds:** 1D 1T 1S **Baths:** 2 En 1 Pr (4)

Planning a longer stay? Always ask for any special rates

Bridge of Cally

NO1351

Bridge Of Cally Hotel, *Bridge of Cally, Blairgowrie, Perthshire, PH10 7JJ.* Small family hotel. Cooking award. Walk over 2000 acres. **Open:** All year (not Xmas)
01250 886231 Mr McCosh **D:** Fr £20.00–£27.50 **S:** Fr £20.00–£27.50 **Beds:** 1F 3D 4T 1S **Baths:** 7 En 2 Pr

Clunie

NO1043

Bankhead, *Clunie, Blairgowrie, Perthshire, PH10 6SG.* Quiet house on small farm, golfing, fishing, walking nearby. **Open:** All year
01250 884281 (also fax) Mrs Wightman *ian@ihwightman.freeserve.co.uk* **D:** Fr £18.00 **S:** Fr £20.00–£21.00 **Beds:** 1F 1T **Baths:** 2 En (3)

Comrie

NN7722

St Margarets, *Braco Road, Comrie, Crieff, Perthshire, PH6 2HP.* Attractive Victorian family house, good fishing, golfing, walking, horse riding. **Open:** Mar to Nov **Grades:** STB 3 Star
01764 670413 Mr & Mrs Paterson **D:** Fr £18.00–£20.00 **S:** Fr £18.00–£20.00 **Beds:** 1D 2T **Baths:** 1 En 1 Sh (3) (4)

Millersfield, *Dalginross, Comrie, Crieff, Perthshire, PH6 2HE.* Modern centrally heated bungalow. Peaceful location, attractive garden and warm welcome. **Open:** All year (not Xmas/New Year)
01764 670073 Mrs Rae **D:** Fr £19.00–£20.00 **S:** Fr £19.00–£20.00 **Beds:** 1D 1T (12) (3)

Crieff

NN8621

Largybeg, *Perth Road, Crieff, PH7 3EQ.* Gaelic speakers catered for, no smoking, modern, high quality accommodation. **Open:** All year
01764 655860 Mrs Mark *largybeg@btinternet.com* www.largybegbandb.co.uk **D:** Fr £18.00–£20.00 **S:** Fr £20.00–£25.00 **Beds:** 1T 2D **Baths:** 2 Sh (3)

James Cottage, *77 Burrell Street, Crieff, PH7 4DG.* Large Victorian family house, warm welcome. Excellent food. Ideal location. **Open:** All year
01764 655814 Mrs Honeyman *s.honeyman@fsmail.com* **D:** Fr £20.00–£25.00 **S:** Fr £23.00–£26.00 **Beds:** 1F 1T 1D **Baths:** 3 En (3)

Merlindale, *Perth Road, Crieff, PH7 3EQ.* **Open:** Feb to Dec **Grades:** STB 4 Star, AA 4 Diamond
01764 655205 (also fax) Mr & Mrs Clifford *merlin.dale@virgin.net* www.merlindale.co.uk **D:** Fr £22.50–£27.00 **S:** Fr £25.00–£35.00 **Beds:** 1F 1T **Baths:** 2 En
Luxury Georgian house, all bedrooms ensuite with tea/coffee-making facilities. We have a jacuzzi bath, garden, ample off-road parking, satellite television, and extensive library. Cordon Bleu cooking is our speciality. A warm welcome awaits you in this non-smoking house.

Crieff Holiday Village, *Turret Bank, Crieff, Perthshire, PH7 4JN.* Within easy walking distance from town centre. Quietly situated modern family home. **Open:** All year
01764 653513 Mrs Sloan **Fax: 01764 655028** *katie@turretbank7.freeserve.co.uk* **D:** Fr £15.00–£19.00 **S:** Fr £19.00–£23.00 **Beds:** 1F 1T 1D **Baths:** 3 En (6)

Dunkeld

NO0243

Niel Gow Cottage, *Inver, Dunkeld, Perthshire, PH8 0JR.* Neil Gow, C18th fiddler, lived here - lovely walks, central for touring. **Open:** Easter to Oct
01350 727278 (also fax) Mrs Lyon **D:** Fr £14.00–£16.00 **S:** Fr £14.00–£16.00 **Beds:** 1T 1D **Baths:** 1 Sh (4)

Taybank Hotel, *Tay Terrace, Dunkeld, Perthshire, PH8 0AQ.* Friendly music bar, spontaneous sessions, beautiful location, tasteful rooms. **Open:** All year
01350 727340 Mr Close **Fax: 01350 728606** *admin@dunkeld.co.uk* **D:** Fr £17.50 **S:** Fr £17.50–£22.50 **Beds:** 2F 1T 1D 1S **Baths:** 2 Sh **cc**

All details shown are as supplied by B&B owners in Autumn 2002

Fearnan

NN7244

Tigh An Loan Hotel, *Fearnan, Aberfeldy, Perthshire, PH15 2PF.* Old C19th inn; beautifully situated overlooking Loch Tay. **Open:** Easter to Oct
01887 830249 Mr Kelloe **D:** Fr £29.00–£31.00 **S:** Fr £29.00–£31.00 **Beds:** 1F 3S **Baths:** 3 En 2 Sh (25) **cc**

Forgandenny

NO0818

Battledown, *Forgandenny, Perth, PH2 9EL.* Explore Scotland from this perfectly situated comfortable C18th cottage. **Open:** All year **Grades:** STB 4 Star
01738 812471 Mr & Mrs Dunsire **Fax: 01738 812 471** *ian@battledown34.freeserve.co.uk* **D:** Fr £25.00 **S:** Fr £25.00 **Beds:** 1T 2D **Baths:** 3 En (3) **cc**

Fortingall

NN7347 *Fortingall Hotel, Kenmore Hotel, Coshieville Hotel, Farley House*

Fortingall Hotel, *Fortingall, Aberfeldy, Perthshire, PH15 2NQ.* Fine food, log fires, comfortable bedrooms and excellent Highland hospitality. **Open:** Mar to Dec
01887 830367 (also fax) *hotel@fortingall.com* www.fortingall.com **D:** Fr £27.50 **S:** Fr £27.50 **Beds:** 2F 4T 4D **Baths:** 10 En (12) **cc**

Kinnighallen Farm, *Duneaves Road, Fortingall, Aberfeldy, Perthshire, PH15 2LR.* Come and have a relaxing stay in this sleepy, rural backwater where wildlife abounds. **Open:** Apr to Nov
01887 830619 (also fax) Mrs Kininmonth *a.kininmonth@talk21.com* www.heartlander.scotland.net/home/kinnighallen.htm **D:** Fr £15.00 **S:** Fr £15.00 **Beds:** 1D 1T 1S **Baths:** 1 Sh (2) (5)

Killiecrankie

NN9162 *Atholl Arms, Tilt Hotel, Claymore Hotel, Killiecrankie Hotel*

Tighdornie, *Killiecrankie, Pitlochry, Perthshire, PH16 5LR.* Modern house in historic Killiecrankie. 2.5 miles from Blair Castle. **Open:** All year
01796 473276 (also fax) Mrs Sanderson *tigh_dornie@btinternet.com* **D:** Fr £22.00–£25.00 **S:** Fr £27.00–£30.00 **Beds:** 1T 2D **Baths:** 3 En (12) (4)

Kinloch Rannoch

NN6658

Dunalastair Hotel, *Kinloch Rannoch, Pitlochry, Perthshire, PH16 5PW.* **Open:** Feb to Dec
01882 632323 & 01882 632218 Paul Edwards **Fax: 01882 632371** *reservations@dunalastair.co.uk* www.dunalastair.co.uk **D:** Fr £27.50 **S:** Fr £27.50 **Beds:** 2F 10D 10T 3S **Baths:** 25 En cc
Set in picturesque Highland Perthshire village. Bedrooms range from cosy feel to romantic four-poster. 'Taste of Scotland' cuisine, walking, fishing and much more. Perfect base for exploring Scotland. This is a genuine discount, come and see for yourself.

Bunrannoch House, *Kinloch Rannoch, Pitlochry, Perthshire, PH16 5QB.* Lovely country house, beautiful views, open fires. Warm welcome and excellent food. **Open:** All year (not Xmas/New Year)
01882 632407 (also fax) Mrs Skeaping *bun.house@tesco.net* www.bunrannoch.co.uk **D:** Fr £22.00–£24.00 **S:** Fr £22.00–£24.00 **Beds:** 2F 3D 2T **Baths:** 5 Pr 2 Sh (10) cc

Kinross

NO1102

Lochleven Inn, *6 Swansacre, Kinross, Fife, KY13 7TE.* Local friendly inn (public bar). **Open:** All year
01577 864185 Mr McGregor **D:** Fr £18.00 **S:** Fr £18.00 **Beds:** 1F 1T 1D **Baths:** 2 Pr (2)

Kirkmichael

NO0860

Curran House, *Kirkmichael, Blairgowrie, Perthshire, PH10 7NA.* Traditional Scottish house. Log fire. Home baking on arrival. **Open:** Jan to Sept
01250 881229 Mr & Mrs Van der Veldt **Fax: 01250 881448** *a.m.vanderveldt@tesco.net* **D:** Fr £18.00–£36.00 **Beds:** 2D 1T **Baths:** 1 Pr 1 Sh

Cnoc Sualtach Guest House, *Kirkmichael, Blairgowrie, Perthshire, PH10 7NS.* Peaceful, comfortable, quality accommodation. Beautiful views. Ideal touring/walking area. **Open:** All year (not Xmas/New Year) **Grades:** STB 4 Star
01250 881329 & 01250 881463 *cnoc_sualtach@compuserve.com* **D:** Fr £20.00 **S:** Fr £20.00–£25.00 **Beds:** 1T 2D **Baths:** 3 En (10)

Meigle

NO2844

Loanhead House, *Dundee Road, Meigle, Blairgowrie, PH12 8SF.* Superb accommodation and food in edge of castle estate location. **Open:** All year (not Xmas/New Year)
01828 640358 Mr Taylor **Fax: 0870 132 9749** *gill@loanheadhouse.co.uk* **D:** Fr £20.00–£24.00 **S:** Fr £20.00–£28.00 **Beds:** 1D 1T **Baths:** 1 En 1 Pr (4)

Methven

NO0226

Lismore, *1 Rorrie Terrace, Methven, Perth, PH1 3PL.* True home-from-home in village 5 miles from Perth. **Open:** All year **Grades:** STB 3 Star
01738 840441 (also fax) Mr Comrie **D:** Fr £13.50–£16.00 **S:** Fr £17.50–£25.00 **Beds:** 1F 1D (8) (2)

Milnathort

NO1204

Hattonburn Farmhouse, *Milnathort, Kinross, Fife, KY13 0SA.* Close to M90. Edinburgh and airport 10 minutes, Perth 20 minutes. **Open:** All year (not Xmas/New Year)
01577 862362 Mrs Todrick **D:** Fr £20.00–£24.00 **S:** Fr £20.00–£24.00 **Beds:** 1T **Baths:** 1 Pr (6)

Perth

NO1123

Achnacarry Guest House, *3 Pitcullen Crescent, Perth, PH2 7HT.* Perfectly situated for exploring Central Scotland and Highlands. Warm welcome. **Open:** All year
01738 621421 David & Allison Golder **Fax: 01738 444110** *info@achnacarry.co.uk* www.achnacarry.co.uk **D:** Fr £22.00–£25.00 **S:** Fr £25.00–£30.00 **Beds:** 1F 1T 2D **Baths:** 4 En (6) cc

The Linn, *3 Duchess Street, Stanley, Perth, PH1 4NF.* **Open:** All year (not Xmas) **Grades:** STB 4 Star
01738 828293 (also fax) Mrs Lundie *ettalundie@hotmail.com* **D:** Fr £20.00–£22.00 **Beds:** 2F 1T **Baths:** 2 En 1 Pr
We warmly invite you to share the comfort of our home; our rooms are prettily furnished & decorated with many thoughtful extras. We are beside the lovely River Tay (5 min walk) the historic Stanley Mill. Perth is only 7 miles away. Ideal base for touring, golfing or fishing. Historic castles, bird watching or walking.

Creswick Guest House, *86 Dundee Road, Perth, PH2 7BA.* A warm welcome is assured in our attractive Edwardian villa. **Open:** Feb to Nov
01738 625896 Mrs Wilson *creswick@lineone.net* **D:** Fr £18.00–£24.00 **S:** Fr £22.00–£25.00 **Beds:** 2D 1T **Baths:** 2 En 1 Pr (4)

The Darroch Guest House, *9 Pitcullen Crescent, Perth, PH2 7HT.* Victorian semi, friendly relaxed atmosphere, ideal base for touring. **Open:** All year
01738 636893 (also fax) Mrs Forsyth *the.darroch@virgin.net* www.thedarroch-guesthouse.co.uk **D:** Fr £19.00–£25.00 **S:** Fr £20.00–£30.00 **Beds:** 1F 2D 1T 2S **Baths:** 3 En 1 Sh (8)

Tigh Mhorag Guest House, *69 Dunkeld Road, Perth, PH1 5RP.* Friendly welcome in Victorian villa close to town centre facilities. **Open:** All year **Grades:** STB 2 Star
01738 622902 *sheilajohn@tinyworld.co.uk* **D:** Fr £19.00–£21.00 **S:** Fr £19.00–£25.00 **Beds:** 1F 1T 2D 2S **Baths:** 3 En 1 Sh (6)

Abercrombie, *85 Glasglow Road, Perth, PH2 0PQ.* Abercrombie is ideally situated near rail/bus stations, leisure pool, ice and bowling rinks. **Open:** All year
01738 444728 Mrs Dewar **Fax: 07138 444728** **D:** Fr £25.00–£30.00 **S:** Fr £25.00–£30.00 **Beds:** 1T 1D 2S **Baths:** 2 En 2 Pr (6) cc

Dunallan Guest House, *10 Pitcullen Crescent, Perth, PH2 7HT.* Well-appointed Victorian villa within walking distance Perth City Centre. **Open:** All year **Grades:** STB 4 Star
01738 622551 (also fax) Mrs Brown *dunallan@aol.com* www.dunallan.co.uk **D:** Fr £21.00–£24.00 **S:** Fr £22.50–£24.00 **Beds:** 1F 1D 2T 3S **Baths:** 7 En (7) cc

Comely Bank Cottage, *19 Pitcullen Cres, Perth, Perthshire, PH2 7HT.* Ten minutes walk to town centre. Enjoy true Scottish hospitality. **Open:** All year (not Xmas)
01738 631118 Mrs Marshall **Fax: 01738 571245** *comelybankcott@hotmail.com* **D:** Fr £18.00–£22.00 **S:** Fr £22.00–£30.00 **Beds:** 1F 1D 1T **Baths:** 3 En (3) cc

Beeches, *2 Comely Bank, Perth, PH2 7HU.* Home-from-home Victorian house. Friendly, relaxing, check web details! **Open:** All year **Grades:** STB 3 Star
01738 624486 Mrs Smith **Fax: 01738 643382** *enquiries@beeches-guest-house.co.uk* www.beeches-guest-house.co.uk **D:** Fr £18.00–£22.00 **S:** Fr £18.00–£22.00 **Beds:** 1D 1T 2S **Baths:** 4 En (4) cc

Parkview Guest House, *22 Marshall Place, Perth, PH2 8AG.* 'B' Listed Georgian town house. Very central, overlooking park. **Open:** All year
01738 620297 (also fax) Mr Farquharson *fiona.farquharson@btinternet.com* **D:** Fr £16.00–£19.00 **S:** Fr £18.00–£20.00 **Beds:** 4F 1T **Baths:** 3 En 1 Sh (4)

Arisaig Guest House, *4 Pitcullen Crescent, Perth, PH2 7HT.* Late-Victorian family-run guest house situated on the A94. **Open:** All year **Grades:** STB 4 Star
01738 628240 Stewart & Wilma Bousie **Fax: 01738 638521** *enquiries@arisaigguesthouse.co.uk* www.arisaigguesthouse.co.uk **D:** Fr £20.00–£22.50 **S:** Fr £25.00–£30.00 **Beds:** 1F 2D 1T 1S **Baths:** 5 En (5) cc

Huntingtower House, *Crieff Road, Perth, PH1 3JJ.* Situated on the western outskirts of Perth, this charming country house with large, secluded garden nestles beside historic Huntingtower Castle. There is easy access to Perth and all main routes throughout Scotland. A friendly welcome and delicious breakfast are assured. **Open:** Feb to Dec
01738 624681 Mrs Lindsay **Fax: 01738 639770** *huntingtowerhouse@btinternet.com* **D:** Fr £22.00–£25.00 **S:** Fr £22.00–£25.00 **Beds:** 1D 2T **Baths:** 1 Pr 1 Sh (11) (3)

Aberdeen Guest House, *Pitcullen Crescent, Perth, PH2 7HT.* Beautiful Victorian house where comfort and care is paramount. **Open:** All year
01738 633183 (also fax) Mrs Buchan *buchan@aberdeenguesthouse.fsnet.co.uk* **D:** Fr £18.00–£22.00 **S:** Fr £18.00–£25.00 **Beds:** 2D 1T **Baths:** 1 En 2 Sh (4)

Pitlochry

NN9458

Claymore Hotel, *162 Atholl Road, Pitlochry, Perthshire, PH16 5AR.* **Open:** All year (not Xmas) **Grades:** STB 3 Star
01796 472888 Mrs Guinn **Fax: 01796 474037** *sue@claymorehotel.fsnet.co.uk* www.claymorehotel.com **D:** Fr £32.00–£42.00 **S:** Fr £50.00–£60.00 **Beds:** 2F 3T 3D 2S **Baths:** 10 En (20) cc
The Claymore stands on the outskirts of Pitlochry in two areas of award-winning gardens, & offers high standards of quality & personal attention. The hotel is renowned for its food, in the restaurant & conservatory. Autumn & spring breaks available.

Auchlatt Steading, *Kinnaird, Pitlochry, Perthshire, PH16 5JL.* **Open:** Easter to Nov
01796 472661 (also fax) Miss Elkins **D:** Fr £19.00 **S:** Fr £19.00 **Beds:** 1T 1D **Baths:** 2 En (2)
Newly converted Scottish barn comfortable beds and a good honest breakfast. Overlooking Pitlochry and surrounding beautiful countryside, good hill walking and fishing. Theatre and historic interest.

Balrobin Hotel, *Higher Oakfield, Pitlochry, Perthshire, PH16 5HT.* Quality accommodation with panoramic views at affordable prices. **Open:** Apr to Oct **Grades:** STB 3 Star, AA 2 Star, RAC 2 Star
01796 472901 Mr Hohman **Fax: 01796 474200** *info@balrobin.co.uk* www.balrobin.co.uk **D:** Fr £25.00–£35.00 **S:** Fr £25.00–£39.00 **Beds:** 1F 10D 3T 1S **Baths:** 15 En (5) (15) cc

Gardeners Cottage, *Faskally, Pitlochry, PH16 5LA.* Centre of Scotland, beautiful views, quiet location, walking, cycling, fishing. **Open:** All year **Grades:** STB 3 Star
01796 472450 Mrs Viner **D:** Fr £19.00–£23.00 **S:** Fr £23.00–£30.00 **Beds:** 1T 2D **Baths:** 1 Pr 1 Sh (7)

Easter Dunfallandy Country House B&B, *Pitlochry, Perthshire, PH16 5NA.* Beautifully presented country house with fine views and gourmet breakfast. **Open:** All year (not Xmas/New Year)
01796 474128 Mr Mathieson **Fax: 01796 473994** *sue@dunfallandy.co.uk* www.dunfallandy.co.uk **D:** Fr £28.00 **S:** Fr £38.00 **Beds:** 1D 2T **Baths:** 3 En (12) (6)

Wellwood House, *West Moulin Road, Pitlochry, Perthshire, PH16 5EA.* The Wellwood is a Victorian mansion house set in 2 acres of splendid gardens. **Open:** Mar to Nov
01796 474288 Ms Herd **Fax: 01796 474299** *wellwood@ukonline.co.uk* www.smouthhound.co.uk/hotels/wellwood.html **D:** Fr £19.50–£25.00 **S:** Fr £25.00–£35.00 **Beds:** 1F 5D 4T **Baths:** 8 En 2 Sh (25)

Lynedoch, *9 Lettoch Terrace, Pitlochry, Perthshire, PH16 5BA.* Stone-built semi-detached villa in beautiful Highland Perthshire, ideally situated for walking, golf, fishing etc. **Open:** Easter to Oct
01796 472119 Mrs Williamson *iwilliamson@talk21.com* **D:** Fr £16.00–£18.00 **S:** Fr £16.00–£18.00 **Beds:** 2D 1T **Baths:** 2 Sh (3)

Atholl Villa, *29 Atholl Road, Pitlochry, Perthshire, PH16 5BX.* 10-bedroom Victorian detached stone house, typical Highland construction, edge of town. **Open:** All year
01796 473820 Mrs Bruce *athollvilla@aol.com* www.s-h-systems.co.uk/hotels/athollvilla.html **D:** Fr £17.50–£25.00 **S:** Fr £17.50–£25.00 **Beds:** 3F 2T 2D **Baths:** 7 En (10) cc

Rattray

NO1845 *Angus Hotel, Victoria Hotel*

Shocarjen House, *Balmoral Road, Rattray, Blairgowrie, Perthshire, PH10 7AF.* New purpose built bed and breakfast. Ideal for all activities in Perthshire. **Open:** All year
01250 870525 & 07801 436662 (M) Mrs Beattie **D:** Fr £17.00–£18.50 **S:** Fr £19.00 **Beds:** 1T 1D **Baths:** 2 En (6)

Planning a longer stay? Always ask for any special rates

Rhynd

NO1520

Fingask Farm, *Rhynd, Perth, Perthshire & Kinross, PH2 8QF.* Spacious accommodation in well-appointed farmhouse in a peaceful part of central Perthshire. **Open:** Easter to Oct
01738 812220 Mrs Stirrat **Fax: 01738 813325** *libby@agstirrat.sol.co.uk* **D:** Fr £19.00–£21.00 **S:** Fr £19.00–£21.00 **Beds:** 1D 1T 1S **Baths:** 2 Pr (10) (3) **cc**

Planning a longer stay? Always ask for any special rates

Stanley

NO1133

Newmill Farm, *Stanley, Perth, PH1 4QD.* Working farm with traditional stone-built farmhouse situated alongside the A9. **Open:** Jan to Nov **Grades:** STB 3 Star
01738 828281 (also fax) Mrs Guthrie *guthrienewmill@sol.co.uk* **D:** Fr £19.00–£22.00 **S:** Fr £25.00–£30.00 **Beds:** 2D 1T **Baths:** 3 En

The Linn, *3 Duchess Street, Stanley, Perth, PH1 4NF.* Share the comfort of our home; our rooms are prettily furnished. **Open:** All year (not Xmas) **Grades:** STB 4 Star
01738 828293 (also fax) Mrs Lundie *ettalundie@hotmail.com* **D:** Fr £20.00–£22.00 **Beds:** 2F 1T **Baths:** 2 En 1 Pr

Beechlea, *Stanley, Perth, Perthshire, PH1 4PS.* Luxury comfortable B&B, beautiful quiet countryside, excellent location off A9. **Open:** All year (not Xmas)
01738 828715 Mrs Lindsay *chaslizlin@aol.com* members.aol.com/chaslizlin/index.html **D:** Fr £20.00–£27.00 **S:** Fr £25.00–£27.00 **Beds:** 1F 1D 1T **Baths:** 3 En (10) (6) **cc**

Shetland

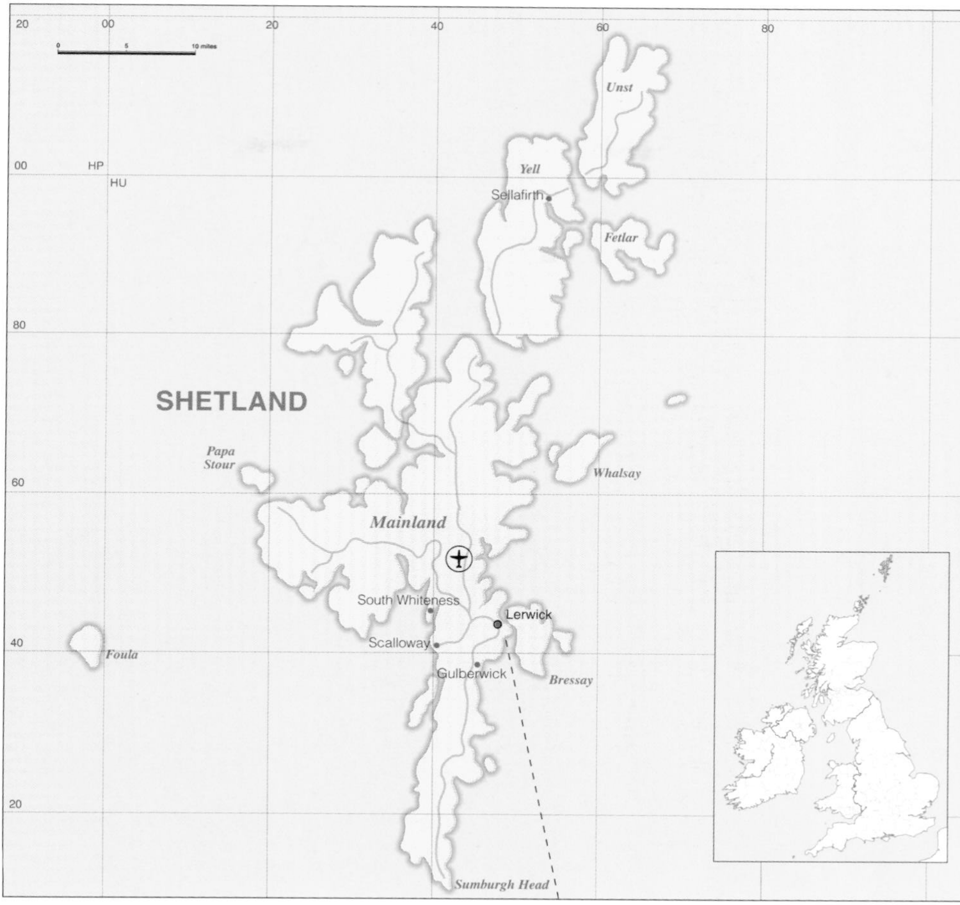

FAIR ISLE Fair Isle

HZ2271

Upper Leogh, *Fair Isle, Shetland, ZE2 9JU.* Working croft, hand spinning demonstration/ tuition available. Local crafts nearby. **Open:** All year
01595 760248 Mrs Coull *kathleen.coull@lineone.net* **D:** Fr £20.00–£22.00 **S:** Fr £20.00–£22.00 **Beds:** 1T 1D 1S (3)

B&B owners may vary rates – be sure to check when booking

MAINLAND Gulberwick

HU4438

Virdafjell, *Shurton Brae, Gulberwick, Shetland, ZE2 9TX.* Peaceful Nordic home overlooking bay. Walks, ponies, bird-watching, good touring base. **Open:** All year **Grades:** STB 4 Star
01595 694336 Mrs Stove **Fax: 01595 696252** *d.stove@talk21.com* **D:** Fr £25.00 **S:** Fr £30.00 **Beds:** 1T 2D **Baths:** 3 En (6)

All details shown are as supplied by B&B owners in Autumn 2002

MAINLAND Lerwick

HU4741

Whinrig, *12 Burgh Road, Lerwick, Shetland, ZE1 0LB.* Private bungalow. Centrally heated. Central to all amenities, warm welcome. **Open:** All year (not Xmas/New Year)
01595 693554 Mrs Gifford *c.gifford@btinternet.com* www.btinternet.com/~C. Gifford/ **D:** Fr £22.00 **S:** Fr £22.00 **Beds:** 2T **Baths:** 1 En 1 Pr (2)

Woosung, *43 St Olaf Street, Lerwick, Shetland,* *ZE1 0EN.* Very central - close to all amenities. Ideal for touring/ walking. **Open:** All year (not Xmas/New Year)
01595 693687 S Conroy *woosung@talk21.com*
D: Fr £17.00 **S:** Fr £22.00 **Beds:** 2T **Baths:** 1 Sh

Breiview, *43 Kantersted Road, Lerwick, Shetland,* *ZE1 0RJ.* Friendly modern accommodation in quiet location. Overlooks bay and Bressay. **Open:** All year (not Xmas/New Year)
01595 695956 (also fax) Mr Glaser *breiview@btopenworld.com* **D:** Fr £25.00–£30.00 **S:** Fr £30.00–£35.00 **Beds:** 1F 2D 3T **Baths:** 6 En (6)

MAINLAND Scalloway

HU4039

Broch Guest House, *Scalloway, Lerwick, Shetland,* *ZE1 0UP.* Comfortable guest house. **Open:** All year (not Xmas)
01595 880767 Mrs Young **D:** Fr £17.00 **S:** Fr £19.00 **Beds:** 3D **Baths:** 3 En (3)

MAINLAND South Whiteness

HU3844

The Inn on the Hill, *The Westings, Whiteness, Shetland,* *ZE2 9LJ.* Country inn with stunning views from all rooms. **Open:** All year
01595 840242 Fax: 01595 840500
westingsinn@aol.com www.westings.shetland.co.uk **D:** Fr £37.50–£40.00 **S:** Fr £37.50–£45.00 **Beds:** 2T 1D 3S **Baths:** 6 En (10) (25) **cc**

YELL Sellafirth

HU5297 *Glenmoriston Hotel*

North Isle Motel, *Sellafirth, Shetland,* *ZE2 9DG.* Beautiful views, overlooking Basta Voe. Wild life, birds. **Open:** All year
01957 744294 **D:** Fr £19.00–£21.00 **S:** Fr £22.00–£25.00 **Beds:** 10T **Baths:** 2 Sh (5) (20)

RATES

D = Price range per person sharing in a double or twin room

S = Price range for a single room

Stirling & the Trossachs

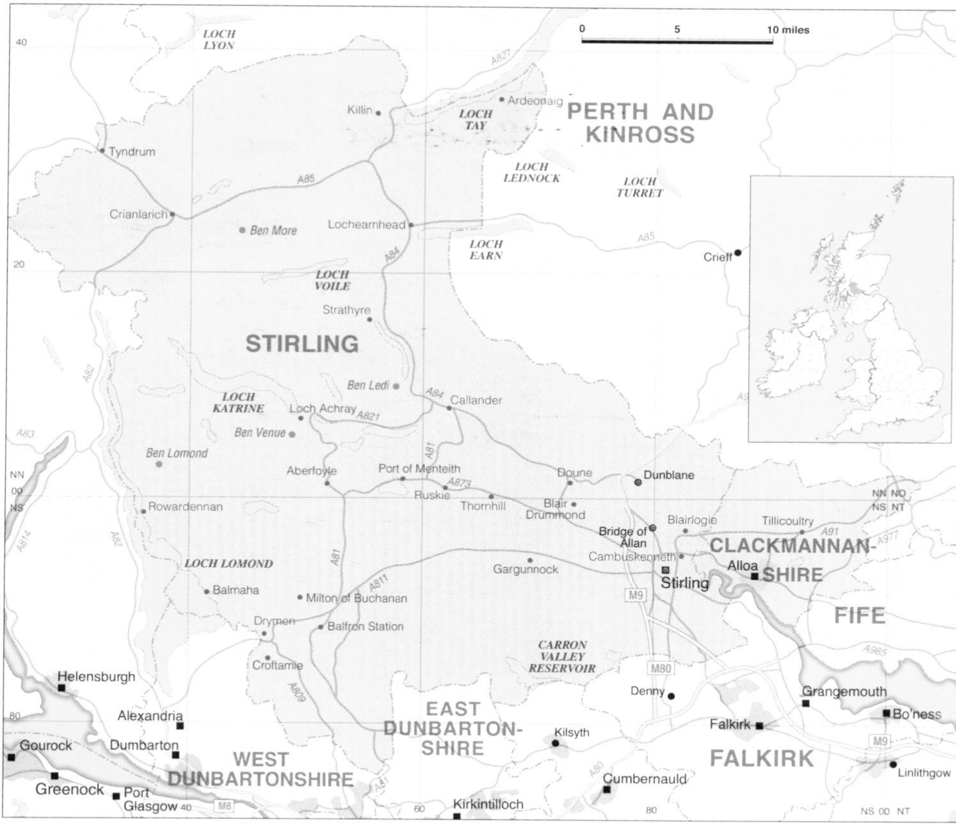

Aberfoyle

NN5200

Creag Ard House B&B, *Aberfoyle, Stirling, FK8 3TQ.* Beautiful Victorian house with superb views over Loch Ard. Magnificent scenery. **Open:** All year **01877 382297** Mrs Wilson *cara@creag-ardhouse.co.uk* www.creag-ardhouse.co.uk **D:** Fr £29.00–£40.00 **S:** Fr £35.00–£70.00 **Beds:** 4D 2T **Baths:** 6 En (7) cc

Ardeonaig

NN6735

Abernethy Trust, *Ardeonaig, Killin, Perthshire, FK21 8SY.* Outdoor activity centre in 20 acre estate overlooking Loch Tay **Open:** Jan to Nov **01567 820523** *at@ardeonaig.org* www.ardeonaig.org **D:** Fr £23.00 **S:** Fr £28.00 **Beds:** 11F 3D **Baths:** 4 Sh (20)

All details shown are as supplied by B&B owners in Autumn 2002

Balfron Station

NS5289

Easter Balfunning Farm, *Drymen, Glasgow, G63 0NF.* A warm welcome awaits you in our attractive farmhouse, idyllically situated. **Open:** All year **01360 440755** Ms Black **D:** Fr £18.00–£21.00 **S:** Fr £21.00–£27.00 **Beds:** 1D 1F **Baths:** 1 Pr 1 En (4)

National Grid References given are for villages, towns and cities – not for individual houses

Loaninghead Farm, *Balfron Station, Glasgow, G63 0SE.* Make this your base. Explore Scotland's first National Park. **Open:** All year
01360 440432 (also fax) Mrs Paterson *paterson.loaninghead@virgin.net* www.visit-lochlomod.com/loaninghead **D:** Fr £18.00–£25.00 **S:** Fr £20.00–£25.00 **Beds:** 1F 1T 1D **Baths:** 1 En 1 Pr 1 Sh

Balmaha

NS4290

Mar Achlais, *Milton of Buchanan, Balmaha, G63 0JE.* Rural setting near Loch Lomond. Excellent touring centre for Scotland. **Open:** All year (not Xmas)
01360 870300 Mr Nichols **Fax: 01360 870444** *marachlais@dial.pipex.com* **D:** Fr £19.00 **S:** Fr £24.00 **Beds:** 1F 1D **Baths:** 2 En (2) cc

Critreoch, *Rowardennan Road, Balmaha, Glasgow, G63 0AW.* Family home quiet location beautiful view over garden to Loch. **Open:** May to Sept
01360 870309 Mrs MacLuskie **D:** Fr £20.00–£22.00 **S:** Fr £25.00–£30.00 **Beds:** 1D 1T **Baths:** 1 En 1 Pr (6)

Conic View Cottage, *Balmaha, Glasgow, G63 0JQ.* Beautifully situated near Loch Lomond and the West Highland Way, surrounded by forest walks. **Open:** Mar to Nov
01360 870297 Mrs Cronin *jenny@balmaha32.freeserve.co.uk* www.geocities.com/jenny_cronin **D:** Fr £15.00–£20.00 **S:** Fr £18.00–£20.00 **Beds:** 1D 1S **Baths:** 1 Sh (2)

Blair Drummond

NS7299 *Lion & Unicorn*

The Linns, *Kirk Lane, Blair Drummond, Stirling, FK9 4AN.* Perfectly situated for exploring central Scotland. Warm welcome. Wholesome breakfast. **Open:** All year (not Xmas/New Year)
01786 841679 Mr Darby **Fax: 01786 842473** *swell@hillview-cottage.com* www.hillview-cottage.com **D:** Fr £21.00–£24.00 **S:** Fr £30.00–£35.00 **Beds:** 2F 1T 2D **Baths:** 5 En (7) cc

Blairlogie

NS8296

Blairmains Farm, *Manor Loan, Blairlogie, Stirling, FK9 5QA.* Traditional stone farmhouse. Working farm, beautiful country location. Coffee shop and farm shop. **Open:** All year (not Xmas/New Year) **Grades:** STB 2 Star
01259 761338 Mrs Logan **D:** Fr £18.00–£20.00 **S:** Fr £20.00–£23.00 **Beds:** 2T 1D **Baths:** 1 Sh

Bridge of Allan

NS7997

Lorraine, *10 Chalton Road, Bridge of Allan, Stirling, FK9 4DX.* Listed building, off main road, lovely views, good walking country. **Open:** All year (not Xmas)
01786 832042 & 07932 140760 (M) B Holliday **Fax: 01786 831066** *101567.2041@compuserve.com* **D:** Fr £18.00–£20.00 **S:** Fr £18.00–£25.00 **Beds:** 1D 1T 1S **Baths:** 2 Sh (4)

Callander

NN6307

Arden House, *Bracklinn Road, Callander, Perthshire, FK17 8EQ.* **Open:** Apr to Oct **Grades:** STB 4 Star, AA 4 Diamond
01877 330235 (also fax) Mr Mitchell & Mr W Jackson *ardenhouse@onetel.net.uk* www.ardenhouse.org.uk **D:** Fr £27.50–£32.50 **S:** Fr £30.00 **Beds:** 3D 2T 1S **Baths:** 6 En (6) cc
Tranquillity in the Trossachs. Peaceful Victorian country house with stunning views. Home of BBC TVs 'Dr Finlay's Casebook'. Comfortable, Elegant ensuite rooms with TV, tea/coffee and many thoughtful touches. Few minutes walk to village. Generous breakfasts and genuine hospitality.

Riverview House, *Leny Road, Callander, Perthshire, FK17 8AL.* Guest-house and self-catering in scenic Trossachs National Park. **Open:** All year (not Xmas)
01877 330635 Mr Little **Fax: 01877 339386** *auldtoll@netscapeonline.co.uk* www.nationalparkscotland.co.uk **D:** Fr £21.00–£22.00 **S:** Fr £22.00–£24.00 **Beds:** 3D 2T 1S **Baths:** 5 En (6)

Lubnaig House, *Leny Feus, Callander, Perthshire, FK17 8AS.* A quiet oasis surrounded by stunning scenery, relax and enjoy. **Open:** May to Sep **Grades:** STB 4 Star, AA 4 Diamond
01877 330376 (also fax) Mr & Mrs Low *info@lubnaighouse.co.uk* www.lubnaighouse.co.uk **D:** Fr £25.00–£32.00 **S:** Fr £25.00–£40.00 **Beds:** 6D 4T **Baths:** 10 En (7) (10)

Annfield House, *North Church Street, Callander, Perthshire, FK17 8EG.* Ideal as an overnight stop for exploring the Highlands. **Open:** All year
01877 330204 Mrs Greenfield **Fax: 01877 330674** **D:** Fr £21.00 **S:** Fr £25.00 **Beds:** 1F 2T 4D 1S **Baths:** 4 En 1 Pr 1 Sh (3) (7)

Waterside House, *South Church Street, Callander, Perthshire, FK17 8HB.* Quiet, quality and comfort by the riverside. Four-poster available. **Open:** All year
01877 331391 *lesley@lesleyedmunds.fsnet.co.uk* **D:** Fr £20.00–£25.00 **S:** Fr £25.00–£35.00 **Beds:** 1T 2D **Baths:** 2 En 1 Pr (2)

East Mains House, *Bridgend, Callander, Perthshire, FK17 8AG.* Comfortable Georgian house with large garden and relaxed atmosphere. **Open:** All year
01877 330535 (also fax) Ms Alexander *east.mains@tesco.net* www.smoothhound.co.uk/hotels/eastm/html **D:** Fr £22.00–£24.00 **S:** Fr £27.00–£29.00 **Beds:** 2F 4D **Baths:** 4 En (6) cc

Glengarry Hotel, *Stirling Road, Callander, Perthshire, FK17 8DA.* Family-run hotel in own grounds. Hearty breakfast, traditional home-cooked evening meals. Easy access. **Open:** All year
01877 330216 *info@glengarryhotel.com* www.glengarryhotel.demon.co.uk **D:** Fr £22.00–£25.00 **Beds:** 3F 1D **Baths:** 4 En (15)

White Cottage, *Bracklinn Road, Callander, FK17 8EQ.* Situated in one acre garden. Magnificent views of Ben Ledi. **Open:** Apr to Nov
01877 330896 Mrs Hughes **D:** Fr £17.50–£19.00 **S:** Fr £20.00–£22.00 **Beds:** 2D **Baths:** 1 Sh (3)

Brook Linn Country House, *Callander, Perthshire, FK17 8AU.* Lovely comfortable Victorian house with magnificent views and personal attention. **Open:** Easter to Oct
01877 330103 (also fax) Mrs House *derek@blinn.freeserve.co.uk* www.brooklinn-scotland.co.uk **D:** Fr £24.00–£30.00 **S:** Fr £23.00–£27.00 **Beds:** 2S 2D 2T **Baths:** 6 En (8) cc

Campfield Cottage, *138 Main Street, Callander, Perthshire, FK17 8BG.* Charming C18th cottage in heart of Callander, down a quiet lane. **Open:** All year (not Xmas/New Year)
01877 330597 Mrs Hunter **D:** Fr £18.00 **S:** Fr £18.00 **Beds:** 2D 1T 1S **Baths:** 1 Sh

Linley Guest House, *139 Main Street, Callander, Perthshire, FK17 8BH.* Comfortable Victorian terraced house close to Callander busy centre. Stirling 25 minutes drive. **Open:** All year
01877 330087 M McQuilton *linley_guesthouse@tinyworld.co.uk* **D:** Fr £16.00–£18.50 **S:** Fr £20.00–£25.00 **Beds:** 1F 1T 3D **Baths:** 2 En 2 Sh (4)

Cambuskenneth

NS8094

Carseview, *16 Ladysneuk Road, Cambuskenneth, Stirling, FK9 5NF.* Quiet conservation village, 15 mins' walk Stirling town centre, panoramic views. **Open:** All year **Grades:** STB 3 Star
01786 462235 (also fax) Mr & Mrs Seaton *bandb@carseview.co.uk* www.carseview.co.uk **D:** Fr £18.00 **S:** Fr £18.00–£20.00 **Beds:** 2T 1S **Baths:** 1 Sh cc

Crianlarich

NN3825

Riverside Guest House, *Tigh-na Struith, Crianlarich, Perthshire, FK20 8RU.* **Open:** All year
01838 300235 Mr & Mrs Chisholm *jansan@btinternet.com* www.riversideguesthouse.co.uk **D:** Fr £18.00–£25.00 **S:** Fr £20.00–£30.00 **Beds:** 2F 1T 2D 1S **Baths:** 3 En 1 Sh (6)
Lovely established guest house in super position on village outskirts. 200 yards off main road with unrestricted views of hills and river. Ideal for fishing, walking and touring by car. Discounts on stays for 3 nights and 5 nights.

Craigbank Guest House, *Crianlarich, Perthshire, FK20 8QS.* Situated one hour's drive from Glen Coe, Loch Lomond, the Trossachs. **Open:** All year (not Xmas)
01838 300279 Mr Flockhart **D:** Fr £17.00–£19.00 **S:** Fr £25.00 **Beds:** 2F 1D 3T **Baths:** 2 En 2 Sh (6)

The Lodge House, *Crianlarich, Perthshire, FK20 8RU.* Superbly located guest house, magnificent views of Crianlarich hills. **Open:** All year **Grades:** STB 4 Star, AA 4 Diamond
01838 300276 Mr Gaughan *admin@lodgehouse.co.uk* www.lodgehouse.co.uk **D:** Fr £25.00–£30.00 **S:** Fr £35.00–£45.00 **Beds:** 1F 3D 2T **Baths:** 6 En (10) cc

Inverherive Cottage, *Crianlarich, Perthshire, FK20 8RU.* Beautifully situated. Private sitting area and entrance. Come and enjoy. **Open:** All year (not Xmas/New Year)
01838 300336 Mr & Mrs Scott *inver@herive.freeserve.co.uk* **D:** Fr £15.00 **S:** Fr £25.00 **Beds:** 1D **Baths:** 1 Pr (6)

Ben More Lodge Hotel, *Crianlarich, Perthshire, FK20 8QS.* Family-run lodge hotel with spectacular setting beneath Ben More. **Open:** All year **Grades:** STB 2 Star
01838 300210 Mr Goodale **Fax: 01838 300218** *john@ben-more.demon.co.uk* www.ben-more.co.uk **D:** Fr £25.00–£34.00 **S:** Fr £28.00–£43.00 **Beds:** 2F 8D 1T **Baths:** 11 En

Croftamie

NS4786

Croftburn, *Croftamie, Drymen, Glasgow, G63 0HA.* Former gamekeeper's cottage in one acre of beautiful gardens overlooking Strathendrick Valley & Campsie Fells. **Open:** All year **Grades:** STB 3 Star, AA 4 Diamond
01360 660796 Mrs Reid **Fax: 01360 661005** *johnreid@croftburn.fsnet.co.uk* **D:** Fr £18.00–£25.00 **S:** Fr £25.00–£30.00 **Beds:** 2D 1T **Baths:** 2 En 1 Pr (12) (20) cc

Doune

NN7301

Inverardoch Mains Farm, *Doune, Perthshire, FK15 9NZ.* Traditional farmhouse on working farm. View of Doune Castle close to Dunblane and Trossachs. **Open:** All year (not Xmas/New Year) **Grades:** STB 2 Star
01786 841268 (also fax) J Anderson **D:** Fr £20.00–£23.00 **S:** Fr £22.00–£28.00 **Beds:** 1F 1T 1D **Baths:** 2 Pr 1 Sh (3) (4)

Drymen

NS4788

Green Shadows, *Buchanan Castle Estate, Drymen, Glasgow, G63 0HX.* **Open:** All year (not Xmas)
01360 660289 & 07775 690855 Mrs Goodwin **D:** Fr £21.00 **S:** Fr £24.00 **Beds:** 1F 1D 1S **Baths:** 2 Sh (8)
Warm, friendly welcome in a beautiful country house with spectacular views over golf course and the Lomond Hills. Buchanan Castle to the rear. 1 mile from Drymen Centre, 2 miles from Loch Lomond. Glasgow Airport 40 mins away.

Easter Drumquhassle Farm, *Gartness Road, Drymen, Glasgow, G63 0DN.* Traditional farmhouse, beautiful views, home-cooking, excellent base on the West Highland Way. **Open:** All year
01360 660893 Mrs Cross **Fax: 01360 660282** *juliamacx@aol.com* members.aol.com/juliamacx **D:** Fr £17.50–£21.00 **S:** Fr £28.00–£39.00 **Beds:** 1F 1D 1T **Baths:** 3 En (10)

The Hawthorns, *The Square, Drymen, Glasgow, G63 0BH.* Built 1873 - The Doctors 'Auld Hoose'. Totally refurbished, all ensuite. **Open:** All year **Grades:** STB 3 Star
01360 660916 Mrs Gallacher **Fax: 01360 661070** *pat@thehawthorns-drymen.com* www.thehawthorns-drymen.com **D:** Fr £25.00–£30.00 **Beds:** 1F 1T 1D **Baths:** 3 En

Croftburn, *Croftamie, Drymen, Glasgow, G63 0HA.* Former gamekeeper's cottage in one acre of beautiful gardens overlooking Strathendrick Valley & Campsie Fells. **Open:** All year **Grades:** STB 3 Star, AA 4 Diamond
01360 660796 Mrs Reid **Fax: 01360 661005** *johnreid@croftburn.fsnet.co.uk* **D:** Fr £18.00–£25.00 **S:** Fr £25.00–£30.00 **Beds:** 2D 1T **Baths:** 2 En 1 Pr (12) (20) cc

Please respect a B&B's wishes regarding children, animals and smoking

Dunblane

NN7801

Mossgiel, *Doune Road, Dunblane, Perthshire, FK15 9ND.* **Open:** Mar to Oct
01786 824325 Mrs Bennett *judy@mossgiel.com*
D: Fr £20.00–£22.00 **S:** Fr £25.00–£30.00
Beds: 2T 1D **Baths:** 2 En 1 Pr (5)
Countryside house situated between Dunblane and Doune Castle. Nearby attractions include Stirling Castle, Wallace Monument and Scotland's first National Park. Good road and rail services into Glasgow and Edinburgh. A full Scottish breakfast and a warm welcome awaits you at Mossgiel.

Gargunnock

NS7094

East Lodge, *Leckie, Gargunnock, Stirling, FK8 3BN.* C19th lodge house tastefully extended. In attractive woodland setting. 'Comfortable, peaceful and elegant'.
Open: All year (not Xmas)
01786 860605 Mrs Currie *jane123456@aol.com*
D: Fr £20.00–£22.00 **S:** Fr £25.00–£28.00
Beds: 1D 1T **Baths:** 1 Pr 1 Sh (3) 1

Killin

NN5732

Falls of Dochart Cottage, *Killin, Perthshire, FK21 8SW.* C17th cottage, overlooking Falls, river. Central for magnificent mountain area. Home cooking. **Open:** All year (not Xmas)
01567 820363 Mr & Mrs Mudd **D:** Fr £18.00
S: Fr £18.00 **Beds:** 1D 1T 1S **Baths:** 2 Sh (1) (4)

Allt Fulieach, *Maragowan, Killin, Perthshire, FK21 8TN.* Comfortable, modern house at the head of Loch Tay. **Open:** All year
01567 820962 Mr Judd **D:** Fr £19.00 **S:** Fr £19.00 **Beds:** 2T 1D **Baths:** 3 En (4)

Main Street, *Killin, Perthshire, FK21 8TP.* Magnificent setting, overlooking River Lochay. Bistro - home-cooked dishes; lounge bar - stock of malt whiskies.
Open: All year
01567 820296 Mr & Mrs Garnier **Fax: 01567 820647** *killinhotel@btinternet.com*
www.killinhotel.com **D:** Fr £19.00–£35.00
S: Fr £19.00–£35.00 **Beds:** 3F 6T 17D 6S
Baths: 32 En (20)
cc

Loch Achray

NN5106

Glenbruach Country House, *Loch Achray, Trossachs, Callander, Perthshire, FK17 8HX.* **Open:** All year
01877 376216 (also fax) Mrs Lindsay
james.lindsay5@btinternet.com
www.nationalparkaccommodation.co.uk
D: Fr £22.00–£25.00 **S:** Fr £22.00–£25.00
Beds: 2D 1T **Baths:** 2 En 1 Pr (12) (3)
Unique country mansion in the heart of Rob Roy country. All rooms with Loch views. Interesting interior design and collections in this Scots-owned home. Situated in the centre of Scotland's First National Park, 1 mile from Loch Katrine.

Lochearnhead

NN5823

Earnknowe, *Lochearnhead, Perthshire, FK19 8PY.* Excellent accommodation in beautiful location overlooking Loch. Ideal touring/walking.
Open: All year (not Xmas/New Year)
01567 830238 (also fax) Mr & Mrs Hopkins
enquiries@earnknowe.co.uk www.earnknowe.co.uk **D:** Fr £19.00–£25.00 **S:** Fr £19.00–£25.00 **Beds:** 1T 1D **Baths:** 1 Sh (4)
cc

Lochearnhead Hotel, *Lochside, Lochearnhead, Perthshire, FK19 8PU.* Small, friendly owner-run hotel on the shores of Loch Earn. **Open:** Easter to Nov **Grades:** AA 2 Star
01567 830229 Fax: 01567 830364 D: Fr £33.00 **S:** Fr £43.00 **Beds:** 1F 5T 4D **Baths:** 10 En (20) **cc**

Milton of Buchanan

NS4490

Mar Achlais, *Milton of Buchanan, Balmaha, G63 0JE.* Rural setting near Loch Lomond. Excellent touring centre for Scotland. **Open:** All year (not Xmas)
01360 870300 Mr Nichols **Fax: 01360 870444**
marachlais@dial.pipex.com **D:** Fr £19.00 **S:** Fr £24.00 **Beds:** 1F 1D **Baths:** 2 En (2)
cc

Ochtertyre

NS7497

Broadford House, *Ochtertyre, Stirling, FK9 4UN.* Lovely country house in 2.5 acres of garden adorned with 300-year-old oak trees.
Open: Easter to Oct
01786 464674 Mrs Littlejohn **Fax: 01786 463256** *simonlittlejohn@compuserve.com* **D:** Fr £20.00–£23.00 **Beds:** 1T 1D **Baths:** 1 En 1 Pr

Port of Menteith

NN5801 *Crown Hotel, Lion & Unicorn*

Inchie Farm, *Port of Menteith, Stirling, FK8 3JZ.* Family farm on shores of Lake Menteith. **Open:** Easter to Oct
01877 385233 (also fax) Mrs Erskine
inchiefarm@ecosse.net **D:** Fr £18.00 **S:** Fr £22.00
Beds: 1F 1T

Rowardennan

NS3598

Anchorage Cottage, *Rowardennan, Drymen, Glasgow, G63 0AW.* Family home on eastern shore of Loch Lomond. Highest standards. **Open:** Easter to Oct
01360 870394 (also fax) D: Fr £26.00–£30.00
S: Fr £36.00–£40.00 **Beds:** 2T 1D **Baths:** 2 En 1 Pr (6)

Ruskie

NN6200 *Crown Hotel, Lion & Unicorn*

Lower Tarr Farm, *Waterfoot, Ruskie, Stirling, Perthshire, FK8 3LG.* Peaceful situation and panoramic views
Open: Easter to Nov
01786 850202 (also fax) Mrs Bain *lowertarr@ecosse.net* **D:** Fr £20.00–£22.00 **S:** Fr £20.00–£25.00 **Beds:** 1F 1D **Baths:** 1 En 1 Pr

Stirling

NS7993

Woodside Guest House, *4 Back Walk, Stirling, FK8 2QA.* **Open:** All year
01786 475470 Mr Drummond **D:** Fr £16.00–£18.00 **S:** Fr £18.00–£20.00 **Beds:** 1F 3D 2T 1S **Baths:** 2 En 2 Pr 2 Sh
Beautifully situated on the old historic Wall of Stirling. Modern, comfortable, friendly, central to all amenities. Five minutes' walk from rail and bus stations. All rooms have private showers.

Anderson House, *8 Melville Terrace, Stirling, FK8 2NE.* **Open:** All year (not Xmas) **01786 465185** Mrs Piggott *m.j.piggott@talk21.com* **D:** Fr £22.00–£24.00 **S:** Fr £25.00–£40.00 **Beds:** 1F 1T 1D 1S **Baths:** 3 En 1 Sh (5)
Welcome to our 200-year-old Georgian home within 2 minutes walk of historic Stirling. Large, bright rooms, antique furnishings, refurbished ensuites, a friendly atmosphere and a great Scottish breakfast will make your stay a memorable one.

Neidpath Guest House, *24 Linden Avenue, Stirling, FK7 7PQ.* Refurbished friendly Edwardian home, 5 minutes walk from town centre. **Open:** All year
01786 469017 & 07710 504998 (M)
kayneidpathbanb@hotmail.com www.smoothhound.co.uk/hotels/neidpath.html **D:** Fr £20.00–£22.00 **S:** Fr £25.00–£35.00 **Beds:** 1F 1T 1D **Baths:** 3 En

Hopeton, *28 Linden Avenue, Stirling, FK7 7PQ.* Ground floor flat of large detached stone building surrounded by attractive gardens. **Open:** All year
01786 473418 Mrs McDonald **D:** Fr £18.00 **S:** Fr £20.00 **Beds:** 1F 1D 1T **Baths:** 1 Pr 1 Sh

16 Riverside Drive, *Stirling, FK8 1XF.* Our small family home in quiet area near to town. **Open:** All year
01786 461105 Mrs Miller **D:** Fr £13.50–£15.00 **S:** Fr £13.50–£15.00 **Beds:** 2S **Baths:** 1 Sh

Wellgreen Guest House, *8 Pitt Terrace, Stirling, FK8 2EZ.* Family-run guest house close to town centre and all its amenities. **Open:** All year
01786 472675 & 07799 135050 (M)
Mrs Mcphail *mcphailwellgreen@hotmail.com* **D:** Fr £19.00 **S:** Fr £19.00 **Beds:** 2F 1T 1S **Baths:** 2 Sh

Linden Guest House, *22 Linden Avenue, Stirling, FK7 7PQ.* Situated in a tree-lined avenue only few minutes' walk to town centre. **Open:** All year **Grades:** STB 3 Star
01786 448850 (also fax) Miss McGuinness *fay@lindenguesthouse.co.uk* www.lindenguesthouse.co.uk **D:** Fr £20.00–£22.00 **S:** Fr £25.00–£35.00 **Beds:** 2F 1D 1T **Baths:** 1 Sh (2)

27 King Street, *Stirling, FK8 1DN.* Comfortable Edwardian town house, convenient bus/rail stations, town centre. **Open:** All year **Grades:** STB 2 Star
01786 471082 (also fax) Mr & Mrs Macgregor *jennifer@sruighlea.com* www.sruighlea.com **D:** Fr £18.00–£22.00 **S:** Fr £22.50–£25.00 **Beds:** 1F 1D 1T **Baths:** 2 Pr

12 Princes Street, *Stirling, FK8 1HQ.* Central for Stirling, buses, trains. Near to Castle and Wallace monument. **Open:** All year
01786 479228 (also fax) Mrs Cairns **D:** Fr £18.00–£20.00 **S:** Fr £18.00–£20.00 **Beds:** 1D 1T 2S **Baths:** 2 En 2 Sh (3)

Ravenscroft, *21 Clarendon Place, Stirling, FK8 2QW.* Beautiful Victorian house in conservation area, views over to castle. **Open:** All year (not Xmas)
01786 473815 Mr & Mrs Dunbar **Fax: 01786 450990** *dunbar@ravenscroft3.freeserve.co.uk* **D:** Fr £23.50 **S:** Fr £35.00 **Beds:** 1D 1T **Baths:** 1 En 1 Pr (2)

Whinwell Cottage, *171 Glasgow Road, Whins of Milton, Stirling, FK7 0LH.* Immaculate, comfortable, accommodation, close to many tourist attractions and amenities. **Open:** All year
01786 818166 **D:** Fr £18.00–£22.00 **S:** Fr £20.00–£30.00 **Beds:** 1F 1T 1D **Baths:** 1 Sh

Strathyre

NN5617

Rosebank House, *Strathyre, Callander, Perthshire, FK18 8NA.* Enjoy the taste of Scotland, 5 Star food and comforts **Open:** All year
01877 384208 Mr & Mrs Moor **Fax: 01877 384201** *rosebank@tinyworld.co.uk* www.rosebankhouse.co.uk **D:** Fr £21.00–£25.00 **S:** Fr £21.00–£25.00 **Beds:** 1F 1T 2D **Baths:** 2 En 1 Sh (3) **cc**

Dochfour, *Strathyre, Callander, FK18 8NA.* Award-winning B&B in scenic glen, specialising in being the best! **Open:** All year
01877 384256 (also fax) Mr & Mrs Ffinch *tony.ffinch@tesco.net* **D:** Fr £17.00–£20.00 **S:** Fr £23.00–£26.00 **Beds:** 2D 1T **Baths:** 2 En 1 Pr (6) **cc**

Thornhill

NS6699

The Granary, *West Moss Side, Thornhill, Stirling, FK8 3QJ.* Recently converted granary. Rooms overlooking gardens with spectacular views. **Open:** All year (not Xmas)
01786 850310 Mrs Cumming **D:** Fr £20.00–£22.00 **S:** Fr £25.00 **Beds:** 2D 1S **Baths:** 2 En 1 Sh (6)

Tillicoultry

NS9197

Wyvis, *70 Stirling Street, Tillicoultry, Clackmannanshire, FK13 6EA.* Converted mill worker's cottage with views to the Ochil Hills. **Open:** All year (not Xmas/New Year)
01259 751513 Mrs Goddard *terrygoddard@netscapeonline.co.uk* **D:** Fr £21.00–£28.00 **S:** Fr £25.00–£28.00 **Beds:** 1T 1D **Baths:** 1 Pr 1 En

Tyndrum

NN3330 *Invervey Hotel*

Glengarry Guest House, *Tyndrum, Crianlarich, Perthshire, FK20 8RY.* Ideal base for touring and outdoor activities. Scottish welcome awaits. **Open:** All year
01838 400224 Mr & Mrs Mailer *glengarry@altavista.net* www.glengarryhouse.co.uk **D:** Fr £18.00–£22.00 **S:** Fr £25.00 **Beds:** 1F 1T 1D **Baths:** 2 En 1 Pr (2) (4)

Tigh na Froach, *Lower Station Road, Tyndrum, Crianlarich, Perthshire, FK20 8RY.* Home cooking a speciality. Ideal for walking, touring and golfing. **Open:** All year (not Xmas/New Year)
01838 400354 & 07776 428508 (M)
Ms Clement *tigh-na-froach@supanet.com* **D:** Fr £17.50 **S:** Fr £22.00 **Beds:** 1T 2D **Baths:** 2 Sh

Western Isles

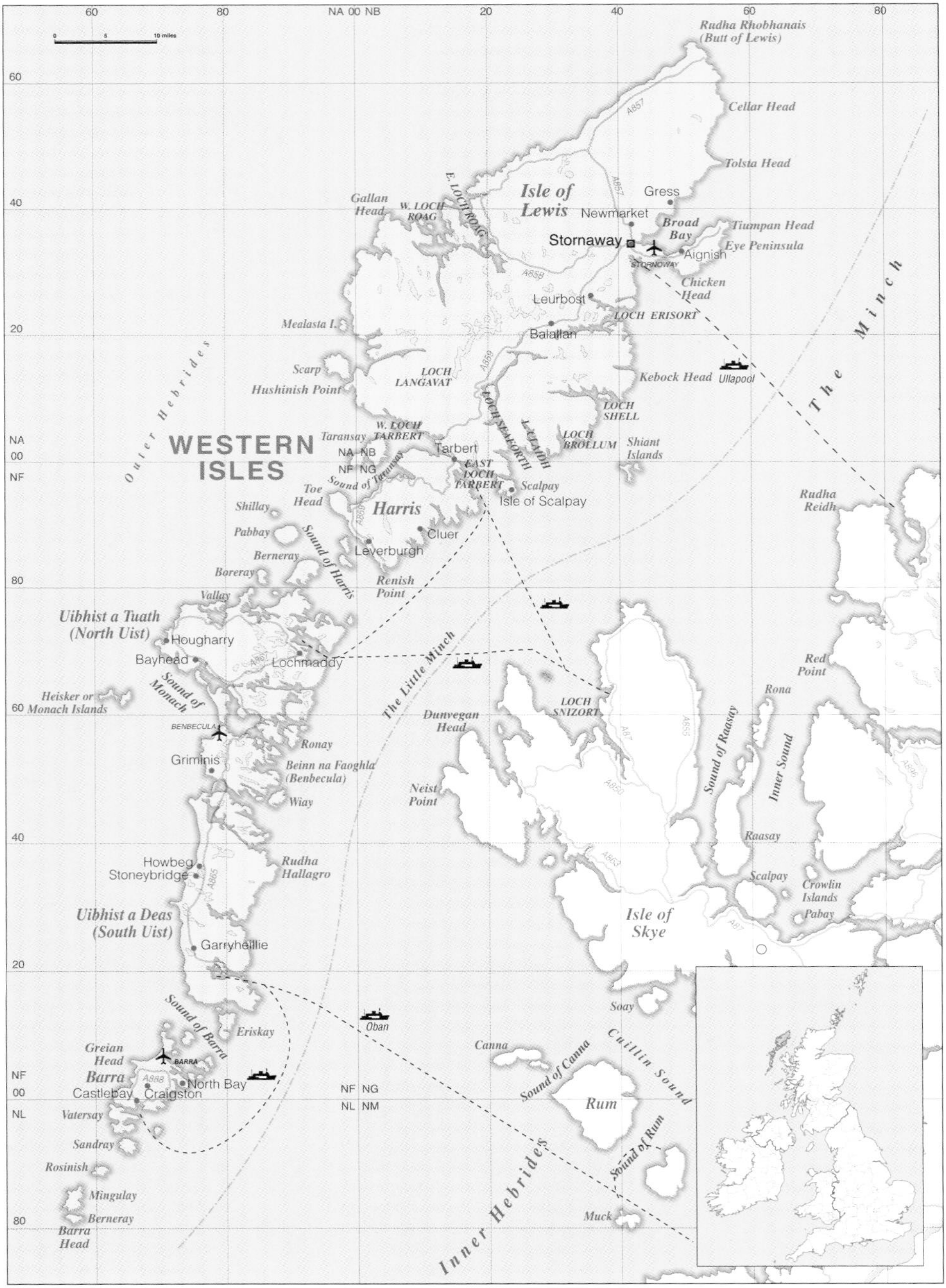

BARRA Craigston

NF6601

Gearadhmor, *123 Craigston, Castlebay, Isle of Barra, HS9 5XS.* Beautiful surroundings. Home cooking a speciality. Traditional Highland hospitality. **Open:** All year

01871 810688 (also fax) Mrs Maclean *archie.b.maclean@tesco.net* **D:** Fr £15.00–£18.00 **S:** Fr £15.00–£20.00 **Beds:** 2F 2T **Baths:** 1 En 3 Sh (6)

BARRA North Bay

NF7203

Northbay House, *Balnabodach, North Bay, Castlebay, Isle of Barra, HS9 5UT.* Attractive former school with comfortable and spacious accommodation. Warm hospitality. **Open:** All year (not Xmas/New Year)

01871 890255 (also fax) Mrs Savory *northbayhouse@isleofbarra.com* **D:** Fr £22.00–£26.00 **S:** Fr £22.00–£26.00 **Beds:** 1T 1D **Baths:** 2 En (4) 1

BENBECULA Griminis

NF7851

Creag Liath, *15 Griminis, Griminish, Isle of Benbecula, HS7 5QA.* Rural working croft, ideal for birdwatching, fishing, cycling and beachcombing. **Open:** All year **Grades:** STB 4 Star

01870 602992 Mrs MacDonald *creagliath@aol.com* **D:** Fr £27.50–£55.00 **S:** Fr £27.50–£55.00 **Beds:** 2F 1T 1D **Baths:** 2 En 2 Pr (5)

HARRIS Cluer

NG1490

Mount Cameron, *2 Cluer, Cluer, Isle of Harris, HS3 3EP.* Mount Cameron is a seven apartment house. Situated within scenic Bays of Harris. **Open:** All year

01859 530356 Mr Mackinnon *calmac2c@aol.com* **D:** Fr £15.00–£20.00 **S:** Fr £20.00 **Beds:** 2D **Baths:** 1 En 1 Pr 1 Sh

HARRIS Isle of Scalpay

NG2395

Seafield, *Isle of Scalpay, Isle of Harris, HS4 3XZ.* Fantastic sea views, homely atmosphere. Free boat trip for two night stay. **Open:** Easter to Nov

01859 540250 Mrs Cunningham *roddy@mjg.sol.uk* **D:** Fr £16.00–£18.00 **S:** Fr £20.00–£22.00 **Beds:** 1F 2D **Baths:** 2 Sh (4)

New Haven, *15 Scalpay, Isle of Scalpay, Isle of Harris, HS4 3XZ.* **Open:** All year **Grades:** STB 3 Star

01859 540325 & 07833 527630 (M) Mrs MacLennan **D:** Fr £20.00–£25.00 **Beds:** 2D **Baths:** 2 En (1) (3)

Spacious, comfortable accommodation with sea view. Ideal for hill-walking, fishing. Short drive to beautiful sandy beaches overlooking Atlantic. Residents' lounge with open fire. 5 miles from ferry terminal.

HARRIS Leverburgh

NG0186

Grimisdale Guest House, *Leverburgh, Isle of Harris, HS5 3TS.* Uniquely situated on peninsula overlooking the natural tranquillity of Harris. **Open:** All year **Grades:** STB 4 Star

01859 520460 Mr MacLeod **Fax: 01859 520461** *farky@grimisdale.co.uk* www.grimisdale.co.uk **D:** Fr £25.00 **S:** Fr £35.00 **Beds:** 1F 2D 1T **Baths:** 3 En 1 Pr (4)

St Kilda House, *Leverburgh, Isle of Harris, HS5 3UB.* Beautiful location, warm welcome, home cooking. Levenburgh ferry 2 minutes. **Open:** All year (not Xmas/New Year)

01859 520419 (also fax) Mrs Macleod **D:** Fr £15.00–£20.00 **S:** Fr £15.00–£20.00 **Beds:** 2D **Baths:** 1 En 1 Pr (2)

HARRIS Tarbert

NB1500

Minchview House, *Tarbert, Harris, Isle of Harris, HS3 3DJ.* 1827 crofthouse overlooking ferry. Skye views, good home cooking. **Open:** Apr to Oct

01859 502140 Mrs Miller *dave-miller@beeb.net* **D:** Fr £20.00–£25.00 **S:** Fr £20.00–£30.00 **Beds:** 1F 1T 1D 1S **Baths:** 1 Sh

Avalon, *12 West Side, Tarbert, Isle of Harris, HS3 3BG.* Magnificent views, 0.75 mile ferry terminal. Excellent base for touring Lewis & Harris. **Open:** All year

01859 502334 Mrs Morrison *info@avalonguesthouse.co.uk* **D:** Fr £20.00 **Beds:** 2T 1D **Baths:** 2 En 1 Pr (4)

LEWIS Aignish

NB4832

Ceol-Na-Mara, *1a, Aignish, Point, Isle of Lewis, Western Isles, HS2 0PB.* Family home, very comfortable and welcoming, rural area near Stornoway. **Open:** All year

01851 870339 (also fax) Mrs MacDonald *sarah@lesmacdonald.freeserve.co.uk* www.lesmacdonald.freeserve.co.uk **D:** Fr £18.00–£20.00 **S:** Fr £20.00–£22.00 **Beds:** 1F 1D 1T **Baths:** 1 Pr 1 Sh (3)

LEWIS Balallan

NB2920

Clearview, *44 Balallan, Balallan, Isle of Lewis, HS2 9PT.* Central location for touring Lewis and Harris. Elevated position, panoramic views. **Open:** All year (not Xmas/New Year) **Grades:** STB 3 Star

01851 830472 Mr & Mrs Mackay *clearview@tinyworld.co.uk* www.witb.co.uk/links/clearview.htm **D:** Fr £20.00–£24.00 **S:** Fr £25.00 **Beds:** 1T 2D **Baths:** 2 En 1 Pr (6)

LEWIS Gress

NB4941

Caladh, *44 Gress, Isle of Lewis, Western Isles, HS2 0NB.* All rooms look overlook river and the sea. Even a talking parrot here. **Open:** All year **Grades:** STB 3 Star

01851 820743 Mrs Evans *Eve@caladh.fsbusiness.co.uk* **D:** Fr £18.00–£20.00 **S:** Fr £19.00–£21.00 **Beds:** 2T **Baths:** 2 En (4)

LEWIS Leurbost

NB3725

Glen House, *77 Liurbost, Leurbost, Lochs, Isle of Lewis, HS2 9NL.* Quiet country residence overlooking scenic sea loch, offering high standard of food and accommodation. **Open:** All year **Grades:** STB 3 Star

01851 860241 Mrs Reid *glenhouse@talk21.com* **D:** Fr £20.00 **S:** Fr £25.00 **Beds:** 2F 1D 1T **Baths:** 2 En 1 Pr (5)

B&B owners may vary rates – be sure to check when booking

LEWIS Newmarket

NB4235

Lathamor, *Bakers Road, Newmarket, Isle of Lewis, HS2 0EA.* Spacious family home overlooking Stornoway. Cycle hire, large gardens. Home cooking. **Open:** All year
01851 706093 (also fax) Mrs Ferguson **D:** Fr £14.00–£20.00 **S:** Fr £14.00–£20.00 **Beds:** 1F 1T 1D 1S **Baths:** 1 Pr (5)

LEWIS Stornoway

NB4232

Dunroamin, *18 Plantation Road, Stornoway, Isle of Lewis, HS1 2JS.* Centrally located Victorian town house, warm welcome assured, hearty breakfasts.
Open: All year
01851 704578 Mrs MacLeod **Fax: 01851 170578 D:** Fr £17.00–£20.00 **S:** Fr £18.00–£25.00 **Beds:** 3F 1D 1T 1S **Baths:** 1 En 1 Sh

BEDROOMS
D = Double
T = Twin
S = Single
F = Family

NORTH UIST Bayhead

NF7468 *Temple View Hotel*

Old Shop House, *Bayhead, Lochmaddy, Isle of North Uist, HS6 5DS.* Bungalow with nice view. Ideal for walking and bird watching. **Open:** All year
01876 510395 Mrs Nicholson **D:** Fr £19.00–£20.00 **S:** Fr £20.00–£25.00 **Beds:** 1F 1T 1D **Baths:** 2 En (4)

NORTH UIST Hougharry

NF7071

Sgeir Ruadh, *Hougharry, Lochmaddy, Isle of North Uist, HS6 5DL.* On top of a deserted sandy beach, with panoramic views across the bay. **Open:** All year
01876 510312 Mrs Simpson *sgeirruadh@aol.com* **D:** Fr £18.50–£22.00 **S:** Fr £20.00–£22.00 **Beds:** 1T 2D **Baths:** 3 En

SOUTH UIST Garryheillie

NF7522

Clan Ranald, *247 Gearraidh Sheile, Garryheillie, Lochboisdale, Isle of South Uist, HS8 5SX.* Working croft, 3 miles from ferry, will collect from terminal. **Open:** Apr to Dec
01878 700263 Mr & Mrs MacDonald **D:** Fr £23.00 **S:** Fr £23.00 **Beds:** 1T 1D 1S **Baths:** 3 En

SOUTH UIST Howbeg

NF7535 *Palachar Inn, Orasay Inn*

6 Tobha Beag, *Howbeg, Lochboisdale, Isle of South Uist, HS8 5SQ.* Situated beside a loch, sandy beaches nearby. Haven for birdwatchers. **Open:** All year (not Xmas/New Year)
01870 620273 Mrs MacEachen **D:** Fr £20.00 **S:** Fr £20.00 **Beds:** 1F 1T **Baths:** 1 Pr

SOUTH UIST Stoneybridge

NF7433

Cross Roads, *Staionebrig, Stoneybridge, Lochboisdale, Isle of South Uist, HS8 5SD.* Ideal for hillwalking, fishing, birdwatching, 2 miles from sandy beaches. **Open:** All year (not Xmas/New Year)
01870 620321 Mrs MacRury **D:** Fr £18.00–£20.00 **S:** Fr £18.00–£20.00 **Beds:** 2D (6)

BATHROOMS
En = Ensuite
Pr = Private
Sh = Shared

Anglesey

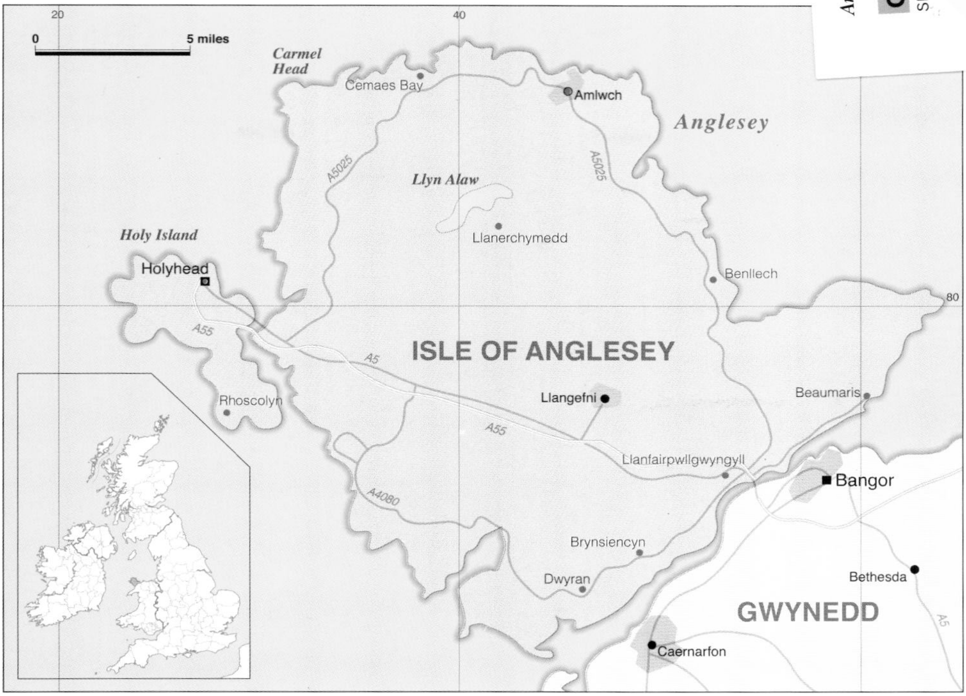

Beaumaris

SH6076

Mor Awel, *Beaumaris, Anglesey, LL58 8NP.* Victorian house, village rural location, nice walks, evening meal. Licensed. **Open:** All year (not Xmas)
01248 490930 Mr Thomas **Fax: 01248 490826** *mor-awel@zetnet.co.uk* **D:** Fr £20.00 **S:** Fr £30.00 **Beds:** 2D 1T 1S **Baths:** 1 En 2 Sh (4)

BEDROOMS
D = Double
T = Twin
S = Single
F = Family

Benllech

SH5182

Bay Court Hotel, *Beach Road, Benllech, Tyn-y-Gongl, Anglesey, LL74 8SW.* 200 yds from sandy beach. Nearby riding, golf, fishing. Handy Snowdonia, ferries.
Open: All year
01248 852573 Mr Threfall **Fax: 01248 852606** **D:** Fr £23.00–£28.00 **S:** Fr £23.00–£28.00 **Beds:** 4F 10D 3T 5S **Baths:** 10 En 3 Sh (50) cc

BATHROOMS
En = Ensuite
Pr = Private
Sh = Shared

Belvoir, *8 Lon Fferam, Benllech, Tyn-y-Gongl, Anglesey, LL74 8RL.* Detached house, pleasant residential locality, quiet, and with stunning seaviews. **Open:** Easter to Oct
01248 852907 Mrs Evans www.belvoirbenllech **D:** Fr £21.50 **S:** Fr £43.00 **Beds:** 2D **Baths:** 2 Pr (2)

Brynsiencyn

SH4867

Fron Guest House, *Brynsiencyn, Llanfairpwllgwyngyll, Anglesey, LL61 6TX.* Traditional high class accommodation with magnificent views of Snowdonia.
Open: Easter to Sept
01248 430310 (also fax) Mr Geldard **D:** Fr £16.00–£17.50 **S:** Fr £16.50–£18.00 **Beds:** 3D **Baths:** 1 En 1 Sh

es Bay

4

Woburn Hill Hotel, *High Street, Cemaes Bay, Anglesey, LL67 0HU.* Popular hotel in old fishing village. Serving local seafood dishes. **Open:** All year
01407 711388 Mrs Potter **Fax: 01407 711190** *brian@woburnhill.freeserve.co.uk* www.woburnhillhotel.com **D:** Fr £27.50–£30.00 **S:** Fr £37.50–£60.00 **Beds:** 5D 2T 1S **Baths:** 5 En 1 Sh (10)

Dwyran

SH4466

Tal-y-Foel, *Dwyran, Llanfairpwllgwyngyll, LL61 6LQ.* Spectacular waterfront location overlooking Snowdonia. Whirlpool baths. Birdwatching, walking, fishing. **Open:** All year (not Xmas/New Year)
01248 430377 Fax: 01248 430977 *hutchings@talyfoel.u-net.com* www.tal-y-foel.co.uk **D:** Fr £25.00 **S:** Fr £25.00–£30.00 **Beds:** 2F 2T **Baths:** 4 En **cc**

Holyhead

SH2482

Monravon Guest House, *Port-y-felin Road, Holyhead, LL65 1PL.* **Open:** All year (not Xmas)
01407 762944 (also fax) *len@monravon.co.uk* www.monravon.co.uk **D:** Fr £15.00–£22.50 **S:** Fr £25.00 **Beds:** 8D **Baths:** 8 En **cc**
Family-run business, 3 minutes to ferry/train terminals. Adjacent to park & beach. Open 24 hours for travellers. All bedrooms have a bathroom and in 2001/2002, we have spent £35,000 refurbishing.

Wavecrest, *93 Newry Road, Holyhead, Anglesey, LL65 1HU.* Ideal ferry stopover for Ireland; close to the South Stack. **Open:** All year (not Xmas)
01407 763637 Mr Hiltunen **Fax: 01407 764862** *cwavecrest@aol.com* www.holyheadhotels.com **D:** Fr £16.00–£20.00 **S:** Fr £18.00–£20.00 **Beds:** 3F 1D 1S **Baths:** 2 En 1 Pr 1 Sh (4)

Roselea, *26 Holborn Road, Holyhead, Anglesey, LL65 2AT.* Good value B&B establishment 29 years, closest to ferry & station. **Open:** All year **Grades:** WTB 2 Star
01407 764391 (also fax) S Foxley *sheila@roselea73.freeserve.co.uk* www.roselea73.freeserve.co.uk **D:** Fr £16.00–£18.00 **S:** Fr £18.00–£20.00 **Beds:** 1F 1T 1D **Baths:** 1 Sh

Tasma, *31 Walthew Avenue, Holyhead, Anglesey, LL65 1AG.* Comfortable accommodation. Conveniently situated for ferries, railway, beaches and shops. **Open:** All year (not Xmas)
01407 762291 Mrs Jones *tasma_99@yahoo.co.uk* **D:** Fr £19.00–£20.00 **S:** Fr £22.00–£28.00 **Beds:** 2F 1S **Baths:** 1 Sh (1)

Llanerchymedd

SH4184 *Ship Inn, Pilot Boat*

Llwydiarth Fawr, *Llanerchymedd, Anglesey, LL71 8DF.* Secluded Georgian mansion set in 850 acres of woodland & farmland. **Open:** All year (not Xmas/New Year)
01248 470321 & 01248 470540 Mrs Hughes **Fax: 01248 470540** *llwydiarth@hotmail.com* llwydiarthfawr.com **D:** Fr £25.00 **S:** Fr £30.00 **Beds:** 1F 1T 1D 1S **Baths:** 4 En (8) **cc**

Planning a longer stay? Always ask for any special rates

Maenaddwyn

SH4584

Tre-Wyn, *Maenaddwyn, Llangefni, LL71 8AE.* A warm welcome. Comfortable accommodation and central to Anglesey's attractions. **Open:** All year (not Xmas/New Year)
01248 470874 Ms Brown **Fax: 01248 470875** *nia@trewyn.fsnet.co.uk* **D:** Fr £20.00–£22.50 **S:** Fr £25.00–£27.00 **Beds:** 1F 2T **Baths:** 3 En

Rhoscolyn

SH2675 *White Eagle, Anchorage Hotel*

Gwynfryn House, *Rhoscolyn, Holyhead, LL65 2EQ.* Rural location. Distant views. Delightful coastal walks within five minutes. **Open:** All year (not Xmas/New Year)
01407 861107 Mr & Mrs Chadwick *ann_dennis@tesco.net* homepages.tesco.net/~Ann_Dennis **D:** Fr £19.00 **S:** Fr £17.50 **Beds:** 2D 2S **Baths:** 1 Sh (10)

Valley

SH2979

Valley Hotel, *London Road, Valley, Holyhead, LL65 3DU.* Superior ensuite accommodation and pub situated 4 miles from ferry. **Open:** All year
01407 740203 K Snape **Fax: 01407 740686** *valleyhotel@tinyworld.co.uk* www.valley-hotel-anglesey.co.uk **D:** Fr £25.00–£49.50 **S:** Fr £37.50 **Beds:** 2F 9T 4D 5S **Baths:** 18 En 1 Sh (40) **cc**

National Grid References given are for villages, towns and cities – not for individual houses

Carmarthenshire

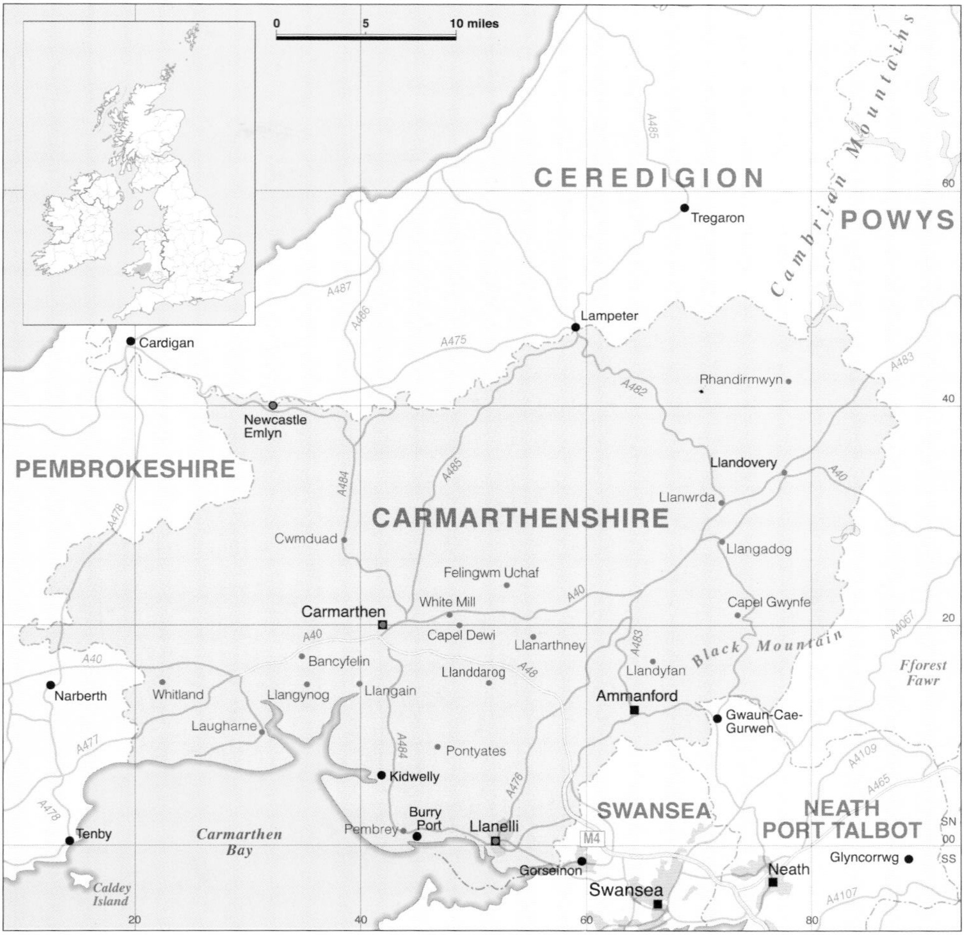

Bancyfelin

SN3217

Sarnau Mansion, *Llysonnen Road, Bancyfelin, Carmarthen, SA33 5DZ.* Beautiful Georgian mansion, large landscaped grounds, tennis court, easy access A40. **Open:** All year

01267 211404 (also fax) Mrs Fernihough **D:** Fr £20.00–£27.50 **S:** Fr £25.00–£35.00 **Beds:** 1F 2D 1T **Baths:** 3 En 1 Pr (10)

Capel Dewi

SN4720

Farm Retreats, *Dewi Uchaf Country House, Capel Dewi, Carmarthen, SA32 8AY.* Large, traditional, comfortable secluded farmhouse. **Open:** All year

01267 290799 F M Burns **Fax: 01267 290003** *uchaffarm@aol.com* walescottageholidays.uk.com **D:** Fr £28.00 **S:** Fr £40.00 **Beds:** 1T 2D **Baths:** 3 En **cc**

Capel Gwynfe

SN7222

Pencrug Farm, *Capel Gwynfe, Llangadog, Carmarthenshire, SA19 9RP.* C17th working farm house. National Park. Quiet. Glorious views. Good food. **Open:** All year (not Xmas/New Year)

01550 740686 (also fax) Mrs Fleming **D:** Fr £14.00 **S:** Fr £14.00 **Beds:** 1D 2T **Baths:** 1 Sh (4)

BEDROOMS
D = Double
T = Twin
S = Single
F = Family

Carmarthen

SN4120

Trebersed Farmhouse, *Travellers Rest, St Peters, Carmarthen, SA31 3RR.* Relax in peaceful countryside staying on friendly working dairy farm. **Open:** All year (not Xmas) **Grades:** WTB 3 Star
01267 238182 Mrs Jones **Fax: 01267 223633** *trebersed.farm@farmline.com* www.trebersed.co.uk **D:** Fr £20.00 **S:** Fr £25.00 **Beds:** 1F 1D 1T **Baths:** 3 En (6) **cc**

Plas Farm, *Llangynog, Carmarthenshire, SA33 5DB.* Ideal touring base for South and West Wales. Easy to find. **Open:** All year
01267 211492 (also fax) Mrs Thomas **D:** Fr £20.00 **S:** Fr £20.00–£25.00 **Beds:** 1F 1D 1T **Baths:** 2 En 1 Pr (4)

53 Parcmaen Street, *Carmarthen, SA31 3DR.* Terraced house, walking distance town centre, bus/train stations, parking. **Open:** All year
01267 238260 & 07779 468675 (M) Mrs Jones **D:** Fr £14.00–£15.00 **S:** Fr £15.00 **Beds:** 1D 1T

Meiros Hall Guest House, *2 Waterloo Terrace, Carmarthen, SA31 1DG.* Homely guest house minutes' walk from centre of quaint market county town of Carmarthen. **Open:** All year (not Xmas/New Year)
01267 222708 J D C Lewis **D:** Fr £17.00 **S:** Fr £17.00 **Beds:** 1F 1T 1D 1S **Baths:** 1 Sh

RATES
D = Price range per person sharing in a double or twin room
S = Price range for a single room

Cwmduad

SN3731

Neuadd Wen Country Guest House, *Cwmduad, Carmarthen, SA33 6XJ.* **Open:** All year **Grades:** WTB 3 Star, AA 4 Diamond
01267 281438 *goodbourn@neuaddwen.plus.com* **D:** Fr £18.00–£22.00 **S:** Fr £18.00–£22.00 **Beds:** 2F 2T 3D 1S **Baths:** 6 En 2 Sh (10)
Peaceful, welcoming, spacious, beamed country guest house set in beautiful wooded valley. Ideal for touring West Wales. Stunning scenery, coastline, crafts & history. Superb home cooking. Collection of 300 jugs in dining room. No single supplement. 2 ground floor rooms.

Felingwm

SN5124

Dolau Guest House, *Felingwm Isaf, Nantgaredig, Carmarthenshire, SA32 7PB.* Peaceful rural riverside location. Luxury accommodation, near Botanic/ Aberglasney gardens. **Open:** All year
01267 290464 Mr Bright *brightdolau@aol.com* www.visit-carmarthenshire.co.uk/dolau **D:** Fr £21.00–£26.00 **S:** Fr £25.00–£30.00 **Beds:** 1F 1D 1T **Baths:** 2 En 1 Pr (6)

Laugharne

SN3010

Swan Cottage, *20 Gosport St, Laugharne, Carmarthen, SA33 4SZ.* Lovely stone cottage, one room only on ground floor, excellent breakfasts. **Open:** All year
01994 427409 Mrs Brown *rob.erts@talk21.com* **D:** Fr £18.00–£20.00 **S:** Fr £18.00–£25.00 **Beds:** 1D **Baths:** 1 En (1)

Castle House, *Market Lane, Laugharne, Carmarthen, SA33 4SA.* Beautiful Georgian house with gardens, overlooking the estuary and castle. **Open:** All year
01994 427616 Mrs Mitchell *charles@laugharne.co.uk* www.laugharne.co.uk/casthous.htm **D:** Fr £25.00–£35.00 **S:** Fr £30.00–£35.00 **Beds:** 1F 2D **Baths:** 2 En 1 Pr (3)

Planning a longer stay? Always ask for any special rates

BEDROOMS
D = Double
T = Twin
S = Single
F = Family

Llanarthney

SN5320 *Old Emlyn Arms*

Central House, *Llanarthney, Carmarthen, SA32 8JE.* Near Botanical Gardens, castles, Towy Valley, market towns. Homely atmosphere. **Open:** All year
01558 668595 Mr & Mrs Jonah *pjonah6442@aol.com* **D:** Fr £18.00 **S:** Fr £18.00 **Beds:** 1F 1T 1D **Baths:** 1 Sh (2)

Llanboidy

SN2123

Castell Pigyn Farm, *Llanboidy, Whitland, Carmarthenshire, SA34 0LJ.* Situated on a peaceful hilltop with fabulous views in all directions. **Open:** Easter to Oct
01994 448391 Mrs Davies **Fax: 01994 448755** **D:** Fr £22.00 **S:** Fr £27.00 **Beds:** 1F 1D 1T **Baths:** 2 En 1 Pr

Llanddarog

SN5016 *White Hart, Butcher's Arms*

Coedhirion Farm, *Llanddarog, Carmarthen, Carmarthenshire, SA32 8BH.* Conveniently situated just off A48 dual carriageway, 5 mins National Botanical Garden of Wales. **Open:** All year
01267 275666 Mr & Mrs Evans *welshfarmhouse@hotmail.com* www.smoothhound.co.uk/hotels/coedhirion.com **D:** Fr £20.00–£22.50 **S:** Fr £27.50–£30.00 **Beds:** 1F 1T 1D 1S **Baths:** 4 En (5)

Llandovery

SN7634

Cwm Rhuddan Mansion, *Llandovery, Carmarthenshire, SA20 0DX.* Unique French chateau-style mansion with original features, antique furnishings. Landscaped gardens with panoramic view. **Open:** All year
01550 721414 (also fax) Mrs Wheadon www.visit-carmarthen-shire.co.uk/cwmrhuddan **D:** Fr £27.50–£30.00 **S:** Fr £30.00 **Beds:** 2F 1D **Baths:** 3 En (10)

Pencerring, *New Road, Llandovery, SA20 0EA.* Victorian house at edge of town. Local shops, pubs, restaurants 5 mins' walk. **Open:** All year
01550 721259 **D:** Fr £19.00 **S:** Fr £19.00 **Beds:** 1D 1T 1S **Baths:** 2 En 1 Pr (1)

Llandyfan

SN6417

Bryncoch Farm, *Llandyfan, Ammanford, SA18 2TY.* **Open:** All year
01269 850480 Mr Richardson **Fax: 01269 850888** *robrich@ntlworld.com* **D:** Fr £17.50 **S:** Fr £20.00 **Beds:** 1F 1T 1D **Baths:** 3 En
Bryncoch, high above the Amman Valley in the Brecons National Park, overlooking Glynher Golf Course. 20 mins from the Botanic Gardens and Aberglasney. Comfortable ensuite bedrooms. English or vegetarian breakfast cooked by your host Graham in a homely atmosphere.

Pen-y-banc Farm, *Llandyfan, Ammanford, SA18 2UD.* In Brecon National Park. Ideal base for touring, SW Wales. **Open:** All year (not Xmas/New Year)
01269 850530 *franhay@freeuk.com* www.penybancbandb.co.uk **D:** Fr £19.00 **S:** Fr £23.00–£25.00 **Beds:** 3D **Baths:** 2 En 1 Pr (6)

Llanelli

SN5000 *Farriers*

Southmead Guest House, *72 Queen Victoria Road, Llanelli, SA15 2TH.* Southmead Guest House, ensuite rooms, car park, town centre. **Open:** All year (not Xmas)
01554 758588 R Fouracre **D:** Fr £15.00–£20.00 **S:** Fr £15.00–£20.00 **Beds:** 1F 2D 2T 2S **Baths:** 4 En 2 Sh

Llangadog

SN7028

Cynyll Farm, *Llangadog, Carmarthenshire, SA19 9BB.* Comfortable C17th farmhouse. Excellent home cooking. Overlooks Black Mountains. **Open:** All year (not Xmas/New Year)
01550 777316 (also fax) Mrs Dare www.visit_camarthenshire.co.uk/cynyll/ **D:** Fr £17.00 **S:** Fr £17.00 **Beds:** 1F 1D **Baths:** 1 En 1 Pr

Llangain

SN3815

Brynderwen, *School Lane, Llangain, Carmarthen, SA33 5AE.* Family-run B&B, quiet village setting. Comfortable rooms, convenient coast, countryside & Irish ferries. **Open:** All year (not Xmas)
01267 241403 M Davies **D:** Fr £20.00–£24.00 **S:** Fr £18.00–£24.00 **Beds:** 1D 1T 1S **Baths:** 2 En 1 Sh (4)

Llangynog

SN3316

Plas Farm, *Llangynog, Carmarthenshire, SA33 5DB.* Ideal touring base for South and West Wales. Easy to find. **Open:** All year
01267 211492 (also fax) Mrs Thomas **D:** Fr £20.00 **S:** Fr £20.00–£25.00 **Beds:** 1F 1D 1T **Baths:** 2 En 1 Pr (4)

Llanwrda

SN7131

Coed Y Brenin, *Llanwrda, SA19 8HD.* High-quality accommodation in beautiful Welsh rural area. Ideal for touring. **Open:** All year
01550 777423 Mrs Rees **D:** Fr £18.00–£22.00 **S:** Fr £18.00–£22.00 **Beds:** 1T 1D 1S **Baths:** 1 En 1 Sh (5)

Newcastle Emlyn

SN3040

Maes Y Derw Guest House, *Newcastle Emlyn, Carmarthenshire, SA38 9RD.* Large Edwardian family house full of original charm and character. **Open:** All year
01239 710860 (also fax) D Davies **D:** Fr £19.00–£20.00 **S:** Fr £25.00–£32.00 **Beds:** 1F 1T 1D **Baths:** 1 En 2 Pr (8) **cc**

Pembrey

SN4201

Four Seasons Guest House, *62 Gwscwm Road, Pembrey, Burry Port, Dyfed, SA16 0YU.* A friendly guest house with ground floor accommodation available. **Open:** All year
01554 833367 (also fax) **D:** Fr £18.00–£20.00 **S:** Fr £22.00–£27.00 **Beds:** 1F 3T 1D **Baths:** 2 En 1 Sh (10)

Pontyates

SN4708

Glynfach Farm, *Pontyates, Llanelli, SA15 5TG.* Warm welcome to our organic small holding. Creative breakfasts; coast & country. **Open:** All year (not Xmas)
01269 861290 (also fax) J Pearce **D:** Fr £18.00 **S:** Fr £18.00 **Beds:** 1D 2T **Baths:** 1 Pr

Rhandirmwyn

SN7843

Nantybai Mill, *Rhandirmwyn, Llandovery, Carmarthenshire, SA20 0PB.* Historic farmhouse dating back to C15th. Spectacular scenery. Relaxing ambience. **Open:** All year
01550 760211 A Jones *nantybai.mill@ukonline.co.uk* **D:** Fr £17.50–£18.50 **S:** Fr £17.50–£18.50 **Beds:** 1T 1D 1S **Baths:** 1 Sh (10)

White Mill

SN4621

Penrhiw Farm Guest House, *White Mill, Carmarthen, SA32 7ET.* Situated 0.25 mile off A40 at Whitemill. Peaceful surroundings overlooking Towy Valley. **Open:** All year
01267 290260 Mrs Jones **D:** Fr £20.00 **S:** Fr £25.00 **Beds:** 2D **Baths:** 1 En 1 Pr (10)

Whitland

SN2016

Fforest Farm, *Whitland, Carmarthenshire, SA34 0LS.* Picturesque peaceful location, easy access to Fishguard(via Ireland). Beautiful walks, fishing available. **Open:** All year (not Xmas/New Year)
01994 240066 Mrs Windsor **D:** Fr £20.00 **S:** Fr £20.00 **Beds:** 2F **Baths:** 2 En

All details shown are as supplied by B&B owners in Autumn 2002

Ceredigion

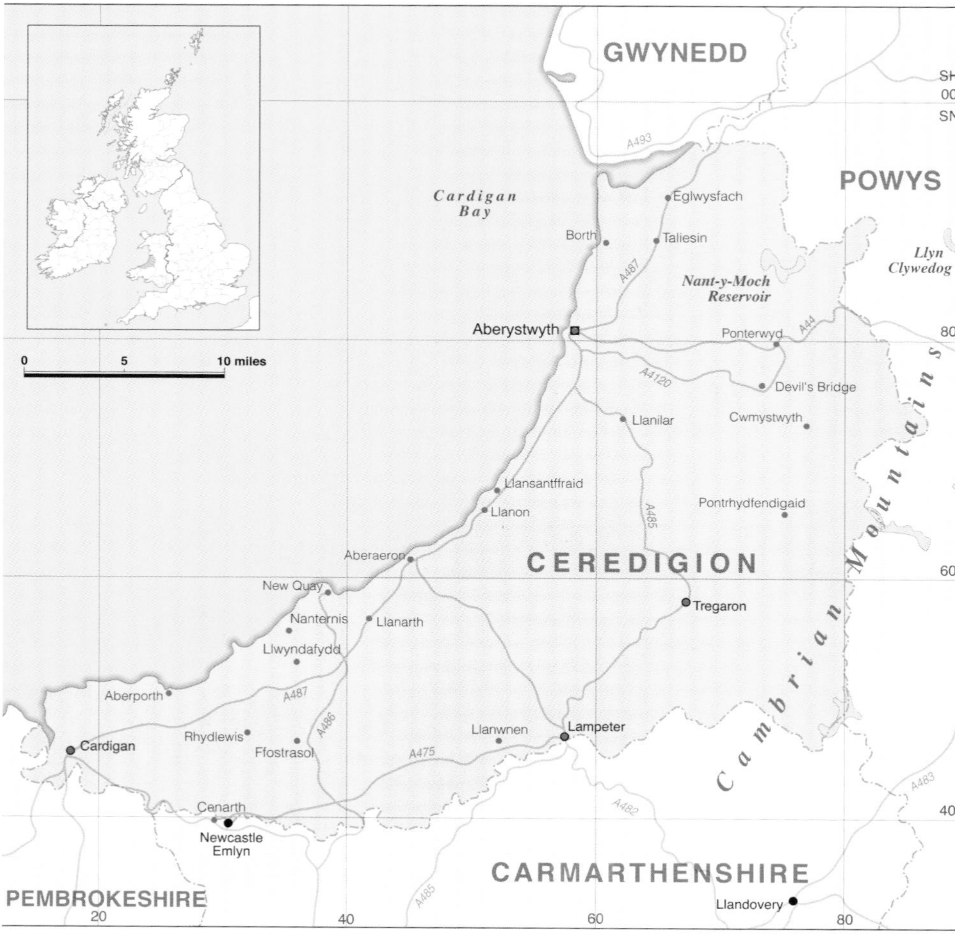

Aberaeron

SN4562

Arosfa, *Harbourside, Aberaeron, Ceredigion, SA46 0BU.* Harbourside. Superb Welsh breakfast with highest AA Grade for 2002. **Open:** All year **Grades:** WTB 3 Star, AA 4 Diamond

01545 570120 Mr Griffiths *arosfabandb@aol.com* www.arosfaguesthouse.co.uk **D:** Fr £20.00–£28.00 **S:** Fr £22.00–£35.00 **Beds:** 1F 2D 1T **Baths:** 4 En 1 Pr (6) (4)

Aberporth

SN2651

Highcliffe Hotel, *School Road, Aberporth, Cardigan, SA43 2DA.* Unspoilt sandy coves, bar, restaurant, waterfalls, dolphins. Kids/pets welcome. **Open:** All year **Grades:** WTB 2 Star, AA 2 Star

01239 810534 (also fax) Mr Conway www.highcliffehotel.co.uk **D:** Fr £22.50–£30.00 **S:** Fr £34.00–£37.00 **Beds:** 4F 6D 4T 1S **Baths:** 14 En 1 Pr (18) **cc**

RATES

D = Price range per person sharing in a double or twin room

S = Price range for a single room

Aberystwyth

SN5881

Llethr Melyn Country Farmhouse, *Crosswood, Aberystwyth, Ceredigion, SY23 4HU.* **Open:** All year
01974 261400 & 07876 685586 (M) Mrs Clements **Fax: 01974 261400** *holidays@welsh-breaks.co.uk* www.welsh-breaks.co.uk **D:** Fr £22.50–£25.00 **S:** Fr £25.00–£30.00 **Beds:** 2D 1S **Baths:** 3 En P (5) TV X V
A 'relaxing rural retreat' situated amongst peaceful countryside. Suites are spacious and very well-presented. Delicious homemade cuisine available. Location suits walking, cycling, fishing, horse-riding and sightseeing. Other facilities include horse riding, accommodation for horses and cycle hire. Brochure available.

Garreg Lwyd Guest House, *Bow Street, Aberystwyth, Ceredigion, SY24 5BE.* On A487. Private parking. Excellent breakfast. Television lounge. Tea & coffee facilities, snacks available. **Open:** All year (not Xmas)
01970 828830 Mrs Edwards **D:** Fr £17.00–£21.50 **S:** Fr £19.00–£23.00 **Beds:** 1F 2D 1T 1S **Baths:** 2 Sh P (6) TV V

Aisling, *21 Alexandra Road, Aberystwyth, Ceredigion, SY23 1LN.* Perfectly situated near train & bus stations, town centre. Warm welcome. **Open:** All year **Grades:** WTB 3 Star
01970 626980 & 07779 594127 (M) Fax: 01970 624921 D: Fr £21.00–£23.00 **S:** Fr £25.00 **Beds:** 1F 1T 1S **Baths:** 1 Sh TV V

Planning a longer stay? Always ask for any special rates

Glyn Garth, *South Road, Aberystwyth, Ceredigion, SY23 1JS.* Family-run Victorian guest house. **Open:** All year (not Xmas/New Year)
01970 615050 (also fax) *glyngarth@aol.com* www.glyngarth.cjb.net **D:** Fr £22.00–£30.00 **S:** Fr £30.00–£40.00 **Beds:** 2F 1T 5D 2S **Baths:** 6 En 1 Sh (10) TV V

Marine Hotel, *Marine Terrace, Aberystwyth, Cardiganshire, SY23 2BX.* Idyllic countryside setting new luxury guest house. Set in peaceful surroundings. **Open:** Jan to Dec
0800 0190020 & 01970 612444 Mrs Evans **Fax: 01970 617435 D:** Fr £20.00–£35.00 **S:** Fr £25.00–£35.00 **Beds:** 7F 14D 13T 5S **Baths:** 38 En 1 Pr (1) P (12) TV X V cc

Talbot Hotel, *Market Street, Aberystwyth, Ceredigion, SY23 1DL.* Newly refurbished hotel, town centre location, conference room. Close to sea front. **Open:** All year
01970 612575 E T Davies **Fax: 01970 412575 D:** Fr £18.00–£30.00 **S:** Fr £25.00–£30.00 **Beds:** 5F 8T 5D **Baths:** 18 En TV X cc

Richmond Hotel, *44-45 Marine Terrace, Aberystwyth, Ceredigion, SY23 2BX.* Seafront family run hotel. Ideal base for touring. **Open:** All year (not Xmas/New Year)
01970 612201 Mr Griffiths *richard@richmondhotel.uk.com* www.richmondhotel.uk.com **D:** Fr £38.00 **S:** Fr £55.00 **Beds:** 4F 4T 4D 3S P TV X V cc

Borth

SN6089

Glanmor Hotel, *High Street, Borth, Ceredigion, SY24 5JP.* Small friendly seaside hotel close to golf course. **Open:** All year **Grades:** WTB 1 Star
01970 871689 Mr Elliot **D:** Fr £22.50 **S:** Fr £22.50 **Beds:** 3F 2D 1T 1S **Baths:** 2 En 2 Sh P (6) TV X V

Maesteg Guest House, *High Street, Borth, Ceredigion, SY24 5JP.* Comfortable, friendly sea front B&B - 2 minutes to village. **Open:** Easter to Oct
01970 871928 Mrs Fiorentino **D:** Fr £16.00–£18.00 **S:** Fr £16.00 **Beds:** 1F 1D 1T 1S **Baths:** 1 Sh TV V

Cardigan

SN1746

Maes-A-Mor, *Park Place, Gwbert Road, Cardigan, SA43 1AE.* Centrally situated opposite the park. Ideal for coast & central Wales. **Open:** All year
01239 614929 (also fax) Mr Jones *maesamor@jejones.demon.co.uk* **D:** Fr £18.00–£20.00 **S:** Fr £20.00–£25.00 **Beds:** 1D 2T **Baths:** 3 En (8) P (3) TV

Brynhyfryd Guest House, *Gwbert Road, Cardigan, SA43 1AE.* 2 miles Cardigan Bay; 6 minutes walk to town centre. **Open:** All year **Grades:** WTB 3 Star, AA 3 Diamond, RAC 3 Diamond
01239 612861 (also fax) Mrs Arcus *g.arcus@btinternet.com* **D:** Fr £18.00–£20.00 **S:** Fr £18.00–£25.00 **Beds:** 1F 3D 1T 2S **Baths:** 3 En 2 Pr (5) TV X V

Cenarth

SN2641 *Nag's Head*

Y Garreg Lwyd, *Cenarth, Newcastle Emlyn, Carmarthenshire, SA38 9RB.* Delightful former farmhouse cottage. **Open:** All year
01239 710230 Mrs Daly **D:** Fr £16.00–£25.00 **Beds:** 1T 1D **Baths:** 1 En 1 Pr (12) P (3) TV V

Cwmystwyth

SN7874

Tainewyddion Uchaf, *Cwmystwyth, Aberystwyth, Ceredigion, SY23 4AF.* Situated at over 1000 ft. Panoramic views overlooking the Ystwyth Valley. **Open:** Easter to Oct
01974 282672 Mrs Liford **D:** Fr £15.00–£18.00 **S:** Fr £15.00–£18.00 **Beds:** 1T 1D 1S **Baths:** 1 En 1 Sh X V

Devil's Bridge

SN7376

Mount Pleasant, *Devil's Bridge, Aberystwyth, Ceredigion, SY23 4QY.* **Open:** All year (not Xmas/New Year) **Grades:** WTB 3 Star
01970 890219 M B Connell **Fax: 01970 890239** *relax@mpleasant.co.uk* www.mpleasant.co.uk **D:** Fr £20.00–£25.00 **S:** Fr £20.00–£33.00 **Beds:** 1T 2D **Baths:** 2 En 1 Pr P (4) TV X V
Relax and enjoy excellent hospitality in our comfortable, well-furnished home, amidst peaceful, stunning scenery. Fully non-smoking, delicious breakfasts and candlelit dinners with menu choice, wine list. Delightful gardens. Ideal for birdwatching, walking, cycling or discovering our many surrounding attractions.

Eglwys Fach
SN6896

Tyglyneiddwen, *Eglwysfach, Machynlleth, Powys, SY20 8SX.* Warm welcome. Excellent breakfast amid beautiful scenery in Dovey Valley. **Open:** All year (not Xmas)
01654 781348 Mrs Greenwood *edna@aber.ac.uk* **D:** Fr £19.00–£22.00 **S:** Fr £18.00–£25.00 **Beds:** 2F 2D 1S **Baths:** 1 En 1 Sh (6)

Ffostrasol
SN3747

Plas Cerdin, *Ffostrasol, Llandysul, Ceredigion, SA44 4TA.* Large modern split-level house. Secluded position with breathtaking views. **Open:** All year
01239 851329 (also fax) Mrs Hicks **D:** Fr £19.00–£20.00 **S:** Fr £20.00–£24.00 **Beds:** 1F 1D 1T **Baths:** 3 En (3) (4)

Lampeter
SN5848

Pantycelyn Guest House, *Llanwnnen, Lampeter, Ceredigion, SA48 7LW.* **Open:** Feb to Oct **Grades:** WTB 3 Star
01570 434455 (also fax) Mrs Jenkins *HuwAnnJ@aol.com* www.pantycelyn-wales.com **D:** Fr £22.00 **S:** Fr £22.00 **Beds:** 1D 1T 1S **Baths:** 3 En (4)
Relax in this peaceful branch of the Teify Valley. Pantycelyn, in 11 acres of meadows, 5 miles west of Lampeter, is ideal for enjoying Cardigan Bay and Ceredigion's many attractions. We promise a warm welcome, memorable breakfasts, plus friendly Welsh Cobs.

Haulfan, *6 Station Terrace, Lampeter, Ceredigion, SA48 7HH.* Central town position, near university, nature reserve and sea. **Open:** Jan to Dec
01570 422718 & 07974 818257 (M) Mrs Williams **D:** Fr £18.00–£22.00 **S:** Fr £20.00–£25.00 **Beds:** 1F 1D 1S **Baths:** 1 En 1 Sh

Penlanmedd, *Llanfair Road, Lampeter, Ceredigion, SA48 8JZ.* Cosy, secluded C18th farmhouse, between coast and mountains. Warm welcome. **Open:** All year (not Xmas)
01570 493438 (also fax) Mrs Coombes *penlanmedd@coombes-e.freeserve.co.uk* **D:** Fr £19.00–£20.00 **S:** Fr £25.00 **Beds:** 1F 1D 1T **Baths:** 3 En (20)

Llanarth
SN4257

Beechwood, *Llanarth, Ceredigion, SA47 0RE.* Friendly family-run bed and breakfast in a quiet village. **Open:** Easter to Sept
01545 580280 Mrs Evans **D:** Fr £14.00 **S:** Fr £16.00 **Beds:** 2F 1T **Baths:** 3 En

Llanilar
SN6275

Glynwern Guest House, *Llanilar, Aberystwyth, Ceredigion, SY23 4NY.* Picturesque riverside house - free fishing, beautiful views, golf, wildlife **Open:** All year (not Xmas/New Year)
01603 782193 Miss Evans **D:** Fr £22.00 **S:** Fr £22.00 **Beds:** 1T 2D **Baths:** 1 En (2)

Llanon
SN5166

The Barn House, *Llanon, Aberystwyth, Ceredigion, SY23 5LZ.* Converted barn in landscaped gardens, sea views. Aromatherapy, reflexology available. **Open:** All year
01974 202581 Mrs Rees **D:** Fr £18.00–£25.00 **S:** Fr £18.00–£25.00 **Beds:** 1F 1T 2S **Baths:** 1 En 1 Pr 1 Sh (6)

Llansantffraid
SN5167

The Haven, *Winllan Road, Llansantffraid, Powys, SY22 6TR.* Detached bungalow, Shropshire-Powys border, with panoramic views. **Open:** All year
01691 828101 Mrs Wilde **D:** Fr £17.00–£19.00 **S:** Fr £20.00–£21.00 **Beds:** 1F 1T **Baths:** 1 En 1 Pr (4) 1

Llanwnnen
SN5347

Pantycelyn Guest House, *Llanwnnen, Lampeter, Ceredigion, SA48 7LW.* Peaceful branch of the Teify Valley. Pantycelyn, in 11 acres of meadows. **Open:** Feb to Oct **Grades:** WTB 3 Star
01570 434455 (also fax) Mrs Jenkins *HuwAnnJ@aol.com* www.pantycelyn-wales.com **D:** Fr £22.00 **S:** Fr £22.00 **Beds:** 1D 1T 1S **Baths:** 3 En (4)

Please respect a B&B's wishes regarding children, animals and smoking

Llwyndafydd
SN3755

Ty Hen Farm Hotel Cottages &, *Leisure Centre, Llwyndafydd, Llandysull, Ceredigion, SA44 6BZ.* Working sheep farm with private indoor pool and fitness room. **Open:** Feb to Nov
01545 560346 (also fax) Mr Kelly *tyhen@ouvip.com* **D:** Fr £25.50–£29.00 **S:** Fr £25.50–£29.00 **Beds:** 1D 1T **Baths:** 2 Pr (20) cc

Nanternis
SN3756 *Crown Inn*

Llainfran House, *Nanternis, New Quay, Ceredigion, SA45 9RR.* Sea views, scenic, secluded 16 acre setting. Warm welcome, lovely accommodation. Victorian country house, modern facilities. Heritage and Gulf Stream Coastline near Cwmtydu Cove. Dolphins, seals, red kites, buzzards, Cornwall without the crowds. Own dining TV lounge. Week holidays a speciality. **Open:** Mar to Oct
01545 561243 **D:** Fr £20.00–£25.00 **Beds:** 1T 1D **Baths:** 2 En (8) (4)

New Quay
SN3859

Brynarfor Hotel, *New Road, New Quay, Ceredigion, SA45 9SB.* Watch dolphins play in the bay, sandy beaches, cliff walks. **Open:** Feb to Dec
01545 560358 Mr Jewess **Fax: 01545 561204** *enquiries@brynarfor.co.uk* www.brynarfor.co.uk **D:** Fr £26.00–£37.00 **S:** Fr £30.00–£37.00 **Beds:** 3F 2D 1T 1S **Baths:** 7 En (10) cc

Ponterwyd
SN7480

The George Borrow Hotel, *Ponterwyd, Aberystwyth, Ceredigion, SY23 3AD.* Famous old hotel set in beautiful countryside, overlooking Eagle Falls & Rheidol Gorge. **Open:** All year (not Xmas)
01970 890230 Mr & Mrs Wall **Fax: 01970 890587** *georgeborrow@clara.net* www.george-borrow.co.uk **D:** Fr £25.00 **S:** Fr £25.00 **Beds:** 2F 3D 2T 2S **Baths:** 9 En (40) cc

Pontrhydfendigaid
SN7366

Red Lion Hotel, *Pontrhydfendigaid, Ystrad Meurig, Ceredigion, SY25 6BH.* Friendly riverside country pub/inn with caravan/camping facilities. **Open:** All year
01974 831232 Mr Earey *red@redlionbont.com* www.redlionbont.com **D:** Fr £18.50 **S:** Fr £18.50 **Beds:** 1F 1T 2D **Baths:** 4 En (50)

Rhydlewis

SN3447

Llwyn-yr-eos, *Rhydlewis, Llandysul, Ceredigion, SA44 5QU.* Organic farm, peaceful, wide-sweeping views, stream, wildlife, beach: 3 miles. **Open:** All year (not Xmas/New Year)
01239 851268 Mrs Lalljee **Fax: 01239 851850** *lalljee@which.net* **D:** Fr £19.00–£20.00 **S:** Fr £19.00–£20.00 **Beds:** 1F 1D **Baths:** 2 En

Rhydlewis House, *Rhydlewis, Llandysul, Ceredigion, SA44 5PE.* Exceptional guest house, once a venue for drovers. Comfort, style, good locally-produced food. **Open:** All year (not Xmas)
01239 851748 (also fax) Ms Russill www.terradat.co.uk/rhydlewis **D:** Fr £20.00–£22.00 **S:** Fr £20.00–£22.00 **Beds:** 1T 1D 1S **Baths:** 2 En 1 Pr (3)

Taliesin

SN6591

Free Trade Hall, *Taliesin, Machynlleth, Powys, SY20 8JH.* Comfortable, welcoming, excellent Welsh breakfasts, coastal views, interesting old shop. **Open:** All year (not Xmas)
01970 832368 (also fax) Ms Regan *info@freetradehall.co.uk* www.freetradehall.co.uk **D:** Fr £18.00–£22.00 **S:** Fr £20.00–£26.00 **Beds:** 1F 2D **Baths:** 1 En 1 Sh (3)

Tregaron

SN6759

Wern Newydd, *Llanio Road, Tregaron, Ceredigion, SY25 6UN.* **Open:** All year
01974 298356 D: Fr £20.00 **S:** Fr £20.00 **Beds:** 1F 1T 1D 1S **Baths:** 1 En 1 Sh
Fantastic view. Good breakfast. Friendly working family farm. Spectacular mountain runs renowned for red kites. Free fishing on Teifi River. Ample parking space. 18 miles from seaside. Perfectly situated to explore rural mid Wales. Opportunity not to be missed.

Lluest Guest House, *Lampeter Road, Tregaron, Ceredigion, SY25 6HG.* Large Victorian house, rambling gardens at the foot of the Cambrian Mountains. **Open:** All year (not Xmas)
01974 298936 (also fax) Mrs Bull *lluest@supanet.com* **D:** Fr £16.00–£19.50 **S:** Fr £16.00–£19.50 **Beds:** 2D 1T 1S **Baths:** 1 En 1 Sh (5)

Talbot Hotel, *The Square, Tregaron, Ceredigion, SY25 6JL.* Olde worlde comfortable family atmosphere, good food and real ales. **Open:** All year (not Xmas)
01974 298208 Mr Williams **Fax: 01974 299059** *talbothotel@btinternet.com* **D:** Fr £21.00–£27.50 **S:** Fr £25.00–£35.00 **Beds:** 1F 3D 8T 1S **Baths:** 10 En 5 Pr (10) **cc**

The Glamorgans

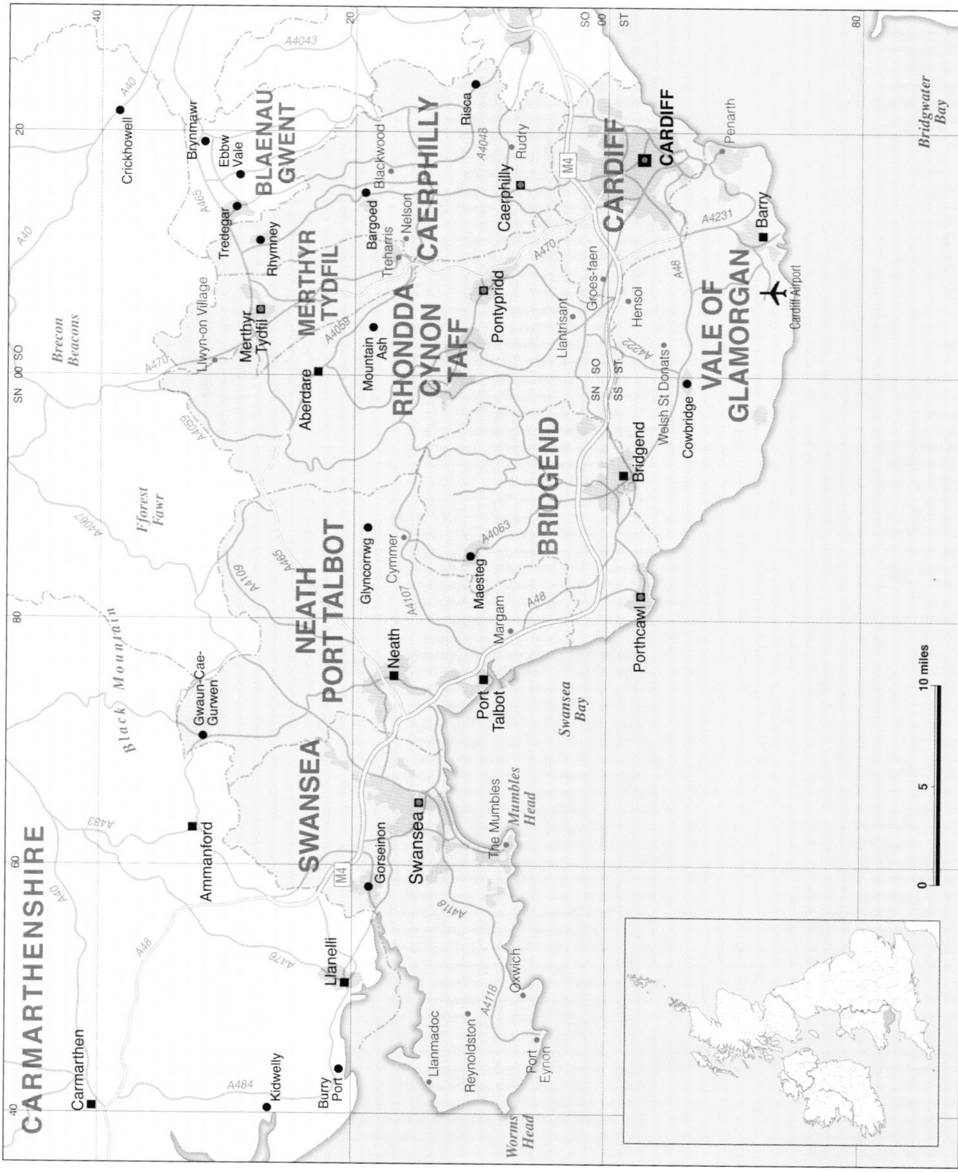

Blackwood

ST1697

Pentre House, *Mynyddislwyn, Blackwood, NP12 2BG.* Beautiful country house set in the heart of rural Wales. **Open:** All year (not Xmas/ New Year)
01495 200864 B Janaway **Fax: 01495 201459** *booking@pentrehouse.co.uk* www.pentrehouse.co.uk **D:** Fr £16.00–£19.00 **S:** Fr £16.00–£19.00 **Beds:** 1T 1d 1S **Baths:** 1 En 1 Sh (4)

Caerphilly

ST1586

The Coach House, *2 Twyn Sych, Rudry, Caerphilly, CF83 3EF.* Located in the heart of the country. 6 miles Cardiff or Newport. **Open:** All year
029 2088 4772 (also fax) Mr Davis **D:** Fr £20.00 **S:** Fr £20.00–£25.00 **Beds:** 2F 1D 3T 4S **Baths:** 1 En 2 Pr 3 Sh

Lugano Guest House, *Hillside Mountain Road, Caerphilly, Mid Glamorgan, CF83 1HN.* Charming character house, residents' own private garden and entrance. Upstairs bedrooms overlook Caerphilly Castle. **Open:** All year (not Xmas)
029 2085 2672 & 07970 906488 (M) *nick@dowson4145freeserve.co.uk* **D:** Fr £21.50–£22.50 **S:** Fr £27.50 **Beds:** 1D 2T **Baths:** 3 En (1) (2)

The Cottage Guest House, *Pwll y Pant, Caerphilly, Mid Glam, CF83 3HW.* 300 year old cottage. Castles, coastline, mountains nearby. Warm welcome. **Open:** All year
029 2086 9160 Mr Giles *thecottage@tesco.net* **D:** Fr £17.00–£20.00 **S:** Fr £26.00–£29.00 **Beds:** 3T **Baths:** 2 En 1 Pr (5)

Cardiff

ST1677

Austins, *11 Coldstream Terrace, City Centre, Cardiff, CF11 6LJ.* In the centre of the city, 300 yards from Cardiff Castle. **Open:** All year
029 2037 7148 Mr Hopkins **Fax: 029 2037 7158** *austins@hotelcardiff.com* www.hotelcardiff.com **D:** Fr £17.50–£19.50 **S:** Fr £20.00–£35.00 **Beds:** 1F 5T 5S **Baths:** 4 En 2 Sh cc

Preste Gaarden Hotel, *181 Cathedral Road, Pontcanna, Cardiff, S Glam, CF11 9PN.* Highly recommended, modernised ex-Norwegian consulate offering olde-worlde charm. **Open:** All year (not Xmas)
029 2022 8607 Mrs Nicholls **Fax: 029 2037 4805** *stay@cosycardiffhotel.co.uk* www.cosycardiffhotel.co.uk **D:** Fr £20.00–£24.00 **S:** Fr £25.00–£30.00 **Beds:** 1F 2D 3T 4S **Baths:** 7 En 3 Pr (3)

Maxines Guest House, *150 Cathedral Road, Cardiff, S Glam, CF1 9JB.* Large Victorian private guest house. **Open:** All year
029 2022 0288 Mr Barrett **Fax: 029 2034 4884** **D:** Fr £20.00–£30.00 **S:** Fr £20.00–£30.00 **Beds:** 4F 2T 2D 2S **Baths:** 5 En 1 Pr 2 Sh (13) cc

Cymmer (Glyncorrwg)

SS8695

Bryn Teg House, *9 Craig-y-fan, Cymmer, Port Talbot, SA13 3LN.* Mountains, biking, cycleways, country walks and fishing in country park. **Open:** All year (not Xmas)
01639 851820 (also fax) **D:** Fr £16.00 **S:** Fr £16.00 **Beds:** 1D 2T **Baths:** 1 Sh

Glyntawe

SN8416

Dderi Farm, *Glyntawe, Penycae, Swansea, W Glam, SA9 1GT.* Modernised C15th farmhouse. Lovely setting. Good walks. Good welcome. **Open:** All year (not Xmas/New Year) **Grades:** WTB 3 Star
01639 730458 Mrs Williams *dderifarm@hotmail.com* **D:** Fr £22.00–£25.00 **S:** Fr £24.00–£26.00 **Beds:** 1T 1D **Baths:** 2 En (6) (3)

Groes-faen

ST0680

Smokey Cottage Guest House, *Groes-Faen, Pontyclun, CF72 8NG.* Family-run guest house offering very best in accommodation. Rural location but close Cardiff M4. **Open:** All year
029 2089 1173 (also fax) *smokeycot@talk21.com* **D:** Fr £20.00–£25.00 **S:** Fr £20.00–£25.00 **Beds:** 1F 2T **Baths:** 3 En

All details shown are as supplied by B&B owners in Autumn 2002

Hensol

ST0478

Llanerch Vineyard, *Hensol, Pendoylan, Vale of Glamorgan, CF72 8JU.* One of Wales' 'Great Little Places'. Most ensuite rooms overlook largest vineyard in Wales. **Open:** All year (not Xmas)
01443 225877 Peter Andrews **Fax: 01443 225546** *llanerch@cariadwines.demon.co.uk* www.llanerch-vineyard.co.uk **D:** Fr £24.00–£30.00 **S:** Fr £38.00–£50.00 **Beds:** 2D 2T **Baths:** 4 En (8) (20) cc

Llanmadoc

SS4493

Tallizmand, *Llanmadoc, Gower, Swansea, W Glam, SA3 1DE.* Tastefully furnished ensuites. Coastal and inland walks, quiet sandy beaches. **Open:** All year (not Xmas) **Grades:** WTB 3 Star
01792 386373 Mrs Main **D:** Fr £22.00 **S:** Fr £25.00 **Beds:** 1D 2T **Baths:** 1 En 2 Pr (5)

Britannia Inn, *Llanmadoc, Gower, Swansea, W Glam, SA3 1DB.* C18th family-owned country inn close to Burry Inley & nature reserve. **Open:** All year (not Xmas/ New Year)
01792 386624 Mr Downie *mikdow@freeuk.com* **D:** Fr £25.00 **S:** Fr £32.50 **Beds:** 1F 1T 3D **Baths:** 5 En (50) cc

Llantrisant

ST0483

The Black Prince Hotel, *Llantrisant Industrial Estate, Llantrisant, Pontyclun, Mid Glam, CF72 8LF.* Friendly, family-run pub. Informal atmosphere but guaranteed a welcome. **Open:** All year
01443 227723 Mr Long **Fax: 01443 228655** **D:** Fr £27.00–£30.00 **S:** Fr £27.00–£30.00 **Beds:** 37F **Baths:** 37 En (100) cc

Llwyn Onn

SO0111

Llwyn Onn Guest House, *Cwmtaf, Merthyr Tydfil, Mid Glam, CF48 2HT.* In the Brecon Beacons National Park, overlooking Llwyn-onn Reservoir and surrounding woodland. Close to Taff Trail, Pen-Y-Fan and Waterfalls. Walking, cycling, fishing, golf, all nearby. Warm Welsh welcome assured. Ideal location for business or leisure. **Open:** All year (not Xmas/New Year)
01685 384384 Mr Evans **Fax: 01685 359310** *reception@llwynonn.co.uk* www.llwynonn.co.uk **D:** Fr £25.00 **S:** Fr £20.00–£28.00 **Beds:** 1D 1T 1S **Baths:** 3 En (4) cc

Manmoel

SO1703

Wyrloed Lodge, *Manmoel, Blackwood, Gwent, NP12 0RW.* Victorian-style home in mountain hamlet. Pub, views, peaceful, walking, touring, home-cooking. **Open:** All year (not Xmas/New Year)
01495 371198 (also fax) Mrs James **D:** Fr £20.00 **S:** Fr £20.00 **Beds:** 1F 2D 1T **Baths:** 4 En (6)

Margam

SS7887

Ty'N-Y-Caeau, *Margam, Port Talbot, W Glam, SA13 2NW.* Original vicarage for Margam Abbey since C17th, in walled gardens. **Open:** Feb to Nov
01639 883897 Mrs Gaen **D:** Fr £22.00–£25.00 **S:** Fr £25.00–£27.00 **Beds:** 1F 2D 4T **Baths:** 6 En 1 Pr (2) (8)

Merthyr Tydfil

SO0506

Maes Y Coed, *Park Terrace, Pontmorlais West, Merthyr Tydfil, Mid Glam, CF47 8UT.* Large comfortable house on edge of Brecon Beacons in 0.25 acre of gardens. **Open:** All year
01685 722246 (also fax) Mr Davies **D:** Fr £16.00–£18.00 **S:** Fr £18.00–£22.00 **Beds:** 4F 5T 1S **Baths:** 4 En (4)

Nelson

ST1195 *Rowan Tree*

Wern Ganol Farm, *Nelson, Treharris, Mid Glam, CF46 6PS.* Working farm with pleasant views across valley. Main A472. **Open:** All year
01443 450413 Mrs Portlock **D:** Fr £20.00 **S:** Fr £21.00–£26.00 **Beds:** 2F 2T 2D

Oxwich

SS4986

Surf Sound Guest House, *Long Acre, Oxwich, Gower, Swansea, W Glam, SA3 1LS.* Secluded, near to beach, ground floor bedrooms available. No-smoking establishment. **Open:** Easter to Oct
01792 390822 Fax: 01792 391230 D: Fr £22.00–£26.00 **S:** Fr £32.00–£40.00 **Beds:** 1F 1T 3D **Baths:** 5 En (6)

Little Haven Guest House, *Oxwich, Swansea, W Glam, SA3 1LS.* Bed and Breakfast open all year in Oxwich, Gower. Close to beach. Ideal walking area. Outdoor heated swimming pool. Large family room ensuite, 2 Doubles and 1 Twin. www.littlehaven.oxwich.btinternet.co.uk **Open:** Jan to Nov
01792 390940 Mrs Lewis www.littlehaven.oxwich.bt.internet.co.uk **D:** Fr £17.00 **S:** Fr £19.00 **Beds:** 2D 1T **Baths:** 1 En 1 Sh (16)

Penarth

ST1871

Glendale Hotel, *8-10 Plymouth Road, Penarth, CF64 3DH.* **Open:** All year **Grades:** WTB 2 Star, RAC 2 Diamond
029 2070 6701 & 029 2070 8302 Fax: 029 2070 9269 www.infotel.co.uk **D:** Fr £29.50–£36.50 **S:** Fr £23.50–£33.50 **Beds:** 20F 9D 8S **Baths:** 18 En 15 Pr 3 Sh cc
Listed building, warm and friendly welcome. Recognised for excellent food, standard, service, fresh fish, meats, traditional Italian dishes, lounge bar, private disco, full on licence, 3 miles from Cardiff train and bus station. Walking distance to Penarth promenade and marina, golf course, Cosmeston Lake.

Alandale Guest House, *17 Plymouth Road, Penarth, S Glam, CF64 3DA.* **Open:** All year **029 2070 9226** Mr Crothers www.alandaleguesthouse.co.uk **D:** Fr £25.00–£28.00 **S:** Fr £20.00–£25.00 **Beds:** 12F 2T 2D 6S **Baths:** 3 En 4 Pr 3 Sh cc
The family-run Alandale Guest House is 5 minutes from the sea front. Cardiff Bay is 10 minutes by car and Cardiff is 10 minutes by train from Penarth station. Ideal guest house for holidays, work or short breaks.

Seacot Hotel, *The Esplanade, Penarth, CF64 3AU.* Family-run, convenient for Cardiff Bay, Millennium Stadium, coastal view. **Open:** All year (not Xmas/New Year)
029 2070 7782 & 029 2070 0333 J & P O'Connell **Fax: 029 2071 0707** *info@seacothotel.co.uk* www.seacothotel.co.uk **D:** Fr £26.00–£37.50 **S:** Fr £30.00–£40.00 **Beds:** 3F 2T 3D 1S **Baths:** 9 En cc

BATHROOMS
En = Ensuite
Pr = Private
Sh = Shared

Penmark

ST0568

The Old Barn, *The Croft, Penmark, Barry, S Glam, CF62 3BP.* Converted C17th barn set in a beautiful rural village. **Open:** All year
01446 711352 (also fax) *enquiries@theoldbarnbedandbreakfast.co.uk* www.theoldbatnbedandbeakfast.co.uk **D:** Fr £20.00–£23.00 **S:** Fr £25.00–£27.00 **Beds:** 1T 1D **Baths:** 2 En

Pontypridd

ST0789

Market Tavern Hotel, *Market Street, Pontypridd, Mid Glam, CF37 2ST.* **Open:** All year (not Xmas) **01443 485331** Mr John **Fax: 01443 491403** *bookings@markettabernhotel.fsbusiness.co.uk* www.markettavernhotel.fsbusiness.co.uk **D:** Fr £21.00–£24.00 **S:** Fr £32.00–£36.00 **Beds:** 4D 3T 4S **Baths:** 11 En cc
All bedrooms ensuite and delightfully furnished. Tavern bar offers good range of ales, wines and food. Chilli Pepper Cocktail Bar and Strads Nightclub are open late Friday and Saturday evenings. Centrally located. Ideal base for Cardiff and the Valleys.

Porthcawl

SS8277

Rockybank Guest House, *15 De Breos Drive, Porthcawl, Mid Glam, CF36 3JP.* First B&B off M4 J37. Quiet, private parking, high-quality 3 star. **Open:** All year (not Xmas) **Grades:** WTB 3 Star
01656 785823 (also fax) Mrs Lewis *rockybank@totalise.co.uk* www.jeanlewis.members.beeb.net **D:** Fr £21.00–£23.00 **S:** Fr £30.00 **Beds:** 1F 1D 1T **Baths:** 3 En (6)

Rossett Guest House, *1 Esplanade Avenue, Porthcawl, CF36 3YS.* Friendly seaside home situated on heritage coastline. Easy access surrounding areas. **Open:** All year (not Xmas)
01656 771664 D: Fr £17.00–£22.00 **Beds:** 1F **Baths:** 2 En 1 Sh (1) (2)

Reynoldston

SS4890

Greenways, *Hills Farm, Reynoldston, Swansea, W Glam, SA3 1AE.* Reynoldston is central to beautiful Tower Bays, Three Cliffs, Rhossili. **Open:** Easter to Nov
01792 390125 Mrs John **D:** Fr £18.00–£20.00 **S:** Fr £20.00–£25.00 **Beds:** 2D 1T (5) (3) cc

King Arthur Hotel, *Higher Green, Reynoldston, Swansea, W Glam, SA3 1AD.* **Open:** All year **Grades:** WTB 3 Star **01792 391099 & 01792 390775 Fax: 01792 391075** *info@kingarthurhotel.co.uk* www.kingarthurhotel.co.uk **D:** Fr £30.00–£45.00 **S:** Fr £35.00–£45.00 **Beds:** 9T 7D 3S **Baths:** 19 En cc
Traditional country inn. Relaxed friendly atmosphere, log fires, cosy restaurant, pleasant ensuite bedrooms. Renowned for delicious home cooked meals & extensive seasonal menus. An ideal centre for exploring Gower. Facilities for small conferences. Self catering cottage available, sleeps six maximum.

Rudry

ST1886

The Coach House, *2 Twyn Sych, Rudry, Caerphilly, CF83 3EF.* Located in the heart of the country. 6 miles Cardiff or Newport. **Open:** All year **029 2088 4772 (also fax)** Mr Davis **D:** Fr £20.00 **S:** Fr £20.00–£25.00 **Beds:** 2F 1D 3T 4S **Baths:** 1 En 2 Pr 3 Sh

Swansea

SS6592

The Coast House, *708 Mumbles Road, The Mumbles, Swansea, W Glam, SA3 4EH.* **Open:** Jan to Nov **Grades:** WTB 3 Star **01792 368702** Mrs Clarke *thecoasthouse@aol.com* **D:** Fr £22.00–£28.00 **S:** Fr £23.00–£35.00 **Beds:** 2F 3D 1S **Baths:** 6 En (3)
Situated on the seafront, most rooms have spectacular views of Swansea Bay. High levels of cleanliness, with ensuite facilities, tv, tea-making, hairdryers and radio alarms. Convenient for Swansea University, Cork ferry and Gower Peninsular. Home-from-home.

Rock Villa Guest House, *1 George Bank, The Mumbles, Swansea, W Glam, SA3 4EQ.* Family-run, friendly guest house. Beautiful view of Swansea Bay. **Open:** All year (not Xmas/New Year) **01792 366794** Mrs Thomas *rockvilla@tiscali.co.uk* users.tinyworld.co.uk/rockvilla **D:** Fr £23.00–£26.00 **S:** Fr £23.00–£33.00 **Beds:** 1F 2T 2D 1S **Baths:** 3 En 2 Sh (3)

The Lyndale, *324 Oystermouth Road, Swansea, W Glam, SA1 3UJ.* Seafront. Central to city amenities. Ideal base for exploring Gower. **Open:** All year (not Xmas/New Year) **01792 653882** H M Williams **D:** Fr £14.00–£18.00 **S:** Fr £16.00–£25.00 **Beds:** 1F 3T 1D 1S **Baths:** 2 Sh (5)

Mirador Guest House, *14 Mirador Crescent, Uplands, Swansea, W Glam, SA2 0QX.* Proximity to university, beaches, Dylan Thomas trail, Gower, city centre & buses. **Open:** All year **01792 466976** Mr Anderson **D:** Fr £20.00–£24.00 **S:** Fr £20.00–£22.00 **Beds:** 1F 2D 1T 1S **Baths:** 3 En 2 Sh

Osprey Guest House, *244 Oystermouth Road, Swansea, W Glam, SA1 3UH.* Sea front location. **Open:** All year (not Xmas/New Year) **01792 642369** Mrs Ellis **D:** Fr £14.00–£16.00 **S:** Fr £16.00–£18.00 **Beds:** 5F 2T 2D **Baths:** 3 Sh

The Mumbles

SS6187

The Coast House, *708 Mumbles Road, The Mumbles, Swansea, W Glam, SA3 4EH.* Situated on the seafront, most rooms have spectacular views of Swansea Bay. **Open:** Jan to Nov **Grades:** WTB 3 Star **01792 368702** Mrs Clarke *thecoasthouse@aol.com* **D:** Fr £22.00–£28.00 **S:** Fr £23.00–£35.00 **Beds:** 2F 3D 1S **Baths:** 6 En (3)

Planning a longer stay? Always ask for any special rates

Rock Villa Guest House, *1 George Bank, The Mumbles, Swansea, W Glam, SA3 4EQ.* Family-run, friendly guest house. Beautiful view of Swansea Bay. **Open:** All year (not Xmas/New Year) **01792 366794** Mrs Thomas *rockvilla@tiscali.co.uk* users.tinyworld.co.uk/rockvilla **D:** Fr £23.00–£26.00 **S:** Fr £23.00–£33.00 **Beds:** 1F 2T 2D 1S **Baths:** 3 En 2 Sh (3)

Treharris

ST0997

Fairmead, *24 Gelligaer Road, Treharris, Nelson, Mid Glam, CF46 6DN.* A small family-run quiet haven, offering a warm welcome. **Open:** All year **01443 411174** Mrs Kedward **Fax: 01443 411430** *fairmeadhouse@aol.com* **D:** Fr £21.50–£35.00 **S:** Fr £27.50–£35.00 **Beds:** 2D 1T **Baths:** 2 En 1 Pr (5)

Welsh St Donats

ST0275

Bryn-y-Ddafad, *Welsh St Donats, Cowbridge, CF71 7ST.* **Open:** All year **01446 774451** Mrs Jenkins **Fax: 01446 771790** *junejenkins@bydd.co.uk* www.bydd.co.uk **D:** Fr £23.00–£27.50 **S:** Fr £30.00–£35.00 **Beds:** 2D 1S 1T 1F **Baths:** 2 En 2 Pr 1 Sh (10) (5)
Surrounded by panoramic views and a network of footpaths, a spacious, secluded comfortable country guest house. First floor residents lounge with balcony overlooking private garden and sun lounge below. Generous breakfast menu, vegetarian and special diet options. A warm welcome assured.

B&B owners may vary rates – be sure to check when booking

Monmouthshire

Abergavenny

SO2914

Pentre House, *Brecon Road, Abergavenny, Monmouthshire, NP7 7EW.* Charming small Georgian award-winning country house in wonderful gardens. **Open:** All year (not Xmas)
01873 853435 Mrs Reardon-Smith **Fax: 01873 852321** *treardonsm@aol.com* **D:** Fr £18.00–£20.00 **S:** Fr £20.00–£25.00 **Beds:** 1F 1D 1T **Baths:** 2 Sh (6)

Kings Head Hotel, *Cross Street, Abergavenny, NP7 5EW.* C16th coaching inn in centre of busy market town. **Open:** All year
01873 853575 (also fax) *kingsheadhotel@hotmail.com* www.kingshead.2ofr.com **D:** Fr £27.50 **S:** Fr £30.00 **Beds:** 2T 2D 1S **Baths:** 5 En

National Grid References given are for villages, towns and cities – not for individual houses

Pentre Court, *Brecon Road, Abergavenny, NP7 9ND.* Spacious, welcoming Georgian house with open fires, set in 3 acres of pretty gardens. **Open:** All year
01873 853545 Mrs Candler *judith@pentrecourt.com* www.pentrecourt.com **D:** Fr £18.00–£24.00 **S:** Fr £18.00–£30.00 **Beds:** 3D **Baths:** 3 En

Planning a longer stay? Always ask for any special rates

Park Guest House, *36 Hereford Road, Abergavenny, NP7 5RA.* **Open:** All year (not Xmas/New Year) **Grades:** WTB 2 Star **01873 853715 (also fax)** *parkguesthouse@hotmail.com* **D:** Fr £17.50–£22.50 **S:** Fr £20.00–£30.00 **Beds:** 1F 1T 3D 1S **Baths:** 3 En 1 Sh (6)
An early Georgian house, a short walk from the town centre. An ideal base for walking, fishing, canal-boating, golf, pony-trekking, climbing & hang-gliding, etc. Also ideal for visiting the numerous border castles, & 'Big-Pit' mining museum.

Black Lion, *Lion Street, Abergavenny, NP7 5PE.* **Open:** All year **01873 853993 Fax: 01873 857885 D:** Fr £20.00–£25.00 **S:** Fr £20.00–£25.00 **Beds:** 1F 3T 5D 3S **Baths:** 1 En 1 Sh cc
Family-run inn, warm Welsh welcome, friendly atmosphere. Hearty breakfast awaits you. Located in market area of town. Music nights, Karaoke Thurs, Fri, Sat. Ideally situated for walkers, cyclists; boating, narrowcast, pony trekking, fishing, hang-gliding, and many more attractions all situated close by.

Tyn-y-bryn, *Deriside, Abergavenny, Monmouthshire, NP7 7HT.* **Open:** All year **01873 856682 & 07855 038969 (M)** Ms Belcham **Fax: 01873 856682** *cbelcham@care4free.net* www.tyn-y-bryn.co.uk **D:** Fr £21.00 **S:** Fr £25.00 **Beds:** 1F 1T 1D **Baths:** 1 En 1 Pr (6)
Farmhouse on slopes of Sugar Loaf Mountain within Brecon Beacons National Park. Spectacular views, idyllic peaceful location yet just one mile from Abergavenny. Friendly hosts. Dogs welcome. Members of Taste of Wales, evening meals by arrangement. Access to the hill from farm.

The Wenallt, *Gilwern, Abergavenny, Monmouthshire, NP7 0HP.* **Open:** All year **01873 830694** Mr Harris **D:** Fr £19.50–£26.00 **S:** Fr £24.00–£28.00 **Beds:** 1F 6D 2T 6S **Baths:** 1 En 6 Pr (20)
C16th Welsh longhouse set in 50 acres of farmland in Brecon Beacons NP, commanding magnificent views over the Usk valley. Retaining its old charm with oak beams, inglenook fireplace, yet offering a high standard; ensuite bedrooms.

Abersychan

SO2603

Mill Farm, *Cwmavon, Abersychan, Pontypool, NP4 8XJ.* **Open:** All year (not Xmas/New Year) **Grades:** AA 4 Diamond **01495 774588 (also fax)** Mrs Jayne **D:** Fr £25.00 **S:** Fr £25.00–£30.00 **Beds:** 1T 2D (6)
Enjoy total relaxation in C15th farmhouse in idyllic setting - antiques, log fires, oak beams, spiral staircases, heated pool in lounge. Breakfast until noon; boules, croquet in garden. Woodland walks. Close to attractions and World Heritage Site. Adults only for complete tranquillity.

Bettws Newydd

SO3605

Thornbury Farm, *Bettws Newydd, Usk, Monmouthshire, NP5 1JY.* Family farm. Warm welcome, beautiful views, attractions - castles, golf, walks. **Open:** All year (not Xmas/New Year) **01873 880598** Mrs Jones **D:** Fr £20.00–£25.00 **S:** Fr £22.00–£25.00 **Beds:** 1T 2D **Baths:** 1 Sh

BATHROOMS
En = Ensuite
Pr = Private
Sh = Shared

Caerleon

ST3390

Great House, *Isca Road, Old Village, Caerleon, NP18 1QG.* C16th, Grade II Listed, delightful village home with clematis garden to river. Comfortable, pretty rooms and very warm welcome. 1.5 miles to M4. Good enroute stop for Ireland and West Wales. 1.25 miles Celtic Manor Golf and Resort Hotel. **Open:** All year (not Xmas) **01633 420216** Mrs Price **Fax: 01633 423492** *price.greathouse@tesco.net* www.visitgreathouse.co.uk **D:** Fr £25.00–£30.00 **S:** Fr £30.00–£32.50 **Beds:** 2T 1S **Baths:** 1 Sh (10) (2)

Caldicot

ST4788

The Lychgate, *47 Church Road, Caldicot, Newport, Monmouthshire, NP26 4HW.* Convenient location within easy reach of Wye Valley and Cardiff. **Open:** All year (not Xmas/New Year) **Grades:** WTB 3 Star **01291 422378** Mrs Welch **D:** Fr £18.00–£19.00 **S:** Fr £25.00 **Beds:** 1T 2D 2S **Baths:** 5 En (5)

Chepstow

ST5393

The First Hurdle, *9-10 Upper Church St, Chepstow, Monmouthshire, NP16 5EX.* **Open:** All year **01291 622189** Ms Cooper **Fax: 01291 628538 D:** Fr £20.00–£25.00 **S:** Fr £25.00–£30.00 **Beds:** 2D 2T 1S **Baths:** 5 En
Warm and homely cottage-style guest house situated in Chepstow's historic quarter. In close proximity to shops, restaurants and the town's famous castle. An ideal walking and touring base for the Forest of Dean, Wye Valley and Offa's Dyke Path.

Afon Gwy Restaurant, *28 Bridge Street, Chepstow, Monmouthshire, NP6 6EZ.* Victorian house overlooking the river Wye, near Chepstow Castle. **Open:** All year **01291 620158 (also fax) D:** Fr £25.00 **S:** Fr £32.00–£37.00 **Beds:** 1F 3D **Baths:** 4 En cc

Planning a longer stay? Always ask for any special rates

Lower Hardwick House, *Mount Pleasant, Chepstow, Monmouthshire, NP16 5PT.* Friendly good quality accommodation. Beautiful views. Great location for walking & cycling. **Open:** All year (not Xmas/New Year)
01291 620515 Valerie Kells **D:** Fr £18.00–£24.00 **S:** Fr £25.00–£45.00 **Beds:** 2F 1D 1T **Baths:** 2 Sh (12)

Clydach
SO2213

Rock & Fountain Hotel, *Clydach, Abergavenny, NP7 0LL.* Family-run hotel within the Brecon Beacons National Park. **Open:** All year
01873 830393 Fax: 01873 730393 *archer@rockandfountain.fsnet.co.uk* **D:** Fr £23.00–£28.00 **S:** Fr £29.50–£33.00 **Beds:** 3F 1T 2D **Baths:** 6 En (20) cc

Cwmbran
ST2894

Springfields, *371 Llantarnam Road, Llantarnam, Cwmbran, Monmouthshire, NP44 3BN.* Large, welcoming Victorian home, family-run for 30 years, Joan Graham. **Open:** All year
01633 482509 Mrs Graham **D:** Fr £17.00–£18.00 **S:** Fr £18.00–£20.00 **Beds:** 2F 4D 3T **Baths:** 6 En 2 Sh (16)

Cwmyoy
SO2923 *Skirrid Inn, Queens Head*

Gaer Farm, *Cwmyoy, Abergavenny, Monmouthshire, NP7 7NE.* A perfect retreat for those wanting peace in the hills. Rooms have private sitting rooms, wonderful views. Our 'Wool Loft' suite has a Rayburn and fridge. Wide breakfast menu and idyllic surroundings in this period farmhouse. **Open:** Easter to Nov
01873 890345 S Judd *judd@farmersweekly.net* abergavenneyfarmholidaygroup.com **D:** Fr £25.00 **S:** Fr £25.00 **Beds:** 3D **Baths:** 3 En (4)

Dingestow
SO4510

Lower Pen-y-Clawdd Farm, *Dingestow, Monmouth, NP5 4BG.* Very attractive house on working farm. Rooms overlook landscaped gardens. **Open:** Mar to Nov
01600 740223 & 01600 740677 Mrs Bayliss **D:** Fr £18.00–£20.00 **S:** Fr £20.00 **Beds:** 1F 1T **Baths:** 1 Sh (1)

Forest Coalpit
SO2821

New Inn Farm, *Forest Coalpit, Abergavenny, Monmouthshire, NP7 7LT.* Peaceful, welcoming mountain farmhouse. Superb views. Walking from the door. **Open:** All year (not Xmas)
01873 890466 (also fax) J Bull *newinn.farm@virgin.net* **D:** Fr £20.00 **S:** Fr £20.00 **Beds:** 1F 1D 1T **Baths:** 1 En 2 Pr (10)

Gilwern
SO2414

The Wenallt, *Gilwern, Abergavenny, Monmouthshire, NP7 0HP.* C16th Welsh longhouse set in 50 acres of farmland in Brecon Beacons NP. **Open:** All year
01873 830694 Mr Harris **D:** Fr £19.50–£26.00 **S:** Fr £24.00–£28.00 **Beds:** 1F 6D 2T 6S **Baths:** 1 En 6 Pr (20)

Grosmont
SO4024

Lawns Farm, *Grosmont, Abergavenny, Monmouthshire, NP7 8ES.* Beautiful C17th farmhouse set in unspoilt countryside. 'A real gem!'. **Open:** Feb to Nov
01981 240298 Mr & Mrs Ferneyhough **Fax: 01981 241275** *edna@ferneyhough8.freeserve.co.uk* www.downourlane.co.uk/7.html **D:** Fr £20.00–£24.00 **S:** Fr £25.00 **Beds:** 2D 1T **Baths:** 2 En 1 Sh

Llandenny
SO4004

The Peargoed, *Llandenny, Usk, Monmouthshire, NP5 1DH.* £15 pppn. Peargoed Farmhouse, Llandenny, Usk, Mon. 01291 690233. **Open:** Easter to Oct
01291 690233 K M James **D:** Fr £15.00 **Beds:** 1D 1S **Baths:** 1 Pr (8) (2)

Llanellen
SO3010

Yew Tree Farm, *Llanellen, Abergavenny, NP7 9LB.* Exceptional self-contained accommodation on secluded farm with far-reaching views. **Open:** Apr to Oct
01873 854307 (also fax) Mrs Rose *groseandcollanellen@ukonline.co.uk* **D:** Fr £20.00 **S:** Fr £25.00 **Beds:** 1F **Baths:** 1 En (2)

Llanfihangel Crucorney
SO3221

Pen-y-dre Farm, *Llanfihangel Crucorney, Abergavenny, Gwent, NP7 8DT.* C17th farmhouse, situated in the picturesque village of Llanfihangel Crucorney. **Open:** All year
01873 890246 (also fax) Mrs Jones **D:** Fr £20.00–£22.00 **S:** Fr £20.00–£25.00 **Beds:** 2D 1D/F **Baths:** 2 En 1 Pr (6) cc

Llanover
SO3107

Ty Byrgwm, *Upper Llanover, Abergavenny, NP7 9EP.* C18th cottage/barn, 26 acres in National Park meadows/woodlands. **Open:** All year
01873 880725 Mrs Bloomfield **D:** Fr £22.50 **S:** Fr £22.00 **Beds:** 1D 2S **Baths:** 2 En 1 Pr (2) (3)

Llantarnam
ST3093

Springfields, *371 Llantarnam Road, Llantarnam, Cwmbran, Monmouthshire, NP44 3BN.* Large, welcoming Victorian home, family-run for 30 years, Joan Graham. **Open:** All year
01633 482509 Mrs Graham **D:** Fr £17.00–£18.00 **S:** Fr £18.00–£20.00 **Beds:** 2F 4D 3T **Baths:** 6 En 2 Sh (16)

Llanthony
SO2827

The Half Moon, *Llanthony, Abergavenny, Monmouthshire, NP7 7NN.* C17th, beautiful countryside. Serves good food and real ales. **Open:** All year (not Xmas)
01873 890611 Mrs Smith *halfmoonllanthony@talk21.com* **D:** Fr £20.00–£25.00 **S:** Fr £22.00–£40.00 **Beds:** 2F 4D 2T 1S **Baths:** 2 Sh (8)

Llantilio Crossenny
SO3914

Glan-Trophy House, *Llantilio Crossenny, Abergavenny, Monmouthshire, NP7 8SU.* Superb accommodation on Offa's Dyke Path. Usk/Wye Valleys closeby. **Open:** All year (not Xmas/New Year) **Grades:** WTB 3 Star
01600 780461 Mrs Barns *carolyn50@btopenworld.com* **D:** Fr £20.00 **S:** Fr £25.00 **Beds:** 2D **Baths:** 1 En 1 Pr (4)

Llantilio Pertholey

SO3116

Werngochlyn Farm, *Llantilio Pertholey, Abergavenny, Monmouthshire, NP7 8DB.* **Open:** All year
01873 857357 Mr Sage **D:** Fr £20.00–£25.00 **S:** Fr £25.00–£30.00 **Beds:** 1F 1D **Baths:** 1 En 1 Pr (1) (7)
C12th listed farmhouse under the Skirrid Mountain, 2.5 miles from Abergavenny. Heated indoor swimming pool, games room, approved riding centre, ensuite bathrooms. Colour tv, coffee & tea facilities, open fires. Many friendly farm animals.

Llantrisant

ST3896

Royal Oak, *Llantrisant, Usk, Monmouthshire, NP15 1LG.* 500-year-old, one-time popular inn and medieval priory boasts beamed bedrooms. **Open:** All year **Grades:** WTB 3 Star
01291 673455 Mr Major **Fax: 01291 673920** *bb@oakroyal.co.uk* www.oakroyal.co.uk **D:** Fr £22.50–£25.00 **S:** Fr £30.00 **Beds:** 1F 1T 1D **Baths:** 2 En 1 Pr (15)

Llanvetherine

SO3617

Great Tre-Rhew Farm, *Llanvetherine, Abergavenny, Monmouthshire, NP7 8RA.* Warm welcome on a Welsh working farm. Peaceful, rural & friendly. **Open:** All year (not Xmas)
01873 821268 Ms Beavan **D:** Fr £17.50–£20.00 **S:** Fr £17.50–£20.00 **Beds:** 1F 2D 1T 1S **Baths:** 2 Sh

Llanvihangel Crucorney

SO3220

Penyclawdd Farm, *Llanvihangel Crucorney, Abergavenny, Monmouthshire, NP7 7LB.* Beef/sheep farm, very large garden. Easy reach Abergavenny, Hereford, Cardiff, Hay-on-Wye. **Open:** All year
01873 890591 (also fax) Mrs Davies **D:** Fr £20.00–£22.00 **S:** Fr £20.00–£22.00 **Beds:** 2F **Baths:** 1 Sh

The Skirrid Mountain Inn, *Llanvihangel Crucorney, Abergavenny, Monmouthshire, NP7 8DH.* An historic country inn of unique character. Wales' oldest inn. **Open:** All year
01873 890258 Miss Grant **D:** Fr £34.50–£39.50 **S:** Fr £34.50–£39.50 **Beds:** 2D

Lower Machen

ST2287

The Forge, *Lower Machen, Newport, NP1 8UU.* Warm welcome, ideal for walking in forests or on mountains. **Open:** All year (not Xmas/New Year)
01633 440226 Mrs Jones **D:** Fr £19.00–£20.00 **S:** Fr £20.00 **Beds:** 1F 1D 1T **Baths:** 1 Sh (3)

Mamhilad

SO3003 *Horseshoe Inn*

Ty-Cooke Farm, *Mamhilad, Pontypool, Monmouthshire, NP4 8QZ.* Spacious C18th farmhouse in cobbled courtyard near Monmouthshire Brecon Canal. **Open:** All year
01873 880382 (also fax) M F Price *ty-cookefarm@hotmail.com* www.downourlane.co.uk **D:** Fr £25.00 **S:** Fr £30.00 **Beds:** 1F 1T 1D **Baths:** 3 En

Mitchel Troy

SO4910

Church Farm Guest House, *Mitchel Troy, Monmouth, NP25 4HZ.* C16th character (former) farmhouse set in large garden with stream. **Open:** All year (not Xmas)
01600 712176 Mrs Ringer **D:** Fr £21.00–£25.00 **S:** Fr £21.00–£30.00 **Beds:** 2F 3D 2T 1S **Baths:** 6 En 1 Sh (12)

Monmouth

SO5012

The Lower Cwm, *Welsh Newton, Monmouth, NP25 5RW.* **Open:** All year (not Xmas/New Year)
01600 713040 (also fax) Mrs Kelly **D:** Fr £20.00–£25.00 **S:** Fr £25.00 **Beds:** 1F 1D **Baths:** 2 Pr (3)
Stone farmhouse with terrace and vine-shaded conservatory, unusual garden, great views. Golf, fishing, canoeing and river swimming nearby. Ideal for exploring mountains and castles of Wales and towns of Hereford, Gloucester, Ross-on-Wye and Forest of Dean.

Riverside Hotel, *Cinderhill Street, Monmouth, NP25 5EY.* Located in the Wye Valley. Warm and friendly ambience. **Open:** All year **Grades:** WTB 2 Star, AA 2 Star
01600 715577 Mr Dodd **Fax: 01600 712668** *riverside.hotel@amserve.net* **D:** Fr £25.00–£34.00 **S:** Fr £40.00–£48.00 **Beds:** 2F 6D 9T **Baths:** 17 En (1) (25) **cc**

Offa's Bed & Breakfast, *37 Brook Estate, Monmouth, NP5 3AN.* Situated in the beautiful Wye Valley, friendly & comfortable family-run B&B. **Open:** Easter to Sep
01600 716934 Mr Ruston & Ms A West *rruston@surfaid.org* www.offas-dyke.co.uk/offasb&b **D:** Fr £18.00 **S:** Fr £21.00 **Beds:** 1F 1D **Baths:** 1 Pr 1 Sh

Newport

ST3188

Caerleon House Hotel, *61 Caerau Road, Newport, Monmouthshire, NP9 4HJ.* **Open:** All year **Grades:** WTB 2 Star
01633 264869 Mr Bushell **Fax: 01633 761012** *caerlonhousehotel@hotmail.com* www.caerlonhousehotel.com **D:** Fr £23.00–£25.00 **S:** Fr £25.00–£30.00 **Beds:** 1F 5T 1D 2S **Baths:** 7 En 2 Sh (8) **cc**
Near centre of Newport, but in quiet area, near civic centre & train station. Beautiful garden for guests' enjoyment. Ample parking, easy access to M4 and major events in Cardiff (10 miles). Ideal touring centre for SE Wales/Wye Valley.

The West Usk Lighthouse, *Lighthouse Road, St Brides Wentlooge, Newport, Monmouthshire, NP10 8SF.* Super B&B in real lighthouse, with water- & four-poster beds. **Open:** All year
01633 810126 & 01633 815860 Mr & Mrs Sheahan *lighthouse1@tesco.net* www.westusklighthouse.co.uk **D:** Fr £45.00 **S:** Fr £50.00–£70.00 **Beds:** 1F 2D **Baths:** 3 En (10)

RATES
D = Price range per person sharing in a double or twin room
S = Price range for a single room

Pentre Tai Farm, *Rhiwderin, Newport, Monmouthshire, NP10 9RQ.* Peaceful Welsh sheep farm in Castle Country close to M4. **Open:** Feb to Nov **Grades:** WTB 2 Star
01633 893284 (also fax) Mrs Proctor *stay@pentretai.f9.co.uk* www.downourlane.co.uk
D: Fr £21.00 **S:** Fr £25.00 **Beds:** 1F 1T
Baths: 2 En (4)

Chapel Guest House, *Church Road, St Brides Wentlooge, Newport, Monmouthshire, NP10 8SN.* Comfortable accommodation in converted chapel situated between Newport and Cardiff. **Open:** All year
01633 681018 Mrs Bushell **Fax: 01633 681431** *chapelguesthouse@hotmail.com* www.chapelguesthouse.com **D:** Fr £23.00
S: Fr £25.00–£30.00 **Beds:** 1F 1D 1T 1S
Baths: 4 En

Craignair, *44 Corporation Road, Newport, Monmouthshire, NP9 0AW.* Friendly guest house. Close to all amenities and shopping centres. **Open:** All year (not Xmas/New Year)
01633 259903 D: Fr £15.00–£18.00 **S:** Fr £16.00–£20.00 **Beds:** 1F 3T 2D 3S **Baths:** 3 Sh (8)

Osbaston

SO5014

Caseta Alta, *15 Toynbee Close, Osbaston, Monmouth, NP25 3NU.* Quiet, comfortable, artistic, upside-down house. Picturesque hillside views. Town - walking distance. **Open:** All year (not Xmas/New Year)
01600 713023 Mrs Allcock **D:** Fr £16.00–£21.00 **S:** Fr £23.00–£30.00 **Beds:** 2F 1T 2D 1S **Baths:** 1 En 1 Sh (2)

Pandy

SO3322

Brynhonddu, *Pandy, Abergavenny, Monmouthshire, NP7 7PD.* Large C16th-C19th country house in great location. **Open:** All year (not Xmas)
01873 890535 Mrs White *kdwhite@clara.net* www.brynhonddu.co.uk **D:** Fr £20.00–£25.00
S: Fr £25.00–£27.50 **Beds:** 1F 1D 1T **Baths:** 1 En 2 Pr (5) (6)

Lancaster Arms, *Pandy, Abergavenny, Monmouthshire, NP7 8DW.* Country pub on Offa's Dyke path, edge of Black Mountains. **Open:** All year (not Xmas/New Year) **Grades:** WTB 2 Star
01873 890699 Mr & Mrs Lyon *lancaster-arms@supanet.com* **D:** Fr £20.00 **S:** Fr £21.00–£23.00
Beds: 2T **Baths:** 2 Pr (10)

Old Castle Court Farm, *Pandy, Abergavenny, Monmouthshire, NP7 7PH.* C13th farmhouse near Offa's Dyke path and River Monnow. **Open:** Feb to Nov
01873 890285 Mrs Probert **D:** Fr £15.00 **S:** Fr £16.00 **Beds:** 1F 1D 1T **Baths:** 3 En 3 Pr (10)

Penallt

SO5210

Cherry Orchard Farm, *Lone Lane, Penallt, Monmouth, NP5 4AJ.* Small C18th working farm situated in Lower Wye Valley. **Open:** All year (not Xmas)
01600 714416 Mrs Beale **Fax: 01600 714447**
D: Fr £18.00 **S:** Fr £18.00 **Beds:** 2D **Baths:** 1 Sh (4)

Rhiwderin

ST2687

Pentre Tai Farm, *Rhiwderin, Newport, Monmouthshire, NP10 9RQ.* Peaceful Welsh sheep farm in Castle Country close to M4. **Open:** Feb to Nov **Grades:** WTB 2 Star
01633 893284 (also fax) Mrs Proctor *stay@pentretai.f9.co.uk* www.downourlane.co.uk
D: Fr £21.00 **S:** Fr £25.00 **Beds:** 1F 1T
Baths: 2 En (4)

Rogiet

ST4687

Court Farm, *Rogiet, Newport, Gwent, NP26 3UR.* Comfortable farmhouse near Usk, Chepstow & Wye Valley. Cardiff 16, Bristol 17 miles. **Open:** All year
01633 880232 S Anstey **D:** Fr £20.00–£25.00
S: Fr £20.00–£25.00 **Beds:** 2F 2T **Baths:** 2 En 1 Pr (10)

St Brides Wentlooge

ST2982

The West Usk Lighthouse, *Lighthouse Road, St Brides Wentlooge, Newport, Monmouthshire, NP10 8SF.* Super B&B in real lighthouse, with water- & four-poster beds. **Open:** All year
01633 810126 & 01633 815860 Mr & Mrs Sheahan *lighthouse1@tesco.net* www.westusklighthouse.co.uk **D:** Fr £45.00
S: Fr £50.00–£70.00 **Beds:** 1F 2D **Baths:** 3 En (10)

Chapel Guest House, *Church Road, St Brides Wentlooge, Newport, Monmouthshire, NP10 8SN.* Comfortable accommodation in converted chapel situated between Newport and Cardiff. **Open:** All year
01633 681018 Mrs Bushell **Fax: 01633 681431** *chapelguesthouse@hotmail.com* www.chapelguesthouse.com **D:** Fr £23.00
S: Fr £25.00–£30.00 **Beds:** 1F 1D 1T 1S
Baths: 4 En

Tintern

SO5300

Holmleigh, *Monmouth Road, Tintern, Chepstow, Monmouthshire, NP6 6SG.* Beautiful old house overlooking the river Wye. **Open:** All year
01291 689521 Mr & Mrs Mark **D:** Fr £16.00
S: Fr £16.00 **Beds:** 2D 1T 1S **Baths:** 1 Sh (3)

Highfield House, *Chapel Hill, Tintern, Chepstow, Monmouthshire, NP6 6TF.* Remarkable house - wondrous views of the Wye Valley. Close Offa's Dyke. **Open:** All year
01291 689838 Mr McCaffery **Fax: 01291 689890 D:** Fr £24.50–£29.50 **S:** Fr £30.00–£37.50 **Beds:** 2F 1D **Baths:** 2 En 1 Pr (10)

Tranch

SO2600

Ty Shon Jacob Farm, *Tranch, Pontypool, NP4 6BP.* Secluded hilltop farm. Panoramic views, home-grown vegetables and good cooking. **Open:** All year
01495 757536 A Harris *tyshonfarm@aol.com* www.s-h-systems.co.uk/hotels/tyshon.html
D: Fr £18.00–£20.00 **S:** Fr £20.00–£22.00
Beds: 2T 1D **Baths:** 2 En 1 Pr (1) (10)

Tregare

SO4110 *Cripple Creek Inn, Hostry Inn*

Court Robert, *Tregare, Raglan, Monmouthshire, NP5 2BZ.* Peaceful C16th home. Comfortable, spacious bedrooms, antique furnishings. **Open:** All year (not Xmas/New Year)
01291 690709 (also fax) Ms Paxton *courtirobert@virgin.net* **D:** Fr £18.00 **Beds:** 2F
Baths: 1 Sh

Trelleck

SO4901

Hollytree House, *Trelleck, Monmouth, NP25 4PA.* A Wye Valley rural village setting with pub and restaurant. **Open:** All year
01600 860181 Mr & Mrs Peckham *gerald.peckham@ic24.net* **D:** Fr £19.50–£21.50
S: Fr £20.50–£22.50 **Beds:** 1F 1T **Baths:** 1 Pr 1 Sh (3) (3)

Please respect a B&B's wishes regarding children, animals and smoking

North East Wales

Bangor-on-Dee

SJ3742

Fraser Cottage, *High Street, Bangor-on-Dee, Wrexham, LL13 0AU.* Pure vegetarian B&B in North Welsh Borderlands; rural village, informal atmosphere. **Open:** All year
01978 781068 (also fax) Ms Knowles *helen@frasercottage.com* www.frasercottage.com **D:** Fr £20.00–£25.00 **S:** Fr £20.00–£25.00 **Beds:** 2D 1T **Baths:** 3 En (3)

Bodfari

SJ0970

Fron Haul, *Sodom, Bodfari, Denbigh, LL16 4DY.* An oasis of calm and taste overlooking the Vale of Clwyd. **Open:** Jan to Dec **Grades:** WTB 3 Star
01745 710301 & 07787 155340 (M) Mrs Edwards **Fax: 01745 710301** *fronhaul@pantglasbodfari.freeserve.co.uk* www.fron-haul.com **D:** Fr £23.00 **S:** Fr £25.00 **Beds:** 1F 1D 1T 1S **Baths:** 1 Pr 2 Sh (12)

Swn Yr Afon, *Mold Road, Bodfari, Denbighshire, LL16 4DP.* Large distinctive house in rural location with extensive views. **Open:** All year (not Xmas/New Year)
01745 710333 (also fax) Mr & Mrs Roberts *swnyrafon@ukonline.co.uk* **D:** Fr £22.00 **Beds:** 1T (4)

Please respect a B&B's wishes regarding children, animals and smoking

Bontuchel

SJ0857

Pantglas Ganol, *Bontuchel, Ruthin, LL15 2BS.* Stay in this beautiful and peaceful location, enjoy the wildlife. **Open:** All year (not Xmas/New Year)
01824 710639 (also fax) Mrs Wilkinson **D:** Fr £20.00–£21.00 **S:** Fr £21.00–£22.00 **Beds:** 1F 1T 1D **Baths:** 1 En 1 Pr

Caerwys

SJ1272

Plas Penucha, *Caerwys, Mold, Flintshire, CH7 5BH.* Peaceful countryside, comfortable farmhouse with large gardens overlooking the Clwydian Hills. **Open:** All year
01352 720210 Mrs Price **Fax: 01352 720881** **D:** Fr £22.00–£25.00 **S:** Fr £22.00–£25.00 **Beds:** 2D 2T **Baths:** 2 En 1 Pr 1 Sh

Chirk

SJ2837

Sun Cottage, *Pentre, Chirk, Wrexham, LL14 5AW.* Welcoming character cottage, 1723. Spectacular woodland views over river valley. **Open:** All year (not Xmas)
01691 774542 Mrs Little *little@suncottage-bb.freeserve.co.uk* **D:** Fr £17.00 **S:** Fr £17.00 **Beds:** 2F 1S **Baths:** 2 Sh (10) (3)

Clawdd-newydd

SJ0852

Bryn Coch, *Clawdd-newydd, Ruthin, LL15 2NA.* Working farm near Clocaenog Forest overlooking Vale of Clwyd. Croeso. **Open:** Easter to Oct
01824 750603 (also fax) Mrs Jones *gaenorjones@hotmail.com* **D:** Fr £18.00–£20.00 **S:** Fr £18.00–£22.00 **Beds:** 1T 1F **Baths:** 1 En 1 Sh

Corwen

SJ0743

Corwen Court Private Hotel, *London Road, Corwen, Denbighshire, LL21 0DP.* Converted old police station/courthouse; six cells, now single bedrooms. **Open:** Mar to Nov
01490 412854 Mr & Mrs Buckland **D:** Fr £17.00–£19.00 **S:** Fr £16.00–£17.00 **Beds:** 4D 6S **Baths:** 4 En 2 Sh (3) (6)

Central Hotel Restaurant & Cafe, *The Square, Corwen, LL21 0DE.* Situated on the River Dee on the A5. Licensed - good foods. **Open:** All year (not Xmas)
01490 412462 Mrs Allsopp *e.thecentral@aol.com* **D:** Fr £19.50–£26.00 **S:** Fr £19.50–£26.00 **Beds:** 1F 3D 3T **Baths:** 7 En

Cynwyd

SJ0541

Pen y Bont Fawr, *Cynwyd, Corwen, LL21 0ET.* **Open:** All year **Grades:** WTB 3 Star
01490 412663 Mr Wivell *robert.wivell@btopenworld.com* **D:** Fr £15.00–£17.00 **S:** Fr £15.00 **Beds:** 1T 2D **Baths:** 2 En 1 Sh (5)
Situated in the Edeyrnion Valley, close to the Berwyn Mountains on the outskirts of Cynwyd Village, near Corwen. Llangollen, Bala, Betws-y-Coed & Snowdonia, are nearby. Ideal for walking, cycling, fishing & horse riding. Water sports in Bala. All rooms have mountain views.

Denbigh

SJ0566

Cayo Guest House, *74 Vale Street, Denbigh, LL16 3BW.* Centrally-situated townhouse. Ideal for viewing N. Wales. Pickup from Bodfari (Offa's Dyke). **Open:** All year (not Xmas/New Year)
01745 812686 Mrs MacCormack **D:** Fr £18.00–£19.00 **S:** Fr £18.00–£19.00 **Beds:** 2D 3T 1S **Baths:** 3 En 1 Pr 1 Sh **cc**

Flint

SJ2472

Oakenholt Farm, *Chester Road, Flint, Flintshire, CH6 5SU.* High quality accommodation with lovely views, ideal base for Deeside and Chester. **Open:** All year
01352 733264 Mrs Hulme *jenny@oakenholt.freeserve.co.uk* www.smoothhound.co.uk/oakenholt.html **D:** Fr £20.00–£25.00 **S:** Fr £20.00–£30.00 **Beds:** 2S 2T 4D 1F **Baths:** 8 En

Please respect a B&B's wishes regarding children, animals and smoking

Froncysyllte

SJ2740

Argoed Farm, *Froncysyllte, Llangollen, LL20 7RH.* Old farmhouse, beamed ceilings, inglenook fireplace in dining room. Idyllic setting. **Open:** All year (not Xmas/New Year) **Grades:** WTB 3 Star
01691 772367 Mrs Landon *llangollen@argoedfm.freeserve.co.uk* **D:** Fr £20.00–£22.00 **S:** Fr £20.00–£22.00 **Beds:** 1F 1D 1T 1S **Baths:** 4 En (6)

Glyn Ceiriog

SJ2038

Pant Farm, *Glyn Ceiriog, Llangollen, LL20 7BY.* Spectacular views, walking, riding on the doorstep, ideal touring base. **Open:** All year (not Xmas)
01691 718534 (also fax) Mrs Tomlinson *chris@pantfarmholidays.com* www.pantfarmholidays.com **D:** Fr £19.00 **S:** Fr £19.00 **Beds:** 2D 1S **Baths:** 2 En (6)

Gwynfryn

SJ2551

Plas Tirion, *Ffordd Bryn Madoc, Gwynfryn, Wrexham, LL11 5UP.* Informal rural accommodation, panoramic mountain views. Interesting touring/walking area. **Open:** All year (not Xmas/New Year)
01978 757497 **S:** Fr £20.00–£25.00 **Beds:** 2S **Baths:** 1 Sh (2)

Hawarden

SJ3165

St Deiniol's Library, *Church Lane, Hawarden, Deeside, CH5 3DF.* William Gladstone's Library, Grade I Listed, building set in own grounds. **Open:** All year (not Xmas)
01244 532350 G P Morris **Fax: 01244 520643** *deiniol.vistors@btinternet.com* www.st-deiniols.org **D:** Fr £22.50–£27.50 **S:** Fr £22.50–£32.50 **Beds:** 5D 3T 14S **Baths:** 10 Sh 4 En (20) **cc**

The Coach House, *Hawarden, Deeside, CH5 3DH.* A converted coaches 5 miles from Chester. Ideal for touring N. Wales. **Open:** All year (not Xmas/New Year)
01244 532328 (also fax) Mrs Jacks **D:** Fr £22.50 **S:** Fr £25.00 **Beds:** 2D 2S **Baths:** 1 Sh (12) (4)

Higher Kinnerton

SJ3261

Green Cottage, *Higher Kinnerton, Chester, CH4 9BZ.* 6 miles from historic Chester, relaxing atmosphere, good food, in a Welsh rural setting. **Open:** All year
01244 660137 & 01244 661369 Mrs Milner **D:** Fr £20.00 **S:** Fr £25.00 **Beds:** 1D 1T **Baths:** 1 Pr

Kinnerton Hall, *43 Main Street, Higher Kinnerton, Chester, CH4 9AJ.* C18th farmhouse, providing luxury accommodation overlooking the Cheshire Plain. **Open:** All year
01244 660213 (also fax) Ms Cannon *gille@kinnertonhall.co.uk* www.kinnerton.co.uk **D:** Fr £17.00–£19.50 **S:** Fr £17.00–£24.50 **Beds:** 1F 1D 2S **Baths:** 1 En 1 Sh

Holywell

SJ1875

Greenhill Farm, *Bryn Celyn, Holywell, Denbigh & Flint, CH8 7QF.* C16th timber framed farmhouse with 'old world' charm. **Open:** Feb to Nov
01352 713270 Mr & Mrs Jones *mary@greenhillfarm.fsnet.co.uk* greenhillfarm.co.uk **D:** Fr £18.50–£20.50 **Beds:** 2F 1D 1T **Baths:** 2 En 2 Sh (6)

Llandegla

SJ1952

Saith Daran Farm, *Llandegla, Wrexham, LL11 3BA.* Ideally placed for touring North Wales, Chester and Offa's Dyke. **Open:** All year (not Xmas/New Year)
01978 790685 Mrs Thompson *ianjoy@saithdaran.freeserve.co.uk* **D:** Fr £18.00 **S:** Fr £18.00 **Beds:** 1T 1S **Baths:** 2 En

Llandrillo

SJ0337

Y Llwyn Guest House, *Llandrillo, Corwen, LL21 0ST.* Enjoy beautiful views of Berwyn Mountains from your bedroom, restaurants in walking distance. **Open:** All year
01490 440455 & 07803 524526 (M) Mrs Jones *aeron@yllwyn39.freeserve.co.uk* www.smoothhound.co.uk/hotels/yllwyn.html **D:** Fr £20.00–£22.00 **S:** Fr £26.00 **Beds:** 1D 1T **Baths:** 1 En 1 Pr (3)

Llanferres

SJ1860

The White House, *Rectory Lane, Llanferres, Mold, Denbighshire, CH7 5SR.* Victorian rectory with recently converted stables set in conservation area. **Open:** All year
01352 810259 *rarmst@hotmail.com* **D:** Fr £19.00–£22.00 **S:** Fr £23.00–£25.00 **Beds:** 2D 1T **Baths:** 3 Pr (6)

Llangollen

SJ2141

Bryn Meirion, *Abbey Road, Llangollen, Clwyd, LL20 8EF.* Edwardian house overlooking Dee, canal, steam railway and surrounding hills. **Open:** All year **Grades:** WTB 3 Star
01978 861911 Mrs Hurle *jhurle@globalnet.co.uk* www.users.globalnet.co.uk/~jhurle **D:** Fr £18.00–£20.00 **S:** Fr £24.00–£35.00 **Beds:** 1F 2D **Baths:** 2 En 1 Pr (4)

Dee Farm, *Rhewl, Llangollen, LL20 7YT.* Comfortable peaceful farmhouse. Llangollen 4 miles. Good walking/touring/sightseeing base. **Open:** Mar to Nov
01978 861598 (also fax) M Harman *harman@deefarm.co.uk* **D:** Fr £22.00–£24.00 **S:** Fr £22.00–£25.00 **Beds:** 2T 1S **Baths:** 1 En 1 Pr (6)

Argoed Farm, *Froncysyllte, Llangollen, LL20 7RH.* Old farmhouse, beamed ceilings, inglenook fireplace in dining room. Idyllic setting. **Open:** All year (not Xmas/New Year) **Grades:** WTB 3 Star
01691 772367 Mrs Landon *llangollen@argoedfm.freeserve.co.uk* **D:** Fr £20.00–£22.00 **S:** Fr £20.00–£22.00 **Beds:** 1F 1D 1T 1S **Baths:** 4 En (6)

River Lodge, *Mill Street, Llangollen, Clwyd, LL20 7UH.* On the banks of the Dee, River Lodge is Llangollen's newest motel lodge. **Open:** Feb to Dec
01978 869019 Mr Byrne **Fax: 01978 861841** *chainbridge@hotmail.com* **D:** Fr £15.00–£35.00 **S:** Fr £15.00–£35.00 **Beds:** 4F 7D 7T **Baths:** 18 En (30) **cc**

Llangynhafal

SJ1263

Esgairlygain (The Old Barn), *Llangynhafal, Ruthin, Denbighshire, LL15 1RT.* Stone barn conversion with original beams & low sloping ceilings. **Open:** Mar to Dec
01824 704047 (also fax) Mrs Henderson **D:** Fr £21.00 **S:** Fr £25.00 **Beds:** 1F 1D 1T **Baths:** 3 En

Lloc

SJ1376

Misty Waters Country Lodge Hotel, *Lloc, Holywell, CH8 8RG.* Country lodge set in peaceful area with a friendly atmosphere. **Open:** All year
01352 720497 (also fax) Mr Edwards www.shepherdscottage.ntb.ore.uk **D:** Fr £20.00 **S:** Fr £30.00 **Beds:** 1F 4D **Baths:** 5 En

Maeshafn

SJ2061

Hafan Deg, *Maeshafn, Mold, Flintshire, CH7 5LU.* **Open:** All year **01352 810465 (also fax)** Mrs Scruton *dave@hafandeg.co.uk* www.hafandeg.co.uk **D:** Fr £22.50 **S:** Fr £25.00 **Beds:** 1F 1T 1D 1S **Baths:** 2 En 1 Pr 1 Sh (4)
A comfortable country home surrounded by woods and hills. Relax on decking or gallery, enjoy home-baked bread for breakfast in the open beamed dining hall with wood burning stove and slate floor. Explore market towns, Roman Chester, castles, mountains.

Minera

SJ2651 *Tyn y Capel*

Butterfields Guest House, *Pen-y-Nant Cottage, Minera, Wrexham, LL13 3DA.* Just outside Minera village, overlooking Minera Mountain. Utilises British sign language. **Open:** All year
01978 750547 (also fax) **D:** Fr £20.00 **S:** Fr £20.00 **Beds:** 5S **Baths:** 1S (3)

Mold

SJ2363

Heulwen, *Maes Bodlonfa, Mold, Flintshire, CH7 1DR.* Spacious rooms. Convenient town centre. Friendly - nothing too much trouble. **Open:** All year (not Xmas) **Grades:** AA 3 Diamond
01352 758785 Mrs Hollywell **D:** Fr £20.00 **S:** Fr £20.00–£25.00 **Beds:** 1F 1S **Baths:** 2 Pr (3)

Northop Hall

SJ2667 *Black Lion*

Brookside House, *Northop Hall, Mold, Flintshire, CH7 6HR.* Relax enjoy the hospitality or our beautifully refurbished cottage. **Open:** All year (not Xmas/New Year)
01244 821146 Mrs Whale *christine@brooksidehouse.fsnet.co.uk* www.brooksidehouse.fsnet.co.uk **D:** Fr £19.00–£22.00 **Beds:** 1F 1T 1D **Baths:** 1 En 1 Pr 1 Sh

Penley

SJ4140

Bridge House, *Penley, Wrexham, LL13 0LY.* Comfortable house, idyllic setting, open views. Landscaped gardens with stream. **Open:** All year (not Xmas)
01978 710763 Mr & Mrs Clarke **D:** Fr £16.00–£18.00 **S:** Fr £18.00–£20.00 **Beds:** 1D 2T **Baths:** 2 Sh

B&B owners may vary rates – be sure to check when booking

Pentre

SJ2940

Pentre Cottage, *Pentre, Chirk, Wrexham, Flintshire, LL14 5AW.* Beautiful Welsh cottage with friendly Lancashire welcome; dog-lovers paradise. **Open:** All year (not Xmas)
01691 774265 Mrs Vant *vant@pentrecott.freeserve.co.uk* **D:** Fr £16.00 **S:** Fr £16.00–£18.00 **Beds:** 1D 1T **Baths:** 1 Pr 1 Sh (3)

Pentre Halkyn

SJ2072 *Glan-yr-Afon Inn, Calcot Arms*

The Hall, *Lygan Y Wern, Pentre Halkyn, Holywell, CH8 8BD.* Delightful cottage in large grounds adjoining Georgian mansion. **Open:** All year
01352 780215 Mrs Vernon **Fax: 01352 780187** *daviniavernon@aol.com* **D:** Fr £20.00 **S:** Fr £25.00 **Beds:** 1T 1D **Baths:** 1 En 1 Sh (5) (4) **cc**

Prestatyn

SJ0682

Traeth Ganol Hotel, *41 Beach Road West, Prestatyn, Denbighshire, LL19 7LL.* Situated on sea front. Recommended by 'Which B&B' guide & other upmarket guides. **Open:** All year **Grades:** WTB 3 Star, AA 2 Star
01745 853594 Mr & Mrs Groves **Fax: 01745 886687** *info@hotel-prestatyn.co.uk* www.hotel-prestatyn.co.uk **D:** Fr £30.00–£35.00 **S:** Fr £40.00–£56.00 **Beds:** 6F 1D 1T 1S **Baths:** 9 En 1 **cc**

Roughsedge House, *26/28 Marine Road, Prestatyn, Denbighshire, LL19 7HG.* Victorian guest house, excellent breakfast. Walkers welcome, friendly atmosphere. **Open:** All year
01745 887359 Mrs Kubler **Fax: 01745 852883** *roughsedge@ykubler.fsnet.co.uk* **D:** Fr £17.00–£20.00 **S:** Fr £17.00–£25.00 **Beds:** 2F 4D 2T 2S **Baths:** 3 Pr 3 Sh **cc**

Rhewl (Llangollen)

SJ1844

Dee Farm, *Rhewl, Llangollen, LL20 7YT.* Comfortable peaceful farmhouse. Llangollen 4 miles. Good walking/touring/sightseeing base. **Open:** Mar to Nov
01978 861598 (also fax) M Harman *harman@deefarm.co.uk* **D:** Fr £22.00–£24.00 **S:** Fr £22.00–£25.00 **Beds:** 2T 1S **Baths:** 1 En 1 Pr (6)

Rhyl

SJ0181

Normaz Guest House, *19 Aquarium Street, Rhyl, LL18 1PG.* Welcoming licensed guest house. Reasonable rates, clean, central and great food. **Open:** Easter to Sept
01745 334761 Mrs Harper *tom@normaz.fsnet.co.uk* **D:** Fr £15.00 **S:** Fr £15.00 **Beds:** 2F 1T 2D 1S **Baths:** 1 Sh

Links Guest House, *20 Beechwood Road, Rhyl, LL18 3EU.* East Parade beach, ground floor available. 3 stars, ensuite **Open:** All year
01745 344381 Mrs Mariner *thelinksgh@cwcom.net* www.virtualrhyl.co.uk/links/index.htm **D:** Fr £15.00–£20.00 **S:** Fr £18.00–£25.00 **Beds:** 3F 4D 2S **Baths:** 6 En 1 Pr (5) **cc**

The Kensington Hotel, *17 East Parade, Rhyl, LL18 3AG.* Traditional Victorian bay property, now family-run hotel. Prominent position on the sea front. **Open:** All year (not Xmas/New Year)
01745 331868 (also fax) Mr Dawson **D:** Fr £20.00–£34.00 **S:** Fr £25.00–£35.00 **Beds:** 10F 4T 10D 10S **Baths:** 10 En 10 Pr **cc**

Rossett

SJ3657

Corner House Farm, *Parkside, Rossett, Wrexham, LL12 0BW.* Suitable for meetings, family gatherings, lovely rural location. 6 miles Chester. **Open:** All year **Grades:** WTB 5 Star
01829 270452 Mrs Coop **Fax: 01829 271260** **D:** Fr £20.00–£28.00 **S:** Fr £25.00–£32.00 **Beds:** 1D 1T 1S **Baths:** 3 En (14) 1

Ruthin

SJ1258

Esgairlygain (The Old Barn), *Llangynhafal, Ruthin, Denbighshire, LL15 1RT.* Stone barn conversion with original beams & low sloping ceilings. **Open:** Mar to Dec
01824 704047 (also fax) Mrs Henderson **D:** Fr £21.00 **S:** Fr £25.00 **Beds:** 1F 1D 1T **Baths:** 3 En

National Grid References given are for villages, towns and cities – not for individual houses

St Asaph

SJ0374

Pen-Y-Bryn Farm, *Boderw, St Asaph, Denbighshire, LL17 0LF.* Comfortable farmhouse in peaceful surroundings overlooking the city. Farmhouse breakfast. **Open:** All year
01745 583213 Mrs Williams **D:** Fr £17.50–£20.00 **S:** Fr £19.00–£20.00 **Beds:** 1F 2D 1S **Baths:** 1 En 1 Sh

Diddanfa, *The Roe, St Asaph, Denbighshire, L17 0LU.* Large Victorian B&B, 2 mins off A55, in lovely Vale of Clwyd. **Open:** All year (not Xmas/New Year)
01745 582849 (also fax) Mr & Mrs Thomas **D:** Fr £15.00–£20.00 **S:** Fr £20.00 **Beds:** 1F 1T 1S **Baths:** 1 Sh

Worthenbury

SJ4146

The Manor, *Worthenbury, Wrexham, LL13 0AW.* Elizabeth and Ian warmly welcome you to a tranquil rural retreat. Relax in country house style and dine on local and home-grown produce. Then retire to a period bedroom and comfy four-poster bed. Explore Cheshire, North Wales and Shropshire. **Open:** Mar to Nov
01948 770342 Mr Taylor **Fax: 01948 770711** **D:** Fr £28.00–£35.00 **S:** Fr £35.00–£45.00 **Beds:** 2D **Baths:** 1 En 1 Pr (12) (4)

Wrexham

SJ3350

Plas Tirion, *Ffordd Bryn Madoc, Gwynfryn, Wrexham, LL11 5UP.* Informal rural accommodation, panoramic mountain views. Interesting touring/walking area. **Open:** All year (not Xmas/New Year)
01978 757497 **S:** Fr £20.00–£25.00 **Beds:** 2S **Baths:** 1 Sh (2)

Plas Eyton, *Wrexham, LL13 0YD.* Easily accessible Victorian house. 3 acre small holding in own private grounds. **Open:** All year
01978 820642 Mrs Davies **D:** Fr £16.00 **S:** Fr £16.00 **Beds:** 1F 1T 1D 2S **Baths:** 1 En 2 Sh (10)

The Windings, *Cea Penty Road, Wrexham, LL12 9TH.* Delightful rural setting. Ideal base for Chester, North Wales, Wrexham. **Open:** All year
01978 720503 Mrs Rooks **Fax: 01978 757372** *windings@enterprise.net* **D:** Fr £20.00 **S:** Fr £20.00 **Beds:** 1T 2D **Baths:** 1 Sh (10)

North West Wales

Aberdovey

SN6196

Sea Breeze Guest House & Tea Room, *6 Bodfor Terrace, Aberdovey, LL35 0EA.* Beautiful village, fabulous sea views, tempting cream teas, clean & friendly. 'Winter breaks' available. **Open:** All year (not Xmas/New Year) **Grades:** WTB 3 Star
01654 767449 *seabreeze@nascr.net* **D:** Fr £21.00–£24.00 **S:** Fr £21.00–£40.00 **Beds:** 2T 3D 1S **Baths:** 4 En 2 Pr cc

Bodfor Hotel, *Sea Front, Aberdovey, LL35 0EA.* Two Star family-run seafront hotel, on main promenade, overlooking sandy beach. **Open:** All year
01654 767475 Mr Evans **Fax: 01654 767679** *davidevans@bodforhotel.co.uk* **D:** Fr £20.00–£29.50 **S:** Fr £20.00–£29.50 **Beds:** 1F 6D 5T 4S **Baths:** 10 En 2 Pr 4 Sh

Post Guest House, *Aberdovey Post Office, Aberdovey, Gwynedd, LL35 0EA.* Friendly, tastefully furnished guest house, enjoying magnificent views. Central position. **Open:** Feb to Nov
01654 767201 M, D & S Prescot **D:** Fr £20.00–£23.00 **S:** Fr £25.00–£35.00 **Beds:** 1F 1D **Baths:** 2 En

Preswylfa, *Balkan Hill, Aberdovey, Gwynedd, LL35 0LE.* Luxury accommodation, breathtaking views, recommended by 'Which? Good B&B Guide'. Organic food. **Open:** All year
01654 767239 Mrs Billingham **Fax: 01654 767983** *info@preswylfa.co.uk* www.preswylfa.co.uk **D:** Fr £30.00 **S:** Fr £50.00–£60.00 **Beds:** 2D 1T **Baths:** 3 En (3)

...ynolwyn

Eisteddfa, *Abergynolwyn, Tywyn, LL36 9UP.* Newly-built bungalow, suitable for disabled in wheelchair, overlooking Tal-y-llyn Railway. **Open:** Mar to Nov
01654 782385 Mrs Pugh **Fax: 01654 782228** **D:** Fr £20.00–£22.00 **S:** Fr £25.00 **Beds:** 2D 1T **Baths:** 2 En 1 Pr

Riverside House, *Abergynolwyn, Tywyn, LL36 9YR.* Victorian former quarry master's house, set in riverside gardens Magnificent views. **Open:** All year
01654 782235 (also fax) Ron Bott *ronbott@talyllyn.freeserve.co.uk* www.snowdonia-wales.co.uk **D:** Fr £18.00–£20.00 **S:** Fr £18.00–£20.00 **Beds:** 1F 3D 1S **Baths:** 1 En 1 Sh (6)

Abersoch

SH3128

Angorfa Guest House, *Lon Sarn Bach, Abersoch, Pwllheli, LL53 7EB.* Newly decorated bedrooms, superb breakfast, great beaches, scenery, walks & activities. **Open:** All year (not Xmas)
01758 712967 (also fax) Mrs Stanworth **D:** Fr £19.00–£25.00 **S:** Fr £22.00–£30.00 **Beds:** 1F 2D 1T **Baths:** 2 Pr 2 Sh (4)

Arthog

SH6414

Graig Wen Guest House, *Arthog, LL39 1BQ.* In 42 acres of woodland leading to Mawddach Estuary. Spectacular view from house. **Open:** All year
01341 250900 & 01341 250482 Mrs Ameson **Fax: 01341 250482** *graig-wen@supanet.com* www.graig-wen.supernet.com **D:** Fr £17.00–£19.00 **S:** Fr £18.00–£24.00 **Beds:** 1F 4D 1T 1S **Baths:** 3 En 2 Sh (4) (20) 2

Bala

SH9235

Traian, *95 Tegid Street, Bala, Gwynedd, LL23 7BW.* Welsh welcome, ideal for walking, sailing, canoeing, cycling. Local produce. **Open:** All year (not Xmas)
01678 520059 Mrs Jones **D:** Fr £18.00–£20.00 **S:** Fr £20.00 **Beds:** 1F 1D 1T **Baths:** 1 Sh

Bangor

SH5771 *The Nelson*

The Guest House, *32 Glynne Road, Bangor, LL57 1AN.* Small, friendly accommodation close to centre. Large choice of breakfasts. **Open:** All year (not Xmas/New Year)
01248 352113 (also fax) Mrs Roberts *ragsroberts@aol.com* **D:** Fr £15.00 **S:** Fr £15.00 **Beds:** 2D 2S **Baths:** 1 Sh (1)

Barmouth

SH6115

Lawrenny Lodge Hotel, *Barmouth, LL42 1SU.* Small quiet family-run hotel. Views over harbour and estuary. **Open:** Mar to Nov
01341 280466 Mr Barber **Fax: 01341 281551** **D:** Fr £22.00–£33.00 **S:** Fr £33.00 **Beds:** 1F 4D 2T 1S **Baths:** 7 En 1 Sh (9) cc

Tal-Y-Don Hotel, *High Street, Barmouth, LL42 1DL.* Families welcome. Home cooking, bar meals and good beer. **Open:** All year (not Xmas)
01341 280508 Mrs Davies **Fax: 01341 280885** **D:** Fr £18.00–£22.00 **S:** Fr £20.00–£25.00 **Beds:** 2F 4D 2T **Baths:** 4 En 2 Sh cc

Endeavour Guest House, *Marine Parade, Barmouth, LL42 1NA.* Sea front location. Beach 75 yards. Railway station 150 yards. **Open:** All year (not Xmas/New Year)
01341 280271 Mr & Mrs Tocker **D:** Fr £20.00–£22.00 **S:** Fr £20.00–£25.00 **Beds:** 7F **Baths:** 4 En 1 Sh (2) (3)

The Gables, *Fford Mynach, Barmouth, Gwynedd, LL42 1RL.* Victorian house of character lovely position near mountains - warm welcome. **Open:** Easter to Nov
01341 280553 Mr & Mrs Lewis **D:** Fr £20.00–£24.00 **S:** Fr £20.00–£24.00 **Beds:** 1F 2D 1S **Baths:** 2 En 1 Sh (4)

Wavecrest Hotel, *8 Marine Parade, Barmouth, North West Wales, LL42 1NA.* Welcoming and relaxing. 'Which?' recommended. Excellent food, wine and whisky. **Open:** Easter to Oct
01341 280330 (also fax) Mr & Mrs Jarman *thewavecrest@talk21.com* www.lokalink.co.uk/wavecrest.htm **D:** Fr £20.00–£28.00 **S:** Fr £23.00–£40.00 **Beds:** 2F 3D 2T 2S **Baths:** 8 En 1 Pr (2)

Bryn Melyn Hotel, *Panorama Road, Barmouth, LL42 1DQ.* Stunning views of mountains, estuary and sea. **Open:** All year (not Xmas/New Year)
01341 280556 Mr Jukes MBII **Fax: 01341 280342** **D:** Fr £27.00–£80.00 **S:** Fr £30.00–£47.00 **Beds:** 2F 2T 5D **Baths:** 8 En 1 Pr (9) cc

Beddgelert

SH5948

The Royal Goat Hotel, *Beddgelert, Caernarfon, LL55 4YE, .* **Open:** Mar to Oct **01766 890224** **Fax: 01766 890422** *info@royalgoathotel.co.uk* www.royalgoathotel.co.uk **D:** Fr £41.00–£49.50 **S:** Fr £41.00–£49.50 **Beds:** 15T 15D **Baths:** 30 En (80) cc
Our 200-year-old Grade II Listed building. 2 restaurants, 2 bars, residents' lounge, set amidst glorious scenery. Beddgelert is a British and European winner for 'Prettiest Village' and 'Bloom in Britain' awards. Foot of Snowdon, yet only 7 miles from the coast.

Plas Colwyn Guest House, *Beddgelert, Caernarfon, LL55 4UY.* Comfortable C17th house, centre of village, river and mountain views. **Open:** All year (not Xmas) **Grades:** WTB 2 Star
01766 890458 Mrs Osmond *plascolwyn@hotmail.com* **D:** Fr £19.00–£22.00 **S:** Fr £19.00–£36.00 **Beds:** 2F 2D 1T 1S **Baths:** 3 En 3 Sh (6) cc

Emrys House, *Beddgelert, Caernarfon, Gwynedd, LL55 4YB.* Friendly, comfortable accommodation at this spacious, centrally situated Victorian house. **Open:** All year
01766 890240 Mrs Gauler *gauler@lineone.net* www.emryshouse.co.uk **D:** Fr £17.50–£20.00 **S:** Fr £25.00 **Beds:** 1T 2D **Baths:** 1 Sh (2)

Ael-y-Bryn, *Caerarfon Road, Beddgelert, Caernarfon, LL55 4UY.* Centrally situated licensed guest house - award-winning village - wonderful views. **Open:** All year
01766 890310 Mrs Duffield *ay.b@virgin.net* www.plastanygraig.co.uk **D:** Fr £15.00–£22.50 **S:** Fr £20.00–£40.00 **Beds:** 4F **Baths:** 1 Pr (2) cc

Betws-y-Coed

SH7956

Bryn Llewelyn Non-Smokers' Guest House, *Holyhead Road, Betws-y-Coed, LL24 0BN.* Attractive Victorian guest house. Village centre, ample private car park. **Open:** All year **Grades:** WTB 2 Star, AA 3 Diamond
01690 710601 (also fax) Mr Rennison *bryn.llewelyn@tiscali.co.uk* www.betws-y-coed-snowdonia.co.uk **D:** Fr £17.50–£27.50 **S:** Fr £19.50–£27.50 **Beds:** 3F 3D 2T 1S **Baths:** 5 En 2 Pr (2) (9) cc

Fron Heulog Country House, *Betws-y-Coed, LL24 0BL.* **Open:** All year **Grades:** AA 4 Diamond, RAC 4 Diamond
01690 710736 Jean & Peter Whittingham **Fax: 01690 710920** *jean&peter@fronheulog.co.uk* www.fronheulog.co.uk **D:** Fr £22.00–£30.00 **Beds:** 2D 1T **Baths:** 3 En
Elegant Victorian stone-built home in peaceful wooded riverside scenery. Excellent modern accommodation - comfort, warmth, style. Ideal Snowdonia location - tour, walk, relax. Enjoy hosts' personal hospitality & local knowledge. In 'Which?'. A5 road, B5106 bridge, turn left, 150 yards ahead. Pay less for longer stays.

Fairy Glen Hotel, *Betws-y-Coed, LL24 0SH.* **Open:** Mar to Oct **Grades:** WTB 2 Star, AA 2 Star
01690 710269 (also fax) Mr & Mrs Youe *fairyglenhotel@amserve.net* www.fairyglenhotel.co.uk **D:** Fr £22.00–£24.00 **S:** Fr £22.00–£36.00 **Beds:** 2F 3D 2T 1S **Baths:** 6 En 2 Pr (10) cc
Family-run 300-year-old small hotel, overlooking River Conwy in the Snowdonia National Park amongst mountains and forest. Private car park and licensed bar. Warm, friendly welcome with fresh home-cooked meals from local produce.

Cwmanog Isaf Farm, *Betws-y-Coed, LL24 0SL.* **Open:** All year **Grades:** WTB 3 Star
01690 710225 & 07808 421634 (M) Mrs Hughes **Fax: 01690 710225** *h.m.hughes@amserve.net* www.cwmanogisaffarmholidays.co.uk **D:** Fr £20.00–£21.00 **S:** Fr £25.00 **Beds:** 1F 2D **Baths:** 3 En (3)
Nestling in the spectacular scenery of the Snowdonia National Park, this traditional Welsh farmhouse enjoys a peaceful homely atmosphere, wonderful views, unforgettable cuisine - situated on a small working farm only 1 mile from the picturesque village of Betws-y-Coed, peace & tranquillity awaits.

Maelgwyn House, *Betws-y-Coed, LL24 0AN.* An architect-designed house in picturesque Welsh village in the National Park. Ideal for mountaineering/mountain biking. **Open:** All year (not Xmas/New Year)
01690 710252 (also fax) Mr Walsh *maesyfedwen@ecossetel.com* **D:** Fr £25.00 **S:** Fr £25.00 **Beds:** 1T 2D **Baths:** 3 En (10) (4)

Park Hill Hotel, *Llanrwst Road, Betws-y-Coed, LL24 0HD.* Informal family-run hotel; our hotel is your castle; views; swimming-pool. **Open:** All year **Grades:** WTB 3 Star, AA 2 Star, RAC 2 Star
01690 710540 (also fax) *parkhill.hotel@virgin.net* www.park-hill-hotel.co.uk **D:** Fr £27.50–£38.00 **S:** Fr £35.00–£47.00 **Beds:** 1F 5D 4T **Baths:** 9 En (10) cc

Afon View 'Non-Smokers' Guesthouse, *Holyhead Road, Betws-y-Coed, LL24 0AN.* Snowdonia, high quality accommodation, ideal walking, touring, mountain biking. **Open:** All year
01690 710726 (also fax) Mr Roobottom *k.roobottom@which.net* www.afon-view.co.uk **D:** Fr £20.00–£25.00 **S:** Fr £25.00–£30.00 **Beds:** 4D 2T 1S **Baths:** 7 En (7)

Llwyn Derw, *Penmachno Road, Betws-y-Coed, Gwynedd, LL24 0PW.* Award winning converted chapel, location ideal base for walking/touring. **Open:** All year (not Xmas/New Year) **Grades:** WTB 3 Star
01690 710289 (also fax) Mrs Pritchard *capel.ebenezer@amserve.net* www.betws-y-coed.co.uk/acc/capel.ebenezer **D:** Fr £19.00–£25.00 **S:** Fr £25.00–£30.00 **Beds:** 2D (2)

Royal Oak Farmhouse, *Betws-y-Coed, LL24 0AH.* Part C13th water mill on beautiful meander of River Llugwy. **Open:** All year (not Xmas)
01690 710427 Mrs Houghton **D:** Fr £22.00–£25.00 **S:** Fr £25.00 **Beds:** 2D 1T **Baths:** 1 En 2 Sh (10)

Bron Celyn Guest House, *Llanrwst Road, Betws-y-Coed, North West Wales, LL24 0HD.* Small Victorian-style guest house on outskirts of picturesque village. **Open:** All year **Grades:** WTB 3 Star
01690 710333 Mr & Mrs Boughton **Fax: 01690 710111** *broncelyn@betws-y-coed.co.uk* www.broncelyn.co.uk **D:** Fr £22.00–£26.00 **S:** Fr £23.00–£50.00 **Beds:** 2F 1T 3D **Baths:** 3 En 2 Pr (7) cc

Swallow Falls Hotel, *Betws-y-Coed, Wales, LL24 0DW.* Perfectly situated for exploring Snowdonia National Park. Opposite Swallow Falls. **Open:** All year
01690 710796 Mr Jones **Fax: 01690 710191** *swallowfalls@virgin.net* **D:** Fr £19.50–£29.50 **S:** Fr £24.50–£34.50 **Beds:** 2F 2T 8D **Baths:** 12 En cc

Royal Oak Farm Cottage, *Betws-y-Coed, LL24 0AH.* Picturesque C17th farmhouse in a quiet riverside setting. **Open:** All year (not Xmas)
01690 710760 Mrs Houghton **D:** Fr £18.00–£20.00 **S:** Fr £20.00–£24.00 **Beds:** 2D 1T **Baths:** 3 Pr (4)

Aberconwy House, *Llanrwst Road, Betws-y-Coed, North West Wales, LL24 0HD.* Victorian guest house, elevated position overlooking the picturesque Snowdonia National Park. **Open:** All year
01690 710202 Mr Jones **Fax: 01690 710800** *aberconwy@betws-y-coed.co.uk* www.betws-y-coed.co.uk/aberconwy/ **D:** Fr £22.00–£50.00 **S:** Fr £22.00–£50.00 **Beds:** 1F 3T 4D **Baths:** 8 En (8) (10) cc

Coed-y-Fron, *Vicarage Road, Betws-y-Coed, LL24 0AD.* Lovely Victorian house & garden in middle of village, superb outlook over Betws-y-Coed. **Open:** All year
01690 710365 Mr & Mrs Mills *mike&beth@coedyfron.enterprise-plc.com* www.coedyfron.co.uk **D:** Fr £18.00–£24.00 **S:** Fr £18.00–£21.00 **Beds:** 1F 3D 2T 1S **Baths:** 3 En 2 Sh (2) (3) cc

Glan Llugwy, *Holyhead Road, Betws-Y-Coed, LL24 0BN.* Perfectly situated for exploring Snowdonia. A warm welcome. Superb breakfast. **Open:** All year
01690 710592 J Brayne *glanllugwy@betws-y-coed.co.uk* **D:** Fr £17.50–£19.00 **S:** Fr £17.50–£19.00 **Beds:** 1F 1T 2D 1S **Baths:** 2 Sh (6) (5)

Riverside, *Betws-y-Coed, LL24 0BN.* Centrally located in centre of village, comfortable accommodation and a superb restaurant. **Open:** All year
01690 710650 (also fax) *riverside4u@talk21.com* **D:** Fr £17.00–£22.00 **S:** Fr £18.00–£22.00 **Beds:** 2D 2T **Baths:** 1 En 1 Pr 1 Sh (10) cc

Please respect a B&B's wishes regarding children, animals and smoking

Dolweunydd Guest House, *Pentre Du, Betws-y-Coed, LL24 0BY.* Runners-up of the North Wales Welcome Host of the Year Awards 2000. Jenny and Rob Shepherd offer guests a warm welcome. Quality ensuite accommodation with colour TV, hospitality tray and central heating. Excellent home cooked food using local produce. **Open:** All year
01690 710693 (also fax) Mrs Shepherd *jenny.dolweunydd@virgin.net* www.snowdonia-dolweunydd.co.uk **D:** Fr £20.00–£28.00 **S:** Fr £25.00–£30.00 **Beds:** 2T 3D **Baths:** 5 En (5) (7)

Betws-yn-Rhos

SH9073

Wheatsheaf Inn, *Betws-yn-Rhos, Abergele, LL22 8AW.* Olde worlde C17th inn in award-winning village. **Open:** All year
01492 680218 D: Fr £22.00 **S:** Fr £26.00 **Beds:** 1F 2D 1S **Baths:** 4 En (1) (3) cc

Blaenau Ffestiniog

SH7045

Cae Du, *Manod, Blaenau Ffestiniog, Gwynedd, LL41 4BB.* **Open:** All year (not Xmas/New Year)
01766 830847 & 07808 090549 (M) S Ashe **Fax: 01766 830847** *caedu@tinyworld.co.uk* **D:** Fr £24.00 **S:** Fr £24.00 **Beds:** 1T 2D **Baths:** 3 En (4)
Picturesque C16th former farmhouse in magnificent mountain setting. Ensuite rooms, stunning panoramic views, home-cooking and a warm, friendly atmosphere make Cae Du an ideal base for exploring the wonders of Snowdonia. It's our home - make it yours.

Bryn Elltyd Guest House, *Tanygrisiau, Blaenau Ffestiniog, Gwynedd, LL41 3TW.* Mountain views: in an acre of peaceful grounds. Guided walking available. **Open:** All year
01766 831356 Mr & Mrs Cole *bob6annie9@aol.com* www.accommodation-snowdonia.com **D:** Fr £17.50–£19.50 **S:** Fr £17.50–£19.50 **Beds:** 1F 2T 1D **Baths:** 4 En (4)

Afallon Guest House, *Manod Road, Blaenau Ffestiniog, LL41 4AE.* Situated in Snowdonia National Park. Clean homely accommodation with Welsh breakfast. **Open:** All year (not Xmas)
01766 830468 Mrs Griffiths **D:** Fr £15.00–£18.00 **S:** Fr £15.00–£18.00 **Beds:** 1D 1T 1S **Baths:** 1 Sh (4)

The Don Guest House, *High Street, Blaenau Ffestiniog, LL41 3AX.* Victorian town house with breathtaking mountain views. Friendly welcome assured. **Open:** All year (not Xmas/New Year)
01766 830403 (also fax) Mr Cotton *allan-cotton@supanet.com* **D:** Fr £14.00–£18.00 **S:** Fr £15.00–£20.00 **Beds:** 3D 2T 1S **Baths:** 2 En 1 Sh (2)

Bontddu

SH6618

Caegoronwy Farm, *Bontddu, Dolgellau, Gwynedd, LL40 2UR.* Historic farmhouse overlooking Cader Idris. Peaceful location for mountain & sea. **Open:** All year (not Xmas/New Year)
01341 430243 (also fax) D: Fr £20.00–£23.00 **S:** Fr £25.00–£30.00 **Beds:** 1F 1D **Baths:** 2 En (4)

Brithdir

SH7618

Llwyn Talcen, *Brithdir, Dolgellau, LL40 2RY.* Enjoy a holiday/short break at our country house in rhododendron gardens. **Open:** Easter to Oct
01341 450276 Mrs Griffiths **D:** Fr £18.00–£20.00 **S:** Fr £18.00–£20.00 **Beds:** 1D 1S **Baths:** 1 En 1 Sh (3) (3)

Bryncrug

SH6003

Gesail Farm, *Bryncrug, Tywyn, Gwynedd, LL36 9TL.* Attractive farmhouse, with fantastic views. Excellent walking, cycling, fishing area. **Open:** All year (not Xmas/New Year)
01654 782286 (also fax) Mrs Jones *wendy-gesail@talk21.com* **D:** Fr £20.00–£25.00 **S:** Fr £25.00 **Beds:** 1F 1D **Baths:** 1 Sh (6)

Peniarth Arms, *Bryncrug, Tywyn, Gwynedd, LL36 9PH.* Cosy village inn Cader Idris. Tal-y-llyn railway nearby. Beautiful scenery. **Open:** All year (not Xmas/New Year)
01654 711505 Mrs Mountford **Fax: 01654 712169 D:** Fr £17.00–£20.00 **S:** Fr £18.00–£25.00 **Beds:** 4D **Baths:** 4 En (1) cc

Planning a longer stay? Always ask for any special rates

Caernarfon

SH4862

The White House, *Llanfaglan, Caernarfon, LL54 5RA.* Quiet, isolated country house. Magnificent views to mountains and sea. **Open:** Mar to Nov
01286 673003 Mr Bayles *rwbayles@sjms.co.uk* **D:** Fr £21.00–£23.00 **S:** Fr £27.00 **Beds:** 2D 2T **Baths:** 3 En 1 Pr (8)

Prince of Wales Hotel, *Bangor Street, Caernarfon, LL55 1AR.* Town location, perfect stopover for Ireland's ferries or exploring Snowdonia. Guest ales. **Open:** All year (not Xmas)
01286 673367 Mrs Minshall **Fax: 01286 676610** *princeofwaleshotel@gofornet.co.uk* www.smoothhound.co.uk/hotels/princewa **D:** Fr £28.00–£35.00 **S:** Fr £28.00–£35.00 **Beds:** 2F 8D 7T 4S **Baths:** 19 En 2 Sh (6) cc

Menai View Guest House & Restaurant, *North Road, Caernarfon, North Wales, LL55 1BD.* Close to Caernarfon Castle, overlooking Menai Straights . Lounge/bar & restaurant. Spa-bath. **Open:** All year (not Xmas/New Year)
01286 674602 (also fax) *menaiview@walesuk4.freeserve.co.uk* menaiviewguesthouse.co.uk **D:** Fr £17.50–£22.50 **S:** Fr £22.50–£27.00 **Beds:** 3F 2T 4D **Baths:** 9 En cc

Swn-Y-Fenai, *8 Church Street, Caernarfon, LL55 1SW.* Perfectly situated, near castle and only 7 miles from Snowdon. **Open:** All year
01286 671677 Mr Newell **Fax: 01745 334513** *philnewell73@hotmail.com* **D:** Fr £14.00–£20.00 **S:** Fr £14.00–£20.00 **Beds:** 1F 4T 1S **Baths:** 2 Sh

Capel Curig

SH7258

Llugwy Guest House, *Capel Curig, Betws-y-Coed, LL24 0ES.* Warm welcome, hearty breakfast, forest and mountain scenery. Easily located. **Open:** All year
01690 720218 Mrs Cousins **D:** Fr £17.50–£18.50 **S:** Fr £19.50–£21.50 **Beds:** 2D 1T 1S **Baths:** 2 Sh (4) cc

Can-yr-Afon, *Capel Curig, Betwys-y-Coed, LL24 0DR.* Situated in the heart of Snowdonia, near the famous Swallow Falls. **Open:** All year (not Xmas/New Year)
01690 720375 Mrs Berry **D:** Fr £18.00 **Beds:** 1F 1T 1D **Baths:** 2 Pr (10) (5)

BATHROOMS
En = Ensuite
Pr = Private
Sh = Shared

Capel Garmon

SH8155

Llannerch Goch C17th Country House, *Capel Garmon, Betws-Y-Coed, North Wales, LL26 0RL.* Peaceful. 2 miles from picturesque Betws-y-Coed. Clear views of Snowdonia. **Open:** All year (not Xmas) **01690 710261** Eirian Ifan *eirianifan@talk21.com* www.croeso-betws.org.uk/acc/bb/llangoch.htm **D:** Fr £20.00–£25.00 **S:** Fr £25.00–£28.00 **Beds:** 3D **Baths:** 3 En (8) (3)

Colwyn Bay

SH8479

Marine Hotel, *West Promenade, Colwyn Bay, LL28 4BP.* Superbly situated seafront hotel offering spacious comfortable ensuite accommodation. **Open:** Easter to Oct **Grades:** WTB 3 Star, AA 2 Star **01492 530295 & 08701 689400 (M)** Mr & Mrs Owen *reservations@marinehotel.co.uk* www.marinehotel.co.uk **D:** Fr £26.00 **S:** Fr £26.00–£31.00 **Beds:** 1F 6D 4T 3S **Baths:** 12 En 2 Pr (10) **cc**

Holly Tree Guest House, *11 Marine Road, Colwyn Bay, LL29 8PH.* Friendly comfortable Victorian house. Modern facilities. Central to everywhere. Parking. **Open:** All year (not Xmas) **01492 533254** Mr Ross **Fax: 01492 532332** *ross@nationwideisp.net* www.avaweb.co.uk/hollytree **D:** Fr £20.00 **S:** Fr £25.00 **Beds:** 2F 4D 3T **Baths:** 9 En (12) **cc**

Cabin Hill Hotel, *College Avenue, Colwyn Bay, LL28 4NT.* Quiet residential area within easy working distance to promenade & shops. **Open:** All year (not Xmas/New Year) **01492 544568** Mrs Ashton **D:** Fr £18.00 **S:** Fr £18.00 **Beds:** 2F 3T 3D 2S **Baths:** 7 En 2 Sh (2)

Edelweiss Hotel, *Lawson Road, Colwyn Bay, LL29 8HD.* C19th house, wooded garden, a slice of countryside by the sea. **Open:** All year **01492 532314** Mr Baker **Fax: 01492 534707** www.hotelvenues.com/edelweiss **D:** Fr £21.00 **S:** Fr £21.00 **Beds:** 4F 10T 10D 3S **Baths:** 27 En (25) **cc**

St Margaret's Hotel, *Princes Drive, Colwyn Bay, LL29 8RP.* Recommended by Which? Good Bed and Breakfast Guide. We are dedicated to the well-being of our guests. We provide excellent food & comfortable bedrooms all with ensuite facilities. Ground floor accommodation available. Own car park. A 'particularly pleasant place to stay'. **Open:** All year **01492 532718** *stmargarets@hotelcb.fsnet.co.uk* www.st-margarets-hotel.co.uk **D:** Fr £21.00–£25.00 **S:** Fr £21.00–£25.00 **Beds:** 1F 5D 3T 2S **Baths:** 11 En (10) **cc**

Llysfaen House, *58 Llysfaen Road, Colwyn Bay, LL29 9HB.* Magnificent sea views. Lovely house. Warm welcome. Good home cooking. Cleanliness assured. **Open:** All year **01492 517859** Mr & Mrs Hooker *views@compuserve.com* **D:** Fr £18.00–£20.00 **S:** Fr £18.00–£20.00 **Beds:** 1T 1D 1S **Baths:** 1 Sh (2)

Conwy

SH7777

Fishermore, *Llanrwst Road, Conwy, LL32 8HP.* Rural setting close to historic town, NT gardens and mountains. **Open:** Easter to Oct **01492 592891** Mrs Dyer *dyers@tesco.net* www.northwalesbandb.co.uk **D:** Fr £19.00–£22.00 **Beds:** 1T 2D 1F **Baths:** 2 En 1 Pr (5)

Henllys Farm, *Llechwedd, Conwy, Gwynedd, LL32 8DJ.* Ideally placed for touring Snowdonia, North Wales coast, Bodnant Gardens. **Open:** Easter to Nov **Grades:** WTB 3 Star Farm **01492 593269** C Roberts **D:** Fr £18.00–£20.00 **S:** Fr £25.00 **Beds:** 1F 1D **Baths:** 2 En

Glan Heulog Guest House, *Llanrwst Road, Conwy, LL32 8LT.* Warm welcome, comfortable beds & a hearty breakfast in a fine Victorian house. **Open:** All year **01492 593845** Mr & Mrs Watson-Jones **D:** Fr £15.00–£20.00 **S:** Fr £18.00–£24.00 **Beds:** 2F 2D 2T **Baths:** 5 En 1 Pr (7) **cc**

Bryn Derwen, *Woodlands, Conwy, LL32 8LT.* Warm welcome to a gracious Victorian home with panoramic views. **Open:** All year **01492 596134** Mr & Mrs Smith **D:** Fr £18.00–£20.00 **S:** Fr £18.00–£25.00 **Beds:** 1F 2D 3T **Baths:** 6 En (8)

Criccieth

SH4938

Mor Heli Guest House, *Min Y Mor, Criccieth, LL52 0EF.* On sea front overlooking 100 miles of coastline. All bedrooms sea views. **Open:** All year (not Xmas) **01766 522802 & 01766 522878** **D:** Fr £22.00 **S:** Fr £25.00 **Beds:** 2F 2D 1T **Baths:** 5 Pr

Awel Mor Hotel, *29 Marine Terrace, Criccieth, LL52 0EL.* Spectacular sea views. An ideal base for touring Snowdonia/Lleyn Peninsula. **Open:** Mar to Nov **01766 522086 (also fax)** Mr & Mrs Petch *sue.petch@virgin.net* www.cricciethaccommodation.com **D:** Fr £21.00–£25.00 **S:** Fr £21.00–£25.00 **Beds:** 3F 2T 2D 2S **Baths:** 8 En 1 Pr **cc**

Min y Gaer, *Porthmadog Road, Criccieth, North West Wales, LL52 0HP.* Comfortable hotel with delightful coastal views. Ideal for touring Snowdonia. **Open:** Easter to Oct **Grades:** WTB 2 Star, AA 4 Diamond, RAC 4 Diamond **01766 522151** Mrs Williamson **Fax: 01766 523540** *info@minygaer.co.uk* www.minygaer.co.uk **D:** Fr £24.00–£26.00 **S:** Fr £24.00–£34.00 **Beds:** 3F 4D 2T 1S **Baths:** 10 En (12) **cc**

Bron Rhiw Hotel, *Caernarfon Road, Criccieth, LL52 0AP.* Cosy, comfortable non-smoking hotel; a truly warm welcome awaits you. **Open:** Mar to Nov **01766 522257** Ms Woodhouse & Ms S C Williams **D:** Fr £22.50–£26.00 **S:** Fr £22.50–£26.00 **Beds:** 7D 1T 1F **Baths:** 7 En 2 Pr (4) **cc**

Dinas Mawddwy

SH8514

The Red Lion Inn, *Dinas-Mawddwy, Machynlleth, Powys, SY20 9JA.* Centuries-old traditional inn. In heart of village amid scenic beauty of southern Snowdonia. **Open:** All year (not Xmas) **01650 531247 (also fax)** Mr Jenkins *rob@llewcoch.co.uk* www.llewcoch.freeserve.co.uk **D:** Fr £20.00–£25.00 **S:** Fr £20.00–£25.00 **Beds:** 3F 1D 1T 1S **Baths:** 3 En 1 Sh (30)

Dolgellau

SH7217

Trem Idris, *Llanelltyd, Dolgellau, LL40 2TB.* **Open:** All year **01341 423776** Ms Jones **D:** Fr £20.00–£23.00 **S:** Fr £25.00–£30.00 **Beds:** 1F 1D **Baths:** 2 En (3) (4)
Homely guest house situated in an elevated position overlooking the beautiful Mawddach estuary. One family ensuite and one double ensuite with own lounge. Both with colour TV, tea/coffee facilities. Ideally situated for exploring the coast and also Snowdonia. Non-smokers, please.

Maesneuadd Farm, *Llanfachreth, Dolgellau, LL40 2DH.* **Open:** All year **Grades:** WTB 3 Star **01341 450256** Mrs Smith **D:** Fr £19.00–£22.00 **S:** Fr £25.00 **Beds:** 1F 1T 1D **Baths:** 3 En (3) (6)
Situated in a peaceful Area of Outstanding Natural Beauty, our 200 year old farmhouse offers excellent accommodation in a friendly relaxing atmosphere. We are surrounded by gardens, flower meadow and woodland with streams and waterfalls and have breathtaking mountain views.

Fronallt, *Dolgellau, LL40 2YL.* Listed cottage, large conservatory, edge of town, mountain views. Orchard/lawns. **Open:** All year (not Xmas/New Year) **01341 422296 & 01341 422286 & 07751 514261 (M)** Mrs Price **Fax: 01341 422286** **D:** Fr £20.00–£25.00 **S:** Fr £20.00–£25.00 **Beds:** 1T 1F **Baths:** 1 En 1 Pr

Tanyfron, *Arran Road, Dolgellau, LL40 2AA.* Modernised, former stone farmhouse, beautiful views. 'Wales in Bloom' Winners 2000. **Open:** Feb to Nov **01341 422638** Mrs Rowlands **Fax: 01341 421251** *rowlands@tanyfron.freeserve.co.uk* www.tanyfron.co.uk **D:** Fr £20.00–£22.50 **Beds:** 1D 2T **Baths:** 3 En (5) (6)

Ivy House, *Finsbury Square, Dolgellau, North West Wales, LL40 1RF.* Attractive country town guest house, good home-made food. **Open:** All year **01341 422535** Mrs Bamford **Fax: 01341 422689** *marg.bamford@btconnect.com* www.ukworld.net/ivyhouse **D:** Fr £19.00–£25.00 **S:** Fr £25.00–£35.00 **Beds:** 1F 3D 2T **Baths:** 3 En 2 Sh **cc**

Arosfyr Farm, *Penycefn Road, Dolgellau, North West Wales, LL40 2YP.* Homely friendly farmhouse, flower gardens, mountainous views, self-catering available. **Open:** All year **01341 422355** Mrs Skeel Jones **D:** Fr £17.00–£18.50 **S:** Fr £19.00–£21.00 **Beds:** 1F 1D 1T **Baths:** 2 Sh (4)

Esgair Wen Newydd, *Garreg Feurig, Llanfachreth Road, Dolgellau, LL40 2YA.* Bungalow, mountain views. Relaxed atmosphere. High standards. Double Award Winners. **Open:** Mar to Nov **Grades:** WTB 3 Star **01341 423952** Mrs Westwood **D:** Fr £19.50 **S:** Fr £21.50 **Beds:** 2D 1T **Baths:** 1 Sh (3) (3)

Gwelafon, *Caedeintur, Dolgellau, Gwynedd, North Wales, LL40 2YS.* Beautiful, high-standard, spacious house. Panoramic views of town and mountains. **Open:** Mar to Oct **Grades:** WTB 3 Star **01341 422634** Mrs Roberts **D:** Fr £20.00–£25.00 **S:** Fr £20.00–£22.00 **Beds:** 1D/T 2S **Baths:** 1 En 1 Sh (7) (3)

Dolgun Uchaf, *Dolgellau, LL40 2AB.* Perfectly situated for exploring beautiful Snowdonia National Park. Warm welcome, farmhouse breakfast. **Open:** All year **01341 422269 Fax: 01341 422285** *dolgunuchaf@guesthousessnowdonia.com* www.guesthousessnowdonia.com **D:** Fr £18.00–£22.00 **S:** Fr £18.00–£25.00 **Beds:** 1F 1T 1D **Baths:** 3 En **cc**

Aber Cottage, *Smithfield Street, Dolgellau, LL40 1DE.* Cosy market town stone cottage (1811) foot of Cader - comfortable welcoming hospitality. **Open:** All year **01341 422460 & 07885 547052 (M)** Mrs Mullin *gmullini@compuserve.com* **D:** Fr £18.00–£20.00 **S:** Fr £18.50–£25.00 **Beds:** 1F 2D 1T 2S **Baths:** 2 En 1 Pr 2 Sh

Please respect a B&B's wishes regarding children, animals and smoking

Dolwyddelan

SH7352

Rhiw Goch, *Pont y Pant, Dolwyddelan, LL25 0PQ.* **Open:** All year (not Xmas/New Year) **01690 750231** Mrs King **D:** Fr £22.00 **S:** Fr £22.00 **Beds:** 3D **Baths:** 2 Sh (4)
A warm welcome awaits you in our comfortable, lovely C17th longhouse. Set in 35 acres with wonderful gardens and marvellous views over Lledr Valley. Perfect for total relaxation and walking, exploring Snowdonia, coastline, castles, Bodnant Gardens, Portmeirion. Choice of traditional or Continental breakfasts.

Bryn Tirion Farm, *Dolwyddelan, LL25 0JD.* C12th Dolwyddelan Castle, 100 yards on the farm, picturesque Lledr Valley. **Open:** All year (not Xmas/New Year) **Grades:** WTB 2 Star **01690 750366** Mrs Price **D:** Fr £25.00 **S:** Fr £25.00 **Beds:** 1F 1D 1T **Baths:** 2 En 1 Pr (12)

Dwygyfylchi

SH7377

Caerlyr Hall Hotel, *Conwy Old Road, Dwygyfylchi, Penmaenmawr, LL34 6SW.* Country house set in natural amphitheatre with sea & mountain views. **Open:** All year **01492 623518** Mr & Mrs Warner **Fax: 01492 622070** www.caerlyrhallhotel.co.uk **D:** Fr £25.00–£30.00 **S:** Fr £25.00–£30.00 **Beds:** 5F 1D 3T **Baths:** 8 En 1 Pr (12) **cc**

Dyffryn Ardudwy

SH5822

Parc yr Onnen, *Dyffryn Ardudwy, Gwnedd, LL44 2DU.* Rural setting; superb sea and mountain views by peaceful lane. **Open:** All year **01341 247033** Mr & Mrs Bethell **D:** Fr £18.00–£20.00 **S:** Fr £20.00 **Beds:** 1D 1T **Baths:** 2 En (3)

National Grid References given are for villages, towns and cities – not for individual houses

Ffestiniog

SH7041

Cae'r Blaidd Country House, *Llan Ffestiniog, Blaenau Ffestiniog, Gwynedd, LL41 4PH.* Secluded tranquil refurbished Victorian country house with panoramic mountain views. **Open:** All year **Grades:** WTB 4 Star **01766 762765 (also fax)** *info@caerblaidd.fsnet.co.uk* www.caerblaidd.fsnet.co.uk **D:** Fr £30.00 **S:** Fr £38.00 **Beds:** 3F **Baths:** 2 En 1 Pr (6)

Friog

SH6112

Einion House, *Friog, Fairbourne, North West Wales, LL38 2NX.* Lovely old house in marvellous walking country. Good home cooking. **Open:** All year (not Xmas/New Year) **01341 250644** Mr Waterhouse *enquiries@einionhouse.freeserve.co.uk* **D:** Fr £20.50 **S:** Fr £22.00–£27.50 **Beds:** 4D 1T 1S **Baths:** 4 En 2 Pr

Gellilydan

SH6839 *Bryn Arms*

Tyddyn Du Farm, *Gellilydan, Blaenau Ffestiniog, Gwynedd, LL41 4RB.* Superb central location. Spectacular scenery. Converted barn and stable suites. **Open:** All year **01766 590281** Ms Williams *stil@snowdonia.farm.com* www.snowdonia.farm.com **D:** Fr £23.00–£35.00 **S:** Fr £25.00 (10)

Gwynfryn, *Gellilydan, Blaenau Ffestiniog, LL41 4EA.* Detached house with character in a small village. Friendly welcome. **Open:** All year **01766 590225** Mrs Jones **D:** Fr £17.00–£18.00 **Beds:** 1T 1D **Baths:** 1 Sh

Glan-yr-afon (Druid)

SJ0242

Llawr-Betws Farm, *Glan-yr-afon, Corwen, LL21 0HD.* Modern, comfortable farmhouse. **Open:** All year **01490 460224** Mr Jones **D:** Fr £15.00 **S:** Fr £10.00 **Beds:** 3F 2D 1S **Baths:** 2 Pr (2)

Glan-yr-afon (Fron-goch)

SH9040

The Old Post Office, *Glan-yr-afon, Corwen, Gwynedd, LL21 0HB.* 7 miles Bala Lake. Incorporating North Wales's only dedicated teddy bear shop. **Open:** All year **01490 460231 (also fax)** H J Jennings **D:** Fr £18.00–£19.50 **S:** Fr £16.00–£19.50 **Beds:** 1F 1D 1T 1S **Baths:** 2 En 1 Sh (2)

Harlech

SH5831

Maes yr Hebog, *Heol y Bryn, Harlech, Gwynedd, LL46 2TU.* Quality bungalow accommodation, great food, spectacular views, mountains and coast. **Open:** Mar to Oct **Grades:** WTB 5 Star **01766 780885** Mr & Mrs Clark www.harlechholidays.co.uk **D:** Fr £23.00–£25.00 **S:** Fr £38.00–£43.00 **Beds:** 2D **Baths:** 2 En (2)

Gwrach Ynys Country Guest House, *Ynys, Talsarnau, North West Wales, LL47 6TS.* Edwardian country house, tranquil rural setting, close sea & mountains in Snowdonia NP. **Open:** Mar to Nov **01766 780742** Mrs Williams **Fax: 01766 781199** *gwynfor@btinternet.com* www.grwachynys.co.uk **D:** Fr £23.00–£28.00 **S:** Fr £30.00–£35.00 **Beds:** 2F 2D 2T 1S **Baths:** 6 En (8)

Tyddyn Y Gwynt, *Harlech, LL46 2TH.* Perfect setting for peaceful holidays; warm welcome, tourist attractions, mountain scenery, beaches. Car essential. **Open:** All year **01766 780298** Mrs Jones **D:** Fr £16.00 **S:** Fr £16.00–£18.00 **Beds:** 1F 1D 1T 1S **Baths:** 1 Sh (8)

Llanbedr

SH5826

Cae Nest Hall Country House Hotel, *Llanbedr, LL45 2NL.* C15th Welsh manor in the magnificent Snowdonia National Park. **Open:** Feb to Nov **Grades:** WTB 3 Star, AA 2 Star **01341 241349 (also fax)** *cae-nest@orbix.uk.net* www.smoothhound.co.uk/hotels/caenest.html **D:** Fr £29.00–£39.50 **S:** Fr £39.00–£54.50 **Beds:** 2F 1T 6D 1S **Baths:** 10 En (10)

Planning a longer stay? Always ask for any special rates

Llanbedr-y-cennin

SH7569

Waen Newydd, *Llanbedr-y-Cennin, Conwy, Gwynedd, LL32 8UR.* Secluded C19th farmhouse. Spacious grounds high above village in open countryside. **Open:** All year **01492 660527** Ms Jeffries **Fax: 01492 660155** *pauline@jeffries.fsnet.co.uk* www.waen-newydd.co.uk **D:** Fr £20.00 **S:** Fr £25.00 **Beds:** 1T **Baths:** 1 En

Llanberis

SH5760

Lake View Hotel, *Tan Y Pant, Llanberis, Caernarfon, LL55 4EL.* **Open:** All year **Grades:** WTB 2 Star, AA 2 Star **01286 870422** Mr & Mrs Sims **Fax: 01286 872591** *reception@lakeviewhotel.com* www.lakeviewhotel.co.uk **D:** Fr £24.00–£34.00 **S:** Fr £30.00–£35.00 **Beds:** 3F 2T 5D **Baths:** 9 En 1 Pr (30) **cc** Welsh country cottage hotel in stunning location, overlooking Lake Padarn and mountains. Many visitor amenities in nearby Llanberis. Warm & cosy hotel, candlelit restaurant with choice of menus & full Welsh breakfast. Meetings room. 'Taste of Wales' accredited. Four-poster beds some rooms.

Mount Pleasant Hotel, *High Street, Llanberis, Caernarfon, LL55 4HA.* Friendly, family-run, foot of Snowdon. Cosy bar, real ale. **Open:** All year **01286 870395 (also fax)** Mrs Waterton *mph@waterton.org.uk* www.waterton.org.uk **D:** Fr £18.00–£22.00 **S:** Fr £18.00–£25.00 **Beds:** 2F 3D 1T 2S **Baths:** 1 En 2 Sh (8)

Beech Bank Guest House, *High Street, Llanberis, Caernarfon, LL55 4EN.* Small friendly lake and mountain views, close to all amenities. **Open:** All year (not Xmas) **01286 870414** Mrs Watson **D:** Fr £17.00 **S:** Fr £17.50 **Beds:** 1F 2D 1T **Baths:** 1 Sh (6)

Marteg, *High Street, Llanberis, Caernarfon, Gwynedd, LL55 4HA.* Within walking distance of Snowdon mountain railway and all amenities. **Open:** Jan to Dec **01286 870207** Mr & Mrs Torr *carol@marteg.freeserve.co.uk* **D:** Fr £22.00–£25.00 **S:** Fr £22.00–£25.00 **Beds:** 2D 1T **Baths:** 3 En (4)

Llandanwg

SH5628

Glan-Y-Gors, *Llandanwg, Harlech, LL46 2SD.* 3 star small guest house near beach, with panoramic views. **Open:** All year
01341 241410 G Evans **D:** Fr £18.00–£19.00 **S:** Fr £19.00

Llandudno

SH7881

Crickleigh Isaf, *37 Lloyd Street, Llandudno, LL30 2YG.* **Open:** All year (not Xmas/New Year)
01492 870271 Mrs Clark-Jones www.crickleighisaf.co.uk **D:** Fr £18.00–£22.00 **S:** Fr £18.00–£22.00 **Beds:** 1T 3D 2S **Baths:** 2 En 2 Pr (10)
Lovingly restored over the last two years, the atmosphere is welcoming, the bedrooms are attractively decorated, have hospitality trays, colour television, bathrobes, hairdryer, new beds and furnishings. Relax in our guest lounge and dine in the elegant dining room.

Hotel Carmen, *4 Carmen Sylva Road, Llandudno, LL30 1LZ.* **Open:** All year
01492 876361 Mr Felton *thehotelcarmen@aol.com* www.hotel-carmen-llandudno.co.uk **D:** Fr £19.50–£25.00 **S:** Fr £19.50–£25.00 **Beds:** 2F 7D 2T 3S **Baths:** 14 En
Hotel Carmen is a non-smoking family-run residence, superbly situated only 100 yds from the promenade. A few minutes from Llandudno town centre, near to theatre/conference centre. Ample parking. Ideal for touring North Wales and its many attractions. Special breaks throughout year.

Karden House Hotel, *16 Charlton Street, Llandudno, LL30 2AA.* Pleasant clean and comfortable family-run hotel. Close to beach, shops, train and coach stations. Vegetarian diets available. **Open:** All year **Grades:** WTB 2 Diamond, RAC 2 Diamond
01492 879347 (also fax) E D & J M Sides *technical@comset.fsnet.co.uk* **D:** Fr £15.00–£17.50 **S:** Fr £15.00–£16.00 **Beds:** 4F 4D 2S **Baths:** 6 En 1 Sh 1 Pr

The Sunningdale, *59 Church Walks, Llandudno, Ll30 2HL.* Superior accommodation with lovely gardens and views. Walk to town and promenade. **Open:** All year (not Xmas/New Year)
01492 875915 (also fax) www.sunningdalebandb.co.uk **D:** Fr £25.00–£32.50 **S:** Fr £35.00–£40.00 **Beds:** 1T 5D **Baths:** 6 En (6)

Hotel Carmen, *4 Carmen Sylva Road, Llandudno, LL30 1LZ.* Non-smoking family-run residence, superbly situated only 100 yds from the promenade. **Open:** All year
01492 876361 Mr Felton *thehotelcarmen@aol.com* www.hotel-carmen-llandudno.co.uk **D:** Fr £19.50–£25.00 **S:** Fr £19.50–£25.00 **Beds:** 2F 7D 2T 3S **Baths:** 14 En

White Lodge Hotel, *Central Promenade, Llandudno, LL30 1AT.* Conveniently-situated, beautifully furnished luxury hotel overlooking sea. Friendly atmosphere. **Open:** All year **Grades:** WTB 3 Star, AA 2 Star
01492 877713 Mr Rigby *whitelodgehotel@llandudno500.fsnet.co.uk* **D:** Fr £28.00–£31.00 **Beds:** 2F 6D 4T **Baths:** 12 Pr (5) (12)

Hafod y Mor Hotel, *Hill Terrace, Llandudno, LL30 2LS.* High quality accommodation, fantastic views, ideal base for Snowdonia/Anglesey. **Open:** All year
01492 876925 www.hafodymor.co.uk **D:** Fr £25.00 **S:** Fr £25.00 **Beds:** 2F 1T 5D 2S **Baths:** 10 En (4)

No. 9 Guest House, *9 Chapel Street, Llandudno, LL30 2SY.* Friendly family-run guest house in a town centre location. **Open:** All year (not Xmas)
01492 877251 *numbernine@34gg.freeserve.co.uk* **D:** Fr £15.00–£19.00 **S:** Fr £15.00–£25.00 **Beds:** 4F 2D 1T 1S **Baths:** 4 En 3 Sh 3

Planning a longer stay? Always ask for any special rates

The Grafton Hotel, *Promenade, Craig y Don, Llandudno, North West Wales, LL30 1BG.* Only 5 mins' walk from North Wales Theatre and Conference Centre. **Open:** All year (not Xmas/New Year)
01492 876814 Derek Griffiths **Fax: 01492 879073** *derek@thegraftonhotel.com* www.hotellink.co.uk/llandudno/grafton.html **D:** Fr £20.00–£28.00 **S:** Fr £22.00–£28.00 **Beds:** 2F 10D 5T 5S **Baths:** 22 Pr (12) 1

Stoneleigh Guest House, *10 St David Road, Llandudno, LL30 2UL.* Family-run seaside guest house offering good home cooking. **Open:** All year
01492 875056 Mr & Mrs Roberts **D:** Fr £20.00–£22.00 **S:** Fr £25.00–£27.00 **Beds:** 1F 1T 2D **Baths:** 4 En (6)

Ty Glandwr, *42 St Mary's Road, Llandudno, Gwynedd, LL30 2UE.* Elegant Edwardian town house, convenient public transport, theatre, castles, Snowdonia. **Open:** All year (not Xmas/New Year)
01492 871802 Mrs Beesley *tyglandwr@talk21.com* **D:** Fr £19.00–£25.00 **S:** Fr £22.00–£25.00 **Beds:** 1T 2D 1S **Baths:** 3 En 1 Pr

Dolwen Guest House, *7 St Mary's Road, Llandudno, LL30 2UB.* A warm welcome awaits you at Dolwen, which is a very comfortable Edwardian house. We are situated in the town centre within easy reach of beach, shops and theatre. Llandudno is ideally situated for exploring Snowdonia and North Wales. **Open:** Mar to Nov
01492 877757 *david.kyffin@tesco.net* **D:** Fr £18.00–£20.00 **Beds:** 1F 1T 1D **Baths:** 1 En 1 Pr 1 Sh

Ashdale Guest House, *3 St Davids Road, Llandudno, LL30 2UL.* Halfway between North and West Shores, ideal for exploring Llandudno. **Open:** All year (not Xmas/New Year)
01492 877089 *bnbmccann@lineone.net* **D:** Fr £19.00–£22.00 **S:** Fr £19.00–£22.00 **Beds:** 2F 2T 4D 1S **Baths:** 7 En 2 Sh (4) (3)

Llanegryn

SH6005

Cefn Coch Country Guest House, *Llanegryn, Tywyn, LL36 9SD.* High-quality accommodation. Spectacular views, peaceful. Birdwatching, walking, cycling, touring. **Open:** Mar to Oct
01654 712193 (also fax) Mrs Sylvester *david@cefncoch.force9.co.uk* www.cefncoch.force9.co.uk **D:** Fr £22.00–£25.00 **S:** Fr £25.00–£28.00 **Beds:** 2D 3T **Baths:** 3 En 2 Sh (11)

Llanelltyd

SH7119

Trem Idris, *Llanelltyd, Dolgellau, LL40 2TB.* Homely guest house situated in an elevated position overlooking the beautiful Mawddach estuary. **Open:** All year **01341 423776** Ms Jones **D:** Fr £20.00–£23.00 **S:** Fr £25.00–£30.00 **Beds:** 1F 1D **Baths:** 2 En (3) P (4) TV V

Llanfachreth

SH7522

Maesneuadd Farm, *Llanfachreth, Dolgellau, LL40 2DH.* 200-year-old farmhouse offering excellent accommodation in a friendly relaxing atmosphere. **Open:** All year **Grades:** WTB 3 Star **01341 450256** Mrs Smith **D:** Fr £19.00–£22.00 **S:** Fr £25.00 **Beds:** 1F 1T 1D **Baths:** 3 En (3) P (6) TV V

Llanfaglan

SH4760

The White House, *Llanfaglan, Caernarfon, LL54 5RA.* Quiet, isolated country house. Magnificent views to mountains and sea. **Open:** Mar to Nov **01286 673003** Mr Bayles *rwbayles@sjms.co.uk* **D:** Fr £21.00–£23.00 **S:** Fr £27.00 **Beds:** 2D 2T **Baths:** 3 En 1 Pr P (8) TV

Llanfairfechan

SH6874

Rhiwiau Riding Centre, *Llanfairfechan, LL33 0EH.* Magnificent views of mountains and sea; riding and walking. **Open:** All year (not Xmas) **01248 680094** Mrs Hill **Fax: 01248 681143** *rhiwiau@aol.com* www.rhiwiau.co.uk **D:** Fr £15.00–£16.50 **S:** Fr £15.00–£16.50 **Beds:** 1F 1D 4T 1S **Baths:** 3 Sh P (12) TV × V

Llanfihangel Glyn Myfyr

SH9949

The Old Rectory, *Llanfihangel Glyn Myfyr, Cerrigydrudion, Corwen, LL21 9UN.* Luxury rural retreat in idyllic surroundings. Perfectly situated for exploring N. Wales. **Open:** All year (not Xmas) **Grades:** WTB 3 Star **01490 420568 & 07850 241795** Mr & Mrs Hughes **Fax: 01490 420773** **D:** Fr £26.00–£30.00 **S:** Fr £26.00–£30.00 **Beds:** 2F **Baths:** 1 En 1 Pr P (3) TV V

Llanfor

SH9336

Melin Meloch (Water Mill) Guest House, *Llanfor, Bala, Gwynedd, LL23 7DP.* One of the most picturesque buildings and water gardens in this area. **Open:** All year **01678 520101** B M Gunn *theoldmill@mac.com* www.melin.co.uk **D:** Fr £20.00–£25.00 **S:** Fr £36.00–£42.00 **Beds:** 1F 3D 2T 2S **Baths:** 4 En 2 Pr 1 Sh (4) P (10) TV V

Llangower

SH9032

Plas Gower, *Llangower, Bala, LL23 7BY.* A warm welcome in an old stone house, beautiful views over Bala Lake, mountains. **Open:** All year (not Xmas) **01678 520431 (also fax)** Mrs Foreman *olwen@plasgower.com* **D:** Fr £19.50–£21.00 **S:** Fr £20.00–£22.00 **Beds:** 1D 1T **Baths:** 1 En 1 Pr P (4) TV V

Llangwnnadl

SH2033

Carrog Farm, *Llangwnnadl, Pwllheli, Gwynedd, LL53 7NL.* Set in beautiful farmland with the sea visible across fields. **Open:** Easter to Oct **01758 770694** Mrs Thomas **D:** Fr £18.00–£20.00 **S:** Fr £18.00–£20.00 **Beds:** 3F 1T 1D 1S **Baths:** 2 Sh TV ×

Llanrwst

SH7961

Nant-Y-Glyn Isaf, *Llanrwst, Gwynedd, LL26 0NN.* Working farm. Spacious, well-appointed rooms. Magnificent views, quiet location. **Open:** All year **01492 640327 (also fax)** Mrs Evans *maievans@farmwales.co.uk* **D:** Fr £19.50–£25.00 **Beds:** 1F 1D 1T **Baths:** 3 En (8) P TV V

Argoed Guest House, *Crafnant Road, Trefriw, Conwy, LL27 0TX.* Comfortable old-fashioned house. Beautiful views of Conwy Valley. Easy access to mountains & coast. **Open:** All year **Grades:** WTB 3 Star **01492 640091** Mr & Mrs Phillips *keithandanne@tiscali.co.uk* www.argoed.co.uk **D:** Fr £21.00 **S:** Fr £29.00 **Beds:** 2D 1T **Baths:** 3 En P (5) TV **cc**

Planning a longer stay? Always ask for any special rates

Llansannan

SH9366

Cleiriach, *Llansannan, Denbigh, Conwy, LL16 5LW.* Beautiful scenery, quiet and peaceful location. Room only available. **Open:** All year (not Xmas/New Year) **01745 870695** Mrs Williams *katycleiriach@aol.com* **D:** Fr £15.00–£22.00 **S:** Fr £15.00–£22.00 **Beds:** 1T 1D **Baths:** 1 Sh P (2) TV × V

Llanuwchllyn

SH8730

Eifionydd, *Llanuwchllyn, Bala, LL23 7UB.* Beautiful location; warm welcome. Enjoy your vacation in well-appointed rooms. **Open:** Easter to Oct **01678 540622 (also fax)** Mr & Mrs Murray *eifionydd@ntlworld.com* www.eifionydd.com **D:** Fr £20.00–£22.00 **S:** Fr £25.00–£27.00 **Beds:** 1F 1T 1D **Baths:** 3 En P TV V

Llanycil

SH9134

Abercelyn Guest House, *Llanycil, Bala, Gwynedd, LL23 7YF.* Georgian residence set in landscaped gardens overlooking Bala Lake. **Open:** All year (not Xmas/New Year) **01678 521109** Mrs Hind **D:** Fr £22.50–£26.50 **S:** Fr £25.00–£28.00 **Beds:** 2F 1T 1D **Baths:** 2 En 1 Pr P (4) TV V **cc**

Llechwedd

SH7676

Henllys Farm, *Llechwedd, Conwy, Gwynedd, LL32 8DJ.* Ideally placed for touring Snowdonia, North Wales coast, Bodnant Gardens. **Open:** Easter to Nov **Grades:** WTB 3 Star Farm **01492 593269** C Roberts **D:** Fr £18.00–£20.00 **S:** Fr £25.00 **Beds:** 1F 1D **Baths:** 2 En P TV ×

RATES

D = Price range per person sharing in a double or twin room

S = Price range for a single room

Maenan

SH7965

Plas Maenan Country House Hotel, *Maenan, Llanrwst, Gwynedd, LL26 0YR.*
Open: All year **Grades:** WTB 2 Star
01492 660232 Fax: 01492 660551 *gillinghams@plasmaenan.fsnet.co.uk* www.plas-maenan-hotel.co.uk **D:** Fr £25.00–£45.00 **S:** Fr £35.00–£55.00 **Beds:** 2F 5D 6T **Baths:** 13 En
With spectacular views of Snowdonia, this Victorian country house stands in extensive grounds in a sunny, elevated position overlooking the Conwy valley. Conservatory restaurant, elegant lounge & cosy bar with open fires. Short breaks throughout the year.

Maentwrog

SH6640

The Old Rectory Hotel, *Maentwrog, Blaenau Ffestiniog, LL41 4HN.* Main house/budget annexe, 3 acre garden. Informal, peaceful. **Open:** All year (not Xmas)
01766 590305 (also fax) Ms Herbert **D:** Fr £22.50–£32.50 **S:** Fr £30.00–£45.00 **Beds:** 2F 6D 2T **Baths:** 10 En

Manod

SH7244

Cae Du, *Manod, Blaenau Ffestiniog, Gwynedd, LL41 4BB.* Picturesque C16th former farmhouse in magnificent mountain setting. **Open:** All year (not Xmas/New Year)
01766 830847 & 07808 090549 (M) S Ashe **Fax: 01766 830847** *caedu@tinyworld.co.uk* **D:** Fr £24.00 **S:** Fr £24.00 **Beds:** 1T 2D **Baths:** 3 En (4)

Morfa Nefyn

SH2840 *Cliffs Inn*

Llys Olwen Guest House, *Morfa Nefyn, Pwllheli, LL53 6BT.* Established 1972. Approximately 500 metres from beautiful cliff walks. **Open:** Mar to Nov
01758 720493 (also fax) *llysolwen@beeb.net* www.llysolwen.co.uk **D:** Fr £21.50 **S:** Fr £21.50 **Beds:** 4F 2T 2D **Baths:** 4 Sh

Mynytho

SH3030

Paradwys, *Mynytho, Pwllheli, Gwynedd, LL53 7SA.* Lovely sea and mountain views. Peaceful ideal walking, golfing, brochure **Open:** All year (not Xmas/New Year)
01758 740876 (also fax) Mrs Roberts **D:** Fr £20.00 **Beds:** 1D **Baths:** 1P (1)

Nant Peris

SH6058

Tyn y Ffynnon, *Nant Peris, Caernarfon, Gwynedd, LL55 4UH.* Beautiful spacious cottage set in 2 acres below Llanberis pass. **Open:** All year (not Xmas/New Year)
01286 871723 Mrs Kelly **D:** Fr £18.00–£20.00 **S:** Fr £20.00–£22.00 **Beds:** 1F 1T 2D **Baths:** 1 Pr 1 Sh (6)

Nantgwynant

SH6250

Pen-Y-Gwryd Hotel, *Nantgwynant, Caernarfon, LL55 4NT.* Famous mountain inn, heart of Snowdonia. Associated with Lord Hunt's Everest team (1953). **Open:** Mar to Nov
01286 870211 Mrs Pullee **D:** Fr £23.00–£28.00 **S:** Fr £33.00–£38.00 **Beds:** 16F 6T 9D 1S **Baths:** 5 En 5 Pr 5 Sh (30)

Nantmor

SH6046

Cwm Caeth, *Nantmor, Caernarfon, Gwynedd, LL55 4YH.* **Open:** All year (not Xmas/New Year) **Grades:** WTB 3 Star
01766 890408 Gay & Tim Harvey *timharvey@ukonline.co.uk* **D:** Fr £22.00–£25.00 **S:** Fr £30.00 **Beds:** 1D **Baths:** 1 En
Typical Welsh farmhouse in Snowdonia, with magnificent views, off the beaten track. Ideal for touring/hiking. Near to Snowdon and Welsh Highland Railway. Comfortable accommodation including own sitting room and access. 2 miles from Beddgelert. 6 miles from Porthmadog. Telephone for brochure.

Pant-glas

SH4747

Hen Ysgol Old School Pant-glas, *Bwlch Derwin, Pant-glas, Garndolbenmaen, LL51 9EQ.* Beautiful mid-C19th Welsh country school. Perfectly situated for the attractions of Snowdonia. **Open:** All year
01286 660701 T J Gibbins *oldschoolpantglas@talk21.com* **D:** Fr £17.00–£20.00 **S:** Fr £20.00–£25.00 **Beds:** 2F 1D 1T **Baths:** 1 En 1 Sh (6)

Penmaenmawr

SH7176

Bodlwyfan, *Conwy Road, Penmaenmawr, LL34 6BL.* Beautiful Victorian house, overlooking the sea and mountains in quiet location. **Open:** All year
01492 623506 Mr Anderton *bodlwyfan@totalise.co.uk* www.bodlwyfan.co.uk **D:** Fr £17.50–£20.00 **S:** Fr £18.00–£21.00 **Beds:** 1F 3T 2D 1S **Baths:** 2 Sh (6)

Pennal

SH6900

Marchlyn, *Aberdovey Road, Pennal, Machynlleth, SY20 9YS.* Quiet location near Aberdovey on a Welsh-speaking working farm. **Open:** All year
01654 702018 **D:** Fr £17.00–£20.00 **S:** Fr £17.00–£20.00 **Beds:** 1F 4D 1T 1S **Baths:** 2 En 1 Pr

Penrhyn Bay

SH8281

Awelfor Guest House, *74 Llandudno Road, Penrhyn Bay, Llandudno, LL30 3HA.* Immaculately presented, close to all amenities. Completely non-smoking establishment. **Open:** All year
01492 549373 *i+s@awelfor.freeserve.co.uk* ukworld.net/awelfor **D:** Fr £20.00–£23.00 **Beds:** 6D **Baths:** 6 Pr

Penrhyndeudraeth

SH6139

Wenallt, *Penrhyndeudraeth, Gwynedd, LL48 6PW.* Award-winning guest house near Portmeirion. Lovely views. Ideal touring base. **Open:** All year (not Xmas/New Year)
01766 770321 (also fax) G Cooper *gh@wenalt.globalnet.co.uk* **D:** Fr £22.00–£25.00 **S:** Fr £27.00–£30.00 **Beds:** 1T 2D **Baths:** 3 En (3) **cc**

Pentrefoelas

SH8751

Maesgwyn Farm, *Pentrefoelas, Betws-Y-Coed, LL24 0LR.* On the edge of Snowdonia National Park in quiet countryside.
Open: Apr to Nov **Grades:** WTB 3 Star
01690 770668 F Jones **D:** Fr £18.00–£20.00 **S:** Fr £18.00–£20.00 **Beds:** 1F 1D **Baths:** 1 Sh

Penygroes

SH4753

Lleuar Fawr, *Penygroes, Caernarfon, Gwynedd, LL54 6PB.* Peaceful location, substantial farmhouse breakfast, comfortable bedrooms. Warm Welsh welcome. **Open:** All year (not Xmas)
01286 660268 (also fax) Mrs Lloyd Jones *user@lleuarfawr.fsnet.co.uk* **D:** Fr £18.00–£20.00 **S:** Fr £25.00 **Beds:** 1D 1T **Baths:** 2 En

Porthmadog

SH5638

35 Madog Street, *Porthmadog, LL49 9BU.* Modern terraced house. **Open:** All year (not Xmas)
01766 512843 Mrs Skellern **D:** Fr £14.00–£15.00 **S:** Fr £14.00–£15.00 **Beds:** 1F 1D 1T 1S **Baths:** 2 Sh (3)

Pwllheli

SH3735

Rhosydd, *26 Glan Cymerau, Pwllheli, Gwynedd, LL53 5PU.* Detached bungalow, outskirts Pwllheli. Near beach, leisure centre, golf, marina. **Open:** All year
01758 612956 S Williams *helen@rhosydd.freeserve.co.uk* **D:** Fr £15.00–£17.50 **S:** Fr £15.00–£17.50 **Beds:** 1T 1D **Baths:** 1 En 1 Sh

Rhos-on-Sea

SH8381

Sunnyside, *146 Dinerth Road, Rhos-on-Sea, Colwyn Bay, LL28 4YF.* Central for sea, country and mountains, golf and cricket, welcoming. **Open:** Easter to Oct
01492 544048 Mrs Pryce **D:** Fr £16.00 **S:** Fr £20.00 **Beds:** 1T 1D **Baths:** 1 Sh

Sunnydowns Hotel, *66 Abbey Road, Rhos-on-Sea, Conwy, LL28 4NU.* Perfectly situated for exploring Snowdonia and North Wales beaches. **Open:** All year
01492 544256 Mr Willington **Fax: 01492 543223** *sunnydowns-hotel@tinyworld.co.uk* www.hotelnorthwales.co.uk **D:** Fr £22.00–£29.00 **S:** Fr £25.00–£35.00 **Beds:** 3F 3T 7D 2S **Baths:** 15 En (12)

Ashmount Hotel, *College Avenue, Rhos-on-Sea, Colwyn Bay, LL28 4NT.* Christian hotel, perfectly situated for beaches and Snowdonia. **Open:** All year
01492 545479 **D:** Fr £20.00–£28.50 **S:** Fr £20.00–£28.50 **Beds:** 3F 3T 4D 2S **Baths:** 11 En 1 Pr (0) (8)

Rhyd

SH6341

Bodlondeb Farm, *Rhyd, Penrhyndeudraeth, LL48 6ST.* In small rural hamlet near Ffestiniog Railway, Portmeirion, mountains & beaches.
Open: Easter to Oct
01766 770640 *bodlondeb.rhyd@virginnet.co.uk* **D:** Fr £17.50–£19.50 **S:** Fr £17.50–£19.50 **Beds:** 1T 2D (2)

Rhyd-Ddu

SH5652

Ffridd Isaf, *Rhyd-Ddu, Caernarfon, LL54 6TN.* Restored C16th Grade II farmhouse, beneath Snowdon. Magnificent views, log fires, good food, muddy boots no problem, secure parking. Last house before the summit on the Rhyd Ddu path. Come and get away from it all. **Open:** All year
01766 890452 Mrs Kent **D:** Fr £15.00 **S:** Fr £15.00 **Beds:** 1T 1D **Baths:** 1 Sh

Rhydymain

SH7921

Rhaeadr Wnion, *Rhydymain, Dolgellau, LL40 2AH.* Victorian house in 3 acres of gardens in beautiful Snowdonia. **Open:** All year **Grades:** WTB 3 Star
01341 450249 Mrs Perkins **D:** Fr £17.00–£19.00 **S:** Fr £20.00–£22.00 **Beds:** 2D 2T **Baths:** 2 En 1 Sh (5)

Rowen

SH7571

Bulkeley Mill, *Rowen, Conwy, Gwynedd, LL32 8TS.* Converted water mill set in beautiful gardens and mountain scenery.
Open: All year
01492 650481 Mrs Seville *SKenseville@cs.com* www.bulkeley-mill.co.uk **D:** Fr £27.00–£29.00 **S:** Fr £32.00 **Beds:** 1F 1D **Baths:** 2 En (4)

Saron (Llanwnda)

SH4658

Gwern, *Saron, Caernarfon, LL54 5UH.* **Open:** Easter to Oct
01286 831337 *ellenpjones@hotmail.com* www.gwernfarm.co.uk **D:** Fr £20.00–£24.00 **S:** Fr £20.00–£24.00 **Beds:** 1F 1D **Baths:** 2 En (3)
Croeso to Gwern, a working beef and sheep farm, set in peaceful countryside amidst spectacular mountain and coastal scenery. Large, beautifully furnished bedrooms with lounge area. Choice of breakfasts using local produce and own eggs. Central to North West Wales.

Pengwern Farm, *Saron, Llanwnda, Caernarfon, LL54 5UH.* Charming, spacious farmhouse of character, beautifully situated between mountains & sea.
Open: Jan to Nov
01286 831500 & 07778 411780 (M) Mr & Mrs Rowlands **Fax: 01286 831500** *jhjgr@enterprise.net* **D:** Fr £24.00–£28.00 **S:** Fr £30.00–£38.00 **Beds:** 1T 2D **Baths:** 3 En cc

Tal-y-llyn

SH7109

Dolffanog Fach, *Tal-y-llyn, Tywyn, North West Wales, LL36 9AJ.* Stone-built farmhouse situated near Tal-y-llyn Lake and Cader Idris mountain. **Open:** Mar to Nov
01654 761235 (also fax) Mrs Pugh *meirwen.pughe@talk21.com* www.walestouristsonline.co.uk **D:** Fr £22.00–£24.00 **S:** Fr £25.00–£30.00 **Beds:** 1T 2D **Baths:** 3 En

Minffordd Hotel, *Tal-y-Llyn, Tywyn, LL36 9AJ.* 400 year old ex-drovers inn.
Open: All year
01654 761665 G Holt **Fax: 01654 761517** *hotel@minffordd.com* www.minffordd.com **D:** Fr £39.00–£61.00 **S:** Fr £47.00–£69.00 **Beds:** 2T 4D 1S **Baths:** 7 En (13) (14) cc

Talsarnau

SH6135

Estuary Motel Y Traeth, *Talsarnau, LL47 6TA.* Snowdonia National Park, near Portmeirion. All modern ground floor rooms. **Open:** All year
01766 771155 Mr King **D:** Fr £16.50–£24.50 **S:** Fr £34.50 **Beds:** 1F 5D 4T **Baths:** 10 En (16) (30) cc

Trawsfynydd

SH7035

Old Mill Farmhouse, *Fron Oleu Farm, Trawsfynydd, Blaenau Ffestiniog, LL41 4UN.* Olde Worlde charm, wonderful scenery, friendly animals, large good breakfasts. **Open:** All year **Grades:** WTB 3 Star
01766 540397 (also fax) Miss Roberts & Mrs P Osborne *penmar@oldmillfarm.spacomputers.com* **D:** Fr £22.00–£30.00 **S:** Fr £25.00–£30.00 **Beds:** 2F 3D 2T **Baths:** 7 En (10)

All details shown are as supplied by B&B owners in Autumn 2002

Trefriw

SH7863

Ty Newydd Guest House, *Ty Newydd, Trefriw, LL27 0JH.* Welcoming, good standard accommodation central for mountains, lakes & coasts. **Open:** All year **Grades:** WTB 3 Star **01492 641210** Mr & Mrs Jones *tynewyddtrefriw@aol.com* www.tynewyddtrefriw.co.uk **D:** Fr £18.00–£20.00 **S:** Fr £20.00–£30.00 **Beds:** 1F 1T 1D 1S **Baths:** 2 En 2 Sh

Argoed Guest House, *Crafnant Road, Trefriw, Conwy, LL27 0TX.* Comfortable old-fashioned house. Beautiful views of Conwy Valley. Easy access to mountains & coast. **Open:** All year **Grades:** WTB 3 Star **01492 640091** Mr & Mrs Phillips *keithandanne@tiscali.co.uk* www.argoed.co.uk **D:** Fr £21.00 **S:** Fr £29.00 **Beds:** 2D 1T **Baths:** 3 En (5) **cc**

Planning a longer stay? Always ask for any special rates

Hafod Country Hotel, *Trefriw, Conwy, LL27 0RQ.* Converted farmhouse on edge of village nestling into heavily wooded Snowdonian foothills. **Open:** Feb to Jan **01492 640029 Fax: 01492 641351** *hafod@breathemail.net* www.hafodhouse.co.uk **D:** Fr £27.50–£40.00 **S:** Fr £32.00–£47.50 **Beds:** 4D 2T **Baths:** 6 En (12) **cc**

Craig y Felin, *Trefriw, Betws-y-Coed, LL27 0RJ.* Beautiful peaceful location. Panoramic views. Close to lakes & mountains. **Open:** All year **01492 640868** *gordon@couperg.freeserve.co.uk* www.snowdonia.org.uk/trefriw **D:** Fr £20.00–£23.00 **S:** Fr £30.00–£32.00 **Beds:** 1F 1T 1D **Baths:** 2 En 1 Pr (5)

RATES

D = Price range per person sharing in a double or twin room

S = Price range for a single room

Tremadog

SH5640

Ty Newydd Guest House, *30 Dublin Street, Tremadog, Porthmadog, Gwynedd, LL49 9RH.* Close to the Ffestiniog Railway, Portmeirion and many other attractions. **Open:** All year (not Xmas/New Year) **01766 512553** *johnjulieo@aol.com* porthmadog.co.uk/tynewydd **D:** Fr £18.50–£21.00 **S:** Fr £28.50–£31.00 **Beds:** 1F 1T 2D **Baths:** 1 Sh (6)

Tywyn (Aberdovey)

SH5800

Hendy Farm, *Tywyn, LL36 9RU.* Comfortable farmhouse near town and beach. Own halt on Tal-y-llyn railway. **Open:** Easter to Oct **01654 710457 (also fax)** Mrs Lloyd-Jones *jones@farmline.com* www.croesocaderidris.co.uk-hendy **D:** Fr £20.00–£24.00 **S:** Fr £24.00–£29.00 **Beds:** 2D 1T **Baths:** 2 En 1 Pr

Pembrokeshire

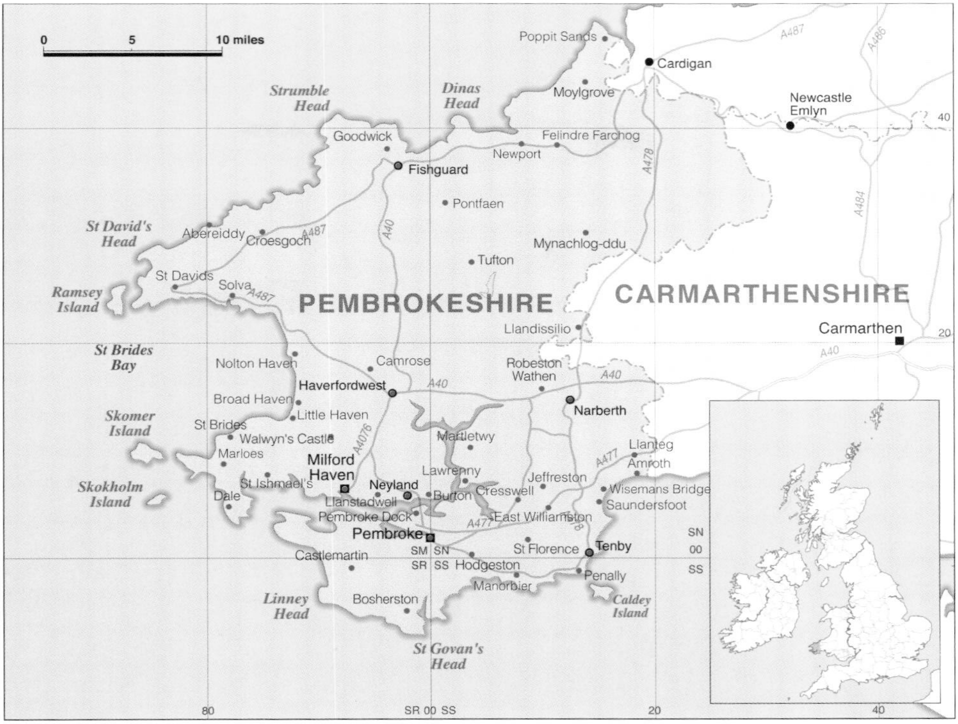

Abereiddy

SM7931 *The Sloop*

Murmur-y-Mor, *Abereiddy, Haverfordwest, Pembs, SA62 6DS.* Beautiful views. Ideal for Coastal Path walkers, near Abereiddy Beach. **Open:** Mar to Oct
01348 831670 L A Thomas **D:** Fr £20.00 **S:** Fr £25.00 **Beds:** 1T 1S **Baths:** 1 En 1 Sh (12) (4)

Amroth

SN1607

Beach Haven Guest House, *Amroth, Narberth, SA67 8NG.* Quiet picturesque location, magnificent sea views, transfers available. **Open:** All year (not Xmas)
01834 813310 Mr Rickards **D:** Fr £15.00–£17.00 **S:** Fr £15.00–£17.00 **Beds:** 2D 1T 1S **Baths:** 2 En 2 Sh (5)

All details shown are as supplied by B&B owners in Autumn 2002

Ashdale Guest House, *Amroth, Narberth, Pembs, SA67 8NA.* Well situated for:- beaches, theme parks, Dylan Thomas, Irish ferries **Open:** Easter to Nov
01834 813853 (also fax) Mrs Williamson **D:** Fr £15.00–£16.00 **S:** Fr £15.00–£16.00 **Beds:** 2F 1T 2D 1S **Baths:** 2 Sh (6)

Bosherston

SR9694

Trefalen Farm, *Bosherston, Pembroke, SA71 5DR.* 100 yards to Broadhaven beach. Short walk to village pub. **Open:** All year
01646 661643 Mr & Mrs Giardelli **Fax: 01646 661626** *trefalen@aol.com* **D:** Fr £19.00 **S:** Fr £22.50 **Beds:** 1S 1T 1D **Baths:** 2 Sh

Cornerstones, *Bosherston, Pembroke, SA71 5DN.* Immaculately contained accommodation. Half mile Broadhaven Beach & Coastal Path. **Open:** All year (not Xmas/New Year)
01646 661660 Mrs James **D:** Fr £20.00–£21.00 **S:** Fr £25.00 **Beds:** 1T 1F **Baths:** 1 En 1 Pr (4)

Broad Haven

SM8613 *Galleon Inn, Royal Hotel, Swan Inn, The Castle, St Brides Inn*

Anchor Guest House, The Sea Front, *Broad Haven, Haverfordwest, Pembs, SA62 3JN.* Opposite sandy beach with magnificent sea views. Adjacent cafe, shop, restaurant. Coastal Path. **Open:** All year (not Xmas/New Year)
01437 781051 Mrs Morgan **Fax: 01437 781050** *anch@bdhn.fsnet.co.uk* www.anchor-guesthouse.co.uk **D:** Fr £18.00–£27.00 **S:** Fr £20.00–£27.00 **Beds:** 8 **Baths:** 8 En

Burton

SM9805

Beggars Reach Hotel, *Burton, Milford Haven, Pembs, SA73 1PD.* Quiet country house hotel. Ideal base for exploring Pembrokeshire. **Open:** All year
01646 600700 W Smallman **Fax: 01646 600560 D:** Fr £26.25 **S:** Fr £32.50 **Beds:** 3F 1T 6D 2S **Baths:** 12 En (25) cc

Camrose
SM9219

The Fold, Cleddau Lodge, *Camrose, Haverfordwest, Pembrokeshire, SA62 6HY.* Converted C17th farmhouse, gardens, woodlands, river with otters, view of Preseli. **Open:** Easter to Oct
01437 710640 Mrs Brookman **Fax: 01437 710663** *cleddau.lodge@btinternet.com* **D:** Fr £15.00–£18.50 **S:** Fr £18.50 **Beds:** 1D **Baths:** 1 Pr (10)

Castlemartin
SR9198

Chapel Farm, *Castlemartin, Pembroke, Pembrokeshire, SA71 5HW.* Large comfortable farmhouse overlooking sea, offers relaxing holidays to unwind. **Open:** All year
01646 661312 (also fax) Mrs Smith *chapelfarm@aol.com* **D:** Fr £20.00–£22.00 **S:** Fr £25.00–£27.00 **Beds:** 1F 1T **Baths:** 1 En 1 Pr (10)

Cresswell Quay
SN0506

Cresswell House, *Cresswell Quay, Kilgetty, Pembs, SA68 0TE.* **Open:** All year
01646 651435 Mr Wright *phil@cresswellhouse.co.uk* www.cresswellhouse.co.uk
D: Fr £25.00–£30.00 **S:** Fr £25.00–£35.00
Beds: 1T 2D **Baths:** 2 En 1 Pr
Set on the banks of the Cleddau Estuary, centrally situated for South Pembrokeshire and coast. Wonderful food, breakfast choices include kedgeree, home-made fishcakes, smoked salmon, scrambled eggs. All rooms with a view, 100 yards from traditional ale house. Four-poster bed available.

Croesgoch
SM8230

Bank House Farm, *Abereiddy Road, Croesgoch, Haverfordwest, Pembs, SA62 6XZ.* Picturesque sea views on country road between Croes-goch and Abereiddy.
Open: All year (not Xmas)
01348 831305 Mrs Lloyd **D:** Fr £15.00–£18.00 **S:** Fr £18.00 **Beds:** 1D 1T **Baths:** 1 Sh

Maes y Ffynnon, *Penygroes, Croesgoch, Haverfordwest, Pembs, SA62 5JN.* Modern large bungalow, private grounds; ideal base for walking or touring. **Open:** Mar to Oct
01348 831319 Mrs Evans **D:** Fr £16.50 **S:** Fr £18.50 **Beds:** 1F 1T **Baths:** 2 En (4)

Dale
SM8005 *The Griffin Inn*

The Post House Hotel, *Dale, Haverfordwest, Pembs, SA62 3RE.* Licensed hotel, ensuite bedrooms, plus suite of rooms, TV lounge, conservatory. **Open:** Mar to Jan
01646 636201 Mr & Mrs Riley *posthousedale@talk21.com* **D:** Fr £24.00–£27.50 **S:** Fr £26.00 **Beds:** 2T 2D 1S **Baths:** 5 En (6)

Point Farm, *Dale, Haverfordwest, Pembs, SA62 3RD.* Large country house on sea front. Adjacent to Pembrokeshire coast.
Open: All year (not Xmas/New Year)
01646 636254 Mrs Webber **D:** Fr £25.00 **Beds:** 1T 2D 1S **Baths:** 2 En (4)

East Williamston
SN0904

Whitehall Lodge, *Green Meadow Close, East Willliamston, Tenby, SA70 8RU.* Perfect location for Pembrokeshire Coast. Warm welcome. Comfortable, quality accommodation.
Open: All year **Grades:** WTB 3 Star
01834 812682 Mrs Keys **Fax: 01834 810077** *ruth.keys@lineone.net* www.whitehall-lodge.co.uk **D:** Fr £20.00–£25.00 **S:** Fr £30.00 **Beds:** 1F 1T 1D **Baths:** 2 En 1 Sh

RATES
D = Price range per person sharing in a double or twin room
S = Price range for a single room

B&B owners may vary rates – be sure to check when booking

Felindre Farchog
SN1039

The Salutation Inn, *Felindre Farchog, Crymych, Pembs, SA41 3UY.* **Open:** All year **Grades:** WTB 3 Star
01239 820564 Fax: 01239 820355 *johndenley@aol.com* www.salutationcountryhotel.co.uk
D: Fr £24.00–£30.00 **S:** Fr £32.00–£38.00
Beds: 2F 2T 4D **Baths:** 8 En
C16th coaching inn in Pembrokeshire Coast National Park. Ground floor rooms with telephones. Ideally situated for walking, riding, golf, beaches etc. Riverside restaurant. Good food served using local produce. Bar meals, good selection of wines and real ales. Friendly staff.

Fishguard
SM9537

Cartref Hotel, *13-19 High Street, Fishguard, Pembs, SA65 9AW.* Friendly, comfortable hotel. Excellent family accommodation. Free garage. Open 24 hours. **Open:** All year **Grades:** WTB 2 Star, AA 2 Star
01348 872430 Mrs Bjorkquist **Fax: 01348 873664** *cartef@themail.co.uk* **D:** Fr £25.00–£28.00 **S:** Fr £32.00–£36.00 **Beds:** 2F 2D 2T 4S **Baths:** 10 En (3) cc

Stanley House, *Quay Road, Goodwick, Fishguard, Pembs, SA64 0BS.* Overlooking Fishguard, ferry terminal and bay and Preseli Hills beyond. **Open:** All year
01348 873024 Mr & Mrs Hendrie **D:** Fr £17.50–£21.50 **S:** Fr £21.50 **Beds:** 2F 2D 2T 1S **Baths:** 1 En 1 Pr 2 Sh (3)

Goodwick
SM9438

Stanley House, *Quay Road, Goodwick, Fishguard, Pembs, SA64 0BS.* Overlooking Fishguard, ferry terminal and bay and Preseli Hills beyond. **Open:** All year
01348 873024 Mr & Mrs Hendrie **D:** Fr £17.50–£21.50 **S:** Fr £21.50 **Beds:** 2F 2D 2T 1S **Baths:** 1 En 1 Pr 2 Sh (3)

Ivybridge, *Drim Mill, Dyffryn, Goodwick, Fishguard, Pembs, SA64 0FT.* **Open:** All year (not Xmas) **Grades:** WTB 2 Star
01348 875366 Mrs Davies **Fax: 01348 872338** *ivybridge@cwcom.net* www.ivybridge.cwc.net
D: Fr £20.50–£24.50 **S:** Fr £19.50–£25.50
Beds: 4F 4D 2T 1S **Baths:** 4 En 2 Pr (12) cc
Friendly family-run guest house. Ensuite rooms with colour TV and hot drinks tray. Good home cooking, heated indoor pool, licensed, vegetarians welcome. Ample off-road parking. 2 minutes ferry port. Early/late visitors welcome.

Haverfordwest

SM9515

East Hook Farm, *Portfield Gate, Haverfordwest, SA62 3LN.* **Open:** All year **Grades:** WTB 4 Star
01437 762211 Fax: 01437 760310 *jen.easthook@virgin.net* www.easthookfarmhouse.co.uk **D:** Fr £24.00–£27.50 **S:** Fr £30.00 **Beds:** 1F 1T 1D **Baths:** 2 En 1 Pr (3)
Unwind in our Georgian farmhouse surrounded by peaceful unspoilt countryside. Large rooms furnished with antiques and all the home comforts you could wish for. Selection for breakfast, local produce used. Evening meals available by arrangement. Perfect place to relax.

College Guest House, *93 Hill Street, Haverfordwest, Pembs, SA61 1QX.* Large Georgian house, good food, central location, lovely countryside, near beach. **Open:** All year **Grades:** WTB 3 Star, AA 3 Diamond
01437 763710 (also fax) Mr Larby *colinlarby@aol.com* www.collegeguesthouse.com **D:** Fr £24.00–£27.00 **S:** Fr £25.00–£27.00 **Beds:** 2F 3T 2D 1S **Baths:** 8 En (8) cc

Planning a longer stay? Always ask for any special rates

Greenways, *Shoals Hook Lane, Haverfordwest, Pembs, SA61 2XN.* Quiet retreat. The best in the west - find peace in our heaven on earth. **Open:** All year
01437 762345 Mr Tuson **Fax: 01437 779190** *keith2son@aol.co.uk* www.greenways-guesthouse.com **D:** Fr £20.00–£25.00 **S:** Fr £20.00–£25.00 **Beds:** 1F 3D 3T 4S **Baths:** 3 En 1 Sh

Cuckoo Mill, *Pelcomb Bridge, St Davids Road, Haverfordwest, Pembs, SA62 6EA.* Central Pembrokeshire. Quietly situated. Excellent food. Genuine welcome. Unrestricted access. **Open:** All year
01437 762139 Mrs Davies **D:** Fr £20.00–£25.00 **S:** Fr £20.00–£25.00 **Beds:** 1F 2D 1T **Baths:** 2 Sh (4)

Hodgeston

SS0399

Rosedene, *Hodgeston, Freshwater East, Pembroke, SA71 5JU.* Peaceful village location, 1 mile Coastal Footpath. Affordable luxury! **Open:** Easter to Nov
01646 672586 E A Fallon **Fax: 01646 672855** *eileen@rosedene85.freeserve.co.uk* www.rosedene85.freeserve.co.uk **D:** Fr £22.00–£27.00 **S:** Fr £32.00–£37.00 **Beds:** 1F 2T 4D **Baths:** 7 En (7) 1 cc

Jeffreston

SN0806

Jeffreyston Grange, *Jeffreyston, Kilgetty, Pembs, SA68 0RE.* **Open:** All year (not Xmas)
01646 650159 Mr & Mrs Hesslegrave **Fax: 01646 651124 D:** Fr £20.00 **S:** Fr £20.00
Beds: 1F 2D 2T **Baths:** 4 En 1 Pr (4)
Warm, friendly, cosy & comfortable, peacefully located opposite the ancient parish church.

Lawrenny

SN0106

Knowles Farm, *Lawrenny, Kilgetty, Pembs, SA68 0PX.* Lovely farmhouse overlooking organic farm on estuary. Birding, walking, boating, relaxing! **Open:** Easter to Oct
01834 891221 (also fax) V Lort-Phillips *ginilp@lawrenny.org.uk* www.lawrenny.org.uk
D: Fr £24.00–£26.00 **S:** Fr £33.00–£35.00
Beds: 1T 2D **Baths:** 2 En 1 Pr (20)

Little Haven

SM8512 *Royal Hotel*

The Bower Farm, *Little Haven, Haverfordwest, Pembs, SA62 3TY.* Friendly farmhouse, fantastic sea views. **Open:** All year
01437 781554 Mr Birt-Llewellin *bowerfarm@lineone.net* www.a1tourism.com/uk/bower.html **D:** Fr £22.00–£29.00 **S:** Fr £25.00–£30.00 **Beds:** 2F 1D 1T 1S **Baths:** 5 En (10)

Whitegates, *Settlands Hill, Little Haven, Haverfordwest, Pembs, SA62 3LA.* Overlooking the sea & lovely fishing village, good eating places within easy walking distance. **Open:** All year (not Xmas)
01437 781386 (also fax) Mr & Mrs Llewellin
D: Fr £20.00–£27.00 **S:** Fr £30.00–£35.00
Beds: 1F 4D 1T **Baths:** 4 En 2 Pr cc

Llandissilio

SN1221

Plas-y-Brodyr, *Rhydwilym, Llandissilio, Clynderwen, Pembs, SA66 7QH.* Peaceful farmhouse in unspoilt valley. Ideal base for exploring Pembrokeshire & West Wales. **Open:** Mar to Nov
01437 563771 Mrs Pogson **Fax: 01437 563294** *janet@farmhols.freeserve.co.uk* www.pfh.co.uk/plasybrodyr **D:** Fr £20.00–£22.00 **S:** Fr £25.00–£27.00 **Beds:** 2D **Baths:** 1 En 1 Pr (4)

Llanstadwell

SM9405 *Ferry House*

Ferry House Inn, *Hazelbeach, Llanstadwell, Milford Haven, Pembs, SA73 1EG.* Watch the yachts and the waves roll by and enjoy fresh fish, real ales, a hearty Welsh breakfast and a warm welcome at our family run riverside village inn, alongside Pembrokeshire's beautiful Coastal Path. **Open:** All year (not Xmas/New Year)
01646 600270 Mr & Mrs Philips **Fax: 01646 600567** *ferryhouseinn@freenet.co.uk* **D:** Fr £20.00–£25.00 **S:** Fr £30.00–£45.00 **Beds:** 2F 2T 1D 1S **Baths:** 6 En (15) cc

The Old Mill, *Hazelbeach, Llanstadwell, Milford Haven, Pembs, SA73 1EG.* Old farmhouse situated on Coastal Path between Milford and Hazelbeach.
Open: Easter to Nov
01646 690190 Mr Johnson *sheila@hickey.ntlworld.com* **D:** Fr £15.00–£20.00 **S:** Fr £15.00–£20.00 **Beds:** 1F 2D **Baths:** 2 Sh (20)

Planning a longer stay? Always ask for any special rates

Llanteg
SN1810

East Llanteg Farm, *Llanteg, Amroth, SA67 8QA.* **Open:** All year (not Xmas/New Year)
Grades: WTB 3 Star
01834 831336 Mrs Lloyd *john@pembrokeshireholiday.co.uk* www.pembrokeshireholiday.co.uk **D:** Fr £18.00–£22.00 **S:** Fr £18.00–£22.00 **Beds:** 1F 1T 1D **Baths:** 2 En 1 Pr (6)
The comfortable farmhouse is ideally located for exploring Pembrokeshire's renowned coastline. Tenby is near at hand and Amroth only minutes away. Comfortable bedrooms with colour televisions and private guests' lounge. Good traditional home-cooking. Guests assured of a warm welcome.

Pen Y Bont Guest House, *Amroth Road, Llanteg, Narberth, Pembs, SA67 8QL.* Licensed guest house, friendly, good food, pleasant 4 acre grounds. **Open:** Easter to Sep
01834 831648 Mrs Maudsley **D:** Fr £18.00–£22.00 **S:** Fr £18.00–£22.00 **Beds:** 2F 1T 2D 1S **Baths:** 1 En 1 Sh

Manorbier
SS0697

Fernley Lodge, *Manorbier, Tenby, Pembs, SA70 7TH.* Victorian house in heart of beautiful coastal village. **Open:** All year (not Xmas)
01834 871226 Mrs Cowper *fernleylodge@yahoo.com* **D:** Fr £20.00–£25.00 **S:** Fr £20.00–£25.00 **Beds:** 1F 1D **Baths:** 2 Pr (2) (7)

Marloes
SM7908

Foxdale, *Glebe Lane, Marloes, Haverfordwest, Pembs, SA62 3AX.* Set in the heart of the Pembrokeshire Coast National Park. Close to cliff path. **Open:** All year
01646 636243 Mrs Roddam-King **Fax: 01646 636982** *foxdale.guest.house@totalise.co.uk* www.foxdale.guest.house.8m.com **D:** Fr £18.00–£25.00 **S:** Fr £23.00–£30.00 **Beds:** 2D 1T **Baths:** 2 En 1 Pr (6)

BEDROOMS
D = Double
T = Twin
S = Single
F = Family

Martletwy
SN0310

The Peacock Tea Garden, *Hoarstone House, Martletwy, Narberth, Pembs, SA67 8AZ.* A country house situated in its own grounds amidst the tranquil countryside of mid-Pembrokeshire. **Open:** Easter to Sept
01834 891707 (also fax) Mrs Mooney *peacock@jpmarketing.co.uk* www.jpmarketing.co.uk/peacock **D:** Fr £20.50–£27.50 **S:** Fr £25.50–£32.50 **Beds:** 1D 1T **Baths:** 1 En 1 Pr (8)

Milford Haven
SM9005

The Heart of Oak, *Hill Street, Halkin, Milford Haven, SA73 3LR.* 200-year-old coaching inn situated in Milford Haven, close to the Marina and Docks. **Open:** All year
01646 698760 Mrs Caddey **D:** Fr £17.50 **S:** Fr £20.00 **Beds:** 4T 2D 2S **Baths:** 4 En (15)

Belhaven House Hotel, *29 Hamilton Terrace, Milford Haven, Pembs, SA73 3JJ.* Hotel on A4076 overlooking marina. Two ground floor bedrooms. **Open:** All year (not Xmas)
01646 695983 Mr Henricksen **Fax: 01646 690787** *HBruceH@businessunmetered.com* **D:** Fr £22.00–£30.00 **S:** Fr £38.50–£40.00 **Beds:** 3F 3D 3S **Baths:** 6 En 1 Pr 2 Sh (8)

Kings Arms, *Hakin Point, Milford Haven, Pembs, SA73 3DG.* Public house, home-cooking. Near marina, railway station. All rooms sea view. **Open:** All year (not Xmas)
01646 693478 Mrs Hutchings **D:** Fr £17.50 **S:** Fr £17.50 **Beds:** 2F 4T **Baths:** 3 En

Moylgrove
SN1144 *Golden Lion, Ferry Inn*

The Old Vicarage, *Moylgrove, Cardigan, Pembrokeshire, SA43 3BN.* Edwardian country house, large lawned garden and glorious sea view. **Open:** Mar to Nov
01239 881231 Patricia & David Phillips **Fax: 01239 881341** *stay@old-vic.co.uk* www.old-vic.co.uk **D:** Fr £24.00–£28.00 **S:** Fr £26.00–£38.00 **Beds:** 1T 2D **Baths:** 3 En (5)

Trewidwal, *Moylegrove, Cardigan, Pembrokeshire, SA43 3BY.* Beautiful ex-farmhouse. Extensive grounds. Outstanding coastal and hill views. Peace. **Open:** All year (not Xmas/New Year)
01239 881651 Mr & Mrs Bloss *alan.bloss@btinternet.com* www.trewidwal.co.uk **D:** Fr £18.00–£22.00 **S:** Fr £20.00–£24.00 **Beds:** 1F 1D **Baths:** 1 En 1 Pr (4)

Mynachlog-ddu
SN1430

Dolau Isaf Farm, *Mynachlog-ddu, Clunderwen, Pembs, SA66 7SB.* Comfort and service in central tranquil settings. Quality farmhouse food. **Open:** All year (not Xmas/New Year)
01994 419327 (also fax) Mrs Lockton *dolau-isaf@pfh.co.uk* **D:** Fr £22.00–£25.00 **S:** Fr £22.00 **Beds:** 1T 2D **Baths:** 2 En 1 Pr

Narberth
SN1014

Highland Grange Farm, *Robeston Wathen, Narberth, Pembs, SA67 8EP.*
Open: All year **Grades:** WTB 3 Star, AA 3 Diamond, RAC 3 Diamond
01834 860952 & 07855 359919 (M) Ms James *info@highlandgrange.co.uk* www.highlandgrange.co.uk **D:** Fr £21.00–£26.50 **S:** Fr £25.00–£30.00 **Beds:** 2F 1D 1T 2S **Baths:** 2 En 2 Sh (6)
Perfect location on A40 in hilltop village. Bordering National Park, walking, castle nearby, country inns 200M. Spacious accommodation, guest lounge, library. Generous Welsh hospitality. Wide choice of breakfast including vegetarian, delicious meals. Child friendly environment, Shetland ponies. IRISH FERRYPORTS 35 minutes.

Great Canaston Farm, *Robeston Wathen, Narberth, Pembrokeshire, SA67 8DE.* River & woodland walks surround comfortable/spacious farmhouse. Breakfasts a speciality. **Open:** All year (not Xmas/New Year)
01437 541254 (also fax) Mrs Lewis *eleanor2@tesco.net* **D:** Fr £18.00–£23.00 **S:** Fr £25.00 **Beds:** 2F **Baths:** 1 Sh (5)

Woods Cross, *Narberth, Pembrokeshire, SA67 8RQ.* Woods Cross is a cottage 8 miles from Tenby, 5 miles from Saundersfoot, 5 minutes from Oakwood. Views overlooking the Preseli Hills. Everyone given a warm, homely welcome. Folly Farm 3 miles. Car essential. **Open:** Mar to Oct
01834 860694 Mrs Logan **D:** Fr £16.50–£17.50 **S:** Fr £20.00 **Beds:** 2D **Baths:** 1 Sh (14) (4)

Newport

SN0539

Treetops, *West Street, Newport, Pembs, SA42 0TD.* Excellent position for exploring countryside and coastal path. Hearty breakfasts. **Open:** All year **Grades:** WTB 4 Star
01239 820048 (also fax) Mr Edser *bandbtreetops@talk21.com* www.bandbtreetops.co.uk **D:** Fr £28.00 **S:** Fr £40.00–£45.00 **Beds:** 1T 1D 1S **Baths:** 2 En 1 Pr (3)

Llysmeddyg Guest House, *East Street, Newport, Pembrokeshire, SA42 0SY.* Listed Georgian house and mews flat and mountain bike hire. **Open:** All year (not Xmas)
01239 820008 Ian & Penny Ross *penny@ipross.freeserve.co.uk* **D:** Fr £22.00–£24.00 **S:** Fr £25.00–£35.00 **Beds:** 1F 1D 2T 1S **Baths:** 2 En 1 Sh (5)

Neyland

SM9605 *Jolly Sailor*

Y Ffynnon, *45 Honeyborough Road, Neyland, Milford Haven, Pembs, SA73 1RF.* Comfortable, private house. Friendly welcome. Irish ferry by prior arrangement. **Open:** All year (not Xmas/New Year)
01646 601369 (also fax) D Hawley **D:** Fr £16.00 **S:** Fr £16.00 **Beds:** 1T 1D 1S **Baths:** 1 Sh (1)

Nolton Haven

SM8618 *Mariners' Inn*

Nolton Haven Farm House, *Nolton Haven, Haverfordwest, Pembs, SA62 4NH.* Beachside farmhouse, working farm. 75 yards village inn, quiet, good walks. **Open:** All year (not Xmas)
01437 710263 (also fax) Mr Canton *stilbb@noltonhaven.com* www.noltonhaven.com **D:** Fr £15.00 **S:** Fr £15.00 **Beds:** 3F 2D 1T 1S **Baths:** 2 Pr 4 Sh (20)

Mariners Inn, *Nolton Haven, Haverfordwest, Pembs, SA62 3NH.* Adjacent to coastal path and beach. Owner managed. **Open:** All year
01437 710469 **D:** Fr £21.00 **S:** Fr £42.00 **Beds:** 1F 6T **Baths:** 7 En cc

Pembroke

SM9801

High Noon Guest House, *Lower Lamphey Road, Pembroke, Pembrokeshire, SA71 4AB.* Clean, comfortable & friendly, in Pembroke town with views over meadowland. **Open:** All year (not Xmas/New Year)
01646 683736 (also fax) C Barnikel *info@highnoon.co.uk* www.highnoon.co.uk **D:** Fr £17.50–£21.50 **S:** Fr £18.50–£26.50 **Beds:** 2F 1T 3D 3S **Baths:** 5 En 4 Sh (9) cc

Pembroke Dock

SM9603

The Old Rectory, *Cosheston, Pembroke Dock, Pembroke, SA72 4UJ.* Large former rectory in 2 acre gardens. **Open:** All year (not Xmas)
01646 684960 Mrs Bailey **D:** Fr £17.50–£20.00 **S:** Fr £17.50–£20.00 **Beds:** 1F 1D 2T 1S **Baths:** 2 Sh (4)

Penally

SS1199

Brambles Lodge, *Penally, Tenby, Pembs, SA70 7QE.* **Open:** All year (not Xmas/New Year)
01834 842393 Peter & Heather Sparks *sparksemail@tiscali.co.uk* www.smoothhound.co.uk/hotels/brambles.html **D:** Fr £18.00–£25.00 **S:** Fr £18.00–£25.00 **Beds:** 1F 2T 4D 1S **Baths:** 5 En 3 Sh (6) (9)
Attractive guest house with homely atmosphere in picturesque coastal village of Penally, only 1.5m Tenby. Coastal Path, beaches, golf course, village pubs/restaurant within easy walking distance. Special rates for long stays. Peter and Heather look forward to meeting you.

Giltar Grove Country House, *Penally, Tenby, Pembs, SA70 7RY.* **Open:** All year
01834 871568 Mrs Diment *giltarbnb@aol.com* www.giltargrovecountryhouse.co.uk **D:** Fr £20.00–£25.00 **S:** Fr £20.00–£25.00 **Beds:** 1F 3D 1T 1S **Baths:** 4 En 1 Pr 1 Sh (10)
Late Victorian Welsh country house, totally refurbished, charm and character retained. Peaceful location; great walks, wildlife, scenery right outside door - Coastal Path 3 mins. All bedrooms ensuite, 2 with four-posters. Mentioned in 'Which?', Sunday Times; Top 20 Finalist, AA Landlady of the Year.

RATES
D = Price range per person sharing in a double or twin room
S = Price range for a single room

Pontfaen

SN0234

Gellifawr Country House, *Pontfaen, Fishguard, Pembs, SA65 9TX.* **Open:** All year
01239 820343 **Fax: 01239 820128** *info@gellifawr.co.uk* www.gellifawr.co.uk **D:** Fr £23.00–£27.50 **S:** Fr £28.00–£35.00 **Beds:** 1F 6D **Baths:** 7 En (20) cc
Welcoming country hotel, seven bedrooms, set in 12 acres in the Preseli National Coastal Park. Comfortable & relaxed, 4 miles to the beaches. Bar and restaurant, with excellent home-cooked food. Excellent walking country or a place to come & relax. 3 star.

Poppit Sands

SN1548

Glan-y-Mor, *Poppit Sands, St Dogmaels, Cardigan, Pembs, SA43 3LP.* Ex-farmhouse with beautiful sea view. Warm & friendly atmosphere. **Open:** All year (not Xmas/New Year)
01239 612329 Mrs Sharp *glanymor79@hotmail.com* **D:** Fr £18.00–£20.00 **S:** Fr £18.00–£20.00 **Beds:** 1D 1S **Baths:** 1 Sh

Robeston Wathen

SN0815

Highland Grange Farm, *Robeston Wathen, Narberth, Pembs, SA67 8EP.* Perfect location on A40 in hilltop village. Bordering National Park, walking, castle nearby. **Open:** All year **Grades:** WTB 3 Star, AA 3 Diamond, RAC 3 Diamond
01834 860952 & 07855 359919 (M) Ms James *info@highlandgrange.co.uk* www.highlandgrange.co.uk **D:** Fr £21.00–£26.50 **S:** Fr £25.00–£30.00 **Beds:** 2F 1D 1T 2S **Baths:** 2 En 2 Sh (6)

Canton House, *Robeston Wathen, Narberth, Pembs, SA67 8EP.* Large peach-coloured country house, panoramic views. Convenient touring, amenities. **Open:** All year (not Xmas/New Year)
01834 860620 Mrs Brown **D:** Fr £20.00 **S:** Fr £20.00–£35.00 **Beds:** 1F 1T 1D 1S **Baths:** 1 Sh (5)

BATHROOMS
En = Ensuite
Pr = Private
Sh = Shared

BATHROOMS
En = Ensuite
Pr = Private
Sh = Shared

Saundersfoot

SN1304

Valley Farm B & B, *Valley Road, Saundersfoot, SA69 9BX.* **Open:** Mar to Oct
01834 813388 *t.pearson4@ntlworld.com* **D:** Fr £20.00–£22.00 **S:** Fr £24.00–£30.00 **Beds:** 2D **Baths:** 2 En (3)
Peacefully situated C19th farmhouse full of character in beautiful Pembrokeshire National Park. Glorious sandy beaches, Coast Path, castles, heritage sites, wonderful walking & bird-watching areas nearby. Vegetarians very welcome. Home made bread. Saundersfoot in Bloom winner. Bargain breaks available.

Solva

SM8024 *Royal George, Harbour House, Ship Inn, Farmers Arms, Grove Hotel*

Pendinas, *St Brides View, Solva, Haverfordwest, Pembs, SA62 6TB.* Glorious sea views from all rooms, good food, warm welcome. **Open:** Easter to Oct
01437 721283 Ms Davies *pendinas.solva@talk21.com* www.pendinas.co.uk **D:** Fr £20.00–£22.00 **S:** Fr £20.00–£22.00 **Beds:** 2D 2S **Baths:** 1 Sh (3)

St Brides

SM8010

Fopston Farm, *St Brides, Haverfordwest, Pembs, SA62 3AW.* C17th working farm of 282 acres with interesting features. Beautiful scenery, lovely safe beaches. **Open:** Easter to Oct **Grades:** WTB 2 Star
01646 636271 (also fax) Mrs Price **D:** Fr £22.00–£25.00 **S:** Fr £28.00–£31.00 **Beds:** 1F 2T 1D **Baths:** 1 En 2 Sh (6)

St Davids

SM7525

Pen Albro Guest House, *18 Goat Street, St Davids, Haverfordwest, Pembs, SA62 6RF.* Cathedral 150 yards, Coastal Path 0.25 hr, pub next door. **Open:** All year
01437 721865 D: Fr £17.00 **S:** Fr £17.00 **Beds:** 1D 1T 1S

Ramsey House, *Lower Moor, St Davids, Haverfordwest, Pembs, SA62 6RP.* **Open:** All year (not Xmas) **Grades:** WTB 4 Star, AA 4 Diamond, RAC 4 Diamond
01437 720321 & 01437 720332 Mac & Sandra Thompson **Fax: 01437 720025** *info@ramseyhouse.co.uk* www.ramseyhouse.co.uk **D:** Fr £32.00–£35.00 **S:** Fr £32.00–£70.00 **Beds:** 3D 3T **Baths:** 5 En 1 Pr (8) **cc**
Superior non-smoking 4 Star guest house exclusively for adults. Convenient location for cathedral and Coast Path. Award winning dinners/wines with Welsh emphasis. Licensed bar and friendly relaxed hospitality completes your enjoyment. Dinner B&B £48–£52 pppn, £288–£312 weekly.

St Florence

SN0801

La Ponterosa, *Eastern Lane, St Florence, Tenby, SA70 8LJ.* Enjoy warm friendly hospitality. Village location. Perfectly situated for exploring Pembrokeshire. **Open:** Mar to Nov
01834 871674 Mrs Mayhew *laponterosa@aol.com* **D:** Fr £19.00–£25.00 **S:** Fr £20.00–£25.00 **Beds:** 1F 1T 4D **Baths:** 6 En (10)

St Ishmael's

SM8307

Skerryback Farmhouse, *Sandy Haven, St Ishmael's, Haverfordwest, Pembs, SA62 3DN.* Welcoming C18th farmhouse, adjoining Coastal Path, relaxed atmosphere, tea/coffee on arrival. **Open:** Mar to Nov
01646 636598 Mrs Williams **Fax: 01646 636595** *williams@farmersweekly.net* www.pfh.co.uk **D:** Fr £22.50–£28.00 **S:** Fr £25.00–£30.00 **Beds:** 1D 1T 1S **Baths:** 1 Sh 2 En

Planning a longer stay? Always ask for any special rates

Tenby

SN1300

Clarence House Hotel, *Esplanade, Tenby, Pembs, SA70 7DU.* **Open:** Jan to Dec
01834 844371 Mr Phillips **Fax: 01834 844372** *clarencehotel@freeuk.com* www.clarencehotel-tenby.co.uk **D:** Fr £19.00–£49.00 **S:** Fr £19.00–£49.00 **Beds:** 8F 19S 16D 31T **Baths:** 74 Pr
Superbly situated in centre of esplanade overlooking South Beach. Steps to beach opposite hotel door. Panoramic views encompassing Castle Hill, Galdey Island and Giltar Point. Golf course short walk away. Town centre short level walk. Lift to all floors.

The Lynmaure, *26 Victoria Street, Tenby, Pembs, SA70 7DY.* Perfectly situated for Pembrokeshire Coastal Path or town centre. **Open:** All year (not Xmas)
01834 842844 (also fax) Mr Egginton **D:** Fr £16.00–£25.00 **S:** Fr £22.00–£30.00 **Beds:** 3F 4T 8D 2S **Baths:** 17 Pr **cc**

Glenthorne Guesthouse, *9 Deer Park, Tenby, Pembs, SA70 7LE.* Situated 250 metres from Tenby's beautiful beaches and coast path. **Open:** All year (not Xmas)
01834 842300 Mr & Mrs Lapham **D:** Fr £14.00–£20.00 **S:** Fr £14.00–£20.00 **Beds:** 2F 5D 1T 1S **Baths:** 5 En 1 Pr 3 Sh (5)

St Oswalds Guest House, *Picton Terrace, Tenby, Pembs, SA70 7DR.* Fifty yards beach, Town two minutes, ensuite rooms, Private parking. **Open:** Apr to Oct
01834 842130 (also fax) Mr Nichols **D:** Fr £17.00–£25.00 **Beds:** 7D 4F **Baths:** 11 En (2) (10)

RATES
D = Price range per person sharing in a double or twin room
S = Price range for a single room

Tufton

SN0428

Golwg-y-Fro, *Tufton, Haverfordwest, Pembrokeshire, SA63 4UB.*
Open: Feb to Oct
01437 532379 Mrs Llewellyn **D:** Fr £18.00–£20.00 **S:** Fr £19.50–£21.00 **Beds:** 1F 2D **Baths:** 1 Sh 1En
Warm welcome awaits you, perfectly situated at the foot of Preseli Mountain. Panoramic view overlooking Llys-y-Fran Reservoir. Ideal, fishing, walks, coastal paths, beaches, oak wood. Peaceful surroundings, comfortable beds for good night's rest. Full breakfast, ample parking. Recommended by guests. Off road.

Walwyns Castle

SM8711

Barley Villa Farm House, *Walwyns Castle, Haverfordwest, Pembs, SA62 3EB.* Spacious modern farmhouse in scenic countryside. Warm welcome awaits you.
Open: Easter to Nov
01437 781254 Mrs Davies *barley-villa@pfh.co.uk* **D:** Fr £18.00–£22.00 **S:** Fr £21.00–£25.00 **Beds:** 2D 1T **Baths:** 2 En 1 Sh (10) (4)

BATHROOMS
En = Ensuite
Pr = Private
Sh = Shared

Wisemans Bridge

SN1406

Pinewood, *Cliff Road, Wisemans Bridge, Narberth, Pembs, SA67 8NU.* Peaceful, comfortable accommodation. Beach: 350 yards. Lounge sea view, on Coastal Path.
Open: All year
01834 811082 Mrs Grecian **D:** Fr £19.50 **S:** Fr £25.00 **Beds:** 1T 2D **Baths:** 3 En (3)

BEDROOMS
D = Double
T = Twin
S = Single
F = Family

Powys

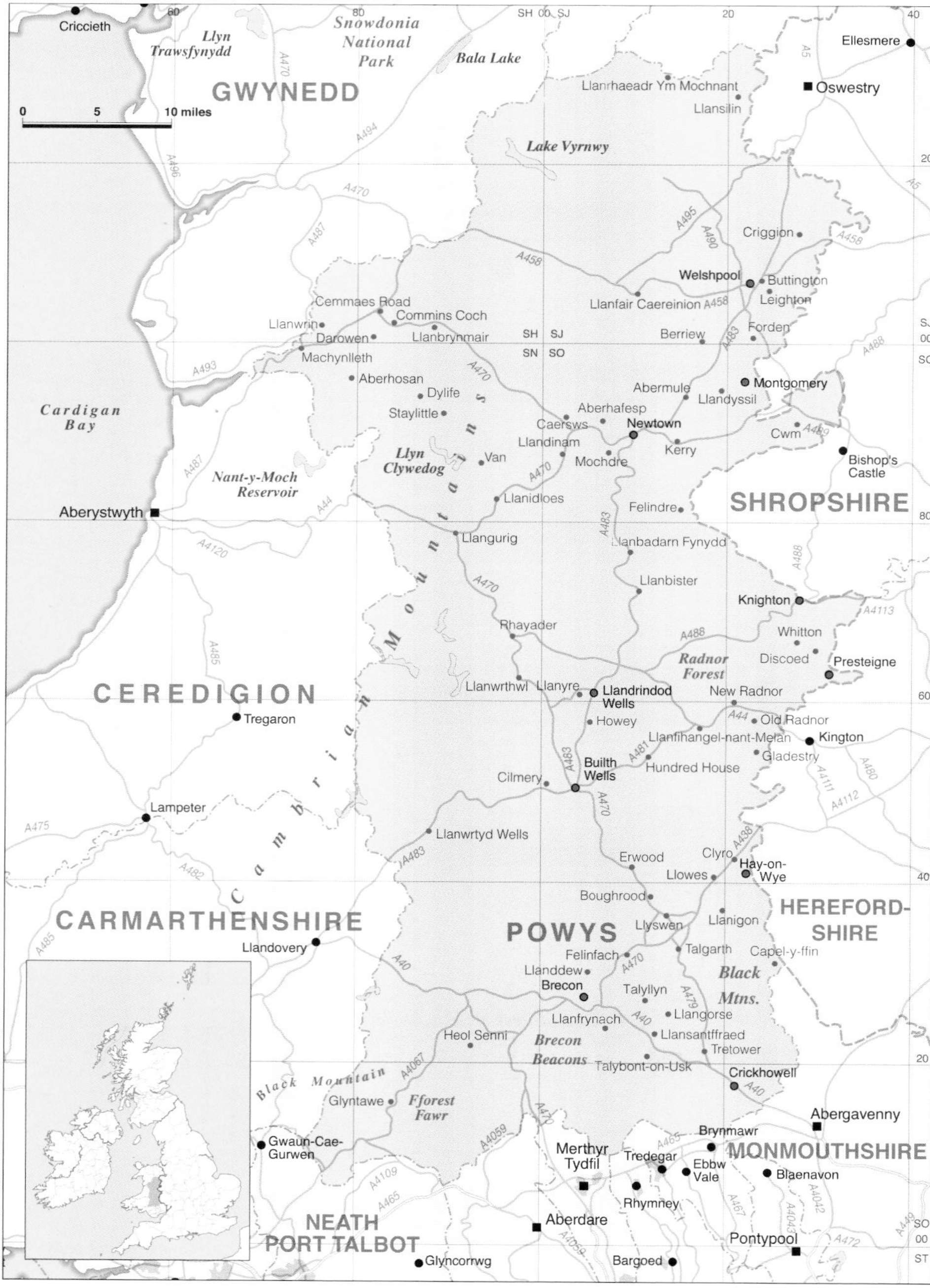
Criccieth
Llyn Trawsfynydd
Snowdonia National Park
Bala Lake
GWYNEDD
0 5 10 miles
Llanrhaeadr Ym Mochnant
Llansilin
Oswestry
Ellesmere
Lake Vyrnwy
Criggion
Welshpool
Buttington
Leighton
Llanfair Caereinion
Forden
Berriew
Cemmaes Road
Commins Coch
Llanwrin
Darowen
Llanbrynmair
Machynlleth
Aberhosan
Dylife
Staylittle
Cardigan Bay
Montgomery
Abermule
Llandyssil
Aberhafesp
Caersws
Newtown
Llandinam
Kerry
Cwm
Bishop's Castle
Mochdre
Van
Llyn Clywedog
Nant-y-Moch Reservoir
Llanidloes
Aberystwyth
SHROPSHIRE
Felindre
Llangurig
Llanbadarn Fynydd
Llanbister
Knighton
Rhayader
Whitton
Discoed
Presteigne
Radnor Forest
Cambrian Mountains
CEREDIGION
Llanwrthwl
Llanyre
Llandrindod Wells
New Radnor
Tregaron
Howey
Old Radnor
Llanfihangel-nant-Melan
Kington
Gladestry
Builth Wells
Hundred House
Cilmery
Lampeter
Llanwrtyd Wells
Erwood
Clyro
Hay-on-Wye
Llowes
Boughrood
CARMARTHENSHIRE
POWYS
Llyswen
Llanigon
HEREFORD-SHIRE
Llandovery
Talgarth
Felinfach
Capel-y-ffin
Llanddew
Brecon
Black Mtns.
Talyllyn
Llangorse
Llanfrynach
Llansantffraed
Heol Senni
Brecon Beacons
Tretower
Talybont-on-Usk
Crickhowell
Black Mountain
Glyntawe
Fforest Fawr
Abergavenny
Brynmawr
Gwaun-Cae-Gurwen
Merthyr Tydfil
Tredegar
Ebbw Vale
MONMOUTHSHIRE
Blaenavon
Rhymney
NEATH PORT TALBOT
Aberdare
Pontypool
Glyncorrwg
Bargoed

B&B owners may vary rates – be sure to check when booking

Aberhafesp

SO0692

Dyffryn Farm, *Aberhafesp, Newtown, Powys, SY16 3JD.* 5 Star accommodation on organic hill farm - walks & nature reserve nearby. **Open:** All year (not Xmas) **01686 688817 & 07885 206412 (M)** Mr & Mrs Jones **Fax: 01686 688324** *dave&sue@clara.net* www.daveandsue.clara.net **D:** Fr £24.00–£25.00 **S:** Fr £24.00–£25.00 **Beds:** 1F 1D 1T **Baths:** 3 En

Aberhosan

SN8097

Bacheiddon Farm, *Aberhosan, Machynlleth, Powys, SY20 8SG.* Working farm. Ideal walking, touring area. Close RSPB and MWT. **Open:** May to Oct **01654 702229** Mrs Lewis **D:** Fr £20.00 **S:** Fr £22.00 **Beds:** 3D **Baths:** 3 En

Abermule

SO1694

Dolforwyn Hall Hotel, *Abermule, Montgomery, Powys, SY15 6JG.* Picturesque country hotel with comfortable ensuite rooms overlooking the Severn Valley. **Open:** All year **01686 630221** K Galvin **Fax: 01686 630360** *enquiries@dolforwyn.co.uk* www.dolforwyn.co.uk **D:** Fr £30.00 **S:** Fr £39.50–£45.00 **Beds:** 1F 2T 3D 2S **Baths:** 8 En (30) cc

Berriew

SJ1800

Plasdwpa Farm, *Berriew, Welshpool, Powys, SY21 8PS.* Magnificent Mountain setting in this very comfortable farmhouse, very tranquil. **Open:** Mar to Nov **01686 640298 (also fax)** Mrs Hughes *plas@care4free.net* **D:** Fr £15.00–£16.00 **S:** Fr £18.00–£20.00 **Beds:** 1F 1D 1T **Baths:** 1 Sh (4)

Boughrood

SO1339

Upper Middle Road, *Boughrood, Brecon, Powys, LD3 0BX.* Quiet location overlooking mountains. Cycle route Hay-On-Wye 7 miles. **Open:** All year (not Xmas/New Year) **01874 754407** K Kelleher *middleroad@lineone.net* www.middleroad.free-online.net **D:** Fr £19.00 **S:** Fr £26.00 **Beds:** 1T 1D **Baths:** 1 En (3)

Brecon

SO0428

Old Ford Inn, *Llanhamlach, Brecon, LD3 7YB.* **Open:** All year **Grades:** WTB 3 Star **01874 665220** *enquiries@theoldfordinn.co.uk* www.theoldfordinn.co.uk **D:** Fr £24.00–£27.00 **S:** Fr £26.00–£35.00 **Beds:** 2F 1T 4D 1S **Baths:** 8 En (16) cc Ancient coaching inn, traditional beamed bars & dining room, alongside the A40, 'twix Brecon & Abergavenny, enjoying a glorious setting with superb southerly views over the Beacons. Ideally situated for pony trekking, Llangorse Lake & hill walking, which are all available nearby.

Cherry Picker House, *9 Orchard Street, Brecon, Powys, LD3 8AN.* **Open:** All year **Grades:** AA 3 Red Diamond **01874 624665** Mr Venner *info@cherrypickerhouse.co.uk* www.cherrypickerhouse.co.uk **D:** Fr £18.00–£25.00 **S:** Fr £20.00–£30.00 **Beds:** 1T 2D **Baths:** 1 Sh 1En (4) Cherrypicker House is a 250-year-old Georgian town house, 500 metres from the town centre. The house maintains many of its original features including an open stone fireplace, twisting old oak stairs and exposed beams throughout. Welcome Host Gold Award.

Glanyrafon, *1 The Promenade, Brecon, Powys, LD3 9AY.* Riverside Edwardian house, view of Beacons, near town centre. **Open:** Easter to Oct **01874 623302 (also fax)** Mrs Roberts *roberts@glanyrafon.zx3.net* www.smoothhound.co.uk/hotels/glanyrafon.html **D:** Fr £20.00 **S:** Fr £25.00 **Beds:** 2D 1T **Baths:** 2 Sh (11) (3)

Tir Bach Guest House, *13 Alexandra Road, Brecon, Powys, LD3 7PD.* Panoramic view of Brecon Beacons. Quiet road near town centre. **Open:** All year (not Xmas) **Grades:** WTB 2 star **01874 624551** Mrs Thomas *tirbach@btclick.com* www.tirbach.co.uk **D:** Fr £18.00–£20.00 **S:** Fr £25.00–£30.00 **Beds:** 1F 1D 1T **Baths:** 1 Sh

Planning a longer stay? Always ask for any special rates

Canal Bridge B&B, *1 Gasworks Lane, Brecon, LD3 7HA.* Spacious and comfortable B&B close to historic town centre, museums, theatre, River Usk. **Open:** Mar to Nov **01874 611088** Ms Lake *janet-lake@care4free.net* **D:** Fr £18.00–£20.00 **S:** Fr £23.00–£25.00 **Beds:** 2F 4D 1T **Baths:** 4 En 3 Pr (6)

Brecon Canal Guest House, *Canal Bank, The Watton, Brecon, Powys, LD3 7HG.* Situated adjacent to Brecon Canal, five minutes walk from town. **Open:** Feb to Nov **01874 623464 Fax: 01874 610930** *brecanal@brecon112.freeserve.co.uk* **D:** Fr £18.00–£21.00 **S:** Fr £18.00 **Beds:** 1D 2T 1S **Baths:** 2 En (6)

Lansdowne Hotel, *39 The Watton, Brecon, Powys, LD3 7EG.* Warm & friendly family-run hotel & restaurant located in centre of Brecon. **Open:** All year **01874 623321** Mrs Mulley **Fax: 01874 610438** *reception@lansdownehotel.co.uk* www.lansdownehotel.co.uk **D:** Fr £23.50–£25.00 **S:** Fr £27.50–£30.00 **Beds:** 2F 5D 2T **Baths:** 9 Pr cc

Flag & Castle Guest House, *11 Orchard Street, Llanfaes, Brecon, Powys, LD3 8AN.* Family-run guest house near to town centre and National Park. **Open:** All year **01874 625860** Mr & Mrs Richards **D:** Fr £20.00–£25.00 **S:** Fr £25.00 **Beds:** 2T 1D **Baths:** 3 En

Tir Bach, *Libanus, Brecon, Powys, LD3 8NE.* Beautiful C17th Welsh longhouse in Brecon Beacons National Park. **Open:** All year (not Xmas) **01874 625675** Mrs Norris **Fax: 01874 611198** *norris.tirbach@talk21.com* **D:** Fr £20.00–£22.00 **S:** Fr £23.00–£25.00 **Beds:** 1T 2D **Baths:** 2 En 1 Pr

Pen-y-Bryn House, *Llangorse, Brecon, LD3 7UG.* Situated in the Brecon Beacons National Park, overlooking Llangorse Lake, large gardens, mountains beyond. **Open:** All year (not Xmas) **01874 658606** Mrs Thomas **Fax: 01874 658215** *jumt@pen-y-bryn79.freeserve.co.uk* **D:** Fr £20.00 **S:** Fr £25.00 **Beds:** 1F 1T 1D **Baths:** 2 En 1 Pr

Builth Wells

SO0350

Rhydfelin, *Builth Road, Builth Wells, Powys, LD2 3RT.* 1725 cosy stone guest house, restaurant, bar and tea garden. **Open:** All year (not Xmas) **01982 552493** E M Moyes *liz@rhydfelinguesthouse.freeserve.co.uk* www.rhydfelinguesthouse.freeserve.co.uk **D:** Fr £19.50–£22.50 **S:** Fr £30.00–£45.00 **Beds:** 1F 2D 1T **Baths:** 1 En 2 Sh (12)

Dollynwydd Farm House, *Builth Wells, Powys, LD2 3RZ.* **Open:** All year (not Xmas)
01982 553660 (also fax) Mrs Williams **D:** Fr £18.00–£20.00 **S:** Fr £18.00–£20.00 **Beds:** 1D 2T 2S **Baths:** 1 En 2 Sh (6)
C17th farmhouse lying beneath Eppynt Hills. Very comfortable house down quiet farm lane. Within easy distance of Elan Valley, Brecon Beacons, Black Mountains, Hay-on-Wye bookshops. Superb area for walking, touring, birdwatching. 1 mile from Builth Wells B4520 - 1st left down lane signed Tregare/Erwood.

The Cedar Guest House, *Hay Road, Builth Wells, Powys, LD2 3AR.* Built 1880, on A470 backing Wye Valley with good views, good food, parking. **Open:** All year
01982 553356 Mr Morris **Fax: 01982 553193** *vmorris@fsnet.co.uk* www.cedars.co.uk **D:** Fr £22.50 **S:** Fr £27.50–£30.00 **Beds:** 1F 1D 3T 2S **Baths:** 5 En 2 Sh (15) **cc**

Halcyon House & Llewelyn Leisure Park, *Cilmery, Builth Wells, Powys, LD2 3NU.* Jacuzzi, snooker, views, hospitality, inn, cows, sheep; self-catering, camping. **Open:** All year
01982 552838 & 07831 101052 Mr Johnson **Fax: 01982 551090** *deejay1010@aol.com* **D:** Fr £18.00–£22.00 **S:** Fr £22.00–£26.00 **Beds:** 2F 1S **Baths:** 2 Sh **cc**

Woodlands, *Hay Road, Builth Wells, Powys, LD2 3BP.* Impressive Edwardian house, with ensuite facilities with secluded parking. **Open:** All year (not Xmas)
01982 552354 & 07967 387718 (M) Mrs Nicholls **Fax: 01982 552354** *HeskethN@aol.com* **D:** Fr £18.00–£20.00 **S:** Fr £22.00–£25.00 **Beds:** 4T **Baths:** 4 En (4)

Buttington

SJ2408

1 Plas Cefn, *Heldre Lane, Buttington, Welshpool, Powys, SY21 8SX.* Quiet private house. **Open:** All year (not Xmas/New Year)
01938 570225 Mr Broxton **D:** Fr £15.00 **S:** Fr £15.00 **Beds:** 1F 1D 1S **Baths:** 1 Sh

Caersws

SO0391

The Talk House (Ty Siarad), *Pontdolgoch, Caersws, Powys, SY17 5JE.* Delightful C19th Inn, completely refurnished in recent years. **Open:** All year (not Xmas/New Year)
01686 688919 Mrs Dawson **D:** Fr £37.50–£47.50 **S:** Fr £65.00 **Beds:** 3D **Baths:** 3 En (14) (30) **cc**

Capel-y-ffin

SO2531

The Grange, *Capel-y-Ffin, Abergavenny, NP7 7NP.* Small Victorian approved ensuite guest house situated in beautiful mountains. **Open:** Easter to Nov
01873 890215 Mrs Griffiths **Fax: 01873 890157 D:** Fr £23.00 **S:** Fr £23.00 **Beds:** 1F 1D 1T 1S **Baths:** 3 En (6) (10)

Cemmaes Road

SH8204

Cefn Coch Uchaf, *Cemmaes Road, Machynlleth, Powys, SY20 8LU.* C14th Dovey Valley farmhouse, lovely views. **Open:** All year (not Xmas)
01650 511552 Mrs Harris **D:** Fr £17.50–£18.00 **S:** Fr £17.50–£18.50 **Beds:** 2D 1T **Baths:** 1 Pr 1 Sh

Cilmery

SO0051

Halcyon House & Llewelyn Leisure Park, *Cilmery, Builth Wells, Powys, LD2 3NU.* Jacuzzi, snooker, views, hospitality, inn, cows, sheep; self-catering, camping. **Open:** All year
01982 552838 & 07831 101052 Mr Johnson **Fax: 01982 551090** *deejay1010@aol.com* **D:** Fr £18.00–£22.00 **S:** Fr £22.00–£26.00 **Beds:** 2F 1S **Baths:** 2 Sh **cc**

Clyro

SO2143

Tump Farm, *Clyro, Hay-on-Wye, Hereford, HR3 6JY.* Comfortable, friendly, peaceful farmhouse in outstandingly beautiful countryside. Near the small, interesting 'book town' of Hay-on-Wye. **Open:** All year (not Xmas)
01497 820912 Mrs Francis *jafrancis20@hotmail.com* **D:** Fr £15.00 **S:** Fr £16.50 **Beds:** 1T 1D **Baths:** 1 Sh (4)

Baskerville Hall Hotel, *Clyro Court, Clyro, Hay-on-Wye, Hereford, HR3 5LE.* Brecon Beacons, mountainous. Indoor pool, sauna, Conan Doyle connections **Open:** All year
01497 820033 *enquiries@baskervillehall.co.uk* www.baskerville.co.uk **D:** Fr £25.00–£37.00 **S:** Fr £35.00–£47.00 **Beds:** 5F 10T 10D 2S **Baths:** 27 En (30) **cc**

Commins Coch

SH8402

Gwalia, *Commins Coch, Machynlleth, Powys, SY20 9PZ.* Peaceful, remote, small farm. Home cooked, wholefood, vegetarian meals. **Open:** All year
01650 511377 Mrs Chandler **D:** Fr £18.00 **S:** Fr £18.00 **Beds:** 1F 1T **Baths:** 1 Sh

Crickhowell

SO2118 *White Hart*

White Hall, *Glangrwyney, Crickhowell, Powys, NP8 1EW.* Comfortable Georgian house next to restaurant, close to Black Mountains. **Open:** All year (not Xmas)
01873 811155 & 01873 840267 Ms Llewelyn **Fax: 01873 840178** *pllewelyn@white-hall.freeserve.co.uk* **D:** Fr £15.00–£20.00 **S:** Fr £20.00–£25.00 **Beds:** 1F 2D 1S **Baths:** 2 En 1 Sh (3)

Bell Inn, *Glangrwyney, Crickhowell, Powys, NP8 1EH.* C17th former coaching inn. Excellent food and ensuite accommodation. **Open:** All year
01873 810247 Mr Llewelyn **Fax: 01873 812155 D:** Fr £25.00–£35.00 **S:** Fr £30.00 **Beds:** 1F 2D 2T 1S **Baths:** 6 En (20) **cc**

Glangrwyney Court, *Crickhowell, Powys, NP8 1ES.* Georgian mansion in 4 acres of established gardens surrounded by parkland. **Open:** All year
01873 811288 C R Jackson **Fax: 01873 810317** *glangrwyne@aol.com* www.walescountryhousebandb.com **D:** Fr £22.50–£27.50 **S:** Fr £55.00 **Beds:** 1F 2T 2D **Baths:** 4 En 1 Pr (10)

Castell Corryn, *Llangenny, Crickhowell, Powys, NP8 1HE.* Above Usk Valley in Brecon Beacons NP. Outstanding views, beautiful restful gardens, homely welcome. **Open:** All year (not Xmas/New Year)
01873 810327 (also fax) Mr Harris *castellcorryn@aol.com* **D:** Fr £20.00–£25.00 **S:** Fr £25.00–£30.00 **Beds:** 2T 1D **Baths:** 2 En 1 Pr (6)

Criggion

SJ2915

Brimford House, *Criggion, Shrewsbury, Shropshire, SY5 9AU.* Elegant Georgian farmhouse in tranquil scenic surroundings between Breidden Hills & River Severn. **Open:** All year
01938 570235 Mrs Dawson *info@brimford.co.uk* www.virtual-shropshire.co.uk/brimford-house **D:** Fr £20.00–£25.00 **S:** Fr £20.00–£30.00 **Beds:** 1T 2D **Baths:** 2 En 1 Sh (4)

Crossgates
SO0561

Guidfa House, *Crossgates, Llandrindod Wells, Powys, LD1 6RF.* Stylish Georgian house offering comfort, good food and a relaxing atmosphere. **Open:** All year **Grades:** WTB 4 Star, AA 4 Diamond
01597 851241 Mr Millan **Fax: 01597 851875** *guidfa@globalnet.co.uk* **D:** Fr £26.50–£29.00 **S:** Fr £31.50–£37.50 **Beds:** 2D 3T 1S **Baths:** 5 En 1 Pr (10) cc

Cwm
SO2590

The Drewin Farm, *Cwm, Church Stoke, Montgomery, Powys, SY15 6TW.* C17th farmhouse with panoramic views. Offa's Dyke footpath on doorstep. **Open:** Easter to Oct
01588 620325 (also fax) C M E Richards *ceinwen@drewin.freeserve.co.uk* **D:** Fr £20.00–£22.00 **S:** Fr £25.00 **Beds:** 1F 1T **Baths:** 2 En (6)

Darowen
SH8201

Cefn Farm, *Darowen, Machynlleth, Powys, SY20 8NS.* Unsurpassable views, good walking. Half-hour drive seaside. Open fire, personal service. **Open:** All year
01650 511336 Mr Lloyd **D:** Fr £20.00 **S:** Fr £20.00 **Beds:** 1F 1D

Discoed
SO2764

Gumma Farm, *Discoed, Presteigne, Powys, LD8 2NP.* Peaceful, 350 acre working farm. All rooms beautifully furnished with antiques. **Open:** Easter to Nov
Grades: WTB 4 Star
01547 560243 Mrs Owens *anne.owens@farming.co.uk* **D:** Fr £23.00 **S:** Fr £30.00 **Beds:** 1D 1T 1S **Baths:** 1 En 1 Pr

Dylife
SN8694

Star Inn, *Dylife, Staylittle, Llanbrynmair, Powys, SY19 7BW.* Beautiful countryside. Fishing, golf, sailing, walking, clay-shooting, quad-biking. **Open:** All year
01650 521345 Mrs Ward -Banks **D:** Fr £20.00–£22.00 **S:** Fr £20.00–£25.00 **Beds:** 1F 3D 1T 2S **Baths:** 2 Pr 1 Sh

BATHROOMS
En = Ensuite
Pr = Private
Sh = Shared

Erwood
SO0942

Trericket Mill Vegetarian Guesthouse, *Erwood, Builth Wells, Powys, LD2 3TQ.* Listed C19th watermill in Wye Valley, friendly and informal. **Open:** All year (not Xmas) **Grades:** WTB 2 Star
01982 560312 Alistair & Nicky Legge *mail@trericket.co.uk* www.trericket.co.uk **D:** Fr £22.00–£25.00 **S:** Fr £32.00–£35.00 **Beds:** 2D 1T **Baths:** 3 En (8)

Hafod-y-Gareg, *Erwood, Builth Wells, Powys, LD2 3TQ.* Secluded medieval farmhouse in idyllic Welsh hillside locality. Rooms overlooking pasture & woodland. **Open:** All year (not Xmas)
01982 560400 Mrs McKay **D:** Fr £13.50–£17.50 **S:** Fr £13.50–£17.50 **Beds:** 1F 2D 1T **Baths:** 3 En (6)

Felindre
SO1681

Trevland, *Felindre, Knighton, Powys, LD7 1YL.* Quiet border village. Warm welcome offered to all. **Open:** All year
01547 510211 Mrs Edwards *marion@trevland.freeserve.co.uk* **D:** Fr £16.50–£17.50 **S:** Fr £16.50–£17.50 **Beds:** 1F 1D 1T **Baths:** 3 En (5)

Felinfach
SO0933 *Griffin Inn*

Llwyncynog Farm, *Felinfach, Brecon, Powys, LD3 0UG.* Peaceful location commanding splendid views of Brecons and Black Mountains. **Open:** Easter to Oct
01874 623475 Mrs Phillips **D:** Fr £18.00–£20.00 **S:** Fr £20.00–£25.00 **Beds:** 1F 1T 1D **Baths:** 2 En 1 Pr (2)

Forden
SJ2200

Church House, *Forden, Welshpool, Powys, SY21 8NE.* Near Powis Castle, Welshpool Light Railway. Quiet, walking/cycling area. **Open:** All year (not Xmas/New Year)
01938 580353 Mrs Bright **D:** Fr £18.50 **S:** Fr £18.50 **Beds:** 1F 1D 1T **Baths:** 1 Pr 1 Sh

All details shown are as supplied by B&B owners in Autumn 2002

Meithrinfa, *Forden, Welshpool, Powys, SY21 8RT.* Large bungalow set in own grounds, elevated position, overlooking Severn Valley. **Open:** Easter to Nov
01938 580458 Mrs Hughes **D:** Fr £18.00–£20.00 **S:** Fr £20.00–£22.00 **Beds:** 1F 1T **Baths:** 2 En (3)

Gladestry
SO2355

Offa's Dyke Lodge, *Gladestry, Kington, Herefordshire, HR5 3NR.* Luxury accommodation, spectacular views, fine cooking, the perfect relaxing break.
Open: All year **Grades:** WTB 4 Star
01544 370341 Steve White **Fax: 01544 370342** *odl@offtec.ltd.uk* www.offas-dyke-lodge.co.uk **D:** Fr £25.00–£29.00 **S:** Fr £35.00–£39.00 **Beds:** 1D 2T/D **Baths:** 2 En 1 Pr (10) 3

Hay-on-Wye
SO2242

Tinto House, *Broad Street, Hay-on-Wye, Hereford, HR3 5DB.* **Open:** All year (not Xmas) **Grades:** AA 4 Diamond
01497 820590 Mr Evans **Fax: 01497 820425** *john@tintohouse.fsnet.co.uk* www.tintohouse.co.uk **D:** Fr £22.50–£27.50 **S:** Fr £30.00–£40.00 **Beds:** 2D 1T **Baths:** 3 En
Comfortable Grade II Listed Georgian town house in the centre of famous book town of Hay-on-Wye, which has a large garden overlooking the River Wye and Radnorshire Hills.

The Old Post Office, *Llanigon, Hay-on-Wye, Hereford, HR3 5QA.* A very special find in Black Mountains, superb vegetarian breakfast. **Open:** All year
01497 820008 Mrs Webb www.oldpost-office.co.uk **D:** Fr £18.00–£28.00 **S:** Fr £20.00–£35.00 **Beds:** 1F 1D 1T **Baths:** 2 En 1 Sh (3)

Lansdowne, *Cusop, Hay-on-Wye, Hereford, HR3 5RF.* Victorian house, pretty garden, beautiful views, spacious bedrooms, quiet location. **Open:** All year (not Xmas/New Year)
01497 820125 (also fax) Mr & Mrs Sheldon *sheldon@lansdowne-bb.co.uk* www.lansdowne-bb.co.uk **D:** Fr £20.00–£25.00 **S:** Fr £27.00–£30.00 **Beds:** 1T 1D **Baths:** 2 En (3)

Fernleigh, *Hardwick Road, Cusop, Hay-on-Wye, Hereford, HR3 5QX.* Quiet location walking distance of the famous book town of Hay-on-Wye. **Open:** Easter to Oct
01497 820459 Mr Hughes **D:** Fr £17.00–£20.00 **S:** Fr £19.00–£20.00 **Beds:** 2D 1S **Baths:** 1 En 1 Sh (4)

Heol Senni
SN9223

Maeswalter, *Heol Senni, Brecon, Powys, LD3 8SU.* 300-year-old farmhouse situated in the picturesque Senni valley. **Open:** All year
01874 636629 Mrs Mayo *maeswalter@talk21.com* **D:** Fr £19.00–£20.00 **S:** Fr £20.00–£25.00 **Beds:** 1F 2D 1T **Baths:** 1 En 2 Sh 1 Pr (1) (8)

Howey
SO0558

Holly Farm, *Howey, Llandrindod Wells, Powys, LD1 5PP.* Comfortable old farmhouse, dates back to Tudor times; bedrooms have lovely views of countryside. **Open:** All year (not Xmas)
01597 822402 Mrs Jones www.smoothhound.co.uk/hotels/hollyfm.html **D:** Fr £20.00–£25.00 **S:** Fr £24.00–£26.00 **Beds:** 1F 2D 2T **Baths:** 3 En 2 Sh (6)

Hundred House
SO1154

Gaer Farm, *Hundred House, Llandrindod Wells, Powys, LD1 5RU.* Converted stone timber barn with panoramic views of surrounding mountains. **Open:** All year (not Xmas)
01982 570208 (also fax) Mrs Harley *relax@gaerfarm.co.uk* www.gaerfarm.co.uk **D:** Fr £18.00–£25.00 **Beds:** 2F 1S **Baths:** 3 En 3

Kerry
SO1489

Greenfields, *Kerry, Newtown, Powys, SY16 4LH.* Comfortable guest house, good food, warm welcome. **Open:** All year (not Xmas) **Grades:** WTB 2 Star
01686 670596 Mrs Madeley **Fax: 01686 670354** *info@greenfields-guesthouse.co.uk* www.greenfields.co.uk **D:** Fr £20.00–£22.00 **S:** Fr £20.00–£22.00 **Beds:** 1F 1D 1T 1S **Baths:** 3 En (4) (6) cc

Knighton
SO2872

The Fleece House, *Market Street, Knighton, Powys, LD7 1BB.* Attractive decorated quality accommodation in converted C18th coaching inn. **Open:** All year **Grades:** WTB 3 Star
01547 520168 Mrs Simmons *info@fleecehouse.co.uk* www.fleecehouse.co.uk **D:** Fr £20.00–£28.00 **S:** Fr £25.00–£36.00 **Beds:** 3T **Baths:** 2 En 1 Pr

9 West Street, *Knighton, Powys, LD7 1EN.* A warm welcome to The Gateway to Mid Wales, perfect for exploring the beautiful Welsh Marches & walking in the foothills. Visit the Offa's Dyke Centre, Elan Valley (Red Kite Country), Shropshire Hills Discovery Centre & other attractions within easy travelling distance. **Open:** All year (not Xmas/New Year)
01547 529021 Mrs Maslen-Jones *maslenjones@btinternet.com.uk* **D:** Fr £18.00 **S:** Fr £20.00 **Beds:** 1T 1D **Baths:** 1 Sh (6) (2)

Offas Dyke House, *4 High Street, Knighton , Powys, LD7 1AT.* Warm friendly B&B situated in the heart of Knighton. **Open:** All year
01547 528634 (also fax) S Ashe **D:** Fr £16.00 **S:** Fr £16.00 **Beds:** 2T 3D 1S **Baths:** 3 Sh (4)

Westwood, *Presteigne Road, Knighton, Powys, LD7 1HY.* Spacious Victorian house in quiet town location. Warm, friendly welcome. **Open:** All year
01547 520317 Mrs Sharratt *sharratt@westwoode.freeserve.co.uk* **D:** Fr £18.00 **S:** Fr £18.00 **Beds:** 1F 1D 1S **Baths:** 1 En 1 Sh (4)

Leighton
SJ2305 *Green Dragon*

Orchard House, *Leighton, Welshpool, Powys, SY21 8HN.* Comfortable, lovely, quiet location, yet close to Welshpool. **Open:** All year
01938 553624 (also fax) Mrs Pearce *pearce@orchardhouse.softnet.co.uk* **D:** Fr £22.00–£23.00 **S:** Fr £22.00–£25.00 **Beds:** 1T 2D **Baths:** 2 En 1 Pr cc

Sycamore Cottage, *Leighton, Welshpool, SY21 8HR.* Perfectly situated for exploring Mid Wales, warm welcome, farmhouse breakfast. **Open:** All year (not Xmas/New Year)
01938 553899 Mr & Mrs Jones **D:** Fr £17.00–£20.00 **S:** Fr £18.00–£22.00 **Beds:** 2F 2D **Baths:** 2 Sh

Llanbadarn Fynydd
SO0977

Hillside Lodge Guesthouse, *Llanbadarn Fynydd, Llandrindod Wells, Powys, LD1 6TU.* Half mile main road, on hillside in private gardens overlooking Ithon Valley. **Open:** Jan to Dec
01597 840364 Mr & Mrs Ainsworth **D:** Fr £20.00 **S:** Fr £25.00 **Beds:** 2F 1T **Baths:** 3 En (6)

Llanbister
SO1073

The Lion, *Llanbister, Llandrindod Wells, Powys, LD1 6TN.* Small country pub set in beautiful countryside overlooking river. **Open:** All year
01597 840244 J E Thomas **Fax: 01597 840601** *lion@llanbister@virgin.net* **D:** Fr £20.00 **S:** Fr £25.00 **Beds:** 3F 1D 1S **Baths:** 5 En (5)

Llanbrynmair
SH8902

Wynnstay Arms Hotel, *Llanbrynmair, Powys, SY19 7AA.* In a walkers' paradise. **Open:** All year (not Xmas)
01650 521431 Mrs Taylor *wynnstayarmsllanbrynmair@barbox.net* **D:** Fr £20.00 **S:** Fr £37.00 **Beds:** 2F 2D 2T **Baths:** 2 Sh

Llanddew
SO0530 *The Oak, Castle Hotel, George Hotel*

The Gables, *23 Alexandra Road, Llanddew, Brecon, Powys, LD3 9SS.* Edwardian house, magnificent view of Brecon Beacons, private parking. **Open:** All year (not Xmas/New Year)
01874 622058 Mrs Williams **D:** Fr £22.00 **S:** Fr £26.00 **Beds:** 1T 2D 1S **Baths:** 1 En 2 Sh

Llandinam
SO0288

Trewythen, *Llandinam, Powys, SY17 5BQ.* Situated in scenic surroundings and ideal for touring Lakes & Wales. **Open:** Easter to Nov
01686 688444 (also fax) Mrs Davies **D:** Fr £22.00–£24.00 **S:** Fr £25.00–£30.00 **Beds:** 1F 1D **Baths:** 2 En

Llandrindod Wells

SO0561

Guidfa House, *Crossgates, Llandrindod Wells, Powys, LD1 6RF.* Stylish Georgian house offering comfort, good food and a relaxing atmosphere. **Open:** All year **Grades:** WTB 4 Star, AA 4 Diamond
01597 851241 Mr Millan **Fax: 01597 851875** *guidfa@globalnet.co.uk* **D:** Fr £26.50–£29.00 **S:** Fr £31.50–£37.50 **Beds:** 2D 3T 1S **Baths:** 5 En 1 Pr (10) cc

Drovers Arms, *Llandrindod Wells, Powys, LD1 5PT.* Quality food & accommodation. Cosy village inn. Beautiful scenery & local attractions. Two course A La Carte dinner £10 per head. **Open:** All year
01597 822508 Joyce Hacking & Henry Torz *info@drovers-arms.co.uk* www.drovers-arms.co.uk **D:** Fr £25.00–£30.00 **S:** Fr £35.00–£40.00 **Beds:** 2D 1T **Baths:** 3 En (3) cc

Greylands, *High Street, Llandrindod Wells, Powys, LD1 6AG.* Handsome Victorian townhouse. Surrounded by beautiful countryside. Secure cycle storage. **Open:** All year
01597 822253 Mrs MacDonald *greylands@csma-netlink.co.uk* **D:** Fr £16.00–£19.00 **S:** Fr £17.00–£20.00 **Beds:** 1F 2D 1T 3S **Baths:** 6 En 1 Sh (5) cc

Llandyssil

SO1995

The Dingle, *Cwminkin, Llandyssil, Montgomery, Powys, SY15 6HH.* Converted barn. Private, peaceful valley, running stream, wildlife. Garaging. **Open:** All year
01686 668838 (also fax) Mrs Nicholson *kaybuzzards@yahoo.co.uk* **D:** Fr £15.00 **S:** Fr £15.00 **Beds:** 1F 1D 1S **Baths:** 1 Sh (8) (6)

Llanfair Caereinion

SJ1006

Cwm Llwynog, *Llanfair Caereinion, Welshpool, Powys, SY21 0HF.* Easy reach Powis Castle, steam railway, garden with unusual plants. **Open:** All year (not Xmas)
01938 810791 (also fax) Ms Cornes **D:** Fr £20.00 **S:** Fr £20.00 **Beds:** 2D 1T **Baths:** 2 Pr 1 Sh

Madogs Wells, *Llanfair Caereinion, Welshpool, Powys, SY21 0DE.* Beautiful valley, watch bird life from your breakfast table. Astronomy holidays. **Open:** All year (not Xmas)
01938 810446 (also fax) Mrs Reed **D:** Fr £17.00 **S:** Fr £17.00 **Beds:** 1F 1D **Baths:** 1 Sh (5)

Llanfihangel-nant-Melan

SO1858

Summergill, *Llanfihangel-nant-Melan, Presteigne, Powys, LD8 2TN.* Surrounded by farm land. Ideal for walking and touring. **Open:** All year
01544 350247 Mrs Griffiths **D:** Fr £15.00–£16.00 **S:** Fr £15.00–£16.00 **Beds:** 1F 1T 1D **Baths:** 2 En 1 Sh (4)

Llanfrynach

SO0725

Llanbrynean Farm, *Llanfrynach, Brecon, Powys, LD3 7BQ.* Beautiful countryside, traditional family farmhouse, ideal location for Brecon Beacons. **Open:** Easter to Nov
01874 665222 Mrs Harpur **D:** Fr £19.00–£21.00 **S:** Fr £20.00–£25.00 **Beds:** 1F 1D 1T **Baths:** 2 En 1 Pr (8)

Llangorse

SO1327 *Castle Inn, Red Lion*

Trefeinon Farm, *Llangorse, Brecon, Powys, LD3 0PS.* Delightful area for exploring. Activities in the National Park. **Open:** Easter to Oct
01874 658607 Mrs Sheppard **D:** Fr £20.00–£25.00 **S:** Fr £20.00–£25.00 **Beds:** 1D 1S **Baths:** 2 Pr

Llangurig

SN9079

The Old Vicarage Guest House, *Llangurig, Llanidloes, Powys, SY18 6RN.* **Open:** Feb to Dec **Grades:** WTB 3 Star, AA 4 Diamond
01686 440280 (also fax) M Hartey *theoldvicarage@llangurig.fslife.co.uk* www.theoldvicaragellangurig.co.uk **D:** Fr £21.00–£23.00 **S:** Fr £25.00–£30.00 **Beds:** 1F 2D 1T **Baths:** 4 En (5) (6)
Homely licensed guesthouse, set in its own grounds. Ideally situated for exploring the lakes & mountains of Mid Wales. Walk the forgotten footpaths or watch the red kite soar above. Coast 25 miles away, warm welcome, good food guaranteed.

RATES
D = Price range per person sharing in a double or twin room
S = Price range for a single room

Llanidloes

SN9584

Esgairmaen, *Van, Llanidloes, Powys, SY18 6NT.* Comfortable farmhouse in unspoilt countryside, ideal for waking & bird-watching. **Open:** Easter to Oct
01686 430272 **D:** Fr £18.00–£20.00 **S:** Fr £18.00–£20.00 **Beds:** 1F 1D **Baths:** 2 En (1) (4)

Lloyds, *Cambrian Place, Llanidloes, Powys, SY18 6BX.* Small, informal, country town hotel with high standards of hospitality. **Open:** Mar to Jan **Grades:** WTB 3 Star Hotel
01686 412284 Mr Lines **D:** Fr £27.50 **S:** Fr £20.00–£35.00 **Beds:** 3D 2T 4S **Baths:** 6 En 1 Sh

Llanigon

SO2139

The Old Post Office, *Llanigon, Hay-on-Wye, Hereford, HR3 5QA.* A very special find in Black Mountains, superb vegetarian breakfast. **Open:** All year
01497 820008 Mrs Webb www.oldpost-office.co.uk **D:** Fr £18.00–£28.00 **S:** Fr £20.00–£35.00 **Beds:** 1F 1D 1T **Baths:** 2 En 1 Sh (3)

Llanrhaeadr-ym-Mochnant

SJ1226

Eirianfa, *Waterfall Road, Llanrhaeadr-ym-Mochnant, Oswestry, Shropshire, SY10 0JX.* Overlooking the village and the Tanat Valley, we offer comfortable warm accommodation. **Open:** All year (not Xmas)
01691 780507 Phil Common & Cathy Laceby *eirianfa@yahoo.com* **D:** Fr £17.50–£20.00 **S:** Fr £25.00–£35.00 **Beds:** 1F 1D **Baths:** 1 Sh (3)

Llansantffraed

SO1223

The Allt, *Llansantffraed, Talybont-on-Usk, Brecon, Powys, LD3 7YF.* C18th farmhouse overlooking River Usk with magnificent mountain views. **Open:** All year (not Xmas)
01874 676310 Mrs Hamill-Keays *anne@theallt.com* www.theallt.com **D:** Fr £17.50–£20.00 **S:** Fr £20.00 **Beds:** 2F 1D 1S **Baths:** 1 En 1 Sh

Llansilin

SJ2028 *Green Inn, Wynnstay Inn*

Lloran Ganol, *Llansilin, Oswestry, Shropshire, SY10 7QX.* Dairy and sheep working farm set in its own Welsh valley. **Open:** All year
01691 791287 Mrs Jones **D:** Fr £15.00 **S:** Fr £15.00 **Beds:** 1D 1T 1S **Baths:** 2 Sh

The Old Vicarage, *Llansilin, Oswestry, Shropshire, SY10 7PX.* Peaceful rural location. Spacious, comfortable rooms with views. Guest lounge. **Open:** All year (not Xmas/New Year)
01691 791345 (also fax) Mrs Johnson *pam@vicarage-guests.co.uk* www.vicarage-guests.co.uk **D:** Fr £22.00–£25.00 **S:** Fr £30.00–£35.00 **Beds:** 1T 2D **Baths:** 2 En 1 Pr (13) (4)

Llanwrin

SH7803 *Penrhos Arms, Black Lion*

Mathafarn, *Llanwrin, Machynlleth, Powys, SY20 8QJ.* Historic farmhouse in beautiful Dovey Valley. Near Centre for Alternative Technology. **Open:** All year (not Xmas/New Year)
01650 511226 (also fax) Mrs Hughes **D:** Fr £20.00–£25.00 **S:** Fr £25.00 **Beds:** 1T 1S **Baths:** 1 En 1 Pr

Llanwrthwl

SN9763 *Vulcan Arms*

Dyffryn Farm, *Llanwrthwl, Llandrindod Wells, Powys, LD1 6NU.* C17th home. Warm and friendly atmosphere. **Open:** Nov to Feb
01597 811017 Mrs Tyler **Fax: 01597 810609** *dyffrynfm@cs.com* **D:** Fr £20.00–£22.00 **S:** Fr £20.00–£22.00 **Beds:** 2D 1S (15) (6)

Llanwrtyd Wells

SN8746 *Stonecroft Inn, Drovers' Rest*

Kilsby Country House, *Llanwrtyd Wells, Powys, LD5 4TL.* Breathtaking views, peaceful surroundings, walkers/cyclists/birdwatchers paradise. Friendly atmosphere. **Open:** All year (not Xmas/New Year)
01591 610281 Ms Cooper **Fax: 01591 610873** *kilsbyBB@aol.com* www.kilsbybb.co.uk **D:** Fr £20.00–£22.00 **S:** Fr £22.00–£28.00 **Beds:** 1F 1T 1D **Baths:** 1 Pr 2 Sh (4)

Llanyre

SO0462

Highbury Farm, *Llanyre, Llandrindod Wells, Powys, LD1 6EA.* Peaceful location with short farm trail. Laundry room. Excellent food. **Open:** Mar to Nov
01597 822716 (also fax) Mrs Evans www.farmbreaks.org.uk **D:** Fr £18.00–£21.00 **S:** Fr £21.00–£24.00 **Beds:** 1F 2D **Baths:** 2 En 1 Pr (1) (3)

Greenglades, *Llanyre, Llandrindod Wells, Powys, LD1 6EA.* Beautiful country house in tranquil setting near village inn. **Open:** All year (not Xmas)
01597 822950 E J Jones **D:** Fr £18.00–£22.00 **S:** Fr £20.00–£24.00 **Beds:** 1F 1D 1T **Baths:** 2 En (3)

Llowes

SO1942

Ty-Bach, *Llowes, Glasbury, HR3 5JE.* Ornamental ponds, woodland garden, breathtaking views, abundant wildlife, birds. Friendly. **Open:** All year (not Xmas/New Year) **Grades:** AA 4 Diamond
01497 847759 J M Bradfield **Fax: 01497 847940** *j.bradfield@btinternet.com* www.hay-on-wye.co.uk/tybach **D:** Fr £22.50–£25.00 **S:** Fr £30.00–£40.00 **Beds:** 1T 1D **Baths:** 2 Pr (6)

Llyswen

SO1337 *Bridge End*

Lower Rhydness Bungalow, *Llyswen, Brecon, Powys, LD3 0AZ.* Upper Wye Valley. Wonderful view. Warm welcome. Farm house breakfast. **Open:** All year
01874 754264 Mrs Williams **D:** Fr £18.00 **S:** Fr £18.00 **Beds:** 1F 1D **Baths:** 2 Sh (2)

Machynlleth

SH7400

Talbontdrain, *Uwchygarreg, Machynlleth, Powys, SY20 8RR.* **Open:** All year (not Xmas)
01654 702192 Ms Matthews *hilary@talbontdrain.co.uk* www.talbontdrain.co.uk **D:** Fr £20.00–£26.00 **S:** Fr £20.00–£22.00 **Beds:** 1D 1T 2S **Baths:** 1 Pr 1 Sh (4)
Talbontdrain is a friendly, family home. We enjoy meeting new people and hope you feel at home. Good, plentiful, home-cooked food. Drying facilities. Trampoline. Fantastic views and masses to do locally for all ages. Great walking & cycling. No snow in summer!

Maenllwyd, *Newtown Road, Machynlleth, Powys, SY20 8EY.* Home-from-home, within walking distance all amenities, safe parking. **Open:** All year (not Xmas) **Grades:** WTB 3 Star
01654 702928 (also fax) Mr Vince *maenlwyd@dircon.co.uk* www.cyber-space.co.uk/maenllwyd.html **D:** Fr £22.00–£23.00 **S:** Fr £28.00 **Beds:** 1F 4D 3T **Baths:** 8 En (10) cc

Wynnstay Arms Hotel, *Maengwyn Street, Machynlleth, Powys, SY20 8AE.* Old coaching inn, in heart of historic market town, in stunning Dovey Valley. **Open:** All year
01654 702941 Mr Dark **Fax: 01654 703884** *info@wynnstay-hotel.com* **D:** Fr £35.00–£50.00 **S:** Fr £45.00–£65.00 **Beds:** 3F 9D 5T 6S **Baths:** 23 En (36) cc

Gwelfryn, *6 Green Fields, Machynlleth, Powys, SY20 8DR.* Quiet but central, fantastic breakfasts, near all tourist attractions. **Open:** Easter to Oct
01654 702532 *bb@gwelfryn.co.uk* www.gwelfryn.co.uk **D:** Fr £19.00–£22.50 **S:** Fr £18.00 **Beds:** 1D 1T 1S **Baths:** 1 En 1 Pr

Milebrook

SO3072

Milebrook House Hotel, *Milebrook, Knighton, Powys., LD7 1LT.* Dower House, once the retreat of Emperor Haile Selassie. **Open:** All year
01547 528632 Fax: 01547 520509 *hotel@milebrook.kc3* **D:** Fr £37.75–£41.75 **S:** Fr £51.00–£55.00 **Beds:** 3T 7D **Baths:** 10 En (8) (30) cc

Mochdre

SO0788

Llettyderyn, *Mochdre, Newtown, Powys, SY16 4JY.* Traditional hospitality in a restored farmhouse, one ground floor room. **Open:** All year
01686 626131 Mrs Jandrell *margaret.jandrell@tiscali.co.uk* **D:** Fr £20.00–£22.00 **S:** Fr £25.00–£27.00 **Beds:** 2D 1T **Baths:** 3 En

Montgomery

SO2296

Little Brompton Farm, *Montgomery, Powys, SY15 6HY.* C17th farmhouse on working farm. Superior quality for discerning visitors. **Open:** All year
01686 668371 (also fax) G Bright *gaynor.brompton@virgin.net* www.littlebrompton.co.uk **D:** Fr £21.00–£23.00 **S:** Fr £25.00 **Beds:** 1F 1T 1D **Baths:** 3 En

Hendomen Farmhouse, *Hendomen, Montgomery, Powys, SY15 6HB.* **Open:** All year (not Xmas/New Year) **Grades:** WTB 2 Star
01686 668004 Jo & Bruce Lawson **Fax: 01686 668319** *bruce.lawson@btinternet.com* www.offasdykepath.com **D:** Fr £18.00–£24.00 **S:** Fr £18.00–£24.00 **Beds:** 1T 1D 1S **Baths:** 1 En 1 Sh (9) (2) cc
Welcome to Montgomery - an undiscovered Georgian gem. 1 mile from Offa's Dyke. Walkers our speciality. Transport (people and luggage) arranged. 1 mile from 5 pubs, hotel, museum and castle (Montgomery) Powis Castle 5 miles. Superb views and breakfasts.

The Dingle, *Cwminkin, Llandyssil, Montgomery, Powys, SY15 6HH.* Converted barn. Private, peaceful valley, running stream, wildlife. Garaging. **Open:** All year
01686 668838 (also fax) Mrs Nicholson *kaybuzzards@yahoo.co.uk* **D:** Fr £15.00 **S:** Fr £15.00 **Beds:** 1F 1D 1S **Baths:** 1 Sh (8) (6)

The Manor House, *Pool Road, Montgomery, Powys, SY15 6QY.* Former house of correction, friendly welcome, private house. **Open:** All year
01686 668736 Mrs Williams **D:** Fr £16.00 **S:** Fr £16.00 **Beds:** 1D 1T 1S **Baths:** 1 En 1 Pr (2)

New Radnor

SO2160

Bache Farm, *New Radnor, Presteigne, Powys, LD8 2TG.* C17th farmhouse in beautiful unspoilt countryside amidst the Welsh Marches. **Open:** All year (not Xmas)
01544 350680 Mrs Hardwick **D:** Fr £18.00–£19.50 **S:** Fr £22.00–£25.00 **Beds:** 2D 1T **Baths:** 1 Sh

Newtown

SO1191

Greenfields, *Kerry, Newtown, Powys, SY16 4LH.* Comfortable guest house, good food, warm welcome. **Open:** All year (not Xmas) **Grades:** WTB 2 Star
01686 670596 Mrs Madeley **Fax: 01686 670354** *info@greenfields-guesthouse.co.uk* www.greenfields.co.uk **D:** Fr £20.00–£22.00 **S:** Fr £20.00–£22.00 **Beds:** 1F 1D 1T 1S **Baths:** 3 En (4) (6) cc

Plas Canol Guest House, *New Road, Newtown, Powys, SY16 1AS.* Quiet, comfortable, friendly accommodation. Cotton sheets, fresh flowers, brochure available. **Open:** All year **Grades:** WTB 3 Star
01686 625598 Mrs Burd **D:** Fr £20.00–£22.00 **S:** Fr £20.00–£28.00 **Beds:** 2T 1D **Baths:** 3 En (3)

Old Radnor

SO2459 *Harp Inn*

Trewern Farm, *Old Radnor, Presteigne, Powys, LD8 2RP.* Georgian farmhouse accommodation in unspoilt countryside. Lovely views and bird watching area. **Open:** All year
01544 350255 Mrs Lewis **D:** Fr £22.00–£25.00 **S:** Fr £18.00–£22.00 **Beds:** 1F 1T 2D 2S **Baths:** 1 En 1 Sh

Pontsticill

SO0611 *Butchers' Arms*

Station House, *Pontsticill, Merthyr Tydfil, CF48 2UP.* Comfortable and carefully converted former railway signal box. The property is on the edge of a reservoir with spectacular views across the water to the Brecon Beacons. The Brecon Mountain Railway and Taff Cycle Trail are adjacent. **Open:** All year
01685 377798 Mrs Hills **Fax: 01685 384854** **D:** Fr £22.50–£25.50 **S:** Fr £22.50–£25.50 **Beds:** 1F **Baths:** 1 Pr (3)

Presteigne

SO3164

Gumma Farm, *Discoed, Presteigne, Powys, LD8 2NP.* **Open:** Easter to Nov **Grades:** WTB 4 Star
01547 560243 Mrs Owens *anne.owens@farming.co.uk* **D:** Fr £23.00 **S:** Fr £30.00 **Beds:** 1D 1T 1S **Baths:** 1 En 1 Pr
Peaceful, 350 acre working farm. Presteigne 1 mile. All rooms beautifully furnished with antiques, overlooking garden, pleasant sitting area. Offa's Dyke 0.5 miles. Ideal for walking, cycling, touring Wales. Superb breakfast using home/locally produced meat/veg.

Willey Lodge Farm, *Presteigne, Powys, LD8 2NB.* Comfortable accommodation, C16th house, working farm amidst Welsh Marches - welcome. **Open:** All year (not Xmas/New Year)
01544 267341 Mrs Davies **D:** Fr £18.00–£20.00 **S:** Fr £18.00–£20.00 **Beds:** 1T 1D **Baths:** 1 Pr

Rhayader

SN9768

Brynafon Country House Hotel, *South Street, Rhayader, Powys, LD6 5BL.* **Open:** All year
01597 810735 Mrs Collins **Fax: 01597 810111** *info@brynafon.co.uk.* www.brynafon.co.uk. **D:** Fr £18.00–£40.00 **S:** Fr £35.00–£50.00 **Beds:** 3F 9D 8T **Baths:** 20 En
A former Victorian workhouse built in 1876, this impressive building is now a comfortable, relaxed, family-run hotel. Set amid glorious hills and mountains near Rhayader and the beautiful Elan Valley with a rare red kite feeding centre next door.

Brynteg, *East Street, Rhayader, Powys, LD6 5EA.* Comfortable Edwardian town house, overlooking hills and gardens. **Open:** All year (not Xmas) **Grades:** WTB 3 Star
01597 810052 Mrs Lawrence *brynteg@hotmail.com* **D:** Fr £18.00 **S:** Fr £18.00 **Beds:** 2D 1T 1S **Baths:** 3 En 1 Pr (4)

Beili Neuadd, *Rhayader, Powys, LD6 5NS.* Award-winning accommodation in farmhouse - secluded position with stunning views. **Open:** All year (not Xmas) **Grades:** WTB 4 Star
01597 810211 (also fax) Mrs Edwards *ann-carl@thebeili.freeserve.co.uk* www.midwalesfarmstay.co.uk **D:** Fr £23.00–£24.50 **S:** Fr £23.00–£26.00 **Beds:** 2D 1T 1S **Baths:** 2 En 2 Pr (8)

Liverpool House, *East House, Rhayader, Powys, LD6 5EA.* Excellent accommodation, very close to beautiful Elan Valley Reservoirs. **Open:** All year (not Xmas)
01597 810706 Mrs Griffiths **Fax: 01597 810964** *ann@liverpoolhouse.net* www.liverpoolhouse.net **D:** Fr £15.50–£17.00 **S:** Fr £18.00–£22.00 **Beds:** 2F 5D 1S **Baths:** 7 En 1 Sh (8) cc

Crown Inn, *North Street, Rhayader, Powys, LD6 5AB.* C16th oak-beamed inn, ideally located for discovering lakeland Wales. Friendly atmosphere. Home-made meals. Cask ales. **Open:** All year
01597 811099 Mrs Giles **D:** Fr £18.00–£20.00 **S:** Fr £18.00–£20.00 **Beds:** 3T **Baths:** 3 En (3)

C

Y

Z